THE ECONOMICS OF IMPERFECT COMPETITION AND EMPLOYMENT: Joan Robinson and Beyond

Also by George R. Feiwel and published by NEW YORK UNIVERSITY PRESS

ARROW AND THE FOUNDATIONS OF THE THEORY OF ECONOMIC POLICY (*editor*)
ARROW AND THE ASCENT OF MODERN ECONOMIC THEORY (*editor*)
JOAN ROBINSON AND MODERN ECONOMIC THEORY (*editor*)

JOAN ROBINSON

From the Ramsey and Muspratt Collection. © Peter Lofts: Anglia Supercolor Studios.

The Economics of Imperfect Competition and Employment

Joan Robinson and Beyond

Edited by
George R. Feiwel

NEW YORK UNIVERSITY PRESS
Washington Square, New York

First published in 1989 in the U.S.A by
NEW YORK UNIVERSITY PRESS
Washington Square
New York, N.Y. 10003

Printed in Hong Kong

Library of Congress Cataloging-in-Publication Data

The Economics of imperfect competition and employment.

Includes bibliographies and index.

1. Robinson, Joan, 1903– . 2. Competition,
Imperfect. 3. Employment (Economic theory) I. Feiwel,
George R.
HB103.R63E27 1989 330.1 88–15136
ISBN 0–8147–2592–9

Contents

Notes on the Contributors

G. C. Archibald is Professor of Economics, University of British Columbia. Formerly Professor of Economics, University of Essex, he has been Visiting Professor, University of California (Berkeley) and Northwestern University, and Senior Scholar, Centre of Economic Research, Athens. A Fellow of the Econometric Society and of the Royal Society of Canada, he has held the Leon Fellowship, London University; Ford Foundation Fellowship, and the Canada Council Killam Fellowship. He has been a member of the editorial board of the *Review of Economic Studies* and the *Canadian Journal of Economics* of which he has also served as managing editor. He has been a member of the executive committee of the Canadian Economic Association and of the Committee on New Fellows, Royal Society of Canada. In his numerous articles he deals primarily with imperfect competition, welfare economics, microeconomics, and incentives. He is also the author of *Introduction to Mathematical Economics* (with R. G. Lipsey, 1976), *The Theory of the Firm* (ed., 1971, 1974), and *Information Incentives, and the Economics of Control* (forthcoming).

Robert L. Bishop is Professor Emeritus, Massachusetts Institute of Technology where he has also served for eight years as Head, Department of Economics and Social Sciences and subsequently for ten more years as Dean, School of Humanities and Social Sciences. A Visiting Professor, Brandeis University and Harvard University, he has also served in various consulting functions on several collective bargaining negotiations, a contract negotiation, and an anti-trust case. His research concerns have centred primarily on demand theory and consumer's surplus, the market classification and welfare aspects of monopolistic competition, bargaining theory in bilateral monopoly and oligopoly, and miscellaneous problems in microeconomics, especially taxation, vertical relationships, factor demand, and monopsony. He is the co-editor of *Readings in Economics* (with P. A. Samelson and S. R. Coleman, 1952, 1958).

David Cass, formerly at Yale and Carnegie-Mellon University(ies), is Professor of Economics, and Director, Center for Analytic Research in Economics, University of Pennsylvania. He was Visiting Professor at the University(ies) of Tokyo, Paris, and Geneva and the Hebrew University of Jerusalem, and Sherman Fairchild Distinguished Scholar, California Institute of Technology. A Fellow of the Econometric Society and a Guggenheim Fellow, he has acted as American editor of *The Review of Economic Studies* and associate editor of *Journal of Economic Theory* and *Journal of Financial Economics*. He has written numerous articles in the pure theory of capital, behavior under uncertainty, money and general equilibrium theory, and intertemporal aspects of general equilibrium theory. He is also the co-editor of *Selected Readings in Macroeconomics from Econometrica* (with L. W. McKenzie, 1974) and *The Hamiltonian Approach to Economic Dynamics* (with K. Shell, 1976).

Dudley Dillard is Professor Emeritus of Economics, University of Maryland. After graduating from the University of California (Berkeley) where he was strongly influenced by Leo Rogin, and brief teaching stints at the University(ies) of Colorado and Delaware, he joined the faculty of the University of Maryland where he has been for more than forty-five years, and where as chairman for twenty-five of those years he has built its economics department. He has been Visiting Professor, Columbia University and University of Southern California. A past president of the Southern Economic Association and the Association for Evolutionary Economics and vice-president of the History of Economics Society, he is president of the Eastern Economic Association. He is also a recipient of the Veblen-Commons Award. A student of the history of economic thought, his numerous publications include *The Economics of John Maynard Keynes* (1948) and *Economic Development of the North Atlantic Economy: Historical Introduction to Modern Economics* (1967).

B. Curtis Eaton, formerly Professor of Economics, University of British Columbia, is Professor of Economics, University of Toronto. A Canada Council Fellow and a Fellow of the Economics Institute, Queens University, he has been Visiting Professor, University of Colorado; Visiting Fellow, Yale University; and National Fellow, Hoover Institution. He is a member of the board of editors of the *Canadian Journal of Economics*. He has written about thirty research papers in mathematical economics, imperfect competition, location theory, labor economics, and industrial organization. He is also the author of *Re-employment Experiences of Defense Workers* (with L. Fishman, J. Allen and B. Bunger, 1968) and *Microeconomics* (with D. Eaton, forthcoming).

Robert Eisner is William R. Kenan Professor of Economics, Northwestern University. Formerly at the University of Illinois, he has been Visiting Distinguished Professor, University of Binghamton, Visiting Professor, Monash University (Australia), and for ten years Senior Research Associate, National Bureau of Economic Research. A Guggenheim Fellow and Fellow of the Center for Advanced Study in the Behavioral Sciences, the Econometric Society, and the American Academy of Arts and Sciences, he is past president of the Midwest Economic Association and president of the American Economic Association. His many articles focus primarily on macroeconomic theory and policy and national income accounting. More specifically he has written on the formulation and estimation of the investment function, the role of expectations and the implications of the permanent income hypothesis on both investment and consumption, extensions of existing concepts of national income, and the impact of fiscal policy. His books include *Factors in Business Investment* (1978) and *How Real is the Federal Deficit?* (1986).

George R. Feiwel is Alumni Distinguished Service Professor and Professor of Economics, University of Tennessee. He has been on several occasions Visiting Professor, Harvard University and University of California (Berkeley), Visiting Professor, University of Stockholm, and on several occasions has been Senior Faculty Visitor, University of Cambridge. He has served on the editorial board of the *Journal of Economic Literature* and has participated in the summer IMSSS Seminars, Stanford University. A Guggenheim Fellow, he is the author of more than fifteen books, including *The Economics of a Socialist Enterprise* (1965), *The Soviet Quest for Economic Efficiency* (1967, 1972), *Industrialization Policy and Planning Under Polish Socialism*, 2 vols (1971), *The Intellectual Capital of Michal Kalecki* (1975), and *Growth and Reforms in Centrally Planned Economies* (1977). He is also a contributor to and editor of *Samuelson and Neoclassical Economics* (1982), *Issues in Contemporary Microeconomics and Welfare* (1985), *Issues in Contemporary Macroeconomics and Distribution* (1985), *Arrow and the Ascent of Modern Economic Theory* (1987), and *Arrow and the Foundations of the Theory of Economic Policy* (1987).

Dietrich Fischer is McArthur Foundation Fellow in International Peace and Security Studies and Visiting Fellow, Center of International Studies, Princeton University, and Associate Professor of Computer Science, Pace University. He has taught at New York University and has been a Visiting Professor at the National Polytechnic Institute (Mexico City). A Research Fellow, Geneva International Peace Research Institute, he has been a Consultant to the United Nations Industrial Development Organization; an Economic Affairs Officer, United Nations Conference on Trade and Development; and Visiting Researcher, Institute for Advanced Study (Berlin). Aside from the important subject of the economics of war and peace, his numerous articles range over such fields as industrial structure, income distribution, price theory, mathematical economics, statistics, and growth and development. He is also the author of *Preventing War in the Nuclear Age* (1984) and *Warfare and Welfare: Integrating Security Policy* (with J. Tinbergen, forthcoming).

Jean J. Gabszewicz is Professor and Chairman of the Department of Economic Science and General Director of the Center for Operations Research and Econometrics, Université Catholique de Louvain. A former

Lecturer, University of Essex, he has been Visiting Professor at numerous institutions, including the University(ies) of Tel-Aviv, Paris-Dauphine, Aix-Marseille II, Bonn, Paris XII, Aix-en-Provence, Lyon, Strasbourg, and Dijon, the Institut Universitaire Européen (Florence), and the Polish Academy of Sciences. A Fellow of the Econometric Society, he is a member of the council of the Centre d' Études Perspectives d' Économie Mathématique Appliquées à la Planification (Paris) and of the European Economic Association; a member of the program committee of the European Doctoral Program in Quantitative Economics (jointly held by the University of Bonn, London School of Economics, and the Université Catholique de Louvain); and was associate editor of the *Journal of Economic Theory* and *European Economic Review*. His research interests center mainly around imperfect competition in the game-theoretic framework. He has also extended the non-cooperative Cournot model to general equilibrium analysis and has done considerable analyses of models with product differentiation 'à la Hotelling' – areas in which he has published nearly forty research papers.

James K. Galbraith is Associate Professor of Economics, Lyndon B. Johnson School of Public Affairs, University of Texas (Austin). He has taught at the University of Maryland and has been a Visiting Scholar at The Brookings Institution, but for ten years he has been 'contaminated' by practical policy issues in the 'corridors of power', first as economist, Committee on Banking, Finance and Urban Affairs, United States House of Representatives and then as Deputy and Executive Director, Joint Economic Committee, Congress of the United States. Among his other distinctions, he was a Marshall Scholar, King's College, Cambridge and is the son of John Kenneth Galbraith. His many publications center primarily on economic policy, theory of organizations, and various aspects of the French economy and policy. He is also the author of *The Economic Problem* (with R. L. Heilbroner, 1987), and the editor of *Monetary Policy, Selective Credit Policy and Industrial Policy in France, Britain, West Germany and Sweden* (1981), *Expectations and the Economy* (with P. B. Manchester, 1981), and *Monetarism, Inflation and the Federal Reserve* (with D. C. Roberts, 1985).

Augusto Graziani is Professor of Economic Policy, University of Naples. He has been Visiting Professor at the University(ies) of Birmingham, Michigan, and Dijon, and the College de France. A member of the Executive Committee, Italian Economic Association, he serves as a member of the Consulting Committee, *Journal of Economic Literature*. A foremost authority on the development of southern Italy, he has published many articles in Italian, French, and English on the subject and also on money, interest rates, and public spending. He is also the author of

Macroeconomia (in its third edition) and the co-editor of *Studi keynesiani* (with B. Jossa, 1981).

Leonid Hurwicz is Regents' Professor of Economics, University of Minnesota. He is a Distinguished Fellow of the American Economic Association, a Fellow of the American Academy of Arts and Sciences, a Member of the National Academy of Sciences, a Member of the Academy of Independent Scholars, and past president of the Econometric Society. He has been Fellow of the Center for Advanced Study in the Behavioral Sciences and Visiting Professor, the Cowles Commission (University of Chicago), Stanford University, Harvard University (where he was also Frank W. Tausig Visiting Research Professor), University of California (Berkeley), Tokyo University, and in 1984–5 was Sherman Fairchild Distinguished Scholar, California Institute of Technology. In 1980 he was awarded an Honorary Doctor of Science Degree from Northwestern University. A frequent participant in the summer seminars, IMSSS (Stanford), in the last few years he has taught at several universities and institutes of economics in the People's Republic of China. He has made notable contributions to general equilibrium theory, design of mechanisms for resource allocation, and general economic theory and statistics. Among his numerous publications are *Studies in Resource Allocation Processes* (with K. J. Arrow, 1977) and *Social Goals and Social Organization* (ed. with D. Schmeidler and H. Sonnenschein). He has also contributed to *Issues in Contemporary Microeconomics and Welfare* (1985), and *Arrow and the Ascent of Modern Economic Theory* (1987) and *Arrow and the Foundations of the Theory of Economic Policy* (1987).

Robert E. Kuenne is Professor of Economics and Director, General Economic Systems Project, Princeton University. A recipient of an honorary degree from the University of Umea (Sweden), associate editor of *Journal of Regional Science* and a member of the board of editors of *Energy Economics* and *Economic Modelling* his numerous publications range over the fields of general equilibrium theory, oligopoly theory, military systems analysis, operations research, and energy economics. They include *The Theory of General Economic Equilibrium* (1963), *The Attack Submarine: A Study in Strategy* (1965), *The Polaris Missile Strike: A General Economic Systems Analysis* (1967), *Microeconomic Theory of the Market Mechanism: A General Equilibrium Approach* (1968), *Monopolistic Competition Theory: Studies in Impact* (ed., 1968) and *Rivalrous Consonance: A Theory of General Oligopolistic Equilibrium* (1986). He has also contributed to *Issues in Contemporary Microeconomics and Welfare* (1985), and to *Arrow and the Ascent of Modern Economic Theory* (1987).

Mordecai Kurz is Professor of Economics and Director of Economics,

Institute for Mathematical Studies in the Social Sciences (IMSSS), responsible for the annual summer seminar, Stanford University. A Ford Faculty Fellow, Guggenheim Fellow, and Fellow of the Institute for Advanced Studies, the Hebrew University of Jerusalem, he is a Fellow of the Econometric Society and an associate editor of the *Journal of Economic Theory*. Among the many important consulting posts he has held was that of Special Economic Advisor, the President's Commission on Pension Policy. He is the author of more than sixty papers in areas ranging over growth and capital theory, general equilibrium theory, public economics, income distribution, game theory, and labor supply and social policy and of *Components of Economic Growth of National Output* (1967) and *Public Investment, the Rate of Return, and Optimal Fiscal Policy* (with K. J. Arrow, 1970). He is also a contributor to *Issues in Contemporary Microeconomics and Welfare* (1985) and to *Arrow and the Foundations of the Theory of Economic Policy* (1987).

Guy Laroque, Member of the Unité de Recherches, Institut National de la Statistique et des Études Économiques and Maître de Conférences, École Polytechnique, was formerly Dean of Studies (economics), École Nationale de la Statistique et de l'Administration Économique; a Visiting Research Fellow, Harvard University; participant in the summer seminars, IMSSS (Stanford), and in 1973–5 he was responsible for the building of the French quarterly national accounts. A Fellow of the Econometric Society and formerly assistant editor of the *Review of Economic Studies*, he is associate editor of *Econometrica*. He has written more than thirty articles in general equilibrium theory, money and banking, national income accounting, imperfect competition, incentives and planning, Keynesian temporary equilibria, and business cycles. One of his contributions, of particular relevance here is the attempt to incorporate imperfect competition as a central feature of a Keynesian-type model.

Paul Milgrom, formerly Williams Brothers Professor of Management Studies and Professor of Economics, Yale University and Professor, Kellogg Graduate School of Management, Northwestern University, is Professor of Economics, and member of IMSSS Stanford University. A fellow of the Econometric Society, of the Society of Actuaries, of the Institute for Advanced Studies, Hebrew University of Jerusalem, and a Guggenheim Fellow; he has held the IBM Research Chair at Northwestern University and was Ford Visiting Professor of Economics, University of California (Berkeley). He is associate editor, *Journal of Economic Theory* and *Rand Journal of Economics*. A member of the distinguished 'gang of four' (which includes David Kreps, John Roberts, and Robert Wilson), his research uses the game-theoretic approach to the study of information, risk, and market behavior – areas in which he has published nearly thirty papers. He is also the author of *The Structure of Information in Competitive Bidding* (1979).

Franco Modigliani is Institute Professor, Massachusetts Institute of Technology. He has taught at a number of US Universities including Northwestern, Carnegie-Mellon, Illinois, Harvard, and the New School for Social Research. A Research Consultant to the Cowles Commission during its heyday in Chicago, he is a permanent member, Conference on Income and Wealth, National Bureau of Economic Research; member, Consiglio Italiano per le Scienze Sociali; academic consultant, Board of Governors, Federal Reserve system; senior advisor, Brookings Panel on Economic Activity; and consultant to the Bank of Italy. He holds honorary degrees from several institutions, including the University of Chicago and the Université Catholique de Louvain. A Fellow of the American Academy of Arts and Sciences and a Member of the National Academy of Sciences, he has served as president of the Econometric Society, American Finance Association, and American Economic Association, and honorary president of the International Economic Association. In 1985 he was awarded the Alfred Nobel Memorial Prize in Economic Science. His landmark contributions are now available in three volumes of *The Collected Papers of Franco Modigliani* (1980). His other books include *National Income and International Trade* (with H. Neisser, 1953), *Planning Production, Inventories and Work Forces* (with C. C. Holt, J. F. Muth and H. S. Simon, 1960), *The Determinants of National Saving and Wealth* (ed. with R. Hemming, 1983), and *The Debate Over Stabilization Policies and Other Macroeconomic Issues* (1986).

Takashi Negishi is Professor of Economics, University of Tokyo. He was a Research Associate, Applied Mathematics and Statistics Laboratories, Stanford University; Visiting Professor, University of New South Wales; Hill Foundation Visiting Professor, University of Minnesota; Canada Council Visiting Professor, University of British Columbia; and Visiting Lecturer, London School of Economics and Political Science. A Fellow and Council Member of the Econometric Society, and a member of the Science Council of Japan, he has won the Nikkei Prize for Best Books in Economics in 1973 and the Matsunaga Science Foundation Prize for the Social Sciences in 1977. He has served as president of the Japanese Association of Economics and Econometrics and associate editor of the *International Economic Review*, *Econometrica*, and the *Journal of International Economics*. His many publications range over the fields of general equilibrium theory, international trade, imperfect competition, welfare economics, and monetary theory. They include *General Equilibrium Theory and International Trade* (1972), *Microeconomic Foundations of Keynesian Macroeconomics* (1979), and *Economic Theories in a Non-Walrasian Tradition* (1985). He has also contributed to *Issues in Contemporary Macroeconomics and Distribution* (1985); and *Arrow and the Ascent of Modern Economic Theory* (1987).

John Roberts is Jonathan B. Lovelace Professor of Economics and Associate Dean for Academic Affairs, Graduate School of Business, Stanford University. Formerly Professor of Managerial Economics and Decision Sciences, Kellogg Graduate School of Management, Northwestern University, he was a Visiting Faculty Research Fellow, Center for Operations Research and Econometrics, Université Catholique de Louvain; a Visiting Lecturer, École Nationale de la Statistique et des Études Économiques; and on two occasions Visiting Fellow, Institute for Advanced Studies, Hebrew University of Jerusalem. A Fellow of the Econometric Society, he is associate editor of the *Journal of Economic Theory* and *Econometrica.* A member of the distinguished 'gang of four' (which includes David Kreps, Paul Milgrom, and Robert Wilson), he uses the game-theoretic approach to study imperfect competition, information, and unemployment; incentives and planning, and public goods – fields in which he has written about fifty research papers. He is also a contributor to *Arrow and the Ascent of Modern Economic Theory* (1987).

Ariel Rubinstein is Professor of Economics, the Hebrew University at Jerusalem. A former Research Fellow, Nuffield College, Oxford, he has also held various visiting positions at Bell Laboratories, Mathematical Sciences Research Institute (Berkeley), London School of Economics, Institute for International Economic Studies (Stockholm), and on several occasions IMSSS (Stanford). A Fellow of the Econometric Society, he is a member of the editorial board of *Review of Economic Studies* and associate editor of *Econometrica* and *Journal of Economic Theory.* A foremost young contributor to game theory, he has written more than thirty scientific papers in diverse areas of the subject including theory of bargaining, strategies of conflict resolution, prisoner's dilemma, risk, incomplete information, and social choice.

Steven M. Sheffrin, a product of MIT, is Professor and Chairman, Department of Economics, University of California (Davis). A Brookings Economic Policy Fellow, he has served in the Office of Tax Analysis, US Treasury. He has written about thirty articles in macroeconomics, human resources, and tax policy. He is also the author of *Rational Expectations* (1983) – a well-received book that has been translated into Spanish, French, and Japanese – and *Macroeconomics* (with D. Wilton and D. Prescott, 1988).

Joaquim Silvestre, a student of John Chipman at the University of Minnesota, formerly at the Universitat Autonoma de Barcelona, is

Professor of Economics, University of California (Davis). He was Visiting Scholar, University of California (Berkeley), and Visiting Professor, University of California (San Diego). He is the author of a number of articles whose focus is primarily imperfect competition, the fix price model, and public goods.

Robert M. Solow is Institute Professor, MIT, where he has taught throughout his career. He was a Senior Staff Economist, President Kennedy's Council of Economic Advisers; Eastman Visiting Professor and Fellow, Balliol College, Oxford; and Overseas Fellow, Churchill College, Cambridge. A recipient of nearly ten honorary degrees (including the University(ies) of Chicago, Paris I, and Geneva) he received the John Bates Clark Medal of the American Economic Association and the 1987 Alfred Nobel Memorial Prize in Economic Science. He has served as president of the Econometric Society, the American Economic Association, and the Eastern Economic Association. He is a Fellow of the American Academy of Arts and Sciences, Corresponding Fellow of the British Academy, and Member, National Academy of Sciences. A worthy opponent of Joan Robinson in the capital controversy, he has contributed significantly to growth theory and macroeconomics. Among his many publications are *Linear Programming and Economic Analysis* (with R. Dorfman and P. A. Samuelson, 1958), *Capital Theory and the Rate of Return* (1965), *The Nature and Sources of Unemployment in the US* (1964), and *Growth Theory: An Exposition* (1969).

Joseph E. Stiglitz is Professor of Economic, Princeton University. Formerly Drummond Professor of Political Economy, Oxford University and Professor of Economics, Stanford University and Yale University, he was Oskar Morgenstern Distinguished Fellow and Visiting Professor, Institute for Advanced Studies and Mathematics; Visiting Fellow, St Catherine's College, Oxford; Visiting Professor, University of Canterbury (New Zealand), and Tapp Research Fellow, Gonville and Caius College, Cambridge. A Guggenheim and Fulbright Fellow, he is a Fellow of the Econometric Society and of the American Academy of Arts and Sciences and recipient of the John Bates Clark medal of the American Economic Association. A former associate editor of the *Journal of Economic Theory* and *American Economic Review* and American editor of the *Review of Economic Studies*, he is associate editor of *Energy Economics* and *Managerial and Decision Economics* and co-editor of the *Journal of Public Economics*. He is the author of nearly two hundred papers in a very broad range of fields covering the economics of information, uncertainty (basic concepts, market equilibrium, risk and agriculture, portfolio analysis, and theory of corporate finance), theory of taxation, public economics, distribution of income and wealth, growth and capital theory, natural resources, development and trade, macroeconomics, and the theory of imperfect competition. He is also the co-author of *The Theory of Commodity Price Stabilization* (with D. Newberry, 1981), *Lectures in Public Economics* (with A. B. Atkinson, 1980), co-editor of *New Developments in the Theory of Market Structure* (with E. Mathewson, 1985) and has recently published a textbook on *Economics of the Public Sector* (1986). He is also a contributor to *Arrow and the Foundations of the Theory of Economic Policy* (1987).

John Sutton is Reader, London School of Economics. He has taught at the University(ies) of Sheffield, Tokyo, and California (San Diego), and has been a Visiting Scholar at MIT. He is a member of the editorial board of *Review of Economic Studies* and an associate editor of *Econometrica*. He has written more than twenty-five papers in the areas of imperfect competition, information, international trade, unemployment and inflation, and income distribution. He is also the author of *Protection and Industrial Policy in Europe* (with J. Pearce, 1986).

Lorie Tarshis is chairman, Department of Economics, Glendon College, York University (Canada). He has taught at Tufts University; Stanford University; and Scarborough College, University of Toronto, and served as Research Director, Ontario Economic Council. A Guggenheim Fellow and Fulbright Fellow, he has been Visiting Professor, University of Washington, University of British Columbia, and Tokyo University. A member of Keynes's Political Economy Club, a student of Keynes, and in touch with the members of the 'Circus' he was a research scholar at Trinity College during the fateful years when the *General Theory* was being written and immediately after its publication. He was one of the first to bring 'Keynes to America' and cooperated (with Emile Despres, Walter Salant, Paul Sweezy, and others) in a tract on fiscal policy *An Economic Program for American Democracy* (1938) which influenced Roosevelt advisors. Soon after the war he published the widely acclaimed Keynesian textbook *Elements of Economics*, a book that came under strong right-wing attack in the McCarthy era and that had a second incarnation as *Modern Economics* in 1966. His many accomplishments include work in international economics and finance. He is also the author of *Mobilizing Resources for War* (with T. Scitovsky and E. S. Shaw, 1951), *International Economics* (1955), and *The US Balance of Payments in 1964* (with W. Salant *et al.*, 1962).

Jacques-François Thisse is Professor of Economics and member of the Center for Operations Research and Econometrics, Université Catholique de Louvain. He has been Visiting Professor at a number of institutions, including the University(ies) of Dijon, Strasbourg, Copenhagen, and Pennsylvania; European Institute for Advanced Studies in Management (Brussels); and Distinguished Visiting Professor, McMaster University (Canada). He is associate editor of *Regional Science and Urban Economics*,

Annales d'Économie et de la Statistique, and *Recherches Économiques de Louvain*. He has authored about about sixty articles in mathematical economics, imperfect competition (especially product differentiation), market structure, location theory, and transportation. He is also the author of *Analyse mathématique pour l'économie* (with L. A. Gérard-Varet and J. Perreur, 1976).

Jan Tinbergen, the first recipient (together with Ragnar Frisch) of the Nobel Memorial Prize in Economic Science (1969), is Professor Emeritus, Erasmus University – the former Netherlands School of Economics where he was Professor of Development Planning until 1973. He was also Claveringa Professor of International Cooperation at Leiden University from 1973 to 1975. He was formerly Director, Central Planning Bureau, Netherlands Government and advisor to various governments and the United Nations on development problems. A recipient of some twenty honorary degrees and many other awards and prizes, he contributed vastly in the areas of econometric business-cycle research, economic policy and welfare economics, development planning, and income distribution. His many books include *Statistical Testing of Business Cycle Theories*, 2 vols (1939, 1968), *Centralization and Decentralization in Economic Policy* (1954), *Economic Policy: Principles and Design* (1956, 1967), *Development Planning* (1967), *Income Distribution: Analysis and Policies* (1975), *Production, Income and Welfare* (1986), *Mathematical Models of Economic Growth* (with H. C. Bos, 1962), and *Warfare and Welfare: Integrating Security Policy into Socio-economic Policy* (with D. Fischer, forthcoming). He is also a contributor to *Issues in Contemporary Macroeconomics and Distribution* (1985), and *Arrow and the Foundations of the Theory of Economic Policy* (1987).

James Tobin is Sterling Professor of Economics, Yale University. He was the first Director of the Cowles Foundation for Research in Economics when it made the crucial move from Chicago to Yale. In 1961–2 he was a Member of President Kennedy's Council of Economic Advisors and over the years has served as consultant to the Council, The Federal Reserve System, and the US Treasury. A recipient of the John Bates Clark medal of the American Economic Association, he was awarded the Alfred Nobel Memorial Prize in Economic Science in 1981. A member of the National Academy of Science, he has served as president of the Econometric Society, the American Economic Association, and the Eastern Economic Association. He was educated at Harvard University where he was elected Junior Fellow of the Society of Fellows, spending the last year of his tenure at the Department of Applied Economics, University of Cambridge. He has written more than two hundred articles in macroeconomics, monetary theory and policy, fiscal policy and public finance, consumption and saving, unemployment and inflation, portfolio theory and asset markets, and econometrics. His rich contributions are only partly reflected in collected volumes entitled *Essays in Economics: Macroeconomics* (1972, 1987), *Essays in Economics: Consumption and Econometrics* (1975), and in *National Economic Policy* (1966), *The New Economics One Decade Older* (1974), and *Asset Accumulation and Economic Activity* (1980). He is also a contributor to *Issues in Contemporary Macroeconomics and Distribution* (1985).

Martin L. Weitzman is Professor of Economics, Massachusetts Institute of Technology where he also holds the Mitsui Professorship. He has taught at Yale University and in 1986–7 has been Visiting Professor at Harvard University. A Fellow of the Econometric Society and Guggenheim Fellow, he is associate editor of *Journal of Comparative Economics*, *Economic Letters*, and *Journal of Japanese Economy*. He has written numerous articles in economic theory and comparative economics (broadly defined) to which he has applied sophisticated mathematical techniques (two of which have been co-authored with Soviet colleagues and published in Russian). More specifically, his work studies economic planning, optimal growth theory, and developments in the Soviet economy (applying production-function analysis). He has analyzed the choice between price and quantity instruments and optimal resource allocation with increasing returns. In his famous *The Share Economy* (1984), he has argued that stagflation essentially results from the wage system and largely disappears in profit-sharing capitalist economies.

John K. Whitaker, a student of R. C. O. Matthews and R. M. Goodwin at the University of Cambridge, is Professor of Economics, University of Virginia. Formerly Professor of Economics, University of Bristol; Visiting Bateman Lecturer, University of Western Australia; and Honorary Research Fellow, Birbeck College, University of London; he has served as President of the History of Economics Society and as assistant editor, *Review of Economic Studies*. He is a member of the editorial board of *History of Political Economy* and *Journal of Economic Literature*. A foremost authority on Alfred Marshall, he has also written on business cycles and growth theory, capital theory, and monetary economics. He is the author of *The Early Economic Writings of Alfred Marshall, 1867–1890*, 2 vols. (1975) and is currently editing two volumes of the correspondence of Alfred Marshall. He is also a contributor to *Arrow and the Foundations of the Theory of Economic Policy* (1987).

Robert Wilson is Atholl McBean Professor of Decision Sciences, Graduate School of Business, Stanford University. He has taught at the University of California (Los Angeles) and was Visiting Professor, Université Catholique de Louvain. A Ford Foundation Faculty Research Fellow and Guggenheim Fellow, he was also a Fellow of the Center for Advanced Study in the Behavioral Sciences. He is a Fellow of the Econometric Society and of the American Academy of Arts and Sciences and an associate editor of *Econometrica*. He has published more than sixty papers in general equilibrium theory, game theory, uncertainty, and information. A member of the distinguished 'gang of four' (which includes David Kreps, Paul Milgrom, and John Roberts), his research studies in particular, the role of information in markets and organizations and its effects on strategic behavior, and the design of efficient institutions. He has also contributed to *Issues in Contemporary Microeconomics and Welfare* (1985) and to *Arrow and the Ascent of Modern Economic Theory* (1987).

Preface

With the passing of Joan Robinson a vital flame has gone out of economics. We are all the poorer for it. We all recognize that there was more than one Joan Robinson. She means different things to different people. There were different Joans at any one time and different Joans in time. The dynamics of change in Joan can be considered an ascending or descending trend or even a growth cycle, given the beholders' preconceptions and predispositions.

There was Joan Robinson who initially was fascinated by economic theory as an essentially tool-making process (the subject matter of economics 'is neither more nor less than its own technique' (Joan Robinson, 1932, p.3)), and who later in life revolted against developing a fully-fledged alternative theory to neoclassical economics on the grounds that it would only be another box of tricks. She stressed that what economic theory needs now is a different way of thinking: 'to eschew fudging, to respect facts and to admit ignorance of what we do not know' (1979, p.119). There was Joan, the challenging critic, asking profound questions, but often providing no more than hints to answers. She said of Myrdal (whom she admired) that he saw problems more clearly than solutions and of Sraffa that he was far more negative than positive. *Mutatis mutandis*, the same could be said of her.

There was Joan Robinson, the great Marshallian, trying to escape Marshall's moralizing and fudging, who broke out of the 'Marshallian incubus' and wrote the neoclassical, tool-making *Economics of Imperfect Competition* in Pigovian tradition, inspired by Sraffa's pregnant suggestions and sacrilegious questioning of Marshall.

There was Joan Robinson who at times showed a remarkable grasp of the grand conception of general economic interdependence and asked searching questions about the limitations of Walrasian general equilibrium theory, while she sometimes downgraded its usefulness and its historical achievement.

There was Joan Robinson, political economist *par excellence* in the best Cambridge tradition, who was inspired and enthused by the unique experience and opportunity of participating in Keynes's Circus and who became a formative figure in the Keynesian revolution. There was Joan who increasingly perceived the Keynesian revolution through Kaleckian eyes. Loyal to Keynes her mentor, she increasingly reinterpreted his great teaching in the Kaleckian mode.

There was Joan Robinson, the contributor and interpreter of the Keynesian revolution on the theoretical plane, who incessantly sought to go beyond the *General Theory*; to generalize it into a long-term theory of employment and to 'open' it to an open economy.

There was the Joan Robinson of *The Accumulation of Capital*, a great model builder, who fully understood the need to simplify drastically and was accused of unnecessary abstraction. There was the Joan of the very formalistic book with at least one foot in the mainstream, who seethed with new ideas and concentrated on large themes, but whose execution fell short of the mark in articulating her conception of the vicissitudes of the capitalist economy. To paraphrase Pigou, when a person has devised a new way of climbing a mountain, we may indeed regret that her way has not led to the top, but for the effort that has advanced her towards the top nothing is due but praise.

There was Joan Robinson who perceived economic processes as a Keynesian (Kaleckian) and was critical of Sraffa's prelude to a critique of economic theory. Yet, she was attracted to and influenced by the Sraffian approach and vacillated between Keynesian and Sraffian themes. There was Joan who reinstated Marx as an economist and made his reproduction schemes respectable, while committing the 'sacrilege' of debunking his labor theory of value.

There was Joan Robinson, the astute theoretician in the Cambridge tradition, innocent of sophisticated mathematics in the age of mathematization of economic theory. As she (1979, p.115) said of herself. 'I had a very literary education and to this day I know only the mathematics that I was able to pick up in the course of trying to formalize economic arguments'. She knew some calculus, was brilliant at geometry, knew elementary differential equations, was at home in ordinary algebra and knew the basics of matrix algebra. She understood elementary statistics and the rudiments of econometrics. (She understood the mathematics of reswitching and she saw it intuitively long before anyone except Sraffa had worked it out. She worked out the Golden Rule geometrically without recourse to differential equations, as she did in her critique of the Solow-Swan approach.)

She was gifted with remarkable intuitive and analytical powers and an exceptionally logical mind. She had the enthusiasm of the creatively destructive innovator and pursued a relentless quest to get the logical arguments right. She emerged as a respected, technically competent analytical economist in an age when progress in economics is frequently measured by the sophistication of the contributions to techniques of economic analysis.

There was Joan Robinson who argued that mathematics is a powerful tool of thought, but that its application to economic theory often consists of putting circular arguments into sophisticated mathematical forms. There was Joan who knew her comparative advantage. When asked by Ragnar Frisch to be vice-president of the Econometric Society, she declined the honor on the grounds that it would do no good for her name to appear on the cover of a journal when she could not understand anything inside it. She was annoyed by the modern neoclassical practitioners who take refuge in building increasingly elaborate mathematical manipulations and who resent anyone asking them what it is they are supposed to be manipulating. In her hostility to sophisticated mathematical economics, she unfortunately did not trouble to differentiate between the trivial niceties and the substantive advances in economic content. She wanted to think about the economic issues and did not want to be distracted by what she considered to be purely mathematical questions which, as a matter of division of labor, she preferred to leave to others. There was Joan who believed that the success of economics depends more on insight than precision and that its affinity must be with history as much as with mathematics.

There was Joan Robinson who criticized economic theory for being far removed from reality, abstract, formalistic, esoteric, and all that, while Joan, the theorist, committed similar sins. She was hypercritical of the pervasive concept of equilibrium in economic theory, while she herself used it to advantage in *The Accumulation of Capital.* She was particularly critical of the drawing of practical conclusions from equilibrium analysis, which she did not do.

There was the unfashionable and fierce Joan Robinson who did not appeal to some fledgeling economists because she did not communicate in their language, while telling them that anyway their language is unsuitable for economics, and/or who irritated them by telling them what they had no wish to hear. But there was also Joan the great teacher who influenced her students in subtle ways. She taught them to think for themselves; she injected them with a healthy dose of scepticism; she showed them how to discuss economic theory without resorting to mathematical symbols; and, above all, she fired them with earnestness for their subject.

There was Joan who, in an age when many of her peers tended to concentrate their energies on narrow subjects amenable to mathematically-complicated 'easy' answers, embarked on difficult broad questions to which she did not always have answers. There was Joan in whose work history, institutions, anthropology, politics, and philosophy all played an important role. She (1979, p.118) admitted that 'history can never give a final knockdown answer to any question. Each generation rewrites its own past in accord with its current ideology'. However, she believed 'that there is a lot of difference between good analysis and bad, apart from ideological tendencies'.

There was Joan who came to economics because she hoped to find in it answers to the plight of the poor and who remained in economics fired by social enthusiasm. She tried to show how orthodox theory fails to understand how the capitalist economy works. She sought to establish that government policy had the capacity to improve economic performance and to make society more humane and just. But in her work there is little directly about policy. The argument is implied. While she had an exaggerated view of the potency of intelligent argument, she increasingly came to realize that economic answers are but political questions.

There was Joan the social critic who, in her search for a better world, aligned herself with alternative social designs that appeared to promulgate a better society. Her critics have made much of this, and it may have lost her the Nobel Prize. But we should respect the fact that even in old age she retained a youthful ability to respond with enthusiasm to the promise of a dream. She did not always see the grim realities at first, but when she came to see them – as she always did, for she was as severe a critic of political ideology as of economic ideology – she was merciless in denouncing them. Like many Europeans, she was revolted by certain aspects of the US establishment (social, political, and intellectual) – a feeling that spilled over into economics. She strongly denounced the creation of prosperity by building up the arsenal of military hardware. And she was critical, even contemptuous of 'Hollywood culture'; unlike the French she could not see any value in its creations.

There was Joan Robinson, the great expositor, truly guilty of 'Koopmans's sin' of lucid and persuasive use of language, who, in a few well-chosen words, could rout her opponents. She was a master of controversy. An apt pupil of Keynes, she was blunt spoken and disregarded the niceties of social intercourse. She was a campaigner and preacher in Cambridge-style earnestness, seeker after truth, incorruptible, fiercely courageous, and honest.

There was Joan Robinson of the mordant sense of humor, the antagonist who did not always play cricket, and the forbidding and austere personality. But there was also Joan, the warm and devoted friend whose limpid and sparkling blue eyes and wicked smile conveyed warmth and often said more than mere words could express.

Yes, she was irritating, irascible, intolerant, impractical, angry, difficult, dictatorial, and domineering. But she was also inspiring, incisive, insightful, ingenious, independent, indomitable, and pertinacious; a shrewd and subtle thinker, dedicated to her cause. She had a special blend of vigor, fervor, tenacity, persuasiveness and polemical brilliance in arguing her position. She represented economics at its best, urged us to think for ourselves, and showed us the strengths and limits of economic theorizing. She also showed us what great satisfaction could be derived when economics is put to higher uses for the betterment of mankind. For this and much more she could serve as an admirable figure for future economists to emulate.

Samuelson (1966, p.1593) aptly noted: 'Cambridge economists, God bless them, also deserve justice; and since they cannot always be counted on to pour it on each other in buckets, it is up to us barbarians to join in the rituals'. It is in this spirit that he (1970, p.397) went on to extol his most faithful and severe critic:

> If an ignoramus in economics says that the current economic system cannot be interpreted as a rational scheme, that is nothing. But if one of the greatest analytical economists of our era says this, she is worth listening to. Joan Robinson ... won fame young as one of the inventors of the theory of imperfect competition. She consolidated her worldwide reputation by becoming one of the leading contributors to the Keynesian macroeconomic literature ... In recent decades Mrs. Robinson has been an important pioneer and critic of growth models. For any of these accomplishments she might well be awarded the Nobel Prize in Economics.

And in his masterly introduction (Chapter 2) to *Joan Robinson and Modern Economic Theory*, Paul shows why Joan was a scholar who will enjoy a permanent niche in the Pantheon of economic science.

Reluctant 'admirer', Bronfenbrenner (1979, p.446), comments:

> Voltaire is supposed to have said "I do not agree with a word you say, but shall defend to the death your right to say it." May I paraphrase him, speaking as a "bastard Keynesian" purveyor of "rubbish" and "stinking fish"? I do not agree with most of what Joan Robinson has been saying these past forty years, but hope she wins a Nobel Prize for saying it." Mrs. Robinson has done more than any other contemporary economist (Milton Friedman being her only rival) to save our discipline from ossified cut-and-driedness; also it occasionally occurs to me that she may be right about some matters in dispute, or that some of my favourite fish may be getting a trifle over-ripe with age.

A far more reluctant 'admirer' – one whose views were the butt of Joan's virulent attacks – Milton Friedman (1986, p.77) mused that for economists 'the most important thing to do if you want to be a Nobel laureate is to be a male'. But, he adds

> the absence of females is not, I believe, attributable to male chauvinist bias on the part of the Swedish Nobel Committee. I believe that the economics profession as a whole would have been nearly unanimous that, during the period in question, only one female candidate met the relevant standards – the English economist Joan Robinson, who has since died. The failure of the Nobel Committee to award her a prize may well have reflected bias but not sex bias.

That Joan Robinson's influence on the development of modern economics is much greater than is commonly recognized, the contributions to these two volumes, coming as they do from different streams of thought, eloquently attest. This is not a forum for only those who agree with Joan to pay her tribute. Indeed, she dedicated one of her books (*What are the Questions?*) to her critics and here is an opportunity for both her admirers and critics to reciprocate. As she was the first to admit, a real compliment to a scholar is paid when his/her work is taken seriously and critically. She would have hated hagiography and would have considered it condescending. While Joan cared not at all for self-promotion and embarked on no ego trips, she cared much for how her ideas were received by those who disagreed with her. In these two volumes we try to pay tribute to her memory by taking her ideas, themes and concerns seriously as they deserve to be taken and to convey the advances, lacunae, and vicissitudes of the subject she made most particularly her own. Joan would have especially appreciated the essays by her critics and we are all saddened that the voice that would have answered them so well is stilled.

INTRODUCTION TO THE TWO VOLUMES

Joan Robinson and Modern Economic Theory

There are many paradoxes in the economics of Joan Robinson. In Chapter 1 we provide some clues to help us solve the riddles. She was one of the original architects of the imperfect competition revolution and a creative participant of the Keynesian revolution whose ideas she later attempted to generalize and reconstruct. In this chapter we make a selective attempt at conveying Joan Robinson's perspective on economic theory and policy and to touch only on the opposing positions. We first look at her formative years as an economist and her first steps in her 'long struggle' to escape from Marshall and Pigou which culminated in her first *magnum opus* and discuss the grounds on which she later repudiated it. We then proceed to some aspects of the Keynesian revolution and her later attempts at extending it to the long run. In the next section we present the gist of the capital controversies. Thereafter we pause only selectively on her views on the state of economic theory, the questions asked by modern economists, and her attitude towards alternative approaches.

It is a distinct privilege to present the reader with a complementary introduction – the masterful and reflective Chapter 2 by Paul Samuelson – one of the main contestants of the capital controversies and the target of much of Joan's ascerbic criticism. This insightful and sympathetic essay, intended by Paul as a scholarly assessment and a tribute to Joan, is quite revealing about the author himself. Samuelson recalls that in his lifetime as an economist 'Joan Robinson was always there at the frontier of science'. He considers Joan's work on Marxian economics as the dividing line between her early work on imperfect competition and the theory of employment and her post-war work in growth, distribution and capital theory. It is 'particularly her work in the foundations of capital theory' that Samuelson regards 'as valuable and constructive'. He also emphasizes Joan's analysis of the rising supply price as a 'first case of a scholar in the Marshallian tradition breaking through to sight the Pacific of general equilibrium analysis'. He discusses Sraffa's 1926 bombshell about increasing returns and his inspiration for the imperfect competition and adds: 'Joan and Piero may not have much liked the Egypt of constant returns to scale, but it was not vouchsafed for them to pass in their lifetimes to the Canaan of increasing returns to scale.' Samuelson touches with first-hand knowledge on the personalities of Chamberlin, Schumpeter, Kahn, Sraffa, Pigou, and, of course, Joan Robinson and his interaction with them. He deplores the fact that Joan Robinson actually did not have a clear-cut income distribution theory. He then undertakes a simplified thought experiment involving the 'ultra surrogate' capital model. Samuelson emphasizes how much he learned from Joan in the capital controversies. 'Beyond the effect of rallying the spirits of economists disliking the market order, these Robinson–Sraffa–Pasinetti–Garegnani contributions deepen our understanding of how a time-phased competitive micro-system works.' He also mentions Joan's political leanings, loyalties, and independence of spirit and reminds us that she 'will be long remembered for her originality and breadth – and for the person she was'.

Part I provides a background for analyzing Joan Robinson's work and an insight into how her critique and work affected that of others. It is gratifying to open it with Arrow – who shares with her 'a critical attitude to the existing structure', though they did not agree in their perspectives on economic analysis. In Chapter 3, Arrow shares with us his profound thoughts on a broad range of subjects. He discusses authoritatively developments in modern economic theory, particularly as they relate to Joan Robinson's work. He speaks of Walrasian intertemporal equilibrium and the steady state and the problems of getting into equilibrium (stability analysis). He clarifies the term equilibrium in the Walrasian, Marshallian, Ricardian, and Keynesian sense. He praises Joan for having forced the question of heterogeneity of capital. He then proceeds to questions of income distribution: he denies a connection between the capital controversies and views on income distribution, he contends that the distributional implications of marginal productivity theory are much weaker than they appear, and he speaks of income inequalities within the labor force – a topic he considers more serious in our times than questions of functional distribution. Arrow is critical of Sraffian economics as a new paradigm. He speaks of the rift between micro and macro economics and of the difficulty of theoretical integration when one is convinced, as he is, 'that there *really* is disequilibrium in the sense of non-market clearing', and criticizes the new classical macroeconomics. Arrow then discusses the difficulties of integrating imperfect competition into the general equilibrium system and the relationship of imperfect competition and imperfect information. He suggests how much economists can learn from the problems of computation and measures of differential complexity of different kinds of computation being debated currently by mathematicians and computer scientists. He then turns to growth theory and casts doubts on the validity of a problem of long-run effective demand. He disputes (Joan Robinson's and others') identification of neoclassical economics with capitalist apologetics. 'As one who has had, and still has, a socialist bias of some not very clear kind . . . I do not feel that I adopted neoclassical economics *because* it defended capitalism.' Arrow then speaks of Joan's criticism of mainstream economics and of the insuperable difficulties in tackling some important problems. Finally, he concentrates on evaluating Joan's approach to economic theory, her attitude as social and economic critic, and offers glimpses of her personality that impressed him.

In Chapter 4, Hammond – a former student of Joan who, though she did not prevent him from becoming a leading neoclassical and welfare economist, at least taught him to doubt and to discuss theory without necessarily using mathematics (though he is adept at both) – casts a critical look at the assumptions underlying his own chosen field. Inspired by the writings of Joan Robinson, especially her books *Economic Philosophy* and *Economic Heresies*, and liberally spiced with relevant quotations from many of her works, Hammond discusses the following assumptions, all of which – except the last – are all too commonly found within neoclassical economics: (1) assumptions are not to be compared with reality; (2) consumer sovereignty; (3) unbounded rationality; (4) unbounded foresight; (5) unbounded cooperation; (6) Pareto efficiency is sufficient for ethical acceptability; (7) the distribution of wealth is ethically acceptable; (8) consumers can survive without trade; (9) income effects are negligible; (10) Pareto efficiency is necessary for ethical acceptability; (11) there is a representative consumer; (12) distortionary taxes create deadweight losses; (13) domestic public expenditure programs are wasteful; (14) transfer programs confer no benefits; (15) capital markets are perfect; (16) anticipated monetary and fiscal policies are ineffective; (17) inflation is caused by an expanding money supply; (18) there is a representative worker; (19) the current level of unemployment is ethically acceptable; (20) there is a representative capital good; (21) product markets are perfectly competitive or at least contestable (22) neoclassical economics need not be theological.

In the next chapter (5), Klein acknowledges that Joan Robinson's claim to fame is for her ingenious handling of intricate and subtle problems of capital theory, employment theory, imperfect competition, Marxian theory, and many other subjects quite beyond the uninitiated. But, Klein contends, Book I of her *Accumulation of Capital* 'is truly a masterful statement of economic principles, especially principles of macroeconomics, that could serve better than almost any other "Principles" textbook in laying bare the fundamental aspects of our subject to the beginner'. Klein stresses that from Joan Robinson the student will learn a great deal about the structure of the capitalist economy, its differences from the socialist one, and how the various macroeconomic departments of the total system fit together. The student could also learn not to be overly pedantic and to settle for some common-sense distinctions. She provides the maximum framework that is still institution-free. She distills the essence of the working of the credit market and castigates unproductive financial speculation. She points to the various sources of personal income and makes the clear distinction between income and wealth. She points to the intrinsic difficulties of measuring wealth and of providing an index number for measuring purchasing power. In discussing financial market strategies, she demonstrates a clear grasp of the fundamentals of portfolio management. She fully recognizes and appreciates the role of profit as a driving force in the capitalist economy. In her consumption and investment schema she clearly perceives the double-edged role of savings and points to the paradoxical nature of the capitalist system and the role of thrift in it. There is also an excellent early appreciation of the role of expectations and their relation to decision making in a dynamic system. She develops the highly abstract and unrealistic conditions of tranquillity, lucidity, and harmony. If such conditions were to prevail, she reasons, there would have been no incentives for entrepreneurs to break out in new directions. But if the disturbances were too severe, the economy would have collapsed. She acknowledges that some coherence is embedded in all the confusion.

In view of Joan Robinson's critical attitude towards the mathematization of economic theory, the explanation of the historical development of mathematical economics by no less an authority than Gerard Debreu is particularly relevant. In Chapter 6, Debreu considers the changes in the mathematical form of theoretic models of an economy during the past four decades, and the growth of mathematical economics in that period in relation to each other and to the development of the profession. He then examines the fit of the mathematical form to the economic content of theoretic models, their separation in a completed axiomatic theory and their interplay in its elaboration. He also analyzes the consequence of the axiomatization of economic theory.

In Chapter 7, Goodwin – a close associate of Joan's during 'the age of capital theory' – aims to put forth in simple, plausible form the dynamics of a capitalist economy. This is what Joan devoted most of the latter half of her life to developing in a new and stimulating way. Chapter 7 is phrased in simple mathematical form – a form Joan neither approved of nor was at ease with. Nevertheless, Goodwin attempts to follow along the path on which Joan strove unceasingly to amplify Keynes's central message. Whilst avoiding the manifold complexities of reality, Goodwin attempts to make precise the basic conception (with some complications) of the notion that investment determines demand which, in turn, determines investment, keeping in mind that this is not always so.

Part II deals with one of Joan Robinson's major critiques of modern economics – the problem of stability or as she called it 'getting into equilibrium'. It opens with Chapter 8 where Gram points to Joan Robinson's arguments that 'the lack of comprehensible treatment of historical time, and the failure to specify the rules of the game in the type of economy under discussion' renders useless the bulk of traditional economic theory. Gram suggests that a perfectly coherent basis for this indictment is to be found within the structure of general equilibrium theory itself, a theory that adroitly finesses the problems raised by Robinson either by treating them as formal difficulties (to be solved by an appropriate choice of assumptions), or by reformulating them in ways that appear to leave them permanently on the agenda for further research. Robinson saw in the fascination with equilibrium analysis a misguided refusal to recognize the unavoidable ideological component in economic analysis and an unwillingness to come to terms with the fact that the present is a break in time between the unpredicted consequences of an irrevocable past and the unpredictable developments of an unknowable future. For these reasons she saw economic theory as cutting itself off from making any useful contribution to the discussion of contemporary problems.

In Chapter 9, Walsh offers a note on Joan Robinson's specific objections to the notion of 'getting into equilibrium', in both short- and long-period contexts. He argues that recent work, of which Robinson might not have approved, nevertheless lends support to some of her contentions. In the short period, what she objected to was a perfectly competitive equilibrium, with all markets clearing, of the sort found in an elementary time interval of a standard neo-Walrasian model. Certain recent models of temporary or quasi-equilibrium, where firms set prices and quantity rationing may arise, may represent the beginnings of a theoretical development ultimately capable of meeting some of her objections. In the context of the long period, Walsh argues that Robinson did not in fact change her views concerning Sraffa at the end of her life. Rather, he suggests, she had *always* accepted the Sraffa system as a snapshot of a model *in* long-period equilibrium, and had *always* rejected the view of it as the culmination of a real world process of gravitation. He argues that certain recent studies of gravitation (or more properly convergence) to equilibrium in the context of formal models show that even in this highly simplified context 'getting into equilibrium,' in the sense of a long-period position with reproduction prices, is highly problematical. He qualifies this argument by noting that work on gravitation has shown that, in the case of certain very simple modern classical models, a formal process of convergence to equilibrium *can* be specified, so that Robinson's claim needs some qualification.

Chapter 10 elucidates the problems of 'getting into equilibrium' by one of the leading modern specialists in stability analysis. Frank Fisher discusses the similarities and differences of stability analysis in microeconomic and macroeconomic settings. He then elaborates on the notion of equilibrium and on the serious difficulties of incorporating *real* dynamics into economic theory. He disputes the notion that the concept of equilibrium is inapplicable to study an economy primarily characterized by change. He stresses the 'big gaping hole in the center of what economists know, namely, the question of what happens out of equilibrium and whether we ever get close to equilibrium'. He considers it an 'important gaping hole because most of what we do depends on assuming that it is not a problem. And we really have very little basis for that'.

In Chapter 11, Nell argues that the concept of 'temporary equilibrium' is defective because it does not allow for the formation of a rate of profit on capital; long-run equilibrium, on the other hand, does. But the same forces that tend to form a rate of profit also require balanced growth; moreover, the rate of growth and the rate of profit are connected through income distribution. Different social classes have different propensities to save, and so will tend to accumulate wealth at different rates. However, long-run equilibrium requires that the relative wealth of the different social classes remain constant; the different components of wealth cannot grow at different rates. If they did, then under plausible assumptions, the rich would become richer, and the poor, relatively poorer. Long-run equilibrium is therefore, according to Nell, not the appropriate concept for the analysis of capitalism, which would be better based on a classical–Marxian examination of the economic structure and its laws of motion.

Perforce in this book Sraffa enters in different guises. In the preface to his *magnum opus*, Sraffa wrote that his book is only a prelude to a critique of economic theory (as the subtitle indicates) and that he leaves it up to others, somewhat younger and better equipped to the task, to attempt a full-scale critique. Though I do not mean to imply that Sraffa had Garegnani in mind, we could not have called on anyone better qualified than Piero Garegnani who in Chapter 12 not only offers us the Sraffian perspective, but differentiates his position from Joan Robinson. Garegnani's dispute with Joan was sparked off in 1976 by his remark about a convergence between her and Samuelson's positions on the impossibility of analyzing changes in the economy by means of the traditional comparison between 'normal positions' of the system. Joan Robinson reacted to this by writing a short comment, reproduced as Appendix I of Chapter 12. Garegnani's reply constitutes the major part of the chapter and her rejoinder is printed as Appendix II. In particular, in the major part of Chapter 12, Garegnani focuses on three issues. The first pertains to the implications of the criticism of the traditional concept of capital. The second deals with Joan Robinson's critique of traditional theory, based on the impossibility of analyzing changes by comparing equilibria and with the methodological status of this critique. The third concerns the legitimacy of Joan Robinson's extension of her critique from the comparison of neoclassical equilibria to the more general method of comparing 'normal positions' of the economic system. The appendices show Joan Robinson's objections to Garegnani's criticism of neoclassical theory. She felt that his argument had conceded to neoclassical theory what it should never have granted; that is, the possibility of analyzing changes in the economy by means of a comparison between equilibria.

I have also prevailed on Garegnani to provide us in Chapter 13 with a non-technical introduction to Sraffa. In many ways this provides a backdrop for his discussion in Chapter 12 and was initially designed as an appendix to that chapter. However, it is included here as a separate entry to call attention to it for the reader who may wish for a more general discussion of Sraffa's contributions and Garegnani's conception of them.

From this 'family quarrel' we pass to Part III which deals with the serious questions of capital, growth, and distribution that preoccupied Joan Robinson in the post-war years. It opens with Chapter 14 where Nell points out that Joan Robinson's views on accumulation developed along with growth theory itself. She rejected the Harrod–Domar picture of instability as too extreme, but she found the neoclassical vision of substitution objectionable on two grounds. First, capital is not a factor of production, but consists of produced means of production, aggregated in value terms, on which profit is earned. There is no reason to expect that the value of produced means of production will vary in any regular way with the rate of return; nor can any useful notion of the marginal product of such a conglomeration of goods be defined. Second, factories and equipment will be established on the basis of beliefs and expectations that will often be mistaken or become quickly outdated. The economy's stock of equipment at any moment of historical time will not be in equilibrium; steady growth must be considered at best a useful fiction – and Joan Robinson had increasing doubts about its usefulness, although she continued to adhere to the view that growth and distribution were connected through the classical savings function. Nell notes, however, that this connection is open to two forms of criticism: one in capital theory – that *relative* price changes may generate pressures in the wrong direction, the other in investment theory – the capacity/acceleration relationship may lead to real wage movements in the wrong direction. He concludes that Joan's instincts in criticizing steady growth may have been sound, but the idea needed to take its place – transformational growth – has hardly been sketched.

Mathur, a student of Joan Robinson, derived the concept of platinum age from her work. In his earlier work he considered various states of steady growth in the long-run path of development and derived in this connection the properties of a turnpike. He imposed the minimum time for reaching the golden age as an optimality condition and determined the choice of turnpike therefrom. In Chapter 15 he conceives of development in a broader context of restructuring the capital stock in response to long-term growth of technical knowledge. According to this concept of development, the relatively more advanced countries are all considered to be underdeveloped (though less so than the ones in the take-off stage). A 'second industrial revolution' would require an efficient long-term path of capital accumulation as pointed out by Dorfman, Samuelson and Solow as far back as 1957. Mathur takes three sectors of heterogeneous capital into consideration and derives the guideposts of an alternative methodology to that pioneered by Dorfman, Samuelson and Solow. He obtains this in the Robinsonian framework, using a structure developed for extending von Neumann and Sraffa models to the field of development problems. Thus he derives an optimal strategy for the so-called advanced countries that can be adopted either in the context of socialist, capitalist or mixed economies as a guideline for encouraging investment into an optimal pattern. Mathur perceives the social advantage of the proposed strategy in combining rapid diffusion of high technology while securing social justice in the sense of a high degree of employment and favorable income distribution.

The next five chapters deal with capital theory in a more 'neoclassical vein'. In Chapter 16, Becker and Majumdar present their view of the major issues and results on optimality and decentralization in the class of deterministic, infinite horizon, discrete time, one sector models of capital accumulation. They focus on the qualitative properties of the solution obtained under alternative optimality criteria, the sensitivity of that solution with respect to variations in the initial data and the underlying parameters of the economy. They discuss decentralization of the optimum by means of competitive prices in terms of both the perfect foresight equivalence principle and an informationally decentralized viewpoint. They also study capital accumulation with heterogeneous households.

In Chapter 17, Mas-Colell points out that the line of research initiated by Joan Robinson culminated in the 1960s with the realization that many of the comparative statics theorems, valid for one capital good, do not generalize for the heterogeneous capital goods case. 'To a sensibility educated on the former, the heterogeneous capital goods case admitted models with behavior that appeared "bizarre", "exotic", "paradoxical".' However, Mas-Colell adds, 'this was no disappointment to Joan Robinson and her followers. It was rather their point and in this they were perceptive.' The central example with which Mas-Colell concerns himself in Chapter 17 is the dependence of steady-state consumption on the interest rate. He restricts himself to a world without population growth and without technological change. A basic and quite general theorem, the golden rule, asserts that the maximum consumption level is associated with a rate of interest equal to the rate of population growth, that is, zero. In addition, the standard one capital good case displays a monotonically decreasing relationship between consumption levels and the rate of interest. This does not generalize and it is now well understood that even with only two capital goods a non-monotone association is possible. The purpose of Chapter 17 is to bring this point to its logical conclusion, or, as Mas-Colell puts it, 'to out-Cambridge Cambridge', by showing that in general there is no other theorem on the association across steady states of consumption levels and rates of interest than a slightly strengthened version of the golden rule. Roughly, the result is that, given any set of consumption and rates of interest pairs, a well-behaved technology can be found having precisely this set as the steady-state comparative static locus. A minor positive pay-off of this research strategy is the uncovering of a slight strengthening of the golden rule.

Joan Robinson argued that neoclassical general equilibrium theory could not determine the rates of interest in an intertemporal model. In Chapter 18, Kehoe, Levine, and Romer consider a production economy with a finite number of heterogeneous, infinitely lived consumers. They show that, for almost all endowments, equilibria that converge to a non-degenerate steady state or cycle are locally unique. They do so by stating the equilibrium conditions that equate spending and income for each consumer entirely in terms of first period factor endowments and derivatives of a social value function.

In Chapter 19, Majumdar, Mitra and Nyarko use the techniques of dynamic programming to analyze a problem of optimal intertemporal allocation under uncertainty. The technology constraining the set of feasible policies is non-convex and also assumed to be subjected to random shocks. The criterion for evaluation of alternative policies is maximization of a discounted sum of expected one period utilities derived from consumption. They show the optimal investment policy function to be monotonically non-decreasing; in fact, it is strictly increasing when the optimal program is characterized by a stochastic Ramsey–Euler condition. They show that non-uniqueness of optimal actions is restricted to the initial period only, and further, that the set of all initial stocks, from which there is a unique optimal action, coincides with the set on which the value function is differentiable. The dynamic process of optimal inputs converges to some steady state that depends on the initial stock. Their exercise provides a convenient overview of the recent literature dealing with non-convexities and uncertainty in the context of capital theory and the theory of renewable resources.

In Chapter 20, Brock, Rothschild, and Stiglitz argue that many problems involving the valuation of assets that evolve stochastically can be formulated as optimal stopping problems. Some of the examples they analyze include the problem of finding the optimum time to erect a plant with a given construction cost and whose profits are generated by a stochastic process. In this case, they seek the market value of the rights to construct such a plant as a function of the current state of profit potential. The optimal stopping time is just the time at which the plant is built. Formally identical is the problem of deciding when to stop accumulating human capital and start working. Here human capital is measured by the discounted value of expected future earnings. What distinguishes Chapter 20 from the existing literature on this problem is that its authors show how to derive comparative statics propositions for optimal stopping problems where the instantaneous mean and variance functions are arbitrary functions of the state variables. Brock, Rothschild, and Stiglitz analyze an asset whose growth follows a discrete time-stochastic process. They pose and solve the optimal stopping problem for assets whose intrinsic value follows a diffusion process with instantaneous mean and instantaneous variance. They show also how the same techniques can be applied to optimal stopping problems where the asset is described by a dimensional diffusion process.

With Chapter 21 we pass into other aspects of growth and distribution. Here Lance Taylor sets up a demand-driven two-sector model to analyze the effects on income distribution and steady-state growth of shifts in demand composition – from Engel effects, changes in social preference, or attempts at income redistribution through tax/transfer policies. He shows that distributional movements depend on labor intensity of the sectors, while growth effects depend on the sectoral sensitivity of investment demand functions to profit rates and technical change. With plausible parameter values, outcomes of either sign can result – a finding that sheds light on asserted causes for stagnation and income concentration that have appeared in the literature for at least 150 years.

In Chapter 22, Baumol and Wolff discuss three basic concepts of productivity growth: growth in welfare productivity, productive capacity and crude productivity. They show that these three concepts have very different meanings and uses. They demonstrate that all three of them are significant, even the crude productivity growth measure that makes no adjustment for quality changes and may seem basically indefensible. They show why any robust scalar representation of growth in productive capacity may be impossible and why explicit adjustments for changes in product quality may be unnecessary. That is, at least in principle, one can hope to deal with the quality change problem through reasonably accurate measurement of growth in welfare productivity, which may be, ultimately, the best measure of productivity growth. They use empirical evidence to show that estimates of both annual and annual average productivity growth over fairly long periods are very sensitive to the choice among productivity concepts. Moreover, estimates of capacity productivity growth are very sensitive to the assumptions used to impose an equiproportionate shift on the production function over time.

Joan Robinson's growth theory was essentially concerned with the relationship between the rate of technical progress and capital accumulation. In Chapter 23 Rymes extends her theory to the case of induced technical progress put in place by 'research and development' capital expenditures. He shows that traditional measures of total factor productivity or technical progress, both by industry and at the aggregate level, will generate measures of productivity change misleading when related to measures of R&D capital expenditure. Joan supported Harrod's conception of technical progress. Rymes also shows that new measures of Harrod–Robinson total factor productivity, when related to the R&D measures, will provide a better empirical foundation for the study of the relationship between induced technical progress and R&D expenditures. Joan's growth theory and conceptions of technical progress, adapted from Harrod, are thus seen to have immediate relevance to some very important contemporary empirical and policy questions in the economics of capital accumulation and technical progress.

Joan Robinson often wrote critically about the labor theory of value. She also subscribed to an elegant model of the real wage in which the wage is related to the average product of labor in the wage-goods sector and to the proportion of the total workforce which is engaged in the production of wage-goods. In the final chapter (24) of Part III, Dixon shows that her model of the real-wage can yield an expression for economy-wide wage-share in terms of the sectoral composition of employment and the (implicit) rate of exchange of labor time. The model is rich in classical and Marxian insights.

Part IV deals with development and international trade, both as they relate more specifically to Joan Robinson's thinking and to the development of modern economics as a whole. Joan Robinson was adamant that models of steady growth are futile and, unless the microeconomics of behavior of producers and consumers are plausible, the macroeconomics of the steady state is meaningless. In the opening chapter (25), Srinivasan shows that some of the radical critiques of neoclassical theory of international trade and its presumption of the optimality of free trade are based on wrong use of steady-state analysis. He shows that a class of models purporting to analyze the commodity trade and capital flow relations between developed and developing countries and arriving at conclusions contrary to neoclassical analysis have made implausible microbehavior assumptions. He discusses recent models of international trade based on increasing returns to scale and product differentiation in production and non-competitive market structure from the point of view of economic development. These models and their rehabilitation of interventionist international trade policy are unlikely to be appropriate for developing countries.

In Chapter 26, Adelman and Sunding examine Joan Robinson's writings on economic development and developing economies from the perspective of mainstream development economics. They argue that Joan's thinking about development may be divided into three periods: during the 1950s and 1960s she focused almost exclusively on growth and capital accumulation. She shared with early development economists a preoccupation with investment in physical capital as the major determinant of economic development, but she was more extreme than the mainstream development economists in her stress on the rate of capital accumulation. The second period was characterized by Joan's reaction against post-war changes in capitalist economies, her awareness of failures in East European countries, and her fascination with Maoist China. She was thus led to recognize agriculture's role in economic development. Finally, in the last years of her life, Joan Robinson expressed some disenchantment with China as a model for developing countries. Adelman and Sunding conclude with an assessment of Joan's writings on economic development in the light of the stylized facts of development reported by Chenery and others and in the light of China's performance since 1952.

Joan Robinson's essay on disguised unemployment analyzes the situation in an advanced industrialized country where, in a depression, people are thrown out of work and crowd into substantially lower productivity occupations. In Chapter 27, Streeten argues that this can be modelled in terms of a two-sector model. In one sector wages are rigid downwards and productivity is high. In the other sector incomes (from self-employment) are flexible downwards and productivity is low, in some cases approaching zero. To restore full employment, all that is needed is an increase in effective demand. When the concept has been applied to low-income countries, it is clear that additional assumptions have to be made. Streeten analyzes these in the context of a low-income rural sector with family farms and a high-income industrial sector with wage employment. He distinguishes a static from a dynamic concept. He spells out differently assumptions about what conditions have to change in the agricultural sector as workers are transferred to the industrial sector, if agricultural output is not to fall.

In Chapter 28, Bronfenbrenner offers us the confessions of a 'sinner' in international economics. He recalls the essence of the macroeconomics of international trade theory forty years ago. He speaks of his first-hand experience of post-war Japan, of the 'structural dollar-shortage' thesis as applied to the reconstruction of Japan, and of the thinking at the same time about exchange rates. He then lists six factors responsible for his misunderstandings and is able to provide a clearer conception of international trade theory: (1) lack of belief in the post-war Japanese policy to raise real-wages, to intensify investment in human capital, and to move 'up-market' in the world economy; (2) an underestimate of the difficulties of shifts or transitions between equilibrium positions; (3) an overestimate of the advantages of exchange-rate stability, even at 'wrong' rates; (4) an underestimate of the rising importance of 'processing economies' in international trade; (5) an underestimate of the international economic consequences for the US of its political commitment to high employment 'at whatever cost'; and possibly (6) some element of racism in his underestimate of the economic potential of Japanese labor.

In Chapter 29, Chipman develops a model where two countries each produce an export good and a non-tradable at constant costs (with a single factor of production); the countries do not produce import-competing goods. Thus, the 'elasticity of supply' of exports is infinite in each country. He shows that if the two countries have identical marginal propensities to consume the two tradables, and if the 'Marshall–Lerner' stability condition holds, then a transfer will improve the receiving country's terms of trade if the non-tradable is a superior good, and worsen it if the non-tradable is an inferior good. If the exchange rate is endogenous and each country pursues a monetary policy so as to stabilize the price of its non-tradable, the real and nominal exchange rates and the terms of trade are all proportional. Hence a transfer will strengthen the receiving country's exchange rate if the non-tradable is superior and stability holds. Chipman analyzes a model of pegged, adjustable exchange rates where the demand for money in each country is proportional to expenditure and the exchange rate is exogenously controlled by country 2. He shows that if the capital flow between the countries is exogenously determined in terms of country 1's currency, and if both the 'orthodox presumption' and stability hold, then a devaluation by country 2 will have no real effect; whereas if the capital flow is exogenously determined in terms of country 2's currency, and if both the 'orthodox presumption' and stability hold, then a devaluation by country 2 will improve or worsen its balance of payments (in country-1 currency) according to whether the initial balance is in deficit or surplus. He thus obtains a sharp contrast between regimes according as the exchange rate is endogenous or exogenous.

It is a striking fact (and, in view of her strong social sympathies, a puzzling one) that during no phase of her long professional career did Joan Robinson seriously interest herself in the economics of labor unions. Although she has made noteworthy, important contributions to the theory of international trade in Chapter 30, Kemp and Shimomura pay tribute to Joan Robinson not by elaborating one of her favorite themes but by plunging into territory she has conspicuously neglected. Their purpose is to outline a theory of international trade that incorporates a powerful labor union. As a more specific but subsidiary objective, they seek to discover whether there are circumstances where a maximizing union, by imposing a minimum wage, may so change the effective factor-endowment ratio of a country as to reverse the direction of its trade.

Joan Robinson and many other economists have considered technical progress and the accumulation of more capital per worker to be the only way to raise *per capita* output and income in the long run. Yet, in a study of British agriculture before its mechanization in the mid-nineteenth century, Clark, in Chapter 31, shows that while output *per capita* more than doubled between 1300 and 1841 the source was mainly an increase in work intensity. Simple hand tasks such as reaping and threshing were being done much more quickly in 1841. This increase of the work pace was not a consequence of economizing on more expensive labor in the latter period. For the price of grain relative to labor changed dramatically from year to year, and after the Black Death in 1349, yet such price fluctuations never caused the work pace to change. An increase in the intensity of labor thus has to be ranked above technical progress and capital accumulation as a source of increased incomes in pre-industrial Britain. Clark has every reason to expect similar results for the rest of Europe.

Part V follows up on topics Joan Robinson has touched upon deftly and with much grace and insight. In Chapter 32, Hausman focuses on Joan Robinson's view of the perennial concern of economists to demonstrate that selfish market behavior is morally acceptable, but that, in fact, there is an irreconcilable conflict between morality and economics. Along the way, he considers the extent to which this moral or ideological burden borne by economics affected the Cambridge controversy in the theory of capital, growth and distribution. Although he finds the moral conflict Joan emphasizes to be real and disturbing, he argues that she overstated her claims for the importance of ideology.

In 1942, Joan Robinson wrote that although she was sympathetic with the egalitarianism Marxism champions, the route to those ends through the labor theory of value, does not properly represent Marxian concerns with capitalist property relations. Marxism has championed exploitation as the labor theory of value does not properly represent Marxian concerns with capitalist property relations. Marxism has championed exploitation as the statistic to measure the distributional injustice of capitalism; the inequality of income due to private ownership of the means of production should be remedied by public ownership. Roemer shows that exploitation, as classically defined, is an imperfect statistic for the distributional and ethical concerns which animate Marxism. He proposes an axiomatic approach to reflect more accurately the debate concerning what kinds of property rights are ethically defensible. He asks: What distributions of final output will respect both the self-ownership of persons (their rights to returns from their differential skills) and public ownership of productive resources in the external world? He presents a model showing that public ownership of the external world nullifies the possible returns to self-ownership. Methodologically, he shows how debates within political philosophy can be studied using tools of mechanism theory on spaces of economies. He intends the theorem in Chapter 33 as a challenge to neo-Lockeanism, an illustration of how Marxian ethical concerns can be represented using modern tools of analysis.

Part VI attempts to provide a composite sketch of Joan Robinson's personality and accomplishments as seen through the eyes of various beholders. No matter how perceptive and written with critical flair, yet with admiration and even affection, as their authors would be the first to admit, these images are but shadowy reflections of the vital flame that was Joan. In the opening chapter (34), Boulding recalls the sense of a 'new dawn' in economics in the 1930s in two aspects: Keynes with a great deal of help from Joan Robinson was throwing light on the dark problem of unemployment, and Joan Robinson herself, with *The Economics of Imperfect Competition*, was releasing us from the absurdities of the pure competition model of pricing. These were not false dawns, Boulding stresses, but they did turn out to be cloudy. Joan Robinson never repudiated Keynesianism, though she did abandon imperfect competition in a lifelong search for an adequate theory of capital and profit, that somehow always eluded her. She was a lonely voice, asking the right questions, in an era contented with easy mathematical answers to the wrong questions. Her sense of the great complexity of capital structures and economic relationships denied her access to simple solutions, but the questions she raised will be with us for a long time.

The next seven chapters constitute a series of vignettes of Joan where (in Chapter 35) Streeten stresses her incomparable quality of *Zivilcourage*; Patel (in Chapter 36) emphasizes her innate kindness and warm heart; Scitovsky (in Chapter 37) recalls the young Joan, her loveliness and her stern insistence that he learn to think for himself; Chipman (in Chapter 38) recalls the two sides of Joan – her kindness and her argumentativeness; Sylos Labini (in Chapter 39) shares with us more than thirty years of frequent contacts, her somewhat overbearing qualities and the essence of her friendliness; Foley (in Chapter 40) highlights the capital controversy he observed as an onlooker and junior member of the MIT economics department (he recalls her aggressive, non-discriminating, and impressive intellectual stance) and his personal exchange with her over the labor theory of value she continued to regard as a 'piece of mystical rubbish'; and Gram (in Chapter 41) remembers the Joan of the 1970s, the increasing terseness of her arguments and her growing disenchantment towards the end of her life.

In the following chapter (42) Walsh shares with us his perceptions of Joan in the last years of her life. He stresses her moral seriousness, her interest in and kindness to young people, her innate natural dignity, her stern purpose, and her mystery, her uncompromising stance, her wicked sense of humor, and the ravages of failing health in her last years. He recalls the perseverance with which she guided and advised him and Gram through the years they worked on their joint book and their points of disagreement with her.

In Chapter 43, Nell recalls Joan's commanding presence, her single-mindedness and partisanship. He stresses that it is as a critic that she will be best remembered. He emphasizes that only a theory can beat another theory. 'Only those protected by the amulet of another theory will be safe ... that is the protection that many of Joan's students and followers sought, but which she never provided.' Yet, she had all the ingredients for such a theory, but the construction was lacking.

In the next three chapters we are offered views of Joan from three colleagues in Cambridge. In Chapter 44, Hahn speaks of certain misconceptions in Joan's critique of neoclassical economics, of her attitude towards equilibrium, of the potentially useful role her criticism could play for modern mathematical theorists, and of the acuteness of her criticism of 'bastard' Keynesians. According to Hahn, 'Joan had a number of very important things to say. If she had been trained in mathematics and had been technically more competent she could really have done more to clinch them.' He considers her work on interest rates and money her 'lasting achievement' and is quite irritated by her work in capital theory. He emphasizes that Joan was 'totally a heterodox upper-class Englishwoman' and 'a part of her personality was simply upper-class refusal to go with the herd'.

In the next chapter (45), Matthews speaks of Joan as a crusader whose work cannot be divorced from her overriding desire to establish the truth and to refute self-interested or lazy fallacies. He mentions that her essential originality lay perhaps in her ability to synthesize those who so profoundly influenced her. He stresses the quality of her criticism: 'she was better at pointing out that the Emperor had no clothes than in supplying him with clothing'. He recalls the exciting days when the 'secret seminar' was discussing capital and growth and muses about the Cambridge atmosphere at the time.

In Chapter 46, Goodwin – who strongly supported Joan and Kahn in Cambridge since the early 1950s – offers us an affectionate glimpse of Joan, the passionate seeker after truth. He recalls his first exposure to her as a student at Oxford: 'I understood little but sat spellbound, and, in a sense have remained so ever since.' He speaks of her 'totally self-abnegating dedication' in pursuit of truth, 'her clarity, her unswerving devotion to unpopular, progressive causes, her total sincerity and integrity, her high seriousness, and her unwillingness to suffer fools gladly'.

The last chapter (47) presents the recollections of Lorie Tarshis who first encountered Joan in the classroom in 1933. 'Her lectures were not only clear and crisp; they were delivered by a very attractive young lady . . . A strong, handsome face, a lovely smile, white teeth and bright blue eyes and a liveliness that sparkled.' Not only as a student himself, but whenever he met her later, Tarshis was impressed by her sincere interest in and encouragement of students who demonstrated an ability for independent thought. He also stresses her commitment to truth, her willingness to fight for it no matter how powerful the opposition and the enmity she aroused on her way. There is no more fitting way of concluding than by citing the last paragraph of Chapter 47:

> Like my fellow contributors in these volumes, I dedicate my essay to her memory, and . . . the hope that her example will be followed by many: her determination to discover how things work, her insistence on writing out her findings directly and clearly, her fierce will to hold her ground, once she was persuaded of its rightness, even if she had to stand alone; and all this combined with an unclouded conscience that recognized the claims of others, the worth of friendship and the beauties that man, women and children can create.

The Economics of Imperfect Competition and Employment: Joan Robinson and Beyond

This volume opens with a two chapter introductory part: the first chapter provides a background on the integration of imperfect competition and the theory of employment that inspired Joan Robinson's post-General Theory work; the second is a notable example of a current attempt at building a model of imperfect competition and unemployment in a game theoretic framework, and as such also fits into Part III.

The imperfect competition revolution had no bearing on the Keynesian revolution, though both of them took place at about the same time and in the same place and both involved at least some of the same *dramatis personae*. This is more than a doctrinal history puzzlement. Had it been otherwise, it would have fundamentally affected the course of the age after Keynes. Whatever the merits of Joan Robinson's *Economics of Imperfect Competition*, one of the reasons she came to reject it is because she was strongly influenced by Kalecki's pioneering integration of imperfect competition and macrodynamics. Throughout Chapter 1 we trace Kalecki's pervasive influence on Joan Robinson and her creative adaptation of his approach to pricing, distribution, and, with some reservation (particularly about the investment function), to growth, thus throwing a light on the key ingredients of the Robinsonian construct. In particular, we trace how Kalecki brought his version of the theory of employment to Cambridge and the reception it received; the differences between Kalecki and Keynes in non-economic dimensions, and their diverse intellectual roots. The major part of Chapter 1 examines the essential differences between the Kaleckian and Keynesian models and how these differences can be traced in Joan Robinson's work. To build a realistic theory, Kalecki explained how industrial prices are formed by mark-ups on costs and distinguished between 'cost-determined' and 'demand-determined' prices. The mark-ups depend on the relative strength of market imperfection he called the 'degree of monopoly'. Together with other distributional factors this is the key for the determination of macrodistribution. Kalecki's theory of profits was based on the principle that wage earners do not save, but spend what they get and that entrepreneurs get what they spend. Entrepreneurs' profits are governed by their propensity to invest and consume and not the other way round. Kalecki's model presented the economic process in motion; that is, how one sequence develops from the preceding ones. The model encompasses long-run dynamics and the capacity effects of investments and some other supply considerations. Kalecki approached the theory of effective demand through the theory of the business cycle which established two basic relations: (1) the impact of effective demand generated by investment on profits and national income; and (2) the investment decision function, where the rate of investment decisions at a given time is roughly determined by the level and the rate of change in economic activity at some earlier time. To Kalecki, the key prerequisite for becoming an entrepreneur is the ownership of capital. Investment decisions are related to the firm's 'internal' accumulation of gross savings. These savings allow the firm to make new investments without facing the problems of the limited capital market or 'increasing risk'. Kalecki dealt with an open system and treated the rate of export surplus as a promoter of prosperity and balance-of-payments difficulties as a factor limiting expansion. Kalecki realized that whatever the rationale of the *economics* of full employment, the *political* problems are formidable. During World War II, while he wrote his masterful policy guidelines of the three ways to full employment, he realized the potential objections to such policies and predicted the emergence of the political business cycle.

The second chapter is an illustration of the most recent revival of interest in imperfect competition within a general equilibrium framework. While in the past this work has not borne the expected fruits, Roberts in Chapter 2 goes far beyond towards an integration of imperfect competition and macroeconomics, using the increasingly more fruitful (and one might add, fashionable) game-theoretic approach – an approach also applied by the contributors to Part III of this volume. Roberts considers a game-theoretic, non-Walrasian, general equilibrium model of price determination, production, and exchange. In this game, firms first select prices and wages, consumers/workers then make input supply and output demand offers, and finally firms select the fractions of these to accept. Equilibrium (pure strategy, subgame perfect, Nash equilibrium) involves each agent acting optimally from each point forward while correctly recognizing the results of taking any given course of action. In particular, firms correctly forecast the quantity responses to different prices and wages. Roberts shows that, with a particular structure of preferences, endowments and technology, for any equilibrium with positive levels of economic activity, there exists another equilibrium at the same prices and wages with lower levels of activity. The latter equilibrium corresponds to involuntary unemployment. This unemployment arises because of a failure of excess demand: expectations of low demand are self-confirming. Further, expectations are such that price and wage changes do not appear profitable, and, by the nature of equilibrium, these expectations are correct. He also considers existence issues.

Part II deals with imperfect competition in historical perspective and throws some light on future developments. In the opening chapter (3), Whitaker explores the intellectual background of Cambridge economics against which Joan Robinson's *The Economics of Imperfect Competition* was written. An extensive analysis of the ideas on monopoly and competition of Marshall, Pigou, and Sraffa paves the way for a reconsideration of the main themes of Joan Robinson's book in relation to the web of ideas from which they arose. Whitaker places Joan Robinson's later strictures on her own early work in historical perspective, and reaches somewhat revisionist conclusions on Pigou's deviation from Marshall, Sraffa's criticisms of the Cambridge school, and the way in which *The Economics of Imperfect Competition* related to Cambridge tradition and Sraffa's critique of it. He assigns a key influence to Gerald Shove as a source through which the Cambridge tradition was transmitted to Joan Robinson.

In Chapter 4, Bishop pays tribute to the scientific importance and specific analytical strengths of Joan Robinson's famous first book and attempts to identify and evaluate some of its principal shortcomings. The central strength is, of course, its presentation of the static equilibrium conditions of several leading types of imperfect competition, both monopolistic and monopsonistic – as a necessary step towards freeing economic analysis from its dependence on the perfectly competitive model. The weaknesses he stresses include the ambiguities of exploitation as an offence against justice or efficiency, the preoccupation with labor as persistently exploited and never exploiting, and some deficiencies in the analysis and evaluation of the removal of market imperfections.

In Chapter 5, Negishi takes us back to Edgeworth and then propels us much beyond. Edgeworth demonstrated the so-called equivalence theorem in which the outcome of an exchange economy where traders act cooperatively is identical to the Walrasian equilibrium of the perfect competition where traders act non-cooperatively as price takers, when the number of traders of the same type is infinitely large. Since the infinity of identical traders is a sufficient condition, however, a natural question Negishi asks is whether it is also a necessary one. According to Farell and Schitovitz, the equivalence theorem holds even in the case of duopoly where there are only two suppliers of a good though the number of demands is infinite. Negishi suggests that the theorem holds in a four-person case of an Edgeworth game of exchange, if indivisible lump-sum transactions are ruled out and competition is assured so as to satisfy Jevon's law of indifference. Finally, the theorem still holds in the case of bilateral monopoly or isolated exchange between two traders, if exchanges are repeated indefinitely through time. All this suggests to Negishi that what is essential for perfect competition is not so much the number of traders or the scale of traders relative to that of the economy as perfect information and no friction, also explicitly assumed by Edgeworth. Walrasian assumptions are vindicated by Edgeworth's theorem. Even though traders are actually not price takers and there are no auctioneers, we could assume that traders act as if they were taking prices set by auctioneers, if the information is perfect and there are no frictions. But, Negishi points out, for the development of non-Walrasian economics to provide microeconomic foundations for Keynesian fixprice economics, on the other hand, one has to assume that information is not perfect and there do exist such frictions as cost of organizing coalitions and cost of trade.

The Economics of Imperfect Competition evoked an initial response which was favorable in the extreme. Within a generation, however, considerable disillusion had set in. In Chapter 6, Sutton argues that the low point of the book's fortunes was reached in the 'Archibald versus Chicago' debate, that appeared in the *Review of Economic Studies* of 1961, in which all protagonists appeared to agree only on one thing: that the theory as it stood was empirically empty. The enormous resurgence of interest in imperfect competition that we have witnessed over the past decade has been built around the notion of putting more structure into the basic theory by specifying some explicit representation of consumer preferences over differentiated products. This has been an impressively fruitful line of development. It has led to important new departures in areas as widely separated as the theory of intra-industry trade, and the analysis of vertical restraints on trade. Yet, for all this progress, Sutton retains a nagging worry: is this theory 'consistent with anything'? In Chapter 6 he addresses himself to these continuing concerns.

Part III, consisting of studies of imperfect competition within the game-theoretic framework, opens with Chapter 7 by one of the ablest practitioners of the science and art of game theory. In it Rubinstein argues that it is a matter of judgment to decide when a market outcome is well described by the competitive price model and to decide what the units appearing on the quantity axis of the demand–supply diagram are. The literature he introduces in this chapter aims to assist us in this judgment. The method Rubinstein uses starts by specifying in detail the process by which the terms of transactions are determined. He describes the process of trade as a game and studies non-cooperative solution concepts. Finally, he checks under what circumstances the solution is close to the competitive outcome.

In Chapter 8, Wilson surveys a part of the recent literature on imperfect competition among firms. The topics he has selected emphasize incumbent firms' strategies of entry deterrence and battles for market share or survival. He describes the roles of pricing, supply, and investment in implementing these strategies. He presents the survey in expository form to convey how game-theoretic methods are used to formulate models of dynamic interactions among firms. Dynamic features reveal that firms' strategies are affected by powers of commitment, such as irreversible investment; and, there can be multiple equilibria depending on the firms' mutual expectations. Also, several models reveal the strong effects of informational asymmetries among the competitors: predation can deter entry, and among incumbents profits can be dissipated in wars of attrition; conversely, informational effects can sustain cooperative endeavors. The gist of the results is a verification of the rich complexity of the strategic aspects of imperfect competition, emphasized by Joan Robinson, and an illustration of the game-theoretic methods that have been developed recently to capture the roles of dynamics and informational asymmetries.

In Chapter 9, Hurwicz examines the effects of entry of new firms in a symmetric differentiated products industry; in particular, the effects on the profits of firms already in the industry. The industry is in equilibrium if additional entry would result in negative profits for everyone, but profits can be at equilibrium. He obtains an upper bound on the number of firms that could coexist in an industry under fairly general assumptions, without presupposing symmetry. Under more specialized assumptions, he shows that the profits of individual firms go down as the number of firms increases. This is the case both in the Cournot and Bertrand models. He confines himself to the study of symmetric equilibrium solutions. He shows that under Cournot duopoly *asymmetric* solutions do not exist, but he does not study the more general aspects of existence of asymmetric oligopoly solutions. Some of the results are also valid for *undifferentiated* commodities that is, where all firms sell identical products.

In Chapter 10, Milgrom makes two contributions to the theory of price discrimination. First, considering a monopolist that produces at constant unit costs, he observes that without some connection such as resale possibilities, laws prohibiting price discrimination, or reputational phenomena, the problem naturally decomposes into a set of bilateral monopoly problems with individual prices determined by bargaining. This view is inconsistent with the usual presumption that price discrimination is profitable for the seller. Indeed, when consortiums of buyers may form to negotiate prices, laws that prohibit price discrimination create a free rider problem that may result in higher prices for all. His second contribution is a new graphical analysis of the problem of third-degree price discrimination. Gabszewicz and Thisse (in Chapter 11) investigate the impact of price discrimination in a vertically differentiated market. They show that: (1) a discriminatory pricing equilibrium exists under rather general conditions; (2) the equilibrium qualities coincide with the Pareto-optimal qualities; and (3) all consumers are better off under discriminatory pricing than under uniform pricing.

Part IV on different approaches to imperfect competition opens with Chapter 12 where Archibald and Eaton remind us that spatial models *are* characteristics models, but not vice versa. In quite standard and general characteristics and spatial models, they deal with the resolution of two main problems: the 'combinability' of goods (or stores) to obtain preferred characteristics mixes; and the measurement of distance between goods (or stores). The resolution of these problems is the same in both models: although the models are not identical, they are easily seen to be particular applications of the general characteristics model. The main analytical tool they use is an indirect characterization of preferences in the appropriate space. For both models they identify the case in which characteristics are not satisfactory primitives. The nature, extent, and role of product differentiation in Joan Robinson's theory of imperfect competition were the major topics of dispute in Chamberlin's unrequited challenge to its realism. In the next chapter (13) Kuenne strives to clarify such questions as a prelude towards a formal incorporation of price and product quality in oligopolistic decision making. He suggests a means of measuring product qualities cardinally and explores the interrelations of price and quality choices in the firm's decisions. He shows the crucial dependence of the response of the firm to rivals' changes in product quality upon the convexity or concavity of its sales function and studies the nature of oligopolistic competition in these dimensions under rivalrous consonance. He develops a framework of analysis to seek the difficult-to-obtain general propositions independent of firm and industry specifics.

Chapter 14 is an investigation of the welfare of the different groups of individuals in unemployment situations. The framework is the familiar three-good model studied among others by Barro and Grossman, Benassy, and Malinvaud. Silvestre assumes that, in situations of less than full employment, some workers are fully employed and some others are totally unemployed. This makes the analysis more complex than in the usual models with representative workers since one must consider separately three welfare magnitudes: the number of workers employed, the welfare of the employed workers, and that of the unemployed. Both the framework and the question fit well in Joan Robinson's view of the economic world. The framework is one where economic activity is carried out at prices not necessarily Walrasian, and where unemployment situations are typical. It can be interpreted as a short-run model, but also as a model where agents have monopoly or monopsony power. This second interpretation actually agrees better with Joan Robinson and Kalecki than with Keynes. The question, on the other hand, is in the spirit of Joan Robinson's study of the monopolistic and monopsonistic exploitation of workers, though it is placed in a set-up where the interaction between the labor market and the output market is explicit and where unemployment plays a central role. Silvestre's results characterize the price–wage pairs with the property that any movement away from them makes someone (an owner of a firm or a worker who is employed or unemployed or marginally employed) worse off. One cannot move away from such a point with unanimous approval. Thus price–wage pairs satisfying this property are states of conflict interests. He shows that price–wage pairs close to what he calls the Keynesian–classical boundary (defined by the presence of unemployment and the equality between price and marginal cost) have this property and that those away from it do not.

Part V deals with imperfect competition in specific markets. In the opening chapter (15) Stiglitz, a student of Joan Robinson, relates his work not only to her *Economics of Imperfect Competition*, but also to her 1951 development of a general portfolio theory, 'A clear predecessor of the later work of Tobin' for which Stiglitz believes 'she may have received insufficient credit'. Stiglitz examines imperfect competition in the capital market, using a simple general-equilibrium portfolio model. He shows that the market economy is not, in general, Pareto efficient. In particular, he investigates whether there are too few or too many risky firms, whether they will be too small or too large, whether there will be 'errors' in the choice of techniques, and the like. He investigates in detail the interpretation that, in the absence of a complete set of securities, the market ought to be viewed as monopolistically competitive. He shows that when the number of firms is not fixed, the market solution will err both with respect to the number and choice of firms, even when all firms take as given their value per unit scale of output. More generally, Stiglitz's second motivation is provided by the analysis of equilibrium in the capital market with entry under competitive conditions. And the third motivation is to understand more fully monopolistic competitive equilibrium. Thus, in Chapter 15, Stiglitz considers a simplified version of the capital market model. He assumes all risky firms to be identical, but perfectly correlated and all safe firms (those whose returns are perfectly certain) to be identical. As one safe security is a perfect substitute for another, the safe firms in this model constitute a perfectly competitive industry and the risky firms a monopolistically competitive industry. He then proceeds to assume the returns to the risky firms to be independently (but identically) distributed and then correlated with a general market factor. He assumes all individuals to be identical and risk averse. This formulation allows him to avoid the pitfalls of previous studies of monopolistic competition: individuals purchase not one but all produced commodities; there is a perfectly competitive sector, so he can enquire into the diversion of resources from the perfectly competitive to the monopolistically competitive sector; and since all individuals are identical and purchase the same portfolio, they are all worse off in the competitive situation than in the optimal. Hence, Stiglitz argues, his results are of interest not only for what they suggest about the workings of the capital market, but for the light they shed on the more general question of resource allocation in economies with a monopolistically competitive sector.

In Chapter 16, Kurz examines the properties of competition in the market for credit when the lender must bear the risk of default by the borrower. In the formal model there are many borrowers and many depositors with an intermediary who lends the depositors' funds to the borrowers but must bear the risk of default. Each borrower provides some of his own equity (i.e. collateral) and, to protect the depositors, the intermediary must also have some equity capital. He shows that when taking into account the possibility of default by the intermediary, a competitive equilibrium will often require rationing. He states the characteristics of rationing equilibria and shows that the intermediary will resist, in equilibrium, offers of a higher interest rate by the rationed-out borrowers, since higher interest rates will induce a reduction in the collateral offered by all the borrowers. This will reduce the expected profits of the intermediary. These results supplement earlier papers where equilibrium in credit markets resulted in non-linear pricing but without an explicit rationing constraint.

Joan Robinson insisted that the existence of considerable unemployed resources should not be viewed as a troublesome problem, but rather as a splendid exploitable opportunity of doing something really useful. As other 'Keynesians', she maintained that capitalism, managed with intelligence and goodwill, can continue to flourish in already developed economies. She had her own predilections about the ways and means to and content of full employment and about the message of the Keynesian revolution on planes of theory and policy. According to the proverbial view of the cup as either half full or half empty, there are considerable similarities and differences between her and the mainstream synthesis of neoclassical and Keynesian theory (and policy) represented in Part VI by some of its most distinguished proponents. At a time when the resurgence of classical macroeconomics attempts to bury Keynes, the differences between the various Keynesian factions seem to be somewhat less important.

In Chapter 17, Solow stresses that he is first and foremost a Keynesian and disparages in some degree the academic discussions of 'what Keynes really meant'. He speaks of the work he is doing (with Frank Hahn) to provide a modern theoretical foundation for Keynes's notion of unemployment equilibrium through the modern developments of multiple equilibria. He suggests that Joan Robinson was a superb critic of neoclassical analysis, but also an apt user of its tools in her own work. He then discusses the meaning of 'neoclassical' and suggests that, according to his understanding of the term, Sraffa was also neoclassical. Solow points out that his vision is not so very different from Joan's. He speaks of his slight differences with Tobin, his major differences with the new classical economists, his attitude to post-Keynesian economics, his view of microfoundations for macroeconomics, his position on the neoclassical synthesis, and finally his perspective on growth theory.

In the second testimony (Chapter 18), Tobin shares with us his interpretation of the Keynesian message on the planes of theory and policy and his view of Keynes and the canons of neoclassical economics, imperfect competition, and microfoundations for macroeconomics. He describes the essence of the neoclassical synthesis and negates the view that it inserted 'a few Keynesian contributions into an existing mainstream; it changed the mainstream altogether'. He emphasizes Joan Robinson's historical approach and agrees with her critique of American Keynesians' distortion of Keynes's investment function and entrepreneurial activity. Tobin elaborates on his views about incomes policy and income redistribution and comments on the relationship between Keynesian economics, monetarism, and the welfare state. He speaks of the ultimate emergence of a new synthesis that will borrow the best from all macro thinking: 'Rather than looking at Keynesian static analysis as something good for now, good for next year, and good for the year after that, one looks at it as a panel in a moving picture. In the dynamic system there are relations between periods, based on intertemporal behavior as well as expectations. There are both stock-flow relations, from past to present, and expectations of future variables, from future to present'. The vision behind the future synthesis 'will deviate from the Keynesian vision by taking more explicitly into account anticipations of government policies and by promoting monopolistic-competition features of markets from the vague background into explicitly modeled relationships'.

In the third testimony (Chapter 19), Modigliani stresses that the main difference between Kahn and himself is the former's belief in absolute wage rigidity and his belief in slow wage adjustment. Modigliani speaks about inflation, the Phillips curve, the deficit, and monetary economics. For him, Hicksian IS-LM distills 'the basic message of the *General Theory* in one easy lesson'. He speaks of the need to stabilize the economy and points to the post-war successes. He returns to the causes and consequences of inflation. He contrasts his vision and approach to economics with Milton Friedman and against this background speaks of his formulation of the life-cycle model. Modigliani also sheds light on the analysis of unemployment through search theory, some aspects of the capital controversy in which he participated, and some personal views of Joan Robinson.

In Chapter 20, Weitzman shares with us the essence of his significant work on profit sharing. He focuses on money labor costs which are too high relative to aggregate demand, in particular in the UK and continental Europe. He contends that if the wage would become more flexible in relation to the firm's performance, this would induce firms to hire more workers, thus alleviating the unemployment problem, particularly among the new entrants into the labor force. Although this would involve some uncertainty about take home pay, it would be a far less harmful uncertainty than the one we face in the wage system which involves inflation and large-scale unemployment. Weitzman also speaks about the acceptance and opposition to profit sharing from employers and workers. He mentions the statistically difficult-to-capture microeconomic benefits of profit sharing, but stresses that his development of the scheme was primarily motivated for macroeconomic reasons. He is somewhat reluctant to admit that his scheme has income distribution effects and perceives some opposition to it on the grounds of misperceptions as to who is going to gain. He perceives the scheme as a *supplement* to Keynesian policies. The model of price formation that underlies his scheme is in a sense Kaleckian. It is a model of 'monopolistic competition where basically the anchor is a payment system that is quasi-fixed in the short run'. In general, he views the present state in macroeconomics as being somewhat 'decadent' in that it does not address itself to real-world problems. In this connection he also muses on methodological problems, on the need to cut into a subject even if all foundations are lacking. He mentions the problem of increasing returns as 'fundamental' to our understanding of involuntary unemployment. Weitzman also shares with us his views of Joan Robinson, Cambridge economics, and critiques of general equilibrium theory.

Part VII deals with the place of money and finance in Joan Robinson's economics and with a comparison of Joan Robinson's and the new classical macroeconomists' critiques of the neoclassical synthesis. In the opening Chapter (21), Dillard considers it paradoxical that Joan Robinson dealt only perfunctorily with money in view of her deep involvement in the preparation of Keynes's *General Theory*. As the title suggests, Keynes explains unemployment in terms of money and a monetary theory of interest. Apart from Richard Kahn, Joan Robinson worked more closely than anyone else in developing and refining the ideas and concepts in the *General Theory*. Prior to and following publication of the *General Theory*, she wrote several books and numerous articles, usually with Keynes's explicit sanction, explaining and defending its ideas. Yet in the post-Keynesian years when Joan Robinson extended Keynesian theory to the long period, money occupied no significant place in her theory. This appears paradoxical in view of her earlier immersion in Keynes's monetary economics. Dillard explores this apparent paradox.

The term finance is often referred to in two totally different meanings, the one being the liquidity needed by firms in order to make current production possible, the second being the yield from the placement of long-term securities on the financial market. In most macroeconomic models the first problem is ignored, while the second is identified with the financing of investment. In Chapter 22, Graziani shows this procedure to be fully legitimate in the framework of a fully neoclassical model. But Joan Robinson's model of income distribution requires a different treatment of finance, where, on the one hand, means of payment supplied by banks to firms are explicitly dealt with, and on the other hand, investment is financed by not only saving out of wage income but also firms' profits. Graziani attempts a reconstruction of the financing of the economy according to Joan Robinson's indications. He provides an analytical support to Joan Robinson's view that investment does not seem to react to changes in the rate of interest.

A very unusual and striking parallel is drawn between Joan Robinson's and the new classical macroeconomists' critiques of the neoclassical synthesis in Chapter 23 by Sheffrin, the well-known specialist on the new classical approach. He argues that the criticisms that Joan Robinson raised against American neoclassical Keynesian macroeconomics are in many ways similar to those of the new classical macroeconomists. Although her substantive ideas differ sharply from the new classicals, their preoccupations are surprisingly similar. Sheffrin contends that Joan Robinson's views on time, history, dynamics and even econometrics echo in the writings of the new classicals.

Part VIII concentrates on the most striking market failure (unemployment), but also deals with some others (financial markets) and the need for public policy to step into the gap. In the opening chapter (24), Laroque presents a model in which rational inventory-holders with perfect foresight are responsible for the business cycle. At the same time, the model provides an explanation of why arbitrage may not force the price system to its competitive value in the long run. Inventories prevent the *tâtonnement* process from converging to the competitive equilibrium. Finally the model gives a rationale for the use of Keynesian fiscal and monetary policies.

In Chapter 25, building on the Cass–Shell notion of 'sunspot' phenomena, Cass explores the implications for competitive market allocation when there are too few financial instruments to guarantee Arrow–Debreu equilibrium. He conducts the analysis in terms of the leading example, where two households only have available a single bond for hedging between two possible future states of the world. The most striking result is that, with such market 'failure', there will generally be a continuum of distinct equilibrium allocations in which sunspots matter – and thus ample justification for government intervention in the financial market.

In the next chapter (26), Tarshis deplores the macroeconomists' inability to forge satisfactory explanations for the sharp movements in interest rates in the last fifty years. He examines three such attempts: an explanation of high interest rates as a consequence of a low saving rate; the doctrine that attributes high interest rates to inflation or expectations of inflation; and an explanation of the level of interest rates by reference to the size of the federal budget. He then proceeds to construct a theory to replace those implicit in the aforementioned three attempts – a theory general enough to deal with day-to-day problems, that takes account of the unique features of money and credit markets, and one that must be consistent with acceptable macroeconomic insights.

In a related chapter (27), Eisner suggests that Keynesian unemployment does not require rigid wages. Where wealth effects of government debt to the private sector cannot maintain or restore full employment equilibrium, a fixed wage serves to define the price level. Money is not neutral where it co-exists with interest-bearing government debt. A government budget deficit involving proportionate increase of non-interest-bearing debt (money) and interest-bearing debt will raise current and planned future consumption demand and thus raise investment demand of rational entrepreneurs as well. Under conditions of less-than-full employment this should increase consumption *and* investment. With market-clearing full employment, a nominal deficit financed by proportionate increases of money and interest-bearing debt will cause inflation but no increase in the real value of money and debt.

Economists often assume that politicians have decided what the goals of economic policy are, while the political habit is merely to list goals without choosing among them. In Chapter 28, Jamie Galbraith reviews the goals of the Employment Act, as amended. He argues that the objective of full employment has lost relevance in a time when people are abandoning high-valued leisure for lower-valued jobs. If so, policy should strive instead to achieve sustainable increases in real household income, a process requiring emphasis on the exploitation of comparative advantage in world trade, and the substitution of fewer good jobs for a larger number of poor ones. Price stabilization, finally, is primarily a political imperative, necessary to reduce distributive conflicts that otherwise tend to overwhelm the limited decision-making resources of the political system.

Part IX picks up a theme closely related to Joan Robinson's critique of the American genus of Keynesian economics – namely, the content of full employment with which she challenged American economists in her Ely Lecture in 1971 as the second crisis in economic theory. It concentrates on Joan Robinson's denunciation of the creation of full employment by means of an armaments build-up and on her concern for ways of avoiding a costly arms race and preserving peace. In Chapter 29, Fischer outlines how economists can contribute to that goal by studying the economic consequences of war, analyzing the decision-making processes by which national governments choose between war and peace, and exploring how increased international trade and other forms of economic cooperation can help reduce tensions and increase each side's stakes in maintaining peace. Fischer argues that economists should begin to address also the crucial issues of war and peace – issues that have affected human welfare more seriously than business cycles, inflation, or trade statistics. He emphasizes that unless we can avoid a nuclear holocaust, all our other concerns would be futile.

In the closing chapter (30), the first Nobel laureate in economic science, Tinbergen enjoins the economic profession to follow in the footsteps of the legal and medical professions in accepting the responsibility of pointing out to the general public the dangers involved in nuclear war. His position is that 'the traditional attitude that warfare decisions are exogenous to the economist's realm can no longer be accepted'. In this 'sketch' of what the economics of warfare might consist of, Tinbergen begins with some spiritual and ideological aspects of warfare and a general historical survey of the subject. He then proceeds to a discussion of the economic and industrial aspects of warfare, followed by a retrospect on economists' contributions to the subject. He proposes the new elements to be added to the economics of warfare and suggests world-wide integration and changes in institutions as alternatives to warfare. 'Modern war is such an irrational activity, requiring such enormous sacrifices from humanity, that its elimination can make an unparalleled contribution to human happiness. Efforts made to further that elimination promise to be highly productive in comparison to many alternative efforts.'

References

Bronfenbrenner, M. (1979) 'Review of Joan Robinson's *Contributions to Modern Economics*', *Economic Journal*, 89 (June): 446–7.

Friedman, M. (1986) in W. Breit and R. W. Spencer (eds), *Lives of the Laureates* (Cambridge, Mass.: MIT Press) pp. 77–92.

Robinson, Joan (1932) *Economics is a Serious Subject* (Cambridge: Heffer).

Robinson, Joan (1979) *Collected Economic Papers*, vol. 5 (Oxford: Blackwell).

Samuelson, P. A. (1966) *The Collected Scientific Papers of Paul A. Samuelson*, ed. by J. E. Stiglitz, 2 vols (Cambridge, Mass.: MIT Press).

Samuelson, P. A. (ed) (1970) *Readings in Economics* (New York: McGraw-Hill).

Acknowledgments

Leo Hurwicz is to be 'blamed' for suggesting this undertaking commemorating Joan Robinson's contributions to economics; Ida and I for its execution. But there are many 'partners in crime' (aside from the obvious ones listed in the table of contents) and I am a bankrupt when it comes to distributing the 'blame' fairly.

It all started with a telephone call from Leo shortly after Joan died. I deeply appreciate his initiative, his 'utopian' system designer's confidence, and his wise counsel. The contributors' product is only partly identified in the table of contents. I am beholden to all of them and at a loss for words to express my gratitude for the spirit of cooperation, good workmanship, and the remarkable intellectual experience it has been.

At the formative stages and throughout the gestation of this project, I have had the good fortune to benefit from the support and advice of Kenneth Arrow, Dick Goodwin, Peter Hammond, Lawrie Klein, Mordecai Kurz, Robin Matthews, Ed Nell, Paul Samuelson, Joe Stiglitz, Lorie Tarshis, Jan Tinbergen, and John Whitaker. A very special thanks is due to Franco Modigliani, Bob Solow, and Jim Tobin who went out of their way to make time in their busy schedules, often at times inconvenient for them, to record their thoughts and for the extraordinary experience and the fun it has been.

It is my pleasant duty to record here my indebtedness to Richard (Lord) Kahn, Sir Austin Robinson, John Kenneth Galbraith, and (the late) Gunnar Myrdal for their encouragement and kind cooperation. Special thanks are also due to George Akerlof, John Hobakkuk, Rolf Henriksson, Sir Brian Hopkins, Ada Kalecki, (the late) Leonid Kantorovitch, Tadeusz Kowalik, Sir Arthur Lewis, Bill Nordhaus, K. N. Raj, Dick Stone, and Paul Sweezy.

I am glad to acknowledge all those who graciously commented on my two introductory chapters and preface. Thanks are due to Irma Adelman, Chris Archibald, Kenneth Arrow, Will Baumol, Bobby Becker, Buz Brock, David Cass, John Chipman, Gerard Debreu, Robert Dixon, Jamie Galbraith, Jean Gabszewicz, Harvey Gram, Augusto Graziani, Peter Hammond, Murray Kemp, Lawrie Klein, Andreu Mas-Colell, Robin Matthews, Ed Nell, Takashi Negishi, John Roberts, Paul Samuelson, Steve Sheffrin, T. S. Srinivasan, Lance Taylor, Vivien Walsh, and John Whitaker. Of course none of the above is responsible for any errors of omission or commission.

I am pleased to acknowledge the superb cooperation of the Head of the Reference Library at the University of Tennessee, Bob Bassett, and of the staff of the Stanford Libraries. Thanks are also due to René Olivieri of

Blackwell for his kind cooperation. It was good to have again Keith Povey's editorial help. As always I appreciate the assistance, advice, and encouragement of Tim Farmiloe of Macmillan. He makes the task easier and enjoyable. What more could one ask of a publisher?

In the process of completing these two volumes, I benefited from a fellowship from the Jerome Levy Economics Institute of Bart College. Their financial assistance is appreciated as is David Levy's and Dimitry Papadimitriou's interest and elegance.

It was my good fortune to have known Joan and some of the 'old guard' in Cambridge reasonably well. I am grateful for the opportunity and privilege. Perhaps I should add that the very special relation I had with Joan emanated from my work on Michał Kalecki during the gestation of which Joan demonstrated her best qualities of supporter, scholar, critic, and friend. Ida and I cherish the memories. Joan set and demanded very high standards of personal and scholarly integrity for herself and her friends. As I am writing these words I cannot help but remember the last time we saw her in 1980. Ida and I entered a room full of people, her eyes lit with a unique spark (probably she was remembering Kalecki). She sat with Ida, was silent for a while, and then said how much she appreciated the 'outstanding' work we had done on Kalecki. These words of Joan and the support of the contributors were a sustaining force in the execution of this fascinating endeavor, not always conducted under the most auspicious circumstances. We can only hope the result would not have disappointed Joan and are deeply grateful to those who have shown us so much kindness, understanding, and encouragement.

There is also another lady near to my heart whose moral fortitude, high standards, and exemplary (unremunerated) labors served as an incessant inspiration, guide, and critic during the long and difficult process of gestation and fruition of this enterprise. My wife, Ida, brought to it her usual dedication, enthusiasm, and desire to do the right thing. Lucky is the person who can 'survive' such an environment.

Our thoughts could not be better expressed than in the words of Richard Goodwin (the note in Chapter 7 of *Joan Robinson and Modern Economic Theory*): We offer these two volumes 'as a tribute to the memory of one of the more remarkable persons' we have ever known.

> Joan Robinson was an embodiment of 'the desire and pursuit of the whole' and her passing is a great loss to her friends, and, though often unacknowledged, to the profession as a whole. She had an uncanny and rare ability to unravel the daunting complexities of economic life by the exercise of logic alone. To this austere activity she dedicated unselfishly the bulk of her adult life. For the many of us who stood in awe and admiration of the purity and power of her devotion to the understanding of our world, a light has been extinguished.

Part I

Two Revolutions Combined: Imperfect Competition and Macroeconomics

1 Towards an Integration of Imperfect Competition and Macrodynamics: Kalecki, Keynes, Joan Robinson

George R. Feiwel

It was Michal Kalecki rather than I who brought imperfect competition into touch with the theory of employment. (Joan Robinson, 1933, 1969, p.viii)

1 INTRODUCTION

In Chapter 1 of the companion volume, I have traced Joan Robinson's contributions to economic theory and philosophy. There, on numerous occasions, I referred to the paramount influence of Keynes and Kalecki on her. As time went by, she became more and more Kaleckian in her interpretation of Keynes and in her perceptions of the great intellectual upheaval associated with his name. As early as 1952, referring to Kalecki's independent 'discovery of the General Theory', Joan Robinson (1952, p.159) wrote that 'by now it is impossible to distinguish what one has learned from which'. In fact, writing in 1948, she (1951, 1978 p.134) admitted that when she refers to the General Theory

> I do not mean simply the book called *The General Theory of Employment, Interest, and Money*, but the whole stream of ideas, or rather the analytical system, to which that book made the main contribution, but which is still in process of developing and perfecting itself, finding new applications and modifying its methods to treat new problems.

To what extent Kalecki really shared in the historical achievement that was the Keynesian revolution and whether he anticipated Keynes's *General Theory* is not the main issue here. What really matters is that in an essential sense, Kalecki's analytical construct was superior to Keynes's and that Joan Robinson perceived it as such and was strongly influenced by it. Thus to understand the dynamics of Joan Robinson's thought and the many influences governing her (particularly her shifting conception of the

Keynesian revolution and the economic, social and policy implications derived therefrom), we have to go to some essentials of Kalecki's analytical construct and, indeed, to her perception and interpretation of it.

The imperfect competition revolution had no bearing on the Keynesian revolution, though both of them took place at about the same time and in the same place and both involved at least some of the same *dramatis personae*. This is more than a doctrinal history puzzlement. Had it been otherwise, it would have fundamentally affected the course of the age after Keynes. Whatever the merits of Joan Robinson's *Economics of Imperfect Competition*, one of the reasons she came to reject it is because she was strongly influenced by Kalecki's pioneering integration of imperfect competition and macrodynamics. For her (1979a, p.193) this was one of the important strands of Kalecki's line of argument. 'Kalecki was able to weave the analysis of imperfect competition and of effective demand together'. She saw this as opening up the way for her own postwar work.

Joan Robinson realized that whatever else Keynes provided, his propensity to leave orthodoxy alone in matters of value theory may lead up a wrong alley. (Keynes 'carried a good deal of Marshallian luggage with him and never thoroughly unpacked it to throw out the clothes he could not wear' (Joan Robinson, 1962, p.79).) She was aware that her *Economics of Imperfect Competition* was not a great improvement. She had nothing effective to put in its place. Thus Kalecki provided her with the answer for which she was groping. For her, Kalecki's integration of imperfect competition and theory of employment (in fact, his entire approach) was the 'joker in the pack' of the Keynesian revolution.

After meeting Kalecki (as discussed in Section 2), Joan Robinson's writings reveal his pervasive influence. For her (1978, p.xvi) Kalecki's 'work was the most original and important of any in the interwar years'. How she herself perceived and acknowledged this influence will be discussed throughout this chapter. As we have noted, Kalecki was instrumental in shifting her perspective on Keynesian theory and policy. So much so that she had a tendency to read into Keynes what was actually in Kalecki and/or to attribute it to Keynes's oral teaching (see Joan Robinson, 1951, 1978, p.136). A passage in her review of Leijonhufvud (1968) is quite revealing. In it she (1969b, p.582) acknowledged that 'there is something' to Leijonhufvud's contention 'that we who worked with Keynes were saved from the misunderstandings rife in America because we had the benefit of oral teaching which was not made clear in the book'. But, she continues, 'I think that there are more important explanations. First Kalecki brought to England his own version of the General Theory, which tightened up some loose threads in Keynes's version and brought it into relation with imperfect competition, supplying a missing link in Keynes's theory of prices. To judge by this survey, Kalecki had very little influence on American doctrines'.

She (1976b, p.8) speculated why Kalecki had so little influence in America. His model lent itself to the introduction of all sorts of reservations and complications. 'Perhaps it was for this reason that Kalecki's version of the theory was smothered in a conspiracy of silence in the USA, while Keynes's was accepted and, in a garbled form, incorporated into current teaching. Both were holding a mirror up to modern capitalism, but Keynes's mirror was somewhat misty while Kalecki's was too bright for comfort'.

As noted in Chapter 1 of the companion volume, one can infer from Joan Robinson's writings (1979a, p.170) that from the beginning she saw more to the *General Theory* and saw it in a different light from that in which Keynes himself had seen it. For her the meeting with Kalecki was a perfect meeting of minds. The perceptive and often hostile critic of Cambridge and Cantabrigians, Harry Johnson (1978, p.158), corroborates our impression of Kalecki's dominant influence: 'The most important key to the transmogrification of Keynesian economics into something intellectually quite different in the hands (and writings, teachings and preachings) of Joan Robinson ... is the understanding that the dominant influence on Joan Robinson's Keynesianism was not Keynes, but the Polish economist Michal Kalecki'. Johnson (p.159) recalls that in the 1950s when Joan Robinson discussed theory she spoke of Keynes with some reverence and some impatience, 'but her eyes lit up with admiration whenever she mentioned Kalecki and his works'. Moreover, 'what Joan Robinson presented as Keynesian economics was as much Kaleckian economics as Keynesian economics, and increasingly Kaleckian as time passed'.

Kalecki's strong influence on Joan is manifest in her approach to economic theory in general. In particular, she creatively adopted his approach to pricing, distribution, and (with some reservations) to growth. Indeed, in the preface to her post war *magnum opus*, *The Accumulation of Capital*, she (1956, 1966, p.vi) classed Kalecki with the pioneers: 'My debt to Keynes, Wicksell and Marshall is the debt we all owe to our progenitors, and will be sufficiently obvious in the following pages. I have referred to them at particular points for the reader's convenience, not by way of acknowledgement of their legacies. Michal Kalecki, though a contemporary, comes into the same category'.

I venture to say that it was not only Kalecki, the theoretical, applied and political economist, who had such an impact on Joan. She also strongly admired his moral fortitude, integrity and independence of spirit[1] – characteristics which she fully shared, as we point out in the preface. By and large Joan Robinson shared with Kalecki a non-dogmatic, critical, and open-minded attitude towards Marx. An attitude developed by her after Kalecki encouraged her to read Marx and Rosa Luxemburg – two authors not on the standard Cambridge reading lists (the former particularly downgraded by Keynes). Like Kalecki, she perceived a fruitful apparatus in Marx's schemes of reproduction and had a strong aversion for the Marxian theory of value (see Chapter 1 (Section 8.2) of the companion volume).[2] Both Kalecki and Joan Robinson were political economists *par excellence*, but Kalecki was more pragmatic and less prone to abstract theory far removed from reality, though his work is more rigorous and cast in the mathematical mode. 'Though Kalecki liked to express his ideas in neat formulae, he was conscious of the limitations of that style of exposition, and set his arguments against the backdrop of history, politics and institutional change' (Joan Robinson, 1979a, p.196). Both Joan Robinson and Kalecki shared a strong commitment to improving the human lot and a radical political outlook, again in Kalecki's case more tempered by his exceptional realism. Both had extraordinarily forceful personalities. Those economists who have known Joan and experienced her tongue-lashings might be surprised to learn that Kalecki's personality was stronger. As she (1973, p.91) admitted 'I learned far more, over thirty-five years, from the arguments with Kalecki that I lost than from those that I won.' Kalecki and Sraffa were probably the only two people whom 'fearless Joan' feared.[3]

As far as it is possible to summarize a complex analytical system such as Kalecki's in a few words, the gist of this chapter is that in the 1930s, outside any world center of learning and without any formal education in economics, Michal Kalecki independently discovered the most essential ingredients that went into the making of what came to be known as the Keynesian revolution. In addition to integrating the theories of aggregate output, price, and distribution, Kalecki's system was dynamic. Indeed, Kalecki's theory of dynamics and fluctuations of national income and its partition between wages and profits is more general than the Keynesian system and more relevant to the present day. Kalecki avoided the distinction between micro and macro theories. He constructed his macroeconomic model on the basis of a more realistic theory of the firm that incorporated imperfect competition and income distribution as integral parts of his analysis. He elucidated the dynamic properties of the economic process and dealt with an open economy.

More specifically, in Section 2, we trace how Kalecki brought to Cambridge his version of the theory of employment and the reception it received. Because of our interest here in the Joan Robinson connection, we refrain from the more general aspects of the reaction to and reception of Kalecki's work. In order to better understand the intrinsic analytical differences and the essential similarities of Kalecki's and Keynes's constructs, the differences between their personalities are discussed in Section 3, followed by an outline of their diverse intellectual roots in Section 4. The next three sections examine the essential differences between the Kaleckian and Keynesian models and how these differences can be traced in Joan Robinson's work. To build a realistic theory, Kalecki explained how industrial prices are formed by mark-ups on costs and distinguished between 'cost-determined' and 'demand-determined' prices. The mark-ups depend on the relative strength of market imperfection he called the 'degree of monopoly' (Section 5). Together with other distributional factors this is the key for the determination of macrodistribution. Kalecki's theory of profits was based on the principle that wage earners do not save, but spend what they get and that entrepreneurs get what they spend. Entrepreneurs' profits are governed by their propensity to invest and consume and not the other way round (Section 6). In Section 7 we see that Kalecki's model presented the economic process in motion; that is, how one sequence develops from the preceding ones. The model encompasses long-run dynamics and the capacity effects of investments and some other supply considerations. Kalecki approached the theory of effective demand through the theory of the business cycle which established two basic relations: (1) the impact of effective demand generated by investment on profits and national income; and (2) the investment decision function (on which Joan Robinson disagreed with him), where the rate of investment decisions at a given time is roughly determined by the level and the rate of change in economic activity at some earlier time. To Kalecki the key prerequisite for becoming an entrepreneur is the ownership of capital. Investment decisions are related to the firm's 'internal' accumulation of gross savings. These savings allow the firm to make new investments without facing the problems of the limited capital market or 'increasing risk'. Kalecki dealt with an open system and treated the rate of export surplus as a promoter of prosperity and balance-of-payments difficulties as a factor limiting expansion. The next section (8) summarizes the differences and similarities examined in the preceding three sections as they shed light on Kalecki's model's and the *General Theory*'s respective places in the history of analysis. In Section 9 we show that Kalecki realized that whatever the rationale of the *economics* of full employment, the *political* problems are formidable. During World War II, while he wrote his masterful policy guidelines of the three ways to full employment, he realized the potential objections to such policies and predicted the emergence of the political business cycle. His analysis of postwar economic policy has had a strong influence on Joan Robinson's own, as we show in Chapter 1 (Section 8.3) of the companion volume.

2. KALECKI AND CAMBRIDGE

This is not the place to recount Kalecki's life (see Feiwel 1975, pp.21–6, 237–40, 293–301, 447–55).[4] But to those of us who believe that biography matters to the understanding of a person's work, a background sketch may be helpful. Born in the industrial city of Lodź, Poland, in 1899, Kalecki studied engineering. Before he graduated he sustained one of the first serious hardships and privations that were to plague his life. His father lost his job and the young Kalecki permanently interrupted his formal studies and sought full-time employment. This, though seemingly a blow to his career, was a distinct gain for economics.

Times were hard in post-Versailles Poland. Jobs were not plentiful. Kalecki tried his hand at economic journalism and in the next few years produced a long series of painstakingly researched and documented articles concerned mainly with market analyses for particular goods. Later, in the employment of the Research Institute of Business Cycles and Prices, he cooperated in studies of Polish national income and cyclical fluctuations in Poland and abroad.

This training in detailed empirical studies, combined with extraordinary theoretical insights, acute mathematical abilities, political astuteness, and a social conscience, served him in good stead when in 1933 he published his outline of a business cycle theory *Próba teorii koniunktury* (Kalecki, 1966)[5] – one of the most original and fundamental economic studies of the twentieth century, even if it was not recognized as such at the time and for many years to come. He presented the theory's basic outlines to the sophisticated audience of the newly formed international Econometric Society in October, 1933 (Kalecki, 1935) where it met with praise from Tinbergen and was critically received by Frisch. But there was still no sign that the world at large had recognized the impact of what the obscure Polish economist had to say. After all he wrote either in Polish (1933) or in mathematics (1935) neither of which was *lingua franca* for the majority of economists at the time.

In 1936, Kalecki traveled to Sweden on a Rockefeller Foundation Fellowship to make contact with the Scandinavian economists who were working along similar lines.[6] It is there that he first read the just published *General Theory*, the making of which, and Joan Robinson's participation in the Circus, are traced in Chapter 1 (Section 5) of the companion volume. Later he admitted that it was an eerie feeling, reading his own thoughts expressed by someone else. As Joan Robinson (1965, 1975, p.95) later attested, the fact that two men, miles apart in space, political outlook, education, and social circumstances (as we point out in the next section) had come to the same conclusions 'was a great comfort' to Keynes's entourage:

> Surrounded by blank misunderstanding, there were moments when we almost began to wonder if it was we who were mad or the others. In the serious sciences, original work is *discovery* – finding connections that were always there, waiting to be seen. That this could happen in economics was a reassurance that what we had discovered was really there.

In the spring of 1936 Kalecki traveled to England and remained some time in London where he attended some LSE seminars. He also made contact with Keynes's entourage (in particular Joan Robinson, Richard Kahn and Piero Sraffa). Joan (1979a, p.186) remembers that soon after the publication of her 'Disguised Unemployment' (1936) she

> received a letter, evidently from a foreigner visiting England, who said that he was interested in my article as it was close to some work of his own. I thought this very strange. Who could claim to be doing work that was close to this – the first fruits of the Keynesian revolution? When Michal Kalecki turned up, I was still more astonished. He cared little for party manners or small talk and plunged directly into the subject. He was perfectly familiar with our brand new ideas and he had invented for himself some of Keynes's fanciful concepts, such as the device of burying bank notes in bottles and setting off a boom in mining them. As we talked, I felt like a character in a Pirandello play, I could not tell whether it was I who was speaking or he. But he could challenge a weak point in Keynes's formulation and quickly subdued my feeble attempt to defend it.

In a letter (16 September (no year; probably 1936), courtesy of Mrs Ada Kalecki) Joan wrote to Kalecki: 'I cannot delay to tell you what a pleasure it is to me to be arguing with someone who is making an advance upon Keynes instead of endlessly disputing with people who have not understood the elementary points. I am now working on a book [1937, 1949] in which "Disguised Unemployment" will reappear, with a number of essays making applications of the General Theory to various problems (including international trade). I think you are one of the ten people in Europe who will understand what I am trying to do'. Kalecki drew Joan's attention to his 1935 article, for in the same letter she wrote: 'Your Econometrica article makes me ashamed. We ought to have welcomed you long ago as a kindred spirit. Unfortunately mathematics is an insuperable obstacle for me, and I never turned to the statement at the end. It must be rather annoying for you to see all this fuss being made over Keynes when so little notice was taken of your contribution'.

Reminiscing about those times, in an Oxford Kalecki Memorial Lecture Joan (1979a, p.187) pointed out that while she wrote in 1933 her so-to-speak interim report on how far the Keynesians had reached by that time (1951, 1978, pp.52–8) and comparing it with Kalecki (1933 and 1935) 'it is now evident that Kalecki had got much further'.

In the fall of 1936 Kalecki met Keynes. Joan Robinson (who as a woman was not a member of the Political Economy Club, founded by Keynes in 1909, which met in his rooms at King's College on alternate Mondays) was especially invited to introduce Kalecki who gave a talk in October 1936 – a session presided over by Keynes. The encounter with Keynes did not produce a real intellectual meeting of minds or a joining of scholarly forces. As we shall see in the next section, there was considerable disparity in their characters and relative positions. Joan Robinson (1973a, p.87) said later that Keynes was aloof, 'temperamentally oil and vinegar would not mix'. Shortly before his death Kalecki recalled that he was then a poor Polish Jew in need of a job, while Keynes was concerned with finding historical analogies to his discovery. He was comparing himself to Newton and searching for reasons why they were both misunderstood.

One of the repercussions of Kalecki's meeting with Joan (and to some extent with the other members of the Circus and Keynes himself) seems to be a shift in Kalecki's attitude. However, the shift was essentially not one of economic substance. Whereas previously he had an understandable tendency to differentiate in certain respects his work from Keynes (see, for example, Kalecki, 1936 and 1937), probably under Joan's influence, and more so upon his own realization that the cause of the Keynesian revolution would be better served if he joined the ranks of Keynes's disciples, he laid more stress on the 'Keynesian' aspects of his work, stressed more the similarities than the differences, and adopted the language and method of presentation used by Keynes – which was after all the language to communicate with mainstream economics.[7]

For example, after two years in England, Kalecki published *Essays in the Theory of Economic Fluctuations* (1939). The sixth essay of the volume, entitled 'A Theory of the Business Cycle', was an altered version of the article published under the same title in 1937. By that time the essay had become, at least in some circles, 'a classic of contemporary business cycle theory' (Lange, 1941, p.283). As compared with the previous expositions, in general the book expounds to a much greater extent on what Kalecki called the Keynesian theory of the multiplier. But elements of the multiplier could be traced to his Polish paper of 1933 (1966). In the foreword to the volume he (1939, p.7) acknowledged his indebtedness to Joan Robinson, whose comments helped him to make various improvements.

Joan Robinson's influence in this respect can be gauged from the comments she made (in the previously quoted letter of 16 September) regarding Kalecki (1937):

> I think it is a pity that you suggest at the beginning of your paper that you are making an attack on Keynes's system, when your real object is to fill a gap in it. I think you are wrong that he does not allow for a 'self-winding-up process'. He is always talking about how a movement 'feeds itself' but his treatment is vague and incomplete, and something on the lines of your paper is needed to give it precision.

As far as the definitions are concerned, I think it is possible to dispute about them till doomsday because in the nature of the case no system can be perfect. Keynes' system, as you say, is unrealistic, but yours is troublesome because marginal prime cost, as you define it, is not equal to marginal revenue, or is only equal to it if entrepreneurs are very foolish. It falls short of marginal revenue by some vague margin corresponding to Keynes' marginal user cost.

The idea of marginal disutility of risk-bearing is subject to the same objection as all utility ideas – that it involves a circular argument.

Why does supply price rise with scale? Because marginal disutility increases. How do you know marginal disutility increases? Because supply price rises!

However, Keynes' method does not get out of this difficulty, and it is one of those awkward points in economic theory that there seems no way out of. I think the idea of a rising supply curve of risk bearing for the individual is very useful, and you might supplement it by a further rise in the general supply curve due to individual differences in willingness to take risks. You then get a composite supply curve exactly analogous with the supply curve of output from land of differing fertility.

How much or how little Keynes was told about Kalecki and his work, why this was so, and whether Keynes was willing to listen will forever remain a mystery. Kalecki himself did not bring the fact of the priority of his publication to Keynes's attention. Shortly before his death, Kalecki admitted to me that he did not regret not having done it himself. He considered that it was up to Keynes's disciples to have brought the matter of his priority of publication to Keynes's attention. Mrs Ada Kalecki (Kalecki's widow) remembers that though neither Joan Robinson nor any member of the Circus told Keynes of Kalecki's priority of publication, they were supposed to do so in connection with Kalecki's writing of *Economic Fluctuations* for which they were going to ask Keynes to write a foreword. During that time Keynes fell ill and presumably the people close to him did not want to upset him. Kalecki acknowledged that Keynes's world-wide reputation and academic and intellectual standing probably contributed significantly to the propagation and acceptance of the Keynesian revolution.[8] But being human, Kalecki undoubtedly resented being relegated to the ranks of Keynes's interpreters. As Joan Robinson (1979a, p.187) remembers it:

When Kalecki came to Cambridge in 1936, we told Keynes about him, but he was not much impressed. His own ideas were in full spate (he was thinking about rewriting the *General Theory* in a completely different way) and he had not patience with anyone else's. He picked on a phrase in the *Econometrica* paper that seemed to him too 'monetarist', though in fact it contained a point of view which he later came to himself. Keynes did not sympathize with Kalecki's political presuppositions and by background and temperament they could not have been further apart. I commented on this once, saying 'oil and vinegar would not mix'. Some critic objected that they are mixed every day, but that needs constant stirring. Neither of these two characters was easy to stir. However, Keynes took the trouble to get a research project set up to provide Kalecki with a job. (This was just before the war and nothing much came of it.)

Although Michal behaved in public with a kind of scholarly dignity which is nowadays all too rare, he was naturally disappointed at lack of recognition. He said to me once: 'In the economics profession, no one notices the difference between good work and rubbish'. (I have been disappointed by this myself.)

Harry Johnson – another 'outsider' who did not feel well accepted in the Cambridge of the 1950s, and whose interpretation may, for that reason, be unfavorably slanted – sheds further light on the Keynes–Kalecki relationship. He (1978, p.159) relates a story whose validity he himself questions 'that Keynes could have found a position for Kalecki in Cambridge (as he had done earlier for Sraffa), but chose not to do so, on the grounds that Kalecki's personality was too different from the conventional for Cambridge to swallow'. And Johnson (p.159) continues:

> The irony is that, through Joan Robinson, Kalecki rather than Keynes shaped postwar Cambridge's 'Keynesian economics'. There is another ironical possibility, that had Kalecki been kept in Cambridge, he would have developed an economics far more relevant to, and capable of handling, Britain's postwar economic difficulties than 'Keynesian economics' as it developed at Cambridge, and more specifically at the Institute of Statistics at Oxford. My reason for thinking this is that, on the one occasion on which I met him in Cambridge (he being *en route* back to Poland), Kalecki delivered a lecture on inflation that employed a simple quantity theory of money together with expectations about the future trend of prices – amd which met with a reception from his former admirers so hostile that he was discouraged from publishing it.

Be that as it may, some clue to Keynes's attitude to Kalecki (and indirectly to Joan and to imperfect competition) is provided in the surviving correspondence (in which Joan Robinson served as intermediary and defender of Kalecki) of Keynes in his capacity as editor of the *Economic Journal* to which Kalecki had submitted three articles. Excerpts of this correspondence can be found in the Appendix for the reader to form his own judgment.

3 KALECKI AND KEYNES: CHARACTERS AND ECONOMISTS

In a biographical sketch of Alfred Marshall written in 1924, Keynes (1963a, pp.140–1) – who in this instance appeared to have been thinking more of himself than of Marshall – contemplated the essential qualities of character, understanding and approach that are the ingredients of greatness in economists:

> The study of economics does not seem to require any specialised gifts of an unusually high order. Is it not, intellectually regarded, a very easy subject compared with the higher branches of philosophy and pure science? Yet good, or even competent, economists are the rarest of birds. An easy subject, at which very few excel! The paradox finds its explanation, perhaps, in that the master-economist must possess a rare *combination* of gifts. He must reach a high standard in several different directions and must combine talents not often found together. He must be mathematician, historian, statesman, philosopher—in some degree. He must understand symbols and speak in words. He must contemplate the particular in terms of the general, and touch abstract and concrete in the same flight of thought. He must study the present in the light of the past for the purposes of the future. No part of man's nature or his institutions must lie entirely outside his regard. He must be purposeful and disinterested in a simultaneous mood; as aloof and incorruptible as an artist, yet sometimes as near the earth as a politician.

If I may quote myself (1975, p.viii), in my biography of Kalecki, I applied this quotation to Kalecki and commented as follows:

> This is a formidable list; and although it is doubtful that all of the requirements have ever been united in one person, some of them were Kalecki's most striking attributes. He did indeed possess a rare combination of gifts. He was not a historian by predisposition, but he had a perception for the economic process in motion and how one sequence develops from the preceding ones. First and foremost he was an essentially original thinker, with an unusual ability to identify and address himself to the most relevant problems. He could forge new tools for the solution of a problem or adapt existing ones. He certainly qualified as a mathematician and philosopher and even as a statesman in the sense that his motivation always was toward solving important public

issues. Still another aspect of the Keynes ideal was probably Kalecki's greatest gift: His analytical power and almost a genius for effective simplification permitted him to move easily and quickly from the highly abstract to the earthily practical. In sum, he was a political economist par excellence. And he was absolutely incorruptible, as his life and his former colleagues will attest.

Keynes and Kalecki came from two radically diverse social, cultural, and economic strata. They differed in almost as many aspects as can distinguish men: background, social position, education, experience, political outlook, and not the least in predisposition and temperament. However, certain similarities linked these two men who, in a world crisis, miles apart, under divergent circumstances. unbeknown to each other, and with a different technical apparatus, came to fairly similar conclusions.

Keynes was a product of Eton and Cambridge, with a tinge of Bloomsbury. He was born into the privileged class of the stable and secure British Empire of the latter part of the nineteenth century. Skidelsky (1983, p.1) refers to him as 'not just a man of establishments; but part of the elite of each establishment of which he was a member. There was scarcely a time in his life when he did not look down at the rest of England, and much of the world, from a great height'. Keynes was brought up in the intellectual atmosphere of Cambridge, where his father, John Neville Keynes, taught logic and political economy but he was primarily a University administrator. His early youth was spent in the enlightened reformist environment of his parents and his friends. By contrast, Kalecki was born into hostile surroundings and financial insecurity. He was born a Jew in a country where there was overt anti-Semitism. He was born a Pole while the country was partitioned among three foreign powers. His early childhood was spent under Russian tsarist occupation. From the very beginning – whereas Keynes's life was well ordered and in accord with the elements, so to speak – Kalecki had to battle an inimical world. Whereas Keynes had observed the havoc wrought by business downturns, the suffering and misery of the unemployed, and the sheer waste of idle resources, Kalecki knew the misery at first hand.

Keynes enjoyed what was probably the best education that the British Empire could provide. After seven years at St Faith's in Cambridge, he was enrolled at Eton. The next step was King's College, Cambridge. At the university he first specialized in mathematics, although his field of interest was very broad. Only later in his studies did he become attracted to economics and imbibed the ideas of the Cambridge school under Alfred Marshall and A. C. Pigou. Kalecki's formal education was in engineering, where he got a solid grounding in mathematics. Apparently when still a student Kalecki was so impressed by the power of mathematical tools applied to economics that he thought of investigating economic laws along the lines of the laws of thermodynamics (see Kalecki, 1979, p.429). Worswick (1977, p.28) who came from mathematics and learned economics from Kalecki, writes 'What I liked about Kalecki was that he used just that amount of mathematics that was needed and no more; it was only later on that I realized that he had far more in the shop then he ever put in the window'. Worswick (p.29) also recalls his overall impression of Kalecki: 'I thought him the best when I knew him in the war, and I still think so'. In economics Kalecki was self-taught. He had read Tugan-Baranovsky, Marx, and Rosa Luxemburg. In contrast with Keynes, who was well steeped in certain aspects of classical and neoclassical economics (but was in some respects ahistorical in his outlook as a scholar), Kalecki observed the phenomena of modern capitalism with a fresh mind unencumbered by traditional modes of thought. In a way, the new economics came much easier to Kalecki.

A large part of the *General Theory* is concerned with shedding the shackles of past fallacies. Apparently, for many years, Keynes was constantly grappling with the constraining effect of inculcated orthodoxy. In developing the theory of effective demand, Kalecki did not have to wrestle with this devil – it simply did not exist for him.[9] In a letter to Harrod (30 August 1936), Keynes (1973c, pp.84–5) drew an interesting parallel between his own need to escape orthodoxy and Harrod's disregard of it – a parallel that could well be applied to Keynes and Kalecki.

> I have been much pre-occupied with the causation, so to speak, of my own progress of mind from the classical position to my present views,—with the order in which the problem developed in my mind. What some people treat as unnecessarily controversial is really due to the importance in my own mind of what I *used* to believe, and of the moments of transition which were for me personally moments of illumination. You don't feel the weight of the past as I do. One cannot shake off a pack one has never properly worn. And probably your ignoring all this is a better plan than mine. For experience seems to show that people are divided between the old ones whom nothing will shift and are merely amazed by my attempts to underline the points of transition so vital in my own progress, and the young ones who have not been properly brought up and believe nothing in particular. The particles of light seen in escaping from a tunnel are interesting neither to those who mean to stay there nor to those who have never been there!

After graduating from the university, Keynes worked in the civil service. Shortly thereafter he began lecturing in economics and later became Fellow of King's College, and subsequently its most gifted bursar. During World War I, he held a responsible position in financial administration. Later he participated in an advisory capacity in the Treaty of Versailles. He moved from the theoretical-teaching plane to the observation of economic phenomena from political-administrative pinnacles. Kalecki's career as an economist had a very humble start. One of the first temporary jobs he found was in credit inquiry. Later he undertook painstaking statistical studies of commodity markets and a large-scale study of Polish national income. His career as an economic theoretician was begun by close observation of life. As Lipiński (who at that time was Kalecki's employer) recalled (1977, p.69):

> Most of his contributions were analyses of particular commodity markets (fifty survey articles being devoted to non-ferrous metals alone). But as well as giving a photographic impression of the market in question, he always tried to detect monopolistic tendencies and linkages and the international contradictions they were breeding. At the Institute Kalecki collaborated with Ludwik Landau on two pioneering studies of national income in Poland. In addition he wrote essays on investment trends and indices, the formation of trusts in Polish industry, consumption indices etc. His monthly analyses of the economic situation published in the Institute's *Bulletin* were always masterly.

In this sense also the new economics came easier to Kalecki than to Keynes. Yet both men had a genius for the realities of life. They had uncanny insight into how things actually work and a keen theoretical mind to extract the essence and the tendencies. This common faculty enabled them to come to similar conclusions and to discover what had always been there, unperceived by others. But Keynes was more intuitive and Kalecki was analytically more gifted.

Keynes, like most academic economists, was well trained in the economic theory of his time – at least that taught in Cambridge; that is, Marshall. Kalecki, on the other hand, was highly suspicious of existing theories. He began his career as a theorist not by studying them, but by observing economic reality; by inductive reasoning. He did not readily accept the theoretical findings of others without verifying them himself. 'Many of us seek inspiration by hunting around through the library to see what others have said but he would never take any idea or theorem for granted: almost invariably he would re-work it himself' (Worswick, 1977, p.28). It appears that the first books in economics Kalecki read attracted him more because of their description of reality than their analytic content. In the 1930s, he apparently re-read these works more carefully from the perspective of his own business cycle theory (see Kalecki, 1979, pp.430–2).

Kalecki and Keynes differed considerably in their style and approach to economic theory. Kalecki's argument is couched in mathematical form. His style is 'terse and to the point. He is near to the optimum from the point of view of communicating his ideas clearly and efficiently' (Johansen, 1978, p.162). Keynes's *General Theory* on the other hand, aroused much controversy at the time of its publication, not only because of the novelty of what he had to say, but also because it left much room for interpretation. To this day, more than fifty years after its publication there is continuing and sometimes growing controversy about what Keynes actually meant, as Solow points out in Chapter 17 in this volume. Johansen (1978, p.162) claims quite appropriately that there should 'hardly ever arise any great controversy about what Kalecki actually meant'.

By the mid-1930s, Keynes had gained worldwide recognition as an economist for his controversial *The Economic Consequences of the Peace*, *A Tract on Monetary Reform*, *A Treatise on Money*, and many original and thoughtful articles in *Economic Journal* and elsewhere. Even before the *General Theory* he was a leading economist of the Cambridge school. An important work by Keynes was certain to create a stir among his peers, whether they embraced or rejected the new ideas. On the other hand, Kalecki was a relatively obscure newcomer to the economic fraternity. His work was published in Polish, hence for a limited readership to start with. Even in his own country he was either not well understood or not given much credence. In 1933, Kalecki expounded his theory to a meeting of the Econometric Society. But it did not even ripple the placid waters of existing theory. In a word, Kalecki lacked status, authority, and influence.

In addition to being recognized as a leading economist, Keynes was at the forefront of the intellectual and artistic movements of his time. The breadth, variety, and enormous spectrum of his interests is truly awesome. Keynes was a 'versatile polymath ... intimate both of "Bloomsbury" and of those that inhabit the corridors of power' (Austin Robinson, 1975, p.9; see Skidelsky, 1983). Admirable though it may be, one wonders whether Keynes's wide range of interests was a plus or minus when it came to analytical economics. Apparently when Keynes was told that Hicks was a student of Dante's *Divine Comedy*, he reacted that Hicks could not be a serious economist.

By contrast, Kalecki revolved in a much narrower circle. He was not the worldly man Keynes was. His overriding passion was social justice, full employment, and an adequate and growing living standard for all. Both men were astute and sharp observers and commentators on the political and social scene of their age. But Kalecki was much more pessimistic (realistic) than was Keynes about the power of intellectual argument to produce change. Joan Robinson (1962, p.80) felt that Keynes went

> out of his way to pick out the interpretation of Marshall most adverse to his own views, to pulverize it, mock it and dance upon the mangled remains, just because he thought it a matter of great importance – of real, urgent, political importance – that people should know that he was saying something fresh. If he had been polite and smooth, if he had used proper scholarly caution and academic reserve, his book would have

> slipped down unnoticed and millions of families rotting in unemployment would be so much the further from relief. He wanted the book to stick in the gizzards of the orthodox, so that they would be forced either to spew it out or chew it properly.

Both men were fond of arguing and of controversies. Both were conscious of their extraordinary intellectual powers and did not suffer fools gladly. Both used wit to great advantage and the depth of their thoughts was often revealed in humor.[10] Both appeared to be arrogant – but that was all in the eyes of the beholder. Joan Robinson (1962, p.79) spoke of Keynes as being 'singularly free of spitefulness because his self-assurance needed no external nourishment'. This characterization could equally well be applied to Kalecki. According to Austin Robinson (1975, p.11). Keynes 'was easier to argue with than many who have entrenched themselves in doctrinal positions today. He was more patient and more prepared to meet argument and to face the difficulties of someone who differed from him'. In many respects the image of Kalecki (see Feiwel, 1975, pp.3–17) comes to mind, and indeed also that of Joan Robinson, when one reads her (1978, pp.xi–xii) perceptive portrait of Keynes:

> It is difficult to convey an impression of Keynes to someone who did not know him. In the world, he was considered arrogant and harsh; this was because he loved to put a pin into any pompous balloon that he encountered. With us in Cambridge he was far from harsh. He had exacting standards but withal he was warm-hearted and generous. He was conscious of being far more intelligent than nearly everyone whom he met, but that was just a fact; he had no need to puff himself up. He had a sense of absolute values; he was willing to argue with anyone on the merits of the case in hand; he could be ferociously obstinate but it never occurred to him to use his authority and eminence to crush a younger disputant and he was ready to take an interest in fresh ideas wherever they came from.

It seems, however, that in speaking of Keynes's receptiveness to new ideas, Joan appears to have glossed over a certain elitism in Keynes, as evidenced at least by his dealings with Kalecki who did not have the right credentials (see Appendix). In another context, she (1973a, p.252) admitted that 'Keynes was a snob. If you had not been to a good school he cut you'.

Aside from the fact that they both possessed superbly clear and sharp minds, a link between Keynes and Kalecki was their profound concern for humanity. True, the concern manifested itself differently; it was more or less intense, and the remedies sought varied. Kalecki was always by far more radical. Keynes was certainly not a radical. He wanted to preserve capitalism and realized that, in order to do that, it needed reforming. The basic idea is conservative – that of preserving the existing order of free private enterprise. The approach is liberal – that of the socially conscious observer of the evils of his time whose aim is only to reform the existing order so as to make it function better, more equitably more humanely. Comparing Marx, Marshall and Keynes, Joan Robinson (1960, 1975, pp.3 and 12) said:

> Marx maintained that capitalism is bound to develop in such a way as to bring about its own destruction, and urged the workers to organize themselves to hasten its overthrow. Marshall argued that, in spite of blemishes, it is a system which promotes the good of all. Keynes shows that it has deep-seated defects which, however, he believed are capable of being remedied. Marx is making propaganda against the system. Marshall is defending it and Keynes is criticizing in order to improve it.
>
> Marx's analysis of capitalism shows its strong points, although his purpose was to attack it. Marshall's argument inadvertently shows the wastefulness of capitalism, although he meant to recommend it. Keynes in showing the need for remedies to the defects of capitalism also shows how dangerous the remedies may be.

And elsewhere she (1979a, p.178) continued:

> Keynes had a high degree of intellectual detachment but he frankly admits to an emotional ambivalence. Morally and aesthetically, capitalism disgusted him, while at the same time he felt that the system was the 'best in sight' and must be defended.

Writing as early as 1926, Keynes questioned the myth of a self-regulating mechanism channelling private interests into a social optimum: 'The world is *not* so governed from above that private and social interests always coincide. It is *not* so managed here below that in practice they coincide. It is *not* a correct deduction from the Principles of Economics that enlightened self-interest always operates in the public interest. Nor is it true that self-interest generally *is* enlightened' (Keynes 1963b, p.312). Keynes was troubled by waste, plain stupidity and mismanagement of resources, and needless poverty. But he concentrated attention on expansion of output and not so much on the problem of resource allocation and who got the output. 'For my part, I believe that there is social and psychological justification for significant inequalities of incomes and wealth, but not for such large disparities as exist to-day' (Keynes 1936, p.374). 'Keynes was, indeed, little interested in income distribution' (Austin Robinson, 1975, p.20).

Both Kalecki and Keynes had a distinct preference for inflation over unemployment and deflation. But they differed in their relative emphasis on how to deploy economic resources to enhance and maintain full employment, and on what full employment is for and who are its beneficiaries; i.e. on the problem of level, content, and distribution of aggregate output. In politics, Keynes was a 'pragmatic' English liberal. In the famous last chapter, Keynes said his *General Theory* was 'moderately conservative in its implications' (Keynes, 1936, p.377). But this last chapter was offered as a paradox, according to Joan Robinson (1979a, p.125). 'All his life he had been treated by the establishment as an *enfant terrible*, so that to present himself as a conservative was partly ironical. Moreover, the preceding chapters of the book were a powerful polemic against received ideas. It was because Keynes was shocked by the force of his own indictment of capitalism that he wrote the last chapter in a mollifying tone'.

Did Kalecki criticize capitalism to destroy or to reform and preserve? This question cannot be answered unambiguously. First of all, Kalecki had no dogmatic commitment to destroy the system. He always associated criticism with finding remedies. Even if one should answer that Kalecki was a reformer, it bears underlining that reform had a different meaning for Kalecki and Keynes. For Kalecki it would entail more fundamental changes in the features of the capitalist economy and society. Above all he was dedicated to a more equitable distribution of national wealth.

Kalecki's political position underwent some shifts under the influence of contemporary developments: (1) In his original articles on the business cycle, Kalecki pointed out very forcefully the absurdities and waste of the capitalist system. He showed how the creation of effective demand by investment could be the very reason for the ensuing slump simply because these investments are useful. He pondered over the paradox of a system where useless investments would be more beneficial. This made a very forceful impression on Joan Robinson and is echoed in many of her writings. (2) During World War II, Kalecki seems to have been caught by the prevailing expectations that a more just world would emerge from the destruction. His writings indicate that he inclined toward reform of the capitalist system. His 'Three Ways to Full Employment' is still a valid and timely reform blueprint. But he was skeptical and predicted the emergence of the political business cycle (see Section 9.1). (3) Kalecki was thoroughly disillusioned by the experience of post-war capitalism. He denounced and repudiated the creation of effective demand and an increased living standard by military production. His disappointment was made evident in his refusal to write a second edition of his full-employment essay. Would Keynes have approved the modern methods of creating effective demand?

Another link between Keynes and Kalecki was the lack of understanding with which their theories were met at first. Outside the small group of his students and close collaborators – the Circus – at first few economists understood where Keynes was heading. Later he gained a number of followers on both sides of the Atlantic. But it is only after World War II that Keynesian economics came into its own and became a respectable subject in economics curricula.

Notwithstanding Keynes's 'moderately conservative' attitude, his scheme for bolstering up the capitalist economy was vigorously opposed by those who stood to gain most by its preservation in a more viable form. This opposition stemmed (and still does) from an ill-conceived concept of the viability of the capitalist order without Keynesian-type government intervention. Also, there was a distorted view of the personal interest of the individual capitalist and of that of the system as a whole (cf. Klein 1966, p.184). Paradoxically, the Keynesian tool-box was often abused on the grounds that it is rampant socialism, or at least was paving the way for a socialist order. Such critics seemed to ignore that *laissez-faire* capitalism could not survive, and without the use of Keynesian prescriptions the two existing alternatives were either socialism or fascism. Without considering humanistic values of these alternative social systems, they both involve a far larger dose of government intervention in the economic system than that foreseen by the Keynesian-type reform. 'The authoritarian state systems of to-day seem to solve the problem of unemployment at the expense of efficiency and of freedom. It is certain that the world will not much longer tolerate the unemployment which is associated ... with present-day capitalistic individualism. But it may be possible by a right analysis of the problem to cure the disease whilst preserving efficiency and freedom' (Keynes 1936, p.381).

Kalecki was just as misunderstood. He (1979, p.496) quipped that any new theory in economics provokes primarily ... new misunderstandings. Among his colleagues, few comprehended the purport of Kalecki's essay.[11] A striking example is that from his two closest collaborators, Ludwig Landau, the statistician, and Marek Breit, the economist, it was the former who grasped immediately the essence of new economics, whereas the latter had to break down numerous barriers of orthodox economic theory to assimilate Kalecki's revolutionary concepts. Kalecki met with similar misunderstanding from the militant left. Instead of using the paradoxes of the capitalist economy that he outlined to bolster up their own criticism of capitalism, they attacked him on the grounds that he attempted to save capitalism, which they claimed was an impossible task. They viewed deficit spending as aggravating the situation. These Marxists did not differ much from the traditional school. On a theoretical plane, Kalecki's Marxist critics misunderstood his method (see Kalecki, 1979, pp.158–69; 450–1, 461–2, and *passim*; Lipiński, 1977, pp.70–1, 74).

4 THE INTELLECTUAL ROOTS OF KALECKI AND KEYNES

That even economists are 'social animals', subject to the many complex interactions and tensions between the individual, group and environment, few would probably deny. Thought and action are full of social interdependencies, feedbacks and conflicts. The individual simultaneously gains knowledge from others and suffers from 'assymetry of information'. One uses ideas and language that are common 'group' knowledge. There are ideas in the air. Through indirect exposure, one is contaminated by the thoughts, concepts, modes of expression, terminology and expository style of those one never read, met or heard of. To paraphrase Keynes, not only practical men, but also economists are partly 'slaves' of some defunct economists. One cannot escape the influence of others, even those one rejects or opposes. Unwittingly one follows the line of others. In order to communicate effectively one's ideas to others, one has to formulate and present one's thoughts in a language and methods currently used by all. No economist is an island. All this verges on the commonplace. Yet one needs to be reminded of it when one enters history of economic thought where 'roots' are all too often taken literally.

Yes, it is a truism that no scientist or researcher works in a vacuum, and that his discovery is not totally new. Our thoughts are moulded and influenced by those who came before us. The discovery consists of many elements, ideas, or interdependencies known before, but really unseen, waiting to be perceived in a new configuration and light. The merit of the discoverer lies in integrating new and old ideas, supplying the missing links in creating an analytical system, and in perceiving new implications. So it was with Keynes and Kalecki. Although they arrived at similar conclusions, the many differences in their approach, perception, and inferences can be traced principally to the fact that they were descended from widely disparate genealogical trees of knowledge. Clearly, comparisons are hazardous. There is a large element of incomparability between economists, for both similarities and differences may be emphasized and a body of evidence can be cited to support each contention. Original minds have common traits with respect to certain ideas and diverge considerably on others. Granted that construction of a family tree is not an easy task, one can detect Keynes's intellectual linkage to Malthus and Marshall and Kalecki's affinity with Marx and Rosa Luxemburg. Any short statement in economics is necessarily wrong, except this one, Marshall reminds us. While there are elements of truth in it, it is probably a gross oversimplification to speak of the 'Marshallian Keynes' and the 'Marxian (Luxemburgian) Kalecki', if for no other reason that both men were exposed to powerful other influences and adopted some parts, but rejected weighty components of the baggage of their progenitors.

The *General Theory* is best understood as the culmination of the intellectual development of the Cambridge school of economics, steeped in the classical tradition, via Marshall. Keynes got almost all his economics from Marshall. His attitude towards Marshall is reflected in his splendid and subtly critical essay on Marshall and in his admiring portrait of Mary Paley Marshall, where in many ways there is implied criticism of her husband (Keynes 1963a, pp.125–217 and 324–47).

Keynes revolted against all those theories familiar to him that did not explain the question of effective demand.[12]

> To me the most extraordinary thing, regarded historically, is the complete disappearance of the theory of demand and supply for output as a whole, i.e. the theory of employment, *after* it had been for a quarter of a century the most discussed thing in economics. One of the most important transitions for me, after my *Treatise on Money* had been published, was suddenly realising this. It only came after I had enunciated to myself the psychological law that, when income increases, the gap between income and consumption will increase – a conclusion of vast importance to my own thinking but not apparently, expressed just like that, to anyone else's. Then, appreciably later, came the notion of interest being the measure of liquidity preference, which became quite clear in my mind the moment I thought of it. And last of all, after an immense amount of muddling and many drafts, the proper definition of the marginal efficiency of capital linked up one thing with another. (Keynes, 1973c, p.85)

Keynes was fascinated by Malthus, downgraded Ricardo, and was distinctly biased against and 'could never make head or tail of Marx' (Joan Robinson 1965, 1975, p.96). 'Classical theory that had come down to Keynes from Marshall was a travesty of Ricardo' (Joan Robinson, 1979a, p.212). Keynes believed that 'the idea that we can safely neglect the aggregate demand function is fundamental to Ricardian economics, which underlie what we have been taught for more than a century. Malthus, indeed, had vehemently opposed Ricardo's doctrine that it was impossible for effective demand to be deficient; but vainly.' Since Malthus was not able to explain satisfactorily 'how and why effective demand could be deficient or excessive, he failed to furnish an alternative construction; and Ricardo conquered England as completely as the Holy Inquisition conquered Spain . . . The great puzzle of Effective Demand with which Malthus had wrestled vanished from economic literature . . . It could only live furtively, below the surface, in the underworlds of Karl Marx, Silvio Gesell or Major Douglas' (Keynes, 1936, p.32).

It seems that in his essay on Malthus, Keynes went much too far in commenting on passages of the famous Malthus–Ricardo correspondence. He appears never to have grasped the problem with which Ricardo was wrestling: 'One cannot rise from a perusal of this correspondence without a feeling that the almost total obliteration of Malthus's line of approach, and the complete domination of Ricardo's for a period of a hundred years has been a disaster to the progress of economics.' Keynes continued, 'If only Malthus, instead of Ricardo, had been the parent stem from which nineteenth-century economics proceeded, what a much wiser and richer place the world would be to-day!' (Keynes, 1963a, pp. 117, 120–1). According to Joan Robinson (1979a, p.213), 'Keynes was right in showing that Ricardo was blind to the nature of effective demand but it was not right to throw him into the same box as Pigou in timeless equilibrium. Ricardo was observing a historical process of accumulation going on through time and, like Keynes, he was applying what he believed to be a realistic analysis of the actual situation to problems of policy'.

To a large extent, Keynes's great achievement was negative in the sense that he undermined orthodox economics and policy. He revolted against the tyranny of Say's Law of the Market from within the citadel of orthodoxy (see also Kalecki, 1979, pp.239–59). At least he shook up orthodox economics and provoked re-examination and reassessment. In this respect, Keynes's achievement is incommensurately greater than that of Kalecki (see Joan Robinson, 1965, 1975, p.98; Kahn, 1984, pp.3–90).

What did Marx and his followers have to offer on the question of effective demand? For Keynes, *Capital* was an obsolete textbook, not only scientifically faulty, but inapplicable to the modern world. 'Keynes himself never studied Marxian economics (he was quite happy to believe the rumour that it is all nonsense)' (Joan Robinson, 1980, p.121). Kalecki believed (1968, pp.78–9):

> That Marx was deeply conscious of the impact of effective demand upon the dynamics of the capitalist system follows clearly from this passage of the third volume of the *Capital*: 'The conditions of direct exploitation and those of the realisation of surplus-value are not identical. They are separated not only by time and space but logically as well. The former are limited merely by the productive capacity of the society, the latter by the proportions of various branches of production and by consumer power of the society.'
>
> However, he did not systematically scrutinize the process described by his reproduction schemes from the point of view of the contradictions inherent in capitalism as a result of the problem of effective demand.
>
> It is one of his most prominent followers, Rosa Luxemburg, who expressed very definite and even extreme views on the subject: she rejected altogether the possibility of long-run expanded reproduction if

no 'external markets' are in existence. By 'external markets' she understood those outside the world capitalist system consisting not only of underdeveloped countries but also the non-capitalist sectors of developed capitalist economies, for instance, peasant agriculture as well as government purchases.

The economic writings of Rosa Luxemburg – one of Marx's most brilliant, original, and unorthodox followers, 'rarest of all rare phenomena – a Marxist critical of Karl Marx' (Stark 1968, p.11) – were neglected by both Marxists and non-Marxists alike (Joan Robinson, 1960, 1975, p.59). She was considered 'the queen of underconsumptionists' (Sweezy, 1942, p.171). Marxist economists generally neglected the underconsumption element in Marx's theory. They treated Luxemburg as a heretic. Although Kalecki rehabilitated Luxemberg's views, she is still treated as *persona non grata* by many orthodox Marxists. Her attitude to *Capital* is revealing:

> We must not look to the last two volumes of *Capital* to provide us with a final and completed solution of all economic problems. In some cases these problems are merely formulated, together with an indication here and there as to the direction in which one must work to arrive at a solution. In accordance with Marx's whole attitude, his *Capital* is not a Bible containing final and unalterable truths, but rather an inexhaustible source of stimulation for further study, further scientific investigations and further struggles for truth. (Luxemburg, 1936, p.371, quoted after Dobb 1967, p.264)

Kalecki himself related his argument to Marx and Rosa Luxemburg in the first English editions of his studies on modern capitalism.[13] After presenting certain macroeconomic relationships by means of equations, Kalecki stated:

> It may be interesting to notice that the above equations are contained in the famous Marxian scheme of 'extended reproduction.' Marx even considers the questions of how to provide 'means' for increased expenditure on investment. It must be added, however, that the problems discussed here are treated by Marx from a rather special point of view. He is interested in finding out, with the help of exchange equations, the pace of investment in investment and consumption goods industries respectively, which is necessary in order to secure a steady expansion of output. (The rates of profit in both divisions of industry are assumed to be equal throughout and on this basis the process of expansion is constructed so as to make investment in each, at the end of every

> 'production-exchange cycle,' equal to its saving so that there is no 'shift of capital' from consumption to investment goods industries or conversely.) He does not pay attention to the problem of what happens if investment is inadequate to secure the moving equilibrium, and therefore does not approach the idea of the key position of investment in the determination of the level of total output and employment.
>
> Exactly the reverse attitude is represented by one of his eminent pupils, Rosa Luxemburg. In her *Akkumulation des Kapitals* she stressed the point that, if capitalists are saving, their profits can be 'realized' only if a corresponding amount is spent by them on investment. She, however, considered impossible the persistence of net investment (at least in the long run) in a closed capitalist economy; thus, according to her, it is only the existence of exports to the non-capitalist countries which allows for the expansion of a capitalist system. The theory cannot be accepted as a whole, but the necessity of covering the 'gap of saving' by home investment or exports was outlined by her perhaps more clearly than anywhere else before the publication of Mr. Keynes's *General Theory*. (Kalecki, 1939, pp.45–6)

Marx spelled out the equilibrium conditions for steady growth. This was particularly important because his predecessors assumed that land would be a limiting factor, so that the steady state would require zero growth. Luxemburg does add something new. By holding that investment in the capitalist economy must be zero in the steady state, she made dramatic the possibility that saving would not equal investment so that there could be no equilibrium. But, of course, as Kalecki notes, the contention of zero investment in the long run is unacceptable.

Keynes's harsh words about *Capital* are a blemish on his scholarly escutcheon. Most modern serious scholars treat Marx positively. For our purposes, we may note that Samuelson (1986, p.263) 'once referred to Karl Marx as "... a minor post-Ricardian ... a not uninteresting precursor of Leontief's input-output ..."' He later felt that 'that was worse than a crime. It was a blunder'. Thereafter he hailed *Capital*'s vol. 2 *Tableaus of Simple and Expanded Reproduction* as Marx's most original contribution. He chided both the critics for missing this achievement and Marx's partisans for 'praising his sterile paradigm'. Samuelson's (p.264) advice to an economic theorist about to go to jail (for what 'crime'? the neoclassical synthesis?) who can take with him 'only two chapters out of the scores of chapters in *Capital*'s three volumes ... is to hold on to the final two chapters in Volume II'. Joan Robinson (1973a, p.28) claimed that the Marxian schemes of reproduction,

> with the necessary corrections and elaborations, are the basis of all modern theories of economic growth; they have been much in vogue

> amongst the academics since Professor Domar rediscovered the model of the Russian economist F'eldman. They were used by Michal Kalecki in his analysis of fluctuations, which is the basis of all modern trade cycle theories. They are the basis of the theory of prices in a socialist economy ... And they are the basis of Professor Leontief's input-output economics.

And, in responding to Findlay's characterization of her lineage in *The Accumulation of Capital* as a descendant of Marx (while Harrod and Domar descend from Keynes and Solow and Swan from Wicksell), she (1965, 1975, p.51) protested:

> This is more epigrammatic than correct. He does not mention what I think is the most interesting and important Marxian idea incorporated in my model – that excess demand for labour speeds technical progress; he himself shows how large a part Wicksell's conceptions play in it (other critics complained, I think more justly, that I made too much fuss about them); the Keynesian elements were spilled out when he stood the model on its head. And he fails to mention Kalecki who provided an essential clue: the workers spend what they get and the capitalists get what they spend. I would prefer to claim all four amongst the progenitors of my model.

4.1 Details

Where does the demand come from which keeps accumulation going? (Joan Robinson, 1960, 1975, p.65).

Rosa Luxemburg's answer to this question was to find a market for surplus goods only outside the world capitalist system (Kalecki, 1971, pp.146–55). The 'external markets' are not only composed of underdeveloped countries but also include the non-capitalist sectors of developed capitalist economies, such as the peasant agriculture and the purchases by the government sector. Only the 'exports' from the capitalist system were considered by Luxemburg as the *spiritus movens* of development. Thus here is the pessimistic view of the future of the capitalist economy: by undermining the non-capitalist mode of production and gradually pervading the whole world, capitalism eliminates simultaneously the possibility of its further development.

To the quantitative exaggeration of the role of 'external markets', Luxemburg contributed a fundamental error, which she perpetuated in her analysis of the impact of these markets on the development of capitalism. In the main core of her argument she considered erroneously that the market for the surplus is created to the extent of total exports to the non-capitalist sector and not only to the extent of surplus of export over import.

Indeed, as Kalecki has shown, 'capturing of new foreign markets is frequently mentioned as a way out of depression. But it is usually not added that what is essential in this context is an increase in the export surplus rather than in absolute exports . . . In order to stimulate the upswing by means of foreign trade, the balance of trade component of profits must increase, i.e. new surplus of exports over imports must be achieved' (Kalecki, 1966, p.16). Imports absorb purchasing power similarly to domestically produced goods, and, to the extent that exports are accompanied by imports, they do not contribute to the expansion of markets for national output. Kalecki showed that Luxemburg unduly stressed the impossibility of the development of a capitalist economy and disregarded expansion owing to certain aspects of technical progress which, however, do not ensure a satisfactory long-run utilization of productive capacity. But despite her slips, the significance of 'external markets' for the development of capitalist economies cannot be dismissed.

Kalecki argued that one of the most interesting elements of Luxemburg's theory, relevant to present-day capitalism, is the treatment of government purchases, especially of armaments, as a form of 'external markets' – markets that play a crucial role in the functioning of modern capitalism. Nor did she envision the possibility of averting crises by the income effect that such expenditures generate. Moreover, as in the case of other 'external markets', she consistently committed the error of treating the total government expenditure as a factor of realizing surplus production; i.e. independently of the means of financing. Government expenditures (armaments), to the extent that they are financed by budgetary deficits or by taxation of capitalists, contribute to solving the problem of effective demand because their effect – in contrast to financing government expenditures by indirect or direct taxation burdening workers who largely spend what they earn – contributes to solving the cardinal problem of effective demand as their effect is not offset by the decline of investment and consumption expenditures.

Luxemburg correctly saw armaments orders as 'external markets' that can absorb a part of accumulation. But she failed to exclude from this type of 'external market' the case in which armaments are financed by taxation of wage and salary earners' incomes. Significantly, Luxemburg did not treat the 'external markets' created by government activity as a problem of paramount importance. She predicted the general crisis of capitalism caused by the exhaustion of non-capitalist markets, but she did not envisage the possibility of counteracting the crisis by 'external markets' of government purchases ('armament markets'). At present the 'external markets' of this particular form are of much greater importance for expanded reproduction than at the time (1913) when the author of *The Accumulation of Capital* propounded her theory.

Luxemburg treated expanded reproduction in the long run without the existence of 'external markets' to be not only far from obvious but outright impossible. But as Kalecki commented, she argued this contention naively, without showing the relevance of the question of effective demand for the development of the capitalist economy. One of the flaws in her reasoning was that identification of investment decisions lies not with individual investors, but somehow with the capitalist class, taking the investment decision as a whole. Kalecki wondered why the capitalist class, frustrated by the knowledge of the absence of final markets for the surplus of goods corresponding to accumulation, should see reason in undertaking such investment.

Kalecki realized that, despite errors in her argument, Luxemburg's skepticism about the possibility of long-term expanded reproduction was valuable since the self-propelled development of the capitalist economy cannot be taken for granted. Kalecki noted that, even though following a different line of reasoning, he also arrived at the conclusion that expanded reproduction is by no means a 'natural' phenomenon, and that he attempted to find the source of expanded reproduction in properties of technical progress ('technical dynamism'). Thus Kalecki maintained that development of capitalism does not depend entirely on 'external markets', but the latter factor is still significant.

In elucidating the problem of effective demand, Kalecki considered juxtaposition of Luxemburg's and Tugan-Baranovsky's views of great interest. He attempted to show where, in fact, both of them committed major errors in their arguments and where they contributed to the understanding of the processes of the 'queer and perverse world in which we are living'.

Michael Tugan-Baranovsky expounded the thesis that the capitalist system has unlimited possibilities of development. In the arguments about the market of national output advanced in terms of the Marxian reproduction scheme, the stands taken by Rosa Luxemburg and Tugan-Baranovsky were diametrically opposed. Tugan-Baranovsky denied altogether that the problem of effective demand may obstruct the development of the capitalist mode of production. The latter depends entirely on the growth in productive capacity. On the other hand, Luxemburg considered expanded reproduction in a closed capitalist system impossible. She attributed its entire development to the possibility of realization in external markets. Kalecki's own views were shaped by the contrast between Luxemburg and Tugan-Baranovsky.

Criticism of Tugan-Baranovsky's theory suggested to Kalecki that (i) as a consequence of the problem of effective demand, expanded reproduction is far from obvious and clearly an 'unnatural' state of the capitalist economy; and (ii) nevertheless, such reproduction does not necessarily depend on 'external markets'. There is still something to be learned from Rosa Luxemburg, both as far as her positive contribution and the errors she committed are concerned. The same is, of course, true of Tugan-Baranovsky.

According to Kalecki (1971, p.146), Tugan-Baranovsky 'rightly stresses the "antagonistic character" of the capitalist regime, as a result of which the production of consumer goods is not its final aim and the demand for them is not the motive force of its development'. The aim of production is not the satisfaction of the needs of the broad spectrum of the population but the pursuit of profits by businessmen. Consequently, it is not at all absurd to base development of the economy on an expansion of 'coal and steel', which serves for the production of more 'coal and steel.' The output of 'coal and steel' is as justified as that of consumer goods if it earns profits.

Kalecki (1971, p.155) pointed to Tugan-Baranovky's focus on

> the paradoxical and absurd character of 'antagonistic systems' whose main task is not catering to human needs. In his vision of future capitalism, machines were to produce machines for production of machines. But making the high level of employment and workers' consumption dependent on production of the means of destruction is even more absurd.

Kalecki observed that the theories of Tugan-Baranovsky and Rosa Luxemburg find something like a point of intersection in post-war capitalism (with particular reference to the US), where a decisive function is performed by the 'armaments market' – a market created by the government for the production of means of destruction (Kalecki, 1971, p.155).

Indeed, the bridge between Rosa Luxemburg's and Joan Robinson's *Accumulation of Capital* was Kalecki. Joan Robinson wrote a thoughtful and critical introduction to the English translation of Rosa Luxemburg where she (1960, 1975, p.73) noted at the end that 'for all its confusions and exaggerations, this book shows more prescience than any orthodox contemporary could claim'. When she began seriously her work on the generalization of the General Theory (see Chapter 1 of the companion volume), Joan Robinson (1952, p.158) acknowledged 'that there are a number of confusions and obscurities' in Rosa Luxemburg's exposition. In order to refute the 'various kinds of nonsense that have been attributed' to Rosa Luxemburg, Joan Robinson (pp.156–58) attempted her own interpretation.

It may be noted that in an essay provocatively entitled 'Who is a Marxist?', Joan Robinson (1979a, pp.252–3) wrote that it is natural enough for Marxists to be suspicious of Keynes, but she finds their objections to Kalecki puzzling.

> Marx's theory of effective demand is mainly in long-run terms. 'Accumulate? Accumulate! That is Moses and the prophets'. So long as businesses

reinvest profits, as they are made, in expanding productive capacity, there is no problem of instability – the economy enjoys a continuous boom. The problem, as Rosa Luxemburg saw, would be how to find outlets, over a long future, for the ever growing flow of profits to be invested. The saying: 'The last cause of all real crises always remains the poverty and restricted consumption of the masses', again, seems to envisage long-run stagnation rather than instability. Marx also offered a number of suggestions to account for a ten-year trade cycle, which contain most of the elements that have been elaborated in modern theories.

All this needs to be sorted out and brought to bear on the experience of the last hundred years. To this task, indispensable contributions have been made by Kalecki, but the verbal Marxists refuse to accept anything that is not expressed entirely in Marx's own terminology.

Reflecting on Kalecki's essay on Tugan-Baranovski and Rosa Luxemburg, Joan Robinson (1973a, p.91) observed that this essay, 'in Kalecki's usual terse style, opens up a huge field of speculation in a few paragraphs. Here my dispute with him comes up again. I do not think that he does justice to Rosa Luxemburg's vision of the long-run problem of investment opportunities drying up when the geographical expansion of capitalism comes to an end'. Yet, 'the process of the realization of surplus – as it has been developed by Kalecki – has laid the foundation for an analysis of employment, distribution and effective demand and of the consequences (though not of the causes) of changing technological knowledge' (Joan Robinson, 1980, p.92).

5 MICROFOUNDATIONS FOR MACRODISTRIBUTION

In current teaching, a sharp distinction is usually made between micro- and macroeconomic problems, each being treated in terms of quite different concepts. It is necessary, of course, as the subject grows more complex, to focus upon particular questions one at a time, but a *general* theory cannot be split into these two parts. Micro questions – concerning the relative prices of commodities and the behaviour of individuals, firms, and households – cannot be discussed in the air without any reference to the structure of the economy in which they exist, and to the processes of cyclical and secular change. Equally, macro theories of accumulation and effective demand are generalizations about micro behaviour: the relation of income to expenditure for consumption, of investment to the pursuit of profit, of the management of placements in which financial wealth is held to rates of interest, and of wages to the level of prices result from the reactions of individuals and social groups to the situations in which they find themselves. (Joan Robinson, 1979a, pp.4–5)

5.1 Keynes and Imperfect Competition

Joan Robinson (1979b, p.xi) argued that the dichotomy between micro and macro departments was alien to Keynes's *General Theory*.

> In Marshall there was compartmentalisation, which Keynes broke down, between "real" and "monetary" problems, but not between global relationships and individual behaviour. There cannot be a macro theory of employment and income in the economy as a whole without a micro picture of its structure—industry, commerce, banking—and of the motives and decisions of its inhabitants: financiers, managers, workers, professionals and housewives. Keynes used global concepts to hack out a new path through the tangle of old doctrines, but he did not intend them to be understood as simple quantities. When he defined aggregate demand as "the proceeds which entrepreneurs expect to receive" from the product of a certain level of employment, he was concerned with the views of individuals and groups appraising the situation in a complex inter-related pattern of businesses, markets and industries, not with a mere number of millions of pounds sterling. When the global lines had been laid out, a great deal of detail remained to be filled in. In this, the latter-day micro theories have been no help.

Austin Robinson (1983, p.260) conveyed the teaching in Cambridge in the 1920s in these words:

> Our economics was exclusively microeconomics; almost exclusively long-term with Marshall's short-term quasi-rents thrown in. There was complete schizophrenia between value theory and monetary theory; I listened to value theory one hour and bicycled across Cambridge to listen to a wholly unrelated monetary theory the next hour. I moved on to lectures on public finance that were equally unrelated to the other two. There was no macro-economics. There was no employment theory. There was no growth theory. There was no real economic dynamics. We lived in a world that fluctuated, which we believed to be uncontrollable but somehow self-righting.

Keynes concentrated his attack on the macroeconomic failure of the system, but did not challenge the established price and distribution theories. Yet he (1936, p.292) also complained of the dichotomy in traditional teaching between the so-called Volume I of Principles of Economics concerned with price theory and Volume II concerned with Theory of Money.

> So long as economists are concerned with what is called the Theory of

> Value, they have been accustomed to teach that prices are governed by the conditions of supply and demand; and, in particular, changes in marginal cost and the elasticity of short-period supply have played a prominent part. But when they pass in volume II, or more often in a separate treatise, to the Theory of Money and Prices, we hear no more of these homely but intelligible concepts and move into a world where prices are governed by the quantity of money, by its income-velocity, by the velocity of circulation relatively to the volume of transactions, by hoarding, by forced saving, by inflation and deflation *et hoc genus omne*; and little or no attempt is made to relate these vaguer phrases to our former notions of the elasticities of supply and demand.

At the time to recall the standard Pigovian teaching was that, under competitive conditions, the firm produces output at the level where marginal cost equals price as long as the latter exceeds average prime cost. Therefore, any operating plant is operating at full capacity. Yet during the depression almost all plants were operating below capacity while prices were not falling to equal prime cost. Joan Robinson (1979a, p.188) reports that the concept of marginal revenue was introduced as an explanation of this phenomenon, but Keynes did not use it. He brought in the idea of 'user cost' (loss of value of equipment when it is used rather than remaining idle) as a means for reconciling the concept of competition with the empirical evidence that even during a depression a profit margin was a part of the supply price. This idea did not catch on and did not become part of the post-war Keynesian tradition.

Keynes's attitude towards received price theory was ambivalent. Indeed, as Shove quipped, the trouble with Keynes was that he did not take the twenty minutes necessary to master the theory of value (Joan Robinson, 1962, p.79). 'Keynes inherited from Marshall the notion of rising short-period marginal costs but this is inessential' (Joan Robinson, 1980, p.79). In fact, 'the theory of markets was in need of a Keynesian revolution just as much as the theory of employment' (1979a, p.52). Elsewhere Joan Robinson (p.17) added that 'Keynes intended to bring the theory of prices back from Volume II, Money to Volume I, the Principles of Economics, but Michal Kalecki ... made a greater contribution than Keynes himself to carrying this programme forward'.

Reflecting on the puzzle that the imperfect competition revolution had no bearing on the Keynesian revolution when both of them took place at about the same time and at the same place and both involved at least some of the same *dramatis personae* (Kahn, Joan Robinson, and Sraffa), Tobin (1981, p.207) takes note of

> Keynes's uncritical acceptance of the neoclassical competitive model. By assuming that firms are price takers in auction markets rather than price

setters in monopolistic competition or oligopoly, he made it harder to sustain his vision of persistent disequilibrium, with failures of coordination, communication, and adjustment. Imperfect competition was the other revolution in economics in the 1930s; one of its sites was Keynes's Cambridge, and two of its agents, Joan Robinson and Sraffa, were in his group. Yet for some mysterious reason the two revolutions were never meshed.

Reacting to the *General Theory* in 1937, Ohlin observed that 'Keynes does not seem to me to have been radical enough in freeing himself from the conventional assumptions. When reading his book one sometimes wonders whether he never discussed imperfect competition with Mrs Robinson' (Keynes, 1973c, p.196). Keynes appeared not to have realized where Ohlin was driving. He (1973c, p.190) replied: 'The reference to imperfect competition is very perplexing. I cannot see how on earth it comes in. Mrs Robinson, I may mention, read my proofs without discovering any connection'. The cross currents between the two revolutions might not have been as strong as we might be led to imagine with more than fifty years' hindsight. Sir Austin (1977, p.27) recalls 'some of us were more involved in one and some of us in the other'.

Joan Robinson (1976, p.28) suggested that Keynes 'did not accept the "perfect competition" of the textbooks but some old-fashioned notion of competition that he never formulated explicitly'. One may also note that in the *General Theory* (p.245) Keynes speaks of 'the degree of competition' among other things that should not be assumed as constant. As pointed out in discussion by W. B. Reddaway, this implies that Keynes did not assume perfect competition, but a 'certain degree of competition' (see Harcourt, 1985, pp.96–7).[14] Surely Keynes was aware of the imperfections of competition in the real world. Nevertheless in the *General Theory* he chose to battle orthodoxy on what he considered the most important ground, disregarding the theory of value. Perhaps his acceptance of some of the 'classical postulates' was tactical only. Perhaps he was not comfortable with the strand of imperfect competition developed by Joan Robinson (1933, 1969). Perhaps in his letter of 25 November 1932 (Keynes 1973a, p.866) to Harold Macmillan (to whom he recommended Joan Robinson's book for publication) we may find further clues to Keynes's attitude to imperfect competition (see also Appendix):

> There has been a very considerable development of the theory of value in the last five years, starting from the basis laid by Marshall and Pigou. The nature of these developments can only be ascertained at the present time by studying a number of scattered articles, largely in *The Economic Journal*, but also in America and Germany. These articles are generally concerned with particular points and rather assume a knowledge of the

technique employed and the general character of the diagrammatic methods in use. At present there is no convenient place where anyone who is interested in these developments can either find a clear statement of the nature of modern technique, or a summary of the recent work on the subject. Mrs Robinson aims at filling this gap, and in my opinion she has done it very well. She would claim, I think, that she has done more than this, namely that she has cleared up a number of obscure and doubtful points, and has made some important contributions of her own to the whole matter. I think that the book does indeed contain a number of discussions which are more or less new; on the other hand I should hesitate a little to stress too much the originality of the work. It appears to me to be predominantly a discussion of the development of ideas which have been started by others and which are now widely current, not only for learned articles, but in oral discussion at Cambridge and Oxford. She is, in a sense, taking the cream off a new movement which has not yet found it's own expositor in print.

Shove, who was deeply interested in the theory of value, wrote to Keynes (on 15 April 1936) complimenting him on the main thrust of the *General Theory*. But he accused him of being too kind to Marshallian analysis

> as applied to the individual industry and firm. Unless very artificial assumptions (e.g. perfect and instantaneous fluidity of resources) are made, it seems to me either wrong or completely jejeune. I have been groping all these years after a re-statement of it on lines similar in some respects to your solution for the system as a whole, stressing in particular 'expectations' and the influence of current and immediately past experience upon them. But I can't make it precise. (Keynes, 1973c, p.1)

Keynes replied (21 April 1936):

> What you say about the classical analysis as applied to the individual industry and firm is probably right. I have been concentrating on the other problem, and have not, like you, thought very much about the elements of the system. But you ought not to feel inhibited by a difficulty in making the solution precise. It may be that a part of the error of the classical analysis is due to that attempt. As soon as one is dealing with the influence of expectations and of transitory experience, one is, in the nature of things, outside the realm of the formally exact. (Keynes, 1973c, p.2)

Furthermore, in a letter to Hawtrey (29 November 1935), Keynes (1973b, p.615) admitted that he did not take into account 'criticisms of the practical applicability of the marginal theory of economics. There are, of course, some qualifications to this theory and some criticisms which can be validly made. But this is not a matter which I could very well go into in this book. I am simply accepting the usual theory of the subject without attempting to refine on it'. As Joan Robinson (1979a, p.173) herself recalled, she could not 'get Maynard to take an interest in "marginal revenue"'. In a recent discussion, Kaldor was reported to have observed that 'Joan often told him that she tried to interest Keynes in imperfect competition for many years, and its relevance to the problem of the insufficiency of effective demand – but she never succeeded' (Worswick and Trevithick, 1983, p.47).

5.2 Kalecki's Construct

In contrast to Keynes, Kalecki was not exposed to the academic teaching of competitive theory. Although he sometimes used perfect competition in exposition (and for purposes of contrasting idealized with monopolistic conditions), when he did so, Kalecki (1971, p.158) usually warned that it is

> a most unrealistic assumption not only for the present phase of capitalism but even for the so called competitive capitalist economy of past centuries: surely this competition was always in general very imperfect. Perfect competition when its actual status of a handy model is forgotten becomes a dangerous myth.

In concluding the first chapter on the distribution of national income in his first English book (1939, pp.40–1), Kalecki noted that

> the results arrived in this essay have a more general aspect. A world in which the degree of monopoly determines the distribution of national income is a world far removed from the pattern of free competition. Monopoly appears to be deeply rooted in the nature of the capitalist system: free competition, as an assumption, may be useful in the first stage of certain investigations, but as a description of the normal state of capitalist economy it is merely a myth.

The road Kalecki travelled in search of an adequate analytical incorporation of imperfect competition (and eventually oligopoly) in his successive recasting of his theory was not a smooth one. But this need not detain us here.[15] For our purposes, the important aspect of Kalecki's approach is that for the author of *The Economics of Imperfect Competition*, who was trying to escape from her own creation (see Chapter 1 of the companion volume), Kalecki's construct, at the time she became acquainted with it, opened up new vistas.

One of the differences between Keynes and Kalecki is that the latter aimed at providing a macrodistribution theory on firmer foundations of a more plausible theory of the firm. He sought to bring the strength of the forces of market imperfection, or degree of monopoly (a term he later regretted), in touch not only with the mode of behavior and pricing policy of the firm and process of price formation in an industry, but to incorporate forces of market imperfection in this model of the economy as a whole. He also sought to demonstrate that the intensity of the degree of monopoly is pertinent to the determination of distributive shares and thus closely tied in with the theory of effective demand and his conception about the typical state of underutilization of productive resources in modern capitalist economy.

> The general discontent with the complacency of text-book economics found its main expression in Keynes' *General Theory*, and the theory of employment was, of course, far more important, both for analysis and for policy, than anything concerned with the theory of individual prices. Keynes himself was not much interested in price theory, but the two streams of thought were combined by Michal Kalecki. (Joan Robinson, 1960, 1975, p.241)

Kalecki's contribution on the role of monopoly pricing is crucial. As we have mentioned in Chapter 1 of the companion volume, Joan Robinson rejected her own version of imperfect competition in favor of Kalecki's. It is also interesting to note that Sraffa and virtually all his disciples have, until very recently, constructed their modern classical models in perfect competition (though they claim that these models embody 'classical' competition; that is, competition as struggle between price-setting capitalists in historical time). But these modern classical models were always in general equilibrium, with a uniform rate of profit which clearly assumes perfect competition. Now, models of gravitation try to recapture the process in Smith and Marx and often embody monopolistic firms that set prices. This is an improvement, but it does not go far enough (see Chapters 9 and 12 of the companion volume; Walsh and Gram, 1980).

To build a realistic theory, Kalecki explained how industrial prices are formed by mark-ups on costs and distinguished between 'cost-determined' and 'demand-determined' prices. The intensity of the 'degree of monopoly' (together with other distributional factors) is a key for the determination of macrodistribution. The distributional factors are essentially pertinent to effective demand and to fluctuations in aggregate output and utilization of resources. Kalecki's theory of profits is most clearly expressed in terms of the principle that wage-earners do not save, but spend what they get, and that entrepreneurs get what they spend. Thus entrepreneurs' profits are governed by their propensity to invest and consume and not the other way round. His model not only describes a wider range of economic phenomena, but also presents the economic process in motion (i.e. how one sequence develops from the preceding ones). The model encompasses long-run dynamics, the capacity effects of investments, and some supply considerations. This model provides a starting point for understanding the contemporary problems of simultaneous occurrence of inflation and recession.

Kalecki made the important distinction between 'cost-determined' and 'demand-determined' prices, some aspects of which are similar to the fix-flex price distinction made by Hicks (1965, ch. 7; 1974, pp.23–8) and prominently featured in Okun (1981, pp.21–2 and *passim*). As Joan Robinson (1979a, p.17) puts it, the Kaleckian 'distinction has recently been rediscovered by Hicks'. This is only partially true for the fix-flex price concept is somewhat different from Kalecki. The fix-flex price concept does not account for the distinction in industrial market structure as Kalecki does.

In the Kaleckian system prices fall essentially into two categories (with some overlapping and borderline cases): cost-plus pricing by firms in the manufacturing sector and the customary supply and demand system in the markets for raw materials and agricultural products. In Kalecki's (1971, p.43) words:

> Short-term price changes may be classified into two broad groups; those determined mainly by changes in cost of production and those determined mainly by changes in demand. Generally speaking, changes in the prices of finished goods are 'cost-determined' while changes in the prices of raw materials inclusive of primary foodstuffs are 'demand-determined'. The prices of finished goods are affected, of course, by any 'demand-determined' changes in the prices of raw materials but it is through the channel of *costs* that this influence is transmitted.

As contrasted with short-run changes in prices of finished products (mainly cost-determined), short-run variations in the prices of primary products are considered largely to reflect variations in demand (demand-determined). The distinction between these two types of price formation arises out of divergent conditions of supply in short periods. The output of finished goods is elastic owing to a prevalence of surplus capacity. A rise in demand is met chiefly by an increase in the rate of production, and the price changes that do occur are caused chiefly by changes in costs of production. While in general prices of finished goods are mainly determined by changes in the cost of production, they are affected, of course, by demand-determined variations in the price of raw materials; but it is through the medium of costs that the impulses are transmitted. The supply of raw materials is usually inelastic in the short run. Increasing the supply of agricultural products takes considerable time. In a more restricted sense, the same statement applies to mining. In supply-constrained activities, in the short run, a rise in demand causes disinvestment in inventories and a consequent rise in price (the initial price movement is frequently accompanied by secondary speculative demand, making it even more difficult in the short period for output to catch up with increased demand). The demand-determined prices of raw materials (inclusive of primary foodstuff) tend to decline considerably during slumps and to rise considerably during upswings in economic activity. The record of the 1970s does not bear this out. However, there were new configurations of political and economic forces at work (see Joan Robinson, 1979a, p.206; Kaldor, 1976; Klein, 1985, particularly Parts 3 and 4).

Thus, in summary form, one can say, as Joan Robinson (1979a, p.188) does, that Kalecki 'divided the price system into two parts. In the trade in raw materials, supply and demand rules. In manufacturing industry, prices are set by the producer; the profit margin that he is able to enjoy (the excess of price over average prime costs) depends upon the "degree of monopoly" in the market where he sells.' It is with this second category of prices that we shall be concerned below.

One of the essential characteristics of Kalecki's theory is his novel approach to the microeconomic behavior of the firm and changed assumptions about the shape of costs curves; the firm's price policy; relevant rates of output; and capacity underutilization. Kalecki proceeded from an unorthodox concept of the theory of the firm. He assumed surplus capacity as a typical phenomenon in manufacturing and perfect competition rather the exception in the economic system as a whole. He then focused attention on the firm's price-*making* opportunities and constraints and the policy decisions that the entrepreneurs actually have to make about prices and other forms of non-price competition and labor contracts under various types of imperfect markets.

5.3 Details

In accordance with his general conception that underutilization of productive capacity is a typical condition of a modern capitalist economy (a conception that is perhaps more relevant to the pre-war depression economy than the post-war period at least until the mid 1960s), Kalecki's special assumptions about microeconomic behavior are:

1. A given plant and equipment operate normally *below* the point of practical capacity. Supply is elastic. 'The capitalist world (except in rare moments of strong boom) is a buyer's market. Normally every industry

has productive capacity for more output than it can sell' (Joan Robinson, 1973a, p.14; see 1956, 1966, chs. 19, 20, and *passim*).

> The sphere where increasing marginal costs prevail is agriculture, where an increment in yield requires a disproportionate outlay of fertilizers and labour. The position is altogether different in industry . . . It is . . . reasonable to assume that in an industrial enterprise the curve of the marginal costs is horizontal over a rather long range of output and starts rising only when full capacity is approached. As experience shows, such full utilization is rather exceptional and therefore the assumption of increasing marginal costs must be dropped. (Kalecki, 1966, pp.50–1).

2. Contrary to the 'customary assumption' in the theory of the firm that cost curves are (or tend to be) U-shaped (see Joan Robinson, 1979a, pp.11 and 188), Kalecki assumes that the underlying cost–price relations are of such a nature that the unit prime (variable) cost is independent of the degree of utilization of plant and equipment (ratio of actual to capacity output), and that the limit of practical capacity of the plant (beyond which marginal cost (MC) curves sharply slope upwards) is not 'normally' reached. Since underutilization of capacity is a typical condition in the greater part of the manufacturing industries, short-period prime costs per unit of output are more or less stable over the 'relevant range of output', up to the point (neighborhood) of practical capacity. Kalecki qualified this statement by acknowledging that in fact unit prime costs tend to fall somewhat in many instances as output increases (short-period increasing returns), but he considered this complication of no major importance. The assumption of constancy of unit prime costs (the reverse L-shaped cost curve) is considered only as a first approximation of reality. Kalecki based it on the following hypotheses, that reflected empirical observations: (i) The short-run MC curve is usually almost horizontal over the relevant range of production (i.e. MC is approximately equal to average prime cost) which the entrepreneur identifies with unit prime costs in the short period. (ii) The main components of MC are (non-overhead) wages (w) and costs of materials (r) per unit of output. The change in cost resulting from producing an additional unit with a given and not fully used plant, is made up of the sum of short-period cost of overhead (o) and wages and raw materials ($MC = w + r + o$). (iii) The cost of overhead manual labor and materials usually accounts for only a very small proportion of the total cost of these cost components, within normal variations in the scale of output, and thus can be treated as negligible in relation to the cost of labor and materials and, consequently, can be discarded. In so far as this is the case, the principal components of MC are cost of materials and (non-overhead) labor, always within the relevant range and below the point of the practical capacity of the plant ($MC = w + r$).

3. In view of the uncertainties faced in the process of price formation, Kalecki (1954, 1965, p.12) explicitly states that 'it will not be assumed that the firm attempts to maximize its profits in any precise sort of manner'. However, he sharply differentiated his theory from the so-called full-cost theory, on the grounds that the degree of monopoly (reflected in the mark-up on prime costs) *may*, but need not necessarily, increase due to a rise in overheads in relation to prime costs; and that the price-setting process is influenced by the prices of rival firms (see Joan Robinson, 1979a, p.189; Asimakopulos, 1975; Kalecki, 1980, pp.521 and *passim*).

The full-cost pricing principle, at least in its original version, maintains that the price a manufacturer will normally quote for a particular product will start from the estimated prime cost per unit taken as the base; a percentage addition is made to cover overheads, and further addition is made for 'customary profits' (see Andrews 1949, especially, ch. 5).[16] The essence of the problem is how the margin is determined, or how the 'standard' volume of output and 'something for profit' or the 'customary profit' are arrived at.

At the expense of oversimplifying Kalecki's austere argument of the influence of the degree of monopoly upon price formation, it can be said that each firm in an industry fixes the price for its product by 'marking up' its average unit prime cost in order to cover overheads and to achieve profits, i.e. prices are formed by adding a proportionate mark-up on the prime cost. Schematically; p is the price per unit of output. Unit prime cost consists of: m, raw materials cost per unit of output; w, wage costs per unit of output; o, overhead per unit of output; r, profit per unit of output; and s, gross profit per unit of output. Then,

$$p = \underbrace{m+w}_{\substack{\text{unit prime}\\ \text{costs } (u)}} + \underbrace{o+r}_{\substack{\text{unit gross}\\ \text{profits } (s)}}$$

$$p = u+s$$

The mark-up is measured as the excess of price per unit of output over unit prime costs to the unit prime costs, $(p-u)/u$. Clearly the mark-up is equal to gross profit margin to cover overhead and achieve profits in relation to prime costs, $(o+r)/u$. Alternatively, the mark-up may be conceived in the form of a coefficient k by which unit prime cost is multiplied in order to obtain price ($p=ku$), where k is generally larger than unity, $k=1+(p-u)/u$. The relationship between the mark-up on prime costs and k is simply $(p-u)/u=k-1$.

The major proposition is that the mark-up depends on the process of industrial concentration; on the vigor and weakness in competition; on market imperfections; on industrial setting; on the morphology of markets; on the degree of freedom and constraints in price setting; and on income distribution.

It is important to stress that Kalecki does not define the mark-up as the degree of monopoly. Rather, the mark-up depends on and is symptomatic of the degree of monopoly or oligopoly.

In self-defense, Kalecki (1971, p.168) noted that

> as long as the resources of the economy are far from being fully utilised – and this I believe to be the typical condition of a developed capitalist economy – the mark-ups are determined by semi-monopolistic and monopolistic factors which I nicknamed 'degree of monopoly.' It is this term, I think, that facilitated the dismissal of the theory as being 'tautological.' However, in the *Theory of Economic Dynamics* I showed, I believe, that in any case no problem of *tautology* is involved.

In her defense of Kalecki, Joan Robinson (1965, 1975, pp.97–8) refutes the tautology argument.[17] She points out that the attack on Kalecki presumed that

> the degree of monopoly is defined as the ratio of gross margins to the value of output, and so is identically equal (on the stated assumptions) to one minus the share of wages. The apparent circularity lies only in the way the argument is set out. When by degree [of] monopoly we mean, not the *ex post* level of gross margins, but the price of firms, then, in slumpy conditions, when all plants are working under capacity, it is clearly true to say that if firms pursue a competitive policy, cutting prices in an attempt to sell more, real-wage rates will be higher, and the utilization of existing plant greater, than if they pursue a monopolistic policy, maintaining or even raising gross margins.

Furthermore,

> the expression degree of monopoly has been misunderstood. Kalecki has been accused of reducing it to circularity by defining the degree of monopoly as the ratio of the gross margins to prices. What it means is the absence of price competition (there are other forms of competition in salesmanship, product differentiation etc.). The weaker is price competition in any market, the greater is the freedom of firms to set prices in excess of costs. The ratio of margins to prices is a symptom of the degree of monopoly. (Joan Robinson, 1979a, pp.188–9)

At this point we may also note Joan Robinson's (1979a, p.189) differences with Kalecki.

> Kalecki at first advanced his theory in strictly short-period terms and he argued that the overall degree of monopoly in industry as a whole is all that is needed to account for the shares of wages and gross profits. I objected that there must be some long-period element in the relation of prices to costs. The ratio of overheads to prime costs, which varies between industries for technical reasons, must have some influence on the gross profits that they require. Kalecki met this by suggesting that firms with high overheads act in tacit agreement to 'protect their profits'. This was an admission of long-period influences on the formation of prices but it was not well integrated into the short-period analysis.

Kalecki views the mark-up as governed by a firm's price-fixing policy in relation to price formation in an industry. Its determination is a key to arriving at class shares of national income, in turn affecting spending propensities and the degree of utilization of resources. True, the margin is a 'catch-all' term, grouping the numerous factors that affect its size. It is *determined* by and *reflects* 'semi-monopolistic and monopolistic influences' resulting from imperfect competition or oligopoly. The widely held view that Kalecki's theory is 'tautological' is a *non sequitur*. Kalecki starts with a definitional equation and manipulates the equation so as to provide a theoretical explanation which, of course, can be proven right or wrong, plausible or logically inconsistent, or can be refuted by economic statistics – but this is a different matter. However, once attention shifts to the major factors underlying changes in the degree of monopoly, a behavioral relationship is introduced.

Here exits tautology – so to speak – and we enter the field of theorizing where the aim is to explain observable reality. The hypothesis could be verified or disproved by facts. The explanatory value of hypotheses depends on the questions raised and propositions advanced that help to illuminate facts and processes. Kalecki offered a hypothesis about the major causes of change in the degree of monopoly, or rather a framework for the study of the chief determinants affecting distribution of national income. True, it might be difficult to quantify the many influences that play on the degree of monopoly. One could argue that Kalecki did not provide quite a satisfactory measure. The problem is not only how much is still to be done and how far Kalecki advanced towards a solution, but whether he took a significant step in the right direction. He never claimed that he solved all the problems of this thorny issue. His several reformulations are *prima facie* evidence that he considered it merely as a first serious attempt to tackle the formidable problem.

In a world of predominant surplus capacity and approximately constant prime costs over the relevant range of output, the firm fixes the price of the product taking into consideration mainly its prime costs per unit of output and the prices of other sellers producing similar products. (Only to a much lesser degree is price-fixing influenced by prices and expected reactions outside the product group or an industry.) Prices are fixed by allowing for the 'mobility of customers' (market imperfections) and the influence of the firm's own prices and expected reactions to those of its rivals (oligopoly). The firm must be satisfied that the price fixed is more advantageous than a higher or lower one. For the firm 'must make sure that the price does not become too high in relation to prices of other firms, for this would drastically reduce sales, and that the price does not become too low in relation to its average prime cost, for this would drastically reduce the profit margin' (Kalecki, 1954, 1965, p.12). Although Kalecki is admittedly oversimplifying, he is on the right track.

When each firm in an industry sets the price of its products in relation to unit prime cost (u), the price-maker exercises care that the ratio of the price set by the firm (p) to the weighted average price of all rival firms constituting the industry ($\bar{p}$) (weighted by the respective outputs of various firms constituting an industry, including the firm in question) does not become excessively high. In reconsidering prices, when wage rates of material costs increase, p can be increased proportionately only if $\bar{p}$ rises proportionately as well. However, if $\bar{p}$ increases less than u, p will also be raised less than u. In other words, in setting p, the firm must satisfy the condition that the mark-up is not out of step with competition, as it depends on the relation of the ensuing p to $\bar{p}$.

Subject to the assumption of elastic supply, the 'ratio of average price to average prime cost is equal to the ratio of aggregate proceeds of industry to aggregate prime costs of industry' and 'the ratio of proceeds to prime costs is stable, increases or diminishes depending on what happens to the degree of monopoly' (Kalecki 1954, 1965, p.16).

Starting from this unorthodox model of price formation, Kalecki linked up the ratio of proceeds to prime costs in an industry with the relative share of wages to output in that industry. The next step in Kalecki's derivation is to proceed from a single industry to manufacturing industry as a whole and to generalize the theorizing to embrace the determinants of the relative share of wages in the economy as a whole. Thus, we can proceed through successive stages of aggregation to a general macrodistribution theorem.

Omitting here the steps, Kalecki concludes that, broadly speaking, the principal determinants of the relative share of wage in gross domestically produced national income are:

(i) the degree of monopoly (or oligopoly);
(ii) the ratio of prices of raw materials to unit wage costs;

(iii) the structural composition of the value of the gross income of the private sector.

There is no *a priori* reason why changes in (i) and (ii), *ceteris paribus*, should exactly counteract each other, or that on balance variations in (i) always nearly counterbalance variations in (ii), in combination with or independently of variations in (iii). Only in the absence of other variations, is the degree of monopoly *the* central determinant of the distribution of national output between wages and profit.

Kalecki employed various forms of the determinants of the wage-share equation to explain the alleged magic stability of the proportion of the national product accruing to labor. But this was only an application of the equation to explain, what appeared then on the basis of generalization of economic facts, the approximate stability of functional shares in advanced capitalist economies. If the facts fit, the magic constant may be explained as a balance between two offsetting tendencies, or because one kind of variation always just serves exactly to compensate for another. But actually a hypothesis is needed to show why this is so, what are the forces operating behind the scene. Kalecki attempted to provide an explanatory hypothesis of the determinants of changes in macrodistribution in the long and short run. But he did not specify the quantitative dimensions and did not argue that (i) and (ii) must necessarily offset each other. Contrariwise, he emphasized that no *a priori* statement is possible as to the long-run trend of the relative share of wages in income. However, it is possible to be more specific about variations in the relative share in the course of cyclical fluctuations. Kalecki (1954, 1965, p.18) maintained that there is a tendency for the degree of monopoly to increase in a depression, while the opposite happens in prosperity.

The process of industrial concentration leading to the formation of corporate giants accounting for a substantial share of an industry's output is among the chief causal factors of changes in the degree of monopoly. Kalecki singles out the development of marketing and high-pressure salesmanship as the second crucial factor underlying the rise in the degree of monopoly. Sales promotion campaigns create or maintain consumer demand, protect the seller, and lead to high prices and profits to the detriment of the public, and account for the bulk of wastefulness of market imperfections. In addition to the above determinants of change in the degree of monopoly, Kalecki considers two other factors: (i) the impact of changes in the level of overheads in relation to prime costs; and (ii) the influence of the trade union.

The degree of monopoly may rise as a consequence of a rise of overheads in relation to prime costs. A substantial rise in the level of overheads in relation to prime costs entails constriction of profits, unless the ratio of proceeds to prime costs is allowed to rise. These various forms of collusion (however brought about and by whatever monopolistic devices, limiting competition), may induce rival sellers to guard profits, thus giving rise to a propensity to increase prices in relation to unit prime costs (see Scherer, 1970).

The profit squeeze is particularly strong during periods of depressed economic activity. However, the reduction of profits is by no means an automatic force, but merely a tendency which may even not materialize. According to Kalecki, the basic tendency operates as follows: aggregate proceeds tend to decline in the same proportion as prime costs if the degree of monopoly remains unaltered. Simultaneously, aggregate overheads, by their very nature (largely independent of the rate of production within a certain range), fall in depression less than prime costs. This situation provides the setting for tacit conspiracy not to lower prices in the same proportion as prime costs. Admittedly, all this merely shows a channel through which overheads may influence price formation, but their influence upon prices is much less definite than that of prime costs. 'The degree of monopoly *may*, but need not necessarily increase as a result of a rise in overheads in relation to prime costs' (Kalecki, 1954, 1965, p.18).

The cost–price relations previously discussed were based on short-period considerations (a firm with a given capital equipment). The coefficients reflecting the degree of monopoly, may, but by no means have to change in the long run. In the absence of such alterations the long-run variations in prices will reflect only the long-period changes in prime costs per unit of output. Technological advance will tend to lower the unit prime cost. However, Kalecki maintained, the *relations* between prices and unit prime costs can be affected by changes in capital goods and production techniques only to the extent to which they affect the degree of monopoly.

On several occasions Kalecki explored the ideologically loaded question of the influence of trade unions as a 'countervailing power' to the degree of monopoly culminating in his posthumous paper in 1971. The existence of powerful trade unions restrains the mark-ups. High mark-ups strengthen the bargaining position of trade unions in the pressures for higher wages as they know that the firms can afford to meet them. If wage increases are granted, prices will also be raised; which in turn provoke a new round of pressures for wage increases. High mark-ups cannot be maintained without 'wage (cost) push' pressures and the process tends to go on with price levels steadily rising. This process adversely affects the competitive position of a firm or an industry (bargaining usually proceeds by industries) and induces adoption of a policy of lower (more reasonable or tolerable) profit margins. To a certain extent the degree of monopoly is restrained by the pressures of organized labor. How strong trade unions are can be gauged by comparing the increases they obtain with those they demand. The change in the degree of monopoly produces a redistribution of national income from profits to wages. But this redistribution effect is much smaller than it could be if prices were stable. The rise in wages is to a great extent shifted to consumers. 'Normal' wage increases will usually leave the degree of monopoly unaffected while otherwise mark-ups may tend to get higher because of the rise in labor productivity. Nevertheless, the daily bargaining process is a significant co-determinant of the division of national product between wage and profits.

The argument Kalecki advanced in his last article on the modern capitalist economy may seem somewhat startling. We are told that trade unions indeed may affect the distribution of income, but in a much more sophisticated fashion than traditionally expounded. A rise (decline) in trade union bargaining power leads to a rise (fall) in employment. Redistribution of income in favor of labor's share is feasible only if surplus capacity exists. But if this is not the case, wages in relation to prices of wage-goods cannot be increased, for prices are determined by demand. Kalecki (1971, pp.163–4) went on:

> a wage rise showing an increase in the trade union power leads – contrary to the precepts of classical economics – to an increase in employment. And conversely, a fall in wages showing a weakening in their bargaining power leads to a decline in employment. The weakness of trade unions in a depression manifested in permitting wage cuts contributes to deepening of unemployment rather than to reviving it . . . trade union bargaining may affect the distribution of national income but in a much more sophisticated fashion than expressed by the crude doctrines: when wages are raised, profits fall *pro tanto*. This doctrine proves to be entirely wrong. Such shifts that occur are: (a) connected with widespread imperfect competition and oligopoly in capitalist system; and (b) they are contained in fairly narrow limits. However, the day-by-day bargaining process is an important co-determinant of the distribution of national income.
>
> It should be noted that it is possible to devise other forms of class struggle than wage bargaining, which would affect the distribution of national income in a more direct way. For instance, actions may be undertaken for keeping down the cost of living. The latter might be achieved by price controls which, however, may prove difficult to administer. But there exists an alternative: subsidizing of prices of wage goods which is financed by direct taxation of profits . . . The same is true of the effect of price controls. And, if such measures cannot be carried out by political parties associated with trade unions in the parliament, the power of the trade unions may be used to mobilize supporting strike movements. The classical day-to-day bargaining for wages is not the only way of influencing the distribution of national income to the advantage of the workers . . . redistribution of income from profits to wages . . . is feasible only if excess capacity is in existence. Otherwise it is impossible

to increase wages in relation to prices of wage goods because prices are determined by demand. Price control of wage goods will lead under the circumstances to scarcities of goods and haphazard distribution. Also subsidizing prices of wage goods (financed by direct taxation of profits) can reduce prices only in the longer run by stimulating investment in wage goods industries.

It should be noted, however, that even contemporary capitalism, where deep depressions are avoided as a result of Government intervention, is in general still fairly remote from such a state of full utilisation of resources. This is best shown by the fact that prices of finished goods *are* fixed on a cost basis rather than determined by demand.

As Joan Robinson (1973a, p.120) points out

> Marx once argued (in *Value, Price and Profit*) that strong trade unions can raise real wages and squeeze profits to any extent. We know that they can sometimes squeeze profits a little bit for a little time, but, in the main rises of money-wages rates are offset by rising prices (percentage gross profit margins vary very much less than the level of money-wage rates). In a general historical sense, obviously, the social, political, and economic forces that determine the workers' bargaining power are of dominant importance, but from day to day in the private-enterprise system profits have the upper hand.

Furthermore, Marxists frequently stumble over the relation of the price level to movements in money wages. It was not difficult for them to accept the argument that in depressed conditions wage reductions will result in lower prices and higher unemployment (see Kalecki, 1979, pp.68–71, 158–69, 317–34, and *passim*).

> But then how could Marx be right in asserting that raising money wages will not raise prices? On the other hand, to preach to the trade unions that raising wage rates does their members no good is clearly a deception . . . Kalecki works out the consequences of continuously rising money-wage rates, and shows that while the main effect is to raise prices, yet it may also to some extent raise real wages. It is of no use to advocate 'income policy' as a remedy for inflation, without taking account of its political content. (Joan Robinson, 1973a, p.90)

On another plane, Kalecki emphasized that changes in the degree of monopoly are not only of decisive significance for the distribution of income between workers and capitalists, but also in some cases affect income distribution among capitalists. When the degree of monopoly rises due to an expansion of larger corporations, there is a relative shift of income to industries where such corporations are concentrated. Income is then redistributed from small to big business.

The probable relations of raw materials prices to wage costs – a function of long-term shifts in the demand and supply situation of raw materials – cannot be easily generalized. It is also difficult to predict changes in industrial and sectoral composition of output. Kalecki remains uncommitted on these points. Indeed, the years after 1973 provide a wealth of interesting experience for various extensions in this area (see, for example, Kaldor, 1976).

In Joan Robinson's (1979a, p.18) interpretation:

> Kalecki observed that prime costs are made up of two independent elements, the wage bill and the cost of materials and power. Here there is an interconnection between the two types of price formation, for costs of materials are strongly influenced by supply and demand. Bargaining for money-wage rates depends upon the balance of forces in the labour market. Assuming a stable pattern of gross profit margins, we can deduce the behaviour of prices to be expected in the short period. A rise in the overall level of activity entails an increase in demand for materials, which raises their prices. The rise in prime costs that this entails leads to a more or less proportional rise in prices. Now real wage rates have been reduced, while profits in money terms have risen. This sets the stage for a rise in money-wage rates. On the other tack, a decline in general industrial activity tends to lower materials prices, but the resistance of organized labour is generally strong enough to prevent money-wage rates from being cut (though unemployment and short-time reduce earnings).

Contrary to Kalecki, Harrod (1936, pp.86–97) argued that what we call the degree of monopoly increases in the boom and falls in the slump. Joan Robinson (1951, 1978, pp.59–60) criticized Harrod for disregarding powerful factors that propel the degree of monopoly in the opposite direction.

> The degree of monopoly does not depend only on the imperfection of the market for a commodity, but also on the number of separate units of control engaged in selling it, and, since the fear of loss is more powerful than the hope of gain, the tendency towards restrictive combinations is stronger in a slump than in a boom. This is a factor tending to amplify the swings of activity, and works against the operation of Mr. Harrod's Law.

In his pre-war essay, Kalecki (1939, p.35) argued that formation of cartels to save profits, price-fixing agreements, and other devices to reduce competition and raise barriers to entry are fostered by the low level of activity. This increases the degree of monopoly and likely more than counteracts the impact of 'Harrod's Law'. On the contrary, when activity revives, the cartels are dissolved because of improving prospects of independent action and the emergence of outsiders. But even more important, despite the decline of raw materials' prices and wages, some prices of finished products display a relative rigidity in the slump. This stickiness of prices is due partly to the fact that firms avoid price cuts because they fear the reaction of their competitors. Subsequently, Kalecki (1954, 1965, p.18) modified his position by stating that the 'tendency for the degree of monopoly to rise in the slump, a tendency which is reversed in the boom' is a basic tendency, but 'in some instances the opposite process of cut-throat competition may develop in a depression'. As a result of accumulated evidence, the concept of the relationship between monopolistic tendencies and the trade cycle has altered. Cartels do not generally disappear in the boom; a depressed economic situation can give rise to tensions within cartels. Although post-World War II experience seems to bear out that the profits share in national income tends to increase in the depression and decrease in the boom, this was not the case in the 1930s (see Phelps Brown, 1968).

The possible influence of changes in the structural composition of output usually tends to reduce the relative share of wages during a slump. In fact, these changes are influenced by a greater reduction in production of investment goods than in the manufacturing industry as a whole. The relative share of wages in the income of the investment goods sector is higher than in the rest of the manufacturing industry. Consequently, the relative decline of output of investment goods during a slump tends to reduce the relative distributive share of labor in the net output of manufacturing as a whole. During a depression there is a tendency for a relative shift in the distribution of national income away from 'wage-paying' industries, and within the 'wage-paying' industries from activities with a higher relative share to those with a lower wage-share in output.

5.4 Concluding remarks

We should note again that Kalecki elaborated his argument under conditions of depression, though he modified some of it during the ensuing years. The applicability of the argument during the boom is in question. In fact, during expansion, plants may be operated at the limit of practical capacity and a further rise in demand may entail price increases above the level indicated by the price-fixing considerations noted previously. Thus, when demand increases in relation to available capacity, the price charged by the firm may be increased so as to bring into equilibrium rising demand with limited supply in spite of the fact that unit costs and the degree of monopoly remain unchanged. However, the price-maker may prefer to maintain the level of the price (mark-up) for some time (fearing adverse effects of rising prices) while the firm allows orders to pile up and delays delivery (on quantity rationing see Chapter 9 of the companion volume).

Empirical research indicates that domestic prices of manufactured products are rather sticky and tend to remain unchanged for months or even years at a time. An important exception is when a raw material, which fluctuates widely in price, constitutes a high share of costs. Under such circumstances, the prices of final products are likely to change when costs of raw materials change appreciably. The above case excepted, short-run price stability is the general case and short-run demand variations do not normally lead to price changes (see Andrews, 1949 and 1964; Silberston, 1970; Godley and Nordhaus, 1972; Scherer, 1970, ch 13; Kalecki, 1980, pp.519–36; Okun, 1981).

As salaries are largely independent of volume of output, they are likely to fall less during the slump and rise less during the boom than wages, taken alone. Admittedly, the application of the theory of income distribution to the analysis of long-term variations in distributive share of wages and salaries combined would encounter difficulties, in view of the growing share of salaries in the sum of overheads and profits due to increasing concentration in industry.

To build a realistic theory of distribution, Kalecki offered an explanation how prices in fact are formed by mark-up on prime costs. This use of mark-up to cover overheads is very important then; though it involves monopoly power, it is not synonymous with it. Kalecki has devised a new way of tackling a formidable problem.

In Joan Robinson's (1976b, p.8) view,

> Kalecki took imperfect competition into account. The ratio of gross margins to direct cost, in manufacturing industry, tends to be lower the more intense the competition between firms. The overall *share* of gross profit in value added depends on the 'degree of monopoly', while the *amount* of profit realised over a year depends upon capitalists' expenditure. All kinds of reservations and complications can be introduced into this model, but its simple form displays the essential relationship between the principle of effective demand and the distribution of income.

Propositions about reality are always great oversimplifications. Further research and theorizing usually expand the number of determinants. Kalecki's theory is a great oversimplification of reality, but its strength lies in clearing the path to identification of crucial forces. Despite its classification as a monopoly theory of distribution Kalecki's distribution theory is broader than this term implies.

Whatever the limitation in Kalecki's working out of the argument, he scored a breakthrough by introducing the degree of monopoly into his dynamic model. His pioneering integration of imperfection and macrodynamic strands of analysis is perhaps one of his most original contributions.

6 DISTRIBUTIVE SHARES AND EFFECTIVE DEMAND

6.1 Prelude

> Ricardo was concerned with the distribution of the product of the earth between the classes of the community. Leaving rent aside, this is the question of the relative shares of wages and profits in net national income. (Joan Robinson, 1979a, p.212)

Kalecki's theory of distribution of the national product between wages and profits is within the Ricardian tradition. His theory is not merely a deviation or departure from the neoclassical marginal productivity theory. *He simply never started from it.* He argued that only by penetrating the real world of industrial and market structures (imperfect competition and oligopoly) can any plausible propositions about determinants of macrodistribution be advanced.

To recall, Kalecki's theory of profits can be summarized by stating that wage-earners do not save, but spend what they get, and that entrepreneurs get what they spend. Thus, capitalists' profits are governed by their propensity to invest and consume and not the other way around. As a result of a rise in the degree of monopoly, the relative share of profits in income increases only by lowering the relative share of labor. The distribution determinants will affect not the real-profits that will remain the same, but rather the real-wages and salaries, effective demand, employment and the level of utilization of capacity. A rise in the degree of monopoly entails a rise in the profit–national income ratio, but real total profits do not change, since they continue to be determined by past investment decisions. With constant investments, there is the same total amount of profits (saving). While profits remain unyielding, the real-wages and real national product will decline purely because of a fall in effective demand for wage-goods, with a consequent fall in output and employment in the sector producing wage-goods. Thus national income will contract just so much that the higher percentage share of profits in output renders an unchanged absolute amount of profits. Here the salient point is that shifts in the distribution of income take place not by way of increase in profits, but through a mechanism of decline in national income. The clue is that an increase in the degree of monopoly and thus a shift from wages to profits will cause greater underutilization of productive capacity.

At the outset we should note Kalecki's distinct treatment of saving (consumption) propensities – so different from Keynes's *General Theory*. (Yet, as Keynes's correspondence in the *Collected Writings* (1973b and c), particularly with Kahn and Collin Clark, indicates he saw distribution as relevant to aggregate MPC.) To wit, Kalecki's treatment is based on spending patterns of classes, rather than on a questionable 'fundamental psychological law'. In Keynes's (1936, p.96) words:

> The fundamental psychological law, upon which we are entitled to depend with great confidence both *a priori* from our knowledge of human nature and from the detailed facts of experience, is that men are disposed, as a rule and on the average, to increase their consumption as their income increases, but not by as much as the increase in their income.

In retrospect Lord Kahn (1984, p.134) admits that Keynes's 'treatment suffers from a defect that no distinction is drawn between saving out of profits and out of wages'. And Kahn goes on:

> Being a psychological 'law' of behaviour, Keynes recognised that its quantitative operation depended on the character of the change under review, and the length of time which had elapsed since it occurred.
>
> The extent to which a man will adjust his standard of life to a rise in his income depends on the length of time which has elapsed since the rise has occurred and the confidence with which it can be felt that it will not be reversed.

In Joan Robinson's (1979a, p.191) view:

> Kalecki's way of setting out the essential principle of effective demand avoids two weak points in Keynes' formulation. The first is the concept of the 'propensity to consume'. Keynes relies upon a psychological law that men are disposed to increase their consumption as their income increases, but not by as much as the increase in their income. Kalecki separates the 'men' into workers and capitalists and incomes into wages, which will be fully spent as they are received, and profits, of which a proportion will be handed over to rentiers (with a time lag) and partly spent by them. For Keynes 'men' and their incomes are undifferentiated, while for Kalecki the overall relation of national income to consumption is strongly influenced by its distribution between work and property.

The emphasis Kalecki placed on distribution of income between wages and profits (and the different propensities to save and consume associated with each class of income earners) had a major influence on Joan Robinson's work, particularly in her *Accumulation of Capital*.[18] In fact, Solow and Stiglitz (1968, p.537), referring to what they call the 'Cambridge theory of distribution' ('argued, in slightly different ways, by Nicholas Kaldor, . . . Joan Robinson, and Luigi Pasinetti'), point out that 'in that theory the distribution of income is made to depend primarily or exclusively on the different propensities to spend and save wage income and profits'.

There are significant similarities and differences among the various contributions to the Cambridge theory of distribution and growth. Going into the particulars here would take us too much afield. For our purposes it is probably fair to observe that at Joan Robinson's hands the theory is essentially Kaleckian (see, for example, 1960, 1975, pp.145–58) – that is, Kalecki creatively adapted and amended. Kalecki's influence on Kaldor is a sensitive issue and not a part of this tale. Whether it was direct or indirect (through Hahn) does not need to detain us here (see Kaldor, 1986; Hahn, 1972). It should be added, however, that Kaldor (1955–6, p.94) traces the roots of his theory to Keynes's passage on profits in the *Treatise on Money* likened to a 'widow's cruse':

> This passage, I think, contains the true seed of the ideas developed in the *General Theory* – as well as showing the length of the road that had to be traversed before arriving at the conceptual framework presented in the latter work. The fact that 'profits', 'savings', etc. were all defined here in a special sense that was later discarded, and that the argument specifically refers to expenditure on consumption goods, rather than entrepreneurial expenditure in general, should not blind us to the fact that here Keynes regards entrepreneurial incomes as being the resultant of their expenditure decisions, rather than the other way round – which is perhaps the most important difference between 'Keynesian' and 'pre-Keynesian' habits of thought.

Of interest here is the comment by Luigi Pasinetti (1961–2, 1974, p.99) (then with Kaldor at King's College), who extended Kaldor's theory. Pasinetti seems to object to Kaldor's reference to his theory as Keynesian and reminds us that 'more than Keynes, a notable precursor of Kaldor is perhaps Michal Kalecki'.

In the famous passage (to which Kaldor refers) Keynes (1971, p.125) says:

> If entrepreneurs choose to spend a portion of their profits on consumption (and there is, of course, nothing to prevent them from doing this) the effect is to *increase* the profit on the sale of liquid consumption goods by an amount exactly equal to the amount of profits which have been thus expended . . . Thus however much of their profits entrepreneurs spend on consumption, the increment of wealth belonging to entrepreneurs remain the same as before. Thus profits, as a source of capital increment for entrepreneurs, are a widow's cruse which remains undepleted however much of them may be devoted to riotous living. When on the other hand, entrepreneurs are making losses, and seek to recoup these losses by curtailing their normal expenditure on consumption, i.e. by saving more, the cruse becomes a Danaid jar which can never be filled up; for the effect of this reduced expenditure is to inflict on the producers of consumption-

goods a loss of an equal amount. Thus the diminutions of their wealth as a class is as great, in spite of their savings, as it was before.

What Sir Austin Robinson aptly named the ' "widow's cruse" fallacy' and the 'Danaid jar fallacy', was heatedly debated by Keynes's Circus. As Lord Kahn (1984, p.107) recalls:

> The complaint of the members of the Circus was that Keynes was here implicitly assuming a fixed output of consumption-goods. If entrepreneurs responded to the abnormal profits by increasing the output of consumption-goods, the price-level of consumption-goods would progressively fall, and abnormal profits would fall, until either entrepreneurs earned no more than normal remuneration or some barrier was encountered – full-capacity utilisation or full employment of labour.

For Kahn (1984, p.107) the remarkable aspect of the 'widow's cruse' fallacy' is that it resulted in Keynes devoting much space in the *Treatise* to fluctuations in the rate of investment and the credit cycle.

How Keynes got from forced savings (widow's cruse, Danaid jars, and the like) as his macro adjustment in the *Treatise* to output adjustment in the *General Theory* is a question whose answer lies in the debates of the Circus (see Keynes 1974b; Kahn, 1984; Patinkin and Leith, 1977; Patinkin, 1976; E. A. G. Robinson, 1985). For our purposes, we may note that Joan Robinson (1933) dealt with some of the points debated by the Circus.[19] She pointed out that Keynes had conceded his error. She sent the proofs of the article to Keynes (asking for suggestions (Keynes, 1971, pp.268–70)). He advised her not to make any substantial changes. But he (1971, p.270) added:

> I think you are a little hard on me as regards the assumption of constant output. It is quite true that I have not followed out the consequences of changes of output in the earlier theoretical part. I admit that this wants doing, and I shall be doing it in my lectures; though that does not absolve me from being criticised for not having done it in my *Treatise*. But in my *Treatise* itself, I have long discussions with [?of] the effects of changes in output; it is only at a particular point in the preliminary theoretical argument that I assume constant output, and I am at pains to make this absolutely clear. Surely one must be allowed at a particular stage of one's argument to make simplifying assumptions of this kind; particularly when, as you agree, the assumption in question does not make a very vital difference to the whole character of the argument. All the same, I do not ask you to make any change in what you have written . . .
>
> My own general reaction to criticisms always is that of course my

treatment is obscure and sometimes inaccurate, and always incomplete, since I was tackling completely unfamiliar ground, and had not got my own mind by any means clear on all sorts of points. But the real point is not whether all this is so, as of course it is, but whether this sort of way of thinking and arguing about the subject is right. And that is what I am grateful to you for defending and expounding.

The discussion around the '"widow's cruse" fallacy' was strongly influenced by Kahn's ingenious and fundamental article on the multiplier (Kahn, 1931). (It is interesting to note Sir Austin Robinson's simple example of the 'fallacy': 'If an entrepreneur, loaded with profits, decided on his way home to have a shoe-shine, was the effect solely to raise the price of shoe-shines? Was it impossible to increase the number of shoes shone?' (Keynes, 1971, p.340).) Lord Kahn (1984, pp.91–104) provides a historical record with a half-century retrospective, on the making, meaning, and influence of the multiplier. For our more limited purposes we turn to Joan Robinson's interpretation. In her (1965, 1975, p.93) restatement Kahn's multiplier is 'the relation of an increase in employment in investment to the total increase in employment that it generates'. In addition, Kahn showed 'how the rise in incomes that accompanies an increase in investment brings about a rise in savings of an equal amount'. As she (p.95) points out further, 'Kalecki did not approach the theory of employment through the multiplier, which makes his version in a way less rich than Keynes, though no less forceful'. Joan Robinson (1976a, p.29) also points out that in his treatment of Kahn's multiplier, Keynes allowed to some extent for the distribution of income between wages and profits. 'But Keynes interpreted the notion of the multiplier in terms of his conception of the propensity to consume' – the 'fundamental psychological law'. The confused debate among Keynesians about the savings equal investment question (see Klein 1966, pp.110–17) – a question to which we return later – can partly be traced to this.

Joan Robinson (1979a, p. 191) recalls that they 'made heavy weather' over the savings-equals-investment proposition 'in the early stages of the Keynesian revolution'. She (1966, p.ix) elaborates (see also 1968, p.40):

> In the English version of the theory there was a lot of unnecessary confusion between the equality of savings and investment as an accounting identity (which requires appropriate definitions of the two quantities and the time period) and the substantive proposition that a decision to increase investment will generate a corresponding net increase in savings, while a decision to increase saving will not. The trouble arose because the careless language of Keynes and his popularisers (amongst whom I must plead guilty) gave an opening to opponents who delighted to interpret a

mistaken formulation as a substantive error at the heart of the new theory.

Kalecki avoided all this pother because he started from the assumption that wage incomes are fully spent (with a negligible time-lag) on consumption, so that the gross overall surplus on the sale of consumer goods is equal to the wage bill of the investment sector *plus* the expenditure of capitalists for consumption. 'The workers spend what they get; the capitalists get what they spend.' An increase in investment increases profits to whatever extent is required to raise saving out of profits to the corresponding extent.

In other words:

> Kalecki simply asserts that a rise in the rate of investment will increase the flow of wages, which will be spent, and if the accompanying rise in profits causes an increase in spending out of dividends, profits will rise by so much the more. Thus there is an increase in retained profits equal to the increased outlay on investment. (Joan Robinson, 1979a, p.191)

Joan Robinson's post-war work (particularly 1956, 1966) is permeated by an emphasis that accumulation is not controlled by savings. The latter is a consequence rather than a cause of accumulation. For instance, she (1965, 1975, p.177) attacks the interpretation that interest is a reward for saving, according to which 'if there were no saving there would be no accumulation, therefore the rate of profit has to be high enough to cover the rate of interest that savers demand. This was spoilt by Keynes' argument that the amount of saving is mainly a function of the level of income and its distribution.' She (p.177) then continues in a Kaleckian vein (although she does not make it clear, and seems to attribute it to Keynes, as she does with other aspects of Kalecki on numerous occasions—see also 1951, 1978, p.136):

> In any given situation, with given productive capacity in existence, a higher rate of investment brings about both a higher level of total gross income (through a higher level of employment of labour and utilization of plant) and a higher share of gross profit in gross income (by pushing up prices relatively to money-wage rates). Thus, within reason, investment generates the saving that it requires.

6.2 Macrodistribution

While Kalecki assumed a two-class society, he noted complications arising out of different propensities to consume within each class. Within the capitalist class he distinguished the entrepreneur from the rentier – later richly elaborated by Joan Robinson (1956, 1966).

It is worthy of note that Pasinetti's contribution (1961–2, 1974) was an extension of Kaldor's model into one where workers save and own capital incorporating returns on the accumulated value of workers savings. Pasinetti shows that if the rate of return is the same on workers' and capitalists' savings, the ultimate growth path of the economy will depend on the capitalists' propensity to save. If the workers' propensity to save increases, the overall savings ratio will increase in the short run, but in the end it will result in a decline in the relative share of capitalists income in aggregate income, thus offsetting the initial impact. Pasinetti (1961–2, 1974, pp.112–13) claims that whatever the workers's propensity to save, the essential thrust of the Cambridge (Kaleckian) model of distribution holds – only the capitalists propensity to save is relevant.

In his simplified model of profits, Kalecki first considers the determinants of profits in a closed, *laissez-faire* economy. He abstracts initially from the influence of the balance of foreign trade on profits and from complications arising out of government expenditure and taxation operations by postulating a balanced state budget. Kalecki assumes a two-class society: workers (including salary-earners as well) and non-workers (property owners or capitalists) where wages and salaries and profits account for the entire national income. There are fundamental differences in the propensities to save (consume) of each class. The propensity to save out of profits markedly surpasses that out of wages. In the limiting case of zero workers' savings, the argument can be based on the equality between profits and gross investment plus capitalists' consumption. Workers' savings complicate the argument considerably, but they do not introduce particular problems of principle. To simplify his exposition, Kalecki assumed away these savings: workers spend what they earn and do not save out of their earnings. Hence attention is concentrated on fundamental issues, and the aggregate saving is identified with capitalists' savings.

Kalecki's argument is couched in terms of the customary conceptual framework of national income accounting, and first certain definitional relationships are established. By definition: Gross national product (Y) is equal to the sum of gross private investment (I) and personal consumption (C). Gross investment consists of newly produced, fixed capital goods plus changes in inventories. The value of gross national product is distributed between two social classes, workers and capitalists, and virtually nothing is paid in taxes (personal income = disposable income). Thus: $Y = C + I$. The income of labor consists of wages and salaries (V), while income accruing to capitalists is in the form of gross profits (P), consisting of depreciation and maintenance allowances and undistributed (retained) profits, dividends, drawings from unincorporated firms, rent, and interest. Thus $Y = V + P$. Gross profits equal gross investments plus capitalists' consumption; i.e. Kalecki establishes the equation between gross profits on the one hand, and profit-earners' outlays on consumption and private investment on the other.

He (1971, pp.78–9) then poses the fundamental question:

> What is the significance of this equation? Does it mean that profits in a given period determine capitalists' consumption and investment or the reverse of this? The answer to this question depends on which of these items is directly subject to the decisions of capitalists. Now, it is clear that capitalists may decide to consume and to invest more in a given period than in the preceding one, but they cannot decide to earn more. It is, therefore, their investment and consumption decisions which determine profits, and not vice versa.

Perhaps one should interject here that Kalecki used the term 'determinant' (like many other economists in the 1930s) somewhat ambiguously. Obviously the difficulty is that we are dealing with a world where everything depends on everything else.

To answer the above posed question, Kalecki states that if the period under consideration is short, the capitalists' investment and consumption are determined by decisions made earlier, partly shaped by certain factors operating in the preceding periods. The time-lag between investment decisions and investments is emphasized, since clearly the execution of investment orders takes considerable time. Also, realistically, it is only after a certain delay that capitalists' consumption expenditures respond to changes in the factors that affect them. Undeniably, there is an appreciable time-lag between income and corresponding consumption of capitalists, contrasted with the close relationships between income and consumption of wage-earners. But the time-lag in consumption spending is obviously of lesser importance than the time-lag between investment decisions and execution – a subject with which we shall deal in Section 7.2.

The interpretation of the above identity equation would have little meaning in a stationary situation, where capitalists would decide repeatedly to consume and to invest in a given period what they had earned in the preceding period, with profits in a given period invariably equal to those in the preceding one. In fact, profits are not stationary but fluctuate, and it is their variability that is the dominant phenomenon to be explained. Despite the fact that profits in the preceding periods are not the key determinants of capitalists' spending propensities, typically capitalists do not consume and invest in a given period exactly what they have earned in the preceding one.

Kalecki introduces two major qualifications:

1. Investment in fixed capital is not the sole important component of investment. The past investment decisions may not completely deter-

mine the volume of investment in a given period, i.e. *ex ante* investment may diverge from *ex post*, owing to unexpected changes in inventories. However, Kalecki maintains that the importance of unexpected accumulation and reduction of inventories 'seems to have been frequently exaggerated' (Kalecki, 1971, p.79). This is not to say that abstracting from changes in inventories would be an acceptable assumption – indeed, it is one of the most drastic simplifications of reality (Kalecki 1971, p.166).
2. Investment and consumption decisions are usually made in real terms. Given the time-lag between the decisions and their final implementation, it is likely that, in the meantime, terms of purchase may change. To overcome these difficulties, Kalecki assumes that profit and spending variables considered are calculated in constant prices; i.e. both sides of the equation are deflated by appropriate price indexes.

Thus incorporating the qualifications, Kalecki (1971, pp.79–80) concludes that 'the real gross profits in a given short period are determined by decisions of capitalists with respect to their consumption and investment shaped in the past, subject to correction for unexpected changes in the volume of stocks'.

Following the Marxian schemes of reproduction, Kalecki provides an exposition of the above from a somewhat different viewpoint. In this manner he (1971, pp.80–1) clarifies the role of factors determining the distribution of income in the theory of profits.

> Given that profits are determined by capitalists' consumption and investment, it is the workers' income (equal here to workers' consumption) which is determined by the 'distribution factors'. In this way capitalists' consumption and investment conjointly with the 'distribution factors' determine the workers' consumption and consequently the national output and employment. The national output will be pushed up to the point where profits carved out of it in accordance with the 'distribution factors' are equal to the sum of capitalists' consumption and investment.

6.3 Investment and saving

In Kalecki's model, since gross profits are equal to gross investment plus capitalists' consumption, by deducting capitalists' consumption from both sides, we obtain the equality: capitalists' gross savings = gross investment. The validity of the saving–investment equality is not confined to the special case considered. (When we relax the assumptions that workers do not save, that the budget is balanced and that there is no foreign trade, the currently non-consumed part of GNP – that is, total gross savings – is composed of capitalists' gross savings and workers' savings. The total is equal to gross investment, export surplus, and budget deficit.) Kalecki stressed that the equality between saving and investment is independent of the level of the interest rate, which in the classical economic theory was considered as the factor equilibrating saving and investment (in contrast to the Keynesian approach in which the equilibrating mechanism is through a variation of income). Here Kalecki and Keynes had the same idea, but Kalecki made it more dependent on class stratification. As Joan Robinson (1956, 1975, pp.95–5) put it:

> Kalecki's statement of the theory avoids the problem of the equality of saving and investment, which plagued us so much, by relying simply on the fact that the equivalent of investment outlay is added to profits. He cuts through another passage where Keynes made heavy weather by taking it for granted that the rate of interest is a monetary phenomenon. When investment, income and saving increase, it is necessary for the supply of the medium of exchange to be increased also; otherwise the rate of interest would rise and a drag be set upon investment.

In the 1930s, Kalecki (1966, p.46) argued that, if at some time the entrepreneurs' optimism rises, their investment activity and thus employment in that sector will expand. The resulting increase in income and consumption of labor will, in turn, be accompanied by an expansion of output of the wage-goods sector. The aggregate output 'will expand to the point where profits will be higher by an amount equal to the value of additional investment – if it is assumed that capitalists' consumption remains unchanged'. But if entrepreneurs' consumption spending expands also, owing to enlarged incomes, the rise in profits will be correspondingly augmented. In any case output (income) will be 'finally pushed up to the point where the increase in profits will be equal to the increase in expenditures on investment and capitalists' consumption'. What would be the sources for financing expansion of investment if capitalists do not simultaneously reduce their consumption and release some spending power for investment activity? 'It may sound paradoxical, but according to the above, investment is "financed by by itself".' In summary form, in Kalecki's (1966, p.14):

> Capitalists, as a whole, determine their own profits by the extent of their investment and personal consumption. In a way they are 'masters of their fate'; but how they 'master' it is determined by objective factors, so that fluctuations of profits appear after all to be unavoidable.

In a simplified model, profits in a given time are the direct outcome of profit-earners' investment and consumption in that period. (For the more elaborate model, see Kalecki 1954, 1965, pp.56–74.) And if investment expands by a certain amount, savings out of profits are *pro tanto* larger. In more concrete terms it means that, if some entrepreneurs increase investment financed by their own liquid assets, the profits of other entrepreneurs will 'rise *pro tanto* and thus the liquid reserves invested will pass into the possession of the latter'. If extra investment is financed by bank credit, the spending of such funds 'will cause equal amounts of saved profits to accumulate as bank deposits. The investing capitalists will thus find it possible to float bonds to the same extent and thus to repay the bank credits. One important consequence of the above is that the rate of interest cannot be determined by the demand for and supply of new capital because investment "finances itself" ' (Kalecki, 1971, p.84).

Reflecting on the controversial question of saving and investment, Joan Robinson (1979a, p.191) points out:

> Nowadays, so much stress is laid upon retained profits as the source of finance for investment that we are in danger of slipping back into a new kind of Say's Law, and forgetting that saving cannot take place without investment to generate an excess of income over consumption. Last year's retained profits may be financing this year's investment, and this year's retentions may be going to finance investment next year, but the profits accruing this year are the result of this year's expenditure on investment and capitalists' consumption.

In the simplified profits equation, Kalecki determines capitalists' consumption in a given year C_t by postulating that it roughly consists of the 'constant part *A*' and a part proportionate to P_{t-v}, disposable profits (net of direct taxes) in real terms, with appropriate time-lag. (The parameter *A* is a slowly changing function of time which, for the sake of simplicity, is treated as a constant in the short period, but is subject to long-run shifts. The magnitude of *A* depends on habits acquired during the past economic and social development process and is considered as a 'semi-autonomous' variable, since no attempt is made to relate it to any other variables entering into the argument.) We obtain the relation between capitalists' consumption and profits: $C_t = bP_{t-v} + A$, where v denotes the time-lag between reaction of capitalists' consumption spending to the change in their current income and the coefficient *b* stands for the capitalists' marginal propensity to consume (MPC), indicating what part of the increment of profit will be directed to consumption. Kalecki maintained that *b* is rather likely to be a small fraction and considerably less than unity. The capitalists' propensity-to-consume equation is considered only as a first approximation that disregards a number of significant determinants (see Kalecki, 1939, pp.56–7).

Gross profits are equal to the sum of investment and capitalists' consumption ($P=I+C$) and I, with whose determinants we are at present not concerned, is equal to the difference between P and C. Making use of the relation between capitalists' consumption and profits, we substitute the propensity-to-consume behavioral equation for the term C, and obtain the profits determinants equation under the hitherto stipulated simplifying assumptions where profits at time t are determined by current investment and profits at the time $t-v$; i.e. $P_t=I_t+bP_{t-v}+A$. Kalecki then derives a simplified profit-determination equation, which reads: $P_t=(I_{t-w}+A)/(1-b)$, where w is the time-lag involved and $1>b>0$ and $A>0$ (Kalecki, 1954, 1965, pp.53–4; see 1939, pp.42–74; and 1966, pp.3–4).

The equation is based on: (1) the equality between profits and investment, plus capitalists' consumption, and (2) the postulated relation between capitalists' consumption and profits at some earlier period (where A is the stable part of capitalists' consumption and b is the coefficient of consumption out of an increment of profit – MPC of profit-earners).

This equation is significant for in it the number of profit determinants are reduced from two to one because the dependence of capitalists' consumption on past profits (as given in the capitalists' propensity-to-consume equation) is taken into account. Profits are determined entirely by investment, subject to a certain time-lag. Furthermore, investment depends on investment decisions, determined by certain factors operating in the previous period. Thus profits are a direct outcome of former investment decisions and are sensitive to the variability of investment in time. The time-lag is not only caused by the length of the gestation period, but *inter alia*, reflects delayed entrepreneurial reactions (Kalecki, 1954, 1965, pp.109–16).

Kalecki (1954, 1965, p.55) concluded that capitalists' savings 'lead' profits. He noted that this result may seem paradoxical, for good common sense would suggest the reverse sequence – namely, that savings are determined by profits. But he was emphatic that this is not so. Capitalists' consumption in a certain period is, *grosso modo*, the consequence of their decisions based on past profits. Since, typically, profits change intermittently, actual savings do not match intended disposal of income. 'Indeed, actual savings which are equal to investment *will* "lead" profits', as shown by the profit determinants equation. Kalecki shows how this can happen in a case where, for some time, both investment (and, therefore, saving) and profits are steady. Suppose a sudden rise in investment occurs. 'Savings will increase immediately together with investment, and profits will rise by the same amount. However, capitalists' consumption will rise only after some time as a result of this primary increase in profits. Thus profits will still be increasing after the rise in investment and savings has already come to a stop.'

Kalecki's next step is to relax some of the simplifying assumptions and introduce an open economy, government operations, and workers' savings.

Gross national product is then composed of gross private investment, consumption, government expenditures on goods and services (including public investment), and the excess of exports over imports. The major claimants against income produced are the capitalists, workers, and government in the form of taxes. Thus gross national product earned equals gross profits after taxes, plus wages net of taxes, plus all taxes siphoned off by the government. By standard procedure of national income accounting it can be shown now that: gross profits after taxes equals gross investment, plus budget deficit, plus export surplus, plus capitalists' consumption, minus workers' savings.

> It should be emphasized that the equality between savings and investment plus export surplus plus budget deficit in the general case – or investment alone in the special case – will be valid under all circumstances. In particular, it will be independent of the level of the rate of interest which was customarily considered in economic theory to be the factor equilibrating the demand for and supply of new capital. In the present conception investment, once carried out, automatically provides the savings necessary to finance it. (Kalecki, 1971, p.83)

Here, instead of simply investment, we have the sum of private investment, export surplus, and budget deficit (denoted by I'), minus workers' savings (S); i.e. $P = I' - S + C$. The simplified profit equation can be modified and generalized to read: $P_t = (I'_{t-w} - S_{t-w} + A)/(1-b)$, where I' differs from I by the amount of export surplus and budget deficit.

The increase in the export surplus component of the expanded profit equation will increase profits *pro tanto*. The same applies to the budget deficit. The existence of the export surplus (budget deficit) permits profits to increase above the level determined by the rate of private investment and capitalists' propensity to consume. In this sense domestic capitalists who succeed in increasing their export surplus to foreign countries are able to reap extra profits at the expense of their foreign rivals. 'It is from this point of view that the fight for foreign markets may be viewed' (Kalecki, 1954, 1965, p.51).

Budget deficit generates saving just as investment does, and it is available to be lent to the government. In a certain sense, the budget deficit can be treated as 'an artificial export surplus'. The important thing is that both export surplus and budget deficit generate profits in a similar way.

6.4 Determination of national income

After examining what determines the share of wages in national income and the determinants of profit, Kalecki proceeds to the determination of national income. There he sets himself the task of establishing the basic relations between national income and investment. The strategic role of investment and differences between the marginal propensities to save (consume) of wage-earners and entrepreneurs are of primary importance.

If both wages and salaries (independent of variations in the rate of output) are largely treated together, the real wage and salary bill (V) is likely to display less pronounced fluctuations during the course of the business cycle than real national income. Kalecki derives the following relationship (in real terms): $V = \alpha Y + B$, where coefficient α is positive and less than unity, and B is a positive constant in the short run, but subject to long-run variations. We get the following formula for the relative share of wages and salaries in national income (V/Y): $V/Y = \alpha + (B/Y)$. The coefficient α denotes that part of the relative share of wages and salaries in Y that is independent of the level of Y; the other part B/Y indicates the impact of the stable part (fixed cost element) in salaries. It follows that V/Y increases when real national income falls – a relationship of considerable importance for explaining the business cycle.

In the simplified case where national income is composed of wages plus salaries and profits, substituting $(Y-P)/Y$ for V/Y, we get: $(Y-P)/Y = \alpha + (B/Y)$, and solving for Y, we obtain: $Y = (P+B)/(1-\alpha)$. The gross national income in time t is: $Y_t = (P_t + B)/(1-\alpha)$. Together with the profits determinants equation, the last given equation serves for the determination of national income Y_t, in terms of I_{t-w}. Subject to simplifying assumptions, it is evident that the gross national income is fully determined by investment with a time-lag. As the first equation *reflects* the determinants of distribution of national income 'we can also say: the gross income, Y_t, is pushed up to a point at which profits out of it, as determined by the "distribution factors", correspond to the level of investment I_{t-w}'. The function of the factors determining the distribution of income (including the degree of monopoly) is therefore 'to determine income or product on the basis of profits which are in turn determined by investment' (Kalecki, 1954, 1965, p.61).

A rise in the degree of monopoly increases the relative share of profits in income only by lowering the relative share of labor. The real wage depends on the degree of monopoly. The distribution determinants will affect not the real profits which will remain the same, but rather the real wages and salaries, effective demand, national income, employment, and the level of utilization of capacity. A rise in the degree of monopoly entails a rise in the P/Y ratio, but real total profits do not change, since they continue to be determined by past investment decisions. With an unchanged amount of investment there is the same total amount of profits (savings). While profits remain unyielding, the real wages and salaries and the real national product will decline partly because of a fall in effective demand for wage-goods, with a consequent fall in output and employment in the sector producing consumption goods for workers. Thus forces will set in to contract aggregate output and income which will adjust itself just so much that the higher percentage share of profits in output renders an unchanged absolute amount of profits. Here the salient point is that shifts in the distribution of income take place not by way of a change (increase) in profits, but through a mechanism of variations (decline) in national output (income). The clue is that with a given level of output and income, an increase in the 'degree of monopoly' and thus a shift from wages to profits will produce a rise in underutilization of productive capacity.

It is important to contrast this with Keynes's (1973c, p.122) explanation of his theory of national income determination (in a piece written in 1937 in reply to criticism by Taussig, Leontief, Dennis Robertson, and Viner):

> The theory can be summed up by saying that, given the psychology of the public, the level of output and employment as a whole depends on the amount of investment. I put it in this way, not because this is the only factor on which aggregate output depends, but because it is usual in a complex system to regard as the *causa causans* that factor which is most prone to sudden and wide fluctuation. More comprehensively, aggregate output depends on the propensity to hoard, on the policy of the monetary authority as it affects the quantity of money, on the state of confidence concerning the prospective yield of capital assets, on the propensity to spend and on the social factors which influence the level of the money wage. But of these several factors it is those which determine the rate of investment which are most unreliable, since it is they which are influenced by our views of the future about which we know so little.

Returning to Kalecki's equations for the determination of national income, the rise in the degree of monopoly will be reflected in the reduction of the coefficient α (a rise in the denominator). Hence, only a reduced volume of national income (Y_t) will be compatible with a given level of maintainable investment (I_{t-w}). Clearly, a rise in investment will increase national income by a multiplied amount owing to the well-known induced effects. The greater the MPC, the higher is the number by which the increase in investment must be multiplied to yield the resulting cumulative increment in income; and the larger the 'saving leakage' (MPS), the smaller is the value of the multiplier. Of course, the final effect of change of investment depends on the postulated functional relation between the spendable income and consumption of each class.

To recall, profits are determined by investment with a time-lag. An increase (change) in investment by ΔI_{t-w} produces with a time-lag an increase (change) in profits in time (t) ΔP_t so that: $\Delta P_t = \Delta I_{t-w}/(1-b)$. Clearly, the ratio of an increment (change) of income of capitalists to the corresponding increment (change) of investment (with a time-lag) is equal to $1/(1-b)$, or the size of the multiplier is equal here to the reciprocal of the MPS out of profits.

But ΔY_t increases more than ΔP_t, owing to the combined effect of the rise of investment on capitalists' and labor's consumption. The entire increment in national income, corresponding to and caused by the increment of investment, consists of an increase in income in the form of profits ΔP_t and the amount paid out (accrued) to the labor in the form of wages and salaries ($\Delta Y_t = \Delta P_t + \Delta V_t$). With assumed zero savings out of V, labor's income equals consumption out of wages and salaries. $V_t = Y_t - P_t$ and $\Delta Y_t - \Delta V_t = \Delta P_t$. Since ΔP_t equals ΔI_{t-w} times the reciprocal of MPS out of profits, by substitution (referring to the right-hand side of the change in investment–profits relation equation), we get: $\Delta Y_t = [\Delta I_{t-w}/(1-b)] + \Delta V_t$. By simple algebraic manipulation, and substituting the coefficient α (denoting that part of change in income that accrues to wages and salaries) for $\Delta V_t/\Delta Y_t$, we obtain $\Delta Y_t = \Delta I_{t-w}/[(1-\alpha)(1-b)]$, where both $(1-\alpha)$ and $(1-b)$ are smaller than one, so that ΔI_{t-w} produces an amplified effect on income: $\Delta Y_t/\Delta I_{t-w} = 1/[(1-\alpha)(1-b)]$. With a given rise in investment, the higher the coefficient b (marginal propensity to consume out of incremental profit), the larger is the resulting increase in ΔP_t; the smaller MPS, the greater is ΔP_t. The higher the value of α, the lower is the share of profits in income, and vice versa. The lower the value of α, the larger is the value of b and the larger the MPS. With a given b, the profit share would be higher (and labor's share lower), the higher is the $\Delta I_{t-w}/Y_t$ ratio. If the assumptions of workers' zero saving, balanced foreign trade, and government balanced budget are relaxed, the general income determination equation becomes more complicated, but the basic principles hold.

Here investment is the driving force and changes income by a factor larger than one. A change in investment entails an equivalent primary change in profits (national income), but it sets into motion a chain reaction; i.e. national income changes more in relation to investment owing to the effect that a change in investment produces on consumption out of profits [factor: $1/(1-b)$] and on wage- and salary-earners' income and consumption [factor: $1/(1-\alpha)$].

It bears underlining that Kalecki's theory of determination of national income clearly rests on the assumption of elastic supply. (Indeed, the equation for the determination of national income reflects Kalecki's approach to the theory of the firm and the special price–cost relationship postulated.) Such repercussions of an increase in investment (or capitalists' consumption) are clearly possible only if there exists idle capacities in the consumer-goods-producing industries. If the capacity output of consumer goods is already produced, a rise in investment will not increase the flow of output of consumer goods, but will merely entail a rise in the prices of these goods. This is an inflationary situation: The result is that real wages will fall compared to the levels that would have been achieved if there existed surplus capacities to produce wage goods. (On the inflation barrier see also Joan Robinson, 1956, 1966, pp.48, 91, 238, 326, 356.)

At about the same time as Kaldor (1955–6) wrote, Joan Robinson (1960, 1975, pp.145–58) identified and tried to reconcile four propositions in the theory of distribution. Two of the four are purely Kaleckian and it is particularly interesting (in contrast with Kaldor) that she identified them as such. To wit, she (pp.145–6) wrote:

> The second proposition was derived by Michal Kalecki from the analysis of imperfect competition. It is that, because in manufacturing industry under-capacity working is normal and competition is never perfect, gross profit margins . . . are governed by the price-policy of firms. The relations of prices to money-wage rates determines real-wage rates. Thus, grouping all the influences that play on gross margins (when there is surplus capacity) under the title of the degree of monopoly, the share of wages in product is determined by how great the degree of monopoly is. The third proposition, again, is due to Kalecki . . . and is to be found less sharply stated also in Keynes. It is that the relative shares are governed by the rate of investment and the propensity to consume of each class. The share of wages tends to be greater the greater the proportion of saving out of profits and of saving out of wages. Given the propensity to consume of each class, the share of wages is lower the greater the ratio of investment to the value of total output.

Joan Robinson's first proposition is that relative distributive shares of wages and profits are governed by supplies of factors and their elasticity of substitution. Her fourth is that relative shares depend on the relative bargaining power of workers and employers.

She (p.149) reconciled the second and third proposition as follows:

> The share of profit in income is determined by the *ratio* of investment to income, but the amount of income associated with a given *rate* of investment is influenced by the amount of capacity in existence and the degree of monopoly. The lower is the level of margins the larger is the output of consumption goods accompanying a given *rate* of investment, and therefore the lower is the *ratio* of investment to income. The proposition that the share of profits in income is a function of the ratio of investment to income is perfectly correct, but capacity and the degree of monopoly have to be brought in to determine what income it is that profits are a share of, and investment is a ratio to.

As the Kaleckian theory of distribution is an important building block of her theory of accumulation and growth, Joan Robinson's interpretation of it is of significance.[20] We have tried to illustrate this in several instances. To sum up in her (1969a, pp.260–1) words:

> There are two elements in Kalecki's theory of distribution. The first is; 'the workers spend what they get and the capitalists get what they spend'. The total gross profit per annum in the economy is the gross investment of the year plus the consumption of profits of the year. The second branch of Kalecki's theory is concerned with prices in the short period. He originally set it out in terms of old-fashioned static marginal and average revenue. It can be more simply (and realistically) expressed in terms of the price policy of firms; profit margins, in each market, settle at the level that yields the expected rate of profit (the best attainable in the given conditions) at an average degree of utilization of plant (permitting super-normal profits in a seller's market and sub-normal profits in a buyer's market to be realised through changes in output at constant prices, instead of through changes in prices, as must be supposed to occur under perfect comptition). In terms of the old-fashioned theory, given the policy of all the rest, each finds a kink in his individual demand curve at his actual rate of sales; there is no advantage for anyone in trying to sell more today, but each finds the kink moving outwards through time so that he can plan to increase sales in the future at the same level of profit margins as he is enjoying today ...
>
> The most important point in Kalecki's analysis is the demonstration that the over-all rate of profit cannot be raised by raising the degree of monopoly. A higher proportion of profit margins leads to lower real wages and lower utilization of plant, not to a higher overall total profit. (Of course, if government guarantees to keep up effective demand by non-productive outlays, the firms, taken as a whole, can extract whatever rate of profit they choose.)

7 *GENERAL THEORY* AND ECONOMIC DYNAMICS

7.1 Some Aspects of Economic Dynamics

In contrast to Keynes's *General Theory* couched in a static framework, Kalecki's model is explicitly dynamic (short-period dynamics in the sense of the trade-cycle theory): it shows economic processes in motion, how present events are the result of preceding development, and they, in turn, condition future development.

In a collection of essays published soon after the war, Joan Robinson attempted to incorporate economic dynamics into her own work. In the introduction she (1952, pp.v–vi) wrote:

The theme of these essays is the analysis of a dynamic economic system. The characteristic of a dynamic analysis, in the sense intended here, is that it cannot explain how an economy behaves, in given conditions, without reference of past history; while static analysis purports to describe a position of equilibrium which the system will reach (or would reach if the given conditions remained unchanged for long enough) no matter where it started from.

Short-period analysis is concerned with the equilibrium of a system with a given stock of capital and with given expectations about the future. Past history is thus put into the initial conditions, so that the analysis is static in itself, and yet is part of a dynamic theory. (This explains the paradox that although Keynes' *General Theory* is strictly static in form, it has opened the way for a great outburst of analysis of dynamic problems.)

We have all been studying dynamic economics all our lives, for no one can refrain from reflecting, from time to time, on actual economic events, and actual events are always dynamic. Only in the sealed vacuum of the classrooms where equilibrium theory is taught can static problems be discussed, and even there the outside air is always leaking in. Most of the results of the following analysis are therefore obvious and familiar. It seems, however, worth while to try to connect the familiar problems with the classroom analysis, for so long as the analysis is static and the problems dynamic the two are for ever at cross-purposes . . .

I offer the argument at the primitive stage as an agenda for discussion, rather than as a completed piece of analysis. Having grown up swaddled in equilibrium theory I find my muscles soft and to venture into dynamic problems induces a tendency to vertigo. Since there may be others in like case, I feel it is worth the attempt to clear up some very simple problems, in the hope that our heads may grow stronger as we go on.

In a review of Harrod (1948), Joan Robinson (1951, 1978, p.155) criticized him for not referring to Kalecki. (It may be noted that later Harrod (1964) acknowledged Kalecki's seminal contribution to economic dynamics.)

No one will disagree with Mr. Harrod that modern economic theory lacks, and badly needs, a system of analysis dealing with a dynamic society. Keynes' *General Theory of Employment* broke through the husk of static analysis, but apart from some *obiter dicta*, scarcely developed any theory of long-run development. Mr. Kalecki's pioneering work has been very little followed up (Mr. Harrod makes no reference to him); many others have shot at a venture into the mists, but we have no systematic body of long-run dynamic theory to supplement the short-period analysis of the General Theory and to swallow up, as a special case, the long-run static theory in which the present generation of academic economists was educated.

Economic dynamics means different things to different people. What it is and is not is an unresolved bone of contention. As Samuelson (1947, p.311) quipped: 'Often in the writings of economist the words "dynamic" and "static" are used as nothing more than synonyms for good and bad, realistic and unrealistic, simple and complex. We damn another man's theory by terming it static, and advertise our own by calling it dynamic'.

Whatever else it may mean, economic dynamics attempts to explain the laws of motion and change of a system. In dynamic theory time appears in a most essential way. The system is evolving: present events are the result of preceding developments; they, in turn, contribute to the further development of the system. It is thus that a dynamic process arises (see Kalecki, 1943a, p.80). Samuelson (1947, p.335) noted that 'of all branches of dynamics the one which has received the greatest attention is that dealing with the fluctuations in employment, income, and general business activity'. And for good reason. Without a study of economic dynamics

> there is little possibility of presenting a reasonably realistic description of such phenomena as speculation, cyclical fluctuations, and secular growth. In addition, dynamic process analysis is an enormously flexible mode of thought, both for pinning down the implications of various hypotheses and for investigating new possibilities. (Samuelson, 1966, p.612)

Economic dynamics aims, *inter alia*, to explain the movement and change in economic magnitudes; that is, for the purposes at hand, the pervasive fluctuations and long-run growth (transformation) in the development of (non)capitalist (or variants thereof) economies.

The literature abounds with treatments of fluctuations separately from growth (traditional trade-cycle theory). There is also a strand that attempts to integrate growth and fluctuations. Initially, Kalecki's work fell into the pure (trendless) trade-cycle theory. In his later work, however, he tried to avoid splitting the argument into the pure cycle and trend compartments and sought to advance theory towards a unified approach:

> I myself approached this problem in my *Theory of Economic Dynamics* and my 'Observations on the Theory of Growth' in a manner which now I do not consider entirely satisfactory: I started from developing a theory of the 'pure business cycle' in a stationary economy, and at a later stage I

modified the respective equations to get the trend into the picture. By this separation of short-period and long-run influences I missed certain repercussions of technical progress which affect the dynamic process as a whole. I shall now try to avoid splitting my argument into two stages just as much as applying the approach of moving equilibrium to the problem of growth. (Kalecki, 1971, pp.165–6)

Dynamic analysis is not a recent invention in economics. Its roots go back at least as far as the classical economists' concerns with the stationary state and Malthus's population theories. But as Samuelson (1966, pp.590–1) argues it is only in the second quarter of this century that real progress in working out specific analytical developments of dynamic processes has been made. He identifies the pioneers of modern dynamic theory as Frisch, Roos, Tinbergen, and Kalecki. (The more recent contributors include not only the heroine of these two volumes, but also many of their contributors.)

7.2 Kalecki's Theory of the Business Cycle

From the very beginning one of the strengths of Kalecki's business cycle model was its deep roots in observable reality – the set from which he erects a rigorous, solvable theoretical model in the mathematical mode. Keynes's approach to the process of determination of national income has now permeated economic textbooks (or is being criticized as the orthodoxy). But Keynes did not have a theory of the business cycle. As we have seen, Kalecki introduced a very different interpretation and analysis of the process by which a rise in investment generates an increase in savings. He did not approach the theory of effective demand by the Kahn–Keynes route of the multiplier which makes his version to some extent less appealing or less rich, but no less forceful. He did go straight to the pure (non-monetary) theory of the business cycle (on which Keynes seems to have been very weak) and his original treatment of the capital–stock adjustment mechanism now constitutes a basis for many business-cycle models. (Whatever the relative merits of either approach, they should not be evaluated independently of the confusion about the equality of savings and investment that arose as Keynesian ideas were integrated into the mainstream.)

The theory of economic fluctuations seeks to explain certain swinging motions in the rate of economic activity, as reflected in the movement of economic variables, and to provide a systematic insight into the type of movement that the economic mechanism can perform (damped or fading out with ever decreasing amplitude of fluctuations; unstable or explosive with ceaselessly increasing amplitude; and oscillations that are of non-explosive and non-dying variety). The fundamental questions to be answered are: what causes the recurrence of fluctuations, in what ways are the swinging movements generated (from within the economic system or externally precipitated), and how is their motion kept alive; i.e. how does one position grow out of the preceding one, how does the cyclical mechanism work and how is it maintained or constrained?

Mathematical or econometric theories of business cycles tend to focus attention on systematic oscillations that spring from the internal structure of the economic mechanism, and attempt to explain how the fluctuating process is produced from the response of the economic mechanism to changes in exogenous variables; i.e. how the economic mechanism responds and adapts itself to the random succession of changes in data. With very few exceptions, all satisfactory explanations are neither purely exogenous nor purely endogenous (Samuelson, 1947, pp.340 ff.).

Cycle theory faces a fundamental difficulty in demonstrating that the oscillations are of a non-dying and a non-exploding variety. The difficulty may be avoided by departing from a purely endogenous model and treating the actual process as a result of the operation of the self-generating mechanism and external impulses – as Kalecki does in his later work or by adopting non-linear models (see Goodwin, 1950; Kaldor, 1960).

In Kalecki's original model (in a closed economy, without government demand), investment determines the level of economic activity. Indeed, 'a happy feature of Kalecki's system is the fact that he places capital goods production in the center. A very remarkable feature is that the very small number of variables included is sufficient to get a closed system' (Tinbergen, 1935, pp.269–70). Fluctuations in investment engender the corresponding fluctuations in aggregate economic activity. It is the volatile fluctuations in investment that generally dominate the ups and downs in economic activity. The accent is on the acute variability of investment, which varies relatively more than consumption. That is, aggregate output (income, expenditure) and consumption show smaller fluctuations than investment activity. Kalecki approached the problem essentially by establishing two basic relations based on: (i) the impact of effective demand generated by investment upon profit and national income; and (ii) the determinants of investment decision. If fluctuations in investment cause fluctuations in economic activity, what determines investment? This is the thorny question that preoccupied Kalecki most of his life. Briefly, in his original presentation, the decision to invest is considered an increasing function of national income (real profit accruing to profit-earners) and a decreasing one of the volume of stock of capital of some time ago.

The preliminary mechanism of business fluctuations can be explained in terms of the mutual interaction of the two principal determinants that induce investment: (i) the stimulating effect of higher income on investment; and (ii) the depressing effect of growth of productive capacity in view of the distinctive relation between investment and the stock of capital (investment decisions once converted into the form of actual investments enlarge the stock of productive capital), and vice versa. 'We see that the question, "What causes periodical crises?" could be answered shortly: the fact that investment is not only produced but also producing.' Investment viewed in its income-generating capacity 'is the source of prosperity, and every increase of it improves business and stimulates a further rise of investment'. Simultaneously, however, additional equipment adds to productive capacity and as soon as it is put into operation it competes with the stock of equipment of older vintage. 'The tragedy of investment is that it causes crisis because it is useful. Doubtless many people will consider this theory paradoxical. But it is not the theory which is paradoxical, but its subject – the capitalist economy' (Kalecki, 1939, pp.148–9; see Joan Robinson 1937, 1949, p.92).[21]

In his original model, Kalecki introduced fundamental and interesting dynamic features into his system, notably: (i) the time-lag between investment decisions (orders) and realization and (ii) the determinants of investment decision relations. Indeed, among the most distinctive and remarkable features of Kalecki's model is the clear separation he makes between the decision to invest and the actual implementation; the difference in timing between the initiation of investment, investment production, income generating expenditures spread out throughout the period of production, and commissioning capital goods; the magnified effective demand and the actual delivery of finished investment goods enlarging the stock of existing productive capital. Investment decisions, once they have been embodied in the form of actual investment, entail growth in the stock of productive capital (the capital-creating effect of investment). Once investments are so absorbed, they discourage further investments. Investment *decisions* in a given period, determined by certain factors operating in that period, are followed by actual investments with a time-lag; i.e. time elapses between the moment when decisions to invest are made and when decisions are completely executed. The length of time necessary for the realization of these decisions depends on technical and organizational conditions prevailing at the time of execution of these decisions. Clearly, the rate of investment in the period must not be confused with the rate of investment decisions of that period; the actual investment at time (t) is the result of past investment decisions. The following relation exists between the rate of investment decisions and deliveries of finished capital goods: the rate of the latter follows the former with a time-lag which is equal to the average period of construction (gestation). The time-lag helps us to understand the cumulative nature of expansionary and contractionary processes.

In later works the time-lag was still largely interpreted as a result of the average period of construction but also reflected such factors as delayed entrepreneurial reaction. Consequently, we have the lagged relation where investment at time $(t+1)$ is equal to the rate of investment decision at time $t(I_{t+1}=D_t)$. The equation expresses the lapse of time between the conversion of the decision to invest into the actual investment. Because of the time delay the variables in the equation need to be dated. The size of investment decisions in period t predetermines the size of completed investment in the following period $(t+1)$, i.e. decisions to invest logically take place in advance of their realization. Kalecki recognized that investment decisions embodied in investment orders are not strictly irrevocable, which further complicates the matter. Cancellations of investment orders, in spite of the considerable loss entailed, do take place, but probably not on a sufficient scale to invalidate the results.

Investment decisions are necessarily forward looking. Kalecki introduced uncertainty and expectations into his argument, although he did not provide a theory of how expectations are formed. The Kaleckian system behaves as if a certain delay were involved in the functional relationship between investment and income. That is, national income is lagging behind investment, and investment behind investment decisions; past investment decisions determine the present national income, which influences current investment decisions, which, in turn, determine future national income.

The level of real national income delimits approximately its distribution among wage-earners and profit-earners, particularly the profits accruing to the capitalist sector. The prospective rate of profit, and, therefore, investment, is determined, *grosso modo*, by the level of national income and stock of capital, with an appropriate time-lag. Therefore, these two factors are treated tentatively as the determinants of investment decisions. With a given stock of capital, the rate of profit that can be obtained under current conditions from a new investment is the greater, the larger the level of national income. But the rate of current profit that can be obtained at present from carrying out a new investment does not represent sufficient basis for estimating the prospective rate of profit, for expected future developments must be taken into consideration. There is great uncertainty about what the future may bring forth, and yet the entrepreneur must make decisions in an uncertain world; thus the present state influences predominantly long-term expectations. Entrepreneurs often act as if they expected the existing situation essentially to continue in the future. Clearly, they tend to be optimistic when business prospers, and pessimistic when it does not. Generally, the prospective rate of profit is a function of the actual rate of profit. Thus, with a given volume of capital, the prospective rate of profit is greater, the greater the national income. For a given volume of capital profits will rise with growth of effective demand; i.e. the rate of profit will rise. Contrariwise with the growth of the stock of capital for a given aggregate demand, profits yielded per unit of capital will decline. The larger the profit and the smaller the stock of existing capital equipment, the larger will be the prospective rate of the profit on new investment. An increase in the volume of capital equipment, if profits are constant, is tantamount to a fall in the rate of profit.

Joan Robinson (1942, 1966, pp.40–1) drew a parallel between Marx's treatment of the falling rate of profit and Kalecki's theory of the cycle. She (p.41) noted, however, that

> the resemblance is superficial, for in Mr. Kalecki's scheme it is the level of effective demand which regulates the total of profits, while in Marx's scheme the total of profits is unable to increase for some other reason, and . . . Marx fails to make out his case that the total of profits is limited, apart from effective demand.

As we have seen, in Kalecki's model if the current rate of investment surpasses that of the proceeding period, the level of current profit will rise, profit expectations will improve, investment demand will increase, and more orders will be placed followed by an increased rate of investment activity and enlarged income. The income-generating capacity of investment is the source of prosperity and encourages a further rise in investment. But investment has also a capacity-creating effect; every completed investment adds to productive capacity, competes with the stock of equipment of older vintage, and discourages more investment. Sooner or later investment stops rising and so does the level of current profit. The rate of profit falls. The rise in investment is transitory and the boom cannot endure. A process of cumulative contraction takes place. The growth of national wealth contains the seeds of retardation.

It should be emphasized that Kalecki's development of his theory of business cycles (over a period of more than thirty-five years), starting from his original 1933 contribution in Polish (1966), and the many revisions thereof as discussed in Feiwel (1975, chs. 5 and 6), has undergone a number of significant alterations.[22] In the introduction to his selected essays, Kalecki (1971, p.viii) wrote:

> It is interesting to notice that the theory of effective demand, already clearly formulated in the first papers, remains unchanged in all the relevant writings, as do my views on the distribution of national income. However, there is a continuous search for new solutions in the theory of investment decisions, where even the last paper represents – for better or for worse – a novel approach.

Here we can do no more than highlight the reformulations and modifications he made as he sought to bring the model closer to reality. Whereas his earlier writings were clearly influenced by the severity of the experience in the early 1930s, in the subsequent development of the argument, he made allowances for the relative weak impact of the capital destruction effect. He introduced a certain 'corrective' – a trend factor that shifts investment upward as the cycle continues. In a growing economy investment fluctuates along the long-run trend line. Innovations raise the prospect of profit, thus stimulating investment and engendering an ascending trend. Innovation becomes another weighty factor in the determination of the investment function, together with the change in the rate of profit, the rate of change in the stock of capital and the 'internal' gross savings (depreciation and undistributed profits) of firms.

The exposition of Kalecki's argument is probably clearest and simplest in his 1939 book. It is not surprising that Cambridge students are always referred to this rather than to its successors. But, whereas the earlier model is superior in its expository powers and its focus on fundamentals, the later developments are closer to reality. Indeed this is also true of some of Joan Robinson's writings.

The two new versions of the model (1943a, and 1954) aimed at generalizing the earlier model in a number of ways and relating Kalecki's theory to some of the models that had been constructed by others in the meantime. A number of important modifications, elaborations, and refinements, particularly regarding the factors determining investment decisions and influencing the investment process, were introduced both in the 1943 and 1954 books. Whereas in his earlier work he dealt with an economy without a secular trend, Kalecki (1943a) introduced in Part 2 two chapters on the pure business cycle and trend, respectively. In the introduction to that part Kalecki (1943a, p.59) wrote: 'I do not now consider only the problem of the "pure" business cycle, but deal in the last essay with the trend superimposed on the cycle.' Kalecki concentrated on the influence of factors from which he had abstracted hitherto in order to obtain a pure business cycle in a trendless economy. For instance, in the investment determinants function additional determinants were introduced, depending on the preceding history and evolution of the developing system. Thus the economy ceased to be trendless. Furthermore, this current trend, being the result of foregoing development, contributes in turn to the future long-run development of the economic system. It is in this way, as Kalecki showed, that the dynamic process arises.

Kalecki (1962) first developed a business-cycle equation of a fairly general character devised to cover: (i) his own theory as formulated in Kalecki (1954); (ii) the business-cycle theory based on the acceleration principle; and (iii) Harrod's (1951) theory. Kalecki generalized the business-cycle equation and dynamized it so as to apply to economic systems subject to a tendency of long-run economic development. Next he argued that the Harrodian rate of growth is ephemeral in the sense that any deviation from the path determined by it renders the system non-expanding; i.e. generating cyclical fluctuations but not subject to growth trends. He maintained that the business-cycle equation arrived at offers two solutions for the rate of balanced growth: one, zero, so that the system is not subject to a long-term trend and another rendering a positive but unstable rate of growth. Thus the system is incapable of a long-run growth (proceeding along an ascending trend line) and merely fluctuates around a static position (horizontal line). Kalecki differed strikingly from Harrod on what constitutes the basic conflict of the capitalist economy. Harrod believed that the antinomy leads to fluctuations around a rising trend line, but Kalecki took the stand that 'the antinomy of the capitalist economy is in fact more far reaching: the system cannot break the *impasse* of fluctuations around a static position unless economic growth is generated by the impact of semi-exogenous factors such as the effect of innovations upon investment. It is only in such a case that cyclical fluctuations do occur around the ascending trend line' (Kalecki, 1962, p.134).

Finally, Kalecki introduced the impact of development factors, such as innovations upon the investment in the business-cycle equation. The system then yields two positive solutions for the rate of growth for which the lower is stable. Consequently, the system is subject to a uniform trend (steady growth), depending on the intensity of innovations. Cyclical fluctuations do occur around the trend line in accordance with the business-cycle equation. Development factors like innovations enable the capitalist system to break the impasse of a stationary state and to expand at a rate depending on the intensity of such factors. Also such factors play a decisive role in determining the utilization of existing capacity. But the approach was not fully satisfactory in tackling the intricate question of the interrelationship of growth and cycles – a deficiency of which he was fully aware.

To sum up, Kalecki aimed at developing a theory integrating growth and cyclical processes. He advanced an original, provocative, but somewhat sketchy theory of long-run development trends, the determinants both of trend and cycle. Innovation plays a cardinal role in transforming the static system subject to fluctuations (cyclical fluctuation around the zero level of capital accumulation) into one subject to growth trend. Kalecki emphasized that he failed to see why the business-cycle approach should be abolished in studying the process of economic development. He now approached the growth rate at a given time as a phenomenon deeply rooted in past economic, social and technological development of the system where, as throughout his work (and throughout Joan Robinson's postwar writings), *the current state is the result of the preceding developments and contributes, in turn, to the future long-run development of the economy*. The two basic relations in the approach to business cycles: (i) the impact of effective demand generated by investment on profits and national income, and (ii) the determination of investment function by the level and the rate of change in income or expenditures, should be so formulated as to yield the trend *cum* business-cycle phenomenon. Such a task is incomparably more exacting than the pure business-cycle model. But the results of such inquiry are closer to the reality of the process of development. (The approach of 'mechanistic' theory is based often on such indefensible assumptions as a constant long-run rate of utilization of capacity.) However, for Kalecki, the difficulty of the task should not be an excuse for disregarding this approach which seems to be the only one for a realistic analysis of the dynamics of a capitalist economy. Of interest here is Joan Robinson's (1979a, p.193) perception of the gist of Kalecki's business-cycle theory:

> Kalecki provided the first coherent model of the mechanism of a self-repeating trade cycle (Kaldor, Goodwin and many others have built on his foundations). The clue to his analysis is the distinction between investment decisions and actual investment outlay. Today, plans are being laid for investment in the light of expectations held today. If prospects are such that investment plans exceed current investment, then current investment will be higher in the next period; consequently profits will be higher, expectations will be brighter, and so the 'self winding up' process of a boom is under way. Meanwhile the stock of productive capacity is gradually growing, and when the growth of capacity overtakes the growth of current production, utilization falls, prospects of profit are dimmed and the boom collapses.
>
> As with all such models, the theory of an automatic recovery from a slump was rather weak, and Kalecki later gave up the search for a 'pure' trade cycle and sought for an analysis combining fluctuations in activity with accumulation over the long run.

In his last reflections on the theory of growth (delivered in a lecture in Cambridge less than a year before he died and published posthumously), Kalecki argued that the institutional framework of a social system is a fundamental component of its economic dynamics and, therefore, of the growth theory relevant to that system. On the subject that concerns us here he (1970, pp.311–12) wrote:

> To my mind the central problem of the *laisser-faire* capitalist system . . . is that of effective demand . . . It is also this problem that in the fifties was still generally in the centre of interest of Western economists . . .
>
> But from the time the discussion of economic dynamics has concentrated on problems of *growth* the factor of effective demand was generally disregarded. Either it was simply *assumed* that in the long run the problem of effective demand does not matter because apart from the business cycle it need not be taken into consideration; or more specifically the problem was approached in two alternative fashions: (a) The growth is at an equilibrium (Harrodian) rate, so that the increase in investment is just sufficient to generate effective demand matching the

> new productive capacities which the level of investment creates. (b) Whatever the rate of growth the productive resources are fully utilized because of the long-run price flexibility: prices are pushed in the long run in relation to wages up to the point where the real income of labour and thus its consumption is adequate to cause the absorption of full employment national product.
>
> I do not believe however in justifying the neglect of the problem of finding markets for the national product at full utilization of resources either in (a) or in (b) fashion. It is generally known that the trend represented by the (a) case is unstable: any small fortuitous decline in the rate of growth involves a reduction of investment, and in consequence of the national income, in relation to the stock of equipment, which affects investment adversely and induces a further fall in the rate of growth. The belief that such disturbance creates merely a downswing followed by an upswing in relation to the growth proceeding at an equilibrium rate i.e. that it yields a trend *cum* business cycle is mathematically indefensible: the underlying equations are uncapable [*sic*] of producing a solution corresponding to a combination of an exponential curve with a sine line. Nor do I subscribe to the long-run price flexibility underlying theories of the (b) type. The monopolistic and semi-monopolistic factors involved in fixing prices – deeply rooted in the capitalist system of all times – cannot be characterized as temporary short period price rigidities but affect the relation of prices and wage costs both in the course of the business cycle and in the long run.

On the other hand, one could interject that monopolies are repeatedly destroyed. If prices are rigid in the long run, then one would expect not merely unemployment but a trend in employment independent of labor supply. But history contradicts it. Unemployment varies cyclically but not secularly, regardless of rates of technological innovation or capital formation. This suggests that there must be some tendency for prices and wages to respond to supply and demand conditions. But to return to Kalecki (pp.312–13):

> The 'pure' business cycle is a special case of the general phenomenon of trend *cum* business cycle where the rate of growth is equal to zero, i.e. where the economy is stationary. In the argument on which the theories of the business cycle are based certain quantities were assumed constant – this was partly linked with inadequate accounting for technical progress – which in an expanding economy must certainly grow. Thus it is necessary to deal with this limitation – which ties down the theory of the business cycle to a stationary economy – and arrive at a movement of the system comprising both the trend and cyclical fluctuations. Or to put it

somewhat differently: the central problem of the dynamics of the *laisser-faire* capitalist system is to show what makes the system expand if the solutions on the lines (a) and (b) are discarded as inadequate. Indeed the mere fact that capital accumulation creating new production potentialities is *feasible* does not prove yet that the investment will be adequately used.

7.3 The Investment Function

Essentially Keynes's *General Theory* dealt not only with a static model, but it was concerned explicitly with the fundamentally Marshallian short-run situation.

> We take as given the existing skill and quantity of available labour, the existing quality and quantity of available equipment, the existing technique, the degree of competition, the tastes and habits of the consumer, the disutility of different intensities of labour and of the activities of supervision and organisation, as well as the social structure including the forces, other than variables set forth below, which determine the distribution of the national income. This does not mean that we assume these factors to be constant; but merely that, in this place and context, we are not considering or taking into account the effects and consequences of changes in them. (Keynes, 1936, p.245)[23]

This interpretation is borne out by Lord Kahn, whom Schumpeter has credited with 'almost co-authorship' of the *General Theory* – a credit that Kahn with his usual modesty (and protective attitude towards Keynes's place in history) disclaims.[24] In Kahn's (1984, p.123) words: 'Most of the exposition is based on the assumption of given stocks of equipment at a moment of time and given technical knowledge. The subject of investigation is the degree of utilisation of the equipment and the labour supply.' Furthermore, Kahn (1984, p.123) testifies that in the *General Theory* there is 'little study of the effects of accumulation with the passage of time as the result of investment'.[25] But the discussion in chapters 11, 12, 16 and 24 (on the marginal efficiency of capital; long-term expectations; the nature of capital; and the concluding notes on social philosophy, respectively) do revolve 'in a fundamental sense' around this subject.

It is important to note, however, that in the previously mentioned 1937 response to the critics of the *General Theory*, Keynes (1973c, pp.121–2) re-expressed some of his views. In particular, he seems to have somewhat changed his focus and adopted the business-cycle viewpoint:

> This that I offer is, therefore, a theory of why output and employment are

so liable to fluctuation. It does not offer a ready-made remedy as to how to avoid these fluctuations and to maintain output at a steady optimum level. But it is, properly speaking, a theory of employment because it explains *why*, in any given circumstances, employment is what it is.

Indeed, Keynes's assumption of the existing quality and quantity of available plant and equipment and existing techniques is very restrictive. Innovations are of key importance for explaining the process of development. In his analysis of the apparatus of Keynes's *General Theory*, Schumpeter (1954, pp.1174–5) emphasized that

> of all aspects of the investment process, it is only the expenditure effect of new investment which enters the *model* (not the book): as Keynes himself rightly emphasized, physical capital (equipment) is assumed to remain constant throughout, both in kind and quantity. This limits the theory to an analysis of the factors that determine the higher or lower degree of utilization of an existing industrial apparatus. Those who look for the essence of capitalism in the phenomena that attend the incessant recreation of this apparatus and the incessant revolution that goes on within it must therefore be excused if they hold that Keynes' theory abstracts from the essence of the capitalist process.

For the purpose of this chapter, we should note that as early as June 1935 (in a letter to Keynes, including comments on the proofs of the *General Theory*) Joan Robinson evinced a disquietude over the narrowness of the Marshallian short-run framework. With reference to p.92, she wrote:

> You mean that the community with less capital will be able to continue investing after the other has stopped. But if so it will soon become like the other community. In what sense is there 'long-period equilibrium' if investment is still going on?
>
> You have stopped rather suddenly in this section out of the short period with fixed equipment to which the rest of the book belongs. I think all you really want is to say that the greater the capital equipment in existence at any moment the greater will be the propensity to save, the lower the m.e. of capital corresponding to each rate of investment, [therefore] the lower must be the rate of interest which will give full employment. (Assuming no inventions – you ought to make that clear.)
>
> As a community accumulates capital it approaches the dangerous situation in which 2 per cent or even 0 per cent won't give full employment.
>
> I think this is all you really need. I have been working out this long-period stuff and I find that to make a proper job of it one needs to bring in several considerations that are not really relevant to your main theme,

> e.g. I find elasticity of substitution is an important factor. I feel that this section is in a limbo between long and short periods; you can make your point without bringing the long period in at all. But if you do I think a definition of 'equilibrium' is essential. (Keynes, 1973b, pp.647–8; see Joan Robinson, 1952, p.69)

This appears to be an indications of how her idea of extending the *General Theory* into the long period germinated, although it might have been already with her for some time. Early in 1936 she published her first attempt at what she later called the generalization of the General Theory (see Joan Robinson, 1937, 1947, pp.75–100)—a story told in Chapter 1 of the companion volume.[26] (She later criticized it, inter alia, for being couched in a stationary state where there are no net savings (see Joan Robinson, 1960, 1975, p.vi; 1979b, pp.ix–xxviii).

Keynes (1936, pp.31–2) considered 'the three major gaps in our existing knowledge' that he had to fill to be the analysis of the propensity to consume, the definition of the marginal efficiency of capital (MEC), and the theory of the rate of interest.[27] In section 6.1 we have called attention to Kalecki's and Keynes's different treatments of the first gap and here we shall point to their differences on the second and third gap, but with particular stress on the second in view of Kalecki's fundamental disagreement with Keynes's treatment, and the position taken by Joan Robinson. To recall, in Section 7.2, we have outlined Kalecki's persistent and unfulfilled quest for a satisfactory theory of investment determinants. At this juncture, we shall briefly sketch Keynes's position and contrast the two.

At the outset Keynes (1936, pp.27–31) traced the main thrust of the theory of employment as follows:

> When employment increases, aggregate real income is increased. The psychology of the community is such that when aggregate real income is increased aggregate consumption is increased, but not by so much as income. Hence employers would make a loss if the whole of the increased employment were to be devoted to satisfying the increased demand for immediate consumption. Thus, to justify any given amount of employment there must be an amount of current investment sufficient to absorb the excess of total output over what the community chooses to consume when employment is at the given level. For unless there is this amount of investment, the receipts of the entrepreneurs will be less than is required to induce them to offer the given amount of employment. It follows, therefore, that, given what we shall call the community's propensity to consume, the equilibrium level of employment, *i.e.* the level at which there is no inducement to employers as a whole either to expand or to contract employment, will depend on the amount of current investment. The amount of current investment will depend, in turn, on what we shall

call the inducement to invest; and the inducement to invest will be found to depend on the relation between the schedule of the marginal efficiency of capital and the complex of rates of interest on loans of various maturities and risks.

Thus, given the propensity to consume and the rate of new investment, there will be only one level of employment consistent with equilibrium; since any other level will lead to inequality between the aggregate supply price of output as a whole and its aggregate demand price. This level cannot be *greater* than full employment, *i.e.* the real wage cannot be less than the marginal disutility of labour. But there is no reason in general for expecting it to be *equal* to full employment . . .

The propensity to consume and the rate of new investment determine between them the volume of employment, and the volume of employment is uniquely related to a given level of real wages – not the other way round. If the propensity to consume and the rate of new investment result in a deficient effective demand, the actual level of employment will fall short of the supply of labour potentially available at the existing real wage, and the equilibrium real wage will be *greater* than the marginal disutility of the equilibrium level of employment.

This analysis supplies us with an explanation of the paradox of poverty in the midst of plenty. For the mere existence of an insufficiency of effective demand may, and often will, bring the increase of employment to a standstill *before* a level of full employment has been reached . . .

Moreover the richer the community, the wider will tend to be the gap between its actual and its potential production; and therefore the more obvious and outrageous the defects of the economic system.

Soon after the publication of the *General Theory*, Kalecki (1936) reviewed it in the leading economics journal in Poland (the organ of the Polish Economic Association). He hailed it as 'undoubtedly a turning point in the history of economics'. He viewed the book as divided into two essential parts: (i) determination of short-run equilibrium, restricted by given productive capacity and a given level of investment (per unit of time); and (ii) determination of the size of investment. He considered that Keynes solved the first question quite satisfactorily though Kalecki had some reservations about the lack of rigor and explicitness in exposition. Moreover, Kalecki questioned the route by which Keynes arrived at his solution and presented an alternative way of doing so – a way that was essentially his own, although he did not explicitly refer to his 1933 or 1935 publications. With reference to the second part, Kalecki questioned not the exposition but, more seriously, the analytical construct itself – a question to which we return presently.

In Lord Kahn's (1984, p.142) retrospective on the *General Theory*, he emphasized that

> the major achievement of the *General Theory* is twofold. First, there is the conception of Effective Demand which, given the conditions of supply, determines the level of output and employment. Second, there is the determination of the rate of investment. While lower than the rate of consumption, this is the constituent of Effective Demand which is mainly responsible for fluctuations, and also for demand being often chronically unduly low – as well as, on occasion, unduly high.

It is in this manner that Kahn (p.142) explains why 'the determination of the rate of investment is the subject to which ... the bulk of the *General Theory* is devoted'.

In Keynes's treatment the inducement-to-invest function depends on the relation between the expected rate of profit on newly produced capital goods (called MEC) and the cost of securing funds. Thus the inducement-to-invest function depends partly on the MEC and partly on the rate of interest (Keynes 1936, pp.135–254).

Keynes argued that the actual rate of current investment will be pushed to the point on the investment–demand schedule where the marginal efficiency of capital in general (to recall, defined in terms of the *expectation of prospective* yields of investment, allowing for risk) and the *current* supply price of the capital asset is equal to the market rate of interest that must be paid to secure financing. As there exists at any time a variety of investment projects that can be arranged in descending order of their expected rate of return over cost (excluding interest, but allowing for risk), the actual rate of investment will be pushed at any time to the point where the spread between the prospective yield and rate of interest is reduced to naught. A fall in the rate of interest relatively to given MEC will rise the rate of investment. MEC for any given type of capital asset during any period of time will fall as the investment in it is increased (movement along the MEC curve)

> partly because the prospective yield will fall as the supply of that type of capital is increased, and partly because, as a rule, pressure on the facilities for producing that type of capital will cause its supply price to increase; the second of these factors being usually the more important in producing equilibrium in the short run, but the longer the period in view the more does the first factor take its place. Thus, for each type of capital we can build up a schedule, showing by how much investment in it will have to increase within the period, in order that its marginal efficiency should fall to any given figure. We can then aggregate these schedules for all the different types of capital, so as to provide a schedule relating the rate of aggregate investment to the corresponding marginal efficiency of capital in general which that rate of investment will establish. We shall call this the investment demand-schedule; or, alternatively, the schedule of the marginal efficiency of capital. (Keynes, 1936, p.136)[28]

Kalecki (1936, pp.18–26) saw serious deficiencies in the MEC concept. It says nothing about the investment *decisions* of the entrepreneur who calculates in *existing* market prices of investment goods in the state of 'disequilibrium'. It only indicates that, if the expected rate of profit, calculated on the basis of that price level, will not equal the rate of interest, a change of the level of investment will take place, transforming the existing situation into one where the expected rate of profit *equals* the rate of interest. One could say that Keynes's theory determines only the *ex post* level of investment and says nothing of *ex ante* investment.

Furthermore, Kalecki argued, let us assume that initially the expected rate of profit was higher than the rate of interest, and that an increase of investment has taken place which has increased the prices of investment goods so that the expected rate of profit, computed at these new prices, and the *initially* anticipated revenue is equal to the interest rate. Kalecki noted that the increase of investment not only raises the prices of investment goods, but that, according to Keynes, it is followed by a general rise in activity, increasing prices and production in all branches. Since, as Keynes remarked, the current situation is strongly overweighed in forming expectations about the future, the expectations will become more optimistic and again a difference between MEC and the rate of interest will appear. Thus equilibrium is not reached and the increase of investment continues (here occurs the Wicksellian cumulative effect).

Kalecki also objected to Keynes's concept (which tells us how large investment will be when a given 'disequilibrium' is transformed into 'equilibrium') on the grounds that the increase is not at all a process that leads the system into 'equilibrium'.

Kalecki found it difficult to accept Keynes's solution of the investment problem as satisfactory. The cause of this lack of success is the essentially static approach to the problem that by its very nature is dynamic. Keynes accepted the state of expectations of returns as datum and deduced therefrom a certain given level of investment, neglecting the influence that, in turn, the investments will have on expectations. It is here that Kalecki sees a clue for reaching a realistic theory of investment and provides pointers to his own position. The starting point of such a theory should be the solution of the problem of *ex ante* investment decisions. Let us assume, argued Kalecki, that, at a certain point in time, we have a given state of expectations of future income; determined prices of investment goods; and, finally, a given rate of interest. How large then would be the intended investment of businessmen for a given period? Let us assume that this problem has been solved (impossible without introducing some special assumptions about business men's psychology, or assumptions about the imperfections of the money market). A further development of the investment theory that Kalecki envisaged would be as follows: investment decisions, corresponding to the initial state, would not generally be equal to the existing level of investment. Therefore, in the following period the size of investment would generally be different and, with it, the short-run equilibrium position would change. Thus we have to deal with a different state of expectations from that in the initial period, different prices of investment goods, and a different rate of interest, from which a new level of investment decisions would result.

Notwithstanding his criticism of Keynes's theory on the grounds that it neglects the dynamic aspects, Kalecki claimed that the first part of Keynes's theory retains its intrinsic value. In the dynamic process investments are continually changing, but to each level of investment there will correspond a level of employment and production, determined according to the first part of Keynes's theory. Kalecki argued that Keynes did not explain precisely what influences the changes of investment, but he analyzed at great length the close relationship between these changes and the general movement of employment, production, and income.

In his fifty-year perspective on the *General Theory*, Kahn (1984, pp.145, 148) acknowledged that, although the subject matter is the most important in the *General Theory*, chapter 11 on the MEC is one of the most confused. Also, Keynes exaggerated the importance of the risk-free role of interest as an influence on the rate of investment. Kahn (p.159) argued that 'Keynes' insistence on the overwhelming importance of expectations, highly subject to risk and uncertainty, was one of his biggest contributions'. This is also the aspect that Joan Robinson has continually emphasized and that has imbued her post General Theory work (see Joan Robinson, 1979a, pp.59, 170–2; 1979b, pp.xv–xvi; Keynes, 1973c, pp.112 and *passim*).

In contrast with Keynes, Kalecki asked a most pertinent question as Joan Robinson (1965, 1975, pp.96–7) reminds us:

> If there are schemes which promise a rate of profit greater than the rate of interest, would not each individual enterprise be willing and anxious to carry out an indefinitely large amount of investment? It was no use to reply that a faster rate of investment would raise the cost of capital goods and so reduce the prospective rate of profit; for the rise in costs would come about as a result of actual investment, *ex post*, while the marginal efficiency of capital concerns investment plans *ex ante*.
>
> Kalecki supplied an answer, first by making clear the separation between investment decisions and actual investment; and second, by introducing into the argument the obvious fact that no individual enterprise can command an indefinitely large amount of finance at a given rate of interest. He took risk over from the demand side (where it lies rather uneasily in Keynes' scheme) to the supply side, and postulated that the amount of finance that each individual enterprise will commit to investment is in an increasing function of the prospective rate of profit, depending upon the ratio of its borrowing to its own capital. Then, with

any given distribution of capital amongst enterprises, there is a particular relation between the total amount of investment plans being drawn up at any moment and the level of prospective profits.

The second difficulty was that, though Keynes himself attached great importance to the idea that the present is always overweighted in forming a view about the future, he treated his schedule of prospective profits as though it was independent of the actual rate of investment. Kalecki shows how a higher level of investment this year than last, means a higher level of current profits, therefore a higher expected rate of profit, therefore enlarged investment plans, therefore a higher rate of investment next year.

Moreover, Kalecki brought into the argument the fact that there are distinct links to the financing of investment at a given rate of interest; i.e. the problem of availability of finance. The outside finance that a firm can secure is largely determined by the amount of capital owned by the firm. Kalecki viewed the limitation of the size of the firm by the availability of entrepreneurial capital as going to the very heart of the capitalist system, which cannot be ignored in the theory of investment decisions. One of the important determinants of such decisions is the accumulation of firms' capital out of current profits (generated by investment in the past). Profit influences the investment–demand function not only by providing a motive to do so, but also by providing the means to be able to perform such an act. Investment decisions are related to the firm's 'internal' accumulation of gross savings. These savings allow the firm to make new investments without facing the problems of the limited capital market or 'increasing risk' (see Kalecki, 1939, pp.128, 95–106).

Thus, with a given expected rate of return, greater availability of credit (improved terms of borrowing) may raise the rate of investment decisions. If it does and the new investment orders are placed, during the gestation period extra purchasing power is generated and propagated both owing to the primary effect of investment outlays and the multiplier effect.

As Lord Kahn (1984, pp.162–4) attests it is only in his post-*General Theory* writings that Keynes brought in availability of funds as a restraint on investment, more important than the rate of interest. The financial restraint then becomes, according to Kahn (1984, p.162),

> a factor in the determination of the rate of investment additional to expectations of future profitability, the physical capacity of the industries producing the capital goods in question, and 'animal spirits'. It provides an answer to all those who are doubtful about the strength of the risk-free rate of interest when set off against expectations of profits, highly subject to risk and uncertainty.

On the important differences between Kalecki and Keynes on the investment function, Joan Robinson took a somewhat ambivalent position. Whereas Kalecki continually sought for a vigorous and formal investment function in terms of economic analysis, Joan Robinson was content to accept a rather vague notion comprised of psychological, sociological, historical, and institutional elements and the real forces of population growth and technical progress. In her post-war *magnum opus*, she (1956, 1966, pp.55–6) pointed out that 'we know very little' about what governs the level of investment.[29]

> We know that it varies widely from period to period and from country to country, but any attempt to identify causes of variation in such influences as a tradition of vigorous competition among entrepreneurs (as opposed to a lethargic spirit of live and let live), a rapid rate of technical progress or a high propensity to retain profits (amassing reserves to finance investment without external borrowing) is in danger of confusing symptoms with causes. On the other hand, it is not very satisfactory to have to rely for an explanation upon a 'capitalist spirit' due to Protestantism or goodness knows what. Economic analysis requires to be supplemented by a kind of comparative historical anthropology which is still in its infancy as a scientific study. Meanwhile economic analysis has by no means completed its own task of clarifying the consequences, and the proximate causes, of differences in, and changes in, the rate of accumulation.

Joan Robinson (1979a, p.196) admitted that she had a 'running argument' with Kalecki on this subject. Kalecki

> maintained that inventions (technical progress) raise the prospects of profit for capitalist firms and so encourage investment. I followed Keynes and Marx in regarding the desire of capitalists to expand their operations as an inherent characteristic of the system. I expressed this view in Keynes' phrase about 'animal spirits' which caused Kalecki to regard it as somehow irrational. I pointed out that technical progress *permits* accumulation to go on faster than the labour force is growing but it cannot *cause* high profits, for if accumulation is actually going on steadily, Kalecki's own theory shows that the rate of profit on capital will be constant. (Joan Robinson, 1973a, p.90)

Joan Robinson (1973a, p.90; see 1979a, p.196) perceived that Kalecki (1971, pp.165–88) compromised with her by

> pointing out that at any particular moment some go-ahead firms are installing equipment embodying the latest inventions in the hope of

> gaining a higher rate of profit than the average at the expense of their rivals. Thus it can both be true that inventions may stimulate investment and that the overall rate of profit may be constant over the long run.

Be that as it may, in her *Accumulation of Capital* and, indeed, in embryo form in her *Introduction to the Theory of Employment* (particularly chapter 12), one of the major relations Joan Robinson uses – the two-sided relation between profit and accumulation – is Kaleckian. She explains the central mechanism of her model of accumulation as the 'desire of firms to accumulate' and she assumes that 'it is influenced by the expected rate of profit'.

> The double-sided relationship between the rate of profit and the rate of accumulation now appears. The accumulation going on in a particular situation determines the level of profits obtainable in it, and thus (on the basis of the type of expectations which we have postulated) determines the rate of profit expected on investment. The rate of profit in turn influences the rate of accumulation. The rate of profit generated by a particular situation may be such as to induce a rate of accumulation greater or less than that which is actually taking place (Joan Robinson, 1968, p.47).

8 KALECKI'S MODEL AND THE *GENERAL THEORY*

In the natural sciences the question of multiple discovery is not a new one. In the social sciences, however, it is not so common. As Joan Robinson (1976a, p.28) points out:

> In the natural sciences it is common enough for the same discovery to come almost simultaneously from two independent sources. As a subject develops it throws up a new problem and two equally original minds find the same answer, which turns out to be validated by further work. In the history of economic thought, there is one notable example of this phenomenon, the discovery of the theory of employment by Maynard Keynes and Michal Kalecki. In the social sciences, experiments are not made in laboratories but thrown up by history. The problem to which both Keynes and Kalecki were searching for an answer was the breakdown of the market economy in the great depression of the 1930s.

Merton (1973, pp.356 and 371) reminds us that the pages of history of science are littered with countless instances of similar discoveries made by scientists working without contact with one another. These are sometimes made almost simultaneously and sometimes years apart but unbeknown to each other. This suggests that the discoveries are fated when the prerequisite knowledge and tools have accumulated and when a number of scientists focus on a problem propelled to the forefront of their attention by emerging social needs and/or by developments within the discipline. Thus multiple discoveries are brought about as a result of scientists' responses to similar social and intellectual forces that influence all of them. In fact, he claims there should be nothing remarkable in such a development. On the contrary, this is the dominant pattern and it is the single discoveries that require explanation.

While in the case of Kalecki and Keynes the catastrophic manifestations of the Great Depression and the helplessness of then orthodox economics to explain the problems were similar, the intellectual stimuli and the available toolboxes were different. Both of these provide clues to the similarities and differences in their theories and policy implications – the main subject matter of this chapter dealt with in Sections 5–7.

As I have argued elsewhere (Feiwel, 1975), Kalecki and Keynes were not rival inventors. Indeed, in some respects the architectonic contributions of these two scholars are complementary and not competitive. It has taken a long time for the economics profession to acknowledge this coincidental discovery. Indeed, some economists still do not recognize it as we shall presently see. One of the first to give due credit to Kalecki was L. R. Klein – the author of *The Keynesian Revolution* – who in a review of Harrod's biography of Keynes pointed out that, 'after having re-examined Kalecki's theory of the business cycle, I have decided that he actually created a system that contains everything of importance in the Keynesian system, in addition to other contributions' (Klein 1951, p.447).

Joan Robinson (1965, 1975, p.95) has many times emphasized that 'Kalecki's claim to priority of publications is indisputable'. But more than that, she has frequently underlined that 'in several respects, Kalecki's version is more robust than Keynes's' (Robinson, 1979a, p.187). In her Ely Lecture to the American Economic Association she (1973a, p.97) reminded us that

> Keynes himself was not very much interested in the theory of value and distribution. Kalecki produced a more coherent version of the General Theory, which brought imperfect competition into the analysis and emphasised the influence of investment on the share of profits. Kalecki's version was in some ways more truly a *general* theory than Keynes'.

Reflecting on the 'striking and interesting differences' between Kalecki's and Keynes's theories, approaches, and presentation, Johansen (1978, p.160) emphasized the basic fact 'that Kalecki developed, in some respects in a more advanced form, some of the basic elements of "Keynesian" macroeconomics before Keynes, while on the other hand Keynes's exposition had a much greater impact and still takes the central position in most expositions of macroeconomic theory'. On the question of Kalecki's priority of publication, Johansen (p.160) claimed that it is equally legitimate to turn the argument around 'and say that it was one of Keynes's greatest achievements to rediscover, independently, some of Kalecki's main macroeconomic ideas so shortly after Kalecki himself'. Harry Johnson (1978, pp.158–9) also speaks of Kalecki's priority of publication 'in some respects theoretically superior to Keynes's *General Theory*', but Kalecki 'was unfortunate enough to publish in Polish, his native language, and doubly unfortunate in that, when he finally arrived in Cambridge, he proved to lack all the social and cultural graces necessary for acceptance in the British academic system and establishment – graces with which Keynes was super-abundantly endowed'. And in a review of Kalecki (1971), Johnson (1973, pp.87–8) noted:

> The blurb ranks Kalecki with Keynes. Technically he was far superior, and his contributions during his period in England probably did more to shape the evolution of Keynesian theorizing over the next decade than those of any other Keynesian. On the other hand he lacked Keynes' personal and cultural advantages in the matter of self-advertisement and flair in presentation to the non-mathematically gifted, as well as Keynes' roots in the mainstream liberal traditions of economics.
>
> Given Kalecki's importance in the formative years of Keynesian theorizing, the question naturally arises why his academic stock dropped so rapidly after the period of his major contributions. His disappearance from sight into the United National Secretariat, and then back to Poland, provides a large part of the explanation: without a professorship in a leading American or British university one is academically dead.
>
> These accidents of personal and professional history should not be allowed to detract from appreciation of the greatness of the man's contribution . . .

It has always been my contention that the question of Kalecki's anticipation of Keynes is of lesser importance than that of the superiority of the Kaleckian construct over the Keynesian one in several crucial aspects. However, since the main theme of Don Patinkin's reflective and controversial *Anticipations of the General Theory?* is as the title indicates, the question of anticipation, we shall pause here briefly on some of the questions raised by him as regards Kalecki's priority of publication over Keynes. That much of the argument depends on the frame of reference used by Patinkin is inarguable. His standpoint is certainly colored by his own (evolving) interpretation of the essence of the 'central message' of the *General Theory* – an interpretation that I dare say is a narrow one. In a most scholarly fashion Patinkin (1982, p.81) admits to that: 'I must admit that my definition has sometimes been criticized as too narrow. This may be true'. One can understand that Patinkin takes Keynes's *General Theory* as a yardstick for measuring Kalecki's performance. To many of us, however (no matter how much we admire Keynes's historical achievement), it is just as legitimate and useful to take Kalecki's achievement as a yardstick to measure Keynes's performance.

If one confines oneself to the questionable comparison of the extent to which Kalecki anticipated the specific analytical innovation of the *General Theory*, one can only repeat after Patinkin (p.5) that there is no unanimity of answer to the question of what that innovation was. 'Clearly the broader the specification of the innovative contribution of the *General Theory* the greater the likelihood of finding this contribution anticipated.' Patinkin expects to disarm his critics by allowing that a broader interpretation of the Keynesian message is acceptable. He (p.18) points out, however, that via this route,

> if it is enough to speak in general terms about aggregate demand and supply, then ... Keynes' 1933 *Means to Prosperity*, Wicksell's 1906 *Lectures*, and perhaps even Malthus' writings almost a century before that constitute the General Theory. Alternatively, if the General Theory can be identified even with an imprecise description of the way a decrease in output decreases saving until it is brought to equality with investment, then Keynes' discovery of it should be dated with his 1931 Harris lecture ... And if the General Theory is the proposition that an increase in investment generates an equal amount of saving, then ... this theory was first presented in an imprecise form by Keynes in his 1929 *Can Lloyd George Do It?* and was then rigorously developed by Richard Kahn in his celebrated 1931 multiplier article.

Patinkin discards several broader interpretations of what constitutes the major contribution of the *General Theory* (see pp.6–7). He considers the 'central message' of the *General Theory* to be the explanation of a state of unemployment equilibrium in a capitalist economy. More specifically, he illustrates his argument by the familiar 45° diagram (see p.10). He (p.9) contends that what he means by the theory of effective demand is 'not only that intersection of the aggregate demand curve ... with the 45° line determines equilibrium real output ... at a level that may be below that of full employment ...; not only that disequilibrium between aggregate demand and supply causes a change in output and not price; but also (and this is the distinctively novel feature) that the change in output (and hence income) itself acts as an equilibrating force. That is, if the economy is in a state of excess aggregate supply ... then the resulting decline in output, and hence income, will depress supply more than demand and thus eventually bring the economy to equilibrium'. Patinkin admits that Keynes did not use this diagram which is adapted from a 1939 article by Samuelson (1966, p.1115). Neither did Keynes use Patinkin's more formal interpretation of Keynes's 'central message'. To wit, that 'the theory of effective demand is concerned not only with the mathematical solution of the equilibrium equation ... but with demonstrating the stability of this equilibrium as determined by the dynamic adjustment equation' (Patinkin 1982, p.10).

By narrowing down to such an extent the central message of a theory, Patinkin reduces the possibility of multiple discoveries to almost nought even in the natural sciences. Indeed, Patinkin's central message is that multiple discoveries, if they do occur at all, are exceedingly rare. He (pp.4 and 91–2) cites, for example, the case of Joan Robinson and Chamberlin as one where an alleged multiple discovery was not one at all. As we have seen in Chapter 1 of the companion volume though Chamberlin's monopolistic competition differed in many respects from Joan Robinson's imperfect competition, the reader of both could be forgiven for drawing similar conclusions and for generally treating them almost interchangeably. As Samuelson (1972, p.19) pointed out, the keen historians of science should not be surprised to find multiple discoveries that appear to be substantially similar, and when carefully examined, they turn out to be substantially different. They are multiple discoveries nevertheless. 'With cogency and pertinacity, Chamberlin has always insisted on differentiating his product from that of Mrs. Robinson. Posterity will agree. But in its typical wayward manner, posterity will amalgamate into an optimal package what it conceives to be the best of the various systems'. Samuelson (pp. 20–21) further explained that 'indeed the time has come when we may permit ourselves to use the terms monopolistic competition and imperfect competition interchangeably, emancipating them from their first associations with the different conceptions of Chamberlin and Mrs. Robinson, and using them as convenient names for the best current models of price theory'.

Patinkin (1982, p.14) argues that the primary concern of the *General Theory* is the explanation of equilibrium at less than full employment. For him (p.70) 'the central message of Kalecki's 1933 booklet is in any event cycles and not a state of continued low-level employment', and that Kalecki's 'central message is in any event concerned with the analysis not of output, but of investment'. As I have emphasized, Kalecki's approach to the theory of effective demand is through the theory of the business cycle where investment and its variability play a central role. While one of Keynes's distinct contributions was the focus on the variability of investment as crucially affecting effective demand (and the *General Theory* is full of insights on the causes and consequences of this variability), it may be argued that even in his initial 1933 publication Kalecki went deeper into the determinants of this determinant. Kalecki addressed himself to the repercussions of fluctuations of investment on output. An elaboration of these arguments can be found in Kalecki's analysis of policies to alleviate depression, what he called creating synthetic prosperity (see Kalecki, 1979, pp.177–260).

Indeed, it is legitimate to claim, as Asimakopulos (1983, p.519) does, that Patinkin's interpretation of the theory of effective demand as explaining the factors determining the equilibrium level of employment and its stability at a given rate of investment is, at best, an incomplete statement of the *General Theory's* central message. But as we shall presently see the narrowness of Patinkin's interpretation of Keynes's central message does not depend only on Patinkin's neglect of the variability of investment.

Like many other scholars, Kalecki tended to deal with and emphasize one crucial point at a time. His 1933 essay does not focus on what Patinkin considers to be the central message of the *General Theory*, although certain passages in Kalecki's presentation could be interpreted as representing the crux of the notion. Patinkin (1982, pp.67–8) does quote some of these passages, though he disclaims that on the basis of these passages one could grant Kalecki independent and prior discovery of Patinkin's narrow conception of the essence of the *General Theory*.

Patinkin (p.71) acknowledges that in a 1935 article (translated and republished as 'The Mechanism of the Business Upswing' in Kalecki 1966, pp.26–33) published in *Polska Gospodarcza*, Kalecki explained the Keynesian equilibrating mechanism. But Patinkin would not grant Kalecki independent and prior discovery of this narrow conception of the central message of the *General Theory* primarily because Kalecki advanced his argument in a non-professional journal and above all because 'this theme of unemployment equilibrium receives little if any attention in Kalecki's professional writings during the pre-*General Theory* period' (p.72). It cannot be overemphasized that Kalecki's writings are terse and laconic. He zeroed in on one subject at a time and seldom tackled the same subject unless it was to present a new approach (as in the case of the investment function). Patinkin eloquently presents the practice of repetition of the same theme, with different variations as in music, as a touchstone for finding the central message of a piece of scholarly writing. This was not Kalecki's style. Indeed, his writings are exemplary in their non-repetition in the best tradition of editors' advice to neophyte writers. Moreover, on the issues of independent discovery and anticipation, to get a complete picture of Kalecki's contributions until 1936, one should take into account the entire body of his work until that date, particularly including the articles published in non-academic journals, especially those he later selected for translation and inclusion in the 1966 edition. One should remember that Kalecki was then not an academic economist. He earned his living as a researcher and as an economic journalist. Publication in *Polska Gospodarcza* provided him with a supplement to his relatively meagre income. Moreover it was a publication of the Ministry of Industry and Trade and the Institute for which Kalecki worked was an arm of that ministry.

At this juncture it bears repeating that, unlike Keynes, Kalecki was not trained in the economic orthodoxies prevailing in the 1930s in the major seats of Western academia. The narrowness of Keynes's training and attitudes to economics need not detain us here. However, the approach in and focus of the *General Theory* has to be understood in the light of the tradition from which Keynes came, the particular brand of orthodoxy he was trying to escape, and the mold in which his readers' minds were cast. On the other hand, Kalecki, as we know, was a neophyte in economics who by 1930 had been exposed primarily to Rosa Luxemburg, Tugan Baranovsky, and Marx. It should be remembered that tradition stressed the business-cycle approach and the strategic role of the volatility of investment. It seems to me that, under these circumstances, it is a misunderstanding to analyze Kalecki's pre-1936 writings through the prism of neoclassical equilibrium analysis. True, Kalecki does not explicitly use the concept of equilibrium in his 1933 essay, yet it is present implicitly as is a concept of the multiplier somewhat different from Kahn's (see Kalecki, 1979, pp.95–107). The latter is particularly elaborated in Kalecki's policy articles, especially in his illuminating paper on foreign trade (reprinted in 1966, pp.16–25).

If one were to insist on the dubious necessity of finding Keynes's short period underemployment equilibrium in Kalecki's 1933 essay one could go the route of reconstructing the national income flow in both Keynes and Kalecki, deriving basically the same theory of effective demand, differences in specifications of workers' and capitalists' propensities to save and consume notwithstanding (see Osiatyński 1985, pp.100–102).

As Kalecki himself noted in his 1936 review of the *General Theory*, Keynes's book represents a revolutionary landmark in the history of economics, but the approach is static. Kalecki's approach is dynamic. He considers an evolving system that consists of a cumulative series of short periods that succeed each other. Whatever the achievements and shortcomings of his dynamic approach, Kalecki's pre-1936 writings take us several steps beyond Keynes. On a purely analytical plane, one could perhaps argue that the *General Theory* represents to some extent a special case of Kalecki's more general construct. Patinkin (1982, p.78) himself can be interpreted to lend support to this statement when he says that 'Kalecki's theory indicates one of the ways of extending the Keynesian system so as to provide a theory of the business cycle'. In the sense that Kalecki's construct is more general, Joan Robinson's generalization of the general theory draws on Kalecki's construct.

If one looks at the mathematical models of Kalecki and Keynes, one can compare, as Klein does (in a letter of 12 October 1987 to the author), the Hicks and Lange versions of Keynes[30] – essentially static (but made dynamic by Samuelson and others) – with Kalecki's writings of that time which can be put into an equation system – as Klein (1964) has done – although Kalecki himself put forward each equation separately. He put them all together in his 1935 article, but, according to Klein, one needs to supply the explicit mathematical model of the Keynesian equivalence class. Each piece of Kalecki's model (including the money sector) can be likened to one of Keynes's; they both determine the same set of variables. The fact that Kalecki's is dynamic and Keynes's is static is not all that important; Kalecki's model can be compared with the dynamic enhancements of the Keynesian system. Neither does it matter that Kalecki's system does not contain employment explicitly because the Hicks-Lange versions do not either. After all, the underemployment equilibrium is a particular aspect of the Keynesian system requiring Keynesian-type policy prescriptions to improve the economy's performance. Kalecki's system needs similar policies in order to raise the average levels of activity about which his system tends to oscillate. Klein concludes: 'As far as I am concerned they are mathematically *equivalent*, were developed *independently*, and at about the *same time*'.

Patinkin (p.77) claims that Kalecki's theory 'fails to integrate value theory with monetary theory and is indeed devoid of the marginal analysis on which the former is based'. Kalecki is, indeed, weak in monetary theory, though his discussions are replete with interesting insights on money and particularly on finance. However, one can hardly accept Patinkin's equation of price theory with marginal analysis. Indeed, reliance on orthodox price theory was a weak link in the *General Theory*; one that has spawned a huge body of literature on microfoundations. As it evolved, Kalecki's theory featured monopolistic price formation dovetailed with the rest of his construct. His integrated micro-macro approach is one of the most persuasive and fruitful attributes of his theory.

If the institutional framework of a social system fundamentally conditions the system's economic dynamics – a view Kalecki stressed strongly in his last lecture in Cambridge in 1969 and one that permeated his analysis from the start – the explanation of the functioning of the modern monopoly capitalism requires a realistic perception of market power. Kalecki considered perfect competition as a dangerous myth. He used it as an analytical device in combatting opponents, for example, when discussing wage cuts as a route to restoring prosperity or when analyzing the class struggle and income distribution. Thus, one cannot sufficiently stress that Kalecki's overall perception of contemporary capitalism differed essentially from Keynes's, if for no other reason than because of their divergent views on the competitive process, price formation, and distributional conflicts. One should also note that there has been an essential transformation in the character of the capitalist economy since Kalecki and Keynes wrote. Of course, some of this transformation is directly traceable to the Keynesian revolution and to policies derived more directly from Keynes than from

Kalecki. Also, Kalecki lived through a good part of this period of transformation which his postwar analyses reflect.

Both Kalecki's and Keynes's writings reflect the traumatic problems of the Great Depression, although they came to their similar conclusions via different routes and analytical apparatuses. True, even the general economic and social conditions they experienced were somewhat different (to wit, the stagnation of the 1920s in the UK). However, Patinkin seems to misunderstand Kalecki's concern for unemployment (probably due to his lack of a reading knowledge of Polish – not a necessary equipment for an economist). He (p.88) writes:

> The phenomenon for which a desperate world in the early 1930s was searching for an explanation was that of the bewildering and seemingly endless depression that was creating untold misery and threatening its political stability. This was the problem to whose solution Keynes – in contrast with the Stockholm School and Kalecki – devoted his central message . . .

Whatever inspiration Kalecki derived from Rosa Luxemburg, Tugan Baranovski, and the Marxian schemes of reproduction, one must again emphasize that before he wrote his 1933 essay he undertook painstaking analysis of various industries, markets, world business conditions, and national income studies. Hence his theoretical writings are partly a generalization of inductive reasoning. In fact, one of Kalecki's strong points is his construction of a rigorous mathematical model on the basis of carefully observed real phenomena. It is, indeed, a misunderstanding to say that unemployment was not a central theme of Kalecki's work. If I may interject a personal recollection at this point, I remember that when I was studying Kalecki's writings of the 1930s in preparation for writing my 1975 book, I had the overwhelming impression that he was *obsessed* with unemployment, in the best meaning of the term (see Kalecki, 1979).

More importantly, however, many of us do not agree that the central message of the *General Theory* is underemployment equilibrium. At best, it is only an effective tool to demonstrate the fundamental and critical role of aggregate effective demand in limiting production and underutilization of resources and capacity. The absence of a powerful and effective endogenous mechanism to generate and sustain near full utilization of productive potential and the need for government intervention to restore and maintain such near full utilization appears to me to be the central message of Keynes. To put it differently, at least in the macroeconomic sense the system is subject to a major pernicious and conspicuous market failure – a failure that can be repaired by an alternative mix of policies. In the main, Kalecki's central message is the same. His analytical methods and policy conclusions differ from Keynes's, in many ways they are superior, but in general they are complementary rather than substitutes – a subject that is the 'central message' of this section.

To some extent, we can find support in Keynes (1936, p.297) for our contention of what the central message of Keynes is and is not. He observed that for him the essential content is far more important than the formal arrangement in which he presented it.

> The object of our analysis is, not to provide a machine, or method of blind manipulation, which will furnish an infallible answer, but to provide ourselves with an organised and orderly method of thinking out particular problems; and, after we have reached a provisional conclusion by isolating the complicating factors one by one, we then have to go back on ourselves and allow, as well as we can, for the probable interactions of the factors amongst themselves. This is the nature of economic thinking.

In fact, in his famous 1937 response to critics, Keynes (1973c, p.111) reiterated this position. He wrote: 'I am more attached to the comparatively simple fundamental ideas which underlie my theory than to the particular forms in which I have embodied them, and I have no desire that the latter should be crystallised at the present stage of the debate'.

One can appreciate that scholars coming from different traditions might prefer Keynes's treatment over Kalecki's or vice versa. Patinkin (1982, p.78) even grants that 'Kalecki's theory enables us to make certain improvements on Keynes' '. Similarly Kaleckians should generally admit that the *General Theory* enables us to make certain improvements on Kalecki's construct. However important the question of independent discovery and anticipation may be for doctrinal history and the vested interests of followers, it is far more important to strive to achieve a new synthesis by integrating what is best in Kalecki and Keynes with the positive achievements in the more than half century since they wrote.

In a sense the *General Theory* is painted in bold strokes rather than the creation of a master economic theoretician. 'Keynes, the propagandist, was always forging ahead of Keynes, the author of theoretical academic works. Indeed, it was Keynes' zeal as a reformer, and his facility in putting his ideas into shape, that set the pace for the writing of the *General Theory*' (Kahn, 1984, p.77). Furthermore, 'in his burning anxiety to convince, he did enormously over-simplify' (p.159). As it behooves a classic, the *General Theory* is both larger and smaller than its author. Whatever just praise can be heaped on this book, its limitations stand out clearly as compared with Kalecki's construct. Kalecki's theory is broader, firmer, and more rigorous and corresponds closer to the realities and institutions of contemporary capitalism. While it is in many respects superior to Keynes's, Kalecki's theory is not complete; it is merely a solid and substantial building block towards such a theory.

9 THE ECONOMICS AND POLITICS OF FULL EMPLOYMENT

9.1 Economic Answers and Political Questions

> What made the *General Theory* so hard to accept was not its intellectual content, which in a calm mood can easily be mastered, but its shocking implications. Worse than private vices being public benefits, it seemed that the new doctrine was the still more disconcerting proposition that private virtues (of thriftiness and careful husbandry) were public vices . . .
>
> By making it impossible to believe any longer in an automatic reconciliation of conflicting interests into a harmonious whole, the *General Theory* brought out into the open the problem of choice and judgement that the neoclassicals had managed to smother. The ideology to end ideologies broke down. Economics once more became Political Economy. (Joan Robinson, 1962, pp.75–6)

Both Keynes and Kalecki succeeded in undermining the major orthodox preconception and presumption that in a private market economy there are strong endogenous forces to move, find, and maintain full employment equilibrium. For Joan Robinson (1976a, p.28), accepting the Keynesian-Kaleckian point of view 'meant admitting that there is a fundamental defect in the *laissez-faire* doctrine and recognizing that household saving is a consequence rather than a cause of capital accumulation. The concept of a natural tendency to equilibrium is untenable in theory as well as untrue in reality'.

Implicitly the Keynes–Kalecki theory (whatever their theoretical differences) assigns a crucial role to deliberate government policy for influencing (if not regulating) effective demand (see Joan Robinson, 1962, pp.84–5).[31] In a broader interpretation, public policy should use whatever instruments are most appropriate to influence and coordinate both demand and supply and to keep the system reasonably close to a desirable full-employment growth path, while minimizing adverse side effects. But this is a very general implication. As we know, Kalecki and Keynes differed personally and philosophically in as many dimensions as men can. This and their theoretical differences undoubtedly colored their respective policy interpretations and prescriptions.

Keynes addressed himself to the fundamental question of agenda and non-agenda for government and challenged Bentham's presumption that state interference is generally superfluous and pernicious (see Keynes, 1963b, pp.312–13). Thus, Keynes (1936, pp.380–1) argued that

> Whilst . . . the enlargement of the functions of government, involved in the task of adjusting to one another the propensity to consume and the inducement to invest, would seem to a nineteenth-century publicist or to a contemporary American financier to be a terrific encroachment on

individualism, I defend it, on the contrary, both as the only practicable means of avoiding the destruction of existing economic forms in their entirety and as the condition of the successful functioning of individual initiative.

For if effective demand is deficient, not only is the public scandal of wasted resources intolerable, but the individual enterpriser who seeks to bring these resources into action is operating with the odds loaded against him.

Whilst such enlargement of the government's field of action entails establishing certain controls in areas previously left to private initiative, two wide fields of activity remain unaffected, according to Keynes (1936, p.378).

> The State will have to exercise a guiding influence on the propensity to consume partly through its scheme of taxation, partly by fixing the rate of interest, and partly, perhaps, in other ways. Furthermore, it seems unlikely that the influence of banking policy on the rate of interest will be sufficient by itself to determine an optimum rate of investment. I conceive, therefore, that a somewhat comprehensive socialisation of investment will prove the only means of securing an approximation to full employment; though this need not exclude all manner of compromises and of devices by which public authority will co-operate with private initiative. But beyond this no obvious case is made out for a system of State Socialism which would embrace most of the economic life of the community. It is not the ownership of the instruments of production which it is important for the State to assume. If the State is able to determine the aggregate amount of resources devoted to augmenting the instruments and the basic rate of reward to those who own them, it will have accomplished all that is necessary. Moreover, the necessary measures of socialisation can be introduced gradually and without a break in the general traditions of society.

As the last chapter of the *General Theory* indicates,

> Keynes liked to believe in the power of ideas to influence the course of history. He sometimes maintained that when the principles of employment policy were understood, economic affairs would be conducted rationally, and he even went so far as to predict a happy future in which our grandchildren could devote themselves entirely to the arts and graces of life. (Joan Robinson, 1976a, p.30)

To what extent was the *General Theory* a 'moderately conservative' book, as Keynes (1936, p.377) maintained, given that the entire book was 'a polemic against established ideas'? (Joan Robinson, 1979a, p.175)

> His own mood swung from left to right. Capitalism was in some ways repugnant to him but Stalinism was much worse. In his last years, certainly, the right predominated. When I teased him about accepting a peerage he replied that after sixty one had to become respectable. But his basic view of life was aesthetic rather than political. He hated unemployment because it was stupid and poverty because it was ugly. He was disgusted by the commercialism of modern life. (It is true he enjoyed making money for his College and for himself but only as long as it did not take up much time.) He indulged in an agreeable vision of a world where economics has ceased to be important and our grandchildren can begin to lead a civilized life.

Kalecki saw that the process of establishing full employment could be used as a vehicle to effect basic changes in the capitalist system in the direction of what he considered a more just distribution of national income and towards advancing the standard of living of the entire population. He saw the opportunity, but he was mindful of the grave problems that this would entail. In Kalecki's interpretation, a policy of full employment not only means to push employment up to the level where unemployment, other than frictional, is abolished, but it is a program for maintaining full employment, founded either on a long-run budget deficit policy or on income redistribution.

The opportunity of state intervention to achieve and maintain full employment is for Kalecki a means of effecting major changes in the character and *modus operandi* of the economic system. Thus in Kalecki's version the Keynesian revolution is distinctly put into service as an engine of economic and social change and progress, where mere mitigation of business fluctuations and maintenance of economic activity around an underemployed equilibrium cease to be the goal of economic policy, and a new pattern of employment and direction of government spending and intervention becomes a crucial test of successful performance of the economy. Thus the aim is not to reproduce 'extensively' the existing capitalist system on a larger scale, unhampered by lack of markets, but to effect intensive-type qualitative changes in the very pattern of economic processes. Surely such an approach is bound to encounter strong opposition from many quarters, including, on the one hand, those who would wish to preserve the present order (subject to relatively minor modifications), and, on the other, those who would prefer to demolish the existing system, in order to set up an entirely different order.

Kalecki (1944) distinguished three major ways of generating effective demand in a modern capitalist economy and reflected upon their adequacy and relative efficiency in effecting and supporting full employment.[32] He concentrated on the relative merits of (i) deficit spending, (ii) stimulating private investment, and (iii) redistributing income from higher to lower income groups. His contention was that, in the main, (ii) is not sufficient and not satisfactory, but both (i) and (iii), subject to an appropriate monetary policy and supporting measures (or neutralizing adverse circumstances), provide adequate (but not necessarily equally satisfactory) means for permanent maintenance of full employment. Kalecki underscored that much will depend on the working arrangements for resource allocation.

Deficit spending can solve the problem of generating effective demand and, if it is sufficiently large, it can ensure full employment. Various ways have similar favorable effects on effective demand, but in addition they may lead to a better or worse allocation of resources, income distribution, structure of the economy and society; and may produce different side-effects. The role of investment in establishing a certain level of national income is not associated with its final destination: whether investment will prove socially useful, useless, or destructive, it generates the same effective demand when it is executed. From the standpoint of creating full employment, the proverbial digging of holes in the ground and filling them again (or the piling up of military hardware) produces the same result as building schools, hospitals, roads, etc., and the induced income is fairly independent of the object of primary expenditure.[33]

In the post-war period Kalecki became very bitter about the unethical use of the tools of the Keynesian revolution. In a 1965 address in Mexico City, he expressed deep concern for the fact that the market economies were still intolerably far from reasonably full employment and utilization of capacity. He was particularly concerned about the adverse composition of output. The question that continued to preoccupy him was how to deploy economic resources to enhance welfare which would be more equitably shared among the various strata of society.

> The main problem of a developed capitalist economy is the adequacy of effective demand. Such an economy possesses a capital equipment which more or less matches the existing labour force, and therefore it could generate a rather high income *per capita* provided that its resources are fully used. This, however, is by no means necessarily the case. It was believed in the past that this occurs automatically, i.e. that such an economy tends to maintain full employment and thus unemployment may be considered merely an accidental short lived deviation from full utilisation of resources, an unimportant friction which may be disregarded. A basic revision in that view occurred during the great depression of the 1930s in which the capitalist system was shaken to its foundations. In fact, it is clear for us today that the problem of under-utilisation of resources is, in a sense, inherent in a developed capitalist economy and that potentially, at least, it may emerge at any time. (Kalecki, 1976, p.20)

After describing the possible ways and means by which government policy could generate adequate effective demand,[34] Kalecki (1976, pp.22–3) went on:

> Let us now consider the direction of government expenditure undertaken in order to maintain full employment. From the point of view of creating effective demand this does not matter ... the most rational course, however ... would be to spend on investment and thus to accelerate the development of the economy; or to contribute through government expenditure (or reduction of taxation) to the increase in consumption of the broad masses of the population. However, under capitalism, this does not necessarily happen. Indeed, at present the available economic surplus is, to a great extent, used to produce armaments.
>
> Thus the economy is kept going by armament expenditures and people are assured of their livelihood through the manufacture of the means of destruction. To an outsider, this looks fairly absurd, because the surplus could have been used to increase either investment or consumption. In fact, however, it is wasted, or worse.
>
> But, absurd though it is, even such a method of maintaining full employment assures modern capitalism of a fair degree of political stability, because although the levels of mass consumption are not as high as they could be, they are still much higher than those that would prevail under conditions of unemployment. Morover, if full employment is consistently maintained and if the relative share of labour in the national income remains constant, there will also be some continuous increase in the real wage because of the rising productivity of labour: if the labour force is continuously employed, if there is a rise in productivity and if the relative share of labour in the national income is unaltered, it is perfectly clear that the real wage is bound to rise.

Joan Robinson shared Kalecki's concerns about the content of full employment. Indeed, in 1971 in the Ely Lecture to the American Economic Association she spoke of two crises in economics. 'The first crisis arose from the breakdown of a theory which could not account for the *level* of employment. The second crisis arises from a theory that cannot account for the *content* of employment' (1973a, pp.99–100). She (p.100) went on:

> Now that we all agree that government expenditure can maintain employment, we should argue about what the expenditure should be for. Keynes did not *want* anyone to dig holes and fill them. He indulged in a pleasant daydream of a world in which, when investment had been kept at the full employment level for thirty years or so, all needs for capital installations would have been met, property income would have been

abolished, poverty would have disappeared and civilized life could begin.[35]

But the post-war reality was something quite different. For twenty-five years serious recessions were avoided. 'The most convenient thing for a government to spend on is armaments. The military–industrial complex took charge. I do not think it plausible to suppose that the cold war and several hot wars were invented just to solve the employment problem . . . So it has come about that Keynes's pleasant daydream was turned into a nightmare of terror' (Joan Robinson, 1973a, pp.100–1; see chapter 1 of the companion volume (section 8.3).)

Joan Robinson (1976a, p.30) has made the striking comment that whereas Keynes was an idealist, Kalecki was a realist.[36] In a discussion in Kahn (1984, p.203) she said:

> The great trouble with Keynes was that he was an idealist. He thought that when people could understand his theory, could understand how the capitalistic system actually works, they would then behave in a reasonable manner and operate the system in such a way as to produce favourable results, to produce in particular a high and stable level of employment.

Whatever the rationale of the *economics* of full employment, the *political* problems are formidable. As we have seen, Kalecki realized that full-employment policies could be used to reform the capitalist system. He saw the opportunity, but was mindful of the grave political problems and, in 1943, predicted the emergence of the political business cycle.[37] He (1971, pp.138–45) argued that opposition by the 'leaders of industry' to full employment stimulated by government spending may be expected because of the inherent fear of government interference (in particular opposition, in principle, to government spending generated by budget deficits), opposition to the objects of government spending (particularly to public investments and the subsidizing of consumption), fear of inflationary pressures, opposition to sustained full employment (as against mere prevention of deep depressions), and the dislike of the social and economic changes resulting from the maintenance of full employment (including laxity of workers' discipline). He felt that business cycles in milder form than hitherto would continue and result in some sort of stop-go. These short-lived and relatively moderate cycles would proceed from a situation where the government would stimulate business activity, then withdrew at the early signs of an upswing under the clamor of an 'unsound' financial situation (and even undertake deflationary policies near the peak) only to re-enter as a stimulating agent when unemployment would again rise beyond an 'acceptable level', thus vacillating between combating unemployment and inflation.

In this way Kalecki (1971, p.144) predicted the pattern of the political business cycle:

> In the slump, either under the pressure of the masses, or even without it, public investment financed by borrowing will be undertaken to prevent large scale unemployment. But if attempts are made to apply this method in order to maintain the high level of employment reached in the subsequent boom a strong opposition of 'business leaders' is likely to be encountered. As has already been argued, lasting full employment is not at all to their liking. The workers would 'get out of hand' and the 'captains of industry' would be anxious to 'teach them a lesson.' Moreover, the increase in the upswing is to the disadvantage of small and big *rentiers* and makes them 'boom tired.'
>
> In this situation a powerful block is likely to be formed between big business and the *rentier* interests, and they would probably find more than one economist to declare that the situation was manifestly unsound. The pressure of all these forces, and in particular of big business – as a rule influential in Government departments – would most probably induce the Government to return to the orthodox policy of cutting down the budget deficit. A slump would follow in which Government spending would come again into its own.[38]

In closing his argument, Kalecki (1943b, pp.330–1) offered a reformist prescription for preventing the occurrence of political business cycles. Perhaps this prescription was not republished thirty years later because Kalecki had become overly bitter and skeptical about the hopes he had voiced then. He appears to have suffered from, for lack of a better expression, what we might call the Einstein syndrome: having shown (together with Keynes) to the capitalist world how it could save (and reform) itself by relieving (and in some sense doing away with) periodic depressions, Kalecki saw that world turning insane; for instead of raising the standard of living to a higher level than that achieved so far by public investment, resources were being wasted on armaments production and periodic small-scale wars that turned into large-scale disasters.

Kalecki stressed that the institutions of post-war capitalism would have to alter considerably. He emphasized that 'a progressive' should strive for lasting full employment and government subsidy of consumption. Slumps should not be mitigated but eliminated. Public investment should only be undertaken to the extent that it is needed, and the balance of government spending required to maintain full employment should go towards subsidizing consumption. 'The opposers of such Government spending say that the Government will then have nothing to show for their money. The reply is that the counterpart of this spending will be the higher standard of living of the masses. Is not this the purpose of all economic activity?' New social and political institutions would have to be developed by such a system which would reflect the increased power of the workers. 'If capitalism can adjust itself to full employment a fundamental reform will have been incorporated in it. If not, it will show itself an outmoded system which must be scrapped'. Kalecki then mused whether the struggle for full employment might not lead to fascism. His answer was negative. 'The fight of the progressive forces for full employment is at the same time a way of *preventing* the recurrence of fascism'.

At about the same time as Kalecki wrote his 1943b article, Joan Robinson herself showed considerable prescience of things to come in an uncharacteristic article about postwar full employment. (The article, 'Planning Full Employment – Alternative Solutions of a Dilemma', *The Times*, 23 January 1943, is unsigned but is generally attributed to Joan Robinson.)

> Unemployment is not a mere accidental blemish in a private-enterprise economy. On the contrary, it is part of the essential mechanism of the system, and has a definitive function to fulfil. The first function of unemployment (which has always existed in open or disguised forms) is that it maintains the authority of masters over men. The master has normally been in a position to say: 'If you don't want the job, there are plenty of others who do'. When the man can say 'If you don't want to employ me there are plenty of others who will' the situation is radically altered . . .
>
> The change in the workers' bargaining position which should follow from the abolition of unemployment would show itself in another and more subtle way. Unemployment in a private enterprise economy has not only the function of preserving discipline in industry, but also indirectly the function of preserving the value of money. If free wage bargaining as we have known it hitherto, is continued in conditions of full employment, there would be a constant upward pressure upon money wage-rates. This phenomena also exists at the present time, and is kept within bound by the appeal of patriotism. In peace-time the vicious spiral of wages and prices might become chronic. (Quoted after Worswick and Trevithick, 1983, pp.4–5)

9.2 Revival of Orthodoxy

Before the great slump of the 1930s, Alfred Marshall was the dominant influence on economics in the English-speaking world. He was a subtle thinker who allowed for exceptions to every rule that he propounded but the effect of his doctrines as they were generally interpreted was to

> support laisser-faire – government intervention in economic life, however well-intentioned, will do more harm than good; belief in a natural tendency to equilibrium in the free-market economy at a level of real wages consonant with full employment of the available labour force; the beneficial effects of free trade; the defence of the gold standard and of sound finance. Many arguments drawn from this complex of ideas are being trotted out again now, as they were in the 1930s; for instance, the view that there cannot be any 'involuntary' unemployment, because any individual could always get a job by offering to work at less than the going wage rate, or that government borrowing draws upon a given fund of savings (or is it of finance?) and so 'crowds out' private-sector investment. However, during the great debate that was broken off by the war in 1939, the arguments of Keynes were gradually prevailing over orthodoxy, and by the end of the war Keynes had become orthodox in his turn. (Joan Robinson, 1979a, p.91)

The Great Depression shook the capitalist system to its very foundations, but it did not collapse. The first twenty-five postwar years were remarkably prosperous – whatever exceptions one may take to the methods of achieving prosperity, to the content and distribution of the cake, and to the long-term effect on productivity, well-being, and quality of life. While the business cycle was neither dead nor obsolete, sharp depressions were avoided as a result of major interventions of the new actor in the 'cycle drama' – the government. For a quarter of a century, capitalism – still fairly far remote from full utilization of resources, but without severe depressions and with relatively mild fluctuations (sometimes generated by the government – the political business cycle) – became a qualitatively new phenomenon. As Joan Robinson (1979a, pp.123–4) observed, a particular feature of the political business cycle 'as it is played out in the United States is that when a political boom is required, it is arms expenditures that expand; when a political recession is required, it is social services that are cut'.

In her inaugural lecture in 1966, Joan Robinson (1973a, pp.4–5) reflected on the postwar development. She stressed the chronic deficiency of demand in modern capitalism and the experience (until then) of almost continuous prosperity which built up a belief in perpetual growth and a high level of employment.

> The great slump is now a half-forgotten nightmare. Ever since the war, partly by good luck, partly by good management and partly by the arms race, overall effective demand has been kept from serious relapses. Nowadays governments are concerned not just to maintain employment, but to make national income grow. Nevertheless, the capitalist world is still always somewhat of a buyer's market, in the sense that capacity to produce exceeds what can be sold at a profitable price. Some countries

> have experienced spells of excessive demand, but this corrects itself only too soon. The chronic condition for industrial enterprise is to be looking round anxiously for prospects of sales. Since the total market does not grow fast enough to make room for all, each government feels it a worthy and commendable aim to increase its own share in world activity for the benefit of its own people.
>
> This is the new mercantilism.

Interestingly, the postwar success story was followed by retrogression in the 1970s – stagflation (see Joan Robinson, 1980, pp.43–53) – recovery from which has proven to be extraordinarily difficult and protracted. This undermined the conviction that in 'post-Keynesian' capitalism a growing and high-employment economy with increasing living standards is the norm. 'Since 1974, the occurrence of a serious world-wide recession accompanied by increased inflation has left the economists gaping. Orthodoxy has nothing to offer and all kinds of fanciful notions are floating around' (Joan Robinson, 1979a, p.90). In the US the mainstream of the economics profession has gone from an exaggerated view about the potency of the 'Keynesian medicine', however misinterpreted and misapplied, to a far-reaching agnosticism. It became fashionable to deprecate the positive contributions of Keynesian economics. The 1970s saw a questioning of the government's good intentions, for the consequences of the government's actions may be quite the reverse, an increasing questioning of the need for and effectiveness of stabilization policy, and assaults on the Keynesian revolution. The challenge was not devoid of positive developments, for it shook the complacency of some economists and forced them to re-examine and rethink what should, can, and cannot be done. It exposed some weak points and stimulated a search for overcoming the shortcomings.

Joan Robinson's (1979a, pp.124–5) advice to the US economists would be to abandon the neoclassical synthesis altogether.

> An American economist might very well reproach me: You call me a bastard, but what would *you* do? I could only answer with the quip about the motorist who asked the way to Oklahoma. The man by the roadside answered: If I wanted to go to Oklahoma I should never start here.
>
> The problem has developed far beyond the point where it makes sense to discuss any simple remedies. Keynes himself did not propose *simple* remedies. It was the bastard Keynesians who concocted the bromides from his acid treatment of orthodox nonsense. Now the old guard, who stood out against him in the thirties, are saying Keynes has failed. We must return to strict laisser-faire and sound finance. If you are uncomfortable in the frying pan you can jump into the fire . . .
>
> On inflation [Keynes] agreed with my deduction from the *General Theory* that rising prices would prove to be the great unsolved problem of

> full-employment policy. When money-wage rates do not rise as fast as productivity, the market economy falls into stagnation through sluggish demand, but when the bargaining power of organized labour is sufficient to keep wages rising enough, it will generally raise them too much to maintain stable prices. Keynes regarded this as a political problem which, when he died, still lay in the future.

And, referring to the need to develop new social and political institutions (mentioned at the end of Section 9.1), she (p.125) added that 'it is precisely because such changes in social and political institutions did not occur that the age of growth has been so uneasy and is now in danger of bringing itself to an end'.

What Friedman called, perhaps over-dramatically, the counter-revolution in monetary theory challenged not only the basic precepts of the *General Theory* and the Keynesian techniques of achieving full employment, but also the fundamental philosophy that such a state and the society to which it gives rise are desirable. Probably the crucial difference between Keynesians (of whatever persuasion) and monetarists (their degree of intensity notwithstanding) is their view of the stability of the economy. (Another important difference is the Keynesians' position that money is endogenous to the economic system.) While the Keynesians essentially perceive the economy as fairly but not fatally unstable and improvable by stabilization policies, the monetarists perceive the economy as inherently fairly stable and monetary disturbances as the major source of instability. Hence the need to restrict the manipulatory ability of the government.[39]

Joan Robinson (1978, p.7) perceived the causes of the popularity of monetarism in the US in these terms:[40]

> The advocates of 'Keynesian' policies accepted only half of Keynes' diagnosis of the instability of capitalism. He described how the level of output is determined (in given technical conditions) by investment and consumption. He described how the level of prices is determined by the level of money-wage rates. It was sufficiently obvious that if continuous near-full employment was maintained without any change in traditional institutions and attitudes in industrial relations, there would be an irresistible pressure to inflation. I think that in the United States this element in Keynes was somehow swept under the carpet. It seems that the extraordinary vogue in recent years of an argument so unplausible as the Quantity Theory of Money was due to a refusal to accept the fact that the main influence on the general price level in money terms is the level of money-wage rates and the level of wage rates at any moment is more or less an historical accident, depending on conditions in the labour market over a long past. This was such a serious blow to notions of equilibrium

and the rationality of a market economy that any theory was better, even a theory that consisted of nothing but a set of incantations.

The second stage of the so-called monetarist counter-revolution was the assault by Lucas, Sargent, and others[41] on (i) the Keynesian revolution in general, and the Samuelsonion neoclassical synthesis in particular both on the planes of theory and policy, (ii) Klein-type macroeconometric models, (iii) Friedman's monetarism[42] and (iv) the neoconservatives like Feldstein and others. Not to mention the new classical macroeconomists' denigration of economics that is not mathematically and statistically sophisticated, and the obvious tension between them and the general equilibrium theorists who are so profoundly aware of the limitations of the theory.[43]

Whether it be considered a revolutionary turnabout, a mere constructive focus on inadequate treatment of expectations in macroeconomic models, a transient fad, or whatever, the so-called 'rational expectations counter-revolution' has generated much enthusiasm, heat, and strong condemnation. While there are many reasons for the clashing attitudes both on the planes of theory and policy, it is probably its widely (mis)perceived policy-ineffectiveness implication that accounts for its notoriety.

However analytically innovative and creatively applied, rational expectations alone does not represent the hallmark, nor is it even the dominant component of the novel approach which is more appropriately identified by its proponents as the new classical macroeconomics (NCM), or by Lucas, the chief theoretician of the 'school', as equilibrium business cycle (EBC) models.

In a nutshell, the differentia specifica of NCM (EBC) resides in *three postulates;* (i) instantaneous and continuous competitive market clearing, with perfectly flexible prices and wages; (ii) optimizing behavior of individuals, with agents' expectations being rational; and (iii) agents' imperfect information not only about future events, but also about the current state.

This approach is a very tight version of neoclassical general equilibrium applied to macroeconomics. It provides a bolder and analytically sophisticated support for pre-Keynesian classical macroeconomics and monetary theory, though in the sense of economic content it is an impoverished version of the latter. In the stronger super-neutrality form, it resuscitates the 'classical dichotomy', and the 'neutrality of money'.

Lucas and Sargent (1978, pp.49–50) perceive the predictions of neoclassical Keynesian economics as 'wildly incorrect' and the doctrine on which they rest as 'fundamentally flawed' These they assert, 'are now simple matters of fact, involving no novelties in economic theory. The task which faces contemporary students of the business cycle is that of sorting through the wreckage, determining which features of that remarkable intellectual event called the Keynesian revolution can be salvaged and put to good use, and which others must be discarded.' The difficulties, they say, are 'fatal' and they (1978, p.50) see modern macroeconomic models as being 'of *no* value in guiding policy'.

In a nutshell, in contrast to the earlier, Friedman-type monetarists, the NCM proponents attribute much stronger perpetual market-clearing properties to our economy and even deny that there is a trade-off to anticipated systematic monetary and fiscal policy in the short run. In fact, essentially in their models the 'ambiguous' distinction between the short and long run is eliminated and long-run results rule universally; that is, they hold in the short run as well.

The EBC protagonists tend to stress that the rational expectations hypothesis is not only the foundation for their models, but that they derive their policy implications from it (or in other versions in combination with the natural rate). It seems, however, that it is the market clearing assumption they make that is a *sine qua non* component of their striking policy-ineffectiveness implication (see Feiwel, 1985, ch.2).

Whatever the analytical merits of the concept of market clearing, it is based on the quixotic assumption of perfect price and wage flexibility and omits some of the most essential properties of the dynamics and *modus operandi* of the mixed capitalist economy. By abstracting from the pervasive phenomenon of the disequilibrium, the market-clearing approach empoverishes economic theory in some essential way. Such an approach does not confront the problems of change; that is, upheavals, resistance, and learning. Thus, such an approach considers disequilibrium as promptly and smoothly eliminated by the forces of excess supply or demand. The impediments to the dynamic adjustment process and the difficulties, efforts, and costs involved are underrated or ignored. It is particularly debatable whether the alleged self-stabilizing and self-correcting economic mechanism is sufficiently forceful when the vulnerability of the economic system to external or random disturbances is considered. Usually the dynamic system can be moved towards equilibrium by some forces while others push it away. Nor is any equilibrium of whatever kind necessarily desirable or socially optimal.

In a broader perspective, the differences between the EBC proponents and their critics revolve around diametrically different perceptions of aggregate demand and supply and the morphology of markets. More specifically, underlying changes in demand and supply may not be translated into price changes; adjustments may lag, be incomplete, or costly; industrial prices tend to respond primarily to variations in costs (cost-plus prices) and underutilized capacity influences price movements; markets are asymmetrical; there are market adjustment frictions and persistent rigidities; prices are sticky to a varied degree; the labour market (a heterogeneous entity by itself) is partly guided by the participants' revealed preferences for long-term contracts, these contracts are staggered, featuring leapfrogging and overtaking and different configurations of inertia and anticipation; intensity of monopoly and trade union power; and markets are generally not impersonal – while the personal relationship and trust can be terminated, they often persist, even if not formalized, for both parties seem to perceive benefits from long-term relationships of mutual trust and reliability.

By imposing an inordinately tight concept of rationality and continuous market clearing as well as super-neutrality of money, the EBC models help to focus their critics' attention on the perplexing question why the real world does not essentially work as the models postulate. This contribution should not be underrated.

Classical economics is superior to its present-day version (NCM) in that it perceives competition as part of a growth process and conceives the allocation problem within the context of a dynamic economy with changing endowment of resources, techniques, and tastes. Furthermore, NCM seems to be a retrogression from the classical view and subsequent neoclassical theorizing on the dynamics of transitional states of stable equilibrium and the dynamic modification of the crude static classical system. The resurrected version of classical economics rests on an implausible and distorted conception of economic processes. It abstracts from the salient features of the realities of modern capitalism. It achieves extraordinary analytical rigor and elegance at an extraordinarily high cost to relevance and usefulness to the real world.

NCM has attracted and continues to attract many bright, technically gifted young economists who have invested their intellectual capital in sophisticated mathematics and statistical techniques and computer technology. It is perhaps to them that the quip that an economist is someone who when observing real events worries whether they can happen in theory, is most applicable.[44] Their forte lies in equilibrium economics, and, as such, a number of them have little or no interest in the economic realities around them, nor do they have any genuine macro policy concerns or motivations. They are largely microeconomic theorists used to dabbling in a world of general equilibrium or statistical probability theory who have applied their (mis)perceived comparative advantages to, or imperialistically invaded, macroeconomics. Often they are impatient and intolerant of those who perceive the complexities of the world and chide NCM for disregarding such complexities and playing with simplistic 'toys'.

The development of economics is hardly along an ascending straight line. There are not only detours, but also streets without exit, cyclical and even backward motions. But even the latter are not totally retrogressive as they shake up complacency and/or throw certain hitherto unperceived or only vaguely perceived aspects into a new light. 'A scientific theory, fortunately, benefits not only from its friends but also from its enemies. And the adversary process of scholarship that has produced the monetarist theories of Milton Friedman and others has helped to sharpen the modern application of Keynes's thoughts rather than to destroy them' (Samuelson, 1986, p.281). The economy and society are usually moving and changing. Inventions and innovations are taking place, though the process of 'creative destruction' might encounter even more resistance in economics than in the economy.

There seem to be deeper social, political, and ideological forces at work that condition and interact with the internal movement in economic thought and influence the acceptability of ideas and make them fashionable. Still, 'it is important . . . to distinguish between the intellectual and the political fortunes of economic doctrine. There is a tendency to mix the two. The intellectual opponents of Keynesian economics claim explicitly or tacitly that the electoral victories of Reagan and Thatcher are somehow evidence of the truth of the monetarist or of the new-classical approach to macroeconomic theory . . . Reciprocally, the political right in both countries claims that its policy choices follow from the truth of monetarism or new-classicism. It is well to treat both claims critically' (Worswick and Tevithick, 1983, p.163).

Whether the conservative offensive and its manifestations in economics is a temporary vogue that will soon pass, whether it is deeply ingrained, or whether it will only shift the boundaries but cannot cause a retreat cannot be analyzed here. What the outcome of the turbulence in macroeconomics will be is not easy to predict. Prediction is always hard, especially of the future, von Neumann used to say. The hard part about predicting the larger movements in economics is to distinguish between the permanent and the transitory and between the long-term trend and the oscillations. However, a good case can be made for the view that cyclical fluctuations affect appreciably the long-term ascent of economic knowledge.

It appears that after a *Sturm und Drang* period, NCM has been losing ground. Even within its ranks more sober and pragmatic voices are increasingly being heard. Many are disenchanted with the imaginary world of rational expectations, market clearing and neutrality of money. But even more, there is growing disillusionment with the technical shortcomings of the models and with their flimsy empirical foundations. Through a variety of experiences and stimuli, some young economists are rediscovering Keynes.

All said and done, the Keynesian revolution has fundamentally and forever transformed the scope, character, and relevance of economics, however critical one might be of the analytical apparatuses or particular details of Keynes, Kalecki, Joan Robinson, the neoclassical Keynesians and other writers in that tradition. The General Theory, conceived of as 'a growing and variegated body of thought, richer and wider than the book of that name' (Joan Robinson, 1980, p.105), stands up reasonably well to powerful and sophisticated attack upon it.[45]

In a preaching mood, Samuelson (1986, p.296) warned 'us Keynesians against the vice of complacency. Let us not be *un*reconstructed Keynesians. Let us be *reconstructed* Keynesians – reconstructed by the reconstruction of the world itself'. On a theoretical plane, the reconstruction will undoubtedly draw on many sources and cross currents. Our aim here is to call attention to the Kalecki–Joan Robinson intellectual capital as a potential major building block in this endeavor. 'The Keynesian revolution still remains to be made both in teaching economic theory and in forming economic policy' (Joan Robinson, 1979a, p.177).[46]

APPENDIX

Kalecki's contacts with Keynes were never very extensive. Some of the surviving correspondence between the two deals primarily with some articles that Kalecki submitted to Keynes in his capacity as editor of *The Economic Journal*. The general tone of Kalecki's letters is deferential; that of Keynes is usually critical, at times harshly so, but Kalecki's responses to the criticism strongly defend his point of view. One of the first such encounters (Keynes 1973a, pp. 789–98) concerned Kalecki's 'A Theory of Commodity, Income and Capital Taxation' which appeared in *The Economic Journal* 47 (September 1937): 444–50. From the first Keynes criticized Kalecki for not stating his assumptions sufficiently clearly and for making them too unrealistic – a theme to which he would return in his subsequent dealings with Kalecki, as we shall see presently. Thus in his letter of 16 February, 1937 Keynes wrote:

> There is only one small suggestion I have to make in the text. I think it would be advisable, in the first part, to make quite explicit your assumption that the consumption of the capitalists is entirely directed to goods other than wage goods. It is clear to a careful reader that you are assuming this, but since the assumption is a very unrealistic one, it is desirable to make it clearly.

Kalecki took this criticism to heed and appended a footnote to that effect. But Keynes was not satisfied. On 30 March 1937 he wrote to Kalecki:

> I am not clear that the top of page 5 is quite satisfactory. If the capitalists assume that their income subject to tax will remain the same, the effect of the tax will surely be to reduce their spending. It is only if they have read your article and are convinced by it that their profit will rise by the amount of the tax that they will maintain their spending as before . . .
>
> You are, I think, assuming throughout that there is a surplus of the factors of production. If this is so, it should perhaps be emphasised.

Modifications might be required as soon as any type of labour or type of equipment is in short supply.

I have, however, one more fundamental point which I should like you to think over. Reading your article again, it appears to me that your assumption to the effect that the consumption of capitalists is entirely directed to goods other than wage goods goes a good deal further than you have admitted in the footnote at the bottom of page 4. Does not your argument require that the factors of production required to produce capitalists' consumption-goods shall be totally distinct from the factors of production required to produce wage goods, no substitution of any kind being possible between the two. If so, this is, of course, a hopelessly unrealistic assumption. It may be that capitalists live in quite different sorts of houses from workers. But this does not prove that they do not both use bricks and mortar and the services of plumbers and painters. And there is the obvious case of raw materials.

If this is right, you are obviously in a very strange world. For example, if you are assuming that every factor of production is in surplus supply and that there is no possible substitution between the factors relevant to capitalists' consumption and the factors relevant to workers' consumption, it follows that, however much the capitalists consume, their incomes will rise correspondingly. I am well aware that there is an element of truth in this paradox applied to the real world. But your conclusions purport to be applicable to affairs and, if I am not mistaken, you ought to make more emphatic the peculiarities of the assumptions.

On 4 April 1937 Kalecki responded to these cricicisms. He first broached the question of his assumption about the behavior of capitalists in response to the introduction of an income tax:

I do not think they must necessarily read my article in order not to curtail at once their expenditure on consumption and investment. The matter is treated at first on page 3 in connection with commodity tax. After the introduction of new tax the entrepreneurs even if they expect their incomes to fall *cannot* immediately reduce their investment because it is the result of previous investment decisions which require a certain time to be completed. Thus their savings remain unaltered in the first period of new taxation régime. Their consumption remains also unaltered, if their propensity to consume is not changed. This latter *is* of course an additional assumption for the expectation of future fall of income can influence the present propensity to consume. I think however that the capitalists' consumption is rather insensitive to *expectation*: and that it is only the *actual* fall of their income which can compel them – and this also often only with a time lag – to reduce their standard of living. (I have now added a footnote on this matter.)

I think that this assumption is essential not only for the problems of taxation, but for the whole of *The General Theory*. If for instance the rise of money wages caused the capitalists to reduce immediately their consumption in expectation of future fall of profits, the result would be rather in accordance with the classical theory. Of course my analysis of taxation problems also must be fundamentally changed if I reject the assumption of insensitiveness of capitalists' consumption to expectations of changes in income. The income taxation for instance is then unlikely to raise employment.

I wonder whether it is necessary to emphasise the existence of a surplus of the factors of production. I do not need this assumption at all for the case of commodity tax. For the case of income tax (and capital tax) I think I have paid due attention to this problem in discussing the influence of the elasticity of supply of wage goods (at the bottom of page 6).

I come now to your last question concerning the assumption about capitalists consuming only goods other than wage goods. I fully agree that this assumption is unrealistic. (As concerns however the problem of connection between prices of wage goods and prices of goods subject to capitalists' consumption through the channel of common raw materials it does not arise if the commodity tax is levied on *finished* wage goods. For as I have shown in the paper the output of these goods is unaffected by such taxation and thus the prices of raw materials remain unaltered.) Therefore I have not only stated in the footnote on page 4 this assumption explicitly but also tried to show what corrections are needed if this special assumption is *dropped.* (I have now altered a little this footnote.)

I think however that [on the] whole this problem is not so important in reality. The commodity taxes are usually levied not on all wage goods but only on some articles e.g. sugar, cigarettes, matches and so on. The effect of such taxes will be similar to the effect of those examined in the paper. The capitalists' consumption of these goods – being a small part of total consumption of them – does not interfere much with the process examined. (I have made a corresponding addition to the footnote on page 4.)

Soon thereafter (on 12 April 1937) Keynes wrote a significant letter to Kalecki, both in his capacity as editor and as a private critic. In his capacity as editor he enjoined Kalecki to preface his article clearly with the following assumptions:

1. It is assumed that within the period in view the volume of investment is unalterable.

2. It is assumed that the consumption of capitalists is insensitive to their expectations as to their future income.

3. It is assumed that there is a surplus of all factors of production.

4. It is assumed that the consumption of capitalists is directed to entirely different articles of consumption from those of workers.

5. In some parts of the argument, but not in all, it is assumed that no substitution is possible between factors of production and raw materials which produce for capitalists and those which produce for workers. I am not sure whether it has to be assumed that factors and raw materials which are used for investment goods cannot be used for consumption goods.

These points ought to be made quite clear and emphatic in the manuscript.

As a private critic I add the following, though please take no notice of this.

1. I regard the assumption that investment is fixed as unplausible. Firstly, because it ignores the possibility of fluctuation in stocks. Secondly, because it ignores the possibility of altering the pace at which existing investment decisions are carried out, and thirdly, because at best it can be overcome after a time lag, which may be very short indeed.

2. I think it unplausible to suppose that capitalists' consumption is insensitive to their expectations for the latter are affected by a change in the taxes on their incomes.

3. Much more important than the above, with all these assumptions you can prove something much more drastic and general than you have put down, from which your particular conclusions can be easily derived. But, of course, these more drastic conclusions would not look very plausible if applied to real life.

4. Whilst some of your conclusions may require these assumptions, I do not believe that your main conclusions do require them. The assumptions are mainly brought in to facilitate the exposition. But as long as they are there, they are there; and very much impair the generality of the argument.

5. I hope you are not right in thinking that my *General Theory* depends on an assumption that the immediate reaction of a capitalist is of a particular kind. I tried to deal with this on page 271, where I assume that the immediate reaction of capitalists is the most unfavourable to my conclusion. I regard behaviour as arrived at by trial and error, and no theory can be regarded as sound which depends on the *initial* reaction being of a particular kind. One must assume that the initial reaction may be anything in the world, but that the process of trial and error will eventually arrive at the conclusion which one is predicting.

At the same time Kalecki sought Keynes's opinion of his 'A Theory of the Business Cycle' of which he sent him a reprint on 20 March 1937. Keynes replied on 30 March:

The first two sections I like very much. But I am not convinced by the section on 'The Inducement to Invest', particularly pages 84 and 85.

In the second complete paragraph on page 84 you seem to be assuming not merely that the current rise of prices will have a disproportionate effect on expectations as to future prices, but that future prices will be expected to rise in exactly the same proportion. Surely this is an extravagant over-emphasis of the effect of the immediate situation on long-term expectations? It appears to me that it is only if future prices are expected to rise *in the same proportion* as present prices that you have established the result that 'equilibrium is not reached and the investment continues to rise'.

In the same way on page 85 you point out that the current increase of wealth does something to diminish the marginal risk. But to establish your conclusion you appear to be making some quantitative assumption that the effect will be just of the right degree, which appears to be unjustified. I might mention, in passing, that the risk relating to prospective profit is already allowed for in my formula for the marginal efficiency of capital.

In general, therefore, I do not feel that you have sufficiently established the conclusion italicised at the bottom of the page 85.

Kalecki's reply was characteristic:

May I yet make some remarks on your criticism on my paper in the *Review*? I think that my statement in the second complete paragraph on page 84 you refer to is independent of *how much* expectations improve under the influence of the present rise of prices. I state in this paragraph only that the increase of prices of investment goods which equates the marginal efficiency based on the *initial* state of expectations to the rate of interest, does not create an 'equilibrium'; for at the same time expectations improve to some extent and thus investment increases further. I do not deny that this increase may be convergent and then the point A in the Fig, 3 corresponding to this 'equilibrium' may be reached without increase of the rate of interest (see the bottom of the page 88); whilst if the reaction of the entrepreneurs to 'the present state of affairs' is strong enough full employment will be reached and then the rise of the rate of interest would perform the task of stopping 'inflation' and create the 'equilibrium' represented by point A.

In any case however the process of reaching this equilibrium will be in general spread over many *r* periods. Thus it is interesting to know what determines the rate of investment decisions *during* this process. I sought of solving this problem by introducing the 'principle' of increasing risk and this enabled me to describe the course of reaching point A (Fig. 6).

I think however that the reference to increasing risk (or something like that) is necessary also for adequate explanation of various positions of 'equilibrium' (positions in which the rate of investment has no tendency to change). For the facts show the prices of new investment goods are relatively rigid. It follows from the statistics of Mr Kuznets about gross capital formation that the prices of new investment goods have fallen in U.S.A. between 1929 and 1932 only by 15 per cent. Thus it is clear that the gap between prospective rate of profit and the rate of interest was much lower in the depression than in the prosperity. But then some thing besides the prices of investment goods is required for the formation of 'equilibrium'.

You question also my explanation of why it is the *rate* of investment decisions which is dependent on the gap between prospective rate of profit and the rate of interest. If in first *r* period all capitalists have decided to invest say, £1,000.000.000 the savings of second *r* period will be £1.000.000.000 too. Thus precisely this amount can be freely reinvested in the second *r* period – if the gap between prospective rate of profit is the same as in the first *r* period – because the investment of *new accumulated capital* does not increase the risk. (The existence of pure rentiers creates some complication but does not affect the argument; if the relation of the net indebtedness of an entrepreneur to his wealth is δ and his saving during a given period s – he can invest without increasing risk the amount $s(1+\delta)$. The sum of this amounts is $\Sigma s(1+\delta)=\Sigma s+\Sigma\delta s$ where Σs is the total saving of entrepreneurs and $\Sigma\delta s$ is the total saving of 'pure' rentiers, or the sum of amounts to be invested without increasing the risk is the total saving S.)

Some four years later Keynes received 'A Theorem on Technical Progress' by Kalecki for publication in *The Economic Journal.* Keynes had some very harsh things to say about this piece (and about Kalecki) and he said them to Joan Robinson who acted as intermediary and defender of Kalecki. In this correspondence between Keynes and Joan Robinson (Keynes 1973a, pp.829–36), Keynes again harped on Kalecki's 'fanciful' assumptions and his failure to state them clearly. Keynes revealed his disaffection for imperfect competition, his misunderstanding of Kalecki's dynamics, and his personal distaste for Kalecki. Excerpts showing Keynes's misgivings and Joan Robinson's defence are very enlightening.

On 4 February, 1941, Keynes wrote to Joan Robinson:

> Here is Kalecki's article. As I said the other night, after a highly rational introduction of a couple of pages my first impression is that it becomes high, almost delirious nonsense, I am ready to believe that there are some assumptions in relation to which his conclusions are correct. But so many of them are latent and tacit that no-one could say, I should have thought, whether he has proved his proposition. Indeed I do not feel perfectly sure whether the hypotheses may not be self-contradictory. Is it not rather odd when dealing with 'long-run problems' to start with the assumption that all firms are always working below capacity.
>
> Or take his final conclusion that technical progress causes a reduction

of output. I imagine that he really means by this that if, as a result of technical progress, two blades of grass grow where one grew before there would nevertheless be no increase in output, either because he measures output in terms of marginal wage cost or because he has made some assumption that leads to the conclusion that only half as many fields would be cultivated, the working day being reduced by half. But, if the former explanation is so, he gives no definition of output.

Has not the whole method been carried to ludicrous lengths?

On the same date she replied:

> I am prepared to stick up for Kalecki. He is making an attempt to extend the *General Theory* beyond the short period – tho' not to the long period in the old sense, since that concept involves the whole Classical theory.
>
> He is not saying that inventions leave output constant, for in his 'reference system' output is increasing as capital accumulates. He needs an indefinitely large reserve of labour in his reference system so that employment can increase as required. But granted that, he is all right. The trick is to make assumptions by which effective demand in terms of commodities is the same in the two systems. Then output is the same, and inventions by increasing output per head, reduce employment (relatively to the reference system). The case which he hints at at the end, where output falls (relatively) arises when inventions increase the share of capital relatively to the share of labour and so increase thriftiness. Two blades of grass grow where one grew before, but the demand for hay falls.
>
> As for under-capacity working – that is part of the usual bag of tricks of Imperfect Competition theory. To say that price normally exceeds marginal prime cost sounds common-place enough, but that is really the same thing.
>
> Where Kalecki *is* barmy is insisting on writing articles in this inhuman style. It is a kind of sinful pride that makes him do it.

Keynes responded on 12 February:

> Thanks for your notes on Kalecki. If he is extending the *General Theory* beyond the short period but not to the long period in the old sense, he really must tell us what the sense is. For I am still innocent enough to be bewildered by the idea that the assumption of all firms always working below capacity is consistent with 'a long-run problem'. To tell me that 'as for under-capacity working that is part of the usual pack of tricks of imperfect competition theory' does not carry me any further. For publication in the *Journal* an article must pass beyond the stage of esoteric abracadabra.

> You tell me that it is a kind of sinful pride which makes Kalecki write like this. I think it is a sort of profound stupidity, though physical and aesthetic, perhaps, rather than intellectual. At any rate, he must write the article in such a style that it is fairly evident on the surface whether or not he is talking through his hat. I do not doubt that he is saying something. But I suspect him of being at one of his old tricks in an extreme form, namely, of taking artificial assumptions which have no possible relation to reality or any other merit except that they happen to lead up to a needed result.

Two days later Joan Robinson was very defensive about imperfect competition:

> I have written to Kalecki as you suggest. I must protest at your calling Imperfect Competition an esoteric doctrine. It may be awful rot – as you have always suspected – but for better or worse it is in all the text books now.
>
> Under Imp. Comp. there is surplus capacity even in full equilibrium. Under perfect comp. any firm which is working at all must be working bang up to capacity even in a deep slump. This is certainly more and not less ridiculous.

On 18 February 1941 Keynes apologized for the unintended slur on imperfect competition:

> Imperfect competition as such has become quite the contrary of esoteric! – indeed one of the most fashionable subjects going, especially in U.S.A.
>
> What I call esoteric is bringing in certain assumptions of this sort tacitly and assuming that the reader can be expected to supply out of his knowledge or imagination, not only the relevant assumptions, but the relevant consequences of them and, above all, the solution of how all this works in the 'long-run conditions' . . .
>
> The esoteric fault is to write subject to a whole contraption of secret knowledge, atmosphere and assumption, quite unknown to above half a dozen readers in the *Journal* at the outside.

On 24 February Joan Robinson sent to Keynes a version that Kalecki had revised at her suggestion. Keynes replied to Joan Robinson (on 4 March 1941) that he was satisfied as to the presentation, but he continued to have serious qualms:

> Now that I believe myself to understand exactly what it says, it all seems plain as a pikestaff. Indeed, so much so that I cannot discover that the

elaborate apparatus of the reference system leads to any conclusion which is not obvious from the start . . .

Does the article tell you anything you did not know before? You say that it proves that capital-using inventions do not reduce the share of labour in the national dividend. Where does it show this? I have not discovered it. Don't you mean that, if it reduces it, it only reduces it through one or other of the agencies mentioned above?

I should like to send it to Kaldor for another opinion.

Joan Robinson was quick to defend Kalecki. On the same day she wrote to Keynes:

Yes, now you have gone to the other extreme. Surely if anyone asked you Do capital-using inventions increase capital per unit of output? You would have said Of course – what a dotty question.

It is the interplay of utilisation of capital with changes in technique that Kalecki brings out.

True it seems rather an elaborate mechanism just to add one point to our analysis, but it seems to me a gallant attempt to deal with the analysis of a developing economy without using pure short-period or full long-period assumptions – neither of which is adequate.

I think you are looking a gift horse in the mouth – after all even one valid proposition, extending the *General Theory*, throwing light on the old problem of the constancy of relative shares is something to be thankful for.

The real advantage of the theorem is to clear out of the way an unnecessary difficulty so that some progress can be made with long-run (but not full equilibrium) analysis. Without this theorem one is held up by thinking one has to allow for effects of changes in technique on thriftiness etc., as I thought when I did my Long-Period Theory. Kalecki is on to something important, and this is a necessary step on the way.

Keynes was not persuaded. On 12 March he wrote to Joan Robinson 'what am I to do about the wretched Kalecki?' He concluded his letter by stating:

Meanwhile I have sent the article to Kaldor and enclose his reply. You will see that, in his judgement, Kalecki has not made out your point; though I do not think Kaldor puts it quite strongly enough, since it might be true that technical progress necessarily raised the degree of oligopoly, and yet did not do so sufficiently to offset the other effects.

So I am inclined to return to the opinion that the article is pretentious, misleading, inconclusive and perhaps wrong. I would rather have cheese

> to a weight equal to the paper it would occupy in 5,000 copies of the *Journal*!

And he wrote to Kaldor on 18 March 1941:

> Thanks very much for your note on Kalecki which fell in with my ideas but not, you will have heard, with Joan's. Indeed I went a little further than you because it seemed to me that, even if Kalecki could establish that the effect of capital-using inventions was to increase the gap between actual output and capacity output, he would still have to show that this was quantitatively large enough to offset the opposite effect. I could not see that he made a trace of an effort to establish this. However, Joan has been able to discover that the article is really about something quite different, which neither you nor I noticed. So she is sending it back to Kalecki in the hope that he will elucidate it further. I do not doubt that in the end she will write quite a good article for him!

The article in question was published in *Review of Economic Studies* 8 (June 1941): 178–84.

On 13 December 1941 Kalecki sent to Keynes for his consideration his article 'A Theory of Profits' which appeared in *The Economic Journal* 52 (June September, 1942); 258–67. The tenor of Keynes's critique was similar to that in the past (Keynes 1973a, pp.837–41). On 2 January 1942 he wrote to Kalecki that he suspected Kalecki made more assumptions than he explicitly stated:

> (a) Are you not in effect assuming constant prices? That would certainly facilitate the argument. If you are not assuming constant prices, then it seems to me a variety of particular assumptions have to be made. For example, suppose there was a policy of work or full maintenance at a constant real reward so that workers' real consumption is constant. Would not that disturb you?
>
> (b) Is it not necessary for you to assimilate doles to capitalists' consumption rather than to workers' consumption? Your conclusions seem to me to relate to the sum of capitalists' consumption *plus* doles rather than to capitalists' consumption alone. For example, suppose a system of unemployed relief paid for by direct taxes on capitalists.
>
> (c) As always in these cases, I am bothered about what assumptions are being made about the independence of factors. A rise in prices might affect the real weight of direct taxes owing to the nature of the tax system, though this particular difficulty you would get round if, as I suggest above, you are assuming constant prices.
>
> My other point is that by the time you have got to the end of the article you seem to have persuaded yourself that you are dealing with the real

world. This makes it all the more important to emphasise the assumptions you are making which distinguish your model from reality.

On 9 January 1942 Kalecki cleared up the points raised by Keynes:

I should like to mention first that throughout the argument I consider profits *net* of direct taxes. (This I state on p. 1 but perhaps I did not stress it sufficiently). Accordingly capitalists' consumption is meant as their *personal* consumption *exclusive* of direct taxes (cf. footnote to p. 1). And the equation profits = capitalists' consumption + investment means that profits *net* of taxes are equal to personal capitalists' consumption + investment. Therefore doles paid by direct taxes on capitalists are *not* included in profits or capitalists' consumption. And the changes in the real weight of taxes dependent on price changes do not affect profits in my sense (they do, however, affect the non-profit incomes).

A system of work or full maintenance at a constant real reward so that workers' real consumption is constant does not disturb my results in any case because it does not affect the equality of profits net of tax and personal capitalists' consumption *plus* investment just as it does not affect the equality of savings and investment.

I am certainly *not* assuming constant prices. Nor am I aware of any assumptions which have not been clearly stated although some are introduced only in chapter 11 ('slowness' of long-run development p. 4, the relation between real capitalists' consumption and real capitalists' income p. 5).

Keynes replied the following day admitting that he did not appreciate the fact that Kalecki was considering profits net of direct taxes. He urged Kalecki to emphasize that point. Kalecki's handling of assumptions continued to bother him:

I will not pursue further the question whether you are making unstated assumptions. The worst of your sort of procedure is that there is no means of knowing what assumptions are involved except by exercising intuition and trying to consider various possible cases.

This was followed by an exchange between the two on the effect on capitalists' consumption and investments in the event of an excess profits tax and excess savings tax – subjects hotly debated during the war period. After lengthy arguments by both, Kalecki wrote on January 27:

My theory is definitely not applicable to a war economy, not only because of my assumption that workers do not save, but also because I postulate a balanced budget.

On the following day Keynes replied along the lines that characterize his criticism of Kalecki's work:

> My letters were not meant to be merely teasing. I appreciate that there are certain assumptions on which your conclusions are correct. But, as I said before, the worst of your technique is that it is impossible for the reader as he goes along to know what those assumptions are. And when the conclusion is reached there is an atmosphere as though it had some application to the real world.
>
> I regard it as a very interesting schematism and a useful tool of thought and I cannot but feel that the article would be a great deal better if it was represented like that. But there is also the point that, even regarded as a schematism, it is not much use unless the reader knows fairly precisely just what the assumptions are.

However, we should note here that Keynes was very impressed by Kalecki's 'brilliant' explanation of Bowley's Law (see Feiwel, 1975, p.467). See also notes 32 (p. 136 below) and 37 (p. 137 below).

Notes

1. This view of Kalecki's characteristics is shared by his employer in the 1930s, E. Lipiński (1977, p.74).

   > Kalecki was a man of quite exceptional intellectual independence. I used to even suspect that his early experiences as a theoretician developed in him the habit of regularly exercising his independence. In the thirties, he belonged to a very small group of economists who had pitted themselves against a number of prejudices that were deeply rooted in the minds of the most highly trained economists. He could scarcely have failed to notice later, however, that the whole Keynesian revolution achieved little more than narrowing the wall of myths enclosing man's thinking about economics; that even the most heavily attacked fallacies lived on, if at a greater distance from the main thoroughfare of economic thought. And thus there was developed in Kalecki a distinctive distrust for all views that were not exposed to the most comprehensive criticism. This is the way I would be inclined to explain his permanently polemical approach to everything, including even his own earlier statements. This seems to explain, for example, the remark made to me by a foreigner after a conversation with Kalecki: 'What a strange fellow! The minute you start agreeing with him, he stops agreeing!' A conversation with Kalecki really was an effort; it was dialectics as Zeno would have understood it. Kalecki's distrust of myths, especially elegant, theoretical myths, was far stronger than his tolerance. One felt his attitude towards views differing from his own was one of at best forbearance.

   On Kalecki's independence see also Eshag, 1977, pp.83–4.
2. Lipiński (p.70) recalled his first postwar impressions of Kalecki at the famous 1956 congress of Polish economists. Most other economists spoke about

reviving the Polish economy and urged a creative, as opposed to dogmatic, approach to Marxism. The contradictions of socialist economy, socialist relations of production, bourgeois economy and Marxist economy, degeneration, apologetics – there was no shortage of forceful language, Kalecki did not take any part in the general debate. Somewhat aloof, he delivered a sober, businesslike report on growth and investment. He did not invoke Marx, but he did use his methods. Though he made no mention of social relations, the latter were implicit in his observations about the contradiction between consumption and accumulation, etc. For me, his paper was a classic example of Marxist analysis of economic phenomena.

Brus (1977, p.59), the one time Party economist in Poland, then a revisionist and now an emigré, observed that

> while recognizing the enormous significance of the Marxist approach and of many Marxian tools of economic analysis, Kalecki never felt that he had to accept every component of Marxian economics or to retain those parts of it which have become obsolete in view of new experiences and of the progress of economic theory. He felt, for example, a strong distaste for the Marxian theory of value, which he considered metaphysical and (if I am not mistaken) never wanted to discuss. Nor was he an institutional Marxist bound by 'authoritative' interpretations of the party leaders of the day, who were only concerned to find a quasi-theoretical justification for every twist in their policies, while at the same time refusing to submit socialism to Marxist dialectical scrutiny of contradictions. For Kalecki, socialism, however distinct from capitalism, was never a conflictless utopia.

3. Leaving aside the merits of the economic argument, in a letter to Joan (dated 17 November 1964, courtesy of Mrs Ada Kalecki), pertaining to her draft of the introduction to his prewar essays (see Joan Robinson, 1966, p.xi), Kalecki wrote:

> You mention the problem of wages in Keynesian theory for the first time ... without referring to the problem of employment. However, to meet your wishes I suggest drafting the paragraph in question as follows:
>
> 'The second theme of the General Theory – the interrelation between money wage rates, prices and employment, was no less important than the first. This theme is clearly sounded in the third essay and elaborated in the first'.
>
> You may find queer that I pester you so much with this passage. But what you advocate in it by implication is in fact a wage-stop in a capitalist system without even commenting on the political and economic problems involved.
>
> If your Chinese friends after having read this passage in the original version did not call you a fascist it would only show how deeply they appreciate your benevolence.

In his enlightening picture of the set-up of Cambridge economics in the late 1920s and early 1930s, Sir Austin Robinson (1977, p.29) characterized Sraffa as follows (see also Kahn, 1984, pp.3–4, 23–6, and *passim*; Chapter 13 of the companion volume):

I find it impossible to describe Piero Sraffa to anyone who does not know him, and I do this with more difficulty because he is still alive and capable of expressing the strongest dissent from anything I may say. It was, as I have said earlier, his arrival in Cambridge in 1927 and his lectures in 1928 that gave Cambridge economics its second wind. As any economist will know, he has remained capable of demanding fundamental rethinking of whole branches of economics. It would be easy to imagine him as an iconoclastic human dynamo, constantly throwing out an endless stream of shocking ideas. In fact he could hardly be more different. His first lectures in Cambridge in 1928–9, devoted to analysing some of the ideas buried in Marshall's *Principles*, shocked him as much as, perhaps more than, they shocked his audience. He found the strain of lecturing almost intolerable (he would sit up all night before a lecture worrying about what he was going to say). In 1930, very soon after Pigou had made me secretary of the Faculty Board and responsible under the Board for organising the staffing and the lectures, Piero Sraffa came to me and begged to be allowed to resign his lectureship. He remained librarian of the Marshall Library and we managed a little later to get him made assistant director of research, with general responsibility for all research students, so that he could have a university post without the need any longer to lecture. He was in one sense always in the thick of the work going on around Keynes. As a member of King's College (he was not yet in those days a Fellow of Trinity) he saw more of Keynes than most of us did. But in all our discussions I remembered him as much more like a kettle on a slow gas-ring. One waited hopefully for it to boil. When one had almost forgotten, it suddenly came to the boil. Piero Sraffa at full pressure, with a torrent of Italianate English, was something to remember, if only for its rarity. I find it extraordinarily difficult to guess his contribution. As a critic it was undeniably very considerable indeed. As an eliminator of mistakes and red-herrings and as a puncturer of other people's over-inflated bright ideas it was immense. I do not myself remember him as a major provider himself of bright new ideas. But that element in a collective operation may easily be overvalued. And of Piero Sraffa's creativity in everything that he himself set out to tackle there can be no possible question.

4. I would like to call attention to the informative and long-awaited collected Polish edition (including editorial notes) of Kalecki's work and to J. Osiatyński's and T. Kowalik's painstaking editorial efforts. An English edition is in preparation by Oxford University Press. See Kalecki, 1979 and 1980.
5. The English translation (Kalecki, 1966) contains only a part of the original Polish version reproduced in its entirety in Kalecki, 1979, pp.93–157. Kalecki (1966, p.2) considered his less technical essays (written in 1935), 'The Mechanism of the Business Upswing' and 'The Business Upswing and the Balance of Payments' (1966, pp.26–39) as a good introduction to the more technical essay written in 1933. Indeed, these are best thought of as complementary, as we discuss in Section 8.
6. Lundberg (1981) recalled that Kalecki did not mix well with the Swedish economists. Only with considerable passage of time did Lundberg himself come to appreciate the full value of Kalecki's contributions. On the Swedish model see also Hanson (1982), Klein (1966) and Patinkin (1982). In reviewing Myrdal's work, Joan Robinson (1980, p.151) observed that 'in 1931, Myrdal

published *Monetary Equilibrium*, which drew out from the heritage of Wicksell the conceptions that became known as the Keynesian Revolution (though here Myrdal's patriotism claims too much)'.

7. Though he was rather stubborn and did not at all share Keynes's proverbial propensity to change his mind, Kalecki had the sober attitude that to communicate with any group, one has to learn its language and operate with the intellectual apparatus familiar to that group. Earlier in his life, he adopted this attitude in his controversies with Polish mainstream economists. For example, see his 1934 paper (Kalecki, 1979, pp.239–59).
8. In Joan Robinson's (1979a, p.258) evaluation, on a theoretical plane, Kalecki's 'version of the general theory of employment is in some respects more coherently argued than Keynes' '. However, on a pragmatic level, one should remember that Keynes has performed a great service. His version 'is more useful in shooting down academic orthodoxy, because he understood it from within'.
9. In Joan Robinson's (1979a, pp.194–5) observation: 'Kalecki was free from the remnants of old-fashioned theory which Keynes had failed to throw off. He could see through these confusions at the first glance. His amendments are completely in line with the main argument of the *General Theory*. Kalecki gets Keynes back onto the rails where his "classical" education had led him astray'.
10. Worswick (1977, pp.28–9) contrasts Kalecki's solemnity and sense of humor as follows: 'Although his writing was often technical and abstract, behind it there was always a very strong moral purpose. In wartime, austerity was the common lot, but for him it meant that his heart and his intellect could be in harmony. I fear I am making him sound very solemn. He did have an acute sense of humour and in later life accumulated a vast store of jokes, especially political jokes, which his wife Ada would encourage him to relate as a form of relaxation. But he used to warn us: "Never make jokes about serious matters: they will always come true" '.
11. 'It gives me a feeling of pride to recall that Kalecki's theory of the trade cycle emerged before my very eyes, if not actually under my observation. This may be a good occasion to acknowledge frankly that I did not fully understand Kalecki's discovery until Keynes' similar theory had made the basis for effective stimulation of market forces' (Lipiński, 1977, p.71).
12. 'Keynes impatiently threw all economics from Adam Smith to Pigou into one box and called them "classical". For him they were all alike for they did not take account of his problem – the influence of effective demand on the level of employment. But this was a solecism' (Joan Robinson, 1973a, p.123).
13. Kalecki (1968) succinctly presented the relationship between (modified) Marxian schemes of expanded reproduction (set out in vol. 2 of Marx's *Capital* – production with accumulating capital) and some modern theories of growth, including his own business cycle theory.
14. One should note here that the use of the term 'perfect competition' for 'Marshallians' of the 1930s is quite different from the use made of the term by modern Walrasians. For an interesting distinction of the various meanings of competition see the paper Joan Robinson wrote in 1934 (1951, 1978, pp.20–34). For her later thoughts on the subject see 1971, 1979a, pp.4–19, 146–67.
15. Although here we are concerned particularly with the version of Kalecki's theory that influenced Joan Robinson, one should actually look at it as it evolved. There is a certain duality in Kalecki's approach. In the 1933 original version of his theory, the argument is couched in terms of 'perfect competi-

tion'. Only in the concluding section did he depart from that assumption. There he showed that his conclusions about cyclical changes in production, employment, investment and profit still held, though to the same fluctuations of gross profitability under monopolistic conditions, corresponded weaker fluctuations in profit margins and stronger fluctuations in capacity utilization. Only in the French version of his 1933 essay (in 1935) did Kalecki first note that in a semi-monopolistic economy, the overall price level depends on the monopolies' policy (Kalecki, 1979, p.457).

Even before leaving Poland, in 1935, in numerous discussions at the Institute, Kalecki insisted that in manufacturing industry unit variable cost is generally constant. He tried to verify this hypothesis in his empirical studies of cartels in Poland. In an article published jointly with Landau in 1935, Kalecki took a critical stand against the traditional concept of the rising marginal cost curve (see Kalecki, 1980, p.518). Thus his later discussions with Sraffa and others in Cambridge merely reinforced his proclivity to assume the reverse L-shaped cost curve. Here the interaction and influences went in both directions. As could be expected, Kalecki both welcomed and was critical of the 'Cambridge imperfect competition theory'. Interestingly Kaldor recently credited Kalecki with the 'very important influence' he 'had in the 1930s on English thinking on this subject through Joan Robinson and myself (and I daresay through Kahn . . .)' (Harcourt, 1985, p.94).

In his writings on business cycles until 1938, Kalecki used the competitive model where the short-run marginal cost curve of firms is upward-sloping. However, from the very beginning, he consistently rejected the assumption of full utilization of productive resources throughout the cycle, which undermined the allocative functions of 'free competition' (Kalecki, 1980, p.514).

The theory of the 'determinants' of the relative shares of wages and profits in national income 'governed' by the degree of monopoly was first developed by Kalecki in 1938 (see Kalecki, 1939). The impulse for formulating the distribution theory on the basis of the degree of monopoly was the need to find adequate tools with which to analyze cyclical and long run changes in wages and profits as constituents of national income and their relative shares in national income under oligopolistic competition (Kalecki, 1980, p.516).

From the very beginning Kalecki's conception of the economic process involved monopoly capitalism. In his more popular articles (written at the same time as the 1933 essay) he emphasized the monopolistic character of the markets. To repeat, to understand Kalecki's approach and development, one cannot stress enough that his vision of the economic process took shape when he was writing the articles on the various industries and markets and not as a result of inculcated theories. His own presentation of his theory was in part developed as a result of his discussions with Polish academic economists. He was an extremely fast learner in using the language of the trade – hence his early use of the competitive model. Troubled by the incongruity between the competitive model and his own conception of the economic process, he groped for an analytical expression of his vision. His early Polish writings portray this.

To summarize, Kalecki's English period (roughly 1936–1944) involved several interactions. Aside from the intellectual baggage he brought with him, he had serious discussions with the Cambridge and London economists. At the same time, in addition to his independent work on consolidating and developing his theory, he was briefly employed on an empirical research project on costs and prices in Cambridge. This, in turn, was more generally related to the then ongoing Oxford–Cambridge controversy on that subject. When he went to the Oxford Institute of Statistics in 1939, he was further influenced by and reacted to the full-cost group. Throughout that period, Kalecki broadened the concept of degree of monopoly, increasingly taking oligopoly (with all its attendant difficulties) into account. Kalecki continually sought for a more precise analytical expression of his conception, though the line he traversed was not always smooth.

16. In the controversial Oxford–Cambridge discussion about price formation and costs, the stand taken by Kalecki (who was more interested in, but still critical of the empirically-based Oxford approach) is of interest. On the differences between his theory and the full-cost theory as he saw them, see Kalecki, 1954, p.18 (see also Kalecki, 1980, pp.522–3). For Joan Robinson (1979a, p.189) the full cost doctrine 'appeared to hold that prices of manufactures are determined solely by average cost, which would imply that prices fall when demand increases because overheads are spread over a larger output. This argument was put forward in ideological terms to defend businessmen from the implications that they behave monopolistically'. (See also 1956, 1966, pp.187–8.)

17. Discussion of Kalecki's price theory has been marred by reference to 'tautology'. I think this criticism has proved infertile and useless. A tautology (or identity, to use a less loaded word) is not necessarily empty or stupid. In fact there are tautologies like Wald's identity which are so fiendishly clever that they produced a prolific stream of ideas and applications in probability theory . . .

Moreover, you often find a system or body of statements which can be interpreted alternatively in two different ways: Either as purely analytical truths or as referring to the world of experience. Euklidean geometry is a purely analytic discipline, an axiomatic system in which consistency is the only criterion of truth. But when it is interpreted by a surveyor who associates the concept of a straight line with the manner of a propagation of light it turns out to be a very efficient means of orientation in empirical space. (Steindl, 1987, p.2)

18. Describing her initial attempts at the generalization of the General Theory, Joan Robinson (1979a, p.77) spoke of Harrod's influence. But 'Harrod assumed what has come to be called Harrod saving . . . I adopted Kalecki's assumption – the workers spend what they get, and the capitalists get what they spend'.

19. There is a curious point connected with this article. The controversy which immediately succeeded the publication of the *Treatise* was largely occupied with what we used to call the 'buckets-in-the-well theory' – that is the theory that when the demand for consumption goods falls (thriftiness increases) the demand for capital goods (investment) rises by an equal amount. I wrote an article (as far as I can recollect, in the summer of 1931) attempting to explain Keynes' answer to this argument (the article is somewhat tedious at this time of day, and is not included in this collection). It was accepted by *Economica* but (I never knew why) it did not appear until February, 1933, a few months before the first number of the *Review of Economic Studies* came out. After Keynes' death Professor Samuelson pointed out . . . that this pair of articles exhibits the transition from the

> *Treatise* to the *General Theory*, and Mr. Klein followed up his hint by an attempt to date the birth of the *General Theory* between February and October 1933 . . . I tell this tale as an awful warning to historians. (Joan Robinson, 1951, 1978, pp.viii–ix)

20. Kalecki reacted to the interpretation that he had two theories of distribution, in a letter (14 March 1966) to M. Lutfalla who translated and wrote the introduction to the French edition of Kalecki (1954). He wrote that Lutfalla should stress that the past decisions of capitalists about the size of their investment and consumption in that period determine the *absolute* amount of profit in this period. Such factors as the degree of monopoly (on which the partition of national income between capitalists and workers depends) designate the relative shares of profits in national income. It is in this manner that profits, together with the 'partition factors', designate the amount of national income, and not the other way round. Kalecki suggested that a misunderstanding of this relatively simple idea has made some economists believe that essentially he had two theories of distribution of national income – a totally unfounded interpretation (Kalecki, 1980, p.528).
21. Referring to Kalecki's more popular writings in Polish in the early 1930s and citing him almost verbatim, Lipiński (1977, p.72) reminds us (see Kalecki, 1979, pp.189–98; and Kalecki, 1966, p.31):

> It is often said: why should we build new factories when the old ones are still not fully exploited? . . . Kalecki replied to this by saying that in order to employ existing capacity, it is necessary that it be expanded. Let us suppose, said Kalecki, that – as is frequently the case in the United States – two towns are connected by two railway lines, both of them little used. What should be done? A third railway line should be built, for then the first two can be put to use carrying men and materials needed for building the third. And what when that third line is completed? Then one should build a fourth. And then a fifth. Kalecki warned his readers that the example was paradoxical in the sense that some other investment near the two railways would obviously be better. Nonetheless, he emphasized, this example 'reflects the laws of overall capitalist development splendidly' . . .
>
> Investments have a stimulating effect on the economy only during the period while they are being carried out. The 'productive' character of investments, on the other hand, tends to check, and finally to reverse the original upswing. Kalecki saw it as being one of the most noteworthy paradoxes of capitalism that the increase of productive capacity, and hence of the community's wealth bears within it the seeds of crisis.

22. Steindl (1981a) traces the three versions of Kalecki's business cycle theory. The initial model is the 1933 Polish version and Kalecki (1935). The successive versions are Kalecki (1943) and Kalecki (1968). The main differences in these versions are almost all in the investment function and Steindl correctly points to Kalecki's innovations in the third version where technical progress is introduced and where the problem of trend is treated as inseparable from cycle. For Kalecki's treatment of the trend and contrast with some of the prevailing growth theories see Steindl 1981b, pp.39–43.

    To recall, in the first version, to make the model manageable, Kalecki (1935) concentrated on a system with constant amplitude of fluctuations (zero damping). In this first version he used the form of a second-order linear difference equation, solved with specification of parameter values. The coefficient of the first-order term determines the cyclical stability of the system. If the coefficient is positive the cyclical movement fades out; if it is negative the motion ceaselessly increases the amplitude. Faced with such a predicament, Kalecki imposed the condition that the movement has zero damping. As Goodwin (1986) points out, Kalecki's carefully chosen solution sensibly combined theoretical necessity with practical convenience. As Kalecki (1935, p.336) noted, the case where the amplitude of fluctuations remains constant is of particular interest for it appears to conform more or less to the real-world conditions where no regular progression or deceleration in the intensity of economic fluctuations is generally found. Frisch sharply protested against Kalecki's imposition of the condition that fluctuations should be undamped (see Feiwel, 1975, p.147; Samuelson, 1947, pp.337 and *passim*). As Goodwin (1986) observes, despite all his efforts, Kalecki (or for that matter Frisch) did not resolve the problem. Goodwin (1986) perceives Kalecki's analytical construct as pioneering – an essentially sound approach. But Kalecki lacked the mathematical equipment to tackle the problem successfully. About the same time as Kalecki presented his 1935 paper, Le Corbeiller wrote a paper about precise specification of non-linearities. This led to Goodwin's own notable contribution (1950). As Goodwin (1985, p.10) recalls, 'I had the good fortune to have as a colleague in my laboratory the French mathematician, Philippe Le Corbeiller, who had specialized in oscillation theory. From him I learned that linear differential equations cannot be used to explain oscillators; he introduced me not only to the van der Pol type oscillator but also to a much wider range of types'. For Goodwin's contributions see Vellupillai (1982).

23. In Joan Robinson's (1979a, p.211) interpretation,

> a short-period is not a length of time but the position at a moment of time. Fixed capital, stocks, the organization of business, the training of workers and the habits of consumers are all whatever they are. In such a situation, a particular level of effective demand determines a particular level of output and flow of incomes; a change in effective demand at that moment brings about a particular change in output. Thus, in that situation, there is a short-period supply curve or utilization function, expressing the relation of the amount of employment to the level of effective demand.

24. In a letter to Beveridge (28 July 1936), Keynes (1973c, p.57) acknowledged that about half of the *General Theory* is about the multiplier. In her memoirs on Kahn, Joan Robinson (n.d.) wrote about Kahn (1931): 'its significance and its influence was immensely enhanced by a "long struggle" to establish it as a corner stone of the Keynesian Revolution' (p.1). According to her (p.2) Kahn came upon the multiplier after reading Keynes's and Henderson's pamphlet *Can Lloyd George Do It?* where they claimed that an investment of a certain amount would bring about an increase in saving equal to a large share of the outlay. 'Kahn, with a training in the exact sciences, could see that there was something wrong. Either the argument was nonsense or it was far more powerful than the authors claimed. In working it out properly, Kahn discovered the principle of the multiplier and the necessary equality of savings and investment (a point which James Meade had come upon by another route)'. As we have pointed out in Chapter 1 of the companion volume, Kahn was the intermediary between the Circus and Keynes. Joan Robinson (p.4) wrote that undoubtedly 'Kahn provided the leading ideas as well as the liaison with Keynes'. She (pp.6–7) raised the puzzling question 'why such a powerful and energetic mind never expressed itself in any large-

scale publication. The answer is partly to be found in the rare generosity with which Kahn gave his time, not only to Keynes and to me, but to innumerable pupils, colleagues, and strangers who submitted work to him. There was another reason – perfectionism. Kahn would take endless trouble to remove errors from other people's books, but in the end, responsibility had to be attached to the name on the title page. He had great repugnance to the thought that there might be an error attached to his name'.

25. 'Keynes hardly ever peered over the edge of the short period to see the effect of investment in making addition to the stocks of productive equipment. He used to say: The long period is a subject for undergraduates' (Joan Robinson, 1979a, p.212).

26. We should note here that Kalecki was critical of the way Joan Robinson (1952) proceeded to generalize the General Theory. Essentially he was puzzled by her treatment of investment decision and what he considered her misunderstanding of his treatment of finance as the bottleneck (her stated chief difference with his analysis), her too restrictive and unsatisfactory identification of the real sources of disturbances, and her not probing sufficiently into the cycle-generating character of the capitalist economy. For example, in a letter dated 16 October 1964 (courtesy of Mrs Ada Kalecki), Kalecki reproached Joan Robinson for misunderstanding certain aspects of his theory. Among a number of technical points, he reminded her that he never said that firms invest all finance they can get. For him the principle of increasing risk means that firms may not be willing to borrow as much as they could.

    We should also note here that the generalization entailed extensions into the open economy as well – a subject that she tackled already in 1935 (1973a, pp.229–40). In the introduction to Kalecki's prewar essays, she (1966, p.xi) noted that 'Keynes' *General Theory* was worked out in terms of a closed system. It was left to me to sketch its extension into the theory of foreign trade in slump conditions. Here also Kalecki's work claims priority'. (See also Joan Robinson, 1973a, pp.1–24, 174–5.)

27. As we know, the place of interest rates in the economic process is highly controversial. The role of liquidity preference theory in Keynes's system as well as its peculiar features have been and continue to be subject to searching scrutiny (see Klein, 1966; Patinkin, 1976, Leijonhufvud, 1968). For instance, Shackle (1965) argued that the liquidity theory itself, though intimately necessary to the *General Theory* can be considered in isolation, and stands as Keynes's most inalienable piece of original economic thought. It is remarkable that in his original formulation, Kalecki did not treat liquidity preference and the interest rate. But shortly after the publication of his original model, he introduced a theory of interest, suggesting that the velocity of circulation of cash balances in fact closely depends on the short-term rate of interest. According to Kalecki, this rate cannot be determined as traditional theory because investment automatically generates an equal amount of saving. If investment 'finances itself', irrespective of the level of the rate of interest, the rate of interest itself is determined by the interplay of other factors. Kalecki proposed that the short-term rate of interest is determined by the value of transactions and the supply of money by the banking system. In turn, the long-term rate is determined by anticipations of the short-term rate based on past experience and by estimates of the risk involved in the possible capital loss of holding long-term assets. Velocity of circulation is not a constant, but depends on the movements of the interest rate. Short-term rate

of interest is closely connected with marginal convenience of holding cash. With a given turnover of cash balances, the smaller the volume of cash balances possessed the greater the convenience derived from holding the marginal unit of cash for transaction purposes. But after the volume of cash holdings drops below a certain level, its further reduction involves a very strong rising marginal inconvenience. If, however, cash is abundant with given turnover, the marginal convenience declines to zero at this level if the supply of cash increases further. Thus, subject to qualification, the marginal convenience of holding cash is an increasing function of the velocity of circulation. If the short-term rate of interest exceeds this marginal convenience, the opportunity cost provides stimuli for lending extra cash; if the interest rate is lower, it becomes beneficial to withdraw from short-term assets and get cash. Thus equilibrium is reached when the short-term rate of interest equals the marginal convenience of holding cash. This theory set forth by Kalecki is an alternative way of looking at the Keynesian theory of liquidity preference. Both theories are alike in assuming that velocity is not a constant and is affected by interest rate movements.

In the *General Theory* the rate of interest is determined by the amount of money 'in conjunction with the liquidity preference function. In essence this is little more than a formal definition, since it follows from it that all influences other than the amount of money are portmanteaued in the liquidity function' (Keynes, 1973c, p.11).

Kalecki's approach differs from the stand and interpretation taken by Kahn (1984, pp.137–41 and *passim*). Joan Robinson (1976) observed that whereas the *General Theory* elaborates on the role of money, finance, and the level of interest rates, Kalecki deals with the subject cursorily. The monetary aspects are elaborated in Joan Robinson (1952). 'In my opinion, Keynes rather exaggerated the influence of the rate of interest, but in any case it was always the rate of interest *relatively* to expected profits that had an influence' (Joan Robinson, 1973a, p.97. See also Johnson, 1978; Parts VI and VII and Chapter 26 in this volume.)

28. On this subject, Joan Robinson (1979a, p.113) accused Keynes of fudging.

> The 'marginal efficiency of capital' is derived from the profits expected from investment, allowing for risk; the level of investment at any moment is said to be such as to equate the marginal efficiency of capital to the rate of interest (the cost of finance). Interest charges represent an obligation to pay certain definite sums of money. What is said to be equated to the rate of interest is an uncertain expectation of profit. But this statement is vacuous, for it is impossible to separate out the expected rate of profit from the allowance for the degree of uncertainty with which expectations are held. Keynes later denounced the conception that uncertainty in economic affairs can be reduced to calculable risks as one of the 'pretty, polite techniques, made for a well-panelled board room and a nicely regulated market' which 'tries to deal with the present by abstracting from the fact that we know very little about the future.'

She (p.113) excused this type of fudging on the grounds that it is a self-defensive mechanism. 'In pursuing one line of argument, it is necessary to block off others, by fair means or foul, or else no question can ever be posed'. (See also Joan Robinson, 1968, pp.36–7; 1962, pp.105–6.)

29. On several occasions Joan Robinson (see 1968, p.37) quotes Keynes (1936,

pp.161–2) on the meaning of animal spirits. (See also Joan Robinson, 1960, 1975, pp.89–90, 146, 155; Keynes, 1973c, p.112.)

30. As mentioned in Chapter 1 of the companion volume, Joan Robinson viewed the Hicksian IS-LM version as shunting the Keynesian revolution on to the wrong track. According to her, Hicks misunderstood Keynes's reaction to IS-LM. As we know, Sir John has had a change of heart. He has 'become disillusioned with the *IS/LM* model with which generations of students have been taught to misinterpret the *General Theory*' (Joan Robinson, 1979a, p.10).

31. Recently Kaldor perceived the originality of Keynes's conception of effective demand to have been in the division of the latter into two components: endogenous and exogenous.

> It is the endogenous component which reflects (*i.e.*, is automatically generated by) production, for much the same reasons as those given by Ricardo, Mill or Say – the difference is only that in a money economy (*i.e.* in an economy where things are not directly exchanged, but only through the intermediation of money) aggregate demand can be a *function* of aggregate supply (both measured in money terms) without being *equal* to it – the one can be some fraction of the other. To make the two equal requires the addition of the exogenous component (which could be one of a number of things, of which capital expenditure – 'investment' – is only one) ... If the relationship between output and endogenous demand (which Keynes called 'the propensity to consume') is taken as given, it is the value of exogenous demand which determines what total production and employment will be. A rise in exogenous demand, for whatever reasons, will cause an increase in production which will be some multiple of the former ... A capitalist economy ... is not 'self-adjusting' in the sense that an increase in potential output will automatically induce corresponding growth of actual output. This will only be the case if exogenous demand expands at the same time to the required degree; and as this cannot be taken for granted, the maintenance of full employment in a growing economy requires a deliberate policy of demand management. (Worswick and Trevithick, 1983, pp. 8–9)

32. In a letter (30 December 1944) Keynes complimented Kalecki on this essay which he found remarkable and instructive. He reflected that when one comes across such an essay, one feels that there is real progress in economics. There was almost nothing in it with which he would not agree. Keynes considered Kalecki's essay as the most interesting and original in the book as well as marvellously concise (Kalecki, 1979, p.573; see also Joan Robinson's review article in 1951, 1978, pp.99–104; and the retrospective reflections by Worswick, 1977 and 1985).

33. It is interesting to note that in an article published in 1933 (Kalecki, 1979, pp.189–98), Kalecki was probably the first to have explicitly stated that in stimulating an upswing the object of the expenditure is not relevant. The point is that the expenditure be made (without reducing other components of effective demand) and that military expenditures financed this way are as effective in stimulating an upswing as are non-military ones (see Kalecki, 1979, pp.484–5).

    In a letter to Beveridge (28 July 1936), Keynes defended himself that he did not advocate digging holes in the ground.

What I advocate is the application of labour to *productive* investment, and, if there were no productive investments left, then I should distribute incomes more equally so as to increase consumption. But, although my passage about digging holes in the ground is written in a sense ironically, it means exactly what it says; namely, that, failing everything else, it would lead to an enrichment of the community as compared with doing nothing, because by repercussion more consumption goods would be produced and consumed than before. In fact, my point is to show how much more sensible it would be to employ labour on constructing useful investments. But to enforce my point as to the value of the repercussions of investment as distinct from the investment itself, I take the extreme case when the investment is worth nothing, so as to show that even in such a case there may still be social benefit. (Keynes, 1973c, p.58)

Similarly, Joan Robinson (1960, 1975, pp.90–1) explained the paradox in Keynes's argument.

In his theory the relevant point about investment is that it generates effective demand. It is the process of investment, not its fruits, that matters. Even if investment is merely 'digging holes in the ground and filling them up again', it will generate demand and lead to an increase in real income. The increase in real income does not come from the holes, but from the process of digging them, which causes money to be spent and idle resources already in existence to be brought into useful activity.

34. In any case, once it is accepted that a 'high and stable level of employment' is going to be provided (leaving aside the question of just how high it should be and whether a few wobbles will not be induced to alleviate the stability) then the question of employment as such ceases to be interesting. It was necessary to argue about it only when the official view was that nothing could be done. Now the argument must be about *what* should be done. (Joan Robinson, 1962, pp.129–30)

35. Keynes did not maintain that everything would be easy once the principles of employment policy were understood, or that simple automatic regulators could be fitted into the system of a private enterprise economy that would dispense with the need for wise judgment. The main message of the General Theory was negative. It struck off the shackles of laisser-faire ideology. Keynes knew that new freedom would raise fresh problems and require fresh solutions. He certainly did not see himself as a quack peddling a panacea. (Joan Robinson, 1979a, p.181)

36. The twenty-five years after the war that passed without a major recession has been called the Age of Keynes, but it was not much like his vision. It turned out closer to Kalecki's sardonic description of the regime of the political trade cycle. (Joan Robinson, 1979a, p.176; see also 1976a)

37. In a post card to Kalecki (20 December, 1943) Keynes wrote that he read with great sympathy and interest the article on the political aspects of full employment. He considered the article to be unusually good and perceptive. He mentioned that had he written it himself, he would have added more about the important influences of the disintegrating and outdated doctrine of sound finance which oppose any kind of public spending and budget deficit (Kalecki, 1979, p.568).

38. Commenting on this passage, Joan Robinson (1962, p.94) observed that 'perhaps more emphasis should have been placed on the City than on big business, and more emphasis on monetary policy than budget deficits, but on the whole the above has proved to have been pretty near the mark'.
39. For a summary of the key tenets of monetarism see Feiwel, 1985, pp.27–8.
40. For the Cambridge assault on the quantity theory of money, see Kahn, 1984, pp.27–59; Joan Robinson, 1971, ch.6; Kaldor, 1982. On Keynes's 'liberation from the corset of the quantity theory of money', see, inter alia, Kahn, 1984, p.78 and passim; Moggridge, 1976; Johnson, 1978; Skidelsky, 1983.
41. For an interesting and unusual comparison between Joan Robinson and the new classical macroeconomists see Chapter 23 in this volume.
42.

> Keynes's 1936 *General Theory* had a revolutionary impact precisely because the novel paradigm that it proposed led to analysis and therapies so different from those of pre-1929 classical and neoclassical economics. The new classical economics of rational expectationists is a return with a vengeance to the pre-Keynesian verities . . .
>
> The 'new classical economics' . . . is truly a counterrevolution and the same cannot be said of [Friedman's] 'monetarism'. If I can believe in Lucas market clearing, then I can no longer believe in the behavior equations and relations of the *General Theory* and this holds both for positivistic description or prediction and for policy diagnosis and therapeutic recommendation. Even Milton Friedman found the new rational expectationism at first unwelcome, since it denied the real evils of systematic mismanagement of money . . .
>
> Like the Bourbons so many of us have learned nothing and forgotten nothing. In my observation the way of the world has changed much since the 1930s. Because I regard myself as a serious Keynesian, a post-Keynesian, I have had continually to modify my paradigms and insights. That is not pleasant to do, or easy to do. But it has to be done in the interest of science and I experience no serious qualms of conscience in constantly adapting my Keynesianism to the new cut of the world. To cease to be an old-fashioned Keynesian is not to become a monetarist: I have lost my faith, not my reason. (Samuelson, 1986, pp.291–2)

43. When I asked Arrow to rank the most significant contributions to economics in the last 50 years, he replied: 'I would still put the developments of Keynesian economics at the top of the list; the vision if not the theory contained therein' (Feiwel, 1987, p.227).
44. There are perennial sources of tensions between pragmatic macroeconomists and those who insist on applying the standard rules of neoclassical theory to macro phenomena. Macro models cannot be made to look like general equilibrium models without weakening them by depriving them of their simplicity, institutional content and definitive conclusions – all of which are part of the reason for which these models were created (see Chapter 18 in this volume). One of the recurring questions is whether or not Keynes succeeded in proving the existence of equilibrium with involuntary unemployment (see Chapter 17 in this volume). However, the larger and more fundamental question is whether it really matters, for historically the Great Depression did take place and there still exists the possibility of protracted unemployment which the natural adjustments of a market economy remedy very slowly, if at all (see Feiwel, 1985, ch. 2).
45. For the Cambridge perspective on the strengths and limitations of the *General Theory*, see, inter alia, Worswick and Trevithick, 1983, pp.1–28 and

Kahn, 1984. The neoclassical Keynesian perspective is argued in Chapters 17, 18 and 19 in this volume. Within the vast and growing literature on the vitality and relevance of Keynesian thinking among the younger generation of economists, one might single out Blinder, 1987 and Akerlof and Yellen, 1987.

To refer here to only one aspect, perhaps one should emphasize that integration of imperfect competition and the theory of employment is one of the necessary steps in the reconstruction of the General Theory (a point also argued in Chapter 18 in this volume). 'The main theoretical ingredient which needs to be incorporated into Keynes' theory is a recognition of the prevalence of imperfect or oligopolistic markets and of the importance of innovation and reorganization of production as a stratetic weapon in this form of competition' (Joan Robinson and Cripps, 1979, p.142). In an illuminating essay on Keynesian economics after 50 years, Kaldor argued that the major problem of the *General Theory* is its disregard of imperfect competition. In a discussion, from a different vantage point, Tobin claimed that imperfection of competition is necessary at some stages of Keynes's argument, but not sufficient to explain Keynes's massive, systematic market failures. Moreover, the 'faithful neoclassics' (be they the orthodox during Keynes's lifetime, the Friedmanian monetarists or the new breed of NCM proponents) dismiss imperfect competition as a trivial exception proving the rule of perfect competition. To them, Keynes's macroeconomic would not be any more attractive had he based it on imperfect competition (Worswick and Trevithick, 1983, pp.14 and 30).

46. It is ironic that after the great technical achievements brought by the age of growth, all we are offered is a return to large-scale unemployment and poverty in the midst of plenty, in an age of frustration. Kalecki was right to be sceptical; the modern economies have failed to develop the political and social institutions, at either domestic or international level, that are needed to make permanent full employment compatible with capitalism. (Joan Robinson, 1979a, p.208)

References

Akerlof, G. A, and J. L. Yellen (1987) 'Rational Models of Irrational Behavior', *American Economic Review* 77 (May): 137–42.

Andrews, P. W. S. (1949) *Manufacturing Business* (London: Macmillan).

Andrews, P. W. S. (1964) *On Competition in Economic Theory* (London: Macmillan).

Archibald, G. C. (ed.) (1971) *The Theory of the Firm* (Harmondsworth: Penguin).

Arrow, K. J. (1967) 'Samuelson Collected', *Journal of Political Economy*, 75: 730–7.

Arrow, K. J. (ed.) (1971) *Selected Readings in Economic Theory from Econometrica* (Cambridge Mass.: MIT).

Arrow, K. J. and Y. Honkapohja (eds) (1985) *Frontiers of Economics* (Oxford: Blackwell).

Asimakopulos, A. (1975) 'A Kaleckian Theory of Income Distribution', *Canadian Journal of Economics*, 8(3): 313–33.

Asimakopulos, A. (1983) 'Anticipations of Keynes's *General Theory*?' *Canadian Journal of Economics*, 16(3): 517–30.

Blinder, A. S. (1987) 'Keynes, Lucas, and Scientific Progress', *American Economic Review* 77 (May): 130–6.

Brus, W. (1977) 'Kalecki's Economics of Socialism', *Oxford Bulletin of Economics and Statistics* (Special Issue: Michal Kalecki Memorial Lectures), 39(1): 57–67.

Dobb, M. H. (1967) *Papers on Capitalism, Development and Planning* (London: Routledge).

Eatwell, J. and M. Milgate (eds) (1983) *Keynes' Economics and the Theory of Value and Distribution* (New York: Oxford University Press).

Eshag, E. (1977) 'Kalecki's Political Economy: 'A Comparison with Keynes', *Oxford Bulletin of Economics and Statistics* (Special Issue: Michal Kalecki Memorial Lectures), 39(1): 79–85.

Feiwel, G. R. (1975) *The Intellectual Capital of Michal Kalecki* (Knoxville: University of Tennessee Press).

Feiwel, G. R. (ed.) (1985) *Issues in Contemporary Macroeconomics and Distribution* (London: Macmillan).

Feiwel, G. R. (ed.) (1987) *Arrow and the Ascent of Modern Economic Theory* (London: Macmillan)

Galbraith, J. K. (1975) 'How Keynes came to America', in M. Keynes (ed.) pp.132–41.

Garnett, D. (1975) 'Maynard Keynes as a Biographer', in M. Keynes (ed.) pp.254–59.

Godley, W. A. H. and W. D. Nordhaus (1972) 'Pricing in the Trade Cycle', *Economic Journal*, 82: 853–82.

Goodwin, R. M. (1950) 'A Non-linear Theory of the Cycle' *Review of Economics and Statistics* 32 (November): 316–20.

Goodwin, R. M. (1985) 'A Personal Perspective on Mathematical Economics', *Banca Nazionale del Lavoro Quarterly Review*, 152 (March): 3–13.

Goodwin, R. M. (1986) 'Kalecki's Economic Dynamics', mimeo.

Hahn, F. H. (1972) *The Share of Wages in National Income* (London: Weidenfeld & Nicolson).

Hansson, B. A. (1982) *The Stockholm School and the Development of Dynamic Method* (London: Croom Helm).

Harcourt, G. C. (ed.) (1985) *Keynes and his Contemporaries* (New York: St Martin's Press).

Harrod, R. H. (1936) *The Trade Cycle* (London: Macmillan).

Harrod, R. F. (1948) *Towards a Dynamic Economics* (London: Macmillan).

Harrod, R. F. (1951a) 'Notes on Trade Cycle Theory', *Economic Journal*, 61: 261–75.

Harrod, R. F. (1951b) *The Life of John Maynard Keynes* (London: Macmillan).

Harrod, R. F. (1964) 'Optimum Investment for Growth', in *Problems of Economic Dynamics and Planning: Essays in Honour of Michal Kalecki* (Warsaw: Polish Scientific Publishers) pp.169–79.

Harrod, R. F. (1973) *Economic Dynamics* (London: Macmillan).

Hayek, F. A. (1944) *The Road to Serfdom* (London: Routledge & Kegan Paul).

Hessian, C. H. (1984) *John Maynard Keynes* (New York: Macmillan).

Hicks, J. R. (1965) *Capital and Growth* (Oxford: Oxford University Press).

Hicks, J. R. (1974) *The Crisis in Keynesian Economics* (New York: Basic Books).

Johansen, L. (1978) 'Review of Feiwel's *Intellectual Capital of Michal Kalecki*', *Journal of Political Economy*, 86: 159–62.

Johnson, E. S. and Johnson, H. G. (1978) *The Shadow of Keynes* (Oxford: Blackwell).

Johnson, H. G. (1973) 'Review of Kalecki's *Selected Essays on the Dynamics of the Capitalist Economy*', *Economica* NS 40: 87–8.

Kahn, R. F. (1931) 'The Relation of Home Investment to Unemployment', *Economic Journal* 41: 173–98; reprinted in Kahn (1972) *Selected Essays on Employment and Growth* (Cambridge: Cambridge University Press) pp.1–27.

Kahn, R. F. (1984) *The Making of Keynes's General Theory* (Cambridge: Cambridge University Press).
Kahn, R. F. (1985) 'The Cambridge "Circus" (1)', in G. C. Harcourt (ed.) pp.42–51.
Kaldor, N. (1955–6) 'Alternative Theories of Distribution', *Review of Economic Studies*, 23: 94–100.
Kaldor, N. (1960) *Essays on Economic Stability and Growth* (London: Duckworth).
Kaldor, N. (1976) 'Inflation and Recession in the World Economy', *Economic Journal*, 86: 703–14.
Kaldor, N. (1982) *The Scourge of Monetarism* (Oxford: Oxford University Press).
Kaldor, N. (1986) 'Recollections of an Economist', *Banca Nazionale del Lavoro Quarterly Review*, 156: 3–26.
Kalecki, M. (1935) 'A Macrodynamic Theory of Business Cycles', *Econometrica* 3: 327–44.
Kalecki, M. (1936) 'Parę uwag o teorii Keynesa', *Ekonomista* 3: 18–26; tr. and rpt. in F. Targetti and B. Kinda-Hass (1982) 'Kalecki's Review of Keynes' *General Theory*', *Australian Economic Papers*, 21: 244–60.
Kalecki, M. (1937) 'A Theory of the Business Cycle', *Review of Economic Studies*, 4: 77–97.
Kalecki, M. (1938) 'the Determinants of Distribution of the National Income', *Econometrica* 6: 97–112, reprinted in K. J. Arrow (ed.) (1971), pp.1–16.
Kalecki, M. (1939) *Essays in the Theory of Economic Fluctuations* (London: Allen & Unwin).
Kalecki, M. (1942) 'A Theory of Profits', *Economic Journal*, 52: 258–67.
Kalecki, M. (1043a) *Studies in Economic Dynamics* (London: Allen & Unwin).
Kalecki, M. (1943b) 'Political Aspects of Full Employment', *Political Quarterly*, 14(4): 322–31, partly rptd. in Kalecki (1971).
Kalecki, M. (1944) 'Three Ways to Full Employment', in *The Economics of Full Employment* (Oxford: Blackwell) pp.39–58.
Kalecki, M. (1950) 'A Note on Long-Run Unemployment', *Review of Economic Studies*, 18(1): 62–4.
Kalecki, M. (1954, 1965) *Theory of Economic Dynamics* (London: Allen & Unwin).
Kalecki, M. (1962) 'Observations on the Theory of Growth', *Economic Journal*, 72: 134–53.
Kalecki, M. (1966) *Studies in the Theory of Business Cycles 1933–1939*, tr. from the first Polish edn by Ada Kalecki (Warsaw: Polish Scientific Publishers).
Kalecki, M. (1968) 'The Marxian Equations of Reproduction and Modern Economics', *Social Science Information*, 6: 73–9.
Kalecki, M. (1970) 'Theories of Growth in Different Social Systems', *Scientia*, 64: 311–16.
Kalecki, M. (1971) *Selected Essays on the Dynamics of the Capitalist Economy* (Cambridge: Cambridge University Press).
Kalecki, M. (1976) *Essays on Developing Economies* (Hassocks: Harvester Press).
Kalecki, M. (1979) *Kapitalizm: Koniunktura i zatrudnienie, Dzieła*, vol. 1, J. Osiatyński (ed.) (Warsaw: Panstwowe Wydawnictwo Ekonomiczne).
Kalecki, M. (1980) *Kapitalizm: Dynamika gospodarcza, Dzieła*, vol. 2, J. Osiatyński (ed.) (Warsaw: Panstwowe Wydawnictwo Ekonomiczne).
Keynes, J. M. (1936) *The General Theory of Employment Interest and Money* (London: Macmillan).
Keynes, J. M. (1963a) *Essays in Biography* (New York: Norton).
Keynes, J. M. (1963b) *Essays in Persuasion* (New York: Norton).
Keynes, J. M. (1971) *The Collected Writings of John Maynard Keynes*, vol. 5 (London: Macmillan)

Keynes, J. M. (1973a) *The Collected Writings of John Maynard Keynes*, vol. 12 (London: Macmillan).

Keynes, J. M. (1973b) *The Collected Writings of John Maynard Keynes*, vol. 13 (London: Macmillan).

Keynes, J. M. (1973c) *The Collected Writings of John Maynard Keynes*, vol. 14 (London: Macmillan).

Keynes, J. M. (1979) *The Collected Writings of John Maynard Keynes*, vol. 29 (London: Macmillan).

Keynes, M. (ed.) (1975) *Essays on John Maynard Keynes* (Cambridge: Cambridge University Press).

Klein, L. R. (1951) 'Review of Harrod's *The Life of John Maynard Keynes*', *Journal of Political Economy*, 59.

Klein, L. R. (1964) 'The Role of Econometrics in Socialist Economics' in *Problems of Economic Dynamics and Planning: Essays in Honour of Michał Kalecki* (Warsaw: PWN).

Klein, L. R. (1966) *The Keynesian Revolution* (London: Macmillan).

Klein, L. R. (1985) *Economic Theory and Econometrics*, ed. by J. Marquez (Philadelphia: University of Pennsylvania Press).

Kowalik, T. (1971) *Roza Luksemburg* (Warsaw: Polska Akademia Nauk).

Lange, O. (1941) 'Review of Kalecki's *Essays in the Theory of Economic Fluctuations*', *Journal of Political Economy*, 49(2): 279–85.

Leijonhufvud, A. (1968) *On Keynesian Economics and the Economics of Keynes* (New York: Oxford University Press).

Levy, J. (1943) *Economics is an Exact Science* (New York: New Economic Library).

Levy, P. (1975) 'The Bloomsbury Group', in M. Keynes (ed.) pp.60–72.

Lipiński, E. (1977) 'Michal Kalecki', *Oxford Bulletin of Economics and Statistics* (Special Issue: Michal Kalecki Memorial Lectures), 39(1): 69–77.

Lucas, R. E. (Jr) (1981) *Studies in Business Cycle Theory* (Cambridge, Mass.: MIT).

Lucas, R. E. (Jr) and T. J. Sargent (1978) 'After Keynesian Economics', in *After the Phillips Curve* (Boston: Federal Reserve Bank of Boston).

Lundberg, E. (1981) 'The Development of Swedish and Keynesian Macroeconomic Theory and the General Impact on Economic Policy', Milano: Mattioli Lectures (mimeo).

Meade, J. (1983) 'Memoirs of Maynard Keynes', in D. Worswick and J. Trevithick (eds) pp.263–66.

Merton, R. K. (1973) *The Sociology of Science* (Chicago: University of Chicago Press).

Minsky, H. (1975) *John Maynard Keynes* (New York: Columbia University Press).

Moggridge, D. E. (ed.) (1974) *Keynes: Aspects of the Man and his Work* (London: Macmillan).

Moggridge, D. E. (1976) *Keynes* (Harmondsworth: Penguin).

Okun, A. M. (1981) *Prices and Quantities* (Washington: Brookings Institution).

Osiatyński, J. (1985) 'Don Patinkin on Kalecki and Keynes', *Oeconomia Polona*, 1: 95–104.

Pasinetti, L. (1961–2) 'Rate of Profit and Income Distribution in Relation to the Rate of Economic Growth', *Review of Economic Studies*, 29: 267–79; repr. in Pasinetti (1974), *Growth and Income Distribution* (Cambridge: Cambridge University Press) pp.103–20.

Pasinetti, L. (1979) 'Kaldor, Nicholas', in D. L. Sills (ed.) *International Encyclopedia of the Social Sciences, Biographical Supplement*, vol. 18 (New York: The Free Press) 366–9.

Patinkin, D. (1976) *Keynes' Monetary Thought* (Durham, NC: Duke).

Patinkin, D. (1982) *Anticipations of the General Theory? And Other Essays on Keynes* (Chicago: Chicago University Press).
Patinkin, D. and J. C. Leith (eds) (1977) *Keynes, Cambridge and 'The General Theory'* (London: Macmillan).
Phelps Brown, E. H. (1968) *A Century of Pay* (London: Macmillan).
Robinson, E. A. G. (1975) 'A personal view', in M. Keynes (ed.) pp.9–23.
Robinson, E. A. G. (1977) 'Keynes and his Cambridge Colleagues' in Patinkin and Leith (eds), pp.25–38.
Robinson, E. A. G. (1983) 'Memoirs of Maynard Keynes', in D. Worswick and J. Trevithick (eds) pp.255–61.
Robinson, E. A. G. (1985) 'The Cambridge Circus (2)', in G. C. Harcourt (ed.) pp.52–7.
Robinson, E. A. G. (1986) 'A Child of the Times', *The Economist*, 20: 65–8.
Robinson, Joan (1933) 'A Parable on Savings and Investment', *Economica* 13: 75–84.
Robinson, Joan (1933, 1969) *The Economics of Imperfect Competition* (London: Macmillan).
Robinson, Joan (1936) 'Disguised Unemployment', *Economic Journal*, 46: 225–37.
Robinson, Joan (1937, 1949) *Introduction to the Theory of Employment* (London: Macmillan).
Robinson, Joan (1937, 1947) *Essays in the Theory of Employment*. (London: Macmillan; Oxford: Blackwell).
Robinson, Joan (1942, 1966) *An Essay on Marxian Economics* (London: Macmillan).
Robinson, Joan (1951, 1978) *Collected Economic Papers*, vol. 1 (Oxford: Blackwell).
Robinson, Joan (1952) *The Rate of Interest and Other Essays* (London: Macmillan).
Robinson, Joan (1956, 1966) *The Accumulation of Capital* (London: Macmillan).
Robinson, Joan (1960, 1975) *Collected Economic Papers*, vol. 2 (Oxford: Blackwell).
Robinson, Joan (1962) *Economic Philosophy* (Chicago: Aldine).
Robinson, Joan (1965, 1975) *Collected Economic Papers*, vol. 3 (Oxford: Blackwell).
Robinson, Joan (1966) 'Introduction' to *Studies in the Theory of Business Cycles 1933–1939* by M. Kalecki (Warsaw: Polish Scientific Publishers).
Robinson, Joan (1967) *Economics: An Awkward Corner* (New York: Pantheon Books).
Robinson, Joan (1968) *Essays in the Theory of Economic Growth* (London: Macmillan).
Robinson, Joan (1969a) 'A Further Note', *Review of Economic Studies*, 36: 260–2.
Robinson, Joan (1969b) 'A Review of Leijonhufvud's *On Keynesian Economics and the Economics of Keynes*', *Economic Journal*, 79: 581–3.
Robinson, Joan (1971) *Economic Heresies* (London: Macmillan).
Robinson, Joan (1973a) *Collected Economic Papers*, vol. 4 (Oxford: Blackwell).
Robinson, Joan (1973b) Foreword to J. Kregel, *The Reconstruction of Political Economy* (New York: Wiley) pp.ix–xiii.
Robinson, Joan (1976a) 'Michal Kalecki: A Neglected Prophet', *New York Review of Books,* 23(3): 28–30.
Robinson, Joan (1976b) Introduction to M. Kalecki, *Essays on Developing Economies* (Hassocks: Harvester Press), pp.7–13.
Robinson, Joan (1978) *Contribution to Modern Economics* (New York: Academic Press).
Robinson, Joan (1979a) *Collected Economic Papers*, vol. 5 (Oxford: Blackwell).
Robinson, Joan (1979b) *The Generalization of the General Theory and Other Essays* (London: Macmillan).

Robinson, Joan (n.d.) 'Introduction' (written for a collection of Kahn's early essays, forthcoming), mimeo.
Robinson, Joan and F. Cripps (1979) 'Keynes Today', *Journal of Post Keynesian Economics*, 2(1): 139–44.
Robinson, Joan and F. Wilkinson (1985) 'Ideology and Logic', in F. Vicarelli (ed.) pp.73–98.
Samuelson, P. A. (1947) *Foundations of Economic Analysis* (Cambridge, Mass.: Harvard University Press).
Samuelson, P. A. (1966) *The Collected Scientific Papers of Paul A. Samuelson*, vols. 1 and 2, ed. by J. E. Stiglitz (Cambridge, Mass.: MIT).
Samuelson, P. A. (1972) *The Collected Scientific Papers of Paul A. Samuelson*, vol. 3, ed. by R. C. Merton (Cambridge, Mass.: MIT Press).
Samuelson, P. A. (1986) *The Collected Scientific Papers of Paul A. Samuelson*, vol. 5, ed. by K. Crowley (Cambridge, Mass.: MIT Press).
Scherer, F. M. (1970) *Industrial Market Structures and Economic Performance* (Chicago: Rand McNally).
Schumpeter, J. A. (1954) *History of Economic Analysis* (New York: Oxford University Press).
Shackle, G. L. S. (1965) 'Recent Theories Concerning the Nature and Role of Interest', in *Surveys of Economic Theory*, vol. 1: *Money Interest and Welfare* (London: Macmillan) pp.108–53.
Silberston, A. (1970) 'Price Behaviour of Firms', *Economic Journal*, 80: 511–82.
Skidelsky, R. (1983) *John Maynard Keynes*, vol. I: *Hopes Betrayed 1883–1920* (London: Macmillan).
Solow, R. M. and J. E. Stiglitz (1968) 'Output, Employment, and Wages in the Short Run', *Quarterly Journal of Economics*, 82(4): 537–60.
Sraffa, P. (1926) 'The Laws of Returns Under Competitive Conditions', *Economic Journal*, 36: 535–50.
Stark, W. (1968) 'A Note on Rosa Luxemburg', in R. Luxemburg, *Accumulation of Capital*. (New York: Monthly Review Press).
Steindl, J. (1981a) 'Some Comments on the Three Versions of Kalecki's Theory of the Trade Cycle', in N. Assorodobraj-Kula *et al.* (eds) *Studies in Economic Theory and Practice* (Amsterdam: North-Holland).
Steindl, J. (1981b) 'Ideas and Concepts of Long Run Growth?, *Banca Nazionale del Lavoro Quarterly Review*, 136 (March): 35–48.
Steindl, J. (1985) 'J. M. Keynes: Society and the Economist', in F. Vicarelli (ed.) pp.99–125.
Steindl, J. (1987) 'Kalecki's Theory of Pricing: Notes on the Margin', in G. Fink, G. Poll, and M. Riese (eds) *Economic Theory, Political Power and Social Justice* (Vienna: Springer-Verlag).
Sweezy, P. M. (1942) *Theory of Capitalist Development*. (New York: Oxford University Press).
Thirwall, A. P. (ed.) (1978) *Keynes and Laissez-Faire* (London: Macmillan).
Tinbergen, J. (1935) 'Annual Survey: Suggestions on Quantitative Business Cycle Theory', *Econometrica*, 3: 241–308.
Tobin, J. (1981) 'Review of Patinkin *Keynes' Monetary Thought*', *Journal of Political Economy*, 89(1): 204–7.
Vellupillai, K. (1982) 'Linear and Nonlinear Dynamics in Economics: The Contributions of Richard Goodwin', *Economic Notes*, 11 (3): 73–91.
Vicarelli, F. (ed.) (1985) *Keynes's Relevance Today* (Philadelphia: University of Pennsylvania Press).

Worswick, D. (1977) 'Kalecki at Oxford, 1940–44', *Oxford Bulletin of Economics and Statistics* (Special Issue: Michal Kalecki Memorial Lectures), 39(1): 19–29.

Worswick, D. (1985) 'Jobs for All?' *Economic Journal*, 95: 1–14.

Worswick, D. and J. Trevithick (eds) (1983) *Keynes and the Modern World* (Cambridge: Cambridge University Press).

2 Involuntary Unemployment and Imperfect Competition: A Game-theoretic Macromodel

John Roberts*

The purpose of this chapter is to suggest that the methodology of non-cooperative game theory, which is so prominent in partial equilibrium analyses of imperfectly competitive markets, can fruitfully be adopted to study traditional macroeconomic issues that have usually been approached via non-strategic general equilibrium models or treated solely as disequilibrium phenomena.

The essence of these game-theoretic methods is to specify much more carefully than is standard in macro- and general equilibrium economics the range of possible actions available to agents, the timing of these actions, the information available at any decision point, and the consequences of *all* possible sets of decisions, not just those that correspond to some notion of equilibrium behavior. The result is models that correspond to quite specific institutional settings and so may appear less general than more traditional treatments. On the other hand, these models can generate, *in equilibrium*, important, interesting features that are inconsistent with equilibrium in traditional models.

To illustrate this claim, I study an extremely simple, closed model in which price formation is explicitly modelled and prices and wages are fully flexible, all agents perceive correctly the exact structure of the economy and hold expectations that are fully rational, and yet equilibrium can involve involuntary unemployment.

By involuntary unemployment, I simply mean that at the current prices and wages, the willingness of firms to hire constrains the amount of labor that some or all workers are able to sell, and these workers would be better off if this constraint did not bind. This preference need not be contingent on the workers' being able to purchase additional output if their employment is increased. In particular, they might be happy to work more even if they

* The encouragement of George Feiwel, the comments of Andrew Atkeson, Jean-Pascal Benassy, Frank Hahn, Guy Laroque, Nancy Stokey, and the participants in the NBER 1986 Summer Institute group on Economic Fluctuations led by Russell Cooper, and the financial support of the National Science Foundation (grants SES 83-08723 and SES 86-05666) are appreciated.

were unable to convert their earnings into normal consumption goods and had to hold them as commodity money.

Unemployment arises here because of a failure of effective demand, which in turn arises out of a coordination failure. Along with the unemployment equilibria there can also be Pareto-superior, full-employment equilibria at the same prices. However, given the unemployment equilibrium, no agent finds it individually worthwhile to shift his or her behavior. In particular, given the prices and wages, no individual incentives exist to increase hiring, because there is no profitable market for additional output. Nor are there individual incentives to alter the prices and wages. Given equilibrium at low levels of activity, full employment can be achieved only by coordinated, concerted action by several agents simultaneously (or by outside intervention); several firms would have to increase their hiring together in order for there to be sufficient income generated to increase demand and justify the extra hiring. But no agent finds it worthwhile to carry out his or her part of such an expansion unless he/she is sufficiently sure that the others will do theirs, and the decentralized institutions of price setting and exchange do not provide a mechanism to coordinate actions in this way.

This approach to generating involuntary unemployment is certainly not new (see, e.g., Clower, 1965; Leijonhufvud, 1968). Moreover, these kinds of ideas have been formally modelled elsewhere. Examples include Barro and Grossman's (1971) disequilibrium analysis or the fix-price analyses originated by Benassy (1973) and Drèze (1975) and discussed in Malinvaud (1977) and Benassy (1982). Indeed, much of the latter sort of analysis reappears within our models. The crucial difference here is that we model these ideas as equilibrium phenomena in a context where prices and wages are not exogenously specified but rather may be freely varied if incentives exist to do so. In particular, prices and wages in our models are directly chosen by individual maximizing agents who accurately forecast the quantity responses that any price–wage vector will elicit. Thus, for example, if lowering wages were profitable in the presence of unemployment, it would occur. The fact that unemployment is an equilibrium phenomenon means such incentives are absent.

The work that is closest in spirit to ours is probably that of Benassy (1977), Hahn (1978), and Negishi (1979), which achieves involuntary unemployment with flexible prices in the context of perceived demand curves. The chief points of contrast are that we model explicitly the formation of these demand perceptions and require that they be correct globally, not just at or near the chosen point.

Our work also relates to the large literature that has appeared recently on coordination failures in non-Walrasian market settings as a source of economic inefficiency. Examples include Diamond (1982), Hart (1982), Weitzman (1982), Bryant (1983), d'Aspremont, Dos Santos Ferreira, and

Gerard-Varet (1984), Cooper and John (1985), Heller (1986), and Roberts (1986). In contrast with most of this work, we obtain actual involuntary unemployment, with workers off their labor supply curves, rather than just equilibria with full but inefficiently low employment.[1] The key to our obtaining such equilibria seems to be our thoroughgoing game-theoretic approach: we do not assume that Walrasian auctioneers set any prices or wages, and we are careful to specify what happens 'out of equilibrium'. This latter specification determines the impact of deviating from the prescribed behavior and ensures that individuals cannot gain by such deviations.

Because prices and wages are choice variables and those choosing them recognize and exploit any monopoly or monopsony power they may have, our analysis is in the spirit of imperfectly competitive (general) equilibrium theory, as well as being an exercise in the theory of macroeconomic equilibrium. Of course, the theories of imperfect competition and of unemployment equilibrium were two of the earliest subjects to which Joan Robinson made important contributions. Thus, it seems fitting to offer an essay on the intersection of these topics for a volume dedicated to her, even though (following Keynes) she did not make imperfect competition a central feature of her macroeconomic theory.

1 OVERVIEW

The specification of a model in the present context is a three-step process. In the first step we describe the fundamental data of the set of agents and their tastes, endowments, technology, and information. This sort of specification of the economic environment is familiar in standard general equilibrium theory. The second step involves specification of the institutions for communication, price determination, and exchange in the economy. This defines the game being played between the agents. Of course, many such specifications could be made, and different models would result. Finally, given this game, we specify a solution concept for it, thereby determining the nature of behavior. Here there seems much less freedom of choice in the specification: if we do not specify Nash equilibrium (or some refinement thereof), we would be positing a theory of behavior which, if understood and accepted by the participants in the economy, would generate behavior contradicting the theory.

The models we consider involve two classes of economic agents, capitalists (or firms) and workers, and three types of goods. The first class of goods consists of types of (labor) inputs, the second consists of consumption-good outputs, and the third of a single, universally desired, non-produced good. Each agent (capitalist or worker) has an endowment of goods, a consumption set, and preferences over this set, just as in the standard Arrow–Debreu model. Capitalists also have direct access to the technology for producing outputs from inputs; we may think of this as arising from their being endowed with unmodelled and unmarketed inputs. Information about how to carry out production is a possible example here.

The institutions we consider involve using the distinguished, universally desired good as both the medium of exchange and the unit of account. Thus, we refer to it as money. All transactions will involve exchange of inputs or outputs for money, and all prices will be in terms of money (whose own price is thus unity); goods do not trade directly against one another. In these institutions, capitalists will first simultaneously and independently announce the prices at which they will sell the outputs they can produce and the wages they will pay for inputs they can employ. Workers, knowing these prices, then make simultaneous and independent announcements regarding the amounts of outputs they wish to purchase from each capitalist and the amounts of their endowments of inputs they wish to sell to each. Given these announcements, the capitalists then simultaneously and independently select the fractions of the amount of input offered by each worker to buy from him or her and the fractions of the stated output demands to fulfil, subject to the constraints of technological feasibility. The chosen amounts of inputs are then delivered, production is instantaneously carried out, outputs are distributed, payments are made in terms of money, and consumption occurs. (We will also discuss some variants of these institutions.)

Given a method of determining the allocation in the event that an agent cannot pay for his or her contracted transactions (a bankruptcy rule), a specification of the actions by each agent at each stage gives rise to an allocation, and the agents' preferences (represented by utility functions) determine the pay-offs. Thus, given a specification of the information available to the agents, we have an extensive form non-cooperative game, and we look for (pure-strategy) subgame perfect Nash equilibria (Selten, 1975) in this game. Such equilibria specify choices for each agent at each decision point which, given the others' strategies, maximize the agent's pay-off as evaluated from that point forward. Thus, agents are forming and executing plans that are best-responses to one another in every eventuality, not just those that arise under some putative equilibrium behavior.

In these games, as in most models of non-cooperative exchange (see Shubik, 1984), it is easy to obtain equilibria in which there is no trade whatsoever because no one expects there to be any demand on any market at any price. While such equilibria are not without interest in the present context, we are also interested in finding equilibria with positive levels of economic activity. Despite the well-known difficulties with existence of (pure-strategy) equilibria in imperfectly competitive models (Roberts and Sonnenschein, 1977), we give conditions under which equilibria with full employment do exist, and we show that involuntary unemployment can arise in the class of economies we consider any time we have an equilibrium under the given institutions.

These examples involve relatively strong assumptions. First, capitalists get utility only from money. This makes profit maximization and utility maximization coincide and eliminates any feedback from the distribution of profits onto workers' incomes and the supply and demand for inputs and outputs.[2] Second, workers alone supply inputs and there is no initial endowment of the outputs. Together with the preceding assumption on capitalists, this means that no agent is ever on both sides of a market. Third, each agent is endowed with 'sufficiently large' amounts of money, and negative money holdings bring very large disutility. This obviates the need for complicated bankruptcy rules. Finally, and most significantly, if a worker can supply an input that is used in producing a particular output, then he or she does not consume that output. Such an assumption is obviously extreme, but it may not be completely unrealistic in a modern advanced economy with millions of different consumption goods, where workers specialize in employment but generalize in their consumption activities. With this assumption, an individual firm cannot increase the effective demand for its product simply by increasing its employment or wage, because these variables do not influence its customers' incomes. Similarly, the amounts of labor offered to the firm are not directly dependent on its output price and production level. These effects seem crucial to obtaining involuntary unemployment in equilibrium.

2 IMPERFECTLY COMPETITIVE UNEMPLOYMENT EQUILIBRIUM

Consider an economy with two capitalists, A and B, two workers, J and K, two inputs, R and S, and two outputs, X and Y, as well as commodity money, M. The capitalists hold endowments $\bar{m}_A$ and $\bar{m}_B$ of money and have utility functions $V_A(x,y,r,s,m) = U_A(m)$ and $V_B(s,y,r,s,m) = U_B(m)$. Capitalist A controls a production function f_A for turning R into X, while B can turn S into Y via the production function f_B. Assume f_A and f_B are both strictly increasing, with $f_A(0) = f_B(0) = 0$. Worker J holds an endowment $\bar{r}_J$ of input R and $\bar{m}_J$ of money and has utility $V_J(x,y,r,s,m) = U_J(y,\bar{r}_J - r,m)$, while K is endowed with $\bar{s}_K$ and $\bar{m}_K$ and has utility $U_K(x,\bar{s}_K - s,m)$. Thus, J can sell input to A and buy output from B, while K can supply input to B and buy from A.

The first and simplest institutions of the economy that we consider are the following. First, A announces a price p_X for output X and a wage w_R for input R, and, simultaneously, B announces p_Y and w_B. Next, J announces amounts of $\hat{y}_J$ output Y and $\hat{r}_J$ of input R and K simultaneously announces

$\hat{x}_K$ and $\hat{s}_K$. These are interpreted as offers to buy and sell. Their values can be conditioned on the announced levels values of p_X, p_Y, w_R, and w_S. Finally, A selects $r_A \leqslant \hat{r}_J$ and $x_A \leqslant \hat{x}_K$ with $x_A \leqslant f_A(r_A)$, while B selects $s_B \leqslant \hat{s}_K$ and $y_B \leqslant \hat{y}_J$ with $y_B \leqslant f_B(s_B)$. These are the amounts of the workers' supplies and demands that are met, and can be conditioned on the price–wage vector as well as the workers' announcements. The resultant distribution of goods is

$$m_A = p_X x_A - w_R r_A + \bar{m}_A;\ m_B = p_Y y_B - w_S s_B + \bar{m}_B;$$

$$y_J = y_B,\ r_J = \bar{r}_J - r_A,\ m_J = \bar{m}_J + w_R r_A - p_Y y_B;$$

$$x_K = x_A,\ s_K = \bar{s}_K - s_B,\ m_K = \bar{m}_K + w_S s_B - p_X x_A.$$

We allow that m_i may be negative, but assume that negative money holdings bring utility that is an arbitrarily large negative number.

These institutions define a game. A strategy for worker J in this game is a map $\sigma_J(p_X,w_R,p_Y,w_S) = (\hat{y}_J(p_X,w_R,p_Y,w_S))$, $(\hat{r}_J(p_X,w_R,p_Y,w_S))$, and, correspondingly, a strategy σ_K for K is a pair of quantity announcements for each price–wage vector. A strategy σ_A for A is a pair (p_X,w_R) and, for each $(p_X,w_R,p_Y,w_S,\hat{x}_K,\hat{y}_J,\hat{r}_J,\hat{s}_K)$, a pair (x_A,r_A) satisfying $x_A \leqslant \hat{x}_K$, $r_A \leqslant \hat{r}_J$, $x_A \leqslant f_A(r_A)$. A strategy σ_B for B is, correspondingly, a price–wage pair (p_Y,w_S) and, for each vector of prices and worker quantity announcements, an input–output pair satisfying the feasibility requirements.

An equilibrium is a strategy for each agent with the following properties:

1. For all $(p_X,w_R,p_Y,w_S,\hat{x},\hat{y},\hat{r},\hat{s})$, the pair (x_A,r_A) specified by σ_A maximizes $p_X x - w_R r$ subject to $x \leqslant \hat{x}$, $r \leqslant \hat{r}$, and $x \leqslant f_A(r)$, and the pair (y_B,s_B) specified by σ_B maximizes $p_Y y - w_S s$ subject to $y \leqslant \hat{y}$, $s \leqslant \hat{s}$, and $y \leqslant f_B(s)$.

2. For all (p_X,w_R,p_Y,w_S), the pair $(\hat{y}_J,\hat{r}_J)$ given by σ_J maximizes $U_J(y,\bar{r}_J - r,m)$, given σ_K and given that actual quantities will be determined by σ_A *and* σ_B *as in 1; similarly, the pair* $(\hat{x}_K,\hat{s}_K)$ given by σ_K maximizes $U_K(x,\bar{s}_K - s,m)$, given σ_J, σ_A, and σ_B.

3. The pair (p_X,w_R) given by σ_A maximizes $U_A(\bar{m}_A + px_A - wr_A)$, given that B selects (p_Y,w_S) according to σ_B and that the quantities x_A and r_A will be determined by σ_A, σ_B, σ_J, and σ_K according to 1 and 2. Similarly, the pair (p_Y,w_S) given by σ_B is optimal for B.

Condition 1 just says each capitalist always makes optimal input–output decisions, given the prices and wages and given the amount of labor offered and output demanded. Condition 2 says that each worker optimizes in his/her quantity choices, given the prevailing price–wage vector, the choices he/she (correctly) expects the other worker to make, and the resultant, correctly forecast, input–output responses from the capitalists. Finally, 3 says that each capitalist optimally selects his/her price and wage pair, while correctly forecasting the other's price–wage decision and the final quantities the various possible choices bring forth.

To find an equilibrium, we start at the last stage. Here A will select x_A and r_A to maximize $p_X x - w_R r$ subject to $x \leqslant x_K$, $r \leqslant \hat{r}_J$, and $x \leqslant f_A(r)$. For example, if $f_A(r) = r$, the optimum is $x_A = r_A = 0$ if $p_X < w_R$; if $p_X > w_R$, it is $x_A = r_A$. $= \min[\hat{x}_K, \hat{r}_J]$; and $p_X = w_R$, then any pair (x_A, r_A) with $x_A = r_A$ and $x_A \leqslant \hat{x}_K$, $r_A \leqslant \hat{r}_J$ is optimizing. Optimal values for (y_B, s_B), given the prices, wages, and workers' choices, are determined correspondingly. Note that there is no real strategic interdependence between the firms at this stage.

Now consider the workers' problems of selecting their quantities. This analysis is more complicated, because each worker must forecast the other's choice in order to determine what choices the capitalists will make and thus how much of any offers and orders will be accepted. The workers' problems do have a simultaneous solution, however, as a simple fixed point argument shows. Note that in many cases this solution will involve rationing. For example, J's offer $\hat{r}_J$ places an upper bound of $f_A(\hat{r}_J)$ on x_A and thus on x_K, while $\hat{y}_J$ places an upper bound of $f_B^{-1}(\hat{y}_J)$ on S_B and s_K. Note too that the workers are, rationing aside, price-takers, just as in Walrasian models. Also, their choices are made in a fix-price environment much like that considered by Benassy (1973), Drèze (1975), Malinvaud (1977), and others.

Finally, at the first stage, the capitalists select the prices and wages, given the output-demand and input-supply correspondences that are defined by the equilibrium quantities in the various subgames induced by different price and wage choices. Such behavior is imperfectly competitive, with each capitalist fully recognizing the demand and supply responses his/her choices generate. However, these responses are a property of the equilibrium, because they depend on the workers' forecasts of one another's offers. This point is seen in the following proposition.

Proposition 1: Let $(\bar{p}_X, \bar{w}_R, \bar{p}_Y, \bar{w}_S)$ be arbitrary. Specify the input–output response of A, $\sigma_A(p_X, w_R, p_Y, w_S, \hat{x}, \hat{y}, \hat{r}, \hat{s})$ as the solution of $\max p_X x - w_R r$ subject to $x \leqslant \hat{x}$, $r \leqslant \hat{r}$, and $x \leqslant f_A(r)$, and specify $\sigma_B(p_X, w_R, p_Y, w_S, \hat{x}, \hat{y}, \hat{r}, \hat{s})$ correspondingly. Let $\sigma_J(p_X, w_R, p_Y, w_S) = \sigma_K(p_X, w_R, p_Y, w_S) \equiv (0,0)$. Then the strategies of A's announcing $(\bar{p}_X, \bar{w}_R)$ and B's announcing $(\bar{p}_Y, \bar{w}_S)$, the workers' responding with σ_J and σ_K, and the firm's responding with σ_A and σ_B constitute an equilibrium.

Proof: Obviously, neither A nor B individually can gain in any situation by altering the hiring and output decision. Further, no matter what the prices and wages, neither worker can gain by unilaterally deviating from the prescribed strategies: Because the firm to whom a worker offers labor receives no demand for output, and the one from whom a worker demands output is offered no labor supply, the firms' choices will still be (0,0). Thus, any price–wage choices result in zero profits, so there is no incentive to change prices or wages.

This sort of equilibrium has been called 'trivial' in other non-cooperative models of exchange (e.g. Shubik, 1984). While it is indeed trivial from the point of view of existence, it is not necessarily without interest because it shows that equilibrium need not involve market clearing. However, it would be uninteresting if this were the only sort of equilibrium which our model admitted, because we want to generate unemployment in a context where non-zero employment is also a possible equilibrium. The following propositions establish conditions for this.

Proposition 2: Suppose there exists (p_X,w_R,p_Y,w_S) and (x_K,s_K,y_J,r_J) satisfying

1. x_K, s_K maximizes $U_K(s,\bar{s}_K-s,\bar{m}_K-p_Xx+w_Ss)$;
2. y_J, r_J maximizes $U_J(y,\bar{r}_J-r,\bar{m}_J-p_Yy+w_Rr)$;
3. x_K, r_J maximizes p_Xx-w_Rr subject to $x\leqslant x_K$, $r\leqslant r_J$, $x\leqslant f_A(r)$;
4. y_J, s_K maximizes p_Yy-w_Ss subject to $y\leqslant y_J$, $s\leqslant s_K$, $y\leqslant f_B(s)$.

Then there exists an equilibrium in which the firms select (p_X,w_r) and (p_Y,w_S), the consumers respond to these prices and wages with (y_J,r_J) and (x_K,s_K), and the firms hire and produce at these full-employment levels.

Proof: Specify the strategies for the firms as selecting the given prices and wages, (p_X,w_R) and (p_Y,w_S), and as responding to any vector of prices and wages and of quantities from consumers by making the profit-maximizing choices given these prices and wages and the constraints implied by the consumers' announcements. For consumers, let them respond to the specified prices and wages with their utility-maximizing choices, (x_K,s_K) and (y_J,r_J), and let each respond to any other values for prices and wages with (0,0). Clearly these strategies constitute an equilibrium with full employment.

Proposition 3: Suppose $\sigma'=(\sigma'_A,\sigma'_B,\sigma'_J,\sigma'_K)$ is an equilibrium with prices and wages (p'_X,p'_Y,w'_R,w'_S) which results in a quantity vector $(x'_K,y'_J,r'_J,s'_K)\gg 0$. Then there exists an equilibrium σ'' with the same prices and wages which yields a quantity vector $(x''_K,y''_J,r''_J,s''_K)\ll(x'_K,y'_J,r'_J,s'_K)$. In particular, $x''_K=y''_J=r''_J=s''_K=0$ is one such.

Proof: Given the equilibrium σ', define the strategies σ''_A and σ''_B by $\sigma''_A=\sigma'_A$ and $\sigma''_B=\sigma'_B$. As well, define $\sigma''_J\equiv(0,0)$ and $\sigma''_K\equiv(0,0)$ for all (p_x,w_R,p_Y,w_S). Then clearly σ'' is an equilibrium.

The equilibrium σ'' in Proposition 3 involves unemployed resources and captures something of the idea of effective demand failure. Given that workers do not expect to find either employment or consumption goods, neither finds it worthwhile to offer to buy output or sell input. Even if one of the workers were to announce, say, his or her competitive input-supply and output-demand at some price vector, the capitalists would still not respond positively, since the one still has no demand for its output, though it is offered input, and the other is offered no input and so cannot meet the demand it is offered.

The unemployment in Propositions 1 and 3 is involuntary in that both workers are off their competitive demand curves at the prevailing prices: each is consuming less output and selling less input than he/she would like. However, involuntary employment in the sense of some workers being constrained in this fashion while others are not is not present here. For a model in which this occurs, see Roberts (1987).

Proposition 2 is not vacuous: for example, if Walrasian prices, wages, and quantities exist they would satisfy its conditions. Perhaps of greater relevance are imperfectly competitive outcomes. For example, Roberts (1986) studies a set-up like the present one in which $f_A(z)=f_B(z)=z$, $\bar{r}_J=\bar{m}_J=\bar{s}_K=\bar{m}_K=\alpha$, and $U_J(z,\alpha-t,m)=U_K(z,\alpha-t,m)=z+\ln(\alpha-t)+\ln(m)$. In this case, the Walrasian price–wage vector is $p_X=p_Y=w_R=w_S=\alpha$ and the activity levels are $x=y=r=s=\alpha-1$ (assuming $\alpha>1$). Now consider the prices and wages defined by

$$p_X=p_Y=p(\alpha)=\frac{\alpha[\Gamma+\sqrt{\Gamma^2-4(2\alpha+4)\Delta}]}{2\Delta}$$

$$w_R=w_S=w(\alpha)=\frac{(2+\alpha)}{2\alpha}p(\alpha)-\frac{1}{2}-\frac{1}{2\alpha}\sqrt{\alpha^2(1-p(\alpha))^2-4\alpha p(\alpha)+4p(\alpha)^2},$$

where

$$\Gamma=5\alpha^2+16\alpha+16$$

and

$$\Delta=(2\alpha^3+5\alpha^2+8\alpha+16).$$

The corresponding quantities from the workers' Walrasian demands and supplies are all equal to

$$[\alpha w(\alpha)-p(\alpha)]/w(\alpha).$$

This outcome is supported by an equilibrium of the form in Proposition 2. Moreover, it also arises from the unique equilibrium when the institutions are modified to require that firms hire all of the output offered to them (see Roberts, 1986). The arguments in Proposition 2 do not apply in this latter context, because at high enough wages workers will supply labor even if they do not expect to be able to buy output. This eliminates the zero-activity outcomes at such wages, and, in some cases at least, means that equilibrium must involve full employment. However, existence of equilibrium becomes problematic because of the possible lack of both concavity and continuity for the profit functions. Finally, the outcome here is also that which would be found in more standard imperfectly competitive models in which each firm is assumed to pick its price and wage to maximize profits, assuming that quantities will be determined by the quantity-unconstrained, Walrasian, labor supply and output demand functions.

It is worth noting that $p(\alpha)$ and $w(\alpha)$ are both less than α for all $\alpha > 1$: imperfect competition leads to lower money prices and wages than does perfect competition, although, of course, the price–wage ratio is increased. For example, when $\alpha = 2$, we obtain $p_X = p_Y = 1.727607$ and $w_R = w_S = 1.106339$, with $x = y = r = s = 0.438447$. In contrast, the Walrasian prices and wages are 2 and the activity level is 1. This occurs because the locus of (p_X, p_Y, w_R, w_S)-values where supplies and demands are equal intersects the plane $p_X = p_Y$, $w_R = w_S$ in a line segment that is upward sloping for $p \geqslant w$. Moreover, as $\alpha \to \infty$, the equilibrium prices converge from above to $p = 2$, wages converge to zero, and the fraction of the endowment of R and S used in production approaches $\frac{1}{2}$, while in the Walrasian allocation, this fraction approaches unity. Thus, as might be expected, the effect of imperfect competition is to reduce the level of economic activity. However, this equilibrium does not involve involuntary unemployment, in that J and K are both unconstrained in equilibrium and consume their competitive, utility-maximizing bundles at the non-competitive prices.

By Proposition 3, for each α there is also a symmetric equilibrium with the same prices as given above, but with $x = y = r = s = 0$. It is interesting to note that the equilibrium value of $(p(\alpha), w(\alpha))$, the common value of the capitalists' price–wage levels, lies in the region which, in the canonical fix-price macromodel (Malinvaud, 1977; Benassy, 1982) is identified with repressed inflation.

While Proposition 3 gives involuntary unemployment in a severe form, it will often be the case that equilibria with less extreme inefficiencies also exist.

Proposition 4: Let $\sigma' = (\sigma'_A, \sigma'_B, \sigma'_J, \sigma'_K)$ be an equilibrium with prices and wages (p'_X, p'_Y, w'_R, w'_S) and activity levels (x', y', r', s'). Let $x'' < x'$, $y'' < y'$, $r'' = f_A^{-1}(x'') < r'$, $s'' = f_B^{-1}(y'') < s'$. Suppose (x'', s'') solves

$$\max_{x,s} U_K(x, \bar{s}_K - s, \bar{m}_K - p'_x x + w'_s s)$$

$$\text{subject to } x \leqslant \min(x'', f_A(r''))$$
$$s \leqslant \min(s'', f_B^{-1}(y''))$$

and, simultaneously, (y'', r'') solves

$$\max_{y,r} U_J(y, \bar{r}_J - r, \bar{m}_J - p'_Y y + w'_R r)$$

$$\text{subject to } y \leqslant \min(y'', f_B(s''))$$
$$r \leqslant \min(r'', f_A^{-1}(x'')).$$

Further, suppose $p'_X \partial f_A(r)/\partial r \geqslant w'_R$ and $p'_Y \partial f_B(s)/\partial s \geqslant w'_S$ for all $r \leqslant r''$ and $s \leqslant s''$. Then there is an equilibrium σ'' with prices (p'_X, p'_Y, w'_R, w'_S) and activity levels (x'', y'', r'', s'').

Proof: The simplest proof involves setting $\sigma''_J(p_X, w_R, p_Y, w_S) = (y'', r'')$ and $\sigma''_K(p_X, w_R, p_Y, w_S) = (x'', r'')$ for $(p_X, p_Y, w_R, w_S) = (p'_X, p'_Y, w'_R, w'_S)$ and zero for all other price--wage vectors. The condition on the values of the marginal products ensures that the firms will choose (x'', r'') and (y'', s'').

Note that Proposition 3 is actually a corollary of Proposition 4, since the zero offers automatically satisfy the requirements on (x'', y'', r'', s''). More generally, what is needed is that, at $(x'', \bar{s}_K - s'', \bar{m}_K - p'_X x'' + w'_S s'')$, we have $\partial U_K/\partial x - p'_X \partial U_K/\partial m > 0$ and $\partial U_K/\partial s - w'_S \partial U_K/\partial m < 0$, and correspondingly for J at $(y'', \bar{r}_J - r'', \bar{m}_J - p'_Y y'' + w'_R r'')$, as well as the conditions on marginal products. Thus, given the anticipated constraints, neither worker wishes to reduce further either his/her output purchases or input sales below their already lower-than-optimal levels, and both firms want to produce up to the constraints they face on inputs and outputs.

3 CONTINUOUS PERCEIVED QUANTITIES

A reasonable complaint regarding the preceding results is the dependence of the arguments on maximally pessimistic beliefs: all price and wage changes are unprofitable because they are expected to yield zero-activity. Of course, these expectations are correct in that zero-activity is an equilibrium response to such price and wage choices. Nevertheless, the strong role played in the proofs by convenient discontinuities in the outcomes as a function of prices and wages is troublesome.

Benassy (1977), Hahn (1978), and Negishi (1979) have provided models of equilibrium unemployment with price-setting in which the perceived price–quantity relationships are continuous (but, in essence, kinked). However, these perceptions are not required to be globally correct: if firms were to change their prices, the resulting quantities might not turn out to be those that had been expected. Thus, equilibrium in these models may rest on fortuitous errors in perceptions.

In this section we begin exploring the extent to which we can obtain unemployment equilibria with perceived price–quantity relationships that are both continuous and globally correct. Throughout the section we will work with the specific example given above, further restricted by assuming $\alpha = 2$.

Proposition 5: Let $0 \leqslant \bar{x} \leqslant q^*$, $0 \leqslant \bar{y} \leqslant q^*$, where $q^* = q(2) \simeq 0.438447$. Let $\bar{x}$, $\bar{y}$ satisfy

$$\bar{x} \leqslant (p^*\bar{y} + 2w^* - 2)/2w^* \text{ and } \bar{y} \leqslant (p^*\bar{x} + 2w^* - 2)/2w^*$$

where $p^* = p(2) \simeq 1.728339$ and $w^* = w(2) \simeq 1.106339$. Then there exists an equilibrium in which $p_X = p_Y = p^*$, $w_R = w_S = w^*$, $x_A = r_A = \bar{x}$ and $y_B = s_B = \bar{y}$. Further, the quantity choices specified by the equilibrium strategies are continuous functions of each firm's price and wage choices, given the equilibrium price and wage announcements of the other firm.

Proof: First, note that if J expects to be able to purchase at most $\bar{y}$ of Y and sell at most $r = \bar{x}$ of R, then for any price p_Y and wage $w_R \geqslant 1$, J will offer at most $(p_Y\bar{y} + 2w_R - 2)/2w_R$ of R and will order at most $(w_R\bar{x} + w_R - p_Y)/p_Y$ of Y, while if $w_R < 1$, then the maximum labor offer is as given above if $\bar{y} \geqslant 2(1 - w_R)/p_Y$, and otherwise it is zero. The expressions for K are exactly parallel.

Then, to yield an equilibrium outcome in the subgame given p_X, w_R, p_Y and w_S with $p_X \geqslant w_R \geqslant 1$, $p_Y \geqslant w_S \geqslant 1$, it is sufficient that the announced quantities x', y', r', and s' satisfy

$$x = r = \min\{x', r'\}$$

$$y = s = \min\{y', s'\}$$

$$r' \leqslant (p_Y y + 2w_R - 2)/2w_R$$

$$y' \leqslant (w_R r + 2 - p_Y)/p_Y$$

$$s' \leqslant (p_X x + 2w_S - 2)/2w_S$$

$$x' \leqslant (w_S s + 2 - p_X)/p_X.$$

To see this, note that the firms' behavior will be optimal if the first two conditions are met, while the consumers are correctly forecasting each other's and the firms' choices if the four inequalities hold.

The set of announcements meeting these conditions for $p_X = p_Y = 1.728707$, $w_R = w_S = 1.10639$ is a convex polyhedron with non-empty interior in the positive orthant of R^4. Further, the constraints on x' and y' do not bind at any point in this set other than $x = r = y = s = q^*$. Thus, given that the firms select $p_X = p_Y = p^*$, $w_R = w_S = w^*$, any vector of choices meeting the conditions assumed in the statement is an equilibrium outcome for the play following the choice of these price and wage levels.

Now we must specify the quantities that arise if one of the producers, say A, charges a price and wage different from $p_X = p^*$, $w_R = w^*$. We must do this in such a fashion that the choices constitute subgame equilibria, that A does not find it profitable to make such a choice in preference to (p^*, w^*), and that the quantities depend continuously on p_X and w_R given $p_Y = p^*$, $w_S = w^*$.

We might naturally ask that the demand curve we define for X in this fashion be decreasing in p_X, that the supply of R be increasing in w_R, and that an increase in w_R coupled with a decrease in p_X would increase A's maximum possible output. However, this last desideratum may turn out to be inconsistent with subgame equilibrium in this economy because of cross-effects of prices on equilibrium labor supply. In particular, although the effective demands and supplies are nicely behaved, if we start from quantities that are close to the full-employment level q^*, then a reduction in p_X may necessitate a fall in activity levels. The reason is that, although lowering p_X increases the maximum amount of X that K would order given his perceived constraints (so that demand slopes down), it also lowers his offer of S. Given that y must equal s, this requires a fall in B's output and thus in the amount J can hope to purchase. This in turn lowers the amount of R that J will supply, thereby reducing the maximum feasible level of production for A.

Moreover, an increase in w_R need not allow any increase in A's activity. Increasing w_R does increase both the maximum amounts of R that J will offer and of Y that he will order. This means that there can be subgame equilibria with higher activity levels, because if J does offer and order more and the constraints on K were strictly binding at the original situation, then in equilibrium K will also demand and supply more. However, at q^*, no such increase would be forthcoming from K, because the constraints on K's choices of X and S were not strictly binding. In any case, the original quantities continue to constitute an equilibrium if w_R is increased.

Given this, we specify that if A raises w_R alone, there is no change in quantities and, if A lowers p_X, then quantities remain constant unless they must fall to satisfy the equilibrium conditions. Obviously, then, there is no advantage either to charging $p_X = p^*$ and $w_R > w^*$ or to charging $p_X < p^*$.

If A raises p_X, K's effective demand for X falls independent of any changes in w_R. As long as we specify that the actual level of X transacted then falls sufficiently rapidly as p_X is increased, there is no incentive to raise price. Note that we can do this because the set of potential equilibrium quantities is convex and contains the origin. Similarly, if A lowers w_R, then J's offer of R falls independent of any changes in p_X, and by the same argument we can specify that the decrease in the amount A actually can produce and sell is sufficiently great to ensure that there is no incentive to deviate.

A parallel construction ensures that B will not deviate from (p^*,w^*), given that A is choosing this price–wage pair. Finally, we can specify any quantities that constitute subgame equilibria for the remaining price–wage vectors, where both firms are deviating from p^*, w^*. This step may perhaps introduce other equilibria, but it does not upset the equilibrium constructed.

The perceived relationship between prices, wages, and quantities in this equilibrium is unconventional in that price cuts reduce quantities. It is worth noting, however, that this is in no sense artificial. The direct effect of the price cut is still to increase effective demand; the effect on final quantities is forced on us by the indirect effects of the price cut working through effective labor supplies. Note too that the difficulties arise only if $\bar{x}$ is close to the full employment level q^*: if $\bar{x}$ is sufficiently below q^*, then we could allow A's production actually to increase as p_A is cut (although, of course, too rapid an increase would be incompatible with equilibrium).

4 RELATIONSHIP TO FIX-PRICE EQUILIBRIA

The explicit introduction of constraints on the worker's choices highlights the connection of this work with that on fix-price, quantity-constrained equilibria. In the present treatment, all agents make their quantity choices in a fixed-price, quantity-constrained context. The capitalists are explicitly constrained by the amounts of labor offered and output demanded from them, while each worker effectively perceives constraints on the transactions he/she can realize as a result of the capitalists' optimizing responses to the quantity choices of the other worker. Note that the constraints in our set-up are thus of two different sorts. Those facing the capitalists in their quantity choices involve feasibility and the voluntary exchange assumption that agents are not obliged to trade greater amounts than they choose. When the capitalists' quantity choices are actually made, these constraints are objective realities. The constraints perceived by the workers, however, depend on the beliefs or conjectures they hold about the actions that are being or will be taken by other agents. Any specification of these conjectures then gives rise to perceived constraints, and it becomes a condition of equilibrium that these conjectures be confirmed, so that perceived and actual limits on choices coincide. In this case, the constraints appear in equilibrium as functions of the actual choices, but their correct status is as functions of the conjectured behavior.

In the standard fix-price, quantity-constraint models, the constraints are expressed as functions only of the agents' actual quantity choices. Thus, it is logically possible in these models for a change in the choice of one worker to affect the constraint perceived by another when making his or her choice. Yet the various workers' choices are usually treated in these models as being made simultaneously, so no worker can know the others' choices until his/hers have already been made. Of course, these informational difficulties are finessed in this literature by specifying what happens only when the agents all make their equilibrium choices. Here they are avoided by making the perceived constraints functions of *conjectured* choices, which, in equilibrium, coincide with those actually made.

A second point of contact/contrast with the fix-price literature should be recognized. Recall that in many of the fix-price models (especially those building on Benassy's work), agents are assumed to announce their 'effective' demands and supplies for the various commodities. This concept is defined for each commodity as the quantity of that commodity that maximizes utility, given the budget constraint and the quantity constraints on all commodities *except* the one in question. Effective demands and actual transactions will differ if the prices do not clear markets. In contrast, agents in our treatment are free to announce any quantities they wish, subject only to feasibility and the voluntary-trade constraints on the capitalists. Thus, in particular, they could announce their effective demands, or even larger quantities, if they so choose. However, they also may simply announce the quantities that are utility-maximizing given the full, actual and perceived, constraints (as in Drèze, 1975). These quantities will clearly be at or below the levels of the constraints, and it is such announcements that are specified in the equilibria in the propositions.

Benassy (1982) has argued that it is appropriate to require agents to announce effective demands. He notes that if willingness to buy or sell beyond the constrained amounts is not communicated, then the information relevant to identifying the existence of mutually beneficial bilateral trades will not be transmitted, and such trades will be missed. In such cases, he suggests, it is too easy to obtain unemployment equilibria.

In the present context, requiring agents to announce effective demands seems quite problematic. First, unless one introduces some sort of monitoring and enforcement agency that has no obvious counterpart in real markets, it is hard to see how agents can be forced to make any specific announcements. In particular, other agents in the economy have no obvious incentive to act as monitors and enforcers, because to do so would typically involve costs to them in deviating from optimal quantity choices. Moreover, in our formulation the very definition of effective demands becomes quite subtle and this makes the monitoring task very complicated.

Recall that the constraints that an agent perceives (and would use in computing effective demands) are functions of the agent's conjectures about the actions others will take, and not of these actions directly. Thus, if one assumes that equilibrium obtains, one can tell if the announcements being made correspond to effective demands, but otherwise one generally will not be able to do so.

Nevertheless, it is worth observing that if one worker's realized transactions in a commodity are constrained by the others' announcements then, given the other's announcements, that agent loses nothing (and also gains nothing) by unilaterally increasing the size of his/her announcement. One wonders then whether there are other equilibrium modes of behavior which would involve announcing quantities in excess of binding perceived constraints, which would somehow seem to represent a more reasonable prediction of behavior, and, finally, which would eliminate involuntary unemployment.

A full analysis of this issue is far beyond the scope of this paper. However, a few points are worth noting.

First, the rationality of announcing quantities that are greater than one hopes to be able to trade requires that marginal search and other transactions costs be essentially zero. Only if these costs are negligible (transportation is free, travel time is worthless, phone calls are costless, disappointment conveys no disutility *per se*) is the behavior we have specified not the uniquely rational response to the perceived constraints. Of course, neither our analysis nor the fix-price models explicitly include such costs, and their inclusion might well have pervasive effects on the nature of equilibria, but their reality cannot be doubted.

Second, it is not obvious that announcing larger quantities will either represent more a plausible pattern of behavior or actually change the equilibrium outcome. For example, suppose in the context of the specific example with endowments of $\alpha=2$ and constant returns to scale with input–output coefficients of unity that the Walrasian prices and wages of $p=w=2$ have been announced. Suppose the workers perceive constraints of zero on both their input sales and output purchases. These are strictly below their Walrasian transaction levels. Yet, even ignoring the perceived constraints on output purchases, ordering zero output is uniquely optimal: neither worker wants to buy output unless he/she can sell input, and effective output demands coincide with expected transaction quantities of zero. Thus, even if agents announce effective demands, the zero-activity equilibrium outcome is maintained.[3]

5 EXTENSIONS, DISCUSSION, AND POLICY IMPLICATIONS

The unemployment equilibria we have obtained rest on workers' pessimistic, self-fulfilling expectations regarding demand conditions. Each worker expects not to be hired to work as much as he/she would like and so limits his/her output demands. This in turn means that there is, in fact, little or no demand facing firms, and so they will not hire, thus confirming the workers' expectations. Moreover, firms do not expect that they can generate enough business by changing prices and wages to justify doing so, and these expectations are justified by the workers' pessimism.

While the centrality of self-confirming expectations in our treatment is appealingly in line with the arguments of such scholars as Clower (1965) and Leijonhufvud (1968), the focus on workers' expectations is not. Instead, it is more standard to think of firms' not hiring because they forecast too low demand. This is not a feature of the treatment given above because firms are assumed to receive both labor supply offers and output demands before making their hiring decisions. However, it is a simple matter to modify the models to have workers first offer labor (knowing prices and wages), firms make hiring decisions and pay the workers, workers then express their output demands, and, finally, have firms decide how much of the stated demands to meet.

Considering such a set-up, it is clear that unemployment can again arise given particular prices and wages. Suppose that, at some particular price and wage levels, workers will purchase output if and only if they are employed. Then each firm knows that it will have positive demand if and only if the other hires. Thus, if neither expects the other to hire, neither will forecast any demand for its output, and consequently, not hiring is optimal. Of course, if they could coordinate, so that each expected a positive demand because the other had hired the given firms' customers, then the unemployment equilibrium would be broken. Meanwhile, unemployment arises because firms' pessimistic projections of demand are self-fulfilling.

The issue is whether such prices and wages can be equilibrium choices. The potential difficulty is that, if prices are low enough, workers may demand positive output levels even if they have sold no labor, while if wages are high, they will supply labor even when they expect not to be able to purchase output. Thus, a firm quoting a low price and a high wage can both hire and sell, even if the other does not hire. The problem then is to ensure that firms find such low prices and high wages to be unprofitable. This can be done in certain contexts (see Roberts, 1987).

While this particular change in the institutions does necessarily prevent unemployment, it is clear that others would. In particular, organization of a centralized Walrasian market in which all goods could trade simultaneously against one another would do the trick if we abstract from incentives to misrepresent demands to influence the auctioneer's determination of prices. But while such a proposal might make formal sense in a toy model with few agents and commodities, it is patently nonsensical to consider it seriously for a real economy.

There is, however, still a serious question of whether other institutional structures might perform better than the ones studied here. I chose these particular ones to study because they seemed not terribly unrealistic, but clearly other specifications of the methods of price and wage determination, of the timing of actions, and of the extent and nature of transmission of information regarding willingness to buy or sell are equally plausible and should be investigated.

One obvious drawback of the present modelling is that it yields so many equilibria. For example, Proposition 3 points to the possibility of continua of unemployment equilibria. While such a vast multiplicity may in fact be a reflection of reality (and multiplicity at some level is fundamentally desirable if one wants both full employment and unemployment), we economists have a strong preference for models giving sharper predictions. The issue is whether we can find models or refinements of the equilibrium concept which yield, say, locally unique equilibria with involuntary unemployment.

Finally, a clear line for further work is to study the possibility of improving upon these equilibria by government policy. To the extent that unemployment results from pessimism, while optimism about the state of demand would yield full employment, 'upbeat' speeches might well be a cheap and effective method to shift conjectures and cure the unemployment. Perhaps more plausible, however, would be (balanced-budget) fiscal policies. In particular, if government demanded goods and paid for them via taxes that did not cause a completely offsetting reduction in demand, then firms would face positive levels of demand and would be prepared to hire even if workers express low demands that reflect fears of unemployment. This might well upset the unemployment equilibria. It is worth noting in this context, however, that introduction of government and of the possibility of these policies changes the game completely to one with an extra player. Thus, one would need to go back to the beginning and reformulate the model, specifying when and how the government can act, what information the private agents have about the government's policies when they make their decisions, and what happens under each possible pattern of behavior including, for instance, situations where the government attempts to collect taxes in excess of individuals' incomes. Thus, policy investigation presents a non-trivial set of problems in these models.

6 CONCLUSION

We have modelled the familiar idea of unemployment as arising from effective demand failures that are in turn induced by pessimistic, self-fulfilling expectations about demand. In doing so, we have represented the institutions of the economy via extensive form games. These games were selected partly on the basis of appearing somewhat realistic. They involve explicit modelling of the determination of prices and wages, which are treated as being selected by profit-maximizing firms that correctly recognize the impact of their choices on quantities demanded and supplied. These firms are thus imperfect competitors, and our models of macroeconomic equilibrium are also ones of general, imperfectly competitive equilibrium.

In these models we have demonstrated the possibility of equilibrium at which some or all of the workers are constrained in the amounts of labor they are able to sell. In these equilibria, workers would be strictly better off if they could work more at the going prices and wages, but firms are unwilling to hire them because they correctly perceive inadequate output demand. Moreover, the firms also have no individual incentive to change prices or wages, even though they are free to do so and may face excess supply of labor at the prevailing rates.

Notes

1. d'Aspremont *et al.* seem to employ a non-standard definition of involuntary unemployment which includes intersection of the demand and supply for labor on a horizontal portion of the latter.
2. This factor is the focus of Heller (1985), where it yields multiple full employment equilibria which are Pareto-ordered by the level of employment. See also Cooper and John (1985).
3. Further, one might note that announcing positive demands exposes the agents to (disequilibrium) risk that they may end up having to pay for these quantities though they have sold no labor. However, given our adherence to equilibrium analysis, we do not wish to make too much of this point.

References

Barro, R. J. and H. I. Grossman (1971) 'A General Disequilibrium Model of Income and Employment', *American Economic Review,* 61: 82–93.

Benassy, J.-P. (1973) *Disequilibrium Theory*, PhD Thesis, University of California, Berkeley.

Benassy, J.-P. (1977) 'A Neokeynesian Model of Price and Quantity Determination in Equilibrium', in G. Schwodiauer (ed.), *Equilibrium and Disequilibrium in Economic Theory* (Dordrecht: D. Reidel) pp.511–44.

Benassy, J.-P. (1982) *The Economics of Market Disequilibrium* (New York: Academic Press).

Bryant, J. (1983) 'A Simple Rational Expectations Keynes-Type Model', *Quarterly Journal of Economics*, 98: 525–9.

Clower, R. W. (1965) 'The Keynesian Counterrevolution: A Theoretical Appraisal', in F. H. Hahn and F. P. R. Brechling (eds), *The Theory of Interest Rates* (London: Macmillan).

Cooper, R. and A. John (1985) 'Coordinating Coordination Failures in Keynesian Models', mimeo, Yale University; forthcoming, *Quarterly Journal of Economics.*

d'Aspremont, C., R. Dos Santos Ferreira and L. A. Gerard-Varet (1984) 'Oligopoly and Involuntary Unemployment', Discussion Paper, Center for Operations Research and Econometrics, Université Catholique de Louvain.

Diamond, P. (1982) 'Aggregate Demand Management in Search Equilibrium', *Journal of Political Economy,* 90: 881–94.

Drèze, J. (1975) 'Existence of an Equilibrium under Price Rigidity and Quantity Rationing', *International Economic Review,* 16: 301–20.

Hahn, F. H. (1978) 'On Non-Walrasian Equilibria', *Review of Economic Studies,* 45: 1–18.

Hart, O. (1982) 'A Model of Imperfect Competition with Keynesian Features', *Quarterly Journal of Economics,* 97: 109–38.

Heller, W. P. (1986) 'Coordination Failure under Complete Markets with Applications to Effective Demand', in W. P. Heller, R. M. Starr and D. A. Starrett (eds) *Equilibrium Analysis: Essays in Honor of Kenneth J. Arrow* (Cambridge: Cambridge University Press) pp. 155–75.

Leijohnhufvud, A. (1968) *Keynesian Economics and the Economics of Keynes* (London: Oxford University Press).

Malinvaud, E. (1977) *The Theory of Unemployment Reconsidered* (Oxford: Blackwell).

Negishi, T. (1979) *Microeconomic Foundations of Keynesian Macroeconomics* (Amsterdam: North-Holland).

Roberts, J. (1986a) 'General Equilibrium Analysis of Imperfect Competition: An Illustrative Example', in G. Feiwel (ed.), *Arrow and The Ascent of Modern Economic Theory* (London: Macmillan) pp. 415–38.

Roberts, J. (1987) 'An Equilibrium Model with Involuntary Unemployment at Flexible, Competitive Prices and Wages', *American Economic Review,* 77: 856–74.

Roberts, J. and H. Sonnenschein (1977) 'On the Foundations of the Theory of Monopolistic Competition', *Econometrica,* 45: 101–13.

Selten, R. (1975) 'A Re-examination of the Perfectness Concept for Equilibrium Points in Extensive Games', *International Journal of Game Theory,* 4: 25–55.

Shubik, M. (1984) *A Game-theoretic Approach to Political Economy* (Cambridge, Mass.: MIT).

Weitzman, M. (1982) 'Increasing Returns and the Foundations of Unemployment Theory', *Economic Journal,* 92: 787–804.

Part II

Imperfect Competition: Retrospects and Prospects

3 The Cambridge Background to Imperfect Competition

John K. Whitaker*

The Economics of Imperfect Competition (Robinson, 1933) is a quintessentially Cambridge book, very much an outgrowth of the economics of Marshall and Pigou as tempered and criticized in the 'Cambridge cost controversies' of the 1920s. So close is the book's dependence on Cambridge tradition, and so limited its reliance on intellectual developments emanating elsewhere, that it is difficult to imagine that it could have been written by anyone but a true product of the Cambridge School of Economics, founded by Marshall and, in the early 1930s, very much at the height of its glory.

The intimate relationship between the book's agenda, method, and character, and the Cambridge background from which it sprang is obvious in a general way, but has not yet received the detailed consideration it deserves – for the book is clearly one of the landmarks of inter-war economic theory.[1] My hope is to make a start on the exploration of this question. Such an enterprise involves two distinct aspects. First, some sketch of the relevant Cambridge background must be given. Second, the detailed contents of *The Economics of Imperfect Competition* must be related to this background. A full and balanced treatment of both aspects would call for a paper of inordinate length and complexity. To avoid this I will focus mainly on the first aspect, dealing with the second one in a tentative and preliminary way only. Even so, none but the major streams contributing to the intellectual background of Cambridge economics in the late 1920s are explored, with minor tributaries left for brief closing comment. Section 1 gives some pertinent biographical background on Joan Robinson and touches on the Cambridge School of the 1920s in a general way. Section 2 deals with the approaches to the theory of competitive supply of Marshall and Pigou, the two patriarchs of the Cambridge School,

*A preliminary version of this paper was presented at the annual meeting of the History of Economics Society, George Mason University, May 1985. I am grateful to R. D. Collison Black, Sam Hollander, Brian Loasby and Frederic Lee for comments and advice. I retain vivid memories of Joan Robinson as a striking and formidable figure on the Cambridge scene of the 1950s, but unfortunately our contacts were slight so that I can add little of interest on a personal level.

while Section 3 discusses their approaches to monopoly and imperfectly competitive markets. Section 4 considers Sraffa's 1926 attack on the Marshall–Pigou tradition in value theory, and his call for resort to monopoly theory in the search for unifying principles. We come at last in Section 5 to *The Economics of Imperfect Competition* itself, embarking, as already indicated, on a very tentative delineation of its relation to the background described in Sections 2–4. The final Section 6 draws some tentative conclusions and suggests further lines of enquiry.

1 SOME BACKGROUND

Joan Maurice (as she then was) came up to Girton to study economics with the 'vague hope that it would help me understand poverty' and 'offer more scope for rational argument than history (my school subject) as it was taught in those days'.[2] She graduated in 1925 with a disappointing second in Part II of the Economics Tripos and in 1926 married E. A. G. Robinson, a young (BA 1921) Cambridge economist and College Fellow. The Robinsons spent the next three years in India, where Austin was tutor to the Maharajah of Gwalior, returning to Cambridge in 1929 when Austin took up a University Lectureship in Economics. For the next two years Joan held no formal position, although she did a certain amount of lecturing and tutoring, but in 1931 she became University Assistant Lecturer in Economics and commenced her lifelong association with the Cambridge Faculty. The appearance of *The Economics of Imperfect Competition* in 1933 rapidly cemented her reputation and position.

In Part I of the Tripos, candidates in the early-to-mid 1920s were required to take a paper on 'Economic theory (Value and Distribution) [which] shall deal with the subject-matter covered by Marshall's *Principles of Economics*' while in Part II there was a required paper on Economic Principles which 'shall deal with the scope and method of Economics, with fundamental ideas, and with the general analysis of demand and supply as illustrated by the broader problems of wages, interest, rent, foreign trade, money, prices, and taxation'. Apart from these, and an optional special subject on the Theory of Statistics in Part II, the degree had a strongly applied flavor, with papers on 'Industry and Labour', 'Trade and Finance', and Economic History (several), in Part I, and on 'Public Finance', 'Structure and Problems of Industry', 'Distribution and Labour', and 'Money, Credit and Prices', in Part II.[3]

It is clear that the undergraduates of Joan Robinson's day were thoroughly exposed to Marshall's *Principles* (Marshall, 1920). As she recalled, 'When I came up to Cambridge in October 1921, and started reading economics, Marshall's *Principles* was the Bible, and we knew little beyond it'. Her thorough mastery of the idiom is revealed in the satirical retelling of

Beauty and the Beast in Marshallian prose, written in this period (with Dorothea Braithwaite). Her command of the Marshallian world view was less firm, however: 'I felt smothered by the moralizing and mystified by the theory: in particular, no one seemed to know what was meant by the "representative firm".'[4]

It is hardly conceivable that undergraduates of that day can have completed Part II of the Tripos without becoming well acquainted with Pigou's *Economics of Welfare* (Pigou, 1920). In any case, *The Economics of Imperfect Competition* displays a full grasp of that work and considerable reliance upon it. As Joan Robinson recalled:

> When I returned to Cambridge in 1929, they were still arguing about the representative firm (*Economic Journal*, March 1930). But meanwhile Piero Sraffa ... was calmly committing the sacrilege of pointing out inconsistencies in Marshall ... My first book, *Economics of Imperfect Competition*, though inspired by a hint from Sraffa, was mainly influenced by Professor Pigou.[5]

That *The Economics of Welfare* was the dominant influence on Joan Robinson's book is the position I will argue for below. It runs, I think, somewhat contrary to the popular perception of the matter.

Cambridge in the later 1920s must have been an exciting place in which to study and practice economics. Marshall had been long retired and had died in 1924, but Keynes, Pigou and Robertson were all at the heights of their powers, and the rising generation, especially Sraffa, Kahn and the Robinsons, was replete with talent and enthusiasm. A vivid retrospective sketch of the economics faculty, seen from the perspective of 1931, has been provided by, Sir Austin Robinson (E. A. G. Robinson, 1978) and captures the aura admirably.

Value theory was not a dominant interest in Cambridge during the 1920s. Keynes, Pigou and Robertson devoted little effort to research and writing in this area, although the two latter recurred to it on occasion – see especially Pigou (1927, 1928) and Robertson (1924, 1930). Of the older generation, it was Gerald Shove who devoted himself strenuously to such matters (see Section 6 below). Keynes's attitude in the early 1920s has been described by Harrod:

> his knowledge of Marshall was very thorough and meticulous. He used to take the view at that time that the content of economic theory was extremely small ... He did not think that wide reading in economic theory was necessary ... His recipe for the young economist was to know his Marshall thoroughly and read his *Times* every day carefully, without bothering too much about the large mass of contemporary publication in book form. He was careful to add that one must read one's Pigou and

anything that came from the pens of the chosen few. (Harrod, 1951, p.324.)

This kind of complacent and insular attitude, which doubtless characterized the Cambridge School as a whole, was disturbed in 1926 by the young Sraffa who brought fresh and iconoclastic perspectives on value theory and precipitated a new and creative ferment in the area (on which see Kahn, 1984, pp. 23–6).

2 MARSHALL AND PIGOU ON THE THEORY OF COMPETITIVE SUPPLY

Although – as always with Marshall – the distinction is blurred, it is, I think, helpful to view him as introducing in the *Principles* two different theories of supply, which I have called elsewhere the 'agricultural' and 'industrial' versions.[6] The essential difference is that the former deals with cases in which there is no product differentiation betwen the firms in an industry and in which, also, the firms do not experience *internal* economies of scale. The industrial case deals with situations in which neither of these conditions is satisfied, and hence the 'representative firm' becomes a crucial element in the analysis. (Cases in which internal economies are associated with product homogeneity lead to either full monopoly or the strategic interdependence of a few firms.)

The agricultural case is much the simpler. Because marketing is routine and the minimum-cost size of firm is small, exceptional business ability is not needed to keep a firm operating efficiently more or less indefinitely. Thus, the industry is characterized, at a given level of industry output, by a fixed population of firms, each with rising marginal cost, both short period and long period, and each remaining much the same from year to year. As industry output expands, new firms may be established and external economies may be generated. The latter help offset the rise in supply price due to limited natural resources, but they do not play any crucial role in the analysis.

The essential characteristic of the agricultural case is that individual firms are in equilibrium when the industry is. In the industrial case, however, this is true only of a short-period equilibrium in which there is a fixed population of firms each with a given plant and organization. By contrast, long-period equilibrium is characterized by an ever-changing population of firms, none of whom remain unchanged, and the equilibrium is only of a statistical or population-average sort. The treatment of the industrial case is crucially dependent on the assumption that firms, like men or machines, have a finite life-cycle and that there is a continual turnover in the population of firms. Each firm starts as a struggling newcomer, rises at maturity to a peak of efficiency, and then eventually languishes and dies. This picture of the firm was based on the prototype of the family business which went, according to the Lancashire adage, 'from clogs to clogs in three generations', and although Marshall in later editions extended the theory's coverage to include joint stock companies 'which often stagnate, but do not readily die', the extension somehow lacks conviction.[7] With a life-cycle of half a century or so, what prevents a firm with internal economies from rapidly expanding, driving out competitors, and converting the industry into a monopoly or oligopoly? The marketing difficulties due to product differentiation, allied with constraints on external financing, play a crucial role here. They protect competitors from *rapid* incursions and meanwhile the high level of business ability required for successful marketing incursions and aggressive exploitation of scale economies is not maintained. Individual firms lack the time, the sustained energy, or both, which would be needed to dominate the industry. But if for any reason they succeed, then the industry is removed from the purview of the normal theory of competitive value. Even when the industry remains nominally competitive, the number of firms may not be large and strategic consideration of possible reactions from specific competitors may inhibit action (see Hague, 1958). Competition is defined broadly, resting fundamentally on the 'openness' of markets rather than on atomistic price-taking behavior.

An industry may be in equilibrium, in the sense that total quantity produced remains unchanged at a constant level of the price index for the industry's differentiated output, while individual firms rise or fall like the proverbial trees in the forest. In such an equilibrium there will be an even age distribution of firms, and the size distribution of firms will reflect the expansion–contraction path of the typical firm over its life-cycle. The equilibrium supply price of a given aggregate output just suffices to induce the birth of enough new firms to sustain this aggregate output, given the lifetime-profit prospects implied in the life-cycle path for each firm when price and industry output are at the levels they are. Evidently, the precise determination of this supply price is a complex matter, perhaps intractably complex. It is here that the representative firm comes in as a conceptual device for analyzing supply price in terms of average cost by supposing that all firms are alike and unchanging, rather than heterogeneous and inexorably progressing through the typical life-cycle. The representative firm is the fiction or artifice which permits this translation. A shrewd observer might be able to discern an actual firm whose costs and scale currently approximate those of the hypothetical firm which is representative at the current level of industry output, but this is a matter of empirical approximation, not of logical necessity. Like the average family with 1.7 children, the representative firm can perform its representational role while differing from any real entity.[8]

The average costs of the representative firm must be recalculated for each level of industry output. If this is larger, each firm will find marketing easier and will be able to grow to a greater size before beginning to stagnate and languish. Thus, on average, firms will enjoy greater *internal* economies of scale, which will tend to lower the average costs of the representative firm. Even without external economies, the industry's long-period supply price will tend to fall as industry output rises. Marshall's argument for subsidizing decreasing-cost 'manufacturing' industries, if necessary by taxing increasing-cost 'agricultural' industries, is not dependent upon the presence of external economies. These can be regarded as an optional extra, added for verisimilitude rather than by conceptual necessity. But the same is not true for Pigou's version of the argument.

Pigou's early work on competitive supply (Pigou, 1910, 1912) made little reference to the individual firm, but took the industry supply curve as a datum. The supply price of any output was interpreted as the industry's average (money) cost of producing that output. *Marginal* supply price was defined as the addition to the industry's total cost due to an increment in output. Evidently this marginal supply price (marginal cost to the industry) exceeds supply price (average cost to the industry) whenever the latter is increasing with output. The inequality is reversed in the decreasing-cost case. Pigou identified marginal supply price as the social cost of changing output, defining the 'ideal output' for the industry as that making marginal supply price equal to demand price, which measures marginal benefit to consumers. It follows that ideal output is less than competitive-equilibrium output for increasing-cost industries, and greater for decreasing-cost industries, leading Pigou to propose a universal tax-subsidy scheme to correct these distortions.[9] This argument was criticized by Young (1913) for its assumption that marginal supply price measures social cost. That portion of marginal cost to the industry representing greater remuneration of inputs already employed in the industry must be regarded as a transfer, not a social cost.[10] When Pigou returned to revise *Wealth and Welfare* (Pigou, 1912) after the war, transforming it into *The Economics of Welfare* (Pigou, 1920), he accepted the Young criticism and put up a defense against it by arguing that the industry was to be regarded as sufficiently small that a change in its output would not affect the prices it had to pay for its inputs, observing that this was analogous to the assumption needed on the demand side to justify constancy of the marginal utility of money (Pigou, 1920, p. 935). The second edition of *The Economics of Welfare* (Pigou, 1924) put up some further defenses, including the argument that extra payments to imported inputs already used by the industry were a social cost from a national rather than a cosmopolitan viewpoint. But the definitive statement of Pigou's theory of competitive supply came only in a 1928 article, the substance of which was incorporated in the third edition of *The Economics of Welfare* (Pigou, 1928, 1929, pp.319–21, 789–807). It is difficult, in reading Pigou's earlier treatments of competitive supply, to avoid the impression of a certain vagueness and confusion of thought, but this mental fog is dissipated in Pigou (1928).[11] Two aspects in particular call for attention: the concept of the equilibrium firm, and the explicit analysis of external economies and diseconomies.

The discussion of the equilibrium firm starts from Marshall's position. When the industry is in equilibrium, 'the tendencies to expand and contract on the part of the individual firms will cancel out; but it is certain that many individual firms will not themselves be in equilibrium and possible that none will be' (Pigou, 1928, p.239). A way of avoiding the resulting analytical complexity is found in the thought that 'when the output of the industry as a whole is adjusted to any given state of demand, the tendencies to expansion and contradiction on the part of individual firms cancel out [and] may properly be regarded as *irrelevant* so far as the supply schedule of the industry as a whole is concerned' (Ibid.). Pigou now postulates that the industry supply schedule may be defined by the costs of a hypothetical equilibrium firm:

> The conditions of the industry are compatible with the existence of such a firm; and the implications about these conditions, which, whether it in fact exists or not, would hold good if it did exist, must be valid. For the purpose of studying these conditions, therefore, it is legitimate to speak of it as actually existing. For any given output, then, of the industry as a whole, the supply price of the industry as a whole must be equal to the price, which, with the then output of the industry as a whole, leaves the equilibrium firm in equilibrium. (Pigou, 1928, p.240).

The equilibrium firm is interpreted as a weakened version of Marshall's representative firm, which, according to Pigou, 'is conceived as an "equilibrium firm". But it is also something more. It is a firm of, in some sense, average size – a "typical" firm, built on a scale to which actual firms tend to approximate' (Pigou, 1928, p. 240n).

The identification of the equilibrium firm with the representative firm is correct, so far as it goes. For both Pigou and Marshall, the costs of this apocryphal firm depend on total industry output as well as the firm's own output. Thus, total costs can be written as $F(x, y)$, where y is industry output and x the firm's output, and both authors require supply price to equal the average cost $F(x, y)/x$. Where Pigou diverges from his master is not so much in the *concept* of the equilibrium firm as in the equilibrium condition it must satisfy. For Marshall, a change in the output of the representative firm, like that of every actual firm is inhibited by difficulties of marketing and finance. The value of x is an arbitrary or, more correctly, an institutionally determined function of y. Strong restrictions do not have to be imposed on $\partial F/\partial x$, simply because x cannot vary independently of y. Pigou, on the other hand, assumes that the equilibrium firm is free to change its output and to sell as much as it chooses at the going price. The supply price, p, for any industry output, y, is determined, therefore, by eliminating x from the pair of conditions:

$$p = \partial F(x,y)/\partial x \tag{1}$$

$$p = F(x,y)/x \tag{2}$$

The first, representing the profit-maximization condition for the equilibrium firm, must be supported by the second-order condition $\partial^2 F/\partial x^2 > 0$. As Pigou makes clear, (1) and (2) can hold simultaneously and yield a maximum of profit only if the equilibrium firm operates, for any fixed value of y, at the minimum point on its average cost curve where marginal cost, $\partial F/\partial x$, equals average cost, F/x, and is rising. The equilibrium firm cannot have unexhausted internal economies, and the possibility that supply price might fall as industry output increases can be attributed only to external economies which lower the average cost curve of the equilibrium firm (i.e. the curve of F/x regarded as a function of x for given y) as industry output increases.[12]

A shift in the average cost curve of the equilibrium firm as y increases might be due to a bidding up of the prices of the inputs used by the industry as well as to external economies or diseconomies. As Pigou showed clearly, the former effect can be eliminated by adjusting for the effects of rising input prices. Let the minimum average cost of the equilibrium firm be $(\Sigma w_i z_i)/x$, where $z_1, z_2, \ldots z_n$ are the quantities of the various inputs used, and $w_1, w_2, \ldots w_n$ their unit prices. Since the industry's supply price is determined by this minimum average cost, total industry revenue must be $y(\Sigma w_i z_i)/x$, which must also equal total industry costs given zero excess profits overall. The marginal cost *to the industry* is therefore

$$\frac{d}{dy}[y(\sum w_i z_i)/x] = \frac{\Sigma w_i z_i}{x} + \sum w_i \frac{d(z_i/x)}{dy} + \Sigma\left(\frac{z_i}{x}\right)\frac{dw_i}{dy} \tag{3}$$

To obtain the marginal cost to *society*, the last term is omitted (apart from components relating to imported inputs if a national rather than cosmopolitan view is taken). Note that the input-price index involved in integrating marginal cost over a finite y-interval is of the Divisia or continually-changing-weight variety.[13]

In Pigou (1928, p.253) the possibility that supply price might rise with industry output, after the indicated input-price adjustment, was dismissed on the grounds that anything feasible on a small scale could be replicated to achieve a larger scale, so that average costs would at worst remain constant as output expanded. On the other hand, the possibility of falling supply price was emphasized:

> The increased specialisation of its component firms made possible by an enlargement in an industry as a whole often involves a large reduction in costs ... an increase in the scale to which an industry is producing frequently alters – in general diminishes – the average (and marginal) costs of the equilibrium firm contained in it, whether or not it also alters its size. There is then no difficulty in seeing that the law of decreasing supply price, as conceived when correction has been made for transfer elements in rates of price change, is not merely formally possible, but is likely to be followed in practice by many manufacturing industries. (Pigou, 1928, p.252)

In the revised version, Pigou (1929, p.220), it was conceded that external diseconomies are conceivable although 'highly improbable'.

As in earlier work, ideal output for an industry continued in Pigou (1928) to be the level making marginal cost equal to demand price (assuming no consumption externalities), but now the marginal cost was to be suitably corrected for induced changes in input prices. After a lapse of fifteen years, the criticism of Young (1913), that increased payments to inputs were a transfer, not a social cost, had been fully adapted to and met. Apart from a qualification concerning imported inputs, all departures of competitive output from ideal output were now attributable to external economies or diseconomies, mainly the former, and tax-subsidy schemes were espoused purely as a means of correcting such externalities. In the struggle to clarify his ideas Pigou had slowly fought his way to a position very different from Marshall's, and come close to a line of argument promulgated much earlier by Cunynghame and Edgeworth.[14] This reconciled competition and decreasing costs by endowing *each* firm with a rising marginal cost curve while allowing *each* firm's marginal and average cost curves to shift as industry output changed, a view which became firmly ensconced in economists' consciousness after the definitive statement by Viner (1931).[15] Pigou supposed such a state of affairs only for the equilibrium firm but, as Newman cogently remarks

> Pigou came perilously close in his exposition to saying that when the equilibrium firm was in equilibrium, so was the industry. And it was very easy for subsequent workers – and textbook writers – to substitute 'typical firm', or even 'each individual firm' for 'equilibrium firm'. (Newman, 1960, p.597)

The implications of this remark deserve to be expanded upon. Imposing equilibrium restrictions only on the equilibrium firm rather than on every firm permits weaker restrictions to be met by the heterogeneous actual firms being represented by the equilibrium firm. These firms need not all be in price-taking equilibrium, so that internal economies accruing to existing or potential new firms need not be wholly exhausted. But any scale economies, whatever their actual source, must be *analytically represented* in Pigou's framework as external economies accruing to the equilibrium firm. Pigou, following Marshall, viewed as external all those economies arising from increased specialization and differentiation of function among constituent firms as an industry expands – indeed, for each author these were the prime source of external economies. Yet, such economies, must rest ultimately on internal economies whose exploitation is inhibited by limitation on firms' markets. They cannot arise if all firms, existing and potential, are always in price-taking equilibrium. This apparent contradiction is resolved by distinguishing the formal or analytical representation from the underlying reality. Specialization economies appear analytically *as if* they were external. For Marshall, whose representative firm is permitted unexhausted scale economies, the decision as to whether a particular real-world source of scale economics is to be represented analytically as external or internal is substantially a matter of convenience. An appealing boundary is to call economies internal if they arise from doing the same things as before on a larger scale, and external if they arise from doing different things. Pigou has no such latitude. In his framework, all economies, whatever their actual source, must be treated analytically as external. The advantage Pigou gains is that stronger restrictions are imposed upon the way in which the industry's supply curve can shift as underlying conditions (e.g. factor supplies) change. For his equilibrium firm is more tightly connected than is Marshall's representative firm to the standard structure of production and cost theory.

Pigou's attempt, in constructing his equilibrium firm, to unite Marshall's approach with one based on a more explicit treatment of individual optimization cannot be judged successful. It has generally been interpreted as a capitulation to the dominant theoretical tendency of the period – founding industry equilibrium on that of all the decision-makers involved – while paying mere lip service to Marshall. Its subtleties have passed unnoticed even by die-hard defenders of the more organic Marshallian approach to industry analysis.

Joan Robinson's *Economics of Imperfect Competition* was an important part of the process by which the view that industry equilibrium requires every firm to be in equilibrium became dominant. But the older Marshallian tradition retained Cambridge supporters even if Pigou is discounted. As early as 1924, Robertson was chiding Pigou for abandoning the representative firm as a means for reconciling competition with unexhausted internal economies (Robertson, 1924, pp.22–4), while in 1930 both Robertson and Shove strove, largely unsuccessfully, to translate Marshall's representative-firm approach for an uncomprehending new generation. Their failures had quite different sources. Robertson (1930, especially pp.87–9) was emphatic as to the centrality of the life-cycle process for firms, but entirely neglected to explain the forces preventing each firm from expanding rapidly to exploit internal economies. On the other hand, Shove (1930, especially pp.105–15) gave a careful analysis of the factors, including market imperfections, inhibiting rapid expansion of one firm at the expense of others. But he abandoned the firm's fixed life-cycle, which he regarded as outmoded and characteristic of an earlier phase of economic history, invoking instead merely random variations in the efficiency and vigor of firms. The result was a complex, opaque discussion, compelling in neither its parsimony nor its realism, for no adequate explanation was given of why firms might not continue indefinitely to expand at *some* rate so long as unexhausted internal economies remained. It was only much later, through the work of Newman and Wolfe that the possibility of analyzing equilibrium in such situations by the general theory of stochastic processes came to be discerned, although Shove can, with the light of hindsight, be represented as groping in that direction.[16] Despite this failure, Robertson in particular continued to cling to the Marshallian tradition and was to become its main repository in the post-war years.

3 MARSHALL, PIGOU AND THE THEORY OF MONOPOLY

Marshall regarded the theory of normal value as including the extremes of monopoly and competition but not the intermediate ground which has come to be termed oligopoly:

> Normal action falls into the background, when Trusts are striving for the mastery of a large market; when communities of interest are being made and unmade; and, above all, when the policy of any particular establishment is likely to be governed, not with a single eye to its own business success, but in subordination to some large stock-exchange manoeuvre, or some campaign for the control of markets. (Marshall, 1920, p.xiv.)

Such issues were postponed to the never-published second volume of the *Principles*, but were touched on to some extent in *Industry and Trade* (Marshall, 1919; see also Marshall, 1890). It is true that Marshall's 'manufacturing' version of the competitive case was far from assuming price-taking perfect competition and entered the largely uncharted middle ground between the extremes of pure monoploy and atomistic competition. It bears an obvious general resemblance to later analyses of imperfect or monopolistic competition, including Joan Robinson's. Indeed, in an oft-quoted footnote, each firm was explicitly envisaged as facing a negatively sloped demand curve:

> When we are considering an individual producer, we must couple his supply curve – not with the general demand curve for his commodity in a wide market, but – with the particular demand curve of his own special market. And this particular demand curve will generally be very steep; perhaps as steep as his own supply curve is likely to be, even when an increased output will give him an important increase of internal economies. (Marshall, 1920, p.458n)

But the full implications of this perspective were never developed. Product differentiation and market imperfection were viewed rather as elements in the frictions inhibiting the rapid expansion of firms during their energetic phase than as permanent features a firm would have to deal with, even given an indefinitely prolonged active life. One might argue that since even 'temporary' obstacles would need to persist for decades rather than years in order to achieve their inhibiting effect, they should have received more careful analysis.

Turning to the extreme case of monopoly, Marshall's analysis (Marshall, 1920, pp.477–95, 856–8) was straightforward and derived directly from the treatment in Cournot (1838, pp.56–66). The monopolist was viewed as selling at a uniform price and choosing that output which maximizes total revenue minus total cost, when the latter includes a normal (competitive) return on capital. The graphical analysis employed curves showing average revenue (the 'demand curve') average cost (the 'supply curve'), and average revenue minus average cost (the 'monopoly-revenue curve') as functions of output. A grid of rectangular hyperbolae, each involving a constant *total* amount of money receipts ('constant-revenue curves') was superimposed, and the maximum-profit output was defined as that at which the monopoly-revenue curve touches the highest attainable constant-revenue curve. Marginal revenue as a function of output is neither defined nor graphed, but its role is quite clearly identified in the mathematical appendix (p.857). Four features of Marshall's treatment particularly call for notice.

1. The explicit contrast of competitive and monopolistic forms for an industry, recognizing that costs will differ because of the differing organization of production, so that it is not necessarily the case that 'the amount produced under a monopoly is always less and its price to the consumer always higher than if there were no monopoly' (Marshall, 1920, p.484).[17]
2. The careful and correct analysis of the effects on a monopolist of various kinds of taxes or subsidies.
3. The pioneering analysis of optimal pricing for a publicly owned

monopoly. This analysis leads to marginal-cost pricing if taxation involves no excess burden, when 'total benefit' is maximized, and to Ramsey pricing if taxation involves an excess burden, when 'compromise benefit' is maximized.[18]

4. The suggestion that long-run profit maximization may cause the monopolist to lower current price in order to build up future demand and profits when demand rises more readily than it falls, due to habituation effects or irreversible investments made by consumers.

In *Industry and Trade* much attention was given to a problem which is in a sense the mirror-image of point 4. This is the need for a monopoly to keep current price low so as to deter potential new competitors and prevent future demand being undermined. This led Marshall to the new concept of 'conditional monopoly':

> absolute monopolies are of little importance in modern business as compared with those which are 'conditional' or 'provisional': that is, which hold their sway only 'on condition' that, or 'provided' that, they do not put prices much above the levels necessary to cover their outlays with normal profits. If they did, then competition would probably make itself felt; unless stayed by authority, as is the case with patents, copyrights, and some rights of way ... many monopolies which seem absolute, are yet to some extent liable to be assailed by indirect routes; and are incomplete and subject to the 'condition' that the monopolist makes no such extreme use of his power as will induce others to force their way through obstacles and set up effective competition. (Marshall, 1919, pp.397–8.)

A consequence of this long-run vulnerability is that:

> a well-managed trust reflects that, if it puts its prices so high as to hold out the prospect of good profits to new rivals, after fighting through the campaign of under selling which it is prepared to arrange, the rivals will appear. That is to say, it adjusts its price rather closely to the cost of production *including profits*, on which a new-comer in an ordinary competitive market would base his calculations. But it adds to this something for the insurance against extra risk which a new-comer into its market would expect to face. (Ibid., p.524)

This sketch of a theory of entry-deterring behavior is particularly interesting in the light of the copious recent work on entry-deterrence and market contestability in situations of oligopoly and natural monopoly. Unfortunately, Marshall's pursuit of these issues was buried in a mass of historical and institutional detail and seems to have had little impact on economic thought in the 1920s and 1930s. *Industry and Trade* appears to have been as little read in the Cambridge of the 1920s as it was elsewhere, being referred to more out of piety than because it was viewed as a fount of new ideas.[19] This was so despite Keynes's view that the book 'contains the suggestions, the starting points for many investigations. There is no better book for suggesting lines of original inquiry to a reader so disposed' (Keynes 1924, p.370).

Pigou's approach to monopoly was dominated by comparisons of the deviation of actual from ideal output under both competitive and monopolistic organization of an industry. His most important contribution was to extend the analysis of ordinary monopoly to cover price discrimination. As is well known, he distinguished three types of discrimination. First-degree or 'ideal' discrimination has the monopolist absorbing the entire consumer surplus by selling each unit at the maximum demand-price the purchaser would be willing to pay for it. (Pigou's argument rests here on Marshall's assumption of approximate constancy of the marginal utility of 'money' to each consumer.) Second-degree price discrimination is an approximation to first-degree discrimination, involving a limited set of different prices with each unit sold at the largest such price not exceeding its demand-price. However, little use was made of this concept. Third-degree price discrimination is the more familiar case in which different prices are charged in different submarkets, between which resale or shifting of demand is difficult (Pigou, 1912, pp.202–3; see also Pigou, 1904). The formal solution to third-degree price discrimination is defined with the utmost conciseness and clarity:[20]

> Let $\varphi_1(x_1), \varphi_2(x_2) \ldots$ represent the demand prices of n separate markets and $f(x)$ the supply price. The prices proper to the several markets under monopoly *plus* discrimination of the third degree are given by the values of $\varphi_1(x_1)$, $\varphi_2(x_2) \ldots$ that satisfy n equations of the form
>
> $$\frac{d}{dx_r}[x_r\{\varphi_r(x_r) - f(x_1 + x_2 + \ldots)\}] = 0$$
>
> These n equations are sufficient to determine the n unknowns. (Pigou, 1912, p.222n.)

The treatment of monopoly in Pigou (1912) was carried forward with little substantive change into various editions of *The Economics of Welfare* and it should suffice to consider the treatment in the third edition (Pigou, 1929).[21] The welfare implications of monopoly are clearest in the case of first-degree price discrimination. This will result in an output such that marginal cost to the industry equals the marginal demand price of consumers. If marginal cost to the industry is the same as marginal social cost – that is, if there are no transfer elements in marginal cost – then the resulting output coincides with the ideal output. By having all production units under common control, any economies which are external to the individual production units, but internal to the industry as a whole, are fully internalized. Wherever such externalities are present discriminating monopoly performs better than competition, which fails to yield the ideal level of output. (But, of course, this comparison ignores questions of distribution). On the other hand, if marginal cost to the industry exceeds marginal social cost, because expansion of the industry's output bids up the prices of some inputs, output under first-degree price discrimination will fall short of the ideal level. The profit-maximizing monopolist will internalize pecuniary externalities as well as real externalities (to use a distinction introduced by Viner, 1931). In other words, he will behave as a *monopsonist* when buying such inputs, thereby inefficiently restricting their use (see Pigou, 1929, pp.281–4).

It is unnecessary to trace out in detail the various twists and turns of Pigou's detailed comparisons of ideal output with output under competition or under various kinds of monopoly, but two points might be emphasized.

1. Comparisons are made on the working assumption that any given output is produced at identical cost in all the alternatives considered (Pigou 1929). But this assumption is logically flawed for a comparison of competition and monopoly whenever monopoly also implies monopsonistic restriction of the use of certain inputs. Joan Robinson (1933, pp.273–8) was to explain this point in detail.
2. Under third-degree price discrimination marginal demand price will differ between submarkets. Even if output as a whole is at the ideal level it may, from a welfare viewpoint, be misallocated among submarkets (Pigou, 1929, pp.288–9).

The middle ground between monopoly and competition was touched on by Pigou in various ways. A short chapter entitled 'Monopolistic Competition' dealt with 'multiple monopoly' (or oligopoly as it would now be termed), concentrating mainly on the duopoly case. Cournot and Edgeworth solutions were described and the indeterminacy, within weak bounds, of individual and combined outputs was emphasized. (See Pigou, 1912, pp.192–4; 1929, pp.267–9.) More original, but not entirely satisfactory, was the treatment of cases where monopolistic pricing is combined with free entry of resources, as when professional organizations enforce standard fees but admit all qualified individuals to membership. The result is that resources enter until average returns are reduced to a normal level, lowering average productivity since total sales and output cannot rise given the fixity of price. But the mechanisms involved were left vague (see Pigou, 1929, pp.273–4). Even more unsatisfactory was the discussion of the one-firm industry – the one serious blot on Pigou 1928 from where it was transferred to Pigou 1929 (pp.799–800, 805–6). Pigou evidently had in mind a case where there is a threat of entry, so that the incumbent firm cannot act as an unrestricted monopolist, but his unexplained assertion that the incumbent firm will set output to make demand price just equal the larger of average or marginal cost seems quite arbitrary.

Thus, while Marshall and Pigou each provide some loose hints, the middle ground between monopoly and competition remained largely uncultivated by the Cambridge tradition. It was left to Sraffa to sow the first seed and for Joan Robinson to reap the first harvest from this neglected territory.[22]

4 SRAFFA'S CHALLENGE

Though frequently cited, Sraffa's classic article (Sraffa, 1926) seldom seems to be read with the close attention needed to grasp its complex train of argument. It has two distinct foci, only tenuously related. First, the validity of the partial equilibrium approach to competitive price determination, espoused by Marshall and especially Pigou, is questioned. Second, there is an attempt, surprisingly complete, to visualize a new (but unnamed) theory of cases intermediate between the traditional extremes of monopoly and competition.[23]

The attack on partial equilibrium methods ('particular' equilibrium is Sraffa's term) is premised on the assumption that unlimited scale economies internal to the firm 'must be put aside as being incompatible with competitive conditions' (Sraffa, 1926, p.186, also see p.183). Sraffa takes for granted the need for every firm to be in equilibrium if the industry is to be in equilibrium, and Marshall's alternative approach goes largely unrecognized. The difficulties with partial equilibrium analysis of industry *A* (let us call it) emanate from the supply side. The basic problem is that expansion of *A*'s output, due say to increased demand, will shift the supply curves for other commodities, either by bidding up the prices of scarce inputs they use in common with *A*, or by generating external economies which affect them as well as *A*. The resulting changes in the prices of other commodities, even though their demands have not altered, will further shift *A*'s two-dimensional demand curve to the extent that the other commodities are related to *A* in demand. Moreover, this induced shift may have effects on the price of *A* too large to be neglected as being of 'the second order of smalls'. In short, the partial-equilibrium independence of the supply and demand curves for *A* cannot be sustained generally. The partial equilibrium method is valid in those rare cases in which inputs whose supply to *A* is less than perfectly elastic are used only by *A* and external economies generated by the firms in *A* remain internal to the industry. Otherwise, the method can be applied only to those cases in which external economies are absent and *A* is too small to bid up the price of any of its inputs, but then the supply curve for *A* is horizontal and price is wholly cost determined. As Joan Robinson was later to opine, Sraffa 'was concerned to show that economists who make use of the competitive [partial equilibrium] analysis of value have a strong unconscious bias in favor of rising and falling supply price, simply because, if supply price is always constant, their analysis has nothing interesting to say' (Robinson, 1933, p.118).

The moral is not that scarce factors or external economies have no significance, but rather that they usually transcend the limits of partial equilibrium analysis. The remedy lies in extending 'the field of investigation so as to examine the conditions of simultaneous equilibrium in numerous industries: a well-known conception, whose complexity, however, prevents it from bearing fruit, at least in the present state of our knowledge' (Sraffa, 1926, p.187).[24]

Given the bankruptcy of partial equilbrium, and the emptiness of general equilibrium, Sraffa saw two possibilities: return to the Ricardian cost-based explanation of value, or 'abandon the path of free competition and turn in the opposite direction, namely, toward monopoly' (Sraffa, 1926, p.187). The latter route was followed in the 1926 paper, although the former was of course pursued elsewhere (Sraffa, 1962) with effects that still reverberate.[25]

One attraction of the monopoly route was that 'if we assume the generality of some element of monopoly, even in the case of a large number of independent producers, we can take into consideration that vital factor of internal economies which Marshall's scheme is obliged to ignore'.[26] However, traditional monopoly theory was seen to be just as limited in applicability as the theory of perfect competition. Sraffa perceived the vast bulk of manufacturing industries as characterized by many competing firms, all producing commodities in a single commodity category, but each able to sell more only by lowering its own price. The received theory of profit-maximizing monopoly could be adapted without difficulty to the behavior of each such firm *given the actions of its rivals.* After all, it should be immaterial to a firm whether the customers it loses by raising its price turn to other commodities (as in traditional monopoly theory) or, partly at least, to other suppliers of the firm's own commodity category. But, as Sraffa saw clearly, the novel element now needed is a theory of the *group* equilibrium of all the firms producing commodities in the given category.

Sraffa's theory of group equilibrium is sketched for the case in which there are identical competing firms. In effect, he assumes that each firm views itself as a price leader whose price decisions will be followd by others, so that each of the *n* firms perceives itself as faced by a demand curve which is simply a scaled down version of the demand curve for the entire commodity group. The result is that (at least if all firms have a common and constant marginal cost) output and price are *exactly* as they would be if the industry were in the hands of a profit-maximizing cartel. This is despite the fact that the demand curve for each individual firm *given the prices set by other firms* may be very (but not perfectly) elastic. Sraffa believes that this outcome will hold as a general approximation and that 'even in actual cases where the conditions of the various undertakings differ . . . the cumulative action of slight obstacles to competition produces on prices effects which approximate to those of monopoly' (Sraffa, 1926, p.196).[27] Sraffa's group equilibrium is limited to a fixed number of firms. He recognizes that supernormal profits might attract new entrants to the industry, but he does not explore this aspect, emphasizing instead the barriers which will inhibit entry.

There are severe logical difficulties with Sraffa's conception of group equilibrium. It is one thing to recognize that the demand curve a firm faces given the prices set by its competitors will shift as these prices are changed. It is quite another to imply, as Sraffa does, that each firm views such shifts as a consequence of its own leadership. An alternative (Bertrand) approach, in which each firm chooses its price on the assumption that other firms' prices are unaffected by its choice, gives rise to a quite different group equilibrium closer to the 'competitive' (i.e. price equals marginal cost) one.[28]

The new kind of *partial equilibrium*, imperfect competition theory sketched by Sraffa could accommodate some degree of scale economies internal to the firm without threatening the existence of equilibrium. This was a distinct advantage, since he saw such economies as widespread. On the other hand, his previous criticisms of the partial equilibrium method in competitive conditions applied equally to its use in imperfectly competitive conditions. The new kind of theory might be more relevant and illuminating but its sphere of applicability remained no less circumscribed, and the ultimate need for a general equilibrium approach had not been averted. That, at least, is the logic of Sraffa's own argument, even though he leaves it implicit.

5 *THE ECONOMICS OF IMPERFECT COMPETITION* IN RELATION TO ITS CAMBRIDGE BACKGROUND

The best known aspect of *The Economics of Imperfect Competition* is doubtless its conception of group equilibrium on the lines first sketched by Sraffa. The problem of entry is now introduced explicitly, indeed becomes the dominant feature, leading to the famous tangency condition (referred to at the time as 'Mr Kahn's theorem') and the associated excess-capacity result. On the other hand, the interdependence of the perceived demand curves of the individual firms, and their relation to the market demand for the entire commodity-category produced by the industry, is, if anything, left in a vaguer state than Sraffa had achieved. The flavor is more 'Bertrandesque', but all questions of strategic interdependence among firms are simply ignored and the question of what constitutes an industry is entirely begged.[29]

In terms of the pages devoted to it, this particular aspect of the book is a quite limited one, moreover, it is hardly integrated at all with the bulk of the book. Eliminating all reference to the new theory of imperfect competition would be quite easy and would still leave a very substantial volume, a volume which would be more unified by always having the industry coterminous with a homogenous commodity.[30] Five main elements may be discerned in this hypothetical 'residual book':

1. A full treatment of the theory of the equilibrium and comparative statics of the profit maximizing single-product firm, possibly with monopoly and monopsony power and the ability to separate markets so as to price-discriminate.
2. A careful and elaborate treatment of the partial equilibrium theory of competitive supply and price determination which admits rising and falling supply price.
3. A tracing of the various consequences of converting an erstwhile competitive industry into a (costlessly managed) cartel which preserves the identity of the individual firms but maximizes group profit.
4. Some fragmentary partial equilibrium discussion of welfare, mainly touching on price discrimination and labor exploitation.
5. An ambitious general equilibrium attempt in the penultimate chapter to consider the welfare consequences of 'a world of monopolies'.

In connection with the prominence of these five elements it is perhaps worth noting that the book still bore the title 'Monopoly' when Keynes recommended it to Macmillan in November 1932.[31]

The first element calls for little comment. It developed, with the aid of the new concept of marginal revenue and a new apparatus of marginal curves, a full and unified treatment of profit-maximizing equilibrium for a firm facing a fixed market environment (not involving strategic interdependence with other firms). The development was more elaborate, especially in connection with monopsony and factor substitution than anything that had gone before, and various special cases were all brought together in a more unified way. Nevertheless, the underlying ideas were familiar from the work of Marshall, Edgeworth, Pigou, Bowley, and others, and were conservative rather than revolutionary in nature.

The second element is particularly interesting because it represents an uncompromising defense of the Cambridge tradition against Sraffa's attack on partial equilibrium methods. The concept of 'efficiency' units of factors, which Joan Robinson introduced in this context as an aid to exposition and graphical analysis was soon disowned by her, justifiably in connection with its employment in the appendix to make all production functions homogeneous of degree one by definition, but less justifiably in connection with its perfectly valid simplifying role elsewhere in the book.

The third element is very much a set of variations on a theme enunciated by Pigou (with roots in Marshall). However, in contrast to what Joan Robinson herself was later to castigate as the 'scholastic' tone of the book, distinct intimations of a concern for contemporary events and problems also creep in here. At issue is the justification for the 'rationalization' movement: one of the major reactions to the depressed market conditions of the early 1930s. Unfortunately, though, the book's contrasts between perfect competition and full cartelization are able to shed only limited light on 'one of the most important practical questions of the present age: the effect of the combination of firms, selling against each other in *imperfect* competition, into a single unit of control' (Robinson, 1933, p.10; stress added). This exemplifies the limited extent to which the new concept of imperfect competition was integrated into a book in which older views and approaches remained deeply entrenched.

The fourth element too was very much a development of Pigovian approaches, but the treatment was scrappy and hampered by the fact that Joan Robinson shared with the other Cambridge economists an unwillingness to push demand theory and welfare economics beyond the point Marshall had taken them. *The Economics of Imperfect Competition* is pervaded by a skepticism that any more can be said, and a sharp contrast between final demands, which are vague and subjective, and input demands, which are sharply defined and objective due to the 'rational' profit-maximization principle which underlies them.

It is in the chapter on 'A World of Monopolies', comprising the fifth element listed above, that the book's most powerful and innovative analysis is to be found (Robinson, 1933, pp.307–26: also see Kahn, 1935). Although represented as 'an excursion into the field of analysis covered by the *Economics of Welfare*' (Robinson, 1933, p.307n) it goes well beyond Pigou in working with a truly general equilibrium setting. It is surprising that this discussion has not had more impact on the subsequent development of welfare economics, but, once again, the vague treatment of final demand made the discussion less compelling than it might have been.

6 CONCLUDING COMMENTS

The Economics of Imperfect Competition can be regarded as both a response to, and a reaction against, Sraffa's challenge to what he perceived as the Marshallian tradition in value theory. It developed, although not entirely satisfactorily, a conception of group equilibrium of the sort called for by

Sraffa, but at the same time it defended the broadly Marshallian tradition against Sraffa's attack on the use of partial equilibrium methods.[32]

The treatment of imperfect competition *per se* was not fully integrated into the book. It remained something of a *jeu d'ésprit*, lacking the seriousness of purpose and concern for real phenomena of the contemporaneous but independent work of Chamberlin (1933) – although Chamberlin's theoretical formulations also proved flawed and unsatisfactory.

Joan Robinson's defense of the Cambridge tradition as to competitive partial equilibrium analysis was equally preoccupied with purely theoretical issues, and indifferent to questionings of empirical applicability such as Clapham (1922).[33] But here, at least, the rules of the game were well established and the kind of justification offered by Pigou (1922) might be taken for granted. Nevertheless, there remains an ambiguity as to just what was being attacked or defended. It was not Marshall's original version. Neither Sraffa nor Joan Robinson showed at this time much comprehension of what Marshall actually said. Was it Pigou's version? This was not clearly formulated in print until Pigou (1928) appeared. Perhaps a previous oral tradition existed, but it seems more likely that Pigou himself had not fully articulated his thought before he wrote this article. It appears that, so far as Joan Robinson, if not Sraffa, is concerned, a new figure – Gerald Shove – must be introduced here.[34] By 1933 Shove had been working for possibly as much as a decade on a major study of value theory. Brief extracts from the manuscript were reproduced in Shove (1930) but – possibly in part because of the appearance of Joan Robinson's book – the work was never published, or perhaps even completed, and very little can be gleaned about its coverage and substance. Nevertheless, it is clear that Shove had an important influence on the younger generation in Cambridge. As Joan Robinson wrote in the preface to *The Economics of Imperfect Competition*:

> Mr Shove's articles [Shove, 1928, 1930] form the basis of my treatment of rent and of the four cost curves. But a reader who is acquainted only with those articles would very much under-estimate my debt to him, for his teaching in Cambridge for many years past has influenced directly and indirectly the whole approach to many problems of economic analysis. (Robinson, 1933, p.xiii–xiv)

Shove, who had a keen critical intelligence and a mastery of the writings of Marshall and Pigou, may well have been the medium through whom Joan Robinson's perception of Cambridge tradition was acquired. Unfortunately, evidence is slight, and a detailed exploration of Shove's influence is too complex and imponderable a question to enter into here. It is also necessary to leave aside any attempt to consider in detail the contributions to *Imperfect Competition* of R. F. Kahn and E. A. G. Robinson. It is clear that Kahn's collaboration in the book was close and that most of the mathematical notes, as well as the tangency theorem, must be attributed to him.

E. A. G. Robinson's *Structure of Competitive Industry* (1931) – ostensibly a student handbook, but actually a significant original contribution – stands in a complemetary relationship to *Imperfect Competition* by providing the necessary elaboration for what lies beneath the firm's cost curves.[35] Finally, it will be clear that almost no attention has been paid to intellectual influences emanating outside Cambridge, although these seem to have been slight (in accordance with Cambridge practice) minor indebtedness to Hicks probably being the most significant obligation (Robinson, 1933, p.xv).

The Cambridge tradition in value theory has a continuous but complex line of evolution from Marshall, through Pigou and Shove, to Joan Robinson's 'residual book'. But though there were threads of continuity, the evolution also transformed the theory in significant ways. Marshall had attempted to harness equilibrium concepts and evolutionary or biological considerations into a loose impressionistic balance, and had worked with a notion of industry equilibrium not requiring the equilibrium of each firm. By the time Joan Robinson wrote it had become almost axiomatic to base the supply side of value theory on the profit-maximizing equilibrium of the individual producer. This development was a consequence of economists' increased concern with logical consistency and rigor, more than a conscious rejection of Marshall's approach. Lacking the analytical tools to develop one side of his uneasy compromise, it was almost inevitable that the balance should tip rapidly to the other side given the tacit methodological imperatives of twentieth-century economics. *Imperfect Competition* marks the culmination of this line of development in the Cambridge approach to the theory of value.

It is well known that Joan Robinson eventually came to repudiate her first book as wrongheaded and misguided. She came to see it as 'scholastic', starting from 'a purely *a priori* set of assumptions – the assumptions that Pigou had distilled from Marshall', and 'based on a fudge – confusing comparisons of possible alternative equilibrium conditions with the analysis of a process taking place through time'.[36] Increasingly, and not entirely accurately, she came to distinguish Marshall's approach to industrial analysis from Pigou's ('a loyal disciple of Marshall's and quite innocent of any knowledge of industry': Robinson, 1979, p.11) and to show an appreciation of its distinctive features quite lacking in *Imperfect Competition* itself.[37] She came eventually to see Marshall as having pointed out a different general approach to economics:

> It seems to me now that I took the wrong turning. Professor Pigou had long since worked the hard core of Marshall's analysis into a logical

> system of static theory. Instead of abandoning the static analysis and trying to come to terms with Marshall's theory of development, I followed Pigou and worked out the *Economics of Imperfect Competition* on static assumptions. (Robinson, 1951, pp.vii–viii)

These growing reservations are not without basis, and other criticisms might be levied too – at the complete neglect of strategic interaction among firms, for example (see Robinson, 1960, pp.228–9). In spite of this, the book stands as a monument to a certain approach to economics which has proved to have considerable power, appeal and longevity. The later Joan Robinson might have come to share Pigou's aversion to 'young women who drew curves and said "therefore"' (E. A. G. Robinson, 1984, p.232) but the young Joan Robinson was a formidable exponent of an approach to economics which still remains dominant.

Notes

1. The fullest extant treatment is that of Shackle (1967) which may be recommended. See also Moss (1984), Loasby (1978; 1985).
2. Robinson (1978, p.ix). For further biographical background see Harcourt (1982).
3. See Cambridge University (1924, pp.358–66). The books on economic theory recommended for Part I were 'Marshall, *Principles of Economics*; Taussig, *Principles of Economics*; Gide and Rist, *History of Economic Doctrines*; Cassel, *The Nature and Necessity of Interest*; Carver, *The Distribution of Wealth*; Henderson, *Supply and Demand*.' No recommendations were made for Part II. Marshall's *Industry and Trade* was recommended for Part I's paper on Industry and Labour, while Pigou's *The Political Economy of War* was listed for the Part I paper on Trade and Finance.
4. Robinson (1978, p.ix). 'Beauty and the Beast' was published in Robinson (1951) and republished in Robinson (1978).
5. Robinson (1978, p.ix). Note, however, that Sraffa had ceased to lecture by the time the Robinsons returned from India.
6. Whitaker (1982), which I hope one day to revise! The account which follows is somewhat stylized and I do not attempt to establish the case in detail. Marshall's views were essentially present in the 1890 first edition of his *Principles*, but all references will be to the eighth edition (Marshall, 1920).
7. Marshall (1920, p.316). On this point see in particular Shove (1942), Hague (1958).
8. For discussions of Marshall's reconciliation of competition and internal economies of scale see Frisch (1950), Wolfe (1954), Newman (1960), Hollander (1961), Levine (1980). The classic attack by Robbins (1928) has not worn well.
9. The version described here is that of Pigou (1912). The somewhat confused earlier version (Pigou, 1910) treated the increasing-cost and decreasing-cost cases asymmetrically. External effects in consumption were also contemplated.
10. A similar criticism was made by Clark (1913) and also hinted by Edgeworth

(1913) in his inimitably elusive style. Marshall's private notes on Pigou (1912) are reproduced and analyzed in Bharadwaj (1972).

11. The contrast with the rather feeble discussion in Pigou (1927) is marked. Pigou (1927; 1928) were both provoked by Sraffa's critique (Sraffa 1926) and the resulting debate, but each is concerned more with clarifying Pigou's own position than responding to Sraffa's attack, and may thus be dealt with independently of the latter.
12. That Pigou was unconscious of the extent of his departure from Marshall is evidenced by his interpreting Marshall's statement that 'an increase in the aggregate volume of production of anything will generally increase the size, and therefore the internal economies' of the representative firm as concerned merely with how the firm's minimum-cost output varies with y. See Marshall (1920, p.318), Pigou (1928, p.252).
13. These arguments were spelled out more fully in Pigou (1929, pp.802–5) but were clearly stated in Pigou (1928, p.251).
14. See Chipman (1965), Whitaker (1982) for further details.
15. Viner introduced the unnecessary restriction that external effects lower the firm's cost curves without changing its minimum-cost output. Robertson (1930, p.86) introduced confusion by coining the term 'external-internal' economies for external economies which raise this output.
16. See Newman (1960) and Newman and Wolfe (1961). The more recent work of Nelson and Winter (1982) might also be mentioned in this connection.
17. The comparison is evidently with the 'manufacturing' version of competition. Costs under monopoly are generally

> less than would have to be incurred if the same aggregate production were distributed among a multitude of comparatively small rival producers. They would have to struggle with one another for the attention of consumers, and would necessarily spend in the aggregate a great deal more on advertising in all its various forms than a single firm would; and they would be less able to avail themselves of the many various economies which result from production on a large scale. (Marshall, 1920, p.484)

18. This point is explained in detail in Whitaker (1986).
19. See especially Marshall (1919, pp.395–506) and Liebhafsky (1955). Liebhafsky provides an extensive description of Marshall's views, but his attempt to draw parallels with the later theories of imperfect and monopolistic competition is not entirely convincing. Marshall himself explained that 'mathematical analysis cannot easily be applied to *conditional* monopoly: it is almost constrained to start with the hypothesis of *pure* monopoly' (Marshall, 1919, p.450n).
20. Ironically, this occurs in the chapter on railway problems, not in that on discriminating monopoly. A typographical error by which $\varphi_2(x_2)$ was written as $(\varphi_2)x_2$ was carried forward into all editions of the *Economics of Welfare* (e.g. Pigou, 1929, p.302n).
21. Compare Pigou (1912, pp.192–214) with Pigou (1929, pp.267–89, 806–10). The two most important changes are the refinement in the concept of marginal social cost, already discussed in Section 2 above, and the dropping of an obviously incorrect argument about discrimination with free entry (Pigou, 1912, pp.213–14). The analysis of a price ceiling on a monopolist appeared in both editions but was less formal in the earlier one (Pigou, 1912, pp.265–6; 1929, pp.806–7).

22. Mention might be made of the fact that both Marshall and Pigou regarded the outcome of bilateral monopoly as indeterminate. In this context Pigou introduced the notion of exploitation of labor as an excess of the marginal product of a worker over the actual wage. See Marshall (1920, pp.493–4, 791–3), Pigou (1929, pp.201–2, 811–12).
23. The background to Sraffa's critique of partial equilibrium methods is set out much more fully in Sraffa (1925). There, he gives a clear exposition of the Edgeworth–Cunynghame reconciliation of competition and falling supply price by means of economies external to firms but internal to the industry. But, remarkably, he attributes this position to Marshall. Neither here nor in Sraffa (1926) did he attempt to come to grips with what Marshall actually wrote.
24. See Sraffa's summary description of his 1925 article in a June 1926 letter to Keynes reproduced in Roncaglia (1978, pp.11–13).
25. See Roncaglia (1978, especially pp.9–17).
26. Sraffa to Keynes, June 1926 (Roncaglia, 1978, p.13). That Marshall's scheme ignores internal economies was disputed in Section 2 above.
27. To similar effect:

> as soon as any imperfection is introduced in a system of competition (and such an imperfection in general takes the form of differentiation between the products of different producers of the same commodity) equilibrium is reached in a way extremely similar to that of monopoly and very far from that of competition. (Sraffa to Keynes, June 1926: Roncaglia, 1978, p.13)

28. It is surprising that Sraffa failed to allude to the proof in Cournot (1838, pp.79–99) that competitive equilibrium is approached as the number of competitors becomes large, since the result is directly counter to his own conjecture.
29. The entire problem of interrelatedness of demand amongst firms is shamelessly evaded: 'The demand curve for the individual firm may be conceived to show the full effect upon the sales of that firm which results from any change in the price which it charges whether it causes a change in the prices charged by the others or not' (Robinson, 1933, p.21).
30. Eliminating pp.85–102 would leave about 330 pages of text containing only passing references to the new theory of imperfect competition.
31. See the interesting letter from Keynes to Macmillan reproduced in Keynes (1973, pp.866–8).
32. There is some self-deception in the claim in the preface to *Imperfect Competition* that 'Mr Sraffa's article must be regarded as the fount from which my work flows, for the chief aim of this book is to attempt to carry out his pregnant suggestion that the whole theory of value should be treated in terms of monopoly analysis' (Robinson, 1933, p.xiii: also see pp.3–4).
33. The posthumously published work of Jones (1933), which began in Cambridge, was the one conspicuous attempt to take up Clapham's challenge, but it seems to have been little regarded in Cambridge and its theoretical chapter verges on incoherence.
34. Sraffa's views seem to have been already fully formed in Italy, where a Marshallian school, of which Pantaleoni and Barone were luminaries, was in competition with the Paretian school to which Sraffa belonged by training. (I am indebted to Mauro Gallegati for advice on these matters.) Thus, it was Sraffa as much as anyone who introduced the Trojan horse of general

equilibrium into the Cambridge citadel – an ironical fact in the light of subsequent developments.

35. 'Mr Robinson's work on the optimum size of firms is the foundation of my treatment of competitive equilibrium, and plays an important part in the Appendix on Increasing and Diminishing Returns' (Robinson, 1933, p.xiii).
36. See Robinson (1960, p.222; 1979, pp.114, 112). More generally for retrospective views see Robinson (1951, pp.vii–viii; 1960, pp.222–45; 1969, pp.v–xii; 1978, pp.ix–xi; 1979, pp.1,155).
37. Compare Robinson (1960, pp.240–1; 1969, pp.v–vi, 1979, pp.10–12, 54) with the rather puzzled allusions to Marshall's approach in Robinson (1933, pp.91, 128n, 168n, 342).

References

Bharadwaj, K. (1972) 'Marshall on Pigou's *Wealth and Welfare*', *Economica*, 39: 32–46.

Cambridge University (1924) *The Student's Handbook to the University and Colleges of Cambridge*, 23rd edn revised to 30 June 1924 (Cambridge: Cambridge University Press).

Chamberlin, E. H. (1933) *The Theory of Monopolistic Competition* (Cambridge, Mass.: Harvard University Press).

Chipman, J. S. (1965) 'A Survey of the Theory of International Trade: Part 2, The Neoclassical Theory', *Econometrica*, 33: 685–760.

Clapham, J. H. (1922) 'Of Empty Economic Boxes', *Economic Journal*, 32: 305–14.

Clark, J. M. (1913) 'Review of *Wealth and Welfare* by A. C. Pigou', *American Economic Review*, 3: 623–5.

Cournot, A. A. (1838) *Mathematical Principles of the Theory of Wealth*, translated 1897 (New York: Macmillan).

Edgeworth, F. Y. (1913) 'Contributions to the Theory of Railway Rates, Part IV', *Economic Journal*, 23: 206–26.

Frisch, R. (1950) 'Alfred Marshall's Theory of Value', *Quarterly Journal of Economics*, 64: 495–524.

Hague, D. C. (1958) 'Alfred Marshall and the Competitive Firm', *Economic Journal*, 68: 673–90.

Harcourt, G. C. (1982) 'Joan Robinson', in G. C. Harcourt. *The Social Science Imperialists* (London: Routledge & Kegan Paul).

Harrod, R. F. (1951) *The Life of John Maynard Keynes* (London: Macmillan).

Hollander, S. (1961) 'The Representative Firm and Imperfect Competition', *Canadian Journal of Economics*, 27: 236–41.

Jones, G. T. (1933) *Increasing Return* (Cambridge: Cambridge University Press).

Kahn, R. F. (1935) 'Some Notes on Ideal Output', *Economic Journal*, 45: 1–35.

Kahn, R. F. (1984) *The Making of Keynes' General Theory* (Cambridge: Cambridge University Press).

Keynes, J. M. (1924) 'Alfred Marshall 1842–1924', *Economic Journal*, 34: 311–72; repr. in J. M. Keynes (1933) *Essays in Biography* (London: Macmillan).

Keynes, J. M. (1973) *Economic Articles and Correspondence: Investment and Editorial, Collected Writings*, Vol.12, edited by D. Moggridge (London: Macmillan).

Levine, A. L. (1980) 'Increasing Returns: the Competitive Model and the Enigma that was Alfred Marshall', *Scottish Journal of Political Economy*, 27: 260–75.

Liebhafsky, H. H. (1955) 'A Curious Case of Neglect: Marshall's *Industry and Trade*', *Canadian Journal of Economics*, 21: 339–53.
Loasby, B. J. (1978) 'Whatever Happened to Marshall's Theory of Value?', *Scottish Journal of Political Economy*, 25: 1–12.
Loasby, B. J. (1985) 'Joan Robinson's Wrong Turning', unpublished paper, University of Stirling.
Marshall, A. (1890) 'Some Aspects of Competition', *Journal of the Royal Statistical Society*, 53: 612–43; repr. in A. C. Pigou (ed.) (1925) *Memorials of Alfred Marshall* (London: Macmillan).
Marshall, A. (1919) *Industry and Trade* (London: Macmillan).
Marshall, A. (1920) *Principles of Economics*, 8th edn (London: Macmillan).
Moss, S., (1984) 'The History of the Theory of the Firm, from Marshall to Robinson and Chamberlin: The Source of Positivism in Economics', *Economica* 51: 307–18.
Nelson, R. R. and S. G. Winter (1982) *An Evolutionary Theory of Economic Change* (Cambridge, Mass.: Belknap).
Newman, P. K. (1960) 'The Erosion of Marshall's Theory of Value', *Quarterly Journal of Economics* 74: 587–600.
Newman, P. K. and J. N, Wolfe (1961) 'A Model for the Long-run Theory of Value', *Review of Economic Studies* 29: 51–61.
Pigou, A. C. (1904) 'Monopoly and Consumers' Surplus', *Economic Journal*, 14: 388–94.
Pigou, A. C. (1910) 'Producers' and Consumers' Surplus', *Economic Journal*, 20: 358–70.
Pigou, A. C. (1912) *Wealth and Welfare* (London: Macmillan).
Pigou, A. C. (1920) *The Economics of Welfare*, 1st edn (London: Macmillan).
Pigou, A. C. (1922) 'Empty Economic Boxes: A Reply', *Economic Journal*, 32: 458–65.
Pigou, A. C. (1924) *The Economics of Welfare*, 2nd edn (London: Macmillan).
Pigou, A. C. (1927) 'The Laws of Diminishing and Increasing Cost', *Economic Journal*, 37: 188–97.
Pigou, A. C. (1928) 'An Analysis of Supply', *Economic Journal*, 38: 238–57.
Pigou, A. C. (1929) *The Economics of Welfare*, 3rd edn (London: Macmillan).
Robbins, L. C. (1928) 'The Representative Firm', *Economic Journal*, 38: 387–404.
Robertson, D. H, (1924) 'Those Empty Boxes', *Economic Journal*, 34: 16–31.
Robertson, D. H. (1930) 'Increasing Returns and the Representative Firm', *Economic Journal*, 40: 80–9.
Robinson, E. A. G. (1931) *The Structure of Competitive Industry* (London: Nisbet).
Robinson, E. A. G. (1978) 'Keynes and his Cambridge Colleagues', in D. Patinkin and J. C. Leith (eds) *Keynes, Cambridge and the General Theory* (London: Macmillan).
Robinson, E. A. G. (1984) 'Comment', in P. Wiles and G. Routh (eds) *Economics in Disarray* (Oxford: Blackwell).
Robinson, J. (1933) *The Economics of Imperfect Competition* (London: Macmillan).
Robinson, J. (1951) *Collected Economic Papers*, Vol.1 (Oxford: Blackwell).
Robinson, J. (1960) *Collected Economic Papers*, Vol.2 (Oxford: Blackwell).
Robinson, J. (1969) *The Economics of Imperfect Competition*, 2nd edn (London: Macmillan).
Robinson, J. (1978) *Contributions to Modern Economics* (Oxford: Blackwell).
Robinson, J. (1979) *Collected Economic Papers*, Vol.5 (Oxford: Blackwell).
Roncaglia, A. (1978) *Sraffa and the Theory of Prices* (New York: Wiley).
Shackle, G. L. S. (1967) *The Years of High Theory* (Cambridge: Cambridge University Press).

Shove, G. F. (1928) 'Varying Costs and Marginal Net Products', *Economic Journal*, 38: 258–66.

Shove, G. F. (1930) 'The Representative Firm and Increasing Returns', *Economic Journal*, 40: 94–116.

Shove, G. F. (1942) 'The Place of Marshall's *Principles* in the Development of Economic Theory', *Economic Journal*, 52: 294–329.

Sraffa, P. (1925) 'Sulle Relazioni fra Costo e Quantita Prodotta', *Annali di Economia*, 2: 277–328.

Sraffa, P. (1926) 'The Laws of Returns under Competitive Conditions', *Economic Journal*, 36: 535–50.

Sraffa, P. (1962) *The Production of Commodities by Means of Commodities* (Cambridge: Cambridge University Press).

Viner, J. (1931) 'Cost Curves and Supply Curves', *Zeitschrift fur Nationalokonomie* 3: 23–46; repr. in American Economic Association (1953) *Readings in Price Theory* (Homewood: Irwin).

Whitaker, J. K. (1982) 'Increasing Returns and External Economics: Some Early Developments', Paper presented to the Annual Meetings of the History of Economics Society, Duke University.

Whitaker, J. K. (1986) 'The Continuing Relevance of Alfred Marshall', in R. D. C. Black (ed.) *Ideas in Economics* (London: Macmillan).

Wolfe, J. N. (1954) 'The Representative Firm', *Economic Journal*, 64: 337–49.

Young, A. A. (1913) 'Review of *Wealth and Welfare* by A. C. Pigou', *Quarterly Journal of Economics*, 27: 672–86.

4 Imperfect Competition After Fifty Years

Robert L. Bishop

Joan Robinson's maiden effort was one of which any economist might have been proud. Had the Nobel committee ever deigned to honor her (which I suspect it might have if Edward Chamberlain had lived long enough to share an award) *The Economics of Imperfect Competition* would deservedly have been a central jewel in her crown.

Her main contribution is well known, even by the more recent generations that may or may not bother to read the original work. It takes a theory to awaken the profession's attention fully to what later appear to be obvious facts; and this was assuredly so in the present instance. Following on Sraffa's pregnant suggestions, Robinson and Chamberlin cured most economists almost instantaneously of the notion that, save for a few islands of monopoly, the world economy was adequately modelled by pure or perfect competition and its central equilibrium condition of supply equal to demand.

To be sure, the cure sometimes took effect only with some delay, and in some other quarters it has been more or less permanently resisted. Keynes, for all his proximity to Robinson and her mentor, R. F. Kahn, still elected to put the *General Theory* into a context of purely competitive product markets: although wage rates were sticky despite labor supply in excess of demand (and subject to a rather dubious money illusion), an expansion of employment was deemed impossible except in conjunction with a reduced real-wage rate – as if the product-market equilibrium were purely competitive. To his credit, Keynes soon conceded that this conclusion was, if not erroneous, at least not obligatory.[1] Indeed, both Keynesian and post-Keynesian macroeconomics are far better served by a microeconomic foundation that explicitly incorporates elements of imperfect competition, in both product and factor markets.

Possibly the principal resistance to according imperfectly competitive elements their rightful role is grounded in the preference of the theorists themselves for the greater definiteness and analytical tractability of perfect competition. This vested interest, which is as widespread today as ever, was once given its classical statement by Hicks (1939, pp.83–5). To meet certain obvious difficulties, he momentarily contemplated 'sacrificing the assumption of perfect competition', but quickly drew back because 'a general abandonment of the assumption of perfect competition, a universal adoption of the assumption of monopoly, must have very destructive consequences for economic theory'. To avoid this 'threatened wreckage . . . of the greater part of economic theory', he preferred to base his analysis on the faith or hope that 'the laws of an economic system working under perfect competition will not be appreciably varied in a system which contains widespread elements of monopoly'. As so often in economics, one is reminded of the old joke about the drunk who, having lost his watch in a dark alley, searches for it on the corner where the light is better.

Robinson was once asked, I am told, what motivated her to write *Imperfect Competition*. She is said to have answered that it was to show how labor was exploited.

To condense her argument, suppose that a firm has a production function, $q = q(L,K)$, and faces the demand-price function, $p = p(q)$ – where q is quantity of output, p is its price, and L and K are the respective quantities of labor and capital. Subject to later comments, assume for the moment a wholly static context in which L and K represent the current services of homogeneous physical factors, hired at a wage rate w and a rent rate r, respectively.[2] Denote the supply–price functions of the factors to the firm as $w = w(L)$ and $r = r(K)$. All functions are twice differentiable; and attention is limited to cases where $dp/dq \leqslant 0$, $dw/dL \geqslant 0$, and $dr/dK \geqslant 0$.

The firm's total revenue (R) and marginal revenue (dR/dq) are:

$$R = p(q)q = R(q) = R[q(L,K)] = R^*(L,K),$$

$$\frac{dR}{dq} = p + q\frac{dp}{dq} \leqslant p.$$

Similarly, the firm's total cost (C) and the marginal costs of its factors ($\partial C/\partial K$) are:

$$C = w(L)L + r(K)K = C(L,K),$$

$$\frac{\partial C}{\partial L} = w + L\frac{dw}{dL} \geqslant w,$$

$$\frac{\partial C}{\partial K} = r + K\frac{dr}{dK} \geqslant r.$$

When the firm maximizes its profit, $\pi = R - C$, the first-order conditions may be written in two ways:

$$\frac{\partial R}{\partial L} = \frac{\partial C}{\partial L} \text{ or } \frac{dR}{dq}\frac{\partial q}{\partial L} = \frac{\partial C}{\partial L},$$

$$\frac{\partial R}{\partial K}=\frac{\partial C}{\partial K} \text{ or } \frac{dR}{dq}\frac{\partial q}{\partial K}=\frac{\partial C}{\partial K}.$$

Departing slightly from Robinson's terminology, let us call $\partial R/\partial L$ the marginal revenue product of labor (MRP_L) and $\partial q/\partial L$ labor's marginal physical product (MPP_L) – and similarly for $\partial R/\partial K$ and $\partial q/\partial K$. Analogous to $MRP_L = (dR/dq)(\partial q/\partial L)$ is labor's value of marginal product, $VMP_L = p(\partial Q/\partial L)$.[3]

Concentrating now on labor, we can summarize all the various types of equilibrium thus:

$$p\frac{\partial q}{\partial L} \geqslant \frac{dR}{dq}\frac{dq}{\partial L}=\frac{\partial C}{\partial L} \geqslant w.$$

Since $p = dR/dq$ in a perfectly competitive product market and $dC/dL = w$ in a perfectly competitive labor market, it then follows that $p(\partial q/\partial L) = w$ and $\partial q/\partial L = w/p$.[4] Alternatively, VMP_L can exceed the money-wage rate and MPP_L can exceed the real-wage rate for either or both of two reasons, because (i) $p > dR/dq$ in the product market so that $VMP_L > MRP_L$ and (ii) $\partial C/\partial L > w$ in the factor market, so that $MRP_L > w$. Labor is exploited, in Robinson's terminology, whenever $VMP_L > w$. The exploitation is called monopolistic in the first case and monopsonistic in the second.[5]

One is left to wonder whether Robinson considered such exploitation an offense against efficiency or justice, or both. She does not help us much with her rather casually parenthetical characterization of exploitation as 'the payment to labour of less than its proper wage' (1933, p.281). More significantly, perhaps, her nearly exclusive preoccupation with labor as the victim of exploitation suggests that her concern was primarily with injustice. Although Book IX is entitled simply 'Exploitation', its only two chapters are limited, as in their titles, to the two kinds of exploitation 'of labour'. Even in the volume's final chapter, 'A World of Monopolies', where the analysis shifts to more anonymous factors of production, their remuneration is characterized as wages (e.g. p.311). Toward the end of the discussion, however, there are references to the comparative exploitation of labor and land (pp.319–20).

No matter what we may conclude about the relationship of Robinsonian exploitation to distributive justice, it surely has a firmer analytical connection with allocational inefficiency. Absent externalities, Pareto efficiency ordinarily requires everywhere such equalities as $w/p = \partial q/\partial L$ and $r/p = \partial q/\partial K$. This is so, for example, whenever there is a labor–leisure choice, in order to insure the equality of $\partial q/\partial L$ to the laborer's marginal rate of substitution of L for q – that is, the ratio of his marginal utility of leisure (or disutility of L) to his marginal utility of q. More generally, the indicated equalities are also required whenever any factor has alternative uses in producing final product and one or more intermediate products, as well as being an object of direct consumption.[6]

Robinson inherited her concept of exploitation from Pigou (1932, pp.556–63), except that he had in mind only the monopsonistic type and she accordingly expanded his concept to embrace the monopolistic type as well. With reference to allocational efficiency, this is fully justified because $w/p < \partial q/\partial L$ is inefficient irrespective of the underlying type of market imperfection.

On the other hand, in the context of distributional 'fairness', with which Pigou was specifically concerned (p.549), and with reference to exploitees as victims, the monopsonistic type is far more relevant than the monpolistic. For example, if a product monopolist and a competitive industry both operate in the same competitive labor market, the resulting equality of wage rates is undoubtedly fair despite the fact that Robinson would deem some of the workers exploited and the others not.

More fundamentally, the victims of product monopoly are the consumers of the product, not the factors hired to produce it (even apart from the fact that the employees of monopolists are often treated more generously than their counterparts in the competitive sector). It was thus rather superficial of Robinson to have concentrated so exclusively on factor suppliers as victims, no matter how the connotation of exploitation is divided between injustice and inefficiency.

As to possible cures of the two types of exploitation, Robinson gets back on the right track; for she sees that, while the appropriate corrective for the monopsonistic exploitation of labor is higher wage rates (1933, p.295), the monopolistic type calls instead for lower prices (p.284). Let us examine these points with some care.

Just as supply exceeds demand whenever a firm is in equilibrium with $p > dC/dq$ (in the sense that the firm would gladly sell more at the current price if it could), it is similarly implied that the firm's demand for labor exceeds the supply whenever $w < MRP_L$. Furthermore, provided that the firm enjoys some surplus income (so that it is not driven from the market by the slightest adverse change[7]), the imposition of a moderately lower price on the monopolist will increase his output and factor employment, and the imposition of a moderately higher wage rate on the monopsonist will increase his labor employment and output.[8] Thus each regulation, while lowering the firm's profit, helps everyone else – consumers and factor suppliers alike. Moreover, in that imaginary analytical world of costless transfers, the beneficiaries could even fully compensate the firm for its reduced profit and still retain positive net benefits – as can be shown on the standard diagrams of the firm's equilibrium output and labor employment, respectively.

By contrast, if a non-monopsonistic monopolist is forced to pay higher wage rates, he reduces both labor quantity employed and output and raises price. We have here a distinction that J. K. Galbraith should have made when he celebrated the countervailing power of unions (1952). There is indeed scope for a socially beneficial countervailing of monopsony power; but once this job is done, any further increase of wage rates hurts everyone except the lucky holders of the reduced number of jobs.

Robinson's analysis of monopsony and its cure reveals her bias that labor is almost always the victim and rarely if ever an offender against efficiency or justice. Consider again the case of the profitable firm that is both a product monopolist and a labor monopsonist. The basic diagram (p.294) consists of three familiar curves: the positively sloped labor supply curve (*AC*), the associated, higher marginal cost of labor (*MC*), and the relevant negatively sloped demand for labor (*D*) – see note 3. A monopsonist with the unilateral power to set the wage-rate maximizes profit at the quantity of *L* where *MC* intersects *D*, and the equilibrium wage rate is the corresponding ordinate of *AC*. A minimum or bargained wage-rate where *AC* intersects *D* would then maximize employment and output, and minimize product price; and it would also imitate a perfectly competitive labor market's equality of labor demand and supply. A still higher wage rate converts the former monopsonistic excess demand for labor into a monopolistic excess of supply; employment and output decline, and product price rises.

This analysis is in no way inconsistent with Robinson's, but hers has a very different emphasis. She considers both the wage increase that maximizes employment and the greater one that keeps employment the same as in the monopsonistic equilibrium. Both cases are rather impartially presented as just two alternative ways of eliminating monopsonistic exploitation. Nothing is said about the exertion of labor-monopoly power as the opposite of monopsony power. Nothing is said about either the injustice or inefficiency when some fully qualified workers are eager to work at a monopolistic wage-rate (or less) but are unable to do so.

Indeed, throughout the entire work, labor monopoly is Banquo's ghost.[9] Labor is either exploited or it is not; it never exploits. Especially on Robinson's level of abstraction, the necessary and sufficient conditions for labor monopsony or monopoly are perfectly symmetrical: the one implies an excess of demand over supply and the other implies the opposite. To give the impression that labor monopsony is a major problem and labor monopoly is not worth discussing is inexcusable – in a world where jobs are universally regarded as inherently scarce, where the creation of new jobs has a high social priority, and where (in primary, as opposed to secondary, labor markets) the queueing of qualified job candidates is taken for granted as the normal state.[10]

The closest that Robinson comes to acknowledging a possibly anti-social effect of unions appears in a rather ambivalent discussion of a situation in which 'the market for the commodity and the market for labour are both perfect', but the industry makes temporarily abnormal profits because new firms have not yet had time to enter (pp.289–91). Since neither monopoly nor monopsony power is present, she recognizes that the situation 'does not conform to our definition of exploitation', but the mere temporary existence of abnormal profits prompts her to call it 'similar' or 'akin' to exploitation (p.289). She then says that this 'quasi-exploitation . . . would be removed, so far as the particular industry was concerned, if wages were raised until the abnormal profits disappeared, so that conditions of full equilibrium were produced'.

Robinson concludes, however, that 'to remove the quasi-exploitation in this way is not necessarily a desirable course' (pp.290–1). The drawback is that it 'must entail the misdirection of resources', as compared to the effects of industry expansion in accordance with 'the perfectly *laissez-faire* conditions of the economic text-books' (p.290). She cannot quite make up her mind about that 'system of the text-books'. Although 'it has some merits', it 'perhaps never existed and perhaps if it did it would not have been a very admirable one'. She also expresses the opinion that profits being 'kept at the normal level by changes in wages' is 'an assumption probably far more realistic than the assumption of the text-books'.

So far we have been concerned primarily with the cases of the isolated product monopolist or labor monopsonist. Additional complications appear in Robinson's analysis of the imperfectly competitive industry composed of a well-defined group of firms. She limits her attention, understandably, to the convenient special case in which all the active firms in the group have a perfectly symmetrical relationship to one another, with zero surplus income in long-run equilibrium (p.286). Whether the firms all have (to the same degree) either product-monopoly or labor-monopsony power, the removal of the imperfection (or exploitation) drives some firms out of the industry, and therefore has a more complex effect on the industry's total output and total employment.

In each instance, the exploitation might be removed in either of two ways: (i) the product-demand or labor-supply data spontaneously change in an appropriate manner, or (ii) without any change of data, costlessly enforced price ceilings or wage floors are imposed. Robinson considers each scenario in turn for labor monopsony, but only the first for product monopoly.

The case of just product monopoly is the simpler. It is assumed that all factor supplies are perfectly elastic and the firms' production functions are independent of industry output (p.286n); so each firm's cost curves, besides being all alike, are unchanged. Robinson recognizes that the monopolistic exploitation 'cannot be removed by raising wages, but . . . would disappear if the market became perfect' (p.284). She seems to mean by this that consumers all suddenly abandon their brand preferences and now regard all the formerly differentiated products as homogeneous. More specifically, each firm's negatively sloped average-revenue (*AR*) curve suddenly becomes horizontal at its initial point of tangency with average cost (*AC*).

In the new long-run equilibrium, the number of firms declines and each still active firm increases *q* as it moves downward to the new tangency point at minimum *AC*. In Robinson's scenario, aggregate *q* necessarily increases (save in the limiting case of perfectly inelastic industry demand); but aggregate *pq* may readily either increase or decrease, according as industry demand is relatively elastic or inelastic.[11]

Characteristically, Robinson's primary concern is with the impact on labor – and, rather superficially in the present case, with the effect on the quantity of *L* employed by the given group of firms. This depends on (i) the effect on aggregate *pq* (which here equals *wL* plus *rK, w* and *r* being constant), and (ii) the change, if any, in the *K*/*L* ratio between the two relevant tangency points on each firm's *AC* curve.[12] Furthermore, when the assumptions of constant *w* and *r* are relaxed in favor of less elastic factor supplies, the effects on *L* and *K* are at least partly converted into effects on *w* and *r*.

Only toward the end of her discussion does she consider the effects of product–market imperfection on consumers. This leads her to say:

> It does not follow that because the labour attached to the industry gains by the imperfection of the market that it is therefore not desirable to remove it. Moreover, if all industries were in this case labour would not gain from the existence of the imperfection since their loss as consumers would more than offset their gain as wage earners. (p.288)

The last sentence is at least partly contradicted, however, in the next paragraph (which also concludes the section) where, if 'exploitation is universal' and 'firms of less than optimum size tend to employ less capital per man than optimum firms, . . . it is possible, though not likely, that labour would lose, on balance, by the removal of exploitation' (p.288).

Robinson's failure to consider the second scenario – that is, removing the exploitation by means of price ceilings – is both regrettable and revealing. It may be that she would have considered such discussion merely repetitious, since it is possible that price ceilings at minimum *AC* would have exactly the same objective effects as in her own scenario. This is all the more plausible, moreover, under an assumption that seems to pervade her whole book – namely, that product differentiation is no more than a superficial phenomenon of consumer myopia or irrationality (as it sometimes arguably is, for example, when various brands of medicines are chemically identical, but unequally priced). On the other hand, when product differences are real and consumer preferences are respected by the analyst, new issues are posed that her approach wholly evades. The main such issue concerns the implications for Pareto efficiency.

Under the second scenario when consumer preferences for the differentiated products are real, even the effect of the price ceilings on aggregate q is uncertain; for, even though consumption is stimulated by the lower prices of the products that survive, it may also be repressed by the unavailability of the products that disappear.[13] More fundamentally, and irrespective of the effect on aggregate q, necessary conditions for Pareto efficiency must now include not only the familiar marginal ones, but also the total ones relating to the availability of an optimal variety of products – see also Chamberlin (1950) and Bishop (1967b, esp. pp.255–60). Finally, because full Pareto efficiency is an unattainable Utopian goal, the practical moral is that, in making second-best judgments, one should give due weight to product variety as well as to prices.[14]

In Robinson's companion case, identical firms with monopsony power in hiring labor sell their outputs in a perfectly competitive market (pp.296ff.). Again it is assumed that the firms' identical production functions are independent of industry output and 'the supply to the industry of factors other than labour is perfectly elastic' (p.297n.). Owing to the assumed coincidence that each firm also faces the same positively sloped labor-supply curve (AC_L), tangent to the relevant curve of labor's average net productivity (ANP), the initial equilibrium again implies zero surplus income for every firm in the large-number group.[15] Each firm's equilibrium also implies that a horizontal $AR \equiv MR$ is tangent to a U-shaped AC curve at its minimum point; but that minimum point will shift to a greater output whenever the positively sloped supply curve of labor is replaced by a horizontal one.

A central ambiguity of the present case concerns the wider labor market of which each firm's own imperfectly competitive labor supply is a part. In general, when a firm changes its labor quantity employed, the laborers may come from or go to other firms in the same industry or to a wide variety of other industries. If the many firms in the perfectly competitive product market are geographically dispersed, there may be little or no overlap of their respective labor markets. At the opposite extreme, the industry's labor supply might conceivably be wholly isolated from the rest of the economy.

Except in the very unlikely latter case, Robinson's first-scenario assumption of a magical disappearance of the market imperfection undermines the relevance of her partial-equilibrium analysis of just the one industry. She evades this problem, however, by focusing on the possibility that the aggregate labor quantity in that industry might remain constant. Its workers are then better or worse off according as their wages rise or fall.

She first considers the dubious case in which 'the physical productivity per man is less when the firms are of optimum size' (p.298).[16] In that event, the lower q/L implies that the constant aggregate L produces a smaller aggregate q at a higher p; so the equilibrium w, equal to $ANP = (pq - rK)/L$, rises even more than it would with constant p.

In the far more likely event that q/L rises, the equilibrium $w = ANP$ may either rise or fall – in the same proportion as the industry's $pq - rK$. Since the change in pq reflects the elasticity of the industry's product demand and since rK changes in the same proportion as rK/L and K/L, it is easy enough to catalogue the possibilities: the equilibrium w tends to rise (fall) when product demand is relatively elastic (inelastic) or when K/L falls (rises). Robinson leaves it at that without adding that consumers are always benefited by the lower p and greater q. The improvement in allocational efficiency is much the same as with any cost-saving innovation, which is always capable of hurting special groups to the still greater benefit of the rest.[17]

In Robinson's second scenario, when the exploitation is removed by a minimum wage rate, the analysis can be more successfully fitted into the partial equilibrium framework, because the wage regulation can be limited to the given industry (for example, as the result of collective bargaining). She says that 'this method is less likely to lead to results favourable to labour' (p.299). That conclusion rests on (i) an argument that employment in the given industry is likely to be reduced, and (ii) an unstated value judgment that this disadvantage counts more than the higher wage rate of those who remain employed in the industry.

Robinson's analysis rests on an implicit assumption that there is zero interdependence of the labor-supply curves facing the individual firms in the given industry, so that AC_L is unchanged for each still active firm throughout the industry's adjustment. As the wage rate is raised by decree, even if only moderately, enough firms must leave so that industry q is reduced and p increased, thereby raising ANP enough so that the remaining firms can again break even. The exploitation of the still employed laborers is wholly removed only when each active firm's ANP curve has been raised sufficiently so that its maximum point lies on the new, horizontal AC_L schedule – at the level of the appropriate minimum wage.

As an alternative assumption, suppose that the given industry is highly concentrated geographically, so that there is a high degree of interdependence of the AC_L curves facing its constituent firms. Even though these curves would all shift to the left if all the firms were to pay the minimum wage, they shift rightward again as some firms depart. Furthermore, if that favorable shift is strong enough, it is possible that the ANP curves of the surviving firms would not have to be shifted upward by a reduced industry q and higher p. In a borderline case with an unchanged ANP curve, the appropriate minimum wage rate would again be at that curve's maximum point. In the normal case of an increased q/L, to be sure, the unchanged q would still imply a decrease in the industry's aggregate employment. In order to keep employment constant, accordingly, the rightward shifts of the

AC_L curves would have to be strong enough to lower p and the ANP curves enough to induce a sufficient increase of aggregate q.

There would still be, however, an important difference from the first scenario even if aggregate L happened to remain constant. Earlier, the spontaneous disappearance of the market imperfection could lower the wage-rate of an unchanged aggregate quantity of L; but that is not possible here, where a minimum wage at or below the initial equilibrium level would be inoperative.

In summary, not only is Robinson's relatively unfavorable judgment as to the likely impact of the second scenario on the welfare of labor highly suspect; but also she here neglects totally the benefits to the economy as a whole that derive from the correction of the monopsonistic distortion. Whether output in the given industry is increased or decreased, it is always produced more efficiently.

This critique may be concluded with a few short comments about the book's other strengths and weaknesses.

Even today, many students could profit from Robinson's excellent treatment of the basic techniques of the static equilibrium of the one-product firm, especially the geometry; and the discussion of monopoly equilibrium, competitive equilibrium, and their comparison can likewise be rewarding.

More substantively, the two chapters on price discrimination are classics. They are especially to be commended for their analysis of the conditions under which discrimination increases or decreases the monopolist's total output. Welfare aspects, however, are only sketchily treated. This topic might have been strengthened by a judicious use of Marshallian consumers' surplus (to speak only of tools available at the time).

Robinson's pioneering analysis (and naming) of monopsony has already been acknowledged. As applied to the consumer, however, the analysis suffers from a weak and confused handling of marginal utility. Even dimensionality is confused, as in the equating of marginal utility to price and marginal cost (e.g. p.216).

As to the central topic, imperfect competition, Robinson's pioneering contributions are obvious. At the same time, she deliberately cut herself off from many major aspects of the problem. In acknowledging that 'complications' attributable to advertising are to be ignored, she says, unhelpfully: 'It may be assumed that expenditure on advertisement necessary to increase the sale of a firm can be treated as equivalent, from the point of view of the entrepreneur, to a reduction in price having the same effect upon sales' (p.21). On the same page is her celebrated recognition and immediate evasion of the oligopoly problem: 'The demand curve for the individual firm may be conceived to show the full effect upon the sales of that firm which results from any change in the price which it charges, whether it causes a change in the prices charged by others or not. It is not to our purpose to consider this question in detail.'

Although product differentiation is not analyzed in any depth either, at least it has a relatively clear and legitimate place in the analysis. The differentiatedness of labor and other factors, however, is not at all adequately treated. The unsatisfactory character of her attempt to reduce differentiated factors to a homogeneous equivalent by means of the concept of 'efficiency units' has been widely recognized and also acknowledged by Robinson herself; so nothing more need be said about it here.[18] In effect, her theory must be interpreted as applying to strictly homogenous units of labor (as she herself sometimes specifies, e.g. p.235) and other factor services. In view of her passionate later crusade against the simplistic concept of capital used here, no more need be said about that either.

Warts and all, however, *Imperfect Competition* remains one of the seminal works of the twentieth century.

Notes

1. To Keynes initially, it was 'an important part of agreement' with the 'classical system' that 'an increase in employment can only occur to the accompaniment of a decline in the rate of real wages' (1936, p.17). Later, prompted by Dunlop's criticism (1938), Keynes acknowledged not only that this need not be so, but also that the contrasting possibility was more agreeable to both his theory and his policy recommendations: 'If we can advance farther on the road towards full employment than I had previously supposed without seriously affecting real hourly wages or the rate of profits per unit of output, the warnings of the anti-expansionists need cause us less anxiety' (1939, pp.40–1).
2. For clarity, though at a sacrivice of apparent relevance, K might better be visualized as Ricardo's 'original and indestructible' (but homogenous) land.
3. As to terminology, there is close correspondence between MPP_L and Robinson's 'marginal physical productivity' (p.236) and likewise between VMP_L and her 'value of the marginal physical product' (p.237). In place of MRP_L, however, she uses the term 'marginal productivity', defined as 'the increment of value of the total output caused by employing an additional man, the total value of other factors remaining unchanged' (p.237). This need not be the same as $\partial R/\partial L$, which implies a constant *quantity* of every other factor.

   To develop a demand schedule for labor, Robinson also employs the associated concepts of the average and marginal net productivities of labor (p.239), which she designates as ANP and MNP (p.246). In the present context where $q = q(L,K)$, define the total net productivity of labor as $R - rK$ such that, for each quantity of L, K is adjusted to maximize $R - rK$. From that function of L we then obtain:

$$ANP = \frac{R - rK}{L} \qquad MNP = \frac{d(R - rK)}{dL}.$$

The firm's long-run demand for labor then coincides with *MNP* where it is less than (or equal to) *ANP*. As this explanation shows, one can dispense altogether with Robinson's otiose concepts of average and marginal gross productivities (pp.243–6).

In that special short run when K is fixed, the analogous short-run demand for labor coincides with $MRP_L = \partial R/\partial L$ when it is less than (or equal to) R/L (labor's average revenue product, ARP_L). At the long-run-equilibrium point where MC_L intersects *MNP*, it also intersects the relevant (and typically steeper) MRP_L – see also Bishop (1967a). When (contrary to present assumptions) production calls for fixed proportions of L and K, MRP_L is indeterminate and the short-run demand for labor is perfectly inelastic in the range where $w < R/L$; but *MNP* remains well behaved owing to the negative slope of product demand.

4. In such an equilibrium, it is important to notice that w and p are the given parameters and $\partial q/\partial L$ is the variable to be determined: the firm adjusts its factor quantities in order to equate $\partial q/\partial L$ to w/p – not the other way around. At the level of the firm or industry, marginal-productivity theory explains only factor demand. It helps explain the distribution of income only in the much broader context of the general equilibrium of the whole economy.
5. The highly useful and now standard term, monopsony, was introduced into economics by Robinson (p.215).
6. When Robinson touches on the question of allocational efficiency, her discussion is limited by assumptions of rigidly fixed factor supplies and (implicitly) fully integrated production (pp.308–9). Hence, when there are equal degrees of monopoly power over all products (pp.309–13) and either equal or unequal degrees of monopsony power over all factors (pp.313–15), she finds only distributional consequences and no effect at all on resource allocation. In her view, accordingly, monpoly distorts allocational efficiency only when ratios of price to marginal cost differ from one industry to another (pp.317–18). In addition, her implied judgment that either equal or unequal degrees of monopsony power do not have adverse allocational consequences is also incorrect.
7. In the context of long-run equilibrium, this surplus income is usually called profit. That is sometimes Robinson's practice, specifically when dealing with isolated monopoly (p.56). But in perfect competition, and presumably imperfect competition as well, she rechristens the surplus income of an intramarginal firm 'entrepreneur's rent' and so includes it in the firm's cost curves (p.125). As a result every firm's average-revenue and average-cost curves are always tangent in long-run equilibrium, whether or not it has any surplus income.

   In the short run, any firm almost always has surplus income, because it need only cover variable costs in order to remain active.
8. The interdependence of the product-market and labor-market diagrams should be noticed. Imposing a price ceiling on a monopolist's product lowers *AR* and raises *MR* in the relevant range; and this also lowers *ANP* and raises *MNP* on the labor diagram. Similarly, imposing a wage-rate floor on a monopsonist raises labor's *AC* and lowers its *MC*; and, on the product diagram, this also raises output's *AC* and lowers its *MC*.
9. Of the many references to the various aspects of monopoly in her index, none relates to labor. Among the few non-indexed references to unions, 'the function of a trade union or a minimum wage law' is identified with 'removing exploitation', because 'it reproduces artificially the conditions of

perfect elasticity of supply of labour to individual employers' (p.282). That is so not only at the point where supply equals demand, but also throughout the entire range where supply exceeds demand.

10. I am reminded of the occasion quite a few years ago when one of the most distinguished of Cambridge University's economists, at an MIT seminar, referred in passing to the labor-market monopsony power of General Motors. One wonders when, save in wartime, that company did not have an excess of job qualified applicants.

11. The concept of 'industry demand' is usually suspect with differentiated products, not only because the boundaries of the relevant group of firms are often ill defined but also, even in a relatively well-defined group, because there are usually very different equilibrium prices and quantities from one firm to another. In the present instance, however, the equilibrium equality of all prices (and quantities) makes the concept a defensible one, even before the differentiation is assumed magically to disappear.

12. Clearly, if K/L is constant, L (like wL and rK) will change in the same proportion as pq, and L will be unchanged if product demand is unit-elastic; but if K/L is increased (decreased), the critical point where L is unchanged will be somewhere in the range where product demand is elastic (inelastic).

Robinson's discussion (pp.285ff.) is more complicated because she catalogues the various possible outcomes with reference to 'physical productivity per man' (q/L) and 'cost per man of the other factors employed' (rK/L). This leads her to describe the case of constant K/L and rK/L as one in which 'the fall in cost per unit of output is due entirely to the increase in physical productivity per man' (p.286). The increases in q/L and q/K are, of course, the same.

She also considers the possibility that q/L may decrease, without adequate attention to the extreme abnormality of such a case. As each still active firm increases q and lowers average cost (AC), L (and wL) increase in greater proportion than q. Hence K and rK must fall sharply, not only enough to offset the increase of wL/q but also to account for the net decrease of $AC = (wL + rK)/q$. One wonders where capital might be so strongly inferior a factor.

13. For example, suppose that two competing newspapers with the same costs and demands are each initially in a Bertrand tangency equilibrium. Price ceilings then drive one out and the other into a new zero-profit equilibrium at some lower point on its AC curve. Formerly, some consumers bought one paper or the other, some bought both, and some bought neither. In the new equilibrium, original patrons of the surviving paper continue to buy just one copy each, some but not all former patrons of the defunct paper now buy the remaining one, former readers of both now can buy only one, and some people who used to buy neither now buy a paper for the first time because it is cheaper. Aggregate q clearly can go either up or down – but probably down.

14. For example, if one could choose only between the two alternative equilibria in the preceding note, the choice might go either way. (For convenience I now assume linear demands and negligible income effects.) In the shift from two newspapers to one, clear gainers are (i) those who formerly bought only the surviving paper (whose monetary gain is an easily measured rectangle), and (ii) those who now buy a paper for the first time (whose aggregate gain is a triangle of consumers' surplus). The only clear losers are those who formerly bought the defunct paper and now buy none (whose loss is another triangle of consumers' surplus). The remaining two groups might be either net gainers or

losers: (i) those who have transferred their custom from the defunct paper to the (now cheaper) survivor, and (ii) whose who formerly bought both papers. In principle, each such individual's gain or loss corresponds to the maximum amount of money he would be willing to pay, if necessary, to maintain or reinstate the preferred situation – or equivalently (income effects being negligible), the minimum payment that would just compensate him for accepting the adverse alternative.

Furthermore, if two newspapers are adjudged better than one, three might be still better. This alternative might be achieved by a price floor (or collusive agreement) high enough to let three firms break even.

15. In Robinson's diagram (p.296), *ANP* and *MNP* are inverted U-shaped – see also above, note 3; and, of course, MC_L cuts *MNP* from below at the labor quantity where AC_L is tangent to *ANP* (I add the *L* subscripts to her notation, in order to avoid confusion with product costs).
16. This case, as Robinson also says, is analogous to the one discussed in the final paragraph of note 12; but it is also rather more complex. Here it is assumed that q/L falls even though $ANP = (pq - rK)/L$ rises. Since p and r are both constant along a given *ANP* curve, the decrease of pq/L must be more than offset by a greater absolute (and a still greater proportional) decrease of rK/L. Each firm becomes markedly more labor-intensive as it moves to its 'optimum size'.
17. Even in the unlikely case considered first, where p rises and q falls, the offsetting gains are not only the greater w for the constant L but also the greater output of other goods attributable to the released K.
18. See the index references in *Imperfect Competition*; also Robinson (1934, p. 402) and Leontief (1937, pp.346–7).

References

Bishop, R. L. (1967a) 'A Firm's Short-Run and Long-Run Demands For a Factor', *Western Economic Journal*, 5: 122–40.

Bishop, R. L. (1967b) 'Monopolistic Competition and Welfare Economics', in R. E. Kuenne, *Monopolistic Competition Theory: Studies in Impact* (New York: Wiley) pp.251–65.

Chamberlin, E. H. (1950) 'Product Heterogeneity and Public Policy', *American Economic Review, Papers and Proceedings* 40: 85–92; repr. in Chamberlin (1957) *Towards a More General Theory of Value* (New York: Oxford University Press) pp.92–102.

Dunlop, J. T. (1938) 'The Movement of Real and Money Wage Rates', *Economic Journal*, 48: 413–34.

Galbraith, J. K. (1952) *American Capitalism: The Concept of Countervailing Power* (Boston: Houghton Mifflin).

Hicks, J. R. (1939) *Value and Capital* (Oxford: Clarendon Press).

Keynes, J. M. (1936) *The General Theory of Employment, Interest and Money* (London: Macmillan).

Keynes, J. M. (1939) 'Relative Movements of Real Wages and Output', *Economic Journal*, 49: 34–51.

Leontief, W. (1937) 'Implicit Theorizing: A Methodological Criticism of the Neo-Cambridge School', *Quarterly Journal of Economics* 51: 337–51.

Pigou, A. C. (1952) *The Economics of Welfare*, 4th edn (London: Macmillan).
Robinson, J. (1933) *The Economics of Imperfect Competition* (London: Macmillan).
Robinson, J. (1934) 'Euler's Theorem and the Problem of Distribution', *Economic Journal* 44: 398–414.

5 Competition and the Number of Participants: Lessons of Edgeworth's Theorem

Takashi Negishi

1

In his *Mathematical Psychics* (1881), Edgeworth demonstrated in so-called Edgeworth equivalence theorem that the outcome of an exchange economy where traders act cooperatively is identical to the Walrasian equilibrium of perfect competition where traders act non-cooperatively as price-takers, when the number of traders of the same type is infinitely large. Certainly it clarifies an implication of Walrasian economics and is a pioneering work of the recent theory of a large economy composed of infinitely many small traders.[1]When the number of traders is limited, Edgeworth argued, traders themselves cannot determine the outcome of an exchange economy cooperatively and the utilitarian principle should be introduced to arbitrate disagreement between traders. Since the infinity of identical traders is a sufficient condition in the proof of Edgeworth's equivalence theorem, however, a natural question is whether it is also a necessary one. If it is not necesary, what is essential for Walrasian economies is not so much the infinity of the number of small traders as perfect information and no friction, also assumed in Edgeworth's theorem.

After we consider the case of infinitely many identical traders, following Edgeworth, in Section 2, we shall argue in Section 3, following Farrell (1970) and Schitovitz (1973), that the equivalence theorem holds even in the case of duopoly where there are only two suppliers of a good, though the number of demanders is infinite.[2] In Section 4, then, we shall summarize our consideration (Negishi, 1982b) in the case of four traders: that the equivalence theorem also holds if indivisible transactions are ruled out and competition is assured, so as to satisfy Jevon's Law of Indifference. Section 5 is devoted to the case of bilateral monopoly or isolated exchange between two traders, where it is argued that the equivalence theorem holds if exchanges are repeated indefinitely through time. Finally, we shall consider what lessons we learned from these considerations of the equivalence theorem from the points of view of Walrasian as well as non-Walrasian economics.

2

Edgeworth (1881, pp.34–42) demonstrated by the use of (the original form of) the Edgeworth box diagram that the only stable outcome of a pure exchange economy is the Walrasian equilibrium of perfect competition and that all the other allocations are blocked by traders cooperatively, when the numbers of traders of the same type is infinitely large.

Figure 5.1 is an Edgeworth box diagram, where the quantity of the first good is measured horizontally, that of the second good, vertically, and the quantities of goods given to trader *A* are measured with the origin at *A*, those given to trader *B*, with the origin at *B*. Point *C* denotes the initial allocation of goods before trade, which implies that the total amount of the first good in the economy is *AC* and that of the second good, *BC*.[3] Curves I, II, etc. are indifference curves of trader *A*, curves 1, 2, etc. are those of trader *B*, and curve *DEF* is the contract curve which is a locus of points

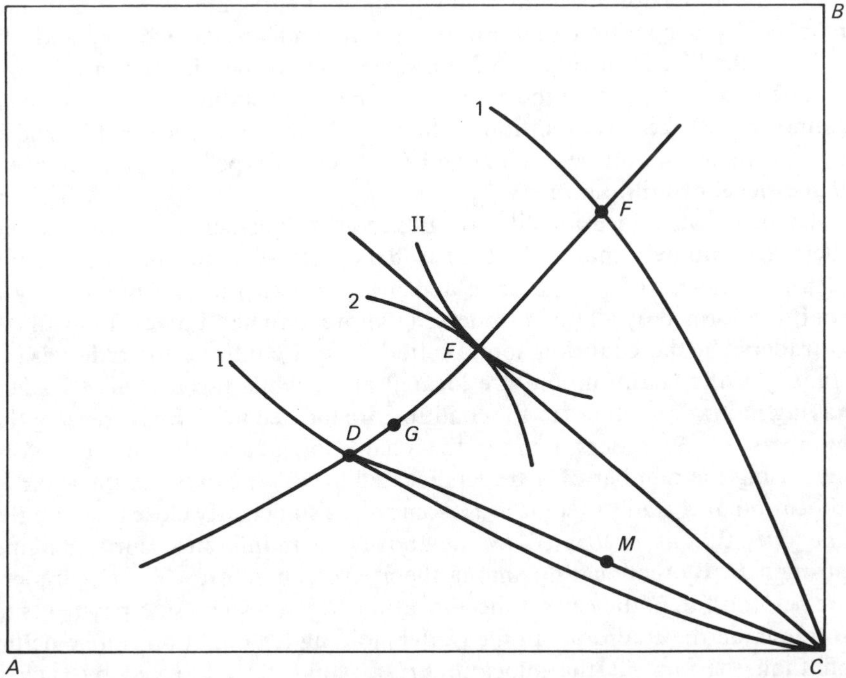

Figure 5.1

where indifference curves of two traders are tangent. Point E is the Walrasian equilibrium of perfect competition, with the common tangent to indifference curves at E passing through point C. It is clear that all the points on the contract curve between D and F are stable outcome if there are only two traders, i.e. trader A and trader B, while Edgeworth insists that all the points except E can be blocked by a coalition of some traders if there are infinitely many identical (in taste and initial holdings) traders of type A and infinitely many identical traders of type B.

Let us first consider the case where there are two traders of type A, i.e. trader A_1 and trader A_2, and two traders of type B, i.e. trader B_1 and trader B_2. It is evident that equal quantities of goods should be allocated to identical traders of the same type, so that we can still consider Figure 5.1.[4] Allocation D can then be blocked by a coalition of A_1, A_2 and either of B_1 and B_2. Suppose A_1 and, say, B_1 keep the contact D between them while A_2 cancels the contract D with B_2 and returns to C. Thus A_1, A_2 and B_1 can arrange by themselves in such a way that, whilst B_1 remains at point D, A_1 and A_2 reach the mid-point M between D and C, thereby achieving a higher level of utility than at D. With some side-payments to B_1, all the traders joining the coalition (A_1, A_2, B_1) can be better off by themselves then they are at D, and the allocation D is blocked. Any allocation on the contract curve and close to D, say, G, can be blocked similarly by the same coalition. Similarly, allocation F or those on the contract curve and close to F can be blocked by a coalition of both B_1 and B_2 and any one of A_1 and A_2. Allocations like H in Figure 5.2, however, cannot be blocked in this way and belong, therefore, to the core, i.e. to the set of stable allocations which cannot be blocked by coalitions. The reason why H cannot be blocked is that at the mid-point between H and C traders of type A cannot achieve a higher level of utility than at H.

To block an allocation like H, Edgeworth considered the case where there are infinitely many identical traders of type A and infinitely many identical traders of type B. The allocation H can then be blocked by a coalition formed by all the A traders and more than half but less than all the B traders. In the coalition some A traders still continue to trade with B traders in the coalition and are located at H, while the rest of A traders having no trade partners in the coalition are located at C. By increasing the numbers of B traders joining the coalition sufficiently and therefore increasing the number of A traders located at H, we can make the average allocation of A traders (some at H, some at C) sufficiently close to H, on the line CH, that it is located like J above the indifference curve passing through H. By reallocating among themselves, therefore, all the A traders are better off than they are at the allocation H. With some side-payments to B traders in the coalition, all the traders joining the coalition can be better off than they are at the allocation H, so that H is blocked by such a coalition. Similarly, any point between D and F where the common tangent

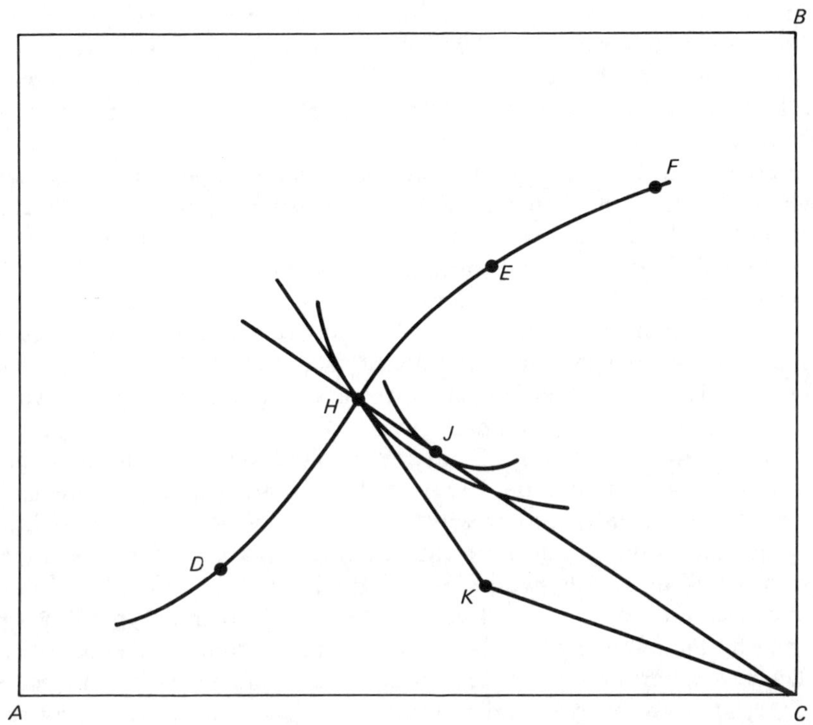

Figure 5.2

to two indifference curves does not pass through the point *C* can be blocked by a coalition of traders, if necessary, by changing the roles of *A* traders and *B* traders from those in the case of the allocation *H*. Obviously only the point *E* belongs to the core, i.e., the set of allocations which are not blocked by such a coalition.

If the number of traders of each type is infinite, therefore, the stable outcome of a pure exchange economy with perfect information and no friction (no restriction of trade, no cost of trade, no cost of organizing coalitions, etc.) can be derived as an equilibrium of perfect competition in which each trader is behaving as if taking prices (the slope of *EC*) as given. The existence of infinitely many identical traders is a sufficient condition for such an equilibrium. But, by no means is it a necessary one, as we shall see.

3

Following Farrell (1970) and Schitovitz (1973), consider next the case of duopoly where there are only two traders of another type, though the total quantities of two goods are finite in the economy. Since equal quantities of goods should be allocated to identical traders of the same type, we can still use the Edgeworth box diagrams, i.e. Figures 5.1 and 5.2, which describe the half of the economy, one of the duopolists and its infinitely many customers.

Suppose first that there are two *B* traders, B_1 and B_2 and infinitely many traders of type *A*. In Figures 5.1 and 5.2, *BC* is the quantity of the second good initially held by a *B* trader and *AC* is the sum of quantities of the first good initially held by the half of *A* traders. Curves I, II, etc. in Figure 5.1 are aggregate indifference curves of *A* traders, as well as individual ones, which can be constructed if the identical individual indifference curves are homothetic, so that the marginal rate of substitution between two goods depends only on the ratio of the quantities of goods and the Engel curve is a line through the origin (Chipman, 1965).

An allocation *H* in Figure 5.2 can now be blocked by a coalition of one *B* trader and more than half but less than all of infinitely many *A* traders. All the *A* traders currently trading with the B_1 trader which joins the coalition also join the coalition and keep the contract *H* with B_1. Some *A* traders currently trading with B_2 (who does not join the coalition) join the coalition and cancel the contract with B_2 to return to the initial point *C*. By decreasing the number of the latter type *A* traders joining the coalition in sufficient numbers and therefore increasing the number of *A* traders located at *H*, relative to those *A* traders located at *C*, we can make the average allocation of individual *A* traders in the coalition sufficiently close to that at point *H*, on the line *CH*, that it is like an allocation at *J* located above the indifference curve passing through *H*.[5] By reallocating among themselves, therefore, all the *A* traders in the coalition are better off than they are at the allocation *H*. With some side-payments to B_1 which is located at *H*, all the traders joining the coalition can be better off than they are at *H*, so that *H* is blocked.

Suppose next that there are two *A* traders, A_1 and A_2 and infinitely many traders of type *B*. In Figures 5.1 and 5.2, then, *AC* is the quantity of the first good initially held by an *A* trader and *BC* is the sum of quantities of the second good initially held by half of the *B* traders. Curves 1, 2, etc. in Figure 5.1 are aggregate indifference curves of *B* traders. In this case, an allocation *H* in Figure 5.2 can be blocked by a coalition of one *A* trader and less than half of infinitely many *B* traders. Suppose A_1 joins the coalition. Those *B* traders also joining the coalition can keep trade with A_1 unchanged so that they can maintain the same level of utility as enjoyed at allocation *H*. A_1 cancels trade with those *B* traders who are not permitted to join the coalition, so that A_1 moves on *HC* from *H* toward *C*. Unless it cancels too many contracts with *B* traders, A_1 can be located as at *J* above the indifference curve passing through *H*. By reallocating among themselves, then, all the traders joining the coalition can be made better off than they are at allocation H, so that H is blocked.[6]

Similarly, any point between D and F on the contract curve where the common tangent to two indifference curves does not pass through point C can be blocked by a coalition of traders, if necessary, by changing the roles of A traders and B traders from those in the case of allocation H. Again, it is point E only which belongs to the core allocation. In other words, even a duopoly market ends up with an equilibrium identical to that of perfect competition, if customers are infinitely many and free to organize coalitions.

4

Let us return to the case where there are two traders of type A, i.e. trader A_1 and trader A_2, and two traders of type B, i.e. trader B_1 and trader B_2. Consider the allocation H on the contract curve DEF in Figure 5.2, which, as we saw in Section 2, cannot be blocked by the coalition of A_1, A_2 and B_1, considered by Edgeworth. We can show, however, that H is not a stable outcome of exchange, if Jevons's Law of Indifference and the trading process are taken into consideration.

> If in selling a quantity of perfectly equal and uniform barrels of flour, a merchant arbitrarily fixed different prices on them, a purchaser would of course select the cheaper ones ... Hence follows what is undoubtedly true, with proper explanations, that in the same open market, at any one moment, there cannot be two prices for the same kind of article. (Jevons, 1888, p.91)
>
> It follows that the last increments in an act of exchange must be exchanged in the same ratio as the whole quantities exchanged. Suppose that two commodities are bartered in the ratio of x for y; then every m-th part of x is given for the m-th part of y, and it does not matter for which of the m-th parts – even an infinitely small part of x must be exchanged for an infinitely small part of y, in the same ratio as the whole quantities. This result we may express by stating that the increments concerned in the process of exchange must obey the equation $dy/dx = y/x$. (Ibid., pp.94–5)

Behind this 'statical view of the question' there must be a dynamic process of trading. What Jevons had in mind is a piecemeal exchange process, since 'dynamically we could not treat the ratio of exchange otherwise than as the ratio of dy and dx, infinitesimal quantities of commodity' (Jevons, 1888, p.94, see also pp.92–3). Let us rule out, therefore, the possibility of an indivisible lump-sum transaction and assume that each single transaction is divisible, so that every portion of a homogenous commodity is treated indifferently, i.e. exchanged against the other commodity at the same rate of exchange. In other words, the dynamic exchange process is a piecemeal one, as considered by Jevons, and finite; i.e. not infinitesimal, transaction is permissible only when it is divisible.

There must be, then, at least two successive transactions and the ratio of exchange should vary in the course of exchange between *C* and *H*, in Figure 5.2, if allocation *H* can ever be reached by exchange starting from *C*. Otherwise, if there is only a single transaction and the exchange ratio remains unchanged throughout the exchange process, it must be equal to the slope of line *CH* and exchange must proceed on line *CH*, starting from *C* and moving toward *H*. Such an exchange process has to be terminated at *J*, however, since the transaction is divisible and it is unfavorable for *A* to go beyond *J*. Further, we can see that the variable ratio of exchange between *C* and *H* must be identical to the slope of the tangent to the indifference curve passing through *H*, for the last infinitesimal or finite transaction arriving at *H*.

Suppose, therefore, that exchange proceeds like *CKH*, i.e. the first transaction to be done with exchange ratio favorable to *B*, and unfavorable to *A*, like *CK*, and the second transaction, with exchange ratio favorable to *A*, and unfavorable to *B*, like *KH*, though the average ratio is *CH*. If we suppose that this is the case, not only with exchange between A_1 and B_1 but also with exchange between A_2 and B_2, allocation *H* can be blocked by the following arbitrage of different exchange ratios: B_1 cancels a part of the transaction with A_1, with the ratio of exchange *KH*, and proposes some new transaction to A_2. Suppose, for the moment, that B_1 offers A_2 the exchange ratio *CK*. A_2 may accept this proposal of B_1 by cancelling a part of his transaction with B_2 at the exchange ratio *CK*, since 'provided that *A* gets the right commodity in the proper quantity, he does not care when it comes, so that we need not . . . distinguish the source or destination' (Jevons, 1888, pp.117–18). In any event, if B_1 offers A_2 an exchange ratio strictly between *CK* and *KH*, both parties can be strictly better off as a result of cancelling parts of their earlier provisional contracts. Not only B_1, but also B_2, A_1 and A_2 may take the initiative to exploit different exchange ratios.

This kind of arbitrage activity is the basis of Jevon's Law of Indifference and allocation *E*; i.e. the solution of Jevons's equation of exchange (Jevons, 1888, pp.95, 99–100) is the only allocation which is not blocked by arbitrage leading to the law of indifference. Edgeworth's equivalence theorem holds if transactions are divisible and the competition between identical traders is assured so as to satisfy Jevon's Law of Indifference.

5

In the case of the bilateral monopoly or the isolated exchange where there is only one *A* trader and one *B* trader, however, Edgeworth was right to insist on the indeterminateness of the outcome of exchanges and to suggest the introduction of the utilitarian principle.

> Thus, proceeding by degrees from the case of two isolated bargainers to the limiting case of a perfect market, we see how contract is more or less indeterminate according as the field is less or more affected with the first imperfection, limitation of numbers. (Edgeworth, 1881, p.42)

> Competition requires to be supplemented by arbitration, and the basis of arbitration between self-interested contractors is the greatest possible sum-total utility. Thus the economical leads up to the utilitarian calculus. (Ibid., p.56)

The utilitarian principle can be justified by the so-called neo-utilitarian arguments which presuppose decision under uncertainty in the situation where individuals do not know what their personal positions would be, but rather have an equal chance of obtaining any of the social positions existing, from the highest down to the lowest (Harsanyi, 1955; Pattanaik, 1968; Vickrey, 1960; and Fleming, 1952).[7] Consider, for example, a prospective immigrant weighting the relative attractiveness of different communities into which he can immigrate. The immigrant is uncertain of the position that he can occupy in the various communities. Under these conditions he may

> make his decision on the basis of maximizing his expected utility, the alternative utilities in question being those of the various members of a given community . . . If we identify the social welfare with the attractiveness of the various communities to this prospective immigrant, we see that the social welfare function takes the form of a weighted sum of the individual utilities. If the immigrant is completely ignorant as to what role he will find in the new community and weights the roles of all individuals equally, we get the Benthamite summation of individual utilities. (Vickrey, 1960)

Both Edgeworth and neo-utilitarians are certainly right if we are concerned with contracts which are once-for-all ones in an essentially timeless situation. If we are interested in contracts which are repeated through time, however, things are different at least in two respects. Firstly, as we argued elsewhere (Negishi, 1982a), neo-utilitarian *ex ante* arguments based on the maximization of expected utility are not applicable, since we cannot neglect the *ex post* problem of envy of the fortunate by the unfortunate. Secondly, as we shall see, it is possible to argue that the equilibrium is determinate and identical to that of perfect competition even in the case of the bilateral monopoly or the isolated exchange.

As is suggested by Walker (1973), Edgeworth himself was interested in contracts repeated through time.

> For Marshall in the passage cited has in view a market in a special sense distinguished from normal, whereas the process which I analyse has much in common with the determination of normal equilibrium. (Edgeworth, 1925, II, p.313)

> They [curves of Demand and Supply] apply also to transactions in factors of production, such as the labour-market; and not only to 'market value' in the sense of the term which refers to short periods, but also to 'natural' or normal value, provided that the periods considered are not so long but that the dispositions, and 'disponibilities' in M. De Foville's phrase, may be supposed constant. We are to conceive two groups of dealers encountering each other, not once only, but from time to time, and ascertaining by repeated tentatives a rate of exchange at which a steady flow of trade is maintained. (Ibid., p.333)

> On the first day in our example a set of hirings are made which prove not to be in accordance with the dispositions of the parties. These contracts terminating with the day, the parties encounter each other the following day, with dispositions the same as on the first day – like combatants *armis animisque refecti* – in all respects as they were at the beginning of the first encounter, except that they have obtained by experience the knowledge that the system of bargains entered into on the first occasion does not fit the real dispositions of the parties. (Edgeworth, 1925, I, p.40)

Let us now consider the problem of two good two trader exchanges which are repeated through time indefinitely. This is done by assuming that the original exchange, say, for a year, is perfectly divisible into exchanges in infinitely many short periods. Initial holdings given at the beginning of the year like manna are assumed to be distributed by traders uniformly over periods, and the unit period utility function as a function of consumed quantities of goods in the period are assumed to be unchanged through time and independent of consumption in other periods so that we can still use Figures 5.1 and 5.2. It is assumed that initial holdings are transferable through periods in either direction with no cost while goods acquired through exchange are storable through periods with no depreciation.

Let us assume that marginal utility is decreasing in the sense that the unit period utility function is concave. Formerly, if c_i is the consumption of the i-th good and $c = (c_1, c_2)$, then the unit period utility function u satisfies

$$a\,u(c^1) + (1-a)\,u(c^2) < u(a\,c^1 + (1-a)\,c^2)$$

for any given a such that $0 \leqq a \leqq 1$, where c^1 and c^2 are different consumption vectors. When $a = 1/2$, this implies that the average of utilities of different consumption vectors is smaller than the utility of the average consumption vector. By assuming away time preference so that multi-period utility is the simple non-weighted sum of unit period utilities, it is assured that an equilibrium series of exchange must be stationary in the sense that each trader consumes unchanged quantities of goods through periods. This is because a contract with non-stationary consumptions is not Pareto-optimal and blocked by two traders cooperatively.[8]

Therefore, we have to consider only contacts between D and F on the contract curve in Figures 5.1 and 5.2, where AC is the amount of the first good given to trader A as the initial holdings and distributed to a unit period, and BC is the amount of the second good initially given to trader B and distributed to the period. Now a stationary contract like H in Figure 5.2 can be blocked by trader A who keeps the trade with trader B unchanged and stays at H in earlier periods and cancels the trade with B and returns to C in later periods. By choosing properly the length of earlier and later periods, transferring the first good (initial holdings) from later periods to earlier periods, and storing the second good (acquired through exchange) from earlier periods to later periods, trader A can locate his stationary consumption at J and be better off than at H. Similarly, any stationary contract between D and F on the contract curve except E can be blocked either by trader A or by trader B. The only maintainable stationary contract is, therefore, E which is identical to the equilibrium of perfect competition even in the case of the bilateral monopoly or the isolated exchange.

6

Edgeworth demonstrated that the existence of infinitely many identical traders is a sufficient condition for the equivalence of the core allocations and Walrasian equilibria of perfect competition for an exchange economy. We have argued above that ,though sufficient, it is not a necessary condition. This suggests that what is essential for perfect competition is not so much the number of traders or the scale of traders relative to that of the economy, as perfect information and no friction which are also explicitly assumed in the proof of Edgeworth's theorem. Let us consider what lessons we can learn from these considerations, not only from the point of view of Walrasian economics but also that of non-Walrasian economics.

In Walrasian economics it is usually assumed that traders are price-takers and prices are 'cried' by auctioneers. Although such auctioneers often exist in organized exchanges, it is highly unrealistic to assume that they exist in all the markets in the economy. Furthermore, in general it is not rational to assume that all the traders are price-takers, since a trader can gain by price-making behavior, i.e. by reducing its supplies to raise prices and by reducing its demands to reduce prices, if all the other traders are price-takers (Roberts and Postlewaite, 1976). To get rid of this difficulty, we have to assume the existence of infinite traders or negligible scale of traders relative to that of the economy, so that the possibility of such gains from price-making behavior can safely be ignored. It must be emphasized, however, that following Edgeworth we are not assuming the price-taking behavior of traders and the existence of an auctioneer. In our cooperative games of exchange, there is no possibility of the price-making behavior of some traders taking advantage of the price-taking behavior of other traders, a problem which may appear in the case of decentralized, i.e. non-cooperative, games of exchange like the Walrasian one.

In a sense Walrasian assumptions are justified by our considerations of Edgeworth's cooperative game of exchange through the equivalence theorem, since the effectiveness of assumptions in a theory should be judged not by the realism of the assumptions themselves, but by the outcome of the theory derived from them. The outcome of a theory of exchange without Walrasian assumptions, i.e. core allocations, is equivalent to the outcome of Walrasian economics, i.e. equilibria of perfect competition. Even though traders are actually not price-takers and there are no auctioneers, we may assume that traders are price-takers and there are auctioneers, provided that information is perfect and there are no frictions.

If information is not perfect and there exist such frictions as cost of organizing coalitions, cost of trade, etc., however, things are quite different. In Walrasian economics, price-taking suppliers perceive infinitely elastic demand curves. Since information is perfect, demand can be increased infinitely by a slight reduction of the price. If information is not perfect, an increase in demand is limited, since a lower price asked by a supplier may not be fully informed to customers who are currently buying from other suppliers. Even if it is informed, some of such customers, who are not informed of the quality of the product of a price-cutting supplier, may not shift their demand to the supplier, unless the reduction of price is considerable. Suppliers have to perceive, then, downward sloping demand curves for the reduction of prices. On the other hand, a higher price charged by a supplier necessarily induces present customers to leave in search of lower priced suppliers, even if such search activities involve some costs. Suppliers have to perceive, therefore, fairly elastic demand curves which are due to the asymmetric behavior of customers (Negishi, 1979, pp.36, 87; Scitovsky, 1976; Reid, 1981, p.97). As in the case of kinked demand curves due to the asymmetric behavior of rival firms (Sweezy, 1939) price rigidity may appear, which can be a microeconomic foundation of Keynesian fix-price economic theory (Negishi, 1979, pp.89–90; Reid, 1981, pp.65–6; Cuddington, Johansson and Löfgren, 1984, pp.41–4).

Notes

1. See, for example, Debreu and Scarf (1963), Hildenbrand (1974) and Hildenbrand and Kirman (1976). See also Negishi (1985) for Cournot's theory of oligopoly which is another pioneering work on the theory of a large economy.
2. Following Edgeworth like us, Farrell used the Edgeworth box diagram, while Schitovitz takes a measured theoretic approach which is certainly more general but has no intuitive appeal like the Edgeworth diagram. See also Negishi (1985) for the Bertrand model of duopoly which generates a perfectly competitive equilibrium.
3. Of course, this is a simplifying assumption and in general C can be anywhere in the box.
4. Otherwise, such an unequal allocation can be blocked by a coalition of the least favored type A trader and the least favored type B trader or a coalition of two equally favored traders with unequal allocations, so that they can be better off by themselves.
5. Though H and J are allocations to half of the traders in the economy, they can be considered as allocations to an A trader, since indifference curves are homothetic. Alternatively, we can argue more generally by the use of Scitovsky indifference curves.
6. This argument is due to Farrell (1970), though he seems to be concerned not so much with the oligopoly with a finite number of firms as with the case of an infinite number of firms. See, however, Friedman (1977), pp.283–5.
7. Creedy (1984) pointed out that Edgeworth himself had the same idea.
8. Since marginal utility is diminishing, the optimal path of the utility of a trader must be stationary through time, while the corresponding consumption stream must be stationary in view of the convexness of indifference curves to the origin.

References

Chipman, J. S. (1965) 'A Survey of the Theory of International Trade', 2, *Econometrica*, 33: 685–760.

Creedy, J. (1984) 'Edgeworth: Utilitarianism and Arbitration', *History of Political Economy*, 16: 609–18.

Cuddington, J. T., P. O. Johansson and K. G. Löfgren (1984) *Disequilibrium Macroeconomics in Open Economies* (Oxford: Blackwell).

Debreu, G. and H. Scarf (1963) 'A Limit Theorem on the Core of an Economy', *International Economic Review*, 4: 235–46.

Edgeworth, F. Y. (1881) *Mathematical Psychics* (London: Kegan Paul).

Edgeworth, F. Y. (1925) *Papers Relating to Political Economy* (London: Macmillan).

Farrell, M. J. (1970) 'Edgeworth Bounds for Oligopoly Prices', *Economica*, 37: 342–61.

Fleming, J. M. (1952) 'A Cardinal Concept of Welfare', *Quarterly Journal of Economics*, 66: 366–84.

Friedman, J. W. (1977) *Oligopoly and the Theory of Games* (Amsterdam: North Holland).

Harsanyi, J. C. (1955) 'Cardinal Welfare, Individualistic Ethics and Interpersonal Comparisons of Utility', *Journal of Political Economy*, 63: 309–21.

Hildenbrand, W. (1974) *Core and Equilibria of a Large Economy* (Princeton: Princeton University Press).

Hildenbrand, W. and A. P. Kirman (1976) *Introduction to Equilibrium Analysis* (Amsterdam: North Holland).
Jevons, W. S. (1888) *The Theory of Political Economy* (London: Macmillan).
Negishi, T. (1979) *Microeconomic Foundations of Keynesian Macroeconomics* (Amsterdam: North-Holland).
Negishi, T. (1982a) 'Edgeworth's *Mathematical Psychics* Considered from the Point of View of Fair Distribution' (in Japanese), *Mita Gakkai Zasshi*, 75–1: 27–38.
Negishi. T. (1982b) 'A Note on Jevons's Law of Indifference and Competitive Equilibrium', *Manchester School*, 50: 220–30.
Negishi, T. (1985) 'Non-Walrasian Foundations of Macroeconomics', in G. R. Feiwel (ed.) *Issues in Contemporary Macroeconomics and Distribution* (London: Macmillan).
Pattanaik, P. K. (1968) 'Risk, Impersonality and the Social Welfare Function', *Journal of Political Economy*. 76: 1152–69.
Reid, G. C. (1981) *The Kinked Demand Curve Analysis of Oligopoly* (Edinburgh: Edinburgh University Press).
Roberts, D. J. and A. Postlewaite (1976) 'The Incentives for Price-Taking Behavior in Large Exchange Economies', *Econometrica*, 44: 115–27.
Schitovitz, B. (1973) Oligopoly in Markets with a Continuum of Traders, *Econometrica*, 41: 467–501.
Scitovsky, T. (1976) 'Asymmetries in Economics', *Scottish Journal of Political Economy*, 25: 227–37.
Sweezy, P. M. (1939) 'Demand under Conditions of Oligopoly', *Journal of Political Economy*, 47: 568–73.
Vickrey, W. (1960) 'Utility, Strategy and Social Decision Rules', *Quarterly Journal of Economics*, 74: 507–35.
Walker, D. A. (1973) 'Edgeworth's Theory of Recontract', *Economic Journal*, 83: 138–49.

6 Is Imperfect Competition Empirically Empty?

John Sutton*

During the past few years, imperfect competition seems to be coming into its own. Models of product differentiation, in particular, are now a standard vehicle in which to discuss many issues in industrial organization and in international trade. Yet this resurgence of interest in the area has failed to dispel a long-standing concern, shared by many economists, that imperfect competition is 'empirically empty' – the particularly pungent dismissal of the theory in George Stigler's Nobel address of 1982 is a recent echo of older debates.

In what follows, I would like to re-explore the basis of these concerns, with reference to the more recent literature. Throughout the chapter, the term 'imperfect competition' is used in a fairly broad and somewhat loose sense, consistent with most of the recent literature, as relating to models which combine the notion that individual firms face downward sloping demand schedules (this being normally attributed to product differentiation across producers), and the idea that free entry leads to zero profit, at least 'approximately'.[1]

1 ARCHIBALD VERSUS CHICAGO

The main virtue of the Robinson–Chamberlin theory lay in its avoidance of certain features of the 'perfect competition' story considered to be patently unrealistic. The argument that the typical firm in manufacturing industry operated under conditions of increasing returns had received widespread support during the 1920s; the *locus classicus* for this view being Sraffa (1926). This in turn was seen as requiring an abandonment of the notion that the firm faced a horizontal demand schedule. What imperfect competition offered was a way in which the notion of a competitive industry might be retained, while relaxing some of the assumptions of the perfect competition model, in the direction of greater realism.[2]

When it came to generating predictions, however, the theory seemed less impressive. One early hope was that it might offer a satisfactory theory of

*David de Meza, Bob Gould, Kurt Klappholz, and Morris Perlman read a preliminary draft of the present essay. Its final form owes much to their extremely helpful and incisive comments.

the cyclical behavior of prices. Despite early enthusiasm,[3] however, the theory has largely been bypassed in discussions of this issue.[4]

The low point in the fortunes of imperfect competition was reached in the 1961 *Review of Economic Studies*, in which Archibald replied to two of the theory's leading critics, George Stigler and Milton Friedman.

The debate centered around two issues. The first of these related to an assertion which had been made in Friedman (1953) and in Stigler (1949). This claimed that the introduction of a new model intermediate between perfect competition and monopoly could only be justified if that model offered us a superior mode of analysis, to that obtainable by a judicious appeal to one or other of the simple polar models. For example, as Friedman argued, the analysis of the effect on cigarette prices of a permanent increase in the rate of indirect tax might be adequately treated by assuming the cigarette industry to be perfectly competitive. On the other hand, to predict the response of cigarette firms to wartime price controls, a monopoly model would be appropriate. For Friedman, the problem is that of specifying the conditions under which either one of the two polar cases will offer an appropriate mode of analysis. Archibald's point was that the lack of adequate criteria, in this respect, vitiated this line of criticism of imperfect competition.[5]

In the light of recent developments in the literature, however, this first line of argument – whatever its merits – would now seem difficult to maintain. Much of the current literature is directed towards the analysis of issues which clearly require us to move beyond a 'monopoly plus perfect competition' framework; the example explored in the next section will serve to illustrate this point.

It is the second of the two issues of the 1961 debate which continues to be a matter of serious concern. This was the issue set out in Archibald's article, and identified as the real problem with imperfect competition. That it was indeed the real problem was not disputed.[6] What Archibald did was to write down a formal representation of an individual firm which faces a demand schedule parameterized by the two choice variables, product quality, and advertizing outlays, and whose cost depends both on product quality and (additively) on advertizing. Archibald showed that no non-trivial comparative static results held good, as to the effects of changing demand parameters, or costs (via taxes, etc.); nor did it help matters to confine oneself to the special cases of the model obtained by assuming 'no advertizing' or 'no quality choice'.

Now it is not surprising that if we enrich the basic monopoly model by adding these additional parameters, then no qualitative results of this Samuelsonian kind are available. It was certainly widely felt, at the time, that it was just such predictions that should be required of a theory. Archibald's paper was widely accepted as the definitive statement of the emptiness of imperfect competition.

Archibald's own conclusion, however, was positive, and indeed appeared a very natural response. What he argued was that only by putting more structure into the theory could one hope to get predictions out. The direction which he favored, and subsequently developed (Archibald and Rosenbluth, 1976), involved specifying consumer tastes over potential product varieties and endogenously determining the (number and possibly type of) products on offer, and in this way pinning down within the model the demand conditions facing each firm at equilibrium.

Whether this is the most appropriate way forward, in respect of empirical testing, is questioned in Section 4 below. As a prediction of the way in which the subject could be fruitfully developed, it has been amply vindicated by the recent literature, in which this approach is now the standard one.

2 PUTTING MORE STRUCTURE IN: AN ILLUSTRATION

Both Robinson and Chamberlin accorded a central role to product differentiation as a motivation for their respective models. Relatively little progress was made until recently, however, in elaborating models that explicitly incorporate product differentiation, as a foundation for the 'imperfect competition' story (notwithstanding the fact that Hotelling's seminal contribution appeared in 1929).[7]

Renewed theoretical interest in such models has, over the past few years, coincided with an expanding range of applications in industrial organization and in trade theory. The latter subject is particularly noteworthy in the present context, since the growing interest in product differentiation models among trade theorists sprang from a specific empirical concern: that the predominant trade flows among the industrial countries are of an *intra-industry* kind (i.e. involving two-way flow of similar products between trading partners) in contrast to the inter-industry flows generated in the traditional 'comparative advantage' framework (where, for narrowly defined industries, we may distinguish a country as either an exporter, or an importer, of a particular good). The predominant part played by intra-industry trade flows came to figure in the empirical literature from the mid-1960s; Balassa's (1966) study of the increase in intra-industry trade flows among European countries following the formation of the EEC was an important early contribution. While several types of models were subsequently advanced to account for such trade (see Grubel and Lloyd, 1975), the main focus of attention in the past few years has been on models in which firms produce differentiated products, within an 'imperfect competition' framework.

The basic mechanism which underlies the many recent models of this kind can be illustrated in a particularly simple way, by using the well known 'circular road' variant of Hotelling's (1929) model.

Imagine the characteristic of a product to be represented by a point on a circle of unit circumference. A consumer's preferences are likewise represented by a point on the circle, corresponding to his 'most preferred' specification. Each consumer aims to buy exactly one unit from some firm. His utility score is given by $u_0 - p - t.d$, where d is the distance between his most preferred specification, and that of his chosen product. The constant t represents the 'intensity' of preferences. Assume that all firms produce at zero marginal cost.

We aim to characterize a Nash equilibrium in prices (Bertrand equilibrium), namely, a set of prices such that each firm, taking his rivals' prices as given, is setting the profit-maximizing price. It can be shown that the only Nash equilibrium in prices is one in which all firms set price $\bar{p} = t/n$. To see that this is in fact a Nash equilibrium, notice that the marginal consumer bounding the firm's market share lies a distance d from the firm, where $u_0 - p - t.d = u_0 - \bar{p} - t(1/n - d)$, for any $p \leqslant 2t/n$, above which price sales are zero. Below this price, the firm's demand schedule is given by

$$x(p) = 2d.s = [1/n - (p - \bar{p})/t].s$$

where $2d$ is its market share, and s denotes the level of total demand (the population of consumers). From this it readily follows that the profit-maximizing price for the firm in question is indeed $p = \bar{p} = t/n$, and so this is an equilibrium. An easy extension shows that this is the only equilibrium. The firm's equilibrium level of output is s/n, and its profits $\pi = s.t/n^2$. An increase in the number of firms thus lowers the level of price, and so total profits.

The easiest way to explore the impact of trade in this setting is to consider two identical markets, initially separated from each other, and each having population s and n equi-spaced products. Suppose the locations of country A's products, and those of country B are 'interleaved', in our circular 'product space', so that when we join the two economies via free trade, the combined economy has $2n$ products which are equi-spaced about the circle. In the new equilibrium, some 'A' consumers will now be closer to some 'B' product, and vice versa, so we generate a two-way trade flow between country A and country B. Moreover, the common price set by all producers in the combined economy is $\bar{p} = t/2n$; and so, while each firm still enjoys sales of s/n, its profits are reduced to $\pi = 2s.t/(2n)^2 = \pi/2$. This, of course, reflects the fact that in the combined economy, each firm faces rivals offering closer substitutes than was the case before.

While the model illustrates this point in a relatively transparent manner, it has some shortcomings. Much effort has been directed at embedding this kind of model into a general equilibrium framework, within which its relationship to conventional trade models can be elaborated more fully (see in particular Krugman, 1981; Helpman, 1981). A more serious shortcoming, in the present context, concerns the fact that the analysis of optimal product choice, which should be dealt with as a separate preliminary game, is notoriously problematic in this model. I will proceed here in a conventional, though not very satisfactory, manner, by looking not for a Nash equilibrium in product locations, but instead for a 'Chamberlinian' configuration in which some number n of firms are placed in symmetric locations, where n is chosen to set profits, net of some sunk 'cost of entry' F, equal to zero.[8]

This allows us to go beyond the 'short-run' picture presented above, by comparing the number of producers present in each autarkic economy, with the number which would be present in the combined economy. Supposing n firms to be active in each of the two separated economies, so that $F = st/n^2$, then in the combined economy we will have a total of N producers, where $F = 2st/N^2$, whence $N = \sqrt{2}n$. Thus the combined economy supports fewer producers than would the two separated economies.

While the precise numbers are, of course, special to the example, the qualitative result is quite a robust one. It follows directly from the central idea which drives these models, and it is this idea which I want to focus on in what follows.

With $2n$ firms present in the enlarged economy, as we saw, (gross) profits per firm are reduced below F; a contraction in the number of firms serves to raise equilibrium prices, by relaxing competition, as the typical firm faces rivals offering less close substitutes for its own product. Were the combined economy to support no more than the n firms (the number present in each of the separated economies) of course prices would be unchanged and gross profits would rise to $2F$. So long as an influx of producers tends to lower equilibrium price, it follows that any increase in industry demand (emanating from an enlargement of the market) will lead to a less than proportionate increase in the number of producers. Each producer then operates at a higher level of output, so that average cost, and price, is lower. The gains from trade are twofold: the typical consumer now enjoys a product closer to his most preferred specification, and prices are lower.

The source of the gains from trade in this model lies in the greater economies of scale available in the enlarged economy. The relationship between product differentiation, and scale economies, is a close one: in the absence of increasing returns, the competitive economy would provide each consumer with his most preferred product – here, product differentiation is present, but innocuous; the 'perfect competition' story works well.[9] It is precisely the limitation on the range of available varieties, reflecting the presence of increasing returns, which adds a new economic dimension.

The purpose of the preceding example is to illustrate how, by importing an explicit 'product differentiation' basis into the imperfect competition structure, we can proceed to a new range of problems, which are otherwise inaccessible. The simple mechanism which we have described above has received a good deal of attention recently, and its novel implications for the analysis of commercial policy have been widely explored in the literature.[10]

3 IS IT EMPTY?

The change of heart towards the use of imperfect competition models in the profession over the past few years has had much to do with the growing awareness that this kind of model enriches our ability to find plausible explanations of well-attested phenomena, which lie outside the reach of a perfect competition, or monopoly, story. This development has coincided with a growing sophistication in the use of oligopoly models, especially in industrial organisation; and both of these closely related developments raise very similar difficulties when it comes to testing theories. Indeed, while these developments seem to have succeeded in rebutting the charge that some amalgam of perfect competition and monopoly will suffice, I will argue in what follows that they make it all the more urgent to address the issue of whether such models are 'consistent with anything'.

A good starting point is afforded by Archibald's conclusion, noted earlier, which asserts that the way out of the difficulty is to put more structure into the model, and so generate more predictions. In offering some comparative static properties of their own model as candidates, Archibald and Rosenbluth (1976) proposed that we should proceed by testing *some specific model* of imperfect competition. While this is quite logically sound, as a way forward, it seems less compelling now than it did a decade ago. For we have recently seen a proliferation of alternative models of imperfect competition, all of them heavily overlapping in respect of their comparative static predictions.

These include, for example, (i) Lancastrian 'characteristics' models (Archibald and Rosenbluth, 1976); (ii) Hotelling models, including the circular road version described above, favored by Lancaster (1979); (iii) models of the kind used by Perloff–Salop (1985) and Hart (1985a,b), which preserve complete symmetry between the several products on offer; (iv) Dixit–Stiglitz (1977) models, in which the product space is bypassed, and firms' products are simply assumed to be 'different' – a very useful simplification, and one nicely exploited by Krugman (1981).

It might still be insisted that we should try to find the 'right' model by letting the many candidates compete against each other. Now it would be possible in principle to do this, in the context of any particular data set (though given the overlap of predictions, it would not be an easy task). But to do so would be to miss the fact that each of these 'product differentiation' models is intended only as a highly stylized representation of real markets. All theories simplify; but these models go a little further in that they aim deliberately to specify a 'space of product attributes' which is chosen mainly for its analytical tractability, and not for its resemblance to some space of characteristics which might be relevant to consumers in a particular market (as the 'circular road' story makes abundantly clear). There is a good reason for this: the 'appropriate' space of characteristics which actually underlie consumer choice must necessarily vary dramatically from one context to another: any model could be the best representation only for an extremely narrow range of applications. And while such a representation may be what we should look for in dealing with some kinds of problem, it is not what we are about, in the present context. Of course, some kinds of distinction between broad classes of attributes are worth maintaining: for instance, there is now a growing literature which concerns the distinction between 'vertical' product differentiation (where products differ in some quality-like attribute, so that all consumers prefer 'more' of this attribute to 'less', *ceteris paribus*), and the kind of 'horizontal' product differentiation embodied in the 'circular road' model of Section 2 above. That said, however, it remains the case that models of product differentiation should be seen as convenient parables; it is inappropriate to expect that any one will be the 'right' model, or even a 'better' model. The choice between these rival forms, as the literature develops further, will continue to depend largely on the relative tractability, and flexibility, of alternative candidates.

But if we are concerned with 'testing' the theory, where does this leave us?

4 PROBLEMS AND PERSPECTIVES

What I would like to argue here is that it seems attractive in this kind of situation to draw out some prediction which is common to all these models. In spite of the controversies recorded above, I would like to argue that this is not a hopeless task.

To provide a point of reference, consider the prediction of the perfect competition model in the following situation: suppose we have a number of (potential) suppliers, all of whom face the same cost conditions. Distinguish the case where their common average cost schedule is (a) U-shaped, (b) falling up to some minimal efficient scale, and then flat. We necessarily exclude the case, (c) where average cost is everywhere falling.

Now suppose the size of the market (number of consumers) increases. Then the long-run supply schedule is flat, and so price is unchanged. The number of firms expands proportionately with the size of the market in case (a), and is indeterminate in case (b).

This contrasts with the mechanism which underlies our 'intra-industry' trade illustration, and much else in the recent imperfect competition literature. To restate our earlier point, we have, in imperfect competition: an expansion in the size of the market leads to (i) a less than proportionate increase in the number of firms, and (ii) a fall in price.

This result relies only on the convexity of the average cost schedule (the distinction (a)–(c) is irrelevant), and the notion that each firm faces a more elastic demand schedule in the new post-entry equilibrium. Now this proposition is an attractive candidate to consider, in trying to frame a testable prediction, in that it is common to almost[11] all of those models which have proved popular in the applied area during the past few years. But should it be viewed as a prediction of the *theory* of imperfect competition? The result derives *inter alia* from an assumption of symmetry between competing firms' brands, which Chamberlin introduced as part of his theory. Robinson's treatment did not invoke this notion, and her discussion of the many possibilities which arise, as to the effect of entry on prices, illustrates well the sort of complication which may occur. The recent literature has extended the list of possibilities further. Following Robinson's discussion, consider for example a market in which each firm's customers comprise two groups, one of which strongly favors its product over rivals' offerings, while the other group is almost indifferent between the firm's product, and other varieties. The presence of this latter group keeps prices 'low', by ensuring each firm's demand is highly elastic at equilibrium. Were each of these latter consumers to be offered a new intermediate good close to his most preferred specification, however, he would strongly prefer the new product. So if firms enter with such new products, all sellers may now find themselves with only 'strongly loyal' consumers, and so prices may rise. A formal analysis of an example in this spirit is provided by Rosenthal (1980).

Other examples abound; of particular interest are a number of examples which depend on a change in the underlying equilibrium concept; for a discussion see note 12 below.

These possibilities may seem rather unlikely, *a priori*, however; in summing up her discussion of the various possibilities, Robinson (1969, p.86) turns last to the case corresponding to the mechanism described above, where

> the new firms were set up, so to speak, in between the old firms (either geographically or in respect of special qualities which appeal in various degrees to different customers). The difference, from the point of view of buyers, between any one firm and the next would thus be reduced, the customers of each firm would become more indifferent, and the elasticity of demand would be increased.

There are some grounds for supposing that the last type of change in demand is the most frequent. It may therefore be considered probable that an increase in total demand will lower price rather than raise it.

What I would like to propose, in what follows, is that a useful way forward may lie in testing imperfect competition theory jointly with the hypothesis, that an increase in the number of suppliers leads to a fall in the elasticity of demand facing each firm. This leads to the testable prediction set out as our above 'proposition'. As a way forward, this might seem at first glance rather unhelpful: after all, if the prediction fails, can we not always rescue the theory by supposing that a 'perverse' elasticity change is at work? Before addressing this central issue, however, I would first like to consider the prior question, of whether such a test is practicable? Can we find a suitable *context* in which the large number of maintained assumptions underlying the above proposition are satisfied in some approximate sense? While we might expect the theory to be relevant over a broad range of industries, the number of cases in which we can hope to isolate the mechanism in question from other influences is highly restricted.

First, we need to find a number of separated markets of varying size, but which can be expected to be substantially similar in respect of cost conditions, and the distribution of consumer types (tastes). To this end, we might look at various towns and cities within the same country, and consider the provision of some service, or of some good whose cost of transport is substantial.

Secondly, we need to consider the well-trodden issue of the 'chain of substitutes'. For some products the market boundaries may be relatively clear; in many instances, the difficulty of defining these boundaries may vitiate the usefulness of such a 'test'.

While the preceding difficulties are intrinsic to the testing of the theory, a further difficulty reflects the present limitations in the development of the theory. For the possible context for testing is severely restricted by the fact that the theory presupposes single product firms.

The difficulty of extending the formal literature to deal adequately with multiproduct firms, already remarked upon by Robinson (1953), remains one of the most serious shortcomings of the literature. Despite some well-known contributions on specific issues,[13] it is not possible on the basis of the existing literature to draw any conclusions as to the circumstances under which an extention of the market would lead merely to a proliferation of new products by existing firms, rather than to the entry of new producers. Our context, then, needs to be one in which – within a given location, at least – single product firms are the norm; or else it needs to be one in which the range of products is not a choice variable for the firm in question.

One final restriction of context is appropriate. This relates to markets in which products are differentiated in terms of some 'vertical' ('quality'-like) attribute, of which all consumers prefer 'more' to 'less'. If firms can increase 'quality' primarily by expenditure on fixed costs (R&D or advertizing) with 'little' increase in unit variable costs, then the above proposition will no longer hold good (for a summary of the recent literature on this issue, see for example Sutton, 1986).

5 FAILING THE TEST

The substance of the present proposal lies in the suggestion that we accept the 'elasticity hypothesis' as a working hypothesis in testing the theory of imperfect competition. The implication of accepting this route is that, should the prediction fail, the theory cannot be 'rescued' simply by assuming a 'perverse' elasticity shift. On the contrary, 'rescuing the theory' requires (i) that an explanation be offered as to why, in this particular market, a 'perverse' elasticity effect is to be expected; and (ii) that the new explanatory hypothesis invented to explain this result should itself generate further novel predictions which can in turn be tested. Even then, the theory is 'rescued' only in the weak sense, that it is shown that some more refined version of the theory may be appropriate to the market in question.

This is best illustrated by turning to a well-known example in which the present prediction fails.

The various contextual restrictions set out above are neatly met by the case of physicians' practices. It is well-known from the empirical literature, however, that an increase in the supply of physicians tends to lead to a *rise* in the price of their services.[14]

Several candidate explanations have been suggested. Some of these rest on the idea that doctors set out to achieve a constant 'target income' in the face of declining patient numbers. One way in which this may happen is through some form of collusive behavior. There is also the possibility that each individual doctor might respond to falling patient numbers by suggesting to some patients that they need to see him more often; this kind of 'supplier-induced demand' (Evans (1974), Evans, Parish and Sully (1973)) is an alternative explanation of how doctors maintain their 'target income'.

Either of these lines of explanation would clearly exclude any variant of the 'imperfect competition' story as being appropriate to this market.

A second type of explanation has been proposed recently by Satterthwaite (1979, p.485). Satterthwaite's explanation is close to the spirit of the 'imperfect competition' story, and can be seen as involving a refinement of that approach, which incorporates the role of incomplete information. The proposed explanation rests on the view that consumers lack information concerning those characteristics of each physician which are relevant to them; and the characteristics which matter to any one consumer (i.e. bedside manner, technical expertise, etc.) may be quite different from those which matter to another. The amount of information a consumer has depends on the size of his 'circle of acquaintances' (each of whom patronizes some particular physician) and not on the number of physicians in the area.

In this context,

> If the number of primary care physicians in a community is small – seven for example – then each physician has a detailed reputation throughout the community. Seven physicians are easy to keep in mind. Each consumer has friends who go to each of the seven, and each consumer can remember what is said about each physician. If the number of physicians is larger – 30, for example – then each physician's reputation is much less distinct. An average consumer cannot accurately catalogue in his mind what he hears about 30 different physicians. Thus, the tendency in communities with a large number of physicians is for each consumer to have accurate information only about his own physician and, perhaps, one or two others. Consequently, the usual response of a friend concerning the qualifications of a particular physician is, 'I have never heard of him'. Therefore, as the number of physicians within the community increases, the quality of information consumers have concerning relative qualifications and prices of physicians declines and searching for new physicians becomes more difficult.

By formally modelling this situation, Satterthwaite establishes the (far from obvious) result that an increase in numbers can lead to a fall in the elasticity of demand facing each seller, as consumer search becomes more costly.

What is of interest, from our present standpoint, is that each of these proposed solutions leads us on to different testable predictions. The results of empirical testing of the 'target income' versus 'incomplete information' predictions are presented in Pauly and Satterthwaite (1981). These results appear to justify, pending further evidence, a tentative conclusion in favor of the 'imperfect information' explanation. If that conclusion is drawn, then it follows that, in this particular market, the basic imperfect competition story is inadequate; and were these factors shown to be important in a range of other markets, the scope and usefulness of the basic model would correspondingly be reduced. But while this, at most, implies a refinement of the theory, acceptance of the 'target income' explanation would exclude the imperfect competition approach, however refined, as an adequate representation for the market(s) in question.

The point which deserves emphasis is that the rejection of the prediction outlined here may reflect the irrelevance of the imperfect competition model; on the other hand, the theory may be 'rescued' by explaining the result as a 'perverse elasticity effect', through adding further structure to the basic model. More structure generates more predictions; what matters is that such a 'rescue' of the theory be admitted only in so far as the added structure generates further novel and successful predictions. Without such a self-denying ordinance, the theory would indeed be 'consistent with anything'.[15]

6 SUMMARY AND CONCLUSION

Once we move beyond the special polar cases of perfect competition and monopoly to a more general imperfect competition framework, comparative static predictions of the Samuelsonian kind will no longer be available, unless we introduce some restrictions. The present essay is concerned with the question of what form these restrictions should take.

Each one of the many models of imperfect competition which are now popular, implicitly embodies various restrictions, and these usually serve to produce a range of comparative static predictions. (For instance, the 'circular road' model developed above yields the prediction that an indirect tax of t pence per unit levied on producers will be passed on fully to consumers (i.e. price rises from p_0 to $p_0 + t$). This result reflects three restrictions embedded in the model, namely, that each consumer buys exactly one unit, that consumers are distributed uniformly in preference space, and that preferences – and so demand schedules – are linear.)

What is of prime interest, however, is what these various models of imperfect competition have in common. Rather than test some particular model, it may be better to focus attention directly on the restrictions themselves. In so doing, we are naturally led to look for restrictions which seem relatively plausible on *a priori* grounds. What I have argued here is that the 'elasticity hypothesis' embodied in Robinson's 'most common case' example affords us the kind of restriction which seems worthy of attention. By setting out to test the theory jointly with the restriction, we are led to predictions which distinguish the theory from the perfect competition model. What I have tried to argue here is that such a route is practicable, and can provide a useful starting point in exploring the empirical content of imperfect competition theory.

Notes

1. While some recent writers would favor a narrower interpretation than this (Hart, 1985a,b), Joan Robinson's later comments (1969) would indicate a much broader, and quite different, reading.
2. Whether this does in fact constitute a virtue, or not, is itself an issue. Friedman's (1953) essay argued that 'the relevant question to ask about the "assumptions" of a theory is not whether they are descriptively "realistic",

for they never are, but whether they are sufficiently good approximations for the purpose in hand. And this question can be answered only by seeing whether the theory works, which means whether it yields sufficiently accurate predictions'. He chose imperfect competition as one of two examples of the neglect of these propositions – its wide acceptance being 'largely explained by the belief that the assumptions of "perfect competiton" or "perfect monopoly" ... are a false image of reality'. But this argument blurs a crucial distinction. All good theories simplify reality by omission and by approximation; if this is all that is meant by the above propositions, it would be hard to disagree. What was at issue for the advocates of imperfect competition was more than this: on their assumption that the typical firm operated under increasing returns, the perfect competition model, which required diminishing returns to make it stand up, could not be defended *even as an approximation.* In fact, if the premise of the 1920s' debate – that average cost falls throughout the relevant range – is accepted, then perfect competition can be excluded on logical grounds, and the success or otherwise of its predictions is irrelevant. For an excellent discussion of this issue, see Nagel (1963).

3. See Dunlop (1938), Tarshis (1939), Keynes (1939), Kalecki (1938).
4. A major focus of the empirical literature concerns the observation that unit costs rise in the downswing (labor hoarding), but this rise is not passed on via prices. (For example, Nordhaus and Godley, 1972; Eckstein and Wyss, 1972). The conventional interpretation is that firms do not pass on cost increases which they see as being temporary in nature. Such a story lies outside the orbit of simple maximizing models, and the literature has tended to bypass such models in favor of a direct application of 'normal-cost pricing equations', which are defended on purely empirical grounds. For a full discussion, see Nordhaus (1972), Phelps and Winter (1970).
5. While I have attempted a fair summary here, it is worth recording that it was in regard to this point that most of the heat of the debate was generated, as Friedman claimed that the view expounded in his (1953) essay was seriously misrepresented by selective quotation in Archibald (1961a).
6. Stigler (1961) remarked, 'Archibald reproaches us for failing to make the real criticism of Chamberlin, "that he does not state what observable, testable predictions may be obtained from his theory". I apologise for having stated this thought in other words'.
7. And unfortunately, contained a central error, which was not noted until recently (d'Aspremont, Gabszewicz and Thisse, 1979), and which vitiates Hotelling's conclusion ('The Principle of Minimal Differentiation'). If this principle was true, it would imply that firms would not find it optimal to differentiate their products at all.
8. It seems clear, as many authors remark, that free entry equilibria in these models might involve 'gaps' between products too small to permit profitable entry, but sufficient to allow positive profits to incumbents. So the 'zero profit' configuration should be seen as only an approximation. While a formal analysis of this point is problematic, it seems unlikely that this difficulty poses a problem for the 'prediction' developed below.
9. For example, imagine the case of competition between rival tailors in offering custom-made suits. Here, we can tell the story in terms of perfect competition in the market for a (homogeneous) product called "tailors' services".
10. For a review of the implications for trade policy, see Pearce and Sutton (1985), chapter 9. A number of relevant papers appear in Kierzkowski (1984).
11. An exception is the Dixit–Stiglitz model, as simplified by Krugman (1981). The reason for this is that here no explicit model of preferences over different

products is introduced; products are simply assumed to be 'different'. So the entry of more products doesn't necessarily imply that each product competes with closer substitutes. That price falls (relative to marginal cost) with entry is ensured by introducing a suitable assumption on demand schedules (preferences). See also note 12 below.

12. A second type of counterexample may be generated by altering the equilibrium concept underlying our 'circular road' example. To see this, notice firstly that a rise in a firm's price causes a loss of sales through two channels: some of its customers switch to rival suppliers, and each of its remaining customers buys less. The latter contribution, which is summarized by the consumers' individual demand schedules, was taken to be zero in our 'circular road' example – each consumer bought exactly one unit at any price. It is the former contribution which leads to the intuition outlined above, for the 'closer' are competing products, the smaller the price rise which leads to a migration of the firm's patrons to rival sellers. Now this argument depends on the idea that a rise in price will not be followed automatically by rival sellers. Suppose, contrary to our earlier 'Nash equilibrium' assumption, that each firm conjectures that any rise in its price will be followed by an equal price rise for neighboring products. Then the 'market boundaries' will be unaffected, and the only sales loss is that associated with diminished purchases by each of its customers. Under these 'Löschian conjectures', each firm behaves as a monopolist *vis-à-vis* the customers in its 'market area'. A change in the number of suppliers narrows the range of this 'market area'. Whether price rises or falls then depends on whether the individual demand schedules of consumers at the margin of the firm's market area are more, or less, elastic than those of intra-marginal consumers. (In the related 'spacial competition' literature, where all firms' products are taken to be identical, but where the consumers pay 'price plus transport cost' on each unit purchased, consumers at different locations are operating at different points along their – identical – individual demand schedules, and the result depends simply on the degree of convexity of these schedules (see Capozza and Van Order, 1978; Benson, 1980).) For another counterexample relying on a change of equilibrium concept, see Salop (1979).
13. See, for example, Schmalensee (1978).
14. For US and Canadian studies, see the several references in Foley *et al.* (1980).
15. That these comments echo Lakatos (1978), in contrast to the views of Friedman and of Popper on falsificationism, which underlay the 1961 debate, will be obvious. A nice discussion of these several views is provided by Mark Blaug's contribution to the Latsis (1976) volume.

References

Archibald, G. C. (1961a) 'Chamberlin versus Chicago', *Review of Economic Studies*, 29: 2–28.

Archibald, G. C. (1961b) 'Reply to Chicago', *Review of Economic Studies*, 29: 68–71.

Archibald, G. C. and G. Rosenbluth (1976) 'The "New" Theory of Consumer Demand and Monopolistic Competition', *Quarterly Journal of Economics*, 89: 569–90.

d'Aspremont, C., J. J. Gabszewicz and J.-F. Thisse (1979) 'On Hotelling's "Stability in Competition"', *Econometrica*, 47: 1145–50.

Balassa, B. (1966) 'Tariff Reductions and Trade in Manufactures Among the Industrial Countries', *American Economic Review*, 56: 466–73.

Benson, B. L. (1980) 'Löschian Competition under Alternative Demand Conditions', *American Economic Review*, 70: 1098–1105.

Bodkin, R. C. (1969) 'Real Wages and Cyclical Variations in Employment: A Re-examination of the Evidence', *Canadian Journal of Economics*, 2: 353–74.

Capozza, D. R. and R. Van Order (1978) 'A Generalized Model of Spacial Competition', *American Economic Review*, 68: 896–907.

Chamberlin, E. H. (1933) *The Theory of Monopolistic Competition*, (Cambridge, Mass.: Harvard University Press).

Dixit, A. and J. Stiglitz (1977) 'Monopolistic Competition and Optimum Product Diversity', *American Economic Review*, 67: 297–308.

Dunlop, J. T. (1938) 'The Movement of Real and Money Wage Rates', *Economic Journal*, 48: 413–34.

Eckstein, O. and D. Wyss (1972) 'Industry Price Equations', in O. Eckstein and D. Wyss (eds), *The Econometrics of Price Determination*, (Washington: Board of Governors of the Federal Reserve System).

Evans, R. G. (1974) 'Models, Markets and Medical Care', in L. M. Officer and L. B. Smith (eds), *Issues in Canadian Economics* (Toronto: McGraw-Hill Ryerson).

Evans, R. G., E. M. A. Parish and F. Sully (1973) 'Medical Productivity, Scale Effects and Demand Generation', *Canadian Journal of Economics*, 6: 376–93.

Foley, P., A. Shaked and J. Sutton (1980) *The Economics of the Professions: An Introductory Guide to the Literature*, ICERD Occasional Paper no. 1, LSE.

Friedman, M. (1953) *Essays in Positive Economics* (Chicago: Chicago University Press).

Friedman, M. (1961) 'More on Archibald versus Chicago', *Review of Economic Studies*, 29: 65–7.

Grubel, H. G. and P. J. Lloyd (1975) *Intra-Industry Trade* (London: Macmillan).

Hart, O. D. (1985a) 'Monopolistic Competition in the Spirit of Chamberlin: A General Model', *Review of Economic Studies*, 52: 529–46.

Hart, O. D. (1085b) 'Monopolistic Competition in the Spirit of Chamberlin: Special Results', *Economic Journal*, 95: 889–908.

Helpman, E. (1981) 'International Trade in the Presence of Product Differentiation, Economies of Scale and Monopolistic Competition', *Journal of International Economics*, 11: 305–40.

Hollander, A. (1987) 'On Price-Increasing Entry', *Economica*, 54: 317–24.

Hotelling, H. (1929) 'Stability in Competition', *Economic Journal*, 39: 41–57.

Kalecki, M. (1938) 'The Determinants of Distribution of the National Income', *Econometrica* (April): 102–12.

Keynes, J. M. (1939) 'Relative Movements of Real Wages and Output', *Economic Journal*, 49: 34–51.

Kierzkowski, H. (ed.) (1984) *Monopolistic Competition and International Trade* (Oxford: Oxford University Press).

Krugman, P. R. (1981) 'Intra-Industry Specialization and the Gains from Trade', *Journal of Political Economy*, 89: 959–73.

Lakatos, I. (1978) *The Methodology of Scientific Research Programmes* (edited by J. Worrall and G. Currie) (Cambridge: Cambridge University Press).

Lancaster, K. (1979) *Variety, Equity and Efficiency* (Oxford: Basil Blackwell).

Latsis, S. (ed.) (1976) *Method and Appraisal in Economics* (Cambridge: Cambridge University Press).

Nagel, E. (1963) 'Assumptions in Economic Theory', *American Economic Review (Papers and Proceedings)*, 53: 211–19.

Nordhaus, W. D. (1972) 'Recent Developments in Price Dynamics', in O. Eckstein and D. Wyss (eds), *The Econometrics of Price Determination* (Washington: Board of Governors of the Federal Reserve System).

Nordhaus, W. and W. Godley (1972) 'Pricing in the Trade Cycle', *Economic Journal*, 82: 853–82.

Pauly, M. V. and M. A. Satterthwaite (1981) 'The Pricing of Primary Care Physicians' Services: A Test of the Role of Consumer Information', *Bell Journal of Economics*, 12: 488–506.

Pearce, J. and J. Sutton (1985) *Protection and Industrial Policy in Europe* (London: Routledge & Kegan Paul).

Perloff, J. and S. Salop (1985) 'Equilibrium with Product Differentiation', *Review of Economic Studies*, 52: 107–20.

Phelps, E. S. and S. G. Winter, Jr (1970) 'Optimal Price Policy under Atomistic Competition', in E. S. Phelps (ed.) *Microeconomic Foundations of Employment and Inflation Theory* (New York: Norton).

Robinson, J. (1953) 'Imperfect Competition Revisited', *Economic Journal*, 63: 579–93.

Robinson, J. (1958) 'Imperfect Competition Today', repr. in *Collected Economic Papers*, Vol.2 (1960) (Oxford: Basil Blackwell).

Robinson, J. (1969) *The Economics of Imperfect Competition*, 2nd edn (London: Macmillan).

Rosenthal, R. J. (1980) 'A Model in Which an Increase in the Number of Sellers Leads to a Higher Price', *Econometrica*, 48: 1575–9.

Salop, S. C. (1979) 'Monopolistic Competition with Outside Goods', *Bell Journal of Economics*, 10: 141–56.

Satterthwaite, M. (1979) 'Consumer Information, Equilibrium Industry Price and the Number of Sellers', *Bell Journal of Economics*, 10: 483–502.

Schmalensee, R. (1978) 'Entry Deterrence in the Ready-to-Eat Breakfast Cereal Industry', *Bell Journal of Economics*, 9: 305–27.

Sraffa, P. (1926) 'The Laws of Returns under Competitive Conditions', *Economic Journal*, 36: 542–50.

Stigler, G. (1949) 'Monopolistic Competition in Retrospect', in *Five Lectures on Economic Problems* (London: Longmans Green).

Stigler, G. (1961) 'Archibald versus Chicago', *Review of Economic Studies*, 28: 63–7.

Stigler, G. (1983) 'Nobel Lecture: The Process and Progress of Economics', *Journal of Political Economy*, 91: 529–45.

Sutton, J. (1986) 'Vertical Product Differentiation: Some Basic Themes', *American Economic Review (Papers and Proceedings)*, 76 (May): 393–8.

Tarshis, L. (1939) 'Changes in Real and Money Wages', *Economic Journal*, 49: 150–4.

Part III

Imperfect Competition: Game-theoretic Approach

7 Competitive Equilibrium in a Market with Decentralized Trade and Strategic Behavior: An Introduction

Ariel Rubinstein*

1 INTRODUCTION

Is there any diagram more familiar to economists than the following?

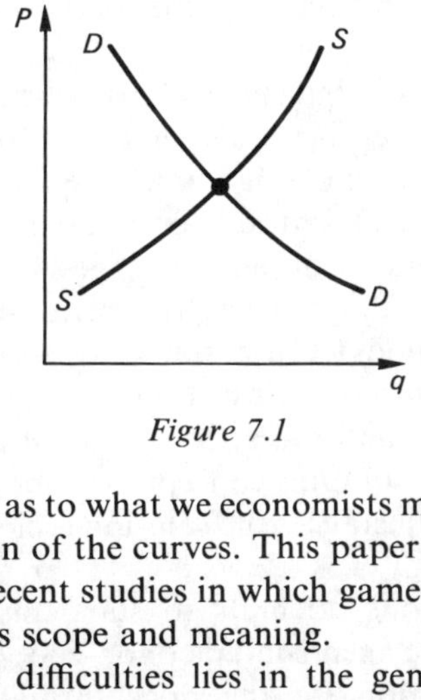

Figure 7.1

Still, I feel puzzled as to what we economists mean by the diagram and by the magic intersection of the curves. This paper is an attempt to introduce the reader to some recent studies in which game-theoretic tools are used to discuss the diagram's scope and meaning.

The origin of the difficulties lies in the generality of the competitive analysis approach. While attempting to cover a wide scope of economic situations, the analysis leaves unspecified the process by means of which the prices are formed. The economic agents are assumed to take the prices as

*My work in this field of the 'mini-micro' foundations for market equilibrium was accomplished together with Asher Wolinsky. Most of the ideas in this paper were developed jointly with Asher. I am deeply grateful to Asher for the many insights I got from him.

I am grateful to Ken Binmore and Ching-to Ma for many valuable suggestions.

It should be clarified that the paper is not an attempt to survey the literature but rather to serve as an introduction. Thus the list of references does not pretend to be comprehensive.

given. The equilibrium prices are announced by a hidden process which equalizes demand and supply of the market commodity. Textbooks tend to use an auctioneer as an example of an institution which justifies competitive price formation. However, the auctioneer story is quite unpersuasive because, first, it is not clear why the agents should take the prices as given – (for any specific auction rules, manipulative behavior may be possible) – and second, the auctioneer is quite a rare institution in the real world.

Time does not appear explicitly in the diagram. When coming to fill in the squares of the supply–demand curves with data about a market for a particular commodity, we must choose the units of the commodities we plug in. But then, are the 'correct' units, units of 'stock' or units of 'flow'? If stock, then over what period? If flow, flow of entrants to the market or flow of agents considering entering the market?

Another source of confusion is in defining the boundaries of a market. Jevons (quoted by Marshall, 1920) says: 'Originally a market was a public place in a town where provisions and other objects were exposed for sale; but the word has been generalized, so as to mean any body of persons who are in intimate business relations and carry on extensive transactions in any commodity.' What are sensible limits to the 'body of persons' included in the analysis?

Obviously it is a matter of judgment to decide when a market outcome is well described by the 'competitive price' model, to decide what the units appearing on the quantity axis of Figure 7.1 are and where to define the boundary of a market. The literature I am speaking about in this paper aims to assist us with this judgment (and to suggest other solution concepts for those cases in which the competitive price seems to be a poor approximation). The method we use starts by specifying in detail the process by which the terms of transactions are determined. Generally speaking, we will describe the process by means of a game. Then game-theoretic, non-cooperative solution concepts will be studied. Finally, we will check under what circumstances the solution is close to the competitive outcome.

There were many previous attempts to start this sort of inquiry by assuming that the economic agents interact non-cooperatively. In many of these attempts the institution for the price formation is a *centralized* mechanism. Clear expositions of this literature may be found in Mas-Colell (1982) and Wilson (1987).

The current paper deals only with models in which the institution of price formation is *decentralized.* Agents are matched and in each match an option for trade is available. The pioneering works of this type are, to my knowledge, those of Diamond–Maskin (1979), Diamond (1981) and Mortensen (1982). In these works, the events after a match occurs are not modelled. Rather, the authors assume that the parties reach an agreement immediately on the terms of the contract suggested by the Nash Bargaining

Solution. A pioneering work in which the negotiation was part of the game is that of Butters (1977).

Our basic image of a market is that of an ocean of traders looking for opportunities to bargain over the exact terms of trade. Throughout the paper, we consider a market in which a single commodity is traded for money. It is assumed that all the sellers in the market are identical. All the sellers have one unit of the good and their reservation price is 0. All the buyers are identical, having the desire to buy one and only one unit of the good and having a reservation price of 1. The special demand–supply diagram we refer to is thus of the type illustrated in Figure 7.2.

We will avoid the assumption that the market operates instantaneously. Rather we will specify the exact relationship between the traders' presence in the market and time. The three main options we are about to consider are:

1. The market is in a steady state in terms of the numbers of sellers and buyers in it. The completion of one transaction is immediately followed by the pairing of a new buyer and seller.
2. All the traders enter the market at one single time and the market continues to operate until all possible transactions are completed.
3. The number of sellers and buyers considering entering the market is constant over time.

The three options correspond to three different interpretations of the quantity axis in the demand–supply diagram.

In the first option, the market operates perpetually and the steady phenomena are the demand and supply opportunities available there.

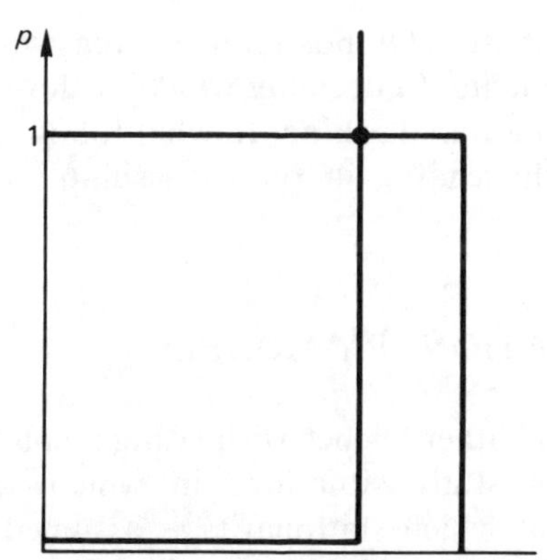

Figure 7.2

Under this option the quantities in the diagram should be interpreted as stock numbers of sellers and buyers existing in the market. This option will be relevant when we wish to consider, say, a market for apartments in a town in which it is known that the number of sellers and buyers searching there remain stable over a long period of time.

In the second option, the market operates only once and during its period of operation demand and supply are not steady. There are no interactions between the market and similar markets taking place in other periods. The markets for flowers in a town on Christmas Eve are more or less the type of markets we have in mind here.

In the third option, the markets operate constantly and the intensities of the flows of sellers and buyers considering entering the market are kept constant over time. A typical illustration is a market for a domestic good which may be imported or exported at prices 0 and 1 respectively. Each trader then has to decide whether he is interested in shopping in the local market or in trading abroad at the given prices.

What are the competitive equilibrium prices under each of the options when, let us say, *the number of the buyers is strictly larger than the number of sellers?*

It may be helpful at this stage if the reader pauses to consider what a competitive equilibrium would be in each of these cases. Is it true that the equilibrium price is equal to unity under all three options?

Before seeking to answer this question, it should be noted that the description of the markets given so far neglects certain important elements. Among them are:

1. the information the traders hold at each point of time;
2. the bargaining procedure used by the agents when they are matched;
3. the matching process.

There are endless reasonable possibilities from which to choose in the selection of these elements. In deciding which of those to study, we face a modelling dilemma of a familiar kind. In what follows, an attempt is made to consider some of the leading alternative assumptions that can be made.

2 TWO BASIC STATIONARY MODELS

In economics as in any other science we investigate phenomena which have some regularity. We study situations in which some stationarity is observed. The level at which stationarity is assumed is a matter for the modeller's good judgment. In this section we demonstrate two different models in which two distinct stationarity assumptions are assumed. There are several common factors shared by the models which will be spelled out first:

Commodity: The subject of the trade is a single indivisible good which is traded for a divisible good (money). At any given time the agents in the economy are split into two groups. In the sellers' group we gather all the agents who hold one unit of the good and wish to sell it. In the buyers' group are included all the agents who are interested in buying the good. The buyers have an unrestricted amount of money in the relevant range.

Time: Time is a discrete and is indexed by the integers. An instant of time is called a period.

Economic agents: Let B and S denote the sets of buyers and sellers. The symbols B and S are also used to denote the number of elements in the corresponding sets. All the agents of a particular type are assumed to have identical preferences. Whenever a seller sells a unit to a buyer at price p, at the t-th period of his life in the market he derives a von Neumann–Morgenstern utility of $p\delta^t$ where δ is a fixed discount factor. For the buyers the utility derived from such an outcome is $(1-p)\delta^t$. The discount factors are equal for all agents in the market.

The asymmetry between sellers and buyers: The only asymmetry between the sellers and the buyers in this model is that; *the sellers are on the short side of the market*. That is, the number of sellers in the market will always be smaller than the number of buyers.

Matching technology: In each period, all the sellers (the short side) active in the market in that period are matched with active buyers. Each agent is matched with at most one agent of the opposite type. The probability that a buyer is matched with a particular seller is not affected by the identity of the seller or of the buyer. This is a very special matching technology. Many of the substantive results in the paper could be extended to other matching technologies. However, in general, the results are sensitive to the specification of the technology.

Bargaining: Whenever a buyer and a seller are matched they hold a bargaining session which is assumed to have the following simple structure:

stage 1: one of the parties is selected (with equal probabilities) to make a proposal, namely to quote a price between 0 and 1;
stage 2: the selected party makes a proposal;
stage 3: the responder says 'Yes' or 'No'.

The previous remark about the choice of matching technology is valid here as well. Some of the results are sensitive to alteration of the bargaining procedure.

Information: At each stage, all the agents have a full record of all the events that occurred in the market up to that stage. This assumption is very powerful and will be discussed later.

We now turn to the differences between the two models:

Model A (constant numbers of sellers and buyers)

The numbers of sellers and buyers in the market is kept constant over time. This assumption has two possible interpretations. The most naive is that, whenever a pair completes a transaction, a new pair springs into existence in the market. A better interpretation is that the numbers of sellers and buyers are kept approximately steady, but the fluctuations are small enough to give the agents the impression that numbers are constant. With our assumption on matching technology, this means that the probability of a match for each period is 1 for a seller and only S/B for a buyer. The probabilities are kept constant through time.

Model B (one entry period)

All the sellers and buyers enter the market at time 0 and no additional agents join the market later. The numbers of sellers and buyers are changed endogenously until all the sellers execute a transaction.

Model A is a variation on models presented by Diamond, Maskin and Mortensen (see, for example, Diamond and Maskin (1979) and Mortensen (1982)). Model B was presented by Binmore and Herrero (1988) and is discussed further by Gale (1987).

We still have to explain what a strategy is in these models. To avoid cumbersome formal notation let us make do with an intuitive definition. A strategy is an agent's plan in which he specifies what offer to make and how to respond to any possible offer whenever it is his turn to act. The action planned will depend on the entire history preceding the relevant decision node.

We turn now to the solution concept. We will be interested in equilibria which satisfy two properties:

(a) All the agents of a particular type use the same strategy.

(b) Strategies depend only on time. More precisely, when a player makes an offer, the offer must depend only on time and on the numbers of buyers and sellers in the market at that time. When a player makes a response to an offer, the response must depend only on the offer, on time and on the numbers of sellers and buyers in the market. Although the players hold full information about the events preceding a decision node, they are assumed to base their behavior only on time. This assumption appears to be crucial and will be discussed in detail later.

By a Market Equilibrium in this context, we mean a pair of strategies, one to be used by all the sellers and one to be used by all the buyers, which constitute a (subgame) Perfect Equilibrium in the sense of Selten. The requirement for such an equilibrium is that the strategies have to generate optimal behavior for each agent at each point of time after every possible history, whether realized or not, given that other sellers and buyers follow the equilibrium strategies.

Remark: For very interesting and thorough discussions of these models with divisible goods see Gale (1986a;1986b). In Gale's model each agent enters the market with an initial bundle (like in Arrow–Debreu economy) and he may make several transactions before he decides to leave it.

3 ANALYSIS OF THE TWO MODELS

In the previous section we required that, in equilibrium, an action at time t depends on time and on the numbers of sellers and buyers only. The analytical advantage of this assumption is that one can talk now about the value of being a buyer (and similarly of being a seller) in the market at time t, given the numbers of sellers and buyers. In Model A, the numbers of sellers and buyers are fixed and thus we can denote by $V_b(t)$ and by $V_s(t)$ the expected utility discounted to period t from optimal behavior to a buyer and to a seller from participation in the market. Model B is more complicated, largely because of the dependence of behavior on the numbers of sellers and buyers. Therefore, in order to simplify the representation we will deal here only with the case $S = 1$. Then for as long as the market remains open we can define $V_s(t)$ and $V_b(t)$ as above.

Model A

The analysis of the model starts with the observation that, for all t, $\delta V_s(t) + \delta V_b(t) < 1$. This follows from the fact that the total surplus to be divided by a pair of one seller and one buyer cannot exceed 1. Therefore, in Market Equilibrium, every match must end with a transaction. Assume this is not the case, then, there is a time t and at least one proposer that suggests a price which, in equilibrium, is to be rejected. But, if the proposer deviates and makes an offer of a price p satisfying both $p > \delta V_s(t+1)$ and $1 - p > \delta V_b(t+1)$, then the responder's best action will be to accept the offer, contradicting the perfectness assumption.

Now, it is clear that, in equilibrium, the price offered by a buyer to a seller at period t will be $\delta V_s(t+1)$ and the price offered by the seller will be $1 - \delta V_b(t+1)$.

Denote by p^* the average price paid by a buyer to a seller. For all t the following three equations must hold:

$$p^*(t) = (1 - \delta V_b(t+1))/2 + \delta V_s(t+1)/2 \tag{1}$$

$$V_s(t) = p^*(t) \tag{2}$$

$$V_b(t) = (S/B)(1 - p^*(t)) + (1 - S/B)\delta V_b(t+1) =$$

$$(S/2B)(1 - \delta V_s(t+1)) + (S/2B)(\delta V_s(t+1)) + (1 - S/B)\delta V_b(t+1) \tag{3}$$

Taking into account the constraint that the price be between 0 and 1, it is possible to show that the only solution to the above set of equations satisfies

$$p^*(t) = 1/[2 - \delta + \delta S/B].$$

Thus the price (and hence the value functions) are stationary. The equilibrium price is sensitive as one would expect: increasing in the ration S/B decreases the price and increasing the discount factor increases the price (and hence V_s). Taking the limit as $\delta \to 1$ leads to the particularly attractive formula $p^* = B/(S+B)$.

Notice that, for $\delta = 1$, there are many equilibria in this model. Actually, all prices between 0 and 1 can be attained as price equilibria.

Notice also that the results depend only on the matching probabilities, $s = 1$ for the seller and $b = S/B$ for the buyer. For other matching technologies with arbitrary probabilities s and b, we get the set of equations (1), (2′) and (3′) where,

$$V_s(t) = sp^*(t) + (1 - s)\delta V_s(t+1) \tag{2′}$$

$$V_b(t) = b(1 - p^*(t)) + (1 - b)\delta V_b(t+1). \tag{3′}$$

It is easy to see that there is a unique solution for this set of equations and the limit of the price as $\delta \to 1$, is $s/(s+b)$.

Model B

Assume $S = 1$. Given a Market Equilibrium, the notion of the value of remaining in the market at time t is well defined here. The case $\delta < 1$ is especially simple here since $\delta V_b(t) + \delta V_s(t) < 1$ for all t. This implies that all matches end with an agreement and that the price is $\delta V_s(t+1)$ if a buyer makes the offer and $1 - \delta V_b(t+1)$ if the seller makes the offer. We get the following sequence of equations (compare it to the set of equations for Model A):

$$V_s(t) = [1 - \delta V_b(t+1)]/2 + \delta V_s(t+1)/2$$

$$V_b(t) = [1 - \delta V_s(t+1)]/2B + \delta V_b(t+1)/2B$$

It is easy to see that this set of equations has a unique solution which is stationary and has the property that $V_s \to 1$ as $\delta \to 1$. That is, the expected price goes to 1 as the impatience of the agents becomes negligible.

The proof for $S > 1$ is done by induction and is omitted.

The existence of a unique equilibrium for a Model B type market remains true under a much wider set of conditions which includes the case of $\delta = 1$ (see Rubinstein and Wolinsky, 1986).

The result for Model A is not consistent with the intuition that price be equal to one. This fact seems at first glance to be disturbing. Here we have a model in which the traditional assumptions about a competitive environment are fulfilled and still, when we take the frictions in the market to be very small, we do not get the competitive outcome.

At second thought there is nothing disturbing in this result. Obviously we do not have to conclude that the competitive approach is wrong but that given an observation that the market's environment is kept constant, the competitive equilibrium solution should not be applied to the data about the demand–supply at each instant.

Model B does lead to a competitive outcome. Thus we may conclude that the analysis supports the idea that given the data about the demand and supply at the beginning of a 'market day' and given that the market is separated from other markets we may apply the formula of the competitive price to this data.

4 MARKET ENTRY

In Section 3, we studied models in which the primitives were the stocks of buyers and sellers in the market. In Model A, the primitives were the stocks at each moment and it was assumed that these stocks are steady over time.

In Model B, the primitives were the stocks at the beginning date of the market.

In many markets we observe a pre-market decision-making problem in which the agents decide whether to enter the market or not. A typical example is a firm production decision. Given that the firm produced a unit of the good, it will appear in the market as a trader trying to get rid of the unit for the best price. The decision to produce is a pre-market decision. We may start the model from the decision of the agents to enter or not to enter the market. Then the primitives should be the volumes of traders who *consider* entering the market.

The origin of the distinction between market behavior and pre-market decision is very old. It appears very clearly in Marshall (1920). Marshall defines 'temporary equilibrium' to be the equilibrium in one market day (book 5, chapter 2). Later (chapter 3), he speaks about the origins of demand and supply curves and defines 'equilibrium' relative to 'pre-market' supply and demand.

Recently, within the literature on strategic behavior in markets, this distinction was made by Douglas Gale (1987). Gale used the distinction mainly to refute a claim that the results of Model A contradict the competitive approach.

Gale analyses a situation where, in each period, there are S sellers and B buyers who consider entering the market. If they do not enter the market, they disappear; that is, there is no accumulation of agents at the 'gates' of the market. A decision to enter the market involves a 'small' cost of $e > 0$. Assume that the market itself is in a steady state; that is, the numbers of sellers and buyers are steady (although they are determined endogenously in the model) and assume that the agents do not believe that their own entry decision influences the market environment. Their decision whether to enter the market or not, will then be just a comparison between e and the value of being in the market.

Obviously, there is a degenerate equilibrium in this model in which all the agents decide not to enter into the market. In order to characterize the other equilibria, denote by S' and B' the (strictly positive) numbers of sellers and buyers who stay in the market at any one time. The formulae for the values and the price in Model A yield that:

$$V_s = s/[2(1-\delta) + \delta s + \delta b]$$

$$V_b = b/[2(1-\delta) + \delta s + \delta b]$$

where $s = \min\{S',B'\}/S'$ and $b = \min\{S',B'\}/B'$. To achieve a steady state in the numbers of sellers and buyers, the number of sellers and buyers entering the market at each period must be equal. Therefore it must be true that both V_s and V_b are at least e. In addition $B > S$ and therefore $V_b = e$. Now we can verify that b, the ratio between numbers of sellers and buyers in the market, must be equal to $[(2-\delta)e]/[1-\delta e]$ and $V_s = [1-\delta e]/[2-\delta]$. When $\delta \to 1$ and $e \to 0$ the limits of V_s and of the average price in the market approach 1 (the competitive price). Notice that the source which generates the ratio b is not explained in this model. It must be created to give consistency to the assumptions in the model.

Thus, Gale's argument claims a coincidence between the strategic approach and the competitive equilibrium concept where the supply–demand curves are interpreted as information about the sellers and buyers who consider entering the market.

We may add a pre-market stage to Model B as well. Assume that before the market starts, the S sellers and the B buyers consider spending the e which is necessary to enter the market. Assume first that the agents who enter the market do not know the actual number of sellers and buyers who enter the market. Then, fixing $e > 0$, and having δ very close to 1, we find that the only equilibrium is one where all the buyers and sellers decide not to enter into the market. Assume next that the agents are notified about the actual number of sellers and buyers who enter the market. Then for all $E \leqslant S$ there is an equilibrium in which E sellers and E buyers enter the market and the expected price is $\frac{1}{2}$.

5 SIMULTANEOUS BARGAINING AND MATCHING

In Section 3 we considered a model in which the bargaining model was extremely simple. One of the agents is selected to make a proposal, the other responds, and a rejection implies a return of the agents to the pool of unmatched agents. This assumption seems to be highly restrictive. In this section we wish to allow the agents to continue the negotiation if they fail to reach an agreement. This section follows Rubinstein–Wolinsky (1985).

We keep the basic structure of Model A with the exception of the bargaining process. We assume that at each period a seller has an exogenous probability, s, to be matched with a new buyer and each buyer has an exogenous probability, b, of being matched with a new seller (s is not necessarily 1). The players are assumed to continue negotiating until either they reach an agreement or they are matched with another partner. When an agent is matched with a new partner he is *forced to leave* his current negotiator and to start bargaining with the new partner.

The exact order of events in each period is the following: first, the matching process determines who is matched with whom. Then, for each matched pair, one of the agents is selected to make a proposal. The selected agent then makes an offer and finally his opponent reacts by accepting or rejecting the offer.

A matched pair faces a sequential bargaining game in which two factors impel an agent to prefer an early agreement: (i) his time preference (as in Model A) and (ii) the fear that his partner will abandon him. Notice that a matched seller at period t, who does not conclude any agreement at time t, starts bargaining with a new partner at period $t+1$ with probability s. With probability $(1-s)(1-b)$ he continues to bargain with his old partner and with probability $(1-s)b$ he finds himself unmatched at period $t+1$. The last possibility is an additional source of pressure on the seller in addition to his impatience with the passage of time.

A candidate for a Market Equilibrium in this model is a pair of strategies, one for each of the sellers and one for each of the buyers, which prescribe the rules of behavior for all the sellers and for all the buyers after all possible personal histories. A pair of strategies is a Market Equilibrium if no agent has a feasible personal history after which he can make a profitable deviation.

It was proved that in this model there is a unique Market Equilibrium (see Rubinstein–Wolinsky (1985) for a proof for 'semi-stationary' strategies and Binmore–Herrero (1988) for non-stationary strategies). There are numbers x^* and y^* such that, in this equilibrium, the sellers always make the offer x^* and the buyers always make the offer y^*. The acceptance policy for the seller is to accept only y^* or more, and for the buyer to accept only x^* or less. Both numbers x^* and y^* tend to $s/(s+b)$ as $\delta \to 1$.

Thus the sequential model leads to pretty much the same outcome as the simpler Model A. Nevertheless, we find the sequential model attractive because it justifies Model A's outcome by being more realistic and furthermore, since the model is richer, it provides us with a tool for answering questions which could not be asked in Model A (see for example Gul, 1986). As is claimed in Wolinsky (1987), the fact that the sequential bargaining market model and Model A lead to the same results is a 'razor edge' fact. Wolinsky (1987) extends the model by allowing all the agents to choose in each period the intensity with which he will pursue the (costly) search for a partner. Then the limit of the Market Equilibrium price is not equal to Model A's price.

The decision to abandon an old agent is not a strategic decision in this model. Nevertheless, it is a rational decision in the sense that an agent would not gain if he decided not to abandon the old partner when he is matched with a new partner. If we allow the breakdown of the negotiation to be a strategic decision in the model, we get more equilibria. In particular we get an equilibrium in which no agent leaves an old partner. Then the bargaining situation between a seller and a buyer is like that in a sequential bargaining game with outside options (see Shaked–Sutton, 1984; and Binmore, 1985) and the average price in the outcome of each bargaining game would be 1/2 independently of the probabilities of matching (this is a by-product of a general phenomenon called by Binmore, Shaked and Sutton 'the outside options principle'). In other words, in this equilibrium, the bargaining outcome is just like that in a bargaining model with a seller and buyer totally isolated from the market.

6 THE ANONYMITY ASSUMPTION

In the analysis of Model B in Section 4, it was assumed that a strategy of an agent must be 'impersonal' in the sense that it depends solely on the number of sellers, the number of buyers and on the date, but not on the agent's personal history. Even without impatience we could derive the result that the only Market Equilibrium is competitive. However, we made quite strong restrictions on the set of possible strategies. We did not allow any equilibrium in which some 'personal' arrangements might emerge in the course of the game. The interactions between the agents were assumed by these restrictions to be impersonal (see Ben-Porath (1980) for a detailed informal discussion of the distinction between personal and impersonal interactions in markets).

This section (which follows section 3 in Rubinstein–Wolinksy (1986)) demonstrates that, if we allow the players' strategies to depend on the entire history, then equilibrium outcomes other than the competitive outcome are possible.

For the sake of simplicity, let us focus on the special case of Model B with $S=1$ and $B>1$. For this model, there is one perfect equilibrium in which the price is the competitive price: the seller always requires price 1 and rejects all other offers. A buyer always offers 1 and accepts all possible offers. Obviously, this is a perfect equilibrium and its outcome is an immediate agreement on the competitive price.

We turn now to a description of a perfect equilibrium in which the equilibrium price is an arbitrary price p^* in the interval [0,1]. In interpreting this equilibrium, it may be helpful to imagine that some buyers may acquire a 'right' (option) to buy the good at price p^*. This is not an exogenously imposed legal 'right' but appears endogenously as an equilibrium phenomenon. Initially this right is 'granted' to some buyer called i^* . The 'right' is transferred to another buyer if the seller makes him an offer strictly greater than p^*. The 'right' will be lost without being transferred if a buyer without a 'right' makes an offer higher than p^*.

As long as one of the buyers is holding the 'right', the seller's offer is p^* to the buyer who holds the 'right' and the seller's offer is 1 to all other buyers. The seller refuses any offer made by all buyers other than the 'right' holder and he accepts no offer less than p^* from the 'right' holder. The holder offers p^* if he is selected to make an offer and he refuses any demand above p^*. The other buyers accept all prices below p^* and they reject any price above p^*. Their offers are 0.

If no buyer holds the 'right', the continuation of the game is as in the equilibrium with the competitive outcome which has been described above.

Notice, that an attempt by a buyer who does not hold the 'right' to compete for the good by making a high offer is interpreted in this equilibrium as a sign that the players are moving to the competitive equilibrium. Otherwise, the market norm suggests that the seller and the right 'holder' settle the transaction between themselves.

Notice also it is essential that the 'right' is transferred from one buyer to another buyer in the equilibrium which supports a non-competitive price. Otherwise, a seller would not be deterred from offering a high price to a buyer who is not supposed to receive the good.

The fact that the players' identities are not suppressed in this model in the sense that they recognize and remember one another, enables us to construct an equilibrium in which a non-competitive price prevails. In Rubinstein–Wolinsky (1986) we showed that even if the agents have only personal recall and the sellers do not identify with buyers, any price could be the outcome of an equilibrium (actually a sequential equilibrium, since the game becomes a game with imperfect information).

Our conclusion from these examples is that the assertion of the competitive price as a good approximation for markets like that of Model B should be qualified when the frictions in the model are very small. Impersonal interactions are required to make this proposition valid.

7 TOWARDS AN ALTERNATIVE MARKET SET-UP

Traditionally, we describe a market of a commodity in terms of the numbers of sellers and buyers and their preference relations. (In the context of this paper the preferences are summarized by their reservation values.) In this section, I would like to speculate on whether there may be another natural framework within which to discuss the market price.

One possible framework is suggested by the previous discussion. The suggested primitives of an alternative model would be descriptions of the sellers' and buyers' 'personal environments'. By a 'personal environment', I refer to the parameters of the random process which creates opportunities to trade, and a specification of the distribution of the potential trading partners.

In the usual framework, it is assumed that the total supply is equally relevant for all buyers. Similarly, it is assumed that the personal environment is common for all buyers (and analogously for all sellers). For the scenario of Model A, a seller's 'personal environment' is the prospect of meeting a buyer with reservation value 1 in every period with probability s. A buyer's 'personal environment' is characterized by the prospect of meeting a seller with probability equal to b in all periods. Recall that for

Model A, given the personal environments (i.e. the probabilities s and b) the solution price is $s/(s+b)$.

Such an approach is not restricted to the case where all the sellers and all the buyers are equal. In Gale (1987) the analysis of Section 3 is extended for all step-wise supply and demand curves. It was shown by Gale that, if the matching probability of an agent of a particular type is proportional to the quantities of agents of each type, then the price will be the number p^* which equates 'supply surplus' with 'demand surplus'. By supply (demand) surplus we refer to the area above (below) the supply (demand) curve and below (above) the horizontal line p^* (see Figure 7.3).

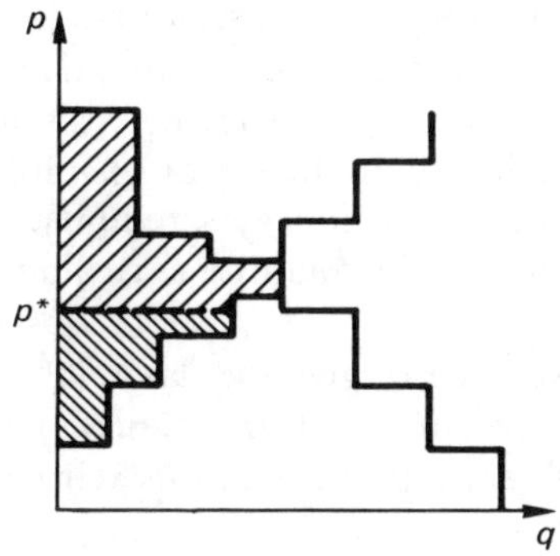

Figure 7.3

I find the alternative set-up plausible for situations where the personal environments remain constant over time. It does not suit models like Model B, where it is difficult to think about the personal environment at subsequent dates without specifying the quantities and the matching technology. However, notice that the traditional framework suffers from a dual problem: if the matching technology is not specified the quantities may give insufficient information for determining the market solution.

8 CONCLUSION

This paper has dealt only with the abstract relationship between strategic market models and competitive equilibrium. However, it should be made clear that a major aim of the strategic approach is also to provide tools for analysis of economic problems which cannot be analyzed by other approaches. (See for example, Shaked and Sutton (1984) on involuntary unemployment, Rubinstein and Wolinksy (1987) on middlemen, and Horn and Wolinksy (1986) and Jun (1986) on the size of the unions.)

As a guide to the user, may I express my impression that simple models based on the Diamond–Mortensen approach (where the Nash Bargaining

Solution is used in place of a detailed bargaining game) are very powerful models. An introduction to the economic uses of this type of model may be found in Diamond (1984). One problem with that approach is that we have to be very careful in the selection of the disagreement point when we apply the static Nash Bargaining Solution (see Binmore, Rubinstein and Wolinksy, 1986; and Sutton, 1986). As explained in the two papers cited above, many applications of the Nash Bargaining Theory suffer from an imprecise use of the very attractive Nash Bargaining Solution.

Needless to say, the strategic decentralized approach is not meant to compete with the competitive approach but is complementary to it. The strategic approach contributes to the understanding of the competitive equilibrium in at least two ways: (i) discussions like Section 6 clarify the limits of the range of applications of the competitive solution, and (ii) when the competitive solution does apply, strategic discussions can clarify the manner in which it should be applied. For example, Gale's argument in Gale (1987) summarized in Section 4 is reminiscent of the question of whether the relevant units on the quantity axis should be units of stocks or units of flows.

In this chapter I have tried to give the flavor of some basic ideas which have appeared in the recent literature. Since the topic stimulates the imagination, I am confident that much more exciting research in the area is still on its way.

References

Ben-Porath, Y. (1980) 'The F-Connection: Families, Friends and Firms and the Organization of Exchange', *Population and Development Review* 6 (1).

Binmore, K. G. (1985) 'Bargaining and Coalitions', in A. Roth (ed.) *Game Theoretic Approaches to Bargaining Theory* (Cambridge: Cambridge University Press).

Binmore, K. G. and M. J. Herrero (1988) 'Matching and Bargaining in Steady Markets', *The Review of Economic Studies*, 55: 17–32.

Binmore, K. G., A. Rubinstein and A. Wolinksy (1986) 'The Nash Bargaining Solution in Economic Modelling', *The Rand Journal of Economics*, 17: 176–88.

Butters, G. (1977) 'Equilibrium Price Distribution in a Random Meetings Market', mimeo, Princeton University.

Diamond, P. A. (1981) 'Mobility Costs, Frictional Unemployment and Efficiency', *Journal of Political Economy*, 89: 798–811.

Diamond, P. A. (1984) *A Search-Equilibrium Approach to the Micro Foundations of Macroeconomics* (Cambridge, Mass.: MIT).

Diamond, P. A. and E. Maskin (1979) 'An Equilibrium Analysis of Search and Breach of Contract', *Bell Journal of Economics* 10: 282–316.

Gale, D. (1987) 'Limits Theorems for Markets with Sequential Bargaining', *Journal of Economic Theory*: 43: 20–54.

Gale, D. (1986a) 'Bargaining and Competition Part I: Characterization', *Econometrica*, 54: 785–806.

Gale, D. (1986b) 'A Simple Characterization of Bargaining Equilibrium in a Large

Market without the Assumption of Dispersed Characteristics', University of Pennsylvania, CARESS, WP 86–05.

Gul, F. (1986) 'Bargaining Foundations of Shapley Value', mimeo, Stanford University.

Horn, H. and A. Wolinksy (1986) 'Worker Substitutability and Patterns of Unionization', mimeo, Institute for International Economic Studies, Stockholm.

Jun, B. H. (1986) 'Non-cooperative Bargaining and Union Formation', mimeo, University of Pennsylvania.

Marshall, A. (1920) *Principles of Economics*, 8th edn (London: Macmillan).

Mas-Collell, A. (1982) 'The Cournotian Foundations of Walrasian Equilibrium Theory: An Exposition of Recent Theory', in W. Hildenbrand (ed.), *Topics in Economic Theory* (Cambridge: Cambridge University Press).

Mortensen, D. T. (1982) 'The Matching Process as a Noncooperative Bargaining Game', in J. J. McCaull (ed.) *The Economics of Information and Uncertainty* (Chicago and London: The University of Chicago Press).

Rubinstein, A. and A. Wolinksy (1985) 'Equilibrium in a Market with Sequential Bargaining', *Econometrica*, 55: 1133–50.

Rubinstein, A. and A. Wolinksy (1987) 'Middlemen', *Quarterly Journal of Economics*, 102: 581–94.

Rubinstein, A. and A. Wolinksy (1986) 'Decentralized Trading, Strategic Behaviour and the Walrasian Outcome', mimeo, University of Pennsylvania and LSE.

Shaked, A. and J. Sutton (1984) 'Involuntary Unemployment as a Perfect Equilibrium in a Bargaining Model', *Econometrica*, 52: 1351–64.

Sutton, J. (1986) 'Non-cooperative Bargaining Theory: An Introduction', *Review of Economic Studies*, 53: 709–24.

Wilson, R. B. (1987) 'Game Theoretic Analysis of Trading Processes', in *Proceedings of the Fifth World Congress of the Econometric Society*, ed. T. Bewley.

Wolinksy, A. (1987) 'Matching, Search and Bargaining', *Journal of Economic Theory*: 42: 311–33.

Wolinksy, A. (1988) 'Dynamic Markets with Competitive Bidding', *The Review of Economic Studies*, 55: 71–84.

8 Entry and Exit

Robert Wilson*

1 INTRODUCTION

Analyses of industrial competition have attained a new vigor with the application of game-theoretic methods. The process of competition is represented in models that reflect genuine struggles for entry, market power, and continuing survival. Dynamics and informational effects are captured explicitly, although so far only in simplified formulations. Recognition of the importance and intricate complexities of competitive processes began a half-century ago in the work of Joan Robinson (1933), and the first game-theoretic formulations were developed by Shubik (1959) a quarter-century later, but the flowering of this approach began in the 1980s with the recognition that informational asymmetries are crucial ingredients to bring the flavor of struggle to the ensuing dynamic processes. Models that admit both dynamics and private information formulate competition as essentially a bargaining process in which credible communication is limited to costly actions. Each firm's claim to survival is signalled by its willingness to offer lower prices longer than others. Firms' struggles for the advantages of monopoly power bring benefits to consumers by dissipating a substantial part of the subsequent profits in the battle to obtain them. This is not the entire story of competition, of course, since also important are, for example, races for cost advantages, product development and differentiation, as well as imposition of search and switching costs on customers to sustain monopoly pricing; nevertheless, it brings theories that describe more realistically the Darwinian aspect of competition.

This chapter presents a few of the models developed recently to study competitive processes that affect a firm's entry into a market, and the decision to exit. The focus is on firms' strategies to gain or protect monopoly power. We omit the ordinary sort of daily battles for market share; the intent is to study battles for survival. That is, we study competition as economic warfare.

The analyses use the methods of game theory, since the key feature is the strategic behavior of the participants as they jockey for position in a game of economic life or death. Some of the theory is adapted from evolutionary biology, and indeed would change little if one were studying two animals competing for prey or a mate. In the economic context, strength derives

* Support from the National Science Foundation (SES 8605666) and the Office of Naval Research (N00014-79C0685) is gratefully acknowledged.

from superior resources, lower costs, etc. Often the overall effect of warfare is simply the discovery of which contestant is stronger, as revealed by the eventual capitulation of the weaker one. Thus, in several of the models described here, the essential ingredient is some initial uncertainty as to which one is the stronger, and the ensuing battle is primarily a demonstration of which one has the greater power to sustain combat. There is no possibility that a battle can be avoided by persuasion: the only credible evidence that one is stronger is the demonstration itself.

We begin with an examination in Section 2 of models of 'predatory' behavior aimed at deterring entry, and this theme is continued in Section 3 where we examine in more detail wars of attrition intended to drive out competitors. Section 4 returns to the theme of entry deterrence via limiting pricing strategies. Section 5 considers the maintenance of monopoly prices by the threat of price wars. In Section 6 we examine firms' incentives to obtain powers of commitment via the timing of capacity additions. Finally, Section 7 establishes the role of reputational effects in collusive situations with incomplete information. Concluding remarks are presented in Section 8 followed by bibliographic references in Section 9.

2 PREDATION

We begin with an examination of the long-standing controversy about the power and motives of large firms to drive out smaller competitors by driving prices below costs. This controversy is associated with the so-called 'deep-pocket' hypothesis and the 'demonstration effect'. The deep-pocket hypothesis refers generally to the proposition that a firm with superior resources can sustain a pitched battle longer, but more particularly it invokes the idea that multi-product conglomerates selling in several markets might be able to subsidize price cuts in one market by drawing on profits from other markets. This idea may seem far-fetched, since surely a firm tries to maximize profits in every market, but in another form it is more plausible: a firm able to retain earnings from other markets can avoid using capital markets in times of stress, and its other earnings can ameliorate shareholders' distress. The deep-pocket hypothesis obtains its strongest form, however, when it is combined with the demonstration effect; namely, the conglomerate's motive to respond aggressively to competition in any one market so as to deter entry in other markets. The notion here is that a stern response in one market is taken as a signal by potential entrants in other markets as to what they might expect if they were to enter. To the extent the demonstration effect is real, it multiplies the conglomerate's incentive to fight: large losses in the entered market can be justified as insignificant compared to the losses incurred if failure to respond now were to initiate a later flood of entries into other markets.

The classic example of predatory behavior is Rockefeller's purported conduct in building the dominant position of the old Standard Oil in the latter part of the nineteenth century. More recent examples, subject to debate, from the late 1960s and early 1970s, include IBM's response to the plug-compatible equipment manufacturers, and Maxwell House's response to Folger's attempt to enter the East coast markets for coffee.

What one means by multiple markets depends on the context. Generally markets are distinct to the degree that the products are not perfect substitutes. This may mean that the products are technically different, but it can also mean that they are sold in geographically separated locales, or that they are targeted to different groups of customers. We do not dwell on such distinctions here but rather take the market segmentation as a datum. Similarly, we do not enter into a detailed analysis of the actual policies that constitute the response to entry (pricing, advertizing, and other marketing devices); rather, we mostly assume that there is a clear-cut distinction between predatory (or aggressive) and acquiescing behavior and that this distinction is manifested in the profits that the firms obtain.

The central difficulty in any analysis of predatory behavior is to illuminate the motives of the incumbent firm and the entrant. Can it possibly be that actions costly for the incumbent in the short run are part of an optimal strategy in the long run? If so, then the incumbent must be investing in something early that will pay off later. That something can be either tangible, such as a monopoly position in the market if it drives out the entrant, or intangible, such as a reputation for being tough that will deter others contemplating entry. For the entrant, a lot hinges on the credibility attached to the incumbent's threat to engage in battle. Is it irrational, a bluff, or is it truly in the incumbent's best interest?

These questions do not have easy answers, and speculation cannot substitute for the particulars of the case, and especially for the personalities peculiar to the leadership of the firms. Our discussion, therefore, focuses on developing sketchy models that capture a few salient aspects to see what they predict a rational, profit-maximizing participant would do.

2.1 Complete Information

To begin we consider two examples involving an incumbent firm, already established in a market, and a potential entrant who is considering entering. Whether or not entry occurs a sequence of events ensues with financial consequences, but here we encapsulate all the follow-on events in a static description that uses present values to represent subsequent income streams. The entrant's choices are simply to enter or not. Following entry the incumbent can either acquiesce (play 'soft') or respond aggressively (play 'tough'). We describe two examples, the second of which is developed in more detail later.

Example 2.1: The War Chest In this first example, suppose that the entrant can survive an aggressive response for only a limited number of periods, say n, which might be very large. Assume that both the incumbent and the entrant know what n is, that the horizon is unlimited, and that the incumbent is surely willing to respond aggressively if the entrant can be driven out in one period. We claim that in this situation the entrant's optimal strategy is not to enter, and if it does it capitulates immediately and exits; for, the incumbent responds aggressively.

To demonstrate this claim we argue by induction. The claim is surely true if the number of periods remaining before the entrant is exhausted is small enough, say not more than $m \geqslant 1$, that the incumbent's losses from fighting are outweighed by the subsequent monopoly profits after the entrant is driven out. So, we conclude that when funds for m periods remain in its war chest the entrant can expect an aggressive response from the incumbent thereafter and therefore its optimal strategy is to exit. But then with $m+1$ periods remaining the incumbent needs to be aggressive for only one period to drive out the entrant, so it will surely fight, and anticipating this the entrant will exit. Continuing this argument for $m+2,\ldots,n$ periods remaining, we conclude that also when all n periods are available to the entrant, it wants to exit – or better, not to enter initially.

The striking paradox inherent in this result is that it holds whatever might be the size n of the entrant's war chest. Later we unravel such paradoxes by showing that the induction argument is invalid if there is even the slightest violation of the assumption that all data of the problem are common knowledge between the incumbent and entrant.

Example 2.2: The Chain Store Game In this example we model the competitive situation somewhat differently. Rather than supposing that the entrant's resources are limited, we assume that the present values of the entrant's and the incumbent's payoffs in the three possible scenarios are those displayed in Table 8.1 below. Notice in the table that without the entrant present the incumbent enjoys monopoly profits of \$3, whereas with the entrant present he can either acquiesce in splitting the market (\$1 each) or respond aggressively to force losses on the incumbent (−\$1) and eliminate his own profits (\$0).

It appears clear in this situation that the entrant wants to enter, expecting the incumbent to act in his own best interest to share the market. Moreover, if this situation is repeated between the same incumbent and entrant then this outcome persists: the two firms adapt to co-existence.

Or is it so clear? Suppose that in fact this market is one of many, say ten, similar ones in which the incumbent operates, and in every one there is a

Table 8.1 Payoffs for the entrant and the incumbent

Actions		*Payoffs*	
Entrant	*Incumbent*	*Entrant*	*Incumbent*
Stays out		\$0	\$3
Enters	Soft	1	1
	Tough	−1	0

potential entrant. If it is true in this market that the incumbent will acquiesce then surely it is so in every market. Playing soft in all markets yields the incumbent \$10. But suppose he were tough in a few, say four, and this salutary action sufficed to deter entry in the other six markets: then his profit would be 6 × \$3 = \$18 – well worth the effort to preserve his dominant position. If the number n of markets is larger, say 100 or 1000, then intuitively one expects the incumbent to establish a reputation for being tough on entrants. The cost of clobbering a few hapless entrants initially is well worth its demonstration effect on the subsequent ones.

How are we to make sense of this seeming contradiction between elementary logic and the intuitive appeal of the 'tough-guy' gambit? There are some ready answers that rely heavily on intuition. Perhaps the incumbent likes to brutalize, maybe he learned rules of thumb ('be tough') at his father's knee, maybe his friends would ridicule any signs of passivity, or maybe his belief in the powers of intimidation transcends accounting statements. The feature shared by all these explanations is the appeal to some *maybe*. Even though this is supposedly a game with complete information, one can conjure uncertainties that allow reputational effects. As long as there is some chance of unobservable psychic or economic factors that could influence the incumbent's choices, then one can interpret tough play as the natural mode of reinforcing in the entrants' perceptions the likelihood that the incumbent has a penchant for snuffing out trespassers. Building a reputation for being tough becomes a sane strategy, even if one is ordinary. It is this approach to the 'paradox' above that we pursue below.

2.2 Uncertainty about Preferences

The simplest way to enable reputational effects is to dispense with the assumption that the features of the situation are common knowledge. To illustrate this we analyze an example in which the incumbent is uncertain whether one of the entrants knows the facts of the situation. For simplicity we suppose that there are only two potential entrants, each of whom has an opportunity to enter one of the incumbent's markets, and these opportunities occur in sequence.

Suppose that it is common knowledge among the entrants that the possible actions and the resulting payoffs are as described in Table 8.1. The incumbent knows these facts too but he is uncertain whether the second entrant knows them. To be specific, suppose that the incumbent assigns a probability 0.6 to the prospect that the second entrant assigns a probability exceeding 0.5 to the notion that the incumbent's predictable or only possible response to entry is to play tough.

The claim we make is that in this circumstance an equilibrium includes the following. The incumbent is prepared to play tough if the first entrant enters, but not if the second enters. The first entrant, anticipating the incumbent's tough response, stays out. The second entrant, on the other hand, anticipates a soft response and decides to enter. Thus, the key result is that the incumbent plays tough against the first entrant although he forgoes an immediate profit of \$1 by doing so. We first explain this equilibrium in an informal way, and then undertake a more complete analysis.

Informal Explanation The entrants' actions are clearly their best choices in response to the incumbent's strategy, so we focus on an explanation of the incumbent's reasoning. If the incumbent meets the first entry by playing tough then his payoff is \$0 plus what he can expect in his match with the second entrant, and, similarly, if he plays soft it is \$1 plus the follow-on profit. He realizes, however, that if he plays soft then the second entrant will recognize that playing tough is not his only feasible action and so the second entrant will surely enter (yielding \$1 for the incumbent, who will respond softly); whereas if he plays tough then (in the incumbent's view) there will remain a 0.6 probability that the second entrant ascribes a high likelihood to the possibility that the incumbent will surely respond to entry by playing tough, and in this event the second entrant will not enter (yielding \$3 for the incumbent). Thus, the incumbent calculates that a tough response to the first entry yields $\$0+0.6\times\$3+0.4\times\$1=\$2.2$, whereas a soft response yields $\$1+\$1=\$2.0$. Choosing between these, the incumbent opts to meet entry the first time with tough play – simply on the chance that this will deter the second entrant. Notice that the incumbent's calculations are wrong, in a sense, since in fact neither entrant assigns any chance to the incumbent's having only the tough response available, and they know that the incumbent is wrong. Nevertheless, the first entrant knows the inexorable consequence of the incumbent's uncertainty about the second entrant's beliefs, which is that he will clobber the first entrant to avoid possibly revealing information to the second entrant; so, the first entrant is deterred from entering.

Formal Analysis To build up a game-theoretic model of this problem, assume that there are three possible states of the world, labelled *A*, *B*, and *C*. The true state happens to be *C*, which the entrants know, but the incumbent knows only that it is one of *B* or *C*, and it is *B* that represents the possibility entertained by the incumbent that the second entrant is unsure whether the incumbent's only feasible action is to play tough, which is represented by *A*. Thus, in *A* the incumbent can only play tough, whereas he has both actions available in *B* and *C*. The incumbent knows only that the true state is *A* or not-*A*; the first entrant knows whether it is *A*, *B*, *or C*; and the second entrant knows whether it is *C* or not-*C*. Assume that the prior probabilities of *A*, *B*, and *C* are 0.5, 0.3, and 0.2, respectively. For example, if the true state were *B* then the second entrant, who would know that it is not-*C*, would assign probability $0.5/[0.5+0.3]=0.625$ to state *A*; and the incumbent would assign probability $0.3/[0.3+0.2]=0.6$ to state *B*, as we initially assumed. The strategies in this setup are:

1. The first entrant stays out in any event.
2. The second entrant enters only if either he knows that *C* obtains or he observed the first entrant to enter and the incumbent to play soft, in which case he infers that state *B* obtains.
3. The incumbent counters the first entry with tough play in any event, and he counters the second entry with tough play only if he knows that *A* obtains.

The second entrant does not enter if he knows only that *C* does *not* obtain, because it yields a negative expected profit: $0.625 \times (-\$1) + 0.375 \times \$1 < \$0$. On the other hand, he enters if the incumbent's play of soft reveals that the state is *B* rather than *A*. Anticipating this, the incumbent, if not-*A* obtains, prefers to play tough against the first entrant, based on the calculation in the previous paragraph.

There is, of course, another equilibrium in which the incumbent threatens to meet all entry with tough play. This threat is not credible, however, since it violates sequential rationality. That is, once the second entrant enters, the incumbent's best strategy in the subgame remaining is to play soft. Realizing this the second entrant who knows that *C* obtains has every incentive to call the incumbent's bluff.

There is, however, another sequentially rational equilibrium in which in states *B* and *C* both entrants enter and the incumbent acquiesces. In this equilibrium, if the second entrant is unsure whether *A* or *B* obtains but he sees the first entrant enter then he infers that the true state is actually *B* and so he enters also. Anticipating this, the first entrant does indeed enter if the state is *B* or *C*, since he realizes that in state *B* the signal to the second entrant that his own entry provides precludes any motive for the incumbent to play tough so as to influence the second entrant's decision. Similarly, if the first entrant's information is the same as the second entrant's, then he enters in state C (but not in not-C) since he anticipates that his entry signals to the incumbent that B is not possible, so tough play to influence the second entrant is useless. However, these equilibria with entry in the first period are eliminated if the first entrant cannot distinguish among the states.

2.3 Incomplete Information

We now elaborate the Chain Store game to explore further aspects of the problem. Keep the same formulation, except suppose that there are n potential entrants, each with a single opportunity to enter in sequence. And, suppose that initially each entrant entertains a small probability p that the incumbent is sure to respond to entry with tough behavior. The origin of this possible adherence to tough is immaterial, but here are several possibilities: (i) the incumbent's payoffs might be reversed, so that tough is more rewarding than soft (possibly for non-financial reasons); (ii) the incumbent might be acting under instructions that commit him to respond aggressively; (iii) he might be irrational, or addicted to a rule-of-thumb, or simply blind to the evident financial consequences. If the probability p is small enough, say $p=0.0001$, perhaps one would be willing to assign that probability to one's twin acting so weirdly. One other ingredient is necessary: assume that if the incumbent ever responds to entry with soft then thereafter each entrant resets p to zero and keeps it there regardless of the incumbent's subsequent actions. This is merely an application of Bayes's Rule if one believes that an incumbent committed to tough can never play soft.

The entrants will employ their observations of the incumbent's behavior to update their probability assessments that the incumbent is committed to tough. We use p_k to indicate this probability assessment when there are k entrants remaining with opportunities to enter. Initially $p_n=p$ and thereafter p_k is a state variable that effectively summarizes the consequences of past history for divining the future. We call p_k the probability that the incumbent is 'strong' (i.e. committed to tough) and then $1-p_k$ is the probability that the incumbent is 'weak' (i.e. an ordinary mortal) when k encounters remain.

Before proceeding we caution the reader that we allow the weak incumbent to randomize his actions between tough and soft. This is done for simplicity in this exposition. In practice no sensible executive flips a coin to choose his action; rather, his choice is decided by recourse to further information, of which there is always plenty (at the very least the choice can depend on his bank account, the contents of the morning paper, etc.). There would be no role here for randomization if we used a model with a finer representation of the incumbent's private information, say allowing a continuum of types for the incumbent instead of just two. In any case the actor need not actually randomize. It is only required that he is indifferent as to which of the 'randomized' actions he takes, and the opponent assesses probabilities for the actions that conform to the randomization.

The use of Bayes's Rule to update the probability assessment is straightforward so long as no events are observed that were assigned zero probability. The rule is that (i) $p_{k-1}=p_k$ if nothing was observed (no entry occurred), (ii) $p_{k-1}=0$ if the incumbent played soft after an earlier entry, and (iii) if the incumbent played tough then $p_{k-1}=p_k/q_k$, where q_k is the marginal probability that an incumbent of either type would have played tough. If x_k is the probability that a weak incumbent would have played tough against the k-th from last entrant, then $q_k=1\cdot p_k+x_k\cdot[1-p_k]$.

We claim that the following are sequentially rational equilibrium strategies:

1. The k-th from the last entrant stays out if $p_k>0.5^k$, enters if $p_k<0.5^k$, and flips a coin to decide if $p_k=0.5^k$.
2. The strong incumbent is always tough on entrants, by assumption. The weak incumbent is tough if $p_k>0.5^{k-1}$ and otherwise he randomizes so that if he were to be tough then the next entrant's probability assessment would be $p_{k-1}=0.5^{k-1}$.

We first trace the ramifications of these strategies. Table 8.2 gives a few values of the critical probability above which the current entrant is deterred from entering. Suppose that the number of entrants is $n=10$ and that initially the probability of a strong incumbent is $p_{10}=0.001$. A weak incumbent will surely be tough on each of the first three entrants if they dare to enter, since $p_k=0.001>0.5^{k-1}$ for $k=10,9,8$. Anticipating this they stay out so the probability that the incumbent is strong remains at 0.001. Indeed, this is true for the fourth entrant as well since he anticipates a probability greater than 0.5 (as explained later) that the incumbent will respond with tough. The fifth entrant enters but he may be met with a tough response; if so then the sixth is indifferent whether he enters (his expected profit is zero, since he sees a 50–50 chance that he will get a tough response). This pattern continues until some entrant enters and is met with a soft response; thereafter, the remaining entrants enter in turn. An interesting feature is that if there were, say, 100 entrants then again it would be the sixth from the last, the ninety-fifth, who would dare enter first.

Now we verify that these strategies are optimal for each firm. An entrant must foresee a probability q_k of a tough response that is less than one-half

Table 8.2 Critical probabilities in the repeated Chain Store game

k	1	2	3	4	5	6	7
0.5^k	0.5	0.25	0.125	0.0625	0.03125	0.015625	0.0078125

to want to enter. Now q_k is less than or greater than one-half according to whether p_k is less or greater than 0.5^k; hence, the k-th from last entrant prefers to enter precisely when $p_k<0.5^k$, as indicated in the equilibrium strategy. For the weak incumbent the choice is whether to forgo \$1 by being tough on the current entrant in exchange for the chance of deterring subsequent entrants. If $p_k>0.5^{k-1}$, then playing tough will surely deter the next entrant, since then $p_{k-1}>0.5^{k-1}$, and this is worth a gain of \$3 − \$1 = \$2. If $p_k \leqslant 0.5^{k-1}$, then there is a 50–50 chance of deterring the next entrant, since after the incumbent plays tough the next entrant will set $p_{k-1}=0.5^{k-1}$ and thereby be led to flip a coin to decide entry. This is worth an expected gain of \$1, and therefore the weak incumbent is indifferent. (There are no subsequent gains to deterrence because the weak incumbent anticipates that thereafter he will be indifferent about responding aggressively.) Thus, the incumbent's strategy is also optimal.

This equilibrium is robust to various amendments in the formulation. If the incumbent discounts his profits from successive engagements by a factor exceeding one-half then the equilibrium is unchanged except that the entrants' randomizations when $p_k=0.5^k$ are altered; if the discount factor is less than one-third, however, the weak incumbent immediately resorts to a soft response. The equilibrium is unchanged also if it is always the same firm that is the potential entrant; in this case the results indicate that the entrant defers entry until near the end of the life of the market. A slight alteration of the equilibrium is required if the incumbent must make his choice before he knows the entrant's decision, assuming as before that playing tough (e.g. cutting price) costs \$1. We discuss in Section 3.3 what happens when the incumbent is uncertain about the entrant's payoffs.

The overriding conclusion from this example is that predatory behavior can be a sane and rational strategy if there is some opportunity for the incumbent to sustain a reputation for aggressive behavior. Typically it is incomplete information, some fuzziness in the entrants' perceptions of the incumbent, that provides this opportunity. The probability assigned to the prospect that the incumbent enjoys or is committed to aggressive behavior can be arbitrarily small provided there are many encounters anticipated, so that the incumbent can fully realize the benefits of a reputation for toughness. That tiny probability suffices because it is the lever that enables the weak incumbent to sutain the entrants' beliefs that he might be strong by imitating the behavior of a strong incumbent.

3 EXIT AND ATTRITION

We now examine more closely a battle for survival between two firms locked in a competition for market share within a single industry, with the possibility that one could be driven out of the market. The aim is to elaborate some of the dynamic features of the competitive process.

The main idea explored is that competition is much like bargaining. Words are cheap in bargaining; what counts is one's willingness to forgo an agreement rather than accept unfavorable terms. Price wars and battles for market share have this feature. What matters is one's ability or willingness to sustain extra costs or lower prices, and the prize goes to the firm that can sustain the struggle longer. Low prices and other costly maneuvers are the language of the negotiation over who wins. They are a meaningful language because the strong – the firm with the better product, the lower costs, or the greater resources – can sustain them longer than can the weak. Often they are the only possible language; few other signals are credible. Tenacity, or the resource advantage that makes it possible, is the ultimate determinant of the outcome. This is not to say that business competition is necessarily or entirely Darwinian, since other modes of encounter are possible, such as product differentiation. Also, more or less collusive behavior is possible, as we study later. But when competition is overtly aggressive it is rare that the weaker firm has a chance to win.

3.1 Attrition and Auctions

To introduce the basic ideas, we start with the simplest war of attrition in which the combatants incur costs (or opportunity costs) until one gives up and the other wins a prize. Here, the two parties are duopolists in a market, giving up means exiting the market, and winning means attaining a monopoly position in the market. The value of the prize is standardized so that it is \$1 for each firm. The feasible choices for the firms at each instant are simply either to fight or to exit; once a firm exits the other receives the prize and the exiting firm gets nothing. As long as they are both fighting each firm incurs a cost that we designate as c_1 for firm **1** and c_2 for firm **2**. These costs are measured in dollars per unit time, so the total cost incurred by firm i if the fighting continues for a time t is $c_i \cdot t$. Neither these costs nor the value of the prize is discounted in this simple formulation.

The key assumption is that the firms' costs are privately known. One can easily see that there is no reason to fight if the costs are common knowledge: the one with the higher cost exits immediately. Assume that each firm assesses a probability distribution for the other firm's costs that has a cumulative distribution function F and a positive density f over an interval of possible costs that are positive. Assume that the firms' costs are independent and that this distribution function is common knowledge.

As the fighting continues each firm learns only that the other firm has not exited, so the time that has elapsed fully summarizes the history of the game so far. A firm's strategy prescribes at each instant whether to continue fighting or not, which can be conveniently summarized by the time at which to exit if the other has not capitulated previously. Since the firms are symmetric, it suffices to consider a symmetric equilibrium. Thus, an equilibrium is specified by a function T that indicates that if one's cost is c then exit at time $T(c)$. One can show that T must be non-increasing, and here we assume that it decreases smoothly. Conversely, use $C(t)$ to denote the cost of a firm that chooses to exit at time t. For example, one firm initially assesses the probability $F(C(t))$ that the other firm will exit after time t, since this is the probability that the other firm has costs low enough to choose an exit time exceeding t.

If firm i expects the other to use the strategy T, and i were to pick the stopping time t, then it would assign probability $1-F(C(t))$ to winning the prize at some time t' before t, and incurring the cost $c_i \cdot t'$, and otherwise that it will exit at t having incurred the cost $c_i \cdot t$. To pick its optimal stopping time it can reason that for each small interval Δ of time that it continues fighting it incurs the cost $c_i \cdot \Delta$ in exchange for the probability that the other firm will exit in that interval. Conditional on the other firm lasting until t, this probability is approximately $-\Delta \cdot f(C(t))C'(t)/F(C(t))$. Thus, it continues until that time t at which $c_i = -f(C(t))C'(t)/F(C(t))$ and then exits. An equilibrium requires, of course, that this value of t is precisely $T(c_i)$ so that the other firm's expectation about its strategy is correct. Using this requirement the condition for an optimal stopping time can be written as

$$T'(c) = -\frac{f(c)}{cF(c)}.$$

This condition defines a differential equation that characterizes the equilibrium strategy T. The appropriate boundary condition is that $T(c^*)=0$ if $F(c^*)=1$, i.e. c^* is the maximum possible cost (possibly infinite) that a firm might have: this is because a firm with the highest possible cost anticipates that it will surely lose if it fights and so it exits immediately. Combining these results, the equilibrium strategy is:

$$T(c) = \int_c^{c^*} \frac{f(x)}{xF(x)} dx.$$

That is, each firm stops at the time that is computed as the area under the portion of the curve $f(x)/xF(x)$ that lies to the right of its cost parameter.

Example 3.1 Suppose that each firm's cost is uniformly distributed between zero and one. Then $T(c)=(1/c)-1$. The stopping times for a few values of the cost parameter are tabulated in Table 8.3. The times are measured in whatever units of time are used to measure the cost, such as dollars per year. Referring to the table, a firm with a cost of \$0.20 per unit

Table 8.3 Stopping times in the war of attrition uniformly distributed costs

c	0	0.2	0.4	0.6	0.8	1.0
$T(c)$	∞	4.00	1.50	0.67	0.25	0
Exp. cost (c)	\$0.00	\$0.32	\$0.37	\$0.31	\$0.18	\$0
Exp. profit (c)	\$1.00	\$0.48	\$0.23	\$0.09	\$0.02	\$0

time plans to exit when four units of time have elapsed, if the other firm has not exited previously. Initially it assesses a probability of 0.8 that it will win the prize, since that is the probability that the other firm's cost is higher, and overall its expected profit is \$0.48.

These stopping times may seem surprisingly large: could it be optimal to sustain losses for so long a duration before calling it quits? The firm with a cost of \$0.20 loses \$0.80 in its quest for the \$1 prize before calling it quits. But such is life: hope springs eternal. Note too that on average a large proportion of the value of the prize is expended by the two firms in their competition to capture it. This proportion is roughly 45 per cent in this example, averaging over the possible types of both firms. This feature, that competition dissipates profits, is the bane of entrepreneurs, but customers benefit, which is a reason it is encouraged socially.

An interesting way of thinking about games of this sort is that a kind of auction is played. Each firm's bid is the maximal time it is willing to endure fighting. The prize is awarded to the highest bidder at the second highest bid; that is, the winning bidder needs to endure fighting only as long as its opponent does. The rub is that the losing bidder also pays the amount of its bid.

3.1.1 Brinkmanship

A war of attrition can also be used to describe competition among firms in various other contexts. An example is the provision of a common good among the firms. Suppose that each firm in an industry obtains a benefit worth $V=\$1$ if some one firm develops a (non-patentable) innovation that becomes available to all firms. In this case one anticipates that each firm plays a waiting game, hoping that another firm will incur the cost of the development. However, if each firm is impatient then a firm's waiting time is limited and at some point it is willing to proceed with the development if no other firm has taken the initiative. We develop briefly one model of this competitive process.

In the interest of simplicity, assume that all firms have the same impatience, represented by an interest rate r. By choosing the units of time appropriately this interest rate can be chosen to be one: $r=1$. The firms are symmetric except that each firm is characterized by its privately known cost c of developing the innovation. Assume that each firm assesses a probability distribution function $F(c)$ that any other firm's cost is less than c, and that the firms' costs are independently distributed. In this case the minimum of the $n-1$ other firms' costs has a probability distribution with the distribution function $1-[1-F(c)]^{n-1}$. All of these features are common knowledge among the firms.

When there are n firms each firm's strategy can be represented by a function T_n indicating that it will stop waiting and supply the innovation at time $T_n(c)$ if its cost is c and no other firm has previously volunteered. One expects that $T_n(0)=0$ and that the function T_n is increasing. If all other firms are using such a strategy, then a firm with the cost c that plans to stop waiting at time t has an expected present value that is the sum of its gains from providing the innovation and from obtaining it free:

$$[1-c]e^{-t}[1-F(C_n(t))]^{n-1}+\int_0^{C_n(t)} e^{-T_n(x)}d\{1-[1-F(x)]^{n-1}\},$$

where $C_n(t)$ is the cost that would lead another firm to stop waiting at t. An equilibrium requires that this expected present value is maximized by choosing $t=T_n(c)$. If the distribution function F has a density function f, then this criterion leads to the following differential equation that characterizes the optimal waiting time strategy:

$$T_n'(c)=[n-1]\frac{c}{1-c}\frac{f(c)}{1-F(c)}.$$

This characterization implies immediately that the n-firm case is related to the two-firm case by the simple relationship that $T_n(c)=[n-1]\cdot T_2(c)$. For example, if a firm has eight competitors then it waits eight times as long as it does with a single competitor. However, as one might expect it can be shown that the expected time until the innovation is completed decreases as the number of firms increases. The least-cost firm is always the one that provides the innovation; consequently, a firm's expected present value is an *increasing* function of its cost of supply.

Example 3.2 Suppose that each firm's cost of development is distributed uniformly between \$0 and \$1. Then the equilibrium waiting time for a firm with the cost c is

$$T_n(c)=[n-1]\left\{c\frac{1}{1-c}-\log\left(\frac{1}{1-c}\right)\right\}.$$

One can then calculate that the expected time until the firm with the lowest cost undertakes the development is $1/n$. The waiting times for the case of two firms are tabulated in Figure 8.1 and Table 8.4. The rather long waiting times when the cost is high reflect the free-rider phenomenon: a high-cost firm waits in hopes that another will take the initiative first.

3.2 Attrition and Selection

The previous examples can be enriched by adding a few ingredients from a realistic situation. Suppose that two firms are in a market that might possibly sustain only one of them with positive profits. Indicate the firms by $i=\mathbf{1}$ and $\mathbf{2}$ and to be specific suppose that at each time t firm i can earn a *gross* profit rate of $M_i(t)$ as a monopolist or $D_i(t)$ as a duopolist. Of course, a firm's duopoly profit is less than its monopoly profit. It may be that these profits vary with time, increasing if the market is expanding or if the firm's costs reflect learning curve effects, or decreasing in the case of a declining industry (for this analysis both firms' profits must move together, up or down). In addition each firm incurs a fixed cost of staying in the market, so many dollars per year: let F_i be firm i's fixed cost. Adopting the convention that a firm earns zero if it drops out of the market, interpret the fixed cost as

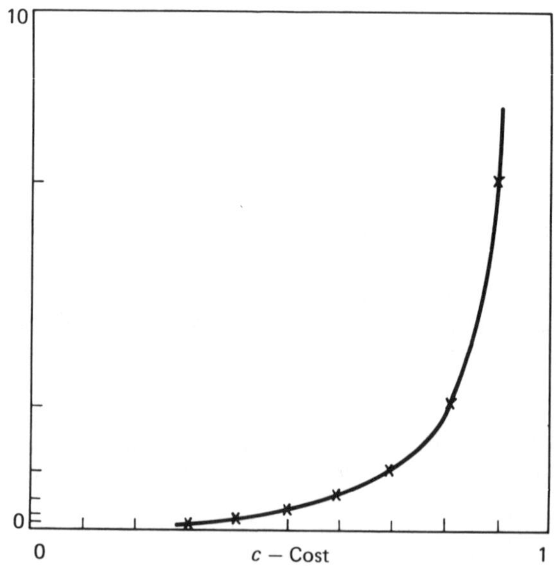

Figure 8.1

Table 8.4 Equilibrium waiting times ($F(c)=c/V$, $r=1$, and $n=2$)

c/V	$T_n(c)\cdot r/[n-1]$
0	0
0.1	0.006
0.2	0.027
0.3	0.072
0.4	0.156
0.5	0.307
0.6	0.584
0.7	1.129
0.8	2.391
0.9	6.697
1.0	∞

cash outlays for overhead, etc., *plus* an opportunity cost reflecting forgone opportunities to engage in other markets.

Thus, if firm **1** drops out after a duration T then its net profit is the present value of the stream $D_1(t)-F_1$ for $0\leqslant t\leqslant T$, whereas **2** gets the stream $D_2(t)-F_2$ over this period *plus* its subsequent monopoly profit $M_2(t)-F_2$ for each time $t>T$. If r is the continuous-time interest rate then **2**'s present value is given by the formula:

$$\int_0^T [D_2(t)-F_2]e^{-rt}dt+\int_T^\infty [M_2(t)-F_2]e^{-rt}dt,$$

of which it obtains only the first term if it drops out at time T. The key feature assumed is that each firm's fixed cost is privately known, whereas all the other data of the situation are common knowledge. This is fairly realistic, since a firm's opportunity cost is often not observable, in contrast to nominal accounting profits. The other firm's probability assessment of firm i's fixed cost can be represented by a distribution function G_i having a density function g_i on an interval of positive fixed costs. For technical reasons, assume this interval is wide enough to allow the possibility that i might be viable as a duopolist were the other firm never to drop out, and possibly not viable as a monopolist. The highest fixed cost that allows a monopoly profit is

$$F_i^*=r\int_0^\infty M_i(t)e^{-rt}dt.$$

A repetition of the reasoning used in the previous example suffices to characterize the firms' equilibrium strategies. At time t firm i's rate of net profit from continuing as a duopoly is $D_i(t) - F_i$, plus the chance that it will win the subsequent monopoly stream with the value

$$V_i(t) = \int_t^{\infty} [M_i(s) - F_i] e^{-rs} ds.$$

This chance has the probability that one computes using Bayes's Rule, to incorporate the information that the other firm has already lasted a duration t, and one's hypothesis about the other's stopping rule. Suppose the other's stopping rule is to stop at time T if its fixed cost is $C_j(T)$, where j indicates the other firm. Then the probability density of its stopping shortly after t (conditional on having lasted to t) is

$$P_j(t) = [1 - G_j(C_j(t))]' / G_j(C_j(t)).$$

Combining these components, firm i wants to stop as soon as its net profit rate declines to zero: namely, when t satisfies

$$D_i(t) - F_i + P_j(t) V_i(t) = 0.$$

An equilibrium requires that this decision to stop occurs at the time t for which $F_i = C_i(t)$ so that the other firm's hypothesis about i's strategy is correct. This condition and a similar one for the other firm specify two different equations that characterize the two firms' strategies. There is also a boundary condition: a firm wants to drop out immediately if its cost exceeds F_i^*, which is the maximal viable fixed cost even with a monopoly.

The form of the equilibrium strategies is represented schematically in Figure 8.2 for the case that the profitability of a presence in the market is increasing over time and the same for both firms.

Similarly, Figure 8.3 depicts the case that profitability is declining over time.

Example 3.3 To illustrate, consider an example in which the firms are symmetric and profits do not depend on time. If the demand curve is linear, say $p = A - Bq$ is the price in excess of the firms' marginal cost when a quantity q is offered, then in a Cournot model the monopoly gross profit is $M = A^2/4B$ (so $F^* = A^2/4B$) and the duopoly gross profit is $D = A^2/9B$. Assume that the fixed costs have a uniform distribution between zero and some upper limit. Computing the symmetric equilibrium stopping-time strategy for the case that the interest rate is $r = 1$ and the choke price is $A = 1$ with $B = 1$ yields the results shown in Table 8.5. Note that the present value is calculated at a time just after zero, so that an opponent who has not immediately dropped out is known to have a standardized fixed cost that is less than 0.25; i.e. $G(F) = F/0.25$.

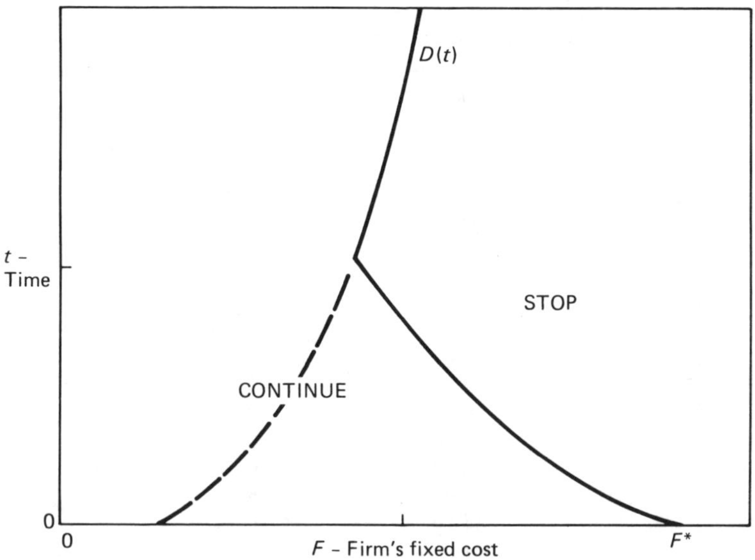

Figure 8.2 Equilibrium strategies: Case I, Increasing profitability

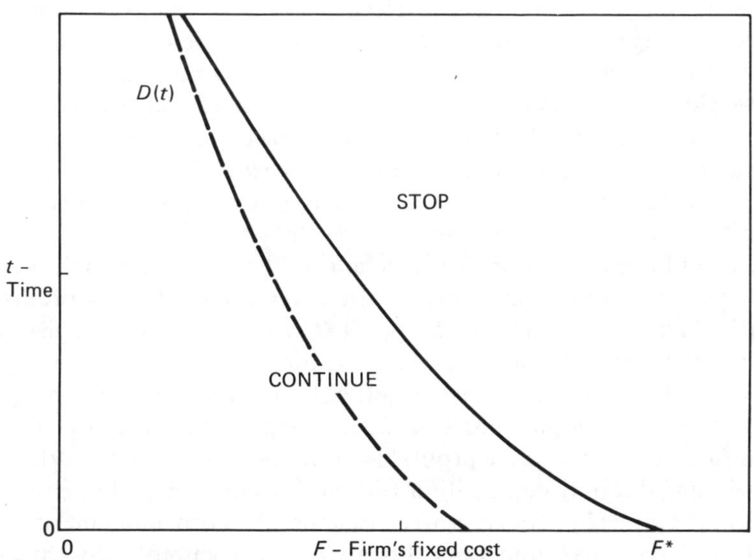

Figure 8.3 Equilibrium strategies: Case II, Decreasing profitability

Table 8.5 Stopping times in the war of attrition ($p=1-q$, $G(F)=F/0.25$, and $r=1$)

Fixed cost $F\cdot B/A^2$	*Stop time* $T\cdot r$	*Present value* $PV\cdot rB/A^2$
.111	∞	.1126
.12	1.024	.0858
.13	.7044	.0661
.14	.5057	.0508
.15	.3659	.0387
.16	.2631	.0290
.17	.1863	.0212
.18	.1287	.0151
.19	.0858	.0103
.20	.0543	.0067
.21	.0318	.0040
.22	.0164	.0021
.23	.0067	.0009
.24	.0016	.0002
.25	0	0

For example, if $A=\$1000$ per unit, the slope is $B=1$, the interest rate is $r=0.1$ per year, and the fixed cost is $F=\$150{,}000$ per year, then $F\cdot B/A^2=0.15$ and according to Table 8.5, $T\cdot r=0.366$, so the indicated stopping time is $T=3.66$ years, yielding an expected present value of \$387,000. Comparing this to the monopoly present value of \$1,000,000 in this case, one sees that again a considerable portion of the prize is dissipated in the competitive process. If the fixed cost were \$200,000 per year the stopping time would be a fraction 0.543 of a year, and the expected present value would be only \$67,000. Note that firms with fixed costs less than \$111,111 per year stay forever and those with fixed costs exceeding \$250,000 per year exit immediately; thus there is a fairly narrow window of fixed costs that generate battles with positive but finite resolutions.

The equilibrium shown in the table allows that the firms might sustain battle forever as a duopoly. This feature is reinforced if gross profits are increasing over time. If the duopoly profit $D(t)$ increases fast enough so that the curve $C(t)$ enters the area in which the present value of continuing net profits as a duopoly are at least zero (i.e. fixed costs are small enough in relation to future duopoly gross profits), then after the time at which it is certain that both can survive profitably as duopolists the firms settle down to continuing duopoly competition with no further chance that either will exit. (In the graph (Fig. 8.4) this area lies under the horizontal line at height 0.1111, and the curve intersects this area only asymptotically, but in a general case this intersection might occur at some finite time.)

The numerical results are fairly sensitive to the assumption that there is a

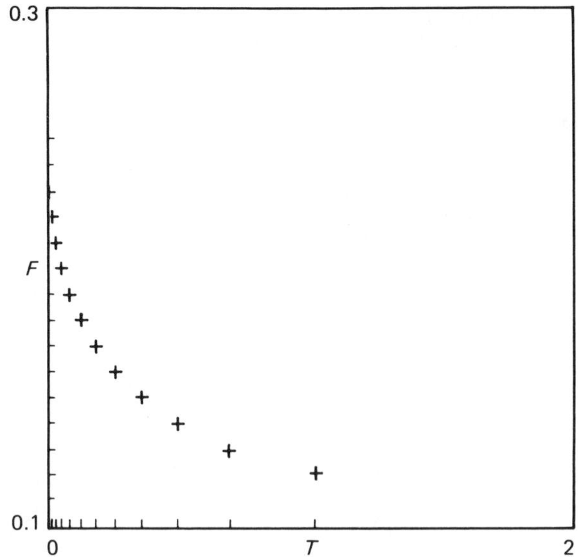

T = Stopping time
F = Fixed cost

Figure 8.4

substantial chance that a competitor has fixed costs low enough to sustain a duopoly forever. Table 8.6 shows the strategies that result when $A = B = r = 1$ and it is known that a firm incurs a cash outflow of 0.10 in addition to a privately known opportunity cost that is uniformly distributed between zero and 0.15 (the technical assumption that represents this feature is that $G(F) = [F - 0.1]/0.15$). Note that in the graph (Fig. 8.5) the scale of the horizontal axis has been compressed compared to the previous graph.

For example, suppose as before that $A = \$1000$ per unit, $B = 1$, and the interest rate is $r = 0.1$. A firm with the fixed cost $F = \$150{,}000$ per year (i.e. a cash outlay of $100,000 plus an opportunity cost of $50,000) now waits $0.7328/0.1 = 7.328$ years before exiting. The expected present value is increased to $959,000. If the opportunity cost were doubled to $100,000 then it would exit after one year; the expected present value is $249,000. The firm's greater patience stems from the greater perceived chance that the opponent will drop out first, given that it has to meet the continuing cash outlay for overhead of $100,000 per year.

Table 8.6 Stopping times in the war of attrition ($p=1-q$, $G(F)=[F–0.1]/0.15$, and $r=1$)

Fixed cost $F \cdot B/A^2$	*Stop time* $T \cdot r$	*Present value* $PV \cdot rB/A^2$
.111	∞	.2242
.12	2.0992	.1806
.13	1.4378	.1470
.14	1.0239	.1194
.15	.7328	.0959
.16	.5198	.0761
.17	.3621	.0594
.18	.2457	.0455
.19	.1607	.0342
.20	.0997	.0249
.21	.0572	.0175
.22	.0290	.0115
.23	.0116	.0068
.24	.0026	.0030
.25	0	0

3.3 Entry and Exit

We turn now to a slightly more realistic depiction of the firms' costs and include as well the decision of the second firm to enter the market and engage in combat. For this purpose we study in more detail the Chain Store game introduced in Section 2. Before we allowed that the incumbent might be either weak or strong, and now we allow also that the entrant might be weak or strong. Assume that there is only a single entrant with repeated opportunities to enter.

Initially the entrant assigns probability p that the incumbent is strong, and the incumbent assigns probability q that the entrant is strong. To represent the idea that the strong incumbent is one with low costs, so that it prefers to price low (i.e. play tough) in response to entry, we use the payoffs in Table 8.7 for each of the possible outcomes in each period. Note that compared to the payoffs used in Section 2 we have subtracted 1 from the incumbent's payoffs and divided the entrant's by 2; since these modifications affect only the origin and scale of the payoffs they have no effect on the equilibria of the game.

Assume that there are n periods in which the situation is repeated and that each firm seeks to maximize the sum of its expected profits (the results are hardly changed if the firms discount future profits moderately).

Note that the strong entrant prefers to enter even if the incumbent plays tough. Following the convention adopted in Section 2, assume that an

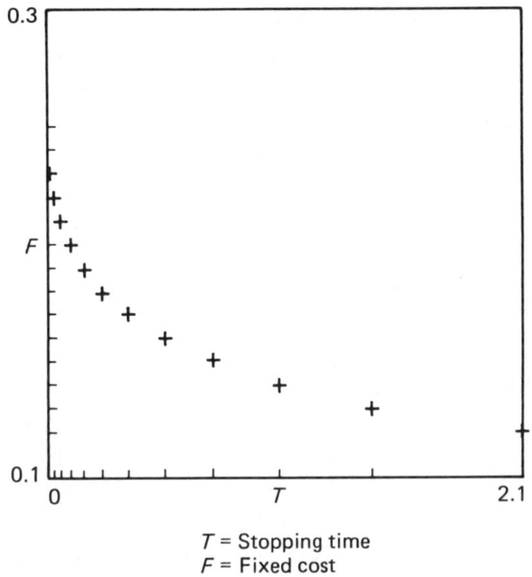

Figure 8.5

incumbent who plays soft or an entrant who fails to enter is thereafter branded as weak, namely his opponent resets $p=0$ or $q=0$ as the case may be, and it remains there regardless of the subsequent actions chosen.

With this convention we study an equilibrium in which the strong entrant always enters and the strong incumbent is always tough. The strategy for the weak entrant therefore specifies whether and when he will enter and for how long he is prepared to fight before exiting if the incumbent has not reverted to soft play by then. Actually, it is easy to see that a weak entrant will either enter immediately or wait until near the end of the game. Waiting, or entering and then exiting, identifies him as weak, so thereafter the game is exactly as described in Section 2 where it was assumed that the entrant was known to be weak. Recall that he may re-enter near the end of the market when the chance increases that a weak incumbent will respond softly.

Table 8.7 Payoffs in the repeated Chain Store game with two-sided uncertainty

	Incumbent's payoffs		*Entrant's payoffs*	
	Weak	*Strong*	*Weak*	*Strong*
No entry	\$2	\$2	\$0	\$0
Enter, soft	0	−1	0.5	1
Enter, tough	−1	0	−0.5	0.5

The strategy for the weak incumbent specifies for how long he is prepared to play tough against an entrant who has entered. Once he capitulates by playing soft he is identified as weak and thereafter the entrant, whether strong or weak, stays in the market and the incumbent's best response is to respond softly, as we saw in the initial analysis of the Chain Store game when the incumbent was known by the entrant to be weak.

In sum, then, the strong entrant and the strong incumbent never stop; the weak ones pick stopping times for how long they are prepared to fight; and lastly, the weak entrant may choose to enter initially or to enter near the end.

Suppose now that the entrant has entered. As the battle continues the firms' probability assessments about each other evolve according to Bayes's Rule. To whatever extent a weak entrant would be likely to have exited, the incumbent assesses an increasingly higher probability that he is facing a strong one; similarly, to whatever extent a weak incumbent would have reverted to a soft response the entrant assesses an increasingly higher probability that he faces a strong one. Thus, if (p_k, q_k) indicates their probability assessments when k encounters remain, then as the fighting continues and k decreases the pair (p_k, q_k) traces a locus of increasing values. If both are strong then eventually $(p_0, q_0) = (1,1)$ when no periods remain (actually before that as it turns out). If one or both are weak, then eventually one gives in: if it is, say, the incumbent who is weak and acquiesces then there is a jump to $(p_k, q_k) = (0, q_k)$ and thereafter the incumbent plays soft in response to the continuing entry; whereas if it is the entrant who is weak and exits then there is a jump to $(p_k, q_k) = (p_k, 0)$ and thereafter the entrant stays out (expecting tough play) until near the end when the entrant may again test the incumbent's response.

As we saw in Section 3, if the firms' possible types are a continuum then each selects a stopping time depending on his type. Here, however, each firm has only two possible types so an equilibrium involves each of the weak types selecting a randomly determined stopping time. Computing these equilibrium strategies is complicated so we will not do it here. The key idea is simple enough to deserve mention. Since the stopping time is random, it must be that the firm is indifferent as to the outcome of the randomization; e.g. whether to stop now or a little later. Thus, each firm's randomization is determined so as to make the other firm indifferent about whether to stop now or a little later, and this is true at all times.

When time is continuous it is considerably easier to compute the firms' strategies; partly this is because with continuous time the weak entrant never re-enters until the last instant. We outline the construction briefly. Assume that the game lasts for a duration T and let the pair (p_t, q_t) be the entrant's and the incumbent's assessed probabilities that the other is strong when a duration t remains. Our aim is to find the locus this pair traces after the entrant enters as t declines from T to 0, and to derive the equilibrium strategies in the form of random stopping times. Suppose that when a duration t remains the entrant assesses a conditional probability $r_t h$ that the weak incumbent will capitulate in the next small interval of time of length h; similarly, the incumbent assesses a conditional probability $s_t h$ that the weak entrant will exit, given that both have been hanging tough so far. Recall that the incumbent gets zero thereafter once he plays soft, whereas he gets $2t$ if the entrant exits with t remaining. Since the weak incumbent is indifferent between continuing tough play or not, it must be that his cost of continuing for the interval h equals his expected profit from the chance that the weak entrant will exit: $h = 2ts_t h(1-q_t)$. Similarly, for the weak entrant we get: $0.5h = 0.5tr_t h(1-p_t)$. Thus, we know that $r_t = 1/t(1-p_t)$ and $s_t = 0.5/t(1-q_t)$, which tells us what the probability distribution of stopping times must be. It remains to describe the locus of probability assessments. If the incumbent continues tough during the interval h then the entrant's posterior probability that he is strong is given by Bayes's Rule: $p_{t-h} = p_t/[1-r_t h(1-p_t)]$; and, similarly, one gets $q_{t-h} = q_t/[1-s_t h(1-q_t)]$. Interpreting h as infinitesimally small, these two equations imply a differential equation that has the unique solution $q_t = \sqrt{p_t}$ satisfying the restriction that $(p_0, q_0) = (1,1)$; this restriction is necessary since if the firms hang tough until the end then surely they are both strong. Thus, we know the locus along which the probability assessments evolve. Further, in order to satisfy the results of the Bayes's Rule calculations above, it must be that these assessments evolve according to the formulas: $p_t = a/t$ and $q_t = \sqrt{a/t}$, where $a = p_T T = q_T^2 T$ is a constant determined from the initial probability assessments from which the process starts. For example, if initially $q < \sqrt{p}$ then the weak entrant randomizes as to whether he will enter, and if he does enter then the battle begins with the initial assessment $(p_T, q_T) = (p, \sqrt{p})$; similarly, if $p < q^2$ then the entrant enters and the weak incumbent randomizes whether to do battle, and if it does respond initially with tough then the process starts from (q^2, q). Note that it becomes certain that the firms are both strong after a time has passed that is less than the full duration T; that is, $(p_t, q_t) = (1,1)$ at $t = a$. At any time before this $(t > a)$ the weak incumbent and the weak entrant have conditional probabilities of stopping (per unit time) of $r_t = 1/(t-a)$ and $s_t = 0.5/(t-\sqrt{at})$, respectively.

These strategies are depicted schematically in Figure 8.6. Recall that if initially (p,q) is below the curve and the entrant enters then there is a jump upwards to the curve, and if it is above the curve and the incumbent plays tough then there is a jump right to the curve; thereafter, the probability assessments move along the curve until one capitulates, producing a jump to the lower boundary if the entrant exits and to the left boundary if the incumbent acquiesces.

This example illustrates several important aspects of such battles for entry. First, each firm's motive is to sustain the fight long enough to induce a relatively weaker opponent to capitulate, but as time passes the evidence

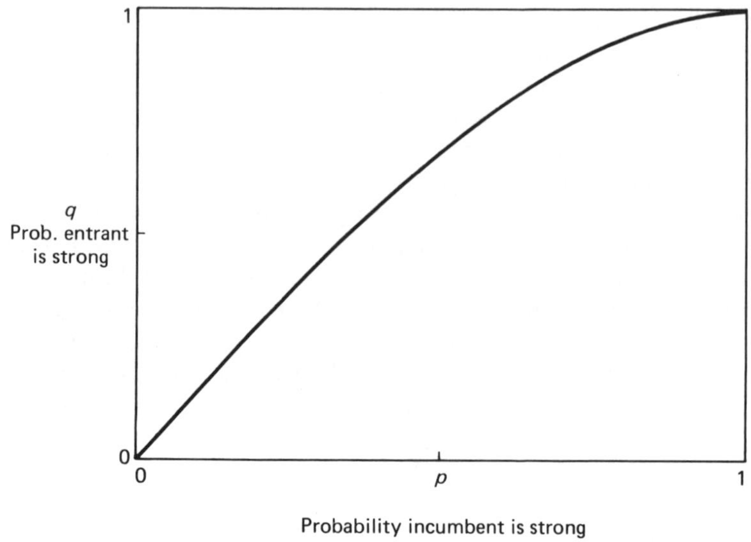

Figure 8.6 Equilibrium locus of probability assessments

accumulates that the other firm is likely to be relatively stronger, the incentive for a weak firm to give up the fight increases until eventually he bows out. Second, the crucial ingredient that initiates the battle is mutual uncertainty about the firms' relative strength; it is this that enables each firm to imitate the behavior of a stronger type so as to intimidate the opposing firm. Third, ordinarily an appreciable portion of the potential profits are dissipated in the battle for the prize.

4 LIMIT PRICING

The discussion of predatory behavior focused on the incumbent's response to entry, aimed at deterring subsequent entrants. Another possibility, however, is that the incumbent can scare off a potential entrant by immediate actions in the market. The primary source of entry is the attraction of perceived profits. If the incumbent can signal that profit margins would be too low to enable an entrant to recoup sunk costs incurred in entering, then perhaps entry can be deterred. Since prices are usually observed by an entrant, and costs are not (if the incumbent is wise), prices are the incumbent's primary instrument to influence a potential entrant's perceptions about the profitability of entry. Setting prices below the monopoly price to discourage entry is commonly called limit pricing. Our aim in this section is to explore how limit pricing works.

A thorough analysis of limit pricing strategies requires a good model of the post-entry competition between the incumbent and the entrant. Here, however, we summarize matters by simply assuming that the firms anticipate how their profits will depend on their pricing strategies, and in turn how their pricing strategies will depend on their costs. This suffices to examine the use of limit pricing to influence the entrant's perceptions about the incumbent's costs, and thereby the profits he anticipates if he enters.

The basic structure of the situation is taken to be the following. There is an incumbent that initially holds a monopoly on its market, and a single potential entrant known to the monopolist. Each firm has some private information about its unit cost of production. In general there are recurrent episodes in which the incumbent first makes a choice about its price or quantity, and then the entrant, having observed this choice more or less precisely, decides whether to enter the market or to defer until the next episode (if any). If he enters then the two firms constitute a duopoly thereafter, or they play out a battle as in Section 3. The incumbent's payoff is the present value of his immediate profit depending on his choice and the subsequent profit depending on the entrant's choice as to whether they continue as a monopoly or a duopoly. In the latter case the entrant's payoff is the present value of his duopoly profit less a sunk cost of entry (discounted by one period to account for the delay in entry), whereas it is zero until he opts for entry. We assume, of course, that the incumbent's profits are always higher in a monopoly, and that the entrant's profits are lower the lower is the incumbent's unit cost.

4.1 Information, Signalling, and Noise

The basic idea of limit pricing can be stated simply as the observation that if the incumbent perceives that the chance of entry increases with his price then he wants to shave his price somewhat below the optimal monopoly price in order to deter entry. This idea is subtle, however, since it is clear that if the entrant knows the incumbent's cost then no observation of the incumbent's action can influence his decision about entry: he enters or not based on his assessment of his profits in a duopoly. Thus, the chance of entry is fixed independently of the incumbent's choice and therefore no limit pricing is worthwhile. Thus, some uncertainty about the profit from entry in the mind of the entrant is essential to the existence of limit pricing.

A second observation is that there may be more entry with limit pricing, in the context we described, than there would be if both firms had perfect information. To see this, suppose that an entrant gets increasingly finer information about the incumbent's cost as he accumulates observations from successive episodes. An entrant that defers entry for a long time gains nearly perfect information and therefore enters or not in precisely the same circumstances (though much later) as it would if it had perfect information initially. On the other hand, an entrant that enters early is likely to make a mistake, so overall there is a greater likelihood of entry. In an extreme case there is only a single episode possible, but suppose that the entrant's observation enables him to infer what cost led the incumbent to make that choice: in this case the entrant enters under precisely the same circumstances as he would with perfect information initially. In sum, then, limit pricing does not necessarily restrict entry below that expected with perfect information.

Why, then, would the incumbent engage in limit pricing? The answer unveils a further subtlety in the basic idea with which we began. If the entrant anticipates that the incumbent will engage in limit pricing, then the incumbent is forced to do so, since otherwise a high price would induce a greater chance of entry. That is, the entrant will take the incumbent's price as a signal about his cost, and a high price signals a high cost and a high duopoly profit for the entrant. On the other hand, the entrant cannot afford to reject the hypothesis of limit pricing, since otherwise it can be used against him to induce him to stay out when in fact entry is profitable. Thus, limit pricing is intrinsic when there is a potential entrant lurking about. The mere potentiality of entry depresses the monopolist's price, and it may even increase the chance of entry above the perfect information case.

If the entrant's observations are noisy (he observes only some portion or some garbled version of the incumbent's decision), then he has an incentive to defer entry until he accumulates enough observations to reduce his risk of entering an unprofitable duopoly. This benefits the incumbent, of course, since he maintains his monopoly longer, but, as mentioned above, noisy observations increase the chance that the entrant will enter mistakenly and decrease both their profits.

After these initial remarks we turn to a worked-out example that illustrates limit pricing.

Example 4.1 Suppose that there is a single episode with two periods. The demand function for the market is assumed to be linear of the form $P = \$100 - \$1 \cdot Q + \varepsilon$, indicating that the expected price declines by one dollar for each unit of output offered by either firm. The noise term ε is uniformly distributed between -20 and $+20$. (One can equally well suppose that the demand function is $P = \$100 - \$1 \cdot Q$, and that ε is a noise term in the entrant's observation of the incumbent's average price. In a model of this sort the incumbent can choose either the price or the quantity.)

The unit cost of the incumbent can be either low (\$10) or high (\$30) and these are perceived by the entrant to be equally likely. The low-cost incumbent's optimal monopoly output is 45 units, yielding an expected profit of \$2025, and for the high-cost incumbent it is 35 units, yielding an expected profit of $1225. The entrant's cost can also be either low ($25) or high ($30) and the incumbent sees these as equally likely. To describe the post-entry profits we will assume for simplicity that the incumbent and the entrant immediately learn each other's costs and then select their supply quantities in the duopoly so that each picks a best response to the other's choice. After some calculation this yields the post-entry profits shown in Tables 8.8a and 8.8b.

Assume also that the entrant incurs a sunk cost of $500 to enter. From these data it is straightforward to see that with perfect information either type of entrant would enter against the high-cost incumbent but not the low-cost one. Also, with incomplete information and unable to make any observation, only the low-cost entrant would enter.

Now suppose that, as in the case of limit pricing, the incumbent chooses the quantity he will supply as a monopolist in the initial period, after which the entrant gets to observe the resulting price (which, due to the noise term, garbles the incumbent's choice) and then to decide whether to enter for the second period. The equilibrium in this case is the following:

— The low- and high-cost incumbents choose to supply 54 and 44 units, respectively. These choices correspond to expected prices of $46 and $56, respectively.
— The low- and high-cost entrants choose to enter only if the price exceeds $36 and $66, respectively.

Table 8.8a Post-entry profit for the incumbent

	Entrant	
Incumbent	*Low cost*	*High cost*
Low cost	$1225	$1344
High cost	469	544

Table 8.8b Post-entry profit for the entrant

	Entrant	
Incumbent	*Low cost*	*High cost*
Low cost	$400	$278
High cost	711	544

Notice that either type of incumbent increases his output by 9 units and lowers his expected price by $9 compared to the optimal monopoly choices.

In order to understand the factors that motivate this behavior we begin by examining the entrant's decision process. The entrant anticipates prices in the range from $26 to $66 from the low-cost incumbent, and in the range from $36 to $76 from the high-cost incumbent. Prices at the low end from $26 to $36 therefore identify the incumbent as one with low costs, and prices at the high end from $66 to $76 identify a high-cost incumbent. In the middle range from $36 to $66 it is equally likely that the price originated from a low-cost or a high-cost incumbent. Since the low-cost entrant is not willing to enter against the low-cost incumbent, but is willing if the odds are 50–50, he will enter if the price is in the mid-range or above. Similarly, the high-cost entrant is willing to enter only against the high-cost incumbent, and not willing if the odds are 50–50, so he will enter only if the price is in the high range above $66.

The low-cost incumbent seeks to maximize the sum of his expected profits from the first and second periods. In the first period his expected profit margin is $\$90-\$1\cdot Q$ per unit, so his marginal profit is $\$90-\$2\cdot Q$ per unit. As for the second period, he thinks there are equal chances that he faces a low-cost entrant who will enter if the first price exceeds $36, in which case the second period profit will be $1225 instead of the maximum monopoly profit of $2025 (i.c. $800 less), and that he faces a high-cost entrant who will enter if the price exceeds $66, in which case the second period profit will be $1344 instead of his hoped-for $2025 (i.e. $681 less). Realizing that the probability of a price realization in excess of $36 declines at the rate of 1/40 as Q increases (i.e. the probability density of the noise term is 1/40), the supply at which his combined marginal profit is driven to zero is the one satisfying the equation

$$90-2Q+\frac{1}{40}\{0.5\cdot 800+0.5\cdot 681\}=0.$$

This yields the solution $Q=54$ and an expected price of $46, exactly as the equilibrium specifies. A similar analysis justifies the high-cost incumbent's choice of the supply quantity $Q=44$ with an expected price of $56. It is important to note that in the above calculation it is the incumbent's anticipation that the entrant's price observation will influence his entry decision that motivates the choice of an expected price below the monopoly price. Otherwise the low-cost incumbent would just choose $Q=45$ units to solve the simple first period marginal profit condition: $90-2Q=0$.

The thrust of this example of limit pricing is to substantiate the intuitive appeal of the argument that limit pricing is intrinsic to situations with threatened entry. Even with noisy observations, the entrant must anticipate limit pricing, lest the incumbent deter profitable entry by misleading actions; and, in turn, the incumbent must price below the monopoly price, lest the entrant infer that entry is more profitable than in fact it is.

5 PRICE WARS

The previous sections studied competitive battles precipitated by entry or, as in wars of attrition, the pressure to cover fixed costs in order to survive profitably. In some cases, however, price wars are precipitated by one firm's misguided efforts to enlarge its market share – or by simple mistakes. In other cases, price wars are undertaken intentionally to police the terms of collusive agreements: deviant members are punished for their attempts to enlarge their share of the pie. In this section we examine some examples that illustrate how such episodes arise. The first example shows the role of mistakes in precipitating price wars.

Example 5.1 Consider a market shared by two firms that are alike in all respects. Demand is such that at a price p the quantity sold is $q=1-p$. We interpret this price as net of the firms' marginal cost, so the industry net revenue is $p[1-p]$. If the firms offer the same price they share the market equally, otherwise the firm with the lower price captures all of the demand. Each firm discounts its profits for all future periods using the discount factor $d<1$. Two special technological features affect this market. First, the firms select their prices alternately, and each firm is committed to its chosen price for two periods. Second, the only feasible prices are \$0, 0.1, 0.2, 0.3, etc. As we shall see these two features combine to enable the two firms to share the monopoly profit.

The optimal monopoly price is $p=\$0.5$ and at this price the profit shared by the two firms is \$0.25 in each period. This allows each firm a profit of \$0.125 and over an infinite horizon this profit stream has a present value of $\$0.125/[1-d]$. To be specific we will specify that $d=0.9$ so that this present value is \$1.25.

In order to show that the firms will maintain the monopoly price we must verify that if one adopts that price then the other's best response is to follow suit. Evidently, one firm can cut its price and gain in the short run, so the incentive to maintain price must lie in the expectation that one price cut will be followed by another. An equilibrium must specify, therefore, how each firm will respond to each possible price of the other firm. Only in this way can one trace the price war that ensues when one firm deviates, thereby establishing the incentive to maintain the monopoly price, as well as trace the process by which the monopoly price is initially attained or subsequently regained. In this simple example it is easy to calculate the equilibrium presented in Table 8.9.

Table 8.9 Equilibrium pricing strategies ($q = 1 - p$ and $d = 0.9$)

Competitor's current price	$0	$0.1	$0.2	$0.3	$0.4	$0.5
Firm's best response	0.5	0.5 or 0.1	0.1	0.1	0.1	0.5
Firm's present value	1.125	1.125	1.17	1.17	1.17	1.25

The calculation of each firm's present value shown in the table will be explained below. Note that in the table there are two best responses if the competitor's price is $0.1, namely, the firm can respond with either the same price or revert to the monopoly price. The equilibrium requires that this choice be 'randomized' (or at least that the competitor entertains a probability assessment as though the choice were randomized). The requisite probability is that the reversion to the monopoly price has probability 0.905. This probability is selected so that either firm is indifferent about reverting to the monopoly price when its competitor's current price is $0.1.

The verification that this strategy is optimal for each firm if the other is using it is displayed in Table 8.10, which shows the firm's present value for each possible response it might choose. The computation assumes that the indicated equilibrium strategy is followed in subsequent periods; clearly, if the strategy were not optimal then some single-period deviation from it would be profitable.

In each row of the table an underlined present value figure indicates the firm's best response to the competitor's price. To see how these figures are obtained, take the example in which the competitor's current price is $0.2 and the firm is contemplating offering the price $0.1. By doing so it gets the whole market this period for an immediate profit of $0.09. It expects the competitor to respond in the next period with either the same price (yielding a profit of $0.045 discounted by the factor 0.9) or the monopoly price (yielding a profit of $0.09 discounted by 0.9). If the price remains at $0.1 then the value of continuation two periods hence is the indicated present value of $1.125 discounted further by 0.9^2; whereas, if the competitor

Table 8.10 Verification of the equilibrium: Present value from each response

	Firm's response				
Competitor's price	$0.1	$0.2	$0.3	$0.4	$0.5
$0.1	<u>1.125</u>	0.91125	0.91125	0.91125	<u>1.125</u>
$0.2	<u>1.17</u>	0.99125	0.91125	0.91125	1.125
$0.3	<u>1.17</u>	1.07125	1.01625	0.91125	1.125
$0.4	<u>1.17</u>	1.07125	1.12125	1.03125	1.125
$0.5	1.17	1.07125	1.12125	1.15125	<u>1.25</u>

reverts to the monopoly price then the value of continuation is \$1.25 again discounted by 0.9^2. All told, then, the present value of offering the price \$0.1 in response to the competitor's price of \$0.2 is

$$\$0.09+0.9\cdot\{0.095\cdot[\$0.045+0.9\cdot\$1.125]+0.905\cdot[\$0.09+0.9\cdot\$1.25]\} = \$1.17.$$

The complexity of this computation stems from the fact that the firms alternate moves and each is committed to its price for two periods.

Now we can see how this equilibrium describes a price war in the event that either firm mistakenly or intentionally deviates from the equilibrium. Suppose that firm **1** cuts its price to \$0.4. Then next period firm **2** will cut its price to \$0.1, following the indicated strategy. Assuming that firm **1** now recognizes its mistake and wants to resume the equilibrium, it is now indifferent between maintaining the current price of \$0.1 or reverting to the monopoly price of \$0.5. If it keeps the current price then firm **2** finds itself in the same situation. Thus, the situation continues until one firm opts to resume monopoly pricing; this costs it in the short run (initially it has no customers) but the deficiency is recouped when the other firm joins in and thereafter they expect to divide the monopoly profit.

The way to imagine this equilibrium is that it is like a yo-yo. The price tumbles down; how long it stays before it pops back up is uncertain. When the price is at the bottom (\$0.1) each firm is indifferent between continuing there (hoping the other firm will take the initiative to raise its price and forgo profits for one period) or venturing to be first to raise its price. The mean time that the price persists at the bottom can be calculated: it is 1.111 periods. Indeed, this is all that really matters: the equilibrium can be described equally well by saying that each firm picks a (random) stopping time indicating how many periods it is willing to persist with the bottom price if the other does not earlier revert to the monopoly price. An intriguing feature is that the firms' ability to commit in alteration for two periods to their prices provides enough stickiness to sustain the monopoly price in equilibrium.

There are, of course, other ways that firms can sustain monopoly prices if commitment is possible. The usual cartel agreement is an example: the firms plan to share the market at a uniform high price until any one member deviates, after which they adopt competitive pricing for some period. The punishment period is chosen long enough to deter deviations; it may be forever if deviation dissolves the cartel. The usual problem with such agreements is familiar from the experience of the OPEC oil cartel: typically it is hard to detect deviations since the price cutting is done secretly to selected customers or in invisible ways such as improvements in product quality. Responding to this problem, cartels adopt policing measures that rely on accessible information; for example, if anticipated demand falls short of expectations then a competitive episode ensues even if no firm was secretly cutting price. Consequently, depending on the noise level in the observations that can be made, there are recurrent episodes of competitive pricing, many of which may be triggered by errors of observation. This scenario is consistent with the view that collusive agreements pose a problem of organizational design, namely, to design detection and enforcement procedures that deter cheating. In most cases a period of competitive pricing is the effective punishment.

6 COMMITMENT AND SUNK COSTS

The pivotal idea in the discussion of predatory behavior in Section 2 was that a firm could plausibly imitate commitment to aggressive behavior when in fact it was not committed. There are other cases in which commitment is real and obvious, and it is to these situations that we now turn. Our focus is on the role of sunk costs in tangible equipment, advertizing, etc.

It is clear that the structure of costs has a lot to do with entry. Economies of scale and indivisibilities in the size of plants can make it unprofitable for newcomers to enter on a small scale. If there are no fixed or sunk costs then an entrant may have little to lose by invading a market: if entry is free then presumably the market will fill up with competitors. On the other hand, asymmetries among firms' fixed and sunk costs can be a major determinant of the outcome of competitive battles. The classic example is the hypothetical battle between a railroad and a shipping line for coastal freight traffic in the absence of regulatory and legal restraints. The railroad's costs are mostly sunk into irreversible investments in track, whereas the shipping line can freely transfer its ships to other routes. With few other options, the railroad is willing to cut prices to the bone to survive; the shipping line presumably must include in its costs the opportunity cost of the profits forgone on other routes for every day it sustains the battle with the railroad. The plausible outcome is that the shipping line will exit this market, or better, never enter in the first place given that it sustains fixed costs in maintaining a presence in the market.

Our interest here is in firms' strategic decisions about commitments to alternative cost structures via choices about capacity. An irreversible commitment to the type and amount of capacity effectively sets the rules of the game that ensues. As before the concern is to elucidate the effects on entry and exit.

6.1 The Incumbent's Defense

We first examine markets that are natural monopolies and study some of the ways that an incumbent firm can deter entry. By a natural monopoly we mean that the present value of monopoly profits more than cover the cost of capital and/or other fixed costs, but a duopolist's profits are insufficient to recover these costs.

A first possibility is that the firm's capital stock is, like the railroad's track, long-lived and irreversible. In this case it is clear that an entrant is deterred from entering by the fact that it cannot recover the requisite capital and fixed costs. But what if capital equipment is short-lived (and for simplicity there are no other fixed costs)? As the time nears for reconstruction of the incumbent's equipment, an entrant could perceive a chance to enter profitably by moving first to install capacity and thereby deter the incumbent from refurbishing its plant. The incumbent in this case is motivated to replace its capital stock early in order to deter the entrant: the optimal time to renew its capital equipment is calculated so that if the entrant were to enter any time sooner its losses in the period of the duopoly would outweigh its subsequent profits were it to gain the monopoly upon the demise of the incumbent's plant. This optimal strategy reveals that the incumbent's profit is precisely the present value of the difference between the monopoly and duopoly profits over the period until replacement of the capital: were it more the entrant could enter profitably and recover its investment by waiting out the incumbent.

An interesting aspect of this analysis is revealed by supposing that the lifetime of equipment is very short (and then so too is the replacement time): in this case the incumbent's profit is nearly zero. This result reflects the general proposition that the profitability derived from the power to make long commitments via irreversible investments diminishes to zero as the period of the commitment shortens. Monopolies in which the brevity of commitments wipes out profits in the attempt to deter entry are said to be perfectly contestable: monopolies they may be, but monopoly profits are precluded by the threat of entry that would eject the incumbent.

The analysis is similar if there are no irreversible capacity costs but there are continuing fixed costs F that must be covered. In this case the market is a natural monopoly if the gross profit of a duopolist is insufficient to cover this fixed cost; here we assume the stronger property that even the monopoly gross profit is insufficient to cover the fixed costs of two firms (to exclude the case where the firms might collude explicitly or implicitly to share the monopoly profit). To represent the power of commitment suppose that each firm commits to its output level for two periods, and in a duopoly they alternate in choosing their output levels. In this case an incumbent monopolist can deter entry by choosing its output level sufficiently large so that an entrant entering in the second period would incur losses that outweigh subsequent profits even were it to succeed in driving out the incumbent. For example, in a symmetric model let $P(q_1,q_2)$ be the period profit of one firm if its output is q_1 and the other's is q_2; and let d be the discount factor. If the discount factor d is not too small, then the output level that deters entry is the largest value of q satisfying:

$$P(q,q)+\frac{d}{1-d}P(q,0)=\frac{F}{1-d}.$$

That is, if q is the optimal output then the entrant will also select q when it enters to deter the incumbent from continuing; consequently, the entrant's profit is $P(q,q)$ the first period it enters (since the incumbent committed for two periods), and $P(q,0)$ thereafter (since the incumbent withdraws), and optimally the present value of this profit stream must be no greater than the present value of the stream of fixed costs (to deter the entrant's entry), and preferably no less (or the incumbent would be sacrificing profits with excessive deterrence). Again we see the feature that if the power of commitment is strong (the discount factor is small, indicating that each period is long) then the incumbent's profit $P(q,0)-F$ per period is large, but if the power of commitment is weak (the discount factor is large, approaching 1) then the incumbent's profit $P(q,0)-F=0$ per period is wiped out and the market is perfectly contestable.

The thrust of these examples is that the threat of entry is a limiting factor on the profitability of even a natural monopoly. The durability of irreversible investments or other possibilities for commitments that affect adversely the profitability of entry can sustain some portion of the potential monopoly profits, but if these deterrents are weak or costly for the incumbent then it is forced to forgo these potential profits to deter entry.

6.2 The Entrant's Gambit

Next we consider an entrant's strategy of limiting its capacity in order to avoid provoking a response from the incumbent firm. If an entrant commits to a capacity that is sufficiently small then the incumbent will not have an incentive to drive out the entrant, or even to engage it directly with duopolistic pricing. It is a common observation that in many industries 'fringe' firms prefer to remain small rather than to risk retaliation by the dominant firms. A useful example is an incumbent hotel in a resort location: an entrant that builds a comparable but small hotel with lower rates (a *pension*) can expect accommodation from the larger hotel, since it is in the larger one's interest to serve the overflow from the smaller one rather than to cut its price to compete directly. This assumes, of course, that the hotel cannot offer selective price discounts to the other's customers, and that the larger hotel is indeed considerably larger.

To explore the logic of this strategy, consider the following example. Assume that the incumbent has installed a very large capacity and it has constant marginal cost c_1, whereas the entrant chooses its capacity K and it has constant marginal cost $c_2 \geqslant c_1$. Demand is a function $Q(p)$ of the price charged: assume that the firm with the lower price captures all of the market that it can serve, but that (reflecting the incumbent's prior advantage) if they charge the same price then the demand goes to the incumbent. If the entrant charges a lower price and limits its capacity then its demand must be rationed.

First, consider the case that the available capacity is rationed randomly among the customers, in which case the entrant serves K customers at its price p_2 and the incumbent serves $[1-K/Q(p_2)]Q(p_1)$ customers at its price p_1, assuming that $p_1 > p_2$. If the incumbent is accommodating it will, of course, choose to charge its optimal monopoly price to the overflow customers it receives; this is the price p_1 that maximizes its profit contribution $[p_1 - c_1]Q(p_1)$, whether or not it obtains the full demand. The entrant's strategy, therefore, must be to curtail its capacity sufficiently to make accommodation better for the incumbent than matching the entrant's price p_2 – in which case the entrant would obtain no sales at all. Thus, the entrant must choose its capacity and price subject to the constraint that

$$[p_1 - c_1][1 - K/Q(p_2)]Q(p_1) > [p_2 - c_1]Q(p_2).$$

This constraint expresses the requirement that the incumbent's profit from accommodation exceeds its profit from matching the entrant's price. Subject to this constraint the entrant can choose its capacity and price to maximize its profit contribution. The effect of this constraint is essentially to induce for the entrant a new demand function $Q^*(p_2 | p_1)$; this new demand function lies below the original demand function by an amount that leaves for the incumbent a sufficient overflow to encourage accommodation. In general, the entrant chooses a limited capacity and a lower price than the incumbent.

Besides a random rationing of its capacity the entrant might be able to ration its capacity to those customers with the highest valuations of the product. In this case the incumbent's overflow demand will be $Q(p_1) - K$ at its price p_1. The incumbent's accommodating response will entail some reduction of its price below the monopoly level, and in turn the entrant's price will be even lower.

A particularly ingenious method of rationing demand to high-valuation customers is for the entrant to issue (transferable) coupons entitling the bearer to service at the price p_2. If this is done the entrant might garner its profits solely from the coupon sales should the incumbent choose to honor the coupons. The incumbent wants to honor the coupons if $p_2 > c_1$, since otherwise it loses this market segment. As for the overflow, the incumbent prefers to accommodate the entrant so long as its optimal price in response exceeds the entrant's price p_2. For example, if $p_1 > c_2 > c_1$ then the entrant can issue K coupons at a price $p_2 > c_1$ for which it charges less than $p_1 - p_2$ per coupon to attract customers.

A useful way to interpret these scenarios is to view the entrant as an extortionist who threatens to produce K units unless it is bought off. Faced with this threat the incumbent purchases the rights to the entrant's output (by honoring the coupons). The way this can work is for the entrant to issue coupons for the K units of capacity at the price (slightly more than) $p_2 = c_1$ by charging (slightly less than) $p_1 - p_2 = p_1 - c_1$ for each coupon. The incumbent then finds it advantageous to honor these coupons (since $p_2 > c_1$). The cost savings for the industry, $[c_2 - c_1]K$, accrues entirely to the entrant via sales of coupons.

In the famous coupon war of 1979 among the major airlines, United issued coupons to recover its market position after a long strike; soon after, the other airlines responded by accepting (and in some cases, issuing) coupons. Eastern did the same in 1980 in its battle with New York Air over the shuttle traffic. Its coupons were valid for a discount on its transcontinental flights as well, and promptly United and American honored the coupons, enabling Eastern to cut back the number of its transcontinental flights in favor of shuttle flights. The airline industry seems particularly suitable for the use of coupons since capacity is mobile: a commitment of capacity to a scheduled route for one period can be reversed later and the equipment redirected to other routes. Thus, the ability to commit capacity for periods of intermediate length may encourage competition via coupons and the like. Contrast this with a resort hotel where a capacity commitment may be permanent, and having issued coupons honored by the incumbent, the facility may stand empty. The cost of a capacity commitment is relatively less in the airline industry than in the hotel industry because the commitment period is much shorter.

6.3 Dynamics of Capacity Expansion

We turn now to an analysis of the incumbent's options in its choice of capacity. In order to examine the dynamic evolution of an industry's capacity levels, we consider a new market in which the incumbent initially has a headstart in the installation of irreversible capacity. The main conclusion will be that the incumbent preserves and exploits its initial advantage by investing more than a subsequent entrant. In the long run, moreover, the entrant is permanently restrained to a lesser capacity by the incumbent's threat to respond to any investment by the entrant with more investment itself.

It is particularly significant that there is a wide range of terminal capacity configurations; indeed, we shall see that the ultimate levels of capacity in the industry depend on the firms' expectations about each other's behavior.

This is a familiar phenomenon in industry: each firm's choice of capacity depends on the anticipated actions or reactions of its competitors.

To keep matters simple, assume that the firms' investment process occurs in an interval of time that is short compared to the projected life of the industry. Thus, the firms' discount rates can be ignored and each is concerned more with the long-run configuration of capacities than with the timing of investments; similarly, depreciation can be ignored. Nevertheless, investment takes time and the rate at which new capacity can be installed is limited, so during the investment phase the firms' decisions interact with one another. Our aim is to analyze this interaction and to identify the final capacities that result.

At any time the firms' two capacities can be plotted as a point (K_1,K_2) as in Figure 8.7. Shown in the figure is the locus R_1 indicating **1**'s preferred capacity depending on **2**'s capacity, and similarly R_2 shows **2**'s preferred capacity depending on **1**'s; e.g. at the intersection of these two loci each firm prefers not to change its capacity. Above both loci neither wants to increase capacity, and neither can reduce it. Below both loci one might imagine that both want to increase capacity, but we will see that this is not necessarily the case, due to the effects of their interaction. Also shown on R_2 is **1**'s preferred point S_1 on that locus, and on R_1 is shown the point S_2 that is **2**'s

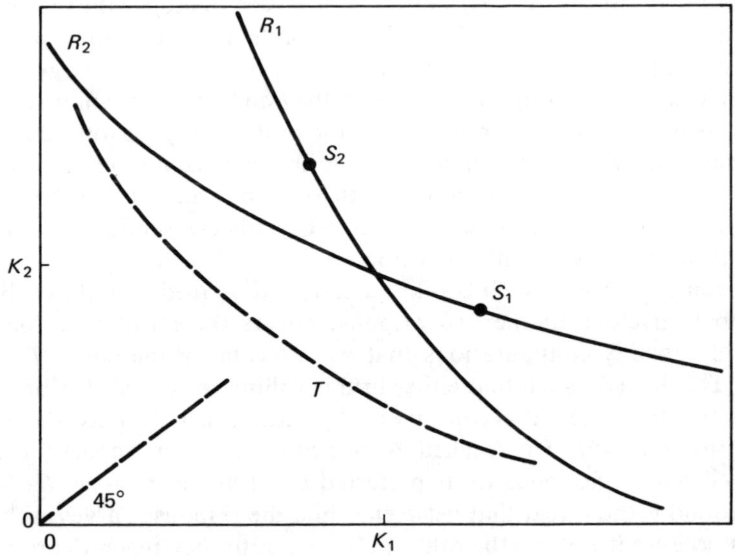

$R_1(K_2)$ = 1's Preferred response to 2
$R_2(K_1)$ = 2's Preferred response to 1

Figure 8.7 The firm's reactions

preferred point on R_1. Assume that from any point (K_1,K_2) there are four possible movements: they can both stop investing, they can both continue (at, say, equal rates), or one can invest while the other stops.

We first argue that if **1** starts initially with a sufficiently large capacity when **2** enters the market then there is an equilibrium that ends up at the point S_1. To see this consider the following strategy for **1**: do not invest if (K_1,K_2) is above both loci; otherwise invest as rapidly as possible, except stop if K_1 reaches or exceeds the level of **1**'s capacity at S_1. The strategy for **2** is similar, except that **2** stops investing when its capacity reaches the level at S_2. With these strategies, starting from a point on the abscissa with $K_1>0$ and $K_2=0$, both firms invest rapidly until, if **1** has a sufficient headstart, **1** reaches its optimal capacity at S_1 and stops to wait for **2** to invest until S_1 is reached and **2** stops as well. That these strategies are in equilibrium (each strategy is a best response to the other) is evident from the fact that below the response curves each expects the other to invest as rapidly as possible to reach its preferred capacity level along its response curve; hence, each must invest rapidly to move the resulting capacity configuration in its preferred direction.

This is not, however, the only equilibrium. To see this, consider the situation that arises when they start at the same time with zero capacities and invest along the 45° line until they reach the intersection of their response curves. In the later stages of this process each is investing because it expects the other to invest: both would prefer to stop with the smaller capacities represented by their preferred points along the line. Indeed, if each expects the other to stop at a smaller capacity (at least as large as both preferred capacities along the line) along the line, then they will invest only up to this point – with the threat that if the other invests beyond this point then they both will and continue on out to the intersection point. Thus, we see that there are many equilibria with outcomes in a range below the response curves, and each equilibrium is described essentially by mutual expectations as to when they will stop.

The general form of such equilibria can be described as follows. Below the upper envelope of the two response curves there will be a locus of terminal capacity configurations that we indicate by the curve T in the figure. This locus is such that either firm is willing to stop at T if the other does. Then, from the initial capacity configuration each firm invests rapidly until either the locus T is reached, or one firm stops if its capacity reaches the level that corresponds to its preferred point along the locus T. In the background is the threat that between T and the response curves each firm invests because it expects the other to invest, until they reach the response curve (as in the previously described equilibrium); and beyond the response curves, of course, neither firm invests.

The important feature of this analysis is that it is indicative of a general feature of capacity expansion over time. Usually there are multiple equilibria representing a range of terminal capacity levels, and each equilibrium corresponds to mutual expectations among the firms as to when they will stop expansion. The formation of these expectations poses a subtle problem of coordination among the firms. In their own interests they would like the terminal locus T to be as low as possible, keeping capacity low to restrain output and keep prices high, but this likely outcome of implicit collusion is only precariously maintained by the mutual threat to expand capacity further if either firm steps beyond the anticipated locus T in a short-sighted attempt to expand its market share.

7 COOPERATIVE BEHAVIOR

Cooperative behavior in the absence of enforcement mechanisms often seems inexplicable on the hypothesis that the participants are rational and interested solely in their own personal gain. Nevertheless, it occurs so frequently in practice that it calls for an explanation. Rather than address the subject generally, here we concentrate on a particular simplified situation that captures the main features in stark form. For historical reasons it is called the repeated prisoners' dilemma game; one can as well think of it as depicting the dilemma faced by two firms trying to sustain high prices. It has been the subject of intensive experimental studies.

In each stage the two players move simultaneously, choosing either to cooperate or not, and each then observes the other's choice. If neither cooperates their payoffs are zero. Each gains 3 from the other's cooperation but it costs the other 1 to cooperate. Each seeks to maximize the sum of his payoffs over n repetitions of this stage game.

The only sequentially rational equilibrium of this game has both players choosing not to cooperate every time, regardless of the number of repetitions. At the final stage cooperation is disadvantageous for both players; at the penultimate stage, therefore, there is no chance that cooperation will be reciprocated in the next stage and so again cooperation is disadvantageous; and so on *ad infinitum*. This sort of reasoning backward from the terminus is familiar from Section 2, and as there it depends on the assumption that the data are common knowledge. We therefore explore what happens when there is some private information.

Suppose that player A entertains a positive probability p, possibly very small, that B is addicted to the strategy tit-for-tat; that is, that B will cooperate unless A does not, in which case his following action will be not to cooperate. Using tit-for-tat, B initially cooperates and thereafter plays whatever A played on the previous round. There are some good reasons for selecting tit-for-tat as a candidate. Besides the ancient rules of 'an eye for an eye' and 'do unto others as they do unto you', there is the interesting fact that in two contests conducted by R. Axelrod tit-for-tat won out. Axelrod

(1981) solicited entries in the form of computer routines that were pitted against each other in a round-robin series. That they were round-robin series is rather important: tit-for-tat has the property that it always obtains cumulative payoffs that are close to whatever its opponents obtain. That is, tit-for-tat always runs a close second, so if its opponents occasionally fare poorly when matched with each other then overall tit-for-tat will tend to win. Indeed, one can show that among a population of rational players an initial minority of tit-for-tat players will tend to survive and grow, in the Darwinian sense. So, tit-for-tat has survival value.

The main result that we verify is that with this small dose of uncertainty, there is a sequentially rational equilibrium in which both players cooperate for all but a relatively few stages. The operative mechanism is that B, whether a tit-for-tat player or not, imitates tit-for-tat, and with this inducement, so does A. The derivation of this result invokes the following argument that we state intuitively and somewhat imprecisely.

Suppose that B is not addicted to tit-for-tat. We argue that for most of the game B will want to imitate tit-for-tat. The first part is trivial: he surely must punish any non-cooperative behavior by A since this yields a short-term advantage and does not alter his reputation that he might be a tit-for-tat player. The key, therefore, is to establish that B will reciprocate A's cooperation if there are many stages remaining. The argument uses the following inequalities, in which $A(r,s)$ and $B(r,s)$ represent A's and B's expected payoffs if they use strategies denoted by r and s, respectively. Also, let t represent B's tit-for-tat strategy, and let (r^0,s^0) be some pair of sequential equilibrium strategies.

1. $B(r^0,s^0) \geqslant B(r^0,t)$, since s^0 is B's optimal response to r^0.
2. $B(r^0,t) \geqslant A(r^0,t) - 4$, since by using tit-for-tat B is assured of a payoff within $1+3$ of A's payoff, regardless of what strategy A uses. Moreover, when using the strategy tit-for-tat B's expected payoff is the same as the contingent payoff depending on B's type, since both types use tit-for-tat.
3. $A(r^0,t) \geqslant A(r^0,s^0)$, since B's use of tit-for-tat can only benefit A. This uses the fact that s^0 punishes A for non-cooperation just as tit-for-tat does, but possibly s^0 does not reciprocate cooperation to the degree that tit-for-tat does.
4. $A(r^0,s^0) \geqslant 2p[n-1] - 2$. If A previously cooperated then by continuing cooperation until B does not A's payoff is at least $2n$ if B is addicted to tit-for-tat and it is at least -1 otherwise. Similarly, if A previously did not cooperate then B is sure to not cooperate, so with this strategy A gets -1 immediately by cooperating plus a continuation value that is at least the corresponding amounts above: $2(n-1]$ or -1. Either way the expected payoff, using the initial probability assessment, is at least the stated amount.

Combining these results, we see that B's expected payoff is at least $2p[n-1]-6$ when his reputation is p and n stages remain. Consequently, when B considers whether to reciprocate cooperation he calculates as follows. He can choose to not cooperate, yielding an immediate payoff of at most 3 but zero thereafter (since his type is revealed the only equilibrium path thereafter has no cooperation). Or he can cooperate, yielding at least -1 immediately and at least $2p[n-2]-6$ in the remaining $n-1$ stages (which he will begin with a reputation that is at least p if he reciprocates cooperation). Thus, if n and p satisfy $-1+2p[n-2]-6>3$, or $n>2+5p$, then B's best choice is to reciprocate cooperation.

This result can be further strengthened to provide a bound, independent of the length of the game, on the number of non-cooperative episodes. The bound we have derived here is quite weak (e.g. if $p=0.01$ then n must exceed 502) but it serves to illustrate the main point. Cooperative behavior from both players prevails for all but a relatively few stages of a long game. In fact, in experimental settings it is commonly observed that most players cooperate a substantial proportion of the time.

This equilibrium stems from the basic observation that each player prefers to play with another who uses tit-for-tat, will respond in kind if the actions taken are consistent with tit-for-tat, and will initiate tit-for-tat if there is some chance the other will play tit-for-tat and there are sufficiently many stages remaining.

What is needed to bootstrap the equilibrium is A's assessment that B might be addicted to tit-for-tat, in which case A is willing to cooperate until it is not reciprocated; in turn, B wants to maintain this belief in A's mind by imitating addiction and thus reaping the long-term rewards of cooperation. The first time B fails to follow tit-for-tat he ruins the prospects for further cooperation, while as long as there is a chance that B is addicted, so that even if he is not addicted he will imitate addiction, A's optimal response is to cooperate until it is not reciprocated.

A striking aspect of this game is that a little private information is good for both parties. Even before B knows his type, both players prefer that this information not be revealed after it is known to B. For example, A prefers that B has an opportunity to imitate an addiction to tit-for-tat.

8 CONCLUSION

The thrust of these examples is to emphasize some of the strategic aspects of competition among firms. Competitive battles are inherently dynamic, and they are severely affected by informational asymmetries. Entry, contests for market share, and struggles for survival are versions of economic warfare. In addition, they involve the features of bargaining, albeit in a language restricted to credible actions, in which tenacity reveals the stronger contestant. Wars of attrition serve the social interest both to select the more efficient firm, and to dissipate monopoly rents in the conflict to obtain or retain them. On the other hand, the threat of price wars can sustain monopoly prices, and capacity limitation and collusive behavior generally can be sustained by expectations of reciprocity. The exercise of monopoly power depends substantially on powers of commitment, but this too can be enforced by irreversible investments in durable equipment.

The complex dynamics of competition among firms with differing information present a far different view than envisaged in the traditional static models with complete information. The recent analyses explore the possibility that economic competition has all the complexity that business strategists ascribe to it: 'it's a jungle out there' and only the strong and the wily survive. The development of this approach relies on game-theoretic models to elaborate the motivation for firms' strategies, and to provide well-specified formulations that explain reputational effects in both competitive and collusive contexts.

9 BIBLIOGRAPHY

Some of the introductory material on predation in Section 2 is adapted from Frederic Scherer (1980, ch.12). This is an excellent reference on the empirical evidence, legal considerations, and analytical studies on this subject and several of the subsequent topics. The War Chest game (Example 2.1) is studied by Benoit (1983, 1984), and the Chain Store game (Example 2.2) is studied by Selten (1978). The apparent contradiction between the complete-information game-theoretic analysis of this finitely repeated game and the intuitive appeal of predatory behavior led Selten to call it a paradox. It is called the Chain Store game after a scenario in which the incumbent is a chain store with shops in several cities, and in each city there is a potential entrant. The idea for the example in Section 2.2 is due to Milgrom and Roberts (1982b), and the analysis of the incomplete-information version of the Chain Store game in Section 2.3 is based on Kreps and Wilson (1982); Milgrom and Roberts (1982b) present a similar model with a continuum of types for both the incumbent and the entrants, and a sequentially rational equilibrium is constructed that uses no randomization.

The example of 'brinkmanship' in Section 3.1.1 is adapted from Bliss and Nalebuff (1984). The analysis of wars of attrition in Section 3.2 is based on Fudenberg and Tirole (1983a).

The analysis of entry and exit in Section 3.3 follows Kreps and Wilson (1982). Kreps and Fudenberg (1985) provide several major extensions to cases in which the incumbent faces several entrants simultaneously or in succession, and depending on whether entrants who have exited can re-enter if the incumbent is revealed to be weak. In general, reputational effects persist and the equilibria have roughly the same form, but the incumbent may be worse off compared to the situation in which contests are not linked informationally by entrants' ability to see how their compatriots are faring or have fared against the incumbent. For example, assuming no re-entry by exited entrants, in the case of sequential play the weak incumbent continues to fight an early strong entrant in order to avoid revealing weakness to later entrants; consequently, depending on whether the chance that an entrant is strong is low (below 2/3 in our example) or high, the weak incumbent's expected profits per entrant increase or decrease as the number of entrants grows, and total profits are bounded in the latter case since the weak incumbent's type is soon revealed. With simultaneous play, and for simplicity a continuum of entrants, the incumbent fights either all or none depending again on whether this chance is high or low.

The material on limit pricing is adapted from Milgrom and Roberts (1982a) and Saloner (1982). An alternative formulation is adopted by Roberts (1985b) for the case that in an initial phase after entry the incumbent has superior information about demand conditions and its supply quantity is not observable by the entrant. Thus, as in a predation context (Section 2), the incumbent drives the price down in order to influence the entrant's decision to exit. In equilibrium the entrant makes the correct inferences so the exit decision is not actually biased, but the entrant's anticipation of this behavior by the incumbent tends to deter entry by reducing expected profits in the initial phase. As in the limit pricing context, the incumbent is forced to lower prices in the initial phase lest he encourage the entrant to stay when in fact it is unprofitable. Fudenberg and Tirole (1985a) note that possession of superior information by the incumbent is not actually necessary to this result: even if both firms are equally uncertain about demand conditions, the incumbent has an incentive to lower prices in order to affect the price signal observed by the entrant and thereby to influence the exit decision.

The example of a price war in Section 5.1 is similar to one devised by Maskin and Tirole (1983, 1985), who develop a wide variety of implications of short-term commitments represented by the firms' alternating actions.

The discussion of the incumbent's defense in Section 6.1 follows Eaton and Lipsey (1980) and Maskin and Tirole (1983); and the entrant's gambit in Section 6.2 follows Gelman and Salop (1983). The discussion of capacity expansion in Section 6.3 is adapted from Fudenberg and Tirole (1983b).

The analysis in Section 7 of the repeated prisoner's dilemma game is based on Kreps, Milgrom, Roberts, and Wilson (1982).

For more comprehensive and detailed surveys than attempted here, but without worked-out examples, and different selections of topics and references, the reader can consult the excellent surveys by Roberts (1985a) and Fudenberg and Tirole (1985b).

References

Axelrod, R. (1981) 'The Emergence of Cooperation Among Egoists', *American Political Science Review*, 75: 306–18.

Benoit, J.-P. (1983) 'Entry with Exit: An Extensive Form Treatment of Predation with Financial Constraints', Institute For Mathematical Studies in the Social Sciences Technical Report 405, Stanford University.

Benoit, J.-P. (1984) 'Financially Constrained Entry in a Game with Incomplete Information', *Rand Journal of Economics*, 15: 490–9.

Bliss, C. and B. Nalebuff (1984) 'Dragonslaying and Ballroom Dancing: The Private Supply of a Private Good', Working Paper, Harvard University.

Eaton, B. C., and R. G. Lipsey (1980) 'Exit Barriers are Entry Barriers: The Durability of Capital as a Barrier to Entry', *Bell Journal of Economics*, 11: 721–9.

Fudenberg, D. and J. Tirole (1983a) 'A Theory of Exit in Oligopoly', Technical Report, Institute for Mathematical Studies in the Social Sciences, Stanford University.

Fudenberg, D. and J. Tirole (1983b) 'Capital as a Commitment: Strategic Investment to Deter Mobility', *Journal of Economic Theory*, 31: 227–50.

Fudenberg, D. and J. Tirole (1985a) 'Predation without Reputation', Working Paper 377, MIT.

Fudenberg, D. and J. Tirole (1985b) 'Dynamic Models of Oligopoly', in J. Lesourne and H. Sonnenschein, *Encyclopedia of Economics* (forthcoming).

Gelman, J. and S. Salop (1983) 'Judo Economics: Capacity Limitation and Coupon Competition', *Bell Journal of Economics*, 14: 315–25.

Kreps, D. M. and D. Fudenberg (1985) 'Reputation and Multiple Opponents', mimeo, Stanford Business School.

Kreps, D. M., P. Milgrom, J. Roberts and R. Wilson (1982) 'Rational Cooperation in the Finitely Repeated Prisoners' Dilemma', *Journal of Economic Theory*, 27: 245–51.

Kreps, D. M. and R. Wilson (1982) 'Reputation and Incomplete Information', *Journal of Economic Theory*, 27: 253–79.

Maskin, E. and J. Tirole (1983) 'A Theory of Dynamic Oligopoly, I: Overview and Quantity Competition with Large Fixed Costs', IMSSS Technical Report 409, Stanford University.

Maskin, E. and J. Tirole (1985) 'A Theory of Dynamic Oligopoly, II: Price Competition', Working Paper 373, MIT.

Milgrom, P. and J. Roberts (1982a) 'Limit Pricing and Entry under Incomplete Information: An Equilibrium Analysis', *Econometrica*, 50: 443–59.

Milgrom, P. and J. Roberts (1982b) 'Predation, Reputation, and Entry Deterrence', *Journal of Economic Theory*, 27: 280–312.

Roberts, J. (1985a) 'Battles for Market Share: Incomplete Information, Aggressive Strategic Pricing, and Competitive Dynamics', Fifth World Congress of the Econometric Society', forthcoming in a volume of proceedings edited by Truman Bewley.

Roberts, J. (1985b) 'A Signalling Model of Predatory Pricing', Research Paper 828, Stanford Business School.

Robinson, J. (1933) *The Economics of Imperfect Competition* (London: Macmillan).

Saloner, G. (1982) *Essays on Information Transmission under Uncertainty*, chapter 2, Ph.D. Dissertation, Stanford Business School.

Scherer, F. (1980) *Industrial Market Structure and Economic Performance*, 2nd edn (Chicago: Rand McNally).

Selten, P. (1978) 'The Chain Store Paradox', *Theory and Decision*, 9: 127–59.

Shubik, M. (1959) *Strategy and Market Structure* (New York: Wiley).

9 Effects of Entry on Profits under Monopolistic Competition

Leonid Hurwicz*

1 INTRODUCTION

The aim of this chapter is to examine the effects of entry of new firms in a symmetric differentiated products industry, in particular the effect on the profits of firms already in the industry. Purposely, our models are kept close to those of a Chamberlinian industry, but with this exception: because of the implicit indivisibilities, it would be only by accident that profits are zero at free entry equilibrium (as they also are in Joan Robinson's models). Typically, the entry of an additional firm would (under symmetry assumptions) result in negative profits for everyone, but if an additional firm does not enter profits at equilibrium are positive.

Two questions are explored. First, we obtain an upper bound on the number of firms that could co-exist in an industry. This result is of a more general nature and does not presuppose symmetry. Second, assuming symmetry,[1] we examine the relationship of profits as a function of the number n of firms in the industry. We show, to no one's surprise, that profits decrease with n. Here our result is in the nature of an example and lacks generality. In particular, the demand side is represented by a single utility function, linear in the numéraire[2] and quadratic in the industry's products. All firms are assumed to have the same (quadratic) average cost function. We investigate both the Bertrand behavior (close to Chamberlin's model) and Cournot behavior on the part of the firms. Unless products are 'independent' (in our model, the utility function parameter $\beta=0$), the conclusion in both cases is that the profits of each individual firm go down as the number of firms n increases. Similar conclusions could undoubtedly be obtained under more general assumptions than those made in the present paper, but it may be of some interest to see how things work out in specific examples – especially since the results obtained are for finite n (rather than asymptotic), and particular attention has been paid to conditions for the existence of equilibria. One reason for constructing specialized examples is to show that it is possible to satisfy the assumptions made in the theorem giving an upper bound on the number of firms in an industry.

* Economics Department, University of Minnesota. This work was supported by National Science Foundation Grants SES-8509547 and IRI-8510042 and earlier NSF grants.

The form of symmetry assumptions is, in part, due to Chamberlin, but it has benefited from formulations in Samuelson (1967, esp. p.129, footnote 23), which may be regarded as a generalization of that in Tun Thin (1967, p.42, eq. (9:2:a)).

I have not investigated the general problem of *asymmetric* solutions, except for Cournot duopoly ($n=2$) where asymmetric positive solutions turn out to be impossible.

Some of the results are valid for the case of undifferentiated commodities as well, i.e., where all firms sell identical products. (In our model this corresponds to the case where the parameters of the utility function satisfy $\beta=\alpha$, or equivalently, $\theta=1$. Since arguments are considerably simplified by assuming $\beta<\alpha$, the case $\beta=\alpha$ is not explicitly covered by all of the results.)

I want to acknowledge the stimulation of K. J. Arrow (1969)[3] and especially, of Shapley and Shubik (1969). Important aspects of my approach follow theirs, but – significantly – we differ in our assumptions concerning the behavior of the utility function as the number of products available to the consumer increases. I also benefited greatly from reading Modigliani's review (1958) and Dewey's book (1969).[4]

2 THE MODEL AND SOME RESULTS

2.1 Notation

$P_i=D_{Ni}^{-1}(x_{i_1},\ldots,x_{i_n})$	the indirect demand function for the i-th product (firm) out of the set $N\equiv\{i_1,\ldots,i_n\}$; i.e., $i\in N$
$c^i=c^i(x_i)$	the average cost function of the i-th firm.
$\mathcal{N}$	the (infinite) set of (potential) products in the given field.

2.2 Assumptions

I. DEMAND BOUNDED FROM ABOVE

$\exists K>0$ such that: $\sum_{i\in N} x_i D_{Ni}^{-1}(x_{i_1},\ldots,x_{i_n})\leqq K$ for all $N\subseteq\mathcal{N}$ and all $x_{i_1},\ldots,x_{i_n}$ (Fig. 9.1a);

II. POSITIVE LOWER BOUND FOR AVERAGE COSTS

$\exists c^*>0$ such that: $c^i(x_i)\geqq c^*$ for all $i\in\mathcal{N}$ and all x_i (Fig. 9.1b);

III. LOSSES AT LOW OUTPUTS

$\exists x^*>0$ such that: $D_{Ni}^{-1}(x_{i_1},\ldots,x_{i_n})-c^i(x_i)<0$ for all $i\in N$, all $N\subseteq\mathcal{N}$, all $x_{i_1},\ldots,x_{i_n}$ such that $x_i<x^*$ (Fig. 9.1c).

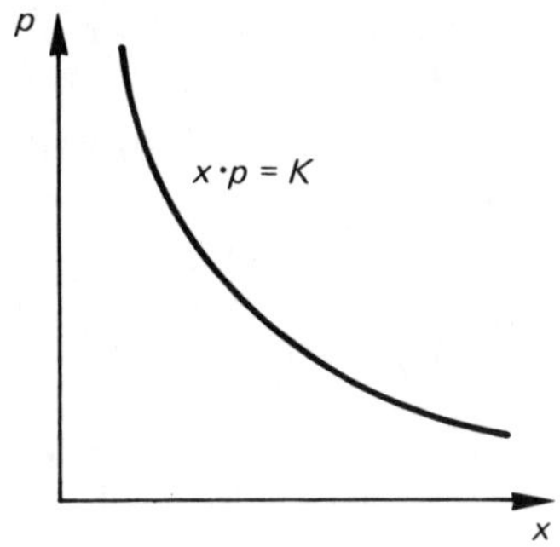

Figure 9.1a

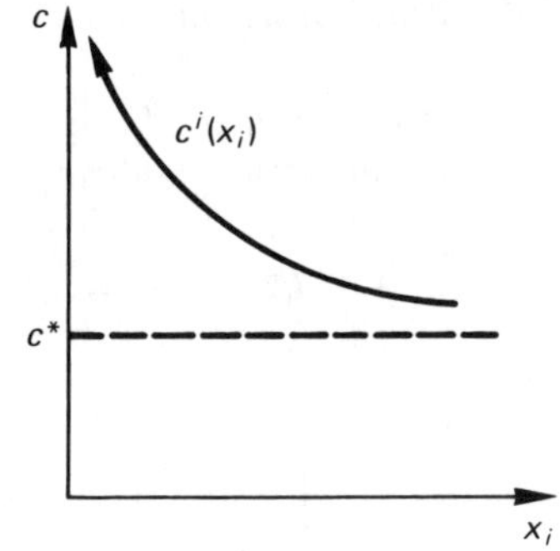

Figure 9.1b

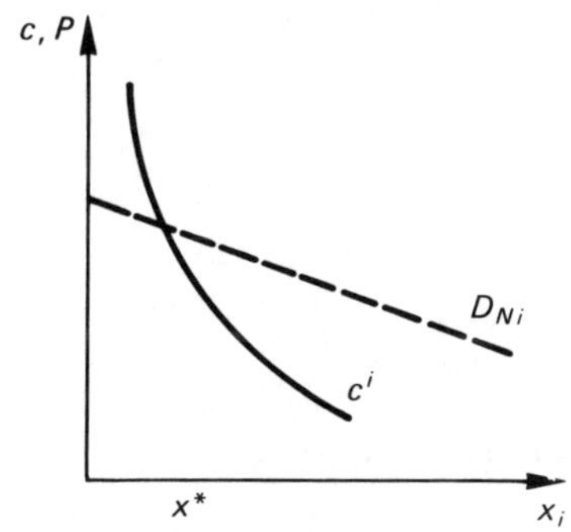

Figure 9.1c

2.3 Theorem 1

(A) Under Assumptions I, II, III, the number of firms with positive outputs and non-negative profits cannot exceed

$$\frac{K}{x^*c^*}.$$

(B) Let Assumption (I) be weakened to Assumption (I′), with K replaced by K_n which may depend on the number of firms n. In order that there be n firms with positive outputs it is necessary that

$$n \leqq \frac{K_n}{x^*c^*}.$$

2.4 Proof of Theorem 1

Let there be n firms (indexed, without loss of generality, as 1,2,...,n) with positive outputs x_i and non-negative profits π_i. By (III),

$$x_i \geqq x^* \quad \text{for all } i \in \{1,\ldots,n\}, \tag{1}$$

and, by (II),

$$p_i \geqq c^* \quad \text{for all } i \in \{1,\ldots,n\}. \tag{2}$$

(If either (1) or (2) were violated for some i, the firms would have negative unit profit $p_i - c^i$, hence negative profit $\pi_i \equiv x_i(p_i - c^i)$, since $x_i > 0$ by hypothesis.)

From (1) and (2), we get

$$\sum_{i=1}^{n} x_i p_i \geqq n \cdot x^* c^*. \tag{3}$$

But, by (I),

$$\Sigma\, x_i p_i \leqq K. \tag{4}$$

The inequalities (3) and (4) together yield

$$n x^* c^* \leqq K, \tag{5}$$

i.e.

$$n \leqq \frac{K}{x^* c^*}, \tag{6}$$

which is the assertion of theorem I(A). The proof of I(B) is analogous.

Remark This theorem applies even in the case of joint monopoly, and also for any type of oligopoly or competition.

2.5 Quadratic Utility with Constant-marginal Utility Numéraire

(Boldface indicates vectors; $\mathbf{x}$ and $\boldsymbol{\sigma}$ are column vectors and the prime indicates transposition; so $\mathbf{x}'$ and $\boldsymbol{\sigma}'$ are row vectors.)

We show that Assumption (I) above holds (with K independent of n for

$n > 1$) for the demand function obtained by the maximization, subject to the budget constraint, of the utility function

$$U = -(\tfrac{1}{2})\mathbf{x}'\Omega\mathbf{x} + \boldsymbol{\sigma}'\mathbf{x} + z,$$

$$\mathbf{x}' = (x_1, x_2, \ldots, x_n),$$

$$\boldsymbol{\sigma}' = (\sigma, \ldots, \sigma),\ \sigma > 0;$$

$$\Omega = (\omega_{ij}),\ \omega_{ii} = \alpha,\ \omega_{ij} = \beta \quad \text{for } i \neq j,$$

$$\alpha > \beta > 0.$$

Proof

1. The above Ω is positive definite (even if $\beta > 0$ is weakened to $\beta \geqq 0$). [It is positive semi-definite if $\alpha \geqq \beta \geqq 0$.]

We have

$$Q(\mathbf{x}) \equiv (\tfrac{1}{2})\mathbf{x}'\Omega\mathbf{x} = (\alpha - \beta)\sum_{i=1}^{n} x_i^2 + \beta \sum_{i=1}^{n}\sum_{j=1}^{n} x_i x_j$$

$$= (\alpha - \beta)\sum_{i=1}^{n} x_i^2 + \beta\left(\sum_{j=1}^{n} x_j\right)^2.$$

Now the second term is always non-negative for $\beta \geqq 0$, while the first term is positive for $\mathbf{x} \neq 0$ provided that $\alpha > \beta$, non-negative for all $\mathbf{x}$ provided $\alpha \geqq \beta$. This proves assertion 1, above.

Remark 1 Thus, for all $\alpha \geqq \beta \geqq 0$, $Q(\mathbf{x})$ is concave; $Q(\mathbf{x})$ is strictly concave for $\alpha > \beta \geqq 0$.

Remark 2 For $\beta < 0$, Ω ceases to be positive semi-definite when n is sufficiently large. This is seen by considering $\mathbf{x}' = (1, \ldots, 1)$ for which $Q = (\alpha - \beta)n + \beta \cdot n^2$; the last expression goes below zero for $\beta < 0$ when n is sufficiently large.

2. The interior maximization of U yields the demand relation

$$\Omega\mathbf{x} = \boldsymbol{\sigma} - \mathbf{p}, \tag{7}$$

so that

$$\mathbf{x}'\mathbf{p} = \mathbf{x}'(\boldsymbol{\sigma} - \Omega\mathbf{x}). \tag{8}$$

We shall now show that, for positive definite Ω and

$$K_n \equiv \frac{\boldsymbol{\sigma}'}{2}\Omega^{-1}\frac{\boldsymbol{\sigma}}{2}, \ n-1, \tag{9}$$

we have the inequality

$$\mathbf{x}'\mathbf{p} \leqq K_n, \tag{10}$$

so that Assumption (I′) is satisfied.

We shall also show that, for $n > 1$ and $\beta > 0$,

$$K_n \leqq \frac{\sigma^2}{4\beta}, \tag{11}$$

so that

$$\mathbf{x}'\mathbf{p} \leqq \frac{\sigma^2}{4\beta} \quad \text{for all } n-1, \tag{12}$$

thus implying Assumption (I) for $n > 1$.

Now, in view of equations (8) and (9), the inequality (10) is equivalent to

$$\frac{\boldsymbol{\sigma}'}{2}\Omega^{-1}\frac{\boldsymbol{\sigma}}{2} - \mathbf{x}'(\boldsymbol{\sigma} - \Omega\mathbf{x}) \geqq 0. \tag{13}$$

But (since $\Omega' = \Omega$) the left-hand side of (13) equals

$$\left(\mathbf{x} - \Omega^{-1}\frac{\boldsymbol{\sigma}}{2}\right)'\Omega\left(\mathbf{x} - \Omega^{-1}\frac{\boldsymbol{\sigma}}{2}\right)$$

and the latter expression is non-negative because Ω is positive definite. Hence (10) is true. It remains to prove (11). Now, since

$$\boldsymbol{\sigma}' = \sigma \cdot \mathbf{1}', \ \mathbf{1}' = (1, \ldots, 1),$$

we have

$$K_n = \frac{\sigma^2}{4}\mathbf{1}'\Omega^{-1}\mathbf{1} = \frac{\sigma^2}{4}\sum_{i=1}^{n}\sum_{j=1}^{n}\omega^{ij}, \tag{14}$$

where $\Omega^{-1} = (\omega^{ij})$.

Hence (11) will follow from

$$\sum_i \sum_j \omega^{ij} \leqq \frac{1}{\beta}, \tag{15}$$

which we now proceed to prove. Note that if $\mathbf{y}$ is the solution of the equation system

$$\mathbf{\Omega y} = \mathbf{1}, \tag{16}$$

then

$$\sum_{i=1}^{n} y_i \equiv \mathbf{1'y} = \mathbf{1'\Omega}^{-1}\mathbf{1} = \sum_i \sum_j \omega^{ij}. \tag{17}$$

Now (16), written out explicitly, is

$$\begin{cases} \alpha y_1 + \beta y_2 + \ldots + \beta y_n = 1 \\ \ldots \quad \ldots \quad \ldots \quad \ldots \quad . \\ \beta y_1 \quad \beta y_2 + \ldots + \alpha y_n = 1 \end{cases}$$

Adding vertically, we get

$$[\alpha + (n-1)\beta] y_1 + [\alpha + (n-1)\beta] y_2 + \ldots \tag{18}$$

$$\ldots + [\alpha + (n-1)\beta] y_n = n,$$

hence

$$[\alpha + (n-1)\beta] \sum_i y_i = n, \tag{19}$$

$$\Sigma\, y_i = \frac{n}{\alpha + (n-1)\beta} \leqq \frac{n}{\beta + (n-1)\beta} = \frac{1}{\beta} \quad \text{for } n > 1, \tag{20}$$

where the inequality follows from $\alpha \geqq \beta$. This completes the proof of (12) for $n > 1$, $\beta > 0$.

Note that, explicitly,

$$K_n = \frac{\sigma^2}{4} \cdot \frac{n}{\alpha + (n-1)\beta},$$

and that

(14) $\quad \beta n \leqq \beta - \alpha + \sigma^2/(4x^*c^*)$

is necessary for the existence of n firms, $n \geqq 1$, with positive outputs. For $n=1$, (14) simplifies to $\alpha \leqq \sigma^2/(4x^*c^*)$. For $n>1$, $\beta>0$, (14) becomes

$$n \leqq 1 + \frac{1}{\beta}\left(\frac{\sigma^2}{4x^*c^*} - 1\right).$$

Remark 3 For later reference, we obtain the elements of Ω^{-1}. Consider the system

$$\Omega \mathbf{y} = \boldsymbol{\rho} \quad \boldsymbol{\rho} = (\rho_1, \ldots, \rho_n). \tag{16'}$$

Then, proceeding as above, we obtain

$$\sum_i y_i = \frac{\Sigma \rho_i}{\alpha + (n-1)\beta}. \tag{20'}$$

Now the first equation of the system (16′) can be written as

$$(\alpha - \beta) y_1 + \beta \Sigma y_i = \rho_1. \tag{21}$$

By (20′), this is equivalent to

$$(\alpha - \beta) y_1 + \beta \frac{\Sigma \rho_i}{\alpha + (n-1)\beta} = \rho_1, \tag{22}$$

and

$$y_1 = \frac{1}{\alpha - \beta}\left[\rho_1 \left(1 - \frac{\beta}{\alpha + (n-1)\beta}\right) - \left(\sum_{k=2}^{n} \rho_k\right) \beta \frac{1}{\alpha + (n-1)\beta}\right] \tag{23}$$

Now let $\boldsymbol{\rho} = (1,0,\ldots,0)$, so that $\rho_1 = 1$ and $\Sigma \rho_i = 1$. Then by (16′), $\mathbf{y}$ is the first column of Ω^{-1} and hence $y_1 = \omega^{11}$.

Then, writing $\theta \equiv \beta/\alpha$, we get from (23)

$$\begin{aligned} y_1 = \omega^{11} &= \frac{1}{\alpha - \beta}\left(1 - \frac{\beta}{\alpha + (n-1)\beta}\right) = \\ &= \frac{1}{\alpha(1-\theta)}\left(1 - \frac{\theta}{1 + (n-1)\theta}\right) = \\ &= \frac{1}{\alpha(1-\theta)} \cdot \frac{1 + (n-2)\theta}{1 + (n-1)\theta} = \\ &= \omega^{ii} \quad \text{for all } i \text{ (by symmetry)}, \end{aligned} \tag{24}$$

[5,6].

Similarly, using the second equation of (16′), we have

$$(\alpha-\beta)y_2+\beta\,\Sigma\, y_i=\rho_2. \tag{20''}$$

Let again $\boldsymbol{\rho}=(1,0,...,0)$ so that $\mathbf{y}$ is the first column of Ω^{-1}. Then $y_2=\omega^{21}$, $\rho_2=0$, $\Sigma\rho_i=1$ and so

$$(\alpha-\beta)\omega^{21}+\frac{\beta}{\alpha+(n-1)\beta}=0. \tag{22'}$$

Hence

$$\omega^{21}=\frac{1}{\alpha-\beta}\cdot\frac{-\beta}{\alpha+(n-1)\beta}= \tag{25}$$

$$=-\frac{1}{\alpha(1-\theta)}\cdot\frac{\theta}{1+(n-1)\theta}$$

$$=\omega^{ij}\quad\text{for all } i\neq j \text{ (by symmetry).}$$

Note that, using (24) and (25), we obtain

$$\sum_{i=1}^{n}\sum_{j=1}^{n}\omega^{ij}=\frac{1}{\alpha-\beta}\left[n-n^2\frac{\beta}{\alpha+(n-1)\beta}\right]=$$

$$=\frac{n(\alpha-\beta)}{(\alpha-\beta)[\alpha+(n-1)\beta]}=\frac{n}{\alpha+(n-1)\beta}\leqq\frac{1}{\beta},$$

as in (20).

2.6 Joint Monopoly (*n* symmetric firms with identical cost functions)

Let p be a scalar and write

$$\mathbf{x}\equiv(x_1,...,x_n),$$

$$G_n(p)=\sum_{i=1}^{n}D_{ni}(p,...,p)\equiv nD_{n1}(p,...,p),$$

so that $G_n(p)$ is the *aggregate demand* when all n firms charge the same price p. Also, denote by Π_i^{Mn} the profit for the i-th individual firm under joint monopoly, when there are n firms. [The superscript M indicates (joint) monopoly.]

ASSUMPTION IV

$$\frac{G_n}{n} < \frac{G_{n-1}}{n-1} \quad \text{for } n=2,3,\dots; \tag{IV.1}$$

(i.e. aggregate demand increases less than in proportion to n); hence

$$G_n < nG_1 \quad \text{for } n=2,3,\dots,;$$

and

$$G_n \textit{ is monotone decreasing in } p. \tag{IV.2}$$

(Hence, so is G_n^{-1}.)

Remark Assumption IV holds for the symmetric quadratic utility function. For in that case (cf. eq. (20′)) (with $y_i = x_i$ and $\rho_i \equiv \sigma - p$)

$$G_n = \Sigma\, x_i = \frac{n(\sigma - p)}{\alpha + (n-1)\beta}$$

Therefore, and since β is positive,

$$\frac{G_n/n}{G_{n-1}/(n-1)} = \frac{\alpha + (n-2)\beta}{\alpha + (n-1)\beta} < 1.$$

Let Π_1^{M1} denote the profit under monopoly and let Π_i^{M2} be the profit of the i-th firm under joint monopoly when there are two firms ($n=2$), with total output divided equally.

Theorem 2

Under Assumption IV,

$$\Pi_1^{M1} \geqq \Pi_i^{M2}.$$

Proof

Let the joint monopoly charge the price p^{M2} and sell the quantity q^{M2}. Assume that each of the two firms produces and sells $x_i = q^{M2}/2$, $i=1,2$.

Denote by $c(\cdot)$ the average cost function common to the two firms.

Then

$$\Pi_i^{M2} = [p^{M2} - c(q^{M2}/2)] \cdot (q^{M2}/2).$$

On the other hand, under profit maximizing monopoly ($n=1$), $\Pi_1^M = [p^{M1} - c(q^{M1})] \cdot q^{M1}$.

Suppose

$$\Pi_i^{M2} > \Pi_1^{M1}.$$

We show that (p^{M1}, q^{M1}) was not profit maximizing for $n=1$, contrary to hypothesis. To see this, consider the situation where there is only one firm in the field, and let this firm produce and sell the quantity $\bar{q} = q^{M2}/2$.

This will sell at $\bar{p}$, where $G_1(\bar{p}) = \bar{q}$. Now, by Assumption (IV.1),

$$G_1(p^{M2}) > \frac{1}{2} G_2(p^{M2}) = \frac{1}{2} q^{M2} = \bar{q}.$$

But

$$\left.\begin{array}{l} G_1(p^{M2}) > \bar{q} \\ \text{and} \\ G_1(\bar{p}) = \bar{q} \end{array}\right\} \Rightarrow \bar{p} > p^{M2},$$

by Assumption (IV.2), i.e. by the monotonicity of G_n.

On the other hand, the average cost remains the same as under the two-firm joint monopoly, i.e., it is $c(\bar{q})$.

Hence the profit now is

$$\bar{\Pi}_1 = [\bar{p} - c(\bar{q})] \cdot \bar{q} > [p^{M2} - c(\bar{q}) \cdot \bar{q} \equiv \Pi_i^{M2}.$$

But from the above supposition that $\Pi_i^{M2} > \Pi_1^{M1}$, it now follows that $\bar{\Pi}_1 > \Pi_i^{M2} \geqq \Pi_i^{M1}$, so that (q^{M1}, p^{M1}) was not profit maximizing for $n=1$, contrary to the hypothesis.

Corollary Under Assumption IV, if monopoly is displaced by symmetric duopoly (of any form), the *individual* profits (i.e. profit rates) cannot go up and may go down.

3 MONOPOLY ($n=1$)

In order to study the behavior of firms as their number n varies, we start by examining the case $n=1$, the monopoly.

Monopoly

The monopolist is assumed to be maximizing profits

$$\pi = xr(x),$$

where x is the level of output, and $r(x)$ the per unit profit; i.e.

$$r(x)=p(x)-c(x),$$

where $p(x)$ is the price received (=average revenue) and $c(x)$ the average cost when x units are produced and sold.

Although much of our analysis can be generalized, we shall confine ourselves to the rather special parametric cases where both the utility function generating demand and the average cost function are quadratic.

Under the assumptions made,

$$p(x)=\sigma-\alpha x,$$

and

$$c(x)=c_2x^2+c_1x+c_0.$$

In order that the cost functions have the usually postulated (U-shape) properties, we make the following assumptions:[7]

(1) $c_2>0$ (a U-shaped curve);

(2) $c_1<0$ (so that the vertex of the 'U' has a positive abscissa $=-[c_1]/[2c_2]$);

(3) $c^*\equiv c\left(-\frac{c_1}{2c_2}\right)=\frac{4c_0c_2-c_1^2}{4c_2}>0$

(*positive* minimum cost as required by Assumption II); i.e.

$$4c_0c_2-c_1^2>0;$$

from (1) and (3), it follows that

(4) $c_0>0$.

Remark For some of the results (e.g. Cournot oligopoly), (3) could be weakened to (3′): $c^*\geqq 0$.

On the demand side, with $n=1$, we have

$$U=-\tfrac{1}{2}\alpha x^2+\sigma x+z \quad \alpha>0, \sigma>0.$$

Hence utility maximization yields

$$\sigma-\alpha x=p,$$

and the demand function is

$$x=\frac{\sigma}{\alpha}-\frac{1}{\alpha}p,$$

or

$$p=\sigma-\alpha x.$$

Here Assumption I is satisfied, with

$$K=\frac{\sigma^2}{4\alpha};$$

i.e.,

$$px\leqq\frac{\sigma^2}{4\alpha}\quad\text{for all } x.$$

We now examine conditions on the parameters that make possible equilibria with a positive level of output. Obviously, such equilibria are impossible if $r(x)<0$ for all $x>0$, since then also $\pi(x)\equiv xr(x)<0$ for all $x>0$ while $x(0)=0$ and so $x=0$ is the unique profit maximizer.

But $r(x)>0$ for all $x>0$ is also impossible because,[8] by $c_2>0$, the unit profit function

$$r(x)\equiv -c_2x^2+Px-Q/c_2$$

is represented by a parabola with vertex upward. Hence a necessary condition for the existence of positive output equilibria is that the quadratic $r(x)=0$ have real roots and that at least one of these roots be positive.

The real roots condition requires that the discriminant be non-negative, i.e.,

$$\Delta^*\equiv P^2-4Q\geqq 0.$$

Denote the real roots of $r(x)=0$ by x^* and x^{**}, with $x^*\leqq x^{**}$.

In order that Assumption III be satisfied (that the lower break-even point be positive) we must have $x^*>0$, hence $x^{**}>0$. But then both the sum and the product of the two roots must be positive, i.e. (since $c_2>0$), hence

$$P>0$$

and

$$Q>0.$$

(In terms of the original parameters,

$$c_1+\alpha<0,$$

$$c_0-\sigma>0.)$$

Consider now the profit function $\pi(x)\equiv xr(x)=-c_2x^3+Px-(Q/c_2)x$. It is a cubic going through the origin. For positive values of x the sign of $\pi(x)$ is the same as that of $r(x)$. Under the assumptions made above, there exist real positive numbers x^*, x^{**} (with $x^*\leqq x^{**}$) such that $\pi(x^*)=\pi(x^{**})=0$, and $\pi(x)<0$ for $x\in(0,x^*)$ and $x>x^{**}$. If $\Delta^*=0$, $x=x^*=x^{**}>0$ is one maximizer of $\pi(\cdot)$ while $x=0$ is the only other. If $\Delta^*>0$, so that $x^*<x^{**}$, then $\pi(x)>0$ for $x^*<x<x^{**}$, and the unique maximizer of $\pi(\cdot)$ is found in the open interval (x^*,x^{**}).

In either case the unique *positive* maximizer is obtained as the greater root of the quadratic

$$\pi'(x)=0,$$

i.e. of

$$-3c_2x^2+2Px-Q/c_2=0.$$

Note that the discriminant Δ of the latter quadratic satisfies

$$\Delta\equiv P^2-3Q=P^2-4Q+Q=\Delta^*+Q.$$

I.e. since we are assuming $\Delta^*\geqq 0$ and $Q>0$, it follows that $\Delta>0$, so that $\pi'(x)=0$ has two distinct real positive roots, to be denoted by ξ_1, ξ_2, with $\xi_1<\xi_2$. Clearly, ξ_2 is the unique *positive* maximizer of $\pi(\cdot)$, although $x=0$ is another maximizer when $\Delta^*=0$.

In fact, ξ_2 is certainly a *local* maximizer since

$$\xi_2=\frac{1}{3c_2}(P+\sqrt{P^2-3Q})>\frac{P}{3c_2}$$

(because $P^2-3Q\equiv\Delta>0$ and $c_2>0$), and hence[9]

$$\pi''(\xi_2)=-6c_2\xi_2+2P<0.$$

Furthermore, it can be shown (see Appendix, pp.320–1) that, under the assumptions made,

$$x^* \leqq \xi_2 \leqq x^{**},$$

with the equalities holding if and only if $\Delta^* = 0$. Hence, whether $\Delta^* = 0$ or $\Delta^* > 0$, ξ_2 is the unique global positive maximizer of $\pi(\cdot)$.

In Figure 9.2 below we show three possible forms of the monopolist's profit function. In Figure 9.2a there are positive profits at the equilibrium point $\xi_2 > 0$. (Here $\Delta^* > 0$.) In Figure 9.2b there is a positive equilibrium output ξ_2 but with zero profits. (Here $\Delta^* = 0$.) In Figure 9.2c profits are negative for all positive outputs although there is a local maximum ξ_2. (Here $\Delta^* < 0$ while $\Delta > 0$.)

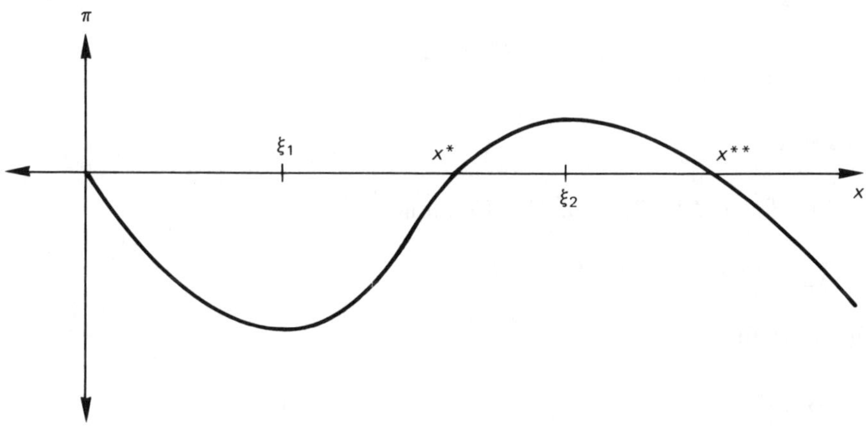

Figure 9.2a

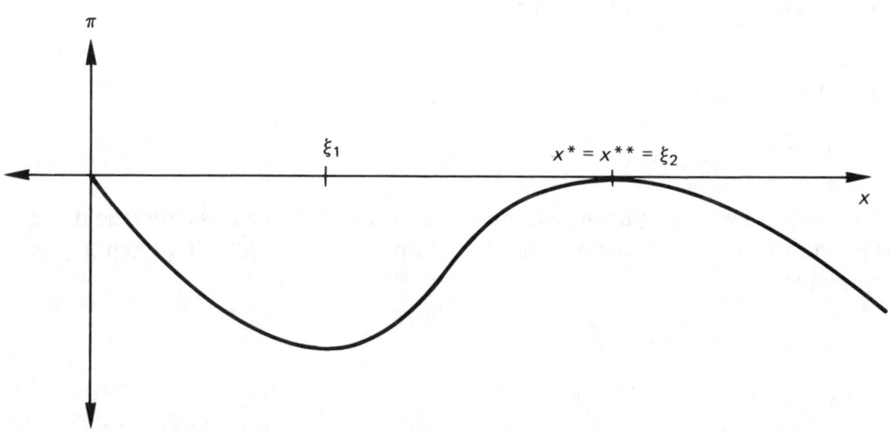

Figure 9.2b

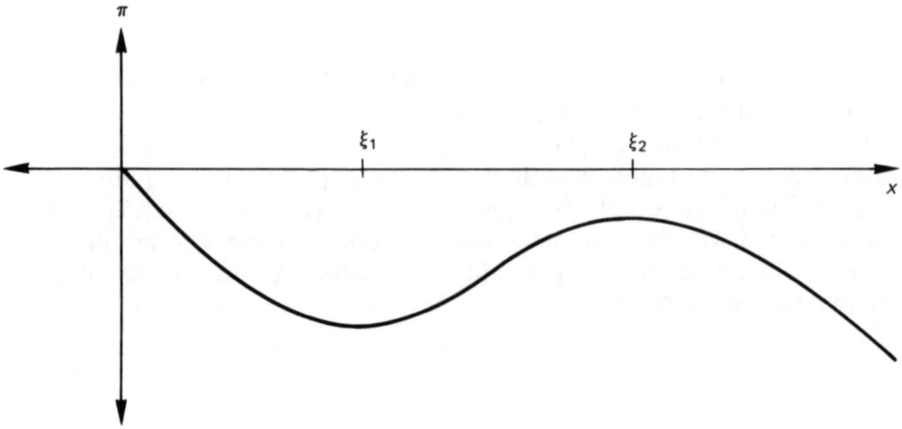

Figure 9.2c

Appendix

1. Proof that $\Delta^* > 0$ (resp. $\Delta^* = 0$) implies

$$\xi_2 > x^* \quad (\text{resp. } \xi_2 = x^*).$$

The inequality

$$\xi_2 \geqq x^*$$

is equivalent to

$$\frac{1}{3c_2}(P + \sqrt{\Delta}) \geqq \frac{1}{2c_2}(P - \sqrt{\Delta^*}),$$

i.e. since $c_2 > 0$, to

$$2\sqrt{\Delta} \geqq P - 3\sqrt{\Delta^*}. \qquad (^0)$$

Now, since $\Delta > 0$ by hypothesis, the inequalities $(^0)$ are necessarily true if the right-hand side is non-positive. So suppose $P - 3\sqrt{\Delta^*} > 0$. Then $(^0)$ is equivalent to

$$4\Delta \geqq (P - 3\sqrt{\Delta^*})^2,$$

i.e. to

$$P\sqrt{\Delta^*} \geqq \Delta^*. \qquad (^{00})$$

Clearly, the equality sign holds when $\Delta^* = 0$, so then $\xi_2 = x^*$. On the other hand, if $\Delta^* > 0$, $(^{00})$ becomes

$$P^2 \geqq \Delta^* \equiv P^2 - 4Q$$

which is equivalent to $0 \geqq -4Q$. But $Q > 0$ by hypothesis, hence $(^{00})$ holds with $>$ sign, thus $\xi_2 > x^*$ when $\Delta^* > 0$.

QED

2. Since $\Delta^* = 0$ if and only if $x^* = x^{**}$, we now know (from **1** above) that $\Delta^* = 0$ implies $x^* = \xi_2 = x^{**}$.

It remains to be shown that, for $\Delta^* > 0$, we have

$$\xi_2 < x^{**}.$$

This inequality is equivalent to

$$\frac{1}{3c_2}(P + \sqrt{\Delta}) < \frac{1}{2c_2}(P + \sqrt{\Delta^*}).$$

In view of $c_2 > 0$, this is equivalent to

$$2\sqrt{\Delta} < P + 3\sqrt{\Delta^*},$$

and – because $\Delta > 0$ by hypothesis – to

$$4\Delta < (P + 3\sqrt{\Delta^*})^2.$$

The latter simplifies to

$$4Q - P^2 < P\sqrt{\Delta^*},$$

i.e.

$$-\Delta^* < P\sqrt{\Delta^*},$$

which is necessarily true when $\Delta^* > 0$ and $P > 0$. Hence $\Delta^* > 0$ implies $\xi_2 < x^{**}$.

QED

Remark

In Chamberlin's model it is necessarily the case that a firm's equilibrium output is below the level minimizing the average cost (in our model

$-[c_1]/[2c_2]$). This is so because profits are assumed zero and so occur at the point of tangency of the average cost curve with the downward sloping average revenue curve which must be to the left of the minimum of the U-shaped average cost curve.

But in our model, despite free entry, there can be equilibrium with positive profits – if an additional entry would result in negative profits. It is therefore of interest to inquire whether equilibrium at or above minimum average cost level is possible. The answer is in the affirmative. We have two illustrative examples.

Example 1 Here $c(x)=3x^2-6x+5$, $\sigma=4$, $\alpha=1$, $c(\cdot)$ is minimized at 1 and monopoly profits are also maximized at 1.

Example 2 With the same cost function and $\sigma=4$, let $\alpha=\frac{1}{2}$. Here again profits are minimized at 1, but monopoly profits are maximized at $x=1.123$, which is to the right of $-(c_1)/(2c_2)=1$. (To make the examples complete one should select additional parameters so that oligopoly for $n\geqq 2$ results in negative profits.)

4 OLIGOPOLY

We now proceed to the study of oligopoly – where $n\geqq 2$. (Much of the analysis will also cover the case $n=1$.)

We consider the two classic versions – those associated with the names of Cournot and Bertrand. In the main, we only consider symmetric solutions. (We do show that for $n=2$ asymmetric Cournot solutions do not exist.)

We start by finding conditions under which any symmetric solution can yield non-negative profits for positive outputs (the same for all firms).

Denote the i-th firm's output by x_i, the price it charges by p_i, unit profit by r_i, and its total profit by π_i. Also, let its average cost at output x_i be denoted by c^i. I.e.,

$$c^i\equiv c(x_i)\equiv c_2x_i^2+c_1x_i+c_0,$$

$$p_i\equiv p_i(\mathbf{x})=\sigma-\alpha x_i-\beta\sum_{j\neq i}x_j$$

$$r_i(\mathbf{x})=p_i-c^i$$

$$\pi_i(\mathbf{x})=x_ir_i(\mathbf{x})$$

where

$$\mathbf{x}=(x_1,\ldots,x_n).$$

The condition that profits be non-negative for positive outputs becomes

$$r_i(\mathbf{x}) \equiv p_i(\mathbf{x}) - c_i(x_i) \geqq 0 \quad \text{for } \mathbf{x} \gg 0.$$

Now assume *symmetry*, so that all outputs x_i are equal, with their common value denoted by x.

Then, for each $i = 1,...,n$, we have

$$p_i(\mathbf{x}) = \sigma - \alpha x - \beta(n-1)x,$$

$$c(x_i) = c_2 x^2 + c_1 x + c_0,$$

and, using the abbreviated notation,

$$\begin{aligned} r_i(\mathbf{x}) &\equiv p_i(\mathbf{x}) - c(x_i) \\ &= -c_2x^2 + [-(c_1+\alpha) - \beta(n-1)]x - (c_0 - \sigma) \\ &= -c_2x^2 + [P - 2M_n]x - Q/c_2 \\ &= r[x], \end{aligned}$$

where

$$M_n = \frac{\beta}{2}(n-1)$$

and, as previously, $P = -(c_1 + \alpha)$, $Q = c_2(c_0 - \sigma)$.

As before, we assume $c_2 > 0$, $P > 0$, $Q > 0$, and also $\alpha > \beta > 0$. (Some of the analysis remains valid when $\alpha = \beta$ or when $\beta = 0$.)

As in the case of monopoly, we require that, for some $x > 0$, we should have $r_i(\mathbf{x}) \geqq 0$ and that the first break-even point be positive (to satisfy Assumption III). This requires that the quadratic $r[x] = 0$ have two real positive roots; $x^* \leqq x^{**}$.[10] Thus, the discriminant Δ_n^* must be non-negative,

$$\Delta_n^* \equiv (P - 2M_n)^2 - 4Q \geqq 0, \tag{26}$$

and the sum of the two roots ($x^* \leqq x^{**}$) must be positive, i.e.

$$P - 2M_n > 0. \tag{27}$$

(Note, that for $n = 1$ (where $M_1 = 0$) these are the previously obtained conditions for the monopoly case.)

We observe that these conditions are 'inherited downward'. Thus,

$$P-2M_{n-1}=P-\beta(n-2)$$
$$=P-\beta(n-1)+\beta=P-2M_n+\beta>P-2M_n,$$

and so $P-2M_n>0$ implies $P-2M_{n-1}>0$. Similarly, when $P-2M_n>0$, we have

$$\Delta^*_{n-1}=[P-2M_{n-1}]^2-4Q$$
$$>[P-2M_n]^2-4Q=\Delta^*_n,$$

so that $\Delta^*_n\geqq 0$ implies $\Delta^*_{n-1}>0$. (Here the inheritance yields a strengthening of the inequality.)

Thus, if non-negative profits (with positive break-even points) are possible at a symmetric output in a market with n firms, then positive profits are possible in markets with any number of firms less than n. This agrees with one's common sense insight.

From now on we must treat separately the Cournot and Bertrand oligopoly models.

4.A Cournot Oligopoly

Here we seek a Nash equilibrium with the x_i as strategy variables and $\pi_i(\mathbf{x})$ as the payoff function. The algebraic situation is similar to that of the monopoly case.

Thus, the i-th firm wishes to maximize $\pi_i(\mathbf{x})$ with respect to $x_i\geqq 0$, treating $\mathbf{x}_{-i}\equiv(x_1,\ldots,x_{i-1},x_{i+1},\ldots,x_n)$ as given. At Cournot equilibrium $\mathbf{x}\equiv(x_1,\ldots,x_n)$, for all i,

$$\pi_i(\mathbf{x})\geqq\pi_i(x_i',x_{-i})\quad\text{for all } x_i'\geqq 0.$$

We shall only be interested in positive output equilibria, and – except in Section 4.A.AS below – only in symmetric equilibria.

Let $\mathbf{x}$ be a positive Cournot equilibrium. Then, for each i,

$$x_i>0,$$

and hence

$$\left.\frac{\partial\pi_i(x_i',x_{-i})}{\partial x_i'}\right|_{x_i'=x_i}=0.$$

Now

$$\frac{\partial \pi_i}{\partial x'_i} = \frac{\partial}{\partial x'_i}[x'_i r_i(x'_i, x_{-i})]$$

$$= r_i(x'_i, x_{-i}) + x'_i[-\alpha - 2c_2 x'_i - c_1]$$

$$= [\sigma - \alpha x'_i - \beta \sum_{j \neq i} x_j - c_2 x'^2_i - c_1 x'_i - c_0] + x'_i[-\alpha - 2c_2 x'_i - c_1]$$

$$= -3c_2 x'^2_i - 2(\alpha + c_1)x'_i - \beta \sum_{j \neq i} x_j - (c_0 - \sigma).$$

Also,

$$\frac{\partial^2 \pi_i}{\partial x'^2_i} = -6c_2 x'_i + 2P.$$

Hence for x'_i to be even a local profit maximizer, it is necessary that

$$x'_i \geqq \frac{P}{3c_2}.$$

4.A.S Symmetric Solutions

4.A.S.1 Local Solutions

Under the assumption of symmetry,

$$x_1 = \ldots = x_n \equiv y \quad (say),$$

hence the above condition

$$\left.\frac{\partial \pi_i}{\partial x'_i}\right|_{x'_i = x_i} = 0$$

becomes

$$\left.\frac{\partial \pi_i}{\partial x'_i}\right|_{\substack{x'_i = x_i = y \\ x_j = y (j \neq i)}} = 0.$$

Thus, we obtain

$$-3c_2 y^2 - 2(c_1 + \alpha)y - \beta(n-1)y - (c_0 - \sigma) = 0.$$

In the abbreviated notation this can be written as

$$\boxed{-3c_2y^2+2[P-M_n]y-Q/c_2=0.}$$

We note that the discriminant Δ_n of this quadratic is given by

$$\Delta_n \equiv (P-M_n)^2-3Q.$$

For a positive solution the roots must be real, i.e. $\Delta_n \geqq 0$, and the second derivative $\partial^2\pi_n/\partial x_i'^2$ non-positive.

Now, at a symmetric solution y, the necessary second-order condition is

$$y \geqq \frac{P}{3c_2}$$

The roots of the preceding quadratic (to be denoted[11] by $\eta_1 \leqq \eta_2$) are given by

$$\eta_1,\eta_2=\frac{1}{3c_2}(P-M_n \pm \sqrt{\Delta_n}).$$

From now on we shall usually omit the subscript n in M_n and in Δ_n. We note that

$$\begin{aligned}\Delta &= (P-M)^2-3Q\\ &= [(P-2M)+M]^2-3Q\\ &= \Delta^* + 4M^2+4MP+Q>\Delta^*,\end{aligned}$$

where the last inequality is due to the fact that M, P, Q are all assumed positive.

Since $\Delta^* \geqq 0 \Rightarrow \Delta > 0$ and $M>0$ for $n>1$, we have

$$\eta_1=\frac{P-M-\sqrt{\Delta_n}}{3c_2}<\frac{P}{3c_2},$$

so η_1 is not even a local positive maximizer. If a positive maximizer exists, it must be η_2.

4.A.S.2 Global Conditions

We now have conditions under which there is a positive point $x^*=x^{**}$ or an interval (x^*,x^{**}), $x^*<x^{**}$, where profits are non-negative, and a candidate η_2 for a symmetric positive profit maximizer.

But in order that η_2 be in fact a global profit maximizer it is necessary (and sufficient) that η_2 be at that point or within that interval, i.e. that (as in the case of monopoly) $x^* \leqq \eta_2 \leqq x^{**}$.

We shall now study conditions under which these inequalities hold.

First, we study conditions under which

$$x^* \leqq \eta_2.$$

This inequality is equivalent to

$$\frac{1}{2c_2}[(P-2M)-\sqrt{\Delta^*}] \leqq \frac{1}{3c_2}[(P-M)+\sqrt{\Delta}].$$

Since $c_2>0$, this is equivalent to

$$3[(P-2M)-\sqrt{\Delta^*}] \leqq 2[(P-M)+\sqrt{\Delta}],$$

or, after simplification,

$$P-4M-\sqrt{\Delta^*} \leqq 2\sqrt{\Delta}. \tag{28}$$

Since $\sqrt{\Delta}>0$ by hypothesis, the preceding inequality is necessarily true if $P-4M-\sqrt{\Delta^*} \leqq 0$. Hence we need only examine the case where

$$P-4M-3\sqrt{\Delta^*}>0, \tag{29}$$

in which case also

$$k \equiv P-4M>0. \tag{30}$$

Since (by (29)) both sides of (28) are positive, the inequality is preserved after squaring. This yields

$$k^2+9\Delta^*-2k\cdot 3\sqrt{\Delta^*} \leqq 4\Delta,$$

or, after cancellation,

$$k^2+2kM-4Q \leqq k\sqrt{\Delta^*}. \tag{31}$$

This inequality necessarily holds if its left-hand side is non-positive.

Hence we only need to consider the case where

$$k^2+2km-4Q>0. \tag{32}$$

In this case, we may square both sides of (31), thus getting

$$(k^2-2kM-4Q)^2 \leqq k^2\Delta^*,$$

Expanding, we get (since $\Delta^*=k^2+4M^2+4kM+-4Q$)

$$k^4+4k^2M^2+16Q^2+4k^3M-8k^2Q-16kMQ$$

$$\leqq k^2(k^2+4M^2+4kM-4Q).$$

After cancellation and simplification this becomes

$$4Q-k^2-4kM \leqq 0,$$

i.e.

$$k^2+4kM-4Q \geqq 0.$$

But the left-hand side is necessarily positive because of (32), and so the last inequality follows. Hence $x^* \leqq \eta_2$ holds whether (32) is true or false. This completes the proof that $x^* \leqq \eta_2$ without any additional conditions.

We now proceed to investigate conditions under which

$$\eta_2 \leqq x^{**}.$$

This inequality may be written as

$$\frac{1}{3c_2}[(P-M)+\sqrt{\Delta}] \leqq \frac{1}{2c_2}[(P-2M)+\sqrt{\Delta^*}].$$

After cancellation and simplification (with $c_2>0$), we get

$$2\sqrt{\Delta} \leqq k+3\sqrt{\Delta^*} \tag{33}$$

where, again,

$$k \equiv P-4M.$$

We now distinguish three cases, depending on the sign of k.

(i) First, let

$$k=0.$$

Then (33) becomes

$$2\sqrt{\Delta} \leqq 3\sqrt{\Delta^*}, \tag{33'}$$

with both sides positive (since $\Delta > 0$ by hypothesis). Squaring both sides

$$4\Delta \leqq 9\Delta^*,$$

i.e. since $k=0$,[12]

$$4(9M^2-3Q) \leqq 9(4M^2-4Q),$$

i.e.

$$-12Q \leqq -36Q,$$

i.e.

$$24Q \leqq 0,$$

which is impossible because $Q > 0$ by hypothesis.

Hence a necessary condition for $\eta_2 \leqq x^{**}$ is that $k \neq 0$; i.e. that

$$P \neq 4M.$$

(ii) Second, consider the case

$$k<0.$$

Here we rewrite (33) as

$$2\sqrt{\Delta}-k \leqq 3\sqrt{\Delta^*} \tag{33''}$$

and square, thus getting

$$4\Delta + k^2 - 4k\sqrt{\Delta} \leqq 9\Delta^*,$$

i.e.

$$9\Delta^* - 4\Delta \geqq k^2 - 4k\sqrt{\Delta}.$$

Now

$$9\Delta^* - 4\Delta = 9[k^2 + 4M^2 + 4kM - 4Q] - 4[k^2 + 9M^2 + 6kM - 3Q] \tag{34}$$

$$= 5k^2 + 12kM - 24Q.$$

So (33″) becomes

$$5k^2 + 12kM - 24Q \geqq k^2 - 4k\sqrt{\Delta}.$$

Since here $k < 0$, we can write this as

$$-24Q - |k| \cdot (5k + 12M) \geqq k^2 + 4 \cdot |k| \text{«} \sqrt{\Delta}. \tag{35}$$

But

$$5k + 12M = 5[(P - 2M) - 2M] + 12M$$

$$= 5(P - 2M) + 2M > 0,$$

since $P - 2M > 0$ by hypothesis (because $x^{**} > 0$). Hence the left-hand side of (35) is negative, while its right-hand side positive, and so (35) cannot be true. We conclude that k cannot be negative when $\eta_2 \leqq x^{**}$.

(iii) It remains to investigate the case

$$k > 0.$$

Here both sides of (33) are positive. After squaring this yields

$$4\Delta \leqq k^2 + 9\Delta^* + 6k\sqrt{\Delta^*},$$

or

$$4\Delta - 9\Delta^* \leqq k^2 + 6k\sqrt{\Delta^*};$$

hence, using (34),

$$-5k^2 - 12kM + 24Q \leqq k^2 + 6k\sqrt{\Delta^*},$$

i.e.

$$-6k^2-12kM+12Q\leqq 6k\sqrt{\Delta^*},$$

or

$$-k^2-2kM+4Q\leqq k\sqrt{\Delta^*}, \tag{36'}$$

$$k^2+2kM-4Q\geqq -k\sqrt{\Delta^*}. \tag{36''}$$

Clearly a sufficient condition for (36″) to hold is that

$$k^2+2kM-4Q\geqq 0, \tag{37}$$

since the right-hand side of (36) is non-positive. It remains therefore to examine the case

$$k^2+2kM-4Q<0. \tag{38}$$

In this case both sides of (36′) are positive. Upon squaring this yields

$$k^4+4k^2M^2+16Q^2+4k^3M-8k^2Q-16kMQ$$

$$\leqq k^2(k^2+4M^2-4kM-4Q)$$

i.e.

$$16Q^2-8k^2Q-16kMQ\leqq k^2 4Q,$$

or

$$16Q^2-4Qk^2-16kMQ\leqq 0.$$

Dividing by $4Q>0$, we get

$$4Q-k^2-4kM\leqq 0.$$

Hence, $\eta_2\leqq x^{**}$, if and only if $k>0$, and either ('the first subcase')

$$k^2+2kM-4Q\geqq 0, \tag{37}$$

or the following two inequalities hold ('the second subcase'):

$$k^2+2kM-4Q<0 \tag{38}$$

and

$$k^2+4kM-4Q\geqq 0. \tag{39}$$

But note that, since $kM>0$, it is the case that (37) implies (39). (This is also the case for $n=1$, where M is replaced by $M_1=0$.)

In fact,

for $\eta_2\leqq x^{**}$, *it is necessary and sufficient that* $k>0$ *and that* (39) *hold.*

Proof

1. Necessity: Let $\eta_2\leqq x^{**}$. We have seen above that $k\leqq 0$ is ruled out. So suppose $k>0$ but (39) is false; then, of course, we do not have the second subcase [(38) with (39)], but neither do we have the first subcase [(37)], since 'not (39)' implies 'not (37)'. Hence $\eta_2\leqq x^{**}$.

2. Sufficiency: Suppose $k>0$ and (39) holds. If (37) also holds, we have the first subcase and $\eta_2\leqq x^{**}$. On the other hand, if (37) is false, then (38) holds and we are in the second subcase. Again, $\eta_2\leqq x^{**}$.

Inheritance

We now proceed to study the problem of inheritance. It was seen already that if $\Delta_n^*\geqq 0$, then $\Delta_n>0$ and also $\Delta_{n-1}^*>0$. Similarly, the positivity of roots is inherited downward. It only remains to check the condition (39) above.

Thus, suppose that $k_n^2+4k_nM_n-4Q\geqq 0$. To prove that downward inheritance obtains, it is enough to show that

$$k_{n-1}^2+4k_{n-1}M_{n-1}\geqq k_n^2+4k_nM_n.$$

But the latter inequality turns out to be equivalent to $M_{n-1}\leqq M_n$, i.e. $n-2\leqq n-1$. This completes the proof.

4.A.S.3 Cournot Profits as a Function of the Size of Industry

We now proceed to study the behavior of an individual firm's profits as more firms enter the market. As was to be expected, these profits do go down.

4.A.S.3.a *The case of non-zero (quadratic) costs; symmetric solutions*

4.A.S.3.a.0 *Main result: profits decrease with n*

Here we consider the situation with

$$\begin{cases} p_i = \sigma_i - \omega_{ii} x_i - \sum_{j \in)i(} \omega_{ij} x_j \\ c^i \equiv c(x_j) = c_0 + c_1 x_i + c_2 x_i^2 \end{cases}$$

$$\pi_i = (p_i - c^i) x_i \quad i = 1, \ldots, n. \tag{40}$$

[We write $)i(= \{1, \ldots, n\} \backslash \{i\}$.]

Again,

$$\sigma_i = \sigma,$$

and

$$\omega_{ik} = \begin{cases} \alpha & (i = k) \\ \beta & (i \neq k) \end{cases}$$

with $\alpha > \beta > 0$.

Maximization yields as a necessary first-order condition (for $x_i > 0$)

$$\frac{\partial \pi_i}{\partial x_i} \equiv (p_i = c^i) + \left(\frac{\partial p_i}{\partial x_i} - \frac{\partial c^i}{\partial x_i} \right) x_i = 0,^{13} \tag{41}$$

i.e.

$$p_i - c(x_i) + [-\alpha - (c_1 + 2c_2 x_i)] x_i = 0. \tag{42}$$

i.e.

$$p_i = c_0 + c_1 x_i + c_2 x_i^2 + [\alpha + (c_1 + 2c_2 x_i)] x_i \tag{43}$$

$$= c_0 + (2c_1 + \alpha) x_i + 3c_2 x_2^2.$$

At a symmetric solution, with $\sigma_i = \sigma$, and $x_1 = \ldots = x_n$, this yields the following quadratic equation for x_i:

$$3c_2 x_2^2 + 2[c_1 + \alpha + (n-1)\beta/2] x_i + (c_0 - \sigma) = 0 \quad i = 1, \ldots, n \tag{44}$$

We make assumptions implying that the roots η_1,η_2 of (44) to be real, positive, and distinct for all n' such that $1 \leqq n' \leqq n$ (see 4.A.S.3.b.2). It is shown in 4.A.S.1 above that the larger root η_2 is the one that maximizes profits.

In what follows we show that, for $x_i > 0$,

$$x_i \frac{d}{dx_i}(p_i - c^i) + (p_i - c^i) > 0 \tag{45}$$

and

$$\frac{dx_i}{dn} < 0. \tag{46}$$

Now,

$$\frac{d\pi_i}{dn} = \frac{d[(p_i - c^i)x_i]}{dn} = \frac{d(p_i - c^i)}{dn} . x_i + (p_i - c^i)\frac{dx_i}{dn} \tag{47}$$

$$= \frac{d(p_i - c^i)}{dx_i} \cdot \frac{dx_i}{dn} . x_i + (p_i - c^i)\frac{dx_i}{dn}$$

$$= \left[x_i \frac{d(p_i - c^i)}{dx_i} + (p_i - c^i) \right] \frac{dx_i}{dn}.$$

Hence, (45), (46), and (47) will yield

$$\frac{d\pi_i}{dn} < 0, \tag{48}$$

since

$$x_i > 0, \tag{49.1}$$

and

$$p_i - c^i > 0. \tag{49.2}$$

4.A.S.3.a.1 *Proof of* (46), *Section 4.A.S.3.a.0: $dx_i/dn < 0$*

At a symmetric equilibrium we have, by eq. (44),

$$3c_2 x^2 (c_1 + \alpha_n)x + (c_0 - \sigma) = 0 \quad i = 1, \ldots, n \tag{50}$$

where

$$\alpha_n \equiv \alpha + \frac{n-1}{2}\beta = \alpha\left(1 + \frac{n-1}{2}\theta\right) \text{ and } \theta = \frac{\beta}{\alpha}, \tag{51}$$

and we write x for x_i.

Note that, from (51),

$$\frac{d\alpha_n}{dn} = \alpha\frac{\theta}{2} = \frac{\beta}{2} > 0. \tag{52}$$

It remains to obtain $dx/d\alpha_n$ from (50), bearing in mind that the larger of the two roots (assumed distinct) is to be used. We differentiate (50) implicitly with respect to α_n, thus obtaining

$$6c_2x\frac{dx}{d\alpha_n} + 2x + 2(c_1 + \alpha_n)\frac{dx}{d\alpha_n} = 0, \tag{53}$$

hence

$$[6c_2x + 2(c_1 + \alpha_n)]\frac{dx}{d\alpha_n} = -2x,$$

so that

$$\frac{dx}{d\alpha_n} = -\frac{x}{3c_2x + c_1 + \alpha_n}. \tag{54}$$

We now show that the denominator in (54) is positive (and hence $dx/d\alpha_n < 0$ when $x > 0$) when the larger (real distinct) root of (50) is used.

The value for the larger root of (50) is

$$x = \frac{1}{3c_2}[-(c_1 + \alpha_n) + \sqrt{\Delta}] \tag{55}$$

where Δ is the discriminant of (50) and $\sqrt{\Delta}$ denotes the absolute value of its square root. Since real distinct roots are assumed.

$$\sqrt{\Delta} > 0. \tag{56}$$

Hence, by (55) and (56),

$$x > \frac{1}{3c_2}[-(c_1 + \alpha_n)], \tag{57}$$

i.e.

$$3c_2x + c_1 + \alpha_n > 0, \tag{58}$$

which shows that the denominator of (54) is positive, and hence, for

$$x > 0, \tag{59}$$

$$\frac{dx}{d\alpha_n} < 0; \tag{60}$$

hence, by (52)

$$\frac{dx}{dn} = \frac{dx}{d\alpha_n} \cdot \frac{d\alpha_n n}{dn} = -\frac{x}{3c_2x + c_1 + \alpha_n} \cdot \frac{\beta}{2} < 0 \tag{61}$$

for $x > 0$.

4.A.S.3.a.2 *Proof of* (45) *in Section 4.A.S.3.a.0*

We want to show that

$$x\frac{d}{dx}(p_i - c^i) + (p_i - c^i) > 0. \tag{45}$$

(We write x for x_i.)

Now, by (42), Section 4.A.S.3.a, at a symmetric equilibrium we have

$$p_i - c^i = -[-\alpha - (c_1 + 2c_2x)]x \tag{62}$$

$$= (\alpha + c_1 + 2c_2x)x.$$

Hence,

$$\frac{d}{dx}(p_i - c^i) = \alpha + c_1 + 4c_2x. \tag{63}$$

Therefore, substituting (42) of Section 4.A.S.3.a and (63) into (45), we get

$$x(\alpha + c_1 + 4c_2x) + x(\alpha + c_1 + 2c_2x) > 0. \tag{45'}$$

Since $x > 0$ by hypothesis, this becomes

$$(\alpha + c_1 + 4c_2 x) + (\alpha + c_1 + 2c_2 x) > 0,$$

i.e.

$$\alpha + c_1 + 3c_2 x > 0. \tag{45''}$$

But, (45″) is equivalent to (58) Section 4.A.S.3.a.1 with $n = 1$, and so it holds by hypothesis. (That is, we assume the roots of (44), Section 4.A.S.3.a.0, to be real, positive, and distinct for all $1 \leqq n' \leqq n$.)

4.A.S.3.b *The special case of zero costs* ($c \equiv 0$)

Here profits are given by

$$\pi_i = p_i x_i \quad (i = 1, 2, \ldots, n) \tag{64}$$

and the (indirect) demand function is

$$p_i = \sigma_i - \omega_{ii} x_i - \sum_{j \in)i(} \omega_{ij} x_j . \tag{65}$$

Therefore, profit maximization yields

$$\frac{\delta \pi_i}{\delta x_i} \equiv p_i + x_i \left(\frac{\delta p_i}{\delta x_i} \right) \equiv p_i + x_i(-\omega_{ii}) = 0 \quad (i = 1, \ldots, n) \tag{66}$$

and

$$\frac{\partial^2 \pi_i}{\partial x_i^2} = -\omega_{ii} - \omega_{ii} = -2\omega_{ii} < 0,$$

where $\omega_{ii} = \alpha > 0$ (see (67), below). So the second-order condition is always satisfied. Let

$$\sigma_i = \sigma \quad \text{for all } i,$$

and

$$\omega_{ik} = \begin{cases} \alpha \text{ for } i = k, \\ \beta \text{ for } i \neq k. \end{cases} \tag{67}$$

Then, at a symmetric equilibrium, we have

$$x_1 = x_2 = \dots = x_n. \tag{68}$$

In the remainder of this section, due to symmetry, we can omit subscripts; thus we shall write $x = x_i$, $p = p_i$, $\pi = \pi_i$ for $i = 1,\dots,n$.

Hence, still at equilibrium, by (66) and (67),

$$\alpha x = p \tag{69}$$

and, by (65) and (67),

$$\alpha x = \sigma - [\alpha + (n-1)\beta]x. \tag{70}$$

From (70), we get (with $\theta \equiv \beta/\alpha$)

$$x = \frac{\sigma}{2\alpha} \cdot \frac{1}{1 + \frac{n-1}{2}\theta} \quad \text{for all } n \geqq 1, \tag{71'}$$

and, by (69),

$$p = \frac{\sigma}{2} \cdot \frac{1}{1 + \frac{n-1}{2}\theta} \quad \text{for all } n \geqq 1. \tag{72''}$$

Thus, both x and p decrease as the number of firms increases from one to two, and so on. Hence so do profits. We can also see it more directly, as follows.

From (69) and (64), at equilibrium,

$$\pi = xp = \alpha x^2, \tag{73}$$

and hence, by (73),

$$\pi = \alpha \left[\frac{\sigma}{2\alpha} \cdot \frac{1}{1 + \frac{n-1}{2}\theta} \right]^2 \quad \text{for all } n \geqq 1. \tag{74}$$

So, equilibrium profits (with zero costs) go down as the number of firms increases.

For latter reference, note that at a symmetric equilibrium (with zero costs), from (73), we have

$$\frac{d\pi}{dn} = 2\alpha x \frac{dx}{dn}, \tag{75}$$

and, by (71′),

$$\frac{d\pi}{dn} = 2\alpha \frac{\sigma}{2\alpha} \frac{1}{1 + \frac{n-1}{2}\theta} \cdot \frac{(-1)}{\left[1 + \frac{n-1}{2}\theta\right]^2} \frac{\theta}{2} < 0. \tag{76}$$

4.A.AS Asymmetric Cournot Solutions ($n = 2$)

In this section we show that, under our assumptions, there are no positive asymmetric solutions for Cournot duopoly.

Proof

Under duopoly, the profit function of the i-th firm is given by

$$\pi_i(x_i, x_j) = x_i r_i(x_i, x_j), \quad j \neq i;\ i, j \in \{1,2\},$$

where the unit profit function $r_i(x_i, x_j)$ of firm i is

$$r_i(x_i, x_j) = p_i(x_i, x_j) - c(x_i),$$

with

$$p_i(x_i, x_j) = \sigma - \alpha x_i - \beta x_j$$

and

$$c(x_i) = c_0 + c_1 x_i + c_2 x_i^2.$$

We assume $c_2 > 0$, $c_0 > \sigma$, $\alpha > \beta > 0$, $\alpha + c_1 < 0$. To make algebra more transparent we find it convenient to use the following notation:

$$-(\alpha + c_1) = P > 0,$$

$$c_2(c_0 - \sigma) = Q > 0,$$

$$\frac{\beta}{2} = M > 0.$$

In this notation we find that

$$\pi_i(x_i,x_j) = -c_2x_i^3 + Px_2^2 - \left(\frac{Q}{c_2} + 2Mx_j\right)x_i, \quad j \neq i;\ i,j \in \{1,2\}. \tag{Δ}$$

Suppose that an asymmetric positive Cournot solution (x_1,x_2) does exist. Then

(i) $0 < x_1$, $0 < x_2$, $x_1 \neq x_2$;

(ii) x_i *maximizes* $\pi_i(x_i,x_j)$ *with respect to* x_i *given* x_j for $i = 1,2$; $j \neq i$;

(iii) $\pi_i(x_i,x_j) \geqq 0, \quad i = 1,2;\ j \neq i.$

Without loss of generality, we shall assume in (i) that

$$x_1 < x_2. \tag{i$'$}$$

Since π_i is differentiable, (i) and (ii) imply

$$\frac{\partial \pi_i}{\partial x_i} = 0,$$

i.e.

$$-3c_2x_i^2 + 2Px_i - \left(\frac{Q}{c_2} + 2Mx_j\right) = 0, \quad i = 1,2.$$

Explicitly,

$$-3c_2x_1^2 + 2Px_1 - \left(\frac{Q}{c_2} + 2Mx_2\right) = 0 \tag{*.1}$$

$$-3c_2x_2^2 + 2Px_2 - \left(\frac{Q}{c_2} + 2Mx_1\right) = 0. \tag{*.2}$$

Subtracting the first equation from the second, we get

$$3c_2(x_1^2 - x_2^2) - 2P(x_1 - x_2) - 2M(x_1 - x_2) = 0,$$

i.e.

$$3c_2(x_1 - x_2)(x_1 + x_2) - 2P(x_1 - x_2) - 2M(x_1 - x_2) = 0.$$

By hypothesis (i), $x_1 - x_2 \neq 0$ and so may be cancelled in the preceding equation, yielding

$$3c_2(x_1 + x_2) - 2P - 2M = 0,$$

so that

$$x_1 + x_2 = \frac{2}{3c_2}(P + M),$$

and

$$x_2 = \frac{2}{3c_2}(P - M) - x_1. \tag{**}$$

Substituting x_2 from (**) into (*), we obtain

$$-3c_2x_1^2 + 2Px_1 - \left[\frac{Q}{c_2} + 2M\left(\frac{2(P+M)}{3c_2} - x_1\right)\right] = 0.$$

Collecting the x_1 terms and changing signs, this gives

$$3c_2x_1^2 - 2(P+M)x_1 + \left[\frac{Q}{c_2} + \frac{4M}{3c_2}(P+M)\right] = 0. \tag{***.1}$$

Carrying out the same exercise for x_2 we find that

$$3c_2x_2^2 - 2(P+M)x_2 + \left[\frac{Q}{c_2} + \frac{4M}{3c_2}(P+M)\right] = 0. \tag{***.2}$$

Since x_1 and x_2 satisfy the same quadratic, our assumption that a positive asymmetric Cournot solution exists implies that x_1 and x_2 are the two distinct real roots of this quadratic, i.e. of

$$3c_2x^2 - 2(P+M)x + \left[\frac{Q}{c_2} + \frac{4M}{3c_2}(P+M)\right] = 0, \tag{****}$$

with the smaller root equal to x_1 by (i'). The existence of distinct real roots implies that the discriminant Δ is positive, i.e. that

$$\Delta \equiv (P+M)^2 = 3Q - 4M(P+M) > 0. \tag{o}$$

[Given that they are real, the positivity of x_1 and x_2 follows from our assumptions which imply that $P+M>0$ (hence the sum of the roots is positive), and also that

$$\frac{Q}{c_2}+\frac{4M}{3c_2}(P+M)>0$$

(hence the product of the roots is positive).]

Solving the quadratic, we have

$$x_1,x_2=\frac{1}{3c_2}(P+M\pm\sqrt{\Delta}). \tag{oo}$$

The discriminant inequality (o) may be written as

$$3Q<P^2-2PM-3M^2.$$

Since $Q>0$ by hypothesis, it follows that

$$P^2-2PM-3M^2>0. \tag{ooo}$$

Defining $\gamma=M/P$, and remembering that $P>0$ by hypothesis, the preceding inequality may be written as

$$-3\gamma^2-2\gamma+1>0.$$

Since the quadratic $-3\gamma^2-2\gamma+1=0$ has roots -1 and $+\frac{1}{3}$, and since γ is necessarily positive, it follows that the last inequality implies

$$\gamma<\frac{1}{3}, \quad \text{i.e. } M<\frac{P}{3}. \tag{+}$$

We now turn to the requirement (iii) that profits be non-negative at the Cournot equilibrium values x_1,x_2. Since $x_i>0$, $i=1,2$, by hypothesis, we must have

$$r_i(x_i,x_j)\geqq 0, \quad i=1,2.$$

Thus, in particular, for $i=1$, we have by (Δ)

$$r_1(x_1,x_2)\equiv -c_2x_1^2+Px_1-\left(\frac{Q}{c_2}+2Mx_2\right)\geqq 0, \tag{Δ.1}$$

and, from maximization,

$$-3c_2x_1^2+2Px_1-\left(\frac{Q}{c_2}+2Mx_2\right)=0. \tag{*.1}$$

Solving (*.1) for $(Q)/(c_2)+2Mx_2$ and substituting into (Δ.1), we get

$$-c_2x_1^2+Px_1-[-3c_2x_1^2+2Px_1]\geqq 0,$$

i.e.

$$2c_2x_1^2-Px_1\geqq 0.$$

Since $x_1>0$ by hypothesis, it follows that

$$2c_2x_1-P\geqq 0,$$

i.e.

$$x_1\geqq\frac{P}{2c_2}.$$

Substituting into the preceding inequality the value of x_1 from (oo), we obtain

$$\frac{1}{3c_2}(P+M-\sqrt{\Delta})\geqq\frac{P}{2c_2}.$$

Cancelling c_2 and moving terms, this can be written as

$$-\frac{P}{6}+\frac{M}{3}\geqq\frac{\sqrt{\Delta}}{3},$$

i.e.

$$-P+2M\geqq 2\sqrt{\Delta}.$$

Since $\Delta>0$ by hypothesis, this implies

$$-P+2M>0,$$

hence

$$\gamma\equiv\frac{M}{P}>\frac{1}{2}.$$

But this contradicts the inequality (+) above which requires that $\gamma<\frac{1}{3}$.

This contradiction shows that there do not exist positive asymmetric Cournot solutions.

QED

In the preceding analysis we sought asymmetric solutions where both firms produced at a positive level of output. It is natural to ask whether there may be asymmetric solutions where one of the firms leaves production. This indeed can be the case.

We have an example where the following is true. If firm 1 operates at its (positive) monopoly level x_1, then $x_2=0$ is the global maximizer of profits for firm 2.

The parameters are chosen as follows: $c_1=1$, $P=4.5$, $M=1$, $Q=1$. The monopoly level of output for firm 1 is $x_1=2.88$, and given this x_1, we find

$$\frac{\partial \pi_2}{\partial x_2} = -3x_2^2 + 9x_2 - 6.77.$$

Clearly,

$$\left.\frac{\partial \pi_2}{\partial x_2}\right|_{x_2=0} < 0.$$

But in fact this quadratic has a negative discriminant, so that

$$\frac{\partial \pi_2}{\partial x_2} < 0$$

for all x_2. Hence $x_2=0$ is the unique global maximizer of profits for firm 2.

4.B Bertrand Oligopoly (symmetric solutions)

Here we seek Nash equilibria with the prices p_i as strategic variables.

We first obtain conditions for the existence of positive symmetric Bertrand solutions and then (in 4.B.3) study the behavior of an individual firm's profits as more firms enter.

4.B.1 Local Conditions

As before, we have

$$\pi_i(\mathbf{x}) = x_i[p_i(\mathbf{x}) - c(x_i)],$$

but now we must express the x_k's as functions of $\mathbf{p}=(p_1,\dots,p_n)$.

We have

$$p_i=\sigma-\sum_{k=1}^{n}\omega_{ik}x_k,$$

with $\omega_{ii}=\alpha$ and $\omega_{ij}=\beta$ for $i\neq j$. As before, we assume $\alpha>\beta>0$, and find it helpful to define $\theta=\beta/\alpha$, so that $0<\theta<1$.

In matrix form, we then have

$$\Omega\mathbf{x}=\boldsymbol{\sigma}-\mathbf{p},$$

where $\Omega=\|\omega_{ik}\|_{i,k=1,\dots,n}$, $\mathbf{x}=\begin{bmatrix}x_1\\ \\ x_n\end{bmatrix}$, $\boldsymbol{\sigma}=\begin{bmatrix}\sigma\\ \\ \sigma\end{bmatrix}$, $\mathbf{p}=\begin{bmatrix}p_1\\ \\ p_n\end{bmatrix}$, so that

$$\mathbf{x}=\Omega^{-1}(\boldsymbol{\sigma}-\mathbf{p}).$$

Writing $\Omega^{-1}=\|\omega^{ij}\|$, we have (see above, Section 2.5, equations (24) and (25)

$$\omega^{ii}=\frac{1}{\alpha(1-\theta)}\cdot\frac{1+(n-2)\theta}{1+(n-1)\theta}\quad\text{for } i\in\{1,\dots,n\},$$

and

$$\omega^{ij}=-\frac{1}{\alpha(1-\theta)}\cdot\frac{\theta}{1-(n-1)\theta}\quad\text{for } i,j\in\{1,\dots,n\},\ i\neq j.$$

Hence at a positive Bertrand equilibrium we have

$$\frac{\partial\pi_i}{\partial p_i}\equiv x_i[1+\omega^{ii}c'(x_i)]-\omega^{ii}[p_i(\mathbf{x})-c(x_i)]=0.$$

At a symmetric equilibrium,

$$p_1=\dots=p_n$$

and

$$x_1=\dots=x_n=z\quad(say).$$

Hence the preceding condition becomes

$$z[1+\omega^{ii}c'(z)]-\omega^{ii}[p_i-c(z)]=0 \tag{76'}$$

where, in our quadratic economy,

$$p_i = \sigma - \alpha x_i - \beta \sum_{j \neq i} x_j$$

$$= \sigma - \alpha z - \beta(n-1)z$$

$$= \sigma - \alpha z[1 + (n-1)\theta], \tag{76''}$$

so that we finally have

$$z[1 + \omega^{ii}(2c_2 z + c_1)] - \omega^{ii}\{\sigma - \alpha z[1 + (n-1)\theta] - c_2 z^2 - c_1 z - c_0\} = 0$$

or

$$z\left[\frac{1}{\omega^{ii}} + (2c_2 z + c_1)\right] - \{\sigma - \alpha z[1 + (n-1)\theta] - c_2 z^2 - c_1 z - c_0\} = 0, \tag{76'''}$$

where ω^{ii} has the value given above. Collecting terms, we get the quadratic

$$3c_2 z^2 + z \left\{ \frac{1}{\omega^{ii}} + 2c_1 + \alpha[1 + (n-1)\theta] \right\} + (c_0 - \sigma) = 0.$$

This can be rewritten as

$$3c_2 z^2 + z \left\{ 2c_1 + 2\alpha - \alpha + \frac{1}{\omega^{ii}} + \alpha[1 + (n-1)\theta] \right\} + Q/c_2 = 0$$

i.e.

$$3c_2 z^2 - 2 \left\{ P - \frac{\beta}{2}(n-1)\left(1 - \frac{\theta}{1 + (n-2)\theta}\right)\right\} z + Q/c_2 = 0$$

or

$$3c_2 z^2 - 2[P - M_n(1 - \theta_n)]z + Q/c_2 = 0 \tag{*}$$

where, for $n \geqq 2$,

$$M_n = \frac{\beta}{2}(n-1), \ \theta_n = \frac{\theta}{1 + (n-2)\theta}.$$

(We may note that, since $0<\theta<1$ and $n \geqq 2$, we have $0<\theta_n<1$. In particular, $\theta_2=\theta$, $M_2=\beta/2$.)

The *second-order condition* turns out to be

$$x_i \geqq \frac{P-\dfrac{\beta\omega^{12}}{\omega^{11}}}{3c_2},$$

i.e.

$$x_i \geqq \frac{P+\beta\dfrac{\theta}{1+(n-2)\theta}}{3c_2} \equiv \frac{P+\beta\theta_n}{3c_2}.$$

As in Cournot model, we assume that (*) has real roots both of which are positive. That is, we assume

$$\Delta'_n \equiv [P-M_n(1-\theta_n)]^2-3Q \geqq 0$$

and

$$P-M_n(1-\theta_n)>0,$$

as well as $c_2>0$, $Q>0$. The roots of (*) will be denoted by $\zeta_1 \leqq \zeta_2$, with superscripts n where necessary.

If a positive profit maximizer exists, it must be a root of (*). But ζ_1 cannot be a maximizer because it violates the second-order condition. In fact, we have (dropping the subscript n)

$$\zeta_1=\frac{1}{3c_2}\{[P-M(1-\theta)]-\sqrt{\Delta'}\}<\frac{P}{3c_2}$$

while the second-order condition requires that $\zeta_1 \geqq P+\beta\theta/3c_2$, hence that $\zeta_1>P/3c_2$, which cannot be true. So, again, *the larger root is the only candidate* for an interior symmetric equilibrium. But in order that this should be the case it is necessary (as well as sufficient) that ζ_2 should be at the point or in the open interval of non-negative unit profits, i.e. that

$$x^* \leqq \zeta_2 \leqq x^{**}.$$

We must therefore investigate conditions under which these inequalities are satisfied.

4.B.2 Global Conditions

It can happen that a Bertrand equilibrium fails to exist although there is a Cournot equilibrium. This is shown by an example with the following parameters: $n=2$, $c_2=1$, $\beta=2$, $\alpha=3$, $c_0-\sigma=0.44$, $c_1=-7.4$. Here three discriminants (Δ^*, Δ, Δ') are positive, $x^*=0.2$, $x^{**}=2.2$, and the Cournot equilibrium $\eta_2=2.2$ yields zero profits (but at a positive output). But the Bertrand positive local maximizer $\zeta_2=2.7$ is in the negative profits area and there is no Bertrand equilibrium.

Hence additional or different conditions (not implied by those for Cournot) must be satisfied for positive Bertrand equilibria to exist.

In fact, it is easily seen that Bertrand equilibria *can* exist in our economies. One such example is obtained by choosing the parameters so that $n=2$, $M=1$, $\theta=0.5$, $P=10$, $Q=0.5$, $c_2=1$. Then $x^*=0.063$, $x^{**}=7.937$, $\zeta_2=6.307$, with profits at ζ_2 equal to $64.193>0$. (The Cournot equilibrium here is $\eta_2=5.972$, with the higher profits 69.341.) Note that here $0<x^*<\eta_2<\zeta_2<x^{**}$.

We also have an example (see below, p.356 and Fig. 9.3) in which there is a positive output Bertrand equilibrium at which the Bertrand profits are exactly zero. (In this example a positive Cournot equilibrium also exists and yields positive profits.)

(i) *First global condition:* $\zeta_2>\eta_2$.

First we show that $\zeta_2>\eta_2$, which implies that $\zeta_2>x^*$ since (as shown above) $\eta_2 \geqq x^*$.[14]

Claim

$$\zeta_2>\eta_2$$

Proof

Suppose (^{0}) is false. Hence (*) $\zeta_2 \leqq \eta_2$ is true. Inequality (*) is equivalent to

$$\frac{1}{3c_2}\{[P-M(1-\theta)]+$$

$$\sqrt{[P-M(1-\theta)]^2-3Q}\} \leqq \frac{1}{3c_2}\{(P-M)+\sqrt{(P-M)^2-3Q}\}$$

$\Leftrightarrow$

$$P-M(1-\theta)+\sqrt{[P-M(1-\theta)]^2-3Q} \leqq P-M+\sqrt{(P-M)^2-3Q}$$

$\Leftrightarrow$

$$M\theta + \sqrt{[P-M(1-\theta)]^2 - 3Q} \leqq \sqrt{(P-M)^2 - 3Q}$$

$\Leftrightarrow$

$$\sqrt{[P-M(1-\theta)]^2 - 3Q} \leqq \sqrt{(P-M)^2 - 3Q} - M\theta < \sqrt{(P-M)^2 - 3Q}$$

So the above implies

$$\sqrt{[P-M(1-\theta)]^2 - 3Q} < \sqrt{(P-M)^2 - 3Q},$$

and since both discriminants are non-negative,

$$[P-M(1-\theta)]^2 - 3Q < (P-M)^2 - 3Q,$$

i.e.

$$[P-M(1-\theta)]^2 < (P-M)^2. \qquad (**)$$

Now we have been *assuming* that

$$P-M(1-\theta) \geqq 0 \quad \text{and} \quad (P-M) \geqq 0.$$

Hence we can take square roots of both sides of (**), which yields

$$P-M(1-\theta) < P-M$$

i.e.

$$P-M+\theta M < P-M$$

i.e.

$$\theta M < 0,$$

which is false. Thus, we have reached a contradiction. It follows that (*) is false, hence (^{0}) is true; i.e. we have proved that

$$\zeta_2 > \eta_2.$$

QED

Under the assumptions made, the condition $\zeta_2^n > \eta_2^n$ implies $\zeta_2^{n-1} > \eta_2^{n-1}$.

This follows from the fact that the proof of the inequality $\zeta_2^n > \eta_2^n$ uses the following two assumptions:

(1) $T_n \equiv P - M_n(1-\theta_n) \geqq 0,$

and

(2) $P - M_n \geqq 0.$

The inheritance property of (2) is easily seen because:

$$(P - M_{n-1}) - (P - M_n) = M_n - M_{n-1} = \beta/2 > 0.$$

Hence:

$$P - M_n \geqq 0 \text{ implies } P - M_{n-1} > 0.$$

The case of (1) is similar but algebraically more complicated. Again, we show that $T_{n-1} - T_n \geqq 0$. In fact, some manipulation yields

$$T_{n-1} - T_n = \frac{\beta}{2}\left(1 - \theta \cdot \frac{1-\theta}{D}\right)$$

where

$$D = [1 + (n-3)\theta] \cdot [1 + (n-2)\theta].$$

For $n \geqq 3$, and $0 < \theta < 1$, clearly $D > 0$ hence $[1 - \theta(1-\theta)]/[D] > 0$, so $T_{n-1} - T_n > 0$. For $n = 2$, $D = 1 - \theta$, hence $[1 - \theta(1-\theta)]/[D] = 1 - \theta > 0$. So $T_{n-1} - T_n > 0$ for all $n \geqq 2$ when $0 < \theta < 1$.

This completes the 'downward inheritance' proof for the inequality $\eta_2^n < \zeta_2^n$.

Furthermore, the results just obtained also establish the inheritance of the reality and positivity of the roots ζ_2^n, ζ_2^n.

The roots are real if and only if the discriminant Δ_n' is non-negative. They are positive when $T_n > 0$ (because $Q > 0$ by hypothesis). Inheritance requires that $\Delta_n' \geqq 0$ and $T_n > 0$ should imply $\Delta_{n-1}' \geqq 0$ and $T_{n-1} > 0$. Let then $\Delta_n' \geqq 0$ and $T_n > 0$. Since it was shown that $T_{n-1} - T_n > 0$, the inequality $T_{n-1} > 0$ follows.

Now $\Delta_m' = T_m^2 - 3Q$ for all $M \geqq 1$. Hence $\Delta_{n-1}' - \Delta_n' = T_{n-1}^2 - T_n^2 = (T_{n-1} + T_n)(T_{n-1} - T_n)$. But $T_{n-1} + T_n > 0$ since $T_n > 0$ implies $T_{n-1} > 0$, and $T_{n-1} - T_n > 0$ as just seen. Hence $\Delta_{n-1}' > \Delta_n'$, and so $\Delta_n' \geqq 0$ implies $\Delta_{n-1}' > 0$.

(ii) *Second global condition:* $\zeta_2 \leqq x^{**}$.

The conditions guaranteeing that $\zeta_2 \leqq x^{**}$ are more complicated. Written out explicitly, this inequality is

$$\frac{1}{3c_2}\{[P-M(1-\theta)]+\sqrt{\Delta'}\} \leqq \frac{1}{2c_2}[(P-2M)+\sqrt{D^*}] \tag{77}$$

where

$\Delta' \equiv [P-M(1-\theta)]^2-3Q$, the discriminant for ζ_2

$\Delta^* \equiv (P-2M)^2-4Q$, the discriminant for x^{**}.

We *assume* $\Delta' \geqq 0$, $\Delta^* \geqq 0$ (so that $x^*>0$). Also $P-2M>0$. (77) is equivalent to

$$2\sqrt{\Delta'} \leqq -R+3\sqrt{\Delta^*}=2\theta M-k \tag{++}$$

or

$$R+2\sqrt{\Delta'} \leqq 3\sqrt{\Delta^*}, \tag{+++}$$

where

$$r \equiv -(P-4M-2\theta M),$$

and we have

$$\Delta'+3Q=[-R+3M(1+\theta)]^2$$

$$\Delta^*+4Q=[-R+2M(1+\theta)]^2.$$

We shall now show that $R<0$. Suppose

$$R \geqq 0.$$

We shall show that this leads to a contradiction.

By the assumptions made above, both sides of $(+++)$ are non-negative and so we may square without changing the inequality.

Hence

$$R^2+4\Delta'+4R\sqrt{\Delta'} \leqq 9\Delta^*,$$

i.e.

$$R^2+4R\sqrt{\Delta'}\leqq 9\Delta^*-4\Delta'$$

$$=9\{[-R+2M(1+\theta)]^2-4Q\}$$

$$-4\{[-R+3M(1+\theta)]^2-3Q\}$$

$$=9\{R^2+4M^2(1+\theta)^2-4RM(1+\theta)-4Q\}$$

$$-4\{R^2+9M^2(1+\theta)^2-6RM(1+\theta)-3Q\}$$

$$=5R^2-12RM(1+\theta)-24Q.$$

That is,

$$4R\sqrt{\Delta'}\leqq 4R^2-12RM(1+\theta)-24Q,$$

i.e.

$$R\sqrt{\Delta'}\leqq R^2-3RM(1+\theta)-6Q.$$

Clearly, this cannot hold for $R=0$ (since $Q>0$ by hypothesis). Hence we may from now on suppose that

$$R>0.$$

The above inequality can then be rewritten as

$$R\sqrt{\Delta'}+6Q\leqq R^2-3RM(1+\theta).$$

Since the left-hand side is positive, it follows that the right-hand side is positive, i.e.

$$R^2-3RM(1+\theta)>0,$$

hence

$$R-3M(1+\theta)>0, \quad (\textit{since } R>0)$$

$$R>3M(1+\theta).$$

Since $R =_{\text{def}} 2\theta M-k=2\theta M-(P-4M)$, the above inequality is

$$2\theta M+4M-P>3M+3\theta M$$

$$M-P>\theta M,$$

where $\theta M>0$.

Hence

$$M-P>0$$

which contradicts the assumption $P-2M>0$.

So we have proved that $R<0$.

Since $-R>0$, the inequality in $(++)$ is preserved under squaring. This yields the equivalent inequality.

$$4\Delta'-R^2-9\Delta^*\leqq 6(-R)\sqrt{\Delta^*}. \qquad (\Delta\Delta)$$

Again, since $-R>0$, either the left-hand side of $(\Delta\Delta)$ is non-positive[15] or the inequality is preserved under squaring. In the latter case the squared inequality $(\Delta\Delta)$ may be written as

$$(A+24Q)^2\leqq B(C-4Q) \qquad (\Delta\Delta\Delta)$$

where

$$A\equiv 4[P-M(1-\theta)]^2-9(P-2M)^2-R^2-24Q,$$

$$B\equiv 36R^2,$$

$$C\equiv (P-2M)^2.$$

It is clear that, under the assumptions made, $B>0$ and $C>0$. It can also be shown that $A<0$. First, it can be calculated that

$$A=-6R[R-2M(1+\theta)].$$

By definition

$$A=(4\Delta'-9\Delta^*)-24Q-R^2.$$

But, it can be calculated that

$$-4\Delta'+9\Delta^*=5R^2-12RM(1+\theta)-24Q.$$

Therefore

$$A = -5R^2 + 12RM(1+\theta) + 24Q - 24Q - R^2$$

$$= -6R^2 + 12RM(1+\theta)$$

$$= -6R[R - 2M(1+\theta)].$$

Now, suppose $A \geqq 0$. Since $R<0$, it must be that $r - 2M(1+\theta) \geqq 0$, which is equivalent to $2M - P$, thus contradicting the assumption $P - 2M > 0$ (needed to have $0 < x^*$).

Now $(\Delta\Delta\Delta)$ is equivalent to

$$24^2Q^2 + 4(12A + B)Q + A^2 - BC \leqq 0. \qquad (***)$$

But it can be shown, using the already established inequalities $R<0$ and $A<0$, that

$$A^2 - BC = 0.$$

Hence we are left with

$$24^2Q^2 + 4(12A + B)Q \leqq 0.$$

Since $Q > 0$, this is equivalent to

$$24 \times 6Q + (12A + B) \leqq 0,$$

i.e.

$$Q \leqq \frac{12A + B}{24 \times 6}.$$

Hence this is a necessary and sufficient condition for $\zeta_2 \leqq x^{**}$.

This inequality can be expressed in terms of the original parameters as

$$Q \leqq \frac{P^2 - 4PM - 4\theta(\theta+2)M^2}{4}.$$

It is to be noted that this property is also 'inherited downward'. That is, $\zeta_2^n \leqq x^{**n}$ implies $\zeta_2^{n-1} \leqq x^{**n-1}$. The proof is analogous to the earlier proofs of inheritance properties and may be sketched as follows.

The inequality for Q guaranteeing that $\zeta_2^m \leqq x_2^{**m}$ can be written as

$$\frac{P^2-4Q}{4} \geqq M_m[P+M_m\theta_m(2+\theta_m)].$$

The inheritance property will follow from

$$M_n[P+M_n\theta_n(2+\theta_n)] \geqq M_{n-1}[P+M_{n-1}\theta_{n-1}(2+\theta_{n-1})]$$

for all $n \geqq 2$. Since $P > 0$ and so $(M_n - M^{n-1})P = [\beta]/[2]P > 0$, it is sufficient to show that, for $n \geqq 2$,

$$M_n^2\theta_n(2+\theta_n) \geqq M_{n-1}^2\theta_{n-1}(2+\theta_{n-1}),$$

which is equivalent to

$$(n-1)^2\theta_n(2+\theta_n) \geqq (n-2)^2\theta_{n-1}(2+\theta_{n-1}).$$

To establish the latter inequality, it is enough to show that

$$(n-1)^2\theta_n \geqq (n-2)^2\theta_{n-1} \tag{78}$$

and

$$(n-1)^2\theta_n^2 \geqq (n-2)^2\theta_{n-1}^2. \tag{79}$$

Now, since $\theta > 0$, (78) is equivalent to

$$(n-1)^2\frac{1}{1+(n-2)\theta} \geqq (n-2)^2\frac{1}{1+(n-3)\theta},$$

which simplifies to

$$2n-3-\theta \geqq 0,$$

which is true for all $n \geqq 2$ since $\theta < 1$.

As for (79), since both sides are squares of non-negative expressions, it is equivalent to

$$(n-1)\theta_n \geqq (n-2)\theta_{n-2},$$

hence (since $\theta > 0$) to

$$\frac{n-1}{1+(n-2)\theta} \geqq \frac{n-2}{1+(n-3)\theta},$$

which simplifies to

$$1-\theta \geqq 0,$$

and so is necessarily true. This completes the proof of downward inheritability for $\zeta_2^n \leqq x^{**n}$.

We have an example where this condition is satisfied with the equality sign, so that $\zeta_2 = x^{**}$ and profits are zero (see Fig. 9.3).

The parameters in this example are chosen as follows: $n=2$, $\beta=2$, $\alpha=4$, $\sigma=30$, $c_0=31.75$, $c_1=-10$, $c_2=1$; hence $M=1$, $\theta=\frac{1}{2}$, $Q=1.75$, $P=6$. We find that $x^{**}=\zeta_2=3.5$, and the Bertrand equilibrium profits are zero.

[We also have $x^{*}=\frac{1}{2}(4-3)=\frac{1}{2}$ and $\eta_2=3.148$. Hence the Cournot profits are positive.]

There is also an example (see 4.B.2 above) where $0<x^{*}<\eta_2<\zeta_2<x^{**}$, and the Bertrand profits are positive but lower than the Cournot profits.

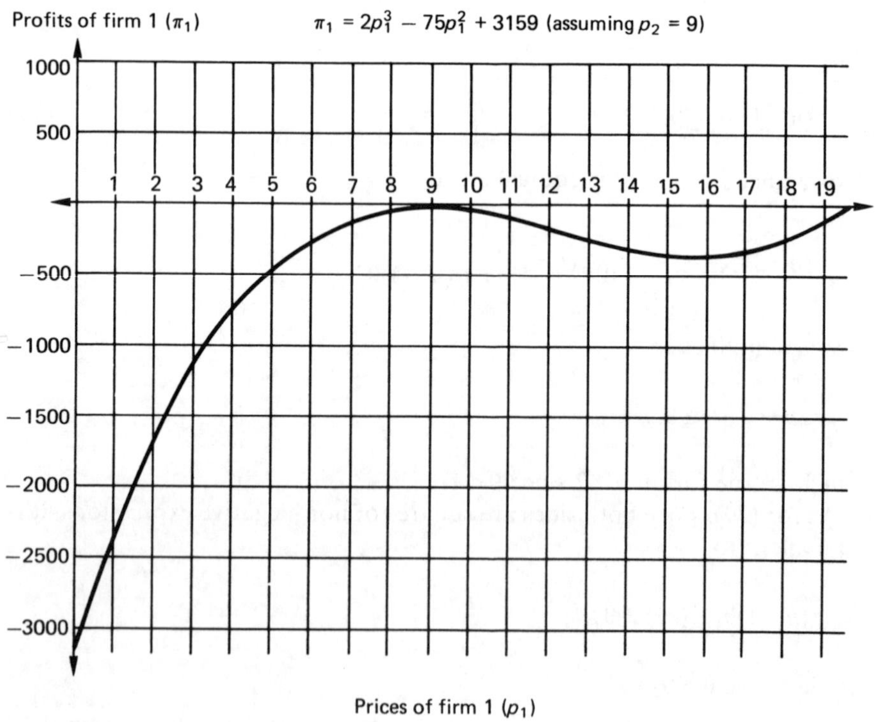

Figure 9.3 Profits of firm 1 as a function of its price (when firm 2 changes the Bertrand equilibrium price)

Thus the Bertrand case is non-vacuous and capable of generating either positive or zero profits.

4.B.3 Bertrand Profits as a Function of the Size of Industry

We now proceed to examine the behavior of profits for an individual firm as a function of n in a Bertrand oligopoly market.

4.B.3.a *The case of quadratic costs*

As in the Cournot case, we shall show that an individual firm's profits π diminish as n increases. For $n \geqq 2$ this will be accomplished by showing that the derivative $d\pi/dn$ is negative. That profits are lower at $n=2$ than at $n=1$ follows from Theorem 2 above.

Since

$$\pi(x) = (p-c)x,$$

we have

$$\frac{d\pi}{dn} = x\frac{d}{dn}(p-c) + (p-c)\frac{dx}{dn}.$$

In what follows we show that $d\pi/dn < 0$ when $x > 0$ by showing that $dx/dn < 0$ and $[d/dn](p-c) < 0$.

4.B.3.a.1

In this section we show that

$$\frac{dx}{dn} < 0 \quad \text{for } n \geqq 2.$$

Using equation (76‴), with $\omega^{ii} = \omega^{11}$ given by eg. (24) and x replacing z, we obtain the quadratic equation satisfied by x, namely,

$$\left[\frac{1}{\omega^{11}} + (c_1 + 2c_2 x)\right] x = \sigma - \alpha[1 + (n-1)\theta]x - c_0 - c_1 x - c_2 x^2, \tag{80}$$

and, as we know, profits are maximized by the larger root (previously denoted by ζ_2). Simplifying, we have

$$3c_2x^2 + \left(2c_1 + \alpha[1+(n-1)\theta] + \frac{1}{\omega^{11}}\right)x + (c_0 - \sigma) = 0. \tag{81}$$

Differentiating implicitly with respect to n we get

$$6c_2x\frac{dx}{dn} + \left(2c_1 + \alpha[1+(n-1)\theta] + \frac{1}{\omega^{11}}\right)\frac{dx}{dn} + x\left[\beta\frac{d}{dn}\left(\frac{1}{\omega^{11}}\right)\right] = 0. \tag{82}$$

Now (82) may be rewritten as

$$\frac{dx}{dn}\cdot\left[2(3c_2x + c_1) + \alpha + \beta(n-1) + \frac{1}{\omega^{11}}\right] = -x\left[\beta + \frac{d}{dn}\left(\frac{1}{\omega^{11}}\right)\right]. \tag{83}$$

But, since x is the larger root of (81), we have

$$x > -\frac{1}{6c_2}\left[2c_1 + \alpha + \beta(n-1) + \frac{1}{\omega^{11}}\right],$$

and therefore, since $c_2 > 0$,

$$6c_2x + 2c_1 + \alpha + \beta(n-1) + \frac{1}{\omega^{11}} > 0. \tag{84}$$

In view of (83), the conclusion $dx/dn < 0$ for $x > 0$ will follow if we show that

$$\beta + \frac{d}{dn}\left(\frac{1}{\omega^{11}}\right) > 0. \tag{85}$$

We note that, by eq. (24),

$$\frac{1}{\omega^{11}} = \frac{\alpha(1-\theta)[1+(n-1)\theta]}{1+(n-2)\theta} \tag{86}$$

and hence

$$\frac{1}{\alpha(1-\theta)}\cdot\frac{d}{dn}\left(\frac{1}{\omega^{11}}\right) = -\frac{\theta^2}{[1+(n-2)\theta]^2}. \tag{87}$$

Substituting from (87) into the left-hand side of (85) we find that

$$\beta+\frac{d}{dn}\left(\frac{1}{\omega^{11}}\right)= \tag{88}$$

$$=\frac{\beta}{[1+(n-2)\theta]^2}\{(1-\theta)+2(n-2)\theta+[(n-2)^2+1]\theta^2\}.$$

It is then seen that, for $n \geqq 2$, and in virtue of the assumption $0<\theta<1$, the right-hand side of (88) is positive, hence (85) is satisfied and $dx/dn<0$ follows.

4.B.3.a.2

In this section we show that

$$\frac{d(p-c)}{dn}<0. \tag{89}$$

Now, according to (76′), we have

$$p-c=\left(\frac{1}{\omega^{11}}+c'(x)\right)x. \tag{78″}$$

Assuming $x>0$ and $p-c \geqq 0$, we also have

$$\frac{1}{\omega^{11}}+c'(x) \geqq 0. \tag{90}$$

Differentiating, we obtain

$$\frac{d}{dn}(p-c)=\left[\frac{1}{\omega^{11}}+c'(x)\right]\frac{dx}{dn}+x\left[\frac{d}{dn}\left(\frac{1}{\omega^{11}}\right)+c''(x)\cdot\frac{dx}{dn}\right].$$

For $n \geqq 2$ and $x>0$, we have seen in Section 4.B.3.a.1 that $dx/dn<0$. This, together with (90), makes the first term in the right-hand side of (91) non-positive. Since $c''(x)=2c_2>0$ by hypothesis, it follows that $xc''(x)[dx/dn]<0$ for $n \geqq 2$ and $x>0$. Finally, as seen in (87),

$$\frac{d}{dn}\left(\frac{1}{\omega^{11}}\right)=-\frac{\alpha(1-\theta)\theta^2}{[1+(n-2)\theta]^2}<0.$$

Hence (89) follows. Thus, $d\pi/dn<0$ for $n \geqq 2$, $x>0$.

4.B.3.b *Special case: zero costs* $(c \equiv 0)$

4.B.3.b.1 Results

Formally, the case of zero costs ($c(x)=0$) is not covered by the preceding proof because c_0, c_1, and c_2 were all assumed to have non-zero values. However, it is not difficult to show directly that the conclusions remain valid.

Writing x, p, σ for x_i, p_i, σ_i we have at a symmetric interior equilibrium,[16] for all $n \geqq 1$,

$$[\alpha+(n-1)\beta]x=\sigma-p \tag{76''.1}$$

and [by (76″), (76′), and $c \equiv 0$]

$$x-p\omega^{11}=0. \tag{76'.1}$$

Substituting x from (76′.1) into (76″.1), we get

$$[\alpha+(n-1)]p\omega^{11}=\sigma-p \tag{91}$$

where [by Section 2.5, eq. (24), p.312], with $\theta \equiv \beta/\alpha$, $0<\theta<1$,

$$\omega^{11}=\frac{1}{\alpha(1-\theta)}\cdot\frac{1+(n-2)\theta}{1+(n-1)\theta}. \tag{24}$$

Hence, (91) becomes

$$[\alpha+(n-1)\beta]p\frac{1}{\alpha(1-\theta)}\cdot\frac{1+(n-2)\theta}{1+(n-1)\theta}=\sigma-p. \tag{92}$$

Upon cancellation, this yields

$$p\cdot\left[1+\frac{1+(n-2)\theta}{1-\theta}\right]=\sigma, \tag{93}$$

i.e.

$$p=\frac{1-\theta}{2+(n-3)\theta}\sigma>0, \quad \text{for all } n \geqq 1. \tag{94}$$

It should be noted, therefore, that p is positive and goes down as n increases for $n \geqq 1$.

It is also the case (see 4.B.3.b.2 below) that x is positive and decreases as n increases for $n \geqq 1$. Now, with $c \equiv 0$, profits are given by

$$\pi = px.$$

Since both factors decrease with n, it follows that π decreases with n, $n \geqq 1$, when costs are zero.

(Note that this is the unique symmetric solution, since there is no other symmetric interior solution and the symmetric solution $x_1 = \ldots = x_n = 0$ would yield lower profits than the positive solution.)

4.B.3.b.2 *The behavior of x as a function of n*

Substituting into (76′.1) the value of p from (94) and that of ω^{11} from (24), we get

$$x = \left(\frac{1-\theta}{2+(n-3)\theta} \cdot \sigma\right) \cdot \frac{1}{\alpha(1-\theta)} \cdot \frac{1+(n-2)\theta}{1+(n-1)\theta},$$

or

$$x = \frac{\sigma}{\alpha} \cdot \frac{1+(n-2)\theta}{[2+(n-3)\theta] \cdot [1+(n-1)\theta]} \quad \text{for all } n \geqq 1. \tag{95}$$

Using $0 < \theta < 1$, we note that $x > 0$ for all $n \geqq 1$. Differentiating with respect to n, we get

$$\frac{\alpha}{\sigma} \cdot \frac{\partial x}{\partial n} = \frac{1}{[\ ]^2 \cdot [\ ]^2} \cdot \{\theta \cdot [2+(n-3)\theta] \cdot [1+(n-1)\theta]$$

$$-[1+(n-2)\theta] \cdot [\theta(1+(n-1)\theta) + \theta(2+(n-3)\theta)]\}$$

i.e. for $\theta > 0$,

$$\frac{\alpha}{\sigma} \cdot \frac{1}{\theta} \cdot \frac{\partial x}{\partial n} =$$

$$[2+(n-3)\theta] \cdot [1+(n-1)\theta] - [1+(n-2)\theta] \cdot [1+(n-1)\theta + 2 + (n-3)\theta]$$

$$= 2+(n-2)\theta + 2(n-1)\theta + (n-3)(n-1)\theta^2 - [1+(n-2)\theta] \cdot [3+(2n-4)\theta]$$

$$= 2+(3n-5)\theta + (n-3)(n-1)\theta^2 - [3+3(n-2)\theta + 2(n-2)\theta + 2(n-2)^2\theta^2]$$

$$= -1-(2n-5)\theta + (-n^2+4n-5)\theta^2$$

$$= -1-(2n-5)\theta-(n^2-4n+5)\theta^2$$

$$= -(1-\theta)-2(n-2)\theta-[(n-2)^2+1]\theta^2<0 \text{ for } n \geqq 2,\ 0<\theta<1.$$

Hence x decreases with n for $n \geqq 2$.

The preceding result does not cover the comparison of the values of x for $n=1$ and $x=2$, to be here denoted by $x^{(1)}$ and $x^{(2)}$. But it can be shown by direct computation that

$$x^{(1)}<x^{(2)}. \tag{96}$$

In fact, from (95), we have

$$x^{(1)}=\frac{\sigma}{\alpha}\cdot\frac{1}{2},$$

and

$$x^{(2)}=\frac{\sigma}{\alpha}\cdot\frac{1}{(1+\theta)(2-\theta)}.$$

But, for $\theta<1$, we have

$$(1+\theta)(2-\theta)>0,$$

which implies (96).

So x is positive and decreases for all $n \geqq 1$.

Remark *Limiting values of* β

The above analysis presupposes $\beta<\alpha$, since otherwise Ω^{-1} does not exist. The conclusion that profits decrease with n is not valid for $\beta=0$, since in that case profits are independent of n.

Notes

1. Except at the transition from monopoly to duopoly, i.e. from $n=1$ to $n=2$ (see Theorem 2). Here symmetry on the demand side is not assumed.
2. So we are in the realm of 'partial equilibrium' analysis.
3. However, Arrow did not study product differentiation, and he assumed the list of monopolists to be given, while for us its variability is central. (See Arrow (1969) pp.45–5, and (1971) p.96.)

4. An earlier mimeographed version of the present paper containing most of these results was circulated in 1971 and used subsequently as a teaching aid in classes. I have not had a chance to see to what extent more recent literature overlaps or covers these results.
5. For $n=1$, this formula yields

$$\omega^{11}=\frac{1}{\alpha(1-\theta)}\cdot\frac{1+(-1)\theta}{1+0\cdot\theta}=\frac{1}{\alpha},$$

which is correct, as can be verified directly, since then $\Omega=\|\alpha\|$.
6. From (24), introducing subscript n, $\omega^{11}_{(n)}$ increases with n, $\omega^{11}_n\uparrow 1/[\alpha(1-\theta)]$. For $\beta=0$ (so that $\theta=0$), $\omega^{11}_n=1/\alpha$ for all n.
7. The *marginal* cost function is given by $d/dx[xc(x)]=c_0+2c_1x+3c_2x^2$. (Thus, we also have a U-shaped marginal cost curve.) Marginal costs are falling to the left of the point $-c_1/3c_2$, as seen by differentiating the marginal cost function and using $c_2>0$, $c_1<0$. (This corresponds to the way Chamberlin draws his diagrams.) The minimal marginal cost value $=(1/3c_2)(3c_0c_2-c_1^2)$. Hence the condition for the vertex of the marginal cost curve to be at or above the x-axis is $3c_0c_2-c_1^2\geqq 0$, somewhat stronger than $4c_0c_2-c_1^2\geqq 0$ for $c^*\geqq 0$ for the average cost curve. (The average and marginal cost curves have the same y-intercept c_0.)
8. Using the abbreviated notation, with $P=-(c_1+\alpha)$, $Q=c_2(c_0-\sigma)$.
9. Since $\pi''(x)=-6c_2x+2P$, it follows that $\pi''(x)<0$ if and only if $x>P/3c_2$.
10. When necessary we use the more complete notation x^{*n}, x^{**n}.
11. We omit the index n. Where necessary we use the more complete notation η^n_1, η^n_2.
12. When $k=0$, $\Delta^*=4M^2-4Q$, $\Delta=9M^2-3Q$.
13. Second-order condition $\delta\pi_i/\delta x_i^2<0$ is $x_i>P/3c_2$ (for all n, without assuming symmetry).
14. It should be noted that $\eta_2\geqq x^*$ is true whether or not $\pi_i(\eta_2)\geqq 0$.
15. This case yields a tighter inequality than the inequality ($\Delta\Delta\Delta$), and hence can be disregarded.
16. At *any* interior solution with $c\equiv 0$, eq. (76′) yields $x_i-p_i\omega^{11}=0$ for all i, while interior utility maximization still yields (in vector notation) $\Omega\mathbf{x}=\boldsymbol{\sigma}-\mathbf{p}$. With $\boldsymbol{\sigma}$ and Ω specified as above, we get $x_1=\ldots=x_n=x$ and also $p_1=\ldots=p_n=p$. This yields (76″.1) and (76′.1).

References

Arrow, K. J. (1969) 'The Firm in General Equilibrium Theory', ONR Technical Report No. 3, Harvard University. Also published in *The Corporate Economy, Growth, Competition, and Innovative Potential*, Marris and Wood (eds) (Cambridge, Mass: Harvard University Press, 1971) pp.68–117.

Bain, J. S. and E. Chamberlin (1954) 'Conditions of Entry and the Emergence of Monopoly', in *Monopoly and Competition and their Regulation* (London: Macmillan).

Bain, J. S. (1956) *Barriers to New Competition* (Cambridge, Mass: Harvard University Press).

Bain, J. S. (1968) *Industrial Organization*, 2nd edn (New York: John Wiley).

Chamberlin, E. H. (1965) *The Theory of Monopolistic Competition*, 8th edn (Cambridge, Mass: Harvard University Press).

Demsetz, H. (1959) 'The Nature of Equilibrium in Monopolistic Competition', *Journal of Political Economy,* 67: 21–30.

Dewey, D. (1958) 'Imperfect Competition No Bar to Efficient Production', *Journal of Public Economy,* 66: 24–33.

Dewey, D. (1969) *The Theory of Imperfect Competition: A Radical Reconstruction* (New York: Columbia University Press).

Farrar, D. E. and C. E. Phillips, Jr (1959) 'New Developments on the Oligopoly Front: A Comment', *Journal of Political Economy,* 67: 414–17.

Fisher, F. M. (1959) 'New Developments on the Oligopoly Front: Cournot and the Bain–Sylos Analysis', *Journal of Political Economy,* 67: 410–13.

Fog, B. (1957) 'Stay-Out Pricing', *Metroeconomica,* 11: 42–51.

Kaldor, N. (1935) 'Market Imperfection and Excess Capacity', *Economica,* N.S. 2: 33–50; repr. in *Essays on Value and Distribution* by Nicholas Kaldor (Glencoe Free Press, 1960) pp.62–80.

Modigliani, F. (1958) 'New Developments on the Oligopoly Front', *Journal of Political Economy,* 66: 215–32.

Negishi, T. (1961) 'Monopolistic Competition and General Equilibrium', *Review of Economic Studies,* 28: 196–201.

Negishi, T. (1962) 'Entry and the Optimal Number of Firms', *Metroeconomica,* 14: 86–96.

Robinson, J. (1933) *The Economics of Imperfect Competition* (London: Macmillan).

Samuelson, P. A. (1967) 'The Monopolistic Competition Revolution', chapter 5 of *Monopolistic Competition Theory: Studies in Impact (Essays in Honor of Edward H. Chamberlin)*, R. E. Kuenne (ed.) (New York: John Wiley).

Shapley, L. and M. Shubik (1969) 'Price Strategy Oligopoly with Product Variation', *Kyklos,* 22: 30–44.

Sherman, R. and T. D. Willett (1967) 'Potential Entrants Discourage Entry', *Journal of Political Economy,* 75: 400–3.

Sylos Labini, P. (1969) *Oligopoly and Technical Progress* (Cambridge, Mass: Harvard University Press; translated from the Italian by Elizabeth Henderson).

Thin, T. (1967) *Theory of Markets* (Cambridge, Mass: Harvard University Press).

Triffin, R. (1940) *Monopolistic Competition and General Equilibrium Theory* (Cambridge, Mass: Harvard University Press).

10 An Essay on Price Discrimination

Paul Milgrom

1 INTRODUCTION

The modern theory of price discrimination began with the work of Pigou (1920). Joan Robinson devoted two chapters of her book *The Economics of Imperfect Competition* (1969) to the problem of ('third degree') price discrimination. Her account examines the conditions that make price discrimination possible, presents a graphical analysis of the discriminating monopolist's pricing decision which has become the standard textbook treatment, and ends with an inquiry into the consequences of price discrimination for both allocative efficiency and distributional equity. Although Pigou's and Robinson's contributions have proved of lasting value, the theory of price discrimination has by no means remained unaltered.[1]

The meaning assigned to the term 'price discrimination' has stretched and changed since Pigou and Robinson wrote, and there is little current consensus on precisely what price discrimination means. Like her predecessors and contemporaries, Robinson defined price discrimination as 'the act of selling the same article, produced under a single control, at different prices to different buyers' (Robinson, 1969, p.179). In the modern view, such a definition is too narrow in its focus on the 'same' article and too broad in holding all price variations to be discriminatory. Even competitive prices for an article would generally vary according to the time and place of delivery, the amount of lead time required, the warranties or auxiliary services demanded, etc. And to the extent that the size of an order affects the cost of filling it, competitive prices would naturally vary with order size, too. Such variations cannot be usefully regarded as exercises of monopoly power, so they are best excluded from any useful definition of price discrimination.

To identify price discrimination, where economists from the early twentieth century had emphasized finding physically identical goods with different prices, modern economists emphasize the motives of the price-setter to create a situation in which the price charged to a customer can be based partly on the value of the good to the customer, rather than just on the cost of producing the good. Although this change sometimes makes the theory less specific and operational, it also achieves an economy of thought and a unity of principles that are important for analyzing the vast and increasing number of ways in which firms seek to exercise their monopoly power.

To illustrate the modern perspective, consider the pricing of air travel. Although first-class air travel differs in seat size and amenities from coach class, the huge fare differentials between the two classes of service are discriminatory. What makes this clear is that the two classes of travel provide essentially the same service at prices (1) that differ far more than proportionately to any cost differences, and (2) that are designed to exploit differences in various travellers' willingness to pay for amenities, or to pass on the costs to others. Moreover, they are part of a complex pattern of pricing in which prices may depend on how long in advance reservations are made, how many days the traveller stays at his destination, whether he stays over a Saturday night, etc. Notice that fares are not made to depend on things that might affect airline costs, such as the need for special meals or whether the customer smokes. Instead, prices are made to depend on factors that are primarily related to the price a buyer might be willing to pay. It is this pattern that identifies the pricing policy as discriminatory.

A full account of the modern concept of price discrimination cannot be given by focusing on pricing alone. Pricing practices are intimately connected with product design decisions, bundling decisions,[2] and other marketing practices. For example, a firm may specialize its product line to make it possible to charge different prices to different customers. The different classes of airline travel cited above are but one instance of this sort of specialization; any product that comes in several varieties from apples and automobiles to video cassette recorders and washing machines is a candidate for this sort of manipulation.[3]

Another example of price discrimination in which non-price practices play a key role is the vertical price squeeze. Thus, suppose that there are two classes of users for a product. Suppose that users in the first class would be willing to pay quite a high price for the product, perhaps because this is the only product that can meet their particular needs. Users in the second class would be willing to pay only a much lower price. The seller would like to charge different prices to the different groups, but suppose that legal restrictions, competition, or the possibility of resale from the low price customers to the high price ones make that sort of discrimination impossible. If the low value user is an industrial customer, the supplier may be able to achieve the desired discriminatory effect by integrating forward and setting the transfer price on supplies transferred to its subsidiary below the market price charged to its customers. Adams and Dirlam (1964) report an instance of such a vertical price squeeze in the steel wire products industry, alleging that integrated steel producers sold certain steel wire products (which faced heavy competition from non-steel alternatives) for nearly the same price as the steel wire used to make it.

The received theory of price discrimination is a part of the theory of monopoly and incorporates that theory's framework and biases. In particular, it incorporates the assumption that sellers set their prices while customers act as price takers, buying whatever quantity suits their tastes at the given prices. In other words, it assumes that the monopolist-seller holds all the bargaining power. In Section 2, I explore the nature of monopoly and price discrimination in the presence of countervailing buying power. I argue against the usual presumption that in markets with a single seller and many buyers, the seller holds a great bargaining advantage.[4] The relative bargaining power of the parties depends on their costs of bargaining, on the ability of the buyers to form coalitions, on the possibilities for resale, and on laws governing price discrimination. Laws against price discrimination, far from benefiting the buyer, may actually enhance a monopolist-seller's bargaining position by making it credible to its negotiating partners that the monopolist will hold out for the same price that other buyers are paying. Of course, this conclusion depends on the customers not forming a coalition or buyers' union to coordinate their bargaining. I comment on the possibilities for a buyers' union as well in Section 2.

In Section 3, I investigate how a firm can design its product line to enhance its ability to engage in price discrimination. Much of the analysis is conducted in terms of a formal model in which customers differ according to how much they are willing to pay for quality. The difficulty the monopolist faces is that products designed for one class of customers may cannibalize the sales of a more profitable product targeted at another class of customers. Some aspects of this problem have been studied before. I give a graphical solution to the problem based on Milgrom (1980) and a parallel analytical treatment. Similar analytical treatments have been given by Harris and Raviv (1981) and Maskin and Riley (1984).

The upshot of the analysis is that the monopolist's product design and pricing decision involves trading off the profits to be earned on direct sales of any particular product against the losses that result in the sales of more profitable products. The design decision is thus distorted away from efficiency, and certain groups who could be economically served by the monopolist might not be served at all. Such distortions do not arise, however, in the design of the most profitable product, since the monopolist is not concerned that customers may switch away from other products to it. Another finding is that an optimal pricing scheme may make the price paid for a given product depend on any random event whose occurrence is correlated with the buyer's willingness to pay. The use in the airline industry of advance purchase requirements with high cancellation fees can be interpreted in this way. That interpretation makes it possible to integrate our analysis with certain related developments in auction theory (Milgrom and Weber, 1982; Milgrom, 1986) and in the theory of contracts (McAfee and McMillan, 1986).

2 DISCRIMINATION AND COUNTERVAILING BUYER POWER

Textbook treatments of monopoly theory and oligopoly theory begin from the premise that the producers can set the prices of their products, and that buyers act as if they were powerless to affect the prices. That premise is by no means self-evident; it needs to be examined both theoretically and empirically. Whether there is a single seller or many, the customer can always *try* to haggle over the price. His success will depend on the relative strength of his bargaining position, which is determined by many factors, including the availability of alternative suppliers and/or alternative customers, the enforceability of restrictions on resale, legal restrictions on price discrimination, and the ability of buyers or sellers to collude or bargain as a group.

The informal arguments most often heard in support of the idea that the monopolist has complete latitude in setting the price rely on the idea that there are other customers who would be willing to buy the marginal unit for the price the monopolist is asking. However, such arguments are erroneous. To see the flaw, suppose that the monopolist produces using a constant returns to scale technology.[5] Then, it will not benefit the seller to offer any refused units to another buyer, so how can the presence of other buyers affect the negotiations with any one buyer? Indeed, how is this monopoly situation different from a collection of unrelated bilateral monopoly problems, in which the seller haggles over the price with each buyer separately?

Let us rephrase the argument to emphasize its cogency. If the monopolist can produce at constant marginal cost over the relevant range of outputs, then the feasible set over which the monopolist and any customer can bargain is independent of the bargains struck with other customers. So, why should the presence or absence of other customers matter? Why should one suppose, as standard textbooks would have us do, that the mere fact that a monopolist is a monopolist makes it immune to attempts at negotiations by its customers? Of course, customers do sometimes bargain with their monopolist-suppliers. That suggests turning the question around: why don't they do so more often?

Answers to these questions in industrial organization should be related to the similar questions that arise in labor economics: how are the negotiations between, say, the United Auto Workers (UAW) and Ford Motor Co. affected by the fact that the union will subsequently negotiate with the other auto-makers? There are two effects at work here. If the auto-makers are to remain competitive, any concessions that the UAW makes to Ford will have to be granted to the others as well. Second, the way the UAW bargains with Ford signals its willingness to hold out for a favorable contract in the subsequent contract negotiations. Then, as arguments in the game-theoretic literature on reputations (introduced by Kreps and Wilson (1982) and Milgrom and Roberts (1982)) make clear, the UAW gains strength in its negotiations with Ford because Ford knows that the union has double reason to carry out its threats – to extract concessions from Ford and to signal its seriousness to its later bargaining partners. Thus, reputation effects make the UAW's threat more credible and may enable it to strike a better bargain.

A general reputation argument would hold that a monopolist can gain leverage in bargaining by linking its negotiations among several customers. Linkages of that sort may be impossible to achieve if, for example, rebates that the seller pays to buyers or special services that the seller provides cannot be observed. Even if linkages could be achieved, the seller might not choose to achieve them. If the UAW thought that Ford was in a strong bargaining position, it might prefer to bargain less aggressively and out of the public eye rather than to be forced into a lengthy strike to demonstrate its resolve to the other auto-makers.[6]

This example of the role of reputations in bargaining illustrates the monopolist's fundamental dilemma: as in many bargaining situations (see Schelling, 1960) its bargaining position is enhanced by commitments that make concessions too costly to grant, but these same commitments and costs also result in a loss of flexibility. The monopolist who charges different prices to different customers cannot claim convincingly that it will not make a price concession to a hard bargaining customer.

As a first, simple example of these ideas, consider the problem of a monopolist who faces a large number of customers each of whom wishes to buy a single unit of his product. Each customer i values a unit at $2V_i$. Suppose the production cost is zero. If (i) the monopolist's product cannot be resold, (ii) there are many customers, and (iii) bargaining is efficient and the bargainers have equal bargaining power in the sense that the gains from trade are to be split equally, then the seller receives a price of V_i from each customer i. Plainly, different customers pay different prices for the same good. However, our story is not the textbook story of price discrimination; although the monopolist does set a different price for each customer, it does not capture all the surplus. The monopolist's profits from this sort of price discrimination are represented in Figure 10.1 with demand curve *BCD* by the area *OAD*.

If the monopolist does not (or cannot) prohibit resale, then all sales will be made at the lowest agreed price. The bargaining outcome in this situation may depend on details of the way bargaining is conducted. One plausible outcome of this situation is that all customers would pay the monopoly price. The monopolist would certainly never want to bargain for a higher price, since to do so would only reduce his profits. And, using our assumption of many buyers and the additional assumption that prices are posted in discrete units, the monopolist could not be swayed to accept a lower price by any single buyer's threat not to buy, since even if the threat were believed it would not pay the monopolist to accommodate the buyer.

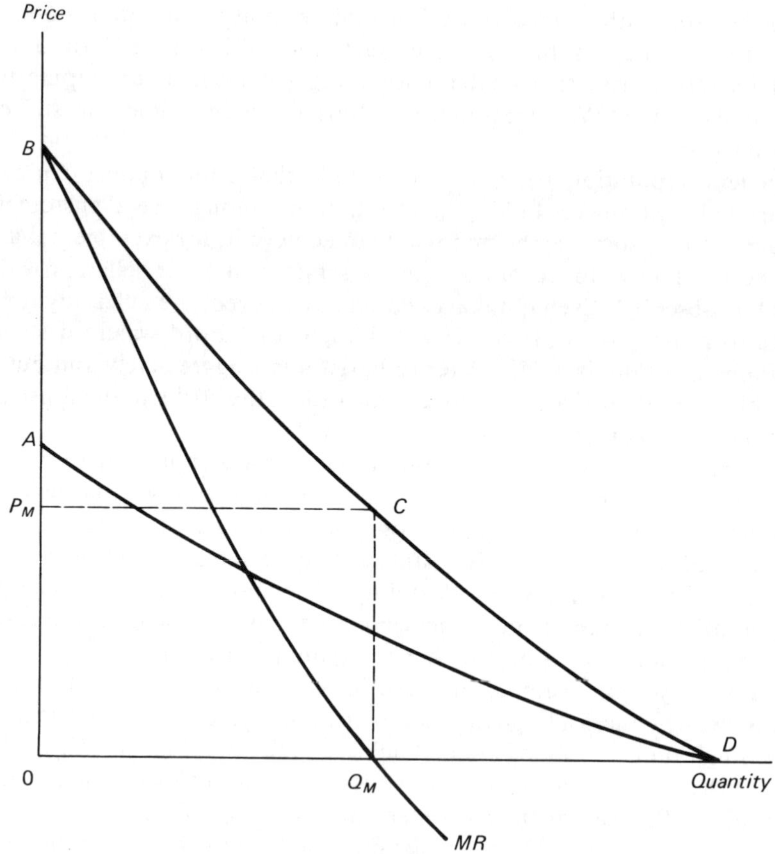

Figure 10.1

In Figure 10.1, the monopolist's profits in this case of simple monopoly pricing are represented by the rectangle OP_MCQ_M. For the case of linear demand, price discrimination leads to the same level of profits as simple monopoly pricing. For general demand, profits may be either higher or lower. Contrary to received theory, the monopolist has no *general* preference to charge individual prices to different customers. And, depending on the demand curve, *the monopolist may actually be better off when he is unable to prohibit resale*!

A similar point could be made in an analysis of reputational effects. There one finds that the monopolist would prefer sometimes to maintain a reputation of never compromising on price and sometimes to sacrifice that reputation in order to be able to haggle with individual customers. A full analysis of reputation issues would take careful account of how much of the monopolist's pricing behavior can be observed, and when. We shall not develop those issues here.

Instead, we return to another question that was raised earlier: why are price negotiations not more common? In retail stores in the Western world, the seller typically sets the price and, except for a few expensive durables like cars and component stereo systems, the customer is given little chance to negotiate. One plausible explanation is that bargaining costs are too high to make it worthwhile to haggle, especially for inexpensive items where large price adjustments are unlikely to be obtainable. To guide the remaining analysis, let us hypothesize that bargaining does not go on over small items in stores and elsewhere due to the costs of bargaining, which are large compared to the purchase price for small purchases. On the buyer's side, these costs are mostly costs of the time consumed in negotiations, combined perhaps with a simple distaste for bargaining. On the seller's side, there are additional costs: those of hiring and training the skilled workers needed for effective bargaining, the costs of monitoring sales workers to ensure that they report the actual price paid, or the resulting loss suffered when the reported price is lower than the actual selling price and the worker pockets the difference. Let us see what implications these bargaining costs have for the theory of price discrimination.

Thus, suppose a monopolist supplier who produces at constant unit cost c faces n buyers. Each buyer desires only a single item, and values the item at unity. For example, if the buyers are manufacturers, the first unit of the input for each buyer has marginal revenue product equal to one; subsequent units have MRP equal to zero. What will be the price?

If the buyers and the seller have equal bargaining power, one might expect that if they do bargain, they will divide the surplus of $1-c$ from their relationship equally. The price negotiated between the seller and each buyer would then be $p=(1+c)/2$. Assume that bargaining costs take the form of a fixed cost b that is smaller than the bargainers' rents on the transaction: $b<p-c=1-p$. If the monopolist posts a price not exceeding $b+p$, buyers will face the choice of accepting that price or incurring the cost b to obtain the price p. They will prefer to accept such a price without haggling, to save on bargaining costs. If the monopolist posts a higher price than $b+p$, buyers will choose to incur the cost and haggle to reach the price p. Thus, the unique (subgame perfect) equilibrium of monopoly pricing game in which the seller sets a price and the buyer then chooses to bargain or not calls for the monopolist to set the price $b+p$ and the buyer to accept that price without haggling. Of course, if buyers differ in their bargaining costs, the price will be set so that some haggle while others do not.

Now suppose that resale is possible or that price discrimination is prohibited, so that any price concession granted to one buyer must be granted to all. The n bargaining problems are now clearly connected. Let us represent that as follows. First, the seller names a price p^*. Then, the buyers decide, independently and simultaneously, whether to bargain and incur the cost b. If the seller sets a price of p^* and k buyers bargain, let p' be the resulting price. Specifying p' is tricky; it depends on how the multilateral interlinked negotiations proceed. For simplicity, let us suppose that the buyers who bargain join together and negotiate as if they were a single party; this plausibly is the best joint strategy for the coalition to follow, since it gives them their most powerful threat to use against the seller. Then, as we shall see, the power of the buyers is limited by a free rider problem – individual buyers are reluctant to join any buyer coalition.

We shall use the Nash bargaining solution to guide our analysis. The 'no agreement' point yields rents of $(p^*-c)(n-k)$ to the monopolist and zero to the k negotiating buyers. If a (non-random) price of p' is agreed upon, the monopolist gets rents of $(p'-c)n$ and the bargainers get $(1-p')k$. Varying p', this identifies the Pareto surface for the bargaining problem. For $k=0$, the solution of the game has $p'=p^*$; otherwise, the Nash bargaining solution sets:

$$p'=p+\frac{(p^*-c)(n-k)}{2n}.$$

Recall that $p=(1+c)/2$ is the price that would prevail in case $k=n=1$. It is evidently also the price that prevails whenever $k=n$, since the buyers then bargain as one.

The marginal reduction in price when a second, third, . . . buyer joins the buyers' coalition is $(p^*-c)/(2n)$. So, at a pure strategy equilibrium, at most one buyer will enter the negotiations unless b is less than that amount, that is, unless p^* exceeds $2nb+c$. No firms will ever enter negotiations at any (subgame perfect) equilibrium if p^* is also less than $p'+b$ for the case $k=1$. Hence, all the downstream firms will buy without entering the negotiations if (i) $p^*\leqslant 1$, (ii) $p^*\leqslant 2nb+c$, and (iii) $p^*\leqslant p'+b$, that is, if

$$p^*\leqslant \mathrm{Min}\left\{1, 2nb+c, \frac{2n(b+p)+(n-1)c}{n+1}\right\}.$$

If the upstream monopolist sets $p^*=\mathrm{Min}(1, 2nb+c)$, at most one firm will bargain at any pure strategy equilibrium. The negotiated price is then:

$$p'=p+\mathrm{Min}\left\{(n-1)b, \frac{(1-c)(n-1)}{2n}\right\}.$$

This price is therefore a lower bound on what the monopolist can expect to get when resale is possible or price discrimination is prohibited. If the bargaining costs b or the number of customers n is large, the negotiated price is at least $1-(1-c)/(2n)$; it is possible that the equilibrium price is even higher. Thus, for n large, the possibility of resale or a restriction against price discrimination assures that the monopolist has all the bargaining power.

Let us summarize our findings in this section. First, the traditional notion that the monopolist sets what price it will while buyers act as price takers has been found to be no better founded in theory than it is in reality: *Buyers bargain when the bargaining costs are sufficiently low relative to the potential gains from negotiations*. Second, the textbook proposition that price discrimination enhances the seller's profits is similarly unfounded: *price variations among customers can reflect variations in their relative bargaining power, with large customers generally getting lower unit prices*. Third, restrictions against price discrimination and against contracts that prohibit resale do not generally serve the interests of buyers. Instead, *legal pricing restrictions can help the seller to commit itself credibly to a policy of not retreating from a very high price*.

3 SEGMENTING A MARKET USING SELF-SELECTION

According to Mrs Robinson's account, a necessary condition for price discrimination is that the monopolist be able to divide its markets into separate parts with different demand elasticities. It must be impossible for a customer in the dear market to make its purchases in the cheap one, or for arbitrageurs to buy in the cheap market for resale in the dear one.

When price discrimination is profitable, sellers cannot be expected to accept passively whatever barriers exist among markets. Instead, they will tailor their product lines and pricing policies to exploit differences among consumers.

Our purpose in this section is to investigate how a monopolist might engage in price discrimination when it holds a hegemony of bargaining power but cannot distinguish low- from high-value users who make their purchases in the *same* market. We consider two devices: product design and linking the effective price paid to a 'random' event that occurs *after* the time of initial purchase.

In general, suppose there are N classes of downstream users whose demands depend on a vector of product attributes $\boldsymbol{a}$. Suppose that each user buys only one grade of the product – or only one grade for each envisioned use. Let $V(Q,\boldsymbol{a},n)$ be the value obtained by a customer of class n from purchasing Q units of a product of grade $\boldsymbol{a}$. Suppose, too, that the different classes of the product are perfect substitutes in production, and are produced using a constant-returns-to-scale technology with unit cost c. Let $M_1, \ldots, M_N$ be the number of buyers in each class. What products would a profit-maximizing monopolist produce? At what prices?

Let us label the product varieties offered by the monopolist and bought by some customer from 1 to N and in such a way that a customer of class j prefers the j-th product. (Some products may have two or more labels.) Given his class n and the menu of product offerings $\boldsymbol{a}_1, \ldots \boldsymbol{a}_j$, the customer will choose a product design j and quantity Q to maximize:

$$V(Q,\boldsymbol{a}_j,n) - Qp_j.$$

By our choice of labelling, the optimal value of j will be $j=n$. Also, let us normalize V so that $V(0,\boldsymbol{a};n)=0$. Notice that our formulation abstracts from discrimination using volume discounts, because the price per unit p_j does not vary with the number of units Q that are bought.

The monopolist takes buyer behavior as given. Its problem is then to choose products $\boldsymbol{a}_j$ and prices p_j to maximize its product. What is the monopolist's optimal choice of product designs and prices? One possibility is for it to design and price products separately for each of the N classes to maximize monopoly profits earned from that class. This may work well if the resulting product variations are sufficiently poor substitutes. However, being variations of the same product, it is likely that some of the variations are good substitutes, so that a buyer of class j might prefer to buy the product designed and priced for another class of buyers. Thus, the monopolist's problem is constrained by the following inequality, which asserts that each buyer must prefer to buy the product 'designed' for its class.

$$\text{(IC)} \quad \max_{Q} V(Q,\boldsymbol{a}_n,n) - Qp_n \geq \max_{Q} V(Q,\boldsymbol{a}_j,n) - Qp_j, \text{ for all } n \text{ and } j.$$

In modern jargon, (IC) is an *incentive constraint*. It requires that if a customer chooses to buy anything, he will buy the intended product. The incentive constraints do not preclude the possibility that a customer will not want to buy anything. The discriminating monopolist may choose not to design any acceptable product for some classes of buyers. Formally, it is simplest to deal with this possibility by including among the possible product specifications $\boldsymbol{a}$ the 'useless' product, for which the optimal quantity is always zero.

Sometimes, the incentive constraints will impose severe limits on the monopolist's freedom in pricing its products without having any product switching among its customers. For example, if the product in question is a chemical compound whose only relevant attribute is its purity, with greater purity being preferred in all uses, erecting barriers between different customer groups may be especially difficult. However, even in that case, the monopolist may be able to exploit variations in customers' marginal willingness to pay for quality to design a profitable product line.

Figure 10.2 displays an example of this kind. It is worked out for the case where the attribute space is one-dimensional ('quality') and the valuation function is $V(Q,q,n) = \text{Min}(Q,1)[b_n q - q^2/2]$. This valuation function ensures that the consumer's optimal quantity choice Q is always either zero or one. That allows us to write the incentive constraints more simply as:

(IC′) $V(1,q_n,n) - p_n \geqslant V(1,q_j,n) - p_j$, for all n and j, and

(PC) $V(1,q_n,n) - p_n \geqslant 0$ for all n.

This last constraint is sometimes called a *participation constraint*, because it reflects the assumption that the buyer can refuse to participate, that is, he can opt not to make any purchase at all.

Suppose that consumer types differ in their marginal valuations of the single attribute – quality. The marginal valuation of quality curve for each

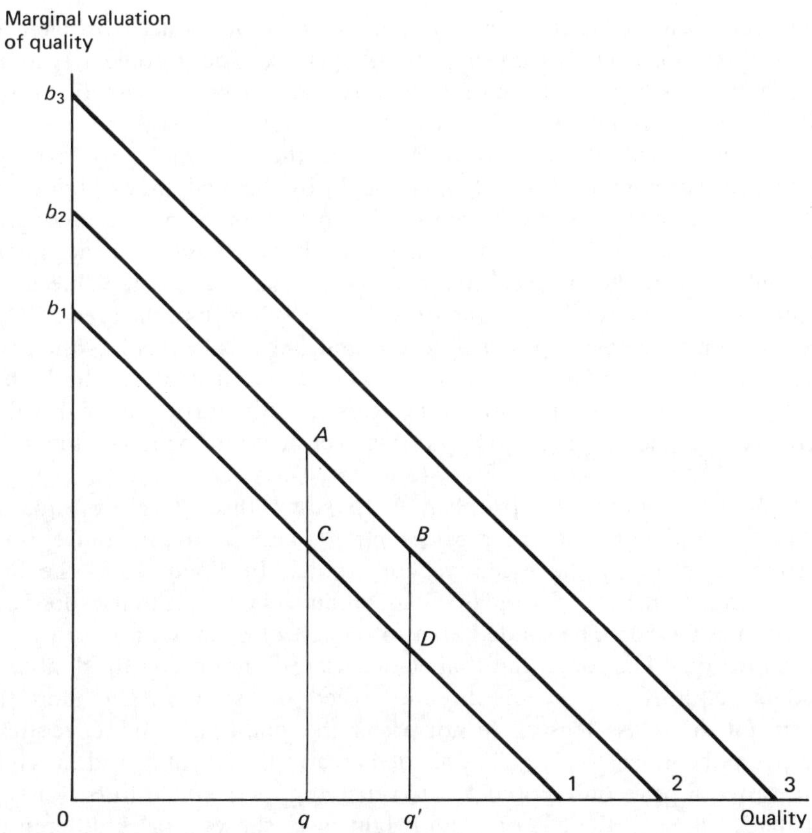

Figure 10.2

class of customer is plotted in the figure. Classes 1, 2, and 3 represent the low value, middle value, and high value users, respectively. In this example, the marginal valuations of quality are shown as linear with slope one. We shall characterize the optimal solution to the product design problem for this specialized example. We shall then recapitulate the general lessons to be learned.

The mathematical statement of the discriminating monopolist's problem is:

$$\max_{p_1,\ldots,p_N,q_1,\ldots q_N} \quad M_1p_1 + \ldots + M_Np_n$$

subject to
(IC′) holds for all n and j, and
(PC) holds for all n.

A mathematical account of the solution to the monopolist's problem in which N is unrestricted is given in the Appendix. The graphical account given below corresponds both in its outline and nearly all its details to the mathematical account. And, for ease of illustration, we set $N=3$.

Consider the question: is it possible for the monopolist to arrange matters so that a good of quality q is bought by the medium or high value users while a good of some higher quality q' is bought by the low value users? The answer is 'No', as can be argued using the figure. The argument uses only two of the six incentive constraints (IC′). The low-value users prefer quality q' to quality q if and only if $p'-p$ is less than the area $qCDq'$. The medium value users prefer q' to q if and only if $p'-p$ is less than the strictly larger area $qABq'$. So medium-value users must prefer the higher quality product whenever low value users do. Similarly, the high-value users prefer higher quality products whenever medium- or low-value users do.

Thus, the monopolist's problem is to select three levels of quality $q_1 \leqslant q_2 \leqslant q_3$ and corresponding prices p_1, p_2, and p_3 to maximize total revenues, subject to the incentive constraints. In Figure 10.3, the first participation constraint for the first class of buyers requires that p_1 does not exceed area $OCFq_1$. The shaded area to the left of q_1 shows a p_1 satisfying that constraint. The constraint that class 2 users do not prefer the quality q_1 product requires that p_2-p_1 do not exceed the area q_1EHq_2, and the constraint that class 1 users do not prefer the quality q_2 product requires that p_2-p_1 be at least q_1FIq_2. The shaded area to the left of q_2 and the right of q_1 shows a price differential p_2-p_1 satisfying these constraints. Finally, the shaded area to the left of q_3 and right of q_2 shows a price differential such that class 2 users do not prefer quality q_2 to q_3 while class 3 users do.

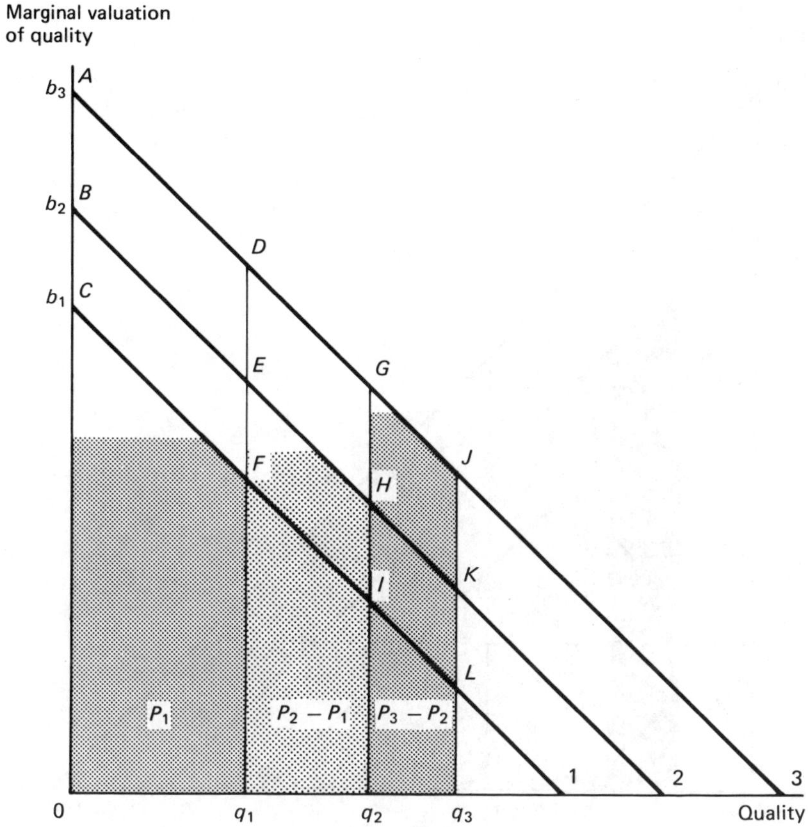

Figure 10.3

Now, because the marginal value of quality increases with increasing class index, all the remaining incentive and participation constraints hold automatically, as can be seen from the figure. Thus, the only constraints of relevance are (i) the participation constraint for the lowest value customer, and (ii) the constraints that limit the price differentials so that a class *i* buyer does not prefer the quality q_{i-1} or quality q_{i+1} product.[7] All the other constraints are implied by these constraints and so can be excised from the problem.

By inspection of the figure, given any qualities q_1, q_2, and q_3, that the monopolist may select, the revenue-maximizing prices for him to set satisfy $p_1 = \text{Area } (OCFq_1)$, $p_2 - p_1 = \text{Area } (q_1EHq_2)$, and $p_3 - p_2 = \text{Area } (q_2GJq_3)$. With the pricing portion of the problem thus solved, our task is reduced to finding the profit-maximizing quality levels.

Given a triple of quality levels, we use Figure 10.4 to analyze the effect of

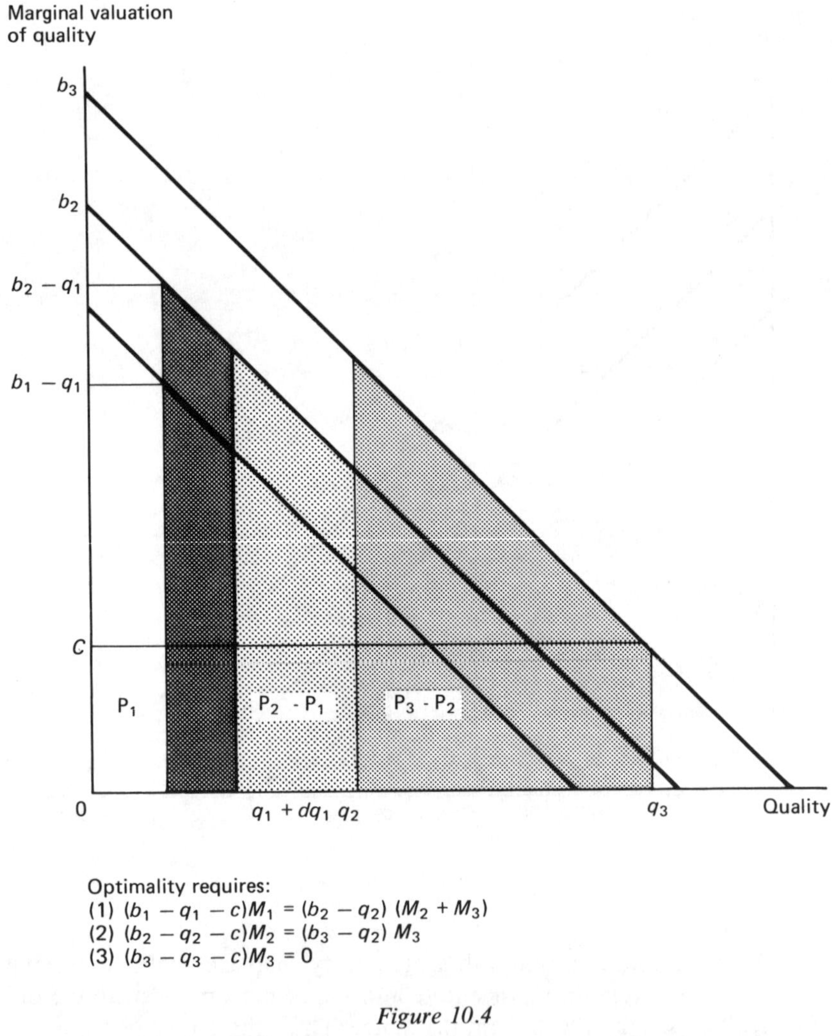

Optimality requires:
(1) $(b_1 - q_1 - c)M_1 = (b_2 - q_2)(M_2 + M_3)$
(2) $(b_2 - q_2 - c)M_2 = (b_3 - q_2)M_3$
(3) $(b_3 - q_3 - c)M_3 = 0$

Figure 10.4

a marginal increase dq_1 in the quality level q_1. The additional quality provided to the M_1 purchasers of quality level q_1 costs the monopolist $M_1 c dq_1$. Also, as the figure shows, the increase in quality leads the monopolist to raise p_1 by approximately $(b_1 - q_1)dq_1$ and to reduce $p_2 - p_1$ by approximately $(b_2 - q_1)dq_1$. Note that $p_3 - p_2$ is unaffected; *the increase in quality of dq_1 forces a price reduction of $(b_2 - q_1)dq_1$ for all higher quality products in the line*. Thus, the change results in additional net revenues from the M_1 customers purchasing quality level q_1 of $M_1(b_1 - q_1 - c)$ and reduced revenues from the $M_2 + M_3$ customers purchasing higher levels of quality of $(M_2 + M_3)(b_2 - q_1)$.

Turning back to the formal problem, if there is an interior optimum (with $0<q_1<q_2\leqslant q_3$), the marginal gains and losses must be equated:

$$M_1(b_1-q_1-c)=(M_2+M_3)(b_2-q_1).$$

It is convenient to rewrite this in the form:

$$\frac{b_2-q_1}{b_1-q_1-c}=\frac{M_1}{M_2+M_3}.$$

Since increasing q_1 beyond b_1-c results in lower net revenues from all groups of purchasers, the optimum requires that $q_1<b_1-c$. Then, since $b_2>b_1$, the left-hand side above is increasing in q_1; it becomes infinite as q_1 approaches b_1-c. If the left-hand side is greater than the right at $q_1=0$, then the optimal q_1 is zero; it does not pay to design a product for the lowest value users. Notice that this happens when the marginal value for the low-value users is quite low relative to higher value users and when the low-value users are relatively few in number. In the case of an interior optimum, there is a unique value of q_1 that satisfies the equality.

Similarly, at an interior optimum, q_2 is set to satisfy:

$$\frac{b_3-q_2}{b_2-q_2-c}=\frac{M_2}{M_3}.$$

The left-hand side is increasing in q_2. If the left-hand side, evaluated at $q_2=q_1$, is less than the right-hand side, then there is a unique $q_2>q_1$ for which the necessary equality holds. If there are too few medium-valuation users, it may happen that the left-hand side is greater than or equal to the right. In that case, $q_2=q_1$ at the optimum, and a single product must be designed for the two groups of consumers. We shall discuss this possibility in more detail below.

Finally, improving the quality q_3 of the highest quality product and increasing its price correspondingly does not affect the pricing of the other products. Its effect is to increase revenues under the pricing rule by $(b_3-q_3)dq_3$ and costs by cdq_3 for each of M_3 customers. Hence, at the optimum, $b_3-q_3=c$. The quality level offered to the third class of users satisfies the first-best efficiency condition.

So far, we have limited attention primarily to the case where the quality levels offered to the several categories of customers are distinct. In our model, this means the case $q_1<q_2<q_3$. We noted, however, that it could happen that $q_1=q_2$ and, in more general problems, two or more consecutive groups may be offered identical products. In the present example, if $q_1=q_2$ at the optimum, then the extra net revenues obtained by raising q_1 (and therefore also q_2) by an amount dq_1 are $(M_1+M_2)(b_1-q_1-c)dq_1$, and these

are offset by a loss of revenues of $M_3(b_3-q_1)dq_1$ from customers purchasing the high quality product. The customer group 2 is most likely to have a product targeted for it at an optimal solution if its members are numerous relative to other groups and if its valuation of quality differs substantially from those who value quality less. It is most likely to be pooled if the reverse conditions hold, that is if it is a relatively small group whose members' preferences are similar to those of consumers who value quality less.

There are several general lessons suggested by our analysis. First, the product designed for one class of buyers imposes limits on the prices set for other classes. This can lead to distortions in the product design decision. In our example, the monopolist set the quality of the product for the customer groups 1 and 2 at a point where the target customer's marginal willingness to pay for quality (b_i-q_i) was greater than the marginal cost.

Second, the monopolist will not always offer a separate product for each customer group. New products are added to the line only if the group of customers they attract are sufficiently large relative to the number of buyers of more profitable products, or if the new product is sufficiently unattractive to buyers of more profitable products. In our model, the profit margin was an increasing function of product quality, so the number of buyers of more profitable products was the same as the number with a higher willingness to pay for quality. This fact simplified both the graphical treatment and the mathematical analysis.

Third, in our model, the design of the top-of-the-line product line was efficient, given the target customer group; the highest valuation customer's marginal willingness to pay for quality (b_3-q_3) was equated to the marginal cost c. This last observation reflects a general principle that holds for a wide variety of product line design problems and has analogues for many other problems as well: The most profitable product in a profit-maximizing line will always be designed efficiently for its intended user group, for it can be designed without concern that purchasers of more profitable products might switch to it.

Throughout this analysis, one product attribute – price – has been given a distinct and special role. This is not because of any special demand attribute of price but because price enters directly into both the seller's profits and the buyer's welfare. A creative seller need not specify a single price for his product, but can charge prices that depend on product usage or related variables.

For an example along these lines, consider the form that price discrimination has taken in the United States airline industry in the 1980s. There, an attempt was made to discriminate between business travellers, who have a relatively inelastic demand for air travel, and vacation travellers, whose demand is much more elastic. Partly, the discrimination has taken the form of restrictive rules on travel, limiting the time of day that certain fares were available or charging lower fares on flights that involved staying over a Saturday night. However, these restrictions still allowed some business travellers to take advantage of the lower fares intended for vacation travellers. The problem, as it would appear to an airline, was to find a way to charge business travellers more for a product with *identical* characteristics, where the usual devices of self-selection are not available.

One device that the airlines found effective was the use of cancellation charges for many types of fares. Vacation travellers typically arrange dates with their employers, or with co-travellers; so they may be expected to cancel infrequently. Business travellers' plans are more subject to last minute changes. Consequently, business travellers pay more cancellation charges more frequently, and so pay a higher average price per flight than vacation travellers.

The device of linking the price paid by a purchaser to some random event over which he has limited control has been found valuable in other applications as well. Milgrom and Weber (1982) labelled a mathematical analogue of this observation the *Linkage Principle*, and applied it to show how certain kinds of auction mechanisms did systematically better than others in terms of the expected price they obtained. The fourth lesson of our analysis is that sellers can generally benefit by applying the Linkage Principle, that is, using information not subject to the buyer's control in setting the price.

Our formal analysis has been highly stylized both in its limited specification of possible demands and in its rarely satisfied assumption that products can be varied on only one dimension. Nevertheless, as we have seen, it suggests general insights and principles and helps to illuminate the trade-offs that a discriminating monopolist faces and to account for the limited quality spectrum offered by individual manufacturers for items ranging from food processors to furniture.

4 CONCLUSION

Half a century ago, Joan Robinson gave the standard treatment of third-degree price discrimination by a monopolist facing separated markets. In the ensuing years, the scope of the theory of price discrimination has grown to include virtually all the practices that a monopolist, protected from entry, might use to increase its profits. Throughout it all, the principles of monopoly theory on which the entire edifice was based have gone unchallenged. Here, we have challenged the basic principles of monopoly and price discrimination theory according to which the seller has full power to set what price it will. We have also advanced the analysis of applications for those cases in which the seller does have unchecked power to set the price. In the latter case, we have emphasized principles of product line analysis design that we expect to apply whenever the monopolist can control his product design, even if he must sometimes negotiate prices for specific customers.

First, and most fundamentally, we have challenged the notion that the monopolist-seller has all the bargaining power and that even first-degree price discrimination allows it to extract all the surplus generated by exchange. The different amounts paid by different users more plausibly represent the natural outcome of individual bargaining between the monopolist and its customers. Generally, bargaining of this sort leads to a sharing of surplus between the buyer and seller. Laws that prohibit price discrimination or restrictions on resale strengthen the seller's hand in bargaining and create a free-rider problem among the buyers. Our analysis is important because it calls into question the foundations of monopoly theory, which pays too little attention to the countervailing strategies available to customers.

Second, we have examined how a firm might discriminate among customers by careful arrangement of its product line. We went on to show how a seller who offers just one product may nevertheless succeed in charging different effective prices to different buyers, by exploiting the Linkage Principle.

Fifty years ago, the theory of monopoly was a subject of lively research controversies, with Robinson as one of its central figures. Today, after a period of relative dormancy, the theory of monopoly is once again in turmoil. One can only hope that some of the new theories will be as fruitful for enhancing our understanding of today's issues as the old were for the issues of their times.

MATHEMATICAL APPENDIX

The monopoly discrimination problem, using the specified forms for $V(Q,a,n)$, is:

$$\max_{p_1,\ldots,p_N,q_1,\ldots,q_N} \quad M_1q_1 + \ldots + M_Np_N$$

subject to, for all n and j,

(IC) $\quad b_nq_n - q_n^2/2 - p_n \geq b_nq_j - q_j^2/2 - p_j$ and

(PC) $\quad b_nq_n - q_n^2/2 - p_n \geq 0.$

Analysis of the Constraints

1. $q_1 \leqslant \ldots \leqslant q_N$.

Proof Choose any i and k between 1 and N. Consider the two constraints (IC) in which i and k play the roles of n and j, respectively. Summing these two constraints leads to:

$$(b_i - b_k)(q_i - q_k) \geqslant 0.$$

By hypothesis, $b_i > b_k$ if and only if $i > k$, so the result is proved.

2. Given the constraints (IC) for $|j-n|=1$, the constraints (IC) for $|j-n|>1$ are redundant.

Proof We prove, by induction, that all the (IC) constraints are satisfied if the ones with $|j-n|=1$ are. Thus, the constraints where $|j-n|=1$ are satisfied by hypothesis. Suppose all the constraints are satisfied for any j and n such that $|j-n| \leqslant k$. Consider the two constraints for i and m where $i-m=k$.

Using the induction hypothesis, (IC) holds for the pair $(i, i-1)$ and the pair $(i-1, m)$. Summing these two yields (IC) for (i, m). Similarly, summing (IC) for the pairs $(m, m+1)$ and $(m+1, i)$ yields (IC) for the pair (m, i).

3. Given the constraints (IC) and the constraints (PC) for $n=1$, the constraints (PC) for $n>1$ are redundant.

Proof The constraint (PC) for any $n>1$ is obtained by summing the corresponding (PC) constraint for $n=1$ and the constraint (IC) for the pair $(n,1)$.

Dropping the constraints identified as redundant in 2 and 3 above, we proceed to study the monopolist's maximization.

Analysis of the Optimal Prices

Fix any non-decreasing set of qualities $q_1, \ldots, q_N$. Let $d_1 = p_1$ and let d_n for $n>1$ be $p_n - p_{n-1}$. The letter 'd' is a mnemonic for price 'differential'. Performing a change of variables in the monopolist's problem, we get:

$$\operatorname*{Max}_{d_1,\ldots,d_N} \quad M_1 d_1 + (M_1 + M_2) d_2 + \ldots + (M_1 + \ldots + M_N) d_N$$

subject to

(IC$^-$) $b_n(q_n - q_{n-1}) - (q_n^2 - q_{n-1}^2)/2 \geqslant d_n$ for all $n > 1$.

(IC$^+$) $b_{n-1}(q_{n-1} - q_n) - (q_{n-1}^2 - q_n^2)/2 \leqslant d_n$ for all $n > 1$.

(PC^1) $b_1 q_1 - q_1^2/2 \geqslant d_1$.

The inequalities (IC$^-$) correspond to (IC) with arguments n and $n-1$. The inequalities (IC$^+$) correspond to (IC) with arguments $n-1$ and n. Since $b_n > b_{n-1}$ and $q_n \geqslant q_{n-1}$ by hypothesis, the inequalities are consistent.

Note that the objective function is increasing in the d_n's. Also, the constraint set consists of one upper bound constraint for each d_n (given by (IC$^-$) and (PC^1)) and one lower bound constraint for d_n for each $n > 1$ (given by (IC$^+$)). It is clear, therefore, that all the upper bound constraints are binding at the optimum, that is, (PC^1) and (IC$^-$) for $n > 1$ hold as inequalities. That completely determines the optimum prices as a function of the qualities.

Analysis of the Optimal Qualities Offered

The price obtained by the monopolist for product n is now $d_1 + \ldots + d_n$, and the d_k's have now been derived for any quality choices $q_1, \ldots, q_N$. Using the foregoing analysis and, for notational simplicity, fixing $q_0 = 0$, the monopolist's optimal quality choice problem can be formulated as follows.

$$\max_{q_1, \ldots, q_N} \sum_{n=1}^{N} M_n \left(\sum_{k=1}^{n} d_k - q_n c \right)$$

subject to:

$$d_n = b_n(q_n - q_{n-1}) - (q_n^2 - q_{n-1}^2)/2 \quad \text{for } n = 1, \ldots, N, \text{ and}$$

$$0 = q_0 \leqslant q_1 \leqslant \ldots \leqslant q_N.$$

Substituting the equality constraints governing the d_n's into the objective yields a quadratic maximization problem. The solution to this problem together with the associated prices determine the monopolist's optimal pricing and product selection strategy.

The case examined in detail in the main text was the 'interior optimum' case, in which the $q_0 \leqslant q_1 \leqslant \ldots \leqslant q_N$ constraints do not bind. Then, the first-order condition corresponding to any quality level q_s is:

$$M_s(b_s - q_s - c) - \sum_{n=s+1}^{N} M_n(b_{s+1} - q_s) = 0 \quad \text{or}$$

$$(b_{s+1}-q_s)/(b_s-q_s-c)=M_s/(M_{s+1}+\ldots+M_N),$$

as derived from the figures in the paper. An analysis of which of the constraints $q_{n-1}\leqslant q_n$ bind, and of when none of these constraints bind, is given by Maskin and Riley (1984).

Notes

1. Philips (1983) provides a survey of the modern theory and evidence on price discrimination, and Wilson (1985) provides an even more complete theoretical account.
2. Bundling is the practice of offering a variety of goods together in a package, or offering goods both individually and in packages with the packages selling at a substantial discount.
3. An example of how far companies might go to achieve discrimination among customers is illustrated by the following example drawn from Scherer (1980), who cited Stocking and Watkins (1946). They reported that Rohm and Haas considered adding arsenic to their industrial plastic moulding powder methyl methacrylate to prevent it from being converted for use in denture manufacture. The industrial version of the compound sold for \$.85 per pound while the version used in denture manufacture sold for \$22 per pound.
4. Others have argued that, sometimes, the monopolist's power to set prices is limited by difficulties of commitment. Coase (1972) has argued that the temptation to engage in price discrimination prevents the monopolist-supplier of a durable good from achieving much more than competitive profits. See Gul, Sonnenschein, and Wilson (1986) for a formalization of this argument, which makes the underlying assumptions and conditions quite clear.
5. The opposite extreme, in which the seller has a fixed supply available, is considered by Milgrom (1987) for the case where there are no restrictions on resale.
6. Fudenberg and Kreps (1986) analyze the costs of benefits of commitment via reputation in a related industrial competition context.
7. This is a special case of the more general result that holds for incentive constraints when the indifference curves in price-quality space satisfy Spence's single crossing condition. For such models, only the 'local' incentive constraints can ever be binding. In models like this one for which making no purchase is like purchasing quality level zero, an additional general conclusion is that the only binding participation constraint is the one for the class of customers with the least willingness to pay for quality.

References

Adams, W. and J. Dirlam (1984) 'Steel Imports and Vertical Integration', *American Economic Review*, 54: 640–6.

Coase, R. (1972) 'Durability and Monopoly', *Journal of Law and Economics,* 15: 143–9.

Debreu, G. (1959) *Theory of Value* (New Haven, Conn.: Yale University Press).

Fudenberg, D. and D. Kreps (1986) 'Reputation and Multiple Opponents, I:

Identical Entrants', Institute of Business and Economic Research Working Paper No. 8602 (Berkeley: University of California).
Gul, F., H. Sonnenschein and R. Wilson (1986) 'Foundations of Dynamic Monopoly and the Coase Conjecture', *Journal of Economic Theory,* 21.
Harris, M. and A. Raviv (1981) 'A Theory of Monopoly Pricing with Uncertain Demand', *American Economic Review,* 71: 347–65.
Kreps, D. and R. Wilson (1982) 'Reputation and Imperfect Information', *Journal of Economic Theory,* 27: 253–79.
McAfee, P. and J. McMillan (1987) 'Competition for Agency Contracts', Working Paper, University of Western Ontario.
Maskin, E. and J. Riley (1984) 'Monopoly with Incomplete Information', *Rand Journal of Economics,* 15: 171–96.
Milgrom, P. (1980) 'Price Discrimination Supported by Quality Variations', unpublished lecture notes, Northwestern University.
Milgrom, P. (1987) 'Auction Theory' in *Advances in Economic Theory, 1985: Invited Papers from the Fifth World Congress of the Econometric Society*, Truman Bewley (ed.).
Milgrom, P. and J. Roberts (1982) 'Predation, Reputation, and Entry Deterrence', *Journal of Economic Theory*, 27: 280–312.
Milgrom, P. and R. Weber (1982) 'A Theory of Auctions and Competitive Bidding', *Econometrica,* 50: 1089–1122.
Philips, L. (1983) *The Economics of Price Discrimination,* (Cambridge: Cambridge University Press).
Pigou, A. (1920) *The Economics of Welfare* (London: Macmillan).
Robinson, J. (1969) *The Economics of Imperfect Competition*, 2nd edn (London: Macmillan).
Scherer, F. (1980) *Industrial Market Structure and Economic Performance*, 2nd edn (Chicago: Rand McNally).
Schelling, T. (1960) *The Strategy of Conflict* (Cambridge, Mass.: Harvard University Press).
Stocking, G. and M. Watkins (1946) *Cartels in Action* (New York: Twentieth Century Fund) pp.402–4.
Wilson, R. (1985) 'Economic Theories of Price Discrimination and Product Differentiation: A Survey', lecture notes, Stanford University.

11 Competitive Discriminatory Pricing

Jean J. Gabszewicz and Jacques-François Thisse*

1 INTRODUCTION

Business practices often take advantage of the heterogeneity in the consumer population: product lines and price schedules are especially designed to discriminate among consumers on the basis of their taste and/or income diversity.

However, because there are many interacting forces, it is not easy to identify the process through which a particular product mix and price schedule emerges on the market.

First, there are cost barriers to brand proliferation: the existence of substantial overhead costs may drastically reduce the ability of firms to adapt their product lines to the spectrum of consumer tastes and incomes. The cost advantage from concentrating productive effort on a restricted number of products may outweigh the increased potential for surplus extraction accruing from increased product variety.

Second, the nature of the product mix also depends on the type of heterogeneity observed in the consumer population. The potential customers of a product may have different opinions about the ranking of its variants, as in the case of the location of firms in geographical space. This means that each variety has its own circle of customers, and a wide range of different substitutes can survive in the market because each of them combines the attributes of the product in a fashion suitable to a particular class of consumers ('horizontal' product differentiation). Alternatively, the potential customers of a product may have a unanimous ranking of the possible substitutes, as in the case of a luxury or standard variant of the product. Then the range of substitutes surviving on the market must rather reflect income differences or different intensity of preferences in the consumer population ('vertical' product differentiation).

Third, the possibility of discriminating in prices and/or product quality between different consumers heavily relies on the ability of firms to identify their income or taste characteristics. In many cases sellers face an 'impersonal' market and, even if they know the distribution of consumer characteristics, they cannot explicitly distinguish one consumer from

* The authors thank S. Anderson for his comments on a first draft.

another. This may well prevent the firms from exploiting full price discrimination among consumers with varying willingness to pay.

Last, but not least, the observed market product mix and price schedule also reflects the competitive context in which firms operate. The possibility for each firm to attract customers around the variants of the product it offers crucially depends on the product constellations and price schedules chosen by its competitors. Accordingly, the way prices are settled and products are designed to sort different consumers among differentiated goods should be widely explained by the underlying competitive process.

Several recent studies have paved the way for better insights into the understanding of the problems raised above. Mussa and Rosen (1978) pioneered the study of the optimal product mix and pricing policy under vertical differentiation, for a monopolist facing a population of consumers of varying intensities of preferences. They assume a continuous quality differentiated spectrum of products with marginal costs increasing in quality, and constant in output for any given quality. They also assume that the monopolist cannot distinguish among buyers, and thereby cannot extract the whole surplus by fully discriminating among them. A similar analysis was conducted by Gabszewicz, Shaked, Sutton and Thisse (1986) when the spectrum of goods is finite and the heterogeneity of consumers follows from income differences. The extension of this approach to duopoly has been recently explored by Champsaur and Rochet (1985).

All the above studies assume that there is no extra set-up cost for the firms to adapt their product lines to consumers' characteristics: product variety may possibly cover the whole spectrum of tastes and incomes. At the other extreme, one assumes that overhead costs are so high that each firm must specialize in the production of a single variant only. Then product competition among firms is drastically weakened since each of them can choose at most a single point in the space of attributes, and not a whole spectrum of variants. Price and product competition under such circumstances was first analyzed by Hotelling (1929) in his pathbreaking contribution on spatial competition. He introduced the prototype of horizontal product differentiation, which constitutes the location model; in this model, each firm charges the same mill price to all consumers, who also bear transportation costs. Hotelling's contribution is at the root of modern theories of monopolistic competition, such as Lancaster (1979), Salop (1979) and Archibald, Eaton and Lipsey (1986). The extension of Hotelling's analysis to the case where firms are allowed to discriminate between consumers according to their location has been initially conducted by Hoover (1937), and recently pursued by MacLeod, Norman and Thisse (1985) and Lederer and Hurter (1986).

Under vertical differentiation, the study of price and product competition between firms each offering a single variant of the product at uniform prices was first introduced by the authors (Gabszewicz and Thisse, 1979;

1980) and pursued by Shaked and Sutton (1982; 1983) and by the authors again (Gabszewicz and Thisse, 1986). In these approaches, oligopolists face a population of consumers ranked by order of increasing income or increasing valuation of the good. Firms choose the particular quality produced from a continuous spectrum of quality variants. Marginal costs are assumed constant in quantity, but increasing with quality. Thus, the model is close to the one proposed by Mussa and Rosen (1978), except that oligopoly has been substituted for pure monopoly, and that firms are allowed to choose only a single variant of the product.

In this chapter, we use a similar model to analyze price and product competition under vertical differentiation, when firms are allowed to discriminate between consumers according to their intensity of desire for the good. Consequently, the present approach can be viewed as the counterpart, for the case of vertical differentiation, of Hoover's contribution for the case of horizontal differentiation. Here two firms each sell a product of different quality to a population of consumers ranked by order of increasing intensities of tastes. We suppose that the firms not only know the distribution of tastes in the market, but can also distinguish among buyers according to their valuations of the good. Then they can engage in price discrimination and possibly charge each buyer a specific price.

Admittedly, in the case of physical goods, there are not many real-world examples where vertical differentiation is combined with discriminatory pricing. This is because consumers can retrade the product among themselves without cost, thus destroying the potential for price discrimination. Furthermore, in practice, it is often difficult for firms to identify consumers by their taste and/or income characteristics. On the other hand, in the case of professional services (doctors, lawyers, psychoanalysts, etc.), arbitrage is impossible and, because of the personal relationships between clients and suppliers, the identification of consumers' characteristics becomes much less problematic. Consequently, price discrimination is feasible and is, indeed, observed.

This chapter is organized as follows: In Section 2, we study the (noncooperative) equilibrium price schedules the firms will set for their products. Using these price patterns, we examine in Section 3 how the firms select a particular product variant. In Section 4, we analyze price competition and the resulting quality profile which arises when firms cannot price discriminate and, instead, charge uniform prices. In Section 5, we characterize the Pareto-optimal selection of qualities (when the products are sold at marginal cost), and compare it with the quality profiles obtained under uniform and discriminatory pricing. Finally, in Section 6, we provide a brief comparison of price discrimination and product selection under vertical and horizontal differentiation.

2 THE EQUILIBRIUM PRICE SCHEDULES

To analyze the impact of discriminatory pricing on quality choice, we shall use a simple model, inspired from Mussa and Rosen (1978), which illustrates the essential features of the solution. However, it is worth noting that the equilibrium price schedules corresponding to a given specification of qualities can be characterized at rather a high level of generality.

Consider a continuum of consumers with taste parameter θ distributed according to a continuous density function $f(\theta)$ on the range [0,1]. Let $q \varepsilon R_+$ be the (one-dimensional) quality index of a differentiated product; for two variants of the product indexed by q_1 and q_2, $q_1 < q_2$ means that the quality of variant 2 is higher than that of variant 1. Let $U(q,x;\theta) = u(q;\theta) + v(x)$ be the utility of a θ-type consumer who consumes a single unit of product q and x units of a (Hicksian) composite commodity. We assume that $U(q,x;\theta)$ is twice continuously differentiable and satisfies the following conditions: (i) $\delta u/\delta q > 0$, i.e. consumers unanimously prefer a high-quality variant to a low-quality variant; (ii) $\delta^2 u/\delta\theta\delta q > 0$, i.e. consumers are ranked in [0,1] by order of increasing marginal utility of quality; and (iii) $\delta v/\delta x > 0$, i.e. consumers prefer to have more of the composite commodity. Income, Y, is the same for all consumers. We suppose that Y is large enough for the equilibrium prices of the variants to be lower than θ-type consumers' reservation prices. Finally, it is supposed that no arbitrage is possible among consumers.

Two firms $i = 1,2$ each sell a variant of fixed quality q_1 and q_2, respectively, with $q_1 < q_2$. The unit cost of producing quality q is $c(q)$. We suppose that $c(q)$ is increasing in quality but constant in quantity for a given quality. Set

$$c_1 \underset{\text{def}}{=} c(q_1) \quad \text{and} \quad c_2 \underset{\text{def}}{=} c(q_2);$$

of course, we have $c_1 < c_2$.

Let $\bar{p}_1(\theta)$ be the unique solution to the equation

$$U(q_2, Y - c_2; \theta) = U(q_1, Y - \bar{p}_1(\theta); \theta), \tag{1}$$

that is, $\bar{p}_1(\theta)$ is the price of variant 1, expressed in units of the composite commodity, for which a θ-type consumer is indifferent between buying variant 2 at cost and variant 1. Similarly, let $\bar{p}_2(\theta)$ be the unique solution such that

$$U(q_2, Y - \bar{p}_2(\theta); \theta) = U(q_1, Y - c_1; \theta) \tag{2}$$

holds. Clearly, both $\bar{p}_1(\theta)$ and $\bar{p}_2(\theta)$ are continuous on [0,1].

In this section, we assume that firms can identify potential customers by their taste characteristic θ and, therefore, can charge specific prices to each type of consumer, even for the same quality item. In particular, both firms know the prices $\bar{p}_1(\theta)$ and $\bar{p}_2(\theta)$ for each type θ.

We define a (non-cooperative) *discriminatory pricing equilibrium* as a pair of price schedules $(p_1^*(\cdot),p_2^*(\cdot))$ assigning a pair of prices $(p_1^*(\theta),p_2^*(\theta))$, for variants 1 and 2, respectively, to each type θ of consumer, such that no firm can increase its profits by unilateral deviation from the chosen price schedule.

Given that firm *i* would refuse to supply consumers at a price lower than its marginal production cost, we assume for simplicity that the admissible price schedules are such that $p_i(\theta) \geqq c_i$ for all θ.[1,2]

We now state our first result.

Proposition 1 If a discriminatory pricing equilibrium exists, then it is unique and given by

$$p_1^*(\theta) = \text{Max}\,\{\bar{p}_1(\theta),c_1\}$$

$$p_2^*(\theta) = \max\,\{\bar{p}_2(\theta),c_2\}.$$

This follows from the lemmas given below; proofs are given in the Appendix.

Lemma 1

Let $(\tilde{p}_1(\cdot),\tilde{p}_2(\cdot))$ be a discriminatory pricing equilibrium. Then

$$U(q_2, Y - \tilde{p}_2(\theta);\theta) = U(q_1, Y - \tilde{p}_1(\theta);\theta).$$

Lemma 2

Let $(\tilde{p}_1(\cdot),\tilde{p}_2(\cdot))$ be a discriminatory pricing equilibrium. Then $\tilde{p}_i(\theta) = c_i$ for at least one value of *i*.

Lemma 3

Let $(\tilde{p}_1(\cdot),\tilde{p}_2(\cdot))$ be a discriminatory pricing equilibrium. Then $\tilde{p}_i(\theta) = \text{Max}\,\{\tilde{p}_i(\theta),c_i\}$ for $i = 1,2$.

It follows from Lemma 1 that, for each θ, θ-type consumers are indifferent between buying variant 1 at $p_1^*(\theta)$ and variant 2 at $p_2^*(\theta)$. Accordingly, the profit functions cannot be defined and, therefore, the existence of an equilibrium cannot be analyzed.

To remove this difficulty, we need a rule specifying how consumers choose between the two variants. To this end, we state some intermediate results (proofs are given in the Appendix).

Lemma 4

$\bar{p}_1(\theta)$ is decreasing and $\bar{p}_2(\theta)$ is increasing on [0,1].

Lemma 5

$p_1^*(\theta)=c_1$ and $p_2^*(\theta)=c_2$ for at most one value of θ.

Lemma 6

If $\bar{p}_1(\theta)=c_1$ at $\bar{\theta}\in]0,1[$, then $\bar{p}_2(\bar{\theta})=c_2$.

The above lemmas imply that the only possible equilibrium configurations are as follows:

(i) $p_1^*(\theta)=c_1$ and $p_2^*(\theta)=\bar{p}_2(\theta)$ for $\theta\in[0,1]$;

(ii) $p_1^*(\theta)=\bar{p}_1(\theta)$ and $p_2^*(\theta)=c_2$ for $\theta\in[0,1]$;

(iii) $\bar{\theta}\in]0,1[$ exists such that $\bar{p}_1(\bar{\theta})=c_1$:

– $p_1^*(\theta)=\bar{p}_1(\theta)$ and $p_2^*(\theta)=c_2$ for $\theta\in[0,\bar{\theta}[$

– $p_1^*(\theta)=c_1$ and $p_2^*(\theta)=\bar{p}_2(\theta)$ for $\theta\in[\bar{\theta},1]$.

Set $\theta^*=0$ in case (i); $\theta^*=1$ in case (ii); and $\theta^*=\bar{\theta}$ in case (iii). Hence, for $\theta\in[0,\theta^*[$, firm 1 can always attract all θ-type consumers by slightly decreasing its price without possible retaliation from firm 2: firm 2 already sells at cost. Similarly, for $\theta\in[\theta^*,1]$, firm 2 can secure all θ-type consumers by applying a marginal price decrease. Consequently, it is natural to assign θ-type consumers to firm 1 when $\theta\in[0,\theta^*[$, and to firm 2 when $\theta\in[\theta^*,1]$. Given this choice rule, profit functions can then be written as follows:

$$\Pi_1(p_1^*(\cdot),p_2^*(\cdot))=\int_0^1 [p_1^*(\theta)-c_1]f(\theta)d\theta$$

$$=\int_0^{\theta^*} [\bar{p}_1(\theta)-c_1]f(\theta)d\theta$$

and

$$\Pi_2(p_1^*(\cdot),p_2^*(\cdot)) = \int_0^1 [p_2^*(\theta) - c_2]f(\theta)d\theta$$

$$= \int_{\theta^*}^1 [\bar{p}_2(\theta) - c_2]f(\theta)d\theta.$$

It is now readily verified that any unilateral change of a price schedule $p_1^*(\cdot)$ or $p_2^*(\cdot)$ on a non-null subset of [0,1] gives rise to a decrease in the firm's profit. In consequence, we have:

Proposition 2 There exists a discriminatory pricing equilibrium.

The intuition behind the above two propositions is rather simple. Since firms are able to discriminate among consumers, they compete in prices on each submarket formed by θ-type consumers. Firm 2 has an advantage over firm 1 in that it sells a product of higher quality. Consequently, by lowering its price, firm 2 can force firm 1 to decrease its own price to the level of unit cost c_1, as long as this does not lead firm 2 to sell at a price lower than c_2. If the relative intensity of preferences for variant 2 is so low that firm 2 cannot attract θ-type consumers at price c_2, then firm 1 is allowed to raise its price above c_1 up to the level where these consumers are indifferent between buying either variant, i.e. $\bar{p}_1(\theta)$. On the other hand, for high θ-values, competition drives down firm 1's price to the unit cost c_1, while firm 2 quotes the highest price that allows it to keep these customers, i.e. $\bar{p}_2(\theta)$. In this case, firm 2 specializes on the segment of consumers whose marginal utility of quality is high; firm 1 sells to consumers with a low marginal utility of quality.

When θ increases from 0 to 1, variant 1 becomes less and less attractive relative to variant 2. Accordingly, on $[0,\theta^*[$, $\bar{p}_1(\theta)$ must decrease to keep θ-type consumers away from variant 2 priced at c_2; on $[\theta^*,1]$, variant 1 is priced at c_1, but firm 2 sells at an increasing price $\bar{p}_2(\theta)$, which expresses firm 2's relative advantage.[3]

To illustrate, let us consider the following specification of the utility function:

$$U(q,x;\theta) = \bar{U} + \theta q + x \tag{3}$$

if a θ-type consumer buys one unit of variant q;

$$U(q,x;\theta) = x,$$

otherwise. In the sequel, we assume that $\bar{U}$ is a constant large enough for θ-type consumers to buy one variant of the differentiated product.

Using (3), we easily derive $\bar{p}_1(\theta)$ and $\bar{p}_2(\theta)$ from (1) and (2):

$$\bar{p}_1(\theta) = -(q_2 - q_1)\theta + c_2 \tag{4}$$

and

$$\bar{p}_2(\theta) = (q_2 - q_1)\theta + c_1. \tag{5}$$

Firm 2 would sell to all consumers if and only if $\bar{p}_2(0) \geqq c_2$. This condition amounts to $c_1 \geqq c_2$ which does not hold since $q_1 < q_2$. Firm 1 does not supply all consumers if and only if $U(q_2, Y - c_2; 1) > U(q_1, Y - c_1; 1)$, i.e.

$$q_2 - q_1 > c_2 - c_1. \tag{6}$$

Consequently, if (6) holds, $\bar{\theta} \in]0,1[$ exists such that

$$U(q_2, Y - c_2; \bar{\theta}) = U(q_1, Y - c_1; \bar{\theta}),$$

that is

$$\bar{\theta} = \frac{c_2 - c_1}{q_2 - q_1}. \tag{7}$$

We are now equipped to describe the equilibrium price schedule: for $\theta \in [0, \bar{\theta}[$,

$$p_1^*(\theta) = -(q_2 - q_1)\theta + c_2 \tag{8a}$$

and

$$p_2^*(\theta) = c_2 \tag{9a}$$

for $\theta \in [\bar{\theta}, 1]$,

$$p_1^*(\theta) = c_1 \tag{8b}$$

and

$$p_2^*(\theta) = (q_2 - q_1)\theta - c_1. \tag{9b}$$

These price schedules are shown in Figure 11.1.

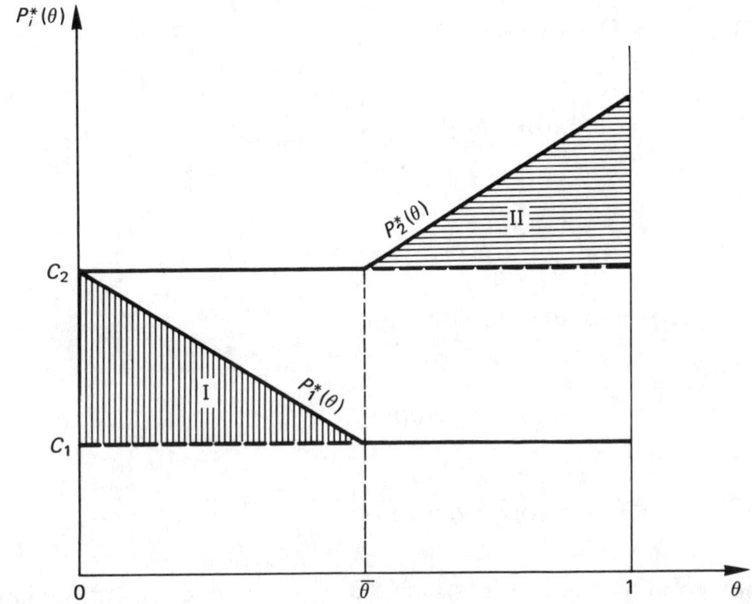

Figure 11.1

3 QUALITY COMPETITION AND DISCRIMINATORY PRICING

Now we turn to the problem of product selection under discriminatory pricing. To this end, we assume that each firm, anticipating the equilibrium price schedules, chooses its most profitable quality, given the quality choice of its competitor. Formally, this means that product selection is made at the first stage of a subgame perfect Nash equilibrium, the second stage of which is the price subgame studied in Section 2.

For simplicity, we consider a specific model in which a θ-type consumer utility function is given by (3), the unit cost of producing quality q is

$$c(q) = q^2/2 \tag{10}$$

and the density function $f(\theta)$ is equal to 1 on [0,1]. Given (10), (7) becomes

$$\bar{\theta} = \frac{q_1 + q_2}{2}. \tag{11}$$

For every given quality pair (q_1, q_2) such that $q_1 < q_2$ and $q_1 + q_2 < 2$, profits of firms 1 and 2 evaluated at the equilibrium price schedules (8*a*,*b*) and (9*a*,*b*) are respectively given by the area of triangles I and II in Figure 11.1:

$$\Pi_1^*(q_1,q_2) = \int_0^{\bar{\theta}} [\bar{p}_1(\theta) - c(q_1)]d\theta$$

$$= \frac{1}{2}\bar{\theta}[\bar{p}_1(0) = c(q_1)]$$

$$= \frac{1}{8}(q_2 - q_1)(q_1 + q_2)^2; \tag{12}$$

$$\Pi_2^*(q_1,q_2) = \int_{\bar{\theta}}^{1} [\bar{p}_2(\theta) - c(q_2)]d\theta$$

$$= \frac{1}{2}(1 - \bar{\theta})[\bar{p}_2(1) - c(q_2)]$$

$$= \frac{1}{8}(q_2 - q_1)(2 - q_1 - q_2)^2. \tag{13}$$

For any given pair of qualities such that $q_1 < q_2$ and $q_1 + q_2 \geqq 2$, we have

$$\Pi_1^*(q_1,q_2) = \int_0^{1} [\bar{p}_1(\theta) - c(q_1)]d\theta$$

$$= \frac{1}{2}[\bar{p}_1(0) - c(q_1)]$$

$$= \frac{q_2^2 - q_1^2}{4}; \tag{14}$$

$$\Pi_2^*(q_1,q_2) = 0; \tag{15}$$

while

$$\Pi_1^*(q_1,q_2) = \Pi_2^*(q_1,q_2) = 0 \tag{16}$$

when $q_1 = q_2$.

The product selection problem is solved at the non-cooperative equilibrium (q_1^*,q_2^*) of the game whose payoff functions are given by (12)–(16) and strategies by qualities q_1 and q_2.

If a quality equilibrium (q_1^*,q_2^*) exists, it must be such that both firms have a positive profit, which implies $q_1^* + q_2^* < 2$ and $\bar{\theta}(q_1^*,q_2^*) < 1$. Accordingly, q_1^* and q_2^* must be the solutions of the first-order conditions:

$$\frac{\delta\Pi_1^*}{\delta q_1}=\frac{1}{8}[-(q_1+q_2)^2+2(q_2-q_1)(q_2+q_1)]=0$$

$$\frac{\delta\Pi_2^*}{\delta q_2}=\frac{1}{8}[(2-q_1-q_2)^2-2(q_2-q_1)(2-q_1-q_2)]=0;$$

that is, $q_1^*=1/4$ and $q_2^*=3/4$.

It remains to be shown that $\Pi_i^*(q_i^*,q_j^*)\geqq\Pi_i^*(q_i,q_j)$ for all $q_i\geqq 0$ and $i=1,2$. Consider firm 1. For $q_1<q_2^*$, we have

$$\frac{\delta^2\Pi_1^*}{\delta q_1^2}=-\frac{1}{4}(3q_1+q_2)<0$$

so that $\Pi_1^*(q_1,q_2^*)$ is maximized at q_1^* on $[0,q_2^*]$. Furthermore, for $q_2^*<q_1<2-q_2^*$, firm 1's profits are given by (13) where indices 1 and 2 are permuted, i.e. $\Pi_1^*(q_1,q_2^*)=1/8(q_1-3/4)(2-q_1-3/4)^2$. A simple argument then shows that $\hat{q}_1=11/12$ is the only maximizer of $\Pi_1^*(q_1,q_2^*)$ on $[q_2^*,2-q_2^*]$. It is easily verified that $\Pi_1^*(q_1^*,q_2^*)>\Pi_1^*(\hat{q}^1,q_2^*)$. As $\Pi_1^*(q_1,q_2^*)=0$ for $q_1>2-q_2^*$, $\Pi_1^*(q_1,q_2^*)$ is therefore maximized at q_1^* on R_+. We now turn to the case of firm 2. We have

$$\left.\frac{\delta\Pi_2^*}{\delta q_2}\right|_{q_1=1/4}>0 \quad \text{if } q_1^*<q_2<q_2^*$$

and

$$\left.\frac{\delta\Pi_2^*}{\delta q_2}\right|_{q_1=1/4}<0 \quad \text{if } q_2^*<q_2<2-q_1^*,$$

so that q_2^* maximizes $\Pi_2^*(q_1^*,q_2)$ on $[q_1^*,2-q_1^*]$. The only maximizer of $\Pi_2^*(q_1^*,q_2)$ on $[0,q_1^*]$ is $\hat{q}_2=1/12$. A direct calculation shows that $\Pi_2^*(q_1^*,q_2^*)>\Pi_2^*(q_1^*,\hat{q}_2)$.

Finally, it is readily verified that (1/4,3/4) is the only equilibrium of the quality game.

In consequence, we have the following result:

Proposition 3 The qualities supplied by firms 1 and 2 under discriminatory pricing are, respectively, $q_1^*=1/4$ and $q_2^*=3/4$.

4 PRICE AND PRODUCT COMPETITION UNDER UNIFORM PRICING

In the previous two sections, we assumed that firms not only knew the distribution of the characteristic θ, but were also able to distinguish consumers on the basis of their characteristics. If, by contrast, firms face an impersonal market in that they only know the distribution of characteristics, each must sell its product at a uniform price. For further comparison we now analyze the non-cooperative market solution under *uniform* pricing.

Denote by p_1 (resp. p_2) the price of firm 1 (resp. 2) selling a product of quality q_1 (resp. q_2). To define the demand function $D_i(p_1,p_2)$ for each firm i, $i=1,2$, let $\tilde{\theta}$ denote the consumer who is indifferent between buying product 1 at price p_1 and product 2 at price p_2, i.e. $\tilde{\theta}$ solves the equation

$$\theta q_1 - p_1 = \theta q_2 - p_2,$$

which implies

$$\tilde{\theta} = \frac{p_2 - p_1}{q_2 - q_1};$$

All consumers θ with $0 \leqq \theta < \tilde{\theta}$ buy from firm 1, while those with $\tilde{\theta} \leqq \theta \leqq 1$ buy from firm 2. Accordingly,

$$D_1(p_1,p_2) = \tilde{\theta}$$

and

$$D_2(p_1,p_2) = 1 - \tilde{\theta},$$

so that, if Π_1 denotes the profits of firm 1, we get

$$\Pi_1(p_1,p_2) = (p_1 - c_1)\tilde{\theta} = \frac{p_2 - p_1}{q_2 - q_1}(p_1 - c_1) \tag{17}$$

and

$$\Pi_2(p_1,p_2) = (p_2 - c_2)(1 - \tilde{\theta}) = \left(1 - \frac{p_2 - p_1}{q_2 - q_1}\right)(p_2 - c_2). \tag{18}$$

In the game with uniform pricing, the strategy space of firm i becomes the set of prices represented by the interval $[c_i, \infty[$. A (non-cooperative) *uniform pricing equilibrium* is then defined as a pair of *prices* $(\tilde{p}_1,\tilde{p}_2)$ such that

$$\Pi_1(\tilde{p}_1,\tilde{p}_2) \geqq \Pi_1(p_1,\tilde{p}_2), \quad \forall p_1 \geqq c_1$$

and

$$\Pi_2(\tilde{p}_1,\tilde{p}_2) \geqq \Pi_2(\tilde{p}_1,p_2), \quad \forall p_2 \geqq c_2.$$

Since the profit functions (17) and (18) are quasi-concave, a uniform pricing equilibrium always exists.

Using first-order conditions the following equations must hold at the uniform pricing equilibrium:

$$\frac{\delta \Pi_1}{\delta p_1} = p_2 - 2p_1 + c_1 = 0$$

and

$$\frac{\delta \Pi_1}{\delta p_2} = q_2 - q_1 + p_1 - 2p_2 + c_2 = 0,$$

so that[4]

$$\tilde{p}_1 = \frac{q_2 - q_1}{3} + \frac{c_2}{3} + \frac{2c_1}{3} \tag{19}$$

and

$$\tilde{p}_2 = \frac{2(q_2 - q_1)}{3} + \frac{2c_2}{3} + \frac{c_1}{3}. \tag{20}$$

Replacing $\tilde{p}_1$ and $\tilde{p}_2$ in $\tilde{\theta}$ shows that $\tilde{\theta}$ is always positive and that $\tilde{\theta} < 1$ iff $q_1 + q_2 < 4$.

To analyze *product* competition under uniform pricing we substitute $\tilde{p}_1$ and $\tilde{p}_2$ from (19) and (20) for p_1 and p_2 in (17) and (18); and replace c_1 and c_2 by $q_1^2/2$ and $q_2^2/2$, respectively. Then profits of firm 1 and 2 only depend on qualities q_1 and q_2 and are written as

$$\tilde{\Pi}_1(q_1,q_2) = \frac{1}{9}(q_2 - q_1)\left(1 + \frac{q_1 + q_2}{2}\right)^2 \tag{21}$$

and

$$\tilde{\Pi}_2(q_1,q_2) = \frac{1}{9}(q_2 - q_1)\left(2 - \frac{q_1 + q_2}{2}\right)^2, \tag{22}$$

respectively. Now we state the following:

Proposition 4

The qualities supplied by firms 1 and 2 under uniform pricing are, respectively, $\tilde{q}_1 = 0$ *and* $\tilde{q}_2 = 4/3$.

(The proof of Proposition 4 is given in the Appendix.)

Comparing Propositions 3 and 4, we see that quality profiles resulting from uniform and discriminatory pricing differ. Before proceeding further with this comparison, it is worth characterizing the optimal qualities examined from a welfare viewpoint; this is done at the beginning of Section 5.

5 PRODUCT COMPETITION AND THE PARETO-OPTIMAL QUALITY PROFILE

To derive the optimal pair of qualities which would be chosen by a social planner, we must assume that quality q is priced at marginal cost $c(q)$, i.e. $q^2/2$. Facing prices $q_1^2/2$ and $q_2^2/2$ for qualities q_1 and q_2, $(q_1 < q_2)$, respectively, all consumers in the interval $[0,\bar{\theta}[$ buy quality q_1 while those in the interval $[\bar{\theta},1]$ buy quality q_2, with $\bar{\theta}$ given by (7) (since $\bar{\theta}$ is constrained to be smaller than or equal to 1, we must have $q_1 + q_2 < 2$). Consumers' surplus $S(q_1,q_2)$ derived from the choice of qualities q_1 and q_2 is thus equal to

$$\int_0^{\bar{\theta}} [U(q_1, Y - c(q_1);\theta)]d\theta + \int_{\bar{\theta}}^1 [U(q_2, Y - c(q_2);\theta)]d\theta.$$

Substituting (10) and (6) in this expression, we get

$$S(q_1,q_2) = \frac{(q_1 + q_2)^2(q_2 - q_1)}{8} + \frac{q_2}{2}(1 - q_2). \tag{23}$$

Differentiating (23) with respect to q_1 and equating to zero yields

$$q_2 = 3q_1. \tag{24}$$

Differentiating (23) with respect to q_2 and using (24) yields

$$\left.\frac{\delta S}{\delta q_2}\right|_{q_1 = 3q_2} = 32q_1^2 - 24q_1 + 4 = 0$$

$$\Leftrightarrow q_1=\frac{1}{4} \quad \text{or} \quad q_1=\frac{1}{2}.$$

Since $\delta^2 S/\delta q_2^2=2q_1-8+6q_2<0$ when $q_1=1/4$, consumers' surplus is maximal when $q_1=1/4$ and $q_2=3/4$. To sum up:

Proposition 5 The Pareto-optimal product selection is given by the pair $(q_1^0,q_1^0)=(1/4,3/4)$, and thus coincides with the pair of qualities supplied by the firms at the discriminatory pricing equilibrium.

Using Propositions 4 and 5, we can now compare the quality profiles resulting from discriminatory and marginal cost pricing on the one hand, and from uniform pricing on the other. It is readily seen that the average quality supplied to consumers under discriminatory or marginal cost pricing is given by:

$$q_1^*\cdot\int_0^{\bar{\theta}(q_1^*,q_2^*)} d\theta+q_2^*\cdot\int_{\bar{\theta}(q_1^*,q_2^*)}^1 d\theta=\frac{1}{4}\cdot\frac{1}{2}+\frac{3}{4}\cdot\frac{1}{2}=\frac{1}{2}$$

where we use the fact that $\bar{\theta}(q_1^*,q_2^*)=\bar{\theta}(q_1^0,q_2^0)=1/2(1/4+3/4)=1/2$. The average quality supplied to consumers under uniform pricing is given by

$$\tilde{q}_1\cdot\int_0^{\tilde{\theta}(\tilde{q}_1,\tilde{q}_2)} d\theta+\tilde{q}_2\cdot\int_{\tilde{\theta}(\tilde{q}_1,\tilde{q}_2)}^1 d\theta=0+[1-\theta(\tilde{q}_1,\tilde{q}_2)]\cdot\frac{4}{3}=\frac{16}{27},$$

where we have used $\tilde{\theta}(\tilde{q}_1,\tilde{q}_2)=5/9$.

It is also interesting to compare the price levels under the three possible alternatives: uniform, discriminatory and marginal cost pricing. First, it is trivial that marginal cost pricing always leads to the lowest prices for all consumers. Perhaps less evident is the fact that each individual consumer is always faced with lower prices, for both qualities, under discriminatory rather than under uniform pricing. To see it, notice that the highest price for quality $q_1^*=1/4$ is borne by consumer $\theta=0$, i.e. $p_1^*(0)=c(q_2^*)=9/32$, while, for quality $q_2^*=3/4$, it is borne by consumer $\theta=1$, i.e. $p_2^*(1)=17/32$. It is then sufficient to check that the equilibrium uniform prices $\tilde{p}_1$ and $\tilde{p}_2$ corresponding to the pair of qualities $(\tilde{q}_1,\tilde{q}_2)=(0,3/4)$ exceed 9/32 and 17/32, respectively. Substituting $\tilde{q}_1$ and $\tilde{q}_2$ in (19) and (20), we get $\tilde{p}_1(\tilde{q}_1,\tilde{q}_2)=20/27$, which is indeed greater than $p_1^*(0)$, and $\tilde{p}_2(\tilde{q}_1,\tilde{q}_2)=40/27$ which is also greater than $p_2^*(1)$.

We may summarize the above comparisons in the following:

Proposition 6 The average quality supplied to the consumers under uniform pricing exceeds the average quality supplied under discriminatory (or marginal cost) pricing. For both qualities, however, the prices paid by consumers are higher under the former than under the latter.

The quality profiles selected by the firms reflect the subsequent pricing mechanism which will be used when this selection is realized. Under discriminatory pricing, prices are low since 'cut-throat' competition operating on each submarket allows each type of consumer to buy at least one of the two variants at marginal cost. Accordingly, firms are not induced to strongly differentiate their products to enjoy the benefits from a higher monopoly power; in fact they differentiate their products exactly as required by the welfare optimum. By contrast, under uniform pricing, product differences strongly influence profits since prices now affect a whole bunch of consumers for each product. Consequently, firms benefit from more substantial vertical differentiation, leading thereby to a weaker price competition. Furthermore, in our example, the combined effects of price and product competition entails a higher average quality than the one observed at the Pareto-optimal (or discriminatory pricing) product selection. However, the price effect more than compensates this quality effect. More specifically, under uniform pricing, consumers buying the standard variant pay a higher price for a lower quality, while consumers purchasing the luxury variant pay a higher price for a higher quality, but the net effect on utility is negative. As a result, *all* consumers are better off under discriminatory than under uniform pricing.

6 CONCLUSION

This paper is the natural complement of Hoover's idea to combine spatial competition and discriminatory pricing. Here, instead, we have assumed a vertically differentiated market. Interestingly enough, we have reached conclusions similar to those derived under horizontal differentiation: (i) There exists a discriminatory pricing equilibrium under rather general conditions (see Lederer and Hurter (1986) for the horizontal differentiation counterpart of this statement). (ii) The equilibrium qualities chosen under price discrimination coincide with the Pareto-optimal qualities (see Lederer and Hurter, 1986). (iii) All consumers are better off (and firms worse off) under discriminatory pricing than under uniform pricing (see Thisse and Vives, 1988). It seems to us that those statements fully justify our interest in combining product competition and discriminatory pricing. Mrs Robinson's contributions have much to say about these problems. We owe her a substantial debt for having guided our steps to that central topic of value theory.

APPENDIX

Proof of Lemma 1

Suppose, on the contrary, that

$$U(q_2, Y - \tilde{p}_2(\theta); \theta) > U(q_1, Y - \tilde{p}_1(\theta); \theta)$$

holds on a non-null subset T of $[0,1]$. As U is continuous in x, we have for $\theta \in T$

$$U(q_2, Y - \tilde{p}_2(\theta) + \varepsilon(\theta); \theta) > U(q_1, Y - \tilde{p}_1(\theta); \theta)$$

when $\varepsilon(\theta) > 0$ is small enough. This implies that θ-type consumers, with $\theta \in T$, would buy from firm 2 at price $\tilde{p}_2(\theta) + \varepsilon(\theta)$. Consequently, firm 2 could increase its profits by selling at price $\tilde{p}_2(\theta + \varepsilon(\theta)$ on T, contrary to the assumption that $(\tilde{p}_1(\cdot), \tilde{p}_2(\cdot))$ is an equilibrium.

Proof of Lemma 2

Suppose, on the contrary, that a non-null subset T of $[0,1]$ can be found such that $\tilde{p}_1(\theta) > c_1$ and $\tilde{p}_2(\theta) > c_2$ for $\theta \in T$. Without loss of generality, we assume that firm 1 supplies a positive fraction $s(\theta)$ of the θ-type consumers on a non-null subset S of T,

Let $\varepsilon(\theta) > 0$ be small enough that $\tilde{p}_2(\theta) - \varepsilon(\theta) > c_2$ and $[\tilde{p}_2(\theta) - \varepsilon(\theta)] f(\theta) > \tilde{p}_2(\theta) f(\theta)[1 - s(\theta)]$ for all $\theta \in S$. As U is increasing in x, Lemma 1 therefore implies

$$U(q_2, Y - \tilde{p}_2(\theta) + \varepsilon(\theta); \theta) > U(q_1, Y - \tilde{p}_1(\theta); \theta).$$

Hence, all θ-type consumers, with $\theta \in S$, would choose to buy from firm 2 at price $\tilde{p}_2(\theta) - \varepsilon(\theta)$. Consequently, firm 2 could increase its profits by selling at price $\tilde{p}_2(\theta) - \varepsilon(\theta)$ on S, a contradiction.

Proof of Lemma 3

Assume that $\tilde{p}_2(\theta) \neq c_2$ on a non-null subset T of $[0,1]$. Then, by Lemma 2, we have $\tilde{p}_1(\theta) = c_1$ for $\theta \in T$. Given Lemma 1, we obtain

$$U(q_2, Y - \tilde{p}_2(\theta); \theta) = U(q_1, Y - c_1; \theta) \quad \text{for } \theta \in T$$

which is precisely the definition of $\bar{p}_2(\theta)$.

Proof of Lemma 4

Differentiating (1) with respect to θ yields

$$\frac{\delta u}{\delta\theta}(q_2;\theta)=\frac{\delta u}{\delta\theta}(q_1;\theta)-\frac{dv}{dx}\cdot\frac{d\bar{p}}{d\theta}.$$

As $\delta/\delta\theta\ [u(q_2;\theta)-u(q_1;\theta)]>0$ and $dv/dx>0$, we have

$$\frac{d\bar{p}_1}{d\theta}=-\frac{1}{\frac{dv}{dx}}\frac{\delta}{\delta\theta}[u(q_2;\theta)-u(q_1;\theta)]<0.$$

A similar argument shows that $d\bar{p}_2/d\theta>0$.

Proof of Lemma 5

Suppose, on the contrary, that $\theta'<\theta''$ exist such that both equalities hold for θ' and θ''. Then, by Lemma 1

$$U(q_2,Y-c_2;\theta')=U(q_1,Y-c_1;\theta') \tag{A.1}$$

and

$$U(q_2,Y-c_2;\theta'')=U(q_1,Y-c_1;\theta''). \tag{A.2}$$

As the marginal utility of quality increases with θ, we have

$$u(q_2;\theta'')-u(q_2;\theta')>u(q_1;\theta'')-u(q_1;\theta'). \tag{A.3}$$

Adding (A.1) and (A.3) yields

$$U(q_2,Y-c_2;\theta'')>U(q_1,Y-c_1;\theta'')$$

which contradicts (A.2).

Proof of Lemma 6

As $\bar{p}_1(\cdot)$ intersects c_1, by Lemma 2, it must be that $\bar{p}_2(\cdot)$ intersects c_2 at $\hat{\theta}\geq\bar{\theta}$. If $\hat{\theta}>\bar{\theta}$, then $p_1^*(\theta)=c_1$ and $p_2^*(\theta)=c_2$ for $\theta\in[\bar{\theta},\hat{\theta}]$, which contradicts Lemma 5.

Proof of Proposition 5

Differentiating (21) and (22) we get

$$\frac{\delta\tilde{\Pi}_1}{\delta q_1}=\left(1+\frac{q_1+q_2}{2}\right)\left(-1+\frac{q_2}{2}-\frac{3q_1}{2}\right)$$

and

$$\frac{\delta\tilde{\Pi}_2}{\delta q_2}=\left(2-\frac{q_1+q_2}{2}\right)\left(2-\frac{3q_2}{2}+\frac{q_1}{3}\right).$$

Since, at equilibrium, it must be that $q_1+q_2<4$, $\delta\tilde{\Pi}_1/\delta q_1$ and $\delta\tilde{\Pi}_2/\delta q_2$ simultaneously cancel iff the system

$$-1+\frac{q_2}{2}-\frac{3q_1}{2}=0$$

$$2-\frac{3q_2}{2}+\frac{q_1}{3}=0$$

has a (positive) solution. It is easily seen that no positive solution to this system exists. On the other hand, since

$$\left.\frac{\delta\tilde{\Pi}_2}{\delta q_2}\right|_{q_1=0}>0 \quad \text{if } 0<q_2<\frac{4}{3}$$

and

$$\left.\frac{\delta\tilde{\Pi}_2}{\delta q_2}\right|_{q_1=0}<0 \quad \text{if } \frac{4}{3}<q_2<4,$$

$\tilde{\Pi}_2(q_2,0)$ is single-peaked so that

$$\left.\frac{\delta\tilde{\Pi}_2}{\delta q_2}\right|_{q_1=0}=0$$

when $q_2=\tilde{q}_2=4/3$ implies that $\tilde{q}_2=4/3$ maximizes $\tilde{\Pi}_2(q_2,0)$. Furthermore,

$$\left.\frac{\delta\tilde{\Pi}_1}{\delta q_1}\right|_{q_2=4/3}<0$$

for $0<q_1<4/3$ so that $\tilde{\Pi}_1(q_1,\tilde{q}_2)$ is maximized at $\tilde{q}_1=0$ over the domain $[0,\tilde{q}_2[$. Finally, since $\tilde{\Pi}_1(0,\tilde{q}_2)>\tilde{\Pi}_1(\hat{q}_1,\tilde{q}_2)$, where $\hat{q}_1=16/9$ is the solution to the problem: Max $\tilde{\Pi}_1(q_1,\tilde{q}_2)$ s.t. $q_1 \in [\tilde{q}_2, 4-\tilde{q}_2]$, $\tilde{q}_1 = 0$ maximizes $\tilde{\Pi}_1(q_1, 4/3)$ in R_+.

Notes

1. All statements concerning the price schedules must be understood as verified almost everywhere in [0,1].
2. Lederer and Hurter (1986) indicate how this assumption can be relaxed without affecting results.
3. For completeness, notice that, for $q_1 = q_2$, we have $p_1^*(\theta) = p_1^*(\theta) = x_1 = c_2$ and $\Pi_1(p_1^*(\cdot), p_2^*(\cdot)) = \Pi_2(p_1^*(\cdot), p_2^*(\cdot)) = 0$.
4. Notice that $\tilde{p}_1$ is always larger than c_1 and that $\tilde{p}_2 \geqq c_2$ holds iff $2(q_2 - q_1) \geqq c_2 - c_1$, an assumption implied by (6).

References

Archibald, G. C., B. C. Eaton and R. G. Lipsey (1986) 'Address Models of Value Theory', in *New Developments in the Analysis of Market Structure*, by J. Stiglitz and F. Matthewson (eds) (Cambridge, Mass: MIT).

Champsaur, P. and J. Ch. Rochet (1985) 'Product Differentiation and Duopoly', CORE Discussion Paper 8515.

Gabszewicz, J. J., A. Shaked, J. Sutton and J.-F. Thisse (1986) 'Segmenting the Market: The Monopolist's Optimal Product Mix', *Journal of Economic Theory*, 39: 273–89.

Gabszewicz, J. J. and J.-F. Thisse (1979) 'Price Competition, Quality and Income Disparities', *Journal of Economic Theory*, 20: 340–59.

Gabszewicz, J. J. and J.-F. Thisse (1980) 'Entry (and Exit) in a Differentiated Industry', *Journal of Economic Theory*, 22: 327–38.

Gabszewicz, J. J. and J.-F. Thisse (1986) 'On the Nature of Competition with Differentiated Products', *Economic Journal*, 96: 160–72.

Hoover, E. M. (1937) 'Spatial Price Discrimination', *Review of Economic Studies*, 4: 182–91.

Hotelling, H. (1929) 'Stability in Competition', *Economic Journal*, 39: 41–57.

Lancaster, K. (1979) *Variety, Efficiency and Equity* (Oxford: Blackwell).

Lederer, P. J. and A. P. Hurter (1986) 'Competition of Firms: Discriminatory Pricing and Locations', *Econometrica*, 54: 623–40.

MacLeod, W. B., G. Norman and J.-F. Thisse (1985) 'Price Discrimination and Equilibrium in Monopolistic Competition', CORE Discussion Paper 8506.

Mussa, M. and S. Rosen (1978) 'Monopoly and Product Quality', *Journal of Economic Theory*, 18: 301–17.

Salop, S. (1979) 'Monopolistic Competition with Outside Goods', *Bell Journal of Economics*, 10: 141–56.

Shaked, A. and J. Sutton (1982) 'Relaxing Price Competition Through Product Differentiation', *Review of Economic Studies*, 49: 3–13.

Shaked. A. and J. Sutton (1983) 'Natural Oligopolies', *Econometrica*, 51: 1469–83.

Thisse, J.-F. and X. Vives (1988) 'On the Strategic Choice of Spatial Price Policy', *American Economic Review*, 78, forthcoming.

Part IV

Imperfect Competition: Different Approaches

12 Two Applications of Characteristics Theory

G. C. Archibald and B. Curtis Eaton*

1 INTRODUCTION

That there is at least some analogy between models of spatial and of monopolistic competition, or even that they are, in some fundamental sense, 'the same', has been commonly thought for many years. It was first suggested (to our knowledge) by Hotelling (1929); Chamberlin (see particularly (1957), pp.7, 23–4, 47–51, 124–9) appears to have regarded them as essentially the same; and many subsequent writers have presumed that a result obtained in one model would have a natural, if unspecified, twin in the other model. The purpose of the present paper is to investigate this presumption.

Although in the last paragraph we referred only to Chamberlin, both he and Robinson were, of course, contemporaneous and independent founders of the theories of 'monopolistic' and 'imperfect' competition. We have used Chamberlinian terminology here largely for convenience and, in part, because he did attempt, albeit with limited success, to 'go behind' the demand curve to consider such matters as product diversity. Robinson, in presenting a geometrically more elegant version of the model, took as a primitive of her analysis a demand curve for a given product constructed, by assumption, to have allowed for all reactions by rivals. (See Robinson (1933) p.21; and for further discussion of the two models, Archibald, 1987.)

We note that there are currently at least two quite different approaches to modelling monopolistic competition. One approach (see, e.g., Dixit and Stiglitz, 1977; Hart, 1979; Spence, 1976) either follows Triffin (1940) in assuming that 'there is nothing between the firm and the whole economy' or relies on cross-elasticities of demand for the usual taxonomy of markets. In these models the set of possible goods is either finite or countably infinite. The goods have no descriptions: they are 'just goods', and there is no well-defined distance between them. A representative consumer buys some of all of them.

This sort of model is in sharp contrast to the usual spatial model in which

* The first author is indebted to the SSHRC for research support. This is a revised version of a paper presented to the Ninth Canadian Economic Theory Conference, University of Western Ontario, 25 May 1984. We are both indebted to R. G. Lipsey for comment and discussion over many years.

a 'market area' is accepted as a primitive which justifies partial equilibrium analysis. In these models the 'addresses' of producers and consumers are usually well defined, as is distance. The space (set of possible addresses) is a continuum. The consumer buys from the nearest store or producer, certainly not from all.

The second approach to monopolistic competition defines preferences on the characteristics of goods rather than goods themselves. Now the space of possible goods is a continuum, and goods, at least, have well-defined addresses. It is assumed that the number of goods exceeds the number of characteristics; and the consumer, of course, buys no more goods than the number of characteristics he wishes to consume. That models in which 'addresses' matter (and there is some increasingness of returns) form an important family, distinct from spaceless value-theory, was argued in Eaton and Lipsey (1977). Archibald, Eaton and Lipsey (1986) (henceforth AEL) made a case for the adoption of address models and discussed some implications (e.g. the possibility of localized competition).

The case for employing these models may be put briefly. There may be goods (and we believe that there are many) such that the name or label of the good does not convey sufficient information: the consumer's choice depends on some vector of 'descriptors', D, say (which we call the address of the good). That is, before choosing, the consumer may need to know, e.g., the location of a good, or its vitamin content, or its protein content, or all three.[1] We may make a simple conceptual experiment. Let the consumer be at a utility-maximizing equilibrium consuming a positive quantity of the good described by D. We now vary one element of D by a small amount ε. We ask if the consumer's utility level can be restored by changing the price of the good by some small amount δ. If it cannot, the two goods, D and what we may describe as $D+\varepsilon$, are somehow unrelated. Our approach is relevant if, corresponding to a small neighborhood round D, there is a small neighborhood round its price such that there are pairs of points in the two neighborhoods at which maximized utility is constant. If this is true, it seems natural to add the requirement that, as ε goes to zero, so does δ (continuity).

That this 'ε–δ' construction holds in spatial models is, of course, properly taken for granted in the spatial literature. If there is to be any close relationship between spatial models and *any* model of monopolistic competition it obviously must hold in that model.

In this chapter we shall argue, not that spatial models and address models of monopolistic competition are 'the same', for indeed they are not, but that they can both be seen as applications, or particular examples, of the characteristics approach.[2] (We might talk of 'attributes', 'descriptors', or 'address models', but it seems convenient to standardize on Lancaster's term 'characteristics'.) Using this approach, it is possible to be quite precise about both similarities and differences. Similarities are most easily seen when we consider the question of the combinability of goods or retail outlets, give indirect representations of preferences, and propose metrics for the measurement of distance (between retail outlets or goods).

The analysis of this chapter is entirely from the consumer's side. In Section 2 we analyze the characteristics approach to monopolistic competition, paying particular attention to apparent dissimilarities to spatial models. In 3 we exhibit the characteristics approach to spatial models. In 4 we offer some conclusions.

2 THE CHARACTERISTICS APPROACH TO MONOPOLISTIC COMPETITION

2.0.1

In this section we shall explore the characteristics model of monopolistic competition, paying particular attention to apparent differences between this model and standard models of spatial competition. The analysis will be entirely from the consumer's point of view.

There appear to be three obvious differences between the characteristics model of monopolistic competition and spatial models.

Combinability

In some characteristics models it is assumed that the consumer may freely combine goods to 'produce' characteristics-mixes that he prefers to those embodied in any single marketed good. It is a standard assumption (sometimes a result) in spatial models that he goes to only one store, the 'nearest' or 'cheapest'. (We shall see below that this apparently obvious result is in fact not a general one.)

Distance

Analysis of spatial competition usually requires specification of a space sufficient to induce an (obvious) metric. Thus the idea of the 'nearest' or 'cheapest' store appears obvious. We shall show below that these naive metrics are adequate only in very crude models, and propose a metric for a more general model. We shall also propose metrics for the characteristics model of monopolistic competition such that one can talk of the 'distance' between two models of automobile or brands of beer.

The Characterization of Diverse Preferences

In spatial models, this appears to be obvious and easy, e.g. consumers located along a road. It is not immediately obvious how it is to be done in a model of monopolistic competition.

We shall investigate the first two of these supposed differences, combinability and the measurement of distance, in turn. Our position is that, except in the case of the simplest and crudest spatial model, they both disappear under careful scrutiny. The third, how to model diverse preferences in both models in a manner both interesting and tractable, appears to be very difficult, and is beyond the scope of this paper.

A fourth apparent difference may be summarily disposed of. It is well known (see Lancaster, 1966; Archibald and Rosenbluth, 1975) that Chamberlinian 'groups' or industries can be unambiguously defined in terms of characteristics (although the corresponding empirical work remains to be done). In spatial theory it is common practice to take a 'market area' as a primitive. There is clearly a difference here (noted in AEL) but its importance is questionable. The similarity is perhaps more important: it is reasonable to carry out partial equilibrium analysis in both cases.

2.1 Combinability

2.1.1

The question of whether or not we should assume that two (or more) distinct goods in a characteristic space are freely combinable appears to be worth investigating in its own right. In the first place, the literature has treated the question in a somewhat cavalier manner. Lancaster (1966; 1971) assumed free combinability without discussion, and was followed by (at least) Lipsey and Rosenbluth (1971) and Archibald and Rosenbluth (1975) (and actually anticipated by Gorman in or about 1956: see Gorman (1980)). Lancaster then adopted the assumption that combining was impossible (1975; 1979), as did Lane (1980). AEL noted that there might be costs to combining but did not pursue the matter. In the second place, there appear to be conceptual difficulties. In what sense might we be said to combine ski-boots and tennis shoes? If we claim to combine their services (on different days) then perhaps all goods (or at least all durables) are trivially combinable. But could anybody want a piece of footwear that embodies a convex combination of the characteristics of a ski-boot and a tennis shoe (if, indeed, the creature can even be defined)? And may not there be costs associated with the combining of at least some goods? We offer below a simple conceptual experiment which will, we hope, clarify these matters. First, we must set out the model.

2.1.2

The primitives are assumed to be the elements of a $1 \times m$ vector of characteristics z on which the utility function is defined. We shall assume here without discussion that our characteristics are 'Lancastrian', that is, they are objectively measurable and continuous. For immediate purposes, we consider only one group of characteristics (for the definition of groups in monopolistic competition, see 2.0.1). We further simplify by assuming that there exist no other marketed goods. Introducing them now adds the complication that we have to consider whether their quantities have been optimally adjusted when we make an experiment within the group. We give below an indirect characterization of preferences which resolves this matter easily: it adds nothing new. Indeed, for present purposes, we need only two characteristics, z_1 and z_2, and a utility function with standard properties defined on them whose image is

$$u = U(z_1, z_2). \tag{1}$$

Marketed goods are represented by a $1 \times n$ vector y. In general, we assume $n > m$. If there are no costs in combining, the consumer may have any mix of characteristics by paying the market price of the required mix of goods: characteristics are 'produced' by goods according to a constant-returns linear technology, $z = Ay$.

The situation is illustrated in Figure 12.1, where we have three goods embodying positive quantities of both characteristics. The length of each vector (in heavy type) shows the quantity of the good that may be bought for a fixed expenditure. If combining is costless, it is well known (Lancaster, 1966) that the market opportunity frontier must be strictly convex: any good which generated a non-convexity would be dominated by a convex combination of the adjoining goods, and not viable. The level surface of $U(z_1,z_2)$ drawn shows that this consumer combines goods 1 and 2 (at Q) if combining is costless. If it is, a consumer with convex preferences always combines (unless his most-preferred characteristics mix happens to be embodied in a marketed good) but never buys more goods than there are characteristics.

2.1.3

Let us consider the possible costs of combining goods. They appear to be of two sorts, transactions costs and costs due to the technology of combining. Transactions costs may be incurred simply as a consequence of buying more individual goods rather than a greater quantity of a single good. The technology of combining may impose costs, perhaps of time and effort (more time in the kitchen to combine more ingredients into a single dish). If rental markets are imperfect, there will clearly be pecuniary costs to combining durables. Whatever the nature of these costs, we assume that they can all be represented by contractions of the feasible set in z-space. Thus in Figure 12.1 the effect of combining costs might be, e.g., to replace the interior of RS with the open line segment $R'S'$: R and S are still attainable but only points within $R'S'$, not within RS. If combining costs are high enough, the consumer will not incur them. Convexity of level sets guarantees that, if the costs of combining are high enough to exclude the whole complement of $R \cup S$ in RST from the feasible set, the consumer will choose one of R,S.

2.1.4

Now we make our first conceptual experiment. We offer the consumer a choice of two regimes, in each of which he receives the same dollar value of marketable goods:

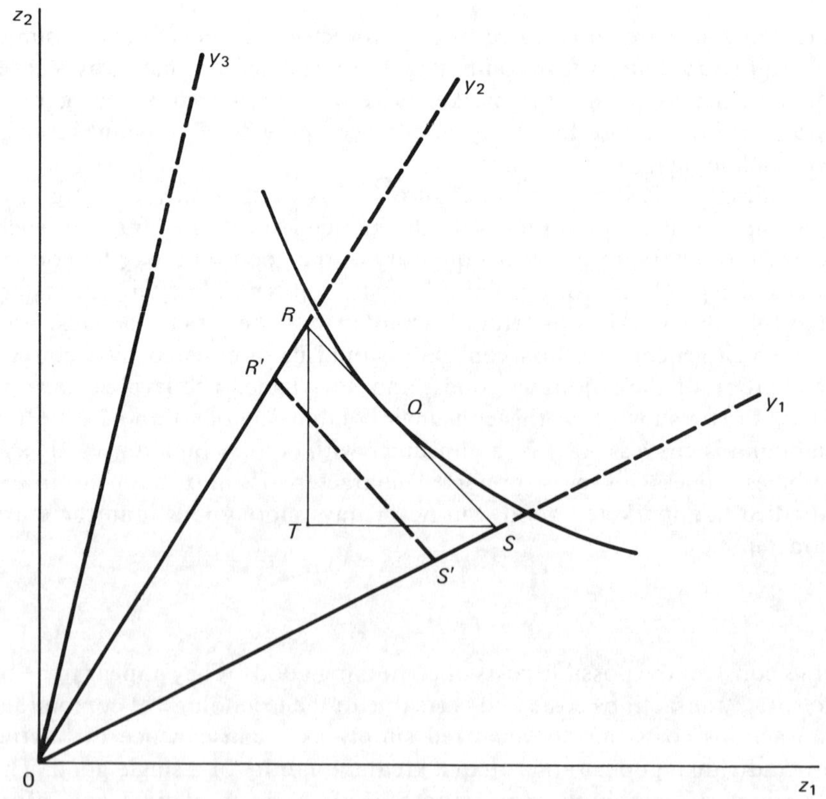

Figure 12.1

(*A*) a convex combination of two goods to produce the desired characteristics-mix (at *Q* in Figure 12.1);
(*B*) a single good embodying the desired characteristics-mix.

(If the goods are indivisible durables, such as automobiles, each regime entails a perfect rental market supplying two goods (*A*) or one good (*B*).)

Writing *I* for indifference, *P* for preference, we have three possibilities:

(i) *AIB*
(ii) *BPA*
(iii) *APB*.

Case (i) is straightforward: the consumer believes that there are no costs to combining. Similarly in case (ii) he believes that there are positive costs. But what about case (iii)?

Case (iii) is clearly inconsistent with the assumption that preferences are convex in z_1–z_2 space. We shall argue, nonetheless, that there is a 'sensible' explanation.

2.1.5

It may be recalled that in his original (1966) paper Lancaster defined the utility function on *activities* rather than characteristics. The characteristics were required as inputs into the activities, and the demands for marketed goods derived at yet another step. As the introduction of activities appeared to add nothing to the analysis,[3] they were subsequently dropped (without further discussion). We need them now to resolve the problem of combinability, and interpret case (iii). We propose that goods be divided into two types:

Type One: goods which serve only one activity, that is, are activity-specific; and
Type Two: goods which serve more than one activity.

To which type an indivisible durable belongs (in the eyes of an individual consumer) may be determined by a second conceptual experiment. Suppose that the good represented by the vector $0Q$ in Figure 12.1 exists. We now offer the individual a choice between (a) $2\,0Q$ and (b) $0R+0S$. We again have three possibilities:

(i) (a)*I*(b)
(ii) (a)*P*(b)
(iii) (b)*P*(a).

In case (i), again, the consumer clearly believes that combining costs are zero, and in case (ii) that they are positive. Both cases are consistent with convex preferences in z_1–z_2 space. Case (iii), again, is not.

Our solution to the problem is that in *both* cases (iii) we are dealing with Type Two goods. The utility function $u = U(z_1,z_2)$ is inappropriate rather than non-concave. Preferences should be defined over the activities rather than the characteristics, even if the activities require the same characteristics as inputs. There is nothing in these experiments to suggest that preferences defined over activities must be 'badly behaved'.

This may be clarified by an illustration. Suppose that a consumer would prefer to drive a sports car when engaged in one activity (perhaps going to work) and a truck when engaged in another (perhaps going fishing). Given indivisibilities and the budget constraint he buys a compromise vehicle, a station wagon. Then in the first experiment, in which we maintain the budget constraint but allow divisibility (perfect rental markets) he gives the case (iii) response: he would 'combine' the truck and the sports car if he could, but 'combine' them in the sense of employing their services in different activities. Similarly, in the second experiment in which we relax the budget constraint he gives the case (iii) response: he prefers a truck plus a sports car to two station wagons. (Evidently ski-boots and tennis shoes are inputs into two different activities!)

We accordingly suggest that if we try to represent preferences in a characteristics space in the case in which goods embodying those characteristics are of Type Two, the preferences will look 'as if' they were non-convex. The error is in defining the preferences on the wrong primitives: activities can obviously be taken as the primitives in analyzing the demand for Type One goods too, but this is the case in which it adds nothing. We evidently need to specify 'combining' in two senses, too. 'Combining one': combining goods in one activity (putting gin and tonic in the same glass). 'Combining two': employing the services of goods in different activities over time (which is only trivially 'combining').

We shall consider a spatial problem in Section 3.1 below in which exactly this problem of combining arises, although the primitives of the problem have different names. Otherwise, we shall confine the analysis to Type One goods, whence we may continue to define preferences on characteristics.

2.2 Distance

2.2.1

It is impossible to maintain that models of monopolistic and spatial competition are 'the same', or even that there is a close analogy between them, unless the distance between goods can be measured. From consideration of Figure 12.1, it is clear that we may define the equivalent and compensating variations in the usual manner, as is done by Morey (1981), as well as the 'compensation function' employed by Lancaster (1975; 1979). All these measures have their uses, but none of them is a metric. Since nearly all spatial models induce a metric, our immediate object is to find a measure of the distance between goods (within an 'industry' or 'market area'). The distance functions we shall propose are all dependent on the individual's preferences, and in various ways on his opportunity set, but we shall see in Section 3 that this is true of the interesting metrics we can define in all but the crudest of spatial models.

We start by proposing a metric (actually, a pseudo-metric) in the primal z-space. We shall then develop an indirect representation of preferences, and propose somewhat more interesting pseudo-metrics on the dual space. For the moment, we confine ourselves to the simple model employed above in which there are only two characteristics and there is no 'outside' good.

2.2.2

We start with Figure 12.1. Let the angle between a vector, showing the characteristics mix embodied in a good, and the horizontal axis be denoted by θ. Then $\tan\theta$ measures the characteristics ratio embodied in a good, and θ may be employed to index goods (whether possible or actually marketed). We might immediately use θ to measure the distance between goods, defining the distance between two goods i and j to be $|\theta_i - \theta_j|$, say. The analogy with simple metrics, e.g. the Euclidean, in spatial models is immediate.[4] It is also immediate that this measure conveys less information about preferences than does the equivalent variation, the compensating variation, or the compensation function: it contains none at all. What we require is a distance function that measures the 'distance' between goods as perceived by the consumer.

Consider Figure 12.2. For some budget M and price vector p, let θ^* be the consumer's preferred characteristics mix and $0Q$ the quantity purchased. Construct the level surface through Q, and consider two less preferred goods (at (p,M)), with mixes θ_i and θ_k. Now define

$$d_1(\theta_i,\theta_k) \equiv \frac{|0S - 0R|}{\max\{0S, 0R\}} \cdot \qquad (2)$$

We now show that $d_1(\cdot)$ has the properties of a pseudo-metric.

(i) $d_1(\theta_r,\theta_s) \geqslant 0$: obvious.

(ii) That $\theta_r = \theta_s \Rightarrow d_1(\theta_r,\theta_s) = 0$ is obvious too.

It is not, however, true that $d_1(\theta_r,\theta_s) = 0 \Rightarrow \theta_r = \theta_s$. For any good more

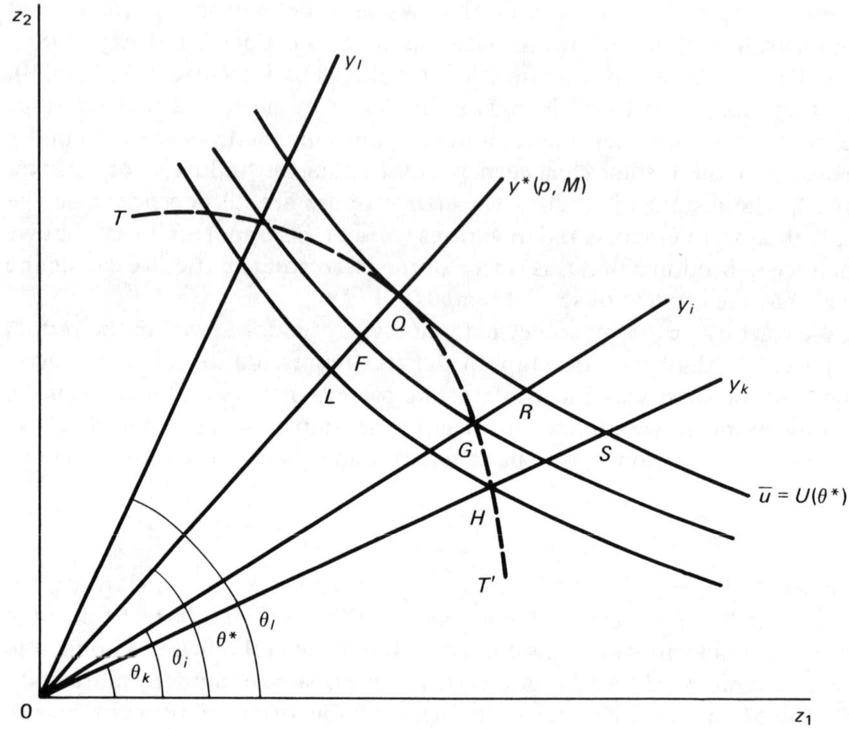

Figure 12.2

intensive in z_1 than y^*, y_i say, there must exist some good less intensive in z_1 than y^*, y_l, say, such that $d_1(\theta_i,\theta_l)=0$ although clearly $\theta_i \neq \theta_l$. Thus, given (iii) and (iv) below, $d_1(\cdot)$ is not a metric but a pseudo-metric. (See Kelley, 1961. The differences between a metric and a pseudo-metric are, in general, unimportant.)

(iii) $d(\theta_r,\theta_s)=d(\theta_s,\theta_r)$ is ensured by use of the mod. in the numerator and max. in the denominator of (2).

(iv) Triangle inequality. We have

$$d(\theta^*,\theta_i)=\frac{OR-OQ}{OR},$$

$$d(\theta_i,\theta_k)=\frac{OS-OR}{OS},$$

and

$$d(\theta^*,\theta_k) = \frac{OS - OQ}{OS},$$

i.e.

$$= \frac{OS - OR}{OS} + \frac{OR - OQ}{OS}$$

and

$$\frac{OR - OQ}{OR} > \frac{OR - OQ}{OS}$$

(by convexity).

Notice that we have employed the level surface defined by $\bar{u} = U(z_1, z_2)$ (which we might write as $\bar{u} = U(Q)$ or $\bar{u} = U(\theta^*)$) given $\theta^*(p,M)$) to define a pseudo-metric on θ. Whether θ is in the interval $[0,\pi/2]$ or in $(0,\pi/2)$, i.e. whether our pseudo-metric space is compact or not, depends on whether the indifference curves have intercepts or are asymptotic to the axes.

2.2.3

Clearly, we could impose this distance measure on any level surface in any space, but would not trouble to, so why bother here? The first answer is simple: we wish to demonstrate that we *can* talk about the distances between differentiated products in a meaningful way. The second is that the function is not without interest. It is a quantity measure: it tells us how much more, proportionately, of the less preferred good is required to keep the consumer at the utility level $\bar{u} = U(Q)$. We cannot, however, interpret it simply as *the* subjective measure of $d(\theta_i, \theta_k)$ since θ^* is a function of (p,M). It will be unique only in the Leontief case, and independent of M (but not p) if preferences are homothetic. Thus the consumer's 'address', θ^*, is in general a function of (p,M), as are all the derived measures of distances: *given* θ^* they depend solely on the shape of the level surface. There must, of course, be values of (p,M) such that θ_i or θ_k would be the most preferred mix.

Consider again the fact that $d_1(\cdot)$, defined on the whole domain of θ, is a pseudo-metric, i.e. that $d_1(y_i, y_l) = 0$. The intuition is simple: if two stores are equidistant from the consumer the distance *between* them is perceived to be zero rather than twice the distance to one of them.

We now turn to the indirect representation of preferences, and the measurement of distance in the dual space.

2.2.4

The model employed so far, while crude, has been sufficient for our purpose. We now introduce a more general model, and a convenient indirect representation of preferences. Let z be an m-vector of characteristics, as before, and x a Hicksian composite good, competitively priced. Preferences are represented by:

$$U: R_+^{m+1} \to R_+$$

with image

$$u = U(z,x). \tag{3}$$

We assume U to have the standard properties of monotonicity and quasi-concavity, and to be continuously twice differentiable. (Monotonicity implies that all characteristics are 'good'. It is easy to allow some of them to be 'bad', as we shall do in Section 3 below.)

If Chamberlinian groups are to be defined, and partial equilibrium analysis to be justified, the utility function must be weakly separable on a partition of $z: z^1, z^2, \ldots, z^k$, $k < m$. Thus we replace (3) with[5]

$$\varphi = \varphi[u^1(z^1), u^2(z^2), \ldots, u^k(z^k), x]. \tag{4}$$

(4) requires further comment. For clarity, interpret the vector z^i as inputs into activity i. (4) is clearly necessary, but not sufficient, for partial equilibrium analysis. Sufficiency requires, in addition, that we rule out Type Two goods – goods which embody characteristics which are inputs into more than one activity.

To rule out Type Two goods, we must add a further assumption on the technology which clearly has nothing to do with preferences. The assumption is that any 'realization' of a subset of the technologically feasible set in the form of a vector of produced goods y can be partitioned conformably with (4). This means that any realized A-matrix, where a_{ij} is the amount of the i-th characteristic produced by the j-th good, can be arranged in block-diagonal form, z partitioned as above, with the corresponding partition induced on y (see Archibald and Rosenbluth, 1975).

Given these assumptions, it is sufficient for our purposes to consider only the one-group, two-characteristics case, whence we can represent preferences by

$$u = U(z_1, z_2, x) \tag{5}$$

with standard properties. It is convenient to refer to any good in the group, embodying quantities of z_1 and z_2, as a 'group good'. For any group good, the ratio in which it embodies the two characteristics is fixed. Let the angle between the vector describing good i in z_1–z_2 space and the horizontal axis be θ_i. Thus $z_2/z_1 = \tan\theta_i$. In the description of a good, we adopt a units convention such that the quantity of each characteristic in a unit of good i is given as a function of θ_i. Thus we let $g(\theta_i)$ and $h(\theta_i)$ be the quantities of z_1 and z_2, respectively, embodied in a unit of good i. Good i is now completely described by two numbers rather than three, namely θ_i and p_i, the price of a unit. We assume that the units convention chosen for the moment gives a parametric description of goods by a convex frontier in z_1–z_2 space. Other varieties of units conventions are, of course, possible: see Section 2.2.6 below.

Employing this units convention, we define an indirect representation of preferences:

$$W(\theta,p,M) \equiv \max_{x,y}\{U[y\cdot g(\theta), y\cdot h(\theta), x] \mid py + x = M\}, \tag{6}$$

where y is the quantity of the group good characterized by (θ,p) and the price of the composite good is normalized to unity. $W(\theta,p,M)$ is decreasing in p and increasing in M. For given (p,M), we can define the consumer's most preferred θ, $\theta^*(p,M)$, as the θ which maximizes $W(\theta,p,M)$. Holding M constant, level surfaces of $W(\theta,p,M)$ are illustrated in Figure 12.3. A level surface in θ–p space will have at most one stationary point. $W(\cdot)$ may or may not be quasi-concave, depending on the units convention chosen: see again 2.2.6 below.

One property of these level surfaces requires special mention: on the assumptions made, they cannot have intercepts on the horizontal axis. Suppose that one did, at θ_l, say, $0 < \theta_l < \pi/2$. Then there is a continuum of (θ,p) values with $p > 0$ indifferent to $(\theta_l,0)$. In the primal space of Figures 12.1 and 12.2, $(\theta_l,0)$ is a vector of positive slope and infinite length. Thus any indifference curve in the indirect space which has an interior intercept corresponds to an indifference curve in the primal space which is at least asymptotic to $(\theta_l,0)$, i.e. has an (infinite) region of positive slope. This is ruled out by the assumption that utility is a non-decreasing function of both characteristics. If indifference curves in the primal space intercept the axes, which is not ruled out, the indifference curves in θ–p space will have corresponding intercepts on the vertical axes. If the indifference curves in the primal space are asymptotic to the axes, then in the indirect space they must all 'converge into the corners' at 0 and $\pi/2$.

Now suppose that the consumer is choosing among n marketed goods in the group and that, whether because of costs or otherwise, he does not combine goods. He will choose to consume good j if

$$W(\theta_j,p_j,M) \geqslant \max_{i \neq j} W(\theta_i,p_i,M). \tag{7}$$

If more than one good satisfies (7), any one of them may be picked. The

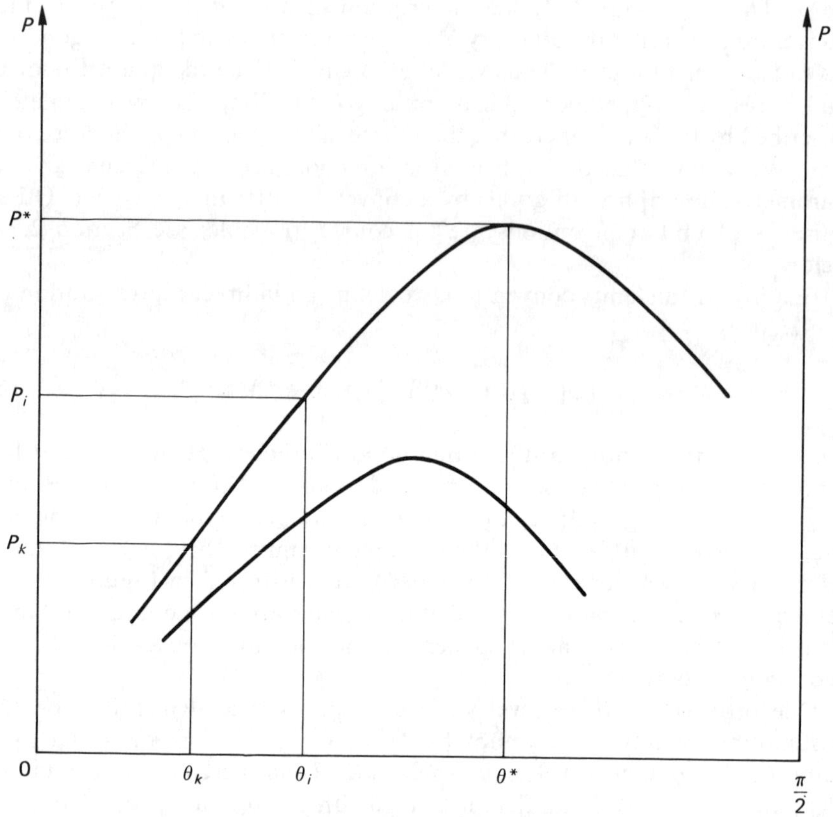

Figure 12.3

quantity demanded can be recovered from the indirect utility function by Roy's Identity.

2.2.5

Now let us see what distance functions on θ we can define with the help of level surfaces of $W(\theta,p,M)$. Consider Figure 12.3. For some M and p^*, θ^* is preferred: θ^* is the 'best', if θ varies continuously while price is held constant at p^*. If, however, utility is to be held constant while θ varies, price must be lower the further θ is from θ^*. How much lower depends on the shape of the level surface. For θ_i it is p_i, for θ_k, p_k. We can define

$$d_2(\theta^*,\theta_i) \equiv \frac{|p^* - p_i|}{\max\{p^*,p_i\}}$$

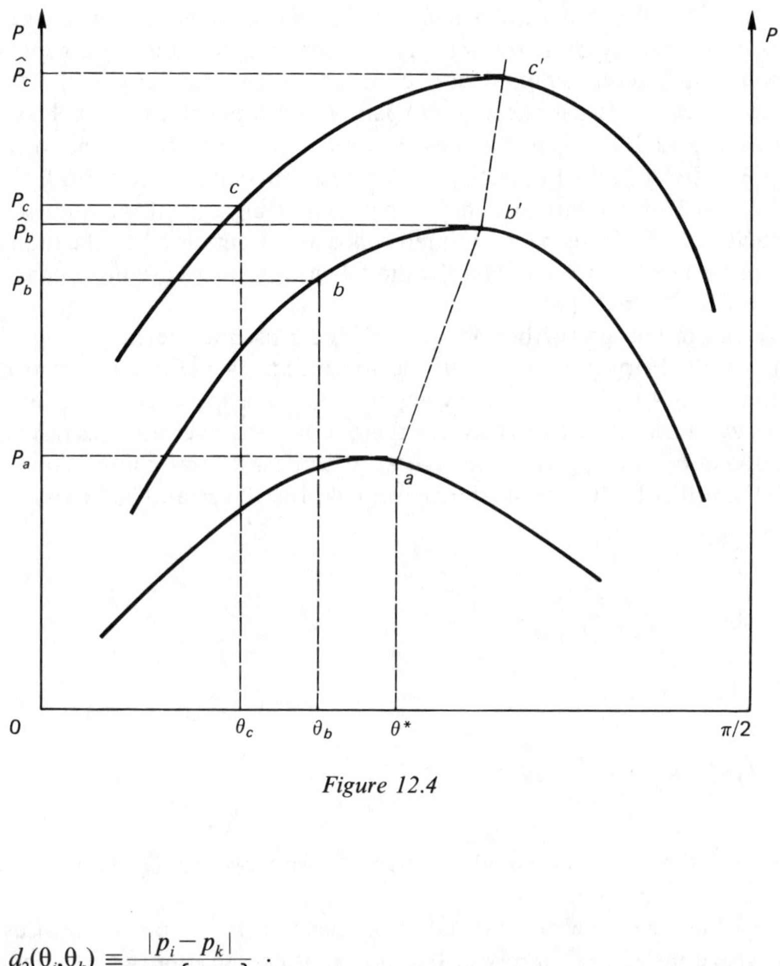

Figure 12.4

and

$$d_2(\theta_i,\theta_k) \equiv \frac{|p_i - p_k|}{\max\{p_i,p_k\}} \ . \tag{8}$$

The proof that this is a pseudo-metric follows that for $d_1(\cdot)$ given in Section 2.2.2 above, whence we repeat only the proof of the triangle inequality. We want

$$d_2(\theta^*,\theta_k) \leqslant d_2(\theta^*,\theta_i) + d_2(\theta_i,\theta_k) \quad \text{or}$$
$$(p^* - p_i)/p^* + (p_i - p_k)/p^* \leqslant (p^* - p_i)/p^* + (p_i - p_k)/p_i \ .$$

This follows from the fact that $p^* > p_i$ (uniqueness of the 'best' θ for given p,M). $d_2(\cdot)$ is again, of course, a pseudo-metric: there exists a $\theta_l, \theta^* < \theta_l < \pi/2$ such that $d_2(\theta_i,\theta_l) = 0$. Once again we have used a constant utility level to induce a measure on θ. The measure is now, however, in terms of a proportional price reduction rather than a quantity increase. $d_2(\cdot)$ differs from $d_1(\cdot)$ in other ways. In constructing $d_2(\cdot)$, M is constant, and the measure is entirely on price. $d_1(\cdot)$ is independent of p and M except in as much as the 'reference mix' θ^* is chosen for some particular pair (p,M). We have no occasion to ask what (p,M) pair would support points such as R or S in Figure 12.2: this is in the sense in which, given θ^*, $d_1(\cdot)$ is independent of (p,M). In $d_2(\cdot)$, the quantity y is 'offstage' (but can be recovered from the indirect by Roy's identity). Finally, in constructing $d_2(\cdot)$ it is assumed that, whatever (p,M), x has been optimally chosen (by definition of the indirect): there is no need to omit it from the model entirely as we did in constructing $d_1(\cdot)$ on the primal space.

We can in fact go further now and define a pseudo-metric on the whole space (θ,p). For some M let θ^* be preferred, as before, at price p_a in Figure 12.4. Now take two arbitrary points in the space, b and c, say, and construct the level surfaces through them. Let these level surfaces have their maxima at b' and c', giving the highest-price/best-θ combination consistent with the utility level. Denote the associated prices by $\hat{p}_b$ and $\hat{p}_c$. We may now define

$$d_3(a,b) \equiv \frac{|p_a - \hat{p}_b|}{\max\{p_a, \hat{p}_b\}}$$

and

$$d_3(b,c) \equiv \frac{|\hat{p}_c - \hat{p}_b|}{\max\{\hat{p}_b, \hat{p}_c\}} \quad . \tag{9}$$

The proof that $d_3(\cdot)$ is a pseudo-metric follows those for $d_1(\cdot)$ and $d_2(\cdot)$ and need not be repeated.

$d_3(\cdot)$, like $d_2(\cdot)$, measures distance in terms of prices, but it metrises the (θ,p) space instead of simply θ. It follows, of course, that we can define a pseudo-metric on any subset of (θ,p), e.g. an opportunity frontier.[6]

Notice that, in defining $d_1(\cdot)$, we employed a 'reference mix' θ^*. Here we employ a 'reference set' of a, b', c', etc. Distances measured by $d_3(\cdot)$ would be the same *wherever* points b and c were chosen on the level surfaces through b' *and* c', or, for that matter, if we chose another point on the level surface through a. For given b,c, $d_3(\cdot)$ is a point-to-set metric. Letting b and c vary along their level sets, it would become a set-to-set metric.

We offer one final example of a pseudo-metric in θ–M space, holding prices constant. Level surfaces in this space are illustrated in Figure 12.5. Given a pair (θ^*, M^O), we define

$$d_M(\theta^*,\theta) = \frac{|M^1 - M^O|}{\max\{M^1, M^O\}}$$

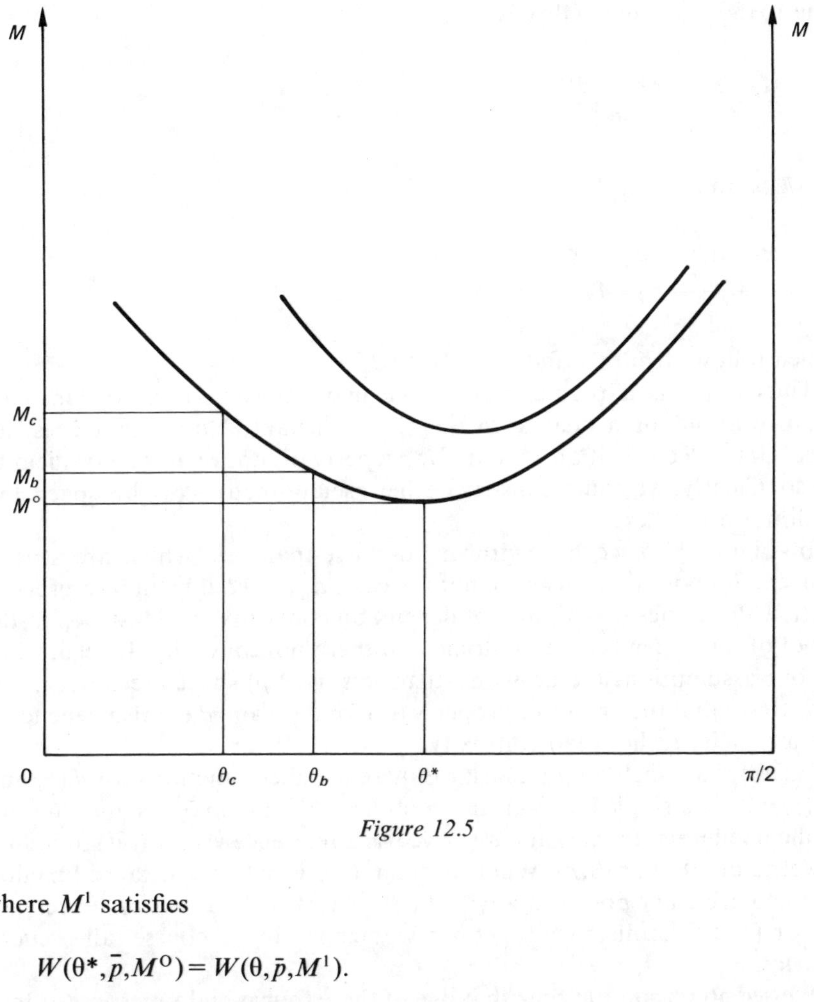

Figure 12.5

where M^1 satisfies

$$W(\theta^*,\bar{p},M^{O}) = W(\theta,\bar{p},M^1).$$

(i) That $d_M(\theta_r,\theta_s) \geqslant 0$ is obvious.

(ii) For any $\theta_i < \theta^*$, there exists $\theta_j > \theta^*$ such that $d_M(\theta_i,\theta_j) = 0$, whence $d_M(\cdot)$ is a pseudo-metric. Of course, $d(\theta_i,\theta_i) = 0$.

(iii) $d_M(\theta_r,\theta_s) = d_M(\theta_s,\theta_r)$ from the definition.

(iv) We want $d_M(\theta^*,\theta_c) \leqslant d_M(\theta^*,\theta_b) + d_M(\theta_b,\theta_c)$ (see Figure 12.5). Thus we want

$$\frac{M_c - M^O}{M_c} \leqslant \frac{M_c - M_b}{M_c} + \frac{M_b - M^O}{M_b}.$$

The LHS of this inequality is

$$\frac{M_c - M_b}{M_c} + \frac{M_b - M^{\mathrm{O}}}{M_c}$$

so we want

$$\frac{M_b - M^{\mathrm{O}}}{M_c} \leqslant \frac{M_b - M^{\mathrm{O}}}{M_b}$$

which follows from the fact that $M_c > M_b$.

Thus $d_M(\cdot)$ is a pseudo-metric. We may interpret it as the income-compensation for a change in θ, prices constant. Notice that it is not necessary to 'centre' it on θ*, but, for property (ii) above, it is convenient to do so. Clearly, we could construct other pseudo-metrics on this space, but shall not do so here.

In Figure 12.5 we have drawn no-worse-than sets which are strictly convex. Suppose that this were not the case. $d_M(\cdot)$ would still be a pseudo-metric. Properties (i)–(iii) do not depend on convexity. The last step in the proof of (iv) depends on monotonicity rather than convexity. Indeed, while on our assumptions the no-worse-than sets in (θ, p) space are convex, it is easy to see that the proofs of property (iv) for $d_2(\cdot)$ and $d_3(\cdot)$ also depend on monotonicity rather than convexity.

We offer a concluding remark on these distance functions. In $d_2(\cdot)$ and $d_M(\cdot)$ we use a single level surface to obtain a metric on θ, whether in price or income terms. In $d_1(\cdot)$ and $d_3(\cdot)$ we use a reference vector (set) to induce a metric on (θ, y) or (θ, p). What we cannot do is define a distance function between arbitrary points in any of these spaces without use of a reference vector (set). The distance functions we define are, of course, all pseudo-metrics.

We see no reason to argue that one of these four pseudo-metrics (or five, counting the one noted in note 5) is 'better' than the others. All are subjective, each entails different restrictions on a subset of utility level, price, income, and quantity. There are three final points to notice. The first is not new, but is nice: we can talk in a meaningful way (or ways) about the distance between a Ford and a Volkswagen. The second is that we shall find, in more general spatial models considered below, metrics with similar properties to those defined here. The third is that it is common, in spatial models, to think of the consumer deciding 'first' which is the nearest store, and 'second' how much to buy at it. We can, if we wish, similarly decompose the consumer's decision in dealing with goods embodying the same characteristics in different proportions: he decides 'first' which is the nearest good and 'second' what quantity to purchase.

2.2.6

For convenience we have worked so far exclusively in two dimensions. It is easy to see that we may measure the distance between two goods in the same ways whatever the dimensionality of the z-space. In each case distance is measured by a scalar: quantity, price, or income. Consider a group of goods embodying m characteristics, $m > 2$. The primal utility function must, of course, be defined over all m characteristics. Proceeding as we have done above, the indirect becomes $\bar{W}(\theta, p, M)$ where θ is a m–1 vector of characteristics-ratios. Distance is, of course, measured in terms of p or M.

So far, we have adopted a units convention which yields a convex frontier in z_1–z_2 space. This convention has served our purpose; but there are others, and the choice is a matter of convenience. Thus we might *define* a unit of y_i such that $g(\theta_i) = 1$ and $h(\theta_i) = \tan \theta_i$. Using standard assumptions on the properties of $U(z_1, z_2, x)$ we should derive monotonic level surfaces, whence we should be able to define metrics instead of pseudo-metrics. Furthermore, using this convention, it is easy to prove quasi-concavity of $W(\cdot)$ in (θ, p). But nothing above hinges upon quasi-concavity (see our proofs of the triangle inequality), whence we shall omit the proof. This convention is, however, useful in discussion of spatial models.

3 THE CHARACTERISTICS APPROACH TO LOCATION THEORY

3.0.1

In this section we show how the consumer's choice problem in standard spatial models may be treated as a characteristics problem, and derive an indirect representation of preferences analogous to that of Section 2 above. We then consider the two subjects analyzed above, combinability and the measure of distance.

It is convenient to start by analyzing a characteristics problem with a 'bad'. Suppose the goods in some group embody one characteristic, z_1, positively valued by the consumer, and another, z_2, which is negatively valued by the consumer. In this case it is convenient to adopt the units convention suggested in Section 2.2.6 above:

$$g(\theta) = 1$$

$$h(\theta) = \tan \theta$$

(where θ is defined as in Section 2 above). The consumer's problem, for arbitrary θ and p, is now

$$\max_{x,y} U(z_1,z_2,x) \quad \text{s.t. (i)} \quad py+x=M$$
$$\text{(ii)} \quad z_1=y$$
$$\text{(iii)} \quad z_2=y\tan\theta. \tag{10}$$

We assume that the partial derivatives of $U(\cdot)$ with respect to z_1 and z_2 are, respectively, positive and negative, and that $U(\cdot)$ is quasi-concave in its arguments.

The maximization problem (10) implicitly defines an indirect representation of preferences, $W(\theta,p,M)$. W is non-increasing in p, non-decreasing in M, and non-increasing in θ. It is non-increasing in θ since, as θ increases, the quantity of the bad, z_2, in a unit of the good increases, while the quantity of z_1 is necessarily constant at unity. Finally, $W(\theta,p,M)$ is quasi-concave in θ and p. We illustrate its θ–p level surfaces in Figure 12.6.

3.0.2

It is usually thought that, in a spatial model, the consumer goes to the 'nearest' outlet (in some obvious sense), and that there is no question of combining outlets in the Lancastrian sense. We introduce a model in which this will prove to be wrong.

We begin by considering a standard choice problem in which transport of some retail good requires expenditure of both time and money by a consumer whose hours of work, whence income, are fixed. His problem is

$$\max_{x,y} \tilde{U}(x,v,y) \quad \text{s.t. (i)} \quad (p+m(\theta))y+x=M$$
$$\text{(ii)} \quad v+t(\theta)y=H \tag{11}$$

where

y is quantity of the retail good
x is a composite good with price normalized to unity, as before, involving no transport costs
v is leisure time
H is total time not spent at work
θ is distance from the retail outlet to the consumer's household

and

$m(\theta)$, $t(\theta)$ are, respectively, the money and time costs of transporting a unit of y a distance θ.

We assume that $m'(\theta)$ and $t'(\theta)$ are non-negative and that $\tilde{U}(\cdot)$ is quasi-concave.

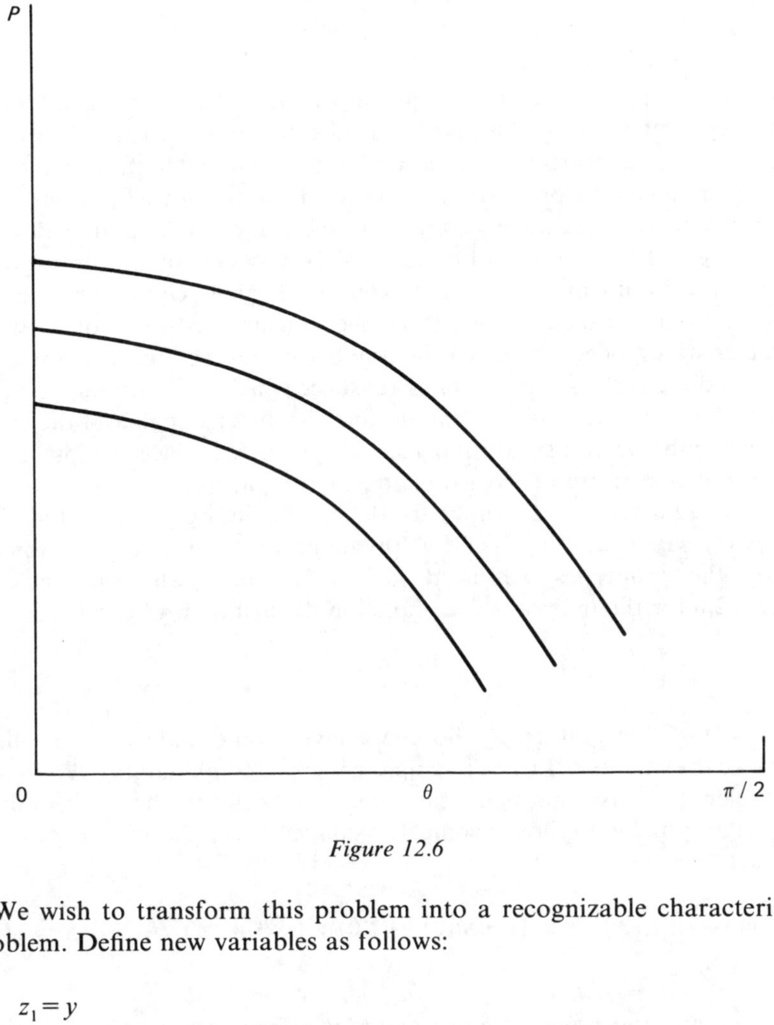

Figure 12.6

We wish to transform this problem into a recognizable characteristics problem. Define new variables as follows:

$$z_1 = y$$

$$z_2 = H - v.$$

Now the consumer's preferences can be written

$$U(z_1,z_2,x) = \tilde{U}(z_1,H - z_2,x)$$

where z_2 is a 'bad', free time devoted to transport and consequently unavailable as leisure. The consumer's choice problem can now be written

$$\max_{x,y} U(z_1,z_2,x) \qquad \text{s.t. (i)} \quad (p + m(\theta))y + x = M$$

$$\text{(ii)}\quad z_1 = y$$
$$\text{(iii)}\quad z_2 = yt(\theta). \tag{12}$$

This is clearly a characteristics problem. In particular, if transport entails no money costs ($m(\theta)=0$ for all θ), it is identical in form to problem (10). The last two constraints in (12) show why it is a characteristics problem. A unit of y, purchased from a firm a distance θ from the household, embodies a unit of something positively valued, z_1, and $t(\theta)$ of the bad, time devoted to fetching it. This jointness of goods and resources devoted to transport is the essential feature of virtually all models of consumer choice in space, and all such models can be seen, from the consumer's point of view, as characteristics models, in which the number of characteristics is (at least) two. The dimensionality of the physical space which the consumer inhabits has nothing to do with this interpretation. The dimensionality of the space, together with the transportation technology in the space, simply define distance, θ, and transport cost functions, $m(\theta)$ and $t(\theta)$.

It is obvious that (12) implicitly defines an indirect utility function, $W(\theta,p,M)$, say. If both $t''(\theta)$ and $m''(\theta)$ are non-negative, this function has exactly the properties we listed in (3.0.2) above, and illustrated in Figure 12.6 for the indirect utility function defined by problem (10).

3.0.3

If hours of work may be freely chosen we have a somewhat simpler problem which we investigate before taking up the issue of combinability. We return to problem (11), assuming now that hours of work may be freely chosen. Then, ignoring non-labor income for convenience, the choice problem becomes

$$\max_{x,v,y} \tilde{U}(x,v,y) \quad \text{s.t.} \quad (p+m(\theta)+wt(\theta))y+x+wv=wH, \tag{13}$$

where w is an exogenous wage rate and H is to be interpreted as total time to be allocated to work, leisure and transport. The indirect utility function defined by (13) has only two arguments, w and $p+m(\theta)+wt(\theta)$, the 'full price' of the good in Becker's terminology. Now, for given w, level surfaces in (θ,p) space are defined by combination of θ and p such that the full price of the good is constant:

$$p+m(\theta)+wt(\theta)=c$$

is a representative level surface. It depends entirely on the parameters p and w, and the 'transportation technology': in particular, it is independent of preferences.

3.1 Combinability

3.1.1

Now we take up the issue of combinability. Let us start with the simple model just presented in (13). Assume that there are two firms or outlets available to the consumer, described by (θ_1,p_1) and (θ_2,p_2). To make the choice problem non-trivial, let $\theta_2<\theta_1$ but $p_2+m(\theta_2)>p_1+m(\theta_1)$: firm Two is closer than firm One but offers a higher price. The consumer's choice in this case depends solely on the full price which, it will be recalled, is independent of preferences. If, for example,

$$p_1+m(\theta_1)+wt(\theta_1)<p_2+m(\theta_2)+wt(\theta_2)$$

the consumer will patronize firm One in spite of the fact that $\theta_2<\theta_1$. The 'nearest' firm, in the effective sense, is not necessarily the one offering the smallest θ but the one offering the smallest full price: 'distance' is to be measured in dollars. If two firms offer the same full price the consumer may, but need not, divide his patronage between them. Combining is simply not an issue in this model.

Suppose, however, that the consumer is not free to choose his hours of work so that we cannot value time spent on transport at the wage rate. Then we return to the model of (12) above in which the 'cost' of transport time, $yt(\theta)$, is subjectively valued. Now combining is a real possibility. To see this, fix the quantity of the composite good at $\bar{x}$ and consider the opportunity set in (z_1,z_2) space. From (12) this is given by

$$\begin{aligned}(p_1+m(\theta_1))y_1+(p_2+m(\theta_2))y_2+\bar{x}&=M,\\ z_1&=y_1+y_2,\\ z_2&=y_1t(\theta)+y_2t(\theta_2).\end{aligned}$$

The upper boundary of this set is illustrated in Figure 12.7. We assume again that $\theta_2<\theta_1$ whereas

$$\hat{p}_2\equiv p_2+m(\theta_2)>p_1+m(\theta_1)\equiv\hat{p}_1,$$

whence the upper boundary is upward sloping. Depending on the shape of the level surfaces, the consumer may prefer a corner solution, at *A* or *B*, or an interior solution, illustrated at *C* in Figure 12.7. The possibility that combining is preferred follows directly from the assumption that the utility function is quasi-concave.

Figure 12.7 is, in fact, nothing but the standard Lancastrian diagram in the case in which z_2 is a bad. The conclusion that the choice problems in space are characteristics problems seems irresistible. Except in the case in

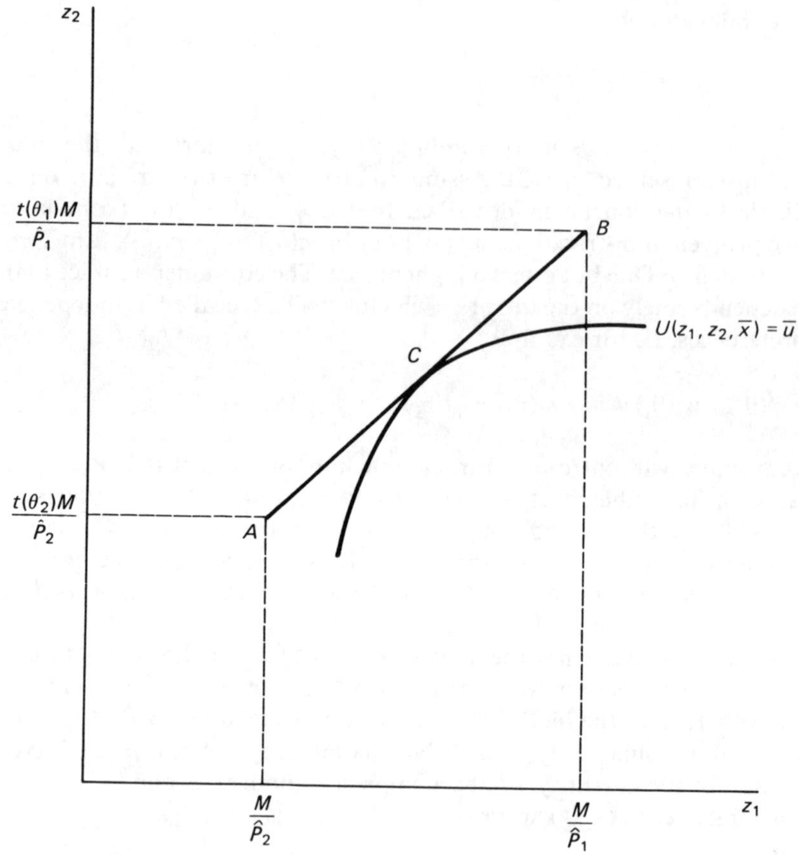

Figure 12.7

which the value of time is exogenous, these problems will display the features of the models of Section 2 above. Judging from the spatial analysis most common in the literature, this point is not well understood.

3.1.2

Nothing has been said about costs of combining. It is not obvious that in the spatial application of the characteristics model there are any costs to combining *per se*. If there are, they can be analysed as before, by shifting the interior of the line AB in Figure 12.7 to the Northwest.

3.1.3

We ask next if there is an analogy in the spatial application to the distinction made in Section 2.1 above between Type One and Type Two goods (or characteristics). Indeed there is, but to see this we must enlarge the space. Let the indirect utility function now be defined on (θ,μ,p,M), where μ is another characteristic, such as waiting time or quality of service. We may repeat the conceptual experiments of 2.1.4 and 2.1.5 above. The question is, would a consumer who combined two outlets described by (θ,μ,p) necessarily prefer a convex combination? The answer, again, is no; and, again, in the case of a 'no' answer, the correct interpretation is not that the utility function is badly behaved, but that it is defined on the wrong primitives. Rather than repeat the whole argument, we offer a simple illustration. A man may go to one bar, close by and with sawdust on the floor (θ, μ, and p all low), for a beer with his mates after work, and to a more distant, more elegant and more expensive establishment when he takes his wife or girlfriend out on a Saturday night. A convex combination would be a less-preferred input into either activity. Thus we can be content with the definition of preferences on characteristics rather than activities in the spatial model only in the Type One case.

3.2 Distance

3.2.1

The physical space in which we locate the consumer necessarily induces a metric. We have measured distance by θ. In neither of the models we have considered, however, is θ the distance measure that determines the consumer's choice. In the model of (12), in which hours of work may be freely chosen, the measure we need is the full price, $\hat{p}+wt(\theta)$: distance is measured in dollars. In the model of (13), in which hours of work are fixed, we may define any of the distance functions $d_2(\cdot)$, $d_3(\cdot)$, or $d_M(\cdot)$ suggested in Section 2.2 above. They are now, of course, metrics rather than pseudometrics since, given the new units convention, $W(\cdot)$ is monotonic in θ. Distance is once again subjective, even in the spatial model with its 'natural' metric. The relevant measure of distance depends on the consumer's personal evaluation of the trade-off between consumption and leisure. Thus we can build a spatial model in which distance depends only on the parameters and the transportation technology, and another in which it (or the several measures of it) depend on preferences, so that distance is again 'in the consumer's eye'.

4 CONCLUSION

Our purpose in this paper has been to use the characteristics – or attributes, or address – approach to exhibit some properties (similarities and dissimilarities) of models of consumer preferences in the applications to diverse goods and locations. We offer a summary of what appear to be the more interesting results.

1. Both models are clearly seen to be particular applications of the more general characteristics model.

2. In both applications, given that we are dealing only with Type One goods (see 2.1.5 above), it is convenient to give an indirect representation of preferences in the space characteristics-parameters-price.

3. The similarity of the indirect representations in the differentiated goods and fixed-hours spatial case is striking. In the variable-hours case the level surfaces are independent of preferences.

4. In the fixed-hours spatial model the economically relevant measure of distance is subjective, as it is in the goods application. The distance functions are defined in the same way in both applications (but, given the units conventions we have chosen, are metrics in the location model, pseudo-metrics in the goods model).

5. In the goods application, the consumer may or may not combine Type One goods, depending on his preferences and the costs of combining. In the fixed-hours case he may or may not combine outlets, but in the variable-hours case he will not. There does not appear to be any reason for introducing into the spatial model the costs of combining *per se*. If we increase the dimensionality of the spatial model we may encounter Type Two goods and characteristics.

6. In both applications the introduction of Type Two goods (or outlets) requires us to replace characteristics with activities as the primitives of our analysis.

7. The problems of characterizing diverse preferences in an interesting and tractable manner in the two models remains, but is beyond the scope of this paper. The problem has been made to 'look' easier in the spatial model by the use of crude and arbitrary special assumptions (e.g. that each consumer buys precisely one unit up to some ceiling price).

8. Many other problems remain, of which we note particularly two. We do not yet know the necessary conditions for competition to be localized in the appropriate space (sufficient conditions are given in AEL). And problems of optimality remain singularly intractable since, in the presence of non-convexities, we cannot conveniently divorce efficiency and distributional considerations without special and very restrictive assumptions.

Notes

1. This approach should not be confused with that of Debreu (1959), in which goods are indexed (subscripted) as necessary to indicate type, quality, location, delivery date, etc. as required. This approach is not applicable if the list of possible goods is a continuum; and it sheds no light on the relationship between goods in a monopolistically competitive group. Debreu's purpose was, of course, quite different.
2. These are not the only applications of the characteristics approach. As Lancaster (1966) originally pointed out, it offers a natural way of modelling job choice. The mean-variance approach to portfolio selection obviously considers two characteristics of an asset. The housing market looks like an obvious candidate for a characteristics approach. Kerr (1984) has successfully applied it to the breeding of 'exotic' cattle, and Morey (1981) to the demand for ski-areas. No one would wish to argue that all these applications are 'the same'.
3. Except additional difficulty: see Pollack and Wachter (1975) where it is argued that, if household production functions are the same, they are not needed in demand analysis, whereas if they differ we cannot compute shadow prices.
4. Hart (1979) suggests that the Euclidean metric be employed to measure the distance between goods in characteristics space. While this can obviously be done, we cannot imagine what the economic interpretation might be.
5. If the range of each u^i is $\mathbb{R}^i$ (u^i), then φ maps the Cartesian product of the $\mathbb{R}^i$ plus one into R_+ (see Blackorby, Primont and Russell, 1978). We assume that, for all i, u^i: $R^s_+ \rightarrow R_+$, where s is the dimensionality of z^i. Thus we have φ: $R^{k+1}_+ \rightarrow R_+$.
6. The compensation function employed by Lancaster (1975; 1979), though not a metric, has the interesting property that the 'compensation' required by an individual who is supplied only with a less-preferred good depends on the shape of the *PPF*. We can give a version of this that has the properties of a pseudo-metric. Let the dashed line TT' in Figure 12.2 be the *PPF* 'scaled down' to the individual (following Lancaster), and let y^*, as before, be the preferred good for this opportunity set. If y^* is not available but y_i is, the consumer is as well off as he would be with OF of y^*; and similarly with y_k and OL. Now define $d(y^*,y_i) \equiv FQ/OQ$ and $d(y_i,y_k) \equiv LF/OF$. The proof that this is a pseudo-metric follows those in 2.2.5 above and need not be repeated. This is really a measure of how much worse off the consumer is, under the resources and technology constraints determining the *PPF*, when less-preferred goods are offered. A measure closer to Lancaster's intention would ask how much he needed to be compensated, i.e. would employ the quantities RG and SH in constructing the distance function. We leave this to the interested reader.

References

Archibald, G. C. (1987) 'Monopolistic Competition' in *The New Palgrave: A Dictionary of Economics*, J. Eatwell, M. Milgate and P. Newman (eds), (London: Macmillan).

Archibald, G. C., B. C. Eaton and R. G. Lipsey (1986) 'Address Models of Value Theory', in *New Developments in the Analysis of Market Structure*, J. E. Stiglitz and G. Frank Mathewson (eds) (Cambridge, Mass.: MIT; London: Macmillan).

Archibald, G. C. and G. Rosenbluth (1975) 'The "New" Theory of Consumer Demand and Monopolistic Competition', *Quarterly Journal of Economics* 80: 569–90.

Blackorby, C., D. Primont and R. R. Russell (1978) *Duality, Separability, and Functional Structures: Theory and Economic Applications* (New York: Elsevier North-Holland).

Chamberlin, E. H. (1957) *Towards a More General Theory of Value* (New York: Oxford University Press).

Debreu, G. (1959) *Theory of Value: An Axiomatic Analysis of Economic Equilibrium* (New York: Wiley).

Dixit, A. K. and J. E. Stiglitz (1977) 'Monopolistic Competition and Optimum Product Diversity', *American Economic Review*, 67: 297–308.

Eaton, B. C. and R. G. Lipsey (1977) 'The Introduction of Space into the Neoclassical Model of Value Theory' in *Studies in Modern Economic Analysis*, M. J. Artis and A. R. Nobay (eds) (Oxford: Blackwell) pp.59–96.

Gorman, W. M. (1980) 'A Possible Procedure for Analysing Quality Differentials in the Egg Market', *Review of Economic Studies*, 47, 843—57.

Hart, O. (1979) 'Monopolistic Competition in a Large Economy with Differentiated Commodities', *Review of Economic Studies*, 46: 1–30.

Hotelling, H. (1929) 'Stability in Competition', *The Economic Journal*, 39: 41–57.

Kelley, J. L. (1961) *General Topology* (Princeton, NJ: van Nostrand).

Kerr, W. A. (1984) 'Selective Breeding, Heritable Characteristics and Genetic-Based Technological Change in the Canadian Beef Cattle Industry', *Western Journal of Agricultural Economics*, 9: 14–25.

Lancaster, K. J. (1966) 'A New Approach to Consumer Theory', *Journal of Political Economy*, 74: 132–57.

Lancaster, K. J. (1971) *Consumer Demand: A New Approach* (New York: Columbia University Press).

Lancaster, K. J. (1975) 'Socially Optimal Product Differentiation', *American Economic Review*, 65: 567–85.

Lancaster, K. J. (1979) *Variety, Equity, and Efficiency* (New York: Columbia University Press).

Lane, W. (1980) 'Product Differentiation in a Market with Endogenous Sequential Entry' *Bell Journal of Economics*, 11: 237–60.

Lipsey, R. G. and G. Rosenbluth (1971) 'A Contribution to the New Theory of Demand: A Rehabilitation of the Giffen Good', *Canadian Journal of Economics*, 4: 131–63.

Morey, E. R. (1981) 'The Demand for Site-specific Recreational Activities: A Characteristic Approach', *Journal of Environmental Economics and Management*, 8: 345–71.

Pollack, R. A. and M. L. Wachter (1975) 'The Relevance of the Household Production Function and Its Implications for the Allocation of Time', *Journal of Political Economy*, 83: 255–77.

Robinson, J. (1933) *The Economics of Imperfect Competition* (London: Macmillan).

Spence, A. M. (1976) 'Product Selection, Fixed Costs, and Monopolistic Competition', *Review of Economic Studies*, 43: 217–35.

Triffin, R. (1940) *Monopolistic Competition and General Equilibrium Theory* (Cambridge, Mass.: Harvard University Press).

13 Price–Quality Competition in Oligopolistic Interdependence

Robert E. Kuenne

1 INTRODUCTION

The nature of product differentiation in Joan Robinson's *Economics of Imperfect Competition* remains unclear fifty-odd years after its publication. Her thinking was shaped by the cost disputes in the British literature of the 1920s that reacted to the recently formalized analysis of the firm in pure competition. Because, it was asserted, decreasing costs were experienced in industry more frequently than not, the limits to the size of the firm must be dictated by a declining demand curve, not rising marginal cost and horizontal demand functions. As Sraffa (1926) argued explicitly in the most influential article in the debate, the analysis of the firm's decision-making must be reformulated in a universal theory of monopoly. Implicitly, the decreasing cost advocates urged that if the inspired fuzziness of Marshallian economics had to be formalized, the monopoly model, not that of pure competition, was the more relevant tool. Robinson's debt to Sraffa is amply recorded in her book.[1]

This must surely be the point of departure in seeking an understanding of the role of product differentiation in her work. Robinson's primary interest lies in the nature, functioning, and – typically – social evils of monopoly. Books IV, V, VI, VIII, IX, and X are devoted exclusively to it and its comparison with pure competition, and they constitute almost 50 per cent of the work. Other chapters, including much of the analysis of perfect (i.e. pure) competition, was to prepare for the departure therefrom of monopoly. Monopoly was the extreme of imperfect *competition*, and the provision and use of tools for its analysis were her primary interests.[2]

The conceptual scaffolding of Robinson's work may be sketched in the following terms. Market structures may be divided into two classes: perfect (i.e. pure) competition and imperfect competition. The two classes are distinguished simply by the firm's demand curve possessing a zero or negative price slope (p.18). All firms are monopolists of their own output, but when, in the production of a 'commodity' they are large in number and 'buyers are all alike in respect of their choice between rival sellers' (p.18, p.170) the first class exists. A commodity is 'a consumable good, arbitrarily demarcated from other kinds of goods, but which may be regarded for practical purposes as homogeneous within itself' (p.17).

Imperfect *competition* is embodied in two types of *markets*: *imperfect* markets, in which buyers reveal preferences for individual firms in well-defined, non-horizontal demand curves, and (borrowing non-Robinsonian terminology) *oligopolistic* markets in which numbers of firms are so small that demand curves are not defined in the absence of explicit reaction patterns (pp.21, 86n.). With these patterned responses such curves may be defined, *mutatis mutandis*, but Robinson explicitly rules out the analysis of oligopoly in the work (pp.21, 86n.). Rather, it is the analysis of imperfect markets by marginalism that constitutes the book, and a more accurate title would have been *The Economics of Imperfect Markets*. As an analysis of *markets* rather than *firms* the focus of her interest was rather definitely the industry, as will be developed below, and it was this dominant interest that led Chamberlin to assert that she failed to meld competition and monopoly at the firm's level.

Imperfect markets span the spectrum in her analysis from Chamberlin's large-group tangency structure through classic monopoly, in each case with buyers expressing their preferences for firms' commodities in demand curves that are not destroyed by fewness. But it is the classic monopoly extreme, as noted above, that is her major interest. Most of the analysis of the large-group case is contained in chapter 6, sections 1 and 2, consisting of only six pages!

Since the basis of existence of imperfect markets is consumer partiality for firms' commodities, what was the nature of these distinctions? The striking feature of Robinson's discussions of these qualities is that they almost invariably are associated with the *seller* rather than the *seller's product*. It is interesting to speculate on the reasons for this view of the phenomenon that seems, to an American economist, to neglect the more prominent product-associated reasons for consumer's distinctions. This neglect of the many dimensions of product qualities and the bases for most advertizing efforts[3] constitutes a deficiency when her analytical contributions are compared with those of Chamberlin.[4]

One contributing factor to this analytical viewpoint may be that fifty years ago branded products in Great Britain were not as dominant a presence in consumer products as they were in America. A more important reason, however, inheres in Robinson's Marshallian indoctrination and the importance it placed upon the industry as a unit of analysis. She realized, more clearly than Chamberlin did at this time, the threat to its existence that non-homogeneous commodities posed. By associating the differentiation with the sellers of an essentially physically similar commodity she did not eliminate that challenge, but in her own mind it substantially lessened it. It permitted her to move from the analysis of the firm in imperfect markets to the analysis of industry demand and supply curves for 'essentially' homogeneous goods.

It was understandable, therefore, that Chamberlin found in Robinson's imperfect market analysis a standard industry monopoly case with essentially competitive firms selling homogeneous products with implied neglect of the firm's product and selling cost decisions. It is, however, another matter to assert, tirelessly and tiresomely, as Chamberlin did, that she failed to meld the concepts into new market structures as he had in the concept of monopolistic competition.[5] It was a difference in emphasis – with a purpose of self-deception – not an omission. The Chamberlinian large-group symmetry case with its tangency solution for the firm is developed explicitly by Robinson, with free entry the profit eliminating mechanism (ch.7). Monopolists fill in the interstices among slightly protected markets for physically homogeneous products, their impacts upon 'industry' demand diffused over their cohabitants. I find Chamberlin's more patient and deeper probing into product differentiation, selling costs, group equilibrium, and oligopoly richer in analytical insight and polished with greater scholarly care. More importantly, it has greater realistic content, once he moved away from the large-group case as he did in his later career.[6] But as a step along the route from perfect (i.e. pure) competition to the monopolized industry analysis that was admittedly her goal, and with the stubborn but pointed refusal to associate differentiation with product, Robinson paused at the market structure featuring the mixture of competition and monopoly that was in essentials indistinguishable from Chamberlin's core large-group case.

This chapter investigates manners of incorporating product differentiation in the decision-making of the firm simultaneously with the price decision. It ignores selling costs, however, to focus upon product qualities. The market structure envisioned is that of differentiated oligopoly under both Cournot neglect of rivals' reactions and a mode of interdependence I have termed 'rivalrous consonance'. In this excursion I am following the lead of Chamberlin in both the choice of variable and market structure, as explained above, but with the guidance of Joan Robinson who saw deeply into the complications of both factors and illuminated them.

Section 2 contains an initial framework for classifying and measuring qualities and attributes of products as they are varied about certain non-appropriable core features. Section 3 analyzes the firm's price–quality decisions in an environment that anticipates no rival reactions, focusing particularly upon the circumstances under which firms move closer together or farther apart on quality scales, and on the trade-offs between price and quality policies.

Section 4 places the firm within an oligopolistic setting to the limited extent of forcing it to adjust to a rival's enhancement of quality. Section 5 moves these decisions into the context of mature differentiated oligopoly using rivalrous consonance as a framework to capture the mixture of competition and cooperation that characterizes such industries. As Chamberlin viewed the pressing task of his period of microeconomic analysis to be the blending of competition and monopoly, I feel that the greatest need of price theory currently is to search for flexible frameworks for the analysis of differentiated oligopoly that permit the fusion of rivalry and tacit cooperation which characterizes such industries. An initial investigation of this quest as it includes both price and quality complexes is contained in this section. Finally, Section 6 contains a brief summary and some conclusions.

2 AN INITIAL FRAMEWORK FOR PRODUCT DIFFERENTIATION ANALYSIS

In prior work, I have quarrelled with the Triffin–Chamberlin notion that the 'product' is not a useful tool of analysis, and that categorization by cross-elasticities that ignores physical properties is preferable.[7] The point is simply that the product is too useful a concept to be abandoned in operational analysis. Joan Robinson's notion of an effectively homogeneous cluster of goods produced by an 'industry' could be defined by isolating a set of goods containing certain 'core' qualities in common, among them physical similarity, as well as diverse 'non-core' qualities which they may or may not possess in common. Certain of these non-core qualities may be *non-appropriable* by rivals – e.g. brand names – but most will lie within the area of competition by imitation. This viewpoint constitutes the point of departure for this paper.

Suppose that in such an industry – or 'product group' – there exist n firms, each associated with a single 'brand', where n is small enough to yield an oligopolistic market structure. Each brand has a complex of non-appropriable qualities, so that no brand can ever merge its identity completely with another through its choice of a quality complex. Through analysis, let us assume we have isolated relevant appropriable qualities $i=1,2,\ldots,m$, the first r of which are variables which can be measured cardinally[8] and the remainder of which are attributes.

2.1 The Derivation of Quality Indifference Premia

Arbitrarily, let us choose Firm (Brand) 1 as an anchor for the analysis. To a large sample of potential customers for the product we address the following set of questions:

Suppose you were given a unit of Brand 1 at no cost to you. If you were offered Brand j instead, how many dollars would you have to receive or give up to make you feel as well off as you feel with Brand 1?

Let us choose some measure of central tendency for the sample responses for $j=2,3,\ldots,n$, and term these the *indifference premia*, I_j, where $I_1 \equiv 0$ and $I_j \gtrless 0$. Next, let us attempt to decompose these I_j into additive components, I_{ij}, $i=1,2,\ldots,m$, by pursuing the following line of questioning for each of the m appropriable qualities:

> Suppose once more you are given a unit of Brand 1. Assume Brand 1's quality i were changed from its present state to that of Brand j's quality i state. How much would you have to receive or pay to feel equally well off as you feel with unchanged Brand 1?

A representative measure of central tendency is once more chosen for the sample responses. We can then record the information obtained in Table 13.1 as the *quality indifference matrix*.

If we assume additivity of the *indifference components*, I_{ij}, and the exhaustiveness of the list of m appropriable qualities, then, for the individual we hypothesize that

$$I_j \equiv \Sigma_i I_{ij} + I_{ej}, \tag{1}$$

where I_{ej} is the indifference component for the non-appropriable qualities. We assume the identity of (1) will be approximated for the central tendency measures of the sample and will neglect sampling error, treating the aggregates as deterministic and consistent (in the sense of identity (1)) measures.

Table 13.1 The quality indifference matrix, I, Brand 1 base

Quality (i)/*Brand* (j)	1	2	...	n
1	0	I_{12}	...	I_{1n}
2	0	I_{22}	...	I_{2n}
.	.	.	...	.
.	.	.	...	.
.	.	.	...	.
m	0	I_{m2}	...	I_{mn}
Non-appropriable ($I_{e,j}$)	0	I_{e2}	...	I_{en}
Indifference Premia	0	I_2	...	I_n

2.2 Conceptual Content

The goal of the exercise in deriving the quality indifference matrix, I, is to obtain an index over qualities which is a ratio scale, i.e. is unique up to a positive multiplicative scalar, measured in monetary units, and to derive it in an operational manner. The derivation of I is independent of prices, but it does mix with quality preferences the attitudes of responding individuals to money, as affected predominantly by money income levels. Because the purpose of isolating the preferences is to gain insights into the firms' decision-making, the intrusion of income into the consumer's quality preferences is not unwelcome since it will influence his decision to buy. However, such preferences do not have the unsullied psychological purity of the indifference map. They are more akin to the preference curve over alternatives under conditions of risk, capturing a relevant attitude to the purpose for which they will be used.

The indifference components, I_{ij}, may be shifted to a base other than Brand 1, say Brand k, by subtracting or adding I_{ik} from each row i element in Table 13.1, so that the Brand k column contains zeroes. Also, several meaningful and potentially useful measures can be obtained from I because of the uniqueness of the measurement. The Euclidean metric may be used to obtain the distances of Brands j and k from each other in quality space:

$$d_{jk} = [\Sigma_i (I_{ij} - I_{ik})^2]^{0.5}, \tag{2}$$

which may be useful in clustering brands into subgroups containing close substitutes in consumers' preferences. A relative measure of qualities' importance can be defined as

$$s_i = \Sigma_j |I_{ij}| / \Sigma_i \Sigma_j |I_{ij}|, \tag{3}$$

which may be used to obtain a weighted distance measure in quality space:

$$d^w_{ij} = [\Sigma_i s_i (I_{ij} - I_{ik})^2]^{0.5}. \tag{4}$$

Several other characteristics of the preference measurement framework are also appealing. It is possible, for example, to include as a brand in Table 13.1 a hypothetical product which does not exist but can be described as a quality complex to consumers. Also, qualities that may not be capable of independent consideration by consumers, being significantly associated physically or psychologically, may be combined into a single quality. And, lastly, the underlying qualities' intensities may be measurable ordinally or cardinally, or may be attributes describable only with a binary 0–1 index: I_{ij} indifference components will be capable of expression in all cases.

But deficiencies in the method provide some drawbacks. First, we have assumed a type of 'additive transitivity'. For quality i, if the consumers indicate that moving from Brand 1 to Brand 2 requires a subsidy of x, and moving from Brand 2 to Brand 3 requires a subsidy of y, then a move from Brand 1 to Brand 3 requires a subsidy of $x+y$. Even if this held for the individual consumer, it is not necessarily true that it will hold for the aggregate measures. And it might not hold for the individual if quality i interacts with other qualities in his preferences. Combining qualities may be useful in such cases, as noted above, but may not always be possible.

Second, we are assuming that the I_{ij} are independent of the quantity taken by consumers. This is a simplification which may or may not be an acceptable approximation, but it is a hypothesis that is at least initially desirable to retain an operational framework.

Third, we have been treating the I_{ij} as aggregate deterministic values obtained by an averaging process. They are more realistically seen as sample estimators of a population value, distributed as a sampling distribution with expected value and variance.

2.3 Quality Scales with Quality-Dollar Units

Consider the row entries of I for quality i. In quality preference space each brand has a location calibrated in dollars for quality i as a distance from Brand 1. When appropriable quality i is a variable that can vary continuously, define

$$I_i = \max_j I_{ij} - \min_j I_{ij}, \tag{5}$$

so that any location for Brand 1 on the scale may be defined as

$$_1x_i = {}_1y_i I_i, \tag{6}$$

where $_1x_i = 0$ for Brand 1's initial state for quality i.

When appropriable quality i is an attribute which can take values only as recorded for existent or hypothetical brands, then acceptable points on the scale for Brand 1 are defined as

$$_1x_i = \Sigma_j y_{ij} I_{ij}, \text{ where } y_{ij}(1-y_{ij}) = 0,\ \Sigma_{ij} y_{ij} = 1. \tag{7}$$

Arbitrarily, again, let us consider Brand 1, and assume the first h appropriable qualities are variables and the remainder are attributes. Then any feasible location for Brand 1 in quality space may be given by the vector $_1X$, with elements defined by (6) and (7).

3 THE FIRM'S DECISION IN AN ASSUMED NON-REACTIVE CONTEXT

Assume that Firm 1 must decide upon a price–quality policy on the assumption that its rivals' prices, p_j, and quality complexes, ${}_jX$, $1<j\leqslant n$, will remain unchanged. The demand for Brand 1 may be written

$$D_1 = D_1(P,X,Y), \tag{8}$$

where $P=[p_1,p_2,\ldots,p_n]$, $X=[{}_1X,{}_2X,\ldots,{}_nX]$, and Y is a vector of unspecified exogenous variables affecting demand that we will treat as fixed over the period of analysis. The average cost of production is a function of the level of output and ${}_1X$:

$$C_1 = C_1({}_1X,D_1). \tag{9}$$

Suppose the first h appropriable qualities are variables as before. Then the firm seeks to

$$\operatorname*{Max}_{p_1,{}_1X} Z = D_1(p_1,{}_1X;\, p_2,p_3,\ldots,p_n,\, {}_2X,{}_3X,\ldots,{}_nX,\, Y) \quad (p_1 - C_1({}_1X,D_1)) \tag{10}$$

subject to

$$1.\quad {}_1x_i = y_i I_i, \quad 1\leqslant i\leqslant h \tag{11}$$

$$2.\quad {}_1x_i = \Sigma_j\, y_{ij} I_{ij}, \quad h+1\leqslant i\leqslant m$$

$$3.\quad y_{ij}(1-y_{ij})=0, \quad h+1\leqslant i\leqslant m,\ 1\leqslant j\leqslant n$$

$$4.\quad \Sigma_j\, y_{ij}=1 \quad h+1\leqslant i\leqslant m.$$

Relations (10) and (11) form a non-linear integer programming problem and may be solved by an algorithm such as SUMT in combination with branch and bound combinatorics. It will not, however, be convex due to the lattice on which the y_{ij}, $h+1\leqslant i\leqslant m$, are defined, and may be too large for practical solution by branch and bound.

To pursue the analysis theoretically, let us therefore assume that all qualities are variables (i.e. $h=m$), and, to reduce notational clutter, let us suppress the subscript 1 on all variables. The first-order conditions for Firm 1's maximum-profit solution are then

$$1.\quad \delta Z/\delta p = D(1-C_D D_p) + (p-C)D_p = 0 \tag{12}$$

$$2.\quad \delta Z/\delta x_i = (p-C)D_i - C_i D - C_D D_i D = 0, \quad 1\leqslant i\leqslant m,$$

where $D_p = \delta D/\delta p$, $D_i = \delta D/\delta x_i$, $C_D = \delta C/\delta D$, and $C_i = \delta C/\delta x_i$. These conditions may be rewritten

$$1.\quad p - C - C_D D = -D/D_p \tag{13}$$

$$2.\quad p - C - C_D D = C_i D/D_i, \quad 1 \leqslant i \leqslant m.$$

The left-hand sides of these equations are the marginal profit per unit of sales expansion by any policy before considering the marginal cost of that policy. The right-hand sides are the marginal costs of the price and quality policies, respectively, per unit of expanded sales by that policy. System (13) implies that a necessary condition for a profit maximum is that the marginal cost of a unit of sales increase be equal for all policies. Therefore, we may rewrite (13) as

$$1.\quad C_i D/D_i = -D/D_p, \quad 1 \leqslant i \leqslant m \tag{14}$$

$$2.\quad p - C - C_D D = -D/D_p.$$

The second-order sufficient conditions for $m = 2$ are that the following Hessian be negative definite either in the neighborhood of the optimum for a local maximum or everywhere for a global maximum:

$$\begin{bmatrix} 2D_p - C_D D_p^2 - D_{pp} D/D_p & D_i - C_D D_p D_i - D_{pi} D/D_p & D_k - C_D D_p D_k - D_{pk} D/D_p \\ D_i - C_D D_p D_i - D_{pi} D/D_p & -(2C_i D_i + C_D D_i^2 + C_{ii} D + D_{ii} D/D_p & 0 \\ D_k - C_D D_p D_k - D_{pk} D/D_p & 0 & -(2C_k D_k + C_D D_k^2 + C_{kk} D + D_{kk} D/D_p) \end{bmatrix} \tag{15}$$

We assume:

1. $D_p < 0$

2. $D_{pp} < 0,\ D_{pi}, D_{pk} \gtreqless 0$

3. $D_{ii}, D_{kk} < 0,\ D_{ik} = 0$

4. $C_D > 0,\ C_{DD} = 0,\ C_i, C_k > 0,\ C_{ii}, C_{kk} \geqq 0.$

Under these conditions, Z is concave in p, x_i, and x_k taken singly, so that the second-order conditions can be overruled by the interaction of the variables only. If all second-order derivatives are assumed near zero in absolute value, p and x_1 and p and x_2 form concave subsystems. Only x_1 and

x_2 interactions jointly interacting with p could upset the conditions, and this is highly unlikely. We conclude that concavity of Z is a highly probable occurrence when second derivatives are not large relative to first-order derivatives.

Let us rewrite (14) in the more convenient form

$$1.\quad D_i/C_i = -D_p, \quad 1 \leqslant i \leqslant m. \tag{16}$$

$$2.\quad p - C - C_D D + D/D_p = 0.$$

For graphic presentation let us assume hereafter that $m = 1$. Then, equation (16.1) yields curves *MBCE* (policy marginal benefit–cost equality) on Figure 13.1 along which policy pairs $[p,x]$ have achieved equal marginal cost per unit of marginal sales. *MCBE* has the slope

$$\left(\frac{dp}{dx}\right)_{MBCE} = \frac{D_{xx} + C_{xx}D_p + C_x D_{px}}{-(D_{xp} + C_x D_{pp})}, \tag{17}$$

which, when $D_{px} \approx 0$ and is ignored, becomes

$$\left(\frac{dp}{dx}\right)_{MBCE} = \frac{D_{xx} + C_{xx}D_p}{-C_x D_{pp}}. \tag{18}$$

Where $D_{xx} < 0$ and $C_{xx} \geqslant 0$ as assumed above, the sign of dp/dx depends upon D_{pp}. It will be negative when $D_{pp} < 0$ and positive when $D_{pp} \geqslant 0$, so that the concavity or convexity of D with respect to p is of great importance to the analysis. As recorded above, we shall assume the normal case is diminishing sales returns to price reductions ($D_{pp} < 0$).

Equation (16.2) yields marginal price policy profit which is zero at the optimum. It shows, in its optimum mode, for any x, the value of p which just equates marginal profit to zero. We will term it the *OPPR* (optimal price policy relation) on Figure 13.1 and, if we continue to ignore D_{px}, its slope will be

$$\left(\frac{dp}{dx}\right)_{OPPR} = \frac{C_x + C_D D_x - D_x/D_p}{2 - C_D D_p - D_{pp}/D_p^2} = \frac{2C_x + C_D D_x}{2 - C_D D_p - D_{pp}/D_p^2}, \tag{19}$$

every term of which will be positive when $D_{pp} < 0$. For $D_{pp} \geqslant 0$, convexity would have to be extreme to make the slope negative.

On Figure 13.1 we have drawn the firm's *MBCE* and *OPPR* functions and its achieved policy optimum. The meaning of these conditions is worth developing. Curve *MBCE* requires that the marginal sales response to the last dollar spent on quality enhancement be equal to the marginal sales

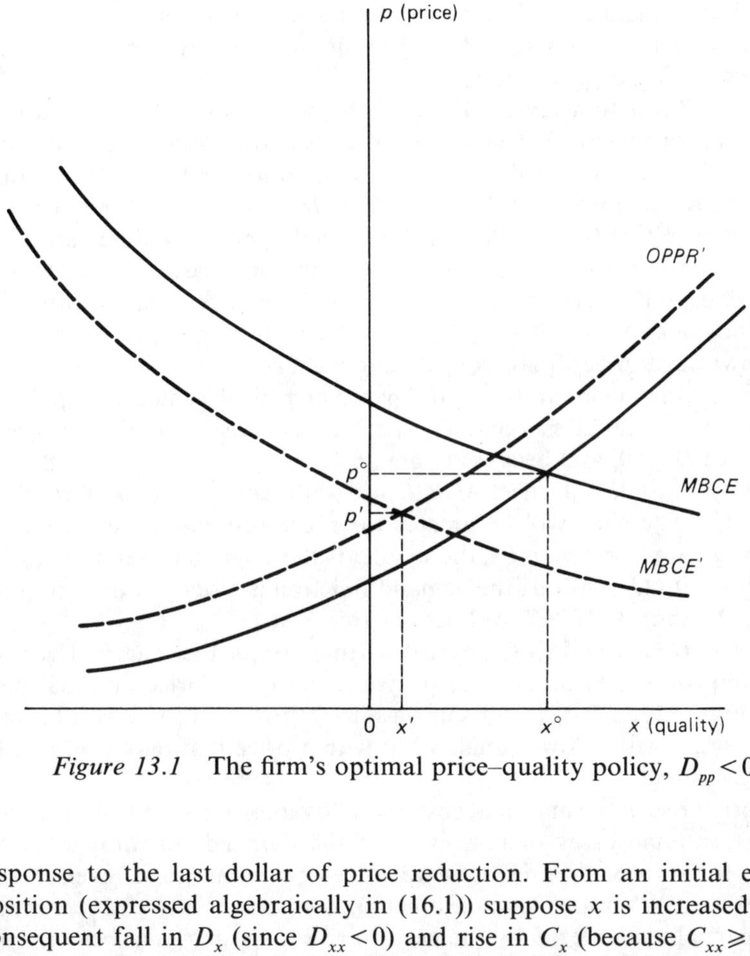

Figure 13.1 The firm's optimal price–quality policy, $D_{pp}<0$

response to the last dollar of price reduction. From an initial equality position (expressed algebraically in (16.1)) suppose x is increased with a consequent fall in D_x (since $D_{xx}<0$) and rise in C_x (because $C_{xx}\geqslant 0$). The absolute value of D_p must fall. With diminishing sales returns to price reductions ($D_{pp}<0$) price must fall to attain the diminished $-D_p$, and hence *MBCE* will slope negatively. But when increasing sales returns to price reductions rule ($D_{pp}\geqslant 0$) – the 'non-normal' case in our presentation – price must rise to reduce $-D_p$, and *MCBE* will be positively sloped.

The slope of *MBCE* reflects the relative effectiveness of price and quality policies as reflected in their marginal benefit–cost ratios displayed in (16.1). When D_{xx} is large absolutely and/or C_{xx} is large, a small rise in x will cause a large fall in the quality policy ratio. When $|D_{pp}|$ is large, a small change in p will restore balance, and the slope of *MBCE* will be shallow. Economically, the numerator of dp/dx is the net effective change in *marginal* sales per unit of dx, consisting of the direct reduction in $D_x(D_{xx})$ and the effective reduction in sales imposed by the rise in cost ($C_{xx}D_x/C_x=-C_{xx}D_p$). This, divided by C_x in the denominator of dp/dx, converts it to the rate of marginal sales change per dollar spent on quality enhancement. The $-D_{pp}$ in the denominator compares this magnitude with the rate of marginal sales change per dollar of price reduction.

The *OPPR* function reveals the price for any x value that will equate marginal profit to zero. When x rises, D rises and C rises, price constant. From (16.2), marginal profit from existing price will fall. Price must therefore rise, to raise p and $-D_p$ (when $D_{pp}<0$) until marginal profit reaches zero. When $D_{pp}\geqslant 0$, D/D_p will become larger in absolute value as p rises, offsetting the direct positive impact of the price rise. Only when this indirect effect outweighs the direct effect will price have to fall to bring the expression back to zero. Hence, *OPPR* will usually slope upward, but may slope downward under 'pathological' circumstances.

Consider, now, comparative static parameter displacements. Suppose a rise in C occurs that affects only C_x, the marginal cost of quality improvement. Since $D_{pp}<0$, and because (from 16.1) the term $-D_p$ must fall for a given D_x, p must fall. Hence, *MBCE* will shift downward to *MBCE′* on Figure 13.1. The shift will be greater the more responsive demand is to price, the greater the rise in C_x, the smaller is the original C_x, and the closer D is to linearity ($D_{pp}=0$). If the demand function is strictly convex in price ($D_{pp}\geqslant 0$) the shift in *MBCE* will be upward.

Similarly, *OPPR* will shift upward when a rise in the marginal cost of quality improvement forces price to rise to re-equate price and marginal cost. In Figure 13.1, *OPPR* shifts upward to *OPPR′*, and a new equilibrium $[p',x']$ emerges with a lower quality but with a price that may rise, fall, or remain the same.

In short, a rise in the marginal cost of quality improvement will, in all but the most extreme cases of convexity of the demand function in price, generate force to move price upward to re-equate marginal revenue and marginal cost. When the demand function is strictly concave ($D_{pp}<0$) this will be partially countered by the need to re-equate marginal benefit–cost ratios of the policies, which will reduce price. When $D_{pp}\geqslant 0$, *MBCE* will slope positively, will shift upward with a rise in C_x, and will reinforce the upward price force from *OPPR*'s shift. When $D_{pp}=0$, *MBCE* will be vertical, and its leftward shift with a rise in C_x will have no effect on the rise in price brought about by *OPPR*'s upward shift.

4 THE FIRM IN A RIVALROUS CONTEXT

4.1 Rival Quality Improvement, Slopes of Demand Function Unaffected

Consider, now, the reaction of a firm to a rise in the quality level of one of its rivals' products when the firm completely neglects any reactions by rivals to its policy response. Suppose, first, that such a change impacts only the position of Firm 1's demand curve, but that D_p and D_x are everywhere unaffected. *MBCE* will not be affected by dx^* (where starred variables denote a rival's policy choices) whereas *OPPR* will shift to the right when D is jointly concave in p and x. Policy will unambiguously consist of a reduction in p and an increase in x. When D is convex in p ($D_{pp} \geqslant 0$) but concave in x, *MBCE* will slope positively, but in non-pathological cases *OPPR* will slope upward. An outward shift of *OPPR*, therefore, will *raise* price as well as quality if the slope of *MBCE* is less than the slope of *OPPR*, and lower both if *OPPR* is less steeply sloped at the equilibrium than *MBCE*.

Assume that $D_{pp} < 0$. From (18) and (19), as D_{pp} becomes larger in absolute value, *MBCE* becomes flatter and *OPPR* becomes steeper. Because demand is less responsive to price changes as $|D_{pp}|$ grows, the firm adjusts to rivals' quality policies by emphasizing the quality of its product. If $D_{xx} < 0$, as it grows in absolute size *MBCE* grows more steeply negative. Lessened responsiveness of sales to quality changes leads the firm to adjust to rivals' quality changes by greater price adjustments. In the limit, as D_{pp} approaches 0, all adjustment is made via price, but as D_{xx} approaches 0 a mix of price and quality adjustments will be used. This latter result occurs because even if D_x does not change with changes in x, C_x does change (in general) and hence a quality adjustment will occur.

When $D_{pp} \geqslant 0$, sales responses to price reductions rise more than linearly and *MBCE* will be positively sloped. As x rises and D_x/C_x in (16.1) falls, $-D_p$ must fall. To effect this, p must rise. Hence, when demand functions are convex in price, equation of marginal policy benefit–cost ratios requires that x and p rise and fall together. So, of course, does the requirement that the marginal profit from price policy be zero. Hence, both *MBCE* and *OPPR* will slope positively.

From (18), the *degree* of positive slope of *MBCE* when $D_{pp} \geqslant 0$ will be greater, (1) the larger the absolute value of D_p, (2) the smaller D_{pp}, (3) the larger the fall in D_x (i.e. $|D_{xx}|$), (4) the larger the rate of rise in the marginal cost of quality as x rises, and (5) the smaller that marginal cost of quality. These are motivated by (16.1). A rise in x leads to a fall in D_x/C_x the greater the rise in C_x and the fall in D_x, and the smaller the initial value of C_x. To match the fall in D_x/C_x, $-D_p$ must fall an equivalent amount, forcing p to rise. The smaller D_{pp}, the greater the price rise required to effect the change in $-D_p$. And, of course, the larger the initial $-D_p$, the higher is initial price, and the greater the required price rise.

The net effect upon the firm's policy responses depends upon the relative sizes of the positive slopes of *MBCE* and *OPPR*. On Figure 13.2a, the case is illustrated where *MBCE* intersects *OPPR* from above because its slope is less steep. In this case the firm increases the quality standard of its product and increases price as well. The rise in a rival's quality shifts D leftward and, if price is maintained, leads to a rise in x to re-equate marginal profit from

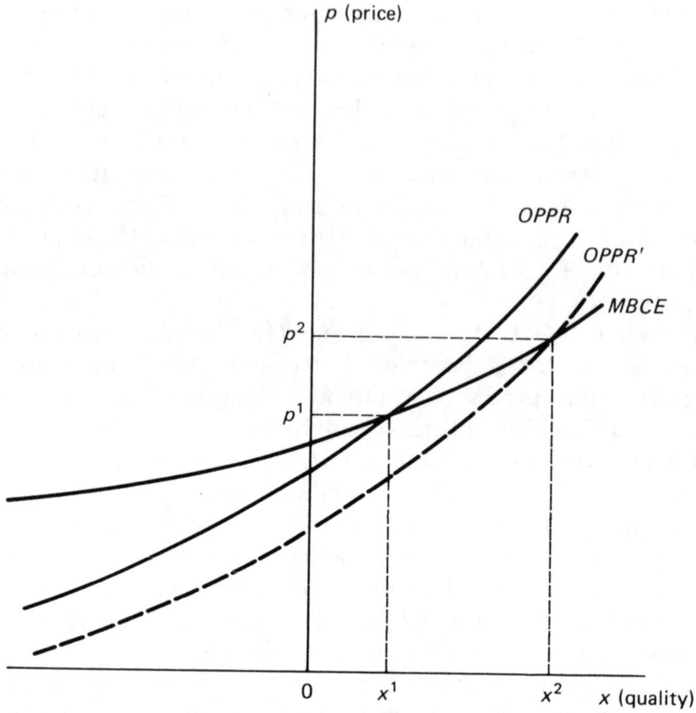

Figure 13.2a Slope of MBCE less than slope of *OPPR*. The firm's policy reaction to a rival's quality enhancement, $D_{pp} \geqslant 0$, when D_p *and* D_x are unaffected

price policy to zero. The rise in x, however, raises C_x and lowers D_x, calling for a rise in p to re-equate marginal policy benefit–cost ratios.

When *MBCE* is below *OPPR*, that rise in p is less than what is required to equate the marginal profit of price policy at the higher x to zero, so quality is enhanced once more to bring that equality about at the higher p. A succession of such adjustments converges to the $[p^2,x^2]$ equilibrium of Figure 13.2a. For any suboptimal x, the p dictated by the need to equate the marginal profit of price policy to zero is 'pulled up' by the need to equate marginal policy benefit–cost ratios.

On the other hand, Figure 13.2b illustrates the adjustment process when *MBCE* intersects *OPPR* from below. The shift downward of *OPPR* resulting from the initial shift in D requires that p fall at x'. The fall in p requires a rise in D_x/C_x obtained by lowering x. But the marginal profit of price policy condition continuously pulls price downward as x falls.

Hence, the final result in the two cases that can occur when $D_{pp} \geqslant 0$ is somewhat paradoxical. In the case where a rise in x requires a weaker rise in

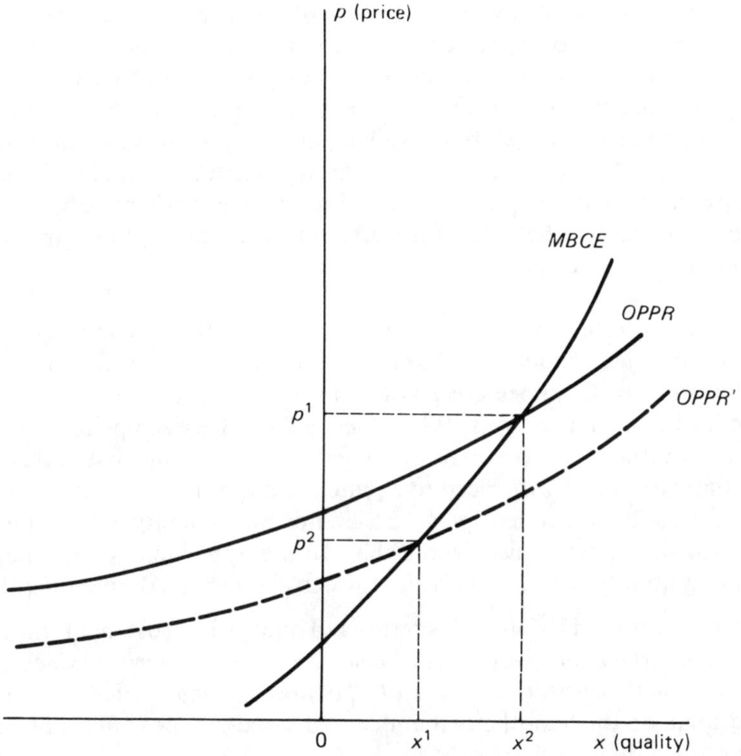

Figure 13.2b Slope of *MBCE* greater than slope of *OPPR*. The firm's policy reaction to a rival's quality enhancement, $D_{pp} \geqslant 0$, when D_p and D_x are unaffected

p to re-equate marginal policy benefit–cost ratios price rises along with quality (Fig. 13.2a). When price must move upward by large amounts to balance marginal policy benefit–cost ratios when x rises, the final response is a fall in both prices and quality (Fig. 13.2b).

But the paradox is readily understood. In the first case price response is weak relative to quality response, so the greater burden of adjustment must fall upon the latter. As it rises by large amounts, the demand curve shifts rightward, requiring p to rise to re-equate marginal profit of price policy to zero. In the second case, price changes must bear the brunt of the adjustment. As p falls by large amounts, D shifts rightward, requiring that quality be lowered to meet the marginal profit condition.

Let us summarize our results for the case of a rival's quality improvement when it does not affect D_p and D_x for Firm 1.

1. In the 'normal' case, when D_{pp} and $D_{xx} < 0$, the intuitive responses will

occur. Firm 1 responds by raising the quality of its product and reducing its price, the exact mix of which policies will depend upon the degree of negative slope of *MBCE*. Price policy will play the larger role when demand is price elastic, closer to linearity in the price dimension, the marginal cost of quality change is small but responds in strong positive fashion to such changes, and D is strongly concave in x, indicating rapidly diminishing sales returns to increases in quality improvement. Oligopolistic quality competition under these conditions should lead to quality improvement and price reductions.

2. In the 'abnormal' case, when $D_{pp} \geqslant 0$ (but $D_{xx} < 0$) increasing sales returns to price reductions characterize Firm 1's demand. Under these conditions two outcomes are possible in both of which price and quality move in the same directions. When the trade-off between price and quality dictated by the need to equate marginal policy benefit–cost ratios is less than that enforced by the need to equate the marginal profit of price policy to zero, quality adjustment plays the greater role. Quality will be improved but price will also be raised somewhat. In the opposite circumstance both price and quality will fall, with the former playing the dominant role.

If we accept diminishing sales returns to quality improvement, *the crucial element in which of these results emerges is the linearity, concavity, or convexity with respect to price of the firm's demand function.* This is conditional on the hypothesis that demand slopes are not affected by rivals' decisions on quality changes.

4.2 Rival Quality Improvement, Slopes of Demand Functions Affected

Suppose, now, that a change in x^*, or a rival's quality position, does affect the slopes of Firm 1's demand function in addition to its position. We assume D_{x^*} (i.e. $\delta D/\delta x^*$) is negative, and that D_{xx^*} can be positive or negative depending upon whether dx^* moves the rival brand in such direction as to become less or more substitutable for Brand 1. And a similar statement holds for D_{px^*} which, under the same conditions, may be positive or negative.

When $D_{pp} < 0$, $D_{xx} < 0$, and $C_{xx} \geqslant 0$, for the most part the impact of a rival's quality change on p and x is ambiguous. When D_{px^*} and D_{xx^*} are positive, making demand more price elastic and quality inelastic, both p and x will rise if

$$\frac{D_{px^*}/D_p}{D_{x^*}/D} < 1 - C_D D_p, \tag{20}$$

or if the ratio of the percentage change in D_p divided by the percentage fall in sales because of dx^* is less than unity plus the marginal cost of D_p. Broadly, then, if dx^* impacts demand more percentagewise than it moves the price slope of demand, Firm 1 will increase both price and quality. Condition (20) is necessary and sufficient to shift *OPPR* upward, and *MBCE* will always move upward with an increase in dx^*.

When D_{px^*} and D_{xx^*} are both negative, *MBCE* and *OPPR* shift down, so that p falls but x moves ambiguously depending upon the degree of shift in both functions. With $D_{px^*} \geqslant 0$ and $D_{xx^*} < 0$, the shifts in *MCBE* and *OPPR* are ambiguous, and thus the movement of p and x not predictable. And when $D_{px^*} < 0$ and $D_{xx^*} \geqslant 0$, *MBCE* will shift down, but *OPPR*'s direction of movement is not determinable.

4.3 The Importance of Second-order Derivatives

Perhaps the most important general result of this analysis of oligopolistic price–quality policy which does not feature rivalrous consonance (to be defined in the next section) is the dominant role played by the second-order partial derivatives D_{pp}, D_{xx}, D_{px^*}, and D_{xx^*}. Their signs and magnitudes determine dp/dx slopes of *MBCE* and *OPPR* and the direction and amounts of shifts in these functions. Because most firms cannot be expected to know the signs and magnitudes of these derivatives or to feel their effects even in the intermediate term, we are entitled to some skepticism that firms' price and quality responses will follow the general patterns outlined above. Rather more rough-hewn patterns of response may be expected to hold in practice, more attuned to first-order effects. And, equally importantly, it is to be expected that many of these first-order swamping effects will be the result of firms' taking into account the impacts of their actions upon rivals' welfares, as well as other goals of their own not exclusively defined by profit maximization.

5 THE FIRM IN RIVALROUS CONSONANCE

It follows that to come to grips with the true complexities of interdependence that characterize oligopolistic market structure, we must extend the firm's decision processes in dimensions that permit the inclusion of the sociological matrix of the industry or product group. Given the non-anonymity that small numbers impose upon rivals, and the expectations of each that others will react to his initiatives, the price–quality choice must be modelled to conform to the compulsions that push the firm simultaneously towards competition and cooperation. The mature oligopoly, at least, must be expected to experience drives in both directions, and the challenge to the theorist is to discover techniques to blend the policy motivations that result from such associations.

Elsewhere, and at some length, I have argued that a framework for experimentation for analysis of such socially conditioned egoism is 'rivalrous consonance' employing crippled optimization techniques.[9] In the modelling, each firm is assumed to maximize the sum of its own and its rivals' profits (or other objectives) when the latter have been discounted by a 'consonance factor', θ_{ij}. In rival i's maximization of such an 'extended profit function', \$1 of rival j's profit (or loss) is treated as the equivalent of θ dollars of rival i's profit (or loss).

In a duopoly, suppose Firms 1 and 2 have primary objectives of maximizing own-profits, but subject to the desire of taking into account the impact of their policies upon the rival's profit. We ignore other goals – expressible as constraints – for simplicity. Continue to suppose only one quality exists for firms to adjust, and let us continue to use unstarred variables and functions for Firm 1 and starred for Firm 2. Then, for example, Firm 1's objective function may be written from (10), after suppressing Y as constant:

$$\text{Max } Z = D(p,x,p^*,x^*)(p - C(x,D)) + \tag{21}$$

$$\theta_{12}[D^*(p^*,x^*,p,x)(p^* - C^*(x^*,D^*)),$$

where Z is Firm 1's *extended profit function*, which includes own-profit and consonance-factor discounted rival-profit. Define the average profit margins, $m = p - C(x,D)$ and $m^* = p^* - C^*(x^*,D^*)$. Then, first-order necessary conditions for an extended profit maximum are:

$$1.\quad D_p(m - C_D D) + \theta_{12} D^*_p(m^* - C^*_{D*} D^*) + D = 0 \tag{22}$$

$$2.\quad D_x(m - C_D D) + \theta_{12} D^*_2(m^* - C^*_{D*} D^*) - C_x D = 0.$$

The expressions in parentheses are the marginal profits on Brands 1 and 2, and we shall symbolize them M and M^* hereafter. Then (22.1) simply requires the marginal extended profit attendant to a slight fall in p to just offset the fall in revenue from previous sales caused by the price drop. And (23.2) requires the marginal extended profit from a slight enhancement of Brand 1's quality to be equal to the increase in cost on previous sales caused by the quality change. As in Section 4, this translates into the requirement that per dollar of direct policy cost, each policy must return the same marginal extended profit. Indeed, Section 4's analysis is a special case of (22) for $\theta_{12} = 0$.

For Firm 1, the analogue of (16.1) – marginal policy benefit–cost equality as captured in *MBCE* of Figure 13.1 – in rivalrous consonance is

$$1. \quad -\frac{D_pC_x + D_x}{D_p^*C_x + D_x^*} = \frac{\theta_{12}M^*}{M}. \tag{23}$$

When $\theta_{12}=0$, (23.1) becomes (16.1). Also, the analogue of (16.2), or *OPPR* in Figure 13.1, is

$$2. \quad D_pM + \theta_{12}D_p^*M^* + D = 0, \tag{23}$$

which simply states the necessity of marginal extended profit on price policy to be zero. And, of course, for Firm 2, the first-order necessary conditions may be written explicitly:

$$1. \quad -\frac{D_{p^*}^*C_{x^*}^* + D_{x^*}^*}{D_{p^*}C_{x^*}^* + D_{x^*}} = \frac{\theta_{21}M}{M^*} \tag{24}$$

$$2. \quad D_{p^*}^*M^* + \theta_{21}D_{p^*}M + D^* = 0.$$

For given values of p^* and x^* (p and x) the analysis of Section 4 holds in its entirety for Firm 1's (Firm 2's) optimal policy-making. The novel elements are the complications introduced in the p/x (p^*/x^*) slopes of the *MBCE* and *OPPR* functions by p^* and x^* (p and x), and the shift effects on those functions of the rival prices and quality values.

For example, for Firm 1, the slope of *MBCE* as defined in (23.1) is

$$\left(\frac{dp}{dx}\right)_{MBCE} =$$

$$-\frac{[D_{xx} + D_pC_{xx}]M + [D_x + D_pC_x]M_x}{[D_{pp}C_x]M + [D_x + D_pC_x]M_p} \; \frac{+\theta_{12}([D_{xx}^* + D_p^*C_{xx}]M^* + [D_x^* + D_p^*C_x]M_x^*)}{+\theta_{12}([D_{pp}^*C_x]M^* + [D_x^* + D_p^*C_x]M_p^*} \tag{25}$$

where we continue to ignore second-order cross-derivatives, and where

$$M_p = 1 - 2C_DD_p > 0 \qquad M_{p^*}^* = 1 - 2C_{D^*}^*D_{p^*}^* > 0$$

$$M_x = -C_x - 2C_DD_x < 0 \qquad M_{x^*}^* = -C_{x^*}^* - 2C_{D^*}^*D_{x^*}^* < 0$$

$$M_{p^*} = -2C_DD_{p^*} < 0 \qquad M_p^* = -2C_{D^*}^*D_p^* < 0$$

$$M_{x^*} = -2C_DD_{x^*} > 0 \qquad M_x^* = -2C_{D^*}^*D_x^* > 0.$$

From (25) it can be seen that two complicating factors intrude when it is compared with the determination in (17) for the non-consonance analysis.

First, because M cannot be factored out, in both numerator and denominator bracketed terms modify M_x and M_p, whose signs are determined by the marginal impacts on amount demanded of price and quality changes as well as the marginal cost of quality change. Second, in numerator and denominator the existence of the second firm's profits in Firm 1's extended profit calculations results in bracketed terms multiplied by θ_{12} which are indeterminate as to sign. On the assumption that $D_{pp}<0$, it is no longer possible to assert unequivocally that *MBCE* slopes negatively in the p–x plane as in Figure 13.1.

However, in the numerator and denominators the first bracketed terms should dominate the second, so that the net sums are negative. This is because (i) M is expected to be greater than M_x, and (ii) the second bracketed terms are opposite in sign and therefore offsetting. In the numerator, within the parentheses, both bracketed terms have offsetting elements signwise; they involve impacts of Firm 1's variables upon Firm 2's demand, which should be weaker than own-demand impacts; and the sum of the terms is multiplied by θ_{12}, which, given realistic values, should reduce the impact of D^* and M^* responses greatly. Hence, it is to be expected that the numerator will be negative.

In the denominator's parenthesized terms, the first bracket should be negative and the second, containing offsetting terms signwise and being multiplied by M_p^*, which may be relatively small, has a high probability of being negative. In any event, after multiplication by θ_{12}, it should pose no threat to the negativity of the denominator.

Therefore, we expect that *MBCE* will retain the negative slope it had in Figure 13.1 (when $(D_{pp}<0,\ D_{xx}<0,\ D_{pp}^*<0,\ D_{xx}^*<0)$. However, we should also expect that rivalrous consonance will reduce the absolute size of the numerator somewhat and increase the absolute size of the denominator, so that the absolute slope value will be smaller. A rise in quality will lead Firm 1 to reduce price less under rivalrous consonance to re-equate the relevant benefit–cost ratios of price and quality policies.

On the other hand, *OPPR*'s slope is unambiguously positive:

$$\left(\frac{dp}{dx}\right)_{OPPR} = -\frac{D_pM_x+\theta_{12}D_p^*M_x^*+D_x}{D_{pp}M+D_pM_p+\theta_{12}D_p^*M_p^*+D_p}\ . \tag{26}$$

The denominator is unambiguously negative and the numerator positive. That is, when x rises, the need to re-equate the marginal extended profit to zero will require price to rise, as in the case of marginal own profit (i.e. $\theta_{12}=0$). However, under rivalrous consonance, the denominator of (26) is expected to rise more in absolute value than the numerator, so the slope of *OPPR* should also be less steep than in the Cournot environment of Section 4.

To make notation a bit more compact, let us define

1. $f_1(D_p,D_x,C_x,D_p^*,M^*,M,\theta_{12}) = M(D_pC_x + D_x) + \theta_{12}M^*(D_p^*C_x + D_x^*)$

2. $f_2(D_p,D_p^*,M^*,M,D,\theta_{12}) = D_pM + \theta_{12}D_p^*M^* + D.$ (27)

Then, defining $\delta f_1/\delta x = f_{1x}$, etc., we may rewrite (25) and (26) more compactly as:

1. $(dp/dx)_{MBCE} = -(f_{1x}/f_{1p})$ (28)

2. $(dp/dx)_{OPPR} = -(f_{2x}/f_{2p}).$

Consider, now, the impact of a change in p^* upon $MBCE$ for constant x when we continue to assume that other-variable second derivatives (D_{pp}^*, etc.) approximate zero:

$$\left(\frac{dp}{dp^*}\right)_{MBCE} = -\frac{AM_{p^*} + \theta_{12}M_{p^*}^*}{AM_p + \theta_{12}M_p^* + (D_{pp}C_xM/(D_p^*C_x + D_x^*))} = -(f_{1p^*}/f_{1p}), \tag{29}$$

where $A = (D_pC_x + D_x)/(D_p^*C_x + D_x^*)$. From (23.1), $A < 0$. Therefore, when $D_p^*C_x + D_x^* \geqslant 0$, $dp/dp^* \geqslant 0$, and $MBCE$ shifts upward when p^* rises. Only when $D_p^*C_x + D_x^* < 0$ and is small enough to make the bracketed term in the denominator positive and larger than the absolute value of the first two terms will $MBCE$ shift down. We treat the first case as more likely, and assume $dp/dp^* \geqslant 0$ for $MBCE$.

For $OPPR$:

$$\left(\frac{dp}{dp^*}\right)_{OPPR} = -\frac{D_pM_{p^*} + \theta_{12}D_p^*M_{p^*}^* + D_{p^*}}{D_{pp}M + (1 + M_p)D_p + \theta_{12}(D_p^*M_p^*)} = -(f_{2p^*}/f_{2p}), \tag{30}$$

which is unambiguously positive.

Hence, a rise in Firm 2's price will raise Firm 1's price in rivalrous consonance. But Firm 1's quality will rise if $MBCE$ rises more than $OPPR$ and fall if the opposite is true, when p^* rises.

As for shifts in $MBCE$ and $OPPR$ when x^* changes, we obtain:

1. $$\left(\frac{dp}{dx^*}\right)_{MBCE} = -\frac{AM_{x^*} + \theta_{12}M_{x^*}^*}{AM_p + \theta_{12}M_p^* + (D_{pp}C_xM/(D_p^*C_x + D_x^*)} = -(f_{1x^*}/f_{1p}) \tag{31}$$

$$2. \quad \left(\frac{dp}{dx^*}\right)_{OPPR} = -\frac{(D_p+\theta_{12}D_p^*)M_{x^*}^*+D_{x^*}}{D_{pp}M+(1+M_p)D_p+\theta_{12}(D_p^*M_p^*)} = -(f_{2x^*}/f_{2p}).$$

Since $f_{1x^*}<0$ and we hypothesize $f_{1p}<0$, *MCBE* should shift down when rival quality is improved. That is, if Firm 1 were constrained to hold its quality constant, the need to re-equate marginal benefit per unit of marginal cost for its policies would lead it to lower price. We expect $f_{2x^*}\geqslant 0$ and $f_{2p}<0$, so *OPPR* should shift up when a rival raises quality of product. If Firm 1 could not change policy, the need to equate the marginal profit from price policy to zero should lead the firm to raise price. Hence x must fall, but p can rise or fall depending upon whether *OPPR* moves up by more or less than *MBCE*, respectively. Since the downward shift is tempered by the consonance term and D_{x^*} in f_{2x^*}, we expect the second alternative to occur.

This result is most dependent upon the sign of f_{2x^*}, and, specifically, assumes that Firm 1's demand is more sensitive to own-price than other-quality. If the reverse is true, and Firm 1's product demand is highly affected by Firm 2's quality, then *OPPR* will shift down when x^* changes, and the shift will be enhanced by consonance. Quality then rises if the absolute size of *OPPR*'s shift is greater than that of *MBCE*, or falls with the reverse, whereas price falls unambiguously.

In Section 4, when rivalrous consonance did not affect Firm 1's responses and other-variable second derivatives were ignored, $dp/dp^*\geqslant 0$, $dx/dp^*<0$, $dp/dx^*<0$, and $dx/dx^*\geqslant 0$. Changes in rivals' parameters shift *MBCE* and, in both rival parameter changes shifted *OPPR* downward. When rivals' profit consequences are taken into account *à la* rivalrous consonance, this determinateness disappears. The problem arises because rivalrous consonance removes the immunity of *MBCE* from feeling the impacts of rival parameter changes. Under the same assumptions in both cases, the signs of $f_{2p}, f_{2x}, f_{1p^*}, f_{2p^*}, f_{1x^*}$, and f_{2x^*} are unambiguous, but where $f_{1p}=f_{1x}=0$ in the non-consonance case, these terms are ambiguously signed in rivalrous consonance.

Thus, rivalrous consonance affects the price–quality policy reaction of a firm by requiring it to re-equate the marginal benefit/marginal cost ratios in response to policy changes by rivals. The movement direction of price and quality to reachieve this equality depends upon the relative strength of the slopes of demand with respect to price and quality and the marginal cost of quality improvements for *both* firms to Firm 1's p and x. If both firms show price-insensitivity in demands, a rise in p^* will require most of the adjustment to be made with a rise in x; quality-insensitivity leads to the opposite result.

6 CONCLUSION

Heuristic methods of measuring quality differentials should be tested empirically as a first step in the analysis of policy-making in differentiated oligopoly. This paper offers some suggested procedures that may have merit. The availability of more than one policy dimension to the oligopolist raises the question of trade-offs between them, and complicates the task of the economist who seeks to interpret realistic oligopolistic behavior. This is especially true when rivalrous consonance frameworks are used to incorporate rivals' concerns for the impacts of their policies upon other industry members.

The crucial relation in the interdependence analysis is the need to trade off price and quality changes to re-equate marginal profit per unit of marginal cost for both policy variables. Explicit results depend upon the first- and second-order partial derivatives of all firms' demand functions to the price–quality complex of the firm under analysis. Industry equilibrium occurs when these marginal benefit/marginal cost ratios are equal and the marginal extended policy profit for either the price or quality is zero for all firms.

The interdependence among firms' sales functions is so entangling that comparative statics analyses of parameter changes in unspecified systems is very difficult even when restrictive assumptions are made concerning relevant partial derivatives. In the general case it will be necessary at this point to examine specific industry relationships and resort to simulative theorizing in order to gain insights.

Notes

1. 'Mr Sraffa's article must be regarded as the fount from which my work flows, for the chief aim of this book is to attempt to carry out his pregnant suggestion that the whole theory of value should be treated in terms of monopoly analysis' (Robinson, 1933, p.v.).
2. Robinson points out the same asymmetry as Chamberlin between the polar analogues of pure competition and pure monopoly, with the latter requiring control over the supply of *all* commodities (Robinson, 1933, p.4).
3. I have discussed this distinction between Chamberlin's product differentiation and its implied interproduct competition versus Robinson's interfirm competition in Kuenne (1967), pp.229–30. In Robinson (1933), see pp.50–1, 86, 89, 90n., 93, and 170. She does refer on p.50 to 'closely similar commodities', and several times she speaks of buyers' preferences for sellers 'for whatever reasons', which would seem to embrace product differentiation. Nonetheless, the reader is struck with her refusal to explicitly relate these preferences to qualities of the product. For example, on pp.89–90 in her most extensive discussion of the issue, she lists as reasons for these preferences transport costs; guarantees of quality through a known seller's name; differences in facilities for service, credit, or customer complaints; and advertizing. All of these are associated with the firm. And, in a curious footnote on p.93, she

compares the producer of a branded product with a pub owner given a limited monopoly by a license whose upper bound on profit is unlimited. This case is obviously not the typical one she has in mind in her analysis of imperfect markets. And, I believe, this emphasis upon the seller and purposeful ignoring of product differentiation is one of the reasons Chamberlin felt (unfairly) that she never truly blended monopoly and competition at the level of the firm.

4. Robinson evinces no interest in the firm's choice of a quality complex for its product and dismisses advertizing as equivalent to a reduction in price (p.21). The comparison above does not imply that Chamberlin made great progress in the analysis of product quality choice of selling costs. But he did introduce them as dimensions of equivalent importance to price in the firm's decision-making.
5. Cf. Chamberlin (1948) pp.204–11; (1957) pp.viii, 26–30, 66–9, 74, 95, 141–2, 221–2, 274, 311–12. Indeed, in chapter 3, where he rewrites monopolistic competition theory as he would if he were to present it in 1951, his presentation in terms of spatially differentiated firms selling a homogeneous product is the Robinson paradigm.
6. Cf. Chamberlin (1957) pp.33, 61–2, 195–6.
7. Kuenne (1967) pp.228–32. To my arguments could be added the lack of clarity about which cross-elasticity measures are appropriate for the task. See Triffin (1940); Bishop (1952), (1953), (1955); Chamberlin (1953); Fellner (1953), (1967); and Heiser (1955).
8. That is, unique up to a linear or a positive multiplicative factor transformation.
9. See, for example, Kuenne (1986) for an extensive discussion of the framework and a motivation for its usage.

References

Bishop, R. L. (1952) 'Elasticities, Cross-Elasticities, and Market Relationships', *American Economic Review,* 42: 781–803.

Bishop, R. L. (1953) 'Reply', *American Economic Review,* 43: 916–24.

Bishop, R. L. (1955) 'Reply', *American Economic Review,* 45: 382–6.

Chamberlin, E. H. (1948) *The Theory of Monopolistic Competition*, 6th edn (Cambridge, Mass.: Harvard University Press).

Chamberlin, E. H. (1953) 'Elasticities, Cross-Elasticities, and Market Relationships: Comment', *American Economic Review,* 43: 910–16.

Chamberlin, E. H. (1957) *Towards a More General Theory of Value* (New York: Oxford University Press).

Fellner, W. (1953) 'Elasticities, Cross-Elasticities, and Market Relationships: Comment', *American Economic Review,* 43: 898–910.

Fellner, W. (1967) 'The Adaptability and Lasting Significance of the Chamberlinian Contribution', in R. E. Kuenne (ed.) *Monopolistic Competition Theory: Studies in Impact* (New York: John Wiley).

Heiser, R. (1955) 'Elasticities, Cross-Elasticities, and Market Relationships: Comment', *American Economic Review,* 45: 373–82.

Kuenne, R. E. (1967) 'Quality Space, Interproduct Competition, and General Equilibrium Theory', in R. E. Kuenne (ed) *Monopolistic Competition Theory: Studies in Impact* (New York: John Wiley).

Kuenne, R. E. (1986) *Rivalrous Consonance: A Theory of General Oligopolistic*

Equilibrium, Contributions to Economic Analysis No. 157 (Amsterdam: North-Holland).

Robinson, J. (1933) *The Economics of Imperfect Competition* (London: Macmillan).

Sraffa, P. (1926) 'The Laws of Returns Under Competitive Conditions', *Economic Journal*, 26: 535–50.

Triffin, R. (1940) *Monopolistic Competition and General Equilibrium Theory* (Cambridge, Mass.: Harvard University Press).

14 Who Benefits from Unemployment?

Joaquim Silvestre*

> But, in fact, unemployment falls more heavily upon some individuals than upon others, and there is no level of employment which can be regarded as the most desirable for all of them. (Joan Robinson, 'Full Employment', in *Essays in the Theory of Employment*)

1 INTRODUCTION

The question addressed here is not very different from the one in chapters 25 and 26 of *The Economics of Imperfect Competition* (1933). There, Joan Robinson defines labor as being 'exploited' when the wage is less than labor's marginal physical product valued at the price at which it is being sold: this occurs because firms either have monopoly power in the output market or monopsony power in the labor market. She then discusses the conditions under which the removal of such market imperfections is beneficial to the workers. One of her conclusions is that the existence of economywide imperfections cannot benefit the workers relative to the competitive outcome, since 'their loss as consumers would more than offset their gain as wage earners' (p.288).

Here, we focus on situations of less than full employment. We adopt the viewpoint that, in such situations, some workers are fully employed and some others are totally unemployed. Thus, the welfare analysis of unemployment situations becomes more complex than in the usual models with a representative worker. There, the welfare of workers can be represented by a (scalar valued) utility index which reflects the effects of prices, wages and the level of unemployment. Here, one must consider separately three welfare magnitudes: the number of workers employed, the welfare of employed workers, and that of the unemployed.

Our viewpoint covers in a more realistic way economies where the labor force is heterogeneous and workers in different groups (defined, e.g., by seniority or citizenship) have different probabilities of being employed.

The analytical set up (see Section 2 below) is a non-Walrasian model with one non-produced good (used as numeraire), one produced good and labor. It is a well-known framework studied among others by Barro-Grossman

* The author is indebted to A. Mas-Colell. He has benefitted from comments by J.-P. Benassy, J.-M. Grandmont, C. Greene and G. Laroque. Some of the present research was reported in Silvestre (1982).

(1976), Benassy (1977, 1982), Malinvaud (1977), Hildenbrand and Hildenbrand (1978) and Hart (1982). The economy is, in the aggregate, identical to the one in Hart (1982), but here we distinguish between shareholders, employed workers and unemployed workers.

The allocation obtained at a non-Walrasian price–wage pair is determined in accordance with fix-price theory,[1] i.e. by the principles of 'voluntary trade' (price no higher than a buyer's marginal benefit and no lower than a seller's marginal sacrifice) and 'frictionless markets' (exhaustion of mutually advantageous market transactions at the given price), together with a rationing rule for situations where several agents are in the long side of a market. The theory (see, e.g., Silvestre, 1986) can be given several interpretations, among them: (i) *competition in the short run*: transactions are carried out at prices which are temporarily out of equilibrium in an otherwise competitive economy; (ii) *imperfect competition*: the agents in one side of the market are price-setters or wage-setters (this corresponds to the imperfections discussed in chapters 25 and 26 of *The Economics of Imperfect Competition*, see Benassy, 1973, 1976, 1977, and Silvestre, 1986, section 3.4–5, for a detailed analysis); (iii) *price controls or guidelines*; and (iv) *price (or wage) negotiation*: representatives of buyers and sellers negotiate prices or wages that are taken as given by individual firms and workers.

We shall be primarily concerned with the following question.[2] Given a price–wage pair that generates unemployment, are there small price-wage changes that make everybody better off? If the answer is 'no', we shall say that the given price–wage pair is 'locally undominated'. Our aim is to characterize the set of locally undominated unemployment price–wage pairs. Our motivation is primarily normative, but the characterization may complement the positive results on the determination of prices and wages in disequilibrium present in the literature (e.g., Hart, 1982). Such positive analyses often adopt a non-cooperative approach. Our results offer a cooperative counterpart to the extent that undominated price–wage pairs can be viewed as natural outcomes of negotiation.

Two types of unemployment appear in this class of models: Keynesian unemployment (where the level of output is determined by effective demand and prices exceed marginal costs), and Classical unemployment (where prices equal marginal costs and output is determined by supply conditions). Keynesian unemployment has perhaps a stronger empirical appeal since evidence supports the view that prices are typically higher than marginal costs (see Hall, 1986, for a recent study). But it has been argued (see, e.g., Malinvaud, 1977, that situations of Classical unemployment do occasionally appear in modern market economies. Both types of unemployment will be studied here. Particularly interesting is the intersection of the two types, i.e. unemployment situations satisfying the 'first fundamental postulate of the classical theory' maintained by Keynes (1936, ch.2) (prices equal marginal costs and the effective demand for output equals competitive supply): the set of such price–wage pairs will be called the Keynesian–Classical boundary.

Our main result is that unemployment price–wage pairs close to the Keynesian–Classical boundary are locally undominated, and those away from it are not. Locally undominated price–wage pairs of the Keynesian unemployment type are states of conflict among the interests of the employed workers, those of the firm's shareholders and the level of unemployment. Lowering prices would increase employment and benefit workers, but it would decrease the welfare of the owners of the firm. One can find, on the other hand, increases in prices and wages which benefit both the shareholders and the employed workers, but they will reduce the level of employment. These results contrast with those obtained in Silvestre (1988) for the case where there is a representative worker: only price–wage pairs on the Keynesian–Classical boundary itself may there be undominated (and only under some conditions).

This chapter is organized as follows: The basic concepts and assumptions are presented in sections 2 and 3. Keynesian (resp. Classical) unemployment is studied in Section 4 (resp. 5). Proofs are relegated to the Appendix.

2 THE MODEL

2.1 The Economy

Three commodities: a non-produced good[3] (k), labor (l) and output (y). Two types of consumers: workers and shareholders, with identical utility function $U(y,k)$. We assume that U is 1-homogeneous, differentiable, strictly quasi-concave and strictly increasing in the strictly positive orthant R^2_{++}. The non-produced good will be used as numeraire. Denote by p (resp. w) the price of output (resp. labor): only strictly positive vectors $(p,w) \varepsilon R^2_{++}$ will be considered. Given $p > 0$, write $(h(p), 1\text{-}ph(p))$ for the unique solution to the program: max $U(y,k)$ subject to $py + k = 1$. It follows that whenever (individual or aggregate) wealth is I, then (individual or aggregate) demand for output is $h(p)I$. We assume that $h(p)\ \varepsilon\ (0,1/p)$, $\forall p > 0$. Write: $v(p) := h(p)/(1\text{-}ph(p))$. Clearly, $v' < 0$, $v \to 0$ as $p \to \infty$ and $v \to \infty$ as $p \to 0$.

Output is produced by a single firm using labor. The inverse production function is $\bar{l}(y) := y^{\alpha}$, $\alpha > 1$.[4]

The set of workers is the closed interval $L = [0,l_0]$. Initial endowments of the non-produced good and leisure are uniformly distributed among workers, μ (resp. 1) being their mean endowment of the non-produced good (resp. leisure). Workers receive no profit income. The set of shareholders is a closed interval S of unit length. Initial endowments and profit shares are uniformly distributed among shareholders, k_S (resp. zero) being their mean endowment of the non-produced good (resp. leisure). Aggregate initial endowments of the non-produced good are therefore: $k_L := \mu l_0$ for the workers, k_S for the shareholders and $k_0 = k_L + k_S$ for the economy. The supply of labor is fixed at l_0.

2.2 Aggregate Output

Denote by $y^* := l_0^{\frac{1}{\alpha}}$ the full employment output. The realized level of output at a given (p,w) will be determined by the following consideration. If output is less than demand and less than y^* and if price exceeds marginal cost, output will expand until it reaches either y^* or the level of demand or the point where price equals marginal cost. Levels of output higher than demand or higher than y^* or with marginal cost higher than price cannot, on the other hand, be realized. Formally, the price of output does not exceed its marginal cost if and only if $y \leqslant y_C(p,w) := (p/\alpha w)^{1/(\alpha-1)}$. Given (p,y), aggregate wealth is $k_0 + py$ and (effective) demand for output is $y_D(p,y) := h(p)(k_0 + py)$. Thus, realized output must satisfy: $y = \min\{y^*, y_C(p,w), y_D(p,y)\}$. This determines output (and hence employment) uniquely for given (p,w).[5] Note that the assumptions on utility and technology guarantee that aggregate output and employment are always positive.

The (p,w) pairs can be classified by the type of the resulting allocation as follows. First, $y^* \leqslant y_C(p,w)$ and $y^* \leqslant y_D(p,y^*)$ if and only if $w/p \leqslant b^* := (1/\alpha)l_0^{(1-\alpha)/\alpha}$ and $p \leqslant p^* := v^{-1}(y^*/k_0)$. These inequalities define the *full employment region E* in the (p,w) plane (see Figure 14.1). Second, price equals marginal cost if and only if $w/p \geqslant b^*$ and $y_C(p,w) \leqslant y_D(p,y_C(p,w))$, i.e. $w \geqslant k(p) := (p/\alpha)(k_0 v(p))^{1-\alpha}$. This defines the *Classical region*, denoted by C (resp. $\mathring{C}$) when its boundaries are (resp. are not) included, and where output is determined by $y_C(p,w)$. Finally, the inequalities $p \geqslant p^*$ and $w \leqslant k(p)$ define the *Keynesian region*, denoted by K (resp. $\mathring{K}$) when boundaries are (resp. are not) included. Output is, in K, determined by demand through the equality $y = y_D(p,y)$, i.e. $y = y_K(p) := k_0 v(p)$.

The curve '$w = k(p)$' describes, to the right of p^*, the Keynesian–Classical boundary $K \cap C$. One may alternatively describe $K \cap C$ as a function $\tilde{w}$ from real-wages greater than b^* to money wages. By the 0-homogeneity of y_C, if $b = w/p, y_C(p,w) = y_C(1,b) := \bar{y}(b)$, with $\bar{y}'(b) < 0$. The equation defining $K \cap C$ can thus be written $H(b,w) := \bar{y}(b) - y_K(w/b) = 0$. Since $\delta H/\delta b < 0$ and $\delta H/\delta w > 0$, and since for any $b > 0$, $\lim H(b,w)$ is positive (resp. $-\infty$) as $w \to \infty$ (resp. $w \to 0$), the equation defines an increasing function $\tilde{w}(b)$ satisfying: $(w = \tilde{w}(b), b > b^*, p = w/b) \Leftrightarrow (p,w) \in K \cap C$. These facts are illustrated in Figure 14.1, where the dashed lines depict typical isoemployment curves (there is full employment in E) and the arrows indicate increasing employment. Point (p^*,w^*) is the unique Walrasian

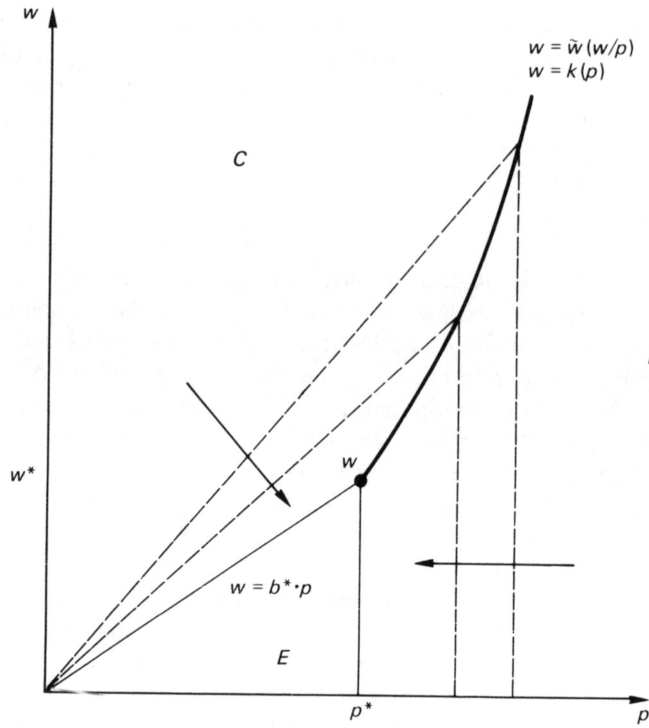

Figure 14.1

equilibrium. Aggregate output is hence independent of the profit shares and the initial distribution (of leisure and the nonproduced good): it is solely determined, as a function of (p,w), by U and the parameters l_0, k_0, and α.

3 INDIVIDUAL CONSUMPTION AND WELFARE

3.1 Rationing in the Labor Market

Let labor demand be $l < l_0$. We shall postulate a queueing rationing scheme: workers in the $[0,l]$ interval work one unit (full time) and those in the interval $[l,l_0]$ are wholly unemployed. One can, for instance, visualize that workers are ordered in the $[0,l_0]$ interval by decreasing seniority.

3.2 Consumption and Utilities in the Keynesian Region

At a $(p,w) \varepsilon K$ there are three groups of consumers: shareholders, employed workers and unemployed workers. Wealth is uniformly distributed within each group. If individual wealth in a given group is I, then the demand vector of a consumer in the group is given by $(h(p), 1 - ph(p))I$. Since demand equals output in the Keynesian region, the same expression gives the individual consumption vector. Write: $\tilde{U}(p) := U(h(p), 1 - ph(p))$. Then in the Keynesian region the utilities of the agents as functions of (p,w) are given by the following expressions, where the subscript S (resp. E, resp. N) denotes a shareholder (resp. an employed worker, resp. an unemployed worker), and where $l_K(p) := \bar{l}(y_K(p))$:

$$
\begin{aligned}
U_S^K(p,w) &= \tilde{U}(p)(k_S + py_K(p) - w(l_K(p))), \\
U_E^K(p,w) &= \tilde{U}(p)(\mu + w), \qquad (1) \\
U_N^K(p,w) &= \tilde{U}(p)\mu.
\end{aligned}
$$

3.3 Rationing in the Output Market

Outside K demand exceeds output. We assume that demand is rationed efficiently. Since leisure does not enter the utility function and since preferences are identical and homogeneous, this implies that all agents consume goods y and k in the same ratio. Taking the budget constraint into account and writing I_A for the individual wealth in group $A(A = S,E,N)$, the individual consumption vector in A, $(x_A, I_A - px_A)$, must satisfy: $x_A/I_A - px_A = y/k_0$, i.e. $x_A(py + k_0) = I_A y$ or: $(x_A, I_A - px_A) = q_A(y,k_0)$, where $q_A = I_A/(py + k_0)$. In the language of the rationing literature, this is the proportional rationing scheme: the amount of output allocated to a group (shareholders, employed workers and unemployed workers) is proportional to its demand, which in turn is proportional to its wealth, and consumption is distributed uniformly within each group.

3.4 Consumption and Utilities in the Classical Region

Write: $Y_C(p,w) := py_C(p,w) + k_0$ (this is national wealth), $\bar{U}(p,w) := U(y_C(p,w),k_0)$, and $l_C(p,w) := \bar{l}(y_C(p,w))$. Given the proportional rationing scheme for output, the utilities of the agents as functions of (p,w) are given in the classical region by:

$$
\begin{aligned}
U_S^C(p,w) &:= \bar{U}(p,w)(py_C - wl_C + k_S)/Y_C, \\
U_E^C(p,w) &:= \bar{U}(p,w)(w + \mu)/Y_C, \qquad (2) \\
U_N^C(p,w) &:= \bar{U}(p,w)\mu/Y_C.
\end{aligned}
$$

The interpretation of the subscripts of U^C is as in 3.2 above.

3.5 The Full Employment Region

It is clear from the discussion in 3.3 above that the allocation obtained at any (p,w) in the full employment region is Pareto optimal. We shall from now on concentrate on pairs (p,w) that generate unemployment, i.e. those in $R^2_{++}\backslash E = (K \bigcup C)\backslash E$. They will not be Pareto optimal (see Silvestre, 1985), and we shall consider a weaker welfare criterion.

3.6 Locally Undominated Unemployment Price–Wage Pairs

Define, for $A = S,E,N$, $U_A: K \bigcup C \rightarrow R$: $U_A(p,w) = U^K_A(p,w)$ if $(p,w) \varepsilon K$, $= U^C_A(p,w)$ if $(p,w) \varepsilon C$. Shareholder a's utility at (p,w) is $U_S(p,w)$. Define $\hat{l}(p,w) = l_K(p)$ if $(p,w) \varepsilon K$, $= l_C(p,w)$ if $(p,w) \varepsilon C$. Worker a's utility at (p,w) is given by:

$$U_a(p,w) = \left\{ \begin{array}{l} U_E(p,w) \text{ if } a \varepsilon [0, \hat{l}(p,w)], \\ U_N(p,w) \text{ if } a \varepsilon [\hat{l}(p,w), l_0]. \end{array} \right\}$$

Definition: A price–wage pair $(p,w) \varepsilon R^2_{++}\backslash E$ is *locally undominated* if there exists an $\in > 0$ such that no (p',w') in the $\in$-neighborhood of (p,w) satisfies $U_a(p',w') \geqq U_a(p,w)$ for all $a \varepsilon S \bigcup L$, with at least one strict inequality. We say that (p,w) is *dominated* if it is not locally undominated.

Theorem 1

A price–wage pair $(p,w) \varepsilon R^2_{++}\backslash E$ is locally undominated iff there exists an $\bar{\mathrm{E}} > 0$ such that no (p',w') in the $\bar{\mathrm{E}}$-neighborhood of (p,w) satisfies simultaneously:

(i) $\hat{l}(p',w') \geqq \hat{l}(p,w)$,

(ii) $U_A(p',w') \geqslant U_A(p,w)(A = S,E,N)$,

with at least one strict inequality.

Proof See Appendix.

Remark: Note that for $(p,w) \varepsilon \mathring{K}$ the level of employment and the welfare of the unemployed depend only on p and move in the same direction. Hence, the consideration of the welfare of the unemployed does not add any restriction to those generated by considering the level of employment when $(p,w) \varepsilon \mathring{K}$.

4 KEYNESIAN UNEMPLOYMENT

The Keynesian region turns out to be partitioned into two subregions: one of the locally undominated (p,w) pairs, which adjoins the Keynesian–Classical boundary, and another one of dominated (p,w) pairs. The boundary of these subregions is a curve '$w = G(p)$' in the (p,w) plane which goes through the Walrasian equilibrium point (see Figures 14.2 and 14.3 below which also illustrate the analysis of the Classical region).

Price–wage pairs below the curve '$w = G(p)$' are dominated. At any point in this subregion one can find a direction of decreasing wages and prices which improves the welfare of employed workers and shareholders and (since it entails lower prices) which also increases employment and the welfare of the unemployed.

Price–wage pairs above the '$w = G(p)$' curve and below the Keynesian–Classical boundary are locally undominated. From any point in this subregion, increasing the utility of both employed workers and shareholders entails higher prices and wages, i.e. a reduction in the level of employment and in the welfare of the unemployed. Conversely, the welfare of the employed workers and the level of employment cannot be simultaneously increased without a deterioration in the welfare of shareholders.

Formally:

Theorem 2

Let p^* denote the Walrasian equilibrium price, and $k(p)$ the curve which defines the Keynesian–Classical boundary (*i.e.* $K \cap C = \{(p,w) \mid p > p^*, w = k(p)\}$). Then there exists a curve $w = G(p)$ such that:

(a) $w^* = G(p^*) = k(p^*)$.
(b) $\forall p > p^*, G(p) < k(p)$.
(c) *If* $p > p^*$ and: $G(p) < w < k(p)$, then (P,w) is locally undominated.
(d) *If* $p > p^*$ and: $0 < w < G(p)$, then (p,w) is dominated.

Proof: See Appendix.

5 CLASSICAL UNEMPLOYMENT

5.1 Locally Undominated (p,w) Pairs

The Classical region also turns out to be partitioned into two subregions:

one of locally undominated (p,w) pairs, adjoining the Keynesian–Classical boundary, and, away from it, a subregion of dominated (p,w) pairs. For (p,w) in the undominated subregion, any change in prices and wages improving employment and the welfare of shareholders and employed workers will necessarily reduce the welfare of the unemployed. The regions are depicted as the (light and dark) shaded areas in Figures 14.2 and 14.3; the different shapes of the locally undominated region correspond to different values of the parameters.

Theorem 3

There exists a continuous function $\hat{w}:[b^*,\infty)\rightarrow R_+$ satisfying: $\hat{w}(b)<\tilde{w}(b)$ whenever $b>b^*$, such that: (i) $w\,\varepsilon\,(\hat{w}(w/p),\ \tilde{w}(w/p)]\Rightarrow(p,w)$ is locally undominated; (ii) $w\,\varepsilon\,(0,\hat{w}(w/p))\Rightarrow(p,w)$ is dominated.

Proof: See Appendix.

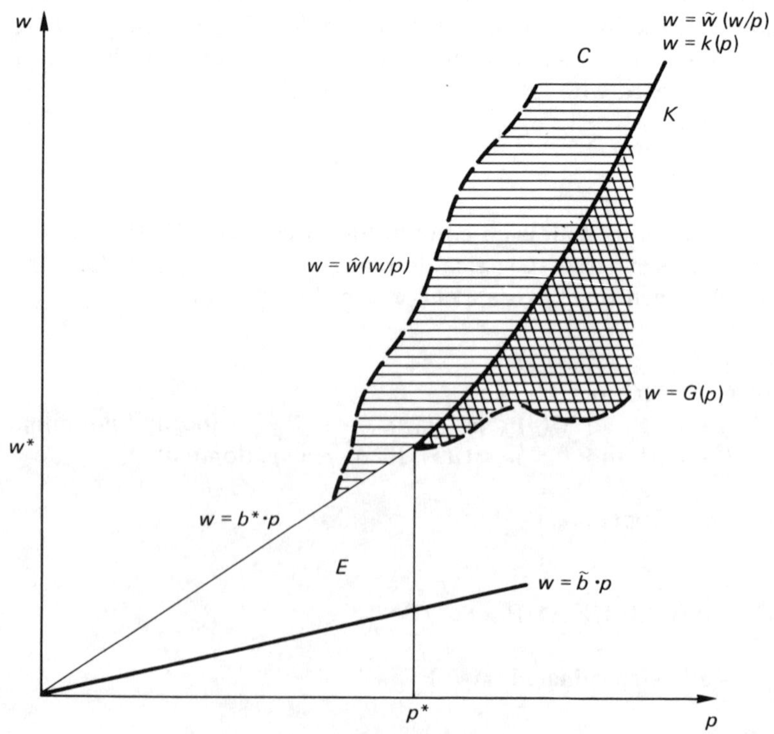

Figure 14.2

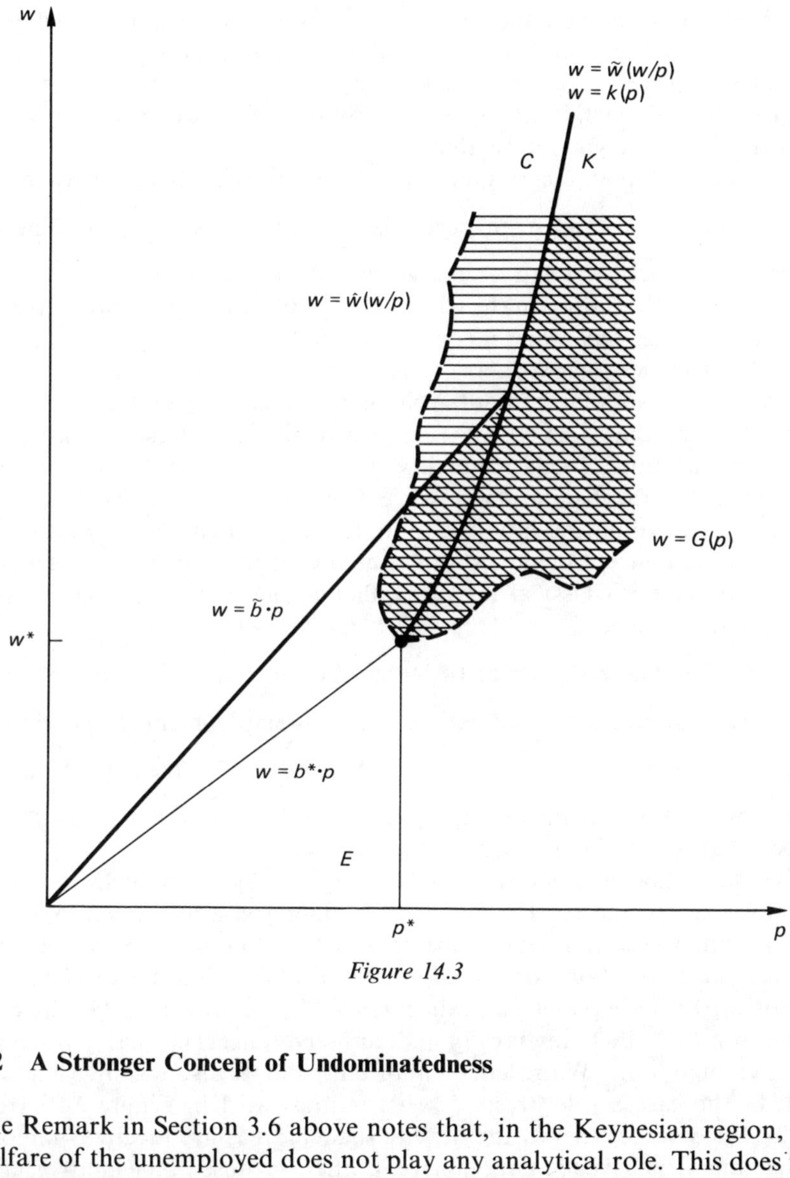

Figure 14.3

5.2 A Stronger Concept of Undominatedness

The Remark in Section 3.6 above notes that, in the Keynesian region, the welfare of the unemployed does not play any analytical role. This does not hold in the Classical region. For some locally undominated (p,w) pairs in the Classical region one can find directions of change of prices and wages which improve everything but the welfare of the unemployed.

This section characterizes among the locally undominated (p,w) pairs in C those for which no movement improving simultaneously the level of employment, the welfare of the employed workers and that of shareholders (disregarding the welfare of the unemployed) can be found. This is clearly a stronger criterion than the previous one. Price–wage pairs satisfying it will be called S-undominated. Formally, the definition of a locally S-undominated price–wage pair (p,w) is obtained by deleting the inequality '$U_N^C(p',w') \geqslant U_N^C(p,w)$' in the previous definition. The two criteria obviously coincide in the Keynesian region.

It turns out that the results depend on the relationship between the parameters k_L, k_0, and α, in particular on whether $k_L/k_0 \gtreqless 1/\alpha$. The first term is the workers' relative endowment of the non-produced good. It is easy to check that, since in the Classical region prices equal marginal costs, the ratio of the real wage income to output is $1/\alpha$. If $k_L/k_0 < 1/\alpha$ (resp. $k_L/k_0 > 1/\alpha$), then the workers' relative endowment in the non-produced good is less (resp. more) than the share of the real wage bill in output: we shall then say that workers are – comparatively – *poor* (resp. *wealthy*).

An implication of this inequality will be useful to interpret our next results. Define the 'balanced real-wage' $\tilde{b}$ by the equation: $\tilde{b} = (\mu/k_0)y_C(1,\tilde{b})$, which has the following interpretation. If $w/p = \tilde{b}$, then: $w/\mu = py_C(p,w)/k_0$, i.e. the ratio (current income)/(money endowment) of an employed worker coincides, in the Classical region, with the one of the economy. Direct computation yields: $\tilde{b} = \alpha^{-(1/\alpha)}(\mu/k_0)^{(\alpha-1)/\alpha}$.

Remember (see e.g., Figure 14.1) that the Walrasian real-wage $b^* := \dfrac{w^*}{p^*}$ is the highest real-wage compatible with full employment. Depending on the values of the data, $\tilde{b} \lesseqgtr b^*$. If $\tilde{b} \leqslant b^*$ (resp. $\tilde{b} > b^*$) then the 'balanced' real wage is (resp. is not) compatible with full employment. It is easy to check that: $\text{sgn}(\tilde{b} - b^*) = \text{sgn}((k_L/k_0) - (1/\alpha))$.

We show that a (p,w) in the Keynesian–Classical boundary is always locally S-undominated. Except for this boundary, a locally undominated (p,w) in the Classical region is also locally S-undominated only if $w/p \leqslant \tilde{b}$. Hence, no locally S-undominated (p,w) exists in the interior of C if $\tilde{b} \leqslant b^*$ (i.e. if workers are poor), since then $w/p > b^* \geqslant \tilde{b}$, $\forall (p,w) \varepsilon C$. On the other hand, if $\tilde{b} > b^*$, then any locally undominated (p,w) such that $w/p < \tilde{b}$ (i.e. close enough to the Walrasian equilibrium point) is also locally S-undominated. The case $\tilde{b} < b^*$ (resp. $\tilde{b} > b^*$) is illustrated in Figure 14.2 (resp. 14.3): price–wage pairs in the heavily shaded areas are locally S-undominated (and hence locally undominated), whereas those in the lightly shaded areas are locally undominated but not locally S-undominated. Formally:

Theorem 4

Let $(p,w) \varepsilon C$ be locally undominated.

(i) $w/p < \tilde{b} \Rightarrow (p,w)$ is locally S-undominated

(ii) $(w/p > \tilde{b}, w < \tilde{w}(w/p)) \Rightarrow (p,w)$ is not locally S-undominated.
(iii) $w = \tilde{w}(w/p) \Rightarrow (p,w)$ is locally S-undominated.

Proof: See Appendix.

APPENDIX: PROOFS

Proof of Theorem 1

Necessity Note that the utility of an employed worker is always higher than that of an unemployed one. Thus, a (p',w') satisfying (i) and (ii) in the statement of the theorem with at least one strict inequality makes nobody worse off and at least one agent better off.

Sufficiency Consider a (p,w) satisfying the condition in Theorem 1. Assume as contradiction hypothesis that (p,w) is not locally undominated. This implies, that, given any $\epsilon \varepsilon (0,\bar{\epsilon})$, there exists a $(p(\epsilon),w(\epsilon))$, such for all $a \varepsilon S \bigcup L$, $U_a(p(\epsilon),w(\epsilon)) \geqq U_a(p,w)$, with strict inequality for some $\bar{a}$. The weak inequalities and the fact that worker 0 (resp. l_0) is employed (resp. unemployed) both at $(p(\epsilon),w(\epsilon))$ and at (p,w) imply that $U_A(p(\epsilon),\ w(\epsilon)) \geqq U_A(p,w)$, $A = S,E,N$. Agent $\bar{a}$ cannot be a worker who is unemployed at (p,w) and employed at $(p(\epsilon),w(\epsilon))$, because then $\hat{l}(p(\epsilon),w(\epsilon)) > \hat{l}(p,w)$, which together with the weak inequalities would contradict the hypothesis that (p,w) satisfies the condition in Theorem 1. If $\bar{a}$ is employed at (p,w) and unemployed at $(p(\epsilon),w(\epsilon))$, then $\hat{l}(p(\epsilon),w(\epsilon)) < \hat{l}(p,w)$. The same inequality obtains if $\bar{a}$ is a shareholder or a worker employed (resp. unemployed) both at $(p(\epsilon),w(\epsilon))$ and at (p,w), since otherwise the hypothesis that (p,w) satisfies the condition in Theorem 1 would be violated. Hence, in any case $\hat{l}(p(\epsilon),w(\epsilon)) < \hat{l}(p,w)$, which together with the fact that nobody is worse off at $(p(\epsilon),w(\epsilon))$ than at (p,w) implies that $U_N(p(\epsilon),w(\epsilon)) \geqq U_E(p,w)$. Let the sequence (ϵ_n) tend to zero. Taking limits we obtain $U_N(p,w) \geqq U_E(p,w)$, a contradiction, since $U_N(p,w) < U_E(p,w)$ whenever $w > 0$. ■

Write U_i, $i = 1,2$, for the partial derivatives of U. Using the fact that $h(p)$ maximizes $U(x,1 - px)$ and 1-homogeneity, one obtains:

Lemma 1

Let $0 \leqslant x \leqslant h(p)$. Then: $U_1(x,1 - px) - pU_2(x,1 - px) \geqslant 0$ and $U_2(x,1 - px) - U(x,1 - px) \leqslant 0$, with equalities *iff* $x = h(p)$, i.e. *iff* $(p,w)\varepsilon K$. ■

Proof of Theorem 2

Define: $G(p){:}= \dfrac{k_L h.(1-(l_K/l_0))}{\bar{l}'\cdot y'_K} + \dfrac{p}{\bar{l}'}$. Since $y'_K < 0$, $G(p) \leqslant p/\bar{l}' = k(p)$ for $y = y_K(p)$, with strict inequality *iff* $l_K < l_0$, i.e. *iff* $p > p^*$. This proves (a) and (b). Using Lemma 1, partial differentiation of (1) in Section 3.2 yields: $\delta U_S^K/\delta p = \tilde{U}\cdot(h\cdot(k_L + wl_K) + (p - w\bar{l}')y'_K)$, $\delta U_S^K/\delta w = -\tilde{U}l_K < 0$, $\delta U_E^K/\delta p = -\tilde{U}h\cdot(\mu + w) < 0$, and $\delta U_E^K/\delta w = \tilde{U} > 0$. One can compute: sgn $((dw/dp)|U_S^K$ cons $-(dw/dp)|U_E^K$ cons$)$ = sgn $(hk_L(1-(l_K/l_0)) + py'_K - w\bar{l}'y'_K)$ = sgn $(w - G(p))$. Hence, if $w < G(p)$, then lowering both prices and wages to $(p - \epsilon_1, w - \epsilon_2)$, where $(\epsilon_1,\epsilon_2) \gg 0$ satisfies: $(dw/dp)|U_S^K$cons $< \varepsilon_2/\varepsilon_1 < (dw/dp)|U_E^K$ cons, will improve the level of employment and the utility of shareholders, the employed and the unemployed. This proves (d). If, on the other hand, $w > G(p)$ then $(dw/dp)|U_S^K$ cons $> (dw/dp)|U_E^K$ cons > 0, and any increase in the utility of both shareholders and the employed would entail higher prices and lower employment. This proves (c). ■

Everything which follows refers to positive price–wage pairs in the Classical region. The proofs of Theorems 3 and 4 will use Lemmas 2–9 below.

For $(p,w)\varepsilon C$, write: $Y_C(p,w){:}= k_0 + py_C(p,w)$, $\bar{U}(p,w){:}= U(y_C(p,w),k_0)$, $\bar{\bar{U}}_i(p,w){:}= U_i(y_C(p,w),k_0)$, $i = 1,2$, and $g(p,w){:}= \bar{\bar{U}}_1 Y_C - p\bar{U}$.

Lemma 2

(*L.2.1*). $g(p,w) \geqslant 0$, with equality *iff* $(p,w)\varepsilon K \cap C$.

(*L.2.2*). Given (p,w), define $\xi(\lambda){:}= g(\lambda.(p,w))/\bar{U}(\lambda.(p,w))$.

Then $\xi' < 0$ and $\lim\limits_{\lambda\to 0}\xi(\lambda) > 0$.

Proof: L.2.1 follows from Lemma 1, since $g = \bar{\bar{U}}_1 py_C + \bar{\bar{U}}_1 k_0 - p\bar{\bar{U}}_1 y_C - p\bar{\bar{U}}_2 k_0 = k_0(\bar{\bar{U}}_1 - p\bar{\bar{U}}_2)$. To prove L.2.2, note that, by 0-homogeneity, $y_C(\lambda.(p,w))$ is constant relative to λ, and hence so are $\bar{U}$ and $\bar{\bar{U}}$. Thus,

$\xi' = (\bar{\bar{U}}_1 y_C - \bar{U})p/\bar{U} = -\bar{\bar{U}}_2 k_0 p/\bar{U} < 0$, and $\lim\limits_{\lambda\to 0}\xi(\lambda)$- $= \bar{\bar{U}}_1 k_0/\bar{U} > 0$. ■

Recall that $y_C(p,w){:}= (p/\alpha w)^{1/(\alpha-1)}$. This yields: $\delta y_C/\delta w = (-p/w)(\delta y_C/\delta p)$ and $(\delta y_C/\delta p)(p/y_C) = 1/(\alpha - 1)$. Lemma 3 below follows from partial differentiation of (2) in 3.4 using these expressions and L.2.1. Write: $q_S{:}= (py_C - wl_C + k_S)/Y_C$, $F_1(p,w){:}= (g/\bar{U}) - p(\alpha - 1)$, and $F_2(p,w){:}= wY_C(\alpha - 1)/((\mu + w)y_C) - (g/\bar{U})$.

Lemma 3

L.3.1. $\dfrac{\delta U_S^C}{\delta p} = \dfrac{1}{Y_C}\left(q_S\dfrac{y_C}{p(\alpha-1)}g + \bar{U}(1-q_S)y_C\right) > 0;$

$$\frac{\delta U_S^C}{\delta w} = \frac{1}{Y_C}\left(-q_S\frac{y_C}{w(\alpha-1)}g - \bar{U}l_C\right) < 0.$$

L.3.2. $\dfrac{\delta U_E^C}{\delta p} = \dfrac{(\mu+w)}{(Y_C)^2}\dfrac{y_C\bar{U}}{p(\alpha-1)}F_1(p,w);\ \dfrac{\delta U_E^C}{\delta w} = \dfrac{(\mu+w)}{(Y_C)^2}\dfrac{y_C\bar{U}}{w(\alpha-1)}F_2(p,w).$

L.3.3. $\dfrac{\delta U_N^C}{\delta p} = \dfrac{\mu}{(Y_C)^2}\dfrac{y_C\bar{U}}{p(\alpha-1)}F_1(p,w);\ \dfrac{\delta U_N^C}{\delta w} = -\dfrac{\mu}{(Y_C)^2}\dfrac{y_C}{w(\alpha-1)}g \leqslant 0.$ ■

See Section 5.2 for the definition and properties of the real wage $\tilde{b}$.

Lemma 4

L.4.1. $\text{sgn}((w/p) - \tilde{b}) = \text{sgn}((w/\mu) - (py_C/k_0))$
$= \text{sgn}((w/p)Y_C/(\mu + w) - y_C).$

L.4.2. $\text{sgn}(F_1(p,w) + F_2(p,w)) = \text{sgn}((w/p) - \tilde{b}).$

L.4.3. If $F_2 > 0$, then: $\text{sgn}((dw/dp)\,|\,U_E^C\text{cons} - w/p) = \text{sgn}(\tilde{b} - (w/p)).$

Proof: The first equality of L.4.1 follows from the fact that, $V(b) := b - (\mu/k_0)y_C(1,b)$ is increasing and, by the definition of $\tilde{b}, V(\tilde{b}) = 0$. For the second one, we compute: $\text{sgn}((w/p)(py_C + k_0)/(\mu + w) - y_C) = \text{sgn}(wpy_C + wk_0 - \mu py_C - wpy_C) = \text{sgn}((w/\mu) - (py_C/k_0))$. L.4.2 follows immediately from L.4.1. By L.3.2, $(dw/dp)\,|\,U_E^C\text{cons} - w/p = -(w/p)((F_1/F_2) + 1)$, and L.4.3 follows from L.4.2. ■

Define: $F_3(p,w) := (g/\bar{U})((py_C/w) - (k_0/\mu) + (l_0 - l_C)) - p(\alpha - 1)(l_0 - l_C).$

Lemma 5

L.5.1. $F_3 = (l_0 - l_C)F_1 + (g/\bar{U})((py_C/w) - (k_0/\mu)).$

L.5.2. $F_3 = \dfrac{(\mu+w)Y_C}{\mu\bar{U}}\left(F_1\dfrac{\delta U_S^C}{\delta w} - \dfrac{p}{w}\dfrac{\delta U_S^C}{\delta p}F_2\right).$

L.5.3. If $F_2 > 0$, then $\text{sgn}((dw/dp)\,|\,U_E^C\text{cons} - (dw/dp)\,|\,U_S^C\text{cons}) = \text{sgn}\ F_3(p,w).$

Proof: L.5.1 is immediate. L.5.3 is an immediate consequence of L.5.2 and L.3.1–2. To prove L.5.2, compute:

$$F_1\frac{\delta U_S^C}{\delta w}-\frac{p}{w}\frac{\delta U_S^C}{\delta p}F_2=$$

$$=\frac{1}{Y_C}\left(\frac{g}{\bar U}-p(\alpha-1)\right)\left(-q_S\frac{y_C}{w(\alpha-1)}g-\bar U l_C\right)$$

$$-\frac{1}{Y_C}\left(\frac{q_S y_C}{w(\alpha-1)}g+\bar U(1-q_S)\frac{py_C}{w}\right)\left(w\frac{Y_C(\alpha-1)}{(\mu+w)y_C}-\frac{g}{\bar U}\right)$$

$$=\frac{1}{Y_C}\left(-gl_C-g\frac{q_S Y_C}{\mu+w}+\frac{py_C g}{w}+p(\alpha-1)\left(\bar U l_C-\bar U(1-q_S)\frac{Y_C}{(\mu+w)}\right)\right)$$

$$=\frac{\mu\bar U}{Y_C(\mu+w)}\left(\frac{g}{\bar U}\left(\frac{-l_C(\mu+w)-q_S Y_C}{\mu}+\frac{py_C(\mu+w)}{\mu w}\right)\right.$$

$$\left.+p(\alpha-1)\left(\frac{l_C(\mu+w)}{\mu}-(1-q_S)\frac{Y_C}{\mu}\right)\right)$$

$$=\frac{\mu\bar U}{Y_C(\mu+w)}\left(\frac{g}{\bar U}\left(\frac{-l_C\mu-l_C w-Y_C+\mu l_0+wl_C}{\mu}+\frac{py_C(\mu+w)}{\mu w}\right)\right.$$

$$\left.+p(\alpha-1)\left(\frac{l_C\mu+wl_C-\mu l_0-wl_C}{\mu}\right)\right)$$

$$=\frac{\mu\bar U}{Y_C(\mu+w)}\left(\frac{g}{\bar U}\left((l_0-l_C)+\frac{-py_C w-wk_0+py_C\mu+py_C w}{\mu w}\right)\right.$$

$$\left.-p(\alpha-1)(l_0-l_C)\right)$$

$$=\frac{\mu\bar U}{Y_C(\mu+w)}F_3.$$

■

Lemma 6

Let $(p,w) \varepsilon C$.

L.6.1. The function $\varphi_1(\lambda) := F_1(\lambda.(p,w))$ is decreasing;

L.6.2. The function $\varphi_2(\lambda) := F_2(\lambda.(p,w))$ is increasing;

L.6.3. If $\tilde{b} > b^*$ and $w/p \varepsilon [b^*, \tilde{b}]$, the function $\varphi_3(\lambda) := F_3(\lambda.(p,w))$ is decreasing.

Proof: L.6.1–2 follow from L.2.2, recalling that y_C is 0-homogeneous. L.6.3 follows from L.2.2 and the facts that $(l_0 - l_C)$ is 0-homogeneous, non-negative, and strictly positive whenever $w/p > b^*$, and that $(py_C/w) - (k_0/\mu)$ is 0-homogeneous, non-negative, and strictly positive whenever $w/p < \tilde{b}$ (by L.4.1). ■

Lemma 7

Given $b \geqslant b^*$, for $i \varepsilon \{1,2\}$ the equation in w "$F_i(w/b,w) = 0$" has a unique solution $w_i(b) > 0$ satisfying: (i) $w_i(b) < \tilde{w}(b)$, $i = 1,2$; (ii) sgn $F_1(w/b,w) = \text{sgn}(w_1(b) - w)$; (iii) sgn $F_2(w/b,w) = \text{sgn}\ (w - w_2(b))$.

Proof: Consider the equation "$F_1(w/b,w) = 0$" first. By L.2.1, $g(\tilde{w}(b)/b, \tilde{w}(b)) = 0$, i.e., $F_1(\tilde{w}(b)/b, \tilde{w}(b)) < 0$. From L.2.2, $\lim_{w \to 0} F_1(w/b,w) > 0$. Thus, there exists a $\bar{\bar{w}}\ \varepsilon\ (0, \tilde{w}(b))$ with $F_1(\bar{\bar{w}}/b, \bar{\bar{w}}) = 0$. Uniqueness and (ii) follow from L.6.1. The case "$F_2(w/b,w) = 0$" is similarly argued using L.6.2.

Lemma 8

Assume that $\tilde{b} > b^*$ and let $b \varepsilon [b^*, \tilde{b}]$. Then the equation in w "$F_3(w/b,w) = 0$" has a unique solution $w_3(b)$ satisfying: (i) sgn $(w_3(b) - \tilde{w}(b)) = \text{sgn}\ (b^* - b)$; (ii) sgn $F_3(w/b,w) = \text{sgn}\ (w_3(b) - w)$.

Proof: From L.5.1, $F_3 = (l_0 - l_C)F_1 + (g/\bar{U})((py_C/w) - k_0/\mu))$. If $(p,w) = (\tilde{w}(b^*)/b^*, \tilde{w}(b^*))$ (i.e., $(p,w) = (p^*,w^*)$), then $l_0 - l_C = 0 = g/\bar{U}$, and the assertion follows from L.6.3. If $b \varepsilon (b^*, \tilde{b}]$, then $F_3(\tilde{w}(b)/b, \tilde{w}(b)) < 0$ (since $l_0 - l_C > 0$, $F_1 < 0$, and $g/\bar{U} = 0$) and $\lim_{w \to 0} F_3(w/b,w) > 0$ (since $\lim_{w \to 0} F_1 > 0$, $\lim_{w \to 0}(g/\bar{U}) > 0$ and $l_0 - l_C$ (resp. $(py_C/w) - (k_0/\mu)$) is 0-homogeneous and positive (resp. non-negative by L.4.1). The proof is concluded as in Lemma 7. ■

Figure 14.4 illustrates some properties of F_i and $w_i(w/p)(i = 1,2,3)$ that can be derived from Lemmas 4–8.

Lemma 9

Let $(p,w)\varepsilon C$ satisfy: $F_3(p,w) < 0$ and $w/p\varepsilon(b^*,\tilde{b})$. Then there exists a neighbourhood N of (p,w) such that: $\{(p',w')\varepsilon N \bigcap C \mid U_A^C(p',w') \geqslant U_A^C(p,w)$ for $A = S,E\} \bigcap \{(p',w')\varepsilon N \bigcap C \mid w'/p' \leqslant w/p\} = \{(p,w)\}$.

Proof: Immediate consequence of the facts that $F_1 < 0$ (by L.4.1 and L.5.1), and hence $F_2 > 0$ (by L.5.2 and L.3.1), and that $w/p < (dw/dp) \mid U_E^C\text{cons} < (dw/dp) \mid U_S^C\text{cons}$ (by L.4.3 and L.5.3). ■

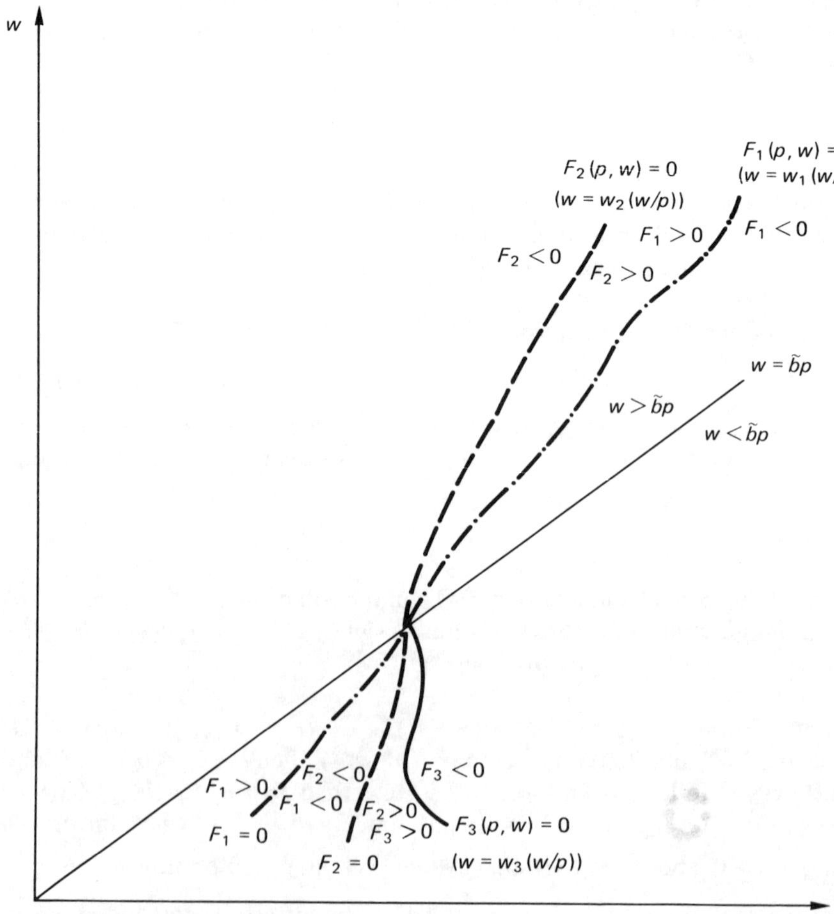

Figure 14.4

Define $\hat{w}$: $[b^*,\infty)\to R$: $\hat{w}(b)=w_1(b)$ if $b\geqslant\tilde{b}$, $\hat{w}(b)=w_3(b)$ if $b<\tilde{b}$. It is easy to check that, by L.4.1, L.5.1, and Lemmas 7–8, $\hat{w}$ is well defined and continuous and satisfies: $\hat{w}(b)\leqslant\tilde{w}(b)$ with equality *iff* $b=b^*<\tilde{b}$.

Proof of Theorem 3

(i) Let $w<\tilde{w}(w/p)$. If $(w/p)<\tilde{b}$, the assertion follows from Lemma 9. If $w/p\geqslant\tilde{b}$, then $w>\hat{w}(w/p)$ implies that $F_1<0$ (by Lemma 7 (ii)), which in turn implies that $F_2>0$ (by L.4.2) and that $F_3<0$ (by L.4.1 and L.5.1). It follows, using L.5.3 and L.3.1, that any local change improving the utilities of workers and shareholders entails higher prices and wages, thus reducing (by L.3.3) the welfare of the unemployed. If $w=\tilde{w}(w/p)$ the assertion is proved by the above argument combined with the one in the proof of Theorem 2 (c).

(ii) If $F_1>0$ (resp. $F_2<0$), then increasing p (resp. reducing w) will increase the welfare of all (see Lemma 3). But $F_1>0$ whenever $w<\hat{w}(w/p)$ and $w/p\geqslant\tilde{b}$. So we are left with the case where $w/p<\tilde{b}$ and $F_2\geqslant 0$. Since now $w<\hat{w}(w/p)=w_3(w/p), F_3>0$ (by Lemma 8) which in turn implies that $F_1<0$ (by L.5.2). If $F_2=0$, write $(dw/dp)\mid U_E^C\text{cons}=+\infty$. If $F_2>0$, then by L.4.3 and L.5.3, and since $F_3>0$, $(dw,dp)\mid U_E^C\text{cons}>$ $\max\{w/p, (dw/dp)\mid U_S^C\text{cons}\}$. Therefore choosing $(\epsilon_1,\epsilon_2)\gg 0$ such that $(dw/dp)\mid U_E^C\text{cons}>\epsilon_2/\epsilon_1>\max\{w/p, (dw/dp)\mid U_S^C\text{cons}\}$ and lowering (p,w) to $(p-\epsilon_1,w-\epsilon_2)$ would increase employment and the utilities of all agents. ■

Proof of Theorem 4

(i) Since (p,w) is locally undominated, by Theorem 3 (ii) $w\geqq\hat{w}(w/p)$, and, since $w/p<\tilde{b}$, by the definition of $\hat{w},\hat{w}(w/p)=w_3(w/p)$; hence, $w\geqslant w_3(w/p)$, i.e. $F_3(p,w)\leqslant 0$. If $F_3<0$ and $w<\tilde{w}(w/p)$, the assertion follows from Lemma 9. If $F_3<0$ and $w=\tilde{w}(w/p)$, the assertion follows from the same argument combined with the one in the proof of Theorem 2 (c). So let $F_3(p,w)=0$. Then, $F_1(p,w)<0$ (by L.5.1 and L.4.1) and hence $F_2(p,w)>0$ (by L.5.2), and $w/p<(dw/dp)\mid U_E^C\text{cons}=(dw/dp)\mid U_S^C\text{cons}$ (by L.4.3 and L.5.3). Moreover, $F_1(p',w')<0<F_2(p',w')$ for (p',w') in a neighborhood N of (p,w). Hence, if $(p'',w'')\varepsilon N$ satisfies: $U_A^C(p'',w'')\geqslant U_A^C(p,w)$, $A=S,E$, $w''/p''\leqslant w/p$ and $(p'',w'')\neq(p,w)$, then $p''<p$, i.e. $U_N^C(p'',w'')>U_N^C(p,w)$. Therefore, if (p,w) is not locally S-undominated, then (p,w) is not locally undominated, contrary to hypothesis.

(ii) By Theorem 3(ii), since (p,w) is locally undominated, $w\geqslant\hat{w}(w/p)$ $=w_1(w/p)$, i.e. $F_1(p,w)\leqslant 0$, which in turn implies that $F_2>0$ (by L.4.2) and

$F_3 < 0$ (by L.4.1 and L.5.1). By L.4.3 and L.5.3, $(dw/dp) \mid U_E^C\text{cons} < \min\ \{w/p,(dw/dp) \mid U_S^C\text{cons}\}$. Therefore choosing $(\epsilon_1,\epsilon_2) \gg 0$ such that: $(dw/dp) \mid U_E^C\text{cons} < \epsilon_2/\epsilon_1 < \min\{w/p,(dw/dp) \mid U_S^C\text{cons}\}$ and changing (p,w) to $(p+\epsilon_1, w+\epsilon_2)$ will improve employment and the utility of shareholders and the employed.

(iii) The case $w/p < \tilde{b}$ is covered in (i) above. If $w/p \geqslant \tilde{b}$, the argument in (ii) above shows (using Lemma 7) that $(dw/dp) \mid U_E^C\text{cons} \leqslant w/p$ and $(dw/dp) \mid U_E^C\text{cons} < (dw/dp) \mid U_S^C\text{cons}$. Hence, for a neighborhood N of (p,w), $\{(p',w') \varepsilon N \cap C \mid U_A^C(p',w') \geqslant U_A^C(p,w), A = S,E\} \cap \{(p',w') \varepsilon N \cap C \mid w'/p' \leqslant w/p\} = \{(p,w)\}$. This together with the argument in the proof of Theorem 2(c) shows that (p,w) is S-undominated. ■

Notes

1. See Laroque (1978, prop. 7.1).
2. See, Benassy (1973, 1975, 1976, 1982), Drèze (1975), Younès (1975). It is shown in Silvestre (1983) that these approaches are equivalent for the economy considered here.
3. See Hart (1982, p.134) for interpreting the non-produced good. In a temporary equilibrium framework, one may view k as 'money', i.e. a proxy for future consumption. But, as long as it enters the utility function in the units in which its initial endowments are measured, this interpretation requires that expectations (of future prices, wealth, etc) be given at the start of the period. See Hildenbrand and Hildenbrand (1978).
4. An alternative interpretation is that there are many firms (such that $\bar{T}(y)$ describes the efficient boundary of the aggregate production set) which are identical in technology and in quantity constraints. See Malinvaud (1977) and Silvestre (1986).
5. See Silvestre (1983, 1986) for deriving this equation from the solution concepts of Benassy (1973, 1975), Drèze (1975) and Younès (1975).

References

Barro, R. J. and H. I. Grossman (1976) *Money, Employment and Inflation* (Cambridge: Cambridge University Press).

Benassy, J. P. (1973) 'Disequilibrium Theory', unpublished Ph.D. Dissertation, University of California, Berkeley.

Benassy, J. P. (1975) 'Neo-Keynesian Disequilibrium Theory in a Monetary Economy', *Review of Economic Studies,* 42(4): 503–23.

Benassy, J. P. (1976) 'The Disequilibrium Approach to Monopolistic Price Setting and General Monopolistic Equilibrium', *Review of Economic Studies,* 43(1): 69–81.

Benassy, J. P. (1977) 'A Neokeynesian Model of Price and Quantity Determination in Disequilibrium', in G. S. Schwödiauer (ed.) *Equilibrium and Disequilibrium in Economic Theory* (Boston: Reidel).

Benassy, J. P. (1982) *The Economics of Market Disequilibrium* (New York: Academic Press).

Drèze, J. (1975) 'Existence of an Exchange Equilibrium Under Price Rigidities', *International Economic Review*, 16.

Hall, R. (1986) 'The Relation Between Price and Marginal Cost in US Industry', NBER Working Paper 1785.

Hart, O. (1982) 'A Model of Imperfect Competition with Keynesian Features', *Quarterly Journal of Economics*, February, 109–38.

Hildebrand, K. and W. Hildenbrand (1978) 'On Keynesian Equilibria with Unemployment and Quantity Rationing', *Journal of Economic Theory*, 18 (2).

Keynes, J. M. (1936) *The General Theory of Employment Interest and Money* (London: Macmillan).

Laroque, G. (1978) 'The Fixed Price Equilibria: Some Results in Local Comparative Statics', *Econometrica*, 46.

Malinvaud, E. (1977) *The Theory of Unemployment Reconsidered*, Yrjö Jahnsson Lectures (Oxford: Blackwell).

Robinson, J. (1933) *The Economics of Imperfect Competition* (London: Macmillan).

Robinson, J. (1937) *Essays in the Theory of Employment* (London: Macmillan).

Silvestre, J. (1982) 'Negotiable Prices and Wages in a Disequilibrium Model', Working Paper 82–37, University of California, San Diego.

Silvestre, J. (1983) 'Fixprice Analysis in Productive Economies', *Journal of Economic Theory*, 30(2): 401–9.

Silvestre, J. (1985) 'Voluntary and Efficient Allocations are Walrasian', *Econometrica*, 53(4): 807–16.

Silvestre, J. (1986) 'The Elements of Fixprice Microeconomics', in L. Samuelson (ed) *Microeconomic Theory* (Cambridge, Mass.: Klüwer-Nijhoff).

Silvestre, J. (1988) 'Undominated prices in the Three Good Model', *European Economic Review*, 32: 161–78.

Younès, Y. (1975) 'On the Role of Money in the Process of Exchange and the Existence of a Non-Walrasian Equilibrium', *Review of Economic Studies*, 42.

Part V

Imperfect Competition: Capital and Credit Markets

15 Monopolistic Competition and the Capital Market

Joseph E. Stiglitz*

1 INTRODUCTION

This essay is related to two topics on which Joan Robinson[1] made important contributions. The first is the theory of imperfect competition. At the time it was written, *The Economics of Imperfect Competition* was heralded (along with Chamberlin's contemporaneous book *The Theory of Monopolistic Competition*[2]) as doing for microeconomics what Keynes had done for macroeconomics. But the revolution to which it was supposed to give rise never occurred, and it was almost forty years before the themes she developed there again became the focus of theoretical research.[3]

The second theme was her development of a general equilibrium portfolio theory in her theory of interest (Robinson, 1952), a clear predecessor of the later work of Tobin.[4]

This chapter examines imperfect competition in the capital market, using a simple general equilibrium portfolio model. It shows that the market economy is not, in general, Pareto-efficient.

It is often suggested that the market for shares in firms is one of the more competitive markets. There are a large number of buyers and sellers, and for most widely held firms – most of the largest firms in the United States – no single individual owns more than a few per cent of the shares. Moreover, shares in one firm are closely competitive with shares in other firms.

On the other hand, it is often alleged that if a firm were to increase its issue of shares, it would face a downward-sloping demand schedule for its shares.

If the former view were correct, then a security which was uncorrelated with the business cycle[5] should be treated as essentially a safe security, and a firm, in evaluating a project, should ignore the variance of the project, but be concerned only with its correlation with the business cycle. There is a widespread view that this is in fact not the case.

These contrasting views would be resolved if the capital market were

* This is a revised version of a paper by the same title, IMSSS Technical Report no. 161, in turn, part of a paper originally presented at the Far Eastern Meetings of the Econometric Society, Tokyo. Financial support from the National Science Foundation, the Ford Foundation, and the Guggenheim Foundation is gratefully acknowledged. I am indebted to A. Dixit and M. Spence for extremely helpful discussions.

monopolistically competitive rather than perfectly competitive: different securities are close but not perfect substitutes for one another.

If different risky securities are not perfectly correlated, then they are imperfect substitutes for one another (in the absence of a full set of Arrow–Debreu securities). If there are many such securities, they will be *close* substitutes for one another, i.e. there are gains from dividing one's assets among $n+1$ risky securities rather than n risky securities, but the marginal gain from the additional diversification allowed by the $n+1^{st}$ security may be relatively small. A risk averse individual will want to hold some of all the available securities, no matter how large the number of firms. As a result, all risky firms will perceive themselves as facing a negatively sloped demand schedule for their securities.

Consider, for instance, the situation where all risky firms are identical but not perfectly correlated; in equilibrium an individual will hold exactly the same amount of all the risky securities. If one of the firms were to contemplate raising its level of investment, it could only induce individuals to hold more of its securities by lowering the price of a unit of its securities. (The amount by which it will be lowered will not necessarily decrease as the number of firms increase; see Stiglitz, 1972a.) Alternatively, assume the firm contemplated raising the price of its shares. This would result in a slight change in the demand for them; in contrast a slight change in the price of one of two commodities that were perfect substitutes (one of two securities that were perfectly correlated) would result in the demand shifting entirely to one or the other of the commodities (securities).

One must then ask, why do individuals hold sufficiently few securities in their portfolios that are not, effectively, perfect substitutes. Several reasons can be put forward: (a) Transaction costs prevent individuals from holding more than a few securities in their portfolios. This is an unconvincing explanation, since with mutual funds, these transaction costs can be made negligible. (b) Information costs make it desirable for individuals to concentrate their portfolios. A quite forceful argument can be made on these grounds – one that is pursued elsewhere.[6] (c) There is only a finite number of firms and the number of states of nature is infinite. The income patterns of any two arbitrarily chosen firms differ in at least some states of nature. Obviously, if there were no costs associated with setting up new firms (creating new assets), then, so long as there is a return from further diversification of risk, additional firms would be created. To explain a limitation on the number of firms there must be some non-convexity in the production process, e.g. some fixed cost associated with setting up a new firm.

It is this view which we wish to pursue in this chapter. In particular, we wish to investigate whether there will be too few or too many risky firms, whether the risky firms will be too small or too large, whether there will be 'errors' in the choice of technique, etc. Interest in these questions is motivated by three considerations:

In our earlier work analyzing the optimality of the stock market (Stiglitz, 1972a), in the context of a mean–variance model, we established that if firms maximized their stock market value, taking the rate of interest and the risk discount factor as given, the equilibrium would not be Pareto-optimal. This result has been the subject of some discussion. One objection raised to our analysis was that under our assumptions there would be a strong motivation for entry. With sufficient entry, as we argued above, different securities with the same correlation with the business cycle will become essentially perfect substitutes. But fixed costs associated with creating firms act as a deterrent to entry. It is therefore important to determine exactly the nature of the equilibrium when the number of firms is endogenous. In particular, there remains the question of how to interpret our earlier result. One interpretation we offered at the time was that in the absence of a complete set of securities, the market ought to be viewed as monopolistically competitive. This chapter investigates in detail that interpretation.[7,8]

Even if firms fail to recognize the effect of their scale of operation on their value (per unit scale) there remains the question of which firms should operate. Earlier analyses with a fixed number of firms, and no firm having any choice of technique, showed that if firms believed that doubling their scale doubled their market value then the equilibrium would be a constrained Pareto-optimal (Diamond, 1971). But if we allow for entry will this still be the case? An example presented in our earlier paper (Stiglitz, 1972a) suggested that this would not in fact be the case, but the generality of this result remained in question. In this paper, we wish to show that *when the number of firms producing is not fixed, the market solution will err both with respect to the number and choice of firms to produce*, even when all firms take their value per unit scale as given. More generally the analysis of equilibrium in the capital market with entry under competitive conditions provides the second motivation for this paper.

Finally, a better understanding of monopolistic competitive equilibrium provides the third motivation for undertaking this study.

It is often asserted that monopolistic competition leads to too much product differentiation and to each firm, as a consequence, producing too little output. It has long been recognized, however, that the usual argument for this, which makes note of the 'excess capacity' in monopolistic competition (i.e. production at levels below the point of minimum average costs) is incorrect, for it fails to take into account the gains from product differentiation:[9] after all, the reason that one commodity is not a perfect substitute for another (that is, the reason that we do not have *perfect* competition) is that at least some individuals perceive there to be a difference in these commodities for which they are willing to pay a price.[10] Thus, what must be compared are the gains from product differentiation with the 'losses' from the inefficiency of producing below minimum average cost. Without some appropriate parameterization of the problem it is difficult to determine whether there will normally be under- or over-diversification, or even to determine conditions under which one would expect one or the other. The most widely studied such parameterization – the Hotelling (1929) formulation of the problem of spatial location, substantially generalized in the recent work of Lovell and Stern[11] – raises some important questions concerning the general validity of the conventional wisdom that in monopolistic competition there are too many firms producing too little output. Although the model of spatial location has an interpretation in the case when products are differentiated by some physical characteristic (say color), that model has a number of features which limits applicability as a description of the general problem of optimal product differentiation. The most important of these is the assumption that individuals purchase from only one store (buy one kind of commodity, e.g. only red balloons, not red balloons, white balloons, and pink balloons). Although this assumption makes sense in the context of the transportation problem, in most other contexts it is not so persuasive. Conventional economics has long embodied the principle of 'Variety is the Spice of Life' in the assumption of quasi-concave indifference curves; the assumption that individuals buy either red or white balloons, but not both, denies the validity of this hypothesis.[12]

A second important limitation is that the analysis is never embedded in a general equilibrium model. For example, consider a simple two-sector model, one sector of which is perfectly competitive, the other of which is described by our monopolistic competition model. Surely, one of the important questions which we wish to answer is, is the effect of monopolistic competition to divert resources from or to the perfectly competitive sector, or are its only consequences felt within the monopolistic competitive sector itself? The conventional location models fail even to address themselves to these questions.

A third difficulty arises in making welfare comparisons. By making firms closer together, individuals who happen to live on the fringes of a market area are made better off, others are made worse off. Hence, stronger welfare criteria than Pareto-optimality are required; conventionally, arguments making use of consumer and producer surplus are employed; compensation could be paid to those who are worse off, but such compensation is never in fact made, for if it were, it would presumably affect the demand curves, and in the analysis, the demand curves are assumed to remain unchanged.[13]

The analysis of monopolistic competition in the capital market provides us with an opportunity to calculate precisely the social benefits and costs of creating a new firm, and to compare the optimal allocation with the market allocation.

In the analysis of this chapter, we shall consider a highly simplified version of the capital market model. All risky firms will be assumed to be identical but not perfectly correlated, and all safe firms (i.e. firms whose returns are perfectly certain) are identical. Since one safe security is a perfect substitute for another safe security, the safe firms will constitute a perfectly competitive industry, the risky firms the monopolistically competitive industry. In Sections 2–5 the returns to the risky firms will be assumed to be independently (but identically) distributed, while in Section 6 they will all be correlated with a general market factor. All individuals will be assumed to be identical and risk averse.

This formulation allows us to avoid the pitfalls of the previous studies of monopolistic competition: individuals purchase not one but all the produced 'commodities'; there is a perfectly competitive sector, so we can enquire into the diversion of resources from the perfectly competitive to the monopolistically competitive sector; and since all individuals are identical and purchase the same portfolio (market basket of goods), they are all worse off in the 'competitive' situation than in the optimal.

Hence, we would argue that the results are of interest not only for what they suggest about the workings of the capital market, but for the light they shed on the more general question of resource allocation in economies with a monopolistically competitive sector.

In other studies, using considerably different parameterizations of the problem, Spence (1976) and Dixit and Stiglitz (1977) have been able to show that the basic results of this study do appear to have more general applicability. In the concluding section of this chapter, we shall comment further on these more general results.

2 THE MODEL[14]

The representative individual evaluates alternative portfolios in terms of their means and variances, i.e.

$$U = U(\mu_Y, \sigma_Y) \tag{1}$$

where μ_Y is his mean income and σ_Y is the standard deviation of his income.

There is a fixed cost, a, of setting up a risky firm.

In this and the immediate following sections we shall assume that the returns to all firms are independently distributed, and that the fixed costs of establishing a risky firm are independent of the number of firms.

The mean and standard deviation of the firm's returns are a function of the 'variable' capital alone. If X_i are the profits available for distribution to shareholders of the i-th firm[15] then

$$\bar{X}_i = EX_i = h_i(I_i) \tag{2}$$

$$\sigma_i = [E(X_i - \bar{X}_i)^2]^{\frac{1}{2}} = g_i(I_i)$$

where I_i is the capital, in excess of the fixed cost of setting up the firm, invested in the *i*-th firm (we shall refer to I_i as 'variable' capital as opposed to, a, the 'fixed' capital). We assume that increasing investment increases both mean and standard deviation of income

$$h_i' > 0, \; g_i' > 0 \tag{3a}$$

$$h_i'' \leqslant 0. \tag{3b}$$

We shall first investigate the case where all risky firms (and potential firms) are identical, i.e. $g_i = g_j$, $h_i = h_j$ all i,j. Accordingly, in this and the immediately following sections we shall drop the subscripts on h and g. The safe firm is assumed to have constant returns to scale with the return given by r.

The total amount available for investment is assumed to be fixed: Let I_R be the total invested in the risky industry, I_S in the safe industry, and n the number of firms in the risky industry;[16]

$$I = I_R + I_S = an + nI_i + I_S. \tag{4}$$

Our problem is the choice of n, I_i, and I_S subject to the resource constraint (4) to maximize utility (1).

One of the main advantages of the mean–variance model is that it allows us to separate out questions of productive efficiency from those of 'portfolio choice based on consumer preferences', that is, we can first describe the efficiency frontier, the allocation of resources (the determination of the number and the size of risky firms) which minimizes risk for given mean and then ask, what point on the efficiency frontier is optimal given the preferences of the representative individual. The market solution may differ from the optimal solution in either or both of these: it may or may not be productively efficient, and even if it is productively efficient, it may not choose the optimal point on the efficiency frontier. Indeed, in our earlier analysis (Stiglitz, 1972a) we showed that with a fixed number of firms, if there were no choice of technique – only a choice of scale – then the economy would be productively efficient, but the market solution resulted in too little allocation of resources to risky investments compared to the optimal allocation. On the other hand, if there were a choice of technique, the economy was not likely to be productively efficient.

Let us first describe, then, the efficiency frontier. We wish to minimize the standard deviation for a given mean. It is easy to show that, given our symmetry assumptions concerning the risky firms, it is optimal to have all firms which produce, produce at the same scale. Thus, we can formulate our problem as

$$\min \sigma_Y = \sqrt{n}\, g(I_i) \tag{5a}$$

subject to

$$\mu_Y = nh(I_i) + r(I - nI_i - an). \tag{5b}$$

Letting θ be the Lagrangean multiplier associated with constraint (5b), we obtain the following order conditions

$$\frac{\delta\sigma_Y}{\delta n} = \frac{1}{2\sqrt{n}} g = \theta[h - r(I_i + a)] = \theta\frac{\delta\mu_Y}{\delta n} \tag{6a}$$

$$\frac{\delta\sigma_Y}{\delta I_i} = \sqrt{n}\, g' = \theta n[h' - r] = \theta\frac{\delta\mu_Y}{\delta I_i}. \tag{6b}$$

Equation (6a) gives the effects of changing the number of firms, keeping the size of each firm constant, while (6b) gives the effects of changing the investment in the risky industry, keeping the total number of firms constant. Dividing (6b) and (6a), we have the result that the mean–standard deviation trade-off, keeping n constant, must be the same as that keeping I_i constant; this implies that, letting I_i^0 be the optimal size of the firm,

$$\frac{g}{2g'} = \frac{h - r(I_i^0 + a)}{h' - r}. \tag{7}$$

Equation (7) has one very strong implication. The optimal size of the risky firm is independent of preferences.

In the special case when there is constant returns to scale to variable capital, i.e. $h'' = g'' = 0$ we can solve explicitly for I_i^0:

$$I_i^0 = \frac{2ra}{h' - r} \tag{7'}$$

which depends only on the relation between the marginal returns in the risky and safe industries and the fixed cost of setting up a new firm.

We may draw the opportunity locus in mean–variance space. In Figure 15.1, we have marked the perfectly safe point by S. If I_R is invested in the risky industry, the mean and variance are given by

$$\sigma_Y = \left(\frac{I_R}{a + I_i^0}\right)^{\frac{1}{2}} g(I_i^0) \tag{8a}$$

$$\mu_Y = \frac{I_R}{a + I_i^0} h(I_i^0) + r(I - I_R) \tag{8b}$$

$$\frac{d\mu_Y}{d\sigma_Y} = \frac{2(\mu_Y - rI)}{\sigma_Y} \tag{8c}$$

$$\frac{d^2\mu_Y}{d\sigma_Y^2} = \frac{2(\mu_Y - rI)}{\sigma_Y^2} > 0. \tag{8d}$$

Because of diversification, the risk increases more slowly than the mean; the opportunity locus is convex. This is true even if there is constant returns to scale to variable capital in the risky industry.

The choice of the optimal point on the opportunity locus is straightforward: it is simply the tangency between the indifference curve and the opportunity locus, as in Figure 15.1. Analytically, we require that

$$\frac{\dfrac{\delta U}{\delta \mu_Y}}{\dfrac{\delta U}{\delta \sigma_Y}} = \theta = \frac{\dfrac{\delta \sigma_Y}{\delta n}}{\dfrac{\delta \mu_Y}{\delta n}} = \frac{\dfrac{\delta \sigma_Y}{\delta I_R}}{\dfrac{\delta \mu_Y}{\delta I_R}} = \frac{2(\mu_Y - rI)}{\sigma_Y} . \tag{9}$$

3 THE MARKET SOLUTION

In our mean–variance model, it is well known that the value of a firm in equilibrium is given by (see Lintner, 1965; Stiglitz, 1972a)

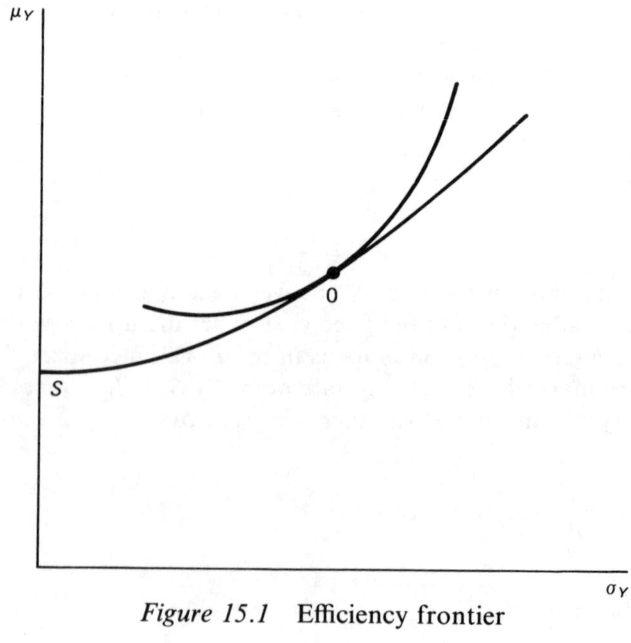

Figure 15.1 Efficiency frontier

$$V_i = \frac{h(I_i) - kg^2(I_i)}{r} \tag{10}$$

where k is the risk discount factor, i.e. we first calculate the certainty equivalence of the risky return by taking the mean and subtracting off a 'risk premium'; the risk premium is simply equal to the risk discount factor times the variance of the security (if the securities are uncorrelated, as we have assumed here). Market equilibrium is characterized by the following two conditions:

(a) Each firm takes k and r as given and maximizes the value of the equity of the original shareholders, i.e.

$$\max V_i - I_i \tag{11}$$

so that

$$h' - r = 2kgg'. \tag{12}$$

(b) Firms enter until there are zero profits for the marginal entrant, i.e.

$$V_i - I_i = a. \tag{13}$$

Substituting (10) into (13) and the result into (12) we obtain upon simplification:

$$\frac{g}{2g'} = \frac{h - r(I_i^c + a)}{h' - r} \tag{14}$$

where I_i^c is the competitive equilibrium size of a risky firm. Equation (14) should be contrasted with (7). The two expressions are identical. The *market solution is efficient.* For any given number of firms, the size is optimal, for any given total investment in the risky industries, the number of firms is optimal.

4 COMPETITIVE VERSUS OPTIMAL SIZE OF RISKY INDUSTRY

In order to compare the competitive versus the optimal size of the risky industry, we must relate the risk discount factor to properties of the utility function. It is easy to show that

$$k = -\frac{U_2}{U_1 \sigma_Y}. \tag{15}$$

Substituting this into (12) we obtain (upon simplification)

$$-\frac{U_2}{U_1} = \frac{h' - r}{2gg'} \sigma_Y = n^{\frac{1}{2}} \frac{h' - r}{2g'} = \frac{1}{2\theta} \left(= \frac{1}{2} \frac{\frac{\delta \mu_Y}{\delta I_i}}{\frac{\delta \sigma_Y}{\delta I_i}} \right). \tag{16}$$

This should be contrasted with the optimal allocation, where, using (10), we have

$$-\frac{U_2}{U_1} = n^{\frac{1}{2}} \frac{(h' - r)}{g'} = \frac{1}{\theta}. \tag{17}$$

The market solution results in the slope of the indifference curve being 1/2 the slope of the opportunity locus, i.e. there is an under-allocation of resources to the risky industry (see Fig. 15.2). This entails that there are too few risky firms, not too many.

Not surprisingly, to operate the risky industry at an optimal level would require some subsidy for the marginal entrant. This follows from substituting (15) into (10), to obtain

$$V_i = \frac{h - (1)/(\theta) n^{\frac{1}{2}} g}{r} \tag{18}$$

then using (6a) to show:[17]

$$V_i < a + I_i^0. \tag{19}$$

Indeed, this will in general be true for all points to the right of C in Figure 15.2: *the monopolistic competition equilibrium is a constrained optimum*, where the government is not allowed to subsidize the fixed costs of establishing private firms.[18]

We would argue that this is not an unreasonable constraint; though production subsidies and taxes are feasible, as are franchise taxes, a subsidy for a firm simply to exist is not. (How, for instance, is the government to stop an individual from declaring himself a 'firm' with high fixed costs? To differentiate such phony firms from real firms would require either detailed

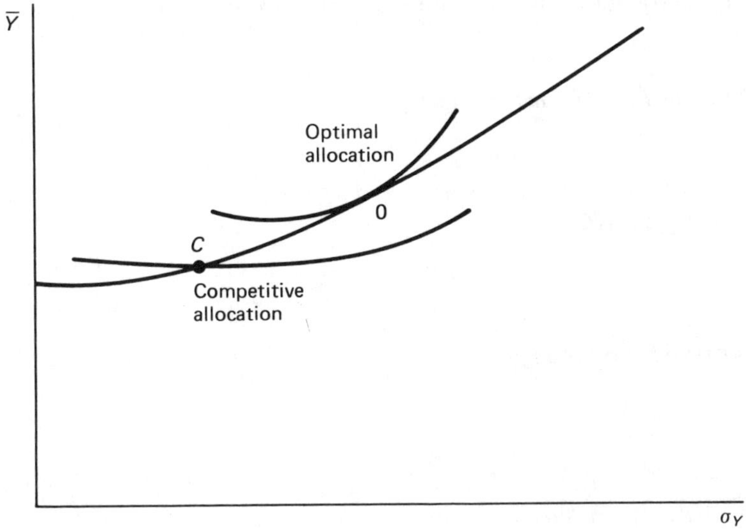

Figure 15.2 Competitive versus optimal allocation of resources

and costly information and administration, or the reliance on easily obtained data, like output, in which case we no longer have a lump-sum subsidy.)

But, as we shall now see, this result as well as the more general result on the productive efficiency (in mean–variance terms) of the monopolistically competitive capital market, do not extend to the case with correlated returns.

5 CORRELATED RETURNS: THE COMPETITIVE ANALYSIS

One widely employed model of the stock market suggests that the returns to a firm, X_i, may be written[19]

$$X_i(I_i,\theta)=h_i(I_i)(1+\beta_i M(\theta)+\varepsilon_i(\theta)) \tag{20}$$

where $M(\theta)$ is the state of the business cycle and

$$E\varepsilon_i\varepsilon_j=E\varepsilon_i=EM(\theta)=\Sigma\,\varepsilon_i M=0.$$

For simplicity, let us again assume all firms are identical. Then 'efficiency' requires

$$\text{Max } nh(I_i) + r[I - n(I_i + a)] \equiv \mu_Y$$

s.t.

$$\sigma_Y = h_i(I_i)b(n) \lesseqgtr \bar{\sigma}_Y$$

where

$$b(n) = \{[E\varepsilon^2 + n\beta^2\sigma_M^2]n\}^{\frac{1}{2}}$$

i.e.

$$\frac{h' - r}{h - r(a + I)} = \frac{h'}{h}\frac{b}{b'n}.$$

Let

$$\frac{b}{b'n} = 1 - \gamma$$

$$\frac{h'}{h} = \frac{r - \gamma h'}{r(1-\gamma)(a + I_i)} \tag{21}$$

or letting

$$\frac{h'I}{h} = \nu \lesseqgtr 1$$

$$I_i = \frac{a\nu(1-\gamma)r}{r - \gamma h' - r(1-\gamma)\nu}. \tag{21'}$$

It has been suggested that in this context, it would be 'reasonable' for firms to assume that their value was proportionate to h_i; if they did, then, with a fixed number of firms, the economy would be efficient. But if the number of firms is variable, the economy will not be efficient: In equilibrium, we have

$$V_i = h_i \frac{\{1 - k[((n-1)h(I^*_i) + h_i)\beta^2\sigma_M^2 + h_i E\varepsilon^2]\}}{r} \equiv h_i\rho \tag{22}$$

I_i is chosen to maximize $V_i - I_i$. Under the hypothesis of constant ρ,

$$\frac{\delta V_i}{\delta I_i} = h_i'\rho = 1 \tag{23}$$

Firms will enter until

$$V_i - I_i = h_i\rho - I_i = a. \tag{24}$$

Hence, instead of (21) we have (using (23) and (24))[20]

$$\frac{h'}{h} = \frac{1}{I_i + a} \tag{25}$$

or

$$I_i = \frac{a}{(1)/(\nu) - 1} \tag{26}$$

Note that if $\gamma = 0$, (26) and (21′) are identical. But

$$\gamma = 1 - \frac{b}{b'n} = 1 - \frac{1}{(1)/(2) + (n\beta^2\sigma^2)/2(E\varepsilon^2 + n\beta^2\sigma_M^2)}$$

$$= -\frac{E\varepsilon^2}{E\varepsilon^2 + 2n\beta^2\sigma_M^2} \leqslant 0$$

Since

$$\frac{r - \gamma h'}{r(1-\gamma)(a+I_i)} - \frac{1}{a+I_i} = -\frac{\gamma(h'-r)}{r(a+I_i)(1-\gamma)}$$

$$I_i^0 < I_i^c \text{ as } \gamma < 0,$$

i.e. the level of investment in each firm in competitive equilibrium exceeds the optimum, unless $\gamma = 0$.

To compare the optimal number of firms with the market solution, we observe that the former requires (at $I = I^0$, $n = n^0$)

$$-\frac{U_2}{U_1} = \frac{(h'-r)}{h'} \cdot \frac{n}{b} \tag{27}$$

while in the latter (using (25))

$$-\frac{U_2}{U_1} = \frac{h'-r}{h'} \cdot \frac{n}{b} \tag{28}$$

at $I = I^c$, $n = n^c$.

Since $[d(h-r)/h']/dI_i = rh''/h^{-2} < 0$, the right-hand side of (28) is always less than the right-hand side of (27), for given n. Since for given n, the mean and standard deviation of income are higher under the market solution, it follows that, with normal indifference maps,[21] the number of firms in the market solution is less than in the optimum, and indeed, the total allocation of resources to the risky sector is small.

This result is intuitive. If each firm believed that its market value per unit scale would remain unchanged, regardless of its scale, then, in a zero profit equilibrium, the firm must be operating at the bottom of its U-shaped cost curve (where the diminishing returns exactly offsets the increasing returns associated with the fixed costs). This entails insufficient diversity: in the optimum, each firm is operating at a scale lower than the bottom of its U-shaped cost curve. Because of the lack of optimal diversity, investing in the risky sector is riskier, and hence the equilibrium level of investment is smaller.

In the case where $\gamma = 0$, there are no gains to diversity, since all firms have perfectly correlated returns and hence the market solution and the optimum coincide with respect to the scale of the representative firm and from (27) and (28) in the total allocation of resources to the risky sector.

The above welfare analysis did not explicitly take into account the constraint that firms be self-financing. If we require that each firm have at least a value equal to its expenditure on investment, i.e.

$$V_i \geqslant I_i + a$$

or

$$h_i(I_i)\rho - I_i \geqslant a \tag{29}$$

we can still show that the market solution is not a constrained optimum.

The behavioral hypothesis employed in this section – that is, firms take the ratio of market value to scale as given[22] – is, however, not totally convincing. At least equally plausible is the hypothesis employed in our earlier analysis where we assumed that firms took the risk discount factor and the rate of interest as given. Accordingly, firms are aware that as they increase their scale, their value per unit scale decreases.

It is worth noting that apart from the differences in behavioral hypothesis, the model analyzed in the previous section is a special case of the model here, with $\beta = 0$, while if $E\varepsilon^2 = 0$, we obtain the standard model with multiplicative uncertainty.

6 INCREASING MARGINAL ENTRANCE COSTS

Thus far in the analysis, we have assumed that all firms face the same fixed costs of entry. We now consider what happens when the fixed costs of entry is an increasing function of the number of firms already in the risky industry, i.e. the firms best suited for the risky industry enter first, and then those less suited enter. For simplicity, we only consider the case of independently distributed firms. We let $f'(n)$ be the fixed cost of establishing the marginal firm; $f''>0$.

Then, instead of equation (7), we obtain for the optimal size of the firm

$$\frac{g}{2g'}=\frac{h-r(I_i^0+f')}{h'-r}$$

which, in the case where this is constant returns to scale to variable capital, reduces to

$$I_i^0=\frac{2\mathrm{rf}'}{h'-r}.$$

Thus, the optimal scale of the firm increases as the number of firms in the risky industry increases.

We still obtain, however, the result that the market solution is efficient when the marginal entrant must pay his (own) fixed cost.

On the other hand, in a number of industries which might be described by a monopolistically competitive model, the cost of entering to the marginal firms is simply the average cost (as in the familiar fisheries or oil well problems). Then, the larger the number of entrants, the larger the fixed cost each must pay. In that case the condition for no entry becomes

$$V_i-I_i=\frac{f(n)}{n}.$$

In that case, as one might expect, the economy does not operate on its mean-variance efficiency frontier.

7 REINTERPRETATION IN PARTIAL EQUILIBRIUM TERMS[23]

The nature of the competitive equilibrium solution can be depicted in terms of the familiar partial equilibrium diagrams. Let $\overline{X}_i$ be our measure of the output for the firm. If $h_i''<0$, the total average cost curve is U-shaped. The 'perceived demand function' giving price per unit of output $V_i/h(I_i)$ is[24]

$$\frac{V_i}{h(I_i)} = \frac{1}{r} - \frac{kg^2(h^{-1}(\overline{X}))}{r\overline{X}_i} .$$

With free entry the equilibrium is given at the tangency of the demand schedule and the average cost schedule. We have also drawn the demand schedule corresponding to the situation where all the risky firms increase their *output* simultaneously. This demand schedule will in general be steeper than that given when only one firm's investment varies, since, at fixed n, as I_i increases for all firms, k will increase (if there is decreasing absolute risk aversion) (see Fig. 15.3).

The gain from the additional diversity resulting from a new firm can be measured by the area under the demand curve. The magnitude of that consumer surplus needs to be compared with the magnitude of the fixed cost. The central result of Section 4 could thus be interpreted as saying that in the market solution, the magnitude of the consumer surplus exceeds the fixed cost, but that additional entry is not possible without providing lump-sum subsidies to pay for the fixed cost.

Let us now consider the model of Section 5, with correlated returns. Then the perceived demand schedule becomes

$$\frac{V_i}{h_i} = \frac{1}{r} - \frac{k\mu_i \Sigma \beta_j h_j(I_j)}{r} - \frac{kh_i}{r}(I_i)[E\varepsilon_i^2 + \beta_i^2 EM^2].$$

The major biases of monopolistic competition, discussed at greater length by Spence (1976) and Dixit and Stiglitz (1977), become evident. The elasticity of the perceived demand schedule is a function of the magnitude of own variance

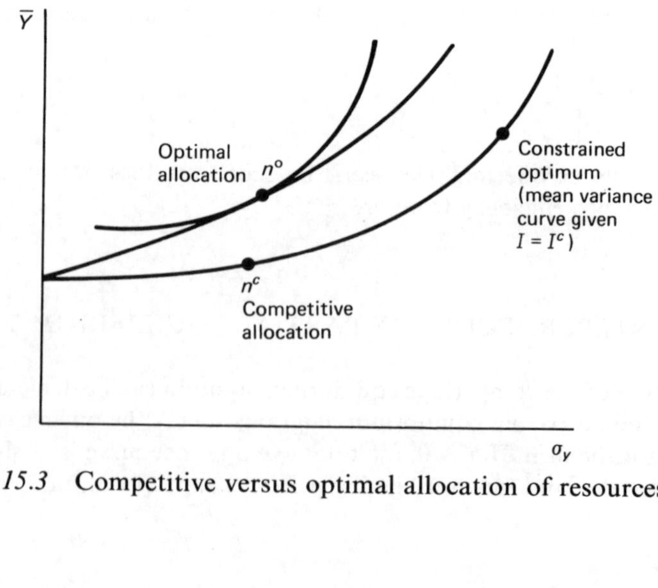

Figure 15.3 Competitive versus optimal allocation of resources

$$[E\varepsilon_i^2 + \beta_i^2 EM^2]h^2$$

relative to covariance with the market

$$h_i\beta_i \Sigma \beta_j h_j(I_j).$$

As Figures 15.4a and 15.4b illustrate, we can find two industries with the same fixed costs, but different ratios of own variance to covariance, such

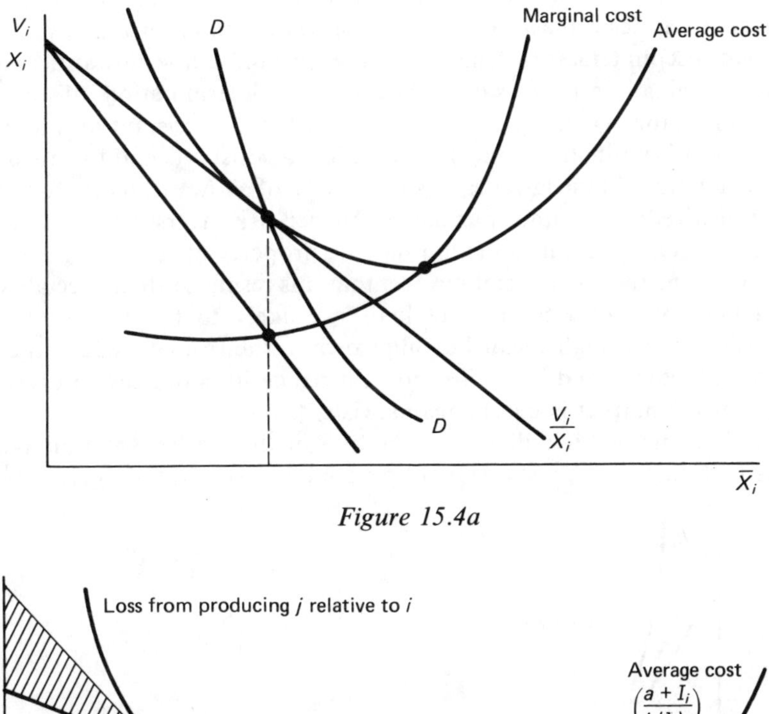

Figure 15.4a

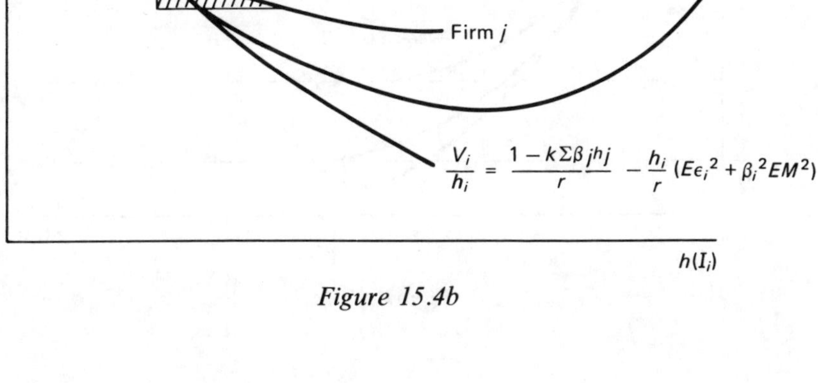

Figure 15.4b

that the firm with the lower own variance is infra-marginal, and the one with the higher own variance is just below the margin, but because of the larger consumer surplus associated with the latter, it would be preferable to produce the latter. (And indeed, if the former were not produced, the latter might even be feasible.) This argues that the market systematically is biased against firms with high own variance, high correlation with the market factor, and biased in favor of those with a low correlation with the rest of the market.

There are additional biases when we take into account the restriction on viability of firms. Since we argued that in the market equilibrium, additional entry is desirable at the margin, there is a social return to lowering k, the risk discount factor. (This shifts the demand curve upward, making some marginal entry feasible.) The precise determination of the risk discount factor is a complex matter, except for the constant absolute risk aversion utility functions (in which case it is a constant) and the quadratic utility function. In the latter case, substitution of a low mean firm for a high mean firm reduces k, and thus makes further risk diversification possible. But the quadratic utility function has the property of increasing absolute risk aversion, and so one might expect that this result is rather special. Since at higher levels of wealth individuals are likely to be less risk averse, securities with a high mean but high own variance may reduce the risk discount factor k, and if this is correct, it strengthens our earlier presumption that the market is biased against risky firms.

Finally, Figure 15.4c illustrates the bias of the market solution against firms with high fixed costs relative to variable costs. In the figure we have

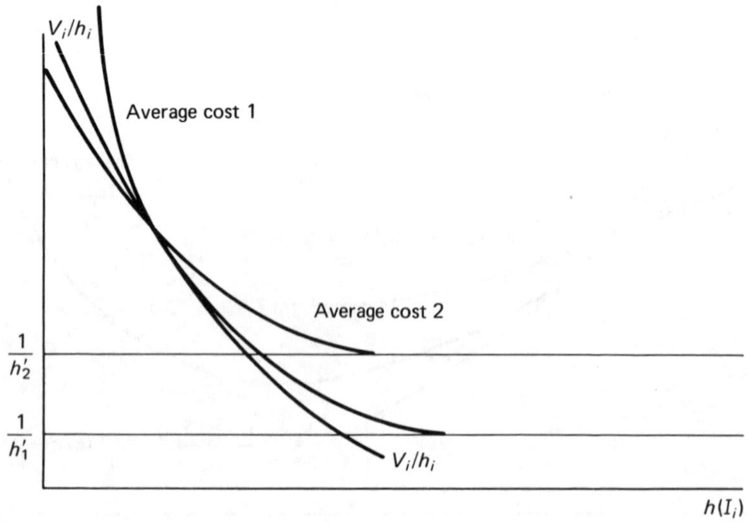

Figure 15.4c

depicted the cost and demand curves for two firms with identical risk properties, with stochastic constant returns to scale, but with one having higher fixed costs ($a_1 > a_2$) but lower marginal costs ($h_1' > h_2'$). Firm 2 is initially viable, firm 1 is not. But if firm 2 is eliminated, firm 1 would be viable, and the switch is clearly desirable.

8 CONCLUDING COMMENTS

We have examined a model where different commodities are close – but not perfect – substitutes for each other. Under normal assumptions of quasi-concave indifference curves, individuals would consume some of all the different varieties of goods produced; if there were no fixed costs to producing a different variety, all the varieties that could be produced would be produced. There are, however, in general, some fixed costs with producing a different commodity, and even if they are small, they will put a limit on the number of different commodities which it is optimal to produce. The question is, how does this optimal allocation compare with that of a monopolistically competitive economy? We have examined this question in the context of a capital market where the different commodities are different securities. We have assumed that individuals evaluate incomes in terms of means and variances, which allows us to derive simple expressions for the valuation (demand) functions for the different securities. We have shown that

(a) If the returns to different securities are independent,

- (i) for any given level of investment in the monopolistically competitive sector (the risky industry), the number of firms and size of each firm is optimal, but
- (ii) there is under-investment in the monopolistically competitive industry; however,
- (iii) the monopolistically competitive allocation is the optimal allocation in the absence of government subsidies for the fixed cost of establishing a new firm.

(b) If the returns to different securities are correlated, the economy will not be operating on its mean–variance efficiency frontier, even if all firms believe that their market value is proportional to their scale. Each firm will be larger than optimal, and there will be too few risky firms. If they recognize the dependence of market value on scale, each firm will be too small. Moreover, the market solution is biased in favor of firms whose own variances are low relative to covariances with respect to the rest of the market, and to low fixed costs–high marginal cost firms.

These results suggest that the misallocations associated with monopolistically competitive industries are far more complicated – and perhaps more important – than much of the conventional wisdom would imply.

Notes

1. I was fortunate enough to have been a student of Joan Robinson while on a Fulbright to Cambridge during 1965–6. Growth theory was the fad of the day, and I had gone to Cambridge partly with the objective of studying under her. She was assigned to be my supervisor. I am afraid that she was convinced that I had already been indoctrinated by MIT, and was past the point of no return. We engaged in lively debates both that year, and during a return visit in 1969–70. Her sense of intellectual commitment, and the passion with which she pursued economics, left a lasting impression on me.
2. There are, of course, important differences between the two works. It would take me beyond the scope of this chapter to discuss these differences.
3. It would be a matter of speculation to try to explain why this was so; while macroeconomists were engaged in trying to explain unemployment, and while the economy was struggling to recover from the Great Depression, a seeming massive failure of the market, microeconomists were busy *proving* that the (competitive) economy was (Pareto) efficient!

   Indeed, the empirical conundrums – how market equilibrium could be reconciled with the obvious presence of significant returns to scale – which motivated some of the early work on imperfect competition were not only not recognized by the competitive equilibrium theorists, they constructed models which explicitly assumed the problems away, by assuming, for instance, convex technologies.

   Professor Robinson's skepticism of neoclassical economics may be well understood in terms of its failure to address what she viewed to be the central economic problems. But she failed to provide a viable alternative theory, and she confused criticisms of neoclassical assumptions with criticisms of the analytical techniques employed by neoclassical economists.

   Those of us trained at MIT during the period were taught the analytical tools and the neoclassical models, but we were also taught not to take these models too seriously: this was the error ascribed to the Chicago economists. I think she would have eventually come to approve of the efforts of these MIT-trained economists to use these tools to understand economies with imperfect competition, incomplete markets, and imperfect information.
4. A contribution for which, I think, she may have received insufficient credit.
5. Assuming for simplicity that the business cycle constitutes the major undiversifiable risk.
6. There are in fact two separate aspects to the argument. If individuals are well informed about a few stocks and uninformed about others, it can be shown that they may own sufficient amounts of the stock about which they are well informed and that they will be risk averse with respect to the actions of those firms. See Stiglitz, 1974, 1982).

   Secondly, because of the fundamental non-convexity associated with information, it is optimal only to obtain information about a limited number of securities. (See Radner and Stiglitz, 1984).
7. It should be emphasized that this is not the only appropriate interpretation. In particular, we argued in our earlier paper that what is 'price taking

behavior' is not unambiguous; in a mean variance model, firms could act as price takers relative to what they consider to be the relevant variables, i.e. they take the rate of interest and the risk discount factor as given. Such an interpretation would have them acting not as monopolistic competitors but as essentially perfect competitors.

It should also be observed that there are other sources of potential inefficiency in the stock market allocation of investment, discussed at greater length in Stiglitz (1972, 1982) and Greenwald and Stiglitz (1986).

8. There are other objections which have been raised concerning our analysis, particularly associated with the choice of the objective function of the firm. As we mentioned briefly in our earlier study and elaborated at greater length in the original version of the paper (presented at the Far Eastern Meetings of the Econometric Society, 1970), the policy which the individual stockholder wishes the firm to pursue depends on whether the individual plans to sell shares (so that he is concerned with market value maximization) or simply to retain his shares. If the ratio of retained shares to shares sold is zero, value maximization is desired, and our earlier analysis is applicable. In the extreme case where no one wishes to change his portfolio, then the policy voted for will be Pareto optimal. These issues are discussed in more detail in Stiglitz (1970) and Grossman and Stiglitz (1977, 1980).
9. Chamberlin himself was careful to avoid this error. See E. W. Chamberlin (1950), pp.85–92. Unfortunately, he never developed a theory of optimal product differentiation. See also R. Bishop. (1967).
10. Some economists have suggested that these are not 'real' differences, only perceived differences – and in fact it is only advertizing which makes individuals think that there is a difference. Why the difference between commodities which are close substitutes should be any less 'real' than differences between other commodities is never made clear in these arguments; the fact that the commodities differ less means that individuals are willing to pay less to have one commodity rather than another, but does not vitiate the fact that these are real differences.
11. See Stern (1972) and Lovell (1970). For a recent survey, see Stiglitz (1986).
12. This may not be an unreasonable assumption for certain large consumer durables, e.g. houses or automobiles. For many everyday commodities, it is clearly inappropriate.
13. This point is, of course, closely related to the previous point that all the analyses are completely partial equilibrium in character.
14. For a more extensive discussion of the basic model, the reader is referred to Stiglitz (1972a).
15. We assume without loss of generality that the firm is entirely financed by equity; under the assumptions of this model, the financial structure of the firm has no consequences.
16. Throughout the discussion, we shall treat n as a continuous variable; the modifications required to take account of the fact that n can take on only integer values are straightforward.
17. I.e.

$$-\frac{1}{2}$$

$$h-\frac{ng}{\theta}<r(a+I_i)$$

17. $\theta[h-r(a+I_i)]=\frac{1}{2}n^{-.5}g<n^{-.5}g$.

18. When I is elasticity supplied, unless a lump sum tax is feasible, the taxes required to obtain the revenue for paying the fixed costs of setting up firms creates distortions; elsewhere, we have shown that if the utility function is additive, then when all individuals are identical, optimal taxation requires that the riskier industry be taxed at a higher (lower) ad valorem rate if the wealth elasticity of the demand for the risky assets is less (greater) than unity. The economy will accordingly operate to the left (right) of the point of tangency of the indifference curve and the efficiency curve (although if I is reduced the whole frontier shrinks down). (See Stiglitz, 1972c).
19. Note that (20) is consistent with 'multiplicative uncertainty', i.e. increasing investment increases returns in all states of nature proportionately.
20. Note that if r is not constant, this may not be a unique solution to (25).
21. That is, where the income consumption loci are negatively sloped.
22. Which is a more 'realistic' hypothesis seems a question of some debate. For a more extended discussion of this issue, see Stiglitz (1972a), pp.55–56.
23. This discussion is meant to be heuristic, to relate our results to the older literature on monopolistic competition. Thus we shall use consumer surplus analysis without rigorously justifying it.
24. This demand schedule assumes that k and r are given.

References

Bishop, R. L. (1967) 'Monopolistic Competition and Welfare Economics', in R. Kuenne (ed.) *Monopolistic Competition Theory* (New York: Wiley).

Chamberlin, E. W. (1933) *Theory of Monopolistic Competition* (Cambridge, Mass.: Harvard University Press).

Chamberlin, E. W. (1950) 'Product Heterogeneity and Public Policy', *American Economic Review*, Papers and Proceedings, 40 (May) pp.85–92.

Diamond, P. (1971) 'A Model of Price Adjustment', *Journal of Economics Theory,* 3: 156–68.

Dixit, A. and J. E. Stiglitz (1977) 'Monopolistic Competition and Optimal Product Diversity', *American Economic Review*, 7 (June): 297–308.

Greenwald, B. C. and J. E. Stiglitz (1986) 'Externalities in Economies with Imperfect Information and Incomplete Markets', *Quarterly Journal of Economics,* 101: 229–64.

Grossman, S. and J. E. Stiglitz (1977) 'On Value Maximization and Alternative Objectives of the Firm', *Journal of Finance,* 32(2): 389–402.

Grossman, S. and J. E. Stiglitz (1980) 'Stockholder Unanimity in the Making of Production and Financial Decisions', *Quarterly Journal of Economics,* 94: 543–66.

Hotelling, H. (1929) 'Stability in Competition', *Economic Journal,* 39(1): 41–57; repr. in Stigler and Boulding (eds), *Readings in Price Theory.*

Kaldor, N. (1935) 'Market Imperfection and Excess Capacity', *Economica*, NS 2(1); 33–50; repr. in Stigler and Boulding (eds), *Readings in Price Theory.*

Lintner, J. (1965) 'The Valuation of Risk Assets and the Selection of Risky Investments in Stock Portfolios and Capital Budgets', *Review of Economics and Statistics* 47 (February).

Lovell, M. C. (1970) 'Product Differentiation and Market Structure', *Western Economic Journal,* 8(2): 120–43.

Radner, R. and J. E. Stiglitz (1984) 'A Non-concavity in the Value of Information', in *Bayesian Models in Economic Theory*, M. Boyer and R. Khilstrom (eds), Elsevier Science Publications.

Robinson, J. (1952) *The Rate of Interest and Other Essays* (London: Macmillan).

Robinson, J. (1969) *The Economics of Imperfect Competition*, 2nd edn (London: Macmillan).

Spence, M. (1976) 'Product Selection, Fixed Costs, and Monopolistic Competition', *Review of Economic Studies*, 43.

Stern, N. H. (1972) 'The Optimal Size of Market Areas', *Journal of Economic Theory*, 4(2): 159–73.

Stiglitz, J. E. (1970) 'On the Optimality of the Stock Market Allocation of Investment', paper presented at the Far Eastern Meetings of the Econometric Society, Tokyo, 27–29 June (mimeo).

Stiglitz, J. E. (1972a) 'On the Optimality of the Stock Market Allocation of Investment', *Quarterly Journal of Economics*, (February) pp.25–60, paper presented to Far Eastern Meetings of the Econometric Society, June 1970, Tokyo.

Stiglitz, J. E. (1972b) 'Some Aspects of the Pure Theory of Corporate Finance: Bankruptcies and Take-Overs', *Bell Journal of Economics and Management Science*, **3** (Autumn): 458–82.

Stiglitz, J. E. (1972c) 'Taxation, Risk Taking, and the Allocation of Investment in a Competitive Economy', in M. Jensen (ed.) *Studies in the Theory of Capital Markets*, pp.294–361.

Stiglitz, J. E. (1974) 'Information and the Capital Market', mimeo.

Stiglitz, J. E. (1982) 'Information and Capital Markets', in *Financial Economics: Essays in Honor of Paul Cootner'*, W. F. Sharpe and Cathryn Cootner (eds) (Englewood Cliffs, NJ: Prentice Hall) pp.118–58.

Stiglitz, J. E. (1986) 'General Theory of Monopolistic Competition', in R. Quandt and M. Peston (eds) *Prices, Competition and Equilibrium* (Oxford: Philip Allan), pp.22–69.

16 Competition, Non-linear Pricing and Rationing in Credit Markets

Mordecai Kurz*

The empirical observation made by most students of credit markets is that rationing is being practiced in those markets. The early developers of the theory of imperfect competition, including Joan Robinson, viewed this as a reflection of monopolistic forces in the credit markets. Research over the past two decades has been suggesting that the credit market possesses some unique features which differentiate it from other markets and this perspective has altered our view of it. Two lines of research have been developed. One observed that lending institutions necessarily need to take the risk of default by their borrowers, and for this reason the interest rate charged by them depends upon the characteristics of the borrower and the amount borrowed. Thus, an upward-sloping interest rate schedule is nothing but a reflection of the ever-present risk of default rather than the imperfection of the credit markets (see Freimer and Gordon, 1965; Stigler, 1967; Stiglitz, 1970; Jaffee, 1971; Baltensperger, 1976; Kurz, 1976; Keeton, 1979; and others). A second line of research focused on the problems generated by the presence of asymmetric information in this market, resulting in either adverse selection of borrowers or in the existence of an incentive for borrowers to take greater risk of default than desired by the lenders (see Jaffee and Russell, 1976; Stiglitz and Weiss, 1981; Hammond, 1986). Naturally, there are critics of both lines of thinking and we shall briefly remark on these below. A consensus does seem to be emerging that the credit market is not an example of monopolistic competition as Joan Robinson thought. Rather, it is an example of market incompletion where incomplete information and/or the non-availability of default insurance are the essential causes of rationing. Thus, our present contribution in honor of Joan Robinson preserves the spirit of professional discussion which she has so perfected.

Stiglitz and Weiss (1981, p.394) criticize the first of the two lines of research, mentioned above, by arguing that it only provides an explanation for why people of different circumstances are offered credit on different

* This work was supported by National Science Foundation Grant IST-8521838 at the Institute for Mathematical Studies in the Social Sciences, Stanford University, Stanford, California. The author thanks his student Luis Cabral for technical assistance.

terms, but it does not give a theoretical justification for credit rationing in the sense in which it is commonly used. Important criticial issues may also be raised against the second line of research. There is no doubt that the lack of complete information has important effects on the credit markets and the work of Stiglitz and Weiss (1981) clearly demonstrates it. However, lending institutions employ many techniques of studying their applicants and the amount of asymmetric information can be substantially reduced by spending resources on gathering information. Moreover, Stiglitz and Weiss (1981, p.401) note that the presence of collateral together with *complete* information on the assets of a borrower will drastically reduce the incentive effects which they analyze and thus remove the need for rationing. This explains why such institutions require, for the approval of any loan, both a complete financial disclosure as well as a business plan which explains the need for funds and specifies the proposed equity of the borrower. We do agree with Stiglitz and Weiss that the studies of the effect of default risk on the behavior of credit markets with complete information (see the earlier citations) have not provided, as yet, an adequate explanation of rationing. The purpose of this chapter is to take the next step and show why rationing will take place even under conditions of complete information.

The view taken here is that even in a world of complete information, a freely competitive credit market without rationing is usually not capable of providing the depositors with full insurance against default. Our analysis will then show that in a market in which a *full* account is taken of the possibility of default, including that of the financial intermediary itself (i.e. the 'bank'), an equilibrium allocation of credit will normally entail credit rationing. The analysis in this paper hinges, in an essential way, on the decomposition of the random nature of the return of any investment in our economy into two components: one which is a random component unique to the firm, and a second which is an economy-wide random component representing the macroeconomic effects of the economy on individual firms, projects, or enterprises.

1 THE MODEL

Our modelling objective is to focus on the interdependence in default of the three agents involved: 'borrowers', financial 'intermediaries' (e.g. banks) and 'depositors'. There is one homogeneous commodity in this economy which is used for consumption, exchange and store of value. The economy is a two-period economy. Each borrower is a regular consumer–entrepreneur with an initial endowment, a utility function defined over random consumptions and a risky 'firm' or 'project' in which he carries out his investment plans. A financial intermediary receives money from 'depositors' and lends it to the 'borrowers' where the difference between the borrowing and the lending rates provides the basis for his profits. 'Depositors' offer the economy labor services used by the firms. However, depositors wish to keep their deposits secure at the hands of the financial intermediary. The distinction between the 'depositors' and the 'entrepreneurs' is artificial and made for analytical convenience. The 'depositors' are identified by the fact that they need money for transactions and for (intertemporal) store of value and do not wish to take any default risk. These agents do not carry out any act of investment and for this reason need a default-free store of value. It is important to note at this point that the demand of the depositors represents a basic social need for a default-free medium of exchange, and store of value and one of the focal points of our analysis is the question of how such a social need can be satisfied in a free competitive economy.

1.1 The Borrowers–Entrepreneurs

There are N borrowers all with the same utility function $u(\cdot,\cdot)$ defined over consumption in period 1 and consumption in period 2. Each entrepreneur has initial assets A and a firm with a random return q. The entrepreneur uses the amount c of his own endowment to invest in the firm and that is viewed as 'collateral'. However, to carry out the production process he also needs labor. As long as he uses his own capital c and his own labor, his income in the second period becomes

$$y_0 = cq. \tag{1}$$

His utility when operating on his own (but depending upon w) is defined by u^*. However, the entrepreneur may borrow the amount b from the intermediary and expand his production into a more advanced operation. The advanced operation is assumed to be a fixed proportion production technology resulting in the revenue of

$$R = \text{Min}\left[I, \frac{1}{\alpha}L\right]q \tag{2}$$

where I is the amount invested in the firm and L is labor employed. If the entrepreneur borrows the amount b, the capital at hand is $(b+c)$. This amount must satisfy

$$b + c = I + Lw \tag{3}$$

where w is the wage-rate. However, the equality of $\alpha I = L$ implies that

$$I=\frac{b+c}{1+\alpha w};\ L=\alpha\frac{b+c}{1+\alpha w}\ . \tag{4}$$

Together (2)–(4) imply that the problem of the entrepreneur is defined by the following maximization problem: select the pair (b,c) to

$$\underset{(b,c)}{\text{Maximize}}\ E_y u(A-c,y) \geqq u^* \tag{5a}$$

where the random variable y is defined by

$$y=\begin{cases} \dfrac{b+c}{1+\alpha w}q-(1+p)b & \text{if } q \geqq \dfrac{b(1+p)}{b+c}(1+\alpha w) \\ \\ 0 & \text{if } q \leqslant \dfrac{b(1+p)}{(b+c)}(1+\alpha w) \end{cases} \tag{5b}$$

and where the function $p(\cdot)$ is an unspecified price function indicating the schedule of fees which the borrower must pay the intermediary for using the capital b for one period. It is important to note that (5b) recognizes explicitly the risk of default when

$$q \leqslant \frac{b(1+p)}{(b+c)}(1+\alpha w).$$

The density $f_q(\cdot)$ and the corresponding distribution $F_q(\cdot)$ of the return q are known by all.

We can introduce a notation for 'leverage' l defined by

$$l=\frac{b}{b+c}(1+\alpha w)$$

and hence

$$c=b\left[\frac{1+\alpha w}{l}-1\right].$$

with the aid of this notation we can restate the maximization problem of the entrepreneur as follows

$$\underset{(b,l)}{\text{Maximize}}\ E_q u\left(A-b\left[\frac{1+\alpha w}{l}-1\right],y\right) \tag{5a$'$}$$

where y is defined by

$$y = \begin{cases} b\left[\frac{q}{l} - (1+p)\right] & \text{if } q \geqq l(1+p) \\ 0 & \text{if } q \leqq l(1+p). \end{cases}$$

For the moment we note that differentiation among the entrepreneurs can be made by considering different values of b and c among them and hence the price function p may be conjectured to be of the form

$$p = \tilde{p}(b,c,x) \tag{6}$$

where x indicates, perhaps, other variables. Given a function like (6) it is clear that each firm will select its demand functions of the form:

$$b = b(w,x) \tag{7a}$$

$$l = l(w,x) \tag{7b}$$

$$c = c(w,x). \tag{7c}$$

An alternative formulation would permit the borrower to construct his portfolio so that the saving c is split into two parts:

(i) λc = amount invested in the risky firm

(ii) $(1-\lambda)c$ = amount put in default-free 'deposits' yielding a return ρ.

With this modification define

$$l = \frac{b}{b+\gamma c}(1+\alpha w)$$

and the maximization of the borrower becomes

$$\underset{(b,l,\lambda)}{\text{Maximize}}\ E_q u\left(A - b\left[\frac{1+\alpha w}{l}\right], y\right) \tag{5a$''$}$$

where y is defined by

$$y = \begin{cases} b\left[\frac{q}{l} + \rho(1-\lambda)\frac{c}{b} - (1+p)\right] & \text{if } q \geqq l\left[(1+p) - \rho(1-\lambda)\frac{c}{b}\right] \\ 0 & \text{if } q \leqslant l\left[(1+p) - \rho(1-\lambda)\frac{c}{b}\right]. \end{cases} \tag{5b$''$}$$

In formulating this problem the borrower is allowed to put aside the amount $(1-\lambda)c$ in the form of default-free deposit. This provides for a reduced probability of default and would be viewed as desirable by the lending financial institution. Under such circumstances the price function should take the form

$$p=\tilde{p}(b,c,\lambda c,x). \tag{6'}$$

It can be shown that the first-order conditions for the borrower would be to select λ^* so that

$$\rho=\frac{\partial \tilde{p}}{\partial(\lambda c)}\,.$$

Although this way of defining the 'collateral' is of interest we shall follow the procedure outlined in (5a')–(5b'). Banks mostly follow the procedure of lending a certain *fraction* of the total required amount, demanding that the investor provide equity ('down payment') capital for the balance. This is the procedure followed in (5a')–(5b'). Figure 16.1 depicts the optimum of a borrower when the price schedule is of the form

$\tilde{p}(b,c)=x$ (x is some constant)

The four curves $E_q u=\alpha_i$ represent the equi-utility curves. Given the price

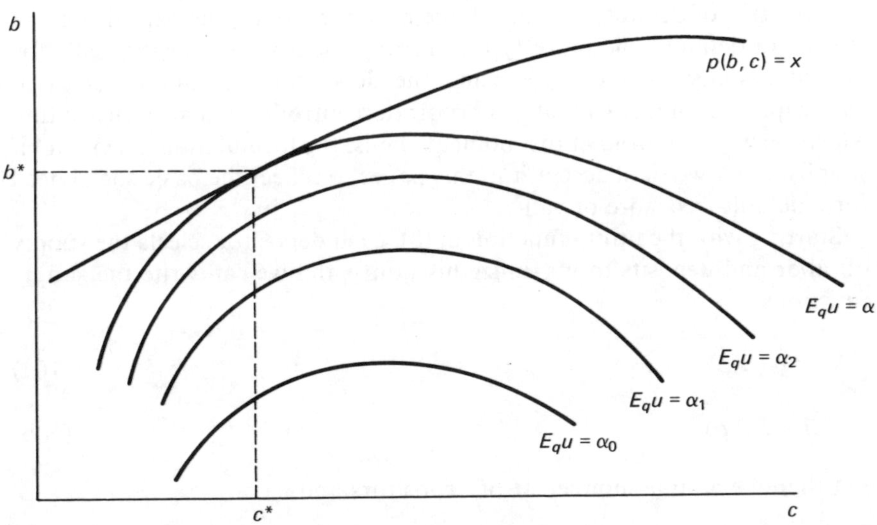

Figure 16.1

schedule ($\tilde{p}(b,c)$ the borrower optimizes by selecting (b^*,c^*) on the price schedule.

1.2 The Depositors

As we stated earlier the depositors provide labor services to the entrepreneurs and deposits to the intermediary. They have a utility function of the form

$$v(e,ew-d,(1+\rho)d) \tag{8}$$

where e = labor effort in period 1
ew = labor income in period 1
d = deposits which are, in fact, savings in period 1
ρ = the *sure* rate of return on deposits, making $(1+\rho)d$ the income earned in the second period.

A more complex formulation of the depositor's problem would allow the depositors to have a fraction λ of their savings in deposits with sure return ρ and $(1-\lambda)$ of their savings in risky investments with a random return denoted by r. Thus, the borrower would want to select (e,d,λ) to maximize

$$E_r v(e,ew-d,(1+\rho)\lambda d+(1+r)(1-\lambda)d). \tag{9}$$

One problem with formulation (9) is that it forces the small depositor to take the risk of default: if r takes large negative values, the depositors will also be in default. The more typical arrangement in our society calls for limited liability so that $r \geqq -1$ and the depositor may not be declared bankrupt. The limited liability corporation introduces a new institution which we want to avoid at the moment. Thus, the formulation in (8) is a bit simplistic but we shall accept it in this paper to reflect the basic social need for a default-free store of value.

Starting with the utility function in (8), each depositor selects the supply of labor and deposits to maximize his utility and we can write the supply functions

$$e=e(w,\rho) \tag{10a}$$

$$d=d(w,\rho). \tag{10b}$$

Let there be a large number M of depositors and let

$$L^s=eM \tag{11a}$$

$$D^s = dM. \tag{11b}$$

We then have the aggregate supply of labor and deposits

$$L^s = L^s(w,\rho) \tag{12a}$$

$$D^s = D^s(w,\rho). \tag{12b}$$

Since the medium of exchange – store of value in this economy is a real commodity, we shall assume that consumers–depositors have a storage-free technology in which any part of their wealth can be stored from period 1 to period 2. This means that depositors will not deposit their money with a financial intermediary if he charges them a fee $\rho < 0$ in order to store their wealth. This assumption of 'free storage' by each depositor can then be formulated as

Assumption A.1 (free storage): $D^s(w,\rho) = 0$ if $\rho < 0$.

Given the above we shall say that the economy is a *Lombard Economy* (or *Lombardian* or '*autarchy*') if $\rho = 0$ and the intermediary ensures the depositor's capital by simply storing it without lending any of the funds to the entrepreneurs–borrowers. Naturally, in a Lombard economy there is no distinction between the intermediary retaining the deposits for the sole purpose of safe-keeping and the depositors storing the money on their own.

1.3 The Intermediary

The intermediary ('bank', 'financial institution', or other such organization) receives the amount B of deposits and lends to each borrower an amount b defined simply by $b = (1/N)B$ where N is the (large) number of entrepreneurs. From the loan to a random entrepreneur i the profits of the intermediary can be defined by

$$\Pi_i = \begin{cases} \dfrac{(b+c)}{1+\alpha w} q_i - b(1+\rho) & \text{if } q_i \leqslant \dfrac{b(1+p)}{(b+c)}(1+\alpha w) \\[2ex] b(1+p) - b(1+\rho) & \text{if } q_i \geqq \dfrac{b(1+p)}{b+c}(1+\alpha w). \end{cases} \tag{13}$$

Equation (13) assumes that the intermediary *guarantees* the depositors a return ρ and if a loan to entrepreneur i is in default (i.e. $q_i \leqslant [b(1+p)/(b+c)](1+\alpha w)$), then it is the intermediary who will repay the depositors the interest and principal. Since the intermediary only transfers capital from depositors to entrepreneurs, it is entirely reasonable to think of the firms as the real agents owing the capital to the borrowers. However, the firms cannot, on their own, *guarantee* the depositors that they will be repaid. It is therefore also useful to think of the intermediary *as providing the firms the generally unavailable default insurance*. This point requires further elaboration.

The most important and unique aspect of the credit market is found in the fact that the institution providing the service of credit intermediation is, in fact, providing two services *simultaneously*: the first is 'credit' and the second is 'default insurance'. If a bank or a savings and loan association loans the funds of their depositors to a borrower, it also gives the borrower bankruptcy insurance in the sense that it will pay the depositors if the borrower defaults. This act of selling a 'basket' of two commodities combined in one package arises since there is no market for bankruptcy insurance and the borrower cannot purchase this service separately. The customary insurance which the intermediary offers does not extend beyond the loans it gives the borrower, so that if the borrower loses everything the intermediary loses only his loan. However, there can be instances in which q_i, the gross return of the firm i, is negative and with $q_i < 0$ it appears in (13) as if the intermediary may insure other obligations of the firm. This would be an unrealistic assumption which we do not wish to make. To avoid it we need to replace q_i in (13) with $\text{Max}\,[0, q_i]$ indicating that the intermediary can take any *positive* assets of the defaulting firm. But then, for mathematical simplicity, we restrict the analysis to $q_i \geqq 0$ and assume:

Assumption A.2: q_i are non-negative random variables.

Using the notation $l = (b/b + c)(1 + \alpha w)$ (13) can be written as

$$\frac{\Pi_i}{b} = \begin{cases} (p - \rho) - \frac{1}{l}[l(1+p) - q_i] & \text{if } q_i \leqslant l(1+p) \\ (p - \rho) & \text{if } q_i \geqq l(1+p) \end{cases} \tag{14}$$

This brings us to the structure of the random variable q_i. The assumption made here is

Assumption A.3: $q_i = z_i s,\ z_i \geqq \underline{z},\ s \geqq \underline{s}$.

z_i is a random variable measuring the outcome of the economic activity which is unique to the firm and s is a random component due to the macroeconomic environment and is common to all firms. The distinction between z_i, measuring the inherent productivity of each firm, and the effect of external, macroeconomic forces impacting the firm is central to this paper. The crucial observation made here is that although the intermediary, acting as a mutual fund, will attempt to *reduce* the risk of his loan portfolio, he cannot *remove* the risk since the q_i are correlated. Assumption 3 simply expresses the structure and reasons for this correlation. To interpret this assumption we may consider two examples. A bank in the South West who lends a great deal to oil operators can easily diversify against the various risks involved in discovering oil and operating oil wells. The main concerns of such a bank are related to the risks which are common to all the operators: lower oil prices, reduction in demand due to a recession, or the discovery of alternate sources of energy, etc. Similarly, a bank lending heavily to farmers can diversify against the risks which are unique to each of the farms but must sustain the risks which are common to all the farms: prices, demand, weather, technology, etc. The crucial assumption made in this paper is that s represents a common risk factor to all firms and as such becomes an uninsurable risk. Our problem is to find out how a competitive economy allocates uninsurable risks.

For simplicity of analysis we shall make the following assumptions:

A.5: Conditional on s the z_i are non-negative random variables i.i.d. with finite variance.

A.6: The joint distribution of z and s is known and it has a density. They are denoted $F_{zs}(\cdot,\cdot)$ and $f_{zs}(\cdot,\cdot)$.

In dividing his total supply of loans B into small loans of size B/N the intermediary diversifies his portfolio and reduces the risk that the default of any small group of projects may endanger the intermediary itself. In essence, the intermediary is using the law of large numbers to diversify the idiosyncratic risks which are unique to the firms. Turning to the lower bounds $\underline{z}$ and $\underline{s}$, we note that it is possible that any particular project will have such a disastrous outcome that z_i should be allowed to be $z_i=0$. The possibility of $z_i<0$ arises since a project may cause damage to other people's properties and such liabilities could arise. For simplicity we ignore $z_i<0$ and allow only $z_i \geqq 0$ by assuming $\underline{z}=0$. The macroeconomic risks are a bit different. There is always the possibility of events such as a nuclear war or a planetary catastrophy which will destroy all economic activity. To allow for such events $s=0$ may be possible. We provide below a brief analysis of the case $\underline{s}=0$ but consider it, perhaps, a bit extreme. Concentrating on the external, macroeconomic causes of default, one notes that even in the Great Depression not all firms in a given industry went bankrupt and to model this, we shall allow $\underline{s}>0$. Under this assumption q_i can take the value 0 only if $z_i=0$ (since $q_i=z_i s$ and $s \geqq \underline{s}>0$).

From (14) we can write the profit of the intermediary from a loan to firm i as

$$\frac{\Pi_i}{b} = \begin{cases} (p-\rho) - \frac{1}{l}(l(1+p) - z_i s) & \text{if } z_i \leqslant \frac{l}{s}(1+p) \\ p-\rho & \text{if } z_i > \frac{l}{s}(1+p). \end{cases} \tag{15}$$

Proposition 1: The aggregate profit function of the intermediary is approximated by the random function

$$\Pi_s = B \left\{ (p-\rho) - \frac{1}{l} \int_0^{(l/s)(1+p)} F_z(x)dx \right\} . \tag{16}$$

Proof: Starting from (15) the profit function is defined by

$$\Pi = \sum_{i=1}^{N} \Pi_i$$

however, conditional on s, the Π_i are i.i.d. so that for large N

$$\sum_{i=1}^{N} \Pi_i \doteqdot NE_{z_i}(\Pi_i|s).$$

But

$$E_{z_i}\frac{(\Pi_i|s)}{b} = (p+\rho) - \frac{1}{l}\int_0^{(l/s)(1+p)} (l(1+p) - z_i s) f_z(z_i)dz_i \tag{17}$$

$$= (p-\rho) - \frac{1}{l}\left[l(1+p)F_z\left(\frac{l}{s}(1+p)\right) + s\int_0^{(l/s)(1+p)} z_i f_z(z_i)dz_i \right].$$

Integration by parts yields

$$\int_0^{(l/s)(1+p)} z_i f_z(z_i)dz_i = \frac{l}{s}(1+p)F_z\left(\frac{l}{s}(1+p)\right) - \int_0^{(l/s)(1+p)} F_z(x)dx. \tag{18}$$

Combining (17), (18) and the condition $Nb = B$ we obtain the desired result. □

Introduce now the following notation

$$\pi_s = \frac{\Pi_s}{B}.$$

Given the profit function (16) of the intermediary we see that the risk he faces is drastically different from the risks of the individual borrowers. Whereas each borrower faces the risk of the random return $q_i = z_i s$ the intermediary faces only the aggregate risk s.

Having established the random profit function of the intermediary we can state his optimization problem. We assume that the owners of the intermediary have a utility function $U(\cdot,\cdot)$ and initial wealth W. The intermediary receives the amount B from depositors, consumes $W-R$ in period 1, and lends to the firms $B+\lambda R$. The amount $(1-\lambda)R$ is left for reserve. Now define

$$C_s = \text{Max}\,[0,(B+\lambda R)\pi_s + (1-\lambda)R] \tag{19}$$

and the intermediary's problem is the maximization of

$$E_s U(W-R, C_s) \tag{20a}$$

subject to

A guarantee to the borrowers that they are certain to receive back their deposits plus interest on their deposits. (20b)

It is restriction (20b) which is the crux of the problem. To see it, we analyze first the case $\underline{s}=0$. As we have stated earlier we regard $\underline{s}=0$ as a bit extreme and present it here mostly as an illustration of the issues involved.

1.4 Equilibrium when $\underline{s}=0$

For the case $\underline{s}=0$ we have the immediate observation:

Proposition 2: Under the postulated conditions, if $\underline{s}=0$, it is not feasible for the intermediary to ensure the safety of all deposits and any competitive economy must necessarily be a Lombard economy.

Proof: From (16), it follows that ensuring the safety of the deposits and the interest on the deposits means that $\Pi_s \geq 0$ for all s. However, for $s=0$ we have

$$\Pi_0 = -(1+\rho)B$$

Hence the intermediary cannot insure against $s=0$. □

Let s^* be defined by

$$\int_0^{(l/s^*)(1+p)} F_z(x)dx = l(p-\rho).$$

It is then clear that $\Pi_s < 0$ for all $s \in [0,s^*]$.

The difficulty of the intermediary in providing default insurance to the depositors is not local to $s=0$. Consider the derivative of Π_s with respect to s at $s=0$. Even if we assume in (17) that z_i and s are independent, it follows that

$$\frac{\partial \pi_s}{\partial s} = \frac{1}{l}\left[(l(1+p) - \frac{l}{s}(1+p)s) f_z\left(\frac{l}{s}(1+p)\right)\right] \frac{l(1+p)}{s^2} +$$

$$+ \frac{1}{l}\int_0^{(l/s)(1+p)} z_i f_z(z_i) dz_i = \frac{1}{l}\int_0^{(l/s)(1+p)} z_i f_z(z_i) dz_i > 0.$$

Hence

$$\frac{\partial \pi_s}{\partial s}\bigg|_{s=0} = \frac{1}{l}\int_0^{\infty} z_i f_z(z_i) dz_i = \frac{\mu_z}{l}.$$

This demonstrates that around $s=0$ the slope of π is modest so that the probability of s falling in the interval $[0,s^*]$ is significant. In Figure 16.2 we show a typical relationship between Π_s and s.

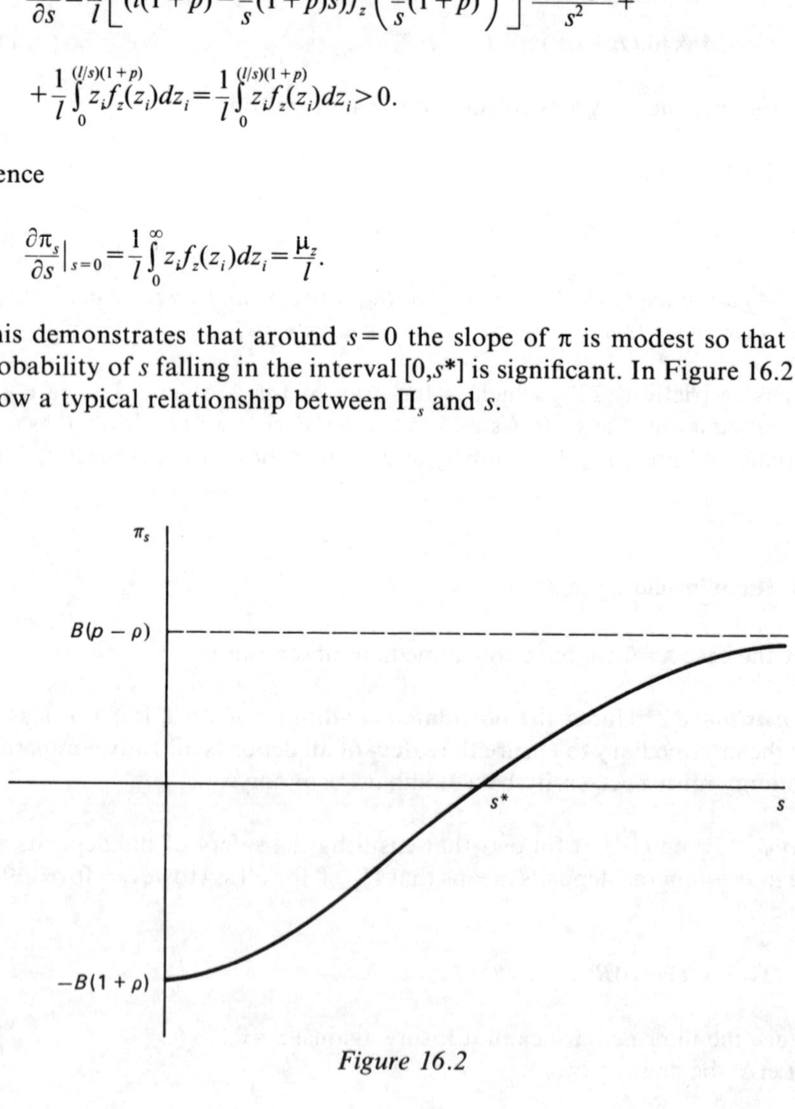

Figure 16.2

It then follows that even if the intermediary wanted to provide the depositors an 'approximate' insurance of their accounts by providing a probability of default 'close' to zero, he may not have enough resources to do so.

Now suppose $\rho = 0$ and assume that the intermediary has some equity capital of his own which we have denoted by R (to indicate the notion of 'reserves'). An examination of these circumstances reveals that even in this case the amount of deposits which the intermediary can ensure is no more than R, but then he does not need to take any of the depositor's capital and could use his own. In such a case the economy is a Lombard economy with $B = 0$ and the intermediary becomes an equity investor in the firms. His problem is the simple optimization

$$\underset{(\lambda, R)}{\text{Max}}\ E_s U(W - R, \lambda R \pi_s + (1 - \lambda R). \tag{21}$$

In such a Lombard equilibrium total investments is $(\lambda R + C)$, where C is the aggregate equity of the borrowers and the amount of labor employed is

$$L = \alpha \frac{\lambda R + C}{1 + \alpha w}. \tag{22}$$

The inability to provide the depositors default insurance has wide-ranging external effects in the economy. In competitive equilibrium $B = 0$, the level of investment is low, the demand for labor and the wage-rate are lower than they would be relative to the economy where default insurance can be available. In the case $\underline{s} = 0$ it is simply not feasible to provide default insurance. Under such circumstances public policy providing insurance to depositors is the only way for society to move from the Lombard economy to an economy with higher level of activity. Note, however, that public insurance under these circumstances is an illusion since society cannot ensure against $s = \underline{s} = 0$. However, if the probability of $s = \underline{s}$ is small, society may prefer to act as if depositors are insured against such an event. We turn now to study the case $\underline{s} > 0$ where it is feasible for society to provide some insurance. The study of competitive equilibrium and the externalities involved is the main objective of our next section.

1.5 Optimum of the Intermediary when $\underline{s} > 0$

We now analyze the more complex case $\underline{s} > 0$ for which it is feasible for the intermediary to offer default insurance to some of the depositors and satisfy constraint (20b). For this it is necessary that

$$(B + \lambda R)\pi_s + (1 - \lambda)R \geqq 0 \quad \text{for all } s. \tag{23}$$

This insurance constraint demands from the intermediary to have adequate reserves even at $\underline{s}$ to meet the obligations to the depositors. Since the idle funds $(1-\lambda)R$ do not earn anything the constraint at $\underline{s}$ is

$$(B+\lambda R)\left[(p-\rho)-\frac{1}{l}\int_0^{l/s(1+p)} f_z(x)dx\right]+(1-\lambda)R=0$$

or

$$(B+\lambda R)=\frac{(1-\lambda)R}{(-\pi_{\underline{s}})} \tag{24}$$

(Note: $\pi_{\underline{s}} \leqslant 0$, otherwise there is no restriction.)

Now, the problem of the intermediary is

$$\underset{(R,B,\lambda)}{\text{Max}}\, E_s U(W-R,(B+\lambda R)\pi_s+(1-\lambda R) \tag{25}$$

subject to the insurance constraint (24). It is clear that this problem can be restated as

$$\underset{(R,\lambda)}{\text{Max}}\, E_s U\left(W-R,(1-\lambda)R\left(\frac{\pi_s}{-\pi_{\underline{s}}}\right)+(1-\lambda)R\right). \tag{26}$$

The first-order conditions of this problem are

$$\frac{\partial E_s U}{\partial R}=-E_s U_1+E_s U_2\left[(1-\lambda)\frac{\pi_s-\pi_{\underline{s}}}{(-\pi_{\underline{s}})}\right] \tag{27a}$$

$$\frac{\partial E_s U}{\partial \lambda}=-E_s U_2 R\left[\frac{\pi_s-\pi_{\underline{s}}}{(-\pi_{\underline{s}})}\right]. \tag{27b}$$

However, $[\pi_s-\pi_{\underline{s}}/(-\pi_{\underline{s}})]>0$ for all s; hence $\partial E_s U/\partial\lambda<0$ for all λ; hence $\lambda^*=0$. We have thus proved:

Proposition 3: The intermediary never takes an equity position in the firms to whom he lends and thus $\lambda^*=0$.

The solution of the optimum problem of the intermediary is now completed and is characterized by the two conditions

optimum $$E_s U_1=E_s U_2\left[\frac{\pi_s-\pi_{\underline{s}}}{-\pi_{\underline{s}}}\right] \tag{28a}$$

insurance $\quad B \leqslant \frac{R}{(-\pi_s)}$ (28b)

This induces the supply function of reserves R and the demand for deposits.

2. EQUILIBRIUM

In setting up the basis for the analysis of equilibrium we need to specify first the allowable equilibrium non-linear price functions $p(\cdot)$ discussed earlier. For this function to provide a signal to borrowers it must depend upon the observed characteristics of the borrowers and parameters demanded by the intermediary. We have already noted that from the optimization of the borrowers we see that p may be selected from the class of functions of the form (we reproduce here):

$$p=\tilde{p}(b,c,x). \tag{6}$$

On the other hand, examination of the profit function of the intermediary from any loan suggests (see (14)) that the expected profits per dollar of loans is defined by

$$E\pi=(p-\rho)-\frac{1}{l}\int_0^{l(1+p)}(l(1+p)-q)f_q(q)dq.$$

If the intermediary requires an expected profit rate π then the equation

$$p-\rho-\frac{1}{l}\int_0^{l(1+p)}(l(1+p)-q)f_q(q)dq=\pi \tag{29}$$

exactly defines a relationship like (6). To put it differently, the solution of (29) can be written

$$p=p(l,\rho+\pi). \tag{30a}$$

The interesting difference between (6) and (30a) is seen as follows: Let ρ^* be an equilibrium deposit rate and π^* be an equilibrium profit rate of the intermediary. In such an equilibrium, each borrower faces a non-linear equilibrium interest rate schedule of the form

$$p-p^*(l,\rho^*+\pi^*)=0$$

where $p^*(\cdot)$ is the solution of (29). The borrower selects optimal l^* as well as an optimal pair (b^*,c^*). However, given that l^* was selected and since

$$l^* = \frac{b}{b+c}(1+\alpha w^*),$$

the non-linear price restriction imposes upon the borrower the requirement of selecting optimal (b,c) from the allowable set

$$b = c\frac{1}{[(1+\alpha w^*/l^*)-1]} \quad 0 \leqslant c \leqslant A. \tag{30b}$$

This means that in drawing Figure 16.1 we need to specify the equilibrium price schedule as *a linear relation between* b *and* c with a slope of $(l^*/1+\alpha w^* - l^*)$. Also note that (30b) implies that the amount of loan granted in equilibrium will be exactly proportional to the collateral of the borrower.

We can rewrite (29) as

$$p = \rho + \pi + \frac{1}{l}\int_0^{l(1+p)}(l(1+p)-q)f_q(q)dq \tag{29'}$$

where in (29′) the interest rate p is decomposed into three components:

(i) ρ – the borrowing cost of the intermediary

(ii) π – the profit rate per unit of borrowed capital to compensate the intermediary for the equity capital R

(iii) $\frac{1}{l}\int_0^{l(1+p)}(l(1+p)-q)f_q(q)dq$ – the premium per unit of deposit to cover the cost of bankruptcy.

2.1 Definition of Equilibrium

To present the definition of equilibrium we recapitulate earlier concepts by taking as given the price function (30a) (in comparison with (6), b is not included and $x = \rho + \pi$).

(a) *Borrowers*

The aggregate demand of borrowers for loans and labor as well as their offered leverage is summarized in the three functions

$$B^d = B^d(w, \rho + \pi) \quad \text{(demand for loans)} \tag{31a}$$

$$B^d + C = \varphi(w, \rho + \pi), \; L^d = \alpha\frac{\varphi(w, \rho+\pi)}{1+\alpha w} \quad \text{(demand for labor)} \tag{31b}$$

$$l = l(w,\rho+\pi). \tag{31c}$$

(b) *The Depositors* define in (12a)–(12b) their supply of labor and deposits

$$L^s = L^s(w,\rho) \quad \text{(supply of labor)} \tag{31d}$$

$$D^s = D^s(w,\rho) \quad \text{(supply of deposits)} \tag{31e}$$

(c) *The Intermediary* defines his supply of equity capital

$$R = R(\rho,\rho+\pi,l), \quad \text{(supply of reserves – defining the supply of loans)} \tag{31f}$$

and consequently his demand for deposits (which equals his supply of loans) is

$$D^d = D^d(\rho,\rho+\pi,l) \quad \text{(demand for deposits).} \tag{31g}$$

We specifically keep l in (31g) to signify *the basic externalities involved in the equilibrium at hand*: the behavior of borrowers influences the profits and thus the behavior of the intermediary.

Definition: An equilibrium is a price function $p^*(l,\rho+\pi)$ and a triple (ρ^*,π^*,w^*) such that

1. $L^s(w^*,\rho^*) = \alpha\dfrac{\varphi(w^*,\rho^*+\pi^*)}{1+\alpha w^*}$

2. $B^d(w^*,\rho^*+\pi^*) = D^d(\rho^*,\rho^*+\pi^*,l(w^*,\rho^*+\pi^*))$

3. $D^s(w^*,\rho^*) \geqq D^d(\rho^*,\rho^*+\pi^*,l(w^*,\rho^*+\pi^*))$

4. $\rho^* \geqq 0$

2.2 Rationing in Equilibrium

There are two factors which have a crucial effect on a competitive equilibrium in this economy. First, $\rho \geqq 0$ otherwise the economy will fall into a Lombard autarchy. Second, the profit rate π^* which can be experienced by the intermediary is severely limited by the incentive structure of depositors and borrowers. To see this let us return to equation (29). Although this equation *defines p*, in equilibrium l itself is also a function of $\rho+\pi$. Hence let $(p^*(\cdot),\rho^*,\pi^*,w^*)$ be an equilibrium. Holding (ρ^*,π^*,w^*) fixed, let us perturb the function p by varying it in the simple linear way

$$p^*(l,\rho^*+\pi^*)+\delta \quad \text{(thus, in fact, raising } \pi^*\text{)}.$$

This reflects the idea of 'raising' or 'lowering' the price when 'the price' is, in fact, a non-linear function. Let $l(\delta)$ be the response of l to the change in p as specified in (32). Now define the profits of the intermediary under the perturbation δ by $\theta(\delta)$:

$$\theta(\delta)=(p^*+\delta)-\rho^*-\frac{1}{l(\delta)}\int_0^{l(\delta)(1+p^*+\delta)}(l(\delta)(1+p^*+\delta)-q)f_q(q)dq. \tag{33}$$

Then

$$\theta'(\delta)=1+\frac{l'(\delta)}{l^2(\delta)}\int_0^{l(1+p^*+\delta)}(l(1+p^*+\delta)-q)f_q dq$$

$$-\frac{1}{l(\delta)}\int_0^{l(1+p^*+\delta)}[l'(1+p^*+\delta)+l]f_q(q)dq.$$

Hence we have

$$\theta'(\delta)=1-F_q(l(1+p^*+\delta))-\frac{l'(\delta)}{l^2(\delta)}\int_0^{l(1+p^*+\delta)}qf_q(x)dx. \tag{34}$$

Lemma 1: $l'(\delta)>0$. Thus, whenever the price p is raised the borrowers increase their desired leverage.

Proof: From (5) the optimization of a borrower is defined by the following problem: let $\zeta=l(1+p^*+\delta)$

$$\max_{(b,l)} \quad u\left(A-b\left(\frac{1+\alpha w}{l}-1\right),0\right)F(\zeta) \tag{35}$$

$$+\int_\zeta^\infty u\left(A-b\left(\frac{1+\alpha W}{l}-1\right),\frac{b}{l}(q+\zeta)\right)f(q)dq$$

Defining the maximand in (35) to be $\psi(l,b,\delta)$, the conditions for maximization imply

$$\psi_l=\psi_b=0$$

$$\psi_{ll}<0 \quad \psi_{bb}<0.$$

Given the maximization we want to compute

$$\frac{dl}{d\delta}=-\frac{\psi_{l\delta}}{\psi_{ll}}$$

but since $\psi_{ll}<0$ the sign of $dl/d\delta$ is determined by $\psi_{l\delta}$. An elementary calculation shows that

$$\psi_{l\delta}=\int_0^{l(1+p^*+\delta)} u_2 f_q(x)dx>0$$

hence

$$\frac{dl}{d\delta}>0. \qquad \square$$

Returning now to (34) we note that

$$\theta'(\delta)\rightarrow 1 \quad \text{as } \delta\rightarrow -(1+p)$$

and

$$\theta'(\delta)\rightarrow -\mu_q\frac{l'(\delta)}{l^2(\delta)}<0 \quad \text{as } \delta \text{ becomes large.}$$

Typically, the curve $\theta(\delta)$ will look like the one depicted in Figure 16.3a. This analysis leads us to our second lemma.

Lemma 2: In any equilibrium (p^*,ρ^*,π^*,w^*) an increase in the interest rate may either increase or decrease the profits of the intermediary. The profit function $\theta(\delta)$ is rising for small δ and falling for large δ, reaching a maximum at $\delta=\delta^*$ (for some δ^*).

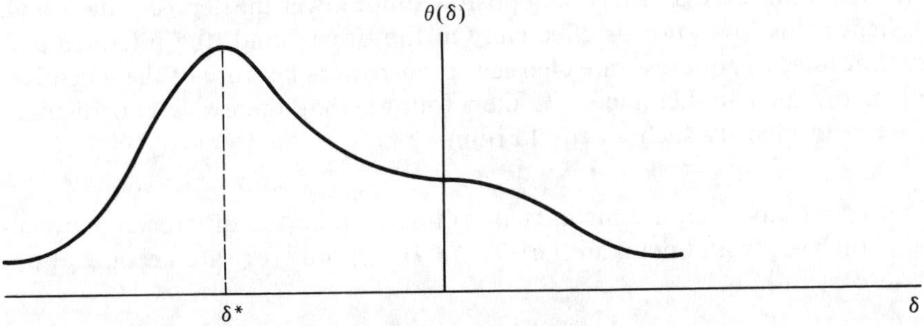

Figure 16.3a

The interpretation of Lemma 2 is of real interest. We have assumed that the firms have constant returns to scale technology and are not facing declining prices for their products. This 'Constant Returns Revenue' environment is modelled to create the best analytical environment for the intermediary to face strong demand for credit. Yet, when we examine (34) we find that even under such conditions $\theta(\delta)$ is composed of three terms:

(i) 1 – indicates that an increase in δ increases π since $\theta=\pi$.

(ii) F_q – indicates the decrease in profit rate due to the fact that increased interest rate increases the direct probability of default.

(iii) $-\dfrac{l'(\delta)}{l^2(\delta)}\int_0^{l(1+p^*+\delta)} qf_q(x)dx$ – indicates the effect of the incentive constraint: as the interest rate increases the borrowers opt for a more leveraged composition of investments and increased leverage always works to reduce the profits of the intermediary (through an *indirect* increase in the probability of default).

Thus, *the crucial factors operating here are the externalities generated by the default possibility of the firm.* These externalities result from the fact that the optimal allocation of the firm influences the profit rate of the intermediary and hence *raising the interest rate may cause profits to rise or fall.* This is obviously the first crucial step in understanding why credit rationing would be necessary in equilibrium.

We now turn to the examination of an equilibrium. In a typical equilibrium the insurance constraint

$$B=\frac{R}{(-\pi_s)}$$

will be binding. This will be the case when the supply of deposits is greater than the amount which the intermediary has the resources to insure. On the one hand, this excess supply of deposits cannot lower the deposit rate below 0, hence this limitation is effective. On the other hand, the intermediary cannot raise the interest rate charged to borrowers because of the incentive effect revealed in Lemma 2. It then follows that there are two distinct criteria to identify such an equilibrium:

(i) $\rho^*=0$ and the intermediary is willing to take the difference between the supply and demand (i.e. $D^s(\cdot)-D^d(\cdot)$) only for safe-keeping at no cost to him.

(ii) Any offer by a rationed borrower to pay a higher price (a higher interest rate than p^*) is not acceptable to the intermediary. This means that in Figure 16.3*a* if $p^*(l^*,\rho^*+\pi^*)$ is an equilibrium then

$$\rho^*=0$$

$$\theta(0)=\pi^*$$

$$\delta^*=0$$

$$\theta'(0)=0$$

and we can draw Figure 16.3b as illustrated. This leads us to the basic proposition of this paper:

Proposition 4: There are two types of equilibria in this economy: unrationed and rationed. In *unrationed* equilibria

(i) $D^s(w^*,\rho^*)=D^d(\rho^*,\rho^*+\pi^*,l(w^*,\rho^*+\pi^*))$

(ii) $\rho^*>0$

(iii) the insurance constraint $R^*\geqq B^*\cdot(-\underline{\pi_s})$ is not binding

(iv) $\pi^*=\theta^*(0)$ but $\theta'(0)\neq 0$.

In *rationed* equilibria

(i) $D^s(w^*,\rho^*)>D^d(\rho^*,\rho^*+\pi^*,l(w^*,\rho^*+\pi^*))$

(ii) $\rho^*=0$

(iii) the insurance constraint $R^*=B^*\cdot(-\underline{\pi_s})$ is binding

(iv) $\pi^*=\theta^*(0)$ and $\theta^{*\prime}(0)=0$.

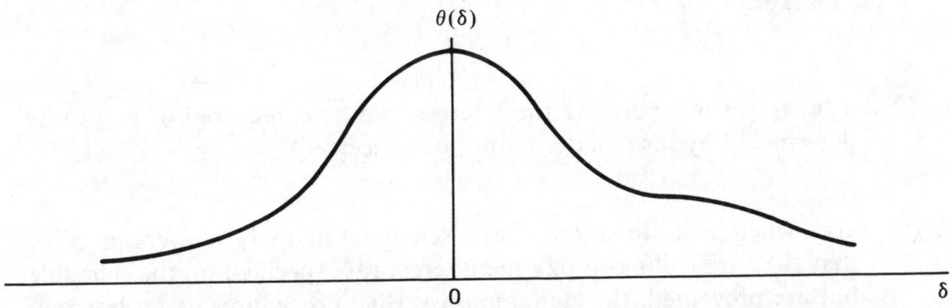

Figure 16.3b

The proposition clarifies the two basic causes of rationing equilibria. On the one hand, the externalities in the credit markets set limits on the effectivness of prices as a rationing device. On the other hand, we attempted to use the depositors in order to model the social need for a default-free store of value and medium of exchange. If the value of $\underline{s}$ is so small that the aggregate loss is too great or the amount of resources available for intermediation is too small, the equilibrium could be nearly a Lombard equilibrium. The social cost in terms of lost investment, employment opportunities, and aggregate output is far greater than the loss perceived by each depositor. To explain this externality, assume for a moment that it is not feasible for depositors to store their own 'gold' at home and the intermediaries are the only vehicle to create a store of value over time. In that case, a competitive equilibrium with $\rho < 0$ may be established and such an equilibrium may not entail rationing. What we are saying is that the depositors may perceive ρ to be a real cost of intertemporal allocation of resources but they may still be better off with $\rho < 0$ than with $\rho = 0$ together with a rationing equilibrium. This is so since with $\rho < 0$ the depositors will end up with a higher wage-rate and the economy will have a higher level of investment and output. Thus, the private optimizations of depositors which result in $\rho \geqq 0$, induce economy-wide externalities which justify the heavy involvement of the Central Bank in deposit insurance, reserve requirement, and equity requirements imposed on the banking system.

On the other side of the market, the intermediary faces a large number of borrowers, each asking for a loan b^*. Since the aggregate supply of funds available is not sufficient for all, some rationing must take place. One interpretation of the rationing is that the intermediary will simply establish a rule for selection of those excluded, while those included are allowed to select the optimal pair (b^*, c^*) as specified above. Alternatively, the intermediary may calculate the equilibrium l^* and select a fixed level of c^{**} and b^{**} consistent with l^* such that every borrower will be *required* to have a collateral c^{**} and each applicant will receive $b^{**} < b^*$. Our theory does not propose any specific rationing device. It does suggest that a borrower will experience two aspects of rationing both of which are explicitly recognized in the market:

(i) a borrower will perceive the interest rate he is required to pay to be determined by his collateral and loan received.

(ii) even when given the interest rate schedule, many borrowers perceive that they are willing to pay the interest rate specified on the schedule but are prevented, through administrative procedures, from borrowing as much as they wanted.

3 PUBLIC POLICY

There are many aspects of banking history in the United States which are supportive of the theory proposed in this chapter. Banks and other intermediaries have traditionally advertized their assets, their past record of stability, and their federal insurance affiliation in order to demonstrate their ability to provide default insurance. In accord with our Proposition 3, banks have generally not taken equity risk positions and such has been the policy followed by the Federal Reserve. Moreover, for a very long time, banks did not offer interest on deposits and thus effectively the default-free nominal interest rate on deposits was zero. These and other empirical observations are consistent with the model without public policy presented in this chapter. However, the deep effects of the public sector in general and the central bank in particular cannot be ignored and any empirical observation made relative to modern time must take these effects into consideration.

In terms of the theory proposed here there are three fundamental effects of the public sector on the functioning of the credit markets in modern times:

(i) The expansion and strengthening of federal insurance to a point where a significant weight of the default insurance of depositors has been shifted to the public sector.

(ii) The great proliferation of near-money *default-free* financial instruments which are issued by the US Treasury and are interest-bearing and easily available in relatively small denominations. These are mostly treasury bills, and short-term notes issued by the US Treasury.

(iii) The post-war public perception that government policy can prevent both depressions like the Great Depression of the 1930s as well as waves of bank defaults even when serious recessions do occur.

These factors are clearly not included in the government-free model presented earlier. On the other hand, the analysis of the important externalities involved provides the important *justification* for the public sector's intervention in this market. But now that public policy is in place, the nature of the equilibrium changed and the evaluation of any empirical observation must take this fact into account. One must recognize that a formal analysis of a complete model with a central bank and public policy is yet to be developed, and for this reason the discussion below is in the nature of conjectures and suggestions for future research.

We start by noting that public policy has been a complex mixture of a policy aiming to protect the banking system from default and monetary policy that aims to regulate the aggregate money supply. Banks have been needing to meet both equity requirements as well as reserve requirements, both of which restrict the credit creation ability of the banking system as well as ensure that banks can honor their default insurance obligations. Both the central bank and the federal insurance corporations came into being only after a long history of massive waves of bank failures. The evidence of such waves suggests that our earlier model excludes a potentially important problem arising from the asymmetric information between the depositors and the intermediary enabling the bank to 'cheat' by violating the no-default constraint. By extending credit beyond the constraint, the banks open the door to simultaneous waves of default. Surely the depositors must have recognized the risk of default under this environment of incomplete information. The equilibrium under such circumstances would, naturally, be different from the one we presented. Under the federal deposit insurance system the bank must still maintain the equity needed for default insurance but in this case the role of the Federal Insurance Corporation is to remove the information imperfection.

It is a well-known fact that although bank failures occur at a regular pace, many such failures are not necessarily arising from lack of equity but, rather, from insufficient liquidity to meet current obligations. Under such circumstances the federal insurance system usually arranges for a merger of the 'defaulting' bank with another institution and neither the depositors nor the federal government sustain any losses. However, another vast area of federal insurance which has expanded at an extremely rapid rate in the post-war period is the program of federal loan guarantees. In this capacity, the government simply replaces the financial intermediary as the provider of default insurance. The government has expanded dramatically its loan guarantees to students, veterans, home buyers, farmers, small businesses, local governments, and many other borrowers. In order to estimate the real public cost of default insurance, one needs to add to the premiums of the federal insurance corporations the actual losses on loan guarantees. These losses have always been significant but in recent years they have become alarmingly large. Interestingly enough, the most dramatic increases in losses occurred in loan guarantees to farmers, resulting precisely from the kind of uninsurable risks central to this paper. The kind of losses sustained by the government on these loans would have caused a major damage to the private banking system had these losses been sustained by it. Needless to add that the enormous potential losses on defaulting foreign loans would have had a devastating effect on the private banks had it not been the expectation that the government is providing some measure of insurance.

The shifting of the default insurance from the private banks to the public sector has occurred at a time when the US Treasury has been providing ever increasing amounts of near-money, default-free financial instruments. This reduction in the externalities of default risk in the private monetary system is surely one of the great achievements of economic policy in the twentieth century. If this proposition is accepted then it is easier to understand the current move to deregulate the banking system and permit banks to pay interest on their deposits. Given that individuals can easily buy treasury bills, banks are no longer only in the intermediary business outlined in our model above. When a bank sells a customer a certificate of deposit for $200,000, that customer, in fact, takes some risk of default since the federal government insures only $100,000 of his deposits. This insurance is hardly sufficient for the checking account of a small corporation. Thus, the bank is in the business of selling risky securities. On the other hand, the banks are now charging extensive fees for various services and small depositors are, in fact, paying a fee for small accounts. In addition, during most of the post-war period, the real rate of return on deposits was negative due to inflation. With these developments, it appears that the effective nominal interest rate paid on insured deposits is close to 0, and the real rate is mostly negative. However, note that the mean nominal return on treasury bills in the post-war period was around 4.6 per cent whereas the mean rate of inflation was 4.2 per cent. This suggests that *even with federal insurance of deposits of intermediaries or deposits in the form of Treasury bills, the real rate of return on default-free deposits in our economy remained essentially equal to 0 or perhaps negative.*

These important developments in financial markets have reduced the perceived private risk of default but are far from having removed it. The reduction in these externalities may very well have contributed to the dramatic expansion of credit institutions and credit instruments in the post-war period. One is tempted to conjecture that this same reason may explain why credit is less tightly rationed and more generally used in our society than a few generations ago. We also suspect that public default insurance may have gone a bit too far and the recent enormous losses on farm and foreign loans raise some intriguing questions regarding the optimal public policy in this area.

References

Baltensperger, E. (1976) 'The Borrower–Lender Relationship, Competitive Equilibrium and the Theory of Hedonic Prices', *American Economic Review*, 66: 401–5.

Freimer, M. and M. J. Gordon (1965) 'Why Bankers Ration Credit', *Quarterly Journal of Economics*, 79: 397–416.

Hammond, P. J. (1986) 'On the Impossibility of Perfect Capital Markets', IMSSS, Stanford University, mimeo.

Jaffee, D. (1971) *Credit Rationing and the Commercial Loan Market* (New York: John Wiley).

Jaffee, D. and T. Russell (1976) 'Imperfect Information and Credit Rationing', *Quarterly Journal of Economics*, 90: 651–66.

Keeton, W. R. (1979) *Equilibrium Credit Rationing* (New York and London: Garland Publishing).

Kurz, M. (1976) 'Quantity Constraints as Substitutes for Inoperative Markets: The Case of the Credit Markets', Technical Report No. 205, IMSSS, Stanford University.

Stigler, G. (1967) 'Imperfections in the Capital Market', *Journal of Political Economy,* 85: 287–92.

Stiglitz, J. E. (1970) 'Perfect and Imperfect Capital Markets', paper presented to the New Orleans meeting of the Econometric Society.

Stiglitz, J. E. (1972) 'Some Aspects of the Pure Theory of Corporate Finance: Bankruptcies and Take-Overs', *Bell Journal of Economics,* 3: 458–82.

Stiglitz, J. E. and A. Weiss (1981) 'Credit Rationing in Markets with Imperfect Information', *American Economic Review,* 71(3): 393–410.

Part VI

Keynes is 'Alive' and 'Well'

17 Testimony I: An interview

Robert M. Solow

Feiwel: Would you reflect on the varieties of Keynesian economics? What do you mean by Keynesian?

Solow: We have realized in the last two dozen years that there is more than one message of Keynesian economics; that the *General Theory* is not a single, unitary, consistent work. Many people write papers and books about what Keynes really meant. Can you imagine anyone writing a book about what Gerard Debreu really meant? No. One could not imagine such a book because there is only one single thing that Gerard Debreu means – and he writes it in such a way that it is unmistakable. I believe that the *General Theory* contains several strands of thought. These strands are often quite independent of one another and they are sometimes not very consistent with one another. Thus it is possible to read the *General Theory* down one line and produce a set of ideas that hang together to a certain extent and then say, 'This is what Keynes meant.' It is equally possible for someone else to dig in the same mine and produce a quite different set of ideas and then say, 'This is what Keynes really meant.' And they are both right! I do not believe it is possible to know what Keynes 'really, really' meant – and what is more, I do not even think it is important to know, except for antiquarian reasons. I think it is more important to remember that any body of scientific thought (I use the word scientific very broadly so that it includes even economics) is a collective product, not an individual product. The Darwinian theory of evolution is not 'what Darwin really meant' or what Darwin said; it is what a century of evolutionary biologists have made of it. I feel the same way about Keynesian economics.

For instance, it is clearly the case that from the point of view of the economics profession as a whole – certainly in North America – the IS-LM model has to a certain extent become Keynesian economics. It is what students read in the elementary and intermediate textbooks; it is what they learn to be Keynesian economics. It is perfectly plain to me that one can dig in Keynes's writings and produce a warrant to take the IS-LM model as one of the things that he did at some moments and in some moods mean (and perhaps in other moments and moods did not). When he saw Hicks's paper he rather approved of it. Joan, I think, used to say that was a moment of weakness; that is to say 'he did not ask me'. Perhaps ... nevertheless it is there. Like a large number of modern Keynesians, I rather approve of the IS-LM model. The IS-LM model is the way I think in practice. It is also the way many of the macro-economists – the day-to-day macroeconomists whom I think of as modern Keynesians – actually think. Suppose you wake up Jim Tobin, Paul Samuelson, or someone else in the middle of the night and say, 'The money supply has just gone up by X per cent, what will happen?' Without hardly waking up we will begin to draw IS-LM models in our minds and we will give answers derived from that. I believe the IS-LM model to be a legitimate version of Keynesian economics. It is crystal clear that it is not all of Keynes. Keynes would have balked dreadfully at the notion that that was all he was talking about.

In relation to the question of wage and price rigidity, Keynes did think that wages were generally rigid. He did not think that was the only reason for unemployment, or even that it was the fundamental reason for unemployment. But he thought that wages were rigid. In fact, in chapter 19 he claimed that it was a good thing that wages were rigid; if wages were flexible things would be worse. Clearly, however, Keynes would not have wanted anyone to say, 'Oh, well, it is just the rigid wage!'

The change of mind that I have had in the last dozen years or so about Keynesian economics is along these lines: in common with most American bastard Keynesians (by the way, I always liked the term 'bastard Keynesian' because it suggests hybrid vigor), I was for many years content to accept that Keynes's claim of having demonstrated the possibility of unemployment equilibrium (that is, equilibrium in a capitalist economy with involuntary unemployment) was a mere exaggeration. He said it because how else could he *épater les bourgeois* but by making this drastic statement? But he had done no such thing. I still believe, by the way, that by anything like modern standards of theoretical rigor, there is nothing remotely like a proof in the *General Theory* of the possibility of equilibrium with involuntary unemployment. There is not even a clear definition of what it could mean. So, I, in common with most bastard Keynesians, said: 'Well, it is enough for our purposes (for practical Keynesianism) even if there is no theory of underemployment equilibrium, that the capitalist economy is subject to very long periods of excessive unemployment, these are disequilibrium states, but disequilibrium states that correct themselves intolerably slowly from the point of view of economic policy. And that is all we need to provide an intellectual foundation for what one thinks of as activist Keynesian macroeconomic (demand-oriented) policy.' I went along with that view for a long time and wrote papers that embodied it. In the last half dozen years I have come around to the view that Keynes was actually wiser; that in some way he had grasped a notion of unemployment equilibrium he did not have the theoretical tools to make precise and to make a convincing case for. Only now are we beginning to have the theoretical tools to make it stick. This rests on modern notions of multiple equilibria. An economy can have several, even an infinity or continuum of, equilibria, some of which are Pareto dominated by others, and some of which have involuntary unemployment. There may also be a full employment equilibrium which the system has no way of achieving because it lacks an auctioneer.

In other words, I think that Keynes had an intuitive notion, that one can now make more precise, of the idea that willingness to trade is an externality. So that one can imagine an economy at rest, at a low level of economic activity, although it would be able to sustain itself at a much higher level of activity, if only there could be a concerted move from the bad equilibrium to the good one. Everybody in the low-level equilibrium produces a small amount because everybody else is producing a small amount and this limits the market. The Walrasian auctioneer could find the higher level equilibrium; the unaided economy cannot. This is now a commonplace amongst high-brow theorists, and even among macro-theorists, because of the experience we have had with Nash equilibrium in non-cooperative game theory. In that context there are often many Nash equilibria, some of which are inefficient, Pareto dominated by other Nash equilibria. Nevertheless, in a non-cooperative game such as the prisoner's dilemma – the most famous example of this – there is no way for the individual agents to achieve improvement except by converting it into a cooperative game. I think one could build a theory of economic policy on that notion of converting a non-cooperative game into a cooperative one. That is one strand in the *General Theory*, but only one strand and one that Keynes was incapable of developing.

This may sound sacrilegious. Keynes was easily the most important and extraordinarily brilliant economist of the twentieth century, but he was not a skilful theorist. Pigou could run rings around Keynes as a theorist, but Pigou lacked the insights that Keynes had. There are more important things than techniques.

Since there are all these parallel Keynesian worlds, I do not know that it makes sense to have real genealogies of modern Keynesians, these distinctions into pre-Keynesian, post-Keynesian, neo-Keynesian, and what not. That verges on idolatry and is never a very good idea. But there are things that anyone who has picked up the spirit in which the *General Theory* was written will believe. Namely, that the unmanaged capitalist system does not behave very well. There is a whole collection of reasons why Keynes thought the economy did not behave well. One of them is the possibility of deficient aggregate demand; in that case demand-oriented policy can do something about it.

Feiwel: Joan Robinson was a severe critic of the mainstream. How unorthodox were her own writings?

Solow: The early Joan, of *Imperfect Competition*, is straightforwardly within the mainstream. There is not *that* much difference between her and Chamberlin – though obviously there were some differences. I think that is why she repudiated it later in her life; because it identified her too much as one of *them*. In *The Accumulation of Capital* there is very little that is fundamentally unorthodox. My picture of Joan is someone using the standard apparatus, but commenting on it cynically from the outside, like a voice-over on a television program. Of course she would never have agreed to this characterization. But her departures from orthodoxy were mainly in the nature of iconoclastic remarks about the silliness or impracticality of the neoclassical intellectual program.

So, there is this image of Joan as a cynical mainstream economist. I rather liked that in her. It is altogether too easy for a modern mainstream economist to get wrapped up in the technical problems. I have done that and so have many of my colleagues ... and sometimes we have not thought enough about what we were actually saying about the economy and the extent to which what we said is belied by what any fool can plainly see happening in the world, and the extent to which there is ideological content in mainstream economics.

Once, at the end of the whole capital controversy, I made the parenthetic remark that to my eye it seems to have run into the sand – there is very little residue in economics today of all that argumentation. At the end of it, when I decided I had had enough, it seemed to me that it was fundamentally an ideological dispute, Joan, who spoke with a lot of resonance, was dominated by the notion that mainstream distribution theory was apologetics for the existing distribution of income. She thought that to say that interest is a return to the productivity of capital goods is somehow, by a piece of sleight of hand, to say that the capitalist deserves what she/he gets. There is no doubt that historically that was the origin of the neoclassical theory of capital. Böhm-Bawerk was after all explicitly replying to Marx. Whether they knew it or not (and they certainly knew it less than Böhm-Bawerk did) the other nineteenth-century economists were providing (amongst other things) an ideological framework for modern industrial capitalism. I have always thought that while mainstream economics does function that way, intellectually speaking, intrinsically it provides just as much raw material for a critique of capitalist distribution. It is not a Marx-like critique, but it certainly suggests that all the nice properties of an idealized capitalist, competitive market system are conditional on original endowments and the theory does not imply any entitlement of existing capitalists to their property, although they have bought it.

So Joan was seized of the notion that to say that interest is in some sense the marginal product of capital is equivalent to saying that just as the laborer is worthy of his hire so is the capitalist worthy of the reward he gets. If you ask 'what was the energy behind this discussion?' I think that is what provided the steam. And that was not something I was prepared to spend any energy on. My interest in the theory of capital owed nothing to apologetics for the distribution of income. Furthermore, the discussion was made much more difficult – and, of course, made me a very guilty party – by Joan's perception at the very beginning that the problem was somehow with the notion of aggregation, with real capital poorly defined as an aggregate and as a physical input into an aggregate production function. I was especially guilty because I was caught red handed. I was a practitioner of that sort of thing.

In fact, of course, if there was to be anything serious about Joan's critique, it had to be about hypothetical *n* commodity, *n* person, Walrasian general equilibrium, modified to allow for capitalistic, intertemporal production. There, for my money, it all ended in mystification; Joan did finally realize that she had to extend her attack to all Walrasian economics and there I *really* could not make head or tail out of what she said. She said things like: 'Walrasian economics is the economics of already existing capital goods.' True, in one sense, so what? You can make a theory of investment ... Walras tried, he did not succeed in making a good one; we still have not succeeded in making a very good one. Nor did Joan. Then the discussion went on into phrases that I simply could not make sense of. Joan, of course, had her own private set of proverbs. One of them was that time is a device to keep everything from happening at once. I do not think that is what time is. Moreover, if that is what time is, it fails because everything (or more than one thing) does happen at once. But, in a sense, these sayings were substitutes for thought on her part.

I take the technologist's point of view that the reason why a truly good theory of capital is so elusive is sheer difficulty. The difficulty takes fundamentally two forms: the first form is that capitalist production – by which I mean intertemporal production – is a terribly complicated event. It is perhaps not impossible to do if one thinks of all capital goods as fixed capital lasting forever. It is perhaps possible to do if one thinks of all capitalist production as Böhm-Bawerkian or Wicksellian tree planting. It is most easy to do if one thinks of all capitalist production as being circulating capital, with inputs provided one period in advance and used up and disappearing at the end of the period. But when you realize that you really need a model of intertemporal production that has all these things happening at once, it is just incomparably difficult. The second form the difficulty takes was something Joan realized full well, but had nothing to say about that I could follow. Namely, that intertemporal production is future-oriented. If it is future-oriented, it is uncertain. And, if it is uncertain then there are moments when one does not really know how to talk about it. One does not know how capital assets are valued at any given hurly-burly moment, when expectations have been disappointed. The hypermodern tendency is to try to reduce everything to diversifiable risk, to expected values. Joan, like Keynes, would have laughed at that – and I think they would be right!

So, the whole thing petered out. The last thing I would like to say is that the sign that it petered out unproductively is how little Robinsonian economics that is positive – something you could teach to students – has survived.

Well, perhaps one more remark, for it would not do to avoid the subject completely. I think the reswitching controversy was fundamentally a red herring. It is an argument against applying simple diminishing-returns arguments to very complex situations. It is a result that shows that one cannot always treat comparisons of steady states as if they were non-steady-state true incremental marginal comparisons. It was obviously an embarrassment to the 'neoclassical' side of this discussion. But that was primarily a tactical byplay. There are no deeper implications.

Feiwel: What do you mean by 'neoclassical'?

Solow: I have never understood very clearly what 'neoclassical' actually means. Neoclassical gets used the way 'static' gets used: dynamic is good, static is bad. In the same sense, neoclassical is bad or foolish. I look at some things from what, I presume, is a neoclassical point of view, but I think of myself as a Keynesian economist, not a post-Keynesian. So, if there is a conflict between Keynesian and neoclassical, I am certainly on the Keynesian side. If there is a conflict between neoclassical and some other kinds of non-neoclassical thought, then I would sometimes find myself on the neoclassical side.

I once suggested in print that what seems to be meant, or at least could be meant, by the word neoclassical is economics that works out the consequences of cost minimization and profit maximization. In that sense I am a neoclassical economist. I think that there are obvious limits to cost minimization and profit maximization as working hypotheses, but on the whole, for a capitalist economy, they are a pretty good place to start. As I remember it, in the same place I also wrote that the possibility of reswitching is a theorem of neoclassical economics – and this goes back to what we were saying before about Joan's work being mostly in the mainstream tradition. The theorem is produced *entirely* within a similar framework to Böhm-Bawerk's. In fact, the first reswitching theorem there ever was was the one that showed that in a Böhm-Bawerkian time-phased economy there could be two or more internal rates of return; there could be more than one interest rate that discounts the stream of inputs and outputs to zero. One of my positive contributions to that whole debate in actual theory, instead of just polemics (resisting, defensive, or aggressive polemics) was to prove that the reswitching that occurs in the Sraffian mechanism is analytically identical to the kind that occurs in the Böhm-Bawerkian mechanism.

Another thought that comes to mind is that the absence of a Robinsonian economics is actually the absence of a Sraffian economics. There is very little in Sraffa's *Production of Commodities by Means of Commodities* that could not be found in David Gale's *The Theory of Linear Economic Models* or Dorfman, Samuelson, and Solow's *Linear Programming and Economic Analysis.* The remarkable thing about Sraffa is that he did it twenty or twenty-five years before with hand-tools, so to speak, and suppressed it. The only non-orthodox, non-neoclassical thing in *Production of Commodities by Means of Commodities* is an erroneous claim that none of the theory in the book has anything to do with virtual change, with the possibility of things being other than they are. Sraffa says it is all just read out of the circulation problem, the reproduction properties. Along with that, Sraffa claims, there is no assumption of constant returns to scale. There are, however, constant returns to scale, for otherwise the zero profit condition has no special interest or meaning. The only other non-orthodox thing in that book is a statement that, in fact, is not even non-orthodox. He winds it down to one degree of freedom along the factor price frontier (or whatever one might wish to call it), and says that where the economy settles on the curve that relates the real interest rate to the real wage is arbitrary; more accurately it is a matter that he does not discuss at all. Neoclassical economists are brought up to think it has something to do with time preferences or savings propensities. Modern Sraffians think it has something to do with power – another tough-guy phrase. That is the sort of thing one says out of the side of one's mouth to indicate that one does not wear a necktie . . . it indicates that one is a cynic about the capitalist system, that one is tough and all that. But it does not provide any positive theory at all, until someone shows how power relations determine the real-wage and the real rate of interest. If one says it is all bargaining, fine, I can agree. Let us now have a theory of bargaining. The only people who have ever tried to make a theory of bargaining, successfully or not, are the mathematical hangers-on of neoclassical economics, like Nash and other game theorists.

Feiwel: Do you see any fundamental differences in vision between yourself and Joan?

Solow: I can give you two answers to that. I would think that Joan's view would have been: 'yes, there is a difference. Bob thinks of the capitalist economy as a smoothly functioning, optimality producing machine, and I think of it as a badly functioning arena for the conflicting interests of different classes, with nonsensical outcomes as likely as optimal outcomes, that sort of thing.' Now, I would say: 'I think that the capitalist economy is a poorly functioning machine, with conflicting interests being resolved in imperfect markets, behind a lot of ignorance, and producing recessions as often as prosperity.' So, where are the differences? This is a true story: Joan did actually once say to me, at the end of a political discussion, 'You are not a reactionary, why don't you agree with me?' What could I tell her? 'No, I am not a reactionary and yes, I do not agree with you'. I think of my view of the capitalist system as being very much like Keynes's view, though with differences of substance that may reflect the fact that I did not come from a confident upper class as he did.

There is something to be said of Joan's view, applied not to me, but to many other modern mainstream economists. When I twit him for having devoted so much of life and effort to refining the Walrasian equations of general equilibrium, my friend Frank Hahn always says: 'You misunderstand completely . . . The *essence* of modern general equilibrium analysis is to show how many strong assumptions we have to make in order for this theory to work.' I am glad that modern general equilibrium theory has produced that insight. But I do not really imagine that all the people who devoted their lives to refining modern Walrasian general equilibrium theory had that in mind. I think that many of them thought of, and continue to think of, competitive general equilibrium as a fair approximation to the modern world. There, of course, I part company with them altogether. Hahn, of course, sees more deeply. But if you are prepared to treat modernized Walrasian economics as the *terra firma* from which Western economics starts, then there is no doubt that in that foundation there is a built-in tendency to view the economy as a smoothly operating machine that grinds out optimality conditions and optimal results in one way or another.

Here we come back to modern macroeconomics. What is called the rational expectations school has its intellectual foundations not in rational expectations (which I think of as a second order hypothesis in this context), but in thinking of the economy as being fundamentally a Walrasian sort of machine. The question then arises: how, on that foundation, can one find an explanation of the apparently non-Walrasian phenomena that one sees, such as business cycles? How can one reconcile the common observation that employment rises and falls by, say, 5 per cent from one year to the next with the belief that what one observes is a Walrasian economy?

I do not have to defend that way of thinking since I have spent a lot of time opposing that view of the economy altogether. If you remember, Milton Friedman's Presidential Address to the American Economic Association (which, in a way, was the beginning of all this) uses the phrase 'the results ground out by the Walrasian equations' in connection with the natural rate of unemployment. So, what I have just described as Joan's view of my picture of the economy might be a legitimate description of Bob Lucas's view of the economy – but not of Bob

Solow's. Did Joan realize that, deep down? Perhaps sometimes; but most of the time she did not really care.

I ended up with a sort of love-hate relationship with Joan. I liked her; I admired her. And, I think, she kind of liked me . . . I enjoyed her company; she enjoyed mine. But she enjoyed my company in the way, I suppose, one rooster enjoys the company of another. And half the time I never knew what was fundamentally dividing us. On the other hand, that did not stop us from fighting very hard . . . much too hard. I am now making a very self-justificatory remark that has to be discounted by at least 80 per cent per year – I do not think of myself as a fundamentally combative person, whereas Joan was. On the other hand, I think of myself as a person who will rise up when baited – *cet animal est très méchant, quand on l'attaque, il se défend*, that sort of thing. I responded . . . and I probably should not have.

Feiwel: How do you perceive Joan's attitude to her American antagonists?

Solow: I think that Joan shared the widespread feeling that 'we happy few in Cambridge are the centre of the economic universe . . . we and Maynard'. Then along come these vulgar Americans who have no education. They carry around this ridiculous mathematics that we never needed and they propose to take over our subject. And we won't let them! We will treat them the way German Jews treat East European Jews – as unworthy intruders. That is a more or less explicit feeling. Richard Kahn once said to me in Cambridge: 'I cannot understand you Americans with these PhD programs. We teach all the economics there is to our undergraduates.'

When you read, for instance, the first volume of Skidelsky's biography of Keynes, what is astonishing is how little economics Keynes knew when he began to lecture on the subject in Cambridge. (I say this as a great admirer of Keynes. I think he was by far the most important economist of our time. As I said, I am a Keynesian, not a post-Keynesian.) Nobody thought that was strange. After all, a graduate of Eton and King's College could master any subject. And if one goes back 300 years in England, one finds people saying of Newton 'who does this man think he is, turning physics into mathematics like this, being technical?' I identify this, tentatively, with the cult of the gentleman. One does not need any of this 'dirty' technical training. An intelligent person, properly educated, can do anything. I think that is at the heart of it. That is why I said at the beginning of this conversation that the 'bastard Keynesian' label is exactly right. It is just what one would say about uneducated rabble.

Perhaps we do overstock the subject with technique. I make that complaint too, but I always feel a little inferior when I make it.

Feiwel: Could you contrast your position with Jim Tobin's?

Solow: As a macroeconomist, you set yourself the task of giving an account of economic fluctuations. You try to understand why employment rises and falls, why capitalist economies have periods of recession. There are two approaches you can take if you are an economist trained in the mainstream tradition. You can say that the underlying equilibrium of the economy is something like a Walrasian equilibrium, but capitalism is unable to achieve the Walrasian equilibrium and whatever is disturbed is likely to stay disturbed and remains in imbalance for a very long time. The other approach is that there is an equilibrium concept according to which a modern capitalist economy can have an equilibrium other than a full-employment one. Keynes, of course, adopted the second of these approaches and, as I mentioned earlier, by logical standards he was unable to make good on that claim. His intellectual descendants, like Jim Tobin and myself, seeing that that claim had not been backed up intellectually, took the tack that the way to model business cycles in the modern capitalist economy is as departures from an equilibrium. Tobin, I think, still continues to take that view.

I (and who knows why?) have come round to the view that Keynes's instinct was right and that it would be worth the effort to do what Keynes did not, that is, provide solid intellectual foundations for the notion of the capitalist economy having (perhaps in addition to a possible Walrasian full-employment equilibrium) other non-Walrasian equilibria. That requires in modern parlance an equilibrium concept other than the Walrasian one. The equilibrium concept we were all taught in school is that supply equals demand in every market and that what makes it so is the finding of a price vector that equates supply and demand in every market. If you envision that the right way to describe the capitalist economy is that it is in equilibrium, *without* all the markets clearing, then you must have another concept of equilibrium. Modern economics has produced several such concepts, the most obvious one (the longest standing one) being the Nash equilibrium concept, that is, that no agent has a strategy superior to that he or she is following, given the strategies other people are following. You can have an equilibrium of that kind. It need have nothing to do with prices. If prices are the strategic variables, then you need a situation where no agent has the desire to change the price. I am now pursuing that line. It remains to be seen which is more successful in producing usable theories of business cycles. Remember the disequilibrium approach had a long and, on the whole, fairly successful track record. (Not wholly successful, mind you.)

Feiwel: Isn't disequilibrium just another side of the equilibrium concept?

Solow: Every equilibrium concept that is worth anything must have a disequilibrium side. You must have some notion as to how the equilibrium is achieved.

Feiwel: What about the new classical macroeconomics in this respect?

Solow: I never know quite how to take their claims. There is a sense in which at every instant of time the whole world is in equilibrium; everyone might have made a different decision a split second ago and did not. For instance, if I utter a sentence to you and then ten seconds later I think it is a wrong sentence, you could refuse to describe it as a disequilibrium sentence since, after all, I chose to speak it. But that is an empty view of things because it does not provide a theory useful for anything. So, if you are going to make a sensible equilibrium theory, you must have a notion as to how the equilibrium is achieved. If it is achieved, there must be potentially observable circumstances where it is not achieved. So, you need a disequilibrium theory.

The new classical macroeconomists do not seem to be willing to talk about disequilibrium. I can tell you what Lucas or Prescott would say if they were here: 'We are able to explain the facts on the hypothesis that every instant is an instance of equilibrium. Why should we not do that?' To which I would reply: 'It is not so clear that you can explain the facts by arbitrarily ruling most of them out of court!' I think that by being unwilling to take on directly the issue of achievement of equilibrium (and, therefore, the allowance for some kind of disequilibrium states) Lucas and company are tying their own hands.

Feiwel: What do you think about the American 'cousins' of Joan – the post-Keynesians?

Solow: I cannot speak judiciously about selfconscious post-Keynesian economics, perhaps because I have not paid enough attention to it, but, for better or worse, I do not detect a coherent school of thought in Minsky, Kregel, Eichner, Davidson *et al.*, not to the extent to which there is a coherent school of thought in Lucas, Prescott, and company, for instance. It is not clear to me how the writings of Paul Davidson, for example, fit with those of Hy Minsky. I do not think they necessarily contradict one another, but that is not the point. I do not know what they are up to. It seems that the selfconscious post-Keynesian economists are an inward-looking group. They talk to one another, but they make no contact with the mainstream. That is not entirely their fault; the mainstream evinces a firm wish not to listen. I guess I am an example of this. On occasion I read what Hy Minsky writes but more because he is my friend (I have known him for forty years or more) than because I think there is something there I *must* pay attention to. There has not succeeded to be any communication . . . and I m a living example of it.

Feiwel: Let me relate my next question to Minsky who, as you know, always speaks about instability. Do macroeconomists mean the same thing by instability as microeconomists?

Solow: I think it is the same (Samuelson–Frisch) notion. I think it is what both Minsky and I have in mind. If I describe the economy as exhibiting instability I mean that when disturbed from equilibrium (by which I do not mean necessarily Walrasian full-employment equilibrium, I only mean a self-sustaining state of affairs without internal pressures to change), there are no strong tendencies to return to it. That is, that there is no internal endogenous economic mechanism that does the job. I would describe the capitalist economy as unstable under those circumstances even if I thought that the government were always intelligent enough to take action that would return the economy to a pre-existing equilibrium. Analogously, I would not say that my dog has no tendency to chase cars if every time the dog makes a move I grab it. So, I am speaking of an internal endogenous economic mechanism; and I think that is what Minsky means. When he speaks of the fragility of modern capitalism – to use his phrase – he means that if the economy is at rest and is disturbed in some way (say, by the defense program), the financial mechanism behaves in such a way that it magnifies or risks magnifying the disturbance rather than diminishing it. And that is exactly the definition of stability in Samuelson's *Foundations of Economic Analysis*.

My complaint about Minsky is only that he exaggerates the instability of capitalism. I think that if I were a man from Mars, who had nothing to read but Hy Minsky's writings, and I were suddenly transported to Earth, I would be astonished if there were not a rampant financial crisis at whatever moment I happened to arrive. To my eye, the state of affairs is not nearly that bad. I feel more comfortable with the notion that the capitalist economy has a kind of neutral equilibrium. If you disturb it, it does not have a strong tendency to magnify the disturbances a lot, but neither does it have a strong tendency to return to its old equilibrium. I think there are many possible equilibria. I cannot back this up; that is, I do not have a well-developed theory. But the feeling I have (and the theory I would like to construct) is one where there is a range of equilibria (not like the Kaldor business-cycle model where there was a low-level equilibrium and a high-level equilibrium and the economy goes from one to the other). The US economy, for instance, now appears to be in something roughly like an equilibrium at 7 per cent unemployment; had things been slightly different in the past, it could have been roughly the same kind of equilibrium at 6 per cent unemployment, or maybe even less.

Feiwel: Here and there you have touched on the work that you are at present doing with Frank Hahn. To use one of his favorite expressions, could you enlarge on the subject?

Solow: What I have described as a feeling and search for a theory is essentially what we are doing. What we rigorously accomplished thus far is, in fact, a vindication of Keynes's statement in chapter 19 of the *General Theory*. As you know, much of the mainstream world regards Keynes as a theorist of rigid wages. And Keynes did, indeed, think that wages were rigid, but he thought that the capitalist system would behave in a worse manner if wages were flexible.

Feiwel: Forgive me for interrupting, this is one of the examples of instability, that in case of wage flexibility, expectations can aggravate the situation?

Solow: Not only expectations. Frank and I have been constructing a model of perfect foresight where the likely equilibrium path followed by a disturbed economy with wage flexibility departs from a good outcome and exhibits genuine, dynamical instability. That we have accomplished. We also have most of what we need to do to ask the question: 'how would such an economy behave if wages were only imperfectly flexible?' This is the 1950s, 1960s Keynesianism that I described Jim Tobin and myself as sharing at that time. We have got that far. Our next step now is to try to carry out the rest of Keynes's program, not necessarily in Keynes's way, and try to provide equilibrium concepts and model economies that would be capable of many equilibria, including undesirable ones. And, what naturally follows, to outline policies capable of moving such an economy from a bad to a good equilibrium. We have ideas about this, but we have not yet embodied them in serious models.

I like to describe our goal as trying to do Keynesian economics in such a way that even a modern mathematical economist can understand it. Whether we will succeed or not is yet an open question.

Feiwel: Of course, when you speak of a bad equilibrium, you presume an exploitable policy that could move the economy to a good one, unlike the new classical macroeconomists?

Solow: Yes, but even Lucas, if he were to face seriously the multiple equilibrium problem and this other question of how the economy gets to equilibrium, would almost be bound to come upon opportunities for policy. If there is a unique equilibrium, Lucas does not face this question, for the economy is in it all the time, and, with rational expectations, no systematic economic policy can have any (non-allocative) effect at all. Remember that even the Lucas group does not exclude the effectiveness of policy; it is only unexpected, unsystematic, erratic policy that is effective.

Feiwel: But what about the assumption of the fast-learning economic actor?

Solow: You are not giving full weight to the significance of the possibility that there are many equilibria for the economy. What does fast learning or fast acting mean then? Suppose the agents understand that the goverment intends to take actions calculated to move the economy from a bad equilibrium to a good equilibrium. Why would individual agents wish to offset those actions? What would they be trying to accomplish? To move to the good equilibrium? Then the policy has been effective merely by announcing it, without even having to do it. Take a strong case. Imagine the economy as being in a Pareto-inferior equilibrium. The government announces a policy that, if the private economy were passive, would move the economy to the Pareto-superior equilibrium. What theory would say 'no, no, that could not possibly happen; the private economy, foreseeing this, would take such actions as would preserve the Pareto-inferior equilibrium'? It would be difficult to know what sort of rationality would govern private agents who would act in such a way. Imagine a prisoner's dilemma situation: the government says: 'We are going to produce a method for you to coordinate your decisions so that you achieve the good outcome for you.' Perhaps there is a game setting where rational prisoners would defeat that. But I do not know of it. I have never seen it described. It is surely not inevitable. It is certainly not something that Lucas and company have ever defended, because they have never faced up to such a situation.

Feiwel: An illegitimate question: why do we need microfoundations for macroeconomics, and, if so, why do they need to be derived from the precepts of neoclassical economics?

Solow: That is a good question to ask of a bastard Keynesian! My opinion about that is well known but it is neither very popular nor convincing. Take the first part: it is clearly not *necessary* to have microfoundations for macroeconomics. There are many subjects where that necessity is not acknowledged. An example I have previously used is the behavior of an airplane. People design airplanes without being able to deduce the behavior of the airplane from microengineering. On the other hand most modern scientifically minded intellectuals are reductionists in one way or another. They think that if big objects are made of small objects, then you cannot have very much confidence in your theory of the big object if it does not correspond to something valid at the micro level, even if it is a good theory of the big object, a successful theory or a practical theory. For instance, I can ride a bicycle perfectly well without understanding the minutiae of the friction of wheels on the road or this or that. But as an intellectual, I would feel better if I were certain that my macrotheory of the bicycle were compatible with the microtheory of the bicycle, And if it were not compatible, I would say 'practical though it may be, it is not the right theory'. So, while it is not necessary to have microfoundations, it is comforting to have them. We all believe that the ultimate theory is a microtheory. There are very few Bergsonian (Henri not Abe) holists amongst modern intellectuals. We may be wrong, but that is our attitude.

Now, given that, I think it was a great tragedy for modern macroeconomics that at the time when the economics profession felt seized with the compulsion to produce microfoundations for macroeconomics, it had no good microfoundations available but Walrasian microeconomics. (I would rather not say 'neoclassical'. One might say that neoclassical economics is identical to Walrasian economics, but then I need another name for Cournot and his descendants.) There is another reason why the microfoundations had to be Walrasian; they were because there was nothing else available. That was too bad! I think it has produced a tremendous amount of waste motion in modern economics. If you were talking to Bob Lucas he would tell you how fortunate we were to have had the right microfoundations available.

Feiwel: How do you feel about the neoclassical synthesis?

Solow: It goes without saying that the sixth edition of Samuelson's *Economics* is not the absolutely final version of what modern macroeconomics will be. That said, let us take the basic statement of the neoclassical synthesis as being a Keynesian synthesis as well. The argument is that the main pathology of the modern capitalist economy is the business cycle, if the business cycle can be taken care of by fiscal and monetary policy, then a capitalist market economy can operate rather as Marshall thought it could. Marshall is more appropriate here because Walras's economy was perfectly competitive. And no one would ever be able to tag Samuelson as a believer that the modern economy is perfectly competitive. But you could begin to use the supply and demand apparatus properly on a market structure when, and only when, macroeconomic policy takes care of the business-cycle problems. In that sense, I am still a day-to-day believer in the neoclassical synthesis. I think that the original statements of the neoclassical synthesis were too optimistic about our understanding of the behavior of the price level and its relationship to expectations. In addition, I think the neoclassical synthesis was a little naive in its equilibrium theory; in not having in mind the modern game-theoretic extensions. So, there is plenty to be done . . . But aside from these two exceptions, I still feel the neoclassical synthesis is by and large right.

Feiwel: May we have your reflections on growth theory, its ups and downs, and particularly on the focus on demand and income distribution?

Solow: My view of the kind of growth theory that I began to do thirty years ago was that it was providing a description of the kind of path a *successful* neoclassical synthesis economy might pursue. I still think that. Certainly my writings on growth theory were not demand-side oriented. Whether I knew it or not (and there is a question of how much one knows when one is doing something), I was trying to describe an economy where demand-side fluctuations had been eliminated.

Let me tell you an illustrative anecdote: when Reaganite supply-side economics began to be publicized by Laffer and company, my colleague, Stan Fischer, reminded me of something I had forgotten: I had gone to give a talk at the University of Chicago in the early days of growth theory. Stan, who had been my student and had been taught by me as a Keynesian, asked me: 'Why are you doing this sort of thing?' And I replied: 'Well, don't you think it is time that the supply side played a role in macroeconomics?' That would have been in the very early 1960s, well before Laffer and company. And as the anecdote suggests I was probably even aware of it at the time.

I was, in fact, describing the supply side of a macromodel. I certainly never achieved any good integration of it with the demand side. Even now I do not know of any clear and successful integration of a growth-theoretic supply side with a demand side capable of describing how shocks to aggregate demand work themselves out. It is an intrinsically difficult thing to do. One important impulse this sort of growth theory gave to macroeconomics was, broadly speaking, to say that a theory of assets had to be part of a complete macroeconomics. Standard Keynesian theory was almost entirely a flow theory. A good integration of growth theory and aggregate demand theory will have to be one that integrates stocks of assets and flows of expenditure. The difficulty is substantive, not technical. What is missing is an understanding of how asset markets behave out of equilibrium. In neoclassical growth theory, there is no problem with asset markets because we can understand asset markets in an economy experiencing a good growth path; it is all present value, that sort of thing. Present value is not well defined off that path and one does not know what to do with it. What I am trying to say is that what is lacking is not some model builder to come along and construct new models, what is lacking is a good, clear, clean hypothesis about how to integrate stocks and flows either out of equilibrium (if you want to think in the disequilibrium mode) or in economies that have many equilibria.

18 Testimony II: An Interview

James Tobin

Feiwel: Can you share with us your interpretation of the Keynesian message on the planes of theory and policy?

Tobin: Keynes really invented the subject of macroeconomics as a distinct topic of analysis. Prior to the *General Theory* there was not that kind of specialization. The substantive message was that there are periods of time when the economy is not operating at an equilibrium at which all markets are cleared; in particular, there is excess supply of labor (involuntary unemployment). There is 'a market failure' in a very important sense, to put it in the terminology of theoretical economics.

Keynes's *principle of effective demand* then comes in: actual demands are limited by the inability of workers to sell as much labor as they want to sell. The resulting variation in output is an equilibrating mechanism ignored by economists before Keynes. Instead of a system where market clearing occurs wholly by adjustment of prices (including futures prices and interest rates), Keynes's system makes income and output also a part of the equilibrating process. When that is so, resources can be unemployed. I think those were Keynes's innovations in analysis of business fluctuations.

The policy implication is that in some circumstances government monetary or fiscal policy can affect aggregate (or as Keynes called it, effective) demand and, in that way, mitigate or possibly eliminate the market failure, the unemployment.

That is, in a nutshell, the major contribution of Keynes.

The question whether to call a situation of underemployment an equilibrium or a disequilibrium was, I think, overrated by Keynes himself. Probably he was too ambitious in claiming that he had discovered an excess supply *equilibrium* in the classical meaning of the term. This does not seem to be terribly important from the point of view of practical policy, or even of theory. Equilibrium can mean a situation where supply and demand are equal in all markets. Keynes's excess supply of labor is obviously not an equilibrium in that sense. Another meaning of equilibrium is a position of rest. Will excess supply persist? Is there an ultimate adjustment that would occur through prices, interest rates, and wealth? This is the issue raised by the real balance or Pigou effect. Maybe there is always an equilibrium in the abstract sense that a sufficiently low price level will restore a balance in labor and product markets. Maybe, but this equilibrium is not of practical importance if the effect is weak and takes a long time.

Price adjustment may not be a stable adjustment mechanism. The *process* of lowering prices and money wages to the values that would restore the Walrasian equilibrium may in itself generate expectations that work the wrong way. The expectation of deflation is equivalent to an increase in the real interest rate, and that is bad for effective demand. A lower level may be good, but the rate of change affects demand in the wrong direction. The same problem arises with disinflation – a reduction in the expected inflation rate.

I realize that rational-expectations theorists would say that since market participants will know the new equilibrium price *level*, the market will establish it right away. There's another unconvincing abstract argument. There will be much disagreement and uncertainty about the new level. The deflation or disinflation is not going to take place all at once, in zero time. While prices or inflation rates are falling, the effects on investment and effective demand are perverse. The mechanism can be shown to be unstable. Rather than waiting it out, Keynesian demand management would be a quicker and surer way of restoring balance in labor and product markets.

Those are the essentials of Keynesian theory and policy. Those ideas were neither understood fully nor systematically expressed prior to the *General Theory*. They become part of mainstream economics since then. That is Keynes's major contribution.

It is an all too common mistake to think that Keynesian theory depends on money wage or price rigidity. It certainly does not depend on any absolute rigidity, only on the fact that adjustments of prices and money wages to demand shocks are so slow that part of the adjustment has to take place simultaneously in income and output. Furthermore, Keynes argued that an effective demand shortfall might not be remediable even by perfect flexibility of money wages and prices. This is where the Pigou effect argument comes in, and so do my objections to it, its weakness and slowness and its potential for perverse and unstable adjustment.

It is true that the Keynesian model is premised on the institution of making wage bargains and setting prices in the monetary unit of account. That is, individual money wages and prices are not completely indexed to overall averages. Nor are bargains between workers and employers made in terms of the products they are producing. As Keynes pointed out, the macroeconomy would be quite different with universal and complete indexation.

Keynes thought it a good idea to have stable rather than fluctuating money wages. His reason was the perversity of the expectations created by very flexible money wages and prices. I believe that he thought of the money-wage path as a policy choice. Governments should by policy stabilize the money wage. He meant 'incomes policy', not demand management. A stable money wage would be the most congenial environment for Keynesian demand management policy and for Keynesian analysis of demand fluctuations from sources other than policy. But the applicability of Keynesian theory is not confined to that situation.

Feiwel: Did Keynes violate the canons of neoclassical economics? Irrespective of whether he did or not, does macroeconomics have to conform to the canons of neoclassical microeconomics?

Tobin: To answer your first question, I do not think that Keynes violated the canons of rational behavior in the sense of attributing to actors in the economy irrational money illusion. That is a common misinterpretation of what he was saying. He was saying that wage bargains are made and prices are set in the monetary unit of account and that they do not move with perfect flexibility in response to new situations.

By the way, even current sympathizers with the counter-revolutions against Keynes commonly treat commodity and labor prices as variables that do not *jump* but move with continuity, in the mathematical sense of the word. This treatment puts into those prices a degree of sluggishness that the same analysts do not attribute to asset prices, which are modelled as capable of jumping in zero time, in a discontinuous way, on new information or new market situations. In one day the Dow Jones stock index may be down 10 per cent. That is a jump! No reasonable person thinks that real-world money wages are going to jump by 10 per cent in one day. Nor do spot prices of most traded commodities behave that way. Future prices of homogenous commodities might jump like that, but for spot prices it would be unusual, and for commodities not traded in organized markets almost inconceivable.

The use of the monetary unit of account as a numeraire for markets is not irrational. It is not money illusion! That is one point. The second point is this: looking at labor markets, Keynes saw workers' principal concerns to be with relative wages rather than absolute money or real wages. There is nothing irrational about concern for relative wages. Interdependent utility functions are perfectly consistent with the neoclassical paradigm. My utility could depend on your real-consumption as well as my own. Such concerns explain why workers might not resist a universal reduction in absolute real wages, in particular a decline accomplished by a rise in the price level relative to existing money wages, while they would resist piecemeal money wage reduction. In a decentralized market economy, workers will not believe that their own money wages reduction will be matched by money-wage reductions of equal proportions in other labor markets. They would fear that their local money-wage reduction will turn out to be a loss of relative status. Empirically, this is an important consideration in the behavior of workers and their unions.

The missing link in Keynes's theory of money wages and employment is his failure to explain why the attitude of employed workers makes any difference to what happens when there is large-scale unemployment. In purely competitive markets, excess supply (that is, workers who do not have jobs) presumably would lower real, relative, and money wages. The fact that workers who are employed do not want to have their relative wages reduced would not prevent the competition of the unemployed outside the factory gates from bringing about wage reduction anyway. Keynes pretends he is speaking of competitive markets, but especially in this case it is clear that he really is not. He cannot help describing labor markets as having enough imperfection of competition so that the workers inside, who already have jobs, have a say about the terms on which new workers can be employed. Keynes did not make it clear that this was a deviation from the assumption of perfect competition he claimed to be making throughout the *General Theory*. The trouble with Keynes's money-wage argument is *not* that he slips in money illusion, but that he fails to put in what is a perfectly reasonable institutional fact about modern capitalist economies, namely, that the employed workers have a bargaining advantage.

Feiwel: Would you be good enough to enlarge on the question of imperfect competition and the Keynesian system?

Tobin: In the labor market, I think, even without unions the workers already employed in mass production industries and firms have bargaining power with respect to the terms on which new workers can be employed. I think it was mistaken of Keynes to try to beat the neoclassicists on their own playing field, so to speak, by saying in effect: 'I shall take all their assumptions about competitive markets and get different conclusions.'

Imperfection of competition in labor markets is associated with imperfect competition in product markets. It strengthens the Keynesian argument in an obvious way when, throughout most of the economy Keynes was talking about and *we* as economists should be talking about today, both prices and money wages are decision variables for firms rather than parameters determined in impersonal auction markets. Obviously if they are decision variables, and they are in the monetary unit of account, then they are not going with the perfect and immediate flexibility assumed in the neoclassical model.

Feiwel: Does macroeconomics need microeconomic foundations? If so, do these foundations need to be derived from the canons of neoclassical economics?

Tobin: My thinking about this is as follows: macromodels should not assume irrationality on the part of the economic actors the results of whose decisions they are trying to describe. Macromodels should not rely on persistent deviations of realized values of the variables in the models from expectations. It would not make sense to think of an intermediate or long-run situation that depends for its continuation on, say, market expectations that the interest rate will be 6 per cent, when the actual interest rate always comes out to be 4 per cent. Eventually people will learn that it is not 6 per cent but 4 per cent.

I do not think that is is necessary to have explicit derivations of the macro equations from individual optimizations, utility maximization or profit maximization. We should have macro equations that are not inconsistent with rational behavior.

A relationship that applies to the economy as a whole – consumption function, investment function, liquidity preference function, demand for money, or demand for other assets – is a combination of two things: the behavior of individuals, and the aggregation of possibly diverse individual behaviors. The aggregation problem is that people are different. They have different tastes; they face different circumstances; they have different attitudes towards risk; and they have different expectations about the future, even about the same variables in the future.

While modern neoclassical economists and new classical macroeconomists insist on seeing relationships explicitly derived from microfoundations, they pay very little attention to the aggregation problem. They evade it by assuming all actors to be identical. I think that assumption is a default from the purposes of macroeconomics. The whole idea of macroeconomics was to examine the coordination mechanisms of the economy and to consider the possibility that they can fail. When one models the whole economy as Robinson Crusoe, acting as the sole consumer, producer, worker, investor, and saver, then obviously one gets a neclassical result. The decision of the one person is going to be the decision of the whole economy, and the welfare of that agent the social welfare. That is a blatant evasion of all the issues of macroeconomics.

Keynes, and those of us who followed him, were aware that equations such as the consumption function or the investment function for the economy as a whole were aggregations of diverse individual behavior. We wrote down those equations, partly thinking about what we knew of individual behavior, partly thinking of what was reasonable and plausible about the distribution of individuals in the dimensions that were important to the macro behavior we were interested in. Then we would ask what the economy would look like if we had that kind of a consumption function or investment function. We did not expect that we could derive the parameters of those equations directly from observations of behavior common to all individuals. We knew we had to use econometrics in order to get estimates of quantitative magnitudes. I do not think that was a wrong methodology. I think the homage paid to microeconomic foundations of macroeconomics is overdone.

Walrasian general equilibrium theory in its full generality allows all kinds of differences in tastes, technologies, and endowments among actors in the economy. Consequently very few propositions of practical significance can be derived from the model. What you can derive are some existence theorems and perhaps some optimization theorems. You cannot do comparative statics or comparative dynamics with those models. They cannot tell you what will happen, for example, if there is a shortage of oil. They cannot even assure you that the price of gasoline will go up. Mathematical economists (Debreu, Sonnenschein, Mantel and others) have shown that almost no imagined market result could be ruled out as inconsistent with rational behavior. That is, you give me an arbitrary market outcome and I can describe a group of individuals with diverse tastes distributed in such a way as to support that particular outcome, even if it is as implausible as the price of gasoline going down because of a shortage of oil. Unrestricted general equilibrium is not fruitful in results of interest for policy. The only way theorists derive meaningful results from explicit microfoundations of rational behavior is by making very strong assumptions about aggregation. I refer to the representative agent fiction, leading to Robinson Crusoe economics, and to the simple two-period overlapping generation model, in which young and old Robinson Crusoes, otherwise identical, coexist and trade.

Feiwel: Rhetoric aside, how do you perceive the essence of the fundamental differences between the American and British Keynesians?

Tobin: I think the fundamental difference is that American Keynesians (by which I mean the dominant stream of American Keynesians, for there are other American Keynesians who follow the British tradition or their own version thereof) think neoclassical analysis is useful in describing the long-run trends of the economy. As I understand it, the British Keynesians regard neoclassical analysis as useless for that purpose as well as for the purpose of analyzing short-run business fluctuations. The major difference then is the view of the roles of saving, interest rates, and investment in the long run.

Feiwel: You have been identified as Paul Samuelson's principal 'partner in crime' in the synthesis of Keynesian and neoclassical economics.

Would you be good enough to share with us the essence of the neoclassical synthesis? To what extent is it consistent with Keynesian economics?

Tobin: First of all, there are a lot of important economic questions in the world to which Keynesian economics is not relevant. There are a lot of pressing economic problems that Keynesian policies are not going to solve. Starvation in Africa and Asia is nothing that Keynesian economics can remedy. What will lift standards of living around the world decade after decade, from one century to the next? The answer, as neoclassical economists have always said, involves accumulation of human and physical capital, technological progress, and enterprise. These are supply-side factors – capacities to produce goods and services – not demand-side variables. Over the long run, supply will generally be the main binding constraint. That is true whether the natural adjustment mechanisms of market economies work in the long run, or policies are endogenously adopted to ensure that resources are used at least to the same degree. That is why I and my 'partners in crime' do not regard it a heresy against Keynesian economics to believe that a neoclassical growth model is a good basis for describing long-run trends.

On the other hand, the neoclassical synthesis accepts the idea that short-run, or even intermediate-run, business fluctuations are largely demand-side, not supply-side. For example, nothing happened between 1979 and 1981 to make the economy less able to produce in 1981 what it was able to produce in 1979 or to make workers less willing or less productive. Supply factors do not change that fast. So, that must be demand. But if we look at 1990 compared to 1950, explanation of the gains must center on what happened to productivity and technological progress, on supply rather than demand. The neoclassical synthesis advocates use of the neoclassical paradigm where it is suited, for long-run analysis and for the allocation of employed resources when the level of utilization is constant. We do not need to apologize.

The synthesis, moreover, applies standard economic reasoning to choices among demand management policies, even in the short run. These choices pertain to the competition of output and to the trend growth of output. According to the synthesis, a full-employment economy does not have to be a high consumption economy. It is not necessary to use fiscal policy to promote public or private consumption in order to remedy unemployment. Keynesian economics has been accused of his bias towards consumption relative to investment and saving, and some of Keynes's language in the *General Theory* invited that criticism. But stabilization at high employment can be achieved with high investment, given an appropriate mix of monetary and fiscal policy. That proposition is another contribution of the neoclassical synthesis.

The synthesis applies standard concepts of welfare economics (like 'opportunity cost') to macroeconomic issues. The argument that there is no social cost in hiring unemployed workers on trivial or useless projects considers only the alternative that the workers will otherwise be idle. But other available alternatives would put them to work on something constructive. If you look at those alternatives, you would choose a different way of increasing demand, more socially useful than digging holes in the ground and filling them up again.

The lessons of the neoclassical synthesis were (i) the importance of supply in the long run and demand in the short run, (ii) the possibility of mixing monetary and fiscal policy in various degrees, and of varying the instruments within those two categories, to affect the composition of output and long-run growth; and (iii) the possibility of remedying demand deficiencies by policies other than sustaining consumption.

Feiwel: Would you care to comment on Joan Robinson as economist?

Tobin: She was a great economist and had many very good ideas. She was one of the leading economists of her generation. That does not mean I agree with everything she wrote or even with some of the main things she wrote. But her writings were always very provocative! Sometimes they were difficult for me to understand, when she started from a different set of tools. But when I made the effort, I could put her ideas in my own framework and understand where she was driving at. The effort was always worthwhile.

Feiwel: In commenting on Modigliani's work, Pasinetti remarked that he perceived the *General Theory* in terms of a number of specific contributions to be inserted into the mainstream of neoclassical theory. Kahn and Joan Robinson, on the other hand, were convinced that they had reached a new global vision of the working of the whole economic system. Personalities aside, may we have your comments and your own position?

Tobin: I do not think Modigliani fits Pasinetti's description of what Modigliani thinks. In any case, I do not agree with what Pasinetti says Modigliani thinks. As for myself, I think the Keynesian view that the economy does not work very well in a macro sense and leaves large amounts of excess supply frequently for long periods of times is not just a minor insertion into the neoclassical framework. If one thinks about what market failures were considered in Pigou's *Economics of Welfare* – pollution from smoke stacks, externalities of that kind – they are very minor compared to having millions of people not working at all for long periods of time. This is a market failure of a much more serious nature.

The neoclassical synthesis, the mainstream that emerged in the post-war period, did not just insert a few Keynesian contributions into an existing mainstream; it changed the mainstream altogether. It may be just as fairly depicted as taking some contributions of neoclassical theory and inserting them into Keynesian macroeconomics.

As for the 'new global vision of the working of the whole economic system' – I do not see it. Nobody would deny that the system is historical rather than stationary, as Joan Robinson argued. Even neoclassical economists, and certainly Keynesian economists, even those who use tools of comparative statics, will recognize that history has brought us to a position that in many respects is irreversible. Moreover, any equilibrium to which the economy converges is not independent of the path followed. This old idea has recently been revived by economists rediscovering the idea of hysteresis. In Newtonian mechanics, a ball in a bowl, for example, goes to the same position of rest wherever it starts. In economics, the path taken affects the eventual position of rest, if any. Most economists agree in principle, but the mathematics is very difficult. Neither of the contending Keynesian factions have solved the formal problems. I have not seen it fruitfully done by the British Keynesians. They say it ought to be done, but they have not done it. I do not think that is the essence of British Keynesian economics, or an important item on the agenda of controversy between the two Keynesian traditions.

Another valid point in the British Keynesians' critique of the 'synthesis' is that American Keynesians have misunderstood and distorted Keynes's message about investment and entrepreneurial activity. American Keynesian economics has swallowed too easily the neoclassical view that there is a stable investment function related in a predictable way to probability calculations and interest rates. Chapter 12 of the *General Theory* says the future investors face is one of true incalculable uncertainty, as in Frank Knight and Keynes's own *Treatise on Probability*, rather than one amenable to a probabilistic risk calculations. Indeed, that is the reason why there is a lot of instability in investment decisions by capitalists. Keynes states the point very clearly in the *General Theory*, and it has not been paid sufficient attention by American Keynesians.

Feiwel: In other words, the essence of the Keynesian theory of investment is that it is the violent shift of the curve rather than the movement along the curve?

Tobin: That is the message of chapter 12 but Keynes does not exclude movements along the curve, which monetary policy could exploit. He thinks that the curve shifts, for reasons hard to understand and difficult for policy to cope with. So, for example, Keynes would endorse a frequent conservative argument, to wit, that if businessmen do not have confidence in the government's policy, that is bad for investment.

Feiwel: And the Council of Economic Advisers destroys business confidence?

Tobin: It might do that . . . Or it might be able to work for a combination of policies with a desirable combination of features, policies that work if people believe in them and people do believe in them. Both features are necessary. Policies that would work if people believe in them can fail if they do not believe in them. Or the business community can believe in policies that will not work, no matter what. It is certainly not true that every set of policies people believe in will work. Businessmen might believe the economy will prosper if taxes are abolished, but that would not make the policy workable. Keynes was very well aware that the task of political leadership is to contrive a set of policies that will work if people believe in them and then induce people to believe in them.

In that sense there is some congruence between Keynes and rational expectationists and their views of what policy is about. Keynes is more general: he is not talking only about monetary policy in a completely neoclassical, Walrasian economy.

Feiwel: Would you be good enough to elaborate on your views on incomes policies?

Tobin: As I mentioned before, Keynes seems to me to have been an advocate of a wage or 'incomes' policy. I too think it would be beneficial, but it is difficult to implement. One cannot expect to make it work under all kinds of pressures, political and economic. One cannot substitute it for demand management policies. But to take the government completely out of the business of worrying about wage and price trends is a mistake. Even guideposts without teeth are better than nothing. I think they worked to some degree in the Kennedy–Johnson years, until the Vietnam War blew everything up.

In a sense, macro demand management policy is itself an incomes policy. When the Federal Reserve says that its policy is going to be restrictive because inflation is too high, and tells business and labor, 'if you do not want a recession, you had better behave yourselves on wages and prices', they are operating an incomes policy. We need more than that. Government needs to work out a consensus with the private economy on the desirable path of wages and prices.

In other countries, there has been more consultation on wage and price behavior among the central bank, the government, and the private sector, designed to concert wage behavior with macropolicy. The Germans, in fact, did that quite successfully for a good many years, and so did the Swedes and Austrians. Their economies are, it is true, very different from ours in other respects. Nation-wide wage bargaining is not possible with our decentralized institutions in the US. But now, we have gone to the other extreme, completely 'hands off'. In Washington today, it is regarded as improper for the government to have an opinion on what should be happening in wage negotiations. I think that is unfortunate.

Feiwel: In *The New Economics One Decade Older* you have said: 'The practitioners of the New Economics did not have to confront distributive issues squarely. It was apparent in advance that if their macroeconomic policies took effect and succeeded, recovery and growth during the 1960s would do much more to lift the incomes of the poor and disadvantaged than any conceivable redistribution and would be much less politically and socially divisive.' Would you be good enough to share with us your present thinking on the question of income distribution?

Tobin: Politicians are likely to judge that it is easier to do good things using the fruits of economic growth than to redistribute what people already have. The idea then was that the objectives of social policy could be accomplished by reallocating the dividends of growth. 'The rising tide lifts all boats'. That idea is congenial to politicians. The War on Poverty was an idea begun during the Kennedy Administration and continued by President Johnson under the slogan of the Great Society. The objective was to improve income distribution, but the reform would be lubricated by economic recovery, growth, and prosperity. Redistributional policy took a back seat in the 1970s when the growth that was meant to be the lubricant of such policies ceased.

One of the ideas of the neoclassical synthesis was that governments could find instruments of policy, within fairly wide limits, that would enable societies to achieve several objectives at once: overall economic growth, stabilization of demand, and distributions of economic welfare thought desirable on grounds of equity. That is an abstract proposition from economists. It says we can have – within limits – progressive taxation, a negative income tax, a welfare state, while we still have full employment and dedicate enough resources to investment and saving to sustain high economic growth. To say all these good things are compatible with each other does not mean that one can put together a consensus that would support all the measures involved in such a package.

Feiwel: Would you care to comment on the relationship between Keynesian economics and the welfare state?

Tobin: Keynesian economics itself, as a macroeconomic analysis and as a set of macroeconomic policies, is not biased towards redistribution in any direction. For instance, one can be a conservative Keynesian and be against the welfare state. One can be a liberal (i.e. social democratic)

Keynesian and advocate the welfare state. And whichever view one takes, one could still advocatc policies that preserve full employment and economic growth. It is not true that Keynesian economics is welfare-state policy. It may be that many individuals who are Keynesians also favor welfare-state measures. Keynesian economics is optimistic, in the sense that it says that we can have welfare-state policy, within limits, without sacrificing important macroeconomic objectives. Both Marxism and some brands of conservative economics claim that capitalism cannot function without a distribution tilted towards high income groups. Theories at both ends of the political spectrum are pessimistic about the ability of capitalism to reduce inequality. Keynesian economics, however, is optimistic that inequality can be diminished without sacrificing the dynamics of prosperity under capitalism.

Feiwel: You have observed that had monetarism not been inextricably linked with the ideology and personality of Milton Friedman and been branded a conservative doctrine, it might be consistent with any other ideology. Would you be kind enough to elaborate?

Tobin: I can imagine that monetarists could be socialists or, to put it differently, that socialists could be monetarists. In fact, some social democratic governments in Europe have been extremely 'conservative' in monetary policy and macroeconomic policy in general. After all, in West Germany there was a social democratic government for a very long time and a generous welfare state, much more extensive than in the US. At the same time the German government has been among the most conservative in macro policy. There is no logically or empirically tight link between conservatism in social policy and in the size-of-government issue and the monetarist approach to macro policy.

The quantity theory of money implies that, at least over some long period of time, the government cannot increase the rate of utilization of resources. That macroeconomic proposition has nothing to do with social security or socialized medicine or any other social policy. New classical macroeconomists think that whether the economy is at 9 or 2 per cent unemployment, the government can do nothing to change the amount of unemployment. That too is a strong proposition about how the macroeconomy works. It is more or less what the Germans believe right now. One can believe that, yet still favor unemployment insurance and children's allowances.

Feiwel: Since you are a student of Schumpeter, allow me to pose the next question in Schumpeterian terms: to what extent has the new classical macroeconomics been creatively destructive of Keynesian economics?

Tobin: In the end I do not think it is going to be destructive of Keynesian economics, creatively or otherwise. Probably a new synthesis will emerge, somewhat different from the older one – a new synthesis that will attempt to deal with some of the valid points of the new classical macroeconomics and incorporate them as well as the essentials of Keynesian economics. There will be a renewed emphasis on the point I made previously and attributed to Keynes, namely, that there has to be some consistency between policy and the beliefs of the private sector about the policy. That is a Keynesian idea to be sure, but it is a new classical idea too. I can imagine that in, say, ten years we can find a new synthesis that will incorporate those ideas of Lucas and others about policy expectations within a Keynesian framework of how the economy works in the short run.

There is a lot of emphasis in new classical macroeconomics on intertemporal choices, particularly the possibilities of substitution between consumption today and consumption tomorrow, and work today and work tomorrow. It is probably considerably overdone, but I expect that Keynesian economics could benefit from multiperiod analyses of the economy that would model these choices more explicitly and fully than was customary heretofore. In other words, it may be that one should look at the IS-LM aggregate supply-aggregate demand framework (a shorthand version of Keynesian economics) as describing a slice of time. The outcomes are the new initial conditions for the next slice of time. Then one goes on to another IS-LM model of the next slice of time, and so on. Thus one has a moving picture, linked together not just by the fact that history determines the future, but also by the fact that what we think about the future determines the present and the future. People are deciding what they are going to do now with some idea of what is going to happen next year and the year after that.

Intertemporal IS-LM models have come up in recent discussions of long-term interest rates. For example, long-term interest rates in recent years rose substantially and usually above short-term rates. A premium of 3 or 4 points developed. Here is an interesting question which not many Keynesian economists thought about before. It is something that back in the 1930s Keynes would have thought about a lot. To what extent could one say that the premium came about because of expectations of, or fears of, policy in the future? For example, fiscal policy: a possible reason for long-term interest rates to be so much higher than short-term rates was that 'the market' thought large deficits would continue, eventually forcing the Fed to crack down on an overstimulated economy and raise real interest rates. Another interpretation pertained to expectations of inflation. Either way, you have an explanation of the premium related to what policy is expected to be a few years from now, rather than what policy is now.

Rather than looking at Keynesian static analysis as something good for now, good for next year, and good for the year after that, one looks at it as a panel in a moving picture. In the dynamic system there are relations between periods, based on intertemporal behavior as well as expectations. There are both stock-flow relations, from past to present, and expectations of future variables, from future to present. The system is not easy to write down in a textbook model with easy diagrams, but that is probably the way we are going.

If so, some progress will have emerged from the divisive controversies in macroeconomics these last few years. Yes, there will have been some destruction. However, I think, there will be more attention to some points underestimated previously by Keynesian believers in the neoclassical synthesis, on the one hand, and more attention by the fancy theorists of the new classical macroeconomics and rational expectations to the facts of the real world. We can already see that. The new classical macroeconomists are already concerned by the fact that they cannot explain the obvious gross facts of economic fluctuations except by very contrived and artificial constructs that no one believes. That is why, I believe, there will be a new synthesis a few years from now.

Feiwel: Granted the need for new synthesis, don't you think that in some very fundamental sense the Keynesian (and Schumpeterian) and Lucasian visions of how the economy works are inconsistent with each other, with, on the one hand the vision of a system in disequilibrium, where changes take place, where adjustments are protracted, and so on, and on the other, the vision of a smoothly functioning, self-adjusting system?

Tobin: Yes, these are two different views of the world. Keynes and Schumpeter think shocks come from nature or the private sector, 'animal spirits' or changing views of the future by businessmen and investors. That is, how much flux is built in to the economy, even when policies are stable. The Lucasian view is that the private economy is naturally stable; the only thing that destabilizes it is the inconstancy and unpredictability of government policy. This implies also stupidity in government policy, for it is hard to understand why the government would behave so irrationally as this theory assumes.

I believe that Keynes and Schumpeter are pretty much on the same side in their views of the world. In fact, the Keynesian ideas of confidence, animal spirits, entrepreneurial risk-taking against an incalculable future – all these are Schumpeterian ideas too. I never thought there was as much difference between Keynes and Schumpeter as Keynes and Schumpeter thought.

Of course, the Lucasian view of the economy is not one without stochastic shocks. He introduces stochastic shocks explicitly, but they are very smooth. They are not the big jumps of Schumpeterian innovation. They are described by fairly tame random processes. For Lucas, the economy is always in equilibrium, subject to those processes. The Invisible Hand writes again. Competitive markets produce the optimal social responses to unavoidable social risks. That is what business cycles are. But the government can exacerbate them by failing to follow consistent policies well understood in private markets.

Those are indeed very different concepts of the way the economy works. In part they arise from differences in assumptions about market structure: imperfect or monopolistic competition, on the one hand, or perfect competition, on the other. They are also associated with different views about the nature of 'markets' and the role of information. Yet I have heard Lucas say that he knows that businessmen *make* prices and do not take prices, but that he does not know how to model price-setting decisions. For the time being, therefore, he goes along with the assumption that prices behave 'as if' they were determined by Walrasian auctioneers. Efforts will surely be intensified to bring monopolistic competition and market imperfections explicitly into macroeconomic models. That is a task that can engage economists from both sides of the macroeconomic debate and challenge their mathematical skills in the process.

Feiwel: Don't you think that it is not only a question of differences of opinion about exogenous shocks and about the environment within which the economy is working, but also about the endogenous economic mechanism (the processes of adjustment), the learning capacity of economic actors, and all that?

Tobin: Yes, they are connected. The reason those things matter is that private agents have more freedom of action, more power than the small, anonymous scattered agents of perfectly competitive markets. These questions of confidence, animal spirits, and price-setting would not matter so much if no one had the discretionary power to engage in those activities.

Feiwel: When you speak of a future synthesis that takes the best of everything, which vision (Keynesian or Lucasian) is going to dominate it?

Tobin: It certainly will not be the Lucasian vision. The vision behind it is going to be more likely that of the neoclassical synthesis of twenty years ago. It will have strong Keynesian elements in it, but it will not be exactly the same as that of twenty years ago. It will deviate from the Keynesian vision by taking more explicitly into account anticipations of government policies and by promoting monopolistic-competition features of markets from the vague background into explicitly modelled relationships.

19 Testimony III: An Interview

Franco Modigliani

Feiwel: Both you and Richard Kahn gave the distinguished Mattioli Lectures. In his comments on Kahn's lectures,* Luigi Pasinetti suggested that there is a divergence between your respective interpretations of Keynes. According to Luigi you, 'a typical Keynesian who came to Keynes, so to speak from the outside – presented Keynes' *General Theory* in terms of a few specific contributions (particularly the theory of liquidity preference, in a context of rigid wages) to be inserted into the main stream of traditional economic theory'. On the other hand, 'Kahn does not even insist on specific contributions. He defines what happened in Cambridge in the early 1930s as "the search for the truth" – a very general term indeed, meant to convey the conviction of having reached a new global version of the working of the whole economic system. For Kahn it would be inconceivable to try to fit any one of the new contributions into the old stream'. And Luigi adds: 'This attitude has also been confirmed by Professor Joan Robinson, who has joined Kahn in underlining their common concern for the search for what they came to call the "general theory" '. May we have your comments?

Modigliani: The key to the question about the differences between Kahn's and my position is in what one makes of wage rigidity. If one believes that wages are rigid, it could be that that leads to a different brand of economics. If, on the other hand, one believes that wages will respond, given some time (not always, but most of the time), then it is clear that Keynesian economics is somewhere between the absolute rigidity and perfect flexibility. Therefore, that one can learn something from the classical formulation of perfect flexibility and that the difference becomes a quantitative one: how fast do wages adjust?

It seems to me that to suppose the wages to be rigid, one first has to specify what kind of rigidity. I think Keynes spoke as if he meant nominal wage rigidity. Of course, in his time it did not make much difference. Since inflation was very small, nominal and real wages were pretty much the same. So he did not have to make the distinction. Nowadays it seems absolutely vital to make the distinction. Anybody

*In Richard F. Kahn, *The Making of Keynes' General Theory* (Cambridge: Cambridge University Press, 1984), pp. 222–3.

who believes wages to be *nominally* rigid, ought to have his head examined; it means he has not looked around. When wages change 3 or 4 per cent and more, a month, as they have in the countries with high inflation, when they change fast as they did in the US during the period of high inflation, it is fairly obvious that nominal wages are not rigid. Nominal wages are quite flexible. What is left then is to interpret Keynes as speaking of real-wage rigidity. Of course, to some extent you can see that Keynes was prepared to recognize upward flexibility; he did make that distinction between upward and downward rigidity. That distinction may even have some validity in terms of later experience, but the main thing is that one has to focus now on real-wage rigidity or flexibility.

I believe that real-wage rigidity – not in the sense that there is no adjustment, but in the sense that the adjustment is slow – is the essence of what is valid in Keynesian economics. Wages do not adjust immediately but take considerable time, and the process involves expectations. This tends to lengthen the process because if people believe certain measures will produce a lower price level, they might go along with lower wages validating the lower price level; but if they do not believe it, these measures will initially generate unemployment which then creates pressures on nominal wages to come down, and gradually one gets there. Adjustments are slow; and sometimes may even be absent. I am willing to admit that. One could argue that, in England, there are really a lot of problems because despite the huge unemployment, there is no indication that real wages are ready to adjust. In general, however, the evidence is that in most countries real wages do adjust. This is even true of countries with strong unions. The unions after all do care for unemployment, even though to a limited extent. We have seen this, for example, in Italy where the unions are quite strong. At first they were not willing to go along with wage moderation and suddenly they lost a lot of their influence because of their inability to protect jobs.

When one has wages adjusting slowly one is back in Keynesian economics where there is room for policy. Take the expectation-augmented Phillips curve, vertical in the long run, which I think is a very good approximation (not always, but in general) to the world. When the rational expectations people describe policy they always have a nice trick: they start from full employment where there is no need for anything; then the government stupidly does something and that ends up being completely ineffective in real terms, because you start at 'full employment' and eventually you end up at full employment. But suppose, instead, you start after a shock has pushed the economy well below full employment. It would then take quite an adjustment of wages and prices before one could get back to full employment. That can be cut short by government intervention which will not succeed in fooling anybody. But, on the contrary, by doing what everybody wants, will make full employment consistent with the initial price and wage level. Since there are contracts, and adjustments are slow, if one can avoid the need for adjustments, make them unnecessary, that is obviously desirable for everybody.

My feeling is that much of Keynes is alive. That the policy prescriptions are valid. What we have completely discarded is the simple Phillips curve which, in fact, was not in Keynes. It is a post-Keynesian addition that for a while seemed to complete the *General Theory* for it provided a theory of wages. That theory (and the implication that one can therefore trade between inflation and unemployment) is something that is gone. I do not think that anyone believes in it seriously any more. But all the rest that deals with fiscal and monetary policies seems to me to stand, of course, enriched by various contributions to the understanding of the Keynesian structure. For example, the balanced budget multiplier is not in Keynes and it is an important thing to understand.

The whole question of the deficit is not discussed much by Keynes; the Keynesian views were that the deficits did not really make any difference. That, I think, is typical of this problem of, say, Kahn versus Modigliani (as you have put it). I say that the deficit makes no difference if you have a lot of slack. But when you have used up the slack (and you can expect that you will always eventually get out of the slack – more rapidly with policy, more slowly without it), then the deficit counts. Even the deficit accumulated during the slack may count. Except that the gains from deficits during the slack may be so large that one would not care. Furthermore, one can always wipe it out later through surplus that quickly follows on the heels of the deficit. Thus, if one starts from the view that there is always unemployment, more or less, that one never is close to full-employment, and there is always slack, then the deficit always produces the saving necessary to take care of the deficit and it does not displace other capital.

Once you allow for the fact that prices and wages are not nominally rigid, then there are various aspects of monetary economics that appear, such as the effect of prices on employment, given a certain monetary policy. You are then ready to discuss phenomena beyond the *General Theory*, such as the theory of stagflation, though my understanding of stagflation is entirely derived from Keynes. I understand stagflation to be a situation where, through the vertical Phillips curve, you get a wage–cost push; everyone trying to maintain his own income. That can either be accommodated or not. If it is accommodated, the inflation continues forever and might get worse. If it is not accommodated, initially you get unemployment and then a gradual adjustment of wages and prices. That is, stagflation. While you have the adjustment you have both unemployment and inflation, though slowly decreasing.

Feiwel: In the comments I quoted in my first question there is an implication that you and Kahn (and Joan Robinson) differ fundamentally in your views of how the economic system works: that whereas Kahn considers Keynes as a diametrically different view of the world, you try to reconcile it with the precepts of neoclassical economics. Can you comment on that?

Modigliani: I have not read Kahn's book so I have some difficulty appreciating precisely what he has to say. One thing, however, is very clear to me: a world where wages are absolutely rigid behaves quite differently from the one where this is not the case. Just take the simplest case. In one kind of world money is not neutral at all. If you decrease money, you will decrease income forever. In the other world, given enough time the quantity theory of money will hold: prices and wages will decline in proportion to money and real quantities will be unchanged. It might take some time. I really do feel that the fundamental difference is in the wage flexibility issue. The question of whether the wages are best regarded as an exogenous given parameter, or whether they are endogenous and are responding to the situation, seems to me to be the fundamental clue. I would say, therefore, that there may be situations where the Keynesian analysis is valid. There may well be situations where wages turn out to be completely rigid, even in nominal terms. Then money would not be neutral and many other consequences would follow. For instance, there will be significant consequences if there is a shift in demand between consumption and saving; that will have more unfavorable long-run repercussions under rigid wages than in a world of long-run wage flexibility. I suspect, however, the short-run implications would not be very different. I think that the classical model is helpful from the standpoint of the longer-run implications (and by no means so long that by then we are all dead).

I would say that studying the consequences of rigid wages is a major contribution especially with respect to its interaction with liquidity preference. I think that the realization that wages may not be flexible and the implications of this are the essence of Keynes. For instance, take again the shift from consumption to saving. In the long run it makes no difference as long as wages adjust. In the short run, however, it does make a difference because unless the supply of money is changed, with slow adjustment it is going to take some time for the system to find its equilibrium again. It is quite a contribution to have investigated wage rigidity even if it is only a short-run phenomenon.

Feiwel: Let me rephrase my question somewhat: is there more to the *General Theory* than the Hicksian *IS-LM?*

Modigliani: In my view the Hicksian paradigm succeeds in distilling the basic message of the *General Theory*. You might call it the essence of the *General Theory* in one easy lesson. Of course, the original has a lot more. It has, for instance, a valuable analysis of the various schedules underlining IS and LM and of the reasons for their instability. But, in addition, Keynes was a wise man with a keen feel for the world, so the book is full of perceptive observations and insights that make it worth reading and rereading.

Feiwel: In your Presidential Address to the American Economic Association you said that the principal messages of Keynes is that a monetary economy '*needs* to be stabilized, *can* be stabilized, and therefore *should* be stabilized by appropriate monetary and fiscal policies'. I have just come from a conference of the National Bureau of Economic Research (on Keynesian and classical economics after fifty years) where all the talk was about the stability and instability of the economy, with much misunderstanding. Setting aside the different connotation of stability as used by the mathematical economists, can you tell us precisely what you meant by the above statement? In what sense do you mean that the economy is unstable?

Modigliani: First of all, in the sense that there are shocks and, secondly that these produce substantial and lasting departures from full employment equilibrium. There are some mechanisms in the system that tend to amplify the effects of shocks. There are also others that tend to dampen them. It seems to me, however, that the evidence is very clear that the economy does go through cycles (by which I do not mean any regular, Kondratiev-type or other, cycles); that it does go through ups and downs. In the post-war period, despite the built-in stabilizers and despite some stabilization attempts, we have had appreciable contractions in 1954, 1958–9, 1969–70, 1974–5 and 1981–2. I maintain that if you did absolutely nothing then the adjustment would be long and painful. I think policy can help in making the adjustment period shorter and less painful. Of course, it is very important to have built-in stabilizers and to understand that expenditures should not be cut or tax rates raised when the economy is in a contraction, and the like. That is all very Keynesian. It is also important to realize that possibly, at some time, there is room for *ad hoc* discretionary measures, and to top that off, monetary policy should always have a discretionary element. A constant rate of monetary growth is just not adequate in the presence of shocks. That the economy *needs* to be stabilized is simply due to the fact that the response to shocks takes a considerable time; the proposition that it *can* be stabilized is, of course, an assertion that has to be demonstrated, but I would say that there are proven policies that will do that.

Feiwel: There are a number of empirical challenges to the statement that the post-war economy is more stable than the pre-war economy (for example, the recent article by Christina Romer in the *JPE* which excludes the Great Depression from the pre-war period and shows that that period was about as stable as the post-war period). How do you react to these claims?

Modigliani: I have not seen the particular study you mentioned. I do know that even Burns admits that the economy was much more stable in the post-war period. By the way, I think that one has to stop the study of the post-war period at 1974. What has happened since then produced a great deal of instability connected with the oil shocks, stagflation, and all the problems that ensued. Such problems never existed before and make comparisons difficult. These problems have had profound effects on growth, on employment, on everything . . . (even though for the US they were not so enormous). It seems to me that if you take the period from 1950 to 1974, the record is one of much greater stability; the fluctuations are further apart and they are smaller. I have recently looked at some data for Italy and I have been very impressed by the same sort of phenomenon. I would think that even without the Great Depression, the pre-war period would be much less stable. There were very sharp contractions in activity, quite unlike what we have had in the post-war period. At that time the contractions were not so dramatic. Nowadays one is rather amused to remember that in 1954 unemployment reached 5.4 per cent and it looked tragic then, and in 1958 it got up to 6.6 per cent. That is where we are now, and glad to be there! My impression is that, leaving out this latest period (which may well have passed; we would have to see what happens to oil; but it may well be a period of history that won't repeat itself), we have had a much more stable economy in the post-war period.

Feiwel: Is this because or despite of stabilization policies?

Modigliani: Of course, very much because of the stabilization policies. Absolutely! I would stress, first of all, built-in flexibility which is a Keynesian inheritance. That was very important and was helped by the much larger role of government which raised taxes, raised expenditures, so that essentially the destabilizing effects of multipliers were reduced. It seems to me that on the whole in many countries measures were taken that were desirable. Measures that on the whole were stabilizing.

Feiwel: You are one of the few eminent 'Keynesian' economists who were very concerned about inflation from the very beginning. What accounts for it?

Modigliani: I am afraid that many of my colleagues were blind in asserting that inflation made no difference. It is a very simple case of confusing the following notions: that the quantity of money in the long run makes no difference, that the price level makes no difference, and that the change in price makes no difference. These are very different propositions. I simply began to be concerned with some of the implications (effects) of inflation. I think that one of the grave errors in this area is to identify neutrality of inflation with whether or not it affects aggregate income and employment. It may well be that inflation need not affect aggregate income and employment. It may well be possible to keep the process going indefinitely by monetary accommodation, though I personally have doubts about that. It seems to me that if one is willing to accommodate any increase in prices, there is no limit to inflation; and if one is not willing to accommodate *any* inflationary impulse, one might as well not accommodate the first, It is one matter to take time and say that one wants to reduce inflation gradually; but it is another matter to say that inflation is of no consequence, and therefore whatever it is, needs to be accommodated. To repeat, it may well be that inflation need not affect aggregate income, except that people do not like inflation – and they have no reason to dislike it if it does not affect aggregate income. Why then stop inflation? If we did not stop it, everything would be fine. I have grave doubts about that scenario.

But even assuming that inflation did not affect aggregate income, I have been concerned with the very large number of distortions that inflation creates. These go everywhere, from the field of taxation (where there are enormous distortions created by inflation) to the field of finance, where the whole housing market has been almost destroyed by high inflation and the very high nominal interest rates that result from it, plus the inability to adopt an appropriate financing instrument in the presence of inflation. It has been one of the disappointments of my life to have created an instrument that is ideally suited for financing housing with high inflation and nobody wants to touch it! There are, at present, very few places where it has been adopted. Given the instruments at hand, inflation has had disastrous effects. It meant an enormous increase in the initial payments of young householders starting life – payments that they could not afford – though this effect has been, in part, offset by another inflation distortion – the deductibility of nominal interest from taxable income.

Incidentally, not only was the financing of mortgages affected, but also the entire private pension system. While the public pensions are indexed, the private ones are not. One can show that inflation, with defined contributions, distorts the annuity payment. You get a nominal annuity that in real terms is very high at the beginning, but gets lower and lower as you get older. And a system with defined benefits actually robs the workers because they are indexed until they retire. At the time they retire, they are no longer indexed.

These are enormous distortions involving millions of people. I am at a loss to understand how one can say that it makes no difference. On top of this you have the whole effect of redistribution from creditors to debtors, again involving many, many people. It has been very destructive, and particularly for older people. It is on these grounds that I find it preposterous to say that inflation has no effect. It has all kinds of most important micro effects, whether or not it has macro effects. Economists cannot dismiss these micro effects. They might ask why we should worry about the redistribution from creditors to debtors as long as it does not affect the aggregate. It seems to me, however, that we ought to be concerned with any large-scale redistributions; that we should be able to point out where and when they occur, and to indicate how painful they are. Possibly, we should also have value judgments regarding the appropriateness of such redistributions. I have often used this parallel: disregarding redistributions due to inflation is very much like saying that robbery is of no consequence. Robbery takes from one person and gives to another; and this kind of redistribution is exactly the same thing. We are concerned with robbery; we have laws against it, and we should be concerned with this kind of robbery as well.

Feiwel: You once said that the differences between you and Milton Friedman can be reduced to the empirical magnitudes of the parameters. With all due respect for your judgment, it seems to me that beyond that there is a fundamentally different perception of how the economy works. Would you care to comment on that?

Modigliani: There is a whole set of value judgments that separates us. First of all, there is the fact that Milton has it from God – something that is not debatable – that everything the government does is wrong; it can never do anything right, except push a button that has been prescribed. If government is allowed any discretion, it uses it poorly, because it is stupid, self-interested, and so on. I have no such preconception. I am ready to admit that governments are sometimes stupid. In the US there is some dishonesty, some stupidity, but on the whole it is not a significant problem. Does government make mistakes? Yes, but not to an extent that would prevent me from ever trusting governments again. Surely, we can argue, for instance, that the Federal Reserve made a big mistake during the Great Depression. It was a mistake in the style of the times and perhaps some mechanical rule would have worked better. But those are the chances one has to take. I think that on the whole we are better off when we allow a certain discretion to the government. Milton's negative view of government is a very good example of a strongly held prior view, so strongly held that it is almost unaffected by observation. This colors Milton's view when he looks at anything. Anything that does involve government intervention, he will be against. This is why he is against discretion. I think if discretion could be entrusted to the angels, he might be in favor of it.

The other thing is that Milton has a strong inclination to think that the outcome produced by the market, basically in terms of distribution and composition, is holy and not to be interfered with. I do not believe this at all. There are some Pareto-optimal points that I prefer to others and I do not believe that the market always produces the best and most desirable ones. I believe in certain redistribution and the like. When I look at the consequences of policy, I may be particularly concerned that unemployment hits the poorest and the least able. The rich people by and large manage. Thus for me unemployment is much more of a calamity than it is for Milton. For him it might be inefficiency, for me it is a human tragedy. These things color our views in different ways.

Of course, when we select material to bolster our points, we select it from our different points of view. For instance, in my last encounter with Milton (which was on TV), he said that there was no reason at all to raise taxes; that the only thing we had to do to mitigate the huge US deficit was to cut expenditure. He justified that on the grounds that in the last few years, contrary to popular belief, taxes had risen but expenditures had risen even more. It turns out that if you look at the situation correctly, his statement was based on taking the government's budget and adding on Social Security. Social Security has increased – we have raised Social Security's contributions and we have spent more in benefits, and the system is still approximately balanced. But, if one looks at the budget of the Federal Government proper, one finds that the receipts have declined and that this is the cause of deficit together with a rise in two items, military expenditure and interest. There has already been a cut in other expenditures. This evidence suggests a strong case for raising taxes and/or cutting military expenditure.

I suspect that Milton was aware of this evidence but chose to ignore the distinction between Social Security and the rest of the government because that served his bias in favor of shrinking the role of government. Though it is also possible that he was so pleased with the behavior of the aggregate figures that he never tested the contribution of various components.

So, we can clash even on empirical evidence!

Feiwel: But beyond the value judgments, the quantitative parameters, and the sources of statistics, you and Friedman differ fundamentally on how the economy works (for instance the speed of adjustment, the endogenous capacity of the system to adjust, the exploitable opportunities, and so on). Am I correct?

Feiwel: Yes, but that is what I mean by differences in the empirical magnitudes of parameters. It is exactly those parameters that lead one to believe in the intrinsic stability or instability of the system. The elasticity of demand for money, the elasticity of investment with respect to interest rates, and so on – these are the crucial parameters. Milton believes that each parameter is in the direction that he would like to see. For instance, he claims that the elasticity of response to interest rates is high, so that if there is just a small movement in interest rates it will provoke a large reaction. There is obviously an ideological bias in assessing the value of parameters. In other words, undoubtedly he exaggerates the values of parameters in the direction that implies a more stable system; I may exaggerate them in my direction, although I try to make careful estimates. In the MPS (The MIT-Penn-Social Science Research Council macro model, constructed in the late 1960s by Ando and me and others for the Federal Reserve), we do have some careful estimates of these responses. On the whole, the multipliers appear to be substantial. Milton would say that there is nothing to worry about because of the shocks; because the response to the shocks is very damped. The MPS, however, suggests that they are substantial; not of the magnitude believed in the past, multipliers of 5 or even 10; they are more like 2 or 3, but they are there! This is what I mean by the difference in parameters.

But I must acknowledge that the difference in parameters is partly the result of prior belief or ideology. That is, Milton as a strong believer in non-intervention, must believe the system to be fairly stable and then the parameters must satisfy certain conditions. I have no such *a priori* beliefs; if anything I tend to believe *a priori* that the system is not that stable. So we end up with somewhat different estimates of the same thing.

Feiwel: Are there major social and policy differences between the position you have taken in your major contribution to consumption theory and that of Friedman?

Modigliani: In a way the only difference between us is the fact that I take life as finite and he takes it as infinite. All the differences come from that, including the fact that I am prepared to acknowledge some role for the bequest motive, which he cannot, because for him life is infinite. Therefore, he is led to believe that at the individual level, the ratio of consumption to (permanent) income is not a function of income at all. I, on the other hand, admit the possibility that the ratio of life saving to life income is a function of income.

Both Milton and I have a sort of social implication, if you will. It is a common one, though stronger in his model than in mine. Namely, that it is not true that the poor have negative savings and the rich have huge positive savings. We both say that every person saves – relative to his permanent income (or life resources). That is the fundamental notion. Even poor people save in the phase of their life when their income is above the normal. That has a general broad implication favorable to a market economy; that it does not generate these inequalities. I do not know that there are other social implications that would be different. As for policy implications, the life-cycle model has several, but they are along lines that Friedman cannot even discuss.

In the life-cycle, the saving rate depends on two things: the profile of wealth by age and the rate of growth of income. Presumably policy cannot do very much about changing the rate of growth. So, the only possible channel is through the life-cycle of wealth. That is something completely foreign to Friedman because he does not have a life-cycle.

In principle, many things could affect the life-profile of wealth. One obvious example is Social Security. This is a subject that has been considerably studied, but it is a difficult one, because of two offsetting effects of Social Security; there is first the replacement effect – Social Security replaces private accumulation of wealth for retirement, thus lowering the wealth profile. But it also tends to make people retire earlier which makes for more saving and wealth over the life-cycle. Other things include family size, which public policy might influence, and the encouragement of bequests. If you could encourage bequests, you might thereby increase the amount of wealth that is bequeathed and thus increase savings. Conceivably taxation could also be used; for instance, taxation of consumption rather than income might lead to a postponement of consumption and thus raise the wealth profile. These are some of the policy implications of the life-cycle that, I think, escape Friedman's Permanent Income formulation.

Feiwel: What do you make of the sometime comments that you never 'understood' the 'anti-Keynesian' implications of the life-cycle?

Modigliani: I certainly do not understand, and, I suspect I never will understand, why the life-cycle hypothesis should be anti-Keynesian. It actually leads to a rather minor modification in the standard Keynesian function, namely, the addition of wealth and the replacement of current income with a measure of expected long-run average income. I cannot see why Keynes would object to either modification for which, anyway, one could easily find hints in the proper chapters of the *General Theory*. To be sure, the life-cycle, in contrast to Keynes's model, derives the aggregate consumption function from household optimizing behavior, but that seems to me to enhance Keynes's propositions. But if, nonetheless, somebody wants to argue that, by embracing the life-cycle, I am betraying Keynes, well, let him make the most of it. For my part, I am not about to renounce the life-cycle or Keynes.

Feiwel: Why do the microfoundations for macroeconomics have to be derived from the optimization principle of neoclassical economics?

Modigliani: My view is that one can really handle unemployment within the framework of rational behavior through the search theory. That is, I fundamentally believe that unemployment (at least within certain bounds that encompass most of the observed fluctuations) is due to the fact that when there are fewer vacancies, search is longer. The pool of unemployed depends on the flow through the labor market and on the length of search. I think that by and large the flow is not much affected by the cycle because of the counteracting forces. That is, in the period of low activity, more people are fired, but fewer people quit, and these two tend to somewhat balance out. The thing is then, if you have more or less demand; you have more or fewer vacancies, and this is what makes for more or less search. Within this framework, the question whether this employment is voluntary or involuntary does not make much sense. It is both: it is involuntary in the sense that the search is long and this protracted process does not reflect anyone's will; it is voluntary in the sense that while one is searching, one is voluntarily not working, though by accepting a downgrading and/or a severe cut in pay, the searchers might have an opportunity of finding a job immediately. To this extent, a person abstains voluntarily from taking a job. Such an attitude can be quite rational because, over the life-cycle, it is much more important to find a good job than to work six months more. There may well be extreme cases where this approach does not help. There are also the effects where unions impose an excessive real or nominal wage (as the case might be). There may then be very few job openings and long unemployment while wages still remain unadjusted. Otherwise, I would expect the adjustment to occur, as the longer the queue, the longer the search time, and the stronger is the pressure on real wages.

I am not very much impressed by the various attempts at modelling implicit contracts and so on. This work is very abstract and it always runs into one difficulty or another. I have never found anything in it that is altogether convincing.

Feiwel: Can you share with us some of your reflections as a participant in the capital controversy?

Modigliani: First of all, my participation in this controversy was rather marginal. It began by my reading Pasinetti's paper, finding some holes in his reasoning, and discussing it with Paul (Samuelson), which led to a joint paper.

As to the substance of the controversy, it seems to me that one can accept the proposition that the frontier does not have to be well behaved.

The only question is whether empirically this is an important matter. In other words, it seems to me that Joan Robinson and her followers take the position that because it is possible that somewhere the frontier is not well behaved, therefore, it is not well behaved, and, therefore, we do not have a theory explaining wages, interest, and so on. I do not see that. It seems to me that all the evidence suggests that the frontier is generally well behaved. The evidence suggests that the stock of capital and the flow of investments are functions of interest rates, adjusted for taxes, and so on, and so forth. In other words the rental rate is an important element in the choice of capital intensity and in the right direction. A high rental rate makes for more labor intensity. So, I do not see why we should worry about the possibility of a perverse frontier, any more than about the possibility of concave utility functions or of global instability.

Feiwel: What is your view of Joan Robinson and her followers' approach to economics?

Modigliani: I have not followed her recent work very closely; I am somewhat acquainted with her capital theory work and I know her earlier work. I think her contributions have been important, though I may find them sometimes irritating. She had strong views as well as very important ideas. I have long felt that her contributions rated a Nobel Prize.

Feiwel: How would you characterize her personally?

Modigliani: That is a very difficult question. She was a difficult person to get along with if you disagreed with her. We had a stormy relationship. She accused me of being impolite and other such things. She had imperious ways; an enormous amount of self-assurance and seeming disdain for her opponents. But, nonetheless, I found her an interesting lecturer and a fascinating person.

20 Profit Sharing – A New 'Keynesian' Alternative? An Interview

Martin L. Weitzman

Feiwel: An essential part of Keynesian economics consists of exploitable opportunities of economic policies and institutional rearrangements. Would you be kind enough to share with us the essence of your significant work on profit sharing?

Weitzman: I share the Keynesian vision of the following sort: if one asks the question, 'what is causing unemployment?' a concise answer is that there is a lack of demand. But that is an incomplete sort of answer. Firms are perceiving a lack of demand, but relative to what? Relative to their marginal costs of production. So, a way to get at the unemployment problem is to increase demand relative to marginal production costs – that was the route Keynes took because reducing marginal costs did not seem practical. It did not seem that wage cuts were possible. There were theoretical and practical difficulties with it. In that world of the 1930s there simply did not seem to be any other kind of realistic alternative.

Of course, the other side of that coin is to try to get at the problem of marginal costs of production. In particular, in the economy as a whole, that means labor costs, because they constitute about three-quarters of the costs throughout the economy. It is a fair generalization, particularly in Europe, that this is the heart of the problem. It appears that now this way of looking at the coin is more accurate: money-labor costs are too high relative to aggregate demand. Employers are reluctant to take on new workers because they are expensive: there is a long-term commitment to keeping them on the job; it is difficult to lay them off, and there is not enough flexibility built into the system. Such flexibility has to be built in. We have to get into the trenches of industrial relations and actually patch up a system where there is some more pay flexibility of the proper sort. I consider this mode of thinking as being in the Keynesian tradition in the broadest sense.

Feiwel: Could you share with us the essence of the profit-sharing scheme you suggest and its theoretical and policy implications?

Weitzman: The essence is actually quite simple. When a British youngster comes of working age (with the enormously high present youth unemployment rates) and comes to an employer, he wears around his neck, so to speak, an implicit sign that says, 'Be very careful before you hire me: my pay is rigid, you will have to pay me a certain amount independent of how well or badly your company is doing, and, furthermore, once you have hired me, it will be very difficult for you to lay me off.' Contrast this with a system where there is more profit sharing – a bonus-kind of system. Perhaps Japan is an example of this sort of thing (and even Korea or Taiwan, although that is controversial, but there are certain elements of it there too). In a profit-sharing system the young worker comes with an implicit sign saying, 'Hire me, I am reasonable: the full commitment you have to me is only the base wage (80 or 90 per cent of my total pay, depending on the particular arrangement), the rest is to some degree a variable package that will depend on how well or badly you are doing.' In such a system, the worker ends up being paid about the same as in the British case or perhaps even more on the average, but his marginal cost is lower. Now, in which system are employers more likely to hire new labor and in which do they avoid that at almost all cost in favor of temporaries, of substituting capital for labor, of almost anything but making a commitment to hiring? That is what it is all about. The base wage essentially represents the marginal cost. If you can pay people the same or even increase their pay on average, but keep the base wage somewhat lower, you can improve macroeconomic performance, perhaps quite significantly.

Feiwel: Do you foresee that the uncertainty associated with flexible wages might destabilize such a system?

Weitzman: I am not quite sure how to answer that. I do not think that for the system as a whole there is any more indeterminacy than for a wage system. Do we really know why wages are what they are? There is a variety of theories, starting with the marginal productivity theory and taking off from there. The same sort of answers could be given for profit sharing. I can see no reason for believing that we would end up with something fundamentally different. There will be more variability for the *tenured* worker. That is an important distinction. There will not be more variability for labor *as a whole*. If we can keep everyone employed (or move closer to a situation where everyone is employed), then labor's *whole* income will be stabilized at a high level and that is generally a good thing. But it will mean some more variability for the nominal pay of already tenured workers. Therein lies a tremendous problem, of course.

In a wage system the majority of workers (or interactants) feel that they are doing well. They are earning a fixed money wage and they are not threatened with unemployment if they are not on the margin. Of course, indirectly they do pay, because the unemployed have to be fed and housed which means expenditure of real resources that come out of the pockets of the employed indirectly. But the majority do not perceive that. They feel they are doing fine. They are getting a fixed number of green pieces of paper. That is an illusion anyway. It is a very useful illusion. It would be hard to see how an economy could be run without such an illusion. But an illusion it is, nevertheless. There are all sorts of uncertainties caused by that.

When you try to stabilize a system that attaches everyone's pay to a fixed number of green pieces of paper at a high level of employment and simultaneously try to keep inflation within reasonable bounds, you end up with all sorts of uncertainties. Unemployment is a prime example, but it is not the only one. Another instance of uncertainty was that introduced by the system itself, namely, the recent US experience where the Fed had to drive up interest rates to record levels in order to fight inflation. What did that do? It created tremendous instability for young people who could not afford homes and the like. We saw all these problems; it was not just statistics, it was a reality. So, all kinds of uncertainties get introduced on a global scale, but no one recognizes that it is coming out of a system that attempts to give people stability in the sense of illusion about the green pieces of paper.

What I am saying is that it is much better for everyone to recognize (to the extent that society is capable of recognizing) from the very beginning that economic life is about uncertainty. Capitalism is certainly about uncertainty. It would be much healthier if a significant fraction of the population would face up to that uncertainty at the very beginning of the process and would let some part (not all, nor even the bulk) of the wage be linked to performance – the profitability of work, or something like that. If one openly recognizes and deals with uncertainty at the beginning, at the end there should be less uncertainty overall, at least a less harmful kind of uncertainty.

Feiwel: Do you envisage any political opposition to the profit-sharing scheme from the employers?

Weitzman: In the US at least I have not noticed any strong opposition. In fact, there is a tendency for them to be in favor of it, though not unanimously. For example, in the 1984 GM-UAW contract talks, General Motors was strongly in favor of profit sharing. They wanted to do more of it than ended up in the contract. So, many employers are looking upon it favorably these days, especially in industries under competitive pressure, because they see it as a way of moderating their wage cost or of allowing them to become automatically more flexible. There are also some employers who are opposed to the scheme. The opposition from employers stems from a desire to keep the workers in their place. These employers get nervous about the possibility of workers asking to look at the books, and then asking to be on boards, having a say in what is produced, and the like. So, there are such fears out there, but I think they can be dealt with.

Such fears seem to be more pervasive in Europe. In Britain, when the profit-sharing scheme was opened up as a policy debate, it came as a surprise, at least for me, to find more opposition from employers and less from labor. Relative to my prior expectations, management has been more fearful of this than I would have thought and labor has been somewhat less fearful than I would have thought. In Britain management feels that it has taken enough of a beating in the last thirty or twenty years from unions telling them what to do and from all sorts of regulations prescribing how they are to run their business, so that the last thing they want now is to open things up to allow labor to tell them even more explicitly how to run their business. That is an actual fear, more so in certain sectors of the economy than in others, and more so in certain economies than in others.

But Europe, where the employers' fear is more intense than in the US, is precisely in a situation where something like a profit-sharing scheme should be instituted. Perhaps not exactly like my idea, but they simply have to introduce some kind of flexibility. So, one way or the other, they will have to face these sorts of issues.

Feiwel: Would not the scheme produce also an additional incentive for the worker to be interested in his job? Would it not induce labor stability?

Weitzman: I think so. I think properly done (and this is a tricky business that involves the most complex aspects of industrial relations, which we understand even more poorly than economics – if such a thing is possible), it can motivate employees because they then have a direct stake in the profitability of the company. It is possible that there are very large externalities here in terms of changing attitudes, in terms of perceiving how there are no 'free lunches', and all that. Perhaps ultimately capital's and labor's fates are intertwined; labor cannot pull out of a company more than the company has in terms of income. It is conceivable that the interactants would come to see these things in a different light. I do not know . . . that is speculative.

Profit sharing (or gain sharing) has been generally touted on the level of the individual firm as a means of improving productivity. But no one has really proven it beyond the shadow of a doubt through some sort of careful study. Indeed, it may well be beyond our means to determine that it actually is true in a statistically significant sense. Many people are guessing . . . Many observers say that that sort of thing happens; that productivity increases, that profitability increases under profit or gain sharing. But I must admit that there have not been any careful studies that have tried to control for all variables. That may be because it is just not possible to study this and control for all the right things.

Feiwel: Are you saying that properly implemented, the profit-sharing scheme might reduce uncertainty, might shift the focus of attention on more long-term policies, on investment, dynamic efficiency, and technical progress?

Weitzman: There is both a microeconomic and a macroeconomic side to profit sharing. The microeconomic side was always out there, although, for a variety of reasons, there is more interest in it now than ever before. What was not out there was the macroeconomic side. From the microeconomic side there seems to be a promise of all sorts of good things. But we do not know enough ... The stories one hears are good. The studies that have been done seem generally favorable. But, as I have indicated, it is simply very difficult to study the effects of profit sharing. One of the problems is cause and effect. If, indeed, one shows that there is a positive correlation between productivity and profit sharing (as most studies seem to indicate), what is causing what? Perhaps good management is causing both. It is bringing in profit sharing at the same time as it is emphasizing productivity. Perhaps good human relations are behind both of these phenomena. So, it is difficult to get conclusions on the micro side.

Looking at profit sharing from the macro side, the big uncertainty from a social point of view are the Okun gaps – the fluctuations in output. The individual uncertainty about personal earnings amounts to Harberger triangle losses. For example, if I take a dollar from you and give it to me, or vice versa, there is some loss that is largely offset. So, there may be some loss, but it is offset. The big loss to society is when you cannot run the economy at (or near) full employment. To the extent that profit sharing would help in the inflation—unemployment trade-off – and I am convinced that it can; the bottom line is that it is hard to see how it can hurt and it is easy to see many ways in which it could help – there could be enormous social gains in the reduction of business-cycle type fluctuations.

Feiwel: To what extent is your scheme concerned with income distribution?

Weitzman: I am not quite sure that I am trying to make much of a statement about income distribution. My scheme is actually pretty narrowly in the standard Keynesian macroeconomic tradition. I am saying, 'Let us get income up for everybody.' This would be my general attitude, but it would depend more specifically upon the country and the times. In Europe that certainly is the major problem. When you have 12 per cent unemployment in the UK, that is a disease! You have to get the patient's fever down and afterwards you worry about the fine tuning. That degree of unemployment is itself causing much deleterious income distribution, simply *ipso facto*. In a way, I am putting income distribution questions off, simply trying to get closer to full employment. That is not to say that measures should not (or cannot) be taken with regard to income distribution, but I am holding them in abeyance.

Feiwel: But are you not concentrating on the effects of income distribution since your scheme aims at dividing income into fixed and variable parts? Is not this, by itself, an income distribution problem *par excellence*? And are you not combining macro and income distribution problems?

Weitzman: In a narrow sense it is addressing certain income distribution problems by saying that more of labor's income should be directly coming out of profits. What my research shows, at least on a theoretical level with the kinds of models I have been playing around with, is that it is not going to do very much to relative shares. That these shares are going to come out about the same. That the quantitative effect on income distribution is not going to be significant.

The major effect will be in improving the employment-inflation tradeoff. The reason is that the wage-system is very unforgiving. If you have a wage-system, then you have to get a certain exact balance between demand and the money wage in order to just hit full employment. This is important. If demand is too low, it is going to cause unemployment. I keep emphasizing this point which I think has not been emphasized nearly enough: these are two sides of the same coin. To say that aggregate demand is too low is the same thing as saying that wages are too high. Aggregate demand is too low relative to what? Relative to money wages. Or wages are too high relative to what? Relative to aggregate demand. It is the same thing! The money wage system as I have said, is very unforgiving because if there isn't this exact balance between the two we have troubles. A profit-sharing system is more forgiving because you can get the wrong profit-sharing coefficients and the wrong base wages (within some degree) and still have full employment without inflationary pressures. You do not have to hit the nail right on the head to get full employment without inflation under a profit-sharing system. I consider that to be the really important attribute of such a system.

To put it somewhat differently, if you think of the wage as a parameter in a wage system, if you do not hit that exactly right relative to aggregate demand, you have problems. If you think of the base wage and the profit-sharing parameter as the basic parameters of the profit-sharing system, they do not have to be 'exactly right' relative to aggregate demand in order to have a relatively good outcome. In this sense, it is a more forgiving system. Without really thinking very carefully about it, we have evolved historically a system that inherently has bad macroeconomic properties. My feeling is that especially in Europe, until we address this in a more fundamental way, there will continue to be major macroeconomic problems. They have to be addressed more fundamentally in terms of this bad design of the wage mechanism.

Feiwel: Does the relative strength of the opposition to profit sharing depend on a misperception of who is going to gain?

Weitzman: Certainly. There is going to be no movement in this direction until there is some sort of perception of crisis; that the system is really malfunctioning in a fairly major way. That is because there never is change of a fundamental sort, no matter how good the theory is – and it could be much better than any that I put forward – unless there is a basic perception that something is fundamentally wrong. Because all change is challenging and all change will end up hurting someone. There is no such basic perception in the US right now (1988). In November 1982, there was something of such a perception, with unemployment rates inching up towards 11 per cent. There actually was a feeling of something basically wrong; that the only way there was to get inflation down and deal with the inflation–unemployment dilemma was to go to unpalatable extremes. There was an outcry for new ideas and a receptivity to them. But that time has passed in the US. It may well come back . . . it probably will come back because I do not think that we have tamed the business cycle.

Right now in Europe there is a perception that there is something fundamentally wrong; that there is a fundamental problem with the economic system that transcends any quick Keynesian patches or any quick monetarist fix-up jobs. That there is something fundamentally wrong on just this kind of level I am talking about. For that reason, I suppose, there is much greater resonance to and receptivity of profit-sharing ideas. The greatest interest has been evinced in the UK, but there is also considerable interest in France, Italy, and other countries. Much more so than in the US, because there is more of an unemployment problem, there is more of a dilemma how to get unemployment rates down and it is felt more keenly that the problem is structural.

Feiwel: Would it be correct to interpret your position as advocating an overhaul of the institutional arrangements of the capitalist system (its wage system), rather than tinkering with fiscal and monetary 'tricks', to mitigate business-cycle fluctuations?

Weitzman: To a certain extent this is correct, but I would not want to phrase it so extremely as to be interpreted as saying that Keynesian policies do not work, or that they are superficial, or anything of this sort. Things work differently in different historical periods. Keynesian policies were working much more effectively until fifteen years ago or so. They still may be the most potent gun in town. For a variety of reasons, it may well be that what I am advocating is not feasible, or has some hidden flaws in it, or whatever. However, I do think the time has come to think more fundamentally and more seriously about the nature of the problem and of all the different ways of getting at it. The Keynesian approach of manipulating financial aggregates of one kind or another, for all the power that it has had and still has, desperately needs, I think, to be supplemented by flexibility on the wage side. To what extent that can replace traditional Keynesian policies or to what extent it only supplements them is an open question that we do not need to answer yet. But such flexibility is needed desperately, especially in certain European economies.

Feiwel: Would you agree with the following oversimplified interpretation: 'Keynes claimed that in the 1930s the problem was not one of wage flexibility, but of flexibility of budgetary policy to adjust itself to more or less rigid wages; Weitzman says that in the 1980s, whatever the track record of the Keynesian policies, we need much more than that'?

Weitzman: Yes, essentially we need to be paying attention to the other side of the coin. Keynes, who did not go deeply into the issue, said that we have to take the wage-level and the wage-system as given; we were not going to be able to change it very much, and it is not clear that we would want to change it. He advocated that we should be actively manipulating the demand side. I am saying that these are two sides of the same coin. It turns out that it is not enough to try to actively influence the demand side; one needs to institute a more forgiving pay system. The two of these together might be a very powerful package, indeed. But right now there should be more emphasis on the cost side, on making it more flexible and more forgiving.

Feiwel: What model of price formation underlies your thinking?

Weitzman: It is Kaleckian in a sense. It is a model of imperfect competition that for macro purposes at least could be summarized as monopolistic competition. (If you wanted to extend it to the microeconomy, you would have to get into oligopoly and all of that.) Basically, it takes the labor–payment mechanism as given in the short run while prices and output are determined in a kind of Nash equilibrium game in order to maximize profits, with the proper income feedbacks taken account of. In other words, the model I have in the back of my mind (and in some of the papers I have written) is one of monopolistic competition where basically the anchor is a payment system that is quasi-fixed in the short run.

Feiwel: A more general question: how do you feel about the recent trends and turmoil in macroeconomics?

Weitzman: I do not know whether it is an advantage or disadvantage, but I am not actually a full-bred macroeconomist and have not become one. Perhaps it is an advantage in that I have had the luxury of being able to sort of stand off to the side and say, 'Look, this is what I believe', and work with that. Someone who teaches macro or is really active and labels himself a macroeconomist is forced to come to grips with all the new developments and try to make some sense of them. Indirectly, I also do, but I have the luxury of not having to try to put it all together.

It is pretty clear to me that macroeconomics is in some sort of state of decadence, to use a strong word. It is perhaps in a state of counterproductivity where what is being produced on the standard frontiers of theoretical macroeconomics does not bear a strong relation, at least in my mind, to the actual problems out there in the world. My viewpoint or my philosophy is actually quite different from someone who thinks of himself as doing research at the frontiers of macroeconomics. I go back to thinking of macroeconomics as starting with Keynes. There was no macro before Keynes. The inspiration and origin of it was very practical: it was a series of problems that arose in the 1930s (and in the UK earlier than that) that needed a solution and Keynes came up with a solution of sorts. In a sense, this remains my attitude towards macroeconomics. It is in a way like a medical attitude: what are the problems of the malfunctioning economy and what are the possible solutions? There are specific problems now and I try to address myself to solving them. As for ultimately understanding at some very deep level what this is all about, I am not quite sure it can be done. I do not think it is being done now, despite a brave attack with hot new mathematical tools. I simply do not see any success to the endeavor; it may not even be possible to mathematize macroeconomics to that degree. The more I get involved in 'real-world' discussions about wage systems or proft sharing or whatever, the more I see that they are tied up with elements of history, with irrationality, with institutions, and with other such 'dirty' words. It may just not be possible to put some of the key elements of this into a neat mathematical package.

I must admit that at some level it bothers me that I do not have a fundamental theory about why wage systems seem to be prevalent. The fact of the matter is that they are not overwhelming. It is questionable to what extent Japan has one; there are many profit-sharing firms out there, so there are a number of exceptions. Yet it does seem to be a fair enough generalization that the wage system is the prevalent payment mechanism. It bothers me somewhat, but not enough to stop me from going ahead. I am content to a certain degree to take the wage mechanism more or less as given as an institution and to ask questions about what would happen if the institution were changed and ask questions about how to get different institutions simply in a common-sense down-to-earth fashion.

Most modern macroeconomists would throw the question out of court right away. They would say, 'If you do not have an answer to this big question about why there is a wage system in the first place, we cannot proceed any further with the discussion because if we do not have that kind of a theory, how are we going to know what would happen if you change it, or what not?'

I do not think it is possible to do economics that way as a general statement. Economics simply is not physics; it is not that precise that you can start off with *really* fundamental axioms and put them all into one box, or you will be doing that forever! You will be doing that for a thousand years and by then the world would have changed. By that time the question you will have answered will be irrelevant because the world would have changed. You simply have to cut in at certain points and take certain institutions as given. That is an art; it is not a science. In certain countries socialism is given, in others capitalism is given. It is all right to say that the system is given. You do not have to have an overall theory explaining what produces capitalism or socialism before you even begin investigating their economic systems. And so it goes down the line. You simply cannot push fundamentalism in economics too far. It becomes counterproductive and economics is not suited to that sort of thing. Economics is an area of study that is at least as closely related methodologically to history, law, and the other social sciences as it is to physics and mathematics. It is some sort of combination. To go too far in one direction or the other one loses the essence of what it is all about.

Essentially, I do not want to push any position too far: let a thousand flowers bloom. If some economists want to do fundamental research of the axiomatic sort, fine, let them! But if they judge nothing as worthwhile until everything is put together in some coherent big picture, then I would definitely oppose that. That is simply not what economics is about! It is the wrong attitude. It is possible to proceed on a wide variety of fronts, but you do not want to exclude the possibility of cutting in at various points and taking the medical kind of approach that says, 'What are the patient's problems, how can we go about making him feel better?' In my view there is nothing methodologically wrong with that kind of approach.

Feiwel: You have written some excellent papers on the implications of increasing returns. Could you share with us the essence of your fundamental arguments?

Weitzman: I think that increasing returns is more fundamental than others do in our understanding of what involuntary unemployment is all about. The models that do not have increasing returns somewhere in there (or imperfect competition which comes close to the same thing because it is hard to visualize imperfect competition without increasing returns) cannot and, in fact, do not get at the essence of what involuntary unemployment is about. All these models, whether rational expectationist or not, built on neoclassical production functions do not actually have involuntary unemployment. They have in effect some sort of voluntary unemployment. If there are constant returns to scale, if you really have a world of blueberry pickers and clam diggers, all kinds of bad signalling problems may arise in fancy enough models or situations. Even in common-sense terms these people can still starve to death if there is a bad harvest or whatever. But in such systems there is never any involuntary unemployment because there is no sense in which the clam digger, who goes out with a minimal amount of equipment, can be called involuntarily unemployed. He is choosing not to employ himself for whatever reason.

To get at the essence of involuntary unemployment, I think you have to have some notion of a larger scale enterprise the worker is deprived from joining. He cannot reproduce in his backyard a 1/10,000-manned automobile plant or something like that. If we had that kind of a world, if we had a real constant-returns-to-scale world, we could not have experienced the Great Depression. That did not occur simply because of bad signals that could be interpreted readily in a constant-returns or diminishing-returns type of world. That was a world where people were losing their comparative advantage that comes from economies of scale; from being a factory worker, from belonging to large-scale teams, and could not replicate the same thing on their own. Now, individuals in the system made desperate attempts to replicate it on their own, but they could not come anywhere near the productivity that comes with large scale. That is, they tried to sell apples at street corners, they tried to shine shoes, they tried to go back to the farm. They tried to do all these things on an individual scale in order to gain employment. I suppose that if the Great Depression had continued for several decades, they would have ultimately had employment. They would have retreated to an earlier mode of production, closer to constant returns to scale. The problem with that is that it is not very productive. The dilemma is that the productive economy is the increasing-returns one, but it is the one where the coordination failures come down tough and have very serious consequences.

I think that increasing returns (and imperfect competition) is actually a very important part of the story in the sense that the *really* big coordination failure is the Okun-gap sort of thing. One can tell other stories of coordination failure, with constant returns to scale, with the wrong signals coming out, as in rational-expectations kinds of worlds, but they typically involve Harberger triangle-type losses. They are not significant economic losses and I do not think that was what the Great Depression was about or that even that is what serious recessions are about. These involve involuntary unemployment. If one wants to tell that story consistently, at some point one has to have increasing returns and imperfect competition. In that sense, it is an important part of microfoundations.

Feiwel: How do you feel about Joan Robinson's work?

Weitzman: I am a great fan of Joan Robinson. Some of her writings, particularly when they get polemical, are difficult to understand. There is a part of her work that I now feel I understand, and for years I did not quite grasp. In a way it was her fault because she made it so polemical. I think she insisted on the distinction between risk and uncertainty that Frank Knight made. While she did not use that kind of language explicitly, I think it was permeating a lot of her thinking. Her complaints about modern neoclassical economics was that their world was assumed to be a risk-like world, rather than an uncertain one. To Joan Robinson, I think this was assuming away most of the problem. She did get polemical about it, however, and it was difficult to decipher exactly what she meant. I have read some of her work more recently and that is what has come across to me.

Feiwel: Joan always insisted on the need to bring in dynamics, time, and history into economic analysis. When you spoke about the development of wage-systems, you spoke in a similar vein. Is it possible to model these things rigorously with the tools available at present and take account of history?

Weitzman: It seems to be awfully difficult. You would want to preclude it; we have to continue researching it. It just seems that at some stage of economics you have to put in certain institutions or attitudes. As I have mentioned before, I do not approach theory with the preconception that it has to be axiomatically based to be any good or that within economics we have to start from building up some complete structure. I do not think that is possible. I feel it is a question of cutting in at a certain point, using some theoretical structure, and gaining some conclusions. How good or effective that is can only be judged by the strength of the results relative to how restrictive the assumptions are. One cannot pass an absolute judgment about how good that kind of performance is. If you ask deep historical economic questions – some of which are very important, like, for instance, why do Germans always seem to succeed (East Germany is the richest state *per capita* in the Eastern Bloc and West Germany is one of the richest in the Western Bloc) – they are at least as important as the more narrow economic questions that we tackle. Why do the Japanese have a quite different labor relations system from ours, including a bonus system? I do not know whether it is possible to model those things. It certainly is not possible now. But whether in principle there is some practically insurmountable obstacle, I do not know.

Feiwel: What is your perception – as a younger generation MIT economist – of the polemics between Joan Robinson (Kaldor, and others) and the neoclassical economists?

Weitzman: I am not quite sure that I qualify to answer that, especially when in your volumes you have contributions by many people who are closer to this sort of thing. I am somewhat too young to have understood what it was all about. It was always a puzzle to me what the intensity of this fight was all about. Someone who was in on it, like Paul Samuelson, Bob Solow, or even Franco Modigliani (although to a somewhat lesser extent) would have much more of a sense of what that battle was about. I never quite grasped why Joan Robinson and the others were so intense in their dislike of what was going on. Perhaps some of it was plain anti-Americanism . . . who knows?

Feiwel: How do you perceive Kaldor's attacks on equilibrium economics?

Weitzman: I certainly can sympathize with part of what Kaldor was saying. I am not sure I liked the way he had it all come out. I think that the more constructive part of his polemic was the attack on constant returns to scale – something that is dear to my heart. As I understood it, he said that that is giving rise to a misleading view of the world. I think that to some extent that is true. To some extent, Walrasian economics is, as Schumpeter called it, the Magna Charta of economics but there are certain misleading views of the world that it gives rise to. To the extent that Kaldor was trying to say that, I have some sympathy for his criticism. But I am not quite sure that that is exactly what he was trying to say. He spoke in such general terms. It is not actually equilibrium that is the problem, it is the particular general equilibrium model based on constant returns and all the rest of that that he seemed to be finding fault with. But he did not actually distinguish between the two. Equilibrium theory does not have to mean the standard constant-returns-to-scale (convexity) model of general equilibrium. That is the one we usually use because it is tractable. But there are others that work in other special cases. There is none that has the kind of general tractability that the convexity model has, but there are other equilibrium models. I never understood why Kaldor did not make that distinction.

Feiwel: Do you mean that there is a tendency by critics to identify the general equilibrium approach with the competitive model?

Weitzman: Exactly. I think that criticisms of the competitive convexity model are one thing. Criticisms of equilibrium methodology are another thing. They tend to get confused.

Part VII

Money, Finance, and the Monetarists

21 The Paradox of Money in the Economics of Joan Robinson

Dudley Dillard*

Is there a paradox in the economics of Joan Robinson in the post-Keynesian period?[1] Apart from Richard Kahn, she worked with Keynes more closely than anyone else during the years of preparation of the *General Theory of Employment, Interest and Money*, a book which explains unemployment in terms of money and interest and which Keynes initially entitled 'The Monetary Theory of Production' (Keynes, 1979, p.49). In the early post-General Theory years, Mrs Robinson published several books and numerous journal articles expounding, with Keynes's approval, the doctrines of the *General Theory*. In her published writings she was always a loyal follower and defender of Keynes's theory. Yet in the post-Keynesian phase (after 1946) of her career money occupies no significant place in her extension of the General Theory to capital accumulation, economic growth, and the distribution of income. There appears to be a paradox in the sense that, after deep immersion in the monetary economics of Keynes, the absence of money as a strategic factor in her theory runs counter to expectations. The present chapter examines this apparent paradox. Section 1 deals briefly with the period prior to the preparation of the *General Theory*; Section 2 with the preparation and early aftermath of the *General Theory*; Section 3 with the post-Keynesian period following Keynes's death in 1946; and Section 4 contains some general observations and conclusions.

1 THE PRE-KEYNESIAN PERIOD

Alfred Marshall's *Principles of Economics* dominated economic thinking at Cambridge University during Joan Robinson's apprenticeship there during the 1920s. Her early work built on foundations laid down by Marshall, but her monumental *The Economics of Imperfect Competition* (1933) was inspired by Piero Sraffa's pathbreaking 1926 article on 'The Laws of Returns under Competitive Conditions' (Sraffa, 1926). In the Foreword to her book she wrote: 'Mr Sraffa's article must be regarded as the fount from

*I am indebted to my wife, Louisa Gardner Dillard, for assistance in the preparation of this paper.

which my work flows, for the chief aim of this book is to attempt to carry out his pregnant suggestion that the whole theory of value should be treated in terms of monopoly analysis' (Robinson, 1933, p.v). The monopoly emphasis is a thread of continuity running through Mrs Robinson's economics from value theory in *Imperfect Competition* to post-Keynesian analysis of the nature of capital in a capitalist economy. The work of Sraffa and Robinson marks the beginning of a Cambridge revolution in value theory that was, in a sense, interrupted by the Keynesian revolution and not completed until Sraffa published his *Production of Commodities by Means of Commodities* (Sraffa, 1960).

'Money' does not appear in the index of Robinson's *Imperfect Competition*, which comes as no surprise in a book in mainstream economic theory. Beginning with Adam Smith, money has been neutralized in classical and neoclassical general principles of economics, including the theory of value, distribution, and growth. Yet it is not logically inevitable that money should be excluded as a significant variable in a theory of imperfect competition. Value theory is a central part of the theory of the firm, and firms in a business enterprise system are primarily concerned with making money. Moreover, firms can make more money under monopolistic conditions by making fewer goods and selling them at higher prices. Business firms normally produce some kind of 'real' product and attempt to realize its value by selling it for money. This is fundamental to all microeconomic activity, and one might assume to microeconomic theory. But Sraffa and Robinson in the tradition of Smith, Ricardo, J. S. Mill, and Marshall ignored the essential properties of money in the money-making process of business firms. Only underworld economists such as Karl Marx and Thorstein Veblen integrated money into general economic theory. The young Joan Robinson probably had not encountered Marx and Veblen at this stage, and even if she had, there is no reason to suppose that her theory of imperfect competition would have been affected. Her intellectual world, however, was on the brink of revolutionary change. The Keynesian revolution was to be the focal point of her professional attention. Money and a monetary theory of interest moved to central stage in this revolution. The primary issue to which the present paper is addressed is whether she ever accepted the central message of Keynes's *General Theory*.

2 THE KEYNESIAN PERIOD

The Foreword of Joan Robinson's *Imperfect Competition* is dated October 1932. By this time she was already deeply immersed in discussions leading from Keynes's *Treatise on Money* (1930) to the *General Theory* (1936), including the Cambridge 'Circus' of the early months of 1931 (Keynes, 1973a, pp.337–43.) In October 1933, she published an important article entitled 'The Theory of Money and the Analysis of Output' (Robinson, 1951). Eighteen years later she said this paper 'gives an outline of Keynes' theory as far as it had got in 1933' (Robinson, 1951, p.viii). Here she distinguishes clearly between changes in output resulting indirectly from changes in prices (the theory of money) and changes in output resulting directly from changes in demand and supply (analysis of output). Lawrence Klein thought this 1933 article so important that he dated the birth of Keynes's *General Theory* from its publication (Klein, 1947, pp.39–40; but see Robinson, 1951, pp.viii–ix). The direct changes in output contain a substantial part of what Don Patinkin calls the unique central message of the *General Theory* (Patinkin, 1982, chapter 4).

Significantly for our purposes, Robinson's 1933 paper contains a clue to the paradox we are seeking to explain. The title of the paper retains the dichotomy of mainstream economics between the theory of prices as the theory of money, on the one hand, and the theory of employment as the theory of output, on the other. Keynes rejects this dichotomy in the *General Theory* (1936, p.293). The content as well as the title of Robinson's 1933 paper fails to capture the spirit of Keynes's 'complete theory of a monetary economy' (1936, p.293). By 1932 Keynes had chosen as the tentative title of the book then in preparation 'The Monetary Theory of Production' (Keynes, 1979, p.49). If Robinson's article had been titled 'The Theory of Money and Monetary Theory of Output', it would have come close to showing an appreciation of what Keynes was striving to achieve. This article, perhaps, foreshadows her non-acceptance of the centrality of money in Keynes's thinking and analysis.

Robinson worked closely with Keynes all the way to the completion of the *General Theory*. She read drafts and proofs and made general and detailed suggestions and criticisms. She is one of only four economists acknowledged in the Preface of the *General Theory*, the others being R. F. Kahn, R. G. Hawtrey, and R. F. Harrod, and only one of two Cambridge colleagues, the other being Kahn (Keynes, 1936, p.viii).

Chapter 17 of the *General Theory*, entitled 'The Essential Properties of Interest and Money', contains the principal statments of the role of money in Keynes's economic theory. When Joan Robinson was reading proofs, Keynes seemed especially anxious to know if she understood chapter 17. At one point he wrote to her:

> You do not say whether the chapter on 'Essential Properties' proved fully intelligible in the long run. If it did, I should be content, since much of the stuff in this chapter, being rather unfamiliar at this stage to the author as well as to the reader, is inevitably more obscure than it will be after the passage of a little time. (Keynes, 1973a, p.645)

In a covering letter accompanying her detailed comments, Mrs Robinson wrote, 'I think I got the "Essential Properties" in the end apart from particular points which I have noted' (Keynes, 1973a, p.646). She included with her letter a five-paragraph statement of her understanding of Keynes's concept of liquidity, and added: 'If I am right about this I don't think I have any further difficulty or disagreement' (Keynes, 1973a, p.646). The fact that Robinson would write a note on liquidity in trying to grasp and clarify the content of chapter 17 is significant because, while liquidity is closely related, chapter 17 attempts to go beyond the liquidity-preference explanation of interest in chapters 13 ('The General Theory of the Rate of Interest') and 15 ('The Psychological and Business Incentives to Liquidity'). If Robinson thought a clear statement about liquidity would clarify chapter 17, she did not fully understand the meaning of that chapter.[2]

The general purpose of chapter 17 of the *General Theory* is to explain what is special about money, what sets it apart from all other assets. Keynes generalizes the problem by explaining, following Sraffa, that all assets have their own-rate of interest. The burden of the chapter is to show why, among all rates of interest, the rate on money is strategically special in relation to involuntary unemployment, Money's special properties include zero carrying costs and zero or neglibible elasticities of production and substitution. Money by its institutional nature in a capitalist economy is the asset for which the liquidity premium is most in excess of its carrying cost. Beyond a certain point, the rate of interest on money 'does not fall in response to an increase in its quantity to anything approaching the extent to which the yield from other assets falls when their quantity is comparably increased' (Keynes, 1936, p.233). Thus in the absence of money the rates of interest would reach equilibrium only at full employment (Keynes, 1936, p.235). This says that involuntary unemployment is caused by interest and money. Keynes restated the argument of chapter 17 in somewhat different terms in a paper entitled 'The Theory of the Rate of Interest', published originally in a *Festschrift* in honor of Irving Fisher (Keynes, 1973b, pp.101–8). In a discussion with Mrs Robinson in 1971, I asked her about the phrases on page 235 of the *General Theory* to the effect that in the absence of money, the rates of interest would reach equilibrium only at full employment. After reading these passages, she said, 'That makes no sense.' I could only conclude that she was not sympathetic to the general thrust of chapter 17. She did not accept Keynes's monetary explanation of involuntary unemployment.

The polarized relation between money and all other assets portrayed in chapter 17 is analogous to Karl Marx's contrast between money and commodities. In section 3 of the first chapter of volume I of *Capital*, Marx shows that money is the logical and necessary outcome of a system of commodity production (Marx, 1936, pp.54–81). Of necessity, according to Marx, in a system of production on private account, there will emerge from the world of commodities, one which will be the general equivalent of all the others. This is money, the universal equivalent of all (other) commodities.

Marx's *Capital*, like Keynes's *General Theory*, may be described as a monetary theory of production in the sense that capitalist firms are primarily concerned with 'making money'. They produce physical output not as an end in itself but as a means toward selling the so-called real output for money, and thereby 'realizing' profits. Money is the universal equivalent in terms of which the exchange value of all commodities is *realized* in the process of being sold for money. Keynes, in an early draft of the *General Theory*, invoked Marx's general formula for capital, *M-C-M′* (Keynes, 1979, p.81). 'An entrepreneur is interested, not in the amount of product, but in the amount of *money* which will fall to his share' (Keynes, 1979, p.82, Keynes's emphasis). Keynes calls Marx's formula for capital a 'pregnant suggestion' (Keynes, 1979, p.81). He continued: 'The firm is dealing throughout in terms of sums of money. It has no object in the world except to end up with more money than it started with. That is the essential characteristic of an entrepreneur economy' (Keynes, 1979, p.89). This concept of a monetary economy was in Keynes's thinking when he wrote chapter 17. Joan Robinson never accepted the message.

Joan Robinson opened her 1961 article on 'Own Rates of Interest' by characterizing Keynes's chapter 17 as 'the mysterious chapter' (Robinson, 1975, p.132). She shuns the use of terms such as 'own-rates of own-interest' and gives a lucid exposition of her contention that Keynes failed to demonstrate why wealth-holders would refuse to lend money at low rates of interest so long as they exceeded zero. A long period of low interest rates in which experience would have shown that interest rates are not going to rise in the future would remove, apart from lenders' risk, any reason for interest rates not to be low. For the long period, she said, 'Keynes had stretched it [liquidity preference] beyond its powers' (Robinson, 1975, pp.135).

In section II of her own-rates paper, Robinson defends Keynes's contention that at some periods in history a strong desire to hold land has kept interest rates high in a manner analogous to Keynes's claim that in modern times the desire to hold money keeps interest rates relatively high (Robinson, 1975, p.135–7).

In a 'postscript' to the own-rates paper, Robinson denies allegations that her intention was to attack the concept of liquidity preference. Instead, she wrote, it was intended to rescue liquidity preference from a misapplication, in chapter 17, by Keynes himself (Robinson, 1975, p.137). Writing a quarter-century after she had read the proofs of chapter 17, Robinson recalls, 'When Keynes was writing that chapter, he admitted that he was groping for ideas that were new to him, and I do not think that he ever quite succeeded in seizing them' (Robinson, 1975, p.138). Certainly she is right that Keynes was groping for new ideas, for a more profound meaning of the role of money in a capitalist economy. His entire career as an economist was devoted to finding progressively subtle insights into the nature of money (Dillard, 1954, p.30).

Robinson offers no clues as to what new ideas Keynes may have been groping for and failed to grasp when he composed chapter 17. But the general problem posed by Keynes in that chapter was by no means novel in the history of economic analysis. As noted above, Marx opened *Capital* with an analysis of the polar relation between money and commodities, the almost precise task undertaken by Keynes in chapter 17. In a discussion with Mrs Robinson in 1971, I asked if she saw any connection between Keynes's chapter 17 and Marx's chapter in which he shows the polarized relation between money and other forms of wealth. She replied that chapter 1 of Marx is 'mysterious', interestingly the identical word she used to describe Keynes's chapter 17 (see above). About Marx's chapter 1, she said, 'I do not understand it.' She seemed unaware of a large body of literature relating money to other assets, such as the labor–money concept developed by the Ricardian socialists, including John Gray in England and P. J. Proudhon in France. Marx's first major undertaking as an economist was the theoretical repudiation of the 'utopian' ideas of the labor–money advocates. References to the labor–money socialists are scattered in the text and footnotes throughout Marx's *Critique of Political Economy* and the early chapters of volume I of *Capital*, and also Marx's *Grundrisse*.

Robinson wrote frequently about Marx, especially in her later years. In addition to her small book, *An Essay on Marxian Economics* (1966), every one of the first five volumes of her *Collected Economic Papers* contains at least one essay on Marx. In all these writings there is no mention or recognition that one of Marx's main contributions to economics was the complete integration of money into his economic theory. The word 'money' is not in the index of *An Essay on Marxian Economics*. Marx's general formula for capital, *M-C-M′*, to which Keynes was attracted (see above), does not appear in Robinson's book on Marx or anywhere else so far as I have discovered. She appears to have been insensitive to 'money' as an important factor in general economic theory.

My long-standing interest in Keynes's concept of 'monetary economy' is indicated by the subtitle, 'The Theory of a Monetary Economy' to my book *The Economics of John Maynard Keynes* (1948). While visiting Cambridge University in the spring of 1971, I prepared a list of questions, all focusing on the general topic of 'monetary economy'. My first question to Mrs Robinson concerned Keynes's contribution to the Spiethoff *Festschrift* (Keynes, 1973a, pp.408–11). This article, entitled 'A Monetary Theory of Production', had been published in Germany during 1933 in a volume that did not circulate widely. Therefore I was not surprised when she said she had never seen the article. I gave her a copy and called attention to the final two paragraphs.[3] Keynes's closing paragraph reads as follows: 'Accordingly I believe that the next task is to work out in some detail a monetary theory of production, to supplement the real-exchange theories which we already possess. At any rate that is the task on which I am now occupying myself, in some confidence that I am not wasting my time' (Keynes, 1973a, p.411). Mrs Robinson's response differed from what I expected. She dismissed the paper with the remark that it referred to the transition from the *Treatise* to the *General Theory*, by which I believe she meant a kind of halfway house between these two important books. My reaction to the Spiethoff piece is quite different. I remember vividly the excitement of discovering that such a statement by Keynes existed as missing evidence to confirm my interpretation of Keynes's theory. I view the Spiethoff paper as Keynes's ambitious agenda for research which he undertook but never completed. He came closest in the groupings contained in chapter 17 on 'The Essential Properties of Interest and Money'. The *General Theory* is an unfinished symphony. In any event, what matters for this chapter is that Joan Robinson showed no enthusiasm for Keynes's idea of a monetary theory of production. Although on that occasion she did not have time for a considered judgment about the Spiethoff paper, her instant reaction was unsympathetic and consistent with her general attitude on this topic. I doubt that her attitude would have been different after longer contemplation.

In two follow-up questions: What do you think Keynes meant by a monetary theory of production? and Is it reasonable to identify a monetary theory of production with a capitalist economy? she had nothing substantive to say; and to a further question: What would a non-monetary economy be? (Keynes, 1936, p.239), she said, 'There is no such thing.' I concluded that a monetary theory of production was of little interest to her, perhaps even that she was hostile to the concept.

In response to yet another question, she said that Keynes had not lectured at Cambridge on own-rates of interest. Chapter 17 was included among early drafts of the *General Theory*, but Donald Moggridge, who was present at the discussion, said the first draft of chapter 17 is not among the 'Keynes papers'. In response to a question concerning A. P. Lerner's point that stickiness of wages and prices is an essential property of money, she did not answer directly but said she agreed with Keynes that unemployment would be worse with fully flexible wages and prices (Lerner, 1952, p.193).

Robinson said she strongly supported G. L. S. Shackle's emphasis on money as 'a medium of postponement', and also his expression 'inherent ignorance concerning the outcome of our actions'. She also felt that Keynes's 1937 response to his critics in the *Quarterly Journal of Economics* is a very important statement of Keynes's basic position (Keynes, 1973b, pp.109–23).

3 THE POST-KEYNESIAN PERIOD

In the post-war, neo-Keynesian phase of her career, Joan Robinson extended the Keynesian system to long-period theories of capital accumulation, growth, and income distribution. Keynes's *General Theory* is primarily short-period analysis. Investment, his strategic factor for determining the volume of employment, disburses effective demand into the economy to supplement the effective demand arising from the income generated by the production of consumer goods and services. Robinson's post-Keynesian efforts take account of the long-term consequences for growth and distribution associated with additions to productive capacity. This led her to explore the *meaning* of capital and to question traditional methods of measuring quantities of capital (Robinson, 1965, p.vi). It also led to inquiry into the theory of profits and the distribution of income between wages and profits.

Joan Robinson's *The Accumulation of Capital* (1965) contains a chapter entitled 'The Meaning of Money'. The traditional dualism rejected by Keynes, between real and money sectors is revealed in the following passage: 'one of the purposes of economic theory is to look through the veil of money to the realities behind it' (Robinson, 1965, p.25). Here she cites the pre-Keynesian work of Professor A. C. Pigou. A reader of this chapter on 'The Meaning of Money' would have no reason to suspect that Keynes's *General Theory* had ever been written, and certainly not that Robinson had been one of its chief architects. The subject matter of this chapter is price levels, purchasing power, and central banks, but nothing about the accumulators of capital being primarily interested in accumulating by selling output for money on an expanding basis. A brief section on liquidity speaks routinely about 'certainty of value' and 'ease of marketability'. A subsequent chapter on 'Money and Finance' in *The Accumulation of Capital* presents nothing to change the picture. Money is never portrayed as playing a part of its own by affecting motives and decisions as one of the operative factors in accumulation. 'Finance' has a place in enabling business firms to gain access to money for adding to their capital assets, but Keynes's type of monetary theory is nowhere to be found in Joan Robinson's extension of Keynes's theory to the long period.

A conceivable rationale for the negligible importance of money in Joan Robinson's post-Keynesian career is that, although money is admittedly important in the short period, real forces take over in her extension of Keynes's short-period analysis to the long period and money fades into insignificance. This argument, however, is not plausible in relation to Keynes's monetary theory of production, where money is the 'realist' of real forces in the long as well as the short period. A monetary (capitalist) economy consists of business firms creating products the values of which are *realized* only after they are sold for money. There is nothing automatic or routine about this institutional process. If products cannot be sold, their values are not realized. If products are sold for less than their cost of production, their values are only partly realized. In Keynes's General Theory, money is an institution of capitalism, and the institution is important in the long as well as the short period.

The unstable and fluctuating conditions of a business enterprise economy are responsible for difficulties of *realizing* monetary values by the sale of 'real' goods. Money as the universal equivalent of private business wealth is clearer in depression than during prosperity because the ability to convert so-called real products into money is more difficult. These products may be real for consumers, but they are not really real for business enterprises. The institutional process, however, remains the same in good times and bad times. Money as the universal equivalent becomes most apparent in financial crises and panics, such as in the United Kingdom in 1931 and the United States in 1932. In these conditions it becomes most apparent that money is the only asset that *really* counts for business firms.

Accumulation of capital constitutes a major part of Joan Robinson's post-Keynesian economic analysis, but there is no reason for money to become less important in the theory of capital accumulation. In Keynes's short-period analysis, investment (capital accumulation) is important only because it supplements the effective demand from consumer spending and increases the level of employment. In taking account of increased productive capacity resulting in the long run from capital accumulation, the difficulty of converting real output into money cumulatively increases. In the long run the accumulation of capital tends to push down the marginal efficiency of capital, weaken the inducement to invest, and render the conversion of unwanted (by business) real products into wanted (by business) money. Thus the minimal importance of money in Robinson's post-Keynesian economics cannot legitimately be explained by her extension of Keynes's short-period analysis to long-period analysis.

The influence of Michal Kalecki and Piero Sraffa in the post-Keynesian period did nothing to attract Joan Robinson's attention to a monetary economy. Kalecki developed monetary aspects of the general theory of employment much less than did Keynes. In 1974, Robinson wrote: 'Kalecki's version of the *General Theory*, rather than Keynes', has been incorporated in the post-Keynesian tradition' (Robinson, 1975, p.xiv). One attraction to her of Kalecki's model was his integration of imperfect competition (degree of monopoly) into the theory of employment. According to Nicholas Kaldor, Robinson tried unsuccessfully to persuade Keynes to incorporate imperfect competition as part of his model when writing the *General Theory* (Worswick and Trevithick, 1983, p.47).

Piero Sraffa exercized the greatest influence on Robinson's thinking in the post-Keynesian period, as he had also during the pre-*General Theory* period (see above, Section 1). The second stage in the Cambridge value revolution culminated with publication, in 1960, of Sraffa's *Production of Commodities by Means of Commodities* (Sraffa, 1960). Starting from a Ricardian base, Sraffa developed a theory of the rate of profit independent of marginal analysis, including the marginal productivity theory of distribution. Although nothing sounds more non-monetary than the 'production of commodities by means of commodities', there is a significant connection between Keynes and Sraffa. In chapter 17 of the *General Theory* Keynes credits Sraffa with the concept 'own rates of interest' and speaks of the desirability of a composite (standard) commodity which would have 'uniquely *the* rate of interest' (Keynes, 1936, 223n and p.225. Keynes's emphasis). In a 1978 article on 'Keynes and Ricardo', Joan Robinson calls for a synthesis of Keynes and Sraffa to provide a general framework of short- and long-period analysis of employment and distribution. She says, 'The post-Keynesians must make use of Sraffa to build up a type of long-period analysis which will prevent neoclassical equilibrium from oozing back into the *General Theory*' (Robinson 1978b, p.15). Recent attempts to integrate the work of Keynes and Sraffa have been done by J. A. Kregel (1983, 1985) and E. J. Nell (1983).

4 SUMMARY AND CONCLUSIONS

What appears at first sight to be a paradox concerning the role of money in Joan Robinson's post-Keynesian economics turns out to be not much of a paradox. Among the economists who most influenced her thinking – Marshall, Sraffa, Keynes and Kalecki – only Keynes had a monetary theory of production. Throughout her career Robinson retained the traditional dualism between real and money factors in economic analysis. Only in Keynes's perspective was money the means as well as the end in the activities of business firms. Keynes's monetary position expressed itself strongly in early drafts of the *General Theory* and in the published version most strongly in chapter 17, the unfinished symphony. Robinson was never sympathetic to chapter 17, a fact that shows through in her comments while reading proofs in 1935, in her paper on own-rates of interest in 1961, and in her conversation with me in 1971. Close association with Sraffa and Kalecki may have made her less sensitive to the role of money in relation to the long-term issues on which she focused in the post-Keynesian period.

Nevertheless, Keynes influenced Robinson in a powerful way on economic theory generally and on money in particular. She accepted Keynes's very monetary-oriented reply to critics in his 1937 summation of the *General Theory* (Keynes, 1973b, pp.108–23). She accepted the important relation between money and uncertainty, money as a link between the present and the future, and the theory of liquidity preference, at least a short-term phenomenon. What she did not accept was Keynes's fundamental conception of a monetary theory of production.

Perhaps what calls for explanation is how Keynes broke from the herd of traditional economists to his theory of a monetary economy. This seems to have been a matter of chance and perceptive insight. At an early date he became, somewhat by chance, an expert on money. Throughout his career his orientation was toward money – Indian currency and finance, a tract on monetary reform, a treatise on money, and finally a general theory explaining unemployment in terms of money and a monetary theory of interest. With large unemployed resources, one needs to abstain from anything in order to make resources available for capital formation. All that need be done is to put the idle resources to work constructing capital assets.

The quality of Keynes's intellect and his social vision enabled him to outdistance his fellow monetary specialists, for example, R. G. Hawtrey and D. H. Robertson. Keynes enjoyed the advantage of relatively little formal training in economics, which kept him relatively free of the classical and neoclassical illusion that capitalism works as if it were a barter economy (Kahn, 1984, p.50; Skidelsky, 1986, p.166). So some combination of chance and insight led Keynes to the 'truth' about the monetary nature of the capitalist economy in which he lived.

The most likely explanation of why Joan Robinson never accepted Keynes's monetary theory of production is that she had her own, somewhat different, vision of economic society and consequently a different theory corresponding to that vision. She was her own person and not just someone's follower. The comparison with Keynes may be put in these terms: Robinson's central emphasis was on the essential properties of capital; Keynes's central emphasis was on the essential properties of money. These two views have much in common, but they also contain important differences.

After many years of discussion and controversy concerning the nature, meaning, and measurement of capital, Robinson embraced Thorstein Veblen's concept of capital (Robinson, 1980, p.116). For Veblen the essence of capital is neither an abstract fund of pecuniary value nor physical assets such as machines used in production, but its essence is in the community's accumulated knowledge of the practical arts used in gaining the community's livelihood (Veblen, 1942a, 1942b). Capital is intangible; it is knowledge. This intangible capital (knowledge) becomes embodied in physical instruments of production. In early stages of society nearly everyone can embody community knowledge of the practical arts in simple instruments such as bows and arrows. In modern times, however, the advanced knowledge is embodied in highly complex and expensive instruments. Ownership of these instruments of production carries with it an exclusive right to the usufruct of the common heritage of society, or in

Veblen's words, 'the profitable engrossing of the community's industrial efficiency' (Veblen, 1942a, p.352). Only community ownership of the expensive instruments would permit the usufruct of the common heritage to be shared by the community that produced the intangible capital (knowledge).

Gram and Walsh, in their admirable summation of Joan Robinson's economics, put the issue as follows:

> Thus, the *meaning* of capital ... which is essential ... to her critique of neoclassical theory, is, in her view, quite simply the *monopoly* by firms on the technology of production. Where such monopoly is abolished, at least in principle by state ownership under socialism, capitalism ceases to exist, but capital goods exist and continue to enhance the productivity of labor. In this sense, *capital* under capitalism is perhaps the most important element in the economics of *imperfect competition*. (Gram and Walsh, 1983, p.530; their emphasis)

This passage makes clear Robinson's consistent perspective from her early treatise on *The Economics of Imperfect Competition* to her mature judgment about the nature of capital under capitalism. This broad vision of economic society is analogous to but not identical with that of Keynes. For Keynes, money as an institution of capitalism, constitutes an institutional monopoly. For Joan Robinson, capital as an institution of capitalism, constitutes an institutional monopoly.

Notes

1. The perfunctory role of money in macroeconomics at Cambridge University was the subject of a paper given by J. A. Kregel at the meetings of the American Economic Association in Dallas, in December 1984. He did not single out Joan Robinson, but she was probably the most important representative of that group. See Kregel's paper, 'Hamlet without the Prince: Cambridge Macroeconomics without Money' (Kregel, 1985).
2. Keynes was more patient with Joan Robinson than with D. H. Robertson. After reading the proofs, Robertson wrote to Keynes that the chapter on 'Essential Properties' was obscure. In response, Keynes acknowledged the obscurity of the chapter and added,

   > A time may come when I am, so to speak, sufficiently familiar with my own ideas to make it easier. But at present I doubt if the chapter is any use except to someone who has entered into, and is sympathetic with, the ideas in previous chapters; to which it has, I think, to be regarded as posterior. For it is far easier to argue the ideas involved in the much simpler way in which they arise in the chapter on liquidity preference. (Keynes, 1973a, p.519)

3. Keynes's article in the Spiethoff *Festschrift* was reprinted in the Autumn 1963

issue of the *Nebraska Journal of Economics and Business* under the title 'On the Theory of a Monetary Economy'. As it appeared initially in the *Festschrift*, it did not have a title. The full title of the book in which it first appeared is *Der Stand und die nachste Zukunft de Konjunkturforschung, Festschrift fur Arthur Spiethoff* (Munich: Duncker & Humblot, 1933).

References

Dillard. D. (1948) *The Economics of John Maynard Keynes* (Englewood Cliffs, NJ: Prentice-Hall).

Dillard, D. (1954) 'The Theory of a Monetary Economy', in K. K. Kurihara (ed.) *Post-Keynesian Economics* (New Brunswick, NJ: Rutgers University Press).

Gram. H. and V. Walsh (1983) 'Joan Robinson's Economics in Retrospect', *Journal of Economic Literature* 21: 518–50.

Kahn, R. F. (1984) *The Making of Keynes' General Theory* (Cambridge: Cambridge University Press).

Kaldor, N. (1983) 'Keynesian Economics after Fifty Years', in D. Worswick and J. Trevithick (eds), *Keynes and the Modern World* (Cambridge: Cambridge University Press).

Keynes, J. M. (1930) *A Treatise on Money*, 2 vols (London: Macmillan).

Keynes, J. M. (1936) *The General Theory of Employment, Interest and Money* (New York: Harcourt, Brace).

Keynes, J. M. (1973a) *The Collected Writings of John Maynard Keynes,* vol. 13, ed. by D. Moggridge (London: Macmillan; New York: St Martin's Press).

Keynes, J. M. (1973b) *The Collected Writings of John Maynard Keynes*, vol. 14, ed. by D. Moggridge (London: Macmillan; New York: St Martin's Press).

Keynes, J. M. (1979) *The Collected Writings of John Maynard Keynes*, vol. 29, ed. by D. Moggridge (London: Macmillan; New York: St Martin's Press).

Klein, L. R. (1947) *The Keynesian Revolution* (New York: Macmillan).

Kregel, J. A. (ed.) (1983) *Distribution, Effective Demand and International Economic Relations* (London: Macmillan).

Kregel, J. A. (1985) 'Hamlet without the Prince: Cambridge Macroeconomics without Money', *American Economic Review*, 75: 133–9.

Lerner, A. P. (1952) 'The Essential Properties of Interest and Money', *Quarterly Journal of Economics*, 66: 172–93.

Marx, K. (1936) *Capital*, vol. I (New York: First Modern Library).

Nell, E. J. (1983) 'Keynes after Sraffa: The Essential Properties of Keynes's Theory of Interest and Money', in Kregel, J. A. (ed.) *Distribution, Effective Demand and International Economic Relations* (London: Macmillan).

Patinkin, D. (1982) *Anticipations of the General Theory? and Other Essays on Keynes* (Chicago: University of Chicago Press).

Robinson, J. (1933) *The Economics of Imperfect Competition* (London: Macmillan)

Robinson, J. (1950) *The Economics of Imperfect Competition* (London: Macmillan; New York: St Martin's Press).

Robinson, J. (1951) *Collected Economic Papers*, vol. I (Oxford: Blackwell).

Robinson, J. (1960) *Collected Economic Papers*, vol. II. (Oxford: Blackwell).

Robinson, J. (1965) *The Accumulation of Capital*, 3rd edn (London: Macmillan; New York: St Martin's Press).

Robinson, J. (1966) *An Essay on Marxian Economics*, 2nd edn (London: Macmillan; New York: St Martin's Press).

Robinson, J. (1968) *Essays in the Theory of Economic Growth* (London: Macmillan; New York: St Martin's Press).

Robinson, J. (1971) *Economic Heresies: Some Old-Fashioned Questions in Economic Theory* (New York: Basic Books).

Robinson, J. (1973) *Collected Economic Papers*, vol. IV (New York: Humanities Press).

Robinson, J. (1975) *Collected Economic Papers*, vol. III (Oxford: Blackwell).

Robinson, J. (1978a) *Contributions to Modern Economics* (New York: Academic Press).

Robinson, J. (1978b) 'Keynes and Ricardo', *Journal of Post Keynesian Economics*, 1 210–16.

Robinson, J. (1979) *The Generalisation of the General Theory and Other Essays* (New York: St Martin's Press).

Robinson, J. (1980) *Collected Economic Papers*, vol. V (Cambridge, Mass.: MIT).

Robinson, J. (1980) *What are the Questions? and Other Essays. Further contributions to Modern Economics* (Armonk, NY: M. E. Sharpe).

Skidelsky, R. (1986) *John Maynard Keynes: Hopes Betrayed, 1883–1920*, vol. I (New York: Viking Press).

Sraffa, P. (1926) 'The Laws of Returns under Competitive Conditions', *Economic Journal*, 36: 535–50.

Sraffa, P. (1932) 'Dr Hayek on Money and Capital', *Economic Journal*, 42: 242–53.

Sraffa, P. (1960) *Production of Commodities by Means of Commodities: Prelude to a Critique of Economic Theory* (Cambridge: Cambridge University Press).

Veblen, T. (1942a) 'Professor Clark's Economics', in *The Place of Science in Modern Civilisation and Other Essays* (New York: Viking Press), pp.186–230.

Veblen, T. (1942b) 'On the Nature of Capital, I and II', in *The Place of Science in Modern Civilisation and Other Essays* (New York: Viking Press), pp.324–80.

Worswick, D. and J. Trevithick (eds) (1983) *Keynes and the Modern World* (Cambridge: Cambridge University Press).

22 Money and Finance in Joan Robinson's Works

Augusto Graziani

1 INTRODUCTORY

A certain amount of ambiguity is still present in the economic literature on the concept of *finance*.

In a simple economy, with no government sector, where only firms and wage-earners are present, the expenditure of wage-earners is financed by their own money incomes, and only firms, who are paying the wage bill in advance, have to meet a problem of finance. The finance problem of firms is manifold:

(a) Firms need an initial provision of liquidity enabling them to pay the wage bill in advance. Such provision has to meet the requirements of output in general, no matter whether consisting of consumption goods or capital goods.

(b) If firms are to be in equilibrium, they must get back through market sales an amount of liquidity equal to their outlays. This can be done in either of two ways, namely, by selling consumption goods to wage-earners, or by issuing securities on the financial market. Sale of consumption goods will bring back the amount of the wage bill that wage-earners have decided to consume while issues on the financial market, if successful, will bring back their money savings. It may seem that in this phase firms are being financed by the market. What in fact they are doing is to try to extract from the market the same money they have injected in it when paying the wage bill.

(c) Finally, firms have to pay interest both on debts incurred towards banks and on bonds issued on the financial market. A provision of finance for such payments is also needed.

For the sake of establishing a clear terminology, we shall denote by *initial financement* the provision of liquidity that firms need in order to cover current costs of output (if we consider a closed economy without government sector, costs for firms taken as a whole will equal the wage bill). We shall denote by *final financement* long-term issues on the financial market (strictly speaking, sales of consumption goods to wage-earners are also a form of final financement, since they also allow firms to get back liquidity anticipated when the wage bill was paid).

The word *financement* therefore will not denote a cash balance or any form of money stock. It will rather denote the act of transmitting liquidity from one agent to the next. When financement is performed by banks, it will also denote a *creation of money*. For the same reason, any repayment by firms to banks will imply an equivalent *destruction of money*.

In current macroeconomic literature, the different aspects of the finance problem are seldom clearly distinguished. In fact it so happens that in most cases:

(a) *initial finance*, as a prior provision of liquidity covering the cost of total output, is totally ignored;

(b) *final finance*, in the form of issue on the financial market, instead of being understood as a means for firms of capturing money savings and of preventing them from going into idle balances, is seen as *financement of investment*. This is, of course, only true if investment equals savings out of wages, which means that self-financing on the part of firms is absent.

The origin of the confusion lies partly in the widespread, and to some extent inevitable, habit of analyzing the properties of an economic model by observing its equilibrium position, and partly in the equally widespread habit of basing the standard Keynesian macroeconomic model on a strictly neoclassical theory of income distribution.

In the equilibrium position, desired liquid balances are equal to the existing money stock. This means that, in so far as the analysis is limited to an inspection of the equilibrium position, the question about how and when the existing stock of money was created need not even be raised, and in fact is never raised. Nothing is said about money creation or about money destruction. The quantity of money simply appears as given from outside. Relationships between firms and banks are not considered worth being analyzed in a macroeconomic context, the banking sector is merged with the productive sector, and banks are considered as a special kind of firm alongside all the others. Nothing is said about money circulation as such, the only problem being one of finding the proper interest rate that brings the demand for money, defined as demand for money balances, into equality with a given money stock.

On the theoretical side, the fact of limiting the analysis to the working of financial markets, thus neglecting any consideration of money creation and destruction, rules out any analysis of how current production is financed, a problem clearly involving firms and banks, but not savers. It also leaves out the fact that all existing money is a debt of firms towards banks, and that on that debt firms have to pay interest. In fact, in the simple structure of current macroeconomic models, the only rate of interest appearing in the model is the rate paid by firms to savers, its level being determined on the financial market. Banks and firms being merged into one sector, the rate of interest paid by firms to banks does not even appear. At the same time, in the equilibrium position of a standard Keynesian model, the money value of investment equals the money value of newly issued securities. This means that savers are the only owners of financial wealth and that, by the ownership of stock, they own the existing productive wealth. In this case, the financial market can be indifferently defined as the market where money savings are captured or the market where new investment is financed. The problem of finance thus reduces to the problem of financing investment.

The fact of working with a model where the financement of output as such is ignored, where profits and self-financement are absent, and where the problem of finance reduces to the long-term financement of investment, brings about the idea that, since long-term finance is supplied by saving, finance should be identified with saving.

Implications on the policy side are even more relevant. The fact of working with a model where the only problem is long-term financement of investment gives a reduced and distorted view of monetary policy. In such models, monetary policy can only work via interest rates on financial markets, and via their effect on investment decisions. It is instead a commonly accepted truth that credit rationing can operate through a more direct and immediate way, by forcing firms to reduce their current outlays, an aspect, however, that current models are not built to deal with.

The theory of money was not always a theory of demand and supply of money balances. In the beginning, it used to be also, if not mainly, a theory of the creation and circulation of money, an approach that was preserved in the Swedish and German traditions (Wicksell, 1898, 1907; Hahn, 1920; Neisser, 1931, 1934). The marginal revolution and the Keynesian revolution, two turning points in the history of economic thought, modified the content of monetary theory.

The marginal revolution, by reducing economics to a theory of simultaneous equilibrium of production and exchange, made necessary, in order to preserve a place for money in the final equilibrium position, to explain why the stock of money could appear as an argument in the utility functions of individuals. In order to achieve this result a long elaboration was necessary, the outcome of which was that money was no longer considered as a source of indirect utility (the utility of the goods that money could buy) but as being endowed with a direct utility of its own. The story of the gradual discovery of the so-called direct utility of money, has been admirably described by Patinkin (1956, chapter 5, sections 1 and 8, supplementary note D).

Keynes's *General Theory* is considered to be the theory of a monetary economy, as contrasted to theories of general equilibrium, which are more in the nature of theories of barter. Also in the *General Theory*, however, the relevance of money lies in its being a store of value and money matters because there is a positive (and, in critical cases, an unlimited) demand for money balances. Thus, beyond all intentions, both the marginal and the Keynesian approach worked in the direction of neglecting what Robertson (1936, p.181) called the forgotten but simple truth that people often acquire money not in order to hold it but in order to use it.

Robertson considered Keynes as mainly responsible for this state of affairs. In spite of Robertson's criticism, it should be recognized that Keynes, while stressing the relevance of money as a store of wealth, had clearly in mind that current production is made possible by money outlays, and that therefore people may want money not for building up money balances but for the purpose of financing production. He brought explicit attention to this point in a famous series of articles published between 1937 and 1939 (Keynes, 1937a and b, 1938, 1939b). What he considered to be 'the most fundamental of [his] conclusions in this field', namely, that 'the investment market can become congested through a shortage of cash. It can never become congested through a shortage of savings', rests exactly on the recognition of the existence and relevance of the problem of current finance, beside and beyond the problems of an equilbrium level of money balances and of long-term financement of investment (Keynes, 1937a, p.669; Kregel, 1984a).

Keynes's 'finance motive for holding money' gave rise to a long debate and to several misunderstandings (Keynes, 1937a, 1937b, 1938, 1939b; Robertson, 1937, 1938a, 1938b; Asimakopulos, 1983; Graziani, 1984). Joan Robinson was the one among his followers who understood the problem most closely. What is to be found in her works is the proof of a clear perception of the nature and working of the problems of finance.

2 THE STRUCTURE OF THE ECONOMY

We shall begin by a simple description of the circulation of money between banks and the non-banking sector. The analysis is cast in the framework of the theory of distribution already to be found in the early writings of Robertson (1926, pp.40–58) and Keynes (1930, chapter 10) and sometimes called the post-Keynesian or Kaleckian model of income distribution (Kalecki, 1942; Robinson, 1962b; Kregel, 1973; Minsky, 1980). The content of this and the following sections tries to follow as closely as possible the model of a monetary economy as sketched by Joan Robinson in *The Accumulation of Capital* (1956, pp.225–35).

We shall consider an economic system consisting of the following three sectors (the economy is closed, and the government sector is ignored):

(a) *Banks*: The banking sector is defined as producing money and granting credit to firms, without taking part in the production of commodities. Since by definition all payments are made in money, and since firms produce no money, firms cannot start production without previously getting credit from the banking system. For the purpose of what follows, it is irrelevant whether banks produce credit on the basis of legal tender supplied by a central bank, or whether the economy is working as a pure credit system.

(b) *Firms*: Firms are engaged in the production of commodities, be it consumer or capital goods. They borrow money from banks, buy labor by paying money wages, sell consumption goods to wage-earners, issue securities on the financial market.

(c) *Households*: Households sell labor services against money wages. Wages are partly spent on consumption goods, partly on buying securities, partly added to money balances.

In such an economy, there are four markets: the *credit market*, where the rate of interest on current loans made by banks is determined, the *labor market*, where the money-wage rate is determined, the *consumption goods market*, where the price of consumption goods is determined, and the *financial market* where the yield of long-term securities is determined. On the other hand, there is no market for capital goods, since firms have been aggregated into one single sector, so that transactions on capital goods become an internal transaction, the production of capital goods appearing as a sort of self-production.

Let us take N for employment, w for the money-wage rate, c for the propensity to consume out of wages, i for the rate of interest on securities. Let the stock of securities issued by firms of the consumers goods and capital goods sectors respectively be equal to:

$$B_c^t = (1 + n)^t wN_c$$

$$B_k^t = (1 + n)^t wN_k$$

$$B = (1 + n)^t wN$$

n being the rate of growth of the stock.

Let us assume a fraction b of total employment to be allocated to the capital goods sector and the remaining $1 - b$ to the consumption goods sector.

It follows that, in the consumption goods market the supply of consumption goods will be equal to:

$$C_s = \pi_c N_c = \pi_c(1 - b)N$$

while demand will be:

$$C_d = c(wN + iB') = cwN[1 + i(1 + n)^t].$$

The price of consumption goods as determined by the equality between supply and demand, will be:

$$p_c = \frac{1 - s}{1 - b} \cdot \frac{1 + i(1 + n)^t}{\pi_c} w.$$

The notional price of capital goods, namely, the price at which capital goods are exchanged inside the firms sector, is such as to level the rate of profit in the two sectors (Robinson, 1971, p.47):

$$p_k = \frac{1 - s}{1 - b} \frac{1 + i(1 + n)^t}{\pi_k} w.$$

If, by accident or calculus, the labor force is allocated between the two sectors in the same proportions as wage-earners allocate their money incomes between consumption and saving (that is, if $b = s$), the prices of consumption and capital goods reduce to:

$$p_c = \frac{1 + i(1 + n)^t}{\pi_c} w, \text{ and: } p_k = \frac{1 + i(1 + n)^t}{\pi_k} w$$

In this case, prices equal unit costs (for firms as a whole, there are no other costs beyond wages and interest paid to savers), and extra-profits are zero.

Gross profits for firms taken as a whole, defined as the difference between the value of output and the sum of wage costs and interest costs are:

$$P_c = \pi_c N_c p_c - wN_c - i(1 + n)^t wN_c$$

$$P_k = \pi_k N_k p_k - wN_k - i(1 + n)^t wN_k$$

$$P = P_c + P_k,$$

which, by substituting the values of p_c and p_k, gives:

$$P = \frac{b - s}{1 - b}[1 + i(1 + n)^t]wN.$$

Two extreme cases deserve to be noted. If $b = s$, *profits are zero* as in neoclassical equilibrium. If the propensity to consume of wage-earners is unity ($s = 0$) we get:

$$p_c = bwN[1 + i(1 + n)^t]$$

namely, profits in the consumption goods sector equal the money cost of capital goods produced.

Profits *in real terms*, defined as the ratio between money profits and the money price of capital goods, are:

$$P_r = P/p_k = \frac{b - s}{1 - s}\pi_k N.$$

Again, if $s = 0$, this reduces to:

$$P_r = \pi_k N_k,$$

namely, total profits equal real investment.

Interest paid on securities issued on the financial market does not enter in the determination of *gross profits*. In fact, any payment made by firms in the form of interest on existing debt will increase the money incomes of households, thereby increasing their expenditure on consumption goods, the level of money prices, and gross profits earned by firms. Savers taken as a whole will never be able to convert their income from capital into higher consumption, unless firms decide on their own to produce a higher amount of consumers goods (Kregel, 1973, p.273). The only use of financial wealth is in fact of allowing single households to alter the time shape of their consumption streams by way of reciprocal loans.

The case of *net profits* is different. Since net profits are defined as gross profits *net of interest paid to the banks*, any increase in interest paid to the banks decreases net profits all around. On the other hand, an increase in interest does not act specifically on the yield of investment.

A possible conclusion is that, if we assume the structure of interest rates to be stable, so that interest on long-term and on short-term loans move together, any increase in the rate of interest, while reducing the profitability of running an enterprise in general, does not act as a specific brake on investment. The working of monetary policy is usually read the other way round: an increase in interest rates is considered to hold up investment decisions and, by reducing investment, to bring about an overall fall in output and employment.

This conclusion is subject to a partial qualification if a single firm, and not firms as a whole, is considered. The reason why interest paid to savers is not a cost to firms as a whole is that, provided there is no change in liquidity preference, savers will spend back on the market their income from capital alongside with their wages. This does not mean, however, that their expenditure will benefit the same firms which have issued new securities. A single firm may therefore be discouraged by higher interest rates on the bond market, for fear of being burdened with higher interest payments without getting higher proceeds. Still if a single firm is incurring losses, there will be at least one other firm earning extra profits, and on the whole investment decisions might be unaltered.

3 THE CIRCULATION OF MONEY

At the beginning of any period, firms get from the banks an amount of finance equal to the wage bill:

$$F_t = w_t N_t.$$

Finance is used to pay wages and therefore transmitted to households. Two possible cases appear:

(a) *An equilibrium situation*: If households spend the whole of their money incomes, no matter whether on consumption goods or on the financial market, and they do not add to their cash balances, finance flows back to firms and firms can repay the banks. The monetary circuit is thus closed, and a new cycle can be started.

The fact of spending the whole of money income does not prevent households from having positive cash balances at each moment of time. If a time interval elapses between the moment wages are paid and the moment they are spent, for the duration of that interval households will hold positive transactions balances. If wages are spent regularly over time, cash balances will be on average equal to one half of the wage bill. We shall assume that cash balances are held in the form of bank deposits (in a pure credit economy there will be no other way of holding money). Since the production process is continuous, new cycles can be started any moment, and a number of monetary cycles coexist over time.

Equilibrium is not altered if we complete the model by introducing in it interest charged by banks on loans made to firms. Let i be the interest rate paid on loans, and r the rate reckoned by banks on deposits. At the end of any period t, firms owe to the banks an amount of money equal to:

$$D_t = [1 + 1/2i]wN_{t-1}$$

on the assumption that money wages are spent regularly over time in the interval between each payment and the next.

Total expenditure of wage-earners, being by assumption equal to income, amounts now to:

$$Y_t = [1 + 1/2r]wN_{t-1}.$$

If $i = r$, receipts of firms are again equal to their debt towards banks. The situation is different if, as it is most likely to be the case, $i > r$. In this case, even if wage-earners spend the whole of their incomes, firms will never be able to repay their debt. A possible way out is given by the fact that banks themselves pay wages to their own employees who spend their incomes on consumption goods or on the financial market, thus adding to the receipts of firms without adding to their outlays. Another way out is the possibility that banks spend on the market profits originating out of the difference between i and r. If this is the case, what in fact happens is that firms are paying their interest debt partly or wholly in kind, by selling goods or securities to banks.

If, i being greater than r, banks do not pay wages high enough or refrain from spending their profits, firms are unable to repay their debt. We are then brought to the second possible case.

(b) *A financial disequilibrium*: If wage-earners decide to add to their transactions balances and to build up speculative balances, the debt of firms will increase from period to period even if wages and employment are constant. As already said, firms can counteract the tendency to build up cash balances by offering higher yields on their debt. But if cash balances are increased, no matter how much the rate of interest on securities is being driven up, firms will be unable to repay wholly their debt to the banks. Since the whole of existing money is a debt of firms to the banks, in so far as money balances increase, the debt of the firms will also increase. As long as the banks accept the situation and let their loans increase, nothing happens in terms of employment and activity levels. When, in the banks' judgement, the situation has become dangerous and they decide to put a brake on the increase in their loans, firms will be unable to keep the level of employment constant, even if no problems on the demand side have appeared.

4 FINANCE AND CASH BALANCES

The economic process gets started as the banking system grants credit to the firms by creating money, thus enabling them to buy labor services and start a production cycle. *Initial finance*, as we may call it, must cover total production costs for the whole of firms, no matter whether they are producing consumption goods or capital goods. Under this viewpoint, consumption and investment are on the same footing.

The economic process comes to its conclusion when firms pay back their loans, which implies a corresponding destruction of money. When firms, by selling output or by placing securities, get returns equal to costs, total output can be said to have found its *final financement*. Final finance for consumption goods originates from sales to households on the commodities market, while final finance for capital goods comes both from sales of securities on the financial market and from firms' profits (as already said, if $b = 1 - c$, sales on the financial market are the only source of finance for investment).

We have already noticed that, if a time interval elapses between the moment wages are paid and the moment they are spent, cash balances of households will automatically have a positive value. We shall now argue that households' balances are the only ones exisiting.

By definition, money balances cannot be held by banks, since money is created the very moment banks grant credit to firms and is destroyed when firms repay their debts to the banks. In principle, the possibility for firms to keep positive cash balances should also be ruled out. Provided there is no uncertainty as to the level of interest rates, firms go into debt the very moment they make a payment, and repay their debt as soon as money flows back through sales on the market. It cannot be ruled out that a single firm, having earned money profits at the expense of other firms, may decide to keep its profits in money form. But this would only give rise to a money balance in the hands of a single firm, whereas firms taken as a whole would still be in debt or at most have a balanced budget towards banks.

In a system such as the one we have described, cash balances are therefore limited to transaction balances held by households. The situation will be different under uncertainty, when firms may find it convenient to go into debt on the financial market before payments come due, if they foresee an increase in interest rates, and for the same reason they anticipate repayment and run down their cash balances when a decrease in interest rates is anticipated. It may be worth remembering that Keynes himself had expressed the view that firms, when building up their cash balances, will rather borrow on the financial market than ask for a bank loan (Keynes, 1937a, p.246).

5 JOAN ROBINSON ON FINANCE

The main findings of the above analysis can be thus summarized:

(a) A sharp distinction should be made between *prior finance*, as the amount of liquidity which is necessary for carrying out production, and *final finance*, as the amount of liquidity that firms get back from the sale of output or from issue of securities, and that is used to repay their debts to the banks. In no way is saving a source of finance. It cannot be prior finance, since saving does not even exist before output is produced and income distributed. Saving cannot be identified with final finance either, since final finance is given by consumption expenditure plus the portion of saving that is spent on securities. To be sure finance is not provided by not spending.

(b) In a closed economy, with no government sector, the money stock is a debt of firms to banks. As a consequence, in normal conditions, firms do not hold cash balances, which are only held by households. Firms will hold cash balances only under uncertainty.

(c) Since proceeds of firms from sale of output or from issue of securities on the financial market can at most equal their outlays, they will never provide money for paying interest to the banks. It is therefore necessary, for firms to be in equilibrium towards banks, that banks, directly or indirectly, spend in the market an amount of money at least equal to interest payments to be made by firms.

(d) High interest rates prevailing on the money market can influence activity levels since a high level of interest levied by the banks reduces net profits of the firms thus reducing the profitability of operating business. On the other hand, interest rates have no specific influence on investment as such.

The four propositions, all coming out of an analysis of the working of finance, can be found clearly stated in Joan Robinson's works.

5.1 The distinction between initial and final finance

A general description of the circulation of money from banks to banks is provided by Joan Robinson in the famous article on 'Own Rates of Interest':

> If we could, so to say, stain a particular volume of *X* units of expenditure and trace it through its future course, we should see it generating income and expenditure on consumption, gradually leaking into savings as it flows its own way ... The process of investment, through saving, is always recreating, with a time lag, the finance that it is absorbing. The new wealth has partly taken the form of gross undistributed profits to firms, and has partly accrued to rentiers. Some is held in cash, some in securities and some has repaid bank loans. (Robinson, 1961, p.133)

The description of the circulation of money, as created by banks and destroyed by the final repayment of bank loans, was surely familiar to Joan Robinson, having been carefully analyzed by Knut Wicksell in *Interest and*

Prices (Wicksell, 1898, chapter IX, sec.B; see also Wicksell, 1907). The same way of describing the economic process must have been transmitted to Joan Robinson by Kalecki, who considered it a sort of basic truth underlying all his analytical thought (Kalecki, 1935; 1939, pp.107–10; see also Feiwel, 1975, pp.35, 39). As Joan Robinson herself relates, Kalecki's 1935 article immediately struck the attention of the Cambridge group and, when shown to Keynes, left him surprised (Robinson, 1977, p.13). In fact, the rather different idea Keynes was pursuing at the time, was that the importance of money lies in its being a possible store of wealth, and that money can act as a brake on real accumulation not because of its being scarce but because it appears to be the most profitable among all possible placements (Kregel, 1984b).

No wonder, therefore, if Joan Robinson, while clearly inheriting Wicksell's tradition and absorbing Kalecki's lesson, remoulds them both in a more Keynesian approach, based on demand and supply of liquidity. In this light, the initial phase of the monetary circuit (firms get finance from banks) is defined as *an addition to the money stock*, while the final phase (firms issue long-term debt on the financial market) is denominated *addition to securities*.

The consequence of the sharp distinction between liquidity and saving is that any concept of 'saving lost in the banking system', or of 'bank credit added to the supply of savings', is refused:

> These two conceptions, 'saving lost in the banking system' and 'an inflationary supplement to saving', cancel each other. For, over an interval of time, the 'excess of savings added to hoards' are represented by the increment of bank deposits held by individual savers, while the 'credits supplementing savings' are represented by the increased loans of the banks. Since the increase in deposits is necessarily equal to the increase in bank assets, the 'excess of saving over investment' is equal to the 'excess of investment over saving'. The two notions have only to be confronted with each other for both to disappear. (Robinson, 1938, pp.66–7; see also Robinson, 1952b, p.80)

As already said, final finance comes from expenditure of wage-earners at the end of the monetary circuit, be it expenditure on consumption goods or on securities:

> It is necessary to guard against the confusion of thinking of rentier thriftness as providing finance for investment. In so far as thrift assists investment it does so by leaving more room within the inflation barrier ... It does not help by providing finance. So far as finance is concerned, rentier expenditure, by generating profits, provides it in a more direct

way than saving, which obliges entrepreneurs to borrow if they want to maintain future investment. (Robinson, 1956, p.276)

The same point had been clearly made by Keynes in the course of a famous debate with Robertson, in which Keynes (1938, p.321; see also 1937b, pp.667–8, and 1939b, p.573) had maintained that 'saving has no special efficacy as compared to consumption in releasing cash and restoring liquidity'. Joan Robinson's conclusion on this point is a total refusal of any concept of 'supply of loanable funds' as an amount of liquidity, available for financing investment and distinct from the existing stock of money and from other forms of financial wealth. (Robinson, 1956, p.403)

5.2 The stock of money as a debt towards banks

As already noted at the outset, in current literature the stock of money is given from outside and considered as a debt of the government, while bank deposits are viewed as an internal transaction of the private sector. If instead, as it should be, banks and firms are considered as belonging to separate sectors, the money stock appears as a debt of the firms to the banks. This point has not escaped the attention of Joan Robinson. In *The Accumulation of Capital*, she rejects as 'very far fetched to regard bankers as belonging to the category of manufacturers of capital goods' (Robinson, 1956, p.227), and sets out a model in which 'bank capital and industrial capital are two water-tight compartments' (Robinson, 1956, p.228).

In her treatment of finance, the fact that the stock of money is in the nature of a debt of firms is clearly stated:

> When employment is increasing (or money wage rates are rising) the entrepreneurs are paying out every week more than they received from last week's sales, so that entrepreneurs, taken as a whole, are continually increasing their indebtedness to banks. (Robinson, 1956, p.227; see also 1962b, p.43; 1971, p.49)

The consequence of this fact is also carefully recognized: in principle, firms should hold no liquid balances. In order to save interest, an entrepreneur, when needing new finance, should only arrange for it in advance, without actually taking it (Robinson, 1952b, p.81n). Hints to this problem are already to be found in Keynes (1937a, p.208), who mentioned the possibility for an entrepreneur of 'arranging overdraft facilities with his bank', without actually going into debt, if not when a payment comes due. If this is true, money is only created the moment a payment is made. Money comes into being at the same time in the form of an asset of wage-earners (we are still taking firms as a whole) and as a liability of entrepreneurs. It is typical of money to need the involvement of at least three agents in order to come into being, a point strongly made in some recent French and Italian literature on the subject (Parguez, 1985; Schmitt, Cencini, 1982; Cencini, 1984, p.126 ff.; Graziani, 1985).

While this is absolutely true in fully stationary conditions, it is no longer true if interest rates fluctuate and changes in rates are anticipated. A firm anticipating an increase in interest rates, might find it convenient to borrow long on the financial market even if no finance is needed for immediate spending (Robinson, 1952b, p.85n., and 1960b, p.130).

5.3 Equilibrium conditions

A further consequence of considering banks and firms ar separate sectors is that firms taken as a whole pay interest to banks on the existing money stock. Now, proceeds of firms from sale of output and from issue of securities on the financial market can at most equal their outlays (the wage bill plus interest on the existing stock of securities). This happens because there is simply no more money in existence than that, if we abstract from possible pre-existing cash balances, which, even if run down, can only make up for a previous higher debt towards banks. Even in the most favorable conditions (namely when savers do not add a penny to their cash balances) firms are therefore unable to repay their debt to the banks, unless banks themselves inject additional money by means other than loans made to firms. This can happen if banks pay wages to their own employees or if they buy finished products directly on the market (for instance, the buildings where their activities are located).

In Joan Robinson's words: 'The whole of the gross proceeds of the banking business (that is the interest paid by the entrepreneurs) returns to industry as quasi-rents arising from the expenditure of their employees' (Robinson, 1956, p.228; see also 1962a, p.44n.).

5.4 Profits and investment

It is a well-known feature of Joan Robinson's model that competition does not eliminate profits but only brings them to a common rate. A clear distinction must therefore be drawn between profits earned by entrepreneurs and interest (or other forms of yield on long-term securities) earned by savers or *rentiers*. As already stated, firms run their business by borrowing money from the banks in order to hire labor, and they pay interest to savers on long-term debt. If wage-earners behave well and do not add to their liquid balances, and if banks spend on the market (through direct purchases or via the expenditure of their employees) the equivalent of interest due by firms, firms are in equilibrium, in that their receipts equal their outlays. The portion of output not sold to wage-earners nor to the banks makes up their net profit. The ratio between the money value of their profits and the initial bank loan (their capital investment) is a measure of the rate of profit.

Profits are therefore measured in relation to circulating capital, or in relation to 'money invested in business', not in relation to existing fixed capital or to current investment. This is most clearly stated in a precious, even if seldom quoted, booklet by Joan Robinson, *Exercises in Economic Analysis*:

> Finance ... will not be forthcoming unless it can secure a *profit*, that is, an excess of product over the payments made to the factors of production ... When a would-be employer does not command finance of his own, he is willing to hire finance provided that he does not have to pay more for it than the difference between the product of labor which it enables him to employ and the wage. (Robinson, 1960a, pp.61–2)

The consequence has been drawn in the preceding analysis, that an increase in interest rates, while discouraging business in general (since it reduces net profits), does not act specifically on investment. While this conclusion is absolutely true for firms taken as a whole, it may not be as true for a single firm taken in isolation. A single firm, faced with higher rates on the bond market, will have to decide whether or not to load its budget with a higher financial burden for a number of years. Higher rates paid to savers mean, as shown above, a higher level of prices and of money profits for firms as a whole, but not necessarily for each single firm. It is therefore reasonable to assume that single firms may refrain from issuing long-term debt when rates are high. The negative influence will be the stronger the more the rise in interest rates is believed to be temporary (Robinson, 1960b, p.129).

If the consequences of a higher rate of interest on investment are debatable, it seems sure on the other hand that investment decisions depend strongly on the level of profits, a point familiar to all readers of Kalecki's works (Kalecki, 1939; see also Feiwel, 1975, p.41). Once the point is recognized that net profits, even if independent of long-term rates paid to savers, do depend instead on short rates paid to banks, a third connection between interest and investment, clearly pointed out by Joan Robinson, comes in the foreground, in that an increase in interest imposed by banks, by reducing net profits of firms, may discourage investment. Since gross profits depend on investment, it would be possible, in principle, for firms to counteract an increase in interest imposed upon them by banks by a corresponding increase in investment such as to keep net profits at the previous level. If firms instead react to an increase in interest by reducing investment, their gross and net profits will go down, and more investment decisions will be postponed:

> In so far as interest rates are discouraging to investment, they tend to retard accumulation, and the slower is the rate of accumulation the lower is the level of profits and the more discouraging any given level of interest rates becomes. (Robinson, 1956, p.242)

References

American Economic Association (1950) *Readings in Business Cycle Theory* (London: Allen & Unwin).

Arena, R. (ed.) *Production, Circulation, et Monnaie* (Paris: Presses Universitaires de France).

Asimakopulos, A. (1983) 'Kalecki and Keynes on Finance, Investment and Saving', *Cambridge Journal of Economics*, 7: 221–33.

Baranzini. M. (ed.) (1982) *Advances in Economic Theory* (Oxford: Blackwell).

Barrère, A. (ed.) (1985) *Keynes Today: Theories and Policies* (London: Macmillan).

Cencini, A. (1984) *Time and the Macroeconomic Analysis of Income* (London: F. Pinter).

Feiwel, G. (1975) *The Intellectual Capital of Michal Kalecki* (Knoxville: University of Tennessee Press).

Graziani, A. (1984) 'The Debate on Keynes' Finance Motive', *Economic Notes*, March: 5–32.

Graziani, A. (1985) 'Monnaie, intéret, dépense publique', *Economies et Sociétés*, Série Monnaie et Production 2 (Paris: Ismea).

Hahn, L. A. (1920; new edn 1930) *Volkswirthschaftliche Theorie des Bankkredits* (Tübingen: J. C. B. Mohr).

Kalecki, M. (1935) 'A Macrodynamic Theory of Business Cycles', *Econometrica*. 3: 327–44.

Kalecki, M. (1937) 'A Theory of the Business Cycle', *Review of Economic Studies*, 4: 77–97.

Kalecki, M. (1939) *Essays in the Theory of Economic Fluctuations* (London: Allen & Unwin).

Kalecki, M. (1942) 'A Theory of Profits', *Economic Journal*, 52: 258–67.

Keynes, J. M. (1930) *A Treatise on Money* (London: Macmillan).

Keynes, J. M. (1937a) 'Alternative Theories of the Rate of Interest', *Economic Journal*, 64: 241–52.

Keynes, J. M. (1937b) 'The "ex-ante" Theory of the Rate on Interest', *Economic Journal*, 47: 663–9.

Keynes, J. M. (1938) 'Comment' [on D. H. Robertson (1938)], *Economic Journal*, 48: 318–22.

Keynes, J. M. (1939a) 'Relative Movements of Real Wages and Output', *Economic Journal*, 49: 34–51.

Keynes, J. M. (1939b) 'The Process of Capital Formation', *Economic Journal*, 49: 569–74.

Kregel, J. (1973) *The Reconstruction of Political Economy. An Introduction to Post-Keynesian Economics* (London: Macmillan).

Kregel, J. (1984a) 'Price and Quantity Constraints on the Expansion of Production: Real or Monetary?' in Arena (ed.).

Kregel, J. (1984b) in 'Monetary Production Economics and Monetary Policy', *Economie et Sociétés*, Séries Monnaie et Production 1 (Paris: Ismea).
Kregel, J. (1985) in 'The Multiplier and Liquidity Preference: Two Sides of the Theory of Effective Demand' in Barrère. (ed.).
Minsky, H. P. (1980) 'Finance and Profits: The Changing Nature of American Business Cycles', US Congress, Joint Economic Committee (Washington: Government-Printing Office).
Minsky, H. P. (1982) *Can it Happen Again*? (New York: Sharpe).
Neisser, H. (1931) *Der Tauschwert des Geldes* (Jena: G. Fischer Verlag).
Neisser, H. (1934) 'General Overproduction. A Study of Say's Law of Markets', *Journal of Political Economy*, 42: 433–65; repr. in *American Economic Association*, 1950 (abridged).
Parguez, A. (1985) 'La Théorie Générale: La Révolution Inachevée dans la Théorie du Capital et de la Monnaie' in Barrère (ed.).
Patinkin, D. (1956; new edn 1965) *Money, Interest and Prices* (New York: Harper & Row).
Robertson, D. H. (1926; new edn 1949) *Banking Policy and the Price Level* (London: King).
Robertson, D. H. (1936) 'Some Notes on Mr Keynes' General Theory of Employment', *Quarterly Journal of Economics*, 51: 168–91; partly integrated in Robertson (1966a).
Robertson, D. H. (1937) 'Alternative Theories of the Rate of Interest: Three Rejoinders, II', *Economic Journal*, 47: 428–36.
Robertson, D. H. (1938a) 'Mr Keynes and "finance"', *Economic Journal*, 48: 314–18.
Robertson, D. H. (1938b) 'Reply' (to Keynes), *Economic Journal*, 48: 555–6.
Robertson, D. H. (1966a) 'Mr Keynes and the Rate of Interest', in Robertson (1966b).
Robertson, D. H. (1966b) *Essays in Money and Interest* (London: Collins).
Robinson, J. (1938) 'The Concept of Hoarding', *Economic Journal*, 48: 231–6; repr. in Robinson (1951).
Robinson, J. (1951) 'The Rate of Interest', *Econometrica*, 19: 92–111; repr. in Robinson (1952); Robinson (1960b) (last section omitted); Robinson (1978) (last section omitted); Robinson (1979a).
Robinson, J. (1952a) 'The Generalisation of the General Theory', repr. in Robinson (1952b), Robinson (1979b).
Robinson, J. (1952b) *The Rate of Interest and Other Essays* (London: Macmillan).
Robinson, J. (1956) *The Accumulation of Capital* (London: Macmillan).
Robinson, J. (1960a) *Exercises in Economic Analysis* (London: Macmillan).
Robinson, J. (1960b) *Collected Economic Papers*, vol.II (Oxford: Blackwell).
Robinson, J. (1960c) 'General Liquidity', *The Banker*, 110: 790–5, in Robinson (1965).
Robinson, J. (1961) 'Own Rates of Interest', *Economic Journal*, 71: 596–600; Robinson (1965).
Robinson, J. (1962a) *Essays in the Theory of Economic Growth* (London: Macmillan).
Robinson, J. (1962b) 'A Model of Accumulation', in Robinson (1962a).
Robinson, J. (1965) *Collected Economic Papers*, vol.III (Oxford: Blackwell).
Robinson, J. (1971) *Economic Heresies* (New York: Basic Books).
Robinson, J. (1977) 'Kalecki and the Economics of Capitalism', *Oxford Bulletin of Statistics*, 39: 7–17; repr. as 'M. Kalecki' in Robinson (1979a).
Robinson, J. (1978) *Contributions to Modern Economics* (Oxford: Blackwell).

Robinson, J. (1979a) *Collected Economic Papers*, vol.V (Oxford: Blackwell).
Robinson, J. (1979b) *The Generalisation of the General Theory and Other Essays* (London: Macmillan).
Schmitt, B. and A, Cencini (1982) 'Wages and Profits in a Theory of Emissions', in Baranzini (ed.).
Wicksell, K. (1898) *Geldzins und Güterpreise* (Jena: G. Fischer Verlag); (English translation (1934) *Interest and Prices*, London: Macmillan).
Wicksell, K. (1907) 'The Influence of the Rate of Interest on Prices', *Economic Journal*, 17: 213–20.

23 Joan Robinson and the New Classical Economists as Critics of Keynesian Economics

Steven M. Sheffrin*

1 INTRODUCTION

Joan Robinson never turned her attention to the writings of the school of new classical economists. It would not be difficult, however, to imagine the nature and tone of a hypothetical essay on such a topic. Her view that the inflation process is largely driven by the evolution of money wages which, in turn, is predominantly influenced by social and political factors, led to a strong rejection of the natural rate hypothesis. The self-conscious application of Walrasian theory which characterizes the new classical economists (not to mention their appellation) would have been particularly galling to her with her well-known views on the sterility of this class of analysis.

It may therefore appear strange and unusual to compare Joan Robinson's criticisms of modern neoclassical Keynesian macroeconomics with those of the new classicals. As one of the earliest Keynesians and the heroine of the post-Keynesian school, her work would be viewed by most of the new classicals as much more extreme than modern American neoclassical Keynesianism which the new classicals made their fame attacking. Yet, as Axel Leijonhufvud and Sir John Hicks have stressed, the ideas associated with the development of the *General Theory* differed in many respects from the research program associated with American neoclassical Keynesian economics.[1] As a colleague of Keynes in Cambridge who read the proofs of the *General Theory* and someone who held back publishing some of her own work on related topics until the publication of the *General Theory*, Joan Robinson thought she knew the true significance of Keynes's breakthroughs. This put her in an ideal position to become a critic of Keynesian economics as it developed.

This paper, however, goes one step further and argues that the criticisms Joan Robinson raised against American neoclassical Keynesian economics are, in many ways, remarkably similar to those of the new classical

*I would like to thank George Feiwel, Kevin Hoover and Thomas Mayer for valuable comments.

economists. Although her substantive ideas differ sharply from the new classicals, their preoccupations are surprisingly similar. This paper highlights these preoccupations and compares and contrasts them to those of the new classicals. As I will demonstrate, her views on time, history, dynamics, and even econometrics echo in the writings of the new classicals.[2]

To avoid any terminological confusions, it is useful to define at the outset what I mean by 'American neoclassical Keynesian economics' or 'Keynesian economics' and 'new classical economics'. By Keynesian economics I refer to the writings, models and thinking associated with the early Franco Modigliani, Lawrence Klein, the Brookings model, the Modigliani of the entire period of the *MPS* model, the work of James Tobin, and the monetarist writings of the 1960s. Thus, the label includes the bulk of conventional macroeconomic thinking, including the natural rate hypothesis, prior to the work of Robert E. Lucas. By the new classical economists, I refer primarily to Lucas and Thomas Sargent both because of their seminal contributions and their attention to the philosophical underpinnings of their work. This includes some but not all of the work associated with rational expectations in the 1970s, excluding the work (typified by Stanley Fischer and John Taylor) which marries rational expectations to wage stickiness.

It will be convenient to break the discussion into four parts. The first part (Section 2) will compare views on the importance of the future and risk and uncertainty. The second part (Section 3) will focus on the inadequacy of dynamic formulations in Keynesian economics. The third part (Section 4) will deal with econometric issues. I conclude with a discussion of the robustness of the common enemy, Keynesian economics, in the face of these persistent attacks, and a brief discussion of some of the overriding methodological differences between Joan Robinson and the New Classical economists.

2 RISK AND UNCERTAINTY

Both Joan Robinson and the new classicals stress the importance that expectations of future events play on the present. Moreover, beliefs about the future affect current actions in ways that are not adequately captured in Keynesian economics.

Joan Robinson argued that not until his *Quarterly Journal of Economics* article of 1937, which was written in response to his critics, did Keynes recognize the key aspect of the revolution begun with the *General Theory*. In her words, the 'revolution lay in the change from the conception of equilibrium to the conception of history; from the principles of rational choice to the problems of decisions based on guess-work and convention' (Robinson, 1979, p.170).

In both Keynes's and Robinson's views, the recognition that savings and investment decisions occur in a fundamentally uncertain world places these actions on a flimsy foundation, subject to sudden and violent changes. Uncertainty in this context is distinguished sharply from calculable risks: 'The uncertainty that surrounds expectations of the outcome of a plan of investment, of the course of technical progress, of the behaviour of future prices, not to mention the effects of natural and political cataclysms, cannot be reduced to a "calculated risk" by applying the theorems of mathematical probability' (Robinson, 1979, p.48.). Keynes stressed that his notion of uncertainty should be distinguished carefully from calculated risks: roulette was not uncertain, the weather was only moderately uncertain, but the price of copper or the rate of interest twenty years in the future was uncertain in the sense that 'there is no scientific basis on which to form any calculable probability whatsoever' (Keynes, 1937, p.214).

How do individuals cope with this uncertainty? In a spirit similar to the experimental psychologists today, such as Tversky and Kahneman (1974), Keynes suggested that individuals use a variety of rules of thumb or practical techniques. In particular, he argued that individuals employ three rules: (i) use the past as a guide to the future even though you recognize the future will differ sharply from the past; (ii) project the existing state of affairs into the future (a concrete application of the first principle); and (iii) fall back on the judgment of others who are perhaps better informed. It is this latter technique that leads to the conventional element about beliefs of the future and makes them susceptible to sudden and violent changes.

Investment decisions which are governed entirely by the future prospects of the firm are thus likely also to be volatile and not easily described by conventional econometric relationships. As the next section of the paper will illustrate, this principle applies not only to aggregate investment but to micro investment decisions and has important implications for intertemporal allocation and the dynamic behavior of the economy.

The prevalence of uncertainty in economic affairs creates a special place for money as a safe asset and repository for uncertainty. In her 1951 *Econometrica* paper, 'The Rate of Interest', Joan Robinson outlined her thoughts on expectations and their importance in portfolio theory. In her view this entire area is problematic: 'The whole subject of expectations bristles with psychological and philosophical difficulties' (Robinson, 1951, p.98.).

Part of the difficulty relates to the following conundrum. If expectations of a future event are held with complete certainty then, they are either fulfilled or not. If they are not then it is hard to believe that individuals will hold expectations the next time with perfect confidence. The same type of conundrum emerges in modern analysis when perfect foresight models are employed but then subjected to 'unanticipated' shocks. Thinking of expectations in terms of probability distributions does not necessarily eliminate the problem. The issue then becomes whether a given realization is from the existing distribution or whether it signals that the distribution is changing.[3] Uncertainty, in Keynes's sense, cannot be eliminated from the topic of expectations.

Joan Robinson suggests an approximate solution to the problem of modelling expectations by asserting that the interest rate will gravitate around its historical average. If the current rate deviates from the average rate, it will be expected to return to the average at some (unknown) time in the future. Persistent deviations from the average rate will lead gradually to revision of the long-run average.

Introducing the notion of an exogenous long-term rate towards which the current long-term rate gravitates brings forward the 'bootstrap' element into interest rates – the current interest rate is largely a function of where individuals think interest rates are likely to be. This theory bears a striking similarity to modern theories of 'sunspot' and multiple equilibria in rational expectations models.[4] In sunspot models, extraneous variables which are not tied to the fundamentals of the problem affect the current equilibrium. In Joan Robinson's theory the long-run equilibrium rate cannot be termed 'extraneous' in that it is a necessary part of an individual's solution to the problem of uncertainty. However, it is not related to the long-term determinants of interest rates (which some would term 'fundamentals') such as productivity and thrift.

In an extensive and striking footnote, Joan Robinson uses the phrase 'rational expectations' in a discussion of Hicks's expectations theory of the term structure but rejects both this notion and Hicks's theory.

> It is true, in a world in which expectations are definite and unanimous, that when we know today's bond rate and today's bill rate, we can reckon what change in the price of bonds is expected over the life of the bills . . . Then the whole pattern of expectations could be described in terms of the expected short rates alone. But all this means is that *rational expectations* must be self-consistent. It certainly does not detach the rate of interest from dependence on its boot straps for, in such a world, the only reason for a difference between short and long rates is the expectation of a change in the long rate. Indeed, one might say that there the short rate is simply an expression of expectations about bond prices. (emphasis added) (Robinson, 1951, p.102)

To understand this argument it is necessary to recall that Joan Robinson believed that expectations were necessarily uncertain and that coping with this uncertainty required individuals to have a belief in a long run normal rate. Rational expectations, or perfect foresight in this example, would only be appropriate in a world with no uncertainty. To put it another way, the 'expectations' hypothesis can never be reduced to an exercise in rational expectations methodology as long as individuals must formulate expectations in a fundamentally uncertain world.

Lucas (1977) also stresses the roles of risk and uncertainty in the decisions that individuals must make. For the most part these decisions involve fundamental choices of actions taken over time, for example, consumption and savings decisions and intertemporal labor supply. These capital theoretic decisions are not taken in an environment of perfect certainty and individuals must be able to formulate decisions in less than fully certain environments.

Lucas contends that individuals must formulate a subjective probability distribution over all unknown random variables that impinge on events. This would appear to put him in substantial disagreement with Joan Robinson and Keynes who insisted that the probability calculus did not apply to 'uncertain' events. However, the apparent disagreement is not substantive at least with respect to the practice of economic theory. It is generally not enough for empirical economists to say that individuals have probability structures; it is necessary to be able to characterize these structures. Thus, Lucas stresses that the *recurrent* nature of business cycles allows the possibility for individuals to conform their probability structures to the 'true' underlying probabilities. Lucas expresses the hope that business-cycle phenomena have enough similarities so that they may be classified as 'risky' rather than 'uncertain' in the sense of Frank Knight, Joan Robinson and Keynes.

Lucas's own remarks on probability theory are sufficiently cryptic so that it is difficult to tell whether, as a matter of pure theory, he would consider himself a Bayesian or a frequentist. For example, in the following description of rational expectations, note the placement of quotations: '(Muth called) the assumed coincidence of subjective and "true" probabilities *rational expectations*' (Lucas, 1978, p.15). However, Lucas's and Muth's theories embody a strict frequentist view of probability. In a rational expectations equilibrium, agents' beliefs conform to the true stochastic processes governing the random variables in the model.

In a recent paper, Lucas (1985) sharply delimits the scope of rational expectation modelling to economic phenomena. Lucas distinguishes between situations in which individuals are still groping to find stable decision rules, situations he terms 'adaptive', and steady-state situations in which individuals have arrived at stable decision rules. Indeed this constitutes the definition of economics: 'Technically, I think of economics as studying decision rules that are *steady-states* of some adaptive process, decision rules that are found to work over a range of situations and hence are no longer revised appreciably as more experience accumulates' (Lucas, 1985, p.2). In this paper, Lucas reviews some of the experimental evidence on how equilibrium prices are determined. One general characteristic of the results is that equilibria that were reached were usually stable but the convergence pattern did not resemble a Walrasian adjustment process or any other readily recognizable process. In an earlier paper, Lucas (1978) also stressed that the process of groping towards an equilibrium is not likely to be simply characterized by economic theory. 'Certainly one would not expect to capture the creativity which is devoted to discovering and gaining from disequilibria in actual economies in *any* mechanical approximation routine' (Lucas, 1978, p.1438). Economic theory, according to Lucas, will be of little use during this transition process.

This inability to describe the adjustment process towards equilibrium fully is troublesome because many, if not most, rational expectations models admit multiple solutions. Lucas (1985) briefly describes some of the research on this topic. There do exist adjustment rules which, in some models, lead to the 'natural' or 'preferred' solution (for example, a zero inflation rate in a model with a constant money stock). However, there is no *a priori* basis from which to choose one adjustment rule over another at this stage and, by the very nature of the topic as Lucas indicates, there may never be.

Abrupt political or economic transitions or a sudden restructuring of rules of the game are not, according to this perspective, useful periods in which to apply economic theory at least in the sense of characterizing individuals' decisions from the environment and previous decision rules. Joan Robinson would have asserted that these situations are precisely the most interesting and important for business cycles. The class of recurrent or repetitive business cycles would be a very small subset of economic fluctuations. Perhaps the difference in their empirical judgments stems from their own economic experience. Joan Robinson's formative period (at least for her macroeconomic thinking) included the stagnation of the 1920s and especially the 1930s which, even today, is often viewed as a distinct or unique event. Lucas, on the other hand, lived through the repeated post-war business recessions which possibly may represent more recurrent phenomena. These psychological thoughts can only be viewed as speculative. Joan Robinson was aware of ongoing work on the trade cycle which suggested repetitive mechanisms. Similarly, Lucas (1972) admits that there are difficulties in explaining unemployment during the 1930s.

Both Robinson and Lucas recognized that theories which stressed uncertainty must address the issue of how individual decision-makers confront the uncertain world. Although their approach was quite different, the extent of their disagreement could, in principle, be reduced to an empirical judgment. For both Robinson and Lucas, their treatments of uncertainty were just preludes to their dynamic theories which directly conflicted with Keynesian theory.

3 DYNAMIC THEORY

Joan Robinson viewed the investment decisions by entrepreneurs as one of the key factors determining cyclical development. Unlike the modern Keynesians (whom she termed 'bastard' Keynesians) she believed that particular decisions of entrepreneurs, not just their sum, was important.

This aspect of her thinking is, of course, tied to her views on capital theory and her critique of the position that capital goods are made of 'putty' and are thereby malleable. But more is at stake:

> There has been a lot of tiresome controversy over this putty. The bastard Keynesians try to make out that it is all about the problem of 'measuring capital'. But it has nothing to do either with measurement or with capital; it has to do with abolishing time. For a world that is always in equilibrium there is no difference between the future and the past, there is no history and there is no need for Keynes. (Robinson, 1979, p.173)

How does bastard Keynesian theory, in her view, abolish time and history?

The key point here is that the composition of investment decisions is important. If one industry has an overoptimistic forecast of demand and invests on these beliefs, then *ex post* there will be too much capital invested in this industry. Workers cannot be immediately moved from one industry to another and the economy will have to digest this misallocation of capital over time. This position is similar to those advanced in recent work, for example, by Lilien (1982) and Sheffrin (1984), emphasizing the links between the micro structure of demand and aggregate performance. Capital is industry specific and investment decisions are not fully reversible. At any time, the economy inherits a vector of capital goods determined by individual entrepreneurs who forecasted demands in an uncertain world. With labor also partially tied to industries, the micro composition of demand also affects the current level of full employment or the natural rate. Thus, it is misleading to speak of a unique level of aggregate investment required to reach full employment without outlining the allocation of this investment.

These views of Joan Robinson were influenced more by the work of Harrod than by Keynes. In particular, the notion that investment spending has a dual role, both stimulating demand and creating capacity, underlies this aspect of her dynamic theory. Keynes, of course, did not focus on the creation of capacity in the *General Theory*.

Lucas (1977) emphasizes similar themes. He associates Keynesian economics with the belief that 'policy could effect immediate, or very short-term, movement of the economy from an undesirable current state, *however arrived at*, to a better state' (Lucas, 1977, p.8). The problem with the Keynesian view, according to Lucas, is that it also ignores history in the sense of the particular determination of the state variables that led to the current undesirable outcome. One concrete example of this phenomenon can be seen in Lucas's (1975) model of money and capital accumulation. In this model, the economy can experience a poor outcome from an 'over-investment' cycle similar to that considered by the Austrian economists. In this model, the steady-state capital stock is constant when the long-run growth rate of money is constant. Monetary shocks, however, can cause the capital stock to temporarily exceed its long-run value. It would be incorrect in an economy experiencing this problem to attempt to stimulate the economy by increasing investment.

These general points can be summarized as an attack on one of Keynesian economics basic concepts, potential output. A very rough characterization of Keynesian policy prescriptions is to stimulate output whenever the forecast for output falls short of potential output. Both Joan Robinson's and Lucas's criticisms of the Keynesians insist that the notion of 'potential output' is a harmful abstraction because it fails to take into account the particular history and configuration of capital (both human and non-human) that has been accumulated on the basis of past decisions taken under uncertainty. These criticisms certainly would apply to any efforts to fine-tune the economy. Joan Robinson, however, would have claimed to be able to recognize 'mass unemployment' when she saw it.

The new classicals derive another fundamental criticism of Keynesian theory from their view of individuals making decisions under uncertainty. Given their objective functions and the stochastic environment, individuals will formulate decision rules which specify what their decision will be when economic variables take on a certain value. Keynesian macro models estimate these decision rules and they become the structural equations in the macro model. The problem with this approach is that the decision rules will depend in an intimate way on the stochastic environment that individuals face. If policy initiatives change the stochastic environment, individual decision rules will change. Keynesian macro models will not embody these changes and give misleading results. The 'Lucas critique' poses a sharp challenge to Keynesian modelling.

4 VIEWS ON ECONOMETRICS

Joan Robinson was very critical of econometrics. Some of her criticisms rest on the sheer difficulties of doing empirical work. She cites Norbert Weiner's point that the categories of economic science change even when they appear unchanged on the surface (Robinson, 1979, p.3). For example, a long time series for steel production will inevitably contain observations for which the nature of the product being produced will undergo substantial revisions. Moreover, there are the inherent difficulties of an empirical science that cannot use controlled experiments. When predictions go astray, it is not always possible to determine if the model was misspecified or the underlying world has changed.

Keynes shared similar thoughts on the practical difficulties of conducting econometrics. These criticisms were detailed in his review of Tinbergen's *A Method and Its Application to Investment Activity* and his rejoinder to Tinbergen's response. The difficulties of applied work were overwhelming even for the best scholars. 'There is no one, therefore, so far as human qualities go, whom it would be safer to trust with black magic. That there is anyone I would trust with it at the present stage or that this brand of statistical alchemy is ripe to become a branch of science, I am not yet persuaded. But Newton, Boyle and Locke all played with alchemy. So let him continue' (Keynes, 1973, p.320)

A more interesting criticism is based on the recognition that individuals respond when the policy environment changes. Joan Robinson's analysis of the econometric problems with the Phillips curve foresaw the 'Lucas critique': 'Perhaps the publicity given to the Phillips curve contributed to falsifying its predictions. It was natural for the trade unions to resolve to demonstrate that it is not true that when a certain proportion of their members are unemployed they are incapable of demanding higher wages' (Robinson, 1979, p.175).

If econometric work is near impossible, how can economic theory be of use in policy situations? Unfortunately, there is no straightforward method; theorists must not study time-series but diagnose how the contemporary economic system operates. Success requires deep intuition and insights. However, the payoffs can be great:

> In 1931, he [Keynes] pointed out that falling prices were putting a great strain on the banks. [In March 1933 the banking system in the United States came to a standstill.] In 1936 [following Keynes] I observed that a period of continuous near-full employment would lead to continued inflation; and (most remarkable of all) Kalecki predicted in 1944 that after the war we should be living under the regime of a political trade-cycle (stop-go). (Robinson, 1979, p.118)

Nevertheless, this raises the spectre that policy prescriptions should only come from great minds and that success in policy analysis may rest on 'tacit knowledge' that cannot be fully communicated.

The new classical Economists did not think that progress in economic science was possible without econometric evidence yet dismissed Keynesian econometrics as susceptible to the Lucas critique. The econometric project of the new classical economists attempts to avoid the Lucas critique by estimating deeper relationships that do not change when the policy environment changes, namely to estimate the tastes and technologies of their economic actors.

Sargent (1985) succinctly describes the methods of the new econometrics. It starts with the assumption that individuals are maximizing an objective function which is completely characterized by a few parameters. The stochastic processes for the variables affecting the decision are also specified tightly up to a small subset of parameters. The econometrician knows the maximization problem that the individual is solving and can calculate the decision rule as a function of the parameters of the objective function (which will include technological constraint) and the stochastic processes. By estimating the decision rule along with the equations for the stochastic processes, the econometrician can, in principle, recover the parameters of the objective function describing tastes and technology. Moreover, this can be accomplished, in principle, without observing *any* fundamental change in the economic environment.

As this bold description of the research program indicates, the new econometrics of 'deep parameters' is very ambitious. The key point is that the econometrician and the economic agent have to be solving the identical problems with identical constraints and stochastic processes for key economic variables. It is not difficult to understand why applications of this procedure to a wide variety of problems have had rather modest to negative results. Most often, the tests of cross-equation restrictions indicate the model does not fit the data.[5]

Faced with the inherent difficulties of their own econometric methods, Lucas and Sargent resorted to alternative methods to document some of their claims. Lucas (1985) uses time-averaged data or low-frequency approaches to document the quantity theory. Sargent (1985) examines the episodes of the great hyperinflations and studies their endings as laboratory experiments of regime changes. However, both these alternative approaches provide results which fail to measure up to the promise of the underlying research program. A modern Keynesian would not find anything surprising in Lucas's finding that inflation rates and money growth rates are related over long periods. Long-period methods cannot contribute to the debate over the transmission mechanism in business cycles or the causality relation between money and prices. Sargent's study that claims disinflation is relatively costless after hyperinflations is subject to the criticism, which he recognizes, that he has studied only episodes in which the price system had effectively stopped functioning so that changing the path of prices was not that disruptive.[6]

5 THE CRITICS AND THE KEYNESIAN TRADITION

What effects did the critics have on the Keynesian tradition? Joan Robinson's criticism of macro theory and her emphasis on the autonomy of money wages have become integral components of the post-Keynesian school of macroeconomics which has had only marginal effects on the mainstream macroeconomic research agenda. Although Robinson's emphasis on the volatility of investment or, in Keynes's phrase, 'animal spirits' is frequently noted, her views have not halted empirical efforts to estimate investment relations.

In another context (Sheffrin, 1983), I assessed the impact of the new classical economics on macroeconomic practice. The information-based theories of business fluctuations have had only limited success and even early supporters of this line of thought have become increasingly critical.[7] Lucas's positive theory of business cycle rested on two pillars: lack of full information about monetary aggregates and the importance of intertemporal substitution. The wealth of information about the most recent behavior of monetary aggregates is difficult to reconcile with the model. Moreover, allowing for contemporaneous information (even observed subject to noise) radically changes the implications of the models. The direct evidence on intertemporal substitution is not terribly persuasive.

The 'Lucas critique', however, has had an important effect on the use and interpretation of econometric models. The effect has been largely negative in that it increased the omnipresent doubts about econometric relations. The econometric of tastes and technology has yet to provide any convincing and enduring results and the prospects for breakthrough along this line diminish with time.

On the other hand, the idea of rational expectations has been taken from the work of the new classical economists and has been increasingly used in what otherwise would be Keynesian style work. Examples include work by Taylor (1980) and Sachs (1985). These economists have appropriated the aspects of the new classical economics that they found appealing (mainly rational expectations) but rejected the market-clearing Walrasian approach. To some extent, therefore, the tools of Lucas and Sargent have been incorporated into a modified Keynesianism which still survives despite the methodological warnings by the new classical economists to avoid unexplained wage and price rigidities.

Joan Robinson and the new classical economists have deflected the Keynesian tradition but not destroyed it. Part of the explanation for this may be that their criticisms were so radical. Joan Robinson would force us to combine the micro nuances of capital theory with aggregate fluctuations. The new classicals would require that econometricians solve identical problems to those faced by economic agents in order to estimate relations that are invariant to policy changes. Both Robinson and the new classicals would force us to confront the limits of the explanatory power of economic reasoning in the face of pervasive risk and uncertainty.

Moreover, Joan Robinson's views on the other matters also tended toward extreme positions. Income policies were necessary to prevent inflation without causing deep recessions; strong centralized governments were necessary to control investment patterns; and sharp changes in our social and political structures were necessary to improve social welfare.

These are radical and far-reaching criticisms and guidelines for research. It is not evident that 'normal' times require such radical approaches. The evidence on the empirical applicability of the Lucas critique is far from persuasive. Although Lucas counts the breakdown of the Phillips curve in the 1970s as evidence for this position, the naive Phillips curve can simply be viewed as an incorrect theory that the Keynesians abandoned. Examinations of the behavior of interest rates and wages and prices during the beginning of the Reagan presidency do not indicate radical breakdowns of the econometric relations.[8] Of course, it could be argued that this period was not truly a 'regime' change yet it would be difficult on this criterion to pinpoint any greater regime changes in the post-war era.

In the face of radical changes in the economic system, it is not evident to pragmatic Keynesians that *any* economic theory will lead to specific predictive results. Even taken on their own terms, Sargent's hyperinflation studies do not pretend to pinpoint the precise empirical developments of the post-inflation periods and the exact mechanics of the transitions.

In summary, the criticisms of Joan Robinson and the new classical economists have not destroyed the Keynesian research program although the new classicals did influence the interpretation and practice of empirical work. Because their approach was so radical, it fell short of convincing 'reasonable' Keynesians that fundamental changes in their full research program was required. It is interesting to note that both Joan Robinson and the new classicals found themselves in intellectual battles with the epitome of the reasonable Keynesian, Robert M. Solow.[9] Being reasonable only guarantees attack from radical, although interesting, perspectives.

Although this chapter has concerned itself with the somewhat surprising theme that the critiques of American neoclassical Keynesian economics by Joan Robinson and the new classical economists were strikingly similar, it is important to recognize the truly significant divergences in their research efforts and vision. The main differences which I wish to highlight concern the role of neoclassical theory in aggregate analysis and methodological individualism.

The entire emphasis of the new classical economists is on the use of microeconomic theory, sufficiently generalized to uncertainty and dynamics, to explain aggregate phenomena. The best single statement of this project is Lucas's 'Understanding Business Cycles' which *defines* this as the principal task of modern aggregate analysis. All the other writings of members of this school share the same premise. Although Lucas recognizes that institutional features in the economy, such as the arrangements to share risk between workers and firms, may affect the appearance of the economy, all fundamental explanations of cyclical phenomenon must rest on explanations based on individual behavior which reflect maximization considerations. There is probably no single better example of social scientists following the research precept of methodological individualism anywhere in social science.

Joan Robinson fundamentally disagreed with the notion that neoclassical theory was valuable for understanding aggregate phenomena and that the principle of methodological individualism was useful. In her view, 'the neoclassical scheme was rather barren of results' and one of Keynes's fundamental contributions was to abandon neoclassical theory for price and wage determinations (Robinson, 1962, p.71). The mark-up theory of prices advanced by Kalecki replaced both the Marshallian and Walrasian theories of price determination.

Even more fundamentally, Joan Robinson stressed the social context of actions taken by individuals. Wage determination by trade unions rather than by the individual haggling of individual workers and employers would be one example. Joan Robinson felt that economics was a branch of moral philosophy and could never be divorced from the larger political or social context.

> The moral problem is a conflict that can never be settled. Social life will always present mankind with a choice of evils. No metaphysical solution that can ever be formulated will seem satisfactory for long. The solutions offered by economists were no less delusory than those of the theologians that they displaced. (Robinson, 1962, p.147)

The latest 'theologians' in her view would be the new classical economists.

Like all great theologians, Lucas offers both a message of hope and despair. A research program based on modelling individual behavior under uncertainty may succeed and thereby ease the economic burden of mankind. But there are no guarantees that this research program will succeed and unfortunately, in the views of the new classical economists, there is no alternative.

Notes

1. This is one of the themes of Leijonhufvud (1968).
2. This chapter does not concentrate on the many areas in which there is fundamental disagreement between Joan Robinson and the New Classicals. Some of these areas include: political prescriptions, methodological individualism, and the value of neoclassical theory for macroeconomic analysis. We return to these themes at the end of the chapter.
3. A related issue is whether the relevant economic time-series can be thought of as stationary.

4. See, for example, Cass and Shell (1983).
5. For a typical example, see Hansen and Singleton (1983).
6. Sargent (1985, p.151) notes that Dornbusch first raised this point with him. Sargent's work on the Poincaré stabilization plan was an attempt to demonstrate his thesis in a less extreme environment.
7. The increased work on real business cycles is part of this reaction.
8. See Blanchard (1984) for some econometric evidence on this point.
9. Solow (1969) debated capital theory problems with Joan Robinson and attacked Lucas's views on unemployment (1980).

References

Blanchard, O. J. (1984) 'The Lucas Critique and the Volker Deflation'. *American Economic Review*, 74 211–15.

Cass, D. and K. Shell (1983) 'Do Sunspots Matter?' *Journal of Political Economy*, 91: 193–227.

Hansen, L. P. and K. J. Singleton (1983) 'Stochastic Consumption, Risk Aversion, and the Temporal Behavior of Asset Returns', *Journal of Political Economy*, 91:249–65.

Keynes, J. M. (1937) 'The General Theory of Unemployment', *Quarterly Journal of Economics*, 51: 209–223.

Keynes, J. M. (1973) *The Collected Writings of John Maynard Keynes*, vol. 14 (London: Macmillan).

Leijonhufvud, A. (1968) *On Keynesian Economics and the Economic of Keynes* (London: Oxford University Press).

Lilien, D. M. (1982) 'Sectoral Shifts and Cyclical Unemployment', *Journal of Political Economy*, 90: 777–93.

Lucas, R. E. (1972) 'Unemployment in the Great Depression: Is There a Full Explanation?' *Journal of Political Economy*, 80: 186–91.

Lucas, R. E. (1975) 'An Equilibrium Model of the Business Cycle', *Journal of Political Economy*, 83: 1113–44.

Lucas, R. E. (1977) 'Understanding Business Cycles', in K. Brunner and A. Meltzer (eds) *Stabilization of the Domestic and International Economy* (Amsterdam: North Holland), pp.7–29.

Lucas, R. E. (1978) 'Asset Prices in an Exchange Economy', *Econometrica*, 46: 1429–46.

Lucas, R. E. (1985) 'Adaptive Behavior and Economic Theory', mimeo.

Robinson, J. (1951) 'The Rate of Interest', *Econometrica*, 19: 92–111.

Robinson, J. (1962) *Economic Philosophy* (New York: Anchor Books).

Robinson, J. (1979) *Collected Economic Papers* vol. 5 (Oxford: Blackwell).

Sachs, J. (1985) 'The Dollar and the Policy Mix: 1985', *Brookings Papers on Economic Actitivy*, 1: 117–98.

Sargent, T. J. (1985) *Rational Expectations and Inflation* (New York: Harper & Row).

Sheffrin, S. M. (1983) *Rational Expectations* (New York: Cambridge University Press).

Sheffrin, S. M. (1984) 'The Dispersion Hypothesis in Macroeconomics', *The Review of Economics and Statistics*, 64: 482–5.

Solow, R. M. (1969) 'The Production Function and the Theory of Capital', in J. Stiglitz and H. Uzawa (eds) *Readings in the Modern Theory of Economic Growth* (Cambridge: MIT) pp.285–92.

Solow, R. M. (1980) 'On Theories of Unemployment', *American Economic Review*, 70: 1–11.

Taylor, J. (1980) 'Aggregate Dynamics and Staggered Contracts', *Journal of Political Economy*, 88: 1–23.

Tversky, A. and D. Kahneman (1974) 'Judgement Under Uncertainty: Heuristics and Biases', *Science*, 185: 1124–31.

Part VIII

Market Failures and Public Policy

At date t, he faces the budget constraint:

$$p_t C_1 + M = p_t Y$$

and he expects the budget constraint at date $t+1$:

$$p_{t+1} C_2 = M$$

(since I shall consider only perfect foresight equilibria, the price p_{t+1} that prevails at date $t+1$ is correctly anticipated by the consumer).

Finally, the consumer may face rationing constraints, noted with upper bars, either on his demand for goods ($C_1 \leqslant \bar{C}_{1t}$, where $\bar{C}_{1t}$ is a non-negative number) or on his supply of labor ($Y \leqslant \bar{Y}_t$). Therefore, the optimal action of the young consumer is given by:

$$\begin{cases} Y_t = \text{Min}\,(Y^*, \bar{Y}_t) \\ C_{1t} = \text{Min}\,(\alpha Y_t, \bar{C}_{1t}) \\ M_{t+1} = p_t(Y_t - C_{1t}) \end{cases} \tag{1}$$

The old consumer enters period t with an initial money holding M_t. In order to avoid the description of inheritance, I shall put assumptions later on on the rationing scheme, so that his demand for goods is never constrained. Thus, his consumption is:

$$C_{2t} = M_t / p_t. \tag{2}$$

The *inventory holders* (or *speculators*) have access to a storage technology which allows them to store up to $\bar{S}$ units of output without cost. They borrow from the bank to finance their activity, and consume their profits in the second period of their life after redemption of their loans. Under perfect foresight, I assume that they do not plan to be bankrupt. The bank lends without interest.

The young speculator chooses the inventory level S_t which maximizes his second-period consumption, and borrows $p_t S_t$ from the bank to finance his acquisition. Furthermore, I assume that when $p_t = p_{t+1}$, i.e. when he is indifferent as far as the level of inventory is concerned, he chooses the value of S_t that minimizes the disequilibrium on the market. He may also face a rationing constraint $\bar{S}_t$ on the quantity of goods that he buys. To summarize, his demand for good is described by:

$$\begin{cases} S_t = 0 & \text{if } p_{t+1} < p_t \\ & \text{or } (p_{t+1} = p_t \text{ and there is an} \\ & \text{excess demand of good)} \\ S_t \text{ belongs to } [0, \text{Min}(\bar{S}, \bar{S}_t)] & \text{if } p_{t+1} = p_t \text{ and the market is} \\ & \text{balanced} \\ S_t = \text{Min}(\bar{S}, \bar{S}_t) & \text{if } p_{t+1} > p_t \\ & \text{or } (p_{t+1} = p_t \text{ and there is an} \\ & \text{excess supply of good)} \end{cases} \tag{3}$$

Let $s_t = -1, 0$, or 1 denote the state of disequilibrium on the market at date t, respectively excess supply, equilibrium, or excess demand. It will be useful for further reference to denote $\sigma(p_{t+1}/p_t, s_t)$ the unconstrained demand correspondence for inventories, i.e. the right-hand side of (3) when $\bar{S}_t = +\infty$. Note that σ is not continuous in (p_{t+1}/p_t) for $s_t = -1$ and $s_t = +1$.

The old speculator redeems his debt $p_{t-1}S_{t-1}$ to the bank, by selling the quantity $p_{t-1}S_{t-1}/p_t$ on the market, and consumes the profit $S_{t-1} - p_{t-1}S_{t-1}/p_t$. I shall consider only equilibria where the old consumer does not meet a rationing constraint on his sales.

Finally, the *bank* receives $p_{t-1}S_{t-1}$ from the old speculator and grants a new loan p_tS_t to the young one. The quantity of money in circulation satisfies therefore:

$$M_{t+1} = M_t - p_{t-1}S_{t-1} + p_tS_t. \tag{4}$$

The quantity of outside money $M_t - p_{t-1}S_{t-1}$ is constant over time. I shall assume that it is strictly positive and equal to M_0 (i.e. $S_{-1} = 0$).

I proceed now with the description of the allocation of resources. What I have in mind is a short period of reference, too short for the price system to equilibrate the market. I assume that the resources at date t are allocated according to the fix-price rule, and that the price system is revised next period in view of the disequilibrium on the market of date t. Quantities adjust infinitely faster than prices.

The equality between supply and demand at date t can be written:

$$C_{1t} + C_{2t} + S_t = Y_t + \frac{p_{t-1}S_{t-1}}{p_t}$$

or equivalently, using (2) and (4):

$$C_{1t} + S_t + \frac{M_0}{p_t} - Y_t = 0. \tag{5}$$

Definition 1: Given the price system p_t and price expectations p_{t+1} a fix-price equilibrium at date t is a vector $e_t=(C_{1t},S_t,Y_t)$ such that there exist quantity constraints $\bar{C}_{1t}\geqslant 0$, $\bar{S}_t\geqslant 0$, $\bar{Y}_t\geqslant 0$ which satisfy (1), (3), and (5) and in addition,

(i) The minimum of supply and demand is traded, i.e.

$$\bar{C}_{1t}=\bar{S}_t=+\infty \quad \text{or } \bar{Y}_t=+\infty.$$

(ii) (Rationing scheme) in the case of excess demand, the inventory holder is served before the consumer-workers:

$$\bar{S}_t<+\infty \quad \text{implies } \bar{C}_{1t}=0.$$

There might not exist a fix-price equilibrium according to the previous definition, because I have not allowed rationing of either the old consumer-worker or of the old speculator in cases of very large imbalances on the market. It is easy to see what restriction on the price system this implies by computing explicitly the fix-price equilibria. This will also provide an explicit formula for the aggregate excess demand which is to determine next period price. To compute the equilibria, one has to distinguish whether the market is in excess supply ($s_t=-1$), balanced ($s_t=0$), or in excess demand ($s_t=+1$).

First, excess supply, i.e. $\bar{C}_{1t}=\bar{S}_t=+\infty$. (1), (3) and (5) give the familiar Keynesian multiplier:

$$\begin{cases} Y_t=\bar{Y}_t=\left(\sigma\left(\dfrac{p_{t+1}}{p_t},-1\right)+\dfrac{M_0}{p_t}\right)/(1-\alpha) \\ C_{1t}=\alpha Y_t \\ S_t=\sigma\left(\dfrac{p_{t+1}}{p_t},-1\right). \end{cases}$$

This will occur only if

$$\sigma\left(\frac{p_{t+1}}{p_t},-1\right)<(1-\alpha)Y^*-\frac{M_0}{p_t}. \tag{6a}$$

Second, supply equals demand, i.e. $\bar{C}_{1t}=\bar{S}_t=\bar{Y}_t=+\infty$. We have:

$$\begin{cases} Y_t = Y^* \\ C_{1t} = \alpha Y^* \\ S_t \in \sigma\left(\dfrac{p_{t+1}}{p_t}, 0\right) \end{cases}$$

This will occur only if

$$(1-\alpha)Y^* - \frac{M_0}{p_t} \in \sigma\left(\frac{p_{t+1}}{p_t}, 0\right) \tag{6b}$$

Finally, excess demand, i.e. $\bar{Y}_t = +\infty$. The rationing scheme implies:

$$\left[\begin{array}{l} Y_t = Y^* \\ C_{1t} = \bar{C}_{1t} = \text{Max}\left[0, \dfrac{M_0}{p_t} + \sigma\left(\dfrac{p_{t+1}}{p_t}, +1\right) - Y^*\right] \\ S_t = \begin{cases} \sigma\left(\dfrac{p_{t+1}}{p_t}, +1\right) & \text{if } \bar{C}_{1t} > 0 \\ Y^* - \dfrac{M_0}{p_t} & \text{if } \bar{C}_{1t} = 0 \end{cases} \end{array}\right.$$

The regime will prevail if $\bar{C}_{1t} < \alpha Y^*$, i.e.:

$$\sigma\left(\frac{p_{t+1}}{p_t}, +1\right) > (1-\alpha)Y^* - \frac{M_0}{p_t} \tag{6c}$$

and one must have $\bar{S}_t \geqslant 0$, i.e.:

$$Y^* \geqslant \frac{M_0}{p_t}. \tag{7}$$

The foregoing analysis leads to

Proposition 1: Given the price system p_t and price expectations p_{t+1}, there is a unique fix-price equilibrium at date t, in a well-defined state s_t of excess demand, balance between supply and demand, or excess supply, if and only if

$$Y^* \geqslant \frac{M_0}{p_t}.$$

Proof of Proposition 1: Given p_{t+1}/p_t, one and only one of the three conditions (6a), (6b), and (6c) is satisfied. In fact the only non-trivial case occurs when $p_{t+1}=p_t$ and the result follows from the definition of σ:

$$\sigma(1,-1)=\bar{S} \quad \sigma(1,0)=[0,\bar{S}] \quad \sigma(1,+1)=0$$

The only situation where an equilibrium does not exist is when $Y^* < M_0/p_t$, which implies that (6c) prevails. Excess demand is so large that one needs to ration the old consumer-workers, something I have ruled out for simplicity to avoid modelling inheritance.

QED

Let $s(p_{t+1}/p_t)$ denote the state of the market at date t. It is now easy to define the *Walrasian excess demand* at date t. It is obtained by relaxing the binding constraints respectively in each state:

$$Z\left(\frac{p_{t+1},p_t}{p_t}\right) = \begin{cases} \sigma\left(\frac{p_{t+1}}{p_t},+1\right)+\frac{M_0}{p_t}-(1-\alpha)Y^* & \text{if } s\left(\frac{p_{t+1}}{p_t}\right) = -1 \\ 0 & \text{if } s\left(\frac{p_{t+1}}{p_t}\right) = 0 \\ \sigma\left(\frac{p_{t+1}}{p_t},+1\right)+\frac{M_0}{p_t}-(1-\alpha)Y^* & \text{if } s\left(\frac{p_{t+1}}{p_t}\right) = -1. \end{cases} \tag{8}$$

Following tradition, I assume that prices adjust to reduce excess demand. The *tâtonnement* process, in linearized form, is taken to be:

$$\frac{p_{t+1}}{p_t}=1+v\frac{Z(p_{t+1}/p_t,p_t)}{Y^*} \tag{9}$$

where $0<v<1$.

The main object of study of this paper can now be defined:

Definition 2: Given an initial price system p_0, an intertemporal equilibrium of the economy with perfect foresight is an infinite sequence $((e_t,p_t)\ t=0,1,\ldots)$ such that, for each $t=0,1,\ldots,e_t$ is a fix-price equilibrium at date t and (9) holds.

We are now in a position to proceed to Section 3 to study the set of intertemporal equilibria.

Remark 1: For the economy without inventories, (9) becomes

$$p_{t+1}=(1-(1-\alpha)v)p_t+\frac{vM_0}{Y^*}.$$

We have taken v in (0,1) so that, in this case, the stationary competitive equilibrium $p^*=M_0/(1-\alpha)Y^*$ is globally stable under the *tâtonnement* process. Note that inventories, in a perfect foresight set-up, introduce the variable p_{t+1} on the right-hand side of the *tâtonnement* process (as would do, in fact, any agent's decision depending on the future). This creates difficulties for the derivation of a well-defined dynamical system. A similar problem was studied in continuous time by Enthoven and Arrow (1956).

Remark 2: One might want to study the intertemporal equilibria where the *tâtonnement* process reacts to *effective* excess demand rather than to *Walrasian* excess demand. The effective demand $\tilde{Z}(p_{t+1}/p_t, p_t)$ is equal to the Walrasian demand when the market is balanced or in excess demand. It differs in cases of excess supply where:

$$\tilde{Z}\left(\frac{p_{t+1}}{p_t}, p_t\right)=C_{1t}+\frac{M_0}{p_t}+\sigma\left(\frac{p_{t+1}}{p_t},-1\right)-Y^*.$$

Since $C_{1t}=\alpha Y_t=\alpha\left(\sigma\left(\frac{p_{t+1}}{p_t},-1\right)+\frac{M_0}{p_t}\right)/(1-\alpha)$, we get:

$$\tilde{Z}\left(\frac{p_{t+1}}{p_t}, p_t\right)=\begin{cases}\dfrac{1}{1-\alpha}Z\left(\dfrac{p_{t+1}}{p_t}, p_t\right) & \text{if } s\left(\dfrac{p_{t+1}}{p_t}\right)=-1\\[2ex] Z\left(\dfrac{p_{t+1}}{p_t}, p_t\right) & \text{if } s\left(\dfrac{p_{t+1}}{p_t}\right)=0 \text{ or } +1\end{cases}\tag{10}$$

The analysis carries forward with minor changes in this case (see Remark 5 below).

Remark 3: A direct inspection of the definitions shows that the quantity theory of money holds for the intertemporal equilibria. In fact take any intertemporal equilibrium $((e_t,p_t))$ associated with an initial quantity of money M_0. Then $((e_t,\lambda p_t))$ is an intertemporal equilibrium of the economy with outside money λM_0.

3 THE PRICE AND INVENTORY CYCLE

While, in the absence of inventories, the *tâtonnement* process converges towards the efficient stationary competitive equilibrium, the properties of the dynamics are deeply affected by the introduction of inventories.

The easiest way to study (9) is to use a diagrammatic analysis. Let:

$$F(p_t)=\frac{M_0}{p_t}-(1-\alpha)Y^*. \tag{11}$$

$F(p_t)$ represents the aggregate excess demand faced by the young speculator. Using (8), it can immediately be seen that the dynamics (9) can be rewritten equivalently

$$F(p_t) \text{ belongs to } \theta\left(\frac{p_{t+1}}{p_t}\right) \tag{12}$$

where θ is the correspondence defined by

$$\theta\left(\frac{p_{t+1}}{p_t}\right)=\begin{cases}\dfrac{Y^*}{v}\left(\dfrac{p_{t+1}}{p_t}-1\right) & \text{if } p_{t+1}<p_t\\[2ex] [0,-\bar{S}] & \text{if } p_{t+1}=p_t\\[2ex] \dfrac{Y^*}{v}\left(\dfrac{p_{t+1}}{p_t}-1\right)-\bar{S} & \text{if } p_{t+1}>p_t\end{cases} \tag{13}$$

The graph of the correspondence θ is drawn on Figure 24.1. For p_{t+1}/p_t smaller than 1, the stock is equal to zero and the graph is a portion of a straight line of slope Y^*/v. At $p_{t+1}/p_t=1$, the inventory can take any value between 0 and $\bar{S}$, and thus the graph is a vertical segment between 0 and $\bar{S}$. Finally, for $p_{t+1}>p_t$, the inventory is equal to $\bar{S}$ and the graph is a half line of slope Y^*/v through the point $(1,-\bar{S})$.

The following characterization is a direct consequence of Proposition 1 and the definition.

Proposition 2: Given an initial price system p_0, the solutions of (12) which satisfy

$$p_t \geqslant M_0/Y^* \quad (\text{or } F(p_t)\leqslant \alpha Y^*) \quad \text{for all } t$$

are in a one-to-one correspondence with the intertemporal equilibria.

It is now easy to find the intertemporal equilibria on the diagram. Put $F(p_t)$ on the vertical axis of Figure 24.1. Select a value for p_{t+1}/p_t. Note that there are three possible choices if $0 > F(p_t) > -\bar{S}$. This indeterminacy hinges on expectations: optimistic, neutral, and pessimistic expectations are all three of them self-fulfilling. When $p_{t+1} < p_t$, $S_t = 0$. When $p_{t+1} = p_t$, $S_t = F(p_t)$ and when $p_{t+1} > p_t$, $S_t = \text{Min}\,[\bar{S}, Y^* - M_0/p_t]$. Given this selection, compute p_{t+1} as $p_t \times (p_{t+1}/p_t)$ and iterate with $F(p_{t+1})$. It is important to remark that, since the quantity of outside money M_0 is strictly positive, the real balance effect implies:

$$\begin{cases} p_{t+1} > p_t & \text{implies } F(p_{t+1}) < F(p_t) \\ p_{t+1} = p_t & \text{implies } F(p_{t+1}) = F(p_t) \\ p_{t+1} < p_t & \text{implies } F(p_{t+1}) > F(p_t). \end{cases} \tag{14}$$

Let me concentrate attention on the set of equilibria starting at $p_0 = M_0/(1-\alpha)Y^*$, the stationary competitive price of the economy without inventories. The evolution of an economy along an intertemporal equilibrium can be partitioned into three types of phases: booms, depressions, and phases of stability.

A boom is an interval of time $[m,n]$ such that $p_{t+1} > p_t$ for all t, between m and n, $m \leqslant t \leqslant n$, $p_m \leqslant p_{m-1}$, and $p_{n+2} \leqslant p_{n+1}$. By definition this is a phase of persistent inflation which corresponds to a path of the dynamical system along the segment AB of Figure 24.1. All along, there is excess demand and full employment. By (14), since $F(p_{t+1}) < F(p_t)$, the rate of inflation decreases over time. The quantity of money in circulation, $M_t = M_0 + p_{t-1}S_{t-1}$, rises.

A depression is an interval of time $[m,n]$ such that $p_{t+1} < p_t$ for all t between m and n, $m \leqslant t \leqslant n$, $p_m \geqslant p_{m-1}$, and $p_{n+2} \geqslant p_{n+1}$. By definition, this is a phase of persistent deflation which corresponds to a path of the dynamical system along the segment CE of Figure 24.1. All along, there is excess supply and unemployment. Again (14) implies that the rate of deflation decreases over time. The output level $Y_t = M_0/(1-\alpha)p_t$ increases through the real-balance effect.

Finally, during a phase of stability $[m,n]$, the price level stays constant. There is full employment and the level of inventories S_t adjusts exactly to the excess demand of the rest of the economy: $S_t = (1-\alpha)Y^* - M_0/p$.

The equations giving the evolution of prices in each of the possible phases can be derived easily from (11) and (13):

$$\begin{cases} p_{t+1} = \left(1 - v(1-\alpha) + v\dfrac{\bar{S}}{Y^*}\right) p_t + v\dfrac{M_0}{Y^*} & \text{during booms if } s_t = +1 \\ p_{t+1} = p_t & \text{during phases of stability if } s_t = 0 \\ p_{t+1} = (1 - v(1-\alpha))p_t + v\dfrac{M_0}{Y^*} & \text{during recessions if } s_t = -1. \end{cases} \quad (15)$$

Proposition 3: Let p_0 be such that $M_0/(1-\alpha)Y^* < p_0 < M_0/[(1-\alpha)Y^* - \bar{S}]$. To any sequence (s_j) $j = 0,1,2,...$, such that $s_j = -1,0$, or 1 is associated a unique intertemporal equilibrium starting at p_0 where the sequence of prices is given by (15), and conversely.

Proof: One has just to apply Proposition 2 and to note that along the sequence:

$$p_t > M_0/Y^*.$$

QED

The booms correspond to the periods where $s_t = +1$, the depressions to periods where $s_t = -1$. The above characterization of the set of intertemporal equilibria with initial condition p_0 shows that there is indeed a lot of equilibria. And one can vary the initial condition. What are the most likely equilibria to prevail in the long run? For the following heuristic discussion, I shall place myself in the situation described in Figure 24.1, where the point B is above the line of ordinate $-\bar{S}$, i.e. under the assumption:

Assumption 1: $\bar{S} < (1-\alpha)Y^*$.

For the assumption of perfect foresight to be meaningful, one must concentrate on easily forecastable equilibria. The equilibria along which it is easier to make forecasts are the ones where the price level stays constant over time. They are represented on the diagram by the points of the line EB. The inventory level is constant at a level S, $0 \leqslant S \leqslant \bar{S}$, and the corresponding price level is $p = M_0/((1-\alpha)Y^* - S)$. E, with $S = 0$, is the stationary competitive equilibrium of the economy without inventories. Consider first the points E and B. At E, an expected temporary increase in demand at constant price pushes $F(p_t)$ to a strictly positive value and therefore induces a price increase (the economy goes to a point above A on the diagram). Similarly, at B, an expected temporary decrease in demand pushes the economy below C. Both E and B are destabilized by *expected temporary shocks* on demand. Consider now the stationary equilibria corresponding to points in the interior of the segment EB. At these points the level of inventories just balances the level of excess demand. Imagine a world with many small uncoordinated inventory holders. If any of them takes a more speculative approach and, say, increases his stock while expecting an increase in price, his expectation will be self-fulfilling and the price will increase. Similarly, if he expects a decrease in price, the price will decrease and all his fellow inventory holders will be bankrupt, if they do not behave similarly. In other words, the equilibria on EB are destabilized by *noise in price expectations*.

On the other hand, booms and depressions are a self-enforcing way of coordinating individual decisions. In fact, during phase AB of the cycle, the speculators make profits linked with inflation. It is not in the interest of any of them to stop his activity. During phase CE of the cycle, it is theoretically possible for the inventory holders, by a sudden increase in their stocks, to bring the economy on AB where they would make profits (their profits are null on CE). But again, if their decisions are not coordinated, taking the risk individually is not worthwhile and leads to bankruptcy. The foregoing argument leads to the conclusion that the most likely intertemporal equilibrium of this economy would be a succession of booms along AB and depressions along CE. The economy would become unstable both at the end of the boom, when it approaches B, and at the end of the depression, when it approaches E. This explains why, although the difference equations (14) predict an infinite time to reach either B or E, random shocks would be responsible for 'catastrophes' that would push the economy from B to C or E to A. Note that this theory of the business cycle is halfway between the two main traditional approaches: it uses both non-linearities *and* random shocks to generate the cycle.

Remark 4: The above discussion is valid under the assumption that $\bar{S} < (1-\alpha)Y^*$ (Assumption 1). Under this assumption, the storage capacity is smaller than the intended consumption level of old agents in a stationary environment. In this circumstance, money has indeed a role in the model, the social contrivance role of money of Samuelson (1958). It enables the agents to reach their optimal intertemporal consumption profile. When $\bar{S} \geqslant (1-\alpha)Y^*$, this optimal allocation can be reached by holding inventories only, and money is superfluous. This is reflected in the set of intertemporal equilibria by the fact that the difference equation which governs the dynamics during the booms (the first equation in (15)) diverges to $+\infty$. On Figure 24.1, starting from A the trajectory hits the line of ordinate $-(1-\alpha)Y^*$ and never gets to B. The economic interpretation of this phenomenon is that, by borrowing more and more to finance their inventories, the speculators get rid of the monetary bubble and p_t tends to $+\infty$ (the price of money in in terms of goods goes to zero).

Remark 5: If the adjustment process is made to react to effective demand rather than Walrasian demand, the only difference with the previous

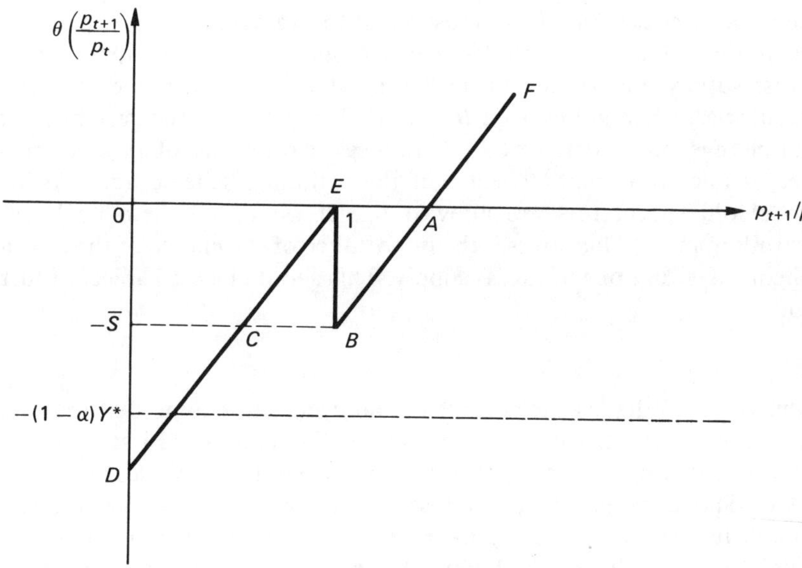

Figure 24.1

analysis is a change in the speed of adjustment during the period of unemployment (see Remark 2 and formula (10)). Equation 13 becomes:

$$\theta\left(\frac{p_{t+1}}{p_t}\right) = \begin{cases} \frac{(1-\alpha)Y^*}{v}\left(\frac{p_{t+1}}{p_t}-1\right) & \text{if } p_{t+1}<p_t \\ [0,-\bar{S}] & \text{if } p_{t+1}=p_t \\ \frac{Y^*}{v}\left(\frac{p_{t+1}}{p_t}-1\right)-\bar{S} & \text{if } p_{t+1}>p_t. \end{cases} \tag{16}$$

On Figure 24.1, point *D* becomes closer to the origin, and the slope of *DE* decreases in absolute value.

Remark 6: It may be useful to point out why the standard argument that rules out inventory cycles in competitive equilibria with perfect foresight does not carry over here. To sketch the argument, suppose that there is a cycle and consider the point where the price level is at a maximum, such as *B* here. Now the young speculators at this point forecast a decrease in price. Thus, they do not store (this is also the case in the present model). In the competitive model this implies that demand is not above average, and thus the price level can only be at most equal to average. Since it is equal to its maximum value one concludes that it is stationary. By contrast here, the excess supply on the current market created by the negative variation of inventories, when going from B to C, does not change the current price (it will change only next period). It induces a rationing of production and creates unemployment. Because of the rationing scheme adopted in the model old speculators are allowed to get rid of all their stock at the prevailing price. This stresses the importance of the choice of the rationing scheme, in situations of excess supply. This should be the subject of further study.

Remark 7: What is the impact of the cycle on income distribution, or preferably on the distribution of welfare in the economy? First, speculators, who would not get a cent at a stationary equilibrium, clearly enjoy the cycle. The consumer-workers lose a lot compared to the competitive equilibrium situation: during the recession, unemployment creates a dead-weight loss and during the boom, they suffer from rationing and inflation (which allows speculators to prosper). As far as the phases of the cycle are concerned, speculators do prefer booms where they consume to recessions where they do not. If one considers the consumer-workers as a whole, there is no clear-cut comparison: a situation with a little loss of income might be preferred to one with a lot of rationing. But in a disaggregated model, unemployment during recessions and rationing during expansions would not be experienced by the same persons.

Remark 8: The previous analysis can be applied with minor changes to a more general non-linear formulation of the *tâtonnement* process. Replace (9) by:

$$\frac{p_{t+1}}{p_t} = 1 + V\left(\frac{Z(p_{t+1}/p_t, p_t)}{Y^*}\right) \tag{17}$$

where V is a strictly increasing function which maps $\mathbb{R}$ into $(-1, +\infty)$ and satisfies $V(0)=0$. It also extends to economies with many consumers with various utility functions. However, it would in general not be possible to get analytic formulas for the cycle. I sketch the argument. Let $\xi(p_{t+1}/p_t, Y^*)$ be the aggregate Walrasian demand of good of the young consumer-workers. Then one has just to replace (3) by:

$$\theta\left(\frac{p_{t+1}}{p_t}\right) = \begin{cases} Y^*V^{-1}\left(\frac{p_{t+1}}{p_t}-1\right) - \xi\left(\frac{p_{t+1}}{p_t}, Y^*\right) & \text{if } p_{t+1}<p_t \\ [-\xi(1,Y^*), -\xi(1,Y^*)-\bar{S}] & \text{if } p_{t+1}=p_t \\ Y^*V^{-1}\left(\frac{p_{t+1}}{p_t}-1\right) - \bar{S} - \xi\left(\frac{p_{t+1}}{p_t}, Y^*\right) & \text{if } p_{t+1}>p_t \end{cases}$$

where V^{-1} is the inverse of V.

The vertical segment EB, associated with the inventory behavior, remains. The stationary competitive equilibrium of the model without inventories corresponds to the price level:

$$p^* = \frac{M_0}{Y^* - \xi(1, Y^*)}.$$

Differentiating (7), it is easy to see that it is locally asymptotically stable if:

$$\frac{\xi_1'(1, Y^*)V'(0)}{Y^*} < 1$$

and

$$\frac{V'(0)(Y^* - \xi(1, Y^*))}{Y^* - V'(0)\xi_1'(1, Y^*)} < 2.$$

Furthermore, if the product $V'\xi_1'/Y^*$ is smaller than 1 on all its domain of definition, the two segments DE and BF of Figure 24.1 would be replaced by increasing curves. The qualitative description of the cycle remains the same. If the condition $V'\xi_1'/Y^* < 1$ is violated, the curves DE and BF may be decreasing in some regions and the analysis becomes more complicated.

Remark 9: The high sensitivity of inventories to price movements is responsible for the inventory cycle in this model. What if the demand for inventory was smoother?

Consider a situation where, because of a diversity of storage costs and storage capacities in the economy, the demand for inventory is a non-decreasing function $\tilde{\sigma}(p_{t+1}/p_t)$, with $\tilde{\sigma}(p_{t+1}/p_t)=0$ for $p_{t+1}/p_t \leqslant 1$, continuously differentiable on $(1, +\infty)$, with a well-defined right derivative at $p_{t+1}/p_t = 1$. The previous analysis extends easily with:

$$\theta\left(\frac{p_{t+1}}{p_t}\right)=\frac{Y^*}{v}\left(\frac{p_{t+1}}{p_t}-1\right)-\tilde{\sigma}\left(\frac{p_{t+1}}{p_t}\right).$$

Let $\tilde{\sigma}'(1)$ be the right derivative of $\tilde{\sigma}$ at $p_{t+1}/p_t=1$. Drawing the diagram, it is immediate to see that if $v\tilde{\sigma}'(1)/Y^*>1$ the stationary competitive equilibrium E is destabilized by an expected temporary increase in demand, as before. If in addition $\tilde{\sigma}$ is concave on $(1,+\infty)$ with an upper limit not greater than $\bar{S}$, the previous analysis can be easily transposed. Note, however, that B should be replaced on Figure 24.1 by the point of $(1,+\infty)$ where $\theta(p_{t+1}/p_t)$ reaches its minimum. Even in the absence of shocks, the boom ends in finite time.

4 STABILIZATION POLICIES AND INTERACTION BETWEEN SHORT-RUN AND LONG-RUN DYNAMICS

During the booms, speculators manage to get a share of output without, it seems, being entitled to it. Are there not competitive forces to destroy this rent? I examine first in this section a very primitive model that might account for the persistence of the cycle in the long run. I then turn to policy considerations. The inventory cycle has very undesirable properties. Remedies should be found to unemployment and the associated loss of output. I study the impact of deficit spending policies, of their implications for the unemployment–inflation trade-off, and I conclude with an examination of the role of monetary policy.

All the discussion of this section is undertaken in the framework of the model where prices react to *effective* demand as in (16).

4.1 Capital Accumulation and the Cycle

Inventory holders enjoy a rent during the cycle, because they are endowed with a fixed storage capacity. In the long run, storage capacity should be determined by cost considerations. We have seen, on the other hand (Assumption 1), that the emergence of the business cycle supposes a not too large storage capacity. I present here a very preliminary qualitative analysis of capital accumulation in the cycle.

To deal with this issue, I modify slightly the model of Section 2. There are now infinite-lived capitalists in the economy who own the storage capacity and rent it to the speculators. The storage technology being linear, competition among the inventory holders brings all the profits to the capitalists. The proceeds serve to maintain storage capacity. Suppose that capacity is produced according to a neoclassical technology. The cost in goods to maintain $\bar{S}$ per unit of time is $C(\bar{S})$, where C is an increasing convex twice continuously differentiable function with $C(0)=0$. The economy has a long-run stationary equilibrium capacity (possibly with inventory cycles) when $C(\bar{S})$ equals the sum, in real terms, of the profits collected along the cycle per unit of time. When profits are higher than cost, new capacity will be added. When profits are smaller than cost the capitalists will face bankruptcy, and capacity will disappear. Note that, in this interpretation of the model, what was previously the consumption of the speculators becomes inefficient investment in storage capacity.

I am going to argue that for a range of cost functions *the economy does not have a stable competitive equilibrium with a stationary allocation of resources.*

The best candidate for a competitive equilibrium with a stationary allocation of resources corresponds to $\bar{S}=0$ and is efficient. We know from the results of Section 3 that if cost of capacity is identically equal to zero in a neighborhood of the origin, this equilibrium is unstable: a small capacity will cost nothing and bring profits.

Proposition 4: For $\bar{S}$ close to 0, the profits collected along a cycle are approximately equal to $\bar{S}^2/(1-\alpha)Y^*$.

Proof of Proposition 4: For small $\bar{S}$ the profits of the speculators occur along phase AB of the cycle and can be computed as (see (15)):

$$\pi(\bar{S})=\sum_{t=0}^{\infty}\bar{S}\left(\frac{p_{t+1}}{p_t}-1\right)$$

where p_t is the solution of the difference equation

$$(p_{t+1}-\bar{p})=(1-\nu(1-\alpha)+\nu\bar{S}/Y^*)(p_t-\bar{p})$$

with initial condition $p_0=M_0/(1-\alpha)Y^*$ and $\bar{p}=M_0((1-\alpha)Y^*-\bar{S})$. Let $k=1-\nu(1-\alpha)+\nu\bar{S}/Y^*$. From the difference equation, we get

$$(p_t-\bar{p})=k^t(p_0-\bar{p})$$

and

$$\left(\frac{p_{t+1}}{p_t}-1\right)=\left(\frac{\bar{p}}{p_t}-1\right)[\nu(1-\alpha)-\nu\bar{S}/Y^*].$$

After some calculation we get:

$$\pi(\bar{S}) = \sum_{t=0}^{\infty} \frac{v\bar{S}^2}{Y^*} \frac{[(1-\alpha)Y^* - \bar{S}]k^t}{(1-\alpha)Y^* - k^t\bar{S}}$$

and thus:

$$\frac{\bar{S}^2}{(1-\alpha(Y^*} \leqslant \pi(\bar{S}) \leqslant \frac{\bar{S}^2}{(1-\alpha)Y^* - \bar{S}} .$$

The result follows.

QED

To get the profits per unit of time, one must divide the profits collected along the cycle through the average length of this cycle. In the presence of random shocks with constant variance, based on the difference equations of the simple model, it seems likely that the number of periods of the cycle is finite for $\bar{S}$ close to zero. Therefore, the profits per unit of time are approximately quadratic, for small $\bar{S}$. They are larger than $C(\bar{S})$ and, consequently, the stationary competitive equilibrium is unstable whenever $C'(0) = C''(0) = 0$. This seems to be a plausible assumption since storage capacity is in practice a joint product with housing or production activities.

What happens, then, when $\bar{S}$ increases? It seems very likely that, when $\bar{S}$ approaches $(1-\alpha)Y^*$, the profits per unit of time tend to zero. Following Remark 4, in fact, prices tend to infinity during the expansion phase which becomes longer and the profit at time t, $\bar{S}(p_{t+1}/p_t - 1)$ becomes very often close to zero.[1] Therefore, the cost curve intersects the profit curve at some $\bar{S}^*$, which corresponds to a stable long-run stationary capacity. These heuristic arguments are very preliminary and further work is needed in this area. I proceed now with the study of government policies.

4.2 Government Spending Financed by Money Creation

Assume that the government commits itself to maintain full employment, by buying good as soon as it sees a prospect for excess supply. Government expenditure is financed by printing money, and it serves to build spacecrafts with minimal direct interaction with the demand of the private sector (except for the income effect). How does that affect the business cycle?

The easiest way to answer the question is to follow the trajectory starting at E with $p_0 = M_0/(1-\alpha)Y^*$, the competitive price, and $S_{-1} = 0$. Along phase AB, there are price increases, excess demand, and full employment. Nothing is changed. Government intervention will take place at B, when speculators forecast a fall in price next period. Recall that, at B, immediately before the catastrophe:

$$p_B = M_0/((1-\alpha)Y^* - \bar{S})$$

$$M_\theta = M_0 + \bar{p}\bar{S},\ Y = Y^*.$$

If the speculators expect a fall in price next period, there will be a variation of inventories equal to $-\bar{S}$ and output, by the multiplier effect, will be reduced to $Y^* - \bar{S}(1-\alpha)$. To restore full employment, the government must buy $G = \bar{S}$, standing for the inventory holders. The creation of money necessary to finance its expenditure is $\Delta M = p_B\bar{S}$. Thus, after government intervention, inventories are equal to zero, $p_I = M_0/((1-\alpha)Y^* - \bar{S})$ and $M_I = M_B + \Delta M - p_B\bar{S}$ (the old speculators redeem their debt). Note that $p_I = M_I/(1-\alpha)Y^*$, and thus the economy is back at point E, with a higher quantity of money and price level than initially. Under this policy, the business cycle reduces to EAB with continuing inflation and increases in the quantity of money. Between two cycles, the gross rate of inflation is constant and equal to:

$$\frac{p_I}{p_0} = \frac{(1-\alpha)Y^*}{(1-\alpha)Y^* - \bar{S}}. \tag{18}$$

This policy is clearly beneficial in the short run to the speculators, who now get to consume most of the time (instead of during half the cycle previously). In a disaggregated model of the consumer-workers (see Remark 7), it is also beneficial to the population subject to unemployment risk, but it hurts the consumers who are rationed during phases of excess demand.

Other, more realistic, forms of government spending, can be analyzed along the same lines. Consider unemployment benefits, often said to be an automatic built-in stabilizer. Assume, for example, that the government compensates the unemployed workers for a fraction β, $0 \leqslant \beta \leqslant 1$, of their loss in wage income. Straightforward calculations show that the first recession period is characterized by the system of difference equations:

$$p_{t+1} = \left(1 - \frac{v(1-\alpha)}{1-\alpha(1-\beta)}\right) p_t + \frac{vM_t}{(1-\alpha(1-\beta))Y^*}$$

$$\frac{M_{t+1}}{Y^*} = \frac{(1-\alpha)\beta}{1-\alpha(1-\beta)} p_t + \left(1 - \frac{\beta}{1-\alpha(1-\beta)}\right) \frac{M_t}{Y^*}$$

with initial condition $\bar{p} = M_0/[(1-\alpha)Y^* - \bar{S}]$. The quantity of money increases to finance the unemployment benefits. This system implies:

$$\left(\frac{M_{t+1}}{Y^*} - (1-\alpha)p_{t+1}\right) = \left[1 - \frac{\beta(1-\alpha)v}{1-\alpha(1-\beta)}\right] \left(\frac{M_t}{Y^*} - (1-\alpha)p_t\right)$$

and it converges since, under my assumptions, $\beta(1-\alpha)v<[1-\alpha(1-\beta)]$. The rest point satisfies $p_I = M_I/(1-\alpha)Y^*$: it corresponds to the point E on the phase diagram (see Fig. 24.2). It is easy to compute the total money creation during the cycle through:

$$M_{t+1}-M_t=\frac{\beta Y^*}{1-\alpha(1-\beta)}\left[(1-\alpha)p_t-\frac{M_t}{Y^*}\right]$$

which gives:

$$M_I-M_0=\frac{\beta Y^*}{\beta+(1-\alpha)v}\left[(1-\alpha)p_0-\frac{M_0}{Y^*}\right]$$

or:

$$\frac{M_I}{M_0}=\frac{p_I}{p_0}=1+\frac{\beta}{\beta+(1-\alpha)v}\frac{\bar{S}}{(1-\alpha)Y^*-\bar{S}}\,. \tag{19}$$

Compared with (18), one sees that the inflation rate between two cycles is always lower when government buys goods. But, of course, here there is still some unemployment. At the trough of the cycle, unemployment is equal to $\bar{S}/(1-\alpha(1-\beta))$ and the unemployment rate u, the ratio of unemployment to Y^* is therefore:

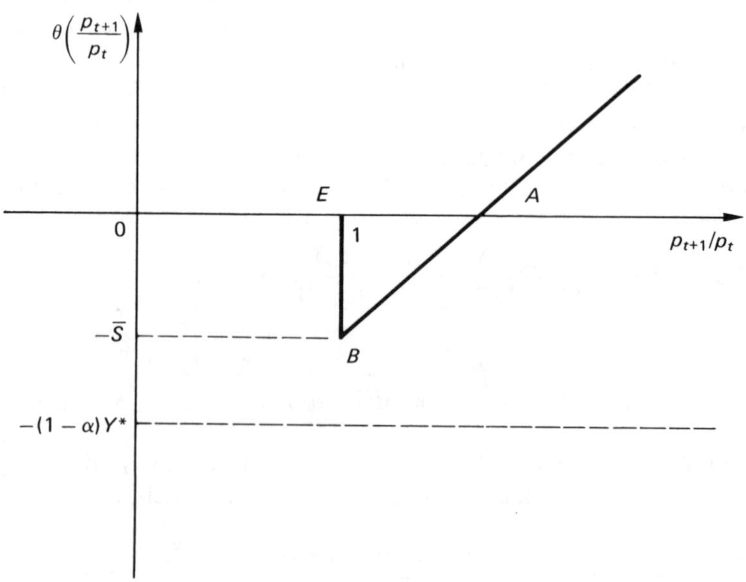

Figure 24.2

$$u = \frac{1}{1-\alpha(1-\beta)} \frac{\bar{S}}{Y^*}. \tag{20}$$

I shall study below (Section 4.3) in more detail the unemployment inflation trade-off.

Deficit spending appears from the preceding analysis to be an ideal tool to drive the economy out of the recession. There is, however, an important caveat. Imagine that the government runs a deficit during the expansion phase, buying a quantity of good G (i.e. trying to reduce unemployment below its 'natural' level). The evolution of the economy is then described by:

$$\frac{p_{t+1}}{p_t} = 1 + \frac{v}{Y^*}\left[G + \frac{M_t}{p_t} + \bar{S}\left(1 - \frac{p_{t-1}}{p_t}\right) - (1-\alpha)Y^*\right]$$

$$M_{t+1} = M_t + (p_t - p_{t-1})\bar{S} + p_t G.$$

This dynamical system has no stationary solution (in fact $p_{t+1} = p_t = p$ implies $G + M_t/p - (1-\alpha)Y^* = 0$, incompatible with $M_{t+1} = M_t + pG$): the price level shoots up to $+\infty$, being always smaller than its competitive value.

4.3 The Unemployment–Inflation Trade-offs

It is of interest to derive specifically the implications of this model for the celebrated macro policy dilemma, the unemployment–inflation trade-off.

First, the short-run unemployment–inflation trade-off follows directly from the postulated process (Fig. 24.3a). When the price level increases, there is full employment. When it decreases, the trade-off is given by a line of slope $-v$. In the absence of government intervention, the unemployment rate at the trough of the cycle is equal to $\bar{S}/(1-\alpha)Y^*$, and during the cycle the economy moves along the line AOC (in fact doing in sequence AO, CO, AO, CO, etc.). Note that the behavior of the speculators is related to the real rate of interest. When the nominal rate of interest is non-zero, one should replace the inflation rate with the real rate of interest on the vertical axis (see Section 4.4 below).

Now government policy creates a long-run trade-off, i.e. a relationship linking the rate of inflation *between* two cycles and the rate of unemployment at the trough of the cycle.[2] Consider, for example, the unemployment benefits policy described in Section 4.2. From (20), unemployment is reduced to $\bar{S}/(1-\alpha(1-\beta))$ at the worst, and the short-run trade-off describes BOC. Therefore, the inflation over the cycle is not any more equal to zero on average, and in fact is given by formula (19). When the government chooses between various values for β, assuming for the time being all other parameters constant, it is confronted with the long-run trade-off, obtained by eliminating β between (19) and (20):

$$\frac{p_I}{p_0}-1=\frac{\bar{S}}{(1-\alpha)Y^*-\bar{S}}\,\frac{\bar{S}-(1-\alpha)Y^*u}{\bar{S}-(1-\alpha)(1-\alpha v)Y^*u} \tag{21}$$

where u varies between $\bar{S}/(1-\alpha)Y^*$ and S/Y^* when β varies between 0 and 1 (Fig. 24.3b).

But an increase in β makes inventory capacity more profitable. In fact it reduces the length of the deflation periods while leaving unchanged that of inflation periods. The negative real-interest rate over the cycle becomes larger in absolute value. This stimulates investment and creates an overac-

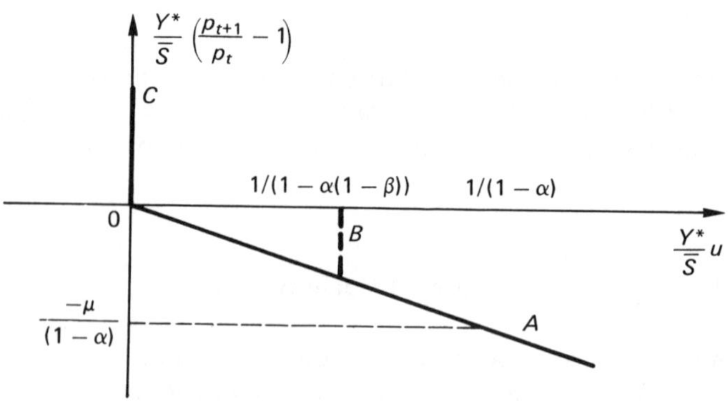

Figure 24.3a The short-run inflation–unemployment trade-off

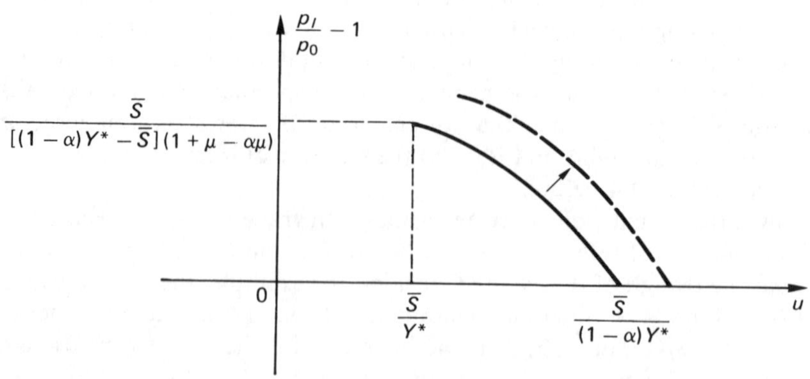

Figure 24.3b The long-run inflation–unemployment trade-off

cumulation of inefficient capital. $\bar{S}$ increases. The point B on the short-run curve moves to the right and the rate of unemployment increases. The long-run curve shifts upward and to the right. When the government policy settles down to a fixed β and capacity reaches its new stationary level, a new long-run equilibrium with cycles prevails. These remarks point to the fact that (21) is *not* the long-run trade-off faced by the government. $\bar{S}$ depends on the government policy β, and this dependence must be made explicit before eliminating β between (19) and (20). The true long-run trade-off might possibly have a positive slope (this will be the case if $\bar{S}(\beta)/(1-\alpha(1-\beta))$ is increasing in β). This, however, should not be the main concern of policy-makers. Unemployment benefits do succeed in transferring resources to the unemployed workers, even though it might in some cases increase the level of unemployment. The inflation–unemployment trade-off hides the more fundamental equity versus efficiency dilemma. One should balance the social equity brought by Keynesian policy against the overaccumulation of capital it creates through inflation (the real cost of inflation). All this should be the subject of further research.

4.4 Monetary Policy

Various institutional set-ups can support the financial side of the model, and sustain the flows of savings of the consumers and the need for credit of the inventory holders. The instruments and the scope of monetary policy depend, of course, on the particular institutional set-up that is considered. But before being more precise, a simple remark is in order. The inventory holders are responsible for the cycle and the ensuing inefficiencies, and the easiest way to get rid of them is to deny them access to credit. In a more realistic model, productive activities in general would also be financed through credit, and the only way to separate noxious speculation from beneficial productive activities would follow from the fact that the latter operate at a non-negative real-interest rate. Therefore a meaningful monetary policy should aim at monitoring this real-interest rate. With this remark in mind, I proceed to the discussion of plausible monetary remedies to unemployment in the inventory cycle.

The simplest institutional set-up compatible with the model at hand is the following. There is a fixed quantity of outside money in circulation (M_0, say gold coins), and the inventory holders can borrow from the consumers by issuing notes, or short-term bonds. There is no default risk for bonds in a perfect foresight equilibrium, and for any strictly positive nominal rate of interest, the demand for loanable funds $(1-\alpha)p_tY^*$ exceeds the supply $p_t\bar{S}$ under Assumption 1. Therefore, the nominal interest rate has to be equal to zero. There is no monetary authority here, and therefore no way to avoid the cycle through monetary manipulation.

A more interesting situation is that in which outside money has the form of bank notes issued by a central bank, which has monopoly power on the credit markets, i.e. it is the only institution allowed to grant credit to the inventory holders. Outside money is backed by government bonds. In order to stabilize the economy, it seems, then, natural that, during the inflationary phase of the cycle, the bank pegs a nominal borrowing rate of interest towards the private sector $r_t, r_t \geqslant 0$, which brings the negative real-rate of interest ρ_t, $\rho_t = (1+r_t)p_t/p_{t+1} - 1$, close to zero. In fact for $\rho_t > 0$, speculation is no longer profitable and the inventory cycle disappears. This is indeed the best way to separate speculative activities from productive activities, the latter being still profitable when the real-interest rate is positive yet small.[3]

This successful monetary policy can only be implemented if the bank has some kind of monopoly power on the credit markets which allows a wedge to be created between the borrowing rate r_t and the lending rate (kept to zero). Note that this wedge need only be small since when the policy succeeds the price level is stabilized.

However, when the bank loses its monopoly power, when the financial system is deregulated, competition implies that the lending rate is equal to the borrowing rate. It is possible to describe the intertemporal perfect foresight equilibria of an economy where such a bank pegs a non-zero nominal interest rate, with a few modifications of the equations of Section 2. First the evolution of the quantity of money (equation 4). At date t, the bank receives $p_{t-1}S_{t-1}(1+r_{t-1})$ units of money from the old speculator that redeems his debt, pays interests $r_{t-1}M_t$ on the previous period deposits and grants a new loan p_tS_t. Therefore (4) becomes:

$$M_{t+1} = M_t - p_{t-1}S_{t-1}(1+r_{t-1}) + r_{t-1}M_t + p_tS_t$$

or:

$$M_{t+1} - p_tS_t = (1+r_{t-1})(M_t - p_{t-1}S_{t-1}) \tag{22}$$

This evolution of the quantity of money is made possible by the interest payments of the private sector $r_{t-1}p_{t-1}S_{t-1}$, paid on inside money, and by the interest payments of the government $r_{t-1}(M_t - p_{t-1}S_{t-1})$, paid on outside money. The quantity of outside money grows at a rate equal to r_{t-1}, like government debt (the debt at date t is equal to that at date $t-1$, plus new public loans contracted to pay the interests during the period). Let:

$$R_t = \prod_{\tau=1}^{t}(1+r_{\tau-1})$$

Then (22) implies:

$$M_{t+1} - p_tS_t = R_tM_0.$$

Straightforward calculations show that the effective excess demand (see (10)) becomes:

$$\tilde{Z}\left(\frac{p_{t+1}}{p_t(1+r_t)}, \frac{p_t}{R_t}\right) =$$

$$= \begin{cases} \left[\sigma\left(\frac{p_{t+1}}{p_t(1+r_t)}, -1\right) + \frac{R_t}{p_t}M_0 - (1-\alpha)Y^*\right]/(1-\alpha) & \text{if } s\left(\frac{p_{t+1}}{p_t(1+r_t)}\right) = -1 \\ 0 & \text{if } s\left(\frac{p_{t+1}}{p_t(1+r_t)}\right) = \ \ 0 \\ \sigma\left(\frac{p_{t+1}}{p_t(1+r_t)}, +1\right) + \frac{R_t}{p_t}M_0 - (1-\alpha)Y^* & \text{if } s\left(\frac{p_{t+1}}{p_t(1+r_t)}\right) = +1. \end{cases} \tag{23}$$

To study the set of intertemporal equilibria, one can construct a diagram analogue to Figure 24.1, replacing (11) and (16) respectively by:

$$F(p_t, R_t) = \frac{R_t}{p_t}M_0 - (1-\alpha)Y^* \tag{24}$$

and

$$\theta\left(\frac{p_{t+1}}{p_t}, r_t\right) = \begin{cases} \frac{(1-\alpha)Y^*}{v}\left(\frac{p_{t+1}}{p_t} - 1\right) & \text{if } p_{t+1} < p_t(1+r_t) \\ [0, -\bar{S}] & \text{if } p_{t+1} = p_t(1+r_t) \\ \frac{Y^*}{v}\left(\frac{p_{t+1}}{p_t} - 1\right) - \bar{S} & \text{if } p_{t+1} > p_t(1+r_t) \end{cases} \tag{25}$$

Now, when the bank pegs a positive nominal interest rate to prevent speculation (to fix ideas, imagine that it follows the rule $p_t(1+r_t)/p_{t+1} = \gamma$, where γ is a constant strictly larger than 1), the quantity of outside money, in line with government debt, increases at a rate equal to the nominal interest rate. This creates a pressure on excess demand through the real-balance effect in the next period. In fact:

$$F(p_{t+1}, R_{t+1}) + (1-\alpha)Y^* = \gamma[F(p_t, R_t) + (1-\alpha)Y^*]$$

and therefore:

$$F(p_{t+1}, R_{t+1}) = \gamma' M_0 - (1-\alpha) Y^*.$$

The policy rule sends the economy on a path of accelerating inflation. The bank cannot maintain the pretense to peg a positive *real* rate of interest without ruining the money. Through competition and deregulation, monetary policy has lost all its powers.

Remark 10: When the bank adopts a policy rule of the type described above, the price adjustment practices as described by the *tâtonnement* process (9) are subject to money illusion. Following Friedman (1968), the agents should index their price-fixing procedures on some indicator of monetary expansion. If the indexation bears on the *current* rate of money growth (equal to the nominal rate of interest), (9) becomes:

$$\frac{p_{t+1}}{p_t(1+r_t)} = 1 + \frac{v}{Y^*} Z\left(\frac{p_{t+1}}{p_t(1+r_t)}, \frac{p_t}{R_t}\right) \tag{26}$$

(25) becomes:

$$\theta\left(\frac{p_{t+1}}{p_t(1+r_t)}\right) = \begin{cases} \dfrac{(1-\alpha)Y^*}{v}\left(\dfrac{p_{t+1}}{p_t(1+r_t)} - 1\right) & \text{if } p_{t+1} < p_t(1+r_t) \\ [0, -\bar{S}] & \text{if } p_{t+1} = p_t(1+r_t) \\ \dfrac{Y^*}{v}\left(\dfrac{p_{t+1}}{p_t(1+r_t)} - 1\right) - \bar{S} & \text{if } p_{t+1} > p_t(1+r_t) \end{cases} \tag{27}$$

Pegging a non-zero interest rate amounts to a change of units. In fact let:

$$\pi_t = \frac{p_t}{R_t}$$

so that:

$$\frac{\pi_{t+1}}{\pi_t} = \frac{p_{t+1}}{p_t(1+r_t)}.$$

With this change of variable, the system (24) and (27) is equal to (11) and (16). With the augmented Phillips curve (26), there is no longer any money illusion.

Notes

1. It is easy to compute from (15) that, along the inflation phase:

$$\frac{p_{t+1}}{p_t} - 1 = \frac{M_0 v}{Y^* p_t} - \frac{v}{Y^*}((1-\alpha)Y^* - \bar{S})$$

with $p_0 = M_0/(1-\alpha)Y^*$. p_t tends to $M_0/((1-\alpha)Y^* - \bar{S})$. At date $t+1$, the profits are at most equal to $\bar{S}(p_{t+1}/p_t - 1)$ (they might be smaller when the demand for inventories is rationed). To make precise the heuristic argument of the text, one needs a better model of the end of the inflation period. This should be the subject of further research.

2. A more appropriate measure might be the *average* level of unemployment along the cycle per unit of time. This would complicate the analysis and is left for further study.

3. When ρ_t is negative, one needs to keep track of the interest income $r_{t-1}p_{t-1}S_{t-1}$ of the bank to describe the intertemporal equilibria of the economy. If the bank distributes its profits to the old consumers, then nothing is changed and the business cycle is still here (in fact, the interest rate policy amounts to a transfer from the speculators to the consumer-workers). In a world of uncertainty, errors in pegging a too high interest rate seem, therefore, less costly than errors on the low side. If the bank sterilizes its interest income, the analysis can be carried forward by replacing (4) with:

$$M_{t+1} - p_t S_t = M_t - p_{t-1}S_{t-1} - r_{t-1}p_{t-1}S_{t-1}.$$

The quantity of outside money decreases at each date by an amount equal to the profits of the bank.

Finally, as noted by Keynes, monetary policy cannot take, by its own means, the economy out of a recession. The bank cannot peg a negative nominal rate of interest, which would induce everyone to speculate against money (the liquidity trap).

References

Blinder, A. S. (1985) 'Can the Production Smoothing Model of Inventory Behavior be Saved?' (mimeo) Princeton University.

Blinder, A. S. and S. Fisher (1981) 'Inventories, Rational Expectations and the Business Cycle', *Journal of Monetary Economics,* 8: 227–304.

Chanut, J. M. and G. Laroque (1979) 'Point de Vue sur les Fluctuations Macroéconomiques de 1949 à 1975', *Economie et Statistique*, June: 73–9.

Enthoven, A. C. and K. J. Arrow (1956) 'A Theorem on Expectations and the Stability of Equilibrium', *Econometrica,* 24: 288–93.

Friedman, M. (1968) 'The Role of Monetary Policy', *American Economic Review,* 58: 1–17.

Goodwin, R. M. (1951) 'The Non-linear Accelerator and the Persistence of Business Cycles', *Econometrica,* 19(1): 1–17.

Grossman, S. J. and L. Weiss (1982) 'Heterogeneous Information and the Theory of the Business Cycle', *Journal of Political Economy,* 90: 699–727.

Samuelson, P. A. (1958) 'An Exact Consumption-loan Model of Interest With or

Without the Social Contrivance of Money', *Journal of Political Economy*, 66: 467–82.

Samuelson, P. A. (1971) 'Stochastic Speculative Prices', *Proceedings of the National Academy of Sciences*.

Scheinkman, J. R. and J. Schechtman (1983) 'A Simple Competitive Model with Production and Storage', *Review of Economic Studies*, 50: 427–41.

25 Sunspots and Incomplete Financial Markets: The Leading Example

David Cass*

1 INTRODUCTION

To even the most casual reader of the daily business pages, it must be fairly obvious that financial markets react (or overreact) to much news which clearly (or, at least, arguably) has little or no direct bearing on 'fundamentals'. Some prominent, current items: the threats issuing from various Middle Eastern factions; the Fed's weekly announcement of previous changes in the money supply; the outcome of this fall's Congressional elections; the great deficit debate. Contrary to one's instinctive reaction as a trained economist, several recent studies have convincingly demonstrated that such market behavior is not necessarily 'non-economic' or 'irrational'. Prices and returns – and hence market allocation itself – may very well consistently depend on purely expectational phenomena. Moreover, self-fulfilling beliefs about market forces may have significant consequences for individual welfare. In short, 'sunspots' may matter, and they may matter very much.[1]

The purpose of this chapter is to advance a further important reason for sunspot effects, namely, that the inherent nature of sunspot beliefs (or, more generally, of uncertainty about the future) militates against ever having a complete array of Arrow–Debreu markets. The logic buttressing this position is simple, but compelling: suppose that, as of today, the range of futures markets were complete. (By this I mean that there is common agreement as to what will 'count' tomorrow, and also full opportunity to hedge against all mutually foreseen events.) Then what prevents some agency from successfully instilling an updated, expanded view of the world? Say, for instance, the 'psychology' of the market, attending to the Ayatullah Khomeini, Paul Volcker, Ronald Reagen or, even, Beryl Sprinkel (the

* This research was undertaken while I was visiting at CEPREMAP and Geneva during a sabbatical leave from Penn. I would like to thank all three institutions for their generous support. Financial assistance from the NSF under grant SOC83-09049 is also gratefully acknowledged.

The final version of the paper itself has benefited substantially from several people's comments and reactions. In particular, an astute observation by Martin Hellwig significantly strengthened the most striking of my results (Proposition 2 below). Of course, I am solely responsible for the ultimate outcome.

present Chairman of the CEA), decides that what will really count tomorrow is some heretofore unrecognized or unimagined aspect of 'reality'. And, honestly, don't we see such revisions being made all the time?

My analysis of the resulting situation, where all conceived market risk cannot be fully covered, is carried out for the simplest possible case; I want to avoid, as much as possible, obscuring the central message with unnecessary technical detail. This intendedly unadorned model is described and investigated in the two following sections. In the first section I introduce the conventional formulation where there are no sunspot beliefs (and markets are complete), while in the second I extend the model to the more plausible and interesting situation where there are sunspot beliefs (but markets are incomplete). Some of my results exactly duplicate those reported earlier in Cass and Shell (1983). In particular, the set of equilibrium allocations when there are no sunspot beliefs is (after a suitable transformation) contained within the set when there are, while equilibrium allocation itself is (in the traditional sense) Pareto optimal if and only if sunspots don't matter. But there are striking differences as well. Thus, except in the unlikely circumstance where there are no incentives to trade, *there always exists a continuum of distinct equilibria in which sunspots matter*, while, for example, *such an equilibrium may be unequivocally Pareto dominated by an equilibrium in which they don't.*

Admittedly, the simple case considered here is just the leading example of a single rationale for sunspot effects. I plan, in a series of subsequent papers, first, to present the general version of these particular results (entailing an extensive analysis of general equilibrium with incomplete or, equivalently, restricted financial markets), and second, to provide a general framework for understanding why sunspots should matter (encompassing my present story, Shell's and my earlier story, and many others as well).

2 THE STANDARD PURE-EXCHANGE MODEL

My basic framework involves pure distribution through competitive markets in a 2×2 economy. This textbook example is so familiar that I only need outline my particular representation.

There are two periods, today and tomorrow, labelled by the superscripts $t=0,1$. In each period there is a single physical commodity, say, the *good*, denoted y^t for $t=0,1$ or $y=(y^0,y^1)$. Today, a single financial instrument, say, *money*, denoted m, is also available. There are spot markets for both goods and money. The spot prices for goods are denoted q^t for $t=0,1$ or $\mathbf{q}=(q^0,q^1)$, while, by convention, money costs, say, one 'dollar' in today's spot market and returns one 'dollar' in tomorrow's. Finally, there are also just two households in the economy, Mr 1 and Mr 2, labelled by the subscripts $h=1,2$.

Mr h is endowed with positive amounts of both goods $e_h=(e_h^0,e_h^1)\gg 0$ and has preferences over non-negative consumption of both goods v_h: $\mathbb{R}^2_+ \to \mathbb{R}$. For simplicity, I will assume throughout that utility functions are differentiable, strictly increasing and strictly concave (on the positive orthant), and that zero consumption of either good is infinitely undesirable, i.e.

$$\text{if } y_h^0=0 \quad \text{or} \quad y_h^1=0, \quad \text{then } v_h(y_h)=-\infty \quad \text{for } h=1,2. \tag{1}$$

Let $\mathbf{y}=(y_1,y_2)$ denote a commodity allocation and $\boldsymbol{m}=(m_1,m_2)$ denote money balances (after today's trading). I will say that an allocation $\boldsymbol{y}$ is (i) *feasible* if it is non-negative, $\mathbf{y}\geqq 0$, and materials balance,

$$\Sigma_h y_h^t=\Sigma_h e_h^t \quad \text{for } t=0,1; \tag{2}$$

(ii) *Pareto optimal* if there is no other feasible allocation $\mathbf{y}'$ which dominates $\mathbf{y}$ in terms of utility,

$$v_h(y_h')\geqq v_h(y_h) \quad \text{for } h=1,2, \text{ with strict inequality for some } h; \tag{3}$$

and (iii) *competitive* if there are some positive spot prices $\boldsymbol{q}\gg 0$ and associated money balances $\boldsymbol{m}$ (which can be of either sign) such that each household optimizes, (y_h,m_h) is the solution to the problem

$$\begin{aligned} &\text{maximize} && v_h(y_h') \\ &\text{subject to} && q^0y_h^{0\prime}+m_h'\leqq q^0e_h^0, \\ &&& q^1y_h^{1\prime}\leqq q^1e_h^1+m_h' \\ &\text{and} && y_h'\geqq 0 \end{aligned} \tag{4}$$

for $h=1,2$, and each market clears,

$$\Sigma_h y_h^t=\Sigma_h e_h^t \quad \text{for } t=0,1 \tag{5}$$

and

$$\Sigma_h m_h=0.$$

It will often be convenient to refer to an equilibrium price–allocation–balance triplet $(\boldsymbol{q},\boldsymbol{y},\boldsymbol{m})$ as a *monetary equilibrium*.

A skeptical reader might reasonably question my emphasis on money. After all, m represents pure inside money, indicating nothing more than borrowing and lending between households. Moreover, it is well known that the 'extended' form (4)–(5) is essentially equivalent to the 'reduced' form obtained by replacing the pair of spot market budget constraints in (4) with the overall contingent market budget constraint

$$\boldsymbol{q}y_h \lesseqgtr \boldsymbol{q}e_h,$$

and then dropping the money (or loan) market clearing equation in (5) to leave just materials balance (2).

The sole reason for my being so explicit – in effect adopting Arrow's (1964) rather than Debreu's (1959) viewpoint about complete markets – is that my formulation permits the most natural introduction of the sunspot beliefs which lead to incomplete markets. However, I should emphasize that I will appeal to this essential equivalence to claim without proof various well-established results, for example, that there always exists at least one monetary equilibrium, and that every competitive allocation generated by a monetary equilibrium is Pareto optimal. In particular, in the sequel I will make generous use of the fact that there is a monetary equilibrium in which households borrow and lend among themselves, i.e. $m_h \neq 0$ for $h = 1,2$, if and only if there are positive incentives to trade, or households' marginal rates of time preference differ at their endowments, i.e.

$$\frac{\partial v_1(e_1)}{\partial y^0} \Big/ \frac{\partial v_1(e_1)}{\partial y^1} \neq \frac{\partial v_2(e_2)}{\partial y^0} \Big/ \frac{\partial v_2(e_2)}{\partial y^1}. \tag{6}$$

3 HOW SUNSPOTS CAN AFFECT ALLOCATION

The basic idea here is very simple; I want to elaborate the standard pure-exchange model to encompass Mr 1's and 2's common belief that some purely extrinsic event, say, *sunspots*, will affect the level of the spot market prices (or, symmetrically, financial market returns) they face tomorrow.

3.1 Sunspots

So suppose now that each household expects tomorrow's spot prices to depend on the observed value of the two possible random events, sunspots or no sunspots, labelled by the superscripts $s = \alpha,\beta$, and having positive probabilities $0 < \pi^\alpha < 1$ and $\pi^\beta = 1 - \pi^\alpha$, respectively. In general, this new situation requires two changes in the description of the underlying market opportunities: on the one hand, surely, spot prices for tomorrow's physical commodities may actually depend on the event s. On the other hand, perhaps, nominal returns on the financial instrument may also depend on the event s. Let the notation $x=(x^0,x^{1\alpha},x^{1\beta})$ (with corresponding prices $\boldsymbol{p}=(p^0,p^{1\alpha},p^{1\beta})$) represent goods, and the notation b (with corresponding non-trivial returns $(r^\alpha,r^\beta)>0$) represent, now say, *bonds*, when there are sunspot beliefs. Also, note that, with such altered market opportunities, Mr h's endowments and preferences will become, say, $\omega_h=(\omega_h^0,\omega_h^{1\alpha},\omega_h^{1\beta})\equiv(e_h^0,e_h^1,e_h^1)$ (independent of the sunspot lottery) and $u_h(x_h)=u_h(x_h^0,x_h^{1\alpha},x_h^{1\beta})\equiv\pi^\alpha v_h(x_h^0,x_h^{1\alpha})+\pi^\beta v_h(x_h^0,x_h^{1\beta})$ (expected over the sunspot lottery), respectively.

Parallel with the previous formulation, let $\boldsymbol{x}=(x_1,x_2)$ denote a commodity allocation and $\boldsymbol{b}=(b_1,b_2)$ denote bond holdings (after today's trading), and say that an allocation $\boldsymbol{x}$ is (i) *feasible* if it is non-negative, $\mathbf{x}\geqq 0$, and materials balance,

$$\Sigma_h\, x_h^0=\Sigma_h\,\omega_h^0 \tag{2^s}$$

and

$$\Sigma_h\, x_h^{1s}=\Sigma_h\,\omega_h^{1s} \quad \text{for } s=\alpha,\beta;$$

(ii) *Pareto optimal* if there is no other feasible allocation $\boldsymbol{x}'$ which dominates $\boldsymbol{x}$ in terms of utility,

$$u_h(x_h')\geqq u_h(x_h) \quad \text{for } h=1,2, \text{ with strict inequality for some } h; \tag{3^s}$$

and (iii) *competitive* if there are some positive spot prices $\boldsymbol{p}\gg 0$ and associated bond holdings $\boldsymbol{b}$ (which can again be of either sign) such that each household optimizes, (x_h,b_h) is the solution to the problem

$$\begin{aligned}
&\text{maximize} \quad u_h(x_h')\\
&\text{subject to} \quad p^0x_h^{0\prime}+b_h'\leqq p^0\omega_h^0,\\
&\qquad\qquad\quad p^{1s}x_h^{1s\prime}\leqq p^{1s}\omega_h^{1s}+r^sb_h' \quad \text{for } s=\alpha,\beta\\
&\text{and} \qquad\quad x_h'\geqq 0
\end{aligned} \tag{4^s}$$

for $h=1,2$, and each market clears,

$$\begin{aligned}
&\Sigma_h\, x_h^0=\Sigma_h\,\omega_h^0,\\
&\Sigma_h\, b_h=0\\
&\text{and}\\
&\Sigma_h\, x_h^{1s}=\Sigma_h\,\omega_h^{1s} \quad \text{for } s=\alpha,\beta.
\end{aligned} \tag{5^s}$$

To distinguish this reformulation, I will refer to an equilibrium price–allocation–holding triplet $(\boldsymbol{p},\boldsymbol{x},\boldsymbol{b})$ as a *financial equilibrium.*

The main issue in this setting is whether such a different view of the world has any real effect on the outcome of market allocation. Following the lead of my earlier joint work, I will say that, for a feasible allocation $\boldsymbol{x}$, *sunspots matter* (resp. *don't matter*) if

$$x_h^{1\alpha} \neq x_h^{1\beta} \text{ (resp. } x_h^{1\alpha} = x_h^{1\beta}\text{) for } h=1,2.$$

The remainder of the chapter then focuses on showing that, though sunspots may not matter, there is strong reason to believe that they invariably will, and even stronger reason, when they do, for active market intervention.[2]

3.2 Equilibrium

It is self-evident that in the presence (or with the advent) of sunspot beliefs, markets are incomplete; there are two possible future states of the world, but only one available financial instrument which can serve to hedge. Putting too much weight on this fact would be, in one important sense, misleading. The first existence result of this section, together with the brief optimality analysis of the next, supports the conclusion that, even when there are sunspot beliefs, the market mechanism is capable of achieving every Pareto optimal allocation (given appropriate endowments). The only problem is that, as the second existence result, also together with the following optimality analysis demonstrates, under these circumstances it will typically do much, much worse (given arbitrary endowments).

Proposition 1: (i) If $(\boldsymbol{q},\boldsymbol{y},\boldsymbol{m})$ is a monetary equilibrium, $r^s>0$ for $s=\alpha,\beta$ or (6) doesn't obtain, and $(x_h^0,x_h^{1s})=(y_h^0,y_h^1)$ for $s=\alpha,\beta$, $h=1,2$, then there are $\boldsymbol{p}$ and $\boldsymbol{b}$ such that $(\boldsymbol{p},\boldsymbol{x},\boldsymbol{b})$ is a financial equilibrium (in which, by definition, sunspots don't matter). (ii) If $(\boldsymbol{p},\boldsymbol{x},\boldsymbol{b})$ is a financial equilibrium in which sunspots don't matter and $(y_h^0,y_h^1)=(x_h^0,x_h^{1s})$ for $s=\alpha,\beta$, $h=1,2$, then there are $\boldsymbol{q}$ and $\boldsymbol{m}$ such that $(\boldsymbol{q},\boldsymbol{y},\boldsymbol{m})$ is a monetary equilibrium.

Proof of Proposition 1: The argument simply involves comparing first-order conditions for the two problems (4) and (4^s). On the one hand, associating the multipliers μ_h^0 and μ_h^1 with the two budget constraints in (4), and then applying the Kuhn–Tucker theorem for concave programming (given the maintained assumptions on endowments and preferences together with (1)) yields the following necessary and sufficient conditions for household maximization when there are no sunspot beliefs:

$$\frac{\partial v_h(y_h)}{\partial y^0} = \mu_h^0 q^0,$$

$$\frac{\partial v_h(y_h)}{\partial y^1} = \mu_h^1 q^1,$$

$$\mu_h^0 = \mu_h^1, \tag{7}$$

$$-q^0(y_h^0 - e_h^0) = m_h$$

and

$$q^1(y_h^1 - e_h^1) = m_h$$

for $h=1,2$. On the other hand, associating the multipliers λ_h^0 and λ_h^{1s} for $s=\alpha,\beta$, with the three budget constraints in (4^s), and then repeating the process (assuming that sunspots don't matter) yields:

$$\frac{\partial v_h(y_h)}{\partial y^0} = \lambda_h^0 p^0,$$

$$\frac{\partial v_h(y_h)}{\partial y^1} = \lambda_h^{1s}(p^{1s}/\pi^s) \quad \text{for } s=\alpha,\beta,$$

$$\lambda_h^{1\alpha} r^\alpha + \lambda_h^{1\beta} r^\beta = \lambda_h^0, \tag{7^s}$$

$$-p^0(y_h^0 - e_h^0) = b_h$$

and

$$p^{1s}(y_h^1 - e_h^1) = r^s b_h \quad \text{for } s=\alpha,\beta$$

for $h=1,2$. Now consider each of the asserted implications in turn.

(i) If $r^s > 0$ for $s=\alpha,\beta$, then choose

$$p^0 = q^0,\ \lambda_h^0 = \mu_h^0,\ p^{1s} = r^s q^1 \text{ for } s=\alpha,\beta,\ \lambda_h^{1s} = (\pi^s/r^s)\mu_h^0 \text{ for } s=\alpha,\beta, \text{ and } b_h = m_h,$$

while if, for example, $m_h = 0$, $r^\alpha > 0$, and $r^\beta = 0$, then choose

$$p^0 = q^0,\ \lambda_h^0 = \mu_h^0,\ \lambda_h^{1\alpha} = (\mu_h^0/r^\alpha),\ p^{1\alpha} = \pi^\alpha r^\alpha q^1,\ \lambda_h^{1\beta} = \mu_h^0,\ p^{1\beta} = \pi^\beta q^1, \text{ and } b_h = m_h.$$

In both cases, direct substitution immediately reveals that (7^s) follows from (7).

(ii) Here, a straightforward calculation (ultimately based on the hypothesis that sunspots don't matter) shows that (7^s) implies that

$$(\lambda_h^{1s}/\lambda_h^0)=\psi^s \quad \text{for } s=\alpha,\beta,\ h=1,2,$$

where

$$\psi^\alpha = 1/(r^\alpha + [(p^{1\alpha}/\pi^\alpha)/(p^{1\beta}/\pi^\beta)]r^\beta) \tag{8}$$

and

$$\psi^\beta = [(p^{1\alpha}/\pi^\alpha)/(p^{1\beta}/\pi^\beta)]\psi^\alpha.$$

So now choose

$$q^0=p^0,\ q^1=\psi^\alpha(p^{1\alpha}/\pi^\alpha)=\psi^\beta(p^{1\beta}/\pi^\beta),\ \mu_h^0=\lambda_h^0, \text{ and } m_h=b_h, \tag{9}$$

noting, in particular, that then (7^s), (8), and (9) imply that

$$\begin{aligned} q^1(y_h^1-e_h^1) &= \pi^\alpha q^1(y_h^1-e_h^1)+\pi^\beta q^1(y_h^1-e_h^1) \\ &= \psi^\alpha p^{1\alpha}(y_h^1-e_h^1)+\psi^\beta p^{1\beta}(y_h^1-e_h^1) \\ &= \psi^\alpha r^\alpha b_h + \psi^\beta r^\beta b_h \\ &= [(\lambda_h^{1\alpha} r^\alpha + \lambda_h^{1\beta} r^\beta)/\lambda_h^0]b_h \\ &= m_h. \end{aligned}$$

Thus, once again, direct substitution immediately reveals that (7) follows from (7^s).

□

In other words, this proposition establishes that there is essentially an equivalence between the competitive allocations generated by monetary equilibria and those generated by just the financial equilibria in which sunspots don't matter. Indeed, the only case in which this relation fails is when there are positive incentives to trade, that is, (6) obtains, but some return is zero, that is (without loss of generality, since the labelling of states is perfectly arbitrary), $r^\alpha>0$ and $r^\beta=0$. And, for the polar case, it turns out that *sunspots always matter*. This special result is worth recording explicitly; among other things, it provides a heuristic rationale for my subsequent analysis: think of the economy as being characterized by returns (as well as preferences and endowments). Then, assuming that the set (or some selected subset) of financial equilibria varies 'regularly' with respect to these particular parameters, there must be – at the very least – many ordinary cases (corresponding to $r^\alpha > 0$, $r^\beta > 0$ but $r^\beta/r^\alpha \sim 0$) in which sunspots matter.[3]

Corollary: Suppose that $r^\alpha > 0$ but $r^\beta = 0$. If (6) obtains, then sunspots always matter in financial equilibrium.[4]

Proof of the Corollary: Suppose that the conclusion is false, i.e. that there is some financial equilibrium $(\boldsymbol{p},\boldsymbol{x},\boldsymbol{b})$ in which $x_h^{1s} = y_h^1$ for $s = \alpha,\beta$, $h = 1,2$. Then from the first-order conditions (7^s) it follows that $p^{1\beta}(y_h^1 - e_h^1) = r^\beta b_h = 0$ or $y_h^1 = e_h^1$ for $h = 1,2$. But then from the second implication in Proposition 1 it also follows that there is a monetary equilibrium $(\boldsymbol{q},\boldsymbol{y},\boldsymbol{m})$ in which $y_h^1 = e_h^1$ or $q^1(y_h^1 - e_h^1) = m_h = 0$ for $h = 1,2$, which contradicts the hypothesis that (6) obtains. □

The essence of this corollary (and its converse) is that, in the polar case when only a single return is positive, financial equilibria in which sunspots don't matter are extremely rare (corresponding to the situations where there are no incentives to trade). Shortly, I will embroider on this basic theme and establish, for the ordinary case where both returns are positive, what is undoubtedly the most fascinating property of this leading example, its superabundance of sunspot equilibria. But first I would like to comment on one feature of my model which has probably not escaped the attention of a perceptive reader, namely, that when $r^\alpha > 0$ and $r^\beta > 0$, I could just as well specify $r^\alpha = r^\beta = 1$, i.e. that bonds are money. (The validity of this claim hinges on the fact that the constraint set in (4^s) is unaffected when each of tomorrow's spot market budget constraints is multiplied by the reciprocal of its corresponding return.) There is, however, purely in terms of interpretation, a good reason for introducing the more general parameterization: the underlying motivation for studying this particular model is probably best reflected by thinking of p^{1s} as (more or less) fixed but r^s as (more or less) variable. Thus, for instance, $r^\alpha < r^\beta$ because ... the report of an 'unexpectedly' large previous increase in the money supply entails a decrease in the current market value of outstanding long-term bonds (and thus their current nominal return), because it signals that 'obviously' future interest rates are going to increase.

Of course, my real reason for introducing such seemingly superfluous generality is somewhat more practical, as we shall now see.

For this purpose it is useful to restrict attention to present value prices

$$P = \{\boldsymbol{p} \gg 0 \colon p^0 = 1\}$$

and unit sum returns

$$R = \{r = (r^\alpha, r^\beta) \gg 0 \colon r^\alpha + r^\beta = 1\}.$$

Proposition 2: Suppose that $r \in R$ and that (6) obtains. Then there is a one-parameter family of financial equilibria yielding distinct competitive allocations for which sunspots matter.

Proof of Proposition 2: The argument is based on a fairly subtle analysis of the structure of the set of financial equilibria, whose details I defer to the Appendix. The central idea of my approach is that competitive allocations can be parameterized by relating financial equilibria in the original model to those in another model where tomorrow's units of account have been adjusted so that Mr 1 acts as if he faces a complete set of Arrow securities, i.e. where x_1 is the solution to the standard problem

$$\begin{aligned} &\text{maximize} && u_1(x_1') \\ &\text{subject to} && \boldsymbol{p}x_1' \lesssim \boldsymbol{p}\omega_1 \\ &\text{and} && x_1' \geqq 0. \end{aligned} \tag{10}$$

In order to implement this approach, define

$$E(r) = \{(\boldsymbol{p},\boldsymbol{x},\boldsymbol{b}): (\boldsymbol{p},\boldsymbol{x},\boldsymbol{b}) \text{ is a financial equilibrium with } \boldsymbol{p} \in P\},$$

$$E_1(r) = \{(\boldsymbol{p},\boldsymbol{x},\boldsymbol{b}) \in E(r): x_1 \text{ is the solution to (10)}\}$$

and

$$\psi(r) = \{\psi = (\psi^\alpha, \psi^\beta) \gg 0: \psi^\alpha r^\alpha + \psi^\beta r^\beta = 1\}$$

for $r \in R$.

Claim. $E_1(r) \neq \phi$ and

$$E(r) = \bigcup_{\psi \in \psi(r)} \{((1, p^{1\alpha}/\psi^\alpha, p^{1\beta}/\psi^\beta), \boldsymbol{x}, \boldsymbol{b}): (\boldsymbol{p},\boldsymbol{x},\boldsymbol{b}) \in E_1(\psi^\alpha r^\alpha, \psi^\beta r^\beta)\}$$

for $r \in R$.

Since exploiting this structure involves varying the returns r by varying the parameters ψ, it will be convenient to denote $r^\psi = (\psi^\alpha r^\alpha, \psi^\beta r^\beta)$. Notice especially that the set of parameters $\psi(r)$ is diffeomorphic to the interval $\{\psi^\alpha: 0 < \psi^\alpha < 1/r^\alpha\}$, and that $r^\psi \in R$ for $\psi \in \psi(r)$. So, in short, the claim simply asserts that, given $r \in R$, the set of financial equilibria, and thus the set of competitive allocations can be parameterized by Mr 1's valuation of his wealth tomorrow in state α relative to his wealth today ψ^α (see the concluding argument in the Appendix).

Assuming its validity, the balance of the proof is straightforward, and consists of showing that, for given $r \in R$, (i) if $\psi' \in \psi(r)$, $(\boldsymbol{p}',\boldsymbol{x}',\boldsymbol{b}') \in E_1(r^{\psi'})$, $\psi'' \in \psi(r)$, $(\boldsymbol{p}'',\boldsymbol{x}'',\boldsymbol{b}'') \in E_1(r^{\psi''})$ and $\boldsymbol{x}'=\boldsymbol{x}''$, then $\psi'=\psi''$ (and, in fact, $(\boldsymbol{p}',\boldsymbol{x}',\boldsymbol{b}')=(\boldsymbol{p}'',\boldsymbol{x}'',\boldsymbol{b}'')$), i.e. the competitive allocations are uniquely related to the parameter ψ^α, while (ii) if $\psi \in \psi(r)$, $(\boldsymbol{p},\boldsymbol{x},\boldsymbol{b}) \in E_1(r^\psi)$ and $x_h^{1\alpha}=x_h^{1\beta}=y_h^1$ for $h=1,2$, then $\psi^\alpha=\pi^\alpha/r^\alpha$, i.e. there is a single value of the parameter ψ^α at which sunspots may not matter.

As in the proof of Proposition 1, my argument here simply involves manipulating the first-order conditions for two different problems, now (10) describing Mr 1's behavior and (4^s) (with r^ψ replacing r) describing Mr 2's behavior. Thus, on the one hand, associating the multiplier λ_1 with the single budget constraint in (10), we have for $h=1$

$$\pi^\alpha \frac{\partial v_1(x_1^0,x_1^{1\alpha})}{\partial x^0}+\pi^\beta \frac{\partial v_1(x_1^0,x_1^{1\beta})}{\partial x^0}=\lambda_1,$$

$$\pi^s \frac{\partial v_1(x_1^0,x_1^{1s})}{\partial x^{1s}}=\lambda_1 p^{1s} \quad \text{for } s=\alpha,\beta \tag{11}$$

and

$$\boldsymbol{p}x_1=\boldsymbol{p}\omega_1.$$

On the other hand, again associating the multipliers λ_h^0 and λ_h^{1s} for $s=\alpha,\beta$ with the three budget constraints in (4^s), we have for $h=2$

$$\pi^\alpha \frac{\partial v_2(x_2^0,x_2^{1\alpha})}{\partial x^0}+\pi^\beta \frac{\partial v_2(x_2^0,x_2^{1\beta})}{\partial x^0}=\lambda_2^0,$$

$$\pi^s \frac{\partial v_2(x_2^0,x_2^{1s})}{\partial x^{1s}}=\lambda_2^{1s} p^{1s} \quad \text{for } s=\alpha,\beta,$$

$$\lambda_2^{1\alpha}(\psi^\alpha r^\alpha)+\lambda_2^{1\beta}(\psi^\beta r^\beta)=\lambda_2^0, \tag{12}$$

$$-(x_2^0-e_2^0)=b_2$$

and

$$p^{1s}(x_2^{1s}-e_2^1)=(\psi^s r^s)b_2 \quad \text{for } s=\alpha,\beta.$$

(i) From the supposition that (6) obtains together with Proposition 1 we know that if $\psi \in \psi(r)$ and $(\boldsymbol{p},\boldsymbol{x},\boldsymbol{b}) \in E_1(r^\psi)$, so $((1,p^{1,\alpha}/\psi^\alpha, p^{1\beta}/\psi^\beta),\mathbf{x},\boldsymbol{b}) \in E(r)$, then $x_h \neq \omega_h$ for $h=1,2$. Moreover, if $\boldsymbol{x}'=\boldsymbol{x}''$, then (11) immediately yields $\boldsymbol{p}'=\boldsymbol{p}''$, so that the last two equations in (12) yield $\psi'=\psi''$.

(ii) The second equation in (11) immediately yields $\pi^\beta/\pi^\alpha = p^{1\beta}/p^{1\alpha}$. But here again from the supposition that (6) obtains together with Proposition 1 we know that $y_h^1 \neq e_h^1$ for $h=1,2$. So the last equation in (12) also yields $p^{1\beta}/p^{1\alpha} = \psi^\beta r^\beta/\psi^\alpha r^\alpha$. Then an obvious calculation (using $\psi \in \psi(r)$) yields the desired conclusion.[5]

□

It appears that, by employing techniques from differential topology (along the basic lines I have just elaborated), this result can be considerably generalized. Be that as it may, the proposition itself in conjunction with Proposition 1 seems to me to establish an overwhelming presumption that, with incomplete financial markets, the raw likelihood of attaining financial equilibria in which sunspots don't matter is practically nil.

3.3 Optimality

Risk averse households will always refuse a lottery in favor of its expected value. For this simple reason, in this world of sunspot beliefs, the criterion of Pareto optimality always rejects financial equilibria in which sunspots matter.

Proposition 3: The competitive allocation generated by a financial equilibrium is Pareto optimal if and only if sunspots don't matter.

Proof of Proposition 3: (i) (necessity) Suppose $\boldsymbol{x}$ is a competitive allocation in which sunspots matter. Then the average allocation $\boldsymbol{x}'$ defined by

$$x_h' = (x_h^0, \pi^\alpha x_h^{1\alpha} + \pi^\beta x_h^{1\beta}, \pi^\alpha x_h^{1\alpha} + \pi^\beta x_h^{1\beta}) \quad \text{for } h=1,2 \tag{13}$$

is feasible (since $\omega_h^{1\alpha} = \omega_h^{1\beta} \equiv e_h^1$ for $h=1,2$) and Pareto dominates $\boldsymbol{x}$ in terms of utility (since v_h is strictly concave for $h=1,2$). That is, $\boldsymbol{x}$ is not Pareto optimal. (ii) (sufficiency) Suppose $\boldsymbol{x}$ is a competitive allocation in which sunspots don't matter. Then, if it isn't Pareto optimal, by the preceding argument it can be dominated by another feasible allocation for which sunspots don't matter. But, in light of the second implication in Proposition 1, this contradicts the first basic theorem of welfare (which applies to the standard pure-exchange model described in Section 2).

□

I almost needn't emphasize that this proposition in conjunction with Proposition 2 tells us that, when perceived market influences outrun available financial instruments, there is very likely to be ample justification for the government to interfere (directly or indirectly) in the operation of financial markets. Perhaps even more interesting is that Propositions 1 and 3 together with Hart's (1975) remarkable analysis of optimality with incomplete markets strongly suggest that a competitive allocation in which sunspots matter might even be Pareto dominated by one in which they don't (for given arbitrary endowments). This intriguing possibility can be readily verified in terms of examples built from additively separable utility functions,

$$v_h(y_h)=f_h^0(y_h^0)+f_h^1(y_h^1) \quad \text{for } h=1,2.$$

I forgo presenting a specific example (since its construction is clear-cut but tedious).[6]

APPENDIX

My only purpose in this appendix is to establish the Claim used in proving Proposition 2. Since I justify a more general statement of the essence of this basic result elsewhere [255(1984)], I permit myself to be somewhat sketchy here (especially regarding the details of various routine 'ε − δ' arguments).

Proof of the Claim. Define the set

$$P^{\varepsilon}=\{p\in P\colon \varepsilon\leqq p^{1s}\leqq 1/\varepsilon \quad \text{for } s=\alpha,\beta\}$$

for $\varepsilon>0$, and pick a bound

$$\bar{x}\gg\omega_1+\omega_2.$$

Now consider the equilibrium model obtained when the solution to (4^s) is replaced by the solution to

$$\begin{aligned}&\text{maximize} && u_1(x_1')\\ &\text{subject to} && px_1'\leqslant p\omega_1 \\ &\text{and} && 0\leqq x_1'\leqq\bar{x}\end{aligned} \tag{A1}$$

and $b_1=-b_2$ for $h=1$, and by the solution to

$$\begin{aligned}&\text{maximize} && u_2(x_2')\\ &\text{subject to} && p^0x_2^{0\prime}+b_2'\leqq p^0\omega_2^0,\\ & && p^{1s}x_2^{1s\prime}\leqq p^{1s}\omega_2^{1s}+r^sb_2' \quad \text{for } s=\alpha,\beta\\ &\text{and} && 0\leqq x_2'\leqq\bar{x}\end{aligned} \tag{A2}$$

for $h=2$. Then the argument proceeds by establishing the following series of results, for given $r\in R$.

(i) If $(\boldsymbol{p},\boldsymbol{x},\boldsymbol{b})$ is a financial equilibrium in this new model, then it is also a financial equilibrium in the original model.

Market clearing (5^s) implies that $x_h \leqq \omega_1+\omega_2 \ll \bar{x}$ for $h=1,2$. So all that needs to be shown is that if x_1 is the solution to (10) and $b_1=-b_2$, then (x_1,b_1) is the solution to (4^s) for $h=1$.

Since $r\in R$, $r^\alpha+r^\beta=1$, so that adding up the constraints in (4^s) for $h=1$ yields the constraint in (10). Hence, feasible solutions to (4^s) for $h=1$ also yield feasible solutions to (10). Moreover, since u_2 is monotone (recall that v_2 is monotone and π^s is positive for $s=\alpha,\beta$), the solution to (4^s) for $h=2$ together with market clearing (5^s) yield

$$p^0(x_1^0-\omega_1^0)=-p^0(x_2^0-\omega_2^0)=b_2=-b_1$$

and

$$p^{1s}(x_1^{1s}-\omega_1^{1s})=-p^{1s}(x_2^{1s}-\omega_2^{1s})=-r^sb_2=r^sb_1 \quad \text{for } s=\alpha,\beta.$$

Hence, (x_1,b_1) is a feasible solution, and thus necessarily also the solution to (4^s) for $h=1$.

(ii) The solution to (A1) [resp. (A2)], say, $x_1(\boldsymbol{p})$ [resp. $(x_2(\boldsymbol{p}),b_2(\boldsymbol{p}))$], is well defined and continuous for $\boldsymbol{p}\in P$ [resp. $\boldsymbol{p}\in P^\varepsilon$ for every $\varepsilon>0$], and these satisfy the appropriate (weak) form of Walras's Law,

$$\boldsymbol{p}x_h(\boldsymbol{p})\leqq \boldsymbol{p}\omega_h, \quad \text{with equality if } x_h(\boldsymbol{p})\ll\bar{x},$$

for $h=1,2$.

Given my strong assumptions on u_h and ω_h, these results are well known for the problem (A1). For the problem (A2), they follow from exactly the same sort of reasoning once it is noted that, when $r\in R$, the feasible solutions to (A2) are uniformly bounded.

(iii) The mapping φ^ε: $P^\varepsilon \to P^\varepsilon$ defined by

$$\boldsymbol{p}\to\{\boldsymbol{p}': \mathbf{p}' \text{ is an optimal solution to the problem } \max_{p''\in P^\varepsilon} \boldsymbol{p}''(x_1(\boldsymbol{p})+x_2(\boldsymbol{p})-\omega_1-\omega_2)\}$$

has a fixed point $\boldsymbol{p}^\varepsilon\in\varphi^\varepsilon(\boldsymbol{p}^\varepsilon)$.

This follows from a standard argument based on the regularity properties asserted in (ii).

(iv) If ε is sufficiently small, then a fixed point $\boldsymbol{p}^{\varepsilon}\in\varphi^{\varepsilon}(\boldsymbol{p}^{\varepsilon})$ yields a financial equilibrium $(\boldsymbol{p},\boldsymbol{x},\boldsymbol{b})=(\boldsymbol{p}^{\varepsilon},(x_1(\boldsymbol{p}^{\varepsilon}),x_2(\boldsymbol{p}^{\varepsilon})),(-b_2(\boldsymbol{p}^{\varepsilon}),b_2(\boldsymbol{p}^{\varepsilon})))$.

This too follows from a standard argument, but now based on Walras's Law and the monotonicity assumption on u_1.

From the equivalence property asserted in (i) together with the existence property asserted in (iv) it follows immediately that, in fact, $E_1(r)\neq\phi$ for $r\in R$. So all that remains to be established is that, again for given $r\in R$,

(v) $E(r)=\bigcup_{\psi\in\psi(r)}\{((1,p^{1\alpha}/\psi^{\alpha},p^{1\beta}/\psi^{\beta}),\boldsymbol{x},\boldsymbol{b})\colon(\boldsymbol{p},\boldsymbol{x},\boldsymbol{b})\in E_1(r^{\psi})\}$.

Consider once again the first-order conditions for (4^s) (given $(\tilde{\boldsymbol{p}},\tilde{\boldsymbol{x}},\tilde{\boldsymbol{b}})\in E(r)$)

$$\begin{aligned}
&\pi^{\alpha}\frac{\partial v_h(\tilde{x}^0_h,\tilde{x}^{1\alpha}_h)}{\partial x^0}+\pi^{\beta}\frac{\partial v_h(\tilde{x}^0_h,\tilde{x}^{1\beta}_h)}{\partial x^0}=\tilde{\lambda}^0_h,\\
&\pi^{s}\frac{\partial v_h(\tilde{x}^1_h,\tilde{x}^{1s}_h)}{\partial x^{1s}}=\tilde{\lambda}^{1s}_h\tilde{p}^{1s}\quad\text{for } s=\alpha,\beta,\\
&\tilde{\lambda}^{1\alpha}_h r^{\alpha}+\tilde{\lambda}^{1\beta}_h r^{\beta}=\tilde{\lambda}^0_h,\\
&-(\tilde{x}^0_h-e^0_h)=\tilde{b}_h
\end{aligned}\tag{A3}$$

and

$$\tilde{p}^{1s}(\tilde{x}^{1s}_h-e^1_h)=r^s\tilde{b}_h\quad\text{for } s=\alpha,\beta$$

for $h=1,2$. Now simply identify ψ^s with $\tilde{\lambda}^{1s}_1/\tilde{\lambda}^0_1$ for $s=\alpha,\beta$. From the equivalence property asserted in (i) it follows that (11) together with $b_1=-b_2$ is equivalent to (A3) for $h=1$ when $\tilde{\boldsymbol{p}}=(1,p^{1\alpha}/\psi^{\alpha},p^{1\beta}/\psi^{\beta})$, $(\tilde{x}_1,\tilde{b}_1)=(x_1,b_1)$ and $(\tilde{\lambda}^0_1,\tilde{\lambda}^{1\alpha}_1,\tilde{\lambda}^{1\beta}_1)=\lambda_1(1,\psi^{\alpha},\psi^{\beta})$ (given $(\boldsymbol{p},\boldsymbol{x},\boldsymbol{b})\in E_1(r^{\psi})$). Similarly, (12) is equivalent to (A3) when $\tilde{\boldsymbol{p}}=(1,p^{1\alpha}/\psi^{\alpha},p^{1\beta}/\psi^{\beta})$, $(\tilde{x}_2,\tilde{b}_2)=(x_2,b_2)$ and $(\tilde{\lambda}^0_2,\tilde{\lambda}^{1\alpha}_2,\tilde{\lambda}^{1\beta}_2)=(\lambda^0_2,\lambda^{1\alpha}_2\psi^{\alpha},\lambda^{1\beta}_2\psi^{\beta})$. In other words, $(\boldsymbol{p},\boldsymbol{x},\boldsymbol{b})\in E_1(r^{\psi})$ is equivalent to $(\tilde{\boldsymbol{p}},\tilde{\boldsymbol{x}},\tilde{\boldsymbol{b}})=((1,p^{1\alpha}/\psi^{\alpha},p^{1\beta}/\psi^{\beta}),\boldsymbol{x},\boldsymbol{b})\in E(r)$ for $\psi\in\Psi(r)$, and the proof is complete.

□

Notes

1. I refer, especially, to my previous papers with Karl Shell (1980) – for an introduction to this basic idea – and (1983) – for an elaboration in terms of a specific model. The excellent paper by Shiller (1978) develops a similar general theme, but in the macroeconometric rather than microequilibrium tradition. The second Cass–Shell paper also contains references to other work based on

our original conception, which, of course, ultimately stems from Keynes (1936).

2. The first of these conclusions requires only minor, additional technical qualification, and the second none at all, even in the most general model of the effects of extrinsic uncertainty when financial markets are incomplete. As I mentioned before, I will justify these claims in forthcoming work.
3. In the original version of this paper, I pursued precisely such a line of reasoning in order to display a host of financial equilibria in which sunspots matter. The specific argument involved demonstrating that a particular subset of financial equilibria (namely, the subset labelled $E_1(r)$ in the proof of Proposition 2 below) varies upper hemi-continuously with respect to returns (when they are restricted, for example, to sum to one).
4. In fact, for this leading example, the opposite statement is also true: If (6) doesn't obtain, then sunspots never matter in financial equilibrium.

   This result follows directly from the easily verified observation that, in the polar case, whether or not there is any competitive allocation for which sunspots matter depends only on whether or not

$$\frac{\partial u_1(\omega_1)}{\partial x^0} \Big/ \frac{\partial u_1(\omega_1)}{\partial x^{1\alpha}} \neq \frac{\partial u_2(\omega_2)}{\partial x^0} \Big/ \frac{\partial u_2(\omega_2)}{\partial x^{1\alpha}},$$

   which is equivalent to (6).
5. Ailsa Röell has suggested a clever alternative to the specific parameterization I have used here. Her central idea – which renders the argument for this leading case (but not for its most interesting generalizations) somewhat more transparent – is the following: let the bond be simply money, so that $r=(1,1)$. Then the budget set in (4^s) is essentially the same as that described by

$$p^0(x_h^0 - e_h^0) + p^{1\alpha}(x_h^{1\alpha} - e_h^1) \leqq 0,$$

$$p^{1\alpha}(x_h^{1\alpha} - e_h^1) = p^{1\beta}(x_h^{1\beta} - e_h^1)$$

   and $x_h \geqq 0$.

   But this means, in particular, that by parameterizing, for instance, $p^{1\alpha} = \theta p^{1\beta}$ with $\theta \in (0,1]$, a subset of the financial equilibria are essentially the same as the ordinary Walrasian equilibria generated by the 2×2 economies for which the two commodities are identified with goods 0 and $(1,\alpha)$, and the two households have preferences and endowments described by

$$u_h^0(y_h^0, y_h^1) = \pi^\alpha v_h(y_h^0, y_h^1) + \pi^\beta v_h(y_h^0, e_h^1 + \theta(y_h^1 - e_h^1))$$

   and e_h, respectively. With this reformulation it is easily shown that, if (6) obtains, then (i) there is (at least) one distinct Walrasian equilibrium associated with each value of the parameter θ while (ii) $y_h^1 = e_h^1 + \theta(y_h^1 - e_h^1)$ for $h=1,2$, i.e. sunspots don't matter, if and only if $\theta = 1$.
6. The specific procedure I have in mind consists of the following steps:
   (i) Pick a positive feasible allocation $\boldsymbol{x} \gg 0$ for which sunspots matter;
   (ii) Pick positive values of the derivatives $f_h^{0\prime}(x_h^0) > 0$ and $f_h^{1\prime}(x_h^{1s}) > 0$ for $s = \alpha, \beta$, $h = 1,2$ (together with probabilities, returns, prices, and multipliers) so that the first-order conditions for (4^s) are satisfied at the chosen

allocation $\boldsymbol{x}$, and these values are consistent with strict concavity; and finally

(iii) Pick positive values of the derivatives $f_h^{1\prime}(\pi^\alpha x_h^{1\alpha}+\pi^\beta x_h^{1\beta})>0$ for $h=1,2$ (now together with just prices and multipliers) so that the first-order conditions for (4^s) are satisfied at the average allocation $\boldsymbol{x}'$ defined by (13) (which are simply (7^s) with $(y_h^1,y_h^1)=(x_h^{0\prime},x_h^{1s\prime})$ for $s=\alpha,\beta$, $h=1,2$), and again these values are consistent with strict concavity.

This construction works because of the fact that, for f: $\mathbb{R}_+\rightarrow\mathbb{R}$ differentiable, strictly increasing and strictly concave, specifying $f'(x')$ and $f'(x'')$ for $x'\neq x''$ leaves great latitude in also specifying $f'(\lambda x'+(1-\lambda)x'')$ for $0<\lambda<1$.

References

Arrow, K. J. (1964) 'The Role of Securities in the Optimal Allocation of Risk-Bearing', *Review of Economic Studies,* 31: 91–6.

Cass, D. (1984) 'Competitive Equilibrium with Incomplete Financial Markets', CARESS Working Paper, University of Pennsylvania.

Cass, D. and K. Shell (1980) 'In Defense of a Basic Approach', in J. H. Kareken and N. Wallace (eds), *Models of Monetary Economies*, Federal Reserve Bank of Minneapolis.

Cass, D. and K. Shell (1983) 'Do Sunspots Matter?', *Journal of Political Economy,* 91: 193–227.

Debreu, G. (1959) *Theory of Value* (New York: Wiley), chapter 7.

Hart, O. D. (1975) 'On the Optimality of Equilibrium When the Market Structure Is Incomplete', *Journal of Economic Theory,* 11: 418–43.

Keynes, J. M. (1936) *The General Theory of Employment, Interest and Money* (London: Macmillan), chapter 12.

Shiller, R. J. (1978) 'Rational Expectations and the Dynamic Structure of Macroeconomic Models: A Critical View', *Journal of Monetary Economics,* 4: 1–44.

26 Debts, Deficits and Interest Rates

Lorie Tarshis

1 INTRODUCTION

Contemporary macroeconomists when asked about points of theory or details of policy, rarely answer with a single voice: the extraordinary diversity of their views is as dismaying to professionals as it is to the public. On only one matter do they all join in the same chorus: lower interest rates would speed up economic growth, reduce unemployment, ease the burden that debtors must now bear and probably reduce the country's trade deficit. Recently, of course, all interest rates from those on overnight loans to those on terms of twenty-five years or more have fallen but they remain very high. Imagine how Keynes, who had anticipated with pleasure further declines in rates from the very low levels of 1935 and a hastening of the 'euthanasia of the rentier', would feel if he knew that in February 1986 long-term corporate bonds in the United States yielded 9.67 per cent (and only 3.4 per cent in 1935) and ninety-day treasury bills, 7.06 per cent (as against 2.25 per cent in 1935).

It is surprising, in view of the sharp changes in interest rates in the last fifty years and more – significant increases from 1929 to 1933, a gradual drop for the next ten years to 1943, little change to 1947–8, then a slow though persistent rise for the next twenty-five years, followed by a spectacular acceleration, punctuated by sharp drops, peaking in 1981 and from then to the spring of 1986, a series of welcome declines – that macroeconomists have been unable to forge explanations for these sharp movements that would command general assent.

Instead the theory of interest has been shattered into a chaos of *ad hoc* explanations – several for every unexpected change and for every failure to change in the desired direction, lacking consistency and internal coherence – a veritable wild-cat well spouting an uncontrollable flood of *ad hoc*'s posing as explanations.

In this chapter, I will begin by examining three such attempts, in the hope that such an examination will not only reveal the inadequacies of contemporary macro theory, but also that it will disclose features responsible for these inadequacies and by so doing that it will help guide efforts to develop an acceptable theory of interest. The first attempt was to explain high interest rates as the consequence of a low saving rate. (This explanation never dies; it has taken a variety of forms down through the years.) Next, we shall examine the doctrine that finds inflation, or expectations of inflation as the cause of high interest rates. (Although I do not contest the possible validity of such a conclusion, the argument usually put forward in its support seems to me to be flawed and to rest upon a faulty model.) My final example – which derives from the title of this piece – very common at present – seeks to explain the level of interest rates by reference to the size of the federal government's budget deficit. Having set out the reasons why the usual argument on its behalf is unacceptable, we digress in order to build up a theory to replace the various theories implicit in these three examples. With that construction we can more readily formulate a judgment as to the validity of the three examples we have examined. In the final stages of the paper, we present some empirical data that bear upon the theory, though they are not able, on their own, to rule out all other 'theories'.

It will be apparent that the theory proposed here is little more than the one presented by Keynes in his *General Theory*, in some degree clarified and somewhat extended to enable it to answer questions that did not interest him. It will be clear too that it rests upon our understanding and appreciation of the role of money that recognizes how essential money is for the functioning of a modern economy. It suggests that to use the model of a *barter* economy is far more likely to *distort* than to *further* an understanding of the operations of today's economy. And deriving from the examination of money's role, it very strongly suggests that an analysis of the forces that determine interest rates must rest on a consideration of the *stocks* of financial assets, rather than of their *flows*.

2 THREE HYPOTHESES ABOUT INTEREST RATES

(a) In the 1930s and at intervals since then, and in various guises, the conventional wisdom has held that interest rates have been so high because 'the saving rate' has been so low, and that if a fall in interest rates is wanted, 'the saving rate' will have to be raised. (The term 'saving rate' has been put in quotes because it can mean several different things. It can, for instance, mean the ratio of personal saving (as a flow) to disposable income (likewise, a flow). Or it can refer to the ratio of personal (or private, or total) savings (a stock) to the GNP (a flow) – though a ratio of stock to flow must sometimes raise questions – or of personal saving (or savings) to the level of investment (flow) or of business wealth (a stock). Or, at the extreme it can refer to the ratio of total saving (= personal and gross business saving and taxes minus transfer payments) to the economy's aggregate output less that part of its output of goods and services taken by consumers.

No doubt some of these ratios look interesting; that some of them are related as cause to the operations of the economy is surely at least plausible. But to spy a plausible connection between one ratio and another seemingly important should not, at all, signify that one or other of these ratios plays a role in determining interest rates; after all, the levels of the various interest rates are implicit in the prices of specific financial assets; not of just anything or everything.

It must be obvious that a choice has to be made from a long list of possible variables, and that choice ought to be guided by 'theory' – by first isolating the variables whose prices imply the level of interest rates. Once those variables have been identified, a detailed examination of the characteristics of the variables must be undertaken because these characteristics can be expected to be important in any analysis of the process of determining their prices.

There is an obvious plausibility to the view that interest rates are somehow influenced by the relative strengths of two flows: (a) of investment, which appears to establish the strength of *demand* for loanable funds needed to finance the investment projects being undertaken; and (b) of saving which appears to establish the corresponding inflow of loanable funds into the market. Their price – the interest rates – should be expected, by analogy with the market for apples, to rise if the level of investment rises relative to saving; and to fall if saving rises relative to investment. And if that is true, it must follow that a deficiency of saving would explain high interest rates; a deficiency of investment would bring interest rates down. But can this plausibility be converted into a general rule? Would it really survive the following doubts?

First, the level of investment – the current rate of spending on capital goods – is not a good proxy for the demand for loanable funds. Business firms are often able to finance at least some of their investment projects without borrowing; their portfolios may hold large stores of money which they can use. Secondly, firms and households may borrow not because they have to buy investment goods but because they want to increase their holdings of highly liquid assets (money) as a safety net against bankruptcy. (Many firms have been forced to seek the protection of the courts because though the value of their assets exceeds their liabilities, they cannot pay their bills or meet their payrolls by offering their suppliers and workers a piece of equipment or a part of the roof on their plant. That form of payment may not be acceptable.) From time to time any firm may face a liquidity crisis and prudence will normally direct it to borrow money – if it is not so readily acquired in other ways – and simply add what it borrows to its bank account. (And at other times, it may hold more than it needs, and it can then pay off loans – thereby making loanable funds available, even though it may be saving nothing.)

Secondly, the level of saving – the current flow of disposable income less spending for consumption together with business saving – the flow of undistributed corporate-profit – is no better a proxy for the flow or supply of loanable funds into the market. The argument here is analogous to that in the paragraph preceding.

Thirdly, and far more important; looking at a single firm or household, it is obvious that its purchases of investment goods can be far larger or smaller than its level of saving. It is then tempting to suppose that for the whole economy the amount of investment can also differ by any margin you wish from the amount of saving. But to suppose that is true is to disregard a central lesson of macroeconomics. Properly defined, the amounts of saving and investment for any period and for any state of the economy – chaos, deep depression, recovery, prosperity, or an explosion boom – the two amounts are identically equal – equal by definition. So what at first glance might have seemed so plausible a cause for changes in interest rates, cannot even come into being. It can no more operate than could the number of heads-up differ from the number of tails-down when a hundred, or two, coins are tossed.

Next, we saw that the demand for loanable funds is not properly measured by the level of investment; and the corresponding supply is not properly measured by the level of saving. However, they can be measured; the former – that is, the demand for loanable funds – by the *stock* of debt instruments which debtors are willing to service, paying interest, when due and repaying the principle when the time comes; and the latter – or the supply of loanable funds – by the stock of such instruments that creditors are willing to hold. The prices of these obligations are subject to almost continuous change so the stocks at any instant play a role, as we shall see, in determining their prices at that same instant. Of course, over a longer period these stocks are likely to change, usually by something less than 1 per cent a month and twelve times that in a year. But for any short period, the stocks outstanding, (as the debtors see them) or the stocks held, (as seen by the creditors), can be thought of as fixed. The flows – which cause the stocks to change over a longer period of time – can be disregarded when the objective of the enquiry is to throw light on their prices at, say, the close of business on Friday, 4 April 1986.

The final point to make in connection with the claim that high interest rates are all the fault of the low saving rate is even more damning. The interest rate moves with the price of a certain type of debt instrument. It can be expressed as the *reward* (a price) paid to the creditor who is willing to hold that debt instrument. It can just as well be described as the price the debtor pays to enable him to hold money – which is what he gets when he sells a debt instrument. But *it is not the reward for, or the price of saving* unless there is no difference in meaning between saving and lending and between purchasing investment goods and borrowing. If the rate of interest is not the price of saving, why should anyone look at the demand for saving and its supply – which I suppose determine its price – as an answer to the determination of the interest rate? (But, incidentally, what is the price of saving? Where is it quoted?)

When the century was young, physicists believed in the existence of the ether – which filled all space not otherwise occupied. Suppose one of them, looking for an explanation for a change in its amount, hypothesized that it would change by the difference between the number of coins that, after being tossed, displayed 'heads-up' and the number of coins that after the same tossing were found with tails-down. Plausible? No less so than the hypothesis about the difference between saving and investment and its effect on interest rates.

(b) A second explanation for high interest rates, borrowed from important insights set out by Irving Fisher into the effects of changes in the value of money upon creditors and debtors, was given a well-advertised rerun after 1970. Fisher noted that creditors lose from inflation; debtors gain. Since both parties would surely recognize these consequences, it is not difficult to believe that creditors would seek compensation; it may not be so easy to believe that debtors would be accommodating unless they were frightened by the prospect of a lender's strike. But this argument seems to imply that the terms of all new issues would be modified in favor of creditors. They would be able to earn more on all new loans. It sounds plausible but once again there is a catch.

At this date creditors in the US own up to $6 trillion of debt instruments. The terms on which these bonds, etc., were issued were frozen into the various loan agreements at the time of issue. A change in the terms of any one of them can only be made binding if authorized by a court of law after it is satisfied that creditors and debtors are willing to accept them; and then only if the court finds that if the changes sought are not made, the debtors would have to act in ways that would jeopardize the existence of the firm, hurting not only its creditors but also its debtors. The process is lengthy and costly and as a result such changes in terms are rarely made.

Hence a new difficulty arises. Once the modified bonds with a yield of, say, 10 per cent have become available, no one would be willing to continue holding the old ones which yielded less – say 9 per cent. Every creditor would accordingly try to exchange his lower yielding bonds for higher yielding ones but, as a class, creditors cannot succeed. They will not find investors so foolish as to be willing to purchase them with their 9 per cent yield, and very soon in order to sell them, they will have to offer them at lower and lower or bargain prices. But as their prices drop their yields rise, even though their terms have not been changed; and the process will continue until the yields on identical bonds – same issuer, approximately the same date of maturity – are the same.

Bearing in mind the point made earlier, that the stock of bonds outstanding is very many times higher than the flow of new issues, it is difficult to believe that their yields would meet at 10 per cent unless the tap of new issues were left open indefinitely. But that is not the end of the story. A more plausible account can be derived by considering investors and their expectations.

Investors will have learned to look ahead; some are quicker in doing so than others. Some will more rapidly come to expect inflation than the rest; and some of them will manage to foresee its consequences for their own portfolios. Specifically they will realize that a rise in interest rates is all too likely and that the prices at which they can, at a later date, sell their longer term bonds will then fall. If any investor were able to sell them *before* their prices fall, he would be able to avoid all the injuries to which inflation will expose other creditors.

As he, and others move to sell, and by so doing abandon their status as creditors (or if they replace their long terms with treasury bills, at least modify that status), prices of long-term debt instruments drop, and their yields, just as quickly rise.

Clearly it pays creditors to be far-sighted. Those able to sell their long-term debt instruments before their prices drop, escape, and that fact puts pressure on all of them to act quickly. But as any sell, others must be buying and they will lose if the sellers' expectations prove to be justified.

Creditors who do not sell out in time will not be compensated by the rise in yields. If they are able to hold them until they mature, their yield will be precisely what they had expected to get when they bought them. But by doing that they may be denying themselves a greater than 'promised yield' because prospective capital gains on those they hold will obviously be reduced in size, even if interest rates subsequently drop, as the length of time to maturity shrinks. And with investors eager to sell before prices drop too far, the decline in their prices will speed up, perhaps even going too far.

As bond prices drop, and their yields rise, newly issued bonds are bound to have higher yields too. If the terms they offer are not altered, their prices must drop too for no one would be willing to buy them at the old price, which would imply a lower yield, when he could purchase the same thing at a lower price and earn more.

The usual argument which implies that the terms of new issues would move in favor of creditors actually operates, in this rendering, through the market for outstanding issues. There is no need to call on debtors to surrender a part of their gains to creditors for whom they are supposed to feel sorry. Unlikely, anyway! The whole mechanism is confined to the credit market which deals almost wholly in bonds, etc., that had been issued earlier. The recognition that inflation will push interest rates higher and the prices of debt instruments down is quite enough to initiate and fuel the whole process as creditors are pressed to sell long-term debt instruments. And it could, and surely it *would,* start even earlier with any upwards revision of expectations of inflation recognized as a factor likely to push interest rates up, because (a) creditors once they recognized the danger to their own interests would be pressed to sell, and (b) the banking system, under the direction of the Central Bank, once inflation had gained in strength, would move to quell it, by tightening the money market.

Several points – some of them implicit in the last few pages – are worth noting for future use:

1. The focus of any acceptable theory of interest has to be on *stocks* rather than *flows*. Had attention been confined to flows the case for a direct relation between a rise in expectations of inflation and interest rates would have been much less persuasive than it seemed. It can be agreed that a potential lender, foreseeing inflation, would have sought (as always) more favorable terms, but holding onto his own money would have exposed him to precisely the same losses from inflation as he would have suffered had he used that money to purchase debt instruments. Money and debt instruments are both, and in the same degree, *wasting* assets during inflation and that knowledge would have weakened the prospective lender's ability to persuade the would-be borrower to accede to the better terms the lender would naturally feel to be his due; at any time and not only when inflation was in prospect.

As to the potential lender, the prospect of inflation does not shift his margin of preference as between money and debt instruments and it therefore would not be expected to alter the price of new issues in terms of money. It is only when *stocks* – the population of already outstanding issues – (which are many times as large as the annual flow into the market) become the center of attention, that a theory of interest is likely to be reasonably complete.

2. A second factor which incidentally underlines the role of stocks arises from the fact that the substitutability of members of new and outstanding issues, and even of members of issues with very different terms is nevertheless very high. (If the 'moral risk' attaching to the various debtors is judged to be very different, their substitutability may be, in the view of an investor who does not share the general judgments of the market as to their relative 'moral risks', rather low; and the same would have to be said of two issues which mature at very different dates – say five years and fifteen years into the future – by an investor whose judgment as to where interest rates are going differed strongly from that reflected in their current prices.) In other words, one investor may prefer to own issue A; another, issue B. But if they mature at approximately the same date and if it is believed that the risk of default is negligible, no investor would have reason for preferring A to B, or B to A.

3. With attention directed towards stock of debt instruments as being far more important in the determination of interest rates, a theory of interest

that makes much of the level of saving is likely to be misleading for two reasons:

(i) Interest rates represent the prices paid by those who choose to hold money in their portfolios. The connection of this choice with decisions about saving must surely be remote. Decisions about saving presumably reflect the relative strengths of the public's preferences for consumption as against accumulating wealth – though their actual rate of accumulation can, of course, turn out to be quite different from their target rate. The investors' *desires* as to the form or composition of their portfolios – so much in real assets and so much as equities, debt instruments and money – is on a completely different plane; and it is difficult to see any connection between them.

(ii) Saving and the desired rate of saving refer to that part of the flow of income that is *not* directed to the purchase of consumer goods. When it actually takes place it implies *an addition* to wealth – perhaps amounting to 5 per cent a year. Borrowing and lending by contrast reflect preferences as to how stocks of wealth and more directly of financial assets are to be held.

Interest rates reflect the prices of debt instruments – presumably of *all* debt instruments – and it scarcely seems reasonable to suppose that these latter prices will be determined, or even that they will be much influenced by the prices of *newly issued* debt instruments – whose value over a year would typically average from 5 per cent to 8 per cent of the whole stock. Of course, the prices of just-issued debt instruments, after allowances have been made for differences in the lengths of time to maturity and 'moral hazards' attaching to the borrower, are bound to be the same as for all other debt instruments, and in particular for that much larger number already outstanding; otherwise, the bond and bill markets would never reach equilibrium. In short, stocks dominate flows when transactions involving the former are far more numerous than those involving the latter.

A related matter: the prices of *all* debt instruments determine *all* interest rates. Apart from differences in the confidence a group of lenders may have in one borrower or another, any issue of debt instruments will be a very good substitute. If so, it is impossible to find any reason for concluding that one *kind* of issue – say long-term government bonds, or long-term corporates – will play a key role in determining interest rates.

(c) Finally, going down our list of hypotheses, we must consider a third, currently the one most strongly favored: interest rates are high, it is argued, or at any rate they will be surprisingly resistant to efforts to lower them, until the federal government's budget deficit has been pared down. Unlike the view that relates interest rates to current expectations of inflation – a view that can be supported – the view that relates interest rates to the federal budget deficit seems neither plausible, as theory, nor does it find significant empirical support in the actual data. Indeed, its theoretical underpinning seems to resemble a black box; no plausible mechanism by which a harder push on the deficit button would generate higher interest rates, can be detected. In effect, for this relationship, one is asked to substitute faith for understanding. (But there have been too many instances in which interest rates have been higher when deficits fell, and vice versa, to encourage faith.)

However, even though the detailed workings of the black box cannot be discerned, enough has been written by those who accept its conclusions to suggest how they would describe its workings, if they were pressed to do so. They appear to accept the following:

(i) a deficit in the federal government's budget pressures it to borrow by floating bonds, bills, etc;
(ii) the higher is that deficit, the greater will be its flotation of debt instruments;
(iii) the pool of funds available for financing the purchase of newly issued debt instruments is limited, though an increase in interest rates would, or at least it *might* enlarge that pool;
(iv) debt instruments issued by the federal government are preferred over all others even though their yield typically is lower than that of most others;
(v) it follows then that any increase in the federal government budget deficit will imply an increased offering of its debt instruments. As a result the funds available for the purchase of those issued by the private sector must decline. The conclusion – that interest rates within the private sector must rise if the public sector's deficit rises – seems a plausible one, unless there are good reasons for rejecting any steps in the argument set out above, or any other points essential for the argument that have not been made explicit.

Before considering them in order, it may be helpful to record some contradictions with the facts.

Interest rates in the United States have scarcely ever been as low as they were in 1942, 1943 and 1944. Long-term corporates yielded from 2.7 per cent to 2.8 per cent and treasury bills earned from 0.3 to 0.4 per cent. Yet the budget deficit, measured as a per cent of the GNP for the same period was about 23 per cent; and that, needless to say is a record that still stands – by a very wide margin. Such data should raise questions about the validity of the hypothesis.

They should not, however, be accepted as completely damning to that view. In those war years, firms were restrained from ordering all the capital goods they wanted and the production of durable consumer goods was severely limited. Firms and households had no reason to issue new debt instruments because they could not use funds borrowed to buy; they were much more likely to be repaying old debt. The prices of these debt instruments were influenced far more by a deficiency in the supply of them than by a deficiency in the demand for them; their prices were, if anything, kept from *falling* and it is easy to understand why their yields scarcely rose.

This experience clearly does not call for a rejection of the theory, though it demands that it be qualified: 'an increase in the government's budget deficit will not call for higher interest rates if private spending is being held back by other constraints'. (But it does not necessarily follow that interest rates would rise if private spending were not so constrained.)

There have, however, been many other instances in which a change in the deficit has not led to the change in interest rates that the hypothesis would suggest. For example, that notorious deficit increased quickly between 1981 and 1986, yet interest rates fell, sometimes very rapidly. They fell especially rapidly between September 1985 and April 1986; while the deficit, already very high, grew 'at an alarming rate'. Those committed to that hypothesis can no doubt explain away that seeming contradiction. They might consider that it is not the deficit so much as the public's expectations of deficits in the future that play the key role – (and, of course, changes in these expectations can be inferred by noting how interest rates have moved). But (a) if a hypothesis usually has to be shunted off the main track to allow a rationalization to come to the rescue, would it not be better to express the hypothesis so that it takes account of the rescuer; and (b) this seems to imply that economic theory and policy can forget fiscal and monetary measures, and other 'hard' facts, and deal only with economic Coué-ism. No government would need more than an 'Expectations Generator' to alter interest rates.

Apart from variations on the theme of expectations, however, most of the rest of the argument set out above must be discarded. Illustrating: the alleged association between the size of the government's budget deficit and the government's debt (and especially the economy's *total* debt) has to be rejected. For one thing, the rules of government bookkeeping – scarcely deserving of the honorific title 'accounting' – have evidently been formulated to provide as unclear and ambiguous a picture of fiscal outgoes and receipts as possible. Transfers to government trust funds from the Treasury are treated as government expenditures whether the fund pays the sums transferred out to its employees, to the public, or instead uses them to buy government securities. Moreover, the figures commonly cited to measure the public (read the Federal Government's) debt usually include as a part of the debt, debt instruments issued and held by the government itself through its own corporations and trust funds and the Federal Reserve banks. Yet you surely would not dream of measuring *your* debt as \$1 000 000 000 087 416.23 after you had written an IOU, payable to bearer for \$1 trillion, signed it and held it securely in your own possession. Why then should the Federal Government count the \$475 billion of its own bonds, bills and notes that *it* holds as a part of *its* debt? And why should it count the interest it pays to the Federal Reserve banks – about $16–17 billion a year – as a part of its expenditures? (Incidentally, the Fed is required to return to the Treasury almost all it receives.)

A third step in the chain of the argument – usually implicit – is that the economy's access to loanable funds is absolutely limited at any date (though it can be expected to grow over time.) That is indeed how the microeconomist would see the matter although that simply reflects the assumption – perfectly appropriate for the consideration of microeconomic problems: that gross income and output are constants. (If saving does grow with a rise in income, what happens to that step?) Alternatively, the economy's access to loanable funds can be thought of as having to do with a stock – either of savings, or money. (Unfortunately, such an assumption as a fixed stock of money has become a commonplace in a consideration of macroeconomic problems. The upwards-tilting *LM*-curve is treated as though it were immutable – a physical constant – rather than as a relation implicitly based upon the behavior of the banking system. Economists have grown so used to it that despite all the evidence to the contrary – in the form of falling interest rates from 1981–6, or 1961–5 – they are rarely prepared, when confronted by a shift to the right in the *IS*-curve and a new intersection with the original *LM*-curve to the North-East of the original one, to acknowledge that the simple-minded increase in the quantity of money that ordinarily accompanies a revival in economic activity would prevent interest rates from rising.)

By the same token, an increase in the supply of money would vitiate the argument – even if it were otherwise plausible – that an increase in public sector's demand for funds would imply that the private sector would face ever-tighter conditions in the market for loans. With the Central Bank behaving as it should, and as it very often would, the nightmares generated by near vertically rising *LM*-curves would be recognized for the phantoms they really are.

Other points worth making require no more than very brief mention. First, the argument that because the yields on debt instruments issued by the public sector are lower than those issued by the private sector, such debt instrument will always find buyers before any issued by the private sector can be placed, is false. At the margin, as influenced by the relative yields on the private and the public sector's debt instruments, buyers or investors are presumably indifferent between them. The demand for one of them will not have absolute priority over the demand for the other; and most of this whole argument in any event must be discarded because it concerns itself with *flows*; and not with *stocks*. In a world in which the level of transactions directly determined by flows were many times as high as those directly influenced by the level of stocks it would be persuasive, but this is *not* the market in which the prices of debt instruments are actually determined, any more than it is the market in which prices of equities, housing or the stock of gold are determined.

3 THE POSITIVE THEORY OF INTEREST

Our purpose in setting out, in such detail, explanations and rationalizations for the behavior of interest rates was only in part – minor at that – to present reasons for questioning the particular arguments here discussed. Its chief aim was to suggest the characteristics required of any theory of interest if it is to be thoroughly acceptable.

Amongst the primary features: the theory must be general enough so that it can deal consistently with such day-by-day topics as: how can their current levels be explained; is that explanation consistent with the one that must be used to account for the world-wide declines in interest rates that began in the fall of 1931, or soon after; and do the measures proposed for getting changes in interest rates flow from the explanation used above?

Secondly, interest rates are set in the money and credit market. A theory of interest that fails to take account of the unique features of money and the points of difference between money and credit cannot be fully acceptable. Thirdly, a theory of interest must be consistent with acceptable macroeconomic insights. A theory of interest that rests upon a divergence of saving and investment may be expressed so as to seem plausible, but unless these terms are defined differently from those used in the various national income concepts, no such discrepancy is possible even when the economy is in a situation of acute disequilibrium or instead in a benign and decidedly stable equilibrium.

Changes in interest rates are signalled by changes in the prices of debt instruments of given characteristics. When the prices of various debt instruments, due to mature in, say, fifteen years, have gone up – and that is precisely what the market will display – the yields on such long-term debt instruments have declined. Such an increase in the prices of bonds of that type may occur whether or not a set of such bonds has just been issued. Debt instruments are being traded in markets all over the world and certainly in the more important capital markets, around the clock, and in the largest markets – say New York – the level of these transactions, in a single day, may reach as much as *$1 trillion*. Such a figure is, of course, absolutely enormous compared to the transactions involving *new* issues – perhaps a few billion dollars a day.

Economists, when faced with problems about the determination of prices, generally rely upon a model involving goods and services. Their prices are generally arrived at through the dealings of potential sellers and buyers with the sellers ready to deliver newly produced outputs and the buyers ready to purchase and use those outputs. The analysis appropriate to such an output is commonly set out in terms of current flows. There is, however, another class of transactions for which such an analysis is not appropriate. Residential housing is one example. While there would be, in the course of, say, a year, some transactions involving newly produced housing, most of them by a wide margin involve houses that had been built earlier and had sported For Sale signs several times from the day they were made ready for occupancy. The same could be said for gold and for antiques (by definition), and other collectibles. They all are unusually durable, and can be stored and maintained readily. But there are other assets even more durable, which can be maintained even more cheaply and are more nearly homogeneous. I mean debt instruments and other financial assets. The color of the bond, and its location are irrelevant. If it has been issued by the Federal Government, it will be regarded as secure beyond question; if by a large and prosperous corporation, as almost secure. A short-term note issued by such a creditor will differ from a long-term bond only in the length of the term to maturity.

Naturally prices of these debt instruments, in a free market – and the money and credit markets are free beyond any others – are determined by the forces of demand and those of supply. And demand – when most transactions involve stocks on hand – comprise the amounts that investors want to hold at various prices (including amounts that borrowers are ready to redeem); supply, subject to the same constraints comprise the stocks of debt instruments presently in existence together with any to be issued that are on offer, again at various prices.

Any change in the attitudes of investors or debtors will affect demand or supply. When holders of debt instruments are persuaded to reduce their holdings and acquire money instead, the demand (for them) drops, their prices fall and their yields must increase. (Keynes treats this as an increase in the liquidity preference function.) If the money supply rises, with no change in relative preferences, efforts to restore portfolio balance will cause the prices of debt instruments to rise: again, lower interest rates. Finally if the stock of debt is increased, the demand for money will rise and interest rates, assuming no other changes, will increase.

There are several ways in which this last process can be explained. Perhaps the most direct is this: an increase in the stock of debt instruments means that the average investor's portfolio holds more bonds, etc., but no more money. But he would then not be in equilibrium, assuming no change in his preference for holding liquid rather than illiquid financial assets. Equilibrium would only be restored – in the sense that he would be content to accept that modified portfolio – if the yield on debt instruments were to rise.

An alternative approach would look at the liquidity preference function in more detail. With more debt instruments in his portfolio, he would have, had he been a bull, a stronger speculative motive for holding money; his precautionary motive for holding money would also increase because, with the same feeling of uncertainty in respect to his expectation that interest rates would not rise, he would, since he has more of his wealth at hazard, feel more urgently the wisdom of diversifying. (By substituting money for some debt instruments.)

This, I thought, was not in the *General Theory*; certainly it is not to be found in chapters 13 and 15 in which Keynes set out his theory of interest. It seemed to me that this could be explained by noting his preoccupation with the short run; a significant change in the stock of debt instruments cannot occur in a couple of months. And my own focus on that stock as an explanatory variable in the determination of interest rates came to me when I was asked to explain the sharp rise in interest rates from the mid 1960s to 1981.

In the course of analyzing this development, I attempted to test for the effect of this variable by comparing changes in the *ratio* of the economy's holdings of debt instruments to the money supply with changes in interest rates. All I can report at this stage with confidence is that, in general, they seem to move together. They both rose from 1929 to 1933. They both fell sharply from 1934 to 1943, stabilized from 1944 to 1948, and then at first gradually but later accelerating, they rose up to 1981. After that the ratio seems to decline; interest rates certainly did.

But I have some doubts: first, another explanation can be found for similar shifts. When interest rates rise, the public will want to hold more debt instruments in their portfolios. (That does not mean that more will be created, however.) My more serious question has to do with measuring the money supply properly. From 1920 to say 1965, M_1 meant pretty much the same thing not only as defined but as to its significant content. But with stronger restraints, banks were encouraged to develop a host of money-hybrids and the border areas between money and debt instruments began to fill up with super-attractive stores of value. From then on, slow growth in M_1 may have meant slow growth in the money supply, but it may also have meant normal growth in the money supply (as defined by investors) with some especially attractive financial assets classified as components of M_2 or M_3 being substituted for a component of M_1.

One final note: a few months ago I was reading Lord Kahn's *The Making of Keynes' General Theory* (Cambridge University Press, 1984). In illustrating Keynes's theory of interest he cited a paragraph from chapter 16 of that book. I quote from it: 'And the current rate of interest depends, as we have seen, not on . . . , but on the strengths of the desires to hold it in liquid and illiquid forms respectively, coupled with the amount of the supply of wealth in the one form relatively to the supply of it in the other' (p.213).

It seems to me that in this passage, Keynes says 'the rate of interest depends upon the liquidity preference function (. . . the relative strengths of the desires for money and debt instruments) and the supplies of money (stock of liquid assets) relative to the supplies of debt instruments (the size of the stocks of illiquid assets)'. If my effort has discovered nothing new, it has, I believe, at least found something worth repeating.

27 Debt and Deficit and Other Illusions

Robert Eisner

Joan Robinson was appropriately contemptuous of the notion that unemployment could be explained by the stubborn refusal of workers to accept the market real wage. In one memorable passage, she wrote,

> [T]he orthodox conception of wages tending to equal the *marginal disutility* of labour, which has its origin in the picture of a peasant farmer leaning on his hoe in the evening and deciding whether the extra product of another hour's work will repay the extra backache, is projected into the modern labour market, where the individual worker has no opportunity to decide anything except whether it is better to work or starve. (Joan Robinson, 1966, p.2)

Joan was, of course, buttressing the argument by Keynes that higher than (full employment) equilibrium real wages were not the *cause* of underemployment. That unemployed workers were not insisting on the market real wage was indicated by the fact that neither they nor their employed brethren would refuse employment at the given money wage if prices were higher. The simultaneous reluctance of employed workers to accept cuts in money wages – in the event, far from an absolute rejection – implied not money illusion but an understandable hostility to forces of immobility and imperfect competition which might force a decline in their *relative* wages.

1 INFLEXIBLE MONEY WAGES AND UNEMPLOYMENT[1]

The role of wage inflexibility in the Keynesian explanation of unemployment has indeed been much misunderstood. The essential Keynesian argument is that, with or without flexible wages, a modern comparative economy may neither endogenously maintain full employment nor correct departures from full employment within any reasonable period of time, if at all.

The problem is the possibility of inadequate effective demand. This is readily demonstrated in the usual elementary text, with wages and hence prices fixed (and with a fixed money supply) in terms of saving and investment demand curves, that intersect at less than the full employment level of output. Allowing the (nominal and real) money supply to increase permits lower rates of interest which increase investment demand. But this may not increase investment demand sufficiently to bring about full employment. On the one hand, investment demand may be insufficiently interest-elastic for moderate declines in the rate of interest to bring about more than moderate increases in investment. On the other hand, more than moderate declines in the rate of interest may be impossible because of the ultimate lower bound (never reached) of the liquidity trap. And if the liquidity trap argument is found to be unappealing, there is finally the bottom stop of zero for the nominal interest rate and hence a similar bottom stop of zero for the real interest rate in an 'equilibrium' situation in which there is no inflation.

But this simple heuristic presentation of the system with prices or wages fixed is not to assert that they are in fact rigid. Much of the *General Theory* involves consideration of what would happen if wages and prices were flexible. The usefulness of the simplifying assumption of fixed wages resides prercisely in Keynes's demonstration that abandonment of the assumption does not invalidate the fundamental conclusion that free markets and full employment equilibrium may not always be compatible.

In a Walrasian model we assume that excess supply of any good or factor of production will generate a decline in its price. But the immediate effects of lower wages on employment must be found in a subsitution of labor for other factors of production or an increase in aggregate demand. For substitution to take place, however, there must be a change in *relative* prices. With perfect competition there is no obvious reason why prices of other factors of production would not decline proportionately with wages if the substitution of labor were to put them in excess supply. Hence there is no direct reason for an excess supply of labor to generate a lower relative price of labor and hence no consequent substitution (Lange, 1952). A substitution of labor for other factors of production would require essentially fortuitous changes in relative prices or expected relative prices, difficult to reconcile with assumptions of perfect competition and lack of rigidities.

The remedy to unemployment must be found in increases in aggregate demand. Flexible prices may in fact permit an increase in aggregate demand. The excess supply of labor would then bring about lower wages and, *a fortiori* with declines in other factor prices, a fall in prices of product such that the *real* value of a fixed nominal quantity of money will be greater. This then will generate lower interest rates.

But here we meet the same obstacle as in the case of an increased real value of money as a consequence of an increase in its nominal quantity. Again, the interest-elasticity of investment demand may not be sufficiently great and the extent to which the rate of interest may be lowered may not be sufficiently large. Credible econometric estimates, including my own, would seem to confirm the investment demand limitation and the lower bound to the rate of interest, if only at zero, may be accepted *a priori*.

There is still another possible role for flexible wages in assuring full employment. Any excess supply of labor, generating a decline in money wages, must be assumed under competitive conditions to generate a fall in the general level of prices. But if the government is a net debtor to the private sector of the economy, that is, the private sector is a net creditor in obligations fixed in money terms, a decline in the general price level increases perceptions by the public of its real wealth, the so-called Pigou effect after the arguments of Haberler and Pigou, well discussed by Patinkin (1948). This argument, it must be noted, loses its foundation in a truly private, competitive economy where there is no government debt, interest-bearing or non-interest-bearing. For here there is no 'outside' asset fixed in money terms that will increase in real value as the price level falls.

And there are further difficulties. As pointed out by Patinkin, they may relate to the dynamic problem of how *declines* in prices, as opposed to a lower level of prices, can be achieved in the face of bankruptcies enroute (cf. Fisher, 1933 and 1936, as discussed by Tobin, 1980, pp.9–12). And there are further dynamic complications in the possibility that elastic price expectations will induce delays in purchases as falling prices generate the view that prices will be still lower in the future.

But finally, refusing to accept the frequently useful assumptions of the Modigliani life-cycle model as fully applicable, the saving function may be such that, as wealth increases, the desire to save or accumulate more may eventually dominate a decreasing marginal utility of consumption. In the short run, given the limited speed at which prices can be expected to fall, the wealth effect may prove inadequate in generating the additional demand necessary to restore full employment. But even in the long run, at least the theoretical possibility remains that the wealth effect will be insufficient. In the words of Patinkin (1948), 'the Pigou effect', that a lower level of prices, *ceterius paribus*, will generate greater effective demand and lower unemployment may be true, but the 'Pigou theorem', that this must imply a return all the way to full employment, may not be true. Hence, in the non-inflationary Keynesian model, price movements may not serve the role of guaranteeing full employment.

If we accept the view that Keynesian unemployment does not require imperfectly flexible wages and prices, what is their role? It is, simply enough, to give definition to the price level. By this view, the intense search for 'microfoundations of macroeconomics' and, in particular, the excellent work on implicit and explicit contracts, do not serve the function of explaining why there is unemployment. Rather, as Keynes suggested, they explain why wages and prices have some stability and do not fall to zero when effective demand is less than the output associated with full employment or, as some would define it, the 'natural' rate of employment. Due to money illusions or not, imperfectly flexible money wages explain not the persistence of unemployment but the survival of a meaningful price system.

2 THE REAL AND NOMINAL MONEY AND DEBT

In the years before inflation came to dominate much of public consciousness, it seemed axiomatic that an increase in the supply of money would bring about a reduction in its rental price, the rate of interest. This in turn, as we taught in all our principles classes, buttressed by the prevailing textbooks, would bring an increase in investment and, with a multiplier generally greater than unity, a further increase in consumption and output. Then came Milton Friedman (1968) in his famed 1967 presidential address to the American Economic Association, telling us we had it all backward. An increase in the rate of growth of the money supply would not lower interest rates. It would raise them! And it would hence have no effect on investment or indeed on output or employment. The latter would remain at its 'natural' rate.

How were propositions that had dominated economic thinking so abruptly negated? Indeed, the counter-revolution rapidly gained new adherence in the profession and, joining forces with rational expectations, caught up much of the new generation of macroeconomists. But there were doubters, and there should have been more.

For one thing, if we have in mind a Walrasian equilibrium with all markets clearing and no interest-bearing government debt, a higher nominal quantity of fiat (outside) money would be compatible with a new equilibrium in which all prices would be higher in the same proportion as the quantity of money was higher. There would therefore be no change in the real quantity of money, no change in interest rates and indeed no real change at all – in investment, output or employment.

This was the old, neoclassical vision of the world, challenged by Keynes and Joan Robinson, clearly presented by Patinkin (1965). Applying Keynes's metaphor, having assumed a Euclidian world in the two dimensions of factor supply and productivity, we had indeed left no room for the crossing of parallel lines or for demand-induced changes in real variables.

Accepting all this, the path of analysis from changes in the supply of money to changes in its rate of growth was easy. A constant money supply would imply a rate of decline of prices exactly equal to the ('natural') rate of increase of output. A money supply increasing at the same rate as output would mean a stable price level. And a rate of growth in the money supply in excess of the natural rate of growth of output would imply a rate of inflation equal to that excess. In no event (except for second-order Tobin–

Mundell effects involving substitution of real assets for money) would there be a change in the real quantity of money.

It is perhaps strange that more voices were not raised to challenge the relevance of all this to a three-dimensional world in which it took more than the *supply* of factors of production and their productivity to determine output, let alone a four-dimensional world explicitly dealing with time without a *deus ex machina* of rational expectations to link present and future where efficient markets and prices to link them do not exist. Perhaps it is hard for economists to see truth beyond the vista of the contemporary scene. For Keynes and Joan Robinson in the 1930s to identify the mass unemployment of their epoch as natural was a crime against nature. In the 1960s, in the United States, with some dedication in high places to high employment and with the surge in demand from the Vietnam War, unemployment due to insufficient effective demand did not seem all that relevant.

But there should have been some further concerns about the relevance of this reincarnation of the neutrality of money. For recall that in indicating above that differences in the nominal quantity of money would not affect any real variables in the Walrasian system, we have stipulated that the government had no interest-bearing debt. If, conversely, the private sector were a net holder of interest-bearing securities, as pointed out long ago by Metzler (1951), a higher nominal quantity of money, with the nominal (face) value of that government debt unchanged, would imply a lower rate of interest. For there would then be substitution of money for bonds as well as for goods. Our new equilibrium would have a higher general level of prices but also more capital-intensive production, induced by the lower interest rates, and whatever changes in relative prices and output that might entail.

Further complications are now introduced when we re-examine the effects of increasing the rate of growth of the money supply. For now, even with the assumption of full employment or clearing markets for output and factors of production, it is, to begin with, no longer clear that an increase in government non-interest-bearing debt in the form of money at a faster rate than output will cause inflation. Suppose the interest-bearing debt of a government is increasing less rapidly than output, perhaps not increasing at all or even declining. The last possibility might be then quite pertinent if, as would be the case in the United States, the money supply is increased by Federal Reserve open market purchases which, in effect, retire government debt. In such a situation the net debt of the government – interest-bearing and non-interest-bearing – might be growing less rapidly than output. But then with net assets of the private sector in the form of this government debt also increasing less rapidly than output, aggregate demand in nominal terms may well be increasing less rapidly than output. Market-clearing prices would have to be declining at a sufficient rate to keep the real debt of the government – again the sum of interest-bearing debt and money – growing sufficiently to keep effective demand equal to the growing rate of output.

But once we get entangled in a world of government debt and changing price levels, the going gets treacherous. A number of widely held positions prove untenable. And many of the usual assertions about the effect of public debt and deficits become misleading at best and, at worst, particularly in presumed policy applications, egregiously wrong. Take the notion, for prime example, that an increase in the public debt will involve a transfer of wealth from the current to a future 'generation'. But surely, this proposition, if true, must relate to an increase in the *real* value of the public debt. Under what circumstances will government budget deficits lead to increases in the real value of the debt?

Assume again a market-clearing, full-employment equilibrium. Then have the government cut taxes, thus producing a budget deficit which is financed by a mixture of interest-bearing debt and fiat money in the same proportions as the already existing value of government interest-bearing debt and money. In this situtation, we should expect a new equilibrium – with rational expectations, an immediate new equilibrium – in which the general level of prices had increased in the same proportion as interest-bearing debt and money. There would hence be no increase in the real public debt or the real quantity of money and no change in any real magnitudes. And, of course, with no change in the real value of public debt, there is no transfer from one generation to another.

Now assume, in good Keynesian fashion that, for whatever reason, markets are not clearing and that there is an excess supply of labor so that output is below its 'natural' rate. The cut in taxes and resultant budget deficit, again financed by a mixture of interest-bearing debt and money in the same proportions as the existing debt and money, will increase effective demand. Output will rise so that prices will rise less than in proportion to the increase in interest-bearing debt and money. Indeed, the increase in wealth that agents in the private sector perceive in the form of their government bonds and money may be viewed, in good neoclassical fashion (cf. Haberler, 1941; Pigou, 1943, 1947) as the forces increasing demand and output.

But with increased output, we can expect more current consumption as a consequence of the increased wealth of households and also plans for more future consumption in accordance with the life-cycle hypothesis (Modigliani and Brumberg, 1954). Then in accordance with a conventional, neoclassical production function and rational expectations, there should be more current investment as well, as agents undertake to acquire the capital to be used in producing the goods and services to meet the expanded future consumption demand.

We find therefore that the deficit and increase in the public debt result in an increase in capital and the provision of more output both currently and in the future. We are not increasing current consumption at the expense of the future generation. We are rather increasing consumption for both generations.

We have thus come full circle. We have turned the argument on the burden of the public debt on its head. A government budget deficit, increasing nominal public debt, as long as the nominal supply of money is increased proportionately, will increase the real debt only to the extent that prices do not increase as rapidly. This is indeed likely to be the situation much of the time where markets do not in fact clear and there is less than full employment. In such a case – where the parallel lines do cross – the impacts of deficits and debt on current capital formation and future welfare are at worst ambiguous, as pointed out by Lange (1938) many years ago. There is an 'optimal propensity to consume' below which the increased current consumption brought on by a fiscal expansion will 'crowd in' investment rather than crowd it out. And in the full-employment, market-clearing equilibrium, somehow fancied by some as the 'long run', greater deficits, bringing faster rates of growth in the nominal values of public debt – as always, interest-bearing and money – will mean a higher rate of inflation, but no change in the real values of debt and money.

3 SOME CURRENT IMPLICATIONS

Where does this leave us in regard to all the recent and current furor about the unprecedented budget deficits in the United States? As I have pointed out elsewhere (Eisner and Pieper, 1984; Eisner, 1986a, *inter alia*), to the extent that inflation serves as a tax on government bonds and money already held by the public, the real deficit is reduced. The deficit is now down considerably, to little over 3 percent of GNP. With income and output growing at 6 or 7 percent rates, the current debt-GNP ratios, around one-half, are thus projected to stabilize.

For those of us committed to full employment, it is hardly obvious that, particularly after the October 1987 stock market shock, tighter fiscal policies that would reduce the debt-GNP ratio are in order. What may better be argued is that our policy mix is wrong and that the money supply or non-interest-bearing debt in the form of private sector claims in the Federal Reserve banks (the 'high-powered') money of federal funds and Federal Reserve notes – should be increasing more rapidly. Consequently, lower real interest rates, as well as a lower value of the dollar in terms of foreign exchange, would then bring the economy to full employment with a lesser increase in the interest-bearing debt and a lesser overall deficit.

But now we are left with the conclusion that with a proper monetary policy, the only cost of 'too large' a deficit is inflation. Once we get to full employment, 'deficits' financed by an appropriate mixture of interest-bearing debt and money will only increase prices in proportion to the increase in debt. There will be no increase in the real value of debt, except that in a growing economy the real value of debt would increase at the same rate as output. We are thus left with the proposition that, without a perverse monetary policy, while the government can create any nominal deficit, it cannot under the popular market-clearing assumptions, run a real deficit which increases the real debt more rapidly than output.

Do these conclusions seem shocking? I cannot believe that Joan Robinson would mind.

APPENDIX[2]

The effects of nominal deficits may be shown in a simple macroeconomic model in which output is a function of effective demand up to the point of full employment. Where aggregate demand exceeds full-employment output, prices rise until a real-balance effect, directly and/or through higher rates of interest, reduces real demand to full-employment output. We can reduce this system to its barest essentials in the following equations:

$$(C/P)_t = C(Y/P,\ K,\ D/P,\ M_x/P,\ i);$$
$$0 < C_1 < 1,\ C_2,\ C_3,\ C_4 > 0,\ C_5 \gtrless 0; \quad (1)$$

$$I/P = I[C(t)/P(t),\ i];\ I_1 > 0,\ I_2 < 0,\ -C_5; \quad (2)$$

$$M/P = L(Y/P,\ K,\ D/P,\ i);\ L_1,\ L_2,\ L_3 > 0,\ L_4 < 0; \quad (3)$$

$$Y/P = C/P + I/P; \quad (4)$$

$$Y/P \gtreqless y_f \quad (5)$$

$$\frac{dP}{dt} > 0 \text{ if } C + I > P\,y_f \quad (6)$$

$$nd = d(D + M_x)/dt \quad (7)$$

$$rd = d[(D + M_x)/P]/dt$$
$$= \frac{d(D + M_x)/dt}{P} - \frac{(dP/dt)(D + M_x)}{P^2} \quad (8)$$

where

C = nominal consumption demand
Y = nominal income or output
K = real capital
D = government interest-bearing debt
M_x = outside money
M = total quantity of money, inside and outside
$D + M_x$ = total government debt
P = the price level
i = the rate of interest
I = nominal investment demand
$C(t)$, $P(t)$ = the expected paths of nominal consumption and prices
y_f = full-employment output
nd = the nominal deficit = the change in the nominal value of total government debt
rd = the real deficit = the change in the real value of government debt

and numerical subscripts indicate partial derivatives with respect to arguments of the behavioral functions.

Thus, real consumption is a function of real output, of wealth in the form of real capital, of total government debt, interest-bearing and non-interest bearing, and of the rate of interest (1). Real investment is a function of the rate of interest and of the expected path of real consumption (2). The rate of interest is determined by the condition that the real supply of money equal the demand for money, which is a function of real output, of the stock of non-monetary wealth, and of the rate of interest (3). Finally, real output equals real consumption plus real investment (4) but is bounded by the supply constraint of full employment (5). If the sum of consumption and investment demand at existing prices exceeds full-employment output, prices rise (6). And while the nominal deficit equals the increase in interest-bearing and non-interest-bearing debt (7), the real deficit equals the increase in the real value of that debt (8).

We have made the customary assumptions regarding partial derivatives. The only crucial one for our argument is that the partial derivative of real consumption with respect to wealth in the form of real government debt to the private sector, C_3, is positive. We thus reject Barro's 'Ricardian equivalence effect', by which government debt is not perceived, either in whole or in part, as a net asset of private agents (Barro, 1974).

Deficits then increase government interest-bearing debt, D, or outside money, M_x, in accordance with (6). Increases in D or M_x in (1) increase both current consumption and planned future consumption (thus expected future consumption). The greater the deficit, the greater the increase in consumption and hence the greater the growth in output, Y/P, up to the point of full employment, y_f. Inflation, by raising the value of P, lowers the real value of total government debt, $(D + M_x)/P$. It hence reduces consumption, both current and planned, or reduces the rate of growth of consumption associated with a given nominal deficit. Increases in current and planned consumption will in turn generate investment, thus further adding to output.

When we reach full-employment output, $(Y/P = y_f)$, the deficit will bring no further change in real variables if $(dM_x/dt)/(dD/dt) = M_x/D$ and M/M_x remains constant, that is, if there is no change in the proportions of money to interest-bearing debt. These proportions might be kept constant, in the United States, by Federal Reserve open market purchases of a proportion of newly issued government interest-bearing debt equal to the proportion that existing outside money (currency and bank deposits with the Fed, essentially corresponding to Fed holdings of Treasury debt in the form of coins, bills, notes, bonds and gold certificates) bears to the existing interest-bearing debt. Banks would then increase the total quantity of money M, in proportion to the increase in outside or 'high-powered' money, M_x (assuming nothing to change equilibrium proportions of public holdings of cash and various kinds of bank liabilities). With D, M_x and M all increased in proportion, if the economy were initially in equilibrium at y_f, it would also be in equilibrium at a new, higher price level P, increased in similar proportion. And with no change in D/P, M_x/P, or M/P there would be no change in i or any of the real variables.

A repeated or continued deficit will eventually bring the sum of consumption and investment demand to equality with full-employment output. If the nominal deficit then continues with $Y/P = Y_f$, prices will rise continuously. In this situation we may then rewrite (8) as

$$rd = \frac{D + M_x}{P}\left[\frac{1}{D + M_x}\,\frac{d(D + M_x)}{dt} - \frac{1}{P}\frac{dP}{dt}\right] \tag{8'}$$

to show the real deficit as the product of the real debt and the difference between the relative rate of increase of the nominal debt and the rate of inflation. But under the conditions of proportionality of D, M_x and P indicated above, these two terms within the brackets are equal. Hence the real deficit is zero.

The system may be extended by the introduction of net Social Security wealth (see Eisner, 1983), defined as the difference perceived by current households between the present value of their expected Social Security benefits and the present value of the taxes that they are paying and expect to pay for Social Security. We may write (1) as

$$C/P = C(Y/P, K, D/P + SSWN/P, M_x/P, I) \tag{1'}$$

Thus, consumption demand would be higher if households perceive greater wealth in the form of holdings of either explicit government debt or implicit government debt in the form of the present value of the excess of Social Security commitments over Social Security taxes. Now, if the introduction of net Social Security wealth increases the total government debt to the private sector, explicit and implicit, consumption demand will rise. If real-output is less than full-employment output, investment may also rise, accommodated of course by a marginal propensity to consume less than one. Just how investment will change will depend upon interest elasticities and the reaction of the money supply. Since, in accordance with the life-cycle hypothesis, increased wealth will generate higher planned consumption not only currently but over the entire life-cycle, rational firms will strive to invest more in anticipation of greater future consumption.

What is the effect of an implicit deficit brought on by the increase in real net contingency obligations such as price-indexed commitments for Social Security if we assume full (or fixed) employment? The answer, at least for the equilibrium or steady-state case, can be remarkably simple. According to equations (1) or (1′), at the existing price level the demand for real consumption would increase. The anticipation that real consumption would increase would generate increased investment demand according to (2). But since real output cannot increase, the price level, P will rise. If the money supply M, is not increased, the new equilibruim will entail a higher rate of interest (associated with a lower ratio of money to total government debt), less investment, and more consumption.

But this result, it should be clear, stems only from the assumption that the money supply is not accommodative. If the initial real value of the explicit government debt, D/P, is sufficiently high, at least higher than the addition of real (indexed) Social Security wealth, there would appear to be no reason why the price level, the money supply and all nominal variables cannot be increased in some proportion, w, such that the sum of explicit and implicit government debt, $D/P + wSSWN/wP$, will equal the original explicit debt, GD/P. Since, with the usual assumption of no money illusion, all real functions are homogenous of degree zero in nominal variables and the price level, if the initial system can be full-employment equilibrium, there is again no reason why there cannot be a corresponding new equilibrium with prices, the money supply (including outside money), and total government explicit and implicit interest-bearing debt all proportionately higher, but the interest rate, real consumption, real investment, real output, and the stock of real capital all unchanged. We are, however, abstracting from the possibility that parameters of $SSWN/P$ would be different from those of D/P in the equation for liquidity preference and for consumption. Agents may well view explicit government debt as much more substantial components of wealth and sources of liquidity than their very uncertain expectations – if they exist – of Social Security benefits in excess of social security taxes.

Notes

1. This section has been adapted from an earlier paper in French (Eisner, 1985), and from a more recent presentation to the Eastern Economic Association (Eisner, 1986b).
2. This appendix has been adapted and expanded from the appendix to chapter 7 in Eisner (1986a).

References

Barro, R. J. (1974) 'Are Government Bonds Net Wealth?' *Journal of Political Economy*, 82: 1095–1117.

Eisner, R. (1983) 'Social Security, Saving and Investment', *Journal of Macroeconomics*, 5: 1–19.

Eisner, R. (1985) 'Chomage Keynésien, prix et effets de richesse de la dette publique', in A. Barrère (ed.) *Keynes aujourd'hui: Théories et politiques* (Paris) pp.413–19.

Eisner, R. (1986a) *How Real Is the Federal Deficit*? (New York: The Free Press).

Eisner, R. (1986b) 'The Revolution Restored: Keynesian Unemployment, Inflation and Budget Deficits', *Eastern Economic Journal*, 12: 217–21.

Eisner, R. and P. J. Pieper (1984) 'A New View of the Federal Debt and Budget Deficits', *The American Economic Review*, 74: 11–29.

Fisher, I. (1933) 'The Debt Deflation Theory of Great Depressions', *Econometrica*, 1: 335–57.

Fisher, I. (1936) *100% Money* (New York: Adelphi).

Friedman, M. (1968) 'The Role of Monetary Policy', *The American Economic Review*, 58: 1–17.

Haberler, G. (1941) *Prosperity and Depression*, 3rd edn (Geneva: League of Nations).

Lange, O. (1938) 'The Rate of Interest and the Optimum Propensity to Consume', *Economica*, NS5: 12–32.

Lange, O. (1952) *Price Flexibility and Employment* (Bloomington, Ind.: Principia).

Metzler, L. A. (1951) 'Wealth, Saving, and the Rate of Interest', *Journal of Political Economy*, 59: 93–116.

Modigliani, F. and R. Brumberg (1954) 'Utility Analysis and the Consumption Function: An Interpretation of Cross-Section Data', in K. J. Kurihara (ed.), *Post Keynesian Economics* (New Brunswick, NJ: Rutgers University Press) pp.388–436.

Patinkin, D. (1948) 'Price Flexibility and Full Employment', *American Economic Review*, 38: 543–64.

Patinkin, D. (1965) *Money, Interest and Prices* (New York: Row Peterson).

Pigou, A. C. (1943) 'The Classical Stationary State', *Economic Journal*, 53: 343–51.

Pigou, A. C. (1947) 'Economic Progress in a Stable Environment', *Economica*, 14: 180–8.

Robinson, J. (1966) *An Essay on Marxian Economics*, 2nd edn (New York: St Martin's Press).

Tobin, J. (1980) *Asset Acumulation and Economic Activity* (Chicago: University of Chicago Press).

28 On the Goals of Economic Policy

James K. Galbraith*

1 QUESTIONS

What are the Questions? Where Do We Go From Here? What Now? Such queries decorate Joan Robinson's later policy essays. Yet the point is critical, not constructive, and one looks in vain there for a program of her own design. For the reader seeking to be led, it is slightly frustrating. Evidently, there is work to do.

Some thinking might well be directed anew to the design of economic goals. Social organizations – political parties, legislatures, administrations – are compulsive goal-setters. There is evidence, surveyed recently in Lindberg and Maier (1985) and by Borooah and Van der Ploeg (1985), that electorates judge governments by economic performance in their tenure. Yet, it is evident that the economic goals of record and the goals of fact are rarely the same. Too often, indeed, governments seem to operate in fine disregard for their legal mandates, especially those that pertain to the long term. For this, it is easy to blame the perfidy (or, equivalently, self-interest) of politicians, and to follow Lucas (1981, p.566) down the path of confining constitutional reform. But perhaps other values, such as that of representative democracy itself, constrain enthusiasm for such a choice. Hence an alternative seems needed, and perhaps one may be found in a judicious redefinition of the appropriate economic goals, and in certain structural reforms that would make their achievement more seriously possible, so as to bring our plans in this sphere into better alignment with our given constitutional rules.

The received goals are handed down to us: enshrined in our legislation, textbooks, models, minds. The political leader finds words for them on ritual occasions, as does the model builder in the first throat-clearing statement of the social welfare function. Neither pays serious attention to their achievement. In 1978 in the United States, for example, after years of legislative struggle, 'full' displaced 'maximum' as the qualifier describing the goal for 'employment' in the law governing such matters, having been denied such status thirty-two years before. Though actual employment rates have not since been as high, the political leaders of the eighties regard

*I thank George Feiwel, Lucy Ferguson and Jim Rebitzer for helpful comments.

their predecessors as failures and themselves as exemplars of success. Meanwhile, the models adjust, estimated Phillips curves shift outward, so that expectations of what can be achieved deteriorate in step with actual achievement.

Consider the Declaration of Policy of the Employment Act of 1946, as amended in 1978 (15 USC 1021):

> The Congress hereby declares that it is the continuing policy and responsibility of the Federal Government to use all practicable means, consistent with its needs and obligations and other essential national policies, and with the assistance and cooperation of both small and larger businesses, agriculture, labor and State and local governments, to coordinate and utilize all its plans, functions, and resources for the purpose of creating and maintaining, in a manner calculated to foster and promote free competitive enterprise and the general welfare, conditions which promote useful employment opportunities, including self-employment, for those able, willing, and seeking to work, and promote full employment and production, increased real income, balanced growth, a balanced Federal budget, adequate productivity growth, proper attention to national priorities, achievement of an improved trade balance through increased exports and improvement in the international competitiveness of agriculture, business and industry, and reasonable price stability as provided in section 5(b) of this Act.

Eight distinct major objectives are specified in this statute. They are, in order listed: (1) full employment and production; (2) increased real income; (3) balanced growth; (4) a balanced Federal budget; (5) adequate productivity growth; (6) proper attention to national priorities; (7) achievement of an improved trade balance through increased exports and improvement in the international competitive position of agriculture, business and industry; and (8) reasonable price stability. Of these, 'balanced growth', and 'proper attention to national priorities', are open to the complaint that they are either too vague or essentially non-economic. A balanced federal budget is an accounting or intermediate rather than a final economic objective. We focus on the remaining five, and ask: could judicious reinterpretation breathe new life into this dead letter?

2 FULL EMPLOYMENT AND PRODUCTION

Full employment became conceptually possible as a policy issue with the Keynesian revolution, and a matter of serious political dialogue only during World War II. Three conditions made the goal of permanent peacetime full employment seem coherent in the 1940s: (i) the achievement of full employment in the war effort and the general technical optimism thereby inspired; (ii) the rise in the power of the state and of labor within the state, and an increasing disesteem of business values, which placed the instruments of attaining full employment in hands that seemed prepared to use them; and (iii) a social conception of full employment that for most people meant male workers in industrial jobs, and hence made the identification of 'full employment' with 'full production' virtually automatic. On this last, note the definition of full employment in *Full Employment in a Free Society*, the Beveridge Report: 'having always more vacant jobs than unemployed *men*, not slightly fewer jobs. It means that the jobs are at fair wages, of such a kind and so located that the unemployed *men* can reasonably be expected to take them' (emphasis added).

Four decades have evidently eroded confidence in these conditions. Today, we feel boxed in by a diminished sense of technical possibility, whether well or poorly founded, and by an undoubted reversal of political fortunes as between business, labor and the state. But these are possibly transitory, matters of confidence and of politics; having turned once the wheel can turn again. The collapse of the sociological stereotype of the industrial worker is by contrast clearly irreversible. So attention should rightly focus first on what this might mean for the objective of full employment.

Rising female labor force participation rates are a longstanding phenomenon, and the received ideas surrounding them appear to have formed under the favorable conditions of the early decades. Over the fifties and sixties, real wages for women were rising, both absolutely and relatively to men, and married women especially were presumed to be substituting market work for homework in response to these favorable incentives. This seemed to explain well the rise in civilian labor force participation rate for women over the first quarter century after the war, from 27 to 36 per cent for all women and from 15 to 34 per cent for married women (Cain, 1966). The higher unemployment experience of such groups could then be said to reflect a larger frictional element in their work lives, transitional oversupply of their relatively undifferentiated skills, discrimination, smaller endowments of search experience and ability. And it was therefore reasonable to regard fluctuations in the raw unemployment rate attributable to rising female or teenage labor force participation as unrelated to the underlying state of demand.

It would seem, however, that the conditions of the most recent fifteen years should call these judgments back into question. Real wages[1] have fallen since 1972, and now stand below the value for 1963. A rising intrinsic attractiveness of work, clearly true in some cases as more interesting jobs open to some women, does not seem to characterize most modern stenographic, retail trades and other service employment where the vast bulk of incremental employment has occurred. Yet, despite all this, the labor force participation rate for women has continued to rise sharply: 53.3 per cent in 1984 compared with 45.9 per cent in 1975.[2]

Perhaps the explanation lies in the dynamics of the household, faced, in 1970 and therafter, for the first time in young memory with the risk of principal-earner unemployment and the prospect of declining real income. The effect of other family income on labor force participation of auxiliary workers is long established. Suppose too that households conceive these things at least partly in relative terms (i.e. in terms of living *standards*), and therefore have stable notions of satisfactory and unsatisfactory consumption possibility sets. In an initial period, say right after World War II, moderate-income households were widely able to meet their standards of consumption by relying on a single earner. So long as the economy grew steadily, the erosion in such arrangements was slow; community consumption standards did not rise sharply above the levels attainable within traditional family employment patterns, opportunities for supranormal household advance, even if where they existed, were checked by routines of community life and patterns of occupational discrimination, while the risk of extraordinary decline was likewise slight.

Recessions, on the other hand, may – and did – induce dramatic change. Suddenly, normal living standards cannot with high certainty be maintained by normal labor force involvement. Those unemployed outright face the most immediate threat. But others, though not immediately hit with direct material loss, are nevertheless worse off. The *risk* of unemployment – a wholly new thing in many people's working lives as recently as 1970 – enters their lives. They fret. And they react to insure against the risk, through the diversification of employment experience within the household, which takes effect after the slump passes and new job opportunities start to become available.

Other reactions follow. Every recession of the post-war period has struck hardest at manufacturing employment, and has led to a subsequent growth of non-manufacturing relative to manufacturing work. Conditions of the labor market are such that the relative wage outside the manufacturing sector must fall as competition for non-manufacturing jobs grows more intense. For those formerly living well on no-longer-available factory employment, the two-income household becomes, after the disruption, the only means to restore household consumption to near its former growth path. As recessions recur, this process continues: each wave of disruption impels more auxiliary workers from previously comfortable, newly insecure families into the labor market.

The process, once started, can be self-reinforcing even if recessions do not recur. As more families acquire second earners, the barriers that previously existed to female labor force participation do erode. Some households whose material living standards were not directly reduced in the recession now perceive an opportunity for advance that was not previously open. Their multiple labor force participation moves them up on the distribution of income. Housing prices, and the prices of other household assets in inelastic supply (college educations, for example), may rise, as these goods are rationed to those who can most afford them. In consequence, families previously satisfied with one earner's income may find their real consumption standards displaced downward as two-earner families move up. Their reaction – which follows a 'tipping' pattern as described by Schelling (1978, pp. 91–115) – would in turn create a powerful incentive for more householders to join the labor pool.

Such labor supply shifts are in the final analysis demand-induced – e.g. by an initial fall in effective demand at the aggregate level, resulting specifically in a decline in the availability of well-paid, secure industrial jobs. The labor market is flexible: people adjust their labor supply to sustained adverse conditions. Intra-household risk-spreading, a desire to maintain consumption standards, and neighborhood effects in asset markets account for the nature of the supply response. Over time, the previously typical family solely supported by the affluent worker diminishes in number, and the multi-earner family achieving comparable consumption standards at a higher level of group market-place effort takes its place. The price of achieving this theoretically harmonious interpretation is a rude admission about social conditions – that for the representative family they were better beforehand.

Now to the main point: the meaning of the conventional unemployment rate as an index of welfare across such changes is murky. In September of 1985, as during all of 1980, the overall unemployment rate was 7.0 per cent. But manufacturing employment was 1 million *less* in the later period (everything else was up by 9 million). By numerous indicators the distribution of income was less equal in 1985. Was the welfare of the working population entirely unchanged by these shifts? It seems doubtful.

The traditional perspective allows the use of the raw unemployment rate as an index of social welfare changes in the short run, while in the longer run adjusting the numbers to filter out the atypically adverse experience of women and teenagers, along the lines pioneered by Perry (1970), so as to concentrate on unemployment clearly identified with the business cycle. This has led, under recent conditions, to the conclusion that 'things are not as bad as they seem' – if it weren't, that is, for all those women and kids. Desirable concomitant changes in social norms and a breakdown of discriminatory barriers reinforce the impression that we should accept higher unemployment rates for women and minorities in the transition to their full integration in the labor market.

The alternative perspective leads to an entirely opposite inference: the women and kids are telling us something about a secular decline in the quality of all available jobs. The men can find work – but it is not always good work, relative to past norms, otherwise fewer women and fewer kids would be out 'on the market' – both those who live within traditional family structures and those outside them. The unemployment rate is misleading, not because it is an inaccurately high reflection of the true state of the labor market, but because it misses a central ingredient of labor market experience, namely the growing underemployment of what used to be called 'heads of household'. Employment is still better than unemployment for any individual at any given moment, but over time higher total employment, and even greater equality both across job types and across households as highly paid manufacturing employment declines in the proportion to the total, can yet result in stagnant production and declining welfare.

3 INCREASED REAL INCOME

If full employment has thus become an uncertain trumpet, what can take its place? The fundamentals of growth theory, of the utilitarian theory of human behavior and of the theory of the household, suggest a candidate. They tell us to focus on the sustainable consumption, on the standard of living – appropriately modified, of course, for ethical, environmental and other long-range or social concerns. Thus the second objective of the Full Employment and Balanced Growth Act, increased real income, is at least firmly rooted in respectable theory.

The objective of increased real income may be pursued in every nation's case in two ways: internally by fostering investment and a high and efficient use of resources, and externally through the development of comparative advantage in international trade. That is, all countries may advance by pursuing balanced development, irrespective of their international position. But, trade theory teaches, those who select a strategy of specialization appropriate to their resource base, physical and human, will advance more quickly.

We may therefore subsume two of the remaining goals, 'adequate productivity growth', and 'achievement of an improved trade balance through increased exports and improvements in the competitiveness of agriculture, business and industry', under the more general rubric of increased real income.

4 PRODUCTIVITY GROWTH

High rates of productivity growth are sought for three basic reasons: to improve living standards, to facilitate price stabilization, and to foster international competitiveness. However, only the first result is analytically reliable, and then only in the context of full utilization of resources.

Achieving the maximum rate of rise in living standards depends on achieving high rates of technological advance to be sure, but only *with* sustained full utilization of resources. Salter understood this point from the first words of his classic study: 'As an almost inevitable consequence of full employment, the post-war decade has witnessed an upsurge of interest in productivity' (1959, p.1). And the converse also holds: from an initial position of underemployment, productivity growth as such is neither necessary nor sufficient for improving the general standard of life. Nothing guarantees that output *per capita* will rise with output per worker, nor that gains will offset losses in the aggregate. All economists know this, of course, but there has been an undoubted tendency, especially in the last fifteen years, to focus on productivity growth as a policy issue *as if* the precondition of sustained full employment had been met, and to neglect the famous conclusion David Ricardo came to in chapter XXXI, 'On Machinery', of the third edition of the *Principles of Political Economy and Taxation*:

> That the opinion entertained by the labouring class, that the employment of machinery is frequently detrimental to their interests, is not founded on prejudice and error, but is conformable to the correct principles of political economy. (1951, p.392)

There is an empirical issue here: is full employment or underemployment in fact the typical initial position? But this question is confused by the aforementioned questions about what is shown by the unemployment rate. It is not resolved either by estimates of the gap between actual and potential national income as in Denison (1979, p.12), which measure only what could actually be produced with the capital stock in existence, not the more nebulous – but yet relevant – question of what *might have been produced* on a former, more successful growth and investment path.

If involuntary displacement to less productive sectors, as well as less-than-wholly voluntary abandonment of domesticity and education for those same sectors, ought, as I have argued, to count as forms of underemployment, then perhaps our internal productivity efforts are misdirected. We should begin to distinguish between the reallocation of resources toward higher productivity growth *sectors* within the bounds of existing technology, and the pursuit of technological improvement primarily through high-volume production, increasing returns and 'learning by doing', on the one hand, and the fostering of rapid capital–labor substitution and displacement in a context of less rapid growth in production, on the other.

A credible strategy for sustained real growth of demand and investment may well be the best strategy for sustained productivity growth. While the slowdown in US productivity growth in the past fifteen years remains, as Denison (1979) observed, 'a mystery', we are now in a position at least to reject the oft-stated view that the rising burden of government – or other well-defined influences on the 'supply side' – is in some sense responsible for it. Furthermore, there is some convergence toward the view that interruptions in the supply of capital services – stemming from the more frequent recessions of the past fifteen years as compared with the previous fifteen – were a significant factor (Baily, 1983; Bruno and Sachs, 1985). Consequently, government actions which forestall recessions may prove the most effective means of boosting productivity growth, even if they contribute nothing to higher productivity directly.[3]

Moreover, an enlarged role of government in the pursuit of sustained demand growth need not be necessarily sterile from the standpoint of the supply side. Some things that government does, surely, are essential to sustaining high rates of general productivity growth. The elementary case for such public complementarities has been made elsewhere (JEC, 1982, pp.107–44; Galbraith, 1984). They include: education, especially technical education; basic scientific research, and infrastructure. Only by maintaining an advanced knowledge and public capital base can a nation hope to remain at the technological frontiers.

Some analysts (for example, Thurow, 1985) equate productivity growth *per se* with competitiveness in international trade. But there is no reason why high productivity growth at the national level is *per se* necessary to trade. One can, for example, have high productivity growth within the traded goods sector, but low productivity growth overall as inputs are released from that sector for less nominally 'productive' uses – and no loss of competitiveness since low-productivity growth outside the traded goods sector is irrelevant to trade. As Denison (1964) pointed out, adoption of new technique proceeds rapidly even if overall rates of investment are low. Or, one may simply have a high degree of product innovation in traded goods, with no measured effect on productivity growth since neither output indices nor input measures change, and yet maintain competitiveness despite low averages all around. Something like this must have happened to the US in the late 1970s, when our current account remained in balance, due to increasing manufactured exports, despite zero or negative aggregate productivity growth, as shown by Lawrence (1984, p.75). For this reason, it seems necessary to distinguish between aggregate productivity enhancements pursued by internal demand and supply management, and the ingredients of a nation's specific success in world markets.

5 EXPORTS AND COMPARATIVE ADVANTAGE

Each nation pursues accumulation by tactics corresponding to its resources and comparative advantage. For expository purposes, we may make the following slightly non-standard classification:

1. Leading Technological Powers (LTPs), with advanced industrial sectors, whose comparative advantage lies in the development of new technologies, and in the production and export of technologically advanced goods, often primarily capital goods, often to a world market.
2. Intermediate Manufacturing Powers (IMPs), capable of exploiting established industrial niches, often with superior labor relations and quality control, but who do not possess the research and development base to develop fundamental new products and processes themselves.
3. Resource-based Less Developed Countries (LDCs), rich and poor, dependent on agriculture, mining, energy.
4. Subsistence economies, backward, miserable, and essentially outside the orbits of world trade.

This classification provides a hierarchy of available standards of living. Nations at each level (like families in the labor market) aspire to move upward to the next: subsistence economies search for bauxite, cobalt and oil, LDCs seek to build a manufacturing sector; IMPs seek to graft onto their industrial successes a self-starting research capability. At the top, suppliers of technical innovation and the capital goods which crystallize such innovation seek – if they are wise – to maintain their lead.[4]

The mid-twentieth-century United States clearly falls in category 1, indeed in its pre-eminent position, despite the strong presence of traditional manufacturing and a rich endowment of resources. It has also, and not by coincidence, enjoyed the world's ranking living standards, certain small economies of Europe and Middle East sheikhdoms excepted. The means of doing so can be thought of at least partly in Schumpeterian terms: as the dynamic monopoly profits that we have reaped by being the sole supplier to the world of innumerable pieces of tangible and intangible capital equipment. The post-war 'Americanization' of the world economy and culture reflects – not the insularity in terms of which Americans sometimes conceive their lot – but their immense weight of influence over the opportunities for development open to everyone else.

We may thus pose the crucial question facing the United States in a tidy way: Do we aspire to sustain the living standards available to countries in category 1, and to avoid falling back to the standards generally available in category 2, diminished as they are by the necessity of paying out rather than being paid the quasi-rents owed to the technological leader? If so, how do we maintain the position of comparative advantage in advanced technology and advanced service trade that secures to us the rents that accrue to the holder of that particular world role?

What is needed here is policy based essentially on Adam Smith, but the Smith, not of the Invisible Hand, but of the principle to which Lord Kaldor returned recently in his third Okun Lecture at Yale University (1985): '*The division of labour is limited by the extent of the market*.'

Now it is perfectly obvious that the extent of the US *consumer* market is fully sufficient to exhaust the division of labor in production of most consumer goods. Thus consumer goods companies, domestic or foreign, can grow to full maturity by selling entirely within or into the US. Capital goods manufacturers cannot do the same. The extent of the US market – or any market of less than global scale – relative to economies of scale and the cost-saving potential of long production runs in capital goods is just much smaller. Companies producing capital goods face the fact that only a global market for their goods fully exhausts the possibilities inherent in the division of labor. US firms in investment goods industries must compete in global markets if they are to remain competive even at home – something that, say, General Motors or Whirlpool Appliances is not obliged to do.

The second point, equally obvious on reflection, is that it is investment goods that pre-eminently embody high technology. In the nature of things the consumer, in contrast to the offshore oil wildcatter or Singapore Airlines, is a consumer of relatively low- and middle-technology goods. Consumers do not buy exotic technologies for a simple reason: they cannot manage them; by the time an exotic technology (lasers, microelectronics) has been packaged for mass consumption it is, virtually by definition, no longer exotic. The high-tech in the personal computer is like nothing compared to the high-tech in the semiconductor manufacturing process. Consumers buy microcomputers but they do not buy (even as hobbyists) silicon-wafer-slicing machines.

Thus the boom among US capital goods producing companies through 1979 corresponded to a boom in high-technology production. It stemmed from a demand surge that went well beyond internal markets. The marginal high-technology markets overseas, in turn, kept US capital good industries – aerospace, electronics, energy equipment – on their technological frontiers, so that technically US aircraft, computers, offshore drilling rigs and so on remained second to none. Thus US high technology balanced our trade through 1979. Moreover, this was no ephemeral success: longer production runs and learning by doing mean falling per unit costs as units cumulated. Had the process gone on long enough, ultimately the dollar could have strengthened without threatening renewed disequilibrium in trade.

But the process was cut off. The Reagan Administration diverted the currency value to the objective of disinflation, producing recession in the US and depression in parts of the world heavily dependent on US trade. Markets where the US had its strongest traditional ties (Latin American in contrast to the Far East) fell most sharply, while the high dollar limited our ability to compete in more distant and more prosperous places. Correspondingly, the world position of US investment goods firms has started to erode.

It will be some time, of course, before the full effects of the declining US relative position on the outward-looking, investment goods, technological frontier are felt in a crisis of those industries with respect to their internal markets. But where an industry stands at the apex of an outward-looking chain (for example in farm equipment) some signs of crisis have already appeared. These will multiply as time goes on. It is not clear, moreover, at what point the damage can no longer be reversed by the device of ending the high dollar exchange-rate regime. Comparative advantage, once lost in the high technology sectors, may not be readily regained.

Thus consideration of trade leads us to a fundamental asymmetry in policy. From an initial position of advantage, a high-technology, investment goods exporting nation need only maintain sensible macroeconomic policies conducive to sustained growth, plus the elementary ingredients of public capital formation, in order to remain in the vanguard. This is what the Brookings economists have repeatedly affirmed. But from a position where leadership has already been lost, things are very different. Catching up requires mobilization of resources, even international mobilization, on a scale that can only be managed by government. The continuing debate between exponents and detractors of industrial policy (and debt policy, affecting international demand) thus ought to turn on an empirical issue: have we or have we not already slipped too far?

6 REASONABLE PRICE STABILITY

We may now turn to the final stated goal. Here the question that needs pining down is, 'Why should we care?'

Most economists dislike inflation[5] but have difficulty explaining, precisely, why. The many stories commonly boil down to uncertainty, imperfect information and adjustment costs, too much acknowledgment of which would conflict with the higher theoretical pursuits of many of the same economists. The closer one's model comes to approximate the perfectly competitive, perfect-information free market economy, the *less* one can say with formal certitude about the costs of inflation.

Those who are both theoretically pure and intellectually honest are left with aesthetics. One witness before the Joint Economic Committee in 1981, in an exchange with Chairman Henry Reuss (JEC, 1981, p.32), put the professional case in pristine form: 'Zero percent inflation is the only inflation makes any sense. You may have wondered why God put a zero in the middle of all the numbers. That's because that's the optimal inflation rate.' On examination, the witness denied that God had set any comparable target for unemployment, 'as far as I know, in the King James version anyway'.

Political leaders, journalists and others, faced with guidance of this order, are understandably at a loss. They persist in the deviant thought that nominal events have real effects. As Professor Hahn (1980, p.80) summarized:

> The government's inconsistent beliefs are widely shared: '. . . reduction in inflation is needed to lay the basis of sustainable growth' (Times Leader, 10 May 1980). Presumably this sort of belief explains why governments all over the world are busy engineering recessions. All this should not stop one from pointing out that the belief has no foundation in general theory and certainly no foundation in any version of the Monetarist theory which these advocates typically embrace.

Left out of the analysis is a related puzzle of which the politicians, at least, are wholly conscious: not why is inflation bad, but why do people think it is bad? Can inflation-aversion rest entirely on money illusion or, worse, on theoretical error? And why do some countries (US, UK, Germany) with inflation have an 'inflation problem' (producing domestic political trauma) while others (France, Japan, Italy) seem not to? The hypothesized costlessness of perfectly anticipated inflation clearly fails to explain this: inflation rates in countries inured to inflation are characteristically not only higher but also more variable than where populations are highly inflation-averse. Are the politicians simply wrongly worried about inflation in some countries (those with strong traditions in economic theory, yet!) and rightly unworried in others?

In sum, the merits of an anti-inflation objective are not clearly thought through, not carefully reconciled with the little that economic theory has to say on the matter. In consequence, we have not paid adequate attention to the character of the polity's aversion to inflation, nor to the subtleties of an anti-inflation policy design tailored to the character of that aversion. What we can say for certain is that simple formulations of the social welfare function in which the instantaneous rate of inflation and the instantaneous rate of unemployment are aggregated lineally (or, worse! quadratically) cannot be right, except, of course, to the extent that they tell you that (in a steady state) less of both is better than more of either, which we already knew.

There is an omitted consideration. *If* maintaining technological superiority – or any other public purpose – requires the attention, planning, commitment and resources of the state, then the state mechanism must be available. Perhaps it is the threatened pre-emption of this ability to act, the threat to the independence or room for maneuver of the state, that constitutes inflation's gravest danger.

Keynes, of course, understood this in 1919: not economic but political instability, not redistribution across class lines but the increasingly speculative character of individual changes in status within the existing class structure, not massive wealth transfers to debtors *per se* but the disruption of financial relations is the threat, while it is the political order not the productive process that is threatened: 'all permanent relations between debtors and creditors, which form the ultimate foundation of capitalism, become so utterly disordered as to be almost meaningless, and the process of wealth-getting degenerates into a gamble and a lottery' (Keynes 1919, p. 149).

Keynes spoke from European experience of his time, but it is obvious that his results are not invariant to political and financial structure. That is, the degree of national inflation-aversion varies with national institutions. It is only under certain types of representative government and certain financial systems, that it seriously disorders political life and disturbs financial security. In others, it does not have this effect.

Democratic systems, indeed all governments with the ability to do so and claims to legitimacy in the modern world, develop ways and means of buffering their populations and the organized constituencies among them from extreme changes in economic condition, including from the increase in the level of undesired uncertainty about prices and capital values, of the speculative element in business life, that inflationary times produce. Democratic systems in the West either have relatively open political systems with a high degree of party competition and viable alternative governments (such as the US, UK and Germany) or not (France before 1981, Japan, Italy). Where the political system is competitive, the forces seeking protection turn to the political arena, and inflation produces political crisis. Where the political system is less competitive, the cooperation between state and business is less politicized, and the buffering function may safely be institutionalized. In Japan this is done through the private banks linked to the large industrial groupings, who assume more long-range financial responsibility for the companies they lend to than do commercial banks in the US or UK (Sakakibara *et al.*, 1982). In France, it is done through state control of the financial sector, equally effective before and after the final nationalizations of 1981 (Cohen, Galbraith and Zysman, 1981). In either case, the political crisis does not occur.

In the United States in the late 1970s, as domestic inflation rose, structural shifts in comparative advantage and pattern of trade created a large amorphous class of self-perceived 'inflation-losers'. Among them were industrial corporations – steel, autos were the trite examples – for whom the lottery had turned out badly. Their chosen path of redress in this instance was proposed reform of the depreciation provisions of the tax code, and their battle-cry was the removal of 'distortions' said to have been induced by the interaction of inflation and historic-cost inventory accounting. Economists could, and did, argue that reform on these grounds made little sense: 'inflation' in the pure sense was not really the culprit behind the relative decline of heavy industry in this period, and anyway there was a private remedy: the corporation could leverage itself so that the depreciation of its debts offset the overstatement of its profits. However, this was an *ex ante* argument; whereas the real debate was over *ex post* public restitution. The arguments were unavailing.

The political system is a limited instrument. Once caught up in a gargantuan struggle over distribution of wealth among the already wealthy, lasting roughly from 1978 through 1982, it could sustain attention on few other issues. Social reform and economic initiative disappeared from the legislative calendars. Tax relief lobbies – for heavy industry and for upper income families, whose share in total income was not actually falling but whose complaint about bracket creep was at least legitimately related to inflation – displaced virtually all other constituency groups from the national agenda. It is not altogether certain, of course, that this would not have happened even if prices had remained stable. Still, inflation tied numerous diverse concerns – business and individual – together for a brief period, allowing the spurious claim (as over depreciation) to combine with the real (as over bracket creep) in a powerful political potion. It is a unity of purpose that lobbies for the powerful have not, in the absence of inflation, succeeded in replicating since.

Hence an argument for price stabilization that is not subject to the nominal-real confusion. Reasonably stable prices are a necessary precondition to calm political consideration of increasing real income, of increasing productivity, of maintaining comparative advantage in high technology capital goods sectors. The United States, as a two-party democracy with a tradition of alternating power, does not have the option of buffering inflation outside the political process. It must therefore seek to bring inflation under satisfactory control through the political process.

In specifying the precise nature of this goal, the dimension of time must be considered. Political crises are not dangerous if they pass quickly. It is the chronic crisis – such as the current one over the deficit – that paralyzes political minds. To put the matter in familiar terms: it takes time for expectations to crystallize into an intractable politico-economic problem. If time can be denied to this process, much will have been achieved.

So, contrary to the economists and their quadratic loss functions, short bursts of high inflation are to be feared *less* than longer, chronic states. It is long periods of price stability, when inflation is below the threshold at which it is thought to be a problem, the expectation of which we should cultivate. It is such periods – even if disrupted occasionally by external shocks – which breed the self-assurance, confidence in government, and sense of resilience which vigorous political institutions require. It is such periods that policy should seek to build, to reinforce, and to return to if they are interrupted. The plain may be subject to an occasional flood, and it is clearly nice to be able to keep the floods small. But, large or small, if floods are not too frequent people will live there nevertheless. What matters for them is how long the plain can be expected to remain dry, not how much water passes over it when it floods.

That being so, anti-inflation policy will succeed – and be perceived as having succeeded – if it only concentrates a given amount of price-level change into a short period of time, and so permits a relatively rapid return to price stability following an external shock. Thus the Japanese ate their oil shock with high inflation in a single year, and thereafter enjoyed decelerating inflation for the rest of the decade, never incorporating fears of accelerating inflation into their expectation. The US, with actual inflation lower in each year than in Japan, talked itself nevertheless into a national neurosis by the end of the decade.

Clearly, the US price stabilization strategy must be changed. This is not a question of trade-offs, but rather of categorical imperatives that must be reconciled through policy design. Moreover, because the world does not sit still while one nation sorts out its internal political difficulties, it is a problem of reconciliation that must be faced within a limited time. The old image of policy as a trade-off between unemployment and inflation is misleading in the present context, because it seems to imply smooth loss functions in the two variables, and because it assumes that ground lost can be more or less readily recovered. In a dynamic world this is not true: the use of recession to fight inflation has irreversible costs, while the pursuit of global technological leadership without price stability cannot succeed because, as the late 1970s showed, it cannot be sustained.

Notes

1. Measured as average weekly earnings in the private nonagricultural sector for production or nonsupervisory employees. Data are from the *Economic Report of the President* (1985, p.277).
2. The actual rise may be contrasted with a projection in Reynolds (1978, p.26) of a 45.9 per cent female participation rate by 1990.
3. This argument is similar to that made by Godley (1985), and greeted with dismay by Salant (1985) and Dillard (1986).
4. The statute does speak, somewhat regrettably given 1978 conditions, of 'an improved trade balance'. Happily, the mercantilist overtone of that usage is diffused by the subsequent clause.
5. There are highly reputable doubters, such as Wood (1978, p.218).

References

Baily, M. N. (1983) 'Will Productivity Growth Recover? Has It Done So Already?', *Brookings Discussion Papers in Economics* (December).

Beveridge, W. (1944) *Full Employment in A Free Society* (London: HMSO).

Borooah, V. K. and F. Van der Ploeg (1983) *Political Aspects of the Economy* (Cambridge: Cambridge University Press).

Bruno, M. and J. Sachs (1985) *The Economics of Worldwide Stagflation* (Cambridge, Mass.: Harvard University Press).

Cain, G. (1966) *Married Women in the Labor Force* (Chicago: University of Chicago Press).

Cohen, S., J. K. Galbraith and J. Zysman (1981) 'Credit Policy and Industrial Policy in France', in *Monetary Policy, Selective Credit Policy and Industrial Policy in France, Britain, West Germany and Sweden*, A Staff Study Prepared for the Use of the Joint Economic Committee (Washington: Government Printing Office).

Denison, E. F. (1964) 'The Irrelevance of the Embodied Question', *American Economic Review*, 54: 90–4.

Denison, E. F. (1979) *Accounting for Slower Economic Growth: The United States in the 1970s* (Washington: Brookings Institution).

Dillard, D. (1986) 'Review of *Keynes and the Modern World*', in *Journal of Economic Issues*, XX: 217–20.

Economic Report of the President (1985) (Washington: Government Printing Office).

Galbraith, J. K. (1984) 'The Debate About Industrial Policy', in Alperovitz and Skurski (eds) *American Economic Policy: Problems and Prospects* (South Bend: University of Notre Dame Press), pp.89–108.

Godley, W. (1985) 'Management of Real National Income and Expenditure', in Worswick and Trevithick (eds) *Keynes and the Modern World* (Cambridge: Cambridge University Press).

Hahn, F. (1980) 'Memorandum', in *Memoranda on Monetary Policy*, House of Commons Treasury and Civil Service Committee, Session 1979–80 (London: HMSO).

Joint Economic Committee (1981) *Outlook for Recession* (Washington: Government Printing Office).

Joint-Economic Committee, *1982 Joint Economic Report* (Washington: Government Printing Office).

Kaldor, N. (1985) 'Cumulative Causation and Interregional Trade', in *Economics Without Equilibrium* (Cardiff: University College Cardiff Press).

Keynes, J. M. (1919) *The Economic Consequences of the Peace* (London: Macmillan).

Lawrence, R. Z. (1984) *Can America Compete?* (Washington: Brookings Institution).

Lindberg, L. N. and C. S. Maier (1985) *The Politics of Inflation and Economic Stagnation* (Washington: Brookings Institution).

Lucas, R. E. (1981) 'Tobin and Monetarism: A Review Article', *Journal of Economic Literature*, 19.

Perry, G. L. (1970) 'Changing Labor Markets and Inflation', *Brookings Papers on Economic Activity*, 3: 411–41.

Reynolds, L. G. (1978) *Labor Economics and Labor Relations*, 7th edn (Englewood Cliffs, NJ: Prentice-Hall).

Ricardo, D. (Sraffa ed.) (1951) *Principles of Political Economy and Taxation* (Cambridge: Cambridge University Press).

Sakakibara, E. *et al.* (1982) *Japanese Financial System in Comparative Perspective*, A Study Prepared for the Joint Economic Committee (Washington: Government Printing Office).

Salant, W. (1985) 'Review of *Keynes and the Modern World*', *Journal of Economic Literature*, XXIII: 1176–85.
Salter, W. E. G. (1959) *Productivity and Technical Change* (Cambridge: Cambridge University Press).
Schelling, T. C. (1978) *Micromotives and Macrobehavior* (New York: W. W. Norton).
Thurow, L. C. (1985) *The Zero-Sum Solution* (New York: W. W. Norton).
Wood, A. (1978) *A Theory of Pay* (Cambridge: Cambridge University Press).

Part IX

The Economics of War and Peace

29 Economic Cooperation as a Means of Improving East–West Relations

Dietrich Fischer*

Joan Robinson was not only interested in economic theory for its own sake, but was deeply concerned with human welfare in all its aspects. She sought to improve the human condition through a better understanding of the interactive forces that move human society. In addition to problems of economic development and fair distribution of income and wealth, she was also particularly concerned with the squandering of resources in the arms race and with ways to reduce international tensions and avoid war.

I had the opportunity to get to know Joan at a week-long Seminar on Economic Theory and Policies for Growth held at the Centro de Investigacion y Docencia Economicas (CIDE) in Mexico City, in September 1977. She once remarked sarcastically that the Egyptians had found a way to create some artificial, inexhaustible demand to stimulate the economy by building pyramids. But modern societies had found something even better, military spending. The more we had, the more we needed!

In the following, I wish to outline how economic motives can serve to help improve international relations and reduce the danger of war, rather than driving us toward mutual extinction through the competitive accumulation of ever more destructive and destabilizing weapons systems.

1 MECHANISMS DRIVING THE ARMS RACE

The nuclear arms race between the United States and the Soviet Union, which has produced the weapons which pose the greatest threat to our survival, has many interwoven causes. One can distinguish between internal and external causes. Among the external causes is mutual fear and the desire to maintain security through military superiority. Of course, if one side has raced ahead of the other (in the past usually the United States), the other is hardly content with a position of military inferiority. It tries to catch up, or to surpass its competitor. (A Russian student wrote as answer to an examination question on the current situation in the United States

*The author is grateful for a Fellowship in International Peace and Security studies from the MacArthur Foundation, which facilitated completion of this chapter.

and the Soviet Union: 'The United States is slowly moving towards the edge of an abyss. The Soviet Union is rapidly catching up with the United States and surpassing it.') The result of this myopic race for superiority, which fails to take into account the effect of a one-sided move on the security of the other side, or even its likely reaction, has brought greater insecurity to both sides.

But external stimulation is not the only cause of the arms race. To deter a nuclear attack, it is not necessary to possess nuclear weapons in equal numbers as a potential opponent. A small fraction would still represent a formidable deterrent. McGeorge Bundy (1982) has stressed that 'the losses that would be sustained in receiving an attack of 100 megatons far outweigh any "gains" in delivering ten times as much to an enemy'. Certainly, to possess 90 per cent of the arsenal of an opponent is ample to deter a nuclear attack, even if one accepts all the assumptions of nuclear strategists. If each side would declare itself satisfied with possessing 90 per cent of the nuclear arsenal of the other side (or if one side would accept 90 per cent and the other side seek strict parity), the arms race would unwind rapidly, even without any mutual agreement, and without any risk to either side's security.

There are powerful economic interests that seek to exaggerate the threat posed by the other side in order to win approval for greater military expenditures, and greater profits. Richard Barnet (1971, p.97) writes that one of the national security managers' greatest fear is that they might run out of enemies. Enemy images need constantly to be recreated.

Selling arms to the government is generally far more profitable than selling products to private consumers. Government officials who can spend public funds have a natural tendency to be more generous than people who have to pay out of their own pocket. Also, officers in charge of signing defense contracts are frequently rewarded later with lucrative posts in the defense industry. They have little desire to spoil their chances of future employment by being too cost conscious. Defense contractors also have a desire to give financial support to election campaigns of representatives who are sympathetic to their interests.

In order to counterbalance these forces which help propel the arms race, it is necessary to nurture economic interests favoring a world at peace. Two sources of such motives are the fear of destruction in case of war, and the profitability of international economic cooperation in peace time.

2 CONTRIBUTIONS OF ECONOMICS TO WAR PREVENTION

Physicists have calculated the consequences of a nuclear war in terms of heat, blast and radiation. Astronomers and climatologists have predicted a prolonged period of cold and dark ('nuclear winter') resulting from the dust and smoke hurled up into the atmosphere by a nuclear war. Physicians have warned of the medical consequences. John Kenneth Galbraith has recently proposed that economists should join their colleagues in other professions and describe what an economy after a 'limited' nuclear war would look like, with the interruption of transportation, the destruction of productive capacity, the areas contaminated through radioactive fallout, etc. Before accepting a cure, a patient must be convinced that he or she has a problem. Similarly, before governments and business interests are prepared to support alternative approaches to securing their perceived interests, they must be convinced that nuclear war is not an option. But fear alone is not a sufficient motivation for change. A patient must be persuaded that an effective cure for his or her ills exists. Similarly, it is necessary to show that better approaches to the defense of nations' vital interests are available than the threat of using nuclear weapons.

Besides adding to the voices warning of danger, economists can also show possible solutions. They can investigate the causes of arms races and ways to escape that vicious circle. They can also explore ways in which both sides' stakes in maintaining peace can be raised, through the development of mutually beneficial economic cooperation.

3 SUPERORDINATE GOALS

A famous experiment in social psychology has shown that among the most effective means to overcome group conflict are 'superordinate goals'. These are goals that are in both side's interest, but cannot be reached by either side alone, only through cooperation. Sherif and Sherif (1969) describe an experiment in which they randomly split a group of boys arriving at a camp in two, with each subgroup choosing its own name and living in a separate cabin. They then led the two groups to play competitive games with each other, such as football and tug of war. The boys began to identify strongly with their own group and hate the other group. They engaged in frequent quarrels and mutual accusations. The researchers tried to improve the situation. First they lectured to the boys about the advantages of mutual cooperation. But this had no measurable effect. Then they put the boys into a situation where they had no other choice but to cooperate if they wanted to achieve a certain goal. After a long hike, when the boys were hungry and tired, they secretly arranged for the food delivery truck to get stuck in a puddle of mud. Neither of the two groups alone was strong enough to get it moving again. Being hungry, the boys reluctantly helped each other and succeeded. That changed the situation totally. From that day on, they finally began to talk to each other, conclude friendships, and saw each other as one larger group solving common problems.

Although international conflicts are usually far more complex and deeply rooted, there are indications that similar mechanisms can help alleviate them. Common enemies have always been a unifying force. For example, when the United States and the Soviet Union faced the common threat of Hitler, they cooperated to defeat Nazi Germany. One factor that helped improve US–Chinese relations in the 1970s was their common perception of a Soviet threat. The United States and the Soviet Union do not face a personalized common enemy today. But they do face a number of common threats, such as world terrorism, resource shortages, pollution and climatic catastrophes, and most of all the danger of mutual annihilation in a nuclear war. Can such impersonal threats have the same effect of facilitating mutual cooperation? If history is any guide, this should indeed be possible. For example, what led to the emergence of the first civilizations in Mesopotamia and Egypt was not the threat of a foreign invader, but the recurrent droughts and floods that were a common threat to all farmers. Yet no individual farmer was able to build a dam for irrigation and flood control. Cooperation on a large scale was required to accomplish such a task, and this led to the creation of highly organized societies. If we are equally smart, we should be able to achieve the minimum of cooperation required to face the far greater common threats of today.

4 POTENTIAL AREAS FOR EAST–WEST COOPERATION

Areas where mutual cooperation is beneficial can be divided into two types: those where cooperation is indispensable to solve a problem, and those where it is not absolutely necessary, but still advantageous.

Examples where cooperation is indispensable are the prevention of nuclear terrorism and the protection of the global environment. As long as a single nation with nuclear technology makes enriched uranium or plutonium available to anyone who can pay, all nations of the earth may face the threat of nuclear terrorism. As long as a single major industrial power continues to release excessive amounts of carbon dioxide, the resulting greenhouse effect can damage agriculture everywhere. If one nation continues to release industrial gases that break down the protective ozone layer, people everywhere will suffer from an increase in the incidence of skin cancer and birth defects. To attack global problems of this nature, world-wide cooperation is indispensable, whether it be tacit, or in the form of an official treaty.

Examples where cooperation is not absolutely necessary, but useful, include economic, scientific and cultural cooperation, the exploration of outer space, the combatting of world hunger, poverty, illiteracy and disease. If the major industrial powers were to undertake a joint research program on the cure and prevention of cancer, they would be in a much better position to conquer that disease than if they all pursue their own projects, with limited coordination and exchange of information. If the United States, the Soviet Union and other nations were to cooperate in the exploration of outer space, instead of devoting much of their efforts to secret military missions, they could substantially improve global communication and expand scientific discoveries, at lower costs to all.

5 AN EXPANSION OF EAST–WEST TRADE

An area that could lead to a reduction of international tensions is increased East–West trade, particularly between the United States and the Soviet Union. Except for some US agricultural exports to the Soviet Union, trade between these two countries is currently very low, at about the level of US trade with Trinidad and Tobago. There are some who doubt whether it would be possible to expand US–Soviet trade significantly. It has been said that while the Soviet Union would like to import more high technology products and processes from the United States, it does not have much to offer in return. The United States does not need to import coal, and Soviet oil or gas is too distant. Neither can Soviet consumer products compete in the US market.

There are two ways in which this situation can be changed. When the United States and China began to increase mutual trade in the early 1970s, China did not produce goods of a design and quality that correspond to American consumers' tastes. But American business people went to China to show local enterprises how to produce goods, such as textiles and other light manufactured products, which could be sold in the United States. If US importers cooperated with Soviet enterprises to sell them technologies used in the production of goods for the US market, this could help increase Soviet exports to the United States. It might also benefit Soviet consumers.

Another way in which US–Soviet trade could be expanded is triangular trade with Japan or Third World countries. Japan is highly dependent on raw material and energy imports. It could make good use of coal and a variety of other minerals and metals from nearby Siberia, possibly by developing new mines in joint enterprises with the Soviet Union. The Soviet Union could then use those foreign-exchange earnings to import from the United States what it desires (provided these goods have no offensive military applications). The added export opportunities would help the United States reduce its huge trade deficit and increase domestic employment. In particular, it would help compensate for Japan's large trade surplus with the United States (exceeding $50 billion in 1985). Thus goods would flow from the United States to the Soviet Union, from the Soviet Union to Japan, and from Japan back to the United States. Foreign exchange would flow in the reverse direction. If prices and quantities are worked out properly, all three countries can draw substantial benefits from such an arrangement, and trade can be balanced in a triangle.

There are also other ways in which trade can be balanced. The United States may not want to import Soviet cars, but Third World countries can use Soviet tractors and a variety of machinery. The United States does import some raw materials, tropical products, textiles and other light manufactures from the Third World. If the United States then increased its exports to the Soviet Union, the circle can be closed. Trade need not be balanced on a bilateral basis.

Even more than trade alone, joint ventures are an instrument to foster mutually beneficial economic cooperation. China used to have a policy of purchasing finished manufacturing plants from abroad. But after it had paid for them, it often could not get them repaired in case they malfunctioned, as the supplier refused any further responsibility. It now prefers joint ventures, where a foreign company building a plant is remunerated with a share of its output. In this way, the supplier of the plant has an incentive to make sure that it remains in good working order, and produces something for which there is a real demand, regardless of whether or not this is specified in the contract.

6 THE IMPROVEMENT IN UNITED STATES–CHINA RELATIONS

An American propaganda film for an anti-ballistic missile (ABM) system made in 1969 pointed out that it was not yet technically feasible to build a 'dense' ABM shield against Soviet missiles, but that was not so important. The Soviet leadership was relatively reasonable and reliable. The great danger were the Chinese, they were so 'fanatic and unpredictable'. Most important was to build at least a 'thin' ABM system to keep out Chinese nuclear missiles.

Today, Americans are no longer afraid of a Chinese nuclear attack, but not because of any 'thin' ABM system. It is because of improved mutual relations. About 15 000 Chinese students are in the United States, and many Americans visit China each year. There is growing trade and cooperation in many areas. China has agreed to launch US communications satellites after a series of US missiles exploded.

If the United States had sent marines and B-52 bombers into China to support a 'moderate' faction during the Cultural Revolution, and had sent ping-pong teams and symphony orchestras into Vietnam, instead of the reverse, its relations with these two countries would probably be the opposite from what they are today: quite friendly relations with Vietnam, and somewhat tense relations with China.

There is no reason why a similar drastic improvement in US–Soviet relations should not be possible, if there is some willingness on both sides.

An American businessman who sells grain to the Soviet Union was once asked, 'Can you trust the Russians? If you sign a contract with them, do they live up to it?' He replied with a smile, 'We do not trust their good will. If we sign a contract, we make sure that if they violate it, they hurt their own interests. We trust their self-interest.' This is no different from the way companies do business with each other within the West.

Many are concerned whether cooperation with a potential opponent is not a form of appeasement, like the 1938 Munich agreement between British Prime Minister Chamberlain and Hitler. But cooperation of the form proposed here is the exact opposite. Appeasement means to yield to aggression and in this way to encourage further aggression. But cooperation in peacetime, while making it clear that such cooperation would end in case of war, increases each side's motivation to keep peace.

Seeking security through cooperation has a significant advantage over seeking security through a military build-up: mutual escalation is welcome! If others seek security by making peaceful cooperation more attractive for us, we are not worried, as we are if they build more arms. On the contrary, such efforts are welcome. But we need not wait for others to make the first move. It is in each side's own interest to begin such a process.

7 AN APPEAL TO ECONOMISTS

Jan Tinbergen (1987) has recently addressed the issue of war prevention from an economist's perspective, and has appealed to fellow economists to help add a chapter on war and peace to economic science. As representatives of the most developed of the social sciences, they ought to begin to address also the urgent question of how decision-makers choose between war and peace. Up to now, economists have generally treated war as an exogenous disturbance that temporarily interrupts the applicability of normal economic reasoning, which can be resumed when peace is restored. But war and peace have had greater impact on human welfare than many other economic variables. With the possibility of human extinction, the prevention of nuclear war has become such an important issue that all professions should contribute their skills to understanding its causes and ways to prevent it. If we could not avoid a nuclear holocaust, all our other preoccupations with business cycles, inflation, and trade statistics would be meaningless. I am confident that this appeal is also in the spirit of Joan Robinson.

References

Barnet, R. J. (1971) *Roots of War* (New York: Penguin Books).

Bundy, M. (1982) ' "No First Use" Needs Careful Study,' *Bulletin of the Atomic Scientists*.

Fischer, D. (1984) *Preventing War in the Nuclear Age* (Totowa, NJ: Rowman & Allanheld).

Galtung, J. (1984) *There Are Alternatives! Four Roads to Peace and Security* (Nottingham: Spokesman).

Sherif, M. and C. Sherif (1969) *Social Psychology* (New York: Harper & Row).

Tinbergen, J. and D. Fischer (1987) *Warfare and Welfare: Integrating Security Policy into Socio-Economic Policy* (Brighton: Wheatsheaf).

30 The Economics of Warfare: Joan Robinson's Challenge

Jan Tinbergen

1 INTRODUCTORY

Modern history seems to be characterized by an *expansion of militarism*. In a series of wars of increasing impact on human society the significance of warfare for human welfare grew to unprecedented dimensions. This is particularly true of the two World Wars, but it also affected the wars of a more regional nature, for instance through the advanced technologies used, sometimes tried out even in the latter type of war. After the Franco-Prussian war of 1870–1 and increasingly after both World Wars, the thought spread that wars had developed into a criminal phenomenon that requires legal regulation. Conflicts between nations should be solved by negotiation or arbitration rather than by the use of violence. Governments should submit their conflicting views to the International Court of Justice and the solution should be formulated by that Court on the basis of international law: Polemology was developed, mainly by scholars with a legal background, as a new branch of science to better understand the emergence of international conflicts.

Thinking about the *criminal character* of warfare accelerated as a consequence of the discovery of *nuclear energy* by the physicists. The application of nuclear energy to armament multiplied the destructive capacity of weaponry and added the phenomenon of radiation. We have reached at present a stage (see also Section 3) when a nuclear war will damage the human environment to such an extent that after some time *life will be impossible*.

Following the legal profession, the *medical* profession (at least some of its members) has recently accepted the responsibility of pointing out to the general public the dangers involved. It told the public that after a nuclear attack even a fraction of the medical aid needed cannot be provided. Moreover, a group of 'medical polemologists' has been established.

A similar responsibility rests on the *economic* profession. Quite clearly *human welfare* is strongly affected – in a negative way – by modern wars both conventional and nuclear, and this makes it the economists' duty to add a chapter on warfare to economic science. The traditional attitude that warfare decisions are exogenous to the economist's realm can no longer be accepted. We, as economists, have to *endogenize* war and peace decisions because of the enormous negative impact of such decisions on human welfare, just as we have endogenized environmental decisions (Hueting, 1980; Myers, 1979). Significant work aiming at endogenizing military phenomena has already been done by Deutsch and his collaborators at the Berlin Science Center (Deutsch, *et al.*, 1980).

In view of the deep interest Joan Robinson took in the subject, in this essay to honor her, an attempt is made to sketch out how a chapter on the economics of warfare might look, although I aim at no more than a very rough sketch. In order to avoid a number of misunderstandings, two preliminary sections must precede, in my opinion, the chapter on economic science. They deal with some spiritual and ideological aspects of warfare (Section 2) and a brief historical survey of fighting and warfare (Section 3). In Sections 4 and 5 we discuss the economic and industrial aspects of warfare respectively, followed by a retrospect on economists' contributions to the subject (Section 6). In Section 7, we sketch briefly the policy aspects of warfare. Then, in Section 8, we outline what new elements should be added to the economics of warfare, on the basis of some of the discussions held in the Netherlands in the first half of 1985. We propose world-wide integration and amendment in institutions as an alternative to warfare in Section 9 and in the final section (10) we offer a summary and some conclusions.

2 SPIRITUAL AND IDEOLOGICAL ASPECTS OF WARFARE

The impact of warfare on human welfare contains (at least for those more immediately and actively involved in warfare) some elements almost alien to other economic activities. These elements are strongly influenced by feelings and philosophies tied into the existence of *nations* or similar groupings of human beings. Often, but by no means always, nations or nation-like groupings are characterized by a particular language. A large number of languages spoken at present are the official language of one particular country, and a large number of countries or nations are characterized by one language. The exceptions to these statements in regions that never knew colonial status, or only knew it centuries ago, are not numerous. Since Europe is the continent that did away with colonial relationships on its own territory first (with minor exceptions), our examples may first be taken from that continent. In Western Europe, Belgium and Switzerland are clearly officially multilingual: Belgium recognizes Dutch, French and German as official languages, Switzerland German, French, Italian and Romanic. Finland has two official languages, Finnish and Swedish. So far France and the United Kingdom have not or only in a very limited way recognized regionally spoken languages (Breton, Welsh), although there is a tendency to yielding to regional claims. In the Netherlands, the use of Frisian makes some progress. In Norway, two versions of Norwegian are recognized. In Eastern Europe the case of the USSR is complicated: many individual republics have their own language but Russian is recognized as the official language everywhere. Outside Europe India gives official status to Hindi and English, Canada to English and French. In fact numerous languages, for instance Bengali, are spoken in India and recognized in one or more of the states.

Outside Europe we find, to begin with, the inverse situation, where one language area covers many nations. In Latin America about twenty nations use Spanish as their official language and in North Africa and West Asia there is a similar number of Arabic speaking nations. In both cases interstate cooperation has appeared to be quite difficult. In the remainder of Africa the previous colonizer's language is maintained as the official languages with English, French and Portuguese as the most important and Italian and Spanish the less important examples.

We went into some detail of this linguistic description because the common people's reaction to *linguistic differences* is very strong; they feel completely helpless in a foreign country. This may be one reason why in the Bible the tower of Babel story is presented as an explanation. Consequently, language differences have such a deep impact on people that *patriotic feelings are a very strong type of emotion*. Together with a common environment and a common history and traditions, patriotic or nationalist emotions can be easily abused by political leaders. They also spur people to efforts rarely attained in performing other spiritual activities. Since motivations can be strengthened in all sorts of directions (including artificial ones) patriotic feelings introduce an *artificial element* into behavior that replaces normal human behavior with many forms of inhuman conduct. One way in which this 'revaluation of all values' (*Umwertung aller Werte* in German) shows its tragic consequences is that many individuals who behaved heroically during a war, cannot find a job in post-war society when the majority of people have come to their senses. The artificial component of nationalism is evident in the belief that one's own nation is abler and nobler than all other nations – and that then is a reason for special loyalty. Of course, this belief cannot be simultaneously correct for all nations concerned. Upon verification it will be shown to be incorrect, however one defines ability or nobility. This is the *differentia specifica* between patriotism or nationalism and other spiritual qualities of human beings. These qualities (intellectual, artistic, or moral, for instance) are generally similar in different nations, although they are not necessarily equally strong. The people of many countries adhere to most spiritual qualities, as is illustrated by the international institutions or associations devoted to their strengthening or joint application such as scientific and artistic associations, churches, philanthropic and other idealistic and (up to a point) political international associations. An international association of nationalists, however, is a *contradictio in terminis*. The tension between such generally human qualities and nationalism is eloquently expressed by the slogan 'right or wrong, my country!'

3 HISTORY OF FIGHTING AND WARFARE

The evolution of warfare from a normal feature of human life to a degenerated criminal activity of frightening dimensions must be kept in mind if we want to shed some light on the necessity to devote a special branch of economic science to this activity.

Conflicts between human beings are part of ordinary life and attempts to solve them by violent action are typical of impatient and strong individuals. Some mild violence in the education of young children may testify to sound common sense. Education without violence may not be optimal and may rest on a misconception of the child's nature. Mild but adequate violence as used by policemen is a *necessary element* of even a perfect democratic society. In olden times fighting with swords and shields was a pastime of knights and contributed to satisfaction – hence, to what in economic science is called welfare or utility – both by the act of fighting itself and, for one of the two combatants by winning. Evidently, the negative contributions from the risk of losing was lower than the contribution from the fun of fighting – at least for those who, on reflection, decided to participate.

A later stage, but still hundreds of years ago, was characterized by fighting between groups who were *paid for their participation* or given the opportunity to loot. They were called soldiers because of their source of income but they did not fight for a personal conflict; here was an institutional change. The fighting activity had an impact on (i) those whose conflict constituted its justification (ii) those hired who did (part of) the fighting, and (iii) citizens who were plundered if not killed or enslaved. There was a possible positive impact on (iv) the citizens of the winning party.

Again a later stage featured the institution of *conscription*, hence the imposition by those in power (monarch or other) on conscripts to fight alongside professional (volunteer) fighters at a pay determined by the ruling group. The tie between fighters and conflict-makers was further loosened.

Alongside these organizational changes *technological* changes increasingly codetermined the nature of 'military production'. Its details (for a macrosketch as presented here) will be discussed in Section 5. Consequently ever larger social groups were affected by the 'production' and in World War II the expression '*total war*' became justified. Not only larger parts of the population were affected but they increasingly experienced a *very strongly negative* impact on their welfare.

In the meantime, this negative impact on both combatants and non-combatants gave rise to *counterforce*. In the early phases of this new development, the process of warfare was assumed to be given and autonomous; it could not be avoided. But a number of 'rules of the game' were proposed to limit some of the worst suffering. Thus, prisoners of war and wounded were given protection and organizations such as the Red Cross (in Islamic countries the Red Crescent) were established. The national organizations were often set up by the International Commission of the Red Cross in Geneva, where coordination and mutual assistance were taken care of. Anti-militarist groupings came into existence; among them some of the smaller Protestant Churches and the Society of Friends ('Quakers'). After World War I several countries introduced the possibility for young men to be 'conscientious objectors' and to do non-military work instead of serving in the military establishments. For instance, when I opted in favor of non-military service (1925–7) in the Netherlands, one year additional service was the price to pay.

4 THE ECONOMIC ASPECTS OF WARFARE

A chapter of economic science dealing with warfare must concentrate on the economic aspects of warfare. The non-economist reader may need a brief explanation of what are economic aspects, or in other words what economic science is about. This can be said in different ways, but some of the main elements are that *scarce resources* are used to *satisfy human needs* in the *best way*. Each of these three elements may be given some more attention in order to clarify their role in economic science. Of the resources used to satisfy human needs, some may be abundantly available or may have been at least in the past; for example fresh air and fresh water were once described as 'free goods'. We all know that unfortunately this is no longer true everywhere on our planet, but as a first appropriate approximation in some regions there are still some 'free goods' such as sand in a desert or seawater in the Pacific. Some forms of energy are still freely available locally, such as wind during a hurricane or geyser hot water in Iceland. The great majority of resources needed is not freely available and can only be obtained at a price: resources are *scarce*. The satisfaction of *human needs* concerns such elements as food, supplied again almost freely in some tropical areas (bananas) or in some seas (fish), protection against too cold or too hot weather (sunshine or shadow), clothing (now very rarely supplied by nature) and health care (at most supplied by some plants). By far the larger part of the needs of today's world population (surpassing 4 billion) is scarce and therefore requires production, that is *processing* of natural resources. Until recently this processing has always required human *labor* and both *natural resources* and labor are called *factors of production.* For an overwhelming part of today's production a third factor, equipment, is needed, often called *capital* or capital goods. It is long ago (or in a few primitive areas on earth) that capital goods were (or are) produced with labor only, applied to natural resources. Today a very extensive stock of capital goods (building, machines, means of transportation, stocks of parts and semi-finished products) is in operation to supply not only the consumer goods (from bread to clothing and pharmaceuticals) but also the investment goods for replacing the worn-out equipment and expanding production capacity.

A link between the multi-faceted production processes mentioned and consumption is the *exchange process*, or *trade*, that takes place in many different forms: wholesale and retail trade, foreign and domestic trade. The place where trade partners meet is called a *market*, but many markets are replaced by *information.* Markets are also the places or the information on available and desired quantities of production factors. Direct exchange or *barter* trade is the smaller part of total trade; the larger part uses *money* as an intermediary. Producers sell their products for money for which they buy the goods or services they wish to obtain.

In the preceding paragraphs a simple sketch of an economy has been given. When it comes to finding the best way of managing such an economy, we must choose a criterion or a policy *aim* and this is often formulated as the *maximization* of that criterion or aim.

It is customary (and also helps to attain economic policy aims) for an economy to be characterized by various forms of *cooperation* between citizens of a nation. We may distinguish *private* cooperation, as occurring in a private enterprise, and *public* cooperation, encompassing public authorities responsible for law and order as required by legislation.

This legislation not only sets a number of rules for the citizens' conduct but also defines a number of *tasks for the authorities.* In differing social systems the number of tasks varies greatly. Some systems are built on the conviction that that number should be *minimal* and other systems are based on the theory that the tasks must together *cover almost all productive activities.* In both systems, however, one of the tasks of public authorities is to maintain 'external security' and here we are back at our main topic: the maintenance of external security is the task of the *military* authorities.

Today's world is subdivided into about 150 *sovereign states* of very unequal size. When expressed in terms of population they vary from about 1 billion (China) to a few tens of thousands. When expressed in production (roughly equal to income, expressed here in 1975 international dollars) the largest country is the USA, whose gross domestic product in 1975 amounted to $1533 billion, followed by Japan $547, Germany $368, France

$310, and India $284; figures for the USSR and China were not available (Kravis, *et al.*, 1982, p.10).

5 WARFARE AS AN INDUSTRY

The economic aspects of warfare will be discussed under two different headings. In this section we consider warfare as an *industry* and in Section 7 as an *economic policy*. These two treatments parallel the two ways of approaching economic science: the explanatory and normative. One aims at an *explanation* of the economic process (the satisfaction of human needs with the aid of scarce resources), where the means of economic policy are considered *given* and the other considers the means of economic policy as the *unknowns*, but assumes the *aims* of that policy to be *given*. Four categories of variables enter into both versions of economic science, *aims* (or when quantitative: target variables), *means* (or when quantitative: instrument variables), *data* (variables determined by other sciences, also called exogenous variables), and *irrelevant* (or 'other') variables (which are of an economic nature but are neither aims nor means). In explanatory economics, means (or instruments) are given and aims (or targets) are the unknowns that result from the means applied. In the theory of economic policy (or normative economics), the aims are given and the means are the unknowns. In both versions of economic science, data (or exogenous variables) and other (or irrelevant variables) are given.

It is natural to start the *explanatory* version of the economics of warfare by describing data and means, that together may be called '*inputs*'. As in economic science we will distinguish between inputs of labor and equipment into the industry considered. We will consider not only military activity in the narrower sense, but integrate the preceding phases such as armament production which increasingly absorbs resources; that is, natural resources, capital and manpower. Total manpower inputs into warfare are not confined to the military, but include manpower engaged in armament production. In war periods usually all the available labor force is mobilized and unemployment is reduced; in the great wars even to zero. This is one of the few positive economic aspects of warfare – positive aspects that should be derived from nobler objectives! The efforts made by military labor are, of course, much more intensive than those of civilian labor: they imply the *devotion of life* or the risk of life-long disablement.

Equipment input into warfare has shown a *strong technological development*. It may even be a stronger development than that of civilian production since, the pressure for higher 'efficiency' is stronger than on civilian production. It is a well-known impression that some technologies (for example aviation) have profited from the war efforts in both World

Wars. Again a brief sketch only will be attempted here as an illustration of the technical development of warfare. Whereas in the Middle Ages hot vegetable oil was a defense against besiegers of a fortress, the invention of gunpowder started a development of *guns* of increasing dimensions and power, with which battleships were also equipped. *Chemical* developments contributed to the introduction of dynamite (Alfred Nobel!) and, later, toxic gases and *biological weapons*. Alongside battleships, the invention of the *submarine* constituted another major innovation to the disadvantage of seafaring nations, especially Britain and Japan. *Tanks* acted as the mechanized carriers of guns and soldiers, parallel with *aircraft*, mentioned before. Gun and carrier were united in the shape of *missiles*, the potential and precision of which have continually been increased. The most dramatic increase in potential was the discovery of *nuclear energy*, as a result of the physical theory of relativity and of the structure of atoms.

While the scale of armaments and the increased speed of the carriers enlarged the war theatre from countries to continents and finally to the world, the most innovating element was, of course, nuclear armament, and especially the radiation therefrom. In principle – and this may hold a promise – the offender may (and will) *also* be threatened with non-survival. This requires a *complete rethinking* of war theories implied by the customary lag – the tendency to derive instructions from last war's experience. One main new feature is that the enormous stock of nuclear weapons, into which annually *billions of dollars* are being invested, *cannot be used*.

Having sketched the nature of direct inputs we must not forget the *negative* input of reduced civilian production, implying a considerable reduction of the standard of life of those who remain alive.

Now what is the *output* obtained with the aid of the huge inputs just listed? Here we shall distinguish the distribution of the output over various groups of recipients.

In the past and in colonial wars material gains may have been obtained as natural resources of the losing party were transferred to the winning party. The value of colonies has been calculated by estimating the addition to national income as a result of the colonial relationship. One of the highest figures presumably is the one obtained for the Netherlands in the period when Indonesia was a colony (Derksen, 1945); a figure of 11 to 18 per cent added to the national income. This type of output from wars ended with colonialism, say around 1960; it need not be discussed further. A considerable material gain may be a *war indemnity* of which the most impressive example is the 5 billion francs paid in cash in 1871 by France to Germany.

Another negative material output is the usual drop in civilian production in both consumer and investment goods. Moreover, the stock of investment goods is destroyed as an immediate consequence of warfare. In World War II the destruction of buildings, and stocks of equipment, semi-finished and finished goods in Germany and Eastern Europe was tremendous.

Two aspects of the *distribution* of the output should be mentioned: the unemployed will find employment, and armament producers will increase sales and profits.

As a negative spiritual output of warfare, *casualties among the non-combatants* have increased more or less parallel to the material destruction just mentioned and have assumed *atrocious dimensions*. These were surpassed considerably by the experiences of the two Japanese cities Hiroshima and Nagasaki hit by a nuclear bomb.

Traditionally, the spiritual output that should justify all the inputs and the net negative outputs is the *glory of the victory* by the winning party. Here the critical analysis of patriotic ideology given in Section 2 applies; and with it, for the last century or so, the dwindling economic justification of warfare as a desirable branch of industry. It may seem desirable during the intoxication of the war period; when they sober up people become conscious of the tremendous suffering and its unnecessary nature, when looked at from a normal human point of view.

6 WHAT HAVE ECONOMISTS CONTRIBUTED IN THE PAST?

A somewhat isolated normative statement was made by G. Cassel, who considers wars undesirable because they cause inflation. An implicit normative statement was the main message of Keynes (1920).

Martin C. McGuire (1965) published in revised form his dissertation (suggested by W. Leontief and supervised by T. Schelling) in which a simple model of two countries and one type of armament (missiles) is developed. War is considered to consist of a succession of alternating attacks from both sides and supposed to stop when no further gains in utility can be expected. The problem is cast in a number of alternative settings, including the search for a Pareto-optimal disarmament solution. Not only variations in quantity but also in quality of missiles are considered. Probabilities of alternative results of the consecutive attacks are introduced. Boulding's Theory of Viability (1962) is mentioned. The subject of secrecy is dealt with in one of the five chapters only. The similarity of the stylized warfare process with Cournot's treatment of duopoly is pointed out.

Russett (1968) is a compilation in which some thirty economists (including the editor) deal with many aspects of international politics. Since war was considered by Von Clausewitz to be 'the continuation of international politics with other means', this book contributes to a number of models of warfare. Important elements dealt with include economic theories of alliances, committee decisions, strategy and market structure, oligopoly stability, technical development, and others. A theoretical model of nationalism constitutes another subject vital to warfare. A number of other phenomena treated are less close to warfare, but pertain to aspects of struggle (discrimination, the propensity to strike). Among the authors we find Shubik, Stigler, Galbraith, Hirschman, Harry Johnson, Anne Krueger, and Lindblom. Also Boulding's Theory of Viability and McGuire's 1965 thesis are among the book's chapters. This publication provides abundant evidence that for quite some time economists have been very close to a number of warfare problems *without* – it seems to me – *taking the final step of internalizing warfare into economic science*. Two authors who have also made important contributions – John von Neumann and Oskar Morgenstern, the creators of the theory of games – are missing, but are quoted several times, illustrating their involvement.

A cluster of publications on warfare by economists appears in 1984, reflecting, no doubt, the impact of President Reagan's policies. A major contribution is by Dietrich Fischer (1984), who explicitly introduces a list of some twenty concepts known from polemology and their relevance to a policy to avoid war. These concepts may be subdivided into three categories: objectives (or motivations), means, and other concepts. As possible *objectives* we may consider defensive and offensive objectives, peaceful social or political change, common security, clear frontiers, stable equilibrium, warning of an attack, military strength. As possible *means* we may list defensive or offensive weapons, fixed or mobile weapons, observable or hidden weapons, strike (or use of weapons), first or second strike (or retaliation), counter-force or counter-value strike, first-strike capability. The remaining concepts are, *inter alia*, policy declarations, treaties, credibility of declarations, observance of treaties, vulnerability, and indulgence.

Next, the author deals with a number of *processes* of human activity and then with a number of *technical relations*. The activities considered are a succession of strikes or attacks, best analyzed by an activity *model*, as described in the theory of games and its predecessors (theories of duopoly or oligopoly and of bargaining). Description and analysis of the complete succession constitutes the *dynamics* of armament or warfare or negotiations. Description of the final result may be seen as the *statics*, at least if the process converges to an equilibrium position.

Although Fischer (1984) does not explicitly distinguish between *factual* and *hypothetical* activities, it seems useful to do so. By hypothetical activities I mean processes playing a role in the build-up of armaments for *deterrence*. Such a build-up aims at non-use of the arms considered. The hypothetical process is used in any attempt to prove that *non-use is the optimal policy*. Among the processes the *creation of new institutions*, especially international ones, is very important. The only long-run solution to the security problem seems to be in the establishment of a real security council. I shall come back to this subject.

Alongside processes directly related to security questions there exist other *indirectly* related processes such as trade policies, transfer of financial means for development financing, or information on technology. We may achieve higher common security by such information.

The *technical relations* considered by Fischer (1984) are, mathematically speaking, closer to inequalities than to equalities. Some examples are: (1) words do not necessarily reflect acts; (2) indulgence may provoke an attack; (3) strength may be insufficient if there is no stability; (4) counter-force capability is less stable than counter-value capability; (5) MIRVs reduce stability; (6) MX as an anti-silo weapon may enhance suspicion of a surprise attack; (7) Cruise missiles are difficult to observe and hence defense against them is difficult; (8) with higher yield of missiles first use becomes more suicidal.

So far Fischer (1984) has been discussed in a way that suggests its use for developing a dynamics of armament or warfare processes. The book's main contribution is at least twofold. Its text yields, in a verbal way, a very clear picture of the main aspects of a peace policy at a world level. And its Table 8.1 provides us with the partly unexpected results of a number of hypothetical warfare processes characterized by the use of various armament systems of two opponents. The unexpected aspects are that both multiple warhead and more accurate missiles contribute to unstable and hence less desirable situations, in contrast to what would be expected. Sometimes a system of greater strength may reduce a nation's security, namely when it reduces stability. The explanation may be that military thinking refers to a war already started, whereas political thinking is more concerned with avoiding war.

MccGwire (1984) (a staff member of Brookings Institution, but not necessarily reflecting that institution's opinion) contains a brief survey of American–Soviet relations after World War II. In leading American circles it was supposed that immediately after that war the USSR was planning an invasion and occupation of Western Europe. In the 1950s and 1960s American military strength surpassed Soviet strength, however, and MccGwire (1984) sees this as explaining what he calls the apparent success of arms control activities, resulting in the SALT I (strategic arms limitation talks I), ABM (antiballistic-missiles treaty) and SALT II. The latter was signed, but not ratified; yet, by mid 1985 it still applied. During the 1970s and until 1982 an increased feeling of being under threat developed in the US, based on increased Soviet armament and military activity (Horn of Africa, Afghanistan). After 1982 this feeling of threat diminished, partly because of increased American armament.

The arguments analyzed by MccGwire (1984) are differences of opinion between the American military leadership and the American experts on the USSR and, similarly, the American government (more influenced by the Pentagon) and European governments (not all to the same degree, more influenced by experts). The subjects on which opinions differ are the choice between deterrence and mutual 'reassurance' (MccGwire's language) and, correspondingly, the choice between more deterrence and more arms control. The military view is seen to be somewhat inconsistent: additional armament is aimed at in a period of decreasing feeling of threat. The military view inverts causality, however: decreasing threat results from increased armament.

Some aspects of the argument are clearly of an economic character. On various occasions, incorrect information is published in order to attain advantages (military authorities overestimate Soviet strength in order to raise their budget, or diplomats underestimate it in order to have a treaty ratified by the Congress). Next, cost considerations induce the government to forgo accuracy of some types of armament or an improved counterforce system. Similarly, but not dealt with by MccGwire, MIRVs (multiwarhead missiles[1]) were introduced because they cost less per warhead, but they are more expensive arms in a broader sense, since they procure less security by destabilizing the military equilibrium. Finally, a patently economic aspect of the peace–war problem comes in when MccGwire rightly states that war is worse than occupation, if we are reminded that today's nuclear war may finish humanity.

The preceding examples of contributions by economists to the problems of peace policies are meant as illustrations; they do not aim at completeness. Contributions were made also to multidisciplinary discussions, increasingly organized in recent years. An excellent example of such a discussion is one organized by the Stanley Foundation and summarized in its publication *Strategy for Peace 1984*.

Finally, a more integrated form of interdisciplinary work should be mentioned, namely the construction of models in which various aspects are combined, usually dealt with by different sciences. Particular attention to this type of model building is being given by the Berlin Scientific Center (*Wissenschaftszentrum Berlin*) and a recent account of its work is given by Deutsch (1984).

7 WARFARE AS A POLICY

We will now take up the second type of scientific economic analysis announced in the beginning of Section 5 and consider as the unknowns the means of warfare or alternative means as a solution of the policy problem characterized by the aim of maximizing an economy's (or nation's) welfare. The interpretation of this maximization is different for an *aggressor* and a *defending* nation, whenever that difference can be made. Famous national leaders of antiquity and the Middle Ages, up to Napoleon Bonaparte had an interpretation of maximizing a nation's welfare in which national glory played an important part. In the case of Hitler, it was the desire to wipe out the 'shame' of Germany's defeat in World War I, strengthened by racism and a form of imperialism. It is this place given to nationalist feelings that we discussed in Section 2 showing its irrational character. A real interest in a country's citizens as human beings and their cultural potentials would have led, and leads today, to an interpretation of social welfare in terms of the happiness derived from health, both physical and spiritual, a good marriage and good friendships and cultural activities (arts and sciences). For religious individuals these values find their climax in contributing to God's glory whereas Humanists believe in them without the spiritual superstructure.

As noted in the policy problem the means are the unknowns. This should be understood in the sense of a *choice* between *alternative* means, ranging from warfare to appearing before a *Court of Justice*, with direct negotiations or mediation as intermediate solutions. These are the alternatives already available now. Applying a somewhat higher degree of creativity one can foresee a solution by means of *supranational agencies as part of the international order*, whose unknowns are in the domains of competence of the various agencies – possibly innovated versions of the International Monetary Fund, the World Bank, the Security Council and several other specialized agencies of the United Nations.

Taking into account the artificial component of nationalism sketched in Section 2, and from the description of the output of warfare as an activity in Section 5 it will be clear that, compared to the alternative means just indicated, warfare as a means to attain maximal welfare *is to be rejected most decidedly*. This conclusion is valid for conventional wars and all the more so for a nuclear war.

8 WHAT NEW ELEMENTS MAY BE ADDED?

During the first half of 1985, we had in the Netherlands lively discussions on the subject and some results of my internalizing the armaments policy into economic science will be presented for comment in this section.

A first subject may be termed the *correction of preferences*. In economic policy (contrary to what some economists think) we do not always take for granted the preferences of individuals. Governments (as well as individual MPs) consider some corrections of preferences a normal element in their policies. An important example is *obligatory schooling*, as a correction of possible myopia in parents or youngsters. Obligatory *social insurance* is another example. A third one is the correction organized by *consumer unions* of distorted quality perceptions of consumer goods – distorted by producer information in advertizing. A relevant addition to this list should be the correction of nationalist or patriotic feelings, *distorted* by nationalist parties, the military establishment or other nationalist groupings. There is a need for correction because nationalism implies the idea that one's own people are better, abler, or nobler than other people. As previously mentioned, this cannot be true simultaneously for any two nations. Still another example of a necessary correction is the *underestimation* of the horrors of war, especially nuclear war, but also conventional war. Among the causes of the underestimation is the obvious fact that the dead cannot inform us. Those who survived hold a biased view. An important task of peace movements of all kinds is to formulate the necessary correction – a task comparable to consumer union tasks, but immensely more important.

A second subject to be added by economics to the discussion of war and peace policies is the *use of models*, in order to explain more completely society's *laws of motion*. Among the social sciences economics probably is ahead in model building, but economic models must be generalized by the introduction of many elements neglected by them. I mentioned the activities in this field of the Berlin Science Center, and will now supplement this information. The theory of games was also mentioned: it characterizes the general method to be used. Fischer (1985) constructed a model (based on an economic model of Von Neumann's) enriched by a military sector. Two countries and two types of weapons are considered, highly threatening and non-threatening arms. This distinction is narrowly related to the one between offensive and defensive weapons. The two sectors' products are civil goods and security. One and the same process may add to one country's and reduce the other country's security. Moreover, the coefficients appearing in the input–output table may reflect high-cost or low-cost production.

The model is used to analyze a number of alternative combinations of processes, and yields, on the one hand, some natural conclusions and, on the other, some quite surprising results that make the model of extreme importance to military and civilian authorities. Alongside the well-known horrifying explosive arms race the possibility of disarmament *even in the absence of any mutual agreement* is known to exist. The latter process becomes more likely, the more non-threatening weapons are opted for and the more cheaply they produce security for both countries. Models of this kind and their results need to be widely publicized and their study should be obligatory reading for all negotiators of the US and the USSR. After having been thoroughly discussed they may *enable governments to show their peaceful intentions*, or a lack of them – which may reduce the prevailing uncertainty about these intentions.

A third subject to be added by economic science to the discussion of peace policy consists of some results of the theory of organizations or *management science*. In these disciplines a crucial problem deals with a hierarchy, consisting of authorities with clearly defined tasks and power, for example armies and civilian administrations. Such hierarchies consist of levels from the lowest to the highest rank. At each level we find a number of decision-makers of equal rank, supervising a number of decision-makers of the next lower rank. That number is sometimes called the span of control. The highest level consists of one decision-making authority. A sovereign country's administration mainly consists of a hierarchy of administrators for geographical subdivisions. The lowest rank authorities may be those accountable for municipalities. The next higher rank may be a district, and the highest rank a state, if states are sovereign for the task considered. This applies to some taxes, decided upon by the state legislature. Other tasks may be federal and then final decisions are made by a federal authority (for example, the Treasury, for taxes).

A central problem in management science is to find the *optimal level of decision-making*. For different tasks the optimal level may vary. If by optimal we mean serving the interests of the population in the best way, the level must be chosen so that all individuals whose interests are affected by the decisions are included. More precisely this means that there must not be so-called 'external effects'; that is, impacts on people outside the area for which the authorities making the decision are responsible.

An important topical example is the task of keeping the environment clean. Recent development of chemical industries has been such that the atmosphere is polluted not only in the immediate neighborhood of a factory, but over thousands of miles. Consequently, national decisions may be suboptimal and continental decisions better. For the pollution of water and the atmosphere world-wide decisions may be optimal. But these are decisions for which no authority exists; the United Nations Environmental Program has neither the competence to make decisions nor the power to have them implemented.

Our main problem, the one of security, also requires decision-making at the world level[2] and here too no authority with sufficient competence and sufficient power exists.

The problem and its solution may be illustrated by *lower level experiences*. Wars have occurred as long as military decisions were made by sovereign governments of parts of the area considered such as wars between provinces of the Netherlands, between princedoms of Germany or states of the US (the Civil War). These wars stopped as soon as a federal government in the true sense was established. Internal wars stopped in Germany after 1870 when a central government was established. Around the same time in Italy and in the US internal wars disappeared. We can be fairly sure that Franco-German wars have ceased after the creation of the European Coal and Steel Community.

Applying this experience to the world level leads to the conclusion that *world-wide integration* constitutes a safe way to prevent war. Integration does not mean that a 'world government' is established, taking over all the tasks of national governments. The *overwhelming part of decisions must remain the tasks of national or lower authorities*. But there are a few, very important, problems whose appropriate solution requires decisions at *world level*, as discussed earlier.

A fourth element to be added by economic science to the discussion of peace policy is the somewhat ironic statement that sometimes military decisions are made on economic grounds in too restricted a sense, namely, neglecting military aspects that the economist now attempts to take more seriously. An example is the introduction of multiwarhead missiles (MIRVs) because their cost per warhead is lower. What has been overlooked – or was not yet clear enough at the time – is that they destabilize the military equilibrium and for that reason reduce security, interpreted by the modern economist as an additional cost, larger than the narrow cost reduction in favor of MIRVs. (We have to find out whether more examples can be found.)

9 INTEGRATION AS AN ALTERNATIVE TO WARFARE

If warfare is to be ruled out, the preceding analysis clearly points to the necessity of creating a world order in which a number of *supranational* and even *world* institutions are *indispensable*. These institutions seem impossible to the usual type of politicians, characterized by a good deal of shortsightedness. Politics being 'the art of the possible', they don't seem to them to deserve consideration. For those with a wider horizon history supplies some support in continuing the process of *integration*. It is only a few centuries ago that wars were fought by what are now provinces of a small country such as the Netherlands. It is 150 years ago that Belgium liberated itself from its imposed union with the 'Northern Netherlands'. After 1945 they voluntarily created a form of cooperation with the latter, known as Benelux. Whereas in 1921 there still were some conservatives in the Netherlands who feared aggression by Belgium, there is nobody left today who considers such a fear to be justified.

More recently, and at a much more important level, France and Germany were designated as arch-enemies. Three wars, in 1870–1, 1914–18 and 1939–45 indicated this. A handful of statesmen – Jean Monnet, Konrad Adenauer, Paul-Henri Spaak, Alcide De Gasperi and others – were the creators of the European Community, which for ever excludes a new military conflict between France and Germany.

In the US, after the Civil War of the 1860s, nobody ever thinks of a military conflict among the states.

Similar processes developed in other parts of the world. Not always smoothly; India's integration did have recessions, but the institutional framework of the subcontinent constitutes a strong counterforce. There is an undeniably clear experience with processes of integration: imposed integration is less effective than integration desired by the people concerned. Switzerland and Scandinavia, although a microcosm in this regard, are interesting examples of a search for the optimal combination of centralization and decentralization of cooperation between their cantons/nations.

The fortieth anniversary of the United Nations organization constitutes a natural and a very necessary occasion for a critical examination of its *operation* and the formulation of necessary *reforms*. Several groups are engaged in such an examination. One source of inspiration for alternative and better ways of operation may be management science, mentioned in the previous section of this chapter. What was said about a hierarchy of decision-making authorities may provide us with an efficient set of institutions that together may constitute the best way of *managing our planet*. And nothing less than such a task is to be performed.

We saw that the bulk of decisions to be made for human life on our planet to operate optimally can be made by national or lower authorities and is outside anyone else's purview. In this respect nations rightly *claim their sovereignty*. We also saw, however, that a few very important problems can only be solved by forms of supranational decision-making, even at a world level. Maintaining a satisfactory quality of the atmosphere and the seas is one example and a reformed United Nations Environmental Program Secretariat is necessary, with the competence and the power to implement its program.

Security is at least as important and requires a similar institutional set-up. National sovereignty cannot be claimed for that aim, except when all national governments convincingly show that their sovereign defense attitude is defensive and in no way offensive. As long as that attitude is not assumed by all governments, only 'common security' will work, as shown by the Independent Commission on Disarmament and Security Issues (Palme Commission) in its 1982 report *Common Security*. By common security we mean a system in which decision-making on all aspects is conducted on the basis of technological data available to all and a decision-making body that exists with the competence and the power to implement its decisions; we may call it a *reformed Security Council*, and it must have no veto, yet the power to implement its decisions.

One feature of an optimal management for our planet deserves particular emphasis. The optimal operation of national authorities can take place only within a *general framework set by world authorities* for the common interest of all in areas such as environment, security and some ten other objectives requiring decisions (trade policies, financial transfers, monetary affairs, etc. for which institutions exist, although not yet in a fully satisfactory form). The feature we emphasized implies that the *national social order* can only be chosen *within* the framework indicated. The system should not exclude changes which previously were only obtained by military power; but these changes must be made peacefully, on the basis of decision of the International Court of Justice. In other well-known terms, changes must fit into a system of *peaceful coexistence*. The choice to establish a socialist order (of whatever variant) can be a national choice, like the choice to establish a liberal order with a few public institutions only, such as Japan or the US.

10 SUMMARY AND CONCLUSIONS

Warfare capacity has expanded and intensified over the last century to such an extent that economic science can no longer consider it as an exogenous variable; it has to be endogenized into economics. Nationalism is based on the assumption that one's own country is abler and nobler than other countries; for different countries these assumptions are mutually contradictory and therefore artificial components of welfare. If the welfare concept is corrected for its artificial component of nationalism, the impact of warfare on welfare is strongly negative. This creates a very powerful argument against warfare as a policy to solve conflicts between nations and in fact characterizes warfare as a crime against humanity. In olden times fighting was an activity only of people involved in a conflict and somewhat contributed to welfare. In a next stage outsiders were drawn in who participated against a payment. Finally conscription drew in also involuntary fighters making a negative contribution to their welfare. Alongside these organizational changes a rapid technological development extended the impact of warfare to increasing numbers of non-combatants, leading to 'total war' in World War II. Counterforces such as the Red Cross and anti-militarist attitudes of some churches and other groupings only marginally influenced these developments. An acceleration was introduced by nuclear energy and this led to a series of innovations of increasingly destructive character. A complete rethinking of the consequences of warfare becomes necessary now that radiation may, in the end, also kill the aggressor's population, and nuclear weapons cannot in fact be used.

It will be clear that the ideas set out in Sections 6 and 8 have a significant impact on the recent international discussions around the war threat. Opinions of the parties involved on the various aspects have to be revised: some opinions on some aspects will be supported, others will find no support. In a general way peace forces will be strengthened and arguments in favor of armament weakened.

More specifically, Professor Fischer's findings constitute strong arguments in favor of more defensive and less threatening weapons, in contrast to offensive and threatening arms. They also show that stability of equilibrium rather than equality of strength (as measured by numbers of warheads, for instance) contributes to security. In addition, Fischer has made it quite clear tht MIRVs are a destabilizing element as may be the higher accuracy of weapons. He also emphasized that economic and technological assistance can work out better than economic and technological isolation. And it follows from his analysis that the superpowers could gain from showing more convincingly their defensive intentions. If they fail to do so some consequences may be drawn and some uncertainties we now face would disappear.

The strongly negative impact of warfare on welfare eliminates warfare as an optimal economic policy to solve conflicts between nations, leaving as alternatives negotiation, arbitration, or bringing the conflict before the International Court of Justice. The best solution lies in an international order in which problems affecting more than one nation have to be treated by supranational agencies endowed with the competence and the power needed to implement the policy to maximize world welfare. History shows a development of integration into units of increasing size and the creation of the world order briefly indicated seems to be the natural goal of an optimal economic policy. More particularly a reform of the UN Security Council, eliminating veto rights of members and making available a strong United Nations Peace Force, must be the subject of urgent discussion.

The contribution to today's discussions that can be made by the internalization of peace policy into economic science constitutes a powerful argument in support of the concept of common security, developed by the Palme Commission; the solution cannot be found by sticking to national sovereignty. In other words, the Strategic Defense Initiative will contribute positively to security, when developed in cooperation with the USSR. This may even be formulated in the provocative way that only the two superpowers together are able to provide the world at large with the security it needs and are able to complete the world integration needed as the last step of all previous acts of integration. This may – or actually should – take the form of a well-organized family of United Nations institutions, the managerial hierarchy the world needs.

In comparison to these macroproblems some other results of internalization into economics of the peace policy we are searching for are minor only, but nevertheless clarify some current issues. Some military decisions made on the basis of economic arguments have erroneously been based on too narrow an interpretation of economics. Thus, MIRVs have been produced because they are 'cheaper' in a restricted economic sense. In fact they are more expensive because they reduce security. Similarly, offensive weapons have sometimes been preferred over defensive weapons 'because they are cheaper'. This again is only true if too narrow an interpretation of economics is adhered to, since offensive weapons produce less security than defensive weapons.

It is my hope that the preceding text illustrates some of the advantages of the expansion of economic science to internalize peace policy. Modern war is such an irrational activity, requiring enormous sacrifices from humanity, that its elimination can make an unparalleled contribution to human happiness. Efforts made to further that elimination promise to be highly productive in comparison to many alternative efforts.

Notes

1. MIRV stands for 'multiple independently targetable re-entry vehicles', where re-entry refers to re-entry into the lower atmosphere; in practice these vehicles are missiles with several warheads.
2. This is not necessary if all governments pursue peaceful changes only; as long as this is uncertain, world-level decisions only can warrant peace.

References

Boulding, K. (1962) *Conflict and Defense* (New York: Harper).

Derksen, J. B. D. and J. Tinbergen (1945) 'Berekeningen over de economische betekenis van Nederlands Oost Indië voor Nederland', *Maandschrift van het Centraal Bureau voor de Statistiek*, 10–12: 210–16 (Dutch; 'Calculations on the Economic Significance of the Netherlands East Indies for the Netherlands', *Monthly Review of the Central Bureau of Statistics*)

Deutsch, K. W. (1980) *Weltmodellstudien: Wachstumsprobleme und Lösungsmöglichkeiten* (with S. A. Bremer, R. Kappel, P. Otto, H. Weck and K. Widmaier) (German; 'World Model Studies: Problems of Growth and Possibilities of their Solution'), quoted in *WZB Mitteilungen*, Special Issue March 1983, p.27.

Deutsch, K. W. (1984), 'Zur Bedeutung von Weltmodellen' (The Importance of World Models), *WZB Mitteilungen* (September): 12–15.

Fischer, D. (1984) *Preventing War in the Nuclear Age* (London: Croom Helm).

Fischer, D. (1985) 'Weapons Technology and the Intensity of Arms Races', *Conflict Management and Peace Science* 8(1).

Hueting, R. (1980) *New Scarcity and Economic Growth* (Amsterdam/North-Holland).

Keynes, J. M. (1920) *The Economic Consequences of the Peace* (London: Macmillan).

Kravis, I. B. *et al.* (1982) *World Product and Income* (Baltimore: Johns Hopkins University Press for the World Bank).

MccGwire, M. K. (1984) 'Peace and War – the Anatomy of an Argument', *Coexistence* 21: 107–22.

McGuire, M. C. (1965) *Secrecy and the Arms Race* (Cambridge, Mass.: Harvard University Press).

Myers, N. (1979) *The Sinking Ark* (Oxford: Pergamon Press).

Russett, B. M. (ed.) (1968) *Conflict Theories of International Policies* (Chicago: Markham).

Index*

*See also the index to *Joan Robinson and Modern Economic Theory*.